AMERICA'S TEST KITCHEN
TWENTIETH ANNIVERSARY
TV SHOW COOKBOOK

Best-Ever Recipes from the Most
Successful Cooking Show on TV

Contents

Acknowledgments

Putting on a cooking show is no small feat. It literally takes an army. Doing it for 20 years, and making it the most successful and longest-running cooking show on TV is a milestone worthy of celebration. This special book is a love letter to the remarkable cast and crew that have brought ATK's recipes to life for millions of home cooks.

In addition to the 11 cast members you know, another 50 people work behind the scenes. For season 20, Executive Producer Kaitlin Keleher conceived and developed each episode with help from Producer Sara Joyner, Associate Producer Caroline Rickert, and Line Producer Diane Knox. The show is edited by Peter Hyzak, Sean Sandefur, and Herb Sevush, being overseen by Post Production Supervisor Chen Margolis. Paul Adams, our science expert, researched the science behind the recipes along with science writer Eric Handler. Along with the on-air crew, executive chefs Erin McMurrer, Keith Dresser, and Andrea Geary helped plan and organize the 26 television episodes shot in May 2019 and ran the "back kitchen," where all the food that appeared on camera originated. Kate Shannon, Miye Bromberg, and Carolyn Grillo organized the tasting and equipment segments.

During filming, chefs Steve Dunn, Matthew Fairman, Andrew Janjigian, Cecelia Jenkins, Tonya Johnson, Lawman Johnson, Lan Lam, Amanda Luchtel, Patrice Lyon, Anne Petito, and Jessica Rudolph cooked all the food needed on set. Assistant Test Kitchen Director Alexxa Benson, Test Kitchen Manager Meridith Lippard, Test Kitchen Facilities Manager Kelly Ryan, Senior Kitchen Assistant Heather Tolmie, and Senior Kitchen Assistant/Shopper Michelle Miller were charged with making sure all the ingredients and kitchen equipment we needed were on hand. Kitchen Assistants Ena Gudiel, Blanca Castanaza, Gladis Campos, and Amarilys Merced also worked long hours. Chefs Allison Berkey, Samantha Block, Camila Chaparro, Afton Cyrus, Natalie Estrada, and Araceli Hintermeister helped coordinate the efforts of the kitchen with the television set by readying props, equipment, and food. Deva Djaafar led all tours of the test kitchen during filming.

Special thanks to director Herb Sevush (our director for all 20 seasons) and director of photography Dan Anderson. We also appreciate the hard work of the production team, including Craig Beck, Mikaela Bloomberg, Fletcher Burns, Phil Burns, Marissa Dianas, Nick Dill, Eric Fisher, Kendra Gahagan, Shawn Gauvain, Eric Goddard, Harlem Logan, Keith McManus, Jay Maurer, Claudia Moriel, Mike Mulvey, Nieves García Perchín, Lisa Roche, Mike Sills, Jennifer Tawa, Charles Turner, Tony Ventura, and Ken Willinger.

We also would like to thank Hope Reed and Karen Fritz and Dani Cook at WETA for managing station relations, and the team at American Public Television that presents the show: Cynthia Fenneman, Shawn Halford, Judy Barlow, and Tom Davison. Thanks also for production support from Zebra Productions, New York.

Sub-Zero, Wolf, and Cove; Kohler; and Pete and Gerry's Organic Eggs sponsored the show, and we thank them for their support. We also thank Sara Domville and Victoria Chin for serving our sponsors.

Meat was provided by T. F. Kinnealey & Co. of Brockton, Massachusetts. Fish was supplied by Wulf's Fish of Boston. Produce was supplied by Sid Wainer & Son.

Welcome to America's Test Kitchen

This book has been tested, written, and edited by the folks at America's Test Kitchen, where curious cooks become confident cooks. Located in Boston's Seaport District in the historic Innovation and Design Building, it features 15,000 square feet of kitchen space including multiple photography and video studios. It is the home of *Cook's Illustrated* magazine and *Cook's Country* magazine and is the workday destination for more than 60 test cooks, editors, and cookware specialists. Our mission is to empower and inspire confidence, community, and creativity in the kitchen.

We start the process of testing a recipe with a complete lack of preconceptions, which means that we accept no claim, no technique, and no recipe at face value. We simply assemble as many variations as possible, test a half-dozen of the most promising, and taste the results blind. We then construct our own recipe and continue to test it, varying ingredients, techniques, and cooking times until we reach a consensus. As we like to say in the test kitchen, "We make the mistakes so you don't have to." The result, we hope, is the best version of a particular recipe, but we realize that only you can be the final judge of our success (or failure). We use the same rigorous approach when we test equipment and taste ingredients.

All of this would not be possible without a belief that good cooking, much like good music, is based on a foundation of objective technique. Some people like spicy foods and others don't, but there is a right way to sauté, there is a best way to cook a pot roast, and there are measurable scientific principles involved in producing perfectly beaten, stable egg whites. Our ultimate goal is to investigate the fundamental principles of cooking to give you the techniques, tools, and ingredients you need to become a better cook. It is as simple as that.

To see what goes on behind the scenes at America's Test Kitchen, check out our social media channels for kitchen snapshots, exclusive content, video tips, and much more. You can watch us work (in our actual test kitchen) by tuning in to *America's Test Kitchen* or *Cook's Country* on public television or on our websites. Download our award-winning podcast *Proof*, which goes beyond recipes to solve food mysteries (AmericasTestKitchen.com/proof), or listen to test kitchen experts on public radio (SplendidTable.org) to hear insights that illuminate the truth about real home cooking. Want to hone your cooking skills or finally learn how to bake—with an America's Test Kitchen test cook? Enroll in one of our online cooking classes. And you can engage the next generation of home cooks with kid-tested recipes from America's Test Kitchen Kids.

Our community of home recipe testers provides valuable feedback on recipes under development by ensuring that they are foolproof. You can help us investigate the how and why behind successful recipes from your home kitchen. (Sign up at AmericasTestKitchen.com/recipe_testing.)

However you choose to visit us, we welcome you into our kitchen, where you can stand by our side as we test our way to the best recipes in America.

facebook.com/AmericasTestKitchen
twitter.com/TestKitchen
youtube.com/AmericasTestKitchen
instagram.com/TestKitchen
pinterest.com/TestKitchen

AmericasTestKitchen.com
CooksIllustrated.com
CooksCountry.com
OnlineCookingSchool.com
AmericasTestKitchen.com/kids

20 Amazing Years

If you watch the show (and if you're reading this book, I assume you do!), you know me as the taste test guy. The cast member who tortures his colleagues with shot glasses of fish sauce at seven in the morning. Along with Adam, Bridget, and Julia, I'm one of the four original cast members featured in all 20 seasons of the show. That's me, below, in 2000 with our director, Herb Sevush, also a 20-year veteran of the show, and a kitchen colleague. For the past four years, I've also been an executive producer of the show and made decisions about new cast members, the new set, and the new show open (which is so much fun).

Working at America's Test Kitchen has been such an honor and privilege because of the way our work impacts your lives. How do I know this? You stop me in the streets, come up to me on planes, and corner me in the supermarket and tell me how watching *America's Test Kitchen* has made you a better cook. Thank you for sharing, and keep on stopping to chat when you see me. My best fan interaction was probably 10 years ago, when our two daughters were young teens. A lovely elderly woman came over to my family and, with a twinkle in her eye, said, "Girls, your dad is in my bedroom every night." She went on to explain how watching episodes of the show was her bedtime ritual and helped her dream up new kitchen adventures in her sleep. My wife patiently listened along and ended up enjoying a good laugh.

Our daily mission in the test kitchen is quite simple. We believe that home cooking is essential. It gives us joy. It keeps us healthy. It makes us human. After all, we are social animals, and what's more social than the preparation and sharing of a good meal? When you tell me our recipes, product reviews, science explainers, and technique demos have given you the confidence to succeed in the kitchen, I know our show is doing its job.

I can't write about the show without talking about the cast and crew. Julia and Bridget are the two best cooking teachers on television. Full stop. Shut the door. Watching them makes me smarter. And their joy for cooking is infectious (in the very best way). Becky, Dan, Elle, Erin, Keith, and Lan are such pros as they cook and succinctly explain what, and why, they are doing in each step of the recipe. I trust Adam and Lisa's product reviews—and so should you. And Dan's science segments make me wish for a do-over on high school chemistry and physics. Finally, the real stars of the show are the people you never see—the producers, camera operators, editors, hair stylists, sound engineers, and wardrobe assistants who turn our recipes into amazing television episodes.

This book is the distillation of 20 years of work, a testament to the 100+ talented cooks who have labored in our test kitchens in quest of culinary perfection. We've developed 20,000 recipes in the past two decades, and the 580 recipes in this volume represent our very best work. So stop reading and get to work—you have a lot of amazing cooking in your future.

—*Jack Bishop*
Chief Creative Officer

Cast Confidential

You've watched them on TV, now you can get to know them up close and personal through their fascinating biographies, fun facts, and recipe commentaries throughout the book.

Julia Collin Davison

Found Her True Passion in the Kitchen

Julia has done just about every job at ATK—from developing recipes and leading the kitchen books team to 20 years of showing America how to cook on camera.

Hometown Rochester, New York

Culinary School The Culinary Institute of America

Favorite Cuisine Indian

Secret Food Craving Sour cream and onion potato chips

Music I Play While Cooking Reggae

Most Beloved Cookbook *The America's Test Kitchen Family Cookbook* (the original red ringbound edition)

Favorite Dinner Party Recipe Grilled Paella from *Cook's Illustrated*

Ingredient I Cannot Live Without Scallions

❝ I come from a long line of great cooks (and good eaters). The best cook of them all is my mother, Winifred, who has always been a bit ahead of her time, growing organic vegetables, grinding meat for hamburger, and steering clear of processed food. My love of cooking really came from hanging out with her in the kitchen growing up.

After graduating from college, I attended the Culinary Institute of America in Hyde Park, New York, and the light bulb went off over my head: I was meant to be a cook. I worked for a variety of restaurants, catering companies, and wineries after graduating from the CIA, but finally landed my dream job at *Cook's Illustrated* in the summer of 1999. At the beginning, I was the last name on the masthead, and my daily work included washing the dishes, helping the editors with their prep, and shopping for groceries, but I didn't mind. I loved the inside look at the process of breaking down recipes to understand how they worked.

Within a few months, I began to develop my own recipes for the magazine, and then in 2000, we filmed our first TV show. I had no idea that the show would be such a success, much less that I'd be the host of the show 20 years later!

The most memorable TV moment for me was in the first week of filming as the new host. I was as nervous as could be, until we shot the sticky bun episode on the third day. At the tasting, Bridget and I completely lost our composure and broke down in fits of laughter in front of the cameras. At first, I worried that our exuberant behavior was unprofessional, but then realized that it was quite the opposite. We were simply being ourselves and enjoying the good cooking, good food, and good company. To me, that's the whole point." ❞

Bridget Lancaster
Hates Winter, Loves Her Job

Good fortune or just a fluke? Bridget reveals how she got her big break in culinary showbiz.

❝ My career at America's Test Kitchen can largely be attributed to being in the right place at the right time. Back in the late 1990s, I was working two jobs in Boston to pay the rent—I'd get up before the crack of dawn to start my job as a pastry chef, and then move to my second job working retail at Williams-Sonoma. One of my coworkers at WS mentioned that they were looking for a new test cook at the magazine that she worked for: *Cook's Illustrated*. I'd been a subscriber to the magazine for a few years (it was the old pecan pie recipe that sealed my allegiance), so I met with the *Cook's Illustrated* folks, performed a few tests to show if I had any kitchen proficiency, and landed the job.

Cut to a couple of years later when there was talk about developing a version of *Cook's Illustrated* for television. We were all curious (OK, skeptical) as to whether people would actually watch a show about how we tear apart a recipe, test each variable, and then build a newer, foolproof version. I mean, we knew we were food nerds, and proud of it—but would America tune in?

And who was going to be on this show? Test cooks? We weren't TV people, we were kitchen people. Were they going to bring in more camera-savvy personalities from the outside? But it was soon revealed that it was very important that the 'cast' should consist of people who were already immersed in the day-to-day recipe testing and methodology. So, if you were working in the test kitchen, guess what? Welcome to TV!

More than 20 years later, *America's Test Kitchen* is at the start of its next 20-year run, and I'm still here. My personal life has changed a lot over the past two decades—my husband and I have two gorgeous sons now, plus George—my big, old sloppy 185-pound Newfoundland dog. My home cooking strategies have changed a bit too—I'm always looking for ways to double recipes, freeze leftovers, make as much ahead as I possibly can. Anything that I can do to make dinner simpler and streamlined, I consider a victory.

But I think I'm still the same person. I continue to drive an old-model, stick-shift car to and from work even though the gridlock reminds me that I should switch to automatic transmission. Despite being told that I would 'get used to them,' I still despise the long New England winters and fantasize about moving down South to escape the cold. But I also still love walking through the doors at ATK and seeing the people that I work with."

Hometown Cross Lanes, West Virginia

Favorite Cuisine Indian

Joined the Show 2001

Food I Will Not Eat Beets (they taste like dirt)

Ingredient I Cannot Live Without None—I like a good challenge

When I'm Not Cooking You'll Find Me Brewing beer or watching old movies

Favorite Food Destination Rome

Secret Food Craving Kale. Just kidding! A bowl of Frosted Flakes

Erin McMurrer

Organizer-in-Chief at America's Test Kitchen

Erin makes our kitchens run like clockwork—but she's also a talented cook and can be seen cooking in front of the cameras, too.

Hometown Scituate, Massachusetts

Culinary School The Culinary Institute of America

Secret Food Craving Jelly Belly jelly beans

Music I Play While Cooking Acoustic guitar (Rodrigo y Gabriela)

Most Beloved Cookbook *Bistro Cooking at Home* by Gordon Hamersley

Ingredient I Cannot Live Without Avocados

First ATK Recipe on Air Baked Stuffed Shrimp

First Recipe Developed at ATK Blueberry Cobbler

" When I look back on my early love of food I'm reminded of just how much home-ec class in high school resonated with me. My teacher, Mrs. Ditommaso, not only taught me the basics of cooking and how to prepare simple meals, but more importantly she taught me how much fun and how satisfying cooking could be. She was my biggest cheerleader in those early days, and was the one who first suggested that I attend culinary school (thank you Mrs. D!).

Throughout high school I worked at a bustling little clam shack. This gave me a taste of the unique and fast-paced world of restaurant kitchens, which I loved. But the real start of my cooking career was at Hamersley's Bistro in Boston, Massachusetts, where I worked for eight years. The owner, Gordon Hamersley, took me under his wing and taught me everything, from how to dress the perfect salad to how to roast the perfect chicken. His menus highlighted seasonal and local high-quality ingredients, which he always prepared in simple and pure ways to allow their natural flavors and textures to shine. That really stuck with me.

For the last 18 years, though, I've been the test kitchen director at ATK. During this time, my role has evolved. In addition to working with my team to manage the 15,000-square-foot test kitchen and all of the systems required to make it run smoothly, I have also developed recipes and co-managed recipe development for *Cook's Illustrated*, I've been overseeing the back kitchen for 19 seasons of *America's Test Kitchen*, and I managed the back kitchen for the first six seasons of *Cook's Country*.

I've also had a role in front of the cameras for both TV shows. Being on camera pushes me out of my comfort zone, so it has forced me to learn some new skills. Watching the true ATK veterans over the years has really helped.

What I love the most about working at America's Test Kitchen are the countless opportunities that have come my way as the company has grown and changed, and the many talented, smart, and fun people that I get to work with on a daily basis—all united in a mission to teach America how to cook. What could be better and more fulfilling than that?"

Keith Dresser

From a Maine Island to Prime-Time TV

Keith is a classically trained chef whose restaurant experience and cooking skills led him to running recipe development at *Cook's Illustrated*.

❝ I grew up on an island in Maine called Arrowsic, near Bath. I was a picky eater (my mother would have stronger words for it). I didn't know how much I liked food until I worked one summer as a prep cook and dishwasher at The Osprey in Robinhood, Maine. I admired the chef, and I loved the feeling at the end of the night when people left satisfied because of the food we made for them. The chef was a celebrity in our small community, but he took me into his kitchen and introduced me to culinary adventures. Like many kids, I had simple tastes and a sweet tooth, but not until I worked at The Osprey did I get hooked on the idea of preparing and exploring food as a career.

I enrolled at New England Culinary Institute in Vermont after high school. Getting up at 3 a.m. for bread baking classes when it was 10 degrees below zero was the biggest challenge. Otherwise, I loved learning every facet of food preparation, from mastering techniques to navigating a professional kitchen, learning about wine, and getting to know the fine points of service. My teachers were mostly French inspired (and French!), and so I would say I am 'classically trained.' But since school, I have always loved diverse cuisines. While I excelled at necessities such as knife skills, butchering, and kitchen logistics, I was a terrible waiter (NECI made us do that too!). This cemented my place in the kitchen.

After culinary school, I worked in restaurants in Cape Cod, Detroit, and Boston for 10 years. I love the teamwork required in restaurant kitchens. It is hard and relentless, but you laugh a lot and friendships run deep in that intense environment. I took time off to get my bachelor's degree, and then started at ATK in 2002. I began as a test cook, wrote my first article in 2003 after some years on the book team, and rose through the ranks at *Cook's Illustrated*. I am now the executive food editor leading recipe development for the magazine. All along, I have been working behind the scenes on the television show. In fact, my first day at ATK was the first day of filming for Season 3. There are a lot of similarities between filming the television show and the high energy and frantic food preparation of restaurant kitchens. I get the best of both worlds at ATK.

I've only been on camera for four seasons, and so now I experience the show from all sides. I am involved with most of the recipes demonstrated on air, I cook much of the food, and now I also get to talk about it with Julia and Bridget on camera."

Hometown Arrowsic, Maine

Culinary School New England Culinary Institute

Secret Food Craving Smoked almonds

Music I Play While Cooking Anything that you can play loud

Most Beloved Cookbook A collection of family recipes that my wife put together

Favorite Dinner Party Recipe Chocolate Pots de Crème from *Cook's Illustrated*

Ingredient I Cannot Live Without Lemons

Becky Hays
Inspired by Julia Child

Becky's lifelong love of cooking started when she began watching *The French Chef.* Now things have come full circle.

Hometown Westfield, Massachusetts

Secret Food Craving Hot artichoke dip and saltines

Joined the Show 2005

First Recipe Developed at ATK Southeast Asian–Style Spring Rolls

When I'm Not Cooking You'll Find Me In my garden

Favorite Cooking Companions My sister, Val, and my son, Nate

Favorite Food Destination Paris

Food I Will Not Eat Durian

❝ My third-grade after-school routine went like this:

Grab a snack, flop down on the couch, and turn on our black-and-white TV to catch my idol, Julia Child, in action. I'd hum along to *The French Chef* theme song, then watch, captivated by the day's preparation. She was everything I wanted to be: smart, confident, and talented in the kitchen. Following her lead and with my mom at my side, I went on to make every recipe I could get my hands on, mostly from my grandmother's 1931 edition of *Joy of Cooking.* Now held together at the spine by duct tape, it was one of the few cookbooks my family owned. Not only did I cook and bake many of its recipes, but I devoured its pages as if it were a novel. Check it out if you ever want to learn how to prepare turtle, squirrel, beaver, raccoon, or even muskrat.

Fast-forward a few years, and I earned degrees in French and economics, helping me to land a job on Wall Street. The work was satisfying and life in New York thrilling, but after five years, I was ready for a change, so I enrolled at the Natural Gourmet Institute, where I learned the whys and hows of what I had been doing in the kitchen for so long. Soon after graduation, a position at *Cook's Illustrated* opened up, and I was delighted to get hired. That was 20 years ago.

My role at America's Test Kitchen has evolved over the past two decades, but two things have remained constant: being surrounded by energetic, intelligent, and passionate colleagues and a never-ending stream of amazing food. These days, I spend my time as the deputy editor of *Cook's Illustrated.* My main task is to edit the copy for the magazine with the goal of providing our readers with everything they need to produce A+ versions of every dish, along with an entertaining account of the recipe development process. And of course, I make it my mission to taste test everything in sight.

When it comes time to film the TV show, my job changes dramatically. I practice my TV recipes for my family beforehand: It's fun to let them taste what I'll be making on camera and to discuss the scenes. Then, it's a stretch of 6 a.m. call times, lots of laughter, and more great food. Even after all these years, I still pinch myself every time I walk onto the set, grateful to follow in Julia's footsteps."

Dan Souza

Making Mom and Dad Proud

Whether in front of the camera or editing the pages of *Cook's Illustrated* magazine, Dan strives to teach and inspire cooks in the same way his family empowered him.

66 My first big break in entertainment came at age 10, when I landed the starring role in my elementary school's production of *Robin Hood*. My dad carved me a wooden sword, giving it coats of gold and silver spray paint and, for durability during battle scenes, a final lacquer of urethane. My mom sewed my kelly-green costume and helped me practice my lines. On opening night I gave it my all on stage trying to hit my marks, screaming my lines, and fake-kissing Maid Marian.

Over the past 27 years this pattern has repeated itself over and over. I go after something big—whether a career change and enrollment in culinary school, a cooking gig at Le Bernardin in New York City, a chance to be a cast member on *America's Test Kitchen*, or the position of editor in chief of *Cook's Illustrated*—and my parents step in with spray paint, sewing kits, love, and deep support.

I've absorbed so much from them. From my mom, I earned a deep curiosity and passion for food. A Mainer and baker by birth, she filled my childhood home with warmth, a glowing energy, and, yes, lots of excellent blueberry pie. From my dad, I gained a sense of pragmatism and an appreciation for things made well, by hand. As a kid I always knew to look for him in his basement workshop, where he'd fix the things my sister and I broke around the house, carve intricate faces into swoopy lengths of driftwood, and build furniture for my mom.

I never imagined my life as a performer would extend much beyond those early days in Sherwood Forest, let alone be a real part of my career in food. Even now, after being a part of the show for seven years, each episode remains a 'someone pinch me' kind of experience.

As editor in chief of *Cook's Illustrated*, I lead the ridiculously talented team that develops and crafts every recipe that appears in the magazine and on *America's Test Kitchen*. Our daily task is to help cooks be successful every time they enter the kitchen. It is, for me, the very definition of a dream job. And if that weren't enough, for three special weeks every May when we film a new season of the show I get to sharpen my knives, put on my pressed navy chef coat, step in front of the cameras, and scream my lines."

Hometown Westford, Massachusetts

Culinary School The Culinary Institute of America

Favorite Cuisine New England coastal cooking

Secret Food Craving Noodles in all forms

Music I Play While Cooking Pop music and cooking both make me feel good, so it's a powerful combination

Most Beloved Cookbook *Pok Pok*, by Andy Ricker

Favorite Dinner Party Recipe Slow-Roasted Pork Shoulder from *Cook's Illustrated*

Ingredient I Cannot Live Without Fish sauce

Lisa McManus

Can't Stay Out of the Kitchen

From her earliest days, our gadget expert has had an obsession with tasting and testing.

Hometown Lincoln, Rhode Island

Joined the Show 2010

Secret Food Craving Freshly baked, crusty baguette with salted butter

When I'm Not Cooking You'll Find Me In the kitchen anyway—it's my happy place.

Thing I Try Not to Say on TV "It's so easy." I jinxed myself by saying this right before I had to demo an electric wine opener. With the cameras rolling, I half-opened a whole case of wine before I got it right.

" I grew up in an Italian American family, with a mom who said she hated cooking. In evidence to the contrary, she drove miles out of her way every week to shop at the fruit market, butcher, baker, and a few different supermarkets, where she'd scout out the best, freshest food. She put a terrific from-scratch meal on the table every night. And she taught me without saying a word that if you buy the right ingredients, good cooking almost takes care of itself. Now that I'm a parent, I have even more appreciation for what she accomplished. Back then, all I knew was that I loved hanging around our kitchen 'helping,' but mostly snagging bites of everything in progress.

Mom was bemused when I would rush home from school to watch PBS where Julia Child cooked and Graham Kerr's knife flew through food like lightning. In junior high, my best friend and I taught ourselves to bake bread, and even brought a fresh loaf to church for communion. (I'd never imagined people coming back for seconds under those circumstances, but they did.)

By college, my friends and I were taking on self-imposed cooking challenges like boning, stuffing, and roasting whole chickens, or making mincemeat or croissants from scratch. I lived at Brown University's French House, where students prepared elaborate dinners every night. I was always in the kitchen, and usually turning in my research papers at the last minute. My editors might say that some things never change.

After college I worked as a journalist for several years, eventually becoming a newspaper food editor before landing my dream job here in the test kitchen. To me, testing equipment is about making sure a product really works for home cooks, and doesn't waste your money, effort, or time. I've always deeply researched my own purchases, so doing it for others comes naturally. (Ask me sometime about how I figured out which car to buy.)

I'm starting my 14th year at ATK, and I've loved every minute of it. I'll never forget my first story, trying out for the job: Tasting apple cider vinegar. I forced staffers to drink 10 different vinegars and they still hired me. A miracle. The best thing about this place is my colleagues. It's wonderful to work with people who have such an incredible depth and breadth of knowledge and skills; people who are full of creativity and curiosity. I'm inspired every day."

Adam Ried

Enjoying the Ride

There was some early career careening, thankfully with a fan-tastic ending!

66 Though I've loved to cook forever, recognizing it as a potential vocation came late. In high school and college I cycled through numerous career ideas (including cartographer!) before settling on architecture. After college I sweet-talked my way into an architecture program in Boston, set up camp here, hit the drafting board… and flamed out in short order. A few more years passed before a colleague, who saw in me what I was missing in myself, pushed me toward cooking school.

The program was a blast, and it changed everything. Along the way I met Anne Tuomey and Doc Willoughby, two editors at *Cook's Illustrated* who helped pave my way toward a freelance gig doing recipe and equipment research, which, to my amazement and delight, became a full-time job in early 1995. By the time *America's Test Kitchen* launched in 2001, I was running the equipment testing program, so I was slotted right into that role on the show, where I have remained happily ever since.

Over the years I've developed rituals around writing and studying my scripts—write, revise twice, and read the final versions five times, highlighting them twice along the way. I haven't been tossed off the show yet, so it's probably a plan worth sticking to. But even after thorough prep, I still get nervous about keeping all the information straight. Once I'm on set though, I relax (a little), essentially ignore the cameras (specific directions from the control room excepted—here's looking at you, Herb!), and simply talk to the host.

Honestly, one of the most enjoyable—and surreal—aspects of having spent 20 years on TV occurs not on set but in the streets, when I get stopped by fans of the show. Though it happens with surprising regularity, I'm always amused that someone would want to talk to me. Aside from a couple of months each year during production, TV isn't a main thrust in my day-to-day existence. Mostly I just live my quiet life, which is why it's such a kick when someone knows who I am and wants to say hi.

The diversity of ATK fans is also a thrill, from a kid of about 5 who spotted me at a classic car show to gruff construction workers to a group of grandmothers at the wedding of one of their granddaughters, where I happened to pass by. As I chatted away with the women, the bride even came over to find out why her grandmother wasn't getting into the pictures at the reception—because she was taking a selfie with me!"

Ingredients I Cannot Live Without Extra-virgin olive oil, lemons, parsley, garlic

Secret Food Craving Cheese puffs, tuna noodle casserole

Food I Will Not Eat Truffle oil

Last Earthly Meal (if I have a choice) Paella or fidueà (allioli mandatory)

First Recipe Developed at ATK Basil Pesto

White or Red? White… Alsatian, please

Mountains or Beaches? Why choose?

Lan Lam

A Line Cook Turned Recipe Developer

Lan spent nine years in fast-paced restaurant kitchens preparing for what she didn't know would ultimately be her dream job.

Hometown Mountain View, California

Culinary School Boston restaurant scene

Favorite Cuisine Vietnamese

Secret Food Craving The fatty nubbin on a rib eye

Ingredient I Cannot Live Without Eggs

Food I Will Not Eat Every so often, I try foods I dislike to see if my tastes have changed. (I no longer avoid beets. Still working on tahini.)

First Recipe Developed at ATK Farmhouse Vegetable and Barley Soup

❝ The summer between junior and senior year of college I worked in the library at Wesleyan University. One of the librarians knew of my interest in food and science, and one day she handed me Harold McGee's *On Food and Cooking*. Two chapters, 'Cooking Methods and Utensil Materials' and 'The Four Basic Food Molecules,' fascinated me. I was a chemistry major, but what I really wanted to do was enroll in culinary school. I spent that summer reading about the science of cooking, and daydreaming about becoming a chef.

It wasn't until a couple of years after graduation that I was ready to give cooking a try. I landed an internship with the pastry team at UpStairs on the Square, a restaurant in Cambridge, Massachusetts. At a time when restaurant kitchens were dominated by men, I happened upon an oasis. UpStairs was owned by two women and its kitchens were led by women, too. Under their tutelage, I realized that culinary school wasn't necessary. I started cooking full-time and eventually transitioned to the savory side of the kitchen.

As my career progressed, I remained enthralled by the high-energy vibe of dinner service, the joy that comes in creating delicious and beautiful food, and most of all the pleasure of working with diverse people—in and out of the kitchen—who are the heart and soul of all restaurants. It was from them that I learned that a discerning palate, exceptional knife skills, or an encyclopedic knowledge of food and technique don't necessarily make you a great cook. They taught me by example that it's more important to know your ingredients and your equipment, and how they interact with each other.

I also learned, ultimately, that the restaurant lifestyle wasn't the best fit for me. Unsure what my next move would be, I applied for a test cook position at America's Test Kitchen. It wasn't long before I realized that I had landed my ideal job. Every day, I am able to combine my love of cooking with the joy of intense collaboration, working alongside people who are equally passionate and curious about food. I've only recently joined the cast of *America's Test Kitchen* and fittingly, I get to work with and learn from another pair of talented women." ❞

Elle Simone Scott

From Behind the Scenes to On the Screen

Elle's culinary road has taken lots of twists and turns, but she's found her niche on camera and in the photo studio at ATK.

❝ I've been cooking as long as I can remember—basically since I was so little I had to sit on phone books to reach the food on the table! I probably could've guessed that I'd be a food stylist, had I known what it was back then. I used to have an assembly line of mud pies, using the pans from my Easy-Bake Oven (once I'd baked all the batters). There was a bush with little red buds that I would pick off to decorate my 'pies.' I remember never wanting to do the same thing twice in a week.

Needless to say, I've been doing this food styling thing for a long time. It's primarily what I do here at ATK when I'm not on camera as a test cook. Styling is my passion and it offers such a variety of projects that it keeps me excited. My favorite styling project to date has been for our upcoming book, *How to Cocktail*. It was my first experience styling cocktails and I'm super-proud of the work.

I came to America's Test Kitchen after living in New York for almost 10 years, where I worked as a freelance food stylist but also produced a host of cooking shows. Oddly enough, even though I had experience similar to what I do here, I was very nervous working on the other side of the camera. It's a lot of pressure to do all the simultaneous tasks that come with being on television—cooking, talking, and teaching— all while being YOURSELF! I ease the pressure by starting the day with lots of hugs, greetings, and high-fives to remind myself that this is a team effort and we're in this together. I also just remain very transparent about my feelings; hey, I'm nervous! I'm also comforted by watching my past episodes (*Snickerdoodles* is my FAVE, btw) and seeing how much I've improved over time.

Even though ATK has millions of fans and followers, I'm still always smitten to meet you all at our Boston and Seattle EATS events. I'm a little shy but I love it when fans want to chat, take pictures, and ask interesting questions about ATK.

Finally, a personal fun fact is that I LOVE BEER and know quite a bit about it."

Hometown Detroit, Michigan

Culinary School Culinary Academy of New York

Favorite Cuisine Caribbean

Secret Food Craving Butter-pecan ice cream

Music I Play While Cooking Jazz

Most Beloved Cookbook *Plantation Row Slave Cabin Cooking: The Roots of Soul Food*, by Patricia Mitchell

Ingredient I Cannot Live Without Sriracha

Jack Bishop
Can Do More than Just Talk

For 20 years, our taste-test expert has been helping home cooks figure out which supermarket ingredients are best—and which ones don't measure up.

Hometown Mountain Lakes, New Jersey

Culinary School Self-taught

Favorite Cuisine Italian

Joined the Show 2001

First On-Air Segment Canned tomatoes

Food I Will Not Eat I'll try anything once

Ingredient I Cannot Live Without Maldon salt

First Recipe Developed at ATK Vanilla Ice Cream

" I'm the only cast member who doesn't 'do' anything.

Julia and Bridget host and cook. Dan demystifies food science and cooks. Elle, Becky, Keith, Erin, and Lan all cook. Adam and Lisa show how kitchen gear works. My job is to talk. Ask my mother and she will tell you I was born to be the taste-test expert. My favorite toddler toys were a pretend phone and a broom (don't ask my wife about my neatness obsession). I also like to 'explain' things (just ask my younger siblings). My parents assumed I would become a lawyer. That's a profession that depends on talking and persuasion, right?

It turned out I was a writer and editor who liked to cook. I owe my love of cooking to my mother, and her mother. When I was 12 years old, my mother, Judith Bishop, went from stay-at-home parent, busy with three kids, to on-air television newsreader and reporter at a local UHF station (this was before cable). The station provided live financial information throughout the day—think CNBC but with fuzzy reception. My mother is an excellent talker and quickly mastered the details of the commodity market and interest rates.

My mother's work hours were long. We could have dinner at 8 p.m. or, as the oldest, I could take charge. (My dad could do many things but cooking wasn't one of them.) So my mother taught me to cook by phone. Remember, we like to talk. She would call from work and walk me through a recipe. I was a quick study and I soon mastered her repertoire: meatloaf, spaghetti with clams (canned), flank steak 'pot roast' (thank you, Lipton Onion Soup Mix).

As my confidence grew, I became more adventurous and looked to my maternal grandmother for inspiration. Katherine Pizzarello made the best lasagna on the planet and her love of vegetables shaped my early culinary sensibilities. I learned to appreciate fennel, radicchio, broccoli rabe, and escarole at my grandparents' dining room table.

So, yes, you know me as the guy on the show who likes to talk. But I'm also a very good home cook. My knife skills can't compare to my colleagues and I never worked in a restaurant. But show up at my home on Thanksgiving and ask my relatives (24 were in attendance last year) what they think. Let's just say they are very happy. Of course, I'm serving many America's Test Kitchen recipes, which always makes me look like a pro."

Breakfast and Brunch

Eggs Benedict with Foolproof Hollandaise

"A humble plate of scrambled eggs was one of the first dishes I learned to cook as a kid, and one of my earliest recipe assignments as a test cook for Cook's Illustrated. It's also one of the easiest ways to make breakfast actually feel like the most important meal of the day. I'll take the purist's form—enriched with a little half-and-half and seasoned generously with salt and pepper—any day of the week, but I certainly don't have to when it's so easy to dress them up. Here we trade dairy for grassy, peppery olive oil and perfectly time our additions of crisp-tender asparagus and silky smoked salmon. The effect is something that feels special, even luxurious. Did I say humble?"

—Dan

Fluffy Scrambled Eggs

Serves 4

WHY THIS RECIPE WORKS Sometimes the simplest things can be the hardest to get right. Scrambled eggs are a good example. Seemingly easy to make, they can easily go wrong, and overcooking is probably the most common problem. We wanted scrambled eggs that turn out of the pan into a mound of large, soft curds—cooked enough to hold their shape but soft enough to eat with a spoon. We learned that beating the eggs too much before cooking them can result in toughness, so we whisked our eggs just until they were combined. Milk was better than water as an addition to scrambled eggs; the sugar, proteins, and fat in milk helped create large curds, which trapped steam for that pillowy texture we were after. A nonstick skillet was a must to prevent sticking, and pan size mattered as well; if the skillet was too large, the eggs spread out in too thin a layer and overcooked. Getting the pan hot was crucial for moist, puffy curds, and constant gentle stirring—really more like pushing and folding—prevented overcooking. Cooked on the stove until they were almost done, which took only a couple of minutes, these eggs finished cooking on the way to the table, remaining moist and meltingly soft. These eggs cook very quickly, so it's important to be ready to eat before you start to cook them.

- 8 **large eggs**
- ½ **cup milk**
- ½ **teaspoon table salt**
  Pinch pepper
- 1 **tablespoon unsalted butter**

1. Whisk eggs, milk, salt, and pepper in bowl until any streaks are gone and color is pure yellow.

2. Melt butter in 10-inch nonstick skillet over high heat, swirling to coat pan. Add egg mixture and, using rubber spatula, cook while gently pushing, lifting, and folding from 1 side of pan to other as eggs form curds. Continue until eggs are nicely clumped into single mound but remain shiny and wet, 1½ to 2 minutes. Serve.

Making Fluffy Scrambled Eggs

Pushing and folding eggs with a rubber spatula helps form large, soft curds.

Hearty Scrambled Eggs with Asparagus and Salmon

SEASON 20 RECIPE

Serves 4

WHY THIS RECIPE WORKS When you want a heartier take on scrambled eggs, it's tempting to round up whatever leftover cooked veggies are stashed in the refrigerator, toss them in a hot skillet with beaten eggs, and stir until curds form. But we wanted a fresh take on scrambled eggs, one that we could actually replicate in the future. This meant staying away from heavy add-ins such as meat and cheese and mundane vegetables such as onions and peppers. We nixed spinach and Swiss chard: They tended to weep after cooking, making the eggs watery. Superdelicate greens were also out: They liked to clump, which made them difficult to disperse evenly. We settled on fresh asparagus, chives, and luxurious smoked salmon. The test kitchen likes to add dairy to beaten eggs, which makes fantastic classic scrambled eggs. But for this fresher take, we wanted to use extra-virgin olive oil for its grassy savoriness. Using oil would also reduce the amount of moisture we were adding to our eggs, ensuring that the asparagus would not get soggy. We beat some oil into the eggs, along with chives, salt, and pepper, and also used the oil, instead of butter, to cook the eggs. Just before they were fully cooked we added the asparagus, which we had quickly rendered crisp-tender first in a skillet. We then transferred our dish to a serving platter, draped it with glossy pieces of smoked salmon, and added more fresh chives. If you can't find thin asparagus, peel the bottom halves of the spears until the white flesh is exposed and then halve each spear lengthwise, before cutting it into ½-inch pieces. If desired, all ingredient amounts can be halved; use a 10-inch skillet.

- 8 **large eggs**
- 3 **tablespoons extra-virgin olive oil, divided**
- 2 **tablespoons minced fresh chives, divided**
- ¼ **teaspoon table salt**
- ¼ **teaspoon pepper**
- 1 **garlic clove, minced**
- 8 **ounces thin asparagus, trimmed and cut into ½-inch lengths**
- 2 **tablespoons water**
- 2 **ounces smoked salmon, torn into ½-inch strips**

1. In medium bowl, beat eggs, 2 tablespoons oil, 1 tablespoon chives, salt, and pepper with fork until no streaks of white remain. Heat 1 teaspoon oil and garlic in 12-inch nonstick skillet over medium heat until fragrant, about 1 minute. Add asparagus and water, cover, and cook, stirring occasionally, until asparagus is crisp-tender, 3 to 4 minutes. Uncover and continue to cook until moisture has evaporated, about 1 minute longer. Transfer asparagus mixture to small bowl and set aside. Wipe skillet clean with paper towels.

2. Heat remaining 2 teaspoons oil in now-empty skillet over medium-high heat until shimmering. Add egg mixture and, using rubber spatula, constantly and firmly scrape along bottom and sides of skillet until eggs begin to clump and spatula just leaves trail on bottom of skillet, 30 to 60 seconds. Reduce heat to low and gently but constantly fold eggs until clumped and just slightly wet, 30 to 60 seconds. Fold in asparagus mixture. Transfer to serving dish, top with salmon, sprinkle with remaining 1 tablespoon chives, and serve.

VARIATIONS

Hearty Scrambled Eggs with Pinto Beans and Cotija Cheese

If cotija cheese is unavailable, you can substitute feta cheese. This recipe can be easily halved, if desired; use a 10-inch skillet. We like to serve these eggs with warm tortillas and hot sauce.

- 8 large eggs
- 3 tablespoons extra-virgin olive oil, divided
- ¼ teaspoon table salt
- ¼ cup jarred sliced jalapeños, chopped coarse
- 2 garlic cloves, minced
- 1 (15-ounce) can pinto beans, rinsed
- ¼ cup chopped fresh cilantro, divided
- 1 ounce cotija cheese, crumbled (¼ cup)

1. In medium bowl, beat eggs, 2 tablespoons oil, and salt with fork until no streaks of white remain. Heat 1 teaspoon olive oil, jalapeños, and garlic in 12-inch nonstick skillet over medium heat until fragrant, about 1 minute. Add beans and 3 tablespoons cilantro and cook, stirring frequently, until moisture has evaporated, about 1 minute. Transfer bean mixture to small bowl and set aside. Wipe skillet clean with paper towels.

2. Heat remaining 2 teaspoons oil in now-empty skillet over medium-high heat until shimmering. Add egg mixture and, using rubber spatula, constantly and firmly scrape along bottom and sides of skillet until eggs begin to clump and spatula just leaves trail on bottom of skillet, 30 to 60 seconds. Reduce heat to low and gently but constantly fold eggs until clumped and just slightly wet, 30 to 60 seconds. Fold in bean mixture. Transfer to serving dish, sprinkle with cotija and remaining 1 tablespoon cilantro, and serve.

Hearty Scrambled Eggs with Shiitake Mushrooms and Feta Cheese

This recipe can be easily halved, if desired; use a 10-inch skillet. Oyster or cremini mushrooms can be substituted for the shiitake mushrooms, if desired; to prepare the oyster or cremini mushrooms, trim the stems but do not remove them. Pre-crumbled feta is often coated with cellulose to keep it from caking. For the best results, buy a block of feta and crumble it yourself.

- 8 large eggs
- 3 tablespoons extra-virgin olive oil, divided
- ¼ teaspoon table salt, divided
- ¼ teaspoon pepper
- 1 shallot, minced
- 1 teaspoon minced fresh thyme
- 8 ounces shiitake mushrooms, stemmed and sliced thin
- ¼ cup water
- 1 ounce feta cheese, crumbled (¼ cup)

1. In medium bowl, beat eggs, 2 tablespoons oil, ⅛ teaspoon salt, and pepper with fork until no streaks of white remain. Heat 1 teaspoon oil, shallot, thyme, and remaining ⅛ teaspoon salt in 12-inch nonstick skillet over medium heat, stirring occasionally, until shallot is softened and beginning to brown, 2 to 3 minutes. Add mushrooms and water, cover, and cook, stirring frequently, until mushrooms are softened, 5 to 8 minutes. Uncover and continue to cook until moisture has evaporated, 2 to 3 minutes longer. Transfer mushroom mixture to small bowl and set aside. Wipe skillet clean with paper towels.

2. Heat remaining 2 teaspoons oil in now-empty skillet over medium-high heat until shimmering. Add egg mixture and, using rubber spatula, constantly and firmly scrape along bottom and sides of skillet until eggs begin to clump and spatula just leaves trail on bottom of skillet, 30 to 60 seconds. Reduce heat to low and gently but constantly fold eggs until clumped and just slightly wet, 30 to 60 seconds. Fold in mushroom mixture. Transfer to serving dish, sprinkle with feta, and serve.

Perfect Fried Eggs

Serves 2

WHY THIS RECIPE WORKS There are two common problems when it comes to fried eggs: undercooked whites and overcooked yolks. A hot nonstick skillet, a touch of butter, and a lid combine to produce perfectly cooked fried eggs—with crisp edges, tender whites, and runny yolks—in just a few minutes. When checking the eggs for doneness, lift the lid just a crack to prevent loss of steam should they need further cooking. When cooked, the thin layer of white surrounding the yolk will turn opaque, but the yolk should remain runny. To cook two eggs, use an 8- or 9-inch nonstick skillet and halve the amounts of oil and butter. You can use this method with extra-large or jumbo eggs without altering the timing.

2 teaspoons vegetable oil
4 large eggs
¼ teaspoon table salt
⅛ teaspoon pepper
2 teaspoons unsalted butter, cut into
   4 pieces and chilled

1. Heat oil in 12-inch nonstick skillet over low heat for 5 minutes. Meanwhile, crack 2 eggs into small bowl and season with salt and pepper. Repeat with remaining 2 eggs and second small bowl.

2. Increase heat to medium-high and heat until oil is shimmering. Add butter to skillet and quickly swirl to coat pan. Working quickly, pour 1 bowl of eggs in 1 side of pan and second bowl of eggs in other side. Cover and cook for 1 minute. Remove skillet from burner and let stand, covered, 15 to 45 seconds for runny yolks (white around edge of yolk will be barely opaque), 45 to 60 seconds for soft but set yolks, and about 2 minutes for medium-set yolks. Slide eggs onto plates and serve.

Making Perfect Fried Eggs

1. Heat oil in nonstick skillet over low heat for 5 minutes.

2. While skillet heats, crack 2 eggs into small bowl. Repeat with remaining eggs and second small bowl.

3. Increase heat. Add butter and swirl to coat pan. Working quickly, position bowls on either side of skillet and add eggs simultaneously.

4. Cover and cook 1 minute. Remove skillet from burner and let stand, covered, until eggs achieve desired doneness.

Perfect Poached Eggs

Serves 2

WHY THIS RECIPE WORKS This is the best method, bar none, for making perfect poached eggs every single time because it solves one of the biggest challenges to poaching eggs—producing a tender, tidy white. It starts with draining the eggs in a colander. This allows the thin, loose whites that would cook up wispy and ragged to slip away before cooking. We transferred the eggs to a liquid measuring cup and deposited them into the water one by one to prevent them from being jostled. Salted water with vinegar helped the whites set up quickly, ensuring that the faster-cooking yolks would still be liquid by the time the whites were cooked through. Poaching the eggs in a Dutch oven filled with just 6 cups of water left plenty of headspace above the eggs so that steam fully cooked the notoriously gooey portion of the white nearest the yolk. We gently poached the eggs by bringing the water to a boil, adding the eggs, covering the pot, and letting them cook off the heat for 3 minutes. Once the cover was removed, we checked the eggs individually, removing them once the white nearest to the yolk was just set. For the best results, be sure to use the freshest eggs possible. This recipe can be used to cook from one to four eggs. To make two batches of eggs to serve all at once, transfer four cooked eggs directly to a large pot of 150-degree water and cover them. This will keep them warm for 15 minutes or so while you return the poaching water to a boil and cook the next batch. We like to serve these eggs on buttered toast or toasted and buttered English muffins or on salads made with assertively flavored greens.

4 large eggs
1 tablespoon distilled white vinegar
   Table salt for cooking eggs

1. Bring 6 cups water to boil in Dutch oven over high heat. Meanwhile, crack eggs, one at a time, into colander. Let stand until loose, watery whites drain away from eggs, 20 to 30 seconds. Gently transfer eggs to 2-cup liquid measuring cup.

2. Add vinegar and 1 teaspoon salt to boiling water. Remove pot from heat. With lip of measuring cup just above surface of water, gently tip eggs into water, one at a time, leaving space between them. Cover pot and let stand until whites closest to yolks are just set and opaque, about 3 minutes. If after 3 minutes whites are not set, let stand in water, checking every 30 seconds, until eggs reach desired doneness. (For medium-cooked yolks, let eggs sit in pot, covered, for 4 minutes, then begin checking for doneness.)

3. Using slotted spoon, carefully lift and drain each egg over Dutch oven. Season with salt and pepper to taste, and serve.

Eggs Benedict with Foolproof Hollandaise

Serves 4

WHY THIS RECIPE WORKS Most people prefer to leave eggs Benedict to the pros, but this recipe makes it easy for a home cook to execute because the hollandaise can be made ahead and the egg poaching method is simple and foolproof. Our unconventional technique for the hollandaise requires whisking butter and egg yolks on the stovetop in a double boiler, creating a strong emulsion stable enough to be chilled and reheated. We served our poached eggs atop toasted English muffins and Canadian bacon, and topped them off with our velvety hollandaise. The hollandaise can be refrigerated in an airtight container for up to three days. Reheat in the microwave on 50 percent power, stirring every 10 seconds, until heated through, about 1 minute.

Hollandaise
- 8 tablespoons unsalted butter, cut into 8 pieces and softened
- 4 large egg yolks
- ⅓ cup boiling water
- 2 teaspoons lemon juice
- Pinch cayenne pepper

Eggs
- 1 tablespoon distilled white vinegar
- Table salt for cooking eggs
- 8 large eggs
- 4 English muffins, split
- 8 slices Canadian bacon

1. For the hollandaise: Whisk butter and egg yolks in large heat-resistant bowl set over medium saucepan filled with ½ inch of barely simmering water (don't let bowl touch water). Slowly add boiling water and cook, whisking constantly, until thickened and sauce registers 160 to 165 degrees, 7 to 10 minutes.

2. Off heat, stir in lemon juice and cayenne and season with salt to taste. Cover and set aside in warm place until serving time.

3. For the eggs: Bring 6 cups water to boil in Dutch oven over high heat and add vinegar and 1 teaspoon salt. Fill second Dutch oven halfway with water, heat over high heat until water registers 150 degrees; adjust heat as needed to maintain 150 degrees.

4. Crack 4 eggs, one at a time, into colander. Let stand until loose, watery whites drain away from eggs, 20 to 30 seconds. Gently transfer eggs to 2-cup liquid measuring cup. Remove first pot with added vinegar from heat. With lip of measuring cup just above surface of water, gently tip eggs into water, one at a time, leaving space between them. Cover pot and let stand until whites closest to yolks are just set and opaque,

about 3 minutes. If after 3 minutes whites are not set, let stand in water, checking every 30 seconds, until eggs reach desired doneness. (For medium-cooked yolks, let eggs sit in pot, covered, for 4 minutes, then begin checking for doneness.)

5. Using slotted spoon, carefully lift and drain each egg over Dutch oven, then transfer to pot filled with 150-degree water and cover. Return Dutch oven used for cooking eggs to boil and repeat steps 4 and 5 with remaining 4 eggs.

6. Adjust oven rack 6 inches from broiler element and heat broiler. Arrange English muffins, split side up, on baking sheet and broil until golden brown, 2 to 4 minutes. Place 1 slice bacon on each English muffin and broil until beginning to brown, about 1 minute. Remove muffins from oven and transfer to serving plates. Using slotted spoon, carefully lift and drain each egg and lay on top of each English muffin. Spoon hollandaise over top and serve.

Eggs in Spicy Tomato and Roasted Red Pepper Sauce (Shakshuka)

SEASON 20 RECIPE

Serves 4

WHY THIS RECIPE WORKS *Shakshuka* is a Tunisian one-pan dish featuring eggs poached in a spiced tomato, onion, and pepper sauce. It's great for a savory breakfast or when you're looking to dress up some eggs for dinner. For the sauce, we blended whole peeled tomatoes and jarred roasted red peppers for a mix of sweetness, smokiness, and acidity. Adding pita bread helped prevent the silky-smooth sauce from weeping. A combination of garlic, tomato paste, and ground spices created the distinct flavor profile we were after. To ensure that the eggs cooked just right, we added them to the skillet off the heat, and covered the whites with sauce to help speed their cooking. Chopped fresh cilantro, crumbled feta, and sliced kalamata olives on top provided brightness, texture, and contrasting flavor.

- 4 (8-inch) pita breads, divided
- 1 (28-ounce) can whole peeled tomatoes, drained
- 3 cups jarred roasted red peppers, divided
- ¼ cup extra-virgin olive oil
- 4 garlic cloves, sliced thin
- 1 tablespoon tomato paste
- 2 teaspoons ground coriander
- 2 teaspoons smoked paprika
- 1 teaspoon ground cumin
- ½ teaspoon table salt
- ¼ teaspoon pepper
- ¼ teaspoon cayenne pepper
- 8 large eggs

½ cup coarsely chopped fresh cilantro
   leaves and stems
1 ounce feta cheese, crumbled (¼ cup)
¼ cup pitted kalamata olives, sliced

1. Cut enough pita bread into ½-inch pieces to equal ½ cup (about one-third of 1 pita). Cut remaining pitas into wedges for serving. Process pita pieces, tomatoes, and half of red peppers in blender until smooth, 1 to 2 minutes. Chop remaining red peppers into ¼-inch pieces and set aside.

2. Heat oil in 12-inch skillet over medium heat until shimmering. Add garlic and cook, stirring occasionally, until golden, 1 to 2 minutes. Add tomato paste, coriander, paprika, cumin, salt, pepper, and cayenne, and cook, stirring constantly, until rust-colored and fragrant, 1 to 2 minutes. Stir in tomato–red pepper puree and reserved red peppers (mixture may sputter) and bring to simmer. Reduce heat to maintain simmer; cook, stirring occasionally, until slightly thickened (spatula will leave trail that slowly fills in behind it, but sauce will still slosh when skillet is shaken), 10 to 12 minutes.

3. Remove skillet from heat. Using back of spoon, make 8 dime-size indentations in sauce (7 around perimeter and 1 in center). Crack 1 egg into small bowl and pour into 1 indentation (it will hold yolk in place but not fully contain egg). Repeat with remaining 7 eggs. Spoon sauce over edges of egg whites so that whites are partially covered and yolks are exposed.

4. Bring to simmer over medium heat (there should be small bubbles across entire surface). Reduce heat to maintain simmer. Cover and cook until yolks film over, 4 to 5 minutes. Continue to cook, covered, until whites are softly but uniformly set (if skillet is shaken lightly, each egg should jiggle as a single unit), 1 to 2 minutes longer. Off heat, sprinkle with cilantro, feta, and olives. Serve immediately, passing pita wedges.

ACCOMPANIMENT
Zhoug (Spicy Middle Eastern Herb Sauce)
Makes 1 cup

This Yemenite hot sauce is often served as an accompaniment to shakshuka or falafel but also adds a kick to roasted or grilled meats, fish, and vegetables or stirred into dips like hummus.

2 cups fresh cilantro leaves and stems
4 Thai chiles, stemmed
3 garlic cloves, peeled
½ teaspoon ground coriander
½ teaspoon ground cumin
½ teaspoon table salt
½ cup extra-virgin olive oil

Pulse cilantro, Thai chiles, garlic, coriander, cumin, and salt in food processor until coarsely chopped, 8 to 10 pulses. Transfer to small bowl. Add oil and stir until sauce has consistency of loose paste. Season with salt to taste. (Sauce can be refrigerated in airtight container for up to 2 weeks. Let come to room temperature before serving).

Soft-Cooked Eggs

Makes 4

WHY THIS RECIPE WORKS Traditional methods for making soft-cooked eggs are hit or miss. We wanted one that delivered a set white and a fluid yolk every time. Calling for fridge-cold eggs and boiling water has two advantages: It reduces temperature variables, which makes the recipe more foolproof, and it provides the steepest temperature gradient, which ensures that the yolk at the center stays fluid while the white cooks through. Using only ½ an inch of boiling water instead of several cups to cook the eggs means that the recipe takes less time and energy from start to finish. Because of the curved shape of the eggs, they actually have very little contact with the water so they do not lower the water temperature when they go into the saucepan. This means that you can use the same timing for anywhere from one to six eggs without altering the consistency of the finished product. Be sure to use large eggs that have no cracks and are cold from the refrigerator. Because precise timing is vital to the success of this recipe, we strongly recommend using a digital timer. You can use this method for one to six large, extra-large, or jumbo eggs without altering the timing. If you have one, a steamer basket makes lowering the eggs into the boiling water easier. We recommend serving these eggs in egg cups and with buttered toast for dipping, or you may simply use the dull side of a butter knife to crack the egg along the equator, break the egg in half, and scoop out the insides with a teaspoon.

Soft-Cooked Eggs with Salad

4 large eggs

1. Bring ½ inch water to boil in medium saucepan over medium-high heat. Using tongs, gently place eggs in boiling water (eggs will not be submerged). Cover saucepan and cook eggs for 6½ minutes.

2. Remove cover, transfer saucepan to sink, and place under cold running water for 30 seconds. Remove eggs from pan and serve, seasoning with salt and pepper to taste.

VARIATIONS
Soft-Cooked Eggs with Salad
Serves 2

Be sure to run the soft-cooked eggs under cold water for 30 seconds before peeling.

Combine 3 tablespoons extra-virgin olive oil, 1 tablespoon balsamic vinegar, 1 teaspoon Dijon mustard, and 1 teaspoon minced shallot in jar, seal lid, and shake vigorously until emulsified, 20 to 30 seconds. Toss with 5 cups assertively flavored salad greens (arugula, radicchio, watercress, or frisée). Season with salt and pepper to taste and divide between 2 plates. Top each serving with 2 peeled soft-cooked eggs, split crosswise to release yolks, and season with salt and pepper to taste.

Soft-Cooked Eggs with Sautéed Mushrooms
Serves 2

Be sure to run the soft-cooked eggs under cold water for 30 seconds before peeling.

Heat 2 tablespoons extra-virgin olive oil in large skillet over medium-high heat until shimmering. Add 12 ounces sliced white or cremini mushrooms and pinch salt and cook, stirring occasionally, until liquid has evaporated and mushrooms are lightly browned, 5 to 6 minutes. Stir in 2 teaspoons chopped fresh herbs (chives, tarragon, parsley, or combination). Season with salt and pepper to taste, and divide between 2 plates. Top each serving with 2 peeled soft-cooked eggs, split crosswise to release yolks, and season with salt and pepper to taste.

Soft-Cooked Eggs with Steamed Asparagus
Serves 2

Be sure to run the soft-cooked eggs under cold water for 30 seconds before peeling.

Steam 12 ounces asparagus (spears about ½ inch in diameter, trimmed) over medium heat until crisp-tender, 4 to 5 minutes. Divide between 2 plates. Drizzle each serving with 1 tablespoon extra-virgin olive oil and sprinkle each serving with 1 tablespoon grated Parmesan. Season with salt and pepper to taste. Top each serving with 2 peeled soft-cooked eggs, split crosswise to release yolks, and season with salt and pepper to taste.

Curry Deviled Eggs with Easy-Peel Hard-Cooked Eggs
SEASON 20 RECIPE

Makes 12 eggs

WHY THIS RECIPE WORKS Deviled eggs make a great appetizer or brunch dish, but the reason most people tend to shy away from them is the hassle of getting the peel off all those eggs. Plus what's the best method for ensuring a hard-cooked egg that's just cooked through with no chalkiness (or greenish tinge) to the yolk? With our method, you no longer need to fear the drudgery of peeling hard-cooked eggs—the shells practically fly off, putting deviled eggs back on the rotation. It turns out that boiled eggs that start in cold water are hard to peel because the proteins in the egg white set slowly, which gives them time to fuse to the surrounding membrane. When you try to remove the shell, parts of the white cling to the membrane, and the surface of the egg is unattractively pockmarked. Instead of a cold-water start, we place cold eggs directly into hot steam (in a steamer basket set over an inch of boiling water in a saucepan), which rapidly denatures the outermost egg white proteins, causing them to form a solid gel that shrinks and pulls away from the membrane. The shell slips off easily to reveal smooth, unblemished hard-cooked eggs. To slice eggs, lay each egg on its side and sweep the blade cleanly down the center. Wipe the knife after each egg. You may use either regular or reduced-fat mayonnaise in this recipe. If preferred, use a pastry bag fitted with a large plain or star tip to fill the egg halves.

- 1 recipe Easy-Peel Hard-Cooked Eggs (recipe follows)
- 3 tablespoons mayonnaise
- 1 tablespoon minced fresh parsley, plus 12 small whole parsley leaves for garnishing
- 1½ teaspoons lemon juice
- 1 teaspoon Dijon mustard
- 1 teaspoon curry powder
- Pinch cayenne pepper

1. Slice each egg in half lengthwise with paring knife. Transfer yolks to bowl; arrange whites on serving platter. Mash yolks with fork until no large lumps remain. Add mayonnaise and use rubber spatula to smear mixture against side of bowl until thick, smooth paste forms, 1 to 2 minutes. Add minced parsley, lemon juice, mustard, curry powder, and cayenne and mix until fully incorporated.

2. Transfer yolk mixture to small heavy-duty plastic bag. Press mixture into 1 corner and twist top of bag. Using scissors, snip ½ inch off filled corner. Squeezing bag, distribute yolk mixture evenly among egg white halves. Garnish each egg half with parsley leaf and serve.

Easy-Peel Hard-Cooked Eggs

Makes 6 eggs

Be sure to use large, cold eggs that have no cracks. You can cook fewer than six eggs without altering the timing, or more eggs as long as your pot and steamer basket can hold them in a single layer. If you don't have a steamer basket, use a spoon or tongs to gently place the eggs in the water; it does not matter if the eggs are above the water or partially submerged. Unpeeled cooked eggs can be stored in the refrigerator for up to 3 days.

6 large eggs

1. Bring 1 inch water to rolling boil in medium saucepan over high heat. Place eggs in steamer basket. Transfer basket to saucepan. Cover, reduce heat to medium-low, and cook eggs for 13 minutes.

2. When eggs are almost finished cooking, combine 2 cups ice cubes and 2 cups cold water in medium bowl. Using tongs or spoon, transfer eggs to ice bath; let sit for 15 minutes. Peel before using.

French Omelets

Serves 2

WHY THIS RECIPE WORKS In contrast to half-moon diner-style omelets, the French omelet is a pristine rolled affair. The temperature of the pan must be just right, the eggs beaten just so, and hand movements must be swift. We decided to ditch the stuffy attitude and come up with a foolproof method for making the ideal French omelet—unblemished golden yellow with an ultracreamy texture, rolled around minimal filling. The classic method requires a black carbon steel omelet pan and a fork, but a nonstick skillet worked fine here. Instead of a fork, which scraped our nonstick pans, bamboo skewers and wooden chopsticks gave us small curds with a silky texture. Preheating the pan

for 10 minutes over low heat eliminated any hot spots. For creaminess, we added very cold butter, which dispersed evenly and fused with the eggs for a moist, rich omelet. To keep the omelet light, we found the perfect number of strokes; excessive beating unravels egg proteins, leading to denseness. We tried different heat levels, but even at medium heat, the omelet cooked so quickly it was hard to judge when it was done, so we turned off the heat when it was still runny and covered it to finish cooking. Finally, for an easy rolling method, we slid the omelet onto a paper towel and used the towel to roll the omelet into the sought-after cylinder. Because cooking these omelets is such a quick process, make sure to have all your ingredients and equipment at the ready. If you don't have skewers or chopsticks to stir the eggs in step 3, use the handle of a wooden spoon. Warm the plates in a 200-degree oven.

2 tablespoons unsalted butter, cut into 2 pieces, divided
½ teaspoon vegetable oil
6 large eggs, chilled, divided
¼ teaspoon table salt, divided
⅛ teaspoon pepper, divided
2 tablespoons shredded Gruyère cheese, divided
4 teaspoons minced fresh chives, divided

1. Cut 1 tablespoon butter in half. Cut remaining 1 tablespoon butter into small pieces, transfer to small bowl, and place in freezer while preparing eggs and skillet, at least 10 minutes. Meanwhile, heat oil in 8-inch nonstick skillet over low heat for 10 minutes.

2. Crack 2 eggs into medium bowl and separate third egg; reserve white for another use and add yolk to bowl. Add ⅛ teaspoon salt and pinch pepper. Break yolks with fork, then beat eggs at moderate pace, about 80 strokes, until yolks and whites are well combined. Stir in half of frozen butter cubes.

3. When skillet is fully heated, use paper towels to wipe out oil, leaving thin film on bottom and sides of skillet. Add half of reserved 1 tablespoon butter to skillet and heat until melted.

Making a French Omelet

1. Add beaten-egg mixture to skillet and stir with chopsticks to produce small curds, which result in a silkier texture.

2. Turn off heat while eggs are still runny; smooth with spatula into even layer.

3. After sprinkling with cheese and chives, cover so residual heat gently finishes cooking omelet.

4. Slide finished omelet onto paper towel–lined plate. Use paper towel to lift omelet and roll it up.

Swirl butter to coat skillet, add egg mixture, and increase heat to medium-high. Use 2 chopsticks or wooden skewers to scramble eggs using quick circular motion to move around skillet, scraping cooked egg from side of skillet as you go, until eggs are almost cooked but still slightly runny, 45 to 90 seconds. Turn off heat and smooth eggs into even layer using rubber spatula. Sprinkle omelet with 1 tablespoon Gruyère and 2 teaspoons chives. Cover skillet with lid and let sit, 1 minute for runnier omelet and 2 minutes for firmer omelet.

4. Heat skillet over low heat for 20 seconds, uncover, and, using rubber spatula, loosen edges of omelet from skillet. Place folded square of paper towel onto warmed plate and slide omelet out of skillet onto paper towel so that omelet lies flat on plate and hangs about 1 inch off paper towel. Roll omelet into neat cylinder and set aside. Return skillet to low heat and heat for 2 minutes before repeating instructions for second omelet starting with step 2. Serve.

Asparagus, Ham, and Gruyère Frittata

Serves 6 to 8

WHY THIS RECIPE WORKS A frittata loaded with meat and vegetables often ends up dry, overstuffed, and overcooked. We wanted a frittata big enough to make a substantial meal for six to eight people—with a pleasing balance of egg to filling, firm yet moist eggs, and a lightly browned crust. We started with a dozen eggs, which we found required 3 cups of cooked vegetables and meat to create the best balance. When we chose our fillings, we needed to be a little selective about the cheese—Gruyère had just the right amount of moisture. Most any vegetable or meat can be added to a frittata, with two caveats: The food must be cut into small pieces, and it must be precooked to drive off excess moisture and fat. A little half-and-half added a touch of creaminess. Given the large number of eggs, we had to shorten the time the frittata spent on the stovetop so the bottom wouldn't scorch. We started the eggs on medium heat and stirred them so they could cook quickly yet evenly. With the eggs still on the wet side, we slid the skillet under the broiler until the top had puffed and browned, but removed it while the eggs in the center were still slightly wet and runny, allowing the residual heat to finish the cooking. A 12-inch ovensafe nonstick skillet is necessary for this recipe. Because broilers vary so much in intensity, watch the frittata carefully as it cooks.

12 large eggs
3 tablespoons half-and-half
½ teaspoon table salt
¼ teaspoon pepper
2 teaspoons extra-virgin olive oil
8 ounces asparagus, tough ends trimmed, spears cut on the bias into ¼-inch pieces
4 ounces (¼-inch-thick) deli ham, cut into ½-inch pieces (¾ cup)
1 shallot, minced
3 ounces Gruyère cheese, cut into ¼-inch cubes (¾ cup)

1. Adjust oven rack about 5 inches from broiler element and heat broiler. Whisk eggs, half-and-half, salt, and pepper together in medium bowl. Set aside.

2. Heat oil in 12-inch ovensafe nonstick skillet over medium heat until shimmering; add asparagus and cook, stirring occasionally, until lightly browned and almost tender, about 3 minutes. Add ham and shallot and cook until shallot softens, about 2 minutes.

3. Stir Gruyère into eggs; add egg mixture to skillet and cook, using rubber spatula to stir and scrape bottom of skillet, until large curds form and spatula begins to leave wake but eggs are still very wet, about 2 minutes. Shake skillet to distribute eggs evenly and cook without stirring to let bottom set, about 30 seconds.

4. Slide skillet under broiler and cook until surface is puffed and spotty brown, yet center remains slightly wet and runny when cut into with paring knife, 3 to 4 minutes. Being careful of hot skillet handle, remove skillet from oven and let stand for 5 minutes to finish cooking; using spatula, loosen frittata from skillet and slide onto platter or cutting board. Cut into wedges and serve.

Quiche Lorraine

Serves 8

WHY THIS RECIPE WORKS A really good quiche should have a smooth, creamy custard in a tender pastry crust. The custard should be rich, but not overwhelmingly so, and moist, not dried out. We aimed to find a way to make this perfect pie. We experimented with multiple combinations of egg and dairy to find the one that would provide just the right balance of richness and lightness. Eggs alone were not rich enough; whole eggs plus yolks provided the degree of richness we wanted. For the dairy component, we found that equal parts of milk and heavy cream worked best. This custard was creamy and smooth. After layering bacon and Gruyère over the bottom of the pie shell—for a classic quiche Lorraine—we poured the custard on top and baked the quiche until it was puffed and set around the edges but still jiggled in the center; the residual heat finished cooking the center without turning the top into a rubbery skin. Before serving the quiche, we let it cool on a wire rack, which is a small but important step; this allows air to circulate under the crust and prevents it from becoming soggy. The center of the quiche will be surprisingly soft when it comes out of the oven, but the filling will continue to set (and sink somewhat) as it cools. If the pie shell has been previously baked and cooled, place it in the heating oven for about 5 minutes to warm it, making sure that it does not burn.

1 recipe Foolproof All-Butter Dough for Single-Crust Pie (page 454), fitted into 9-inch pie plate and chilled
8 slices bacon, cut into ½-inch pieces
2 large eggs plus 2 large egg yolks
1 cup whole milk
1 cup heavy cream
½ teaspoon table salt
½ teaspoon white pepper
  Pinch ground nutmeg
4 ounces Gruyère cheese, shredded (1 cup)

1. Adjust oven rack to middle position and heat oven to 375 degrees. Line chilled crust with double layer of foil and fill with pie weights. Bake until pie dough looks dry and is light in color, 25 to 30 minutes. Transfer pie plate to wire rack and remove weights and foil.

2. Cook bacon in 12-inch nonstick skillet over medium heat until crisp, about 5 minutes. Using slotted spoon, transfer bacon to paper towel–lined plate. Whisk eggs, yolks, milk, cream, salt, pepper, and nutmeg together in medium bowl.

3. Spread Gruyère and bacon evenly over bottom of warm pie shell and set shell on oven rack. Pour custard mixture into pie shell (it should come to about ½ inch below crust's rim). Bake until light golden brown and knife blade inserted about 1 inch from edge comes out clean and center feels set but still soft, 32 to 35 minutes. Transfer quiche to wire rack and cool. Serve warm or at room temperature.

Home Fries for a Crowd

Serves 6 to 8

WHY THIS RECIPE WORKS Making home fries the traditional way requires constant monitoring while standing over a hot skillet, after which you get only three servings at most. We wanted a quicker, more hands-off method for making a larger amount. To speed things up, we developed a hybrid cooking technique: First, we parboiled diced russet potatoes, and then we coated them in butter and cooked them in a very hot oven. We discovered that boiling the potatoes with baking soda quickly broke down their exterior while leaving their insides nearly raw, ensuring home fries with a crisp, brown crust and a moist, fluffy interior. We added diced onions in the last 20 minutes of oven time and finished the home fries with chives to reinforce the onion flavor. Don't skip the baking soda in this recipe. It's critical for home fries with just the right crisp texture.

3½ pounds russet potatoes, peeled and cut into ¾-inch pieces
½ teaspoon baking soda
3 tablespoons unsalted butter, cut into 12 pieces
2 teaspoons kosher salt, divided
  Pinch cayenne pepper
3 tablespoons vegetable oil, divided
2 onions, cut into ½-inch pieces
3 tablespoons minced fresh chives

1. Adjust oven rack to lowest position, place rimmed baking sheet on rack, and heat oven to 500 degrees.

2. Bring 10 cups water to boil in Dutch oven over high heat. Add potatoes and baking soda. Return to boil and cook for 1 minute. Drain potatoes. Return potatoes to Dutch oven and place over low heat. Cook, shaking pot occasionally, until any surface moisture has evaporated, about 2 minutes. Remove from heat. Add butter, 1½ teaspoons salt, and cayenne; mix with rubber spatula until potatoes are coated with thick, starchy paste, about 30 seconds.

3. Remove baking sheet from oven and drizzle with 2 tablespoons oil. Transfer potatoes to baking sheet and spread into even layer. Roast for 15 minutes. While potatoes roast, combine onions, remaining 1 tablespoon oil, and remaining ½ teaspoon salt in bowl.

4. Remove baking sheet from oven. Using thin, sharp metal spatula, scrape and turn potatoes. Clear about 8 by 5-inch space in center of baking sheet and add onion mixture. Roast for 15 minutes.

5. Scrape and turn again, mixing onions into potatoes. Continue to roast until potatoes are well browned and onions are softened and beginning to brown, 5 to 10 minutes. Stir in chives and season with salt and pepper to taste. Serve immediately.

Everyday French Toast

SEASON 20 RECIPE

Serves 4

WHY THIS RECIPE WORKS French toast is a humble dish, not much more than bread married with an eggy custard and browned until crisp in a skillet. But, as with many simple dishes, there are things that can wrong. Add to this the fact that if you want to make French toast for more than a couple of people, all the dipping and flipping becomes cumbersome. So we set our sights on a recipe for French toast that could transform ordinary sandwich bread into a creamy, crisp-crusted treat. No fuss. No mess. No wasted egg mixture. To start, we learned that staggering the order of ingredients added to the eggs not only made it easier to whisk them together but also made the mixture more cohesive. So first we beat the eggs with the vanilla, sugar, salt, and cinnamon until smooth, and then simply stirred the milk in. But after our first batch, we wanted more richness and depth. Melted butter made it more luxurious; adding it before the milk prevented the butter from clumping. Next we moved on to how long to soak the bread—too little time and the custard didn't penetrate the bread enough, but too long and the bread was too delicate. Then in true test kitchen fashion we measured the exact soaking depth for best results: ¼ inch. This led us to our breakthrough discovery: pouring the custard onto a rimmed baking sheet, adding the bread and then baking and then broiling it, which made things better and easier all around—no flipping required. We developed this recipe to work with presliced supermarket bread that measures 4 by 6 inches and is ¾ inch thick. Our favorite is Arnold Country Classics White Bread. Top with maple syrup or confectioners' sugar, if desired.

3 large eggs
1 tablespoon vanilla extract
2 teaspoons packed brown sugar
½ teaspoon ground cinnamon
¼ teaspoon table salt
2 tablespoons unsalted butter, melted
1 cup milk
8 slices hearty white sandwich bread

1. Adjust 1 oven rack to lowest position and second rack 5 to 6 inches from broiler element. Heat oven to 425 degrees. Generously spray bottom and sides of 18 by 13-inch rimmed baking sheet with vegetable oil spray. Whisk eggs, vanilla, sugar, cinnamon, and salt in large bowl until sugar is dissolved and no streaks of egg remain. Whisking constantly, drizzle in melted butter. Whisk in milk.

2. Pour egg mixture into prepared sheet. Arrange bread in single layer in egg mixture, leaving small gaps between slices. Working quickly, use your fingers to flip slices in same order you placed them in sheet. Let sit until slices absorb remaining custard, about 1 minute. Bake on lower rack until bottoms of slices are golden brown, 10 to 15 minutes. Transfer sheet to upper rack and heat broiler. (Leave sheet in oven while broiler heats.) Broil until tops of slices are golden brown, watching carefully and rotating sheet if necessary to prevent burning, 1 to 4 minutes.

3. Using thin metal spatula, carefully flip each slice. Serve.

Making French Toast on a Baking Sheet

1. Pour custard into rimmed baking sheet that has been generously coated with vegetable oil spray (to prevent slices from sticking during baking). Custard will spread into even layer.

2. Add 8 slices of bread, 1 slice at a time, in 2 rows of four. Once last slice is added, first slice is ready to be flipped to soak on its second side.

3. One minute after all 8 slices have been flipped, custard will be completely absorbed.

Blueberry Pancakes

Makes 16 pancakes; serves 4 to 6

WHY THIS RECIPE WORKS Blueberry pancakes sound appetizing, but they are often tough and rubbery or dense and soggy. And they inevitably take on an unappealing blue-gray hue. We wanted pancakes that cooked up light and fluffy and were studded with sweet, tangy bursts of summer's best berry. Starting with the pancakes themselves, we determined that all-purpose flour, sugar, a little salt, and both baking powder and baking soda were essential for the dry ingredients. One egg added just enough structure and richness without making the pancakes overly eggy. Buttermilk was the preferred dairy component, but since our ground rules were to use only what most home cooks would be likely to have on hand, we searched for a substitute. Lemon juice thickens milk almost to the consistency of buttermilk and adds a similar tang that tasters actually preferred. Some melted butter added to the mix prevented our pancakes from being dry and bland. Mixing the batter too strenuously leads to tough pancakes; it's time to stop mixing when there are still a few lumps and streaks of flour. Once we had great-tasting pancakes, we turned to the blueberries. Stirring them into the batter would obviously lead to smashing and those blue-gray streaks, so rather than incorporating the berries, we simply dropped some onto the batter after we'd ladled it into the skillet. Smaller wild berries are sweeter than the larger ones, but frozen berries work as well as fresh, which means we can have great blueberry pancakes any time of the year. To make sure that frozen berries do not bleed, rinse them under cool water in a mesh strainer until the water runs clear, and then spread them on a paper towel–lined plate to dry. If you have buttermilk on hand, use 2 cups instead of the milk and lemon juice. To keep pancakes warm while cooking the remaining batter, hold them in a 200-degree oven on a greased rack set over a baking sheet.

- 2 **cups milk**
- 1 **tablespoon lemon juice**
- 2 **cups (10 ounces) all-purpose flour**
- 2 **tablespoons sugar**
- 2 **teaspoons baking powder**
- ½ **teaspoon baking soda**
- ½ **teaspoon table salt**
- 1 **large egg**
- 3 **tablespoons unsalted butter, melted and cooled slightly**
- 1–2 **teaspoons vegetable oil, divided**
- 1 **cup fresh or frozen blueberries, preferably wild, rinsed and dried, divided**

1. Adjust oven rack to middle position and heat oven to 200 degrees. Spray wire rack set in rimmed baking sheet with vegetable oil spray; place in oven. Whisk milk and lemon juice together in medium bowl or large measuring cup; set aside to thicken while preparing other ingredients. Whisk flour, sugar, baking powder, baking soda, and salt together in bowl.

2. Whisk egg and melted butter into milk until combined. Make well in center of flour mixture and pour in milk mixture; whisk very gently until just combined (few lumps should remain). Do not overmix.

3. Heat 12-inch nonstick skillet over medium heat for 3 to 5 minutes; add 1 teaspoon oil and brush to coat skillet bottom evenly. Using ¼-cup measure or 2-ounce ladle, portion batter into pan in 3 places, leaving 2 inches between portions; sprinkle 1 tablespoon blueberries over each pancake. Cook pancakes until large bubbles begin to appear, 1½ to 2 minutes. Using thin, wide spatula, flip pancakes and continue to cook until second side is golden brown, 1 to 1½ minutes. Serve pancakes immediately or transfer to wire rack in preheated oven. Repeat with remaining batter, using remaining oil if necessary.

Lemon Ricotta Pancakes

Makes 12 pancakes; serves 3 to 4

WHY THIS RECIPE WORKS Light, fluffy ricotta pancakes are sophisticated enough for special occasions, but getting the balance of ingredients just right is essential for pancakes that are puffy and tender, not dense and wet. To compensate for the extra weight of the ricotta, we decreased the amount of flour and stirred 4 whipped egg whites into the batter. Baking soda provided extra rise and aided with browning. Bright, tangy lemon juice complemented the rich, creamy ricotta, and lemon zest enhanced the citrus flavor without watering down the batter. A touch of vanilla extract brought depth and subtle sweetness. For a company-worthy finishing touch, we draped the pancakes with a warm fruit compote. An electric griddle set at 325 degrees can also be used to cook the pancakes. We prefer the flavor of whole-milk ricotta, but part-skim will work, too; avoid nonfat ricotta. Serve with confectioners' sugar or a fruit compote.

- ⅔ **cup (3⅓ ounces) all-purpose flour**
- ½ **teaspoon baking soda**
- ½ **teaspoon table salt**
- 8 **ounces (1 cup) whole-milk ricotta cheese**
- 2 **large eggs, separated, plus 2 large whites**
- ⅓ **cup whole milk**
- 1 **teaspoon grated lemon zest plus 4 teaspoons juice**

½ teaspoon vanilla extract
2 tablespoons unsalted butter, melted
¼ cup (1¾ ounces) sugar
1–2 teaspoons vegetable oil, divided

1. Adjust oven rack to middle position and heat oven to 200 degrees. Spray wire rack set in rimmed baking sheet with vegetable oil spray; place in oven. Whisk flour, baking soda, and salt together in medium bowl and make well in center. Add ricotta, egg yolks, milk, lemon zest and juice, and vanilla and whisk until just combined. Gently stir in melted butter.

2. Using stand mixer fitted with whisk, whip egg whites on medium-low speed until foamy, about 1 minute. Increase speed to medium-high and whip whites to soft, billowy mounds, about 1 minute. Gradually add sugar and whip until glossy, soft peaks form, 1 to 2 minutes. Transfer one-third of whipped egg whites to batter and whisk gently until mixture is lightened. Using rubber spatula, gently fold remaining egg whites into batter.

3. Heat 1 teaspoon oil in 12-inch nonstick skillet over medium heat until shimmering. Using paper towels, wipe out oil, leaving thin film on bottom and sides of pan. Using ¼-cup measure or 2-ounce ladle, portion batter into pan in 3 places, leaving 2 inches between portions. Gently spread each portion into a 4-inch round. Cook until edges are set and first side is deep golden brown, 2 to 3 minutes. Using thin, wide spatula, flip pancakes and continue to cook until second side is golden brown, 2 to 3 minutes. Serve pancakes immediately or transfer to wire rack in preheated oven. Repeat with remaining batter, using remaining oil if necessary.

ACCOMPANIMENTS
Apple-Cranberry Topping
Makes 2½ cups

3 Golden Delicious apples, peeled, cored, halved, and cut into ¼-inch pieces
¼ cup dried cranberries
1 tablespoon sugar
1 teaspoon cornstarch
   Pinch table salt
   Pinch ground nutmeg

Combine all ingredients in bowl and microwave until apples are softened but not mushy and juices are slightly thickened, 4 to 6 minutes, stirring once halfway through microwaving. Stir and serve.

Pear-Blackberry Topping
Makes 3 cups

3 ripe pears, peeled, halved, cored, and cut into ¼-inch pieces
1 tablespoon sugar
1 teaspoon cornstarch
   Pinch table salt
   Pinch ground cardamom
5 ounces (1 cup) blackberries, berries more than 1 inch long cut in half crosswise

Combine pears, sugar, cornstarch, salt, and cardamom in bowl and microwave until pears are softened but not mushy and juices are slightly thickened, 4 to 6 minutes, stirring once halfway through microwaving. Stir in blackberries and serve.

Plum-Apricot Topping
Makes 2½ cups

1½ pounds plums, halved, pitted, and cut into ¼-inch pieces
¼ cup dried apricots, chopped coarse
1 tablespoon sugar
1 teaspoon cornstarch
   Pinch table salt
   Pinch ground cinnamon

Combine all ingredients in bowl and microwave until plums are softened but not mushy and juices are slightly thickened, 4 to 6 minutes, stirring once halfway through microwaving. Stir and serve.

"Pancakes are my family's favorite breakfast (and not just on weekends), so we fancy ourselves experts on the topic. This is our favorite recipe, bar none. We were thrilled when Andrea Geary developed these sweet, nutty, and fluffy gems. Not only are they entirely foolproof (you just can't overmix them), but it means that our breakfast habit now includes whole grains. My 10-year-old son never gets tired of mixing up the batter, manning the griddle, and then slathering his creation with Nutella. I'm a purist, which means plenty of maple syrup and butter."

–Becky

100 Percent Whole-Wheat Pancakes

Makes 15 pancakes; serves 4 to 6

WHY THIS RECIPE WORKS Most recipes for whole-wheat pancakes call for a mix of white and whole-wheat flours, and they also call for a host of extra flavorings like spices, vanilla, fruit juice, or fruit. Why not just whole-wheat flour? We discovered that using all whole-wheat flour actually delivers light, fluffy, and tender pancakes—not the dense cakes you'd imagine—because whole-wheat flour contains slightly less gluten-forming protein than white flour and because the bran in whole-wheat flour cuts through any gluten strands that do form. Recipes for pancakes made with white flour advise undermixing to avoid dense, tough pancakes, but with whole-wheat flour we were guaranteed light and tender cakes even as we whisked our batter to a smooth, thick consistency. We saw no need to cover up whole wheat's natural flavor with other add-ins; its earthy, nutty taste proved to be the perfect complement to maple syrup. As long as we used a bag of fresh or properly stored (in the freezer) whole-wheat flour, it had just the buttery, nutty flavor we wanted. An electric griddle set at 350 degrees can be used in place of a skillet. If substituting buttermilk powder and water for fresh buttermilk, use only 2 cups of water to prevent the pancakes from being too wet. Serve with maple syrup and butter.

- 2 cups (11 ounces) whole-wheat flour
- 2 tablespoons sugar
- 1½ teaspoons baking powder
- ½ teaspoon baking soda
- ¾ teaspoon table salt
- 2¼ cups buttermilk
- 5 tablespoons plus 2 teaspoons vegetable oil, divided
- 2 large eggs

1. Adjust oven rack to middle position and heat oven to 200 degrees. Spray wire rack set in rimmed baking sheet with vegetable oil spray; place in oven.

2. Whisk flour, sugar, baking powder, baking soda, and salt together in medium bowl. Whisk buttermilk, 5 tablespoons oil, and eggs together in second medium bowl. Make well in center of flour mixture and pour in buttermilk mixture; whisk until smooth. (Mixture will be thick; do not add more buttermilk.)

3. Heat 1 teaspoon oil in 12-inch nonstick skillet over medium heat until shimmering. Using paper towels, carefully wipe out oil, leaving thin film on bottom and sides of pan. Using ¼-cup measure or 2-ounce ladle, portion batter into pan in 3 places. Gently spread each portion into 4½-inch round. Cook until edges are set, first side is golden brown, and bubbles on surface are just beginning to break, 2 to 3 minutes. Using thin, wide spatula, flip pancakes and continue to cook until second side is golden brown, 1 to 2 minutes. Serve pancakes immediately or transfer to wire rack in oven. Repeat with remaining batter, using remaining oil if necessary.

Ten-Minute Steel-Cut Oatmeal

Serves 4

WHY THIS RECIPE WORKS Most oatmeal fans agree that the steel-cut version of the grain offers the best flavor and texture, but many balk at the 40-minute cooking time. We decreased the cooking time to only 10 minutes by stirring steel-cut oats into boiling water the night before. This enabled the grains to hydrate and soften overnight. In the morning, more water (or fruit juice or milk) was added and the mixture was simmered for 4 to 6 minutes, until thick and creamy. A brief resting period off the heat ensured the perfect consistency. The oatmeal will continue to thicken as it cools. If you prefer a looser consistency, thin the oatmeal with boiling water. Customize your oatmeal with toppings such as brown sugar, toasted nuts, maple syrup, or dried fruit.

- 4 cups water, divided
- 1 cup steel-cut oats
- ¼ teaspoon table salt

1. Bring 3 cups water to boil in large saucepan over high heat. Remove pan from heat; stir in oats and salt. Cover pan and let sit overnight.

2. Stir remaining 1 cup water into oats and bring to boil over medium-high heat. Reduce heat to medium and cook, stirring occasionally, until oats are softened but still retain some chew and mixture thickens and resembles warm pudding, 4 to 6 minutes. Remove pan from heat and let sit for 5 minutes. Stir and serve, passing desired toppings separately.

VARIATIONS

Apple-Cinnamon Steel-Cut Oatmeal

Increase salt to ½ teaspoon. Substitute ½ cup apple cider and ½ cup whole milk for water in step 2. Stir ½ cup peeled, grated sweet apple, 2 tablespoons packed dark brown sugar, and ½ teaspoon ground cinnamon into oatmeal with cider and milk. Sprinkle each serving with 2 tablespoons coarsely chopped toasted walnuts.

Carrot-Spice Steel-Cut Oatmeal

Increase salt to ¾ teaspoon. Substitute ½ cup carrot juice and ½ cup whole milk for water in step 2. Stir ½ cup finely grated carrot, ¼ cup packed dark brown sugar, ⅓ cup dried currants, and ½ teaspoon ground cinnamon into oatmeal with carrot juice and milk. Sprinkle each serving with 2 tablespoons coarsely chopped toasted pecans.

Cranberry-Orange Steel-Cut Oatmeal

Increase salt to ½ teaspoon. Substitute ½ cup orange juice and ½ cup whole milk for water in step 2. Stir ½ cup dried cranberries, 3 tablespoons packed dark brown sugar, and

⅛ teaspoon ground cardamom into oatmeal with orange juice and milk. Sprinkle each serving with 2 tablespoons toasted sliced almonds.

Banana-Coconut Steel-Cut Oatmeal

Increase salt to ½ teaspoon. Substitute 1 cup canned coconut milk for water in step 2. Stir ½ cup toasted shredded coconut, 2 diced bananas, and ½ teaspoon vanilla extract into oatmeal before serving.

Peanut, Honey, and Banana Steel-Cut Oatmeal

Increase salt to ½ teaspoon. Substitute ½ cup whole milk for ½ cup water in step 2. Stir 3 tablespoons honey into oatmeal with milk and water. Add ¼ cup of peanut butter and 1 tablespoon unsalted butter to oatmeal after removing from heat in step 2. Stir 2 diced bananas into oatmeal before serving. Sprinkle each serving with 2 tablespoons coarsely chopped toasted peanuts.

British-Style Currant Scones

Makes 12 scones

WHY THIS RECIPE WORKS Compared to American scones, British scones are lighter, fluffier, and less sweet—perfect for serving with butter and jam. Rather than leaving pieces of cold butter in the dry ingredients as we would with American scones, we thoroughly worked in softened butter until it was fully integrated. This protected some of the flour granules from moisture, which in turn limited gluten development and kept the crumb tender and cakey. For a higher rise, we added more than the usual amount of leavening and started the scones in a 500-degree oven to boost their lift before turning the temperature down. We brushed some reserved milk and egg on top for enhanced browning, and added currants for tiny bursts of fruit flavor throughout. We prefer whole milk in this recipe, but low-fat milk can be used. The dough will be quite soft and wet; dust your work surface and your hands liberally with flour. For a tall, even rise, use a sharp-edged biscuit cutter and push straight down; do not twist the cutter. These scones are best served fresh, but leftover scones may be stored in the freezer and reheated in a 300-degree oven for 15 minutes before serving. Serve these scones with jam as well as salted butter or clotted cream.

- 3 cups (15 ounces) all-purpose flour
- ⅓ cup (2⅓ ounces) sugar
- 2 tablespoons baking powder
- ½ teaspoon table salt
- 8 tablespoons unsalted butter, cut into ½-inch pieces and softened

- ¾ cup dried currants
- 1 cup whole milk
- 2 large eggs

1. Adjust oven rack to upper-middle position and heat oven to 500 degrees. Line rimmed baking sheet with parchment paper. Pulse flour, sugar, baking powder, and salt in food processor until combined, about 5 pulses. Add butter and pulse until fully incorporated and mixture looks like very fine crumbs with no visible butter, about 20 pulses. Transfer mixture to large bowl and stir in currants.

2. Whisk milk and eggs together in second bowl. Set aside 2 tablespoons milk mixture. Add remaining milk mixture to flour mixture and, using rubber spatula, fold together until almost no dry bits of flour remain.

3. Transfer dough to well-floured counter and gather into ball. With floured hands, knead until surface is smooth and free of cracks, 25 to 30 times. Press gently to form disk. Using floured rolling pin, roll disk into 9-inch round, about 1 inch thick. Using floured 2½-inch round cutter, stamp out 8 rounds, recoating cutter with flour if it begins to stick. Arrange scones on prepared sheet. Gather dough scraps, form into ball, and knead gently until surface is smooth. Roll dough to 1-inch thickness and stamp out 4 rounds. Arrange scones on prepared sheet. Discard remaining dough.

4. Brush tops of scones with reserved milk mixture. Reduce oven temperature to 425 degrees and bake scones until risen and golden brown, 10 to 12 minutes, rotating sheet halfway through baking. Transfer scones to wire rack and let cool for at least 10 minutes. Serve scones warm or at room temperature.

Blueberry Muffins

Makes 12 muffins

WHY THIS RECIPE WORKS Blueberry muffins should be packed with blueberry flavor and boast a moist crumb. But too often, the blueberry flavor is fleeting, thanks to the fact that the berries in the produce aisle have suffered from long-distance shipping. We wanted blueberry muffins that would taste great with blueberries of any origin, even the watery supermarket kind. To intensify the blueberry in our muffins, we tried combining blueberry jam with fresh supermarket blueberries. The muffins baked up with a pretty blue filling, but tasters thought the jam made them too sweet. To solve this, we made our own fresh, low-sugar berry jam by simmering fresh blueberries on the stovetop with a bit of sugar. Adding our cooled homemade jam to the batter along with fresh, uncooked berries gave us the best of both worlds: intense blueberry flavor and the liquid burst that only fresh berries could provide. As for the muffin base, we found that the quick-bread method—whisking together eggs and sugar before adding milk and melted butter, and then folding in the dry ingredients—produced a substantial crumb that could support a generous amount of fruit. Equal amounts of butter and oil gave us just the right combination of buttery flavor and tender texture. To make the muffins even richer, we swapped the whole milk for buttermilk. For a nice crunch, we sprinkled lemon-scented sugar on top of the batter just before baking.

Lemon-Sugar Topping
⅓ cup (2⅓ ounces) sugar
1½ teaspoons grated lemon zest

Muffins
2 cups (10 ounces) fresh blueberries, divided
1 teaspoon plus 1⅛ cups (8 ounces) sugar, divided
2½ cups (12½ ounces) all-purpose flour
2½ teaspoons baking powder
1 teaspoon table salt
2 large eggs
4 tablespoons unsalted butter, melted and cooled slightly
4 tablespoons vegetable oil
1 cup buttermilk
1½ teaspoons vanilla extract

1. For the lemon-sugar topping: Stir sugar and zest together in small bowl until combined; set aside.

2. For the muffins: Adjust oven rack to upper-middle position and heat oven to 425 degrees. Spray muffin tin with vegetable oil spray. Bring 1 cup blueberries and 1 teaspoon sugar to simmer in small saucepan over medium heat. Cook, mashing berries with spoon several times and stirring frequently, until berries have broken down and mixture is thickened and reduced to ¼ cup, about 6 minutes. Transfer to bowl and let cool to room temperature, 10 to 15 minutes.

3. Whisk flour, baking powder, and salt together in large bowl. Whisk remaining 1⅛ cups sugar and eggs in medium bowl until thick and homogeneous, about 45 seconds. Slowly whisk in butter and oil until combined. Whisk in buttermilk and vanilla until combined. Using rubber spatula, fold egg mixture and remaining 1 cup blueberries into flour mixture until just moistened. (Batter will be very lumpy with few spots of dry flour; do not overmix.)

4. Using ⅓-cup measure or ice cream scoop, divide batter equally among prepared muffin cups (batter should completely fill cups and mound slightly). Spoon 1 teaspoon cooked berry mixture into center of each mound of batter. Using chopstick or skewer, gently swirl berry filling into batter using figure-8 motion. Sprinkle lemon sugar evenly over muffins.

5. Bake until muffin tops are golden and just firm, 17 to 19 minutes, rotating muffin tin halfway through baking. Let muffins cool in muffin tin for 5 minutes, then transfer to wire rack and let cool for 5 minutes before serving.

Swirling Jam Into Blueberry Muffins

1. Place 1 teaspoon of cooled berry jam in center of each batter-filled cup, pushing it below surface.

2. Using chopstick, swirl jam into the batter following figure-8 pattern.

Corn Muffins

Makes 12 muffins

WHY THIS RECIPE WORKS A corn muffin shouldn't be as sweet and fluffy as a cupcake, nor should it be dense and "corny" like cornbread. It should taste like corn, but not overpoweringly so, and should be moist with a tender crumb and a crunchy top. Our mission was to come up with a recipe for these seemingly simple muffins that struck just the right balance in both texture and flavor. The cornmeal itself proved to be an important factor, and degerminated meal just didn't have enough corn flavor. A fine-ground, whole-grain meal provided better flavor and texture. Our first batches of muffins were too dry, so we experimented with various ways to add moisture; butter, sour cream, and milk provided the moisture, fat (for richness), and acidity (for its tenderizing effect) that we wanted. We tried mixing the ingredients with both the quick-bread and creaming methods; not only was the former the easier way to go, but it also resulted in less airy, cakey muffins. We got our crunchy top from a 400-degree oven. All in all, we'd resolved all of our issues with corn muffins; these were subtly sweet, rich but not dense, and with a texture that was neither cake nor cornbread. Whole-grain cornmeal has a fuller flavor than regular cornmeal milled from degerminated corn. To determine what kind of cornmeal a package contains, look closely at the label.

- 2 cups (10 ounces) all-purpose flour
- 1 cup (5 ounces) fine-ground whole-grain yellow cornmeal
- 1½ teaspoons baking powder
- 1 teaspoon baking soda
- ½ teaspoon table salt
- 2 large eggs
- ¾ cup (5¼ ounces) sugar
- 8 tablespoons unsalted butter, melted
- ¾ cup sour cream
- ½ cup milk

1. Adjust oven rack to middle position and heat oven to 400 degrees. Spray muffin tin with vegetable oil spray.

2. Whisk flour, cornmeal, baking powder, baking soda, and salt together in medium bowl; set aside. Whisk eggs in second medium bowl. Add sugar to eggs; whisk vigorously until thick and homogeneous, about 30 seconds; add melted butter in 3 additions, whisking to combine after each addition. Add half of sour cream and half of milk and whisk to combine; whisk in remaining sour cream and milk until combined. Add wet ingredients to dry ingredients; mix gently with rubber spatula until batter is just combined and evenly moistened. Do not overmix. Using ⅓-cup measure or ice cream scoop, divide the batter evenly among prepared muffin cups, dropping batter to form mounds. Do not level or flatten surface of mounds.

3. Bake until muffins are light golden brown and skewer comes out clean, about 18 minutes, rotating muffin tin halfway through baking. Let muffins cool in muffin tin for 5 minutes, then transfer to wire rack and let cool for 10 minutes before serving.

VARIATION
Corn and Apricot Muffins with Orange Essence
Makes 12 muffins

1. In food processor, process ⅔ cup granulated sugar and 1½ teaspoons grated orange zest until pale orange, about 10 seconds. Transfer to small bowl and set aside.

2. In food processor, pulse 1½ cups dried apricots until finely chopped, about 10 pulses. Transfer to medium bowl; add ⅔ cup orange juice to apricots, cover bowl tightly with plastic wrap, and microwave until simmering, about 1 minute. Let apricots sit, covered, until softened and plump, about 5 minutes. Strain apricots, discarding juice.

3. Follow recipe for Corn Muffins, substituting ¼ cup packed dark brown sugar for equal amount granulated sugar and stirring ½ teaspoon grated orange zest and strained apricots into wet ingredients before adding to dry ingredients. Before baking, sprinkle portion of orange sugar over each mound of batter.

New York–Style Crumb Cake

Serves 8 to 10

WHY THIS RECIPE WORKS The original crumb cake was brought to New York by German immigrants; sadly, the bakery-fresh versions have all but disappeared, and most people know only the preservative-laden commercially baked type. We wanted a recipe closer to the original version that could be made at home. Most modern recipes use butter cake rather than the traditional yeast dough, which made our job that much easier. The essence of this cake is the balance between the tender, buttery cake and the thick, lightly spiced crumb topping. Starting with our favorite yellow cake recipe, we realized we needed to reduce the amount of butter or the richness would be overwhelming. We compensated for the resulting dryness by substituting buttermilk for milk, which also helped make the cake sturdy enough to support the crumbs, and we left out an egg white so the cake wouldn't be rubbery. We wanted our crumb topping to be soft and cookie-like, not a crunchy streusel, so we mixed granulated and brown sugars and melted the butter for a dough-like consistency, flavoring the mixture only with cinnamon. Broken into little pieces and sprinkled over the cake batter, our topping held together during baking and made a thick layer of moist crumbs with golden edges that didn't sink into the cake. Don't be tempted to substitute all-purpose flour for the cake flour; doing so will make a dry, tough cake. If you can't find buttermilk, you can use an equal amount of plain low-fat yogurt, but do not substitute powdered buttermilk because it will make a sunken cake. When topping the cake, take care to not push the crumbs into the batter. This recipe can be easily doubled and baked in a 13 by 9-inch baking pan. If doubling, increase the baking time to about 45 minutes.

Crumb Topping

- ⅓ cup (2⅔ ounces) granulated sugar
- ⅓ cup packed (2⅓ ounces) dark brown sugar
- ¾ teaspoon ground cinnamon
- ⅛ teaspoon table salt
- 8 tablespoons unsalted butter, melted and still warm
- 1¾ cups (7 ounces) cake flour

Cake

- 1¼ cups (5 ounces) cake flour
- ½ cup (3½ ounces) granulated sugar
- ¼ teaspoon baking soda
- ¼ teaspoon table salt
- 6 tablespoons unsalted butter, cut into 6 pieces, softened
- 1 large egg plus 1 large yolk
- ⅓ cup buttermilk
- 1 teaspoon vanilla extract
  Confectioners' sugar

1. For the crumb topping: Whisk sugars, cinnamon, salt, and melted butter in medium bowl to combine. Add flour and stir until mixture resembles thick, cohesive dough; set aside to cool to room temperature, 10 to 15 minutes.

2. For the cake: Adjust oven rack to upper-middle position and heat oven to 325 degrees. Cut 16-inch length parchment paper or aluminum foil and fold lengthwise to 7-inch width. Spray 8-inch square baking pan with vegetable oil spray and fit parchment into pan, pushing it into corners and up sides; allow excess to overhang edges of pan.

3. In bowl of stand mixer fitted with paddle attachment, mix flour, sugar, baking soda, and salt on low speed to combine. With mixer running at low speed, add butter 1 piece at a time; continue beating until mixture resembles moist crumbs, with no visible butter pieces remaining, 1 to 2 minutes. Add egg, yolk, buttermilk, and vanilla; beat on medium-high speed until light and fluffy, about 1 minute, scraping down sides of bowl once if necessary.

4. Transfer batter to prepared pan; spread batter into even layer. Break apart crumb topping into large pea-size pieces, rolling them between your thumb and forefinger to form crumbs, and spread in even layer over batter, beginning with edges and then working toward center. Bake until crumbs are golden and toothpick inserted into center of cake comes out clean, 35 to 40 minutes. Let cool on wire rack for at least 30 minutes. Remove cake from pan by lifting parchment overhang. Dust with confectioners' sugar before serving.

Cream Cheese Coffee Cake

Serves 12 to 16

WHY THIS RECIPE WORKS This brunch staple is fraught with pitfalls—from dry, bland cake to lackluster fillings that sink to the bottom as they cook. We wanted a rich, moist cake with a texture that could support a tangy swirl of cream cheese filling. We assembled a batter of flour, granulated sugar, salt, butter, eggs, whole milk, and baking powder and settled on a straightforward creaming method: Beat softened butter with sugar, then add the eggs, milk, and dry ingredients. The resulting cake was full of flavor and capable of supporting our cheese filling—but it was also a bit dry. To add moisture, we replaced the milk with rich sour cream, added baking soda, and upped the amount of butter. Our cake now had a lush texture as well as subtle acidity—a perfect backdrop for the cheese filling. We settled on a base mixture of softened cream cheese and sugar and added lemon juice to cut the richness and a hint of vanilla extract for depth of flavor. To prevent graininess, we incorporated some of the cake batter into the cheese. The filling not only stayed creamy, but it fused to the cake during baking, eliminating gaps that had afflicted our earlier tests. For a topping, we decided upon a crisp yet delicate coating of sliced almonds, sugar, and lemon zest. As it baked, the topping formed a glistening, crackly crust on our now-perfect coffee cake. Leftovers should be stored in the refrigerator, covered tightly with plastic wrap. For optimal texture, allow the cake to return to room temperature before serving.

Lemon Sugar–Almond Topping
- ¼ cup (1¾ ounces) sugar
- 1½ teaspoons finely grated lemon zest
- ½ cup sliced almonds

Cake
- 2¼ cups (11¼ ounces) all-purpose flour
- 1⅛ teaspoons baking powder
- 1⅛ teaspoons baking soda
- 1 teaspoon table salt
- 10 tablespoons unsalted butter, softened
- 1⅛ cups (7¾ ounces) plus 5 tablespoons sugar, divided
- 1 tablespoon finely grated lemon zest plus 4 teaspoons juice
- 4 large eggs
- 5 teaspoons vanilla extract, divided
- 1¼ cups sour cream
- 8 ounces cream cheese, softened

1. For the topping: Adjust oven rack to middle position and heat oven to 350 degrees. Stir together sugar and lemon zest in small bowl until combined and sugar is moistened. Stir in almonds; set aside.

2. For the cake: Spray 10-inch tube pan with vegetable oil spray. Whisk flour, baking powder, baking soda, and salt together in bowl; set aside. In stand mixer fitted with paddle attachment, beat butter, 1 cup plus 2 tablespoons sugar, and lemon zest at medium speed until light and fluffy, about 3 minutes, scraping down sides and bottom of bowl as necessary. Add eggs one at a time, beating well after each addition, about 20 seconds, and scraping down beater and sides of bowl as necessary. Add 4 teaspoons vanilla and mix to combine. Reduce speed to low and add flour mixture in 3 additions, alternating with sour cream in 2 additions, mixing until incorporated after each addition for 5 to 10 seconds and scraping down bowl as needed. Remove bowl from mixer and fold batter once or twice with rubber spatula to incorporate any remaining flour.

3. Measure out 1¼ cups batter and set aside. Spoon remaining batter into prepared pan and smooth top. Return now-empty bowl to mixer and beat cream cheese, remaining 5 tablespoons sugar, lemon juice, and remaining 1 teaspoon vanilla on medium speed until smooth and slightly lightened, about 1 minute. Add ¼ cup of reserved batter and mix until incorporated. Spoon the cheese filling mixture evenly over batter, keeping filling about 1 inch from edges of pan; smooth top. Spread remaining 1 cup reserved batter over filling and smooth top. With butter knife or offset spatula, gently swirl filling into batter using figure-8 motion, being careful not to drag filling to bottom or edges of pan. Firmly tap pan on counter 2 or 3 times to dislodge any bubbles. Sprinkle lemon sugar–almond topping evenly over batter and gently press into batter to adhere.

4. Bake until top is golden and just firm and skewer inserted into cake comes out clean (skewer will be wet if inserted into cheese filling), 45 to 50 minutes. Remove pan from oven and firmly tap on counter 2 or 3 times (top of cake may sink slightly). Let cake cool in pan on wire rack for 1 hour. Gently invert cake onto rimmed baking sheet (cake will be topping side down); remove tube pan, place wire rack on top of cake, and invert cake topping side up. Let cool to room temperature, about 1½ hours, before serving.

Making Cream Cheese Coffee Cake

1. Reserve 1¼ cups of batter, then fill pan with remaining batter; smooth top.

2. Beat ¼ cup of reserved batter with filling ingredients; spoon filling evenly over batter.

3. Top filling with remaining 1 cup reserved batter; smooth top.

4. Using figure-8 motion, swirl filling into batter. Tap pan on counter.

5. Sprinkle lemon sugar–almond topping onto batter, then gently press to adhere.

Perfect Sticky Buns

Makes 12 buns

WHY THIS RECIPE WORKS Many recipes for sticky buns call for a firm, dry dough that's easy to manipulate into the required spiral, simple to slice, and sturdy enough to support a generous amount of topping. But firm, dry sticky buns aren't very appealing. To make a softer, more tender, and moist sticky bun, we added a cooked flour-and-water paste to the dough. The paste traps water, so the dough isn't sticky or difficult to work with, and the increased hydration converts to steam during baking, which makes the bread fluffy and light. The added water also keeps the crumb moist and tender. To ensure that the soft bread wouldn't collapse under the weight of the topping, we strengthened the crumb by adding a resting period and withholding the sugar and salt until the gluten was firmly established. Dark corn syrup plus water was the key to a topping that was substantial enough to sit atop the buns without sinking in but not so firm that it presented a danger to our teeth. These buns take about 4 hours to make from start to finish. For dough that is easy to work with and produces light, fluffy buns, we strongly recommend that you measure the flour for the dough by weight. The slight tackiness of the dough aids in flattening and stretching it in step 6, so resist the urge to use a lot of dusting flour. Rolling the dough cylinder tightly in step 7 will result in misshapen rolls; keep the cylinder a bit slack. Bake these buns in a metal, not glass or ceramic, baking pan. We like dark corn syrup and pecans here, but light corn syrup may be used, and the nuts may be omitted, if desired.

Flour Paste
⅔ cup water
¼ cup (1⅓ ounces) bread flour

Dough
⅔ cup milk
1 large egg plus 1 large yolk
2¾ cups (15⅛ ounces) bread flour
2 teaspoons instant or rapid-rise yeast
3 tablespoons granulated sugar
1½ teaspoons table salt
6 tablespoons unsalted butter, softened

Topping
6 tablespoons unsalted butter, melted
½ cup packed (3½ ounces) dark brown sugar
¼ cup (1¾ ounces) granulated sugar
¼ cup dark corn syrup
¼ teaspoon table salt
2 tablespoons water
1 cup pecans, toasted and chopped (optional)

Filling
¾ cup packed (5¼ ounces) dark brown sugar
1 teaspoon ground cinnamon

1. *For the flour paste:* Whisk water and flour together in small bowl until no lumps remain. Microwave, whisking every 25 seconds, until mixture thickens to stiff, smooth, pudding-like consistency that forms mound when dropped from end of whisk into bowl, 50 to 75 seconds.

2. *For the dough:* In bowl of stand mixer, whisk flour paste and milk together until smooth. Add egg and yolk and whisk until incorporated. Add flour and yeast. Fit stand mixer with dough hook and mix on low speed until all flour is moistened, 1 to 2 minutes. Let sit for 15 minutes. Add sugar and salt and mix on medium-low speed for 5 minutes. Stop mixer and add butter. Continue to mix on medium-low speed for 5 minutes longer, scraping down dough hook and sides of bowl halfway through (dough will stick to bottom of bowl).

3. Transfer dough to lightly floured counter. Knead briefly to form ball and transfer seam side down to lightly greased bowl; lightly coat surface of dough with vegetable oil spray and cover bowl with plastic wrap. Let dough rise until just doubled in volume, 40 minutes to 1 hour.

4. *For the topping:* While dough rises, grease 13 by 9-inch metal baking pan. Whisk melted butter, brown sugar, granulated sugar, corn syrup, and salt together in medium bowl until smooth. Add water and whisk until incorporated. Pour mixture into prepared pan and tilt pan to cover bottom. Sprinkle evenly with pecans, if using.

5. *For the filling:* Combine sugar and cinnamon in small bowl and mix until thoroughly combined; set aside.

6. Turn out dough onto lightly floured counter. Press dough gently but firmly to expel air. Working from center toward edge, pat and stretch dough to form 18 by 15-inch rectangle with long edge nearest you. Sprinkle filling over dough, leaving 1-inch border along top edge; smooth filling into even layer with your hand, then gently press mixture into dough to adhere.

7. Beginning with long edge nearest you, roll dough into cylinder, taking care not to roll too tightly. Pinch seam to seal and roll cylinder seam side down. Mark gently with knife to create 12 equal portions. To slice, hold strand of dental floss taut and slide underneath cylinder, stopping at first mark. Cross ends of floss over each other and pull. Slice cylinder into 12 portions and transfer, cut sides down, to prepared baking pan. Cover tightly with plastic wrap and let rise until buns are puffy and touching one another, 40 minutes to 1 hour. (Buns may be refrigerated immediately after shaping for up

to 14 hours. To bake, remove baking pan from refrigerator and let sit until buns are puffy and touching one another, 1 to 1½ hours.) Meanwhile, adjust oven racks to lowest and lower-middle positions. Place rimmed baking sheet on lower rack to catch any drips and heat oven to 375 degrees.

8. Bake buns on upper rack until golden brown, about 20 minutes. Tent with aluminum foil and bake until center of dough registers at least 200 degrees, 10 to 15 minutes. Let buns cool in pan on wire rack for 5 minutes. Place rimmed baking sheet over buns and carefully invert. Remove pan and let buns cool for 5 minutes. Using spoon, scoop any glaze on baking sheet onto buns. Let cool for at least 10 minutes before serving.

Making Sticky Buns

1. Pour topping mixture into prepared baking pan and tilt pan to cover bottom. Sprinkle evenly with pecans, if using.

2. Smooth filling into even layer on dough rectangle and roll dough loosely into cylinder. Pinch seam to seal and roll cylinder seam side down.

3. Slice cylinder into 12 equal portions. Transfer slices, cut sides down, to prepared baking pan. Let rise, then bake buns until golden brown and center of dough registers at least 200 degrees.

4. Let buns cool in pan on wire rack. Place rimmed baking sheet over buns and carefully invert. Remove pan and let buns cool. Using spoon, scoop any glaze on baking sheet onto buns.

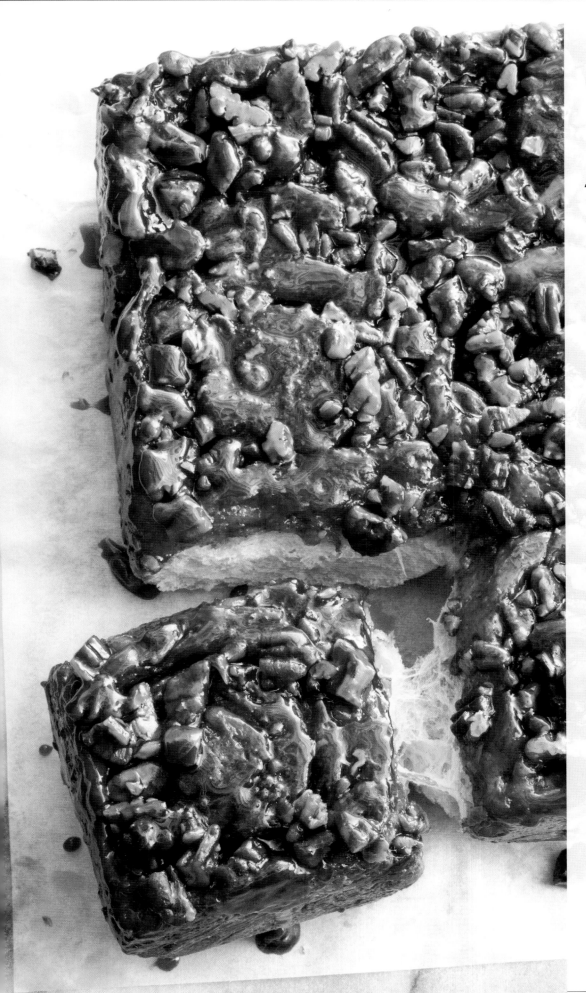

"These are the best sticky buns that I have ever eaten, but this recipe itself is an example of how much I learn at work. I'd baked breads and worked with yeasted doughs for decades, but had never heard of the Japanese bread-baking technique of tangzhong, which my coworker Andrea Geary introduced to the test kitchen. She used it here to solve the problem of making moist and light buns that could somehow support the heavy, sticky topping. The resulting buns are just sturdy enough, yet as soft and plush as velvet.

This was also the TV recipe over which Julia and I lost it on camera, unable to control our laughter. Let me explain. It was our first year as hosts, on a Friday at the end of a very long week of shooting episodes. We were spent—mentally, emotionally, physically—and after a few bites of the buns, the rush of sugar and carbs was overwhelming. I think my eyes rolled into the back of my head—like a shark biting down on its kill. The crew kept the cameras rolling, not sure what was happening but very sure they wanted to capture it all. Next time you watch that episode (or the blooper video!), know that we were having as much fun as it looked, and I ate three buns in about 15 minutes."

—*Bridget*

Soups, Stews, Chilis, and Curries

Thai Hot and Sour Noodle Soup with Shrimp

Hearty Chicken Noodle Soup

Serves 4 to 6

WHY THIS RECIPE WORKS Sometimes we prefer a simple bowl of chicken soup—a brothy soup modestly enriched with chicken, noodles, and vegetables. Other times, a heartier version of chicken noodle soup is what we crave—one chock-full of chicken, noodles, and vegetables—a true meal in a bowl. We began by jump-starting the flavor of our soup with a mixture of store-bought chicken broth and water, but the broth-and-water base had a distinctly flat flavor. A few pounds of chicken parts created a rich stock, but browning the parts and then simmering them was just too fussy for what we wanted. Instead, we turned to a somewhat unlikely but more convenient substitute—store-bought ground chicken. Ground chicken offers more surface area and exponentially more flavor, providing a great-tasting stock when sautéed with aromatics and then simmered with the broth and water. All the stock needed was some body and thickening, which we got from a little cornstarch. With our broth down, we were ready to add the chicken (breasts that had been poached in the stock until just cooked through and then shredded), vegetables, and noodles. Along with onion, celery, and carrots, we further enriched the soup with potato and Swiss chard. Our streamlined hearty chicken noodle soup was now rich and satisfying. When skimming the fat off the stock, we prefer to leave a little bit on the surface to enhance the soup's flavor.

Stock

- 1 tablespoon vegetable oil
- 1 pound ground chicken
- 1 small onion, chopped
- 1 carrot, peeled and chopped
- 1 celery rib, chopped
- 8 cups chicken broth
- 4 cups water
- 2 (12-ounce) bone-in, skin-on chicken breast halves, halved crosswise
- 2 teaspoons table salt
- 2 bay leaves

Soup

- ¼ cup cold water
- 3 tablespoons cornstarch
- 1 small onion, halved and sliced thin
- 2 carrots, peeled, halved lengthwise, and cut crosswise into ¾-inch pieces
- 1 celery rib, halved lengthwise and cut crosswise into ½-inch pieces
- 8 ounces russet potato, peeled and cut into ¾-inch pieces
- 1½ ounces egg noodles (1 cup)
- 4–6 Swiss chard leaves, ribs removed, torn into 1-inch pieces (2 cups; optional)
- 1 tablespoon minced fresh parsley

1. *For the stock:* Heat oil in Dutch oven over medium-high heat until shimmering. Add ground chicken, onion, carrot, and celery. Cook, stirring frequently, until chicken is no longer pink, 5 to 10 minutes (do not brown chicken).

2. Reduce heat to medium-low. Add broth, water, chicken breasts, salt, and bay leaves; cover and cook for 30 minutes. Remove lid, increase heat to high, and bring to boil. (If liquid is already boiling when lid is removed, remove chicken breasts immediately and continue with recipe.) Transfer chicken breasts to large plate and set aside. Continue to cook stock for 20 minutes, adjusting heat to maintain gentle boil. Strain stock through fine-mesh strainer into container, pressing on solids to extract as much liquid as possible; discard solids. Allow liquid to settle for about 5 minutes and skim off fat. (Strained stock can be refrigerated in airtight container for up to 2 days or frozen for up to 3 months. Chicken breasts can be refrigerated in zipper-lock bag with air squeezed out for up to 2 days.)

3. *For the soup:* Return stock to Dutch oven set over medium-high heat. In small bowl, combine water and cornstarch until smooth slurry forms; stir into stock and bring to gentle boil. Add onion, carrots, celery, and potato and cook until potato pieces are almost tender, 10 to 15 minutes, adjusting heat as necessary to maintain gentle boil. Add egg noodles and continue to cook until all vegetables and noodles are tender, about 5 minutes.

4. Meanwhile, using 2 forks, shred chicken; discard skin and bones. Add shredded chicken; Swiss chard, if using; and parsley to soup and cook until heated through, about 2 minutes. Season with salt and pepper to taste, and serve.

Avgolemono

Serves 4 to 6

WHY THIS RECIPE WORKS Avgolemono, or Greek chicken and rice soup, gets its name from the egg-lemon mixture that thickens and flavors it. Our version contains tender shreds of chicken that are poached to perfection by sitting off the heat in hot broth. We flavored the broth with citrusy coriander and lemon zest, which gave it savory depth and enhanced the soup's lemon flavor. Processing eggs, yolks, and a portion of the cooked rice in a blender and then stirring this puree into the hot broth gave our avgolemono a velvety consistency. If you have homemade chicken broth, we recommend using it in this recipe, as it gives the soup the best flavor and body. Our preferred commercial chicken broth is Swanson Chicken Stock. Use a vegetable peeler to remove strips of zest from the lemons.

"This recipe for tortilla soup, developed by Becky Hays in 2005, is an oldie but goodie: It's one of my all-time favorites that I make religiously throughout the year. Long ago, I ordered this soup just about every day while vacationing in Puerto Vallarta, Mexico, and Becky's version is as authentic as it comes. Its smoky and spicy broth, tender chunks of chicken, and crisp corn tortilla strips— all topped off with creamy avocado, fresh cilantro, salty cotija cheese, tangy crema, and a healthy squeeze of lime juice—never fail to bring me right back to sunny Mexico. Don't forget to serve it with bottles of ice-cold Mexican lager!"

–Erin

1½ pounds boneless, skinless chicken breasts, trimmed
1¾ teaspoons table salt
12 (3-inch) strips lemon zest plus 6 tablespoons juice, plus extra juice for seasoning (3 lemons)
2 sprigs fresh dill, plus 2 teaspoons chopped
2 teaspoons coriander seeds
1 teaspoon black peppercorns
1 garlic clove, peeled and smashed
8 cups chicken broth
1 cup long-grain rice
2 large eggs plus 2 large yolks

1. Cut each chicken breast in half lengthwise. Toss with salt and let sit at room temperature for at least 15 minutes or up to 30 minutes. Cut 8-inch square of triple-thickness cheesecloth. Place lemon zest, dill sprigs, coriander seeds, peppercorns, and garlic in center of cheesecloth and tie into bundle with kitchen twine.

2. Bring broth, rice, and spice bundle to boil in large saucepan over high heat. Reduce heat to low, cover, and cook for 5 minutes. Turn off heat, add chicken, cover, and let sit for 15 minutes.

3. Transfer chicken to large plate and discard spice bundle. Using 2 forks, shred chicken into bite-size pieces. Using ladle, transfer 1 cup cooked rice to blender (leave any liquid in pot). Add lemon juice and eggs and yolks to blender and process until smooth, about 1 minute.

4. Return chicken and any accumulated juices to pot. Return soup to simmer over high heat. Remove pot from heat and stir in egg mixture until fully incorporated. Stir in chopped dill and season with salt, pepper, and extra lemon juice to taste. Serve.

Tortilla Soup

Serves 6

WHY THIS RECIPE WORKS By breaking the classic tortilla soup recipe down to its three main components—the flavor base (tomatoes, garlic, onion, and chiles), the chicken stock, and the garnishes (including fried tortilla strips)—we found that we could devise techniques and substitute ingredients to make our own compelling version of tortilla soup. To achieve maximum flavor for our tortilla soup recipe, we composed a puree made from chipotle chiles, tomatoes, onions, garlic, jalapeños, and a cilantro-oregano substitute for the Mexican ingredient *epazote*, and then fried the puree in oil over high heat. We then added the puree to store-bought chicken broth, which we strained after poaching chicken in it and infusing it with onions, garlic, cilantro, and oregano. Turning to the garnish, we oven-toasted our lightly oiled

tortilla strips instead of frying them and substituted sour cream and Monterey Jack cheese for the harder-to-find Mexican crema and cotija cheese. Despite its somewhat lengthy ingredient list, this recipe is very easy to prepare. If you desire a soup with mild spiciness, trim the ribs and seeds from the jalapeño (or omit the jalapeño altogether) and use the minimum amount of adobo sauce (1 teaspoon, pureed with the tomatoes in step 3). Our preferred brand of chicken broth is Swanson Chicken Stock. (The soup can be completed short of adding the shredded chicken to the pot at the end of step 3. Return the soup to a simmer over medium-high heat before proceeding. The tortilla strips and the garnishes are best prepared the day of serving.)

Tortilla Strips
8 (6-inch) corn tortillas, cut into ½-inch-wide strips
1 tablespoon vegetable oil

Soup
2 split bone-in, skin-on chicken breasts (1½ pounds) or 4 bone-in, skin-on chicken thighs (1¼ pounds), skin removed and trimmed of excess fat
8 cups chicken broth
1 pound white onion, trimmed of root end, quartered, and peeled, divided
4 cloves garlic, peeled, divided
2 sprigs fresh epazote, or 8 to 10 sprigs fresh cilantro plus 1 sprig fresh oregano
1⅛ teaspoons table salt, divided
2 tomatoes, cored and quartered
½ jalapeño chile
1 canned chipotle chile, plus up to 1 tablespoon adobo sauce
1 tablespoon vegetable oil

Garnishes
Lime wedges
1 avocado, diced fine
Fresh cilantro leaves
8 ounces cotija cheese, crumbled, or Monterey Jack cheese, diced fine
Minced jalapeño chile
Mexican crema or sour cream

1. *For the tortilla strips:* Adjust oven rack to middle position; heat oven to 425 degrees. Spread tortilla strips on rimmed baking sheet; drizzle with oil and toss until evenly coated. Bake until strips are deep golden brown and crisped, about 14 minutes, rotating pan and shaking strips (to redistribute) halfway through baking time. Season strips lightly with salt; transfer to plate lined with several layers paper towels.

2. *For the soup:* While tortilla strips bake, bring chicken, broth, 2 onion quarters, 2 garlic cloves, epazote, and ½ teaspoon salt to boil over medium-high heat in large saucepan; reduce heat to low, cover, and simmer until chicken is just cooked through, about 20 minutes. Using tongs, transfer chicken to large plate. Pour broth through fine-mesh strainer; discarding solids. When cool enough to handle, shred chicken into bite-size pieces; discard bones.

3. Puree tomatoes, remaining 2 onion quarters, remaining 2 garlic cloves, jalapeño, chipotle, and 1 teaspoon adobo sauce in food processor until smooth. Heat oil in Dutch oven over high heat until shimmering; add tomato mixture and ⅛ teaspoon salt and cook, stirring frequently, until mixture has darkened in color, about 10 minutes. Stir strained broth into tomato mixture, bring to boil, then reduce heat to low and simmer to blend flavors, about 15 minutes. Taste soup; if desired, add up to 2 teaspoons additional adobo sauce. Add shredded chicken and simmer until heated through, about 5 minutes. To serve, place portions of tortilla strips in bottom of individual bowls and ladle soup into bowls; pass garnishes separately.

Thai-Style Chicken Soup

Serves 6 to 8

WHY THIS RECIPE WORKS Replicating the complex flavors of Thai chicken soup at home can be difficult, since it relies on such exotica as galangal, makrut lime leaves, lemon grass, and bird chiles. We wanted a plausibly authentic version of Thai chicken soup that could be prepared with more readily available (i.e., supermarket) substitutes. We started by making a classic version of the soup and substituting one ingredient at a time. We developed an acceptably rich and definitely chicken-flavored broth by using equal parts chicken broth and coconut milk (adding the coconut milk in two stages: at the beginning and just before serving). We couldn't fake the flavor of lemon grass, but it proved to be easy enough to find. Our most exciting find was a "magic bullet" substitution: jarred red curry paste included all the other exotic ingredients we were missing. Just adding a dollop at the very end of cooking and whisking it with pungent fish sauce and tart lime juice allowed all the classic flavors to come through loud and clear. To make slicing the chicken easier, freeze it for 15 minutes. Although we prefer the richer, more complex flavor of regular coconut milk, light coconut milk can be substituted for one or both cans. For a spicier soup, add additional red curry paste to taste.

Soup
- 1 teaspoon peanut or vegetable oil
- 3 stalks lemon grass, trimmed to bottom 6 inches, sliced thin
- 3 large shallots, chopped (¾ cup)
- 8 sprigs fresh cilantro, chopped
- 3 tablespoons fish sauce, divided
- 4 cups chicken broth
- 2 (14-ounce) cans coconut milk, divided
- 1 tablespoon sugar
- 8 ounces white mushrooms, trimmed and sliced ¼ inch thick
- 1 pound boneless, skinless chicken breasts, trimmed, halved lengthwise, and cut on bias ⅛ inch thick
- 3 tablespoons lime juice (2 limes)
- 2 teaspoons Thai red curry paste

Garnishes
- ½ cup fresh cilantro leaves
- 2 Thai, serrano, or jalapeño chiles, stemmed, seeded, and sliced thin
- 2 scallions, sliced thin on bias
  Lime wedges

1. Heat oil in large saucepan over medium heat until just shimmering. Add lemon grass, shallots, cilantro sprigs, and 1 tablespoon fish sauce and cook, stirring frequently, until just softened but not browned, 2 to 5 minutes.

2. Stir in broth and 1 can coconut milk and bring to simmer over high heat. Cover, reduce heat to low, and simmer until flavors meld, about 10 minutes. Pour broth through fine-mesh strainer, discarding solids. (At this point, soup can be refrigerated in airtight container for up to 1 day.)

3. Return strained soup to clean saucepan and bring to simmer over medium-high heat. Stir in sugar and remaining can of coconut milk and bring to simmer. Reduce heat to medium, add mushrooms, and cook until just tender, 2 to 3 minutes. Add chicken and cook, stirring constantly, until no longer pink, 1 to 3 minutes. Remove soup from heat.

4. Whisk remaining 2 tablespoons fish sauce, lime juice, and curry paste together, then stir into soup. Ladle soup into individual bowls and garnish with cilantro, chiles, and scallions. Serve with lime wedges.

Thai Hot and Sour Noodle Soup with Shrimp (Guay Tiew Tom Yum Goong)

SEASON 20 RECIPE

Serves 4 to 6

WHY THIS RECIPE WORKS The hot and sour soup called *tom yum* is a bold example of the energetic flavors that Thai cuisine is famous for. The heat comes from chiles and galangal (also known as Thai ginger), the sour from lime juice and tamarind (a dark, tart fruit). But tom yum also serves up saltiness courtesy of fish sauce and sweetness via a touch of sugar. Lemon grass, makrut lime leaves, cilantro, and Thai basil round out the fragrant bowl. There are many versions of tom yum soup, but one of our favorites, known as *guay tiew tom yum goong*, is chock-full of shrimp, rice noodles, and sometimes mushrooms and/or tomatoes and topped with a deeply savory, sweet, and spicy chili jam. To infuse the broth (we chose chicken broth as our starting point) with some of Thailand's signature aromatics, we found that simply slicing them and simmering them in the broth took more than an hour to extract sufficient flavor. Ultimately, it made sense to do as Thai cooks do: slice the aromatics and then lightly smash them to partially break them down. Now the broth developed a heady perfume after just 15 minutes of simmering, and the pieces could easily be removed using a slotted spoon. Sugar and fish sauce rounded things out with sweetness and saltiness. To bulk up the soup, we stirred in fresh oyster mushrooms and the grassy green parts of the scallions. Next, we slipped a pound of peeled large shrimp into the steaming broth off the heat for 5 minutes. The residual heat ensured that the shrimp gently cooked through with little risk of turning rubbery. Halved cherry tomatoes added pops of color and another layer of acidity and sweetness, and a healthy squeeze of lime juice delivered the sour flourish that is a hallmark of guay tiew tom yum goong. As for the rice noodles, we first soaked them in boiling water and then ladled the fragrant soup over them. In a final nod to authenticity, we topped each bowl with a crimson dollop of *nam prik pao* (Thai chili jam, so called because of its jammy consistency), a rich, sweet, savory, and slightly spicy condiment of fried garlic, shallots, and dried chiles cooked down with fish sauce and brown sugar. Whole shrimp are traditional in this soup, but you can halve them crosswise before cooking to make them easier to eat. If galangal is unavailable, substitute fresh ginger. Makrut lime leaves (sometimes sold as kaffir lime leaves) add a lot to this soup. If you can't find them, substitute three 3-inch strips each of lemon zest and lime zest. We prefer vermicelli made from 100 percent rice flour to varieties that include a secondary starch such as cornstarch. If you can find only the latter, soak them longer—up to 15 minutes.

- 4 ounces rice vermicelli
- 2 lemon grass stalks, trimmed to bottom 6 inches
- 4 scallions, trimmed, white parts left whole, green parts cut into 1-inch lengths
- 6 makrut lime leaves, torn if large
- 2 Thai chiles, stemmed (1 left whole, 1 sliced thin), divided, plus 2 Thai chiles, stemmed and sliced thin, for serving (optional)
- 1 (2-inch) piece fresh galangal, peeled and sliced into ¼-inch-thick rounds
- 8 cups chicken broth
- 1 tablespoon sugar, plus extra for seasoning
- 8 ounces oyster mushrooms, trimmed and torn into 1-inch pieces
- 3 tablespoons fish sauce, plus extra for seasoning
- 1 pound extra-large shrimp (21 to 25 per pound), peeled, deveined, and tails removed
- 12 ounces cherry tomatoes, halved
- 2 tablespoons lime juice, plus extra for seasoning, plus lime wedges for serving
- ½ cup fresh cilantro leaves
- ¼ cup fresh Thai basil leaves, torn if large (optional)
- 1 recipe Thai Chili Jam (Nam Prik Pao) (optional) (page 50)

1. Bring 4 quarts water to boil in large pot. Remove from heat, add vermicelli, and let sit, stirring occasionally, until vermicelli are fully tender, 10 to 15 minutes. Drain, rinse with cold water, drain again, and distribute evenly among large soup bowls.

2. Place lemon grass, scallion whites, lime leaves, whole Thai chile, and galangal on cutting board and lightly smash with meat pounder or bottom of small skillet until mixture is moist and very fragrant. Transfer lemon grass mixture to Dutch oven. Add broth and sugar and bring to boil over high heat. Reduce heat and simmer for 15 minutes. Using slotted spoon, remove solids from pot and discard.

3. Add mushrooms, fish sauce, scallion greens, and sliced Thai chile and simmer for 3 to 4 minutes. Stir in shrimp. Cover and let sit off heat until shrimp are opaque and cooked through, 4 to 5 minutes. Stir in tomatoes and lime juice. Season with extra sugar, extra fish sauce, and extra lime juice to taste.

4. Ladle soup into bowls of noodles; sprinkle with cilantro and Thai basil, if using. Serve, drizzled with Thai Chili Jam, if using, and passing lime wedges and extra sliced Thai chiles, if using, separately.

ACCOMPANIMENT
Thai Chili Jam (Nam Prik Pao)
Makes ¾ cup

The sweet, savory, and spicy condiment called nam prik pao is the classic garnish for guay tiew tom yum goong, *but it's too good to be relegated to a single use. Thai cooks also use it on fried eggs, noodles, and white rice; in stir-fries; or even as a sandwich spread. Slice the shallots to a consistent thickness to ensure even cooking. For a spicier jam, add more chile seeds.*

- ½ **cup vegetable oil**
- 2 **large shallots, sliced thin**
- 4 **large garlic cloves, sliced thin**
- 10 **dried arbol chiles, stemmed, halved lengthwise, and seeds reserved**
- 2 **tablespoons packed brown sugar**
- 3 **tablespoons lime juice, plus extra for seasoning (2 limes)**
- 2 **tablespoons fish sauce, plus extra for seasoning**

1. Set fine-mesh strainer over heatproof bowl. Heat oil and shallots in medium saucepan over medium-high heat, stirring frequently, until shallots are deep golden brown, 10 to 14 minutes. Using slotted spoon, transfer shallots to second bowl. Add garlic to hot oil and cook, stirring constantly, until golden brown, 2 to 3 minutes. Using slotted spoon, transfer garlic to bowl with shallots. Add arbols and half of reserved seeds to hot oil and cook, stirring constantly, until arbols turn deep red, 1 to 2 minutes. Strain oil through prepared strainer into bowl; reserve oil and transfer arbols to bowl with shallots and garlic. Do not wash saucepan.

2. Process shallot mixture, sugar, and lime juice in food processor until thick paste forms, 15 to 30 seconds, scraping down sides of bowl as needed.

3. Return paste to now-empty saucepan and add fish sauce and 2 tablespoons reserved oil. Bring to simmer over medium-low heat. Cook, stirring frequently, until mixture is thickened and has jam-like consistency, 4 to 5 minutes. Off heat, season with extra lime juice, extra fish sauce, and salt to taste. (Jam can be refrigerated for up to 1 month.)

Classic French Onion Soup

Serves 6

WHY THIS RECIPE WORKS The ideal French onion soup combines a satisfying broth redolent of sweet caramelized onions with a slice of toasted baguette and melted cheese. We wanted a foolproof method for achieving extraordinarily deep flavor from the humble onion—the star of this classic soup. The secret to a rich broth was to caramelize the onions fully. The good news was that caramelizing the onions, deglazing the pot, and then repeating this process dozens of times kept ratcheting up the flavor. The bad news was what a laborious, hands-on process this proved to be. Fortunately, we found that if we first cooked the onions, covered, in a hot oven for 2½ hours, we only needed to deglaze the onions on the stovetop three or four times. Just one type of onion (yellow) was sufficient, but a combination of three different liquids (water, chicken broth, and beef broth) added maximum flavor. For the topping, we toasted the bread before floating it on the soup to ward off sogginess and added only a modest sprinkling of nutty Gruyère so the broth wasn't overpowered. Use a Dutch oven that holds 7 quarts or more for this recipe. Sweet onions, such as Vidalia or Walla Walla, will make this dish overly sweet. Use broiler-safe crocks and keep the rims of the bowls 4 to 5 inches from the heating element to obtain a proper gratinée of melted, bubbly cheese. If using ordinary soup bowls, sprinkle the toasted bread slices with Gruyère and return them to the broiler until the cheese melts, then float them on top of the soup. For the best flavor, make the soup a day or two in advance. Alternatively, the onions can be prepared through step 1, cooled in the pot, and refrigerated for up to three days before proceeding with the recipe.

Soup
- 3 **tablespoons unsalted butter, cut into 3 pieces**
- 4 **pounds onions, halved and sliced through root end ¼ inch thick**
- 1½ **teaspoons table salt, divided**
- 2 **cups water, plus extra for deglazing, divided**
- ½ **cup dry sherry**
- 4 **cups chicken broth**
- 2 **cups beef broth**
- 6 **sprigs fresh thyme, tied together with kitchen twine**
- 1 **bay leaf**

Cheese Croutons
- 1 **small baguette, sliced ½ inch thick on bias**
- 8 **ounces Gruyère cheese, shredded (2 cups)**

1. *For the soup:* Adjust oven rack to lower-middle position and heat oven to 400 degrees. Generously spray inside of large Dutch oven with vegetable oil spray. Add butter, onions, and 1 teaspoon salt to pot. Cook, covered, for 1 hour (onions will be moist and slightly reduced in volume). Remove pot from oven (handles will be hot) and stir onions, scraping bottom and sides of pot. Return pot to oven with lid slightly ajar and

continue to cook until onions are very soft and golden brown, 1½ to 1¾ hours, stirring onions and scraping bottom and sides of pot after 1 hour.

2. Being careful of hot handles, remove pot from oven and place over medium-high heat. (Do not turn off oven.) Cook onions, stirring frequently and scraping bottom and sides of pot, until liquid evaporates and onions brown, 15 to 20 minutes, reducing heat to medium if onions are browning too quickly. Continue to cook, stirring frequently, until pot bottom is coated with dark crust, 6 to 8 minutes, adjusting heat as necessary. (Scrape any browned bits that collect on spoon back into onions.) Stir in ¼ cup water, scraping pot bottom to loosen crust, and cook until water evaporates and pot bottom has formed another dark crust, 6 to 8 minutes. Repeat process of deglazing 2 or 3 more times, until onions are very dark brown. Stir in sherry and cook, stirring frequently, until sherry evaporates, about 5 minutes.

3. Stir in remaining 2 cups water, chicken broth, beef broth, thyme, bay leaf, and remaining ½ teaspoon salt, scraping up any final bits of browned crust on bottom and sides of pot. Increase heat to high and bring to simmer. Reduce heat to low, cover, and simmer for 30 minutes. Discard thyme and bay leaf; season with salt and pepper to taste.

4. *For the croutons:* While soup simmers, arrange baguette slices in single layer on rimmed baking sheet. Bake until dry, crisp, and golden at edges, about 10 minutes. Set aside.

5. Adjust oven rack 6 inches from broiler element and heat broiler. Set individual broiler-safe crocks on baking sheet and fill each with about 1¾ cups soup. Top each bowl with 1 or 2 baguette slices (do not overlap slices) and sprinkle evenly with Gruyère. Broil until cheese is melted and bubbly around edges, 3 to 5 minutes. Let cool for 5 minutes; serve.

Quick Beef and Vegetable Soup

Serves 4 to 6

WHY THIS RECIPE WORKS Rich and hearty beef and vegetable soup with old-fashioned flavor is a snap to make—if you have a few hours free and several pounds of beef and bones hanging around. We wanted to find another way to develop the same flavors and textures in under an hour. We knew the key to this recipe would be finding the right cut of meat, one that had great beefy flavor and that would cook up tender in a reasonable amount of time. Tender cuts, like strip steak and rib eye, became tough, livery, and chalky when simmered in soup. Sirloin tip steak was the best choice—when cut into small pieces, the meat was tender and offered the illusion of being cooked for hours; plus, its meaty flavor imparted richness to the soup. In place of labor-intensive homemade beef broth, we doctored store-bought beef broth with aromatics and lightened its flavor profile with chicken broth. To further boost the flavor of the beef, we added cremini mushrooms, tomato paste, soy sauce, and red wine, ingredients that are rich in glutamates, naturally occurring compounds that accentuate the meat's hearty flavor. To mimic the rich body of a homemade meat stock (made rich through the gelatin released by the meat bones' collagen during the long simmering process), we relied on powdered gelatin. Our beef and vegetable soup now had the same richness and flavor as cooked-all-day versions in a whole lot less time. Choose whole sirloin tip steaks over ones that have been cut into small pieces for stir-fries. If sirloin tip steaks are unavailable, substitute blade or flank steak, removing any hard gristle or excess fat. Button mushrooms can be used in place of the cremini mushrooms, with some trade-off in flavor. If you like, add 1 cup frozen peas, frozen corn, or frozen cut green beans during the last 5 minutes of cooking. For a heartier soup, add 10 ounces red potatoes, cut into ½-inch pieces (2 cups), during the last 15 minutes of cooking.

1 **pound sirloin tip steaks, trimmed and cut into ½-inch pieces**
2 **tablespoons soy sauce**
1 **teaspoon vegetable oil**
1 **pound cremini mushrooms, trimmed and quartered**
1 **large onion, chopped**
2 **tablespoons tomato paste**
1 **garlic clove, minced**
½ **cup red wine**
4 **cups beef broth**
1¾ **cups chicken broth**
4 **carrots, peeled and cut into ½-inch pieces**
2 **celery ribs, cut into ½-inch pieces**
1 **bay leaf**
1 **tablespoon unflavored gelatin**
½ **cup cold water**
2 **tablespoons minced fresh parsley**

1. Combine beef and soy sauce in medium bowl; set aside for 15 minutes.

2. Heat oil in Dutch oven over medium-high heat until just smoking. Add mushrooms and onion; cook, stirring frequently, until onion is browned and dark bits form on pan bottom, 8 to 12 minutes. Transfer vegetables to bowl.

3. Add beef and cook, stirring occasionally, until liquid evaporates and meat starts to brown, 6 to 10 minutes. Add tomato paste and garlic; cook, stirring constantly, until fragrant, about 30 seconds. Add red wine, scraping bottom of pot to loosen any browned bits, and cook until syrupy, 1 to 2 minutes.

4. Add beef broth, chicken broth, carrots, celery, bay leaf, and browned mushrooms and onion; bring to boil. Reduce heat to low, cover, and simmer until vegetables and meat are tender, 25 to 30 minutes. While soup is simmering, sprinkle gelatin over cold water and let sit.

5. Remove pot from heat and discard bay leaf. Add gelatin mixture and stir until completely dissolved. Stir in parsley, season with salt and pepper to taste, and serve.

Vietnamese Beef Pho

Serves 4 to 6

WHY THIS RECIPE WORKS Traditional versions of this Vietnamese beef and noodle soup call for simmering beef bones for hours to make a deeply flavorful broth. We wanted to make this soup suitable for the home cook, which meant that beef bones were out of the question. Instead, we simmered ground beef in spiced store-bought broth, which gave us the complexity and depth we were after in a fraction of the time. To serve the soup, we poured our broth over thinly sliced strip steak and gathered a variety of essential garnishes, such as lime wedges, hoisin and chile sauces, and bean sprouts. Use a Dutch oven that holds 6 quarts or more for this recipe. Our favorite store-bought beef broth is Better Than Bouillon Roasted Beef Base. An equal weight of tri-tip steak or blade steak can be substituted for the strip steak; make sure to trim all connective tissue and excess fat. One 14- or 16-ounce package of rice noodles will serve four to six. Look for noodles that are about ⅛ inch wide; these are often labeled "small." Don't use Thai Kitchen Stir-Fry Rice Noodles since they are too thick and don't adequately soak up the broth.

- 1 pound 85 percent lean ground beef
- 2 onions, quartered through root end, divided
- 12 cups beef broth
- 2 cups water, plus extra as needed
- ¼ cup fish sauce, plus extra for seasoning
- 1 (4-inch) piece ginger, sliced into thin rounds
- 1 cinnamon stick
- 2 tablespoons sugar, plus extra for seasoning
- 6 star anise pods
- 6 whole cloves
- 2 teaspoons table salt, plus extra for seasoning
- 1 teaspoon black peppercorns
- 1 (1-pound) boneless strip steak, trimmed and halved
- 14–16 ounces (⅛-inch-wide) rice noodles
- ⅓ cup chopped fresh cilantro
- 3 scallions, sliced thin (optional)

  Bean sprouts
  Sprigs fresh Thai or Italian basil
  Lime wedges
  Hoisin sauce
  Sriracha sauce

1. Break ground beef into rough 1-inch pieces and drop in large Dutch oven. Add water to cover by 1 inch. Bring mixture to boil over high heat. Boil for 2 minutes, stirring once or twice. Drain ground beef in colander and rinse well under running water. Wash out pot and return ground beef to pot.

2. Place 6 onion quarters in pot with ground beef. Slice remaining 2 onion quarters as thin as possible and set aside for garnish. Add broth, 2 cups water, fish sauce, ginger, cinnamon, sugar, star anise, cloves, salt, and peppercorns to pot and bring to boil over high heat. Reduce heat to medium-low and simmer, partially covered, for 45 minutes.

3. Pour broth through colander set in large bowl; discard solids. Strain broth through fine-mesh strainer lined with triple thickness of cheesecloth; add water as needed to equal 11 cups. Return broth to pot and season with extra sugar and salt (broth should taste overseasoned). Cover and keep warm over low heat.

4. While broth simmers, place steak on large plate and freeze until very firm, 35 to 45 minutes. Once firm, cut against grain into ⅛-inch-thick slices. Return steak to plate and refrigerate until needed.

5. Place noodles in large container and cover with hot tap water. Soak until noodles are pliable, 10 to 15 minutes; drain noodles. Meanwhile, bring 4 quarts water to boil in large pot. Add drained noodles and cook until almost tender, 30 to 60 seconds. Drain immediately and divide noodles among individual bowls.

6. Bring broth to rolling boil over high heat. Divide steak among individual bowls, shingling slices on top of noodles. Pile reserved onion slices on top of steak slices and sprinkle with cilantro and scallions, if using. Ladle hot broth into each bowl. Serve immediately, passing bean sprouts, basil sprigs, lime wedges, hoisin, Sriracha, and extra fish sauce separately.

Caldo Verde

Serves 6 to 8

WHY THIS RECIPE WORKS This soup of sausage, potatoes, and hearty greens is a staple in many Portuguese households. While the flavors are rich, it's not a heavy soup. Without changing the soup's essentially light character, we wanted to create a slightly heartier result—something that could function as a main course. To start, we replaced the hard-to-find Portuguese linguiça sausage with widely available Spanish-style chorizo, which boasts a similar garlicky profile. We sautéed the sausage right in the Dutch oven in just 1 tablespoon of olive oil, eliminating the need to dirty an extra skillet. For deeper flavor, we split the water with an equal amount of chicken broth. Collard greens offered a more delicate sweetness and a meatier bite than kale, and chopping the leaves into bite-size pieces made them more spoon-friendly. Finally, we swapped out starchy russet potatoes for sturdy Yukon Golds, which held their shape during cooking. Pureeing some of the potatoes and a few tablespoons of olive oil into our soup base made a creamier, heartier dish. A bit of white wine vinegar brightened the pot. We prefer collard greens, but kale can be substituted. Serve this soup with hearty bread and, for added richness, a final drizzle of extra-virgin olive oil.

¼ cup extra-virgin olive oil, divided
12 ounces Spanish-style chorizo sausage, cut into ½-inch pieces
1 onion, chopped fine
4 garlic cloves, minced
1¼ teaspoons table salt
¼ teaspoon red pepper flakes
2 pounds Yukon Gold potatoes, peeled and cut into ¾-inch pieces
4 cups chicken broth
4 cups water
1 pound collard greens, stemmed and cut into 1-inch pieces
2 teaspoons white wine vinegar

1. Heat 1 tablespoon oil in Dutch oven over medium-high heat until shimmering. Add chorizo and cook, stirring occasionally, until lightly browned, 4 to 5 minutes. Transfer chorizo to bowl and set aside. Reduce heat to medium and add onion, garlic, salt, and pepper flakes and season with pepper to taste. Cook, stirring frequently, until onion is translucent, 2 to 3 minutes. Add potatoes, broth, and water; increase heat to high and bring to boil. Reduce heat to medium-low and simmer, uncovered, until potatoes are just tender, 8 to 10 minutes.

2. Transfer ¾ cup solids and ¾ cup broth to blender jar. Add collard greens to pot and simmer for 10 minutes. Stir in chorizo and continue to simmer until greens are tender, 8 to 10 minutes longer.

3. Add remaining 3 tablespoons oil to soup in blender and process until very smooth and homogeneous, about 1 minute. Remove pot from heat and stir pureed soup mixture and vinegar into soup. Season with salt and pepper to taste, and serve. (Soup can be refrigerated for up to 2 days.)

"This soup, developed by my colleague Dan Souza, is the perfect example of using flavor science to build a better recipe. The technique is dead simple yet inventive. The end result is a luxurious puree that captures the essence of cauliflower. Don't skip the garnish—the crispy little florets and browned butter make the dish beautiful and delicious. This soup is the perfect first course for a dinner party because it's both light and special. For the same reasons, this is my favorite first course for Thanksgiving. I make the soup the day before and then prepare the garnish right before serving. I enlist some help to serve 18 or more portions (yes, our house is very crowded on Thanksgiving). I ladle the soup into white bowls, someone else artfully arranges the browned cauliflower–butter garnish, and a third helper sprinkles chives on top."

–*Jack*

Creamy Cauliflower Soup

Serves 4 to 6

WHY THIS RECIPE WORKS For a creamy cauliflower soup that tasted first and foremost of cauliflower, we did away with the distractions—no cream, flour, or overpowering seasonings. Cauliflower, simmered until tender, produced a creamy, velvety smooth puree, without the aid of any cream, due to its low insoluble fiber content. For the purest flavor, we cooked it in salted water (instead of broth), skipped the spice rack entirely, and bolstered it with sautéed onion and leek. We added the cauliflower to the simmering water in two stages so our soup offered the grassy flavor of just-cooked cauliflower and the sweeter, nuttier flavor of long-cooked cauliflower. Finally, we fried a portion of the florets in butter until both the cauliflower and butter were golden brown and used each as a separate, richly flavored garnish. White wine vinegar may be substituted for the sherry vinegar. For the best flavor and texture, trim the core thoroughly of green leaves and leaf stems, which can be fibrous and contribute to a grainy texture in the soup.

- 1 head cauliflower (2 pounds)
- 8 tablespoons unsalted butter, cut into 8 pieces, divided
- 1 leek, white and light green parts only, halved lengthwise, sliced thin, and washed thoroughly
- 1 small onion, halved and sliced thin
- 1½ teaspoons table salt
- 4½ cups water
- ½ teaspoon sherry vinegar
- 3 tablespoons minced fresh chives

1. Pull off outer leaves of cauliflower and trim stem. Using paring knife, cut around core to remove; slice core thin and reserve. Cut heaping 1 cup of ½-inch florets from head of cauliflower; set aside. Cut remaining cauliflower crosswise into ½-inch-thick slices.

2. Melt 3 tablespoons butter in large saucepan over medium-low heat. Add leek, onion, and salt; cook, stirring frequently, until onion is softened but not browned, about 7 minutes.

3. Increase heat to medium-high; add water, sliced core, and half of sliced cauliflower; and bring to simmer. Reduce heat to medium-low and simmer gently for 15 minutes. Add remaining sliced cauliflower, return to simmer, and continue to cook until cauliflower is tender and crumbles easily, 15 to 20 minutes.

4. While soup simmers, melt remaining 5 tablespoons butter in 8-inch skillet over medium heat. Add reserved florets and cook, stirring frequently, until florets are golden brown and butter is browned, 6 to 8 minutes. Remove skillet from heat and use slotted spoon to transfer florets to small bowl. Toss florets with vinegar and season with salt to taste. Pour browned butter in skillet into small bowl and reserve for garnishing.

5. Process soup in blender until smooth, about 45 seconds. Rinse out pan. Return pureed soup to pan and return to simmer over medium heat, adjusting consistency with up to ½ cup water as needed (soup should have thick, velvety texture, but should be thin enough to settle with a flat surface after being stirred) and seasoning with salt to taste. Serve, garnishing individual bowls with browned florets, drizzles of browned butter, and chives and seasoning with pepper to taste.

Carrot-Ginger Soup

Serves 6

WHY THIS RECIPE WORKS The coupling of sweet carrots and pungent ginger has the potential to produce an elegant, flavorful soup. But in most versions, the hapless addition of other vegetables, fruits, or dairy makes it difficult to truly taste the starring flavors. Another common problem is a grainy consistency. We wanted to bring this soup to its full potential and produce a version with a smooth, silken texture and pure, clean flavors. For unadulterated carrot flavor, we used water in place of vegetable broth, eliminating the blurred vegetable background. Swapping ¾ cup of carrot juice for some of the water and stirring in another ¾ cup right before serving gave us intense carrot flavor. We also used peeled and sliced carrots; the earthy, sweet cooked carrots and the bright, raw carrot juice provided a well-balanced depth of flavor. To amp up the ginger flavor, we used a combination of fresh and crystallized ginger, with the former supplying spiciness and the latter delivering the almost citrusy freshness that ginger is prized for. For the silkiest possible consistency, we turned to one of the test kitchen's secret weapons: baking soda. Just ½ teaspoon of baking soda helped to break down the cell walls of the carrots for a soup that was downright velvety—without the need for lengthy cooking or fussy straining. As finishing touches, a sprinkle of fresh chives and a swirl of sour cream provided subtle onion flavor and mild tang. In addition to sour cream and chives, serve the soup with Buttery Croutons if desired (recipe follows).

2 tablespoons unsalted butter
2 onions, chopped fine
¼ cup minced crystallized ginger
1 tablespoon grated fresh ginger
2 garlic cloves, peeled and smashed
2 teaspoons table salt
1 teaspoon sugar
2 pounds carrots, peeled and sliced ¼ inch thick
4 cups water
1½ cups carrot juice, divided
2 sprigs fresh thyme
½ teaspoon baking soda
1 tablespoon cider vinegar
  Chopped chives
  Sour cream

1. Melt butter in large saucepan over medium heat. Add onions, crystallized ginger, fresh ginger, garlic, salt, and sugar; cook, stirring frequently, until onions are softened but not browned, 5 to 7 minutes.

2. Increase heat to high; add carrots, water, ¾ cup carrot juice, thyme sprigs, and baking soda and bring to simmer. Reduce heat to medium-low and simmer, covered, until carrots are very tender, 20 to 25 minutes.

3. Discard thyme sprigs. Working in batches, process soup in blender until smooth, 1 to 2 minutes. Return soup to clean pot and stir in vinegar and remaining ¾ cup carrot juice. (Soup can be refrigerated for up to 4 days.) Return to simmer over medium heat and season with salt and pepper to taste. Serve with sprinkle of chives and dollop of sour cream.

ACCOMPANIMENT
Buttery Croutons
Makes about 2 cups

3 tablespoons unsalted butter
1 tablespoon extra-virgin olive oil
3 slices hearty sandwich bread, cut into
  ½-inch pieces (2 cups)

Heat butter and oil in 12-inch skillet over medium heat until butter is melted. Add bread pieces and cook, stirring frequently, until golden brown, about 10 minutes. Transfer croutons to paper towel–lined plate and season with salt to taste.

Super Greens Soup with Lemon Tarragon Cream
Serves 4 to 6

WHY THIS RECIPE WORKS We wanted a deceptively delicious, silky-smooth soup that delivered a big dose of healthy greens. Our ideal would be packed with all the essential nutrients of hearty greens and boast a deep, complex flavor brightened with a garnish of lemon and herb cream. First, we built a flavorful foundation of sweet caramelized onions and earthy sautéed mushrooms. We added broth, water, and lots of leafy greens (we liked a mix of chard, kale, arugula, and parsley), and simmered until the greens became tender before blending them smooth. We were happy with the soup's depth of flavor, but it was watery and too thin. Many recipes we found used potatoes as a thickener, but they lent an overwhelmingly earthy flavor. Instead, we tried using Arborio rice. The rice's high starch content thickened the soup to a velvety, lush consistency without clouding its bright, vegetal flavors. For a vibrant finish, we whisked together heavy cream, sour cream, lemon zest, lemon juice, and tarragon and drizzled it over the top. Our favorite brand of Arborio rice is RiceSelect.

¼ cup heavy cream
3 tablespoons sour cream
½ teaspoon plus 2 tablespoons extra-virgin olive oil, divided
¼ teaspoon finely grated lemon zest plus
  ½ teaspoon juice
½ teaspoon minced fresh tarragon
1¼ teaspoons table salt, divided
1 onion, halved through root end and sliced thin
¾ teaspoon light brown sugar
3 ounces white mushrooms, trimmed and sliced thin
2 garlic cloves, minced
  Pinch cayenne pepper
3 cups water
3 cups vegetable broth
⅓ cup Arborio rice
12 ounces Swiss chard, stemmed and chopped coarse
9 ounces kale, stemmed and chopped coarse
¼ cup fresh parsley leaves
2 ounces (2 cups) baby arugula

1. Combine cream, sour cream, ½ teaspoon oil, lemon zest and juice, tarragon, and ¼ teaspoon salt in bowl. Cover and refrigerate until ready to serve.

2. Heat remaining 2 tablespoons oil in Dutch oven over medium-high heat until shimmering. Stir in onion, sugar, and remaining 1 teaspoon salt and cook, stirring occasionally, until onion releases some moisture, about 5 minutes. Reduce heat to low and cook, stirring often and scraping up any browned

red potatoes were perfect; they kept their shape and didn't become waterlogged during cooking. To pump up the flavor of the soup, we used a substantial amount of leeks and sautéed both the white and light green parts in butter. Leeks and potatoes require different cooking times, so we staggered the cooking—leeks first, then potatoes—and then we removed the pot from the stove so the potatoes could gently cook through in the hot broth without becoming mushy. We also added a bit of flour with the sautéed leeks to give our broth some body. At last, we had a flavorful, oniony soup, full of perfectly cooked potatoes and sweet, tender leeks. Leeks can vary in size; if your leeks have large white and light green parts, use the smaller amount of leeks.

- 6 tablespoons unsalted butter
- 4–5 pounds leeks, white and light green parts only, halved lengthwise, sliced crosswise 1 inch thick, and rinsed thoroughly (11 cups)
- 1 tablespoon all-purpose flour
- 5¼ cups chicken broth
- 1¾ pounds red potatoes, peeled and cut into ¾-inch pieces
- 1 bay leaf

1. Melt butter in Dutch oven over medium-low heat. Add leeks, increase heat to medium, cover, and cook, stirring occasionally, until leeks are tender but not mushy, 15 to 20 minutes; do not brown them. Add flour and cook, stirring constantly, until thoroughly combined, about 2 minutes.

2. Increase heat to high; whisking constantly, gradually add broth. Add potatoes and bay leaf, cover, and bring to boil. Reduce heat to medium-low and simmer, covered, until potatoes are almost tender, 5 to 7 minutes. Remove pot from heat and let sit, covered, until potatoes are tender, 10 to 15 minutes. Discard bay leaf, season with salt and pepper to taste, and serve. (Soup can be refrigerated for up to 2 days. Warm over low heat until hot; do not boil.)

Sweet Potato Soup

Serves 4 to 6

WHY THIS RECIPE WORKS The secrets to a creamy sweet potato soup are to use the peels and turn off the heat. Most recipes call for so many other ingredients that the sweet potato flavor ends up muted and overpowered. By cutting back to shallot, thyme, and butter and using water instead of broth, we put the focus on the main ingredient. For extra earthiness, we also pureed some of the potato skins into the soup. However, the real key to intensifying the sweet potato flavor was to use only a minimal amount of flavor-diluting water.

bits, until onion is deeply browned and slightly sticky, about 30 minutes. (If onion is sizzling or scorching, reduce heat. If onion is not browning after 15 to 20 minutes, increase heat.)

3. Stir in mushrooms and cook until they have released their moisture, about 5 minutes. Stir in garlic and cayenne and cook until fragrant, about 30 seconds. Stir in water, broth, and rice, scraping up any browned bits, and bring to boil. Reduce heat to low, cover, and simmer for 15 minutes.

4. Stir in chard, kale, and parsley, 1 handful at a time, until wilted and submerged in liquid. Return to simmer, cover, and cook until greens are tender, about 10 minutes.

5. Off heat, stir in arugula until wilted. Working in batches, process soup in blender until smooth, about 1 minute per batch. Return pureed soup to clean pot and season with salt and pepper to taste. Drizzle individual portions with lemon tarragon cream and serve.

Rustic Leek and Potato Soup

Serves 6

WHY THIS RECIPE WORKS Rustic potato-leek soup often disappoints with soft, mealy potatoes and dingy, overcooked leeks. We wanted to perfect this soup so both ingredients would be at their best and the dish would retain its textural integrity and bright flavor. We quickly eliminated potatoes with high or medium starch levels because they broke down too quickly in the chicken broth. Waxy, low-starch

To do so, we let the sweet potatoes sit in hot water off heat to make use of an enzyme that converts their starch content to sugar. Less starch meant we could create a soup with less water, keeping the sweet potato flavor in the forefront. To highlight the flavor of the sweet potatoes, we incorporated a quarter of the skins into the soup. In addition to the chives, serve the soup with one of our suggested garnishes (recipes follow). The garnish can be prepared during step 1 while the sweet potatoes stand in the water.

4 tablespoons unsalted butter
1 shallot, sliced thin
4 sprigs fresh thyme
4¼ cups water, plus extra as needed
2 pounds sweet potatoes, peeled, halved lengthwise, and sliced ¼ inch thick, ¼ of peels reserved
1 tablespoon packed brown sugar
½ teaspoon cider vinegar
1½ teaspoons table salt
¼ teaspoon pepper
Minced fresh chives

1. Melt butter in large saucepan over medium-low heat. Add shallot and thyme sprigs and cook until shallot is softened but not browned, about 5 minutes. Add water, increase heat to high, and bring to simmer. Remove pot from heat, add sweet potatoes and reserved peels, and let sit uncovered for 20 minutes.

2. Add sugar, vinegar, salt, and pepper. Bring to simmer over high heat. Reduce heat to medium-low, cover, and cook until potatoes are very soft, about 10 minutes.

3. Discard thyme sprigs. Working in batches, process soup in blender until smooth, 45 to 60 seconds. Return soup to clean pot. Bring to simmer over medium heat, adjusting consistency with extra water if desired. Season with salt and pepper to taste. Serve, topping each portion with sprinkle of chives.

ACCOMPANIMENTS
Buttery Rye Croutons
Makes 1½ cups
The croutons can be made ahead and stored in an airtight container for up to one week.

3 tablespoons unsalted butter
1 tablespoon extra-virgin olive oil
2 slices light rye bread, cut into ½-inch pieces (1½ cups)

Heat butter and oil in 10-inch skillet over medium heat until butter is melted. Add bread pieces and cook, stirring frequently, until golden brown, about 10 minutes. Transfer croutons to paper towel–lined plate and season with salt to taste.

Candied Bacon Bits
Makes about ¾ cup
Break up any large pieces before serving.

4 slices bacon, cut into ½-inch pieces
2 teaspoons packed dark brown sugar
½ teaspoon cider vinegar

Cook bacon in 10-inch nonstick skillet over medium heat until crisp and well rendered, 6 to 8 minutes. Using slotted spoon, remove bacon from skillet and discard fat. Return bacon to skillet and add brown sugar and vinegar. Cook over low heat, stirring constantly, until bacon is evenly coated. Transfer to plate in single layer. Let bacon cool completely.

Maple Sour Cream
Makes ⅓ cup
Maple balances the sweet potatoes' earthiness.

⅓ cup sour cream
1 tablespoon maple syrup

Combine ingredients in bowl.

Creamless Creamy Tomato Soup

Serves 6

WHY THIS RECIPE WORKS Creamy tomato soup boasts a bright, sweet tomato flavor when done right, but not everyone is a fan of rich cream soups. We wanted to keep the sharp tomatoey flavor in this classic soup, but ditch the dairy and tame the tartness in other ways. Our first step was to choose canned tomatoes over fresh tomatoes—canned are simply more consistent in flavor than your average supermarket tomato. We mashed whole tomatoes (preferred over diced or crushed for their concentrated flavor) with a potato masher, then combined them with aromatics sautéed in extra-virgin olive oil, not butter, which guaranteed bright, clean flavor. Stirring in some olive oil before pureeing our soup added back vital flavor that was lost when we cooked the oil. To combat the acid in the tomatoes, we added full-flavored brown sugar. And for an ultracreamy texture without the cream, we pureed sandwich bread into the soup. For a final touch, we stirred chicken broth into the pot and simmered the soup briefly to give our creamless creamy tomato soup a rich and velvety feel. If half of the soup fills your blender more than halfway, process the soup in three batches, but do not add more olive oil for the third batch. You can also use a handheld blender to process the soup directly in the pot. Serve this soup topped with Classic Croutons (recipe follows), if desired. For an even smoother soup, strain the pureed mixture through a fine-mesh strainer before stirring in the chicken broth in step 2.

- ¼ cup extra-virgin olive oil, plus extra for drizzling, divided
- 1 onion, chopped
- 3 garlic cloves, minced
  Pinch red pepper flakes (optional)
- 1 bay leaf
- 2 (28-ounce) cans whole tomatoes
- 3 slices hearty white sandwich bread, crusts removed, torn into 1-inch pieces
- 1 tablespoon packed brown sugar
- 2 cups chicken broth
- 2 tablespoons brandy (optional)
- ¼ cup chopped fresh chives

1. Heat 2 tablespoons oil in Dutch oven over medium-high heat until shimmering. Add onion, garlic, pepper flakes (if using), and bay leaf. Cook, stirring frequently, until onion is translucent, 3 to 5 minutes. Stir in tomatoes with their juice. Using potato masher, mash until no pieces bigger than 2 inches remain. Stir in bread and sugar and bring soup to boil. Reduce heat to medium and cook, stirring occasionally, until bread is completely saturated and starts to break down, about 5 minutes. Discard bay leaf.

2. Transfer half of soup to blender. Add 1 tablespoon oil and process until soup is smooth and creamy, 2 to 3 minutes. Transfer to large bowl and repeat with remaining soup and remaining 1 tablespoon oil. Return soup to clean pot. Stir in chicken broth and brandy, if using. Return soup to boil and season with salt and pepper to taste. Ladle soup into bowls, sprinkle with chopped chives, drizzle with oil, and serve. (Soup can be refrigerated for up to 2 days. Warm over low heat until hot; do not boil.)

ACCOMPANIMENT
Classic Croutons
Makes about 1½ cups

- 3 slices hearty white sandwich bread, crusts removed, cut into ½-inch pieces (1½ cups)
- 1½ tablespoons extra-virgin olive oil

1. Adjust oven rack to upper-middle position and heat oven to 400 degrees. Combine bread pieces and oil in medium bowl and toss to coat. Season with salt and pepper to taste.

2. Spread bread cubes in even layer on rimmed baking sheet and bake, stirring occasionally, until golden, 8 to 10 minutes. Let cool on baking sheet to room temperature. (Croutons can be stored in airtight container or plastic bag for up to 3 days.)

Classic Gazpacho

Serves 8 to 10

WHY THIS RECIPE WORKS Spain's famous chilled soup, gazpacho, boasts bright flavors, distinct pieces of vegetables, and a bracing tomato broth. But all too often, gazpacho is either grainy with the addition of too much bread (a common thickener) or watery from an abundance of macerated vegetables. We were after a chunky gazpacho that was well seasoned with vibrant tomato flavor. We had to figure out the best method for preparing the vegetables. Although it was a breeze to use, the blender broke down our vegetables beyond recognition. Next, we tried the food processor, but even this machine pulverized some of our tomatoes, and the resulting soup was closer to a slushie than a good gazpacho. For the best texture, we had to chop the vegetables by hand. Tomatoes are the star player in this dish, and early on we decided that full, ripe beefsteaks were the best option. As for peppers, we preferred red over green for their sweeter flavor. Onion and garlic are usually too overpowering in gazpacho, so we kept to modest levels. A combination of tomato juice and ice cubes—to help chill the soup—provided the right amount of liquid for our broth. And instead of using bread as a thickener, we saved it to make croutons. Now our gazpacho was nice and chunky, and brightly flavored. This recipe makes a large quantity, but it can be easily halved if you prefer. Traditionally, the same vegetables used in the soup are also used as garnish. If that appeals to you, cut additional vegetables while you prepare those called for in the recipe. Other garnish possibilities include Garlic Croutons (recipe follows), chopped pitted black olives, chopped Easy-Peel Hard-Cooked Eggs (page 26), and finely diced avocado.

1½ pounds ripe beefsteak tomatoes, cored and
   cut into ¼-inch pieces (4 cups)
1 pound red bell peppers, stemmed, seeded,
   and cut into ¼-inch pieces (2 cups)
2 small cucumbers (1 peeled and 1 unpeeled;
   both halved lengthwise, seeded, and cut into
   ¼-inch pieces) (2 cups)
½ small sweet onion (such as Vidalia, Maui, or
   Walla Walla) or 2 large shallots, minced
2 garlic cloves, minced
⅓ cup sherry vinegar
2 teaspoons table salt
5 cups tomato juice
8 ice cubes
1 teaspoon hot pepper sauce (optional)
   Extra-virgin olive oil

1. Combine tomatoes, peppers, cucumbers, onion,
garlic, vinegar, salt, and pepper to taste in large nonreactive
bowl. Let sit until vegetables just begin to release juices,
about 5 minutes. Stir in tomato juice, ice cubes, and hot
pepper sauce, if using. Cover tightly and refrigerate to let
flavors meld, at least 4 hours or up to 2 days.

2. Season with salt and pepper to taste and remove
and discard any unmelted ice cubes. Serve cold, drizzling
each portion with about 1 teaspoon oil.

ACCOMPANIMENT
Garlic Croutons
Makes about 3 cups

3 tablespoons extra-virgin olive oil
3 garlic cloves, minced
¼ teaspoon table salt
6 slices hearty white sandwich bread,
   cut into ½-inch pieces (3 cups)

1. Adjust oven rack to middle position and heat oven
to 350 degrees. Combine oil, garlic, and salt in small bowl;
let sit 20 minutes, then pour through fine-mesh strainer into
medium bowl, discarding garlic. Add bread pieces to bowl
with oil and toss to coat.

2. Spread bread cubes in even layer on rimmed baking
sheet and bake, stirring occasionally, until golden, about
15 minutes. Let cool on baking sheet to room temperature.
(Croutons can be stored in airtight container or plastic bag
for up to 1 day.)

Provençal Vegetable Soup (Soupe au Pistou)

SEASON 20 RECIPE

Serves 6

WHY THIS RECIPE WORKS Provençal vegetable
soup is a classic French summer soup with a delicate broth
that is intensified by a dollop of pistou, the French equivalent
of Italy's pesto. We wanted a simple version that focused on
fresh seasonal vegetables. Leeks, green beans, and zucchini
all made the cut; we like their summery flavors, different
shapes, and varying shades of green. We added canned white
beans (which were far more convenient than dried in this
quick-cooking soup) and orecchiette for its easy-to-spoon
shape. Using the liquid from the canned beans added much-
needed body to the broth. For the pistou, we just whirred
basil, Parmesan, olive oil, and garlic together in our food
processor. For the best flavor, we prefer broth prepared from
our Vegetable Broth Base (page 88), but you can use store-
bought broth.

Pistou
¾ cup fresh basil leaves
1 ounce Parmesan cheese, grated (½ cup)
⅓ cup extra-virgin olive oil
1 garlic clove, minced

Soup
1 tablespoon extra-virgin olive oil
1 leek, white and light green parts only,
   halved lengthwise, sliced ½ inch thick,
   and washed thoroughly
1 celery rib, cut into ½-inch pieces
1 carrot, peeled and sliced ¼ inch thick
½ teaspoon table salt
2 garlic cloves, minced
3 cups vegetable broth
3 cups water
½ cup orecchiette or other short pasta
8 ounces haricots verts or green beans,
   trimmed and cut into ½-inch lengths
1 (15-ounce) can cannellini or navy beans
1 small zucchini, halved lengthwise, seeded,
   and cut into ¼-inch pieces
1 large tomato, cored, seeded, and cut into
   ¼-inch pieces

1. *For the pistou:* Process all ingredients in food
processor until smooth, scraping down sides of bowl as
needed, about 15 seconds. (Pistou can be refrigerated
for up to 4 hours.)

"A lot of cooks stop making soup with the first signs of spring. It's too bad because they are likely missing out on this light, fresh vegetable soup. Our version of this southern French classic incorporates many early summer vegetables, but what I like about this recipe is that it can be varied to suit your taste and what is available. No haricots verts? Try asparagus. Don't like zucchini? Try adding Swiss chard. The variations are endless. The only 'must-have' is the pistou. This vibrant pesto-like sauce adds richness and zip and makes this soup unlike any other."

—*Keith*

2. *For the soup:* Heat oil in Dutch oven over medium heat until shimmering. Add leek, celery, carrot, and salt and cook until vegetables are softened, 8 to 10 minutes. Stir in garlic and cook until fragrant, about 30 seconds. Stir in broth and water and bring to simmer

3. Stir in pasta and simmer until slightly softened, about 5 minutes. Stir in haricots verts and simmer until bright green but still crunchy, 3 to 5 minutes. Stir in cannellini beans and their liquid, zucchini, and tomato and simmer until pasta and vegetables are tender, about 3 minutes. Season with salt and pepper to taste. Serve, topping individual portions with generous tablespoon pistou.

Farmhouse Vegetable and Barley Soup

Serves 6 to 8

WHY THIS RECIPE WORKS Most recipes for hearty winter vegetable soups, it turns out, are neither quick nor easy. For a satisfying soup that wouldn't take the better part of a day to make, we started with canned chicken broth. To this we added soy sauce and ground dried porcini mushrooms. These ingredients added a savory, almost meaty flavor to the soup base. To make the soup more filling, we added barley to the hearty combination of carrots, potatoes, leeks, cabbage, and turnips. We prefer an acidic, unoaked white wine such as Sauvignon Blanc for this recipe. We love the richness added by the Lemon-Thyme Butter and the crunch of Herbed Croutons (recipes follow), but the soup can also be garnished with crisp bacon or crumbled cheddar cheese.

⅛ ounce dried porcini mushrooms, rinsed
8 sprigs fresh parsley plus 3 tablespoons minced, divided
4 sprigs fresh thyme
1 bay leaf
2 tablespoons unsalted butter
1½ pounds leeks, white and light green parts sliced ½ inch thick and washed thoroughly
2 carrots, peeled and cut into ½-inch pieces
2 celery ribs, cut into ¼-inch pieces
⅓ cup dry white wine
2 teaspoons soy sauce
2 teaspoons table salt
6 cups water
4 cups chicken or vegetable broth
½ cup pearl barley
1 garlic clove, peeled and smashed
1½ pounds Yukon Gold potatoes, peeled and cut into ½-inch pieces
1 turnip, peeled and cut into ¾-inch pieces
1½ cups chopped green cabbage
1 cup frozen peas
1 teaspoon lemon juice

1. Grind mushrooms with spice grinder until they resemble fine meal, 10 to 30 seconds. Measure out 2 teaspoons porcini powder; reserve remainder for another use. Using kitchen twine, tie together parsley sprigs, thyme sprigs, and bay leaf.

2. Melt butter in Dutch oven over medium heat. Add leeks, carrots, celery, wine, soy sauce, and salt. Cook, stirring occasionally, until liquid has evaporated and celery is softened, about 10 minutes.

3. Add water, broth, barley, garlic, porcini powder, and herb bundle; increase heat to high and bring to boil. Reduce heat to medium-low and simmer, partially covered, for 25 minutes.

4. Add potatoes, turnip, and cabbage; return to simmer and cook until barley, potatoes, turnip, and cabbage are tender, 18 to 20 minutes.

5. Off heat, remove herb bundle. Stir in peas, lemon juice, and minced parsley; season with salt and pepper to taste. Serve.

Lemon-Thyme Butter
Makes 6 tablespoons

- 6 tablespoons unsalted butter, softened
- 1 tablespoon minced fresh thyme
- ¾ teaspoon finely grated lemon zest plus ¼ teaspoon juice
- Pinch table salt

Combine all ingredients in bowl.

Herbed Croutons
Makes about 2½ cups
Our favorite brand of sandwich bread is Arnold Country Classics White Bread.

- 1 tablespoon unsalted butter
- 1 teaspoon minced fresh parsley
- ½ teaspoon minced fresh thyme
- 4 slices hearty white sandwich bread, cut into ½-inch pieces

Melt butter in 10-inch skillet over medium heat. Add parsley and thyme; cook, stirring constantly, for 20 seconds. Add bread and cook, stirring frequently, until light golden brown, 5 to 10 minutes. Season with salt and pepper to taste.

Italian Pasta and Bean Soup (Pasta e Fagioli)

Serves 8 to 10

WHY THIS RECIPE WORKS The American version of this hearty Italian bean-and-vegetable stew—sometimes called "pasta fazool"—often turns out bland, with mushy beans and pasta and too much tomato. And it can take hours to prepare. We wanted rich broth, perfectly cooked beans and pasta, and complex flavors—and we wanted to prepare it in a reasonable amount of time. Substituting canned beans for dried would save the most preparation time, and we found cannellini beans to be the closest to the dried cranberry beans used in authentic recipes. We started to build deep flavor by sautéing pancetta (though bacon also works) and, for aromatics, onion, garlic, and celery. Tomatoes (diced worked better than crushed or sauce) went in next. A small amount of minced anchovies was unidentifiable but added complexity. Chicken broth diluted with water was our cooking liquid; chicken broth alone made the dish taste too much like chicken soup. A Parmesan rind

added another layer of flavor. Last into the pot went the pasta. The flavors of our thick, hearty soup harmonized perfectly and, best of all, we had spent less than an hour at the stove. This soup does not hold well because the pasta absorbs the liquid, becomes mushy, and leaves the soup dry. You can, however, make the soup in two stages. Once the beans are simmered with the tomatoes, before the broth and water are added, the mixture can be cooled and refrigerated for up to three days. When ready to complete the soup, discard the Parmesan rind (otherwise it will become stringy), add the liquid, bring the soup to a boil, and proceed with the recipe.

- 1 tablespoon extra-virgin olive oil, plus extra for drizzling
- 3 ounces pancetta or bacon, chopped fine
- 1 onion, chopped fine
- 1 celery rib, chopped fine
- 4 garlic cloves, minced
- 1 teaspoon dried oregano
- ¼ teaspoon red pepper flakes
- 3 anchovy fillets, minced to paste
- 1 (28-ounce) can diced tomatoes
- 1 Parmesan cheese rind, plus grated Parmesan for serving
- 2 (15-ounce) cans cannellini beans, rinsed
- 3½ cups chicken broth
- 2½ cups water
- 1 teaspoon table salt
- 8 ounces small pasta such as ditalini, tubetini, conchiglietti, or orzo
- ¼ cup chopped fresh parsley, divided

1. Heat oil in Dutch oven over medium-high heat until shimmering. Add pancetta and cook, stirring occasionally, until it begins to brown, 3 to 5 minutes. Add onion and celery and cook, stirring occasionally, until vegetables are softened, 5 to 7 minutes. Add garlic, oregano, pepper flakes, and anchovies and cook, stirring constantly, until fragrant, about 30 seconds. Add tomatoes with their juice, scraping up any browned bits. Add cheese rind and beans; bring to boil, then reduce heat to low and simmer to meld flavors, 10 minutes. Add chicken broth, water, and salt; increase heat to high and bring to boil. Add pasta and cook until tender, about 10 minutes.

2. Discard cheese rind. Off heat, stir in 3 tablespoons parsley; season with salt and pepper to taste. Ladle soup into individual bowls; drizzle each serving with oil and sprinkle with remaining 1 tablespoon parsley. Serve immediately, passing grated Parmesan separately.

"This is the recipe that I prepared for my 2005 screen test with Herb Sevush, the director of America's Test Kitchen, who filmed me using a handheld camera. I remember sweating things out before we started to roll, but the recipe is so simple to make that once I started cooking, my nerves faded away and I just had fun talking about my favorite topic: food! Dried beans are one of the ingredients I use most often in the kitchen. They are economical and healthful, and with the right kind of attention, boy do they ever taste good. Here, lots of heady cumin and a smoky ham steak give the soup meatiness whereas a soffrito brings vegetal complexity. A word of advice: Offer plenty of garnishes. Along with adding loads of personality to the soup, they make dinnertime more fun: Each person can customize their bowl, choosing from an array of colors, flavors, and textures."

—*Becky*

Black Bean Soup

Serves 6

WHY THIS RECIPE WORKS Making traditional black bean soup used to be an all-day affair. Generating full flavor required hours of simmering soaked beans with numerous ingredients, including parsnips, carrots, beef bones, and smoked ham hocks. But quicker versions developed for modern kitchens often produce watery, bland, and unattractive soups. We wanted a simplified procedure that would result in an attractive, dark-colored soup full of sweet, spicy, smoky flavors and brightened with fresh garnishes. Though convenient, canned beans couldn't compare in flavor to dried, which imparted good flavor to the broth as they simmered, and we discovered that we didn't have to soak them. A touch of baking soda in the cooking water kept the beans from turning gray. Homemade stock would be time-consuming to prepare, so we focused on adding flavor to prepared broth. Ham steak provided the smoky pork flavor of the more conventional ham hock and more meat as well. We spiced up our aromatics—carrot, celery, onion, and garlic—with lots of cumin and some red pepper flakes. We wanted a chunky texture in our soup, so we pureed it only partially, thickening it further with a slurry of cornstarch and water. Some lime juice added brightness. The customary garnishes of sour cream, avocado, red onion, cilantro, and lime wedges topped our richly flavored but easy-to-make black bean soup. Dried beans tend to cook unevenly, so be sure to taste several beans to determine their doneness in step 1. For efficiency, you can prepare the soup ingredients while the beans simmer and the garnishes while the soup simmers. Though you do not need to offer all of the suggested garnishes, do choose at least a couple; garnishes are essential for this soup, as they add not only flavor but texture and color as well.

Beans

- 1 pound (2 cups) dried black beans, picked over and rinsed
- 5 cups water
- 4 ounces ham steak, trimmed of rind
- 2 bay leaves
- 1/8 teaspoon baking soda
- 1 teaspoon table salt

Soup

- 3 tablespoons extra-virgin olive oil
- 2 large onions, chopped fine
- 3 celery ribs, chopped fine
- 1 large carrot, chopped
- 1/2 teaspoon table salt
- 5–6 garlic cloves, minced
- 1 1/2 tablespoons ground cumin
- 1/2 teaspoon red pepper flakes
- 6 cups chicken broth
- 2 tablespoons cornstarch
- 2 tablespoons water
- 2 tablespoons lime juice

Garnishes

- Lime wedges
- Minced fresh cilantro
- Red onion, diced fine
- Avocado, peeled, pitted, and diced
- Sour cream

1. *For the beans:* Place beans, water, ham, bay leaves, and baking soda in large saucepan with tight-fitting lid. Bring to boil over medium-high heat; using large spoon, skim foam as it rises to surface. Stir in salt, reduce heat to low, cover, and simmer briskly until beans are tender, 1 1/4 to 1 1/2 hours (if necessary, add 1 cup more water and continue to simmer until beans are tender); do not drain beans. Discard bay leaves. Remove ham steak (ham steak darkens to color of beans) and cut it into 1/4-inch pieces; set aside.

2. *For the soup:* Heat oil in Dutch oven over medium-high heat until shimmering but not smoking; add onions, celery, carrot, and salt and cook, stirring occasionally, until vegetables are soft and lightly browned, 12 to 15 minutes. Reduce heat to medium-low and add garlic, cumin, and pepper flakes; cook, stirring constantly, until fragrant, about 3 minutes. Stir in beans, bean cooking liquid, and broth. Increase heat to medium-high and bring to boil, then reduce heat to low and simmer, uncovered, stirring occasionally, to blend flavors, about 30 minutes.

3. *To finish the soup:* Ladle 1 1/2 cups beans and 2 cups liquid into food processor or blender, process until smooth, and return to pot. Stir cornstarch and water in small bowl until combined, then gradually stir half of cornstarch mixture into soup; bring to boil over medium-high heat, stirring occasionally, to fully thicken. If soup is still thinner than desired once boiling, stir remaining cornstarch mixture to recombine and gradually stir mixture into soup; return to boil to fully thicken. Off heat, stir in lime juice and reserved ham; ladle soup into bowls and serve immediately, passing garnishes separately. (Soup can be refrigerated for up to 3 days.)

Red Lentil Soup with North African Spices

Serves 4 to 6

WHY THIS RECIPE WORKS Red lentils are one of our favorite legumes. They cook quickly and don't require any presoaking or brining. One of their best qualities, however, is that they disintegrate when cooked, forming a creamy, thick puree—perfect for a satisfying soup. Their mild flavor does require a bit of embellishment, so we started by sautéing onions in butter and used the warm mixture to bloom some fragrant North African spices. Tomato paste and garlic completed the base before the addition of the lentils, and a mix of chicken broth and water, gave the soup a full, rounded character. After only 15 minutes of cooking, the lentils were soft enough to be pureed with a whisk. A generous dose of lemon juice brought the flavors into focus, and a drizzle of spice-infused butter and a sprinkle of fresh cilantro completed the transformation of commonplace ingredients into an exotic yet comforting soup.

4 tablespoons unsalted butter, divided
1 large onion, chopped fine
1 teaspoon table salt
¾ teaspoon ground coriander
½ teaspoon ground cumin
¼ teaspoon ground ginger
¼ teaspoon pepper
⅛ teaspoon ground cinnamon
   Pinch cayenne pepper
1 tablespoon tomato paste
1 garlic clove, minced
4 cups chicken broth
2 cups water
10½ ounces (1½ cups) red lentils, picked over and rinsed
2 tablespoons lemon juice, plus extra for seasoning
1½ teaspoons dried mint, crumbled
1 teaspoon paprika
¼ cup chopped fresh cilantro

1. Melt 2 tablespoons butter in large saucepan over medium heat. Add onion and 1 teaspoon salt and cook, stirring occasionally, until softened but not browned, about 5 minutes. Add coriander, cumin, ginger, pepper, cinnamon, and cayenne and cook until fragrant, about 2 minutes. Stir in tomato paste and garlic and cook for 1 minute. Stir in broth, water, and lentils and bring to simmer. Simmer vigorously, stirring occasionally, until lentils are soft and about half are broken down, about 15 minutes.

2. Whisk soup vigorously until it resembles a coarse puree, about 30 seconds. Stir in lemon juice and season with salt and extra lemon juice to taste. Cover and keep warm. (Soup can be refrigerated for up to 3 days. Thin soup with water, if desired, when reheating.)

3. Melt remaining 2 tablespoons butter in small skillet over medium-low heat. Remove from heat and stir in mint and paprika. Ladle soup into individual bowls, drizzle each portion with 1 teaspoon spiced butter, sprinkle with cilantro, and serve.

Best Chicken Stew

Serves 6 to 8

WHY THIS RECIPE WORKS While recipes for chicken stew are few and far between, the ones we've come across are either too fussy or too fancy, or seem more soup than stew, with none of the complexity and depth we expect from the latter. We wanted to develop a chicken stew recipe that would satisfy like the beef kind—one with succulent bites of chicken, tender vegetables, and a truly robust gravy. To start, we created an ultraflavorful gravy using chicken wings, which we later discarded. Browning the wings lent deep chicken flavor to the stew, and since wings are more about skin and bones than about meat, discarding them after they'd enriched the gravy didn't seem wasteful. A few strips of bacon, crisped in the pot before we browned the wings in the rendered fat, lent porky depth and just a hint of smoke. Soy sauce and anchovy paste, though unusual ingredients for chicken stew, lent more savory depth (without making the stew taste salty or fishy). Reducing the liquid with the aromatics at the beginning of cooking and then cooking the stew uncovered further concentrated the flavor. To finish our hearty, savory stew, we added a splash of fresh white wine for a touch of brightness and a sprinkle of parsley for freshness. Mashed anchovy fillets (rinsed and dried before mashing) can be used instead of anchovy paste. Use small red potatoes measuring 1½ inches in diameter.

2 pounds boneless, skinless chicken thighs, halved crosswise and trimmed
½ teaspoon table salt
¼ teaspoon pepper
3 slices bacon, chopped
1 pound chicken wings, halved at joint
1 onion, chopped fine
1 celery rib, minced
2 garlic cloves, minced
2 teaspoons anchovy paste
1 teaspoon minced fresh thyme
5 cups chicken broth, divided
1 cup dry white wine, plus extra for seasoning
1 tablespoon soy sauce
3 tablespoons unsalted butter, cut into 3 pieces
⅓ cup all-purpose flour
1 pound small red potatoes, unpeeled, quartered
4 carrots, peeled and cut into ½-inch pieces
2 tablespoons chopped fresh parsley

1. Adjust oven rack to lower-middle position and heat oven to 325 degrees. Arrange chicken thighs on baking sheet and lightly season both sides with salt and pepper; cover with plastic wrap and set aside.

2. Cook bacon in Dutch oven over medium-low heat, stirring occasionally, until crispy, 6 to 8 minutes. Using slotted spoon, transfer bacon to medium bowl. Add chicken wings to pot, increase heat to medium, and cook until well browned on both sides, 10 to 12 minutes; transfer wings to bowl with bacon.

3. Add onion, celery, garlic, anchovy paste, and thyme to fat in pot; cook, stirring occasionally, until dark fond forms on pan bottom, 2 to 4 minutes. Increase heat to high; stir in 1 cup broth, wine, and soy sauce, scraping up any browned bits; and bring to boil. Cook, stirring occasionally, until liquid evaporates and vegetables begin to sizzle again, 12 to 15 minutes. Add butter and stir to melt; sprinkle flour over vegetables and stir to combine. Gradually whisk in remaining 4 cups broth until smooth. Stir in wings and bacon, potatoes, and carrots; bring to simmer. Transfer to oven and cook, uncovered, for 30 minutes, stirring once halfway through cooking.

4. Remove pot from oven (handles will be hot). Use wooden spoon to draw gravy up sides of pot and scrape browned fond into stew. Place over high heat, add thighs, and bring to simmer. Return pot to oven, uncovered, and continue to cook, stirring occasionally, until chicken offers no resistance when poked with fork and vegetables are tender, about 45 minutes. (Stew can be refrigerated for up to 2 days.)

5. Discard wings and season stew with up to 2 tablespoons extra wine. Season with salt and pepper to taste, sprinkle with parsley, and serve.

Chicken and Dumplings

Serves 6 to 8

WHY THIS RECIPE WORKS Chicken and dumplings make chicken pot pie look easy: There's no disguising a leaden dumpling. Our goals were to develop a dumpling that was light yet substantial, and tender yet durable; and to develop a well-rounded recipe that, like chicken pot pie, included vegetables, therein providing the cook with a complete meal in one dish. Dumplings can contain myriad ingredients, and there are just as many different ways to mix them. We tried them all—with disastrous results. But when we stumbled on a unique method of adding warm liquid rather than cold to the flour and fat, our dumplings were great—firm but light and fluffy. The reason? The heat expands and sets the flour so that the dumplings don't absorb liquid in the stew. The best-tasting dumplings were made with all-purpose flour, whole milk, and the chicken fat left from browning the chicken. For the stew, we chose bone-in, skin-on chicken thighs for their deep flavor and added enough vegetables to make this dish into a meal. After browning the chicken and vegetables separately, we simmered them in the sauce until the chicken was done and the sauce thickened. We added some peas and parsley, then steamed the dumplings on top of everything until the dumplings turned light and tender. Don't use low-fat or fat-free milk in this recipe. Be sure to reserve 3 tablespoons of chicken fat for the dumplings in step 4; however, if you prefer not to use chicken fat, unsalted butter can be substituted. Start the dumpling dough only when you're ready to top the stew with the dumplings.

Stew
- 5 **pounds bone-in, skin-on chicken thighs**
- 1¾ **teaspoons table salt, divided**
- ¾ **teaspoon pepper**
- 4 **teaspoons vegetable oil, divided**
- 4 **tablespoons unsalted butter**
- 4 **carrots, peeled and sliced ¼ inch thick**
- 2 **celery ribs, sliced ¼ inch thick**
- 1 **onion, chopped fine**
- 6 **tablespoons all-purpose flour**
- ¼ **cup dry sherry**
- 4½ **cups chicken broth**
- ¼ **cup whole milk**
- 1 **teaspoon minced fresh thyme**
- 2 **bay leaves**
- 1 **cup frozen peas**
- 3 **tablespoons minced fresh parsley**

Dumplings
- 2 cups all-purpose flour
- 1 tablespoon baking powder
- 1 teaspoon table salt
- 1 cup whole milk
- 3 tablespoons reserved chicken fat

1. *For the stew:* Pat chicken dry with paper towels, then season with 1½ teaspoons salt and pepper. Heat 2 teaspoons oil in Dutch oven over medium-high heat until just smoking. Add half of chicken and cook until golden on both sides, about 10 minutes. Transfer chicken to plate and remove skin. Pour off chicken fat and reserve. Return pot to medium-high heat and repeat with remaining 2 teaspoons oil and remaining chicken. Pour off and reserve any chicken fat.

2. Add butter to Dutch oven and melt over medium-high heat. Add carrots, celery, onion, and remaining ¼ teaspoon salt and cook until softened, about 7 minutes. Stir in flour. Whisk in sherry, scraping up any browned bits and smoothing out any lumps. Stir in broth, milk, thyme, and bay leaves. Nestle chicken, with any accumulated juices, into pot. Cover and simmer until chicken is fully cooked and tender, about 1 hour.

3. Transfer chicken to carving board. Discard bay leaves. Allow sauce to settle for 5 minutes, then skim fat from surface using wide spoon. Using 2 forks, shred chicken; discard bones. Return chicken to stew.

4. *For the dumplings:* Stir flour, baking powder, and salt together. Microwave milk and chicken fat in bowl until just warm (do not overheat), about 1 minute. Stir warmed milk mixture into flour mixture until incorporated and smooth.

5. Return stew to simmer, stir in peas and parsley, and season with salt and pepper to taste. Drop golf ball–size dumplings over top of stew, about ¼ inch apart (you should have about 18 dumplings). Reduce heat to low, cover, and cook until dumplings have doubled in size, 15 to 18 minutes. Serve.

Chicken and Sausage Gumbo

Serves 6

WHY THIS RECIPE WORKS Most recipes for the beloved Louisiana soup, gumbo, start with a wet roux, a cooked paste of flour and fat that can take an hour or more to make. We streamlined this process by using a dry roux of oven-toasted flour, which gave the same effect as a wet roux but without the oil. To flavor our gumbo we used easy-to-work-with boneless, skinless chicken thighs and andouille sausage, rounding out the dish with garlic, thyme, bay leaves, and spices. We stirred in white vinegar rather than hot sauce at the end for acidity without adding heat to an already well-seasoned dish. This recipe is engineered for efficiency:

Get the flour toasting in the oven and then prep the remaining ingredients before you begin cooking. We strongly recommend using andouille, but in a pinch, kielbasa can be substituted. The salt level of the final dish may vary depending on the brand of sausage, so liberal seasoning with additional salt at the end may be necessary. Serve over white rice.

- 1 cup (5 ounces) all-purpose flour
- 1 tablespoon vegetable oil
- 1 onion, chopped fine
- 1 green bell pepper, chopped fine
- 2 celery ribs, chopped fine
- 3 garlic cloves, minced
- 2 bay leaves
- 1 tablespoon minced fresh thyme
- 1 teaspoon paprika
- ½ teaspoon cayenne pepper
- ¼ teaspoon table salt
- ¼ teaspoon pepper
- 4 cups chicken broth, room temperature, divided
- 2 pounds boneless, skinless chicken thighs, trimmed
- 8 ounces andouille sausage, sliced into ¼-inch-thick half-moons
- 6 scallions, sliced thin
- 1 teaspoon distilled white vinegar
  Hot sauce

1. Adjust oven rack to middle position and heat oven to 425 degrees. Place flour in 12-inch skillet and bake, stirring occasionally, until color of ground cinnamon or dark brown sugar, 40 to 55 minutes. (As flour approaches desired color it will take on very nutty aroma that will smell faintly of burnt popcorn and it will need to be stirred more frequently.) Transfer flour to medium bowl and cool. (Toasted flour can be stored in airtight container for up to 1 week.)

2. Heat oil in Dutch oven over medium heat until shimmering. Add onion, pepper, and celery and cook, stirring frequently, until softened, 5 to 7 minutes. Stir in garlic, bay leaves, thyme, paprika, cayenne, salt, and pepper and cook until fragrant, about 1 minute. Stir in 2 cups broth. Add chicken thighs in single layer (they will not be completely submerged by liquid) and bring to simmer. Reduce heat to medium-low, cover, and simmer until chicken is fork-tender, 15 to 17 minutes. Transfer chicken to plate.

3. Slowly whisk remaining 2 cups broth into toasted flour until thick, batter-like paste forms. (Add broth in small increments to prevent clumps from forming.) Return pot to medium heat and slowly whisk flour paste into gumbo, making sure each addition is incorporated before adding next. Stir sausage into gumbo. Simmer, uncovered, until gumbo thickens slightly, 20 to 25 minutes.

4. Once cool enough to handle, using 2 forks, shred chicken into bite-size pieces. Stir chicken and scallions into gumbo. Remove pot from heat and stir in vinegar and season with salt to taste. Discard bay leaves. Serve, passing hot sauce separately. (Gumbo can be refrigerated for up to 24 hours.)

Hungarian Beef Stew

Serves 6

WHY THIS RECIPE WORKS The Americanized versions of Hungarian goulash served in the United States bear little resemblance to the authentic dish. Sour cream has no place in the pot, nor do mushrooms, green peppers, or most herbs. We wanted the real deal—a simple dish of tender braised beef packed with paprika flavor. To achieve the desired spicy intensity, some recipes call for as much as half a cup of paprika per 3 pounds of meat, but that much fine spice gave the dish a gritty, dusty texture. The chefs at a few Hungarian restaurants introduced us to paprika cream, a condiment as common in Hungarian cooking as the dried spice—but hard to find in the States. Instead, we created our own quick version by pureeing dried paprika with roasted red peppers and a little tomato paste and vinegar. This mixture imparted vibrant paprika flavor without any offensive grittiness. As for the meat, after settling on chuck-eye roast, we bought a whole roast and cut it ourselves into uniform, large pieces to ensure even cooking. Since searing the meat first—normally standard stew protocol—competed with the paprika's brightness, we referred back to a trend we noticed in the goulash recipes gathered during research: skipping the sear. We tried this, softening the onions in the pot first, then adding paprika paste, carrots, and meat before placing the covered pot in the oven. Sure enough, the onions and meat provided enough liquid to stew the meat, and the bits of beef that cooked above the liquid line browned in the hot air. A bit of broth added near the end

of cooking thinned out the stewing liquid to just the right consistency. Do not substitute hot, half-sharp, or smoked Spanish paprika for the sweet paprika in the stew, as they will compromise the flavor of the dish. Since paprika is vital to this recipe, it is best to use a fresh container. We prefer chuck-eye roast, but any boneless roast from the chuck will work. Cook the stew in a Dutch oven with a tight-fitting lid. (Alternatively, to ensure a tight seal, place a sheet of foil over the pot before adding the lid.) Serve the stew over boiled potatoes or egg noodles.

3½ pounds boneless chuck-eye roast, trimmed and cut into 1½-inch pieces
2 teaspoons table salt, divided
1 cup jarred roasted red peppers, rinsed
⅓ cup paprika
2 tablespoons tomato paste
1 tablespoon distilled white vinegar, divided
2 tablespoons vegetable oil
6 onions, chopped fine
4 large carrots, peeled and sliced 1 inch thick
1 bay leaf
1 cup beef broth, warmed
¼ cup sour cream (optional)

1. Adjust oven rack to lower-middle position and heat oven to 325 degrees. Sprinkle meat evenly with 1 teaspoon salt and let sit for 15 minutes. Process roasted peppers, paprika, tomato paste, and 2 teaspoons vinegar in food processor until smooth, 1 to 2 minutes, scraping down sides as needed.

2. Combine oil, onions, and remaining 1 teaspoon salt in Dutch oven; cover and set over medium heat. Cook, stirring occasionally, until onions have softened but have not yet begun to brown, 8 to 10 minutes. (If onions begin to brown, reduce heat to medium-low and stir in 1 tablespoon water.)

3. Stir in paprika mixture; cook, stirring occasionally, until onions stick to bottom of pan, about 2 minutes. Add beef, carrots, and bay leaf; stir until beef is well coated. Scrape down sides of pot. Cover pot and transfer to oven. Cook until meat is almost tender and surface of liquid is ½ inch below top of meat, 2 to 2½ hours, stirring every 30 minutes. Remove pot from oven (handles will be hot) and add enough beef broth that surface of liquid is ¼ inch from top of meat (beef should not be fully submerged). Return covered pot to oven and continue to cook until fork slips easily in and out of beef, about 30 minutes.

4. Skim fat off surface using wide spoon; stir in remaining 1 teaspoon vinegar and sour cream, if using. Discard bay leaf, season with salt and pepper to taste, and serve. (Stew can be refrigerated for up to 2 days; wait to add optional sour cream until after reheating. Before reheating, skim hardened fat from surface and add enough water to stew to thin it slightly.)

Catalan-Style Beef Stew

Serves 4 to 6

WHY THIS RECIPE WORKS Supremely meaty and complexly flavored, Spanish beef stew is a little different than its American counterpart. It starts with a *sofrito*, a slow-cooked jamlike mixture of onions, spices, and herbs that builds a flavor-packed base. We normally use chuck eye for stew, but swapped it out for boneless beef short ribs, determining that they gave us a beefier-tasting stew. We finished the stew with a mixture of toasted bread, toasted almonds, garlic, and parsley. This mixture, called a picada, brightened the stew's flavor and thickened the broth. While we developed this recipe with Albariño, a dry Spanish white wine, you can also use a Sauvignon Blanc. Remove the woody base of the oyster mushroom stems before cooking. An equal amount of quartered white mushrooms may be substituted for the oyster mushrooms. Serve the stew with boiled or mashed potatoes or rice.

Stew
- 2 tablespoons extra-virgin olive oil
- 2 large onions, chopped fine
- ½ teaspoon sugar
- 2 teaspoons table salt, divided
- 2 plum tomatoes, halved lengthwise, pulp grated on large holes of box grater, skins discarded
- 1 teaspoon smoked paprika
- 1 bay leaf
- 1½ cups dry white wine
- 1½ cups water
- 1 large sprig fresh thyme
- ¼ teaspoon ground cinnamon
- 2½ pounds boneless beef short ribs, trimmed and cut into 2-inch pieces
- ½ teaspoon pepper

Picada
- ¼ cup whole blanched almonds
- 2 tablespoons extra-virgin olive oil, divided
- 1 slice hearty white sandwich bread, crusts removed, torn into 1-inch pieces
- 2 garlic cloves, peeled
- 3 tablespoons minced fresh parsley
- 8 ounces oyster mushrooms, trimmed
- ½ teaspoon table salt
- 1 teaspoon sherry vinegar

1. For the stew: Adjust oven rack to middle position and heat oven to 300 degrees. Heat oil in Dutch oven over medium-low heat until shimmering. Add onions, sugar, and ½ teaspoon salt; cook, stirring often, until onions are deeply caramelized, 30 to 40 minutes. Add tomatoes, paprika, and bay leaf; cook, stirring often, until darkened and thick, 5 to 10 minutes.

2. Add wine, water, thyme sprig, and cinnamon to pot, scraping up any browned bits. Season beef with remaining 1½ teaspoons salt and pepper and add to pot. Increase heat to high and bring to simmer. Transfer to oven and cook, uncovered. After 1 hour stir stew to redistribute meat, return to oven, and continue to cook, uncovered, until meat is tender, 30 minutes to 2 hours.

3. For the picada: While stew is in oven, heat almonds and 1 tablespoon oil in 10-inch skillet over medium heat; cook, stirring often, until almonds are golden brown, 3 to 6 minutes. Using slotted spoon, transfer almonds to food processor. Return now-empty skillet to medium heat, add bread, and cook, stirring often, until toasted, 2 to 4 minutes; transfer to food processor with almonds. Add garlic and process until mixture is finely ground, about 20 seconds, scraping down bowl as needed. Transfer mixture to bowl, stir in parsley, and set aside.

4. Return again-empty skillet to medium heat. Heat remaining 1 tablespoon oil until shimmering. Add mushrooms and salt; cook, stirring often, until tender, 5 to 7 minutes. Transfer to bowl and set aside.

5. Discard bay leaf and thyme sprig. Stir picada, mushrooms, and vinegar into stew. Season with salt and pepper to taste, and serve.

Modern Beef Burgundy

Serves 6 to 8

WHY THIS RECIPE WORKS We wanted to update the French classic *boeuf bourguignon* to have tender braised beef napped with a silky sauce with bold red wine flavor—without all the work that traditional recipes require. To eliminate the time-consuming step of searing the beef, we cooked the stew uncovered in a roasting pan in the oven so that the exposed meat browned as it braised. This method worked so well that we also used the oven, rather than the stovetop, to render the salt pork and to caramelize the traditional mushroom and pearl onion garnish. Salting the beef before cooking and adding some anchovy paste and porcini mushrooms enhanced the meaty savoriness of the dish without making our recipe too fussy. If the pearl onions have a papery outer coating, remove it by rinsing them in warm water and gently squeezing individual onions between your fingertips. Two minced anchovy fillets can be used in place of the anchovy paste. To save time, salt the meat and let it stand while you prep the remaining ingredients. Serve with mashed potatoes or buttered noodles.

"'Game changing' is a perfect descriptor for this Catalan beef stew, which changed the way that I make stew. Until this recipe came along, our stewing method always started by batch-browning pieces of meat. Yes, that's a great way to develop flavor, but the process is admittedly tedious. The revelation that the meat could brown if left directly exposed to the oven's heat was, frankly, mind-blowing.

The flavors are intensely beefy and complex, as we used the ultimate beef stew meat (short ribs) and peppered in warm spices such as smoked paprika and cinnamon. The verdant, bright picada—a Catalonian pesto that's traditional to the dish—is the perfect punctuation to finish the slow-cooked stew. I use the same picada recipe to stir into bean soups, chicken braises, and more."

–Bridget

1 (4-pound) boneless beef chuck-eye roast, trimmed and cut into 1½- to 2-inch pieces, scraps reserved
1½ teaspoons table salt
6 ounces salt pork, cut into ¼-inch pieces
3 tablespoons unsalted butter, divided
1 pound cremini mushrooms, trimmed, halved if medium or quartered if large
1½ cups frozen pearl onions, thawed
1 tablespoon sugar
⅓ cup all-purpose flour
4 cups beef broth
1 (750-ml) bottle red Burgundy or Pinot Noir, divided
5 teaspoons unflavored gelatin
1 tablespoon tomato paste
1 teaspoon anchovy paste
2 onions, chopped coarse
2 carrots, peeled and cut into 2-inch lengths
1 garlic head, cloves separated, unpeeled, and crushed
2 bay leaves
½ teaspoon black peppercorns
½ ounce dried porcini mushrooms, rinsed
10 sprigs fresh parsley, plus 3 tablespoons minced
6 sprigs fresh thyme

1. Toss beef and salt together in bowl and let stand at room temperature for 30 minutes.

2. Adjust oven racks to lower-middle and lowest positions and heat oven to 500 degrees. Place salt pork, beef scraps, and 2 tablespoons butter in large roasting pan. Roast on upper rack until well browned and fat has rendered, 15 to 20 minutes.

3. While salt pork and beef scraps roast, toss cremini mushrooms, pearl onions, remaining 1 tablespoon butter, and sugar together on rimmed baking sheet. Roast on lower rack, stirring occasionally, until moisture released by mushrooms evaporates and vegetables are lightly glazed, 15 to 20 minutes. Transfer vegetables to large bowl, cover, and refrigerate.

4. Remove roasting pan from oven and reduce temperature to 325 degrees. Sprinkle flour over rendered fat and whisk until no dry flour remains. Whisk in broth, 2 cups wine, gelatin, tomato paste, and anchovy paste until combined. Add onions, carrots, garlic, bay leaves, peppercorns, porcini mushrooms, parsley sprigs, and thyme sprigs to pan. Arrange beef in single layer on top of vegetables. Add water as needed to come three-quarters up side of beef (beef should not be submerged). Return roasting pan to oven and cook until meat is tender, 3 to 3½ hours, stirring after 1½ hours and adding water to keep meat at least half-submerged.

5. Using slotted spoon, transfer beef to bowl with cremini mushrooms and pearl onions; cover and set aside. Strain braising liquid through fine-mesh strainer set over large bowl, pressing on solids to extract as much liquid as possible; discard solids. Stir in remaining wine and let cooking liquid settle, 10 minutes. Using wide, shallow spoon, skim fat off surface and discard.

6. Transfer liquid to Dutch oven and bring mixture to boil over medium-high heat. Simmer briskly, stirring occasionally, until sauce is thickened to consistency of heavy cream, 15 to 20 minutes. Reduce heat to medium-low, stir in beef and mushroom-onion garnish, cover, and cook until just heated through, 5 to 8 minutes. Season with salt and pepper to taste. Stir in minced parsley and serve. (Stew can be made up to 3 days in advance.)

Daube Provençal

Serves 4 to 6

WHY THIS RECIPE WORKS Daube Provençal, also known as daube niçoise, has all the elements of the best French fare: tender beef, a luxurious sauce, and complex flavors. So why does it usually end up as beef stew with a few misplaced ingredients instead of being its own, coherent dish? We wanted to translate the flavors of Provence—olive oil, olives, garlic, wine, herbs, oranges, tomatoes, mushrooms, and anchovies—to an American home kitchen, and create a bold, brash, and full-flavored beef stew, with ingredients that married into a robust but unified dish. We started with the test kitchen's reliable set of techniques to turn tough but flavorful beef into a tender stew: Brown the beef; add the aromatics; sprinkle some flour in the pan to thicken the braising liquid;

deglaze with cooking liquid; add the meat back to the pot; and finally, cover and cook slowly in the oven until tender. Technique established, we concentrated on selecting and managing the complex blend of ingredients that defines this dish. We chose briny niçoise olives, bright tomatoes, floral orange peel, and the regional flavors of thyme and bay leaf. A few anchovies added complexity without a fishy taste, and salt pork contributed rich body. A whole bottle of wine added bold flavor and needed just a little cooking to tame its raw bite. Finally, to keep the meat from drying out during the long braising time required to create a complex-tasting sauce, we cut it into relatively large 2-inch pieces. Serve this French beef stew with egg noodles or boiled potatoes. If niçoise olives are not available, kalamata olives, though not authentic, can be substituted. Cabernet Sauvignon is our favorite wine for this recipe, but Côtes du Rhône and Zinfandel also work. Our favorite cut of beef for this recipe is chuck-eye roast, but any boneless roast from the chuck will work. Because the tomatoes are added just before serving, it is preferable to use canned whole tomatoes and dice them yourself—uncooked, they are more tender than canned diced tomatoes. Once the salt pork, thyme, and bay leaves are removed in step 4, the daube can be cooled and refrigerated in an airtight container for up to four days. Before reheating, skim the hardened fat from the surface and then continue with the recipe.

 2 **cups water, divided**
 ¾ **ounce dried porcini mushrooms, rinsed**
 1 **(3½-pound) boneless beef chuck-eye roast, trimmed and cut into 2-inch pieces**
1½ **teaspoons table salt**
 1 **teaspoon pepper**
 ¼ **cup extra-virgin olive oil, divided**
 5 **ounces salt pork, rind removed**

 2 **onions, halved through root end and sliced ⅛ inch thick**
 4 **large carrots, peeled and sliced 1 inch thick**
 2 **tablespoons tomato paste**
 4 **garlic cloves, peeled and sliced thin**
 ⅓ **cup all-purpose flour**
 1 **(750-ml) bottle bold red wine**
 1 **cup chicken broth**
 1 **cup pitted niçoise olives, divided**
 4 **(3-inch) strips orange peel, sliced thin lengthwise**
 2 **anchovy fillets, minced**
 5 **sprigs fresh thyme, tied together with kitchen twine**
 2 **bay leaves**
 1 **(14.5-ounce) can whole tomatoes, drained and cut into ½-inch pieces**
 2 **tablespoons minced fresh parsley**

1. Combine 1 cup water and mushrooms in small bowl; cover with plastic wrap, cut 3 vents for steam with knife, and microwave for 30 seconds. Let sit until mushrooms soften, about 5 minutes. Lift mushrooms from liquid with fork and chop into ½-inch pieces (you should have about ¼ cup). Strain liquid through fine-mesh strainer lined with paper towel into medium bowl. Set mushrooms and liquid aside.

2. Adjust oven rack to lower-middle position and heat oven to 325 degrees. Dry beef thoroughly with paper towels, then season with salt and pepper. Heat 2 tablespoons oil in Dutch oven over medium-high heat until just smoking; add half of beef. Cook without moving pieces until well browned, about 2 minutes per side, for total of 8 to 10 minutes, reducing heat if fat begins to smoke. Transfer meat to medium bowl. Repeat with remaining 2 tablespoons oil and remaining beef.

3. Reduce heat to medium and add salt pork, onions, carrots, tomato paste, and garlic to now-empty pot; cook, stirring occasionally, until light brown, about 2 minutes. Stir in flour and cook, stirring constantly, about 1 minute. Slowly add wine, gently scraping up any browned bits and smoothing out any lumps. Add broth, remaining 1 cup water, and beef with any accumulated juices. Increase heat to medium-high and bring to simmer. Add mushrooms and their liquid, ½ cup olives, orange peel, anchovies, thyme, and bay leaves, distributing evenly and arranging beef so it is completely covered by liquid; partially cover pot and place in oven. Cook until fork inserted in beef meets little resistance (meat should not be falling apart), 2½ to 3 hours.

4. Discard salt pork, thyme, and bay leaves. Add tomatoes and remaining ½ cup olives; warm over medium-high heat until heated through, about 1 minute. Cover pot and allow stew to settle, about 5 minutes. Using wide, shallow spoon, skim excess fat from surface of stew. Stir in parsley and serve.

Carbonnade

Serves 6

WHY THIS RECIPE WORKS Most recipes for this Belgian beef, onion, and beer stew go in one of two directions: In one version, the recipe masks its genuine flavors, and in others the recipes rigidly adhere to the "three ingredients only" rule, so the stew is pale and tasteless. We wanted hearty chunks of beef and sliced sweet onion in a thickened broth, laced with the malty flavor of beer. We found that top blade steak, which has a fair amount of marbling, provided the best texture and a "buttery" flavor that worked well alongside the onions and beer. White and red onions were too sweet in our stew; yellow onions worked better. The onions should be browned only lightly; overcaramelization caused them to disintegrate. Tomato paste gave the stew depth, as did garlic. Fresh thyme and bay leaves provided seasoning, and a splash of cider vinegar added the right level of acidity. Beer is a staple of Belgian cooking, and we found that it's less forgiving than wine when used in a stew. The light lagers we tried resulted in pale, watery stews; better were dark ales and stouts. But beer alone often made for bitter-tasting stew, so we included some broth; a combination of chicken and beef broth gave us more solid and complex flavor. Top blade steaks (also called blade or flat-iron steaks) are our first choice, but any boneless roast from the chuck will work. If you end up using a chuck roast, look for the chuck-eye roast, an especially flavorful cut that can easily be trimmed and cut into 1-inch pieces. Buttered egg noodles or mashed potatoes make excellent accompaniments to carbonnade.

3½ pounds top blade steaks, 1 inch thick, trimmed and cut into 1-inch pieces
1½ teaspoons table salt, divided
½   teaspoon pepper
3   tablespoons vegetable oil, divided
2   pounds onions, halved and sliced ¼ inch thick
1   tablespoon tomato paste
2   garlic cloves, minced
3   tablespoons all-purpose flour
¾   cup chicken broth
¾   cup beef broth
1½ cups dark beer or stout
4   sprigs fresh thyme, tied with kitchen twine
2   bay leaves
1   tablespoon cider vinegar

1. Adjust oven rack to lower-middle position and heat oven to 300 degrees. Pat beef dry thoroughly with paper towels, then season with 1 teaspoon salt and pepper. Heat 2 teaspoons oil in Dutch oven over medium-high heat until just beginning to smoke; add about one-third of beef to pot. Cook without moving beef until well browned, 2 to 3 minutes; turn each piece and continue cooking until second side is well browned, about 5 minutes. Transfer browned beef to medium bowl. Repeat with 2 teaspoons more oil and half of remaining beef. (If drippings in bottom of pot are very dark, add ½ cup of chicken or beef broth and scrape pan bottom with wooden spoon to loosen browned bits; pour liquid into bowl with browned beef, then proceed.) Repeat once more with 2 teaspoons more oil and remaining beef.

2. Add remaining 1 tablespoon oil to now-empty Dutch oven; reduce heat to medium-low. Add onions, tomato paste, and remaining ½ teaspoon salt; cook, scraping bottom of pot with wooden spoon to loosen browned bits, until onions have released some moisture, about 5 minutes. Increase heat to medium and continue to cook, stirring occasionally, until onions are lightly browned, 12 to 14 minutes. Stir in garlic and cook until fragrant, about 30 seconds. Add flour and stir until onions are evenly coated and flour is lightly browned, about 2 minutes. Stir in broths, loosening any browned bits and smoothing out any lumps; stir in beer, thyme, bay leaves, vinegar, browned beef with any accumulated juices, and salt and pepper to taste. Increase heat to medium-high and bring to full simmer, stirring occasionally; cover partially, then place pot in oven. Cook until fork inserted into beef meets little resistance, 2 to 2½ hours.

3. Discard thyme and bay leaves. Season with salt and pepper to taste, and serve. (Stew can be refrigerated for up to 3 days.)

Trimming Blade Steaks

To trim blade steaks, halve each steak lengthwise, leaving gristle on 1 half. Then simply cut gristle away.

Cioppino

Serves 4 to 6

WHY THIS RECIPE WORKS Brought to San Francisco by Italian immigrants, the earliest versions of cioppino were uncomplicated affairs made by fishermen with the day's catch. Today's restaurant versions showcase a variety of fish and shellfish piled high in a bright, complex broth. Cioppino is an indulgence for a seafood lover—but many recipes are intimidating for home cooks. We wanted a restaurant-worthy cioppino in which every component was perfectly cooked but that could be on the table quickly and with minimal fuss. First, we scaled down the seafood. For the fish, halibut fillets worked perfectly—they were tender and had just enough heft. As for the shellfish, a combination of briny littleneck clams and savory-sweet mussels had the flavors we were looking for. The only way to perfectly cook three varieties of seafood was to cook each one separately and bring them all together in the hot broth to serve. We poached the halibut in the broth while the clams and mussels steamed in a separate pan. Removing the shellfish as they opened ensured ideal doneness for each one, and using a shallow skillet made the task easy. We used white wine to steam the mussels and clams, and then added the briny cooking liquid to the stew for a boost of intense seafood flavor. Bottled clam juice improved the broth even further. Any firm-fleshed, ¾- to 1-inch-thick white fish (such as cod or sea bass) can be substituted for the halibut. Discard clams or mussels with unpleasant odors, cracked shells, or shells that won't close. If littlenecks are not available, substitute Manila or mahogany clams, or use 2 pounds of mussels. If using only mussels, skip step 3 and cook them all at once with the butter and wine for 3 to 5 minutes.

- ¼ cup vegetable oil
- 2 large onions, chopped fine
- ½ teaspoon table salt
- ½ teaspoon pepper
- ¼ cup water
- 4 garlic cloves, minced
- 2 bay leaves
- 1 teaspoon dried oregano
- ⅛–¼ teaspoon red pepper flakes
- 1 (28-ounce) can whole peeled tomatoes, drained with juice reserved, chopped coarse
- 1 (8-ounce) bottle clam juice
- 1 (1½-pound) skinless halibut fillet, ¾ to 1 inch thick, cut into 6 pieces
- 1 pound littleneck clams, scrubbed
- 1¼ cups dry white wine
- 4 tablespoons unsalted butter
- 1 pound mussels, scrubbed and debearded
- ¼ cup chopped fresh parsley
  Extra-virgin olive oil

1. Heat vegetable oil in Dutch oven over medium-high heat until shimmering. Add onions, salt, and pepper; cook, stirring frequently, until onions begin to brown, 7 to 9 minutes. Add water and cook, stirring frequently, until onions are soft, 2 to 4 minutes. Stir in garlic, bay leaves, oregano, and pepper flakes and cook for 1 minute. Stir in tomatoes and reserved juice and clam juice and bring to simmer. Reduce heat to low, cover, and simmer for 5 minutes.

2. Submerge halibut in broth, cover, and gently simmer until fish is cooked through, 12 to 15 minutes. Remove pot from heat and, using slotted spoon, transfer halibut to plate, cover with aluminum foil, and set aside.

3. Bring clams, wine, and butter to boil in covered 12-inch skillet over high heat. Steam until clams just open, 5 to 8 minutes, transferring them to pot with tomato broth as they open.

4. Once all clams have been transferred to pot, add mussels to skillet, cover, and cook over high heat until mussels have opened, 2 to 4 minutes, transferring them to pot with tomato broth as they open. Pour cooking liquid from skillet into pot, being careful not to pour any grit from skillet into pot. Return broth to simmer.

5. Stir parsley into broth and season with salt and pepper to taste. Divide halibut among serving bowls. Ladle broth over halibut, making sure each portion contains both clams and mussels. Drizzle with olive oil and serve immediately.

Brazilian Shrimp and Fish Stew (Moqueca)

Serves 6

WHY THIS RECIPE WORKS For a bright, fresh, and filling version of this traditional Brazilian stew, we started with the seafood. Cod and shrimp made for a nice balance of flavor and texture, and both were easy to find. After tossing the seafood with garlic, salt, and pepper, we looked to the other components of the stew. To balance the richness and sweetness of the coconut milk with the bright, fresh flavor of the aromatics, we blended the onion, tomatoes, and a portion of the cilantro in the food processor until they had the texture of a slightly chunky salsa, which added body to the stew. We diced the bell peppers for contrasting texture and bite. To ensure that the seafood was properly cooked, we brought the broth to a boil so that the pot was superhot, added the seafood and lime juice, covered the pot, and removed it from the heat, allowing the seafood to gently cook in the residual heat. To finish our *moqueca*, we added more cilantro and a couple of tablespoons of homemade pepper sauce, which elevated the stew with its bright, vinegary tang. Pickled hot cherry peppers are usually sold jarred, next to the pickles or jarred roasted red peppers at the supermarket. Haddock or other firm-fleshed, flaky white fish may be substituted for the cod. We prefer untreated shrimp, but if your shrimp are treated with sodium, do not add salt to the shrimp in step 2. Our favorite coconut milk is made by Aroy-D. Serve with steamed white rice.

Pepper Sauce

- 4 pickled hot cherry peppers (3 ounces)
- ½ onion, chopped coarse
- ¼ cup extra-virgin olive oil
- ⅛ teaspoon sugar

Stew

- 1 pound large shrimp (26 to 30 per pound), peeled, deveined, and tails removed
- 1 pound skinless cod fillets (¾ to 1 inch thick), cut into 1½-inch pieces
- 3 garlic cloves, minced
- 1½ teaspoons table salt, divided
- ¼ teaspoon pepper
- 1 onion, chopped coarse
- 1 (14.5-ounce) can whole peeled tomatoes
- ¾ cup chopped fresh cilantro, divided
- 2 tablespoons extra-virgin olive oil
- 1 red bell pepper, stemmed, seeded, and cut into ½-inch pieces
- 1 green bell pepper, stemmed, seeded, and cut into ½-inch pieces
- 1 (14-ounce) can coconut milk
- 2 tablespoons lime juice

1. *For the pepper sauce:* Process all ingredients in food processor until smooth, about 30 seconds, scraping down sides of bowl as needed. Season with salt to taste and transfer to separate bowl. Rinse out processor bowl.

2. *For the stew:* Toss shrimp and cod with garlic, ½ teaspoon salt, and pepper in bowl. Set aside.

3. Process onion, tomatoes and their juice, and ¼ cup cilantro in food processor until finely chopped and mixture has texture of pureed salsa, about 30 seconds.

4. Heat oil in Dutch oven over medium-high heat until shimmering. Add red and green bell peppers and ½ teaspoon salt and cook, stirring frequently, until softened, 5 to 7 minutes. Add onion-tomato mixture and remaining ½ teaspoon salt. Reduce heat to medium and cook, stirring frequently, until puree has reduced and thickened slightly, 3 to 5 minutes (pot should not be dry).

5. Increase heat to high, stir in coconut milk, and bring to boil (mixture should be bubbling across entire surface). Add seafood mixture and lime juice and stir to evenly distribute seafood, making sure all pieces are submerged in liquid. Cover pot and remove from heat. Let sit until shrimp and cod are opaque and just cooked through, 15 minutes.

6. Gently stir in 2 tablespoons pepper sauce and remaining ½ cup cilantro, being careful not to break up cod too much. Season with salt and pepper to taste. Serve, passing remaining pepper sauce separately.

Hearty Tuscan Bean Stew

Serves 8

WHY THIS RECIPE WORKS Unlike *pasta e fagioli*, where beans and pasta share the spotlight, Tuscan bean soup boasts creamy, buttery cannellini beans in the starring role. Ideally, the beans should have a uniformly tender texture, but too often the skins are tough and the insides mealy—or the beans turn mushy. We wanted to fix the bean problem and convert this Italian classic into a hearty, rustic stew for a deeply flavorful one-pot meal. Since the beans are the centerpiece of this stew, we concentrated on cooking them perfectly. After testing a variety of soaking times, we settled on soaking the beans overnight, a method that consistently produced the most tender and evenly cooked beans. But none of the methods we tested properly softened the skins. The answer was to soak the beans in salted water. Brining the beans, rather than the conventional approach of soaking them in plain water and then cooking them in salt water, allowed the salt to soften the skins but kept it from penetrating inside, where it could make the beans mealy. Tests showed that gently cooking the beans in a 250-degree oven produced perfectly cooked beans that stayed intact. The final trick was to add the tomatoes toward the end of cooking, since their acid interfered with the softening process. To complete our stew, we looked for other traditional Tuscan flavors, including pancetta, kale, lots of garlic, and a sprig of rosemary. And to make it even more substantial, we served the stew on a slab of toasted white bread, drizzled with fruity extra-virgin olive oil. We prefer the creamier texture of beans soaked overnight for this recipe, so brine the beans for at least 8 hours or up to

24 hours. If you're short on time, however, you can quick-soak them: Place the rinsed beans in a large heat-resistant bowl. Bring 2 quarts water and 3 tablespoons salt to a boil. Pour the water over the beans and let them sit for 1 hour. Drain and rinse the beans well before proceeding with step 2.

- 3 tablespoons table salt, for brining
- 1 pound (2 cups) dried cannellini beans, picked over and rinsed
- 1 tablespoon extra-virgin olive oil, plus extra for drizzling
- 6 ounces pancetta or bacon, cut into ¼-inch pieces
- 1 large onion, chopped
- 2 celery ribs, cut into ½-inch pieces
- 2 carrots, peeled and cut into ½-inch pieces
- 8 garlic cloves, peeled and crushed
- 4 cups chicken broth
- 3 cups water
- 2 bay leaves
- 1 pound kale or collard greens, stemmed and chopped into 1-inch pieces
- 1 (14.5-ounce) can diced tomatoes, drained
- 1 sprig fresh rosemary
- 8 slices hearty white bread, each 1¼ inches thick, broiled until golden brown on both sides and rubbed with garlic clove (optional)

1. Dissolve salt in 4 quarts cold water in large bowl or container. Add beans and soak at room temperature for at least 8 hours or up to 24 hours. Rinse beans well.

2. Adjust oven rack to lower-middle position and heat oven to 250 degrees. Heat oil and pancetta in Dutch oven over medium heat. Cook, stirring occasionally, until pancetta is lightly browned and fat has rendered, 6 to 10 minutes. Add onion, celery, and carrots. Cook, stirring occasionally, until vegetables are softened and lightly browned, 10 to 16 minutes. Stir in garlic and cook until fragrant, about 1 minute. Stir in broth, water, bay leaves, and soaked beans. Increase heat to high and bring mixture to simmer. Cover pot, transfer to oven, and cook until beans are almost tender (very center of beans will still be firm), 45 minutes to 1 hour.

3. Remove pot from oven and stir in kale and tomatoes. Return pot to oven (handles will be hot) and continue to cook until beans and greens are fully tender, 30 to 40 minutes.

4. Remove pot from oven and submerge rosemary sprig in stew. Cover and let sit for 15 minutes. Discard bay leaves and rosemary sprig and season stew with salt and pepper to taste. If desired, use back of spoon to press some beans against side of pot to thicken stew. Serve over toasted bread, if using, and drizzle with oil.

Our Favorite Chili

Serves 6 to 8

WHY THIS RECIPE WORKS Our goal in creating an "ultimate" beef chili was to determine which of the "secret ingredients" recommended by chili experts around the world were spot-on—and which were expendable. We started with the beef. Most recipes call for ground beef, but we preferred meaty blade steaks, which don't require much trimming and stayed in big chunks in our finished chili. For complex chile flavor, we traded in the commercial chili powder in favor of ground dried ancho and arbol chiles; for a grassy heat, we added fresh jalapeños. Dried beans, brined before cooking, stayed creamy for the duration of cooking. Beer and chicken broth outperformed red wine, coffee, and beef broth as the liquid components. For balancing sweetness, light molasses beat out other offbeat ingredients (including prunes and Coca-Cola). And finally, for the right level of thickness, flour and peanut butter didn't perform as promised; instead, a small amount of ordinary cornmeal sealed the deal, providing just the right consistency in our ultimate beef chili. A 4-pound chuck-eye roast, well trimmed of fat, can be substituted for the blade steak. Because much of the chili flavor is held in the fat of this dish, refrain from skimming fat from the surface. Dried New Mexican or guajillo chiles make a good substitute for the anchos; each dried arbol may be replaced with ⅛ teaspoon cayenne pepper. If you prefer not to work with any whole dried chiles, the anchos and arbols can be replaced with ½ cup commercial chili powder and ¼ to ½ teaspoon cayenne pepper, though the texture of the chili will be slightly compromised. Serve with your favorite chili toppings.

- 3 tablespoons table salt, for brining
- 8 ounces dried pinto beans (1¼ cups), picked over and rinsed
- 6 dried ancho chiles, stemmed, seeded, and torn into 1-inch pieces
- 2–4 dried arbol chiles, stemmed, seeded, and split into 2 pieces
- 3 tablespoons cornmeal
- 2 teaspoons dried oregano
- 2 teaspoons ground cumin
- 2 teaspoons cocoa powder
- 1½ teaspoons table salt, divided
- 2½ cups chicken broth, divided
- 2 onions, cut into ¾-inch pieces
- 3 small jalapeño chiles, stemmed, seeded, and cut into ½-inch pieces
- 3 tablespoons vegetable oil, divided
- 4 garlic cloves, minced
- 1 (14.5-ounce) can diced tomatoes
- 2 teaspoons light molasses
- 3½ pounds blade steak, ¾ inch thick, trimmed and cut into ¾-inch pieces
- 1 (12-ounce) bottle mild lager, such as Budweiser, divided

1. Combine 3 tablespoons salt, 4 quarts water, and beans in Dutch oven and bring to boil over high heat. Remove pot from heat, cover, and let sit for 1 hour. Drain and rinse well.

2. Adjust oven rack to lower-middle position and heat oven to 300 degrees. Place ancho chiles in 12-inch skillet over medium-high heat and toast, stirring frequently, until flesh is fragrant, 4 to 6 minutes, reducing heat if chiles begin to smoke. Transfer to food processor and cool. Do not wash out skillet.

3. Add arbol chiles, cornmeal, oregano, cumin, cocoa, and ½ teaspoon salt to food processor with toasted ancho chiles; process until finely ground, about 2 minutes. With processor running, slowly add ½ cup broth until smooth paste forms, about 45 seconds, scraping down sides of bowl as necessary. Transfer paste to small bowl. Place onions in now-empty processor and pulse until roughly chopped, about 4 pulses. Add jalapeños and pulse until consistency of chunky salsa, about 4 pulses, scraping down bowl as necessary.

4. Heat 1 tablespoon oil in now-empty Dutch oven over medium-high heat. Add onion mixture and cook, stirring occasionally, until moisture has evaporated and vegetables are softened, 7 to 9 minutes. Add garlic and cook until fragrant, about 1 minute. Add chile paste, tomatoes, and molasses; stir until chile paste is thoroughly combined. Add remaining 2 cups chicken broth and beans; bring to boil, then reduce heat to simmer.

5. Meanwhile, heat 1 tablespoon oil in now-empty 12-inch skillet over medium-high heat until shimmering. Pat beef dry with paper towels and sprinkle with remaining 1 teaspoon salt. Add half of beef and cook until browned on all sides, about 10 minutes. Transfer meat to Dutch oven. Add half of beer to skillet, scraping up any browned bits, and bring to simmer. Transfer beer to Dutch oven. Repeat with remaining 1 tablespoon oil, remaining beef, and remaining beer. Stir to combine and return mixture to simmer.

6. Cover pot and transfer to oven. Cook until meat and beans are fully tender, 1½ to 2 hours. Let chili sit, uncovered, for 10 minutes. Stir well, season with salt to taste, and serve. (Chili can be refrigerated for up to 3 days.)

Beef Chili with Kidney Beans

Serves 8 to 10

WHY THIS RECIPE WORKS Many basic chili recipes yield a pot of underspiced, underflavored chili reminiscent of Sloppy Joes. We wanted an easy recipe for a basic chili, made with supermarket staples, that would have some heat and great flavors—chili that would please almost everyone. To start, we added the spices to the pan with the aromatics (bell peppers, onion, and lots of garlic) to get the most flavor,

"This chili isn't just good, it's competition-winning good. No joke—I've witnessed several family members win friendly chili cookoffs (nothing professional, mind you) with this recipe. The trick is in the homemade chile paste, which uses ancho and arbol chiles that you grind up along with a few other seasonings, including cocoa powder and cornmeal. You just can't buy chili powder that tastes this good. The blade steaks offer a big beefy flavor and tender texture to the chili, but what's even better is how easy they are to prep— there's no bones and no serious trimming required. Now, this chili does include pinto beans, which some chili enthusiasts will scoff at, but I like beans in chili, so there. It's also worth mentioning that this chili is easy to personalize and over the years, I've made a few killer variations that add bourbon, grilled onions, and even kale!"

–*Julia*

and used commercial chili powder with a boost from more cumin, oregano, cayenne, and coriander. For the meat, we found that 85 percent lean ground beef gave us full flavor. A combination of diced tomatoes and tomato puree gave our chili a well-balanced saucy backbone. We added quick-cooking canned red kidney beans with the tomatoes so that they heated through and absorbed flavor. For a rich, thick consistency, we cooked the chili with the lid on for half of the cooking time. If you are a fan of spicy food, consider using a little more of the red pepper flakes or cayenne—or both. The flavor of the chili improves with age; if possible, make it a day or up to three days in advance and reheat before serving. Serve with your favorite chili toppings.

- 2 tablespoons vegetable oil
- 2 onions, chopped fine
- 1 red bell pepper, stemmed, seeded, and cut into ½-inch pieces
- 6 garlic cloves, minced
- ¼ cup chili powder
- 1 tablespoon ground cumin
- 2 teaspoons ground coriander
- 1 teaspoon red pepper flakes
- 1 teaspoon dried oregano
- ½ teaspoon cayenne pepper
- 2 pounds 85 percent lean ground beef, divided
- 2 (15-ounce) cans dark red kidney beans, rinsed
- 1 (28-ounce) can diced tomatoes
- 1 (28-ounce) can tomato puree
- ½ teaspoon table salt
  Lime wedges

1. Heat oil in Dutch oven over medium heat until shimmering. Add onions, bell pepper, garlic, chili powder, cumin, coriander, pepper flakes, oregano, and cayenne and cook, stirring occasionally, until vegetables are softened and beginning to brown, about 10 minutes. Increase heat to medium-high and add half of beef. Cook, breaking up pieces with wooden spoon, until no longer pink and just beginning to brown, 3 to 4 minutes. Add remaining beef and cook, breaking up pieces with wooden spoon, until no longer pink, 3 to 4 minutes.

2. Add beans, tomatoes with their juice, tomato puree, and salt. Bring to boil, then reduce heat to low and simmer, covered, stirring occasionally, for 1 hour. Uncover and continue to simmer for 1 hour, stirring occasionally (if chili begins to stick to bottom of pot, stir in ½ cup water and continue to simmer), until beef is tender and chili is dark, rich, and slightly thickened. Season with salt to taste. Serve with lime wedges. (Chili can be refrigerated for up to 3 days.)

Best Vegetarian Chili

Serves 6 to 8

WHY THIS RECIPE WORKS Vegetarian chilis are often little more than a mishmash of beans and vegetables. To create a robust, complex-flavored chili—not just a bean and vegetable stew—we found replacements for the different ways in which meat adds depth and savory flavor to chili. Walnuts, soy sauce, dried shiitake mushrooms, and tomatoes added hearty savoriness. Bulgur filled out the chili, giving it a substantial texture. The vegetable oil and nuts lent a richness to the chili, for full, lingering flavor. We prefer to use whole dried chiles, but the chili can be prepared with jarred chili powder. If using chili powder, grind the shiitakes and oregano and add them to the pot with ¼ cup of chili powder in step 4. Pinto, black, red kidney, small red, cannellini, or navy beans can be used in this recipe, either a single variety or a combination of beans. For a spicier chili use both jalapeños. Serve with your favorite chili toppings.

- 1 pound (2½ cups) dried beans, rinsed and picked over
- 3 tablespoons table salt, for brining
- 2 dried ancho chiles
- 2 dried New Mexican chiles
- ½ ounce dried shiitake mushrooms, chopped coarse
- 4 teaspoons dried oregano
- ½ cup walnuts, toasted
- 1 (28-ounce) can diced tomatoes, drained with juice reserved
- 3 tablespoons tomato paste
- 1–2 jalapeño chiles, stemmed and chopped coarse
- 3 tablespoons soy sauce
- 6 garlic cloves, minced
- ¼ cup vegetable oil
- 2 pounds onions, chopped fine
- 1¼ teaspoons table salt
- 1 tablespoon ground cumin
- 7 cups water
- ⅔ cup medium-grain bulgur
- ¼ cup chopped fresh cilantro

1. Bring 4 quarts water, beans, and 3 tablespoons salt to boil in Dutch oven over high heat. Remove pot from heat, cover, and let stand for 1 hour. Drain and rinse beans well.

2. Adjust oven rack to middle position and heat oven to 300 degrees. Arrange ancho and New Mexican chiles on rimmed baking sheet and toast until fragrant and puffed, about 8 minutes. Transfer to plate and let cool, about 5 minutes. Stem and seed toasted chiles. Working in batches, grind toasted chiles, shiitakes, and oregano in spice grinder or with mortar and pestle until finely ground.

3. Process walnuts in food processor until finely ground, about 30 seconds. Transfer to bowl. Process drained tomatoes, tomato paste, jalapeño(s), soy sauce, and garlic in food processor until tomatoes are finely chopped, about 45 seconds, scraping down bowl as needed.

4. Heat oil in Dutch oven over medium-high heat until shimmering. Add onions and 1¼ teaspoons salt; cook, stirring occasionally until onions begin to brown, 8 to 10 minutes. Reduce heat to medium, add ground chile mixture and cumin, and cook, stirring constantly, until fragrant, about 1 minute. Add rinsed beans and water and bring to boil. Cover pot, transfer to oven, and cook for 45 minutes.

5. Remove pot from oven (handles will be hot). Stir in bulgur, ground walnuts, tomato mixture, and reserved tomato juice. Return to oven and cook until beans are fully tender, about 2 hours.

6. Remove pot from oven, stir chili well, and let stand, uncovered, for 20 minutes. Stir in cilantro and serve. (Chili can be refrigerated for up to 3 days.)

Thai Chicken Curry with Potatoes

Serves 4 to 6

WHY THIS RECIPE WORKS Warm-spiced, savory-sweet massaman curry is a Thai specialty, but it presents problems for the home cook with difficult-to-find ingredients and work-intensive processes. We set out to streamline the traditional recipe. To make a deeply flavorful curry paste, we toasted chiles, garlic, and shallots per tradition, but we replaced galangal with readily available ginger and traded out toasted, ground whole spices for preground five-spice powder. Coconut milk and lime juice rounded out the flavor of our curry. We stuck with potatoes, onion, chicken, and peanuts, simmered in the sauce until they were tender; a garnish of lime zest and cilantro added color and brightness. Serve the curry with jasmine rice. The ingredients for the curry paste can be doubled to make extra. Refrigerate the paste for up to one week or freeze it for up to two months.

Curry Paste
- 6 dried New Mexican chiles
- 4 shallots, unpeeled
- 7 garlic cloves, unpeeled
- ½ cup chopped fresh ginger
- ¼ cup water
- 1½ tablespoons lime juice
- 1½ tablespoons vegetable oil
- 1 tablespoon fish sauce
- 1 teaspoon five-spice powder
- ½ teaspoon ground cumin
- ½ teaspoon pepper

Curry
- 1 teaspoon vegetable oil
- 1¼ cups chicken broth
- 1 (14-ounce) can coconut milk
- 1 pound Yukon Gold potatoes, unpeeled, cut into ¾-inch pieces
- 1 onion, cut into ¾-inch pieces
- ⅓ cup dry-roasted peanuts
- ¾ teaspoon table salt
- 1 pound boneless, skinless chicken thighs, trimmed and cut into 1-inch pieces
- 2 teaspoons grated lime zest
- ¼ cup chopped fresh cilantro

1. *For the curry paste:* Adjust oven rack to middle position and heat oven to 350 degrees. Line rimmed baking sheet with aluminum foil. Arrange chiles on prepared sheet and toast until puffed and fragrant, 4 to 6 minutes. Transfer chiles to large plate. Heat broiler.

2. Place shallots and garlic on foil-lined sheet and broil until softened and skin is charred, 6 to 9 minutes.

3. When cool enough to handle, stem and seed chiles and tear into 1½-inch pieces. Process chiles in blender until finely ground, about 1 minute. Peel shallots and garlic. Add shallots, garlic, ginger, water, lime juice, oil, fish sauce, five-spice powder, cumin, and pepper to blender. Process to smooth paste, scraping down sides of blender jar as needed, 2 to 3 minutes. You should have 1 cup paste.

4. *For the curry:* Heat oil in large saucepan over medium heat until shimmering. Add curry paste and cook, stirring constantly, until paste begins to brown, 2½ to 3 minutes. Stir in broth, coconut milk, potatoes, onion, peanuts, and salt, scraping up any browned bits. Bring to simmer and cook until potatoes are just tender, 12 to 14 minutes.

5. Stir in chicken and continue to simmer until chicken is cooked through, 10 to 12 minutes. Remove pan from heat and stir in lime zest. Serve, passing cilantro separately.

Thai Green Curry with Chicken, Broccoli, and Mushrooms

Serves 4

WHY THIS RECIPE WORKS This herbacious green curry is the perfect partner to chicken and vegetables. Like most Thai food, Thai curries embrace a delicate balance of tastes, textures, temperatures, and colors that come together to create a harmonious whole. Unlike Indian curries, Thai curries almost always contain coconut milk. Also, they tilt the spice balance toward fresh aromatics, which are added in the form of a paste. We wanted an authentic Thai green curry, perfumed with lemon grass, hot chiles, and coconut milk, that could be made easily by the home cook. A food processor made quick work of blending together the green curry paste, the flavors of which were rounded out with shallots, lemon grass, cilantro stems, garlic, ginger, coriander, and cumin. To approximate the flavor of makrut lime leaves, we added grated lime zest to the curry paste. To make the curry, we skimmed the coconut cream off the coconut milk and cooked it with the curry paste, which gave our curry silky body and intense, rich flavor. We paired the curry with chicken, broccoli, mushrooms, and bell pepper. All that we needed now was rice to soak up the flavorful sauce. To make slicing the chicken easier, freeze it for 15 minutes. Serve with white rice.

2 (14-ounce) cans unsweetened coconut milk, not shaken, divided
1 recipe Green Curry Paste (recipe follows) or 2 tablespoons store-bought green curry paste
2 tablespoons fish sauce
2 tablespoons packed brown sugar
1½ pounds boneless, skinless chicken breasts, trimmed and sliced thin
½ teaspoon table salt
8 ounces broccoli florets, cut into 1-inch pieces
4 ounces white mushrooms, trimmed and quartered
1 red bell pepper, stemmed, seeded, and cut into ¼-inch strips
1 Thai chile, stemmed, seeded, and quartered lengthwise (optional)
½ cup fresh basil leaves
½ cup fresh mint leaves
1 tablespoon lime juice

1. Carefully spoon off about 1 cup of top layer of cream from 1 can of coconut milk. Whisk coconut cream and curry paste together in Dutch oven, bring to simmer over high heat, and cook until almost all of liquid evaporates, 5 to 7 minutes. Reduce heat to medium-high and continue to cook, whisking constantly, until cream separates into puddle of colored oil and coconut solids, 3 to 8 minutes. Continue cooking until curry paste is very aromatic, 1 to 2 minutes.

2. Whisk in remaining coconut milk, fish sauce, and sugar, bring to simmer, and cook until flavors meld and sauce thickens, about 5 minutes. Season chicken with salt, stir into sauce, and cook until evenly coated, about 1 minute. Stir in broccoli and mushrooms and cook until vegetables are almost tender, about 5 minutes. Stir in bell pepper and chile, if using, and cook until bell pepper is crisp-tender, about 2 minutes. Off heat, stir in basil, mint, and lime juice. Serve.

Green Curry Paste
Makes about ½ cup
We strongly prefer the flavor of Thai chiles here; however, serrano and jalapeño chiles are decent substitutes. For more heat, include the chile seeds and ribs when chopping.

⅓ cup water
12 green Thai, serrano, or jalapeño chiles, stemmed, seeded, and chopped coarse
8 garlic cloves, peeled
3 shallots, peeled and quartered
2 stalks lemon grass, trimmed to bottom 6 inches, sliced thin
2 tablespoons grated lime zest (2 limes)
2 tablespoons vegetable oil
2 tablespoons minced fresh cilantro stems
1 tablespoon minced fresh ginger
2 teaspoons ground coriander
1 teaspoon ground cumin
1 teaspoon table salt

Process all ingredients in food processor to fine paste, about 3 minutes, scraping down sides of bowl as needed.

Cutting Lemon Grass
Because of its tough outer leaves, lemon grass can be difficult to slice or mince. We like this method, which relies on a sharp knife.

1. Trim all but bottom 6 inches of lemon grass stalk.

2. Remove tough outer sheath from trimmed lemon grass. (If lemon grass is particularly thick or tough, you may need to remove several layers to reveal tender inner portion of stalk.)

3. Thinly slice trimmed lemon grass on slight bias.

"Curry dishes can come across as very intimidating, but had I known how easy they were to make back in my New York dwelling days, I would've saved a ton of money on carryout! This panang beef curry was developed by test cook Anne Petito. We became friends while we were both living in New York, years before we crossed paths again at America's Test Kitchen. This recipe is very authentic and easy to execute, and your friends will be impressed by your bold use of flavors."

—Elle

Panang Beef Curry

Serves 6

WHY THIS RECIPE WORKS Made with an orange-red paste that usually includes ground peanuts, panang curry is a sweeter, more unctuous derivative of red curry. We wanted a panang curry just as flavorful as traditional versions but quicker to make, so we turned to jarred red curry paste. We doctored the paste with the distinct flavors of this dish: makrut lime leaves, fish sauce, sugar, fresh chile, and peanuts. We cooked the beef separately in plain water until tender to ensure that its flavor didn't overpower the other flavors in the dish. Once the beef was cooked (which can be done well in advance), we added it to the coconut milk–based sauce and simmered it briefly. Red curry pastes from different brands vary in spiciness, so start by adding 2 tablespoons and then taste the sauce and add up to 2 tablespoons more. Makrut lime leaves are sometimes sold as kaffir lime leaves. If you can't find them, substitute three 3-inch strips each of lemon zest and lime zest, adding them to the sauce with the beef in step 2 (remove the zest strips before serving). Do not substitute light coconut milk. Serve with rice and vegetables.

- 2 **pounds boneless beef short ribs, trimmed**
- 2 **tablespoons vegetable oil**
- 2–4 **tablespoons Thai red curry paste**
- 1 **(14-ounce) can unsweetened coconut milk**
- 4 **teaspoons fish sauce**
- 2 **teaspoons sugar**
- 1 **red Thai chile, halved lengthwise (optional)**
- 6 **makrut lime leaves, middle vein removed, sliced thin**
- ⅓ **cup unsalted dry-roasted peanuts, chopped fine**

1. Cut each rib crosswise with grain into 3 equal pieces. Slice each piece against grain ¼ inch thick. Place beef in large saucepan and add water to cover. Bring to boil over high heat. Cover, reduce heat to low, and cook until beef is fork-tender, 1 to 1¼ hours. Using slotted spoon, transfer beef to bowl; discard water. (Beef can refrigerated for up to 24 hours.)

2. Heat oil in 12-inch nonstick skillet over medium heat until shimmering. Add 2 tablespoons curry paste and cook, stirring frequently, until paste is fragrant and darkens in color to brick red, 5 to 8 minutes. Add coconut milk, fish sauce, sugar, and chile, if using; stir to combine and dissolve sugar. Taste sauce and add up to 2 tablespoons more curry paste to achieve desired spiciness. Add beef, stir to coat with sauce, and bring to simmer.

3. Rapidly simmer, stirring occasionally, until sauce is thickened and reduced by half and coats beef, 12 to 15 minutes. (Sauce should be quite thick, and streaks of oil will appear. Sauce will continue to thicken as it cools.) Add lime leaves and simmer until fragrant, 1 to 2 minutes. Transfer to serving platter, sprinkle with peanuts, and serve.

Lamb Curry

Serves 4 to 6

WHY THIS RECIPE WORKS For many home cooks Indian cooking is a mystery, full of exotic spices and unfamiliar techniques. We hoped to bring Indian curry to the American home kitchen with a complex but not heavy-flavored curry that wouldn't take all day to prepare. Allowing the spices to cook completely provided the intense flavor we were after. We used a combination of whole spices—cinnamon sticks, cloves, green cardamom pods, black peppercorns, and a bay leaf—and toasted them in oil before adding aromatics, jalapeño, and ground spices. Instead of browning the meat, we stirred it into the pot along with crushed tomatoes and cooked the mixture until the liquid evaporated and the oil separated. This is a classic Indian technique that allows the spices to further develop their flavors in the oil, flavors which are then cooked into the meat. We then added water and simmered the mixture until the meat was tender, then stirred in the spinach and *channa dal* (yellow split peas) and cooked the dish until all the ingredients were melded and tender. If desired, 1½ pounds boneless, skinless chicken thighs, trimmed and cut into ¾-inch chunks, can be substituted for the lamb. For more heat, add the jalapeño seeds and ribs when mincing. For a creamier curry, choose yogurt over the crushed tomatoes. Serve with Onion Relish (page 88) and Cilantro-Mint Chutney (page 88).

Spice Blend
- 1½ **cinnamon sticks**
- 4 **whole cloves**
- 4 **green cardamom pods**
- 8 **black peppercorns**
- 1 **bay leaf**

Curry
- ¼ **cup vegetable oil**
- 1 **onion, halved and sliced thin**
- 5 **garlic cloves, minced**
- 1 **tablespoon minced fresh ginger**
- 1 **jalapeño chile, halved lengthwise, stemmed, and seeded**
- 2 **teaspoons ground cumin**
- 2 **teaspoons ground coriander**
- 1 **teaspoon ground turmeric**
- ½ **teaspoon table salt**
- 1½ **pounds boneless leg of lamb, trimmed and cut into ¾-inch pieces**
- ⅔ **cup crushed tomatoes or ½ cup plain low-fat yogurt**
- 2 **cups water**
- 1½ **pounds spinach, stemmed and chopped (optional)**
- ½ **cup channa dal (yellow split peas)**
- ¼ **cup chopped fresh cilantro**

1. *For the spice blend:* Combine all ingredients in small bowl and set aside.

2. *For the curry:* Heat oil in Dutch oven over medium heat until shimmering. Add spice blend and cook, stirring frequently, until cinnamon sticks unfurl and cloves pop, about 5 seconds. Add onion and cook, stirring occasionally, until softened, 5 to 7 minutes. Stir in garlic, ginger, jalapeño, cumin, coriander, turmeric, and salt and cook until fragrant, about 30 seconds.

3. Stir in lamb and tomatoes. Bring to simmer and cook, stirring frequently, until liquid evaporates and oil separates and turns orange, 5 to 7 minutes. Continue to cook until spices are sizzling, about 30 seconds.

4. Stir in water and bring to simmer over medium heat. Reduce heat to medium-low, cover, and cook until lamb is almost tender, about 40 minutes.

5. Stir in spinach, if using, and channa dal and cook until channa dal is tender, about 15 minutes. Season with salt to taste, stir in cilantro, and serve.

Thai Red Curry with Shrimp, Pineapple, and Peanuts

Serves 4

WHY THIS RECIPE WORKS This fragrant curry pairs briny shrimp with sweet chunks of pineapple, red bell pepper, snow peas, an abundance of fresh herbs, and a perfectly spiced and balanced homemade red curry paste. Most Thai curries blend coconut milk and curry paste on the stovetop to form the base of the dish, adding a hefty dose of fish sauce and other ingredients and then the protein and vegetables. When we simply added all the coconut milk first, we found the resulting sauce to be rather thin. Instead, we removed a cup of the creamy top of the coconut milk and heated that with the curry paste for a base that was superrich and silky. We used a food processor to blend together the red curry paste, which features small dried red chiles and a fresh red jalapeño. Shallots, lemon grass, cilantro stems, garlic, ginger, and coriander rounded out the flavors of this paste. The combination of snow peas and sweet pineapple paired perfectly with the briny shrimp and spicy curry paste. Unsalted roasted cashews can be substituted for the peanuts. For a more authentic appearance, leave the shells on the shrimp tails. Serve with white rice.

2 (14-ounce) cans unsweetened coconut milk, not shaken, divided
1 recipe Red Curry Paste (recipe follows) or 2 tablespoons store-bought red curry paste
2 tablespoons fish sauce
2 tablespoons packed brown sugar
1½ pounds medium shrimp (41 to 50 per pound), peeled and deveined
½ teaspoon table salt
1 pound peeled and cored pineapple, cut into 1-inch pieces
4 ounces snow peas, strings removed
1 red bell pepper, stemmed, seeded, and cut into ¼-inch strips
1 Thai chile, stemmed, seeded, and quartered lengthwise (optional)
½ cup fresh basil leaves
½ cup fresh mint leaves
1 tablespoon lime juice
½ cup unsalted roasted peanuts, chopped

1. Carefully spoon off about 1 cup of top layer of cream from 1 can of coconut milk. Whisk coconut cream and curry paste together in Dutch oven, bring to simmer over high heat, and cook until almost all liquid evaporates, 5 to 7 minutes. Reduce heat to medium-high and continue to cook, whisking constantly, until cream separates into puddle of colored oil and coconut solids, 3 to 8 minutes. Continue cooking until curry paste is very aromatic, 1 to 2 minutes.

2. Whisk in remaining coconut milk, fish sauce, and sugar, bring to simmer, and cook until flavors meld and sauce thickens, about 5 minutes. Season shrimp with salt, add to sauce with pineapple, and cook, stirring occasionally, until shrimp are almost opaque, about 4 minutes. Stir in snow peas, bell pepper, and chile, if using, and cook until vegetables are crisp-tender, about 2 minutes. Off heat, stir in basil, mint, and lime juice. Sprinkle with peanuts and serve.

Red Curry Paste
Makes about ½ cup
If you can't find a red jalapeño chile, you can substitute a green jalapeño. For more heat, include the jalapeño seeds and ribs when chopping.

8 dried small red chiles, such as bird chiles, japonés, or arbol
⅓ cup water
4 shallots, peeled and quartered
2 stalks lemon grass, trimmed to bottom 6 inches, sliced thin

6 garlic cloves, peeled
1 red jalapeño chile, stemmed, seeded, and chopped
2 tablespoons minced fresh cilantro stems
2 tablespoons vegetable oil
1 tablespoon grated lime zest
2 teaspoons ground coriander
1 teaspoon ground cumin
1 teaspoon minced fresh ginger
1 teaspoon tomato paste
1 teaspoon table salt

1. Adjust oven rack to middle position and heat oven to 350 degrees. Place dried red chiles on baking sheet and toast in oven until fragrant and puffed, about 5 minutes. Remove chiles from oven and set aside to cool. When cool enough to handle, stem and seed chiles, then break into small pieces.

2. Process chile pieces with water, shallots, lemon grass, garlic, jalapeño, cilantro, oil, lime zest, coriander, cumin, ginger, tomato paste, and salt in food processor to fine paste, about 3 minutes, scraping down sides of bowl as needed.

Indian Curry with Potatoes, Cauliflower, Peas, and Chickpeas

Serves 4 to 6

WHY THIS RECIPE WORKS Vegetable curries can be complicated affairs, with lengthy ingredient lists and fussy techniques meant to compensate for the lack of meat. We wanted a curry we could make on a weeknight in less than an hour—without sacrificing flavor or overloading the dish with spices. Although initially reluctant to use store-bought curry powder, we found that toasting the curry powder in a skillet turned it into a flavor powerhouse. Further experimentation proved that adding a few pinches of garam masala added even more spice flavor. To build the rest of our flavor base we started with a generous amount of sautéed onion, vegetable oil, garlic, ginger, fresh chile, and tomato paste for sweetness. When we chose our vegetables (chickpeas and potatoes for heartiness and cauliflower and peas for texture and color), we found that sautéing the spices and main ingredients together enhanced and melded the flavors. Finally, we rounded out our sauce with a combination of water, pureed canned tomatoes, and a splash of heavy cream or coconut milk. This curry is moderately spicy when made with one chile. For more heat, include the chile seeds and ribs when mincing. Serve with Onion Relish (page 88) and Cilantro-Mint Chutney (page 88).

2 tablespoons sweet or mild curry powder
1½ teaspoons garam masala
¼ cup vegetable oil, divided
3 garlic cloves, minced
1 tablespoon minced fresh ginger
1 serrano chile, stemmed, seeded, and minced
1 tablespoon tomato paste
1 (14.5-ounce) can diced tomatoes
2 onions, chopped fine
12 ounces red potatoes, unpeeled, cut into ½-inch pieces
1¼ pounds cauliflower, trimmed, cored, and cut into 1-inch pieces
1¼ cups water
1 (15-ounce) can chickpeas, rinsed
1 teaspoon table salt
1½ cups frozen peas
¼ cup heavy cream or coconut milk

1. Toast curry powder and garam masala in small skillet over medium-high heat, stirring constantly, until spices darken slightly and become fragrant, about 1 minute. Transfer spices to small bowl; set aside. In separate small bowl, stir 1 tablespoon oil, garlic, ginger, serrano, and tomato paste together. Pulse tomatoes with their juice in food processor until coarsely chopped, 3 or 4 pulses.

2. Heat remaining 3 tablespoons oil in Dutch oven over medium-high heat until shimmering. Add onions and potatoes and cook, stirring occasionally, until onions are caramelized and potatoes are golden brown around edges, about 10 minutes. (Reduce heat to medium if onions darken too quickly.)

3. Reduce heat to medium. Clear center of pot, add garlic mixture, and cook, mashing mixture into pan, until fragrant, 15 to 20 seconds. Stir garlic mixture into vegetables. Add toasted spices and cook, stirring constantly, for 1 minute. Add cauliflower and cook, stirring constantly, until spices coat florets, about 2 minutes.

4. Add tomatoes, water, chickpeas, and salt, scraping up any browned bits. Bring to boil over medium-high heat. Cover, reduce heat to medium, and cook, stirring occasionally, until vegetables are tender, 10 to 15 minutes. Stir in peas and cream and continue to cook until heated through, about 2 minutes. Season with salt to taste, and serve.

ACCOMPANIMENTS

Onion Relish

Makes 1 cup

If using a regular yellow onion, increase the sugar to 1 teaspoon. This relish can be refrigerated in an airtight container for up to 24 hours.

- 1 Vidalia onion, chopped fine
- 1 tablespoon lime juice
- ½ teaspoon paprika
- ½ teaspoon sugar
- ⅛ teaspoon table salt
  Pinch cayenne pepper

Combine all ingredients in small bowl.

Cilantro-Mint Chutney

Makes 1 cup

This chutney can be refrigerated in an airtight container for up to 24 hours.

- 2 cups packed fresh cilantro
- 1 cup packed fresh mint leaves
- ⅓ cup plain yogurt
- ¼ cup finely chopped onion
- 1 tablespoon lime juice
- 1½ teaspoons sugar
- ½ teaspoon ground cumin
- ¼ teaspoon table salt

Process all ingredients in food processor until smooth, about 20 seconds, scraping down sides of bowl as needed.

Vegetable Broth Base

Makes about 1¾ cups base, or about 1¾ gallons broth

WHY THIS RECIPE WORKS Our vegetable broth base offers both great flavor and convenience. The broth bases found on supermarket shelves promise an economical alternative to liquid broth, but they usually deliver harsh, overwhelming flavors. To make a vegetable concentrate that would pack bold but balanced flavor, we started with a classic mirepoix of onion, carrots, and celery. However, the celery gave the broth a bitter flavor, and the onion was too pungent. We swapped in celery root and leeks, which lent similar but milder flavors. Some parsley added a fresh, herbal note. To amp up the savory flavor and give the broth more depth and complexity, we added dried onion, tomato paste, and soy sauce. A hefty dose of salt ensured that the broth was well seasoned and kept the base from freezing solid, so we could store it in the freezer for months and easily remove a tablespoon at a time without having to thaw the container. For the best balance of flavors, measure the prepped vegetables by weight. Kosher salt aids in grinding the vegetables.

- 2 leeks, white and light green parts only, chopped, and washed thoroughly (2½ cups or 5 ounces)
- 2 carrots, peeled and cut into ½-inch pieces (⅔ cup or 3 ounces)
- ½ small celery root, peeled and cut into ½-inch pieces (¾ cup or 3 ounces)
- ½ cup (½ ounce) fresh parsley leaves and thin stems
- 3 tablespoons dried minced onion
- 2 tablespoons kosher salt
- 1½ tablespoons tomato paste
- 3 tablespoons soy sauce

1. Process leeks, carrots, celery root, parsley, dried minced onion, and salt in food processor, pausing to scrape down sides of bowl frequently, until paste is as fine as possible, 3 to 4 minutes. Add tomato paste and process for 1 minute, scraping down sides of bowl every 20 seconds. Add soy sauce and continue to process for 1 minute. Transfer mixture to airtight container and tap firmly on counter to remove air bubbles. Press small piece of parchment paper flush against surface of mixture and cover tightly. Freeze for up to 6 months.

2. *To make 1 cup broth:* Stir 1 tablespoon fresh or frozen broth base into 1 cup boiling water. If particle-free broth is desired, let broth steep for 5 minutes, then strain through fine-mesh strainer.

Salads

Wilted Spinach Salad with Warm Bacon Dressing

Salad with Herbed Baked
Goat Cheese and Vinaigrette

Foolproof Vinaigrette

Makes about ¼ cup, enough to dress 8 to 10 cups lightly packed greens

WHY THIS RECIPE WORKS Vinaigrettes often seem a little slipshod—harsh and bristling in one bite, dull and oily in the next. We were determined to nail down a formula for the perfect vinaigrette, one that would consistently yield a homogeneous, harmonious blend of bright vinegar and rich oil in every forkful. We found that top-notch ingredients are crucial. Balsamic vinegar worked best with more assertive greens. We preferred fruity extra-virgin olive oil as an all-purpose oil option, while walnut oil was best for nuttier vinaigrettes. As for mixing methods, whisking together the ingredients only got us so far. A key ingredient—mayonnaise—was necessary to emulsify (bind together) the oil and vinegar for a stabilized, smooth dressing. Red wine, white wine, or champagne vinegar will work in this recipe; however, it is important to use high-quality ingredients. Our favorite white wine vinegar is Napa Valley Naturals Organic White Wine Vinegar. Our favorite red wine vinegar is Laurent du Clos Red Wine Vinegar. Our favorite extra-virgin olive oil is California Olive Ranch Everyday Extra Virgin Olive Oil. This vinaigrette works with nearly any type of green (as do the walnut and herb variations). For a hint of garlic flavor, rub the inside of the salad bowl with a cut clove of garlic before adding the lettuce.

   1   tablespoon wine vinegar
1½ teaspoons very finely minced shallot
 ½ teaspoon regular or light mayonnaise
 ½ teaspoon Dijon mustard
 ⅛ teaspoon table salt
  3 tablespoons extra-virgin olive oil

   1. Combine vinegar, shallot, mayonnaise, mustard, salt, and season with pepper to taste in small bowl. Whisk until mixture is milky in appearance and no lumps of mayonnaise remain.

   2. Whisking constantly, very slowly drizzle oil into vinegar mixture. If pools of oil gather on surface as you whisk, stop adding oil and whisk mixture well to combine, then resume whisking in oil in slow stream. Vinaigrette should be glossy and lightly thickened, with no pools of oil on surface.

VARIATIONS
Foolproof Lemon Vinaigrette
This vinaigrette is best for dressing mild greens.

Substitute lemon juice for vinegar, omit shallot, and add ¼ teaspoon grated lemon zest and pinch sugar along with salt and pepper.

Foolproof Balsamic-Mustard Vinaigrette
This vinaigrette is best for dressing assertive greens. Our favorite balsamic vinegar is Bertolli Balsamic Vinegar of Modena.

Substitute balsamic vinegar for wine vinegar, increase mustard to 2 teaspoons, and add ½ teaspoon chopped fresh thyme along with salt and pepper.

Foolproof Walnut Vinaigrette
Substitute 1½ tablespoons roasted walnut oil and 1½ tablespoons vegetable oil for extra-virgin olive oil.

Foolproof Herb Vinaigrette
Add 1 tablespoon minced fresh parsley or chives and ½ teaspoon minced fresh thyme, tarragon, marjoram, or oregano along with salt and pepper.

Salad with Herbed Baked Goat Cheese and Vinaigrette

Serves 6

WHY THIS RECIPE WORKS Warm goat cheese salad has been a fixture on restaurant menus for years, featuring artisanal cheeses, organic greens, barrel-aged vinegars, and imported oils. We wanted to bring this restaurant favorite home with creamy cheese rounds infused with the flavor of fresh herbs and surrounded by crisp, golden breading, all cradled by lightly dressed greens. Ground Melba toasts (those ultradry and crispy crackers) made the crispiest crust for the goat cheese. After dipping the cheese rounds in beaten egg and herbs, we coated them with the crumbs, shaped them into attractive disks, and froze them to set the cheese and the crust. With the oven superhot and the cheese very cold, the cheese developed a crispy crust (with no oozing) and kept its shape, and a quick brush of olive oil on the outside of the disks lent flavor to the crumbs without turning them oily. A mix of greens paired well with the tangy flavor of the goat cheese, and a simple, light vinaigrette was all that was needed to finish this elegant salad. The baked goat cheese should be served warm. Prepare the salad components while the cheese is in the freezer; then toss the greens and vinaigrette while the cheese cools a bit after baking.

Goat Cheese
  3 ounces white Melba toasts (about 2 cups)
  1 teaspoon pepper
  3 large eggs
  2 tablespoons Dijon mustard
  1 tablespoon chopped fresh thyme
  1 tablespoon chopped fresh chives
12 ounces goat cheese
     Extra-virgin olive oil

Salad

- 6 tablespoons extra-virgin olive oil
- 2 tablespoons red wine vinegar
- 1 tablespoon Dijon mustard
- 1 teaspoon minced shallot
- ¼ teaspoon table salt
- 14 cups mixed delicate and spicy salad greens, such as arugula, baby spinach, and frisée

1. For the goat cheese: In food processor, process Melba toasts to fine, even crumbs, about 1½ minutes; transfer crumbs to medium bowl and stir in pepper. Whisk eggs and mustard in second medium bowl until combined. Combine thyme and chives in small bowl.

2. Using dental floss or kitchen twine, divide cheese into 12 equal pieces by slicing log lengthwise through middle and each half into 6 even pieces. Roll each piece of cheese into ball; roll each ball in herbs to coat lightly. Transfer 6 pieces to egg mixture and turn each piece to coat; transfer to Melba crumbs and turn each piece to coat, pressing crumbs into cheese. Flatten each ball gently with your fingertips into disk about 1½ inches wide and 1 inch thick and set on baking sheet. Repeat with remaining 6 pieces of cheese. Transfer baking sheet to freezer and freeze disks until firm, about 30 minutes. Adjust oven rack to top position and heat oven to 475 degrees.

3. For the salad: Meanwhile, whisk oil, vinegar, mustard, shallot, and salt in small bowl until combined; season with pepper to taste; set aside.

4. Remove cheese from freezer and brush tops and sides evenly with oil. Bake until crumbs are golden brown and cheese is slightly soft, 7 to 9 minutes (9 to 12 minutes if cheese is completely frozen). Using thin metal spatula, transfer cheese to paper towel–lined plate and let cool for 3 minutes.

5. Place greens in large bowl, drizzle vinaigrette over, and toss to coat. Divide greens among individual plates; place 2 rounds of goat cheese on each salad and serve.

Arugula Salad with Figs, Prosciutto, Walnuts, and Parmesan

Serves 6

WHY THIS RECIPE WORKS Unlike everyday iceberg lettuce, spicy arugula is more than just a leafy backdrop for salad garnishes. But arugula's complex, peppery flavor also makes it something of a challenge to pair with other ingredients. We wanted a truly outstanding arugula-based salad with co-starring ingredients that would stand up to these spicy greens. Salad combinations with harsh, one-dimensional flavor

profiles (adding radishes and lemon-buttermilk dressing to arugula, for example) struck out, with too much abrasive flavor. What we did like were the salads containing fruit and cheese, so we decided to pair our arugula with sweet and salty ingredients. Fried prosciutto strips and shaved Parmesan fit the bill when it came to upping the saltiness of our salad. A spoonful of jam added to the vinaigrette helped to emulsify the dressing and provided a sweet contrast to arugula's peppery bite. For additional sweetness, dried figs worked well and toasted walnuts delivered just the right amount of crunch. Although frying the prosciutto adds crisp texture to the salad, if you prefer, you can simply cut it into ribbons and use it as a garnish. Honey can be substituted for the jam in the vinaigrette.

- ¼ cup extra-virgin olive oil, divided
- 2 ounces thinly sliced prosciutto, cut into ¼-inch-wide ribbons
- 3 tablespoons balsamic vinegar
- 1 tablespoon raspberry jam
- 1 small shallot, minced
- ¼ teaspoon table salt
- ⅛ teaspoon pepper
- ½ cup dried figs, stemmed and chopped
- 8 ounces (8 cups) baby arugula
- ½ cup walnuts, toasted and chopped
- 2 ounces Parmesan cheese, shaved

1. Heat 1 tablespoon oil in 10-inch nonstick skillet over medium heat. Add prosciutto and cook, stirring often, until crisp, about 7 minutes. Using slotted spoon, transfer prosciutto to paper towel–lined plate; set aside.

2. Whisk vinegar, jam, shallot, salt, and pepper together in large bowl. Stir in figs, cover, and microwave until steaming, about 1 minute. Whisking constantly, slowly drizzle in remaining 3 tablespoons oil. Let sit until figs are softened and vinaigrette has cooled to room temperature, about 15 minutes.

3. Just before serving, whisk vinaigrette to re-emulsify. Add arugula and gently toss to coat. Season with salt and pepper to taste. Serve, topping individual portions with prosciutto, walnuts, and Parmesan.

Kale Caesar Salad

Serves 4

WHY THIS RECIPE WORKS We weren't willing to sacrifice flavor in order to make a healthier version of classic Caesar salad. It had to include a rich, creamy dressing, but we did want to eliminate some of the usual fat. A thick mayonnaise-based dressing stood up to the hearty kale. Using that as a starting point, we cut out half the mayonnaise, replacing it with low-fat yogurt. We found we only needed ½ cup of Parmesan to get the satisfying, nutty flavor so

3. In large bowl whisk mayonnaise, yogurt, ¼ cup Parmesan, lemon juice, vinegar, Worcestershire, mustard, anchovies, garlic, remaining ½ teaspoon salt, and remaining ½ teaspoon pepper together until well combined. Whisking constantly, drizzle in remaining 1 tablespoon oil until combined.

4. Toss kale with dressing and refrigerate for at least 20 minutes or up to 6 hours. Toss dressed kale with croutons and remaining ¼ cup Parmesan. Serve.

Classic Greek Salad

Serves 6 to 8

WHY THIS RECIPE WORKS Most versions of Greek salad consist of iceberg lettuce, chunks of green pepper, and a few pale wedges of tomato, sparsely dotted with cubes of feta and garnished with one forlorn olive of questionable heritage. We wanted a salad with crisp ingredients and bold flavors—married with a lively, herb-infused dressing. A combination of lemon juice, red wine vinegar, garlic, and olive oil made a rich, zesty vinaigrette, and oregano lent it fresh herb flavor. To give our salad a flavorful foundation, we marinated onion and cucumber slices in the vinaigrette. This step also served to mute the sting of raw onion in the salad. We swapped in crisp, flavorful romaine for the iceberg. And along with sliced tomatoes, we added jarred roasted red peppers for a bit of sweetness. A handful of kalamata olives and tangy feta cheese lent the traditional touches, and torn mint and parsley leaves gave our salad a fresh finish. For efficiency, prepare the other salad ingredients while the onion and cucumber marinate.

Vinaigrette
- 6 tablespoons extra-virgin olive oil
- 3 tablespoons red wine vinegar
- 2 teaspoons minced fresh oregano
- 1½ teaspoons lemon juice
- 1 garlic clove, minced
- ½ teaspoon table salt
- ⅛ teaspoon pepper

Salad
- ½ red onion, sliced thin
- 1 cucumber, peeled, halved lengthwise, seeded, and sliced ⅛ inch thick
- 2 romaine hearts, torn into 1½-inch pieces (about 8 cups)
- 2 tomatoes, cored, seeded, and each tomato cut into 12 wedges
- 6 ounces jarred roasted red bell peppers, cut into 2 by ½-inch strips (about 1 cup)
- ¼ cup fresh parsley leaves, torn
- ¼ cup fresh mint leaves, torn
- 20 large pitted kalamata olives, quartered
- 5 ounces feta cheese, crumbled (about 1¼ cups)

essential to Caesar dressing. The addition of anchovy fillets provided rich umami notes. A 10-minute soak in warm water tenderized the kale. We swapped the usual white bread croutons for croutons made from whole-grain bread, as the hearty greens paired well with the more rustic croutons.

- 12 ounces curly kale, stemmed and cut into 1-inch pieces (16 cups)
- 3 ounces rustic whole-grain bread, cut into 2-inch pieces (1½ cups)
- 2 tablespoons extra-virgin olive oil, divided
- ⅛ teaspoon plus ½ teaspoon table salt, divided
- ⅛ teaspoon plus ½ teaspoon pepper, divided
- 3 tablespoons mayonnaise
- 3 tablespoons plain low-fat yogurt
- 1 ounce Parmesan cheese, grated (½ cup), divided
- 1 tablespoon lemon juice
- 2 teaspoons white wine vinegar
- 2 teaspoons Worcestershire sauce
- 2 teaspoons Dijon mustard
- 3 anchovy fillets, rinsed and minced
- 1 garlic clove, minced

1. Adjust oven rack to middle position and heat oven to 350 degrees. Place kale in large bowl and cover with warm tap water (110 to 115 degrees). Swish kale around to remove grit. Let kale sit in warm water bath for 10 minutes. Remove kale from water and spin dry in salad spinner in multiple batches. Pat leaves dry with paper towels if still wet.

2. Toss bread, 1 tablespoon oil, ⅛ teaspoon salt, and ⅛ teaspoon pepper together in bowl. Spread on rimmed baking sheet and bake until golden and crisp, about 15 minutes. Let croutons cool completely on sheet. (Cooled croutons can be stored in airtight container at room temperature for up to 24 hours.)

1. For the vinaigrette: Whisk oil, vinegar, oregano, lemon juice, garlic, salt, and pepper in large bowl until combined.

2. For the salad: Add onion and cucumber to vinaigrette and toss; let sit to meld flavors, about 20 minutes.

3. Add romaine, tomatoes, bell peppers, parsley, and mint to bowl with onions and cucumbers; toss to coat with vinaigrette.

4. Transfer salad to serving bowl or platter; sprinkle olives and feta over salad and serve.

Mediterranean Chopped Salad

Serves 4 to 6

WHY THIS RECIPE WORKS Chopped salads are often little better than a random collection of cut-up produce from the crisper drawer exuding moisture that turns the salad watery and bland. We wanted lively, thoughtfully chosen compositions of lettuce, vegetables, and perhaps fruit—cut into bite-size pieces—with supporting players like nuts and cheese contributing hearty flavors and textures. Salting some of the vegetables—cucumbers and tomatoes—to remove excess moisture was an important first step. As for the dressing, most recipes we tried called for a ratio of 3 parts oil to 1 part vinegar, but we found that a more assertive blend of equal parts oil and vinegar was far better at delivering the bright, acidic kick needed in salads boasting hearty flavors and chunky textures. We also found that marinating ingredients such as bell peppers, onions, and fruit in the dressing for 5 minutes before adding cheese and other tender components brought a welcome flavor boost. Our favorite feta cheese is made by Real Greek Feta.

  1   **cucumber, peeled, halved lengthwise, seeded, and cut into ½-inch pieces**
 10 **ounces grape tomatoes, quartered**
  1   **teaspoon table salt**
  3   **tablespoons red wine vinegar**
  1   **garlic clove, minced**
  3   **tablespoons extra-virgin olive oil**
  1   **(15-ounce) can chickpeas, rinsed**
  ½   **cup pitted kalamata olives, chopped**
  ½   **small red onion, chopped fine**
  ½   **cup chopped fresh parsley**
  1   **romaine lettuce heart (6 ounces), cut into ½-inch pieces**
  4   **ounces feta cheese, crumbled (1 cup)**

1. Toss cucumber and tomatoes with salt and let drain in colander for 15 minutes.

2. Whisk vinegar and garlic together in large bowl. Whisking constantly, slowly drizzle in oil. Add cucumber-tomato mixture, chickpeas, olives, onion, and parsley and toss to coat. Let sit for at least 5 minutes or up to 20 minutes.

3. Add lettuce and feta and gently toss to combine. Season with salt and pepper to taste. Serve.

Wilted Spinach Salad with Warm Bacon Dressing

Serves 4 to 6

WHY THIS RECIPE WORKS Traditional wilted spinach salad, tossed with warm bacon dressing, makes for an appealing and elegant salad. But too often, this salad is a soggy mess of slimy spinach, bogged down from too much oil and too much heat. We wanted perfectly wilted spinach, a rich, balanced dressing, and crisp pieces of meaty bacon throughout. Baby spinach was preferred over the mature variety for its tender, sweet qualities. Fried thick-cut bacon provided more textural interest than regular sliced bacon. And using the bacon fat left in the skillet to cook our onion and garlic gave the finished salad a smoky flavor. For the vinaigrette, a generous amount of cider vinegar, enhanced with sugar, cut the richness of the bacon fat. We found that pouring the hot vinaigrette right over the baby spinach provided enough heat to wilt the spinach without saturating it. With wedges of hard-cooked egg for some heartiness, this wilted spinach salad delivers on all fronts. This salad comes together quickly, so have the ingredients ready before you begin cooking. When adding the vinegar mixture to the skillet, step back from the stovetop—the aroma is quite potent.

6 ounces baby spinach (6 cups)
  3 tablespoons cider vinegar
  ½ teaspoon sugar
  ¼ teaspoon pepper
    Pinch table salt
  8 slices thick-cut bacon, cut into ½-inch pieces
  ½ red onion, chopped
  1 garlic clove, minced
  3 hard-cooked eggs (page 26), peeled and quartered

1. Place spinach in large bowl. Whisk vinegar, sugar, pepper, and salt in small bowl until sugar dissolves; set aside.

2. Fry bacon in 10-inch skillet over medium-high heat, stirring occasionally, until crisp, about 10 minutes. Using slotted spoon, transfer bacon to paper towel–lined plate. Pour off all but 3 tablespoons bacon fat left in pan. Add onion to skillet and cook over medium heat, stirring frequently, until softened, about 3 minutes. Stir in garlic and cook until fragrant, about 15 seconds. Add vinegar mixture, then remove skillet from heat. Working quickly, scrape bottom of skillet to loosen browned bits. Pour hot dressing over spinach, add bacon, and toss gently until spinach is slightly wilted. Divide salad among individual plates, arrange egg quarters over each, and serve.

Italian Bread Salad (Panzanella)

Serves 4

WHY THIS RECIPE WORKS When the rustic Italian bread salad *panzanella* is done well, the sweet juice of the tomatoes mixes with a bright-tasting vinaigrette, moistening chunks of thick-crusted bread until they're soft and just a little chewy—but the line between lightly moistened and unpleasantly soggy is very thin. Toasting fresh bread in the oven, rather than using the traditional day-old bread, was a good start. With this method, the bread lost enough moisture in the oven to absorb the dressing without getting water-logged. A 10-minute soak in the flavorful dressing yielded perfectly moistened, nutty-tasting bread ready to be tossed with the tomatoes, which we salted to intensify their flavor. A thinly sliced cucumber and shallot for crunch and bite plus a handful of chopped fresh basil perfected our salad. The success of this recipe depends on high-quality ingredients, including ripe, in-season tomatoes and fruity olive oil. Fresh basil is also a must. Your bread may vary in density, so you may not need the entire loaf for this recipe.

  1 (1-pound) loaf rustic Italian or French bread, cut or torn into 1-inch pieces (6 cups)
  ½ cup extra-virgin olive oil, divided
  ¾ teaspoon table salt, divided
  1½ pounds tomatoes, cored, seeded, and cut into 1-inch pieces
  3 tablespoons red wine vinegar
  ¼ teaspoon pepper
  1 cucumber, peeled, halved lengthwise, seeded, and sliced thin
  1 shallot, sliced thin
  ¼ cup chopped fresh basil

1. Adjust oven rack to middle position and heat oven to 400 degrees. Toss bread pieces with 2 tablespoons oil and ¼ teaspoon salt; arrange bread in single layer on rimmed baking sheet. Toast bread pieces until just starting to turn light golden, 15 to 20 minutes, stirring halfway through baking. Let cool to room temperature.

2. Gently toss tomatoes and remaining ½ teaspoon salt in large bowl. Transfer to colander set over bowl; set aside to drain for 15 minutes, tossing occasionally.

3. Whisk remaining 6 tablespoons oil, vinegar, and pepper into tomato juices. Add bread pieces, toss to coat, and let sit for 10 minutes, tossing occasionally.

4. Add tomatoes, cucumber, shallot, and basil to bowl with bread pieces and toss to coat. Season with salt and pepper to taste, and serve immediately.

"This is my idea of the perfect salad. Instead of watery lettuces, it's got an abundance of intensely flavored herbs and greens. Cucumbers and tomatoes are lightly coated with lemon juice and a hint of garlic, not drowned with a gloppy dressing. And the best part? Every bite features crunchy bits of seasoned pita."

—Lan

Pita Bread Salad with Tomatoes and Cucumber

Serves 4

WHY THIS RECIPE WORKS This Middle Eastern salad is at its best when it combines fresh, flavorful produce with crisp pita and bright herbs. Many recipes eliminate excess moisture from the salad by taking the time-consuming step of seeding and salting the cucumbers and tomatoes. We skipped that process, favoring the crisp texture of the cucumber (the English variety, which has fewer seeds) and the flavorful seeds and jelly of the tomato. We fended off soggy bread by making the pita moisture-repellent, brushing its craggy sides with plenty of olive oil before baking. The oil soaked into the bread and prevented the pita chips from absorbing the salad's moisture while still allowing them to take on some of its flavor. A fresh, summery blend of mint, cilantro, and peppery arugula comprised the salad's greenery and a vinaigrette of lemon juice, garlic, salt, and olive oil lent it an uncomplicated, bright finish. The success of this recipe depends on ripe, in-season tomatoes. A rasp-style grater makes quick work of turning the garlic into a paste.

- 2 (8-inch) pita breads
- 3 tablespoons plus ¼ cup extra-virgin olive oil, divided
- 3 tablespoons lemon juice
- ¼ teaspoon garlic, minced to paste
- ¼ teaspoon table salt
- 1 pound tomatoes, cored and cut into ¾-inch pieces
- 1 English cucumber, peeled and sliced ⅛ inch thick
- 1 cup arugula, chopped coarse
- ½ cup chopped fresh cilantro
- ½ cup chopped fresh mint
- 4 scallions, sliced thin

1. Adjust oven rack to middle position and heat oven to 375 degrees. Using kitchen shears, cut around perimeter of each pita and separate into 2 thin rounds. Cut each round in half. Place pita bread, smooth side down, on wire rack set in rimmed baking sheet. Brush 3 tablespoons oil over surface of pita. (Pita does not need to be uniformly coated. Oil will absorb and spread as it bakes.) Season with salt and pepper. Bake until pita is crisp and pale golden brown, 10 to 14 minutes. Let cool to room temperature.

2. While pita toasts, whisk lemon juice, garlic, and salt together in small bowl. Let sit for 10 minutes.

3. Place tomatoes, cucumber, arugula, cilantro, mint, and scallions in large bowl. Break pita into ½-inch pieces and place in bowl with vegetables. Add lemon-garlic mixture and remaining ¼ cup oil and toss to coat. Season with salt and pepper to taste. Serve immediately.

Creamy Buttermilk Coleslaw

Serves 4

WHY THIS RECIPE WORKS Order barbecue down South, and you won't just get coleslaw on the side, you'll get buttermilk coleslaw. Unlike all-mayonnaise coleslaw, buttermilk coleslaw is coated in a light, creamy, and refreshingly tart dressing. We wanted a recipe that showcased the best attributes of this side salad: a pickle-crisp texture and a tangy dressing. To prevent watery coleslaw, we salted, rinsed, and dried our shredded cabbage. This also gave us the texture we wanted—as the salted cabbage sat, moisture was pulled out of it, wilting it to the right crispy texture. For a tangy dressing that clung to the cabbage and didn't pool at the bottom of the bowl, we supplemented the buttermilk with mayonnaise and sour cream. For finishing touches, we added shredded carrot, which contributed both color and sweetness. The mild flavor of shallot was a welcome addition, and sugar, mustard, and cider vinegar amped up the slaw's tanginess. To serve the coleslaw immediately, rinse the salted cabbage in a large bowl of ice water, drain it in a colander, pick out any ice cubes, then pat the cabbage dry before dressing.

- 1 pound red or green cabbage, shredded (6 cups)
- 1¼ teaspoons table salt, divided
- 1 large carrot, peeled and shredded
- ½ cup buttermilk
- 2 tablespoons mayonnaise
- 2 tablespoons sour cream
- 1 small shallot, minced
- 2 tablespoons minced fresh parsley
- ½ teaspoon cider vinegar
- ¼ teaspoon Dijon mustard
- ½ teaspoon sugar
- ⅛ teaspoon pepper

1. Toss cabbage with 1 teaspoon salt in colander set over medium bowl. Let sit until cabbage wilts, at least 1 hour or up to 4 hours. Rinse cabbage under cold running water (or in large bowl of ice water if serving immediately). Press, but do not squeeze, to drain; pat dry with paper towels. Transfer cabbage to large bowl; add carrot.

2. Combine buttermilk, mayonnaise, sour cream, shallot, parsley, vinegar, mustard, sugar, pepper, and remaining ¼ teaspoon salt in small bowl. Pour buttermilk dressing over cabbage and carrot and toss to coat. Serve chilled or at room temperature. (Coleslaw can be refrigerated for up to 2 days.)

Confetti Cabbage Salad with Spicy Peanut Dressing

Serves 6

WHY THIS RECIPE WORKS Cabbage makes a great salad—not just as coleslaw but as a crunchy, flavorful, dress-up kind of salad. We aimed to develop an Asian-inspired cabbage salad that incorporated spicy, sweet flavors for a salad side dish that was a refreshing change from the same old slaw. Salting the cabbage and setting it over a colander helped to extract excess liquid, which otherwise would dilute the potent flavors of the dressing. Shredded carrot gave the salad some sweetness, and radishes brought a peppery crunch. For the dressing, we started with smooth peanut butter for its rich flavor and velvety texture. Rice vinegar and soy sauce provided bright, tangy notes. White sugar would have contributed too much sweetness, but a small amount of honey was just right. Last touches to the dressing came in the form of a spicy jalapeño chile and fresh ginger. Processed to a smooth consistency, our spicy peanut dressing provided the perfect lush coating to the crisp vegetables. Serve this Asian-inspired cabbage salad with simple pork or chicken dishes. To serve the salad immediately, rinse the salted cabbage and carrot in a large bowl of ice water, drain them in a colander, pick out any ice cubes, then pat the vegetables dry before dressing.

- 1 pound red or green cabbage, shredded (6 cups)
- 1 large carrot, peeled and shredded
- 1 teaspoon table salt
- 2 tablespoons smooth peanut butter
- 2 tablespoons peanut oil
- 2 tablespoons rice vinegar
- 1 tablespoon soy sauce
- 1 teaspoon honey
- 2 garlic cloves, minced
- 1½ tablespoons grated fresh ginger
- ½ jalapeño chile, seeded
- 4 radishes, halved lengthwise and sliced thin
- 4 scallions, sliced thin

1. Toss cabbage and carrot with salt in colander set over medium bowl. Let sit until cabbage wilts, at least 1 hour or up to 4 hours. Rinse cabbage and carrot under cold running water (or in large bowl of ice water if serving immediately). Press, but do not squeeze, to drain; pat dry with paper towels.

2. Process peanut butter, oil, vinegar, soy sauce, honey, garlic, ginger, and jalapeño in food processor until smooth. Combine cabbage, carrot, radishes, scallions, and dressing in medium bowl; toss to coat. Season with salt to taste. Cover and refrigerate; serve chilled. (Salad can be refrigerated for up to 2 days.)

Shredding Cabbage

1. Cut cabbage into quarters, then trim and discard hard core.

2. Separate cabbage into small stacks of leaves that flatten when pressed.

3. Use chef's knife to cut each stack of cabbage leaves into thin shreds.

Chopped Carrot Salad with Fennel, Orange, and Hazelnuts

SEASON 20 RECIPE

Serves 4 to 6

WHY THIS RECIPE WORKS We were inspired by a recipe by Joan Nathan to create a finely chopped carrot salad that delivered the vegetable's juicy, earthy sweetness but offered a texture that's more like grains, with a pleasant crunch. Finely chopping carrots in the food processor, instead of grating them by hand, produced the delicately crunchy, light-textured base we were after. The food processor broke down the carrots in seconds, and we saved even more time by not peeling the carrots; scrubbing them was sufficient, and the skins contributed a subtle but pleasant bitterness. We added bulk and contrasting flavor to the carrots with lots of fresh chives (chopped by hand to avoid overprocessing the leaves in the food processor), toasted hazelnuts, and chopped fennel. A bright dressing bound it all together. We prefer the convenience and the hint of bitterness that leaving the carrots unpeeled lends to this salad; just be sure to scrub the carrots well before using them.

¾ cup hazelnuts, toasted and skinned
¼ cup extra-virgin olive oil
2 tablespoons white wine vinegar
1 teaspoon table salt
½ teaspoon pepper
¼ teaspoon orange zest plus ⅓ cup juice
1 fennel bulb, stalks discarded, bulb halved, cored, and cut into 1-inch pieces
1 pound carrots, trimmed and cut into 1-inch pieces
½ cup finely chopped fresh chives, divided

Pulse hazelnuts in food processor until coarsely chopped, 10 to 12 pulses; transfer to small bowl. Whisk oil, vinegar, salt, pepper, and orange zest and juice in large bowl until combined. Pulse fennel in now-empty processor until coarsely chopped, 10 to 12 pulses; transfer to bowl with dressing. Process carrots in again-empty processor until finely chopped, 10 to 20 seconds, scraping down sides of bowl as needed. Transfer carrots to bowl with fennel mixture. Add ¼ cup chives and half of hazelnuts and toss to combine. Season with salt to taste. Transfer to serving platter, sprinkle with remaining ¼ cup chives and remaining hazelnuts, and serve.

VARIATIONS
Chopped Carrot Salad with Mint, Pistachios, and Pomegranate Seeds
Omit hazelnuts, fennel, orange zest, and orange juice. Substitute 3 tablespoons lemon juice for vinegar. Add 1 tablespoon honey, ½ teaspoon smoked paprika, and ⅛ teaspoon cayenne pepper with oil. Substitute toasted pistachios for hazelnuts. Add 1 cup pomegranate seeds along with carrots. Substitute mint for chives.

Chopped Carrot Salad with Celery and Raisins
Omit hazelnuts, fennel, orange zest, and orange juice. Substitute 3 tablespoons lemon juice and 1 tablespoon honey for vinegar. Add 3 celery ribs, trimmed and sliced thin, and ¾ cup raisins along with carrots.

Chopped Carrot Salad with Radishes and Sesame Seeds
Omit hazelnuts, fennel, orange zest, and orange juice. Substitute 3 tablespoons vegetable oil and 2 teaspoons toasted sesame oil for olive oil. Add 2 tablespoons honey with oil. Substitute 3 tablespoons rice vinegar for wine vinegar. Increase salt to 1¼ teaspoons and add 1½ teaspoons Korean pepper flakes with salt. Before processing carrots, pulse 8 ounces radishes, trimmed and halved, in food processor until coarsely chopped, 10 to 12 pulses; add with carrots to dressing. Add ¼ cup sesame seeds along with carrots. Substitute cilantro for chives.

Smashed Cucumbers (Pai Huang Gua)
Serves 4

WHY THIS RECIPE WORKS Smashed cucumbers, or *pai huang gua*, is a Sichuan dish that is typically served with rich, spicy food. We started with English cucumbers, which are nearly seedless and have a thin, crisp skin. Placing them in a zipper-lock bag and smashing them into large, irregular pieces sped up a salting step that helped to expel excess water. The craggy pieces also did a better job of holding on to the dressing. Using black vinegar, an aged rice-based vinegar, added a mellow complexity to the soy and sesame dressing. We recommend using Chinese *Chinkiang* (or *Zhenjiang*) black vinegar in this dish because of its complex flavor. If you can't find it, you can substitute 2 teaspoons of rice vinegar and 1 teaspoon of balsamic vinegar. A rasp-style grater makes quick work of turning the garlic into a paste. We like to drizzle the cucumbers with Sichuan Chili Oil (recipe follows) when serving them with milder dishes such as grilled fish or chicken.

2 English cucumbers (about 14 ounces each)
1½ teaspoons kosher salt
4 teaspoons Chinese black vinegar
1 teaspoon garlic, minced to paste
1 tablespoon soy sauce
2 teaspoons toasted sesame oil
1 teaspoon sugar
1 teaspoon sesame seeds, toasted

1. Trim and discard ends from cucumbers. Cut cucumbers crosswise into 3 equal lengths. Place pieces in large zipper-lock bag and seal bag. Using small skillet or rolling pin, firmly but gently smash cucumbers until flattened and split lengthwise into 3 to 4 spears. Tear spears into rough 1- to 1½-inch pieces and transfer to colander set in large bowl. Toss pieces with salt and let sit for at least 15 minutes or up to 30 minutes.

2. While cucumbers sit, whisk vinegar and garlic together in small bowl; let sit for at least 5 minutes or up to 15 minutes.

3. Whisk soy sauce, sesame oil, and sugar into vinegar mixture until sugar has dissolved. Transfer cucumber pieces to medium bowl and discard any extracted liquid. Add dressing and sesame seeds to cucumbers and toss to combine. Serve immediately.

ACCOMPANIMENT
Sichuan Chili Oil
Makes about 1½ cups

The hallmark of Sichuan chili oil is a balance between la—*the concentrated heat from dried chiles—and* ma—*the numbing effect of Sichuan peppercorns. Blooming the aromatics (ginger, bay leaves, star anise, and cardamom) in vegetable oil brought out their flavor and built a pungent base. This hot oil was then poured over the chili powder, which helped build a deep, savory toasted chili flavor. Asian chili powder is similar to hot red pepper flakes but is milder and more finely ground. A Sichuan chili powder is preferred, but Korean red pepper flakes, called* gochugaru, *are a good alternative.*

- ½ cup Asian chili powder
- 2 tablespoons sesame seeds
- 2 tablespoons Sichuan peppercorns, crushed, divided
- ½ teaspoon table salt
- 1 cup vegetable oil
- 1 (1-inch) piece ginger, unpeeled, sliced into ¼-inch rounds and smashed
- 2 bay leaves
- 3 star anise pods
- 5 green cardamom pods, crushed

Place chili powder, sesame seeds, half of peppercorns, and salt in heatproof bowl. Heat oil, ginger, bay leaves, star anise, cardamom pods, and remaining peppercorns in small saucepan over low heat. Cook, stirring occasionally, until spices have darkened and mixture is very fragrant, 25 to 30 minutes. Strain oil mixture through fine-mesh strainer into bowl with chili powder mixture (mixture may bubble slightly); discard solids in strainer. Stir well to combine. Once cool, transfer mixture to airtight container and let sit for at least 12 hours before using. (Oil can be stored at room temperature for up to 1 week or refrigerated for up to 3 months.)

Mexican-Style Corn Salad (Esquites)
Serves 6 to 8

WHY THIS RECIPE WORKS There's nothing like the sweet, nutty flavor of charred corn right off the grill, but we wanted a simpler route to enjoying Mexican street corn (*elote*) that didn't require firing up the grill, and we wanted it in salad form (*esquites*) so it wouldn't be messy to eat. First, we looked to the stovetop and cooked our kernels in a little oil in a covered skillet. The kernels that were in contact with the skillet's surface browned and charred, and the lid prevented the kernels from popping out of the hot skillet and trapped steam, which helped cook the corn. To maximize flavorful browning, we cooked the corn in two batches, which allowed more kernels to have contact with the skillet. Once the corn was perfectly toasted and cooked through, we used the already-hot skillet to bloom chili powder and lightly cook minced garlic, which tempered its bite. To tie everything together, we made a simple crema with mayonnaise, sour cream, and lime juice, which we tossed with the charred corn and spices before adding crumbled cotija, chopped cilantro, and sliced scallions. Letting the corn cool before adding the cilantro, scallions, and cheese preserved their fresh flavors. If desired, substitute plain Greek yogurt for the sour cream. We like serrano chiles here, but you can substitute a jalapeño chile that has been halved lengthwise and sliced into ⅛-inch-thick half-moons. Adjust the amount of chiles to suit your taste. If cotija cheese is unavailable, substitute feta cheese.

- 3 tablespoons lime juice, plus extra for seasoning (2 limes)
- 3 tablespoons sour cream
- 1 tablespoon mayonnaise
- 1–2 serrano chiles, stemmed and cut into ⅛-inch-thick rings
- ¾ teaspoon table salt, divided
- 2 tablespoons plus 1 teaspoon vegetable oil, divided
- 6 ears corn, kernels cut from cobs, divided
- 2 garlic cloves, minced
- ½ teaspoon chili powder
- 4 ounces cotija cheese, crumbled (1 cup)
- ¾ cup chopped fresh cilantro
- 3 scallions, sliced thin

1. Combine lime juice, sour cream, mayonnaise, serrano(s), and ¼ teaspoon salt in large bowl. Set aside.

2. Heat 1 tablespoon oil in 12-inch nonstick skillet over high heat until shimmering. Add half of corn and spread into even layer. Sprinkle with ¼ teaspoon salt. Cover and cook, without stirring, until corn touching skillet is charred, about 3 minutes. Remove skillet from heat and let stand, covered, for 15 seconds, until any popping subsides. Transfer corn to bowl with sour cream mixture. Repeat with 1 tablespoon oil, remaining ¼ teaspoon salt, and remaining corn.

Mexican-Style Corn Salad

"Over the years, I have grilled, fried, baked, and roasted countless pounds of eggplant in order to use up the inevitable glut that is produced by our family garden. Of all the recipes I've tried, this salad is at the top of the list. What makes it special is the texture of the eggplant. We use the microwave to dehydrate cubes of eggplant before quickly frying them. The result is golden brown cubes of eggplant with crispy edges and silky interiors that soak up the pungent dressing. Finished with tomatoes, a lot of fresh herbs, and crispy fried shallots, this salad exemplifies the varied colors, tastes, and textures of Thai cooking."

—*Keith*

3. Return now-empty skillet to medium heat and add remaining 1 teaspoon oil, garlic, and chili powder. Cook, stirring constantly, until fragrant, about 30 seconds. Transfer garlic mixture to bowl with corn mixture and toss to combine. Let cool for at least 15 minutes.

4. Add cotija, cilantro, and scallions and toss to combine. Season salad with salt and up to 1 tablespoon extra lime juice to taste. Serve.

Crispy Thai Eggplant Salad
SEASON 20 RECIPE

Serves 2 to 3

WHY THIS RECIPE WORKS For this salad, we took elements from Sicilian caponata—eggplant, tomatoes, herbs, and vinegary notes—and married them with intense Thai flavors. We first dehydrated the eggplant in the microwave and then shallow-fried it before marinating it in *nam prik*—a bright Thai condiment made with lime juice, fish sauce, rice vinegar, ginger, garlic, and chile. We tossed in juicy cherry tomatoes, a healthy amount of fresh herbs, and crispy fried shallots for a dish that delivered all of the five tastes and as many different textures. Japanese eggplant was our unanimous favorite when we tested this recipe, but globe or Italian eggplant can be substituted if necessary. Palm sugar yields the best results for this recipe, but an equal amount of light brown sugar can be substituted. Traditional Genovese basil is a fine substitute for the Thai basil. Chopped roasted peanuts make for a crunchy, on-theme substitute for the fried shallots. Depending on the size of your microwave, you may need to microwave the eggplant in two batches. Be sure to remove the eggplant from the microwave immediately so that the steam can escape. Serve this salad with sticky rice, grilled steak, or both.

2 tablespoons fish sauce
2 tablespoons unseasoned rice vinegar
2 tablespoons lime juice
2 tablespoons (⅞ ounce) palm sugar
1 (1-inch piece) ginger, peeled and chopped coarse
2 garlic cloves, chopped coarse
½ red Thai chile, seeded and sliced thin
1 cup cherry tomatoes, halved
2 large Japanese eggplants (1½ pounds), sliced in half lengthwise, then cut crosswise into 1½-inch pieces
1 teaspoon kosher salt
2 cups vegetable oil
½ cup fresh cilantro leaves
½ cup fresh mint leaves
½ cup fresh Thai basil leaves
½ cup Fried Shallots (recipe follows)

1. Process fish sauce, vinegar, lime juice, palm sugar, ginger, garlic, and chile in blender on high until ginger, garlic, and palm sugar are broken down and dressing is mostly smooth, about 1 minute. Transfer to medium serving bowl and stir in tomatoes. Set aside while preparing eggplant.

2. Toss eggplant and salt together in medium bowl. Line entire surface of large microwave-safe dish with double layer of coffee filters and lightly spray with nonstick cooking spray. Spread eggplant in even layer over coffee filters. Microwave until eggplant feels dry and pieces shrink to about 1 inch, about 10 minutes, flipping halfway through to dry sides evenly. Remove eggplant from microwave and immediately transfer to paper towel–lined plate.

3. Heat oil in Dutch oven over high heat to 375 degrees. Fry eggplant, stirring occasionally, until flesh is deep golden brown and edges are crispy, 5 to 7 minutes. Transfer to paper towel–lined baking sheet or plate and blot to remove excess oil. Transfer to bowl with nam prik (fish sauce mixture) and toss to evenly dress.

4. Toss cilantro, mint, and basil together in small bowl. Thoroughly fold half of herb mixture into eggplant. Top eggplant mixture with remaining herb mixture and sprinkle with fried shallots. Serve.

ACCOMPANIMENT
Fried Shallots and Fried Shallot Oil
Makes about 1½ cups fried shallots and about 1¾ cups fried shallot oil
Crispy fried shallots are one of our all-time favorite garnishes. Once you get used to having them on hand, they start to infiltrate your cooking in many delicious ways—try them in sandwiches, on salads, and on top of pureed soups, just to start. But this recipe is for Fried Shallot Oil as much as it is for Fried Shallots. Most oil used for home frying is destined for the trash, but this golden oil is infused with rich fried shallot flavor and is great in stir-fries and curries or as a garnish for soups and stews. If the shallots are not sliced to a consistent thickness, they will cook and brown unevenly. We tested slicing the shallots by hand and using the disk blade on a food processor, but only a mandoline provided the consistent thickness required for this recipe. It is crucial to strain the shallots from the oil while they are still deep golden—not brown—to prevent them from turning bitter. Finishing the shallots in a low oven removes their excess moisture without the risk of overbrowning. This recipe can be halved and cooked in a small saucepan.

1 pound shallots, peeled
2 cups vegetable oil
½ teaspoon kosher salt

1. Adjust oven rack to middle position and heat oven to 200 degrees. Using mandoline, slice shallots 1/16 inch thick. Set fine-mesh strainer over heatproof bowl. Line baking sheet with double layer of paper towels.

2. Combine shallots and oil in medium saucepan and heat over high heat, stirring frequently, until shallots wilt and lose bright pink color and oil is bubbling vigorously over entire surface of pot, about 4 minutes. Continue to cook over high heat, stirring frequently, until few shallots turn golden, 8 to 11 minutes. Reduce heat to medium-low so that oil is bubbling gently, and continue to cook, stirring frequently, until shallots are deep golden, 2 to 4 minutes.

3. Immediately strain oil into prepared bowl. Quickly spread shallots onto prepared sheet and sprinkle evenly with salt; stir shallots to incorporate salt and blot oil on paper towel. Slide shallots off paper towel directly onto sheet; discard paper towel. Bake until shallots are dry and firm to touch, 15 to 25 minutes. Let shallots and oil cool completely and store separately in airtight containers. (Shallots can be stored at room temperature for up to 1 month; shallot oil can be stored in refrigerator for up to 1 month.)

Lentil Salad with Olives, Mint, and Feta

Serves 4 to 6

WHY THIS RECIPE WORKS The most important step in making a lentil salad is perfecting the cooking of the lentils so they maintain their shape and firm-tender bite. It turns out there are two key steps. The first is to brine the lentils in warm salt water. With brining, the lentils' skins soften, which leads to fewer blowouts. The second step is to cook the lentils in the oven, which heats them gently and uniformly. Once we had perfectly cooked lentils, all we had left to do was to pair the earthy beans with a tart vinaigrette and boldly flavored mix-ins. French green lentils, or *lentilles du Puy*, are our preferred choice for this recipe, but it works with any type of lentil except red or yellow. Brining helps keep the lentils intact, but if you don't have time, they'll still taste good without it. The salad can be served warm or at room temperature.

1 cup lentils, picked over and rinsed
1 teaspoon table salt, for brining
6 cups water, divided
2 cups chicken broth
5 garlic cloves, lightly crushed and peeled
1 bay leaf
½ teaspoon table salt
5 tablespoons extra-virgin olive oil
3 tablespoons white wine vinegar

½ cup pitted kalamata olives, chopped
½ cup finely chopped fresh mint
1 large shallot, minced
1 ounce feta cheese, crumbled (¼ cup)

1. Place lentils and 1 teaspoon salt in bowl. Cover with 4 cups warm water (about 110 degrees) and soak for 1 hour. Drain well. (Drained lentils can be refrigerated for up to 2 days before cooking.)

2. Adjust oven rack to middle position and heat oven to 325 degrees. Combine drained lentils, remaining 2 cups water, broth, garlic, bay leaf, and ½ teaspoon salt in ovensafe medium saucepan. Cover and bake until lentils are tender but remain intact, 40 minutes to 1 hour. Meanwhile, whisk oil and vinegar together in large bowl.

3. Drain lentils well; discard garlic and bay leaf. Add drained lentils, olives, mint, and shallot to dressing and toss to combine. Season with salt and pepper to taste. Transfer to serving dish, sprinkle with feta, and serve.

VARIATIONS
Lentil Salad with Spinach, Walnuts, and Parmesan Cheese
Substitute sherry vinegar for white wine vinegar. Place 4 ounces baby spinach and 2 tablespoons water in bowl. Cover and microwave until spinach is wilted and volume is halved, 3 to 4 minutes. Remove bowl from microwave and keep covered for 1 minute. Transfer spinach to colander; gently press to release liquid. Transfer spinach to cutting board and chop. Return to colander and press again. Substitute chopped spinach for olives and mint and ¾ cup coarsely grated Parmesan cheese for feta. Sprinkle with 1/3 cup chopped toasted walnuts before serving.

Lentil Salad with Hazelnuts and Goat Cheese
Substitute red wine vinegar for white wine vinegar and add 2 teaspoons Dijon mustard to dressing in step 2. Omit olives and substitute ¼ cup chopped parsley for mint. Substitute ½ cup crumbled goat cheese for feta and sprinkle with 1/3 cup chopped toasted hazelnuts before serving.

Lentil Salad with Carrots and Cilantro
Substitute lemon juice for white wine vinegar. Toss 2 carrots, peeled and cut into 2-inch-long matchsticks, with 1 teaspoon ground cumin, ½ teaspoon ground cinnamon, and 1/8 teaspoon cayenne pepper in bowl. Cover and microwave until carrots are tender but still crisp, 2 to 4 minutes. Substitute carrots for olives and ¼ cup finely chopped fresh cilantro for mint. Omit shallot and feta.

Cool and Creamy Macaroni Salad

Serves 8 to 10

WHY THIS RECIPE WORKS Macaroni salad seems simple enough—toss elbow macaroni and a few seasonings with a mayo-based dressing. So why does this picnic salad often fall short, with mushy pasta and a bland, ho-hum dressing? We set out to make a picnic-worthy macaroni salad with tender pasta and a creamy, well-seasoned dressing. First we had to get the pasta texture just right. To do this, we didn't drain the macaroni as thoroughly as we could have; the excess water was absorbed by the pasta as it sat and this prevented the finished salad from drying out. Also, cooking the macaroni to a point where it still had some bite left meant the pasta didn't get too soft when mixed with the mayonnaise. For the most flavor, we seasoned the pasta first—before adding the mayonnaise—so that the seasonings could penetrate and flavor the macaroni. Garlic powder added flavor to the salad (fresh garlic was too harsh), and lemon juice and Dijon mustard enlivened the creamy dressing. Don't drain the macaroni too well before adding the other ingredients—a little extra moisture will keep the salad from drying out.

1. pound elbow macaroni
   Table salt for cooking pasta
½ cup finely chopped red onion
1 celery rib, finely chopped
¼ cup finely chopped fresh parsley
2 tablespoons lemon juice
1 tablespoon Dijon mustard
⅛ teaspoon garlic powder
   Pinch cayenne pepper
1½ cups mayonnaise

1. Bring 4 quarts water to boil in large pot. Add macaroni and 1 tablespoon salt and cook, stirring often, until tender. Drain macaroni, rinse with cold water, and drain again, leaving macaroni slightly wet.

2. Toss macaroni, onion, celery, parsley, lemon juice, mustard, garlic powder, and cayenne together in large bowl and let sit until flavors meld, about 2 minutes. Stir in mayonnaise and let sit until salad is no longer watery, 5 to 10 minutes. Season with salt and pepper to taste. Serve. (Salad can be refrigerated for up to 3 days; loosen with warm water as needed before serving.)

Italian Pasta Salad

Serves 8 to 10

WHY THIS RECIPE WORKS We wanted to give this summertime staple a makeover, which would involve improving the texture of the noodles, picking the perfect mix-ins, and creating a flavorful dressing that would cling well. First, we opted for corkscrew-shaped fusilli pasta, as the shape has plenty of nooks and crannies for capturing dressing and is easy to spear with a fork. We purposefully cooked the pasta until it was a little too soft so that as it cooled and firmed up, it would have just the right tender texture. Rather than toss raw vegetables into the mix, we took inspiration from Italian anti-pasto platters and used intensely flavored jarred ingredients like sun-dried tomatoes, kalamata olives, and pepperoncini—a mix of textures that didn't overshadow the pasta. For heartiness, we included salami, and to balance the salt and tang, we added chunks of creamy mozzarella, fresh basil, and peppery arugula. To ensure the pasta itself was just as flavorful as the rest of the dish, we made a thick, punchy dressing by process-ing some of the salad ingredients themselves—capers and pepperoncini plus their tangy liquid—with olive oil infused with garlic, red pepper flakes, and anchovies. The pasta firms as it cools, so overcooking is key to ensuring the proper texture. We prefer a small, individually packaged, dry Italian-style salami such as Genoa or *soppressata*, but unsliced deli salami can be used. If the salad is not being eaten right away, don't add the arugula and basil until right before serving.

1 pound fusilli
  Table salt for cooking pasta
¼ cup extra-virgin olive oil
3 anchovy fillets, rinsed, patted dry, and minced
3 garlic cloves, minced
¼ teaspoon red pepper flakes
1 cup pepperoncini, stemmed, plus 2 tablespoons
  reserved liquid
2 tablespoons capers, rinsed
½ cup oil-packed sun-dried tomatoes, sliced thin
½ cup pitted kalamata olives, quartered
8 ounces salami, cut into ⅜-inch dice
8 ounces fresh mozzarella cheese, cut into
  ⅜-inch dice and patted dry with paper towels
2 cups (2 ounces) baby arugula
1 cup chopped fresh basil

1. Bring 4 quarts water to boil in large pot. Add pasta and 1 tablespoon salt and cook, stirring often, until pasta is tender throughout, 2 to 3 minutes past al dente. Drain pasta and rinse under cold water until chilled. Drain well and transfer to large bowl.

2. Meanwhile, combine oil, anchovies, garlic, and pepper flakes in 1-cup liquid measuring cup. Cover and microwave until oil is bubbling and fragrant, 30 to 60 seconds. Set aside.

3. Slice half of pepperoncini into thin rings and set aside. Transfer remaining pepperoncini to food processor. Add capers and pulse until finely chopped, 8 to 10 pulses, scraping down sides of bowl as necessary. Add 2 tablespoons reserved pepperoncini liquid and warm oil mixture and process until combined, about 20 seconds.

4. Add dressing to pasta and toss to combine. Add sun-dried tomatoes, olives, salami, mozzarella, arugula, basil, and reserved pepperoncini rings and toss well. Season to taste with salt and pepper. Serve. (Salad can be refrigerated for up to 3 days.)

Pasta Salad with Pesto

Serves 8 to 10

WHY THIS RECIPE WORKS Pasta salad with pesto should be light and refreshing, not dry and dull. We decided to perfect pesto pasta salad—and keep it fresh, green, garlicky, and full of herbal flavor. Using a pasta shape with a textured surface, like farfalle, guaranteed that the pesto wouldn't slide off. To ensure that the pesto coated the pasta, we didn't rinse the pasta after cooking. Instead, we spread the pasta to cool in a single layer on a baking sheet; a splash of oil helped prevent the pasta from sticking. For the pesto, we blanched the garlic to tame its harsh bite. Lots of basil made for vibrant herb flavor, and to keep the green color from fading, we added mild-tasting baby spinach, which lent the salad a vivid green color but didn't overpower the basil. For a creamy, not greasy, pesto, we enriched it with mayonnaise. Lemon juice brightened the pesto's flavor, and extra pine nuts, folded into the salad, provided an additional hit of nutty flavor and a pleasant crunchy texture. This salad is best served the day it is made; if it's been refrigerated, bring it to room temperature before serving. The pesto can be made a day ahead—just cook the garlic in a small saucepan of boiling water for 1 minute.

2 garlic cloves, unpeeled
  Table salt for cooking pasta
1 pound farfalle
¼ cup plus 1 tablespoon extra-virgin olive oil, divided
3 cups packed fresh basil
1 ounce (1 cup) baby spinach
¾ cup pine nuts, toasted, divided
2 tablespoons lemon juice
1 teaspoon table salt
½ teaspoon pepper
1½ ounces Parmesan cheese, finely grated (¾ cup),
  plus extra for serving
6 tablespoons mayonnaise
1 pint cherry tomatoes, quartered, or grape tomatoes,
  halved (optional)

1. Bring 4 quarts water to boil in large pot. Add garlic to boiling water and let cook for 1 minute. Remove garlic with slotted spoon and rinse under cold water; set aside to cool. Stir 1 tablespoon salt and pasta into boiling water and cook, stirring often, until pasta is just past al dente. Reserve ¼ cup pasta cooking water, drain pasta, toss with 1 tablespoon oil, spread in single layer on rimmed baking sheet, and cool to room temperature, about 30 minutes.

2. Peel and mince garlic. Process garlic, basil, spinach, ¼ cup pine nuts, lemon juice, 1 teaspoon salt, pepper, and remaining ¼ cup oil in food processor until smooth, scraping down sides of bowl as necessary. Add Parmesan and mayonnaise and process until thoroughly combined. Transfer mixture to large serving bowl. Cover and refrigerate until ready to assemble salad.

3. Toss pasta with pesto, adding reserved pasta water, 1 tablespoon at a time, until pesto evenly coats pasta. Fold in remaining ½ cup nuts and tomatoes, if using. Serve, passing extra Parmesan separately.

"It may be a stretch, but I like to think I had an influence on this pasta salad. You see, pesto was the first recipe I ever developed for **Cook's** Illustrated in the mid-1990s. Even though that was… gasp!... about 25 years ago, I recall making more than 50 batches to arrive at a recipe that included two techniques still at play here—blanching the garlic to mitigate its raw bite, and adding a little extra chlorophyll in the form of spinach (or parsley, way back when) to help preserve the color vibrancy.

Pairing the pesto with room-temperature pasta and a touch of mayo for silkiness came later. With just a little extra Parm, a sprinkling of toasted pine nuts, and some cherry or grape tomatoes if you choose, the duo makes a suave salad indeed."

—Adam

American Potato Salad with Hard-Cooked Eggs and Sweet Pickles

Serves 4 to 6

WHY THIS RECIPE WORKS Few salads make a splash at potlucks or picnics the way potato salad does—this classic, all-American side always seems to disappear first. We wanted a recipe for a traditional, creamy (read: mayonnaise-based) potato salad that looked good—no mushy, sloppy spuds—and tasted even better. We began by choosing red potatoes. The skin adds color to a typically monochromatic salad. We boiled them whole for best flavor and then used a serrated knife to cut the potatoes into fork-friendly chunks—the serrated edge helps prevent the skins from tearing for a nicer presentation. While the potatoes were still warm, we drizzled them with vinegar and added a sprinkle of salt and pepper; this preseasoning gave the finished salad more flavor. When the potatoes were cool, we folded in the final traditional touches—mayonnaise, pickles, and red onion—for a perfect potluck potato salad, with a creamy dressing and firm bites of potato. Use sweet pickles, not relish, for the best results. For potatoes that cook through at the same rate, buy potatoes that are roughly the same size.

- 2 **pounds red potatoes, unpeeled**
- ¼ **cup red wine vinegar**
- ½ **teaspoon table salt**
- ¼ **teaspoon pepper**
- ½ **cup mayonnaise**
- ¼ **cup sweet pickles, chopped fine**
- 3 **hard-cooked eggs (page 26), peeled and cut into ½-inch pieces**
- 1 **celery rib, chopped fine**
- 2 **tablespoons minced red onion**
- 2 **tablespoons finely chopped fresh parsley**
- 2 **teaspoons Dijon mustard**

1. Place potatoes in large saucepan, cover with 1 inch water, and bring to boil over medium-high heat. Reduce heat to medium and simmer, stirring occasionally, until potatoes are tender (paring knife can be slipped in and out of potatoes with little resistance), 25 to 30 minutes.

2. Drain potatoes and let cool slightly; peel if desired. Using serrated knife, cut potatoes into ¾-inch pieces while still warm, rinsing knife occasionally in warm water to remove starch.

3. Combine potatoes, vinegar, salt, and pepper in large bowl and toss gently. Cover and refrigerate until cool, about 20 minutes.

4. Meanwhile, combine remaining ingredients. Add potatoes, stir gently to combine, season with salt and pepper to taste, and serve. (Salad can be refrigerated for up to 1 day.)

Classic Chicken Salad

Serves 4 to 6

WHY THIS RECIPE WORKS Making a great chicken salad is an art. And if you are going to the trouble to make one, it may as well be good. We found that recipes for chicken salad are only as good as the chicken itself. If the chicken is dry or flavorless, no amount of dressing or add-ins will camouflage it. To ensure silky, juicy, and flavorful chicken, we used a method based on sous vide cooking (submerging vacuum-sealed foods in a temperature-controlled water bath). Our ideal formula was four chicken breasts and 6 cups of cold water heated to 170 degrees and then removed from the heat, covered, and left to stand for about 15 minutes. This yielded incomparably moist chicken that was perfect for chicken salad. To ensure that the chicken cooks through, don't use breasts that weigh more than 8 ounces or are thicker than 1 inch. Make sure to start with cold water in step 1. We like the combination of parsley and tarragon, but 2 tablespoons of one or the other is fine. This salad can be served in a sandwich, but also is great just simply spooned over leafy greens.

- 2 **tablespoons table salt**
- 4 **(6- to 8-ounce) boneless, skinless chicken breasts, trimmed and pounded to 1 inch thick**
- ½ **cup mayonnaise**
- 2 **tablespoons lemon juice**
- 1 **teaspoon Dijon mustard**
- ¼ **teaspoon pepper**
- 2 **celery ribs, chopped fine**
- 1 **shallot, minced**
- 1 **tablespoon finely chopped fresh parsley**
- 1 **tablespoon finely chopped fresh tarragon**

1. Dissolve salt in 6 cups cold water in Dutch oven. Submerge chicken in water. Heat pot over medium heat until water registers 170 degrees. Turn off heat, cover pot, and let sit until chicken registers 165 degrees, 15 to 17 minutes.

2. Transfer chicken to paper towel–lined baking sheet. Refrigerate until chicken is cool, about 30 minutes. While chicken cools, whisk mayonnaise, lemon juice, mustard, and pepper together in large bowl.

3. Pat chicken dry with paper towels and cut into ½-inch pieces. Transfer chicken to bowl with mayonnaise mixture. Add celery, shallot, parsley, and tarragon; toss to combine. Season with salt and pepper to taste. Serve. (Salad can be refrigerated for up to 2 days.)

VARIATIONS
Curried Chicken Salad with Cashews
Microwave 1 teaspoon vegetable oil, 1 teaspoon curry powder, and ⅛ teaspoon cayenne pepper together, uncovered, until oil is hot, about 30 seconds. Add curry oil to mayonnaise and substitute lime juice for lemon juice and 1 teaspoon grated fresh ginger for mustard in step 2. Substitute 2 tablespoons finely chopped fresh cilantro for parsley and tarragon, and add ½ cup chopped toasted cashews and ⅓ cup golden raisins to salad with celery.

Waldorf Chicken Salad
Add ½ teaspoon ground fennel seeds to mayonnaise mixture in step 2. Substitute 1 teaspoon finely chopped fresh thyme for parsley and add 1 peeled Granny Smith apple, cut into ¼-inch pieces, and ½ cup chopped toasted walnuts to salad with celery.

Chicken Salad with Red Grapes and Smoked Almonds
Add ¼ teaspoon grated lemon zest to mayonnaise mixture in step 2. Substitute 1 teaspoon finely chopped fresh rosemary for tarragon, and add 1 cup quartered red grapes and ½ cup coarsely chopped smoked almonds to salad with celery.

Classic Tuna Salad

Makes about 2 cups, enough for 4 sandwiches

WHY THIS RECIPE WORKS Most people don't think they need a recipe for tuna salad—just open up the can, add mayo and chopped celery, and you're done. But in reality, most tuna salads are pretty bad, either sogged out by too much mayo or too dry from not enough. Not to mention the fact that most aren't very interesting or well flavored. We wanted a tuna salad that was evenly textured, moist, and well seasoned.

We learned that there are three keys to a great tuna salad. The first is to drain the tuna thoroughly in a colander; don't just tip the water out of the can. Next, instead of using a fork, break up the tuna with your fingers for a finer, more even texture. Finally, season the tuna before adding the mayonnaise for maximum flavor. Some additions to tuna salad are a matter of taste, but we thought that small amounts of garlic and mustard added another dimension, and minced pickle was a piquant touch. In addition to classic tuna salad, we developed a few variations that include tuna with balsamic vinegar and grapes, another with curry and apples, and a third with lime and horseradish. Our favorite canned tuna is Wild Planet Wild Albacore.

- 2 (6-ounce) cans solid white tuna in water
- 1 small celery rib, chopped fine
- 2 tablespoons lemon juice
- 2 tablespoons finely chopped red onion
- 2 tablespoons finely chopped dill or sweet pickles
- 2 tablespoons finely chopped fresh parsley
- ½ garlic clove, minced
- ½ teaspoon table salt
- ¼ teaspoon pepper
- ½ cup mayonnaise
- ¼ teaspoon Dijon mustard

Drain tuna in colander and shred with fingers until no clumps remain and texture is fine and even. Transfer tuna to medium bowl and mix in celery, lemon juice, onion, pickles, parsley, garlic, salt, and pepper until evenly blended. Fold in mayonnaise and mustard until tuna is evenly moistened. (Tuna salad can be refrigerated for up to 3 days.)

VARIATIONS
Tuna Salad with Balsamic Vinegar and Grapes
Omit lemon juice, pickles, garlic, and parsley and add 2 tablespoons balsamic vinegar, 6 ounces halved red seedless grapes, ¼ cup toasted slivered almonds, and 2 teaspoons finely chopped fresh thyme to tuna along with salt and pepper.

Curried Tuna Salad with Apples and Currants
Omit pickles, garlic, and parsley and add 1 apple, cut into ¼-inch pieces, ¼ cup currants, and 2 tablespoons finely chopped fresh basil to tuna along with lemon juice, salt, and pepper; mix 1 tablespoon curry powder into mayonnaise before folding into tuna.

Tuna Salad with Lime and Horseradish
Omit lemon juice, pickles, and garlic and add 2 tablespoons lime juice, ½ teaspoon lime zest, and 3 tablespoons prepared horseradish to tuna along with salt and pepper.

Poultry

Crispy Pan-Fried Chicken Cutlets

Perfect Poached Chicken Breasts

Serves 4

WHY THIS RECIPE WORKS Poaching can be a perfect way to gently cook delicate chicken breasts, but the standard approach can be fussy and it offers little in the way of flavor or pizzazz. To up the flavor ante, we added salt, soy sauce, garlic, and a small amount of sugar to the poaching liquid for meaty, rich-tasting chicken. We found that our salty poaching liquid could double as a quick brine, simplifying the recipe and infusing the chicken with flavor all the way through. To ensure that the chicken cooked evenly, we used plenty of water and raised the chicken off the bottom of the pot in a steamer basket. Taking the pot off the heat partway through cooking allowed the delicate meat to cook through using gentle, residual heat and prevented overcooking. A couple of simple, flavorful sauces made the perfect accompaniment to our tender, moist chicken. To ensure that the chicken cooks through, don't use breasts that weigh more than 8 ounces each. If desired, serve the chicken with one of our sauces (recipes follow) or in a salad or sandwiches.

4 (6- to 8-ounce) boneless, skinless chicken breasts, trimmed
½ cup soy sauce for cooking chicken
¼ cup table salt for cooking chicken
2 tablespoons sugar for cooking chicken
6 garlic cloves, smashed and peeled, for cooking chicken

1. Cover chicken breasts with plastic wrap and pound thick ends gently with meat pounder until ¾ inch thick. Whisk 4 quarts water, soy sauce, salt, sugar, and garlic in Dutch oven until salt and sugar are dissolved. Arrange breasts, skinned side up, in steamer basket, making sure not to overlap them. Submerge steamer basket in brine and let sit at room temperature for 30 minutes.

2. Heat pot over medium heat, stirring liquid occasionally to even out hot spots, until water registers 175 degrees, 15 to 20 minutes. Turn off heat, cover pot, remove from burner, and let stand until meat registers 160 degrees, 17 to 22 minutes.

3. Transfer breasts to cutting board, cover tightly with aluminum foil, and let rest for 5 minutes. Slice each breast on bias into ¼-inch-thick slices, transfer to serving platter or individual plates, and serve.

ACCOMPANIMENTS

Warm Tomato-Ginger Vinaigrette
Makes about 2 cups
Parsley may be substituted for the cilantro.

¼ cup extra-virgin olive oil, divided
1 shallot, minced
1½ teaspoons grated fresh ginger
⅛ teaspoon ground cumin
⅛ teaspoon ground fennel
12 ounces cherry tomatoes, halved
¼ teaspoon table salt
1 tablespoon red wine vinegar
1 teaspoon packed light brown sugar
2 tablespoons chopped fresh cilantro

Heat 2 tablespoons oil in 10-inch nonstick skillet over medium heat until shimmering. Add shallot, ginger, cumin, and fennel and cook until fragrant, about 15 seconds. Stir in tomatoes and salt and cook, stirring frequently, until tomatoes have softened, 3 to 5 minutes. Off heat, stir in vinegar and sugar and season with salt and pepper to taste; cover to keep warm. Stir in cilantro and remaining 2 tablespoons oil just before serving.

Cumin-Cilantro Yogurt Sauce
Makes about 1 cup
Mint may be substituted for the cilantro. This sauce is prone to curdle and thus does not reheat well; prepare it just before serving.

2 tablespoons extra-virgin olive oil, divided
1 shallot, minced
1 garlic clove, minced
1 teaspoon ground cumin
⅛ teaspoon red pepper flakes
½ cup plain whole-milk yogurt
⅓ cup water
1 teaspoon lime juice
2 tablespoons chopped fresh cilantro

Heat 1 tablespoon oil in small skillet over medium heat until shimmering. Add shallot and cook until softened, about 2 minutes. Stir in garlic, cumin, and pepper flakes and cook until fragrant, about 30 seconds. Remove from heat and whisk in yogurt, water, lime juice, and remaining 1 tablespoon oil. Season with salt and pepper to taste, and cover to keep warm. Stir in cilantro just before serving.

Quick Sun-Dried Tomato Sauce
Makes about 1 cup
For the best taste and texture, make sure to rinse all the dried herbs off the sun-dried tomatoes.

½ slice hearty white sandwich bread, cut into ½-inch pieces
¼ cup pine nuts
2 tablespoons extra-virgin olive oil, divided
2 garlic cloves, sliced thin
1 small tomato, cored and cut into ½-inch pieces
½ cup oil-packed sun-dried tomatoes, rinsed
2 tablespoons coarsely chopped fresh basil
2 tablespoons balsamic vinegar
½ teaspoon table salt

Heat bread, pine nuts, and 1 tablespoon oil in 12-inch skillet over medium heat; cook, stirring constantly, until bread and pine nuts are lightly toasted, 2½ to 3 minutes. Add garlic and cook, stirring constantly, until fragrant, about 30 seconds. Transfer bread mixture to food processor and pulse until coarsely chopped, about 5 pulses. Add tomato, sun-dried tomatoes, basil, vinegar, salt, and remaining 1 tablespoon oil to processor. Pulse until finely chopped, 5 to 8 pulses. Transfer to bowl and let sit for at least 10 minutes.

Pan-Seared Chicken Breasts

Serves 4

WHY THIS RECIPE WORKS A boneless, skinless chicken breast doesn't have the bone and skin to protect it from the intensity of a hot pan. Inevitably, it emerges moist in the middle and dry at the edges, with an exterior that's leathery and tough. We wanted a boneless, skinless chicken breast that was every bit as flavorful, moist, and tender as its skin-on counterpart. We decided to utilize a technique that we've used successfully in the test kitchen with thick-cut steaks, where we gently parcook the meat in the oven and then sear it on the stovetop. First, we salted the chicken to help it retain more moisture as it cooked. To expedite the process we poked holes in the breasts, creating channels for the salt to reach the interior of the chicken as it parcooked. We then placed the breasts in a baking dish and covered it tightly with foil. In this enclosed environment, any moisture released by

the chicken stayed trapped under the foil, keeping the exterior from drying out without making it so overly wet that it couldn't brown quickly. The next step was figuring out how to achieve a crisp, even crust on our parcooked breasts. We turned to a Chinese cooking technique called velveting, in which meat is dipped in a mixture of oil and cornstarch to create a thin protective layer that keeps the protein moist and tender, even when exposed to ultrahigh heat. We replaced the oil with butter (for flavor) and mixed flour in with the cornstarch to avoid any pasty flavor. The coating helped the chicken make better contact with the hot skillet, creating a thin, browned, crisp veneer that kept the breast's exterior as moist as the interior. For the best results, buy similarly sized chicken breasts. If your breasts have the tenderloin attached, leave it in place and follow the upper range of baking time in step 1. For optimal texture, sear the chicken immediately after removing it from the oven.

4 (6- to 8-ounce) boneless, skinless chicken breasts, trimmed
1 teaspoon table salt
1 tablespoon vegetable oil
2 tablespoons unsalted butter, melted
1 tablespoon all-purpose flour
1 teaspoon cornstarch
½ teaspoon pepper
1 recipe Lemon and Chive Pan Sauce (optional; recipe follows)

1. Adjust oven rack to lower-middle position and heat oven to 275 degrees. Use fork to poke thickest half of each breast 5 or 6 times, then sprinkle each breast with ¼ teaspoon salt. Place chicken, skinned side down, in 13 by 9-inch baking dish and cover tightly with aluminum foil. Bake until chicken registers 145 to 150 degrees, 30 to 40 minutes.

2. Remove chicken from oven and transfer, skinned side up, to paper towel–lined plate and pat dry with paper towels. Heat oil in 12-inch skillet over medium-high heat until smoking. While pan is heating, whisk melted butter, flour, cornstarch, and pepper together in small bowl. Lightly brush tops of chicken with half of butter mixture. Place chicken in skillet, coated side down, and cook until browned, 3 to 4 minutes. While chicken browns, brush second side with remaining butter mixture. Flip chicken, reduce heat to medium, and cook until second side is browned and chicken registers 160 degrees, 3 to 4 minutes. Transfer chicken to platter and let rest while preparing pan sauce (if not making pan sauce, let chicken rest for 5 minutes before serving).

ACCOMPANIMENT

Lemon and Chive Pan Sauce
Makes about ¾ cup

1 shallot, minced
1 teaspoon all-purpose flour
1 cup chicken broth
1 tablespoon lemon juice
1 tablespoon finely chopped fresh chives
1 tablespoon unsalted butter, chilled

Add shallot to now-empty skillet and cook over medium heat until softened, about 2 minutes. Add flour and cook, stirring constantly, for 30 seconds. Add broth, increase heat to medium-high, whisk and bring to simmer, scraping up any browned bits and smoothing out any lumps. Simmer rapidly until reduced to ¾ cup, 3 to 5 minutes. Stir in any accumulated chicken juices, return to simmer, and cook for 30 seconds. Off heat, whisk in lemon juice, chives, and butter; season with salt and pepper to taste. Spoon sauce over chicken and serve immediately.

Better Chicken Marsala

Serves 4

WHY THIS RECIPE WORKS In revisiting chicken Marsala, we took a new approach to fabricating and cooking chicken cutlets. First, we cut each chicken breast in half crosswise. Then, we cut the thicker half in half horizontally to make three identically sized pieces that could easily be pounded into cutlets. We salted the cutlets briefly to boost their ability to retain moisture and then dredged them in a light coating of flour, which accelerated browning and helped prevent the meat from overcooking. We seared the cutlets quickly on both sides and set them aside while we made the sauce. Our Marsala sauce used reduced dry Marsala and chicken broth, along with cremini and dried porcini mushrooms

for rich flavor and gelatin for a silky texture. Once the Marsala and mushroom sauce was complete, we returned the cutlets to the pan to cook them through and wash any excess starch into the sauce, eliminating gumminess. It is worth spending a little extra for a moderately priced dry Marsala ($10 to $12 per bottle). Serve the chicken with potatoes, white rice, or buttered pasta.

2¼ cups dry Marsala, divided
  4 teaspoons unflavored gelatin
  1 ounce dried porcini mushrooms, rinsed
  4 (6- to 8-ounce) boneless, skinless chicken breasts, trimmed
  2 teaspoons table salt
  ½ teaspoon pepper
  2 cups chicken broth
  ¾ cup all-purpose flour
  ¼ cup plus 1 teaspoon vegetable oil, divided
  3 ounces pancetta, cut into ½-inch pieces
  1 pound cremini mushrooms, trimmed and sliced thin
  1 shallot, minced
  1 tablespoon tomato paste
  1 garlic clove, minced
  2 teaspoons lemon juice
  1 teaspoon finely chopped fresh oregano
  3 tablespoons unsalted butter, cut into 6 pieces
  2 teaspoons finely chopped fresh parsley

1. Bring 2 cups Marsala, gelatin, and porcini mushrooms to boil in medium saucepan over high heat. Reduce heat to medium-high and vigorously simmer until reduced by half, 6 to 8 minutes.

2. Meanwhile, cut each chicken breast in half crosswise, then cut thick half in half again horizontally, creating 3 cutlets of similar thickness. Place cutlets between sheets of plastic wrap and pound gently to even ½-inch thickness. Place cutlets in bowl and toss with salt and pepper. Set aside for 15 minutes.

3. Strain Marsala reduction through fine-mesh strainer, pressing on solids to extract as much liquid as possible; discard solids. Return Marsala reduction to saucepan, add broth, and return to boil over high heat. Lower heat to medium-high and simmer until reduced to 1½ cups, 10 to 12 minutes. Set aside.

4. Spread flour in shallow dish. Working with 1 cutlet at a time, dredge cutlets in flour, shaking gently to remove excess. Place on wire rack set in rimmed baking sheet. Heat 2 tablespoons oil in 12-inch skillet over medium-high heat until just smoking. Place 6 cutlets in skillet and lower heat to medium. Cook until golden brown on 1 side, 2 to 3 minutes. Flip and cook until golden brown on second side, 2 to 3 minutes. Return cutlets to wire rack. Repeat with 2 tablespoons oil and remaining 6 cutlets.

Better Chicken Marsala

5. Return now-empty skillet to medium-low heat and add pancetta. Cook, stirring occasionally, scraping pan bottom to loosen any browned bits, until pancetta is brown and crisp, about 4 minutes. Add cremini mushrooms and increase heat to medium-high. Cook, stirring occasionally and scraping pan bottom, until liquid released by mushrooms evaporates and mushrooms begin to brown, about 8 minutes. Using slotted spoon, transfer cremini mushrooms and pancetta to bowl. Add remaining 1 teaspoon oil and shallot to pan and cook until softened, about 1 minute. Add tomato paste and garlic and cook until fragrant, about 30 seconds. Add reduced Marsala mixture, remaining ¼ cup Marsala, lemon juice, and oregano and bring to simmer.

6. Add cutlets to sauce and simmer for 3 minutes, flipping halfway through simmering. Transfer cutlets to platter. Off heat, whisk in butter. Stir in parsley and cremini mushroom mixture. Season with salt and pepper to taste. Spoon sauce over chicken and serve.

Sweet and Tangy Oven-Barbecued Chicken

Serves 4

WHY THIS RECIPE WORKS Smoky, tender, and tangy, barbecued chicken is a real crowd pleaser. What do you do when a craving for this summertime favorite strikes in midwinter? Oven-barbecued chicken is the obvious solution. We started with boneless, skinless chicken breasts; the mild white meat is a perfect backdrop for the sauce. (Skinless breasts also meant that we wouldn't have to deal with the problem of flabby skin.) We lightly seared the chicken breasts in a skillet, then removed them from the pan to make a simple but flavorful barbecue sauce with pantry ingredients like grated onion, ketchup, Worcestershire sauce, mustard, molasses, and maple syrup. When we returned the chicken to the pan, the sauce clung nicely to the meat, thanks to the light searing we had given the chicken. We slid the chicken and sauce, still in the skillet, into the oven to cook through. Finally, for a nicely caramelized coating on the sauce, we finished the chicken under the high heat of the broiler. The result? Juicy chicken, thickly coated with a pleasantly tangy barbecue sauce. Real maple syrup is preferable to imitation syrup, and "mild" or "original" molasses is preferable to darker, more bitter types. Use a rasp-style grater or the fine holes of a box grater to grate the onion. Make this recipe only in an in-oven broiler; do not use a drawer-type broiler. Broiling times may differ from one oven to another, so we urge you to check the chicken for doneness after only 3 minutes of broiling. You may also have to lower the oven rack if your broiler runs very hot. It is important to remove the chicken from the oven before switching to the broiler setting to allow the broiler element to come up to temperature.

1 cup ketchup
3 tablespoons molasses
3 tablespoons cider vinegar
2 tablespoons finely grated onion
2 tablespoons Worcestershire sauce
2 tablespoons Dijon mustard
2 tablespoons maple syrup
1 teaspoon chili powder
¼ teaspoon cayenne pepper
4 (5- to 6-ounce) boneless, skinless chicken breasts, tenderloins removed, trimmed
½ teaspoon table salt
¼ teaspoon pepper
1 tablespoon vegetable oil

1. Adjust oven rack to upper-middle position, and heat oven to 325 degrees. Whisk ketchup, molasses, vinegar, onion, Worcestershire, mustard, maple syrup, chili powder, and cayenne together in bowl; set aside. Pat chicken dry with paper towels and season with salt and pepper.

2. Heat oil in 12-inch ovensafe skillet over high heat until just smoking. Add chicken, skinned side down, and cook until very light golden, 1 to 2 minutes; flip chicken and cook until very light golden, 1 to 2 minutes. Transfer chicken to plate; set aside.

3. Discard fat in skillet; off heat, add sauce mixture, scraping up any browned bits. Simmer sauce over medium heat, stirring frequently, until sauce is thick and glossy and spatula leaves trail in sauce, about 4 minutes. Off heat, return chicken to skillet, skinned side up, and turn to coat thickly with sauce; spoon extra sauce over each piece to create thick coating.

4. Place skillet in oven and cook until chicken registers 130 degrees, 8 to 12 minutes. Remove skillet from oven, turn oven to broil, and heat for 5 minutes. Place skillet back in oven and broil until chicken registers 160 degrees, 3 to 8 minutes. Transfer chicken to serving platter and let rest for 5 minutes. Meanwhile, whisk sauce in skillet to recombine and transfer to small bowl. Serve chicken, passing extra sauce separately.

Chicken Piccata

Serves 4 to 6

WHY THIS RECIPE WORKS Chicken piccata is one of those appealing Italian recipes that taste complex but are actually easy to prepare. Our goal was properly cooked chicken with a streamlined sauce that really tasted of lemons and capers. Many recipes suggest breading cutlets for chicken piccata, but we found that flour alone was sufficient; there was no point building a crisp crust that would end up drenched in sauce. After browning the chicken and sautéing aromatics, we deglazed the pan with chicken broth alone; although wine

3. Spread flour in shallow dish. Working with 1 cutlet at a time, dredge cutlets in flour, shaking gently to remove excess. Place on wire rack set in rimmed baking sheet. Heat 2 tablespoons oil in 12-inch skillet over medium-high heat until smoking. Place 6 cutlets in skillet, reduce heat to medium, and cook until golden brown on 1 side, 2 to 3 minutes. Flip and cook until golden brown on second side, 2 to 3 minutes. Return cutlets to wire rack. Repeat with 2 tablespoons oil and remaining 6 cutlets.

4. Add remaining 1 teaspoon oil and shallot to skillet and cook until softened, 1 minute. Add garlic and cook until fragrant, 30 seconds. Add broth, reserved lemon juice, and reserved lemon slices and bring to simmer, scraping up any browned bits.

5. Add cutlets to sauce and simmer for 4 minutes, flipping halfway through simmering. Transfer cutlets to platter. Sauce should be thickened to consistency of heavy cream; if not, simmer 1 minute. Off heat, whisk in butter. Stir in capers and parsley. Season with salt and pepper to taste. Spoon sauce over chicken and serve.

is sometimes suggested, we found it to be too acidic for this dish. We simmered slices from half a lemon in the broth for a few minutes; this was easier than grating the zest. For maximum lemon flavor in the sauce, we used a generous ¼ cup of lemon juice, added when the sauce was nearly done so as not to blunt its impact. Butter gave the sauce body and was preferable to flour, which made it overly thick. Plenty of capers and a bit of parsley finished our ultralemony piccata. To make slicing the chicken easier, freeze it for 15 minutes. If you like, use thinly sliced cutlets available at many supermarkets. These cutlets don't have any tenderloins and can be used as they are.

- 4 **(6- to 8-ounce) boneless, skinless chicken breasts, tenderloins removed, trimmed**
- 2 **teaspoons kosher salt**
- ½ **teaspoon pepper**
- 2 **large lemons**
- ¾ **cup all-purpose flour**
- ¼ **cup plus 1 teaspoon vegetable oil, divided**
- 1 **shallot, minced**
- 1 **garlic clove, minced**
- 1 **cup chicken broth**
- 3 **tablespoons unsalted butter, cut into 6 pieces**
- 2 **tablespoons capers, drained**
- 1 **tablespoon minced fresh parsley**

1. Cut each chicken breast in half crosswise, then cut thick half in half again horizontally, creating 3 cutlets of similar thickness. Place cutlets between sheets of plastic wrap and gently pound to even ½-inch thickness. Place cutlets in bowl and toss with salt and pepper. Set aside for 15 minutes.

2. Halve 1 lemon lengthwise. Trim ends from 1 half, halve lengthwise again, then cut crosswise into ¼-inch-thick slices; set aside. Juice remaining half and whole lemon and set aside 3 tablespoons juice.

Crispy Pan-Fried Chicken Cutlets (Chicken Katsu)

Serves 4 to 6

WHY THIS RECIPE WORKS Chicken cutlets coated in bread crumbs and pan-fried are a staple weeknight meal: They're quick cooking and a crowd pleaser. But the three-step breading process of flour, egg, and crumbs is fussy, so we set out to make a streamlined version. We ditched the flour step, which made for a more delicate coating. Instead of the usual homemade bread crumbs, we swapped Japanese-style panko that we poured into a zipper-lock bag and crushed with a rolling pin, creating a perfectly even coating. To avoid any spotty browning or burned bits of panko with our second batch of cutlets, we discarded the cooking oil from the first batch and started over with fresh oil. Once done cooking, we transferred the cutlets to a paper towel–lined rack, which helped to wick away excess oil while preventing the underside from turning soggy. To punch up the flavor, we turned east for inspiration and made a Japanese-style barbecue sauce with ketchup, Worcestershire sauce, Dijon mustard, and soy sauce. Be sure to remove any tenderloins from the breasts before halving. The cutlets will be easier to slice in half if you freeze them for about 15 minutes. If you are working with 8-ounce cutlets, the skillet will initially be crowded; the cutlets will shrink slightly as they cook. The first batch of cutlets can be kept warm in a 200-degree oven while the second batch cooks. These cutlets can be sliced into ½-inch-wide strips Japanese-style and served over rice with sauce (recipe follows). They can also be served in a sandwich or over a green salad.

2 cups panko bread crumbs
2 large eggs
1 teaspoon table salt
4 (6- to 8-ounce) boneless, skinless chicken breasts, tenderloins removed, trimmed
½ cup vegetable oil, divided

1. Place panko in large zipper-lock bag and finely crush with rolling pin. Transfer crushed panko to shallow dish. Whisk eggs and salt in second shallow dish until well combined.

2. Cut each chicken breast in half horizontally. Place cutlets between sheets of plastic wrap and gently pound to even ¼-inch thickness. Working with 1 cutlet at a time, dredge cutlets in egg mixture, allowing excess egg to drip off, then coat all sides with panko, pressing gently so crumbs adhere. Transfer cutlets to rimmed baking sheet.

3. Set wire rack in second rimmed baking sheet and line with layer of paper towels. Heat ¼ cup oil and small pinch panko in 12-inch skillet over medium-high heat. When panko has turned golden brown, place 4 cutlets in skillet. Cook without moving them until bottoms are crispy and deep golden brown, 2 to 3 minutes. Using tongs, carefully flip cutlets and cook on second side until deep golden brown, 2 to 3 minutes. Transfer cutlets to prepared rack and season with salt to taste. Wipe out skillet with paper towels. Repeat with remaining ¼ cup oil and remaining 4 cutlets. Serve immediately.

ACCOMPANIMENTS
Tonkatsu Sauce
Makes about ⅓ cup
You can substitute yellow mustard for the Dijon, but do not use a grainy mustard.

¼ cup ketchup
2 tablespoons Worcestershire sauce
2 teaspoons soy sauce
1 teaspoon Dijon mustard

Whisk all ingredients together in bowl.

Garlic-Curry Sauce
Makes about ½ cup
Full-fat and nonfat yogurt will both work in this recipe.

⅓ cup mayonnaise
¼ cup plain yogurt
2 tablespoons ketchup
2 teaspoons curry powder
1 teaspoon lemon juice
¼ teaspoon minced garlic

Whisk all ingredients together in bowl.

Best Chicken Parmesan

Serves 4

WHY THIS RECIPE WORKS Classic chicken Parmesan should feature juicy chicken cutlets with a crisp pan-fried breaded coating, complemented by creamy mozzarella and a bright, zesty marinara sauce. But more often it ends up dry and overcooked, with a soggy crust and a chewy mass of cheese. To prevent the cutlets from overcooking, we halved them horizontally and pounded only the fatter halves thin. Then we salted them for 20 minutes to help them hold on to their moisture. To keep the crust crunchy, we replaced more than half of the sogginess-prone bread crumbs with flavorful grated Parmesan cheese. For a cheese topping that didn't turn chewy, we added some creamy fontina to the usual shredded mozzarella and ran it under the broiler for just 2 minutes to melt and brown. Melting the cheese directly on the fried cutlet formed a barrier between the crispy crust and the tomato sauce. Our preferred brand of crushed tomatoes is SMT. This recipe makes enough sauce to top the cutlets as well as four servings of pasta. Serve with pasta and a simple green salad.

Sauce
2 tablespoons extra-virgin olive oil, divided
2 garlic cloves, minced
¾ teaspoon kosher salt
¼ teaspoon dried oregano
Pinch red pepper flakes
1 (28-ounce) can crushed tomatoes
¼ teaspoon sugar
2 tablespoons coarsely chopped fresh basil

Chicken

- 2 (6- to 8-ounce) boneless, skinless chicken breasts, trimmed
- 1 teaspoon kosher salt
- 2 ounces whole-milk mozzarella cheese, shredded (½ cup)
- 2 ounces fontina cheese, shredded (½ cup)
- 1 large egg
- 1 tablespoon all-purpose flour
- 1½ ounces Parmesan cheese, grated (¾ cup)
- ½ cup panko bread crumbs
- ½ teaspoon garlic powder
- ¼ teaspoon dried oregano
- ¼ teaspoon pepper
- ⅓ cup vegetable oil
- ¼ cup torn fresh basil

1. For the sauce: Heat 1 tablespoon oil in medium saucepan over medium heat until just shimmering. Add garlic, salt, oregano, and pepper flakes; cook, stirring occasionally, until fragrant, about 30 seconds. Stir in tomatoes and sugar; increase heat to high and bring to simmer. Reduce heat to medium-low and simmer until thickened, about 20 minutes. Off heat, stir in basil and remaining 1 tablespoon oil; season with salt and pepper to taste. Cover and keep warm.

2. For the chicken: Meanwhile, cut each chicken breast in half horizontally, then place cutlets between sheets of plastic wrap and gently pound to even ½-inch thickness. Sprinkle each side of each cutlet with ⅛ teaspoon salt and let sit at room temperature for 20 minutes. Combine mozzarella and fontina in bowl; set aside.

3. Adjust oven rack 4 inches from broiler element and heat broiler. Whisk egg and flour together in shallow dish or pie plate until smooth. Combine Parmesan, panko, garlic powder, oregano, and pepper in second shallow dish or pie plate. Pat chicken dry with paper towels. Working with 1 cutlet at a time, dredge cutlet in egg mixture, allowing excess to drip off. Coat all sides in Parmesan mixture, pressing gently so crumbs adhere. Transfer cutlet to large plate and repeat with remaining cutlets.

4. Heat oil in 10-inch nonstick skillet over medium-high heat until shimmering. Carefully place 2 cutlets in skillet and cook without moving them until bottoms are crispy and deep golden brown, 1½ to 2 minutes. Using tongs, carefully flip cutlets and cook on second side until deep golden brown, 1½ to 2 minutes. Transfer cutlets to paper towel–lined plate and repeat with remaining cutlets.

5. Place cutlets on rimmed baking sheet and sprinkle cheese mixture evenly over cutlets, covering as much surface area as possible. Broil until cheese is melted and beginning to brown, 2 to 4 minutes. Transfer chicken to serving platter and top each cutlet with 2 tablespoons sauce. Sprinkle with basil and serve immediately, passing remaining sauce separately.

Thai-Style Chicken with Basil

Serves 4

WHY THIS RECIPE WORKS In Thailand, street vendors have mastered an alternative to traditional Chinese high-heat stir-fry, using low flames to produce complex and flavorful dishes like chicken and basil—chopped pieces of moist chicken in a bright, basil-infused sauce. For our version, we started with the aromatics. Because Thai stir-fries are cooked over a low heat, the aromatics are added at the very beginning of cooking, where they infuse the oil with their flavors. To prevent scorching, we started our aromatics (garlic, chiles, and shallots) in a cold skillet. To ensure moist meat, we added fish sauce to the food processor when we ground the chicken, then rested the meat in the refrigerator. The fish sauce acted as a brine, seasoning the chicken and sealing in moisture. We spiced up the flavor of Chinese-style oyster sauce by adding a reserved tablespoon of the raw garlic-chile mixture at the end of cooking. And for intense, bright basil flavor, we cooked a portion of chopped basil with the garlic, chile, and shallot mixture, and stirred in whole basil leaves just before serving. Since tolerance for spiciness can vary, we've kept our recipe relatively mild. For a very mild version, remove the seeds and ribs from the chiles. If fresh Thai chiles are unavailable, substitute two serranos or one medium jalapeño. In Thailand, crushed red pepper and sugar are passed at the table, along with extra fish sauce and vinegar. You do not need to wash the food processor bowl after step 1. Serve with white rice and vegetables, if desired.

- 2 cups fresh basil leaves, divided
- 3 garlic cloves, peeled
- 6 green or red Thai chiles, stemmed
- 2 tablespoons fish sauce, divided, plus extra for serving
- 1 tablespoon oyster sauce
- 1 tablespoon sugar, plus extra for serving
- 1 teaspoon distilled white vinegar, plus extra for serving
- 1 pound boneless, skinless chicken breasts, trimmed and cut into 2-inch pieces
- 3 shallots, peeled and sliced thin
- 2 tablespoons vegetable oil
  Red pepper flakes

1. Pulse 1 cup basil, garlic, and chiles in food processor until chopped fine, 6 to 10 pulses, scraping down sides of bowl once during processing. Transfer 1 tablespoon basil mixture to small bowl; stir in 1 tablespoon fish sauce, oyster sauce, sugar, and vinegar and set aside. Transfer remaining basil mixture to 12-inch nonstick skillet.

2. Pulse chicken and remaining 1 tablespoon fish sauce in food processor until meat is chopped into ¼-inch pieces, 6 to 8 pulses. Transfer chicken to medium bowl and refrigerate for 15 minutes.

"What's the point of eating chicken if it doesn't come with nicely browned skin? This recipe produces perfectly cooked chicken breasts with perfectly rendered, perfectly crisp skin. And all that perfection comes with a pretty perfect side, too. While the chicken rests, you can quickly cook a vegetable in the dirty pan— all that 'gunk' in the pan is, of course, pure chicken flavor. Pairing carrots with big North African flavors solves the 'chicken can be boring' problem. A main plus a side, all in an hour, and with just one pan to wash—that's my definition of smart weeknight cooking."

–Jack

3. Stir shallots and oil into basil mixture in skillet. Heat mixture over medium-low heat (mixture should start to sizzle after about 1½ minutes; if it doesn't, adjust heat accordingly), stirring constantly, until garlic and shallots are golden brown, 5 to 8 minutes.

4. Add chicken, increase heat to medium, and cook, stirring and breaking up chicken with potato masher or rubber spatula, until only traces of pink remain, 2 to 4 minutes. Add reserved basil–fish sauce mixture and continue to cook, stirring constantly, until chicken is no longer pink, about 1 minute. Stir in remaining 1 cup basil and cook, stirring constantly, until basil is wilted, 30 to 60 seconds. Serve immediately, passing extra fish sauce, sugar, vinegar, and pepper flakes separately.

Skillet-Roasted Chicken Breasts with Harissa-Mint Carrots

SEASON 20 RECIPE

Serves 4

WHY THIS RECIPE WORKS When you roast bone-in, skin-on chicken breasts in a skillet, fat is rendered from the skin, juices seep from the flesh, and bits of meat stick to the pan. Tradition dictates that you use these drippings to whip up a pan sauce. But we wanted to make a one-pan meal by cooking a vegetable in them to create a rich, savory side. First, we seasoned bone-in, skin-on chicken breasts under the skin with salt. We placed them skin side down in a cold skillet and then turned on the heat to slowly render and brown the skin without overcooking the delicate flesh just beneath it. Once the skin was well browned, we flipped the breasts and placed them in a 325-degree oven for about 30 minutes to cook through. While the cooked chicken breasts rested, we added shallot and harissa to the skillet and cooked them until the chicken juices reduced and the aromatics began to sizzle in the fat and release flavor. We then added carrots along with a little water to the pan, covered the pan, and let the carrots cook through. With the skillet uncovered, the savory, chicken-y liquid thickened to coat the carrots.

- 4 (10- to 12-ounce) bone-in split chicken breasts, trimmed
- 2½ teaspoons kosher salt, divided
  Vegetable oil spray
- 1 shallot, sliced thin
- 2 teaspoons harissa
- 1½ pounds carrots, peeled and sliced ¼ inch thick on bias
- ½ cup water
- 1 tablespoon chopped fresh mint, divided
- 2 teaspoons lemon juice

1. Adjust oven rack to lower-middle position and heat oven to 325 degrees. Working with 1 breast at a time, use your fingers to carefully separate skin from meat. Peel back skin, leaving skin attached at top and bottom of breast and at ribs. Sprinkle 1½ teaspoons salt evenly over chicken (⅜ teaspoon per breast). Lay skin back in place. Using metal skewer or tip of paring knife, poke 6 to 8 holes in fat deposits in skin of each breast. Spray skin with oil spray.

2. Place chicken, skin side down, in 12-inch ovensafe skillet and set over medium-high heat. Cook, moving chicken as infrequently as possible, until skin is well browned, 7 to 9 minutes.

3. Carefully flip chicken and transfer skillet to oven. Roast until chicken registers 160 degrees, 25 to 30 minutes.

4. Transfer chicken to plate; do not discard liquid in skillet. Add shallot, harissa, and remaining 1 teaspoon salt to skillet and cook over medium-high heat, stirring occasionally and scraping up any browned bits, until moisture has evaporated and mixture begins to sizzle, 2 to 4 minutes. Add carrots and water and bring to simmer. Cover skillet, reduce heat to medium, and cook until carrots are tender, 10 to 12 minutes, stirring halfway through cooking. Uncover and continue to cook, stirring frequently, until sauce begins to coat carrots, 2 to 4 minutes. Add any accumulated chicken juices, 1½ teaspoons mint, and lemon juice to skillet and toss to combine. Season with salt to taste. Transfer carrots to serving platter and sprinkle with remaining 1½ teaspoons mint. Top with chicken and serve.

Crispy-Skinned Chicken Breasts with Vinegar-Pepper Pan Sauce

Serves 2

WHY THIS RECIPE WORKS Perfectly cooked chicken with shatteringly crispy, flavorful skin is a rare find, so we set out to develop a foolproof recipe that would work every time. Boning and pounding the chicken breasts was essential to creating a flat, even surface to maximize the skin's contact with the hot pan. We salted the chicken to both season the meat and dry out the skin; poking holes in the skin and the meat allowed the salt to penetrate deeply. Starting the chicken in a cold pan allowed time for the skin to crisp without overcooking the meat. Weighting the chicken for part of the cooking time with a heavy Dutch oven encouraged even contact with the hot pan for allover crunchy skin. Finally, we created silky, flavorful sauces with a bright, acidic finish, which provided the perfect foil to the skin's richness. This recipe requires refrigerating the salted meat for at least 1 hour before cooking.

Crispy-Skinned Chicken Breasts
with Lemon-Rosemary Pan Sauce

Two 10- to 12-ounce chicken breasts are ideal, but three smaller ones can fit in the same pan; the skin will be slightly less crispy. A boning knife or sharp paring knife works best to remove the bones from the breasts. To maintain the crispy skin, spoon the sauce around, not over, the breasts when serving.

Chicken
- 2 (10- to 12-ounce) bone-in split chicken breasts
- 1 teaspoon kosher salt, divided
- ½ teaspoon pepper, divided
- 2 tablespoons vegetable oil

Pan Sauce
- 1 shallot, minced
- 1 teaspoon all-purpose flour
- ½ cup chicken broth
- ¼ cup chopped pickled hot cherry peppers, plus ¼ cup brine
- 1 tablespoon unsalted butter, chilled
- 1 teaspoon finely chopped fresh thyme
- Salt and pepper

1. For the chicken: Place 1 chicken breast, skin side down, on cutting board, with ribs facing away from knife hand. Run tip of knife between breastbone and meat, working from thick end of breast toward thin end. Angling blade slightly and following rib cage, repeat cutting motion several times to remove ribs and breastbone from breast. Find short remnant of wishbone along top edge of breast and run tip of knife along both sides of bone to separate it from meat. Remove tenderloin (reserve for another use) and trim excess fat, taking care not to cut into skin. Repeat with second breast.

2. Using tip of paring knife, poke skin on each breast evenly 30 to 40 times. Turn breasts over and poke thickest half of each breast 5 to 6 times. Cover breasts with plastic wrap and pound thick ends gently with meat pounder until ½ inch thick. Evenly sprinkle each breast with ½ teaspoon kosher salt. Place breasts, skin side up, on wire rack set in rimmed baking sheet, cover loosely with plastic, and refrigerate for 1 hour or up to 8 hours.

3. Pat breasts dry with paper towels and sprinkle each breast with ¼ teaspoon pepper. Pour oil in 12-inch skillet and swirl to coat. Place breasts, skin side down, in oil and place skillet over medium heat. Place heavy skillet or Dutch oven on top of breasts. Cook breasts until skin is beginning to brown and meat is beginning to turn opaque along edges, 7 to 9 minutes.

4. Remove weight and continue to cook until skin is well browned and very crispy, 6 to 8 minutes. Flip breasts, reduce heat to medium-low, and cook until second side is lightly browned and meat registers 160 degrees, 2 to 3 minutes. Transfer breasts to individual plates and let rest while preparing pan sauce.

5. For the pan sauce: Pour off all but 2 teaspoons oil from skillet. Return skillet to medium heat and add shallot; cook, stirring occasionally, until shallot is softened, about 2 minutes. Add flour and cook, stirring constantly, for 30 seconds. Increase heat to medium-high, add broth and brine, and bring to simmer, scraping up any browned bits and smoothing out any lumps. Simmer until thickened, 2 to 3 minutes. Stir in any accumulated chicken juices; return to simmer and cook for 30 seconds. Remove skillet from heat and whisk in peppers, butter, and thyme; season with salt and pepper to taste. Spoon sauce around breasts and serve.

VARIATIONS
Crispy-Skinned Chicken Breasts with Lemon-Rosemary Pan Sauce
In step 5, increase broth to ¾ cup and substitute 2 tablespoons lemon juice for brine. Omit peppers and substitute rosemary for thyme.

Crispy-Skinned Chicken Breasts with Maple–Sherry Vinegar Pan Sauce
In step 5, substitute 2 tablespoons sherry vinegar for brine, 1 tablespoon maple syrup for peppers, and sage for thyme.

Boning a Split Chicken Breast

1. With chicken breast skin side down, run tip of boning or sharp paring knife between breastbone and meat, working from thick end of breast toward thin end.

2. Angling blade slightly and following rib cage, repeat cutting motion several times to remove ribs and breastbone from breast.

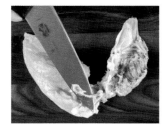

3. Find short remnant of wishbone along top edge of breast and run tip of knife along both sides of bone to separate it from meat.

Chicken Enchiladas with Red Chile Sauce

Serves 4 to 5

WHY THIS RECIPE WORKS Chicken enchiladas are a complete meal that offers a rich and complex combination of flavors, textures, and ingredients. The problem with preparing enchiladas at home is that traditional cooking methods require a whole day of preparation. We wanted a recipe for an Americanized version of chicken enchiladas that could be made in 90 minutes from start to finish. To save time preparing the tortillas, we sprayed them with vegetable oil spray and warmed them on a baking sheet in the oven. We created a quick chile sauce with onions, garlic, spices, and tomato sauce, and to further enhance the sauce's flavor, we poached the chicken right in the sauce. This step also made for moist, flavorful meat. And cheddar cheese spiked with canned jalapeños and fresh cilantro made a rich, flavorful filling. Monterey Jack can be used instead of cheddar or, for a mellower flavor and creamier texture, try farmer's cheese. Be sure to cool the chicken before filling the tortillas; otherwise the hot filling will make the enchiladas soggy.

Sauce and Filling

- 1½ tablespoons vegetable oil
- 1 onion, chopped fine
- 3 garlic cloves, minced
- 3 tablespoons chili powder
- 2 teaspoons ground coriander
- 2 teaspoons ground cumin
- 2 teaspoons sugar
- ½ teaspoon table salt
- 12 ounces boneless, skinless chicken thighs, trimmed and cut into ¼-inch-wide strips
- 2 (8-ounce) cans tomato sauce
- ¾ cup water
- 8 ounces sharp cheddar cheese, shredded (2 cups)
- ½ cup chopped fresh cilantro
- 1 (4-ounce) can pickled jalapeño chiles, drained and chopped (about ¼ cup)

Tortillas and Toppings

- 10 (6-inch) corn tortillas
  Vegetable oil spray
- 3 ounces sharp cheddar cheese, shredded (¾ cup)
- ¾ cup sour cream
- 1 avocado, diced
- 5 romaine lettuce leaves, shredded
  Lime wedges

1. *For the sauce and filling:* Heat oil in medium saucepan over medium-high heat until shimmering. Add onion and cook, stirring occasionally, until softened and beginning to brown, about 5 minutes. Add garlic, chili powder, coriander, cumin, sugar, and salt and cook, stirring constantly, until fragrant, about 30 seconds. Add chicken and cook, stirring constantly, until coated with spices, about 30 seconds. Add tomato sauce and water, stir to separate chicken pieces, and bring to simmer. Reduce heat to medium-low and simmer, uncovered, stirring occasionally, until chicken is cooked through and flavors meld, about 8 minutes. Pour mixture through medium-mesh strainer into medium bowl, pressing on chicken and onions to extract as much sauce as possible; set aside. Transfer chicken mixture to large plate; place in freezer for 10 minutes to cool, then combine with cheddar, cilantro, and jalapeños in medium bowl.

2. Adjust oven racks to upper-middle and lower-middle positions and heat oven to 300 degrees.

3. *To assemble:* Smear bottom of 13 by 9-inch baking dish with ¾ cup chili sauce. Place tortillas in single layer on 2 baking sheets. Spray both sides of tortillas lightly with vegetable oil spray. Bake until tortillas are soft and pliable, about 4 minutes. Transfer warm tortillas to work surface. Increase oven temperature to 400 degrees. Spread ⅓ cup filling down center of each tortilla. Roll each tortilla tightly by hand and place, seam side down, side by side on sauce in baking dish. Pour remaining chili sauce over top of enchiladas. Use back of spoon to spread sauce so it coats top of each tortilla. Sprinkle cheese down center of enchiladas.

4. Cover baking dish with aluminum foil. Bake enchiladas on lower rack until heated through and cheese is melted, 20 to 25 minutes. Uncover and serve immediately, passing sour cream, avocado, lettuce, and lime wedges separately.

Three-Cup Chicken

Serves 4

WHY THIS RECIPE WORKS Originating in Dadu (modern Beijing), three-cup chicken, or *san bei ji*, was named for its sparse ingredient list, with a sauce made up of just 1 cup each of soy sauce, sesame oil, and rice wine. Now adopted by neighboring Taiwan, it has evolved into a national dish of sorts. Its robust, aromatic flavors seemed ideal for adapting for the American kitchen. While traditional recipes involve butchering a whole bird into smaller pieces, we opted for boneless, skinless thighs, which didn't require using a cleaver. The rich flavor of the thighs would stand up to the potent sauce better than that of milder breasts. Marinating the chicken in the sauce helped build deep flavor with minimal effort. We found that scallions, ginger, garlic, and red pepper flakes added even more flavor and complexity to this dish. We prefer the flavor of Thai basil, but common sweet basil can be substituted. For a spicier dish, use the larger amount of red pepper flakes. Serve with white rice.

"Sometimes you need a good recipe shortcut. And by 'good' I mean that it's going to cut down on cooking time, kitchen work, or even grocery shopping, without cutting down quality. This recipe has just the right shortcuts built in. Now, I would never argue that dried chili powder straight out of the jar is a fine substitute for the toasted dried chiles that are the very foundation of an authentic red chile sauce, but when you bloom that same chili powder in hot oil—along with ground coriander—the flavors take a dramatic turn from dusty to developed, dull to deepened.

Braising strips of chicken thighs right in the sauce provides a moment of reciprocity, with each taking on the flavor of the other. Pickled jalapeños offer their one-two punch of heat and brightness to the dish as well. If you like the dish spicier than your family does, do as I do and add more jalapeños to a couple of enchiladas before rolling. I mark these with an extra jalapeño ring on the top of the spicier ones."

—Bridget

- ⅓ cup soy sauce
- ⅓ cup dry sherry
- 1 tablespoon packed brown sugar
- 1½ pounds boneless, skinless chicken thighs, trimmed and cut into 2-inch pieces
- 3 tablespoons vegetable oil
- 1 (2-inch) piece ginger, peeled, halved lengthwise, and sliced into thin half-rounds
- 12 garlic cloves, peeled and halved lengthwise
- ½–¾ teaspoon red pepper flakes
- 6 scallions, white and green parts separated and sliced thin on bias
- 1 tablespoon water
- 1 teaspoon cornstarch
- 1 cup Thai basil leaves, large leaves halved lengthwise
- 1 tablespoon toasted sesame oil

1. Whisk soy sauce, sherry, and sugar together in medium bowl. Add chicken and toss to coat; set aside.

2. Heat vegetable oil, ginger, garlic, and pepper flakes in 12-inch nonstick skillet over medium-low heat. Cook, stirring frequently, until garlic is golden brown and beginning to soften, 8 to 10 minutes.

3. Add chicken and marinade to skillet, increase heat to medium-high, and bring to simmer. Reduce heat to medium-low and simmer, stirring occasionally, for 10 minutes. Stir in scallion whites and continue to cook until chicken registers about 200 degrees, 8 to 10 minutes.

4. Whisk water and cornstarch together in small bowl, then whisk into sauce; simmer until sauce is slightly thickened, about 1 minute. Remove skillet from heat. Stir in basil, sesame oil, and scallion greens. Transfer to platter and serve.

Kung Pao Chicken

SEASON 20 RECIPE

Serves 4 to 6

WHY THIS RECIPE WORKS Spicy chiles and tingly Sichuan peppercorns team up with lightly sauced chicken and peanuts in a stir-fry that's literally sensational. We started our version by toasting peanuts in a skillet to maximize their crunch before setting them aside to cool. Next we toasted crushed Sichuan peppercorns and arbol chiles that we'd halved lengthwise to release their heat. We stirred in plenty of garlic and ginger and then added marinated diced chicken thighs. We covered the skillet to facilitate quick and even cooking of the chicken. When it was almost cooked through, we added some celery for crisp freshness and then a quick and concentrated sauce mixture that cooked down to a glaze. Stirring in the scallions and toasted peanuts last ensured that they retained their all-important crunch. Kung pao chicken

should be quite spicy. To adjust the heat level, use more or fewer chiles, depending on the size (we used 2-inch-long chiles) and your taste. Have your ingredients prepared and your equipment in place before you begin to cook. Use a spice grinder or mortar and pestle to coarsely grind the Sichuan peppercorns. If Chinese black vinegar is unavailable, substitute sherry vinegar. Serve with white rice and a simple vegetable such as broccoli or bok choy. Do not eat the chiles.

Chicken and Sauce

- 1½ pounds boneless, skinless chicken thighs, trimmed and cut into ½-inch pieces
- ¼ cup soy sauce, divided
- 1 tablespoon cornstarch
- 1 tablespoon Chinese rice wine or dry sherry
- ½ teaspoon white pepper
- 1 tablespoon Chinese black vinegar
- 1 tablespoon packed dark brown sugar
- 2 teaspoons toasted sesame oil

Stir-Fry

- 2 tablespoons plus 1 teaspoon vegetable oil, divided
- 3 garlic cloves, minced
- 2 teaspoons grated fresh ginger
- ½ cup dry-roasted peanuts
- 10–15 dried arbol chiles, halved lengthwise and seeded
- 1 teaspoon Sichuan peppercorns, ground coarse
- 2 celery ribs, cut into ½-inch pieces
- 5 scallions, white and light green parts only, cut into ½-inch pieces

1. *For the chicken and sauce:* Combine chicken, 2 tablespoons soy sauce, cornstarch, rice wine, and white pepper in medium bowl and set aside. Stir vinegar, sugar, oil, and remaining 2 tablespoons soy sauce together in small bowl and set aside.

2. For the stir-fry: Stir 1 tablespoon oil, garlic, and ginger together in second small bowl. Combine peanuts and 1 teaspoon oil in 12-inch nonstick skillet over medium-low heat. Cook, stirring constantly, until peanuts just begin to darken, 3 to 5 minutes. Transfer peanuts to plate and spread into even layer to cool. Return now-empty skillet to medium-low heat. Add remaining 1 tablespoon oil, arbols, and peppercorns and cook, stirring constantly, until arbols begin to darken, 1 to 2 minutes. Add garlic mixture and cook, stirring constantly, until all clumps are broken up and mixture is fragrant, about 30 seconds.

3. Add chicken and spread into even layer. Cover skillet, increase heat to medium-high, and cook, without stirring, for 1 minute. Stir chicken and spread into even layer. Cover and cook, without stirring, for 1 minute. Add celery and cook uncovered, stirring frequently, until chicken is cooked through, 2 to 3 minutes. Add soy sauce mixture and cook, stirring constantly, until sauce is thickened and shiny and coats chicken, 3 to 5 minutes. Stir in scallions and peanuts. Transfer to platter and serve.

Chicken Provençal

Serves 4

WHY THIS RECIPE WORKS Chicken Provençal represents the best of rustic peasant food—bone-in chicken is simmered all day in a tomatoey, garlicky herb broth. But all too often, this formula results in dry, rubbery chicken, watery or overly thick sauce, and dulled or muddied flavors. We wanted to rejuvenate this dish and create a chicken dish that was meltingly tender, moist, and flavorful, napped with an aromatic, garlicky tomato sauce that we could mop up with a good loaf of crusty bread. For the best flavor and most tender texture, we used bone-in chicken thighs and browned them in a sheer film of olive oil. Skinless thighs stuck to the pan, and skin-on thighs developed a flabby texture when braised later on. So we settled on a compromise—browning the thighs with the skin on (to develop rich flavor and leave browned bits in the pan), then ditching the skins prior to the braising (to avoid flabby skin). To keep the sauce from becoming greasy, we spooned off the excess fat left behind from browning the chicken, but kept enough to sauté our garlic and onion. Diced tomatoes, white wine, and chicken broth also went into the sauce. We then braised the chicken until it was meltingly tender. As for flavor enhancers, a small amount of niçoise olives added an essential brininess to the dish, and some minced anchovy made the sauce taste richer and fuller. This dish is often served with rice or slices of crusty bread, but soft polenta is also a good accompaniment. Niçoise olives are the preferred olives here; the flavor of kalamatas and other types of brined or oil-cured olives is too potent.

8 (5- to 6-ounce) bone-in chicken thighs, trimmed
1 teaspoon table salt
½ teaspoon pepper
1 tablespoon extra-virgin olive oil, divided
1 small onion, chopped fine
6 garlic cloves, minced
1 anchovy fillet, minced
⅛ teaspoon cayenne pepper
1 cup dry white wine
1 cup chicken broth
1 (14.5-ounce) can diced tomatoes, drained
2½ tablespoons tomato paste
1½ tablespoons finely chopped fresh thyme
1 teaspoon finely chopped fresh oregano
1 teaspoon herbes de Provence (optional)
1 bay leaf
1½ teaspoons grated lemon zest, divided
½ cup pitted niçoise olives
1 tablespoon finely chopped fresh parsley

1. Adjust oven rack to lower-middle position and heat oven to 300 degrees. Season chicken with salt and pepper. Heat 1 teaspoon oil in Dutch oven over medium-high heat until shimmering. Add half of chicken, skin side down, and cook, without moving, until skin is crisp and well browned, about 5 minutes. Flip chicken and brown on second side, about 5 minutes; transfer to plate. Repeat with remaining chicken, transfer to plate, and set aside. Discard all but 1 tablespoon fat from pot.

2. Add onion to pot and cook, stirring occasionally, over medium heat until softened and browned, about 4 minutes. Add garlic, anchovy, and cayenne; cook, stirring constantly, until fragrant, about 1 minute. Add wine, scraping up any browned bits. Stir in chicken broth; tomatoes; tomato paste; thyme; oregano; herbes de Provence, if using; and bay leaf. Discard skin from chicken thighs, then add chicken along with any accumulated juices to pot, submerging chicken in liquid. Increase heat to high, bring to simmer, cover, and transfer pot to oven; cook until chicken offers no resistance when poked with knife but is still clinging to bones, about 1¼ hours.

3. Using slotted spoon, transfer chicken to serving platter and tent with aluminum foil. Discard bay leaf. Set pot over high heat, stir in 1 teaspoon lemon zest, bring to boil, and cook, stirring occasionally, until slightly thickened and reduced to 2 cups, about 5 minutes. Stir in olives and cook until heated through, about 1 minute. Combine remaining ½ teaspoon zest and parsley. Spoon sauce over chicken, drizzle chicken with remaining 2 teaspoons oil, sprinkle with parsley mixture, and serve.

Filipino Chicken Adobo

Serves 4

WHY THIS RECIPE WORKS Adobo is the national dish of the Philippines, and chicken adobo is among the most popular versions. The dish consists of chicken simmered in a mixture of vinegar, soy sauce, garlic, bay leaves, and black pepper. The problem with most recipes we found was that they were aggressively tart and salty. Our secret to taming both of these elements was coconut milk. The coconut milk's richness tempered the bracing acidity of the vinegar and masked the briny soy sauce, bringing the sauce into balance. But the fat from the coconut milk and the chicken skin made the sauce somewhat greasy. To combat this, we borrowed a technique used in French bistros. We placed the meat skin side down in a cold pan and then turned up the heat. As the pan gradually got hotter, the fat under the chicken's skin melted away while the exterior browned. Light coconut milk can be substituted for regular coconut milk. Serve this dish over rice.

8 (5- to 7-ounce) bone-in chicken thighs, trimmed
⅓ cup soy sauce
1 (14-ounce) can coconut milk
¾ cup cider vinegar
8 garlic cloves, peeled
4 bay leaves
2 teaspoons pepper
1 scallion, sliced thin

1. Toss chicken with soy sauce in large bowl. Refrigerate for at least 30 minutes or up to 1 hour.

2. Remove chicken from soy sauce, allowing excess to drip back into bowl. Transfer chicken, skin side down, to 12-inch nonstick skillet; set aside soy sauce.

3. Place skillet over medium-high heat and cook until chicken skin is browned, 7 to 10 minutes. While chicken is browning, whisk coconut milk, vinegar, garlic, bay leaves, and pepper into soy sauce.

4. Transfer chicken to plate and discard fat in skillet. Return chicken to skillet skin side down, add coconut milk mixture, and bring to boil. Reduce heat to medium-low and simmer, uncovered, for 20 minutes. Flip chicken skin side up and continue to cook, uncovered, until chicken registers 175 degrees, about 15 minutes. Transfer chicken to platter and tent loosely with aluminum foil.

5. Remove bay leaves and skim any fat off surface of sauce. Return skillet to medium-high heat and cook until sauce is thickened, 5 to 7 minutes. Pour sauce over chicken, sprinkle with scallion, and serve.

Skillet-Roasted Chicken in Lemon Sauce (Rao's Famous Lemon Chicken)

Serves 4

WHY THIS RECIPE WORKS Inspired by Rao's famous roast lemon chicken in New York City, we aspired to re-create this popular dish, while making it more accessible to home cooks. Instead of the small birds Rao's uses, which can be difficult to find, we used a mixture of white and dark meat bone-in chicken parts. Searing the chicken before transferring it to the oven provided flavorful fond for a pan sauce. Browning the dark meat on both sides ensured the white and dark meats cooked evenly. To get the right amount of lemony flavor, we introduced zest to the sauce right before the chicken was added. The most successful way to thicken the sauce was with flour, added to the aromatics in the beginning of cooking, which provided a full-bodied gravy. A last-minute sprinkle of oregano, parsley, and more lemon zest finished the dish, adding a fruity brightness that complemented the crisp skin, moist meat, and silky sauce. We serve our version of Rao's chicken with crusty bread, but it can also be served with rice, potatoes, or egg noodles. To ensure crisp skin, dry the chicken well after brining and pour the sauce around, not on, the chicken right before serving.

up any browned bits and smoothing out any lumps, and bring to simmer. Cook until sauce is slightly reduced and thickened, 2 to 3 minutes. Stir in 1 tablespoon zest and remove skillet from heat. Return chicken, skin side up (skin should be above surface of liquid), along with any accumulated juices to skillet and transfer to oven. Cook, uncovered, until breasts register 160 degrees and thighs and legs register 175 degrees, 10 to 12 minutes.

4. While chicken cooks, chop parsley, oregano, and remaining 1 teaspoon zest until finely minced and well combined. Remove skillet from oven (handles will be hot) and let chicken sit for 5 minutes.

5. Transfer chicken to serving platter. Whisk sauce, incorporating any browned bits from sides of pan, until smooth and homogeneous, about 30 seconds. Whisk half of herb-zest mixture into sauce and sprinkle remaining half over chicken. Pour some sauce around chicken. Serve, passing remaining sauce separately.

- ½ cup table salt, for brining
- 3 pounds bone-in chicken pieces (2 split breasts cut in half crosswise, 2 drumsticks, and 2 thighs), trimmed
- 1 teaspoon vegetable oil
- 2 tablespoons unsalted butter
- 1 large shallot, minced
- 1 garlic clove, minced
- 4 teaspoons all-purpose flour
- 1 cup chicken broth
- 4 teaspoons grated lemon zest, divided, plus ¼ cup juice (2 lemons)
- 1 tablespoon fresh parsley leaves
- 1 teaspoon fresh oregano leaves

1. Dissolve salt in 2 quarts cold water in large container. Submerge chicken in brine, cover, and refrigerate for 30 minutes to 1 hour. Remove chicken from brine and pat dry with paper towels.

2. Adjust oven rack to lower-middle position and heat oven to 475 degrees. Heat oil in ovensafe 12-inch skillet over medium-high heat until just smoking. Place chicken skin side down in skillet and cook until skin is well browned and crisp, 8 to 10 minutes. Transfer breasts to large plate. Flip thighs and legs and continue to cook until browned on second side, 3 to 5 minutes. Transfer thighs and legs to plate with breasts.

3. Discard fat in skillet. Return skillet to medium heat; add butter, shallot, and garlic and cook until fragrant, about 30 seconds. Sprinkle flour evenly over shallot-garlic mixture and cook, stirring constantly, until flour is lightly browned, about 1 minute. Slowly stir in broth and lemon juice, scraping

Braised Chicken with Mustard and Herbs

SEASON 20 RECIPE
Serves 4 to 6

WHY THIS RECIPE WORKS Chicken is great for braising. It's got skin that renders loads of fat and collagen, which adds flavor and lush body to the sauce, and meat that turns tender and gives up savory juices. We put the classic method under the microscope, starting with 4 pounds of split breasts and leg quarters; to shorten the cooking time and make it easier to arrange everything in the pot, we separated the leg quarters into drumsticks and thighs. First, we browned the chicken skin side down to create a deeply savory fond. Out came the chicken and in the rendered fat we sautéed onion with aromatics, added flour, and deglazed it all with white wine and water, creating the perfect braising liquid. Given that white meat is done at 160 degrees and dark meat turns succulent at 195 degrees when braised, we needed a strategy for cooking the pieces. Instead of starting all the chicken together and removing the breasts when done, we placed the browned legs and thighs in the simmering liquid and cooked them to 140 degrees, which took about 8 minutes. The breasts went in next, at which point we moved the pot to a 300-degree oven, where everything cooked at a leisurely pace until the dark meat and the thickest parts of the breasts hit 195 degrees and 160 degrees, respectively. But the tapered ends of the breast pieces were dry and chalky. The next time around, we halved the breasts crosswise, separating the thinner tapered ends from the thicker broad ends so that we

Braised Chicken with Mustard and Herbs

could add the thin pieces to the pot last. We also brined the chicken before cooking, which, while unusual when braising, ensured that all the meat stayed moist. After giving the dark meat a short head start we nestled the broad ends of the breasts into the pot and then finally added the tapered ends (unbrowned to prevent overcooking). Finally, we covered the pot and transferred it to the oven; after roughly 20 more minutes, all three cuts of chicken were as tender and juicy as could be. Whole-grain mustard, fresh parsley, and lemon juice gave our classic sauce a bright punch of flavor. Chicken breasts are broader at one end than the other, so cut more than halfway up each breast to create two pieces of equal mass. There's no need to take the temperature of the dark meat; it will be properly cooked by the time the white meat reaches its target temperature. If you prefer not to serve the skin, wait until step 6 to remove it; browning the skin produces flavorful compounds that add complexity to the sauce, and braising it releases gelatin, which gives the sauce a rich texture.

½ cup table salt, for brining
1½–2 pounds bone-in split chicken breasts, trimmed and each cut crosswise into 2 pieces of equal mass
1½–2 pounds chicken leg quarters, separated into drumsticks and thighs, trimmed
1 tablespoon vegetable oil
1 onion, chopped fine
3 garlic cloves, minced
1 tablespoon finely chopped fresh thyme
1 teaspoon pepper
1 tablespoon all-purpose flour
1¼ cups water
⅓ cup dry white wine
3 tablespoons finely chopped fresh parsley
1½ tablespoons whole-grain mustard
2 teaspoons lemon juice

1. Dissolve salt in 2 quarts cold water in large container. Submerge chicken in brine, cover, and refrigerate for 30 minutes to 1 hour. Remove chicken from brine and thoroughly pat dry with paper towels. Set aside tapered breast pieces.

2. Adjust oven rack to middle position and heat oven to 300 degrees. Heat oil in Dutch oven over medium-high heat until just smoking. Place all chicken except reserved tapered breast pieces skin side down in pot and cook until skin is well browned, 5 to 8 minutes. (Reduce heat if pot begins to scorch.) Transfer chicken to plate. Pour off all but 2 tablespoons fat from pot, then reduce heat to medium.

3. Add onion and cook, stirring occasionally, until softened, 5 to 7 minutes. Stir in garlic, thyme, and pepper and cook until fragrant, about 30 seconds. Stir in flour and cook, stirring constantly, for 1 minute. Stir in water and wine, scraping up any browned bits.

4. Place thighs and drumsticks skin side up in pot and bring to simmer over medium heat. Cover and cook for 8 minutes. (Sauce will have consistency of thick gravy but will thin as chicken cooks.) Add broad breast pieces, skin side down, along with any accumulated juices. Cover and cook until broad breast pieces register 105 to 115 degrees, 3 to 5 minutes. Remove pot from heat.

5. Using tongs, flip broad breast pieces skin side up. Add tapered breast pieces, skin side up, to pot and cover. Transfer pot to oven and cook until breast pieces register 160 to 165 degrees, 15 to 30 minutes.

6. Transfer chicken to serving dish. Discard skin from tapered breast pieces (or all skin, if desired). Sauce should thinly coat back of spoon; if necessary, simmer until slightly thickened, 1 to 2 minutes. Stir parsley, mustard, and lemon juice into sauce. Season with salt and pepper to taste. Pour sauce over chicken and serve.

VARIATION
Braised Chicken with Basil and Tomato
Increase garlic to 4 cloves and add ¼ teaspoon red pepper flakes with garlic. Substitute 2 tablespoons tomato paste for thyme and dried oregano for pepper. Substitute chopped fresh basil for parsley and red wine vinegar for lemon juice. Sprinkle chicken with additional 1 tablespoon chopped fresh basil before serving.

Spice-Rubbed Picnic Chicken

Serves 8

WHY THIS RECIPE WORKS Cold barbecued picnic chicken presents numerous challenges: the meat may be dry, the skin flabby, and the chicken covered with a sticky, messy sauce. We wanted a recipe for chicken that would be easy to pack (and eat) for a picnic; chicken with moist, tender meat flavored with robust spicy and slightly sweet barbecue flavors. We first threw out the idea of a sticky sauce, substituting a robust dry rub (brown sugar, chili powder, paprika, and pepper) that reproduced the flavors of a good barbecue sauce. We partly solved the flabby skin problem by diligently trimming the chicken pieces as well as by slitting the skin before cooking (which allowed it to render excess fat). But the skin was still flabby from the moisture contributed by our traditional brine (we brine most poultry for better flavor and moister meat). We tried eliminating the brine, adding salt to the rub, and applying it the night before. Sure enough, when we oven-roasted the chicken the next day, we found the meat well seasoned throughout and very moist. Best of all, the skin was flavorful, delicate, and definitely not flabby. If you plan to serve the chicken later on the same day that you cook it, refrigerate it immediately after it has cooled, then let it come back to room temperature before serving. On the breast pieces, we use toothpicks to secure the skin, which otherwise shrinks considerably in the oven, leaving the meat exposed and prone to drying out. We think the extra effort is justified, but you can omit this step. This recipe halves easily.

5 pounds bone-in chicken pieces (split breasts, thighs, drumsticks, or a mix, with breasts cut into 3 pieces or halved if small), trimmed
3 tablespoons packed brown sugar
2 tablespoons chili powder
2 tablespoons paprika
2 tablespoons kosher salt
2 teaspoons pepper
¼–½ teaspoon cayenne pepper

1. Use sharp knife to make 2 or 3 short slashes in skin of each piece of chicken, taking care not to cut into meat. Combine sugar, chili powder, paprika, salt, and pepper in small bowl and mix thoroughly. Coat chicken pieces with spices, gently lifting skin to distribute spice rub underneath but leaving it attached to chicken. Transfer chicken, skin side up, to wire rack set in rimmed baking sheet, lightly tent with aluminum foil, and refrigerate for at least 6 hours or up to 24 hours.

2. If desired, secure skin of each breast piece with 2 or 3 toothpicks placed near edges of skin.

3. Adjust oven rack to middle position and heat oven to 425 degrees. Roast chicken until it registers 140 degrees, 15 to 20 minutes. Increase oven temperature to 500 degrees and continue roasting until chicken is browned and crisp and breasts register 160 degrees, 5 to 8 minutes, removing pieces from oven and transferring them to clean wire rack as they finish cooking. Continue to roast thighs and/or drumsticks, if using, until chicken registers 175 degrees, about 5 minutes. Remove from oven, transfer chicken to rack, and let cool completely before refrigerating or serving. (Chicken can be refrigerated for up to 2 days.)

Tandoori Chicken

Serves 4

WHY THIS RECIPE WORKS We weren't going to let a 24-hour marinade or the lack of a 900-degree oven keep us from turning this great Indian classic into an easy weeknight dinner. We set out to reinvent this traditional dish as a recipe that could be made year-round in a home oven. Traditional tandoors produce moist, smoky meat because the fierce heat allows protein molecules on the meat's surface to cross-link and contract, trapping moisture inside. Juices fall on the coals along with rendered fat, creating smoke that flavors the food. Trying to mimic the tandoor by cooking chicken in a very hot oven gave us disappointing results. Instead we turned to a technique we have used to preserve the juiciness of thick-cut steaks. We baked the chicken in a low-temperature oven until almost done, then gave it a quick broil to char the exterior. To get flavor into the meat, we turned to a salt-spice rub made with garam masala, cumin, and chili powder bloomed in oil with ginger and garlic. We massaged the rub into chicken pieces to lock in juices and infuse flavor, then left them to sit. Following a dunk in yogurt flavored with the same spice mix, the chicken was ready for the oven. The results? Juicy, lightly charred, well-seasoned meat with just the right degree of tenderness. We prefer this dish with whole-milk yogurt, but low-fat yogurt can be substituted. It is important to remove the chicken from the oven before switching to the broiler setting to allow the heating element to come up to temperature. Serve with Onion Relish (page 88), Cilantro-Mint Chutney (page 88), and white rice.

2 tablespoons vegetable oil
6 garlic cloves, minced
2 tablespoons grated fresh ginger
1 tablespoon garam masala
2 teaspoons ground cumin
2 teaspoons chili powder
1 cup plain whole-milk yogurt
¼ cup lime juice (2 limes), divided, plus lime wedges for serving
2 teaspoons table salt
3 pounds bone-in chicken pieces (split breasts cut in half, drumsticks, and/or thighs), trimmed and skin removed

1. Heat oil in 8-inch skillet over medium heat until shimmering. Add garlic and ginger and cook until fragrant, about 1 minute. Stir in garam masala, cumin, and chili powder and cook until fragrant, about 30 seconds. Transfer half of garlic-spice mixture to medium bowl, stir in yogurt and 2 tablespoons lime juice; set aside.

2. In large bowl, combine remaining garlic-spice mixture, remaining 2 tablespoons lime juice, and salt. Using sharp knife, lightly score skin of each piece of chicken, making 2 or 3 shallow cuts about 1 inch apart and about ⅛ inch deep, taking care not to cut into meat. Transfer chicken to bowl and gently rub with salt-spice mixture until evenly coated. Let sit at room temperature for 30 minutes.

3. Adjust oven rack to upper-middle position and heat oven to 325 degrees. Set wire rack in aluminum foil–lined rimmed baking sheet.

4. Pour yogurt mixture over chicken and toss until chicken is evenly coated with thick layer. Arrange chicken pieces, scored side down, on prepared rack. Discard excess yogurt mixture. Bake chicken until breasts register 125 degrees and legs and thighs register 130 degrees, 15 to 25 minutes. (Smaller pieces may cook faster than larger pieces.) Transfer chicken to plate.

5. Turn oven to broil and heat for 10 minutes. Flip chicken pieces scored side up and broil until lightly charred in spots and breasts register 165 degrees and legs and thighs register 175 degrees, 8 to 15 minutes.

6. Transfer chicken to serving platter, tent with foil, and let rest for 5 minutes. Serve with lime wedges.

Tandoori Chicken Without the Tandoor

1. Massage chicken pieces with salt-spice rub to lock in juices and infuse flavor.

2. Toss chicken in spiced yogurt for another layer of flavor.

3. To ensure juicy meat, bake chicken slowly in 325-degree oven until not quite cooked through.

4. For smoky flavor, briefly broil chicken until lightly charred and fully cooked.

Slow-Roasted Chicken Parts with Shallot-Garlic Pan Sauce

Serves 8

WHY THIS RECIPE WORKS For ultramoist roast chicken that boasted the shatteringly crisp skin we loved, we bypassed a whole chicken and turned to parts. We seared leg quarters and then split breasts in oil, rendering some of the fat and giving the crisping a head start. We moved the parts to a 250-degree oven, keeping the slower-cooking thighs on the back portion of the wire rack–lined sheet, facing the

hotter side of the oven. While the chicken rested, we whisked together a simple pan sauce with butter, shallots, garlic, and coriander, adding a little powdered gelatin and cornstarch to give it the rich body of a jus. Before serving, we gave the skin a final crisping under the broiler. To serve four people, halve the ingredient amounts.

> 5 pounds bone-in chicken pieces (4 split breasts and 4 leg quarters), trimmed
> 2 teaspoons kosher salt
> ¼ teaspoon vegetable oil
> 1 tablespoon unflavored gelatin
> 2¼ cups chicken broth
> 2 tablespoons water
> 2 teaspoons cornstarch
> 4 tablespoons unsalted butter, cut into 4 pieces
> 4 shallots, sliced thin
> 6 garlic cloves, sliced thin
> 1 teaspoon ground coriander
> 1 tablespoon finely chopped fresh parsley
> 1½ teaspoons lemon juice

1. Adjust 1 oven rack to lowest position and second rack 8 inches from broiler element. Heat oven to 250 degrees. Set wire rack in aluminum foil–lined rimmed baking sheet. Sprinkle chicken pieces with salt and season with pepper (do not pat chicken dry).

2. Heat oil in 12-inch skillet over medium-high heat until shimmering. Place leg quarters skin side down in skillet; cook, turning once, until golden brown on both sides, 5 to 7 minutes total. Transfer to prepared sheet, arranging legs along 1 long side of sheet. Pour off fat from skillet. Place breasts skin side down in skillet; cook, turning once, until golden brown on both sides, 4 to 6 minutes total. Transfer to sheet with legs. Discard fat; do not clean skillet. Place sheet on lower rack, orienting so legs are at back of oven. Roast until breasts register 160 degrees and legs register 175 degrees, 1 hour 25 minutes to 1 hour 45 minutes. Let chicken rest on sheet for 10 minutes.

3. While chicken roasts, sprinkle gelatin over broth in bowl and let sit until gelatin softens, about 5 minutes. Whisk water and cornstarch together in small bowl; set aside.

4. Melt butter in now-empty skillet over medium-low heat. Add shallots and garlic; cook until golden brown and crispy, 6 to 9 minutes. Stir in coriander and cook for 30 seconds. Stir in gelatin mixture, scraping up any browned bits. Bring to simmer over high heat and cook until reduced to 1½ cups, 5 to 7 minutes. Whisk cornstarch mixture to recombine. Whisk into sauce and simmer until thickened, about 1 minute. Off heat, stir in parsley and lemon juice; season with salt and pepper to taste. Cover to keep warm.

5. Heat broiler. Transfer sheet to upper rack and broil chicken until skin is well browned and crisp, 3 to 6 minutes. Serve, passing sauce separately.

"My husband, Ian, and I know this recipe by heart, as it's our go-to method for roasting a whole chicken. It's just so easy and foolproof. Plus, I love telling the backstory of how this recipe was developed in the test kitchen. It all started when the power went out one day, wrecking a number of recipe tests as the ovens went down. A few half-cooked chickens were in some of the ovens and although the test was ruined, the test cook left the chickens in the still warm but off ovens to finish cooking so that the food didn't go to waste. Bingo: The best method for roast chicken was born. I will warn you that the skin doesn't get supercrisp on this roast chicken (which I don't really care much about), but the drippings left behind in the pan are the best and the fat has already risen to the top for easy skimming."

–Julia

Weeknight Roast Chicken

Serves 4

WHY THIS RECIPE WORKS When you want a hands-off, absolutely foolproof way to roast a chicken, this is the recipe to use. In fact, we think everyone should memorize it—it's that good. Rather than fussing with a V-rack or flipping the chicken, we simply preheated a skillet in the oven. Direct contact with the superhot pan jump-started the thighs' cooking. Roasting the chicken in a 450-degree oven and then turning the oven off allowed the more delicate white meat to remain moist and tender as the bird finished cooking in the oven's residual heat. We prefer to use a 3½- to 4-pound chicken for this recipe. If roasting a larger bird, increase the time when the oven is on in step 2 to 35 to 40 minutes. You will need a 12-inch ovensafe skillet for this recipe. Serve with a pan sauce (recipes follow), if desired. If making a sauce, be sure to save 1 tablespoon of the pan drippings.

- 1 tablespoon kosher salt
- ½ teaspoon pepper
- 1 (3½- to 4-pound) whole chicken, giblets discarded
- 1 tablespoon extra-virgin olive oil

1. Adjust oven rack to middle position, place 12-inch skillet on rack, and heat oven to 450 degrees. Combine salt and pepper in bowl. Pat chicken dry with paper towels and rub entire surface with oil. Sprinkle evenly all over with salt mixture and rub in mixture with your hands to coat evenly. Tie legs together with kitchen twine and tuck wing tips behind back.

2. Transfer chicken, breast side up, to preheated skillet in oven. Roast chicken until breast registers 120 degrees and thighs register 135 degrees, 25 to 35 minutes. Turn off oven and leave chicken in oven until breast registers 160 degrees and thighs register 175 degrees, 25 to 35 minutes.

3. Transfer chicken to carving board and let rest, uncovered, for 20 minutes. Carve and serve.

ACCOMPANIMENTS

Tarragon-Lemon Pan Sauce
Makes about ¾ cup

- 1 shallot, minced
- 1 cup chicken broth
- 2 teaspoons Dijon mustard
- 2 tablespoons unsalted butter
- 2 teaspoons finely chopped fresh tarragon
- 2 teaspoons lemon juice

Being careful of hot skillet handle, while chicken rests, pour off all but 1 tablespoon fat from now-empty skillet, leaving any browned bits and juices in skillet. Place skillet over medium-high heat; add shallot and cook until softened, about 2 minutes. Stir in broth and mustard, scraping up any browned bits. Cook until reduced to ¾ cup, about 3 minutes. Off heat, whisk in butter, tarragon and lemon juice. Season with pepper to taste; cover and keep warm.

Thyme–Sherry Vinegar Pan Sauce
Makes about ¾ cup

- 1 shallot, minced
- 2 garlic cloves, minced
- 2 teaspoons finely chopped fresh thyme
- 1 cup chicken broth
- 2 teaspoons Dijon mustard
- 2 tablespoons unsalted butter
- 2 teaspoons sherry vinegar

Being careful of hot skillet handle, while chicken rests, pour off all but 1 tablespoon fat from now-empty skillet, leaving any browned bits and juices in skillet. Place skillet over medium-high heat; add shallot, garlic, and thyme and cook until softened, about 2 minutes. Stir in broth and mustard, scraping up any browned bits. Cook until reduced to ¾ cup, about 3 minutes. Off heat, whisk in butter and vinegar. Season with pepper to taste; cover and keep warm.

Carving a Whole Chicken

1. Cut chicken where leg meets breast, then pull leg quarter away. Push up on joint, then carefully cut through it to remove leg quarter.

2. Cut through joint that connects drumstick to thigh. Repeat on second side to remove other leg.

3. Cut down along 1 side of breastbone, pulling breast meat away from bone. Remove wing by cutting through wing joint. Slice breast.

Peruvian Roast Chicken with Garlic and Lime

Serves 3 to 4

WHY THIS RECIPE WORKS When you want to roast a chicken but you're looking to infuse it with bold exotic flavors, this Peruvian chicken fits the bill. We treated the meat and skin with a paste of salt, garlic, fresh mint, oregano, paprika, and habanero chile to deliver this dish's signature spicy, smoky flavor, and refrigerated the rubbed bird for at least 6 hours to deeply season the meat. We placed the chicken on a vertical roaster for allover browning and employed two different oven temperatures to get the crisp skin and perfectly cooked meat we were after. Starting out in a 325-degree oven produced tender, juicy meat, but before the chicken was fully cooked, we pulled it from the oven, upped the heat to 500 degrees, and gave the chicken a final 20 minutes to brown its skin. If habanero chiles are unavailable, 1 tablespoon of minced serrano chile can be substituted. Wear gloves when working with hot chiles. Note that this recipe requires refrigerating the rubbed chicken for at least 6 hours or up to 24 hours before cooking (a longer time is preferable). If using kosher chicken, omit the salt in step 1. This recipe calls for a vertical poultry roaster; our favorite is the Vertical Roaster with Infuser by Norpro. If you don't have one, you can substitute a 16-ounce can of beer. Open the can and pour out about half of the liquid. Spray the can lightly with vegetable oil spray and proceed with the recipe.

¼ cup fresh mint leaves
6 garlic cloves, chopped
3 tablespoons extra-virgin olive oil
1 tablespoon table salt
1 tablespoon pepper
1 tablespoon ground cumin
1 tablespoon sugar
2 teaspoons smoked paprika
2 teaspoons dried oregano
2 teaspoons finely grated lime zest plus ¼ cup juice (2 limes) plus lime wedges
1 teaspoon minced habanero chile
1 (3½- to 4-pound) whole chicken, giblets discarded
1 cup Spicy Mayonnaise (recipe follows)

1. Process mint, garlic, oil, salt, pepper, cumin, sugar, paprika, oregano, lime zest and juice, and habanero in blender until smooth paste forms, 10 to 20 seconds. Use your fingers to gently loosen skin covering breast and thighs; place half of paste under skin, directly on meat of breast and thighs. Gently press on skin to distribute paste over meat. Spread entire exterior surface of chicken with remaining paste. Tuck wings behind back. Place chicken in 1-gallon zipper-lock bag and refrigerate for at least 6 hours or up to 24 hours.

2. Adjust oven rack to lowest position and heat oven to 325 degrees. Place vertical roaster on rimmed baking sheet. Slide chicken onto vertical roaster so drumsticks reach down to bottom of roaster, chicken stands upright, and breast is perpendicular to sheet. Roast chicken until skin just begins to turn golden and thickest part of breast registers 140 degrees, 45 to 55 minutes. Carefully remove chicken and sheet from oven and increase oven temperature to 500 degrees.

Flavoring Peruvian Roast Chicken

1. Use your fingers to gently loosen chicken skin from over thighs and breast and rub half of paste directly over meat.

2. Spread remaining paste over skin of entire chicken.

3. Place chicken in gallon-size zipper-lock bag; refrigerate for at least 6 hours or up to 24 hours.

3. Once oven has reached 500 degrees, pour 1 cup water into baking sheet and continue to roast until entire chicken skin is browned and crisp, breast registers 160 degrees, and thighs register 175 degrees, about 20 minutes, rotating pan halfway through roasting. Check chicken halfway through roasting; if top is becoming too dark, place 7-inch square piece of aluminum foil over neck and wingtips of chicken and continue to roast (if sheet begins to smoke and sizzle, add additional water).

4. Carefully remove chicken from oven and let rest, still on vertical roaster, for 20 minutes. Using 2 large wads of paper towels, carefully lift chicken off vertical roaster and onto carving board. Carve chicken and serve, passing mayonnaise and lime wedges separately.

ACCOMPANIMENT
Spicy Mayonnaise
Makes about 1 cup

If you have concerns about consuming raw eggs, ¼ cup of an egg substitute can be used in place of the egg.

- 1 large egg
- 2 tablespoons water
- 1 tablespoon minced onion
- 1 tablespoon lime juice
- 1 tablespoon finely chopped fresh cilantro
- 1 tablespoon minced jarred jalapeños
- 1 garlic clove, minced
- 1 teaspoon yellow mustard
- ¼ teaspoon table salt
- 1 cup vegetable oil

Process egg, water, onion, lime juice, cilantro, jalapeños, garlic, mustard, and salt in food processor until combined, about 5 seconds. With machine running, slowly drizzle in oil in steady stream until mayonnaise-like consistency is reached, scraping down bowl as necessary.

Roast Chicken with Warm Bread Salad

Serves 4 to 6

WHY THIS RECIPE WORKS When the late, renowned chef Judy Rodgers of Zuni Café in San Francisco put her roast chicken with warm bread salad on the menu in the late '80s, it was a real hit. Now, some 30 years later, it still is. We wanted our own take on Zuni Café's roast chicken with bread salad, so we started by butterflying a whole chicken and salting it overnight; this would allow it to cook quickly and evenly and be juicy and well seasoned. Before roasting the chicken in a 475-degree oven, we covered the bottom of a skillet with bread cubes that we had moistened with oil and

broth and then draped the chicken on top. The bread cubes toasted and browned beneath the bird while absorbing its juices to create a mix of moistened, crispy-fried, and chewy pieces all packed with savory flavor. To finish the dish, we built a vinaigrette of champagne vinegar, oil, currants, thinly sliced scallions, Dijon mustard, and chicken drippings that we tossed with peppery arugula and the toasted bread. To ensure the greens didn't wilt, we served the salad alongside the carved chicken. Note that this recipe requires refrigerating the seasoned chicken for 24 hours. This recipe was developed and tested using Diamond Crystal Kosher Salt. If you have Morton Kosher Salt, which is denser than Diamond Crystal, put only ½ teaspoon of salt onto the cavity. Red wine or white wine vinegar may be substituted for champagne vinegar, if desired. For the bread, we prefer a round rustic loaf with a chewy, open crumb and a sturdy outer crust.

- 1 (4-pound) whole chicken, giblets discarded
- 3½ teaspoons kosher salt, divided
- 4 (1-inch-thick) slices country-style bread (8 ounces), bottom crust removed, cut into ¾ to 1-inch pieces (5 cups)
- ¼ cup chicken broth
- 6 tablespoons plus 2 teaspoons extra-virgin olive oil, divided
- ½ teaspoon pepper, divided
- 2 tablespoons champagne vinegar
- 1 teaspoon Dijon mustard
- 3 scallions, sliced thin
- 2 tablespoons dried currants
- 5 ounces (5 cups) baby arugula

1. Place chicken, breast side down, on cutting board. Using kitchen shears, cut through bones on either side of backbone; discard backbone. Do not trim off any excess fat or skin. Flip chicken over and press on breastbone to flatten.

French Chicken in a Pot

2. Using your fingers, carefully loosen skin covering breast and legs. Rub ½ teaspoon salt under skin of each side of breast, ½ teaspoon under skin of each leg, and 1 teaspoon salt onto bird's cavity. Tuck wings behind back and turn legs so drumsticks face inward toward breast. Place chicken on wire rack set in rimmed baking sheet or on large plate and refrigerate, uncovered, for 24 hours.

3. Adjust oven rack to middle position and heat oven to 475 degrees. Spray 12-inch skillet with vegetable oil spray. Toss bread with broth and 2 tablespoons oil until pieces are evenly moistened. Arrange bread in skillet in single layer, with majority of crusted pieces near center, crust side up.

4. Pat chicken dry with paper towels and place, skin side up, on top of bread. Brush 2 teaspoons oil over chicken skin and sprinkle with ¼ teaspoon salt and ¼ teaspoon pepper. Roast chicken until skin is deep golden brown and breast registers 160 degrees and thighs register 175 degrees, 45 to 50 minutes, rotating skillet halfway through roasting.

5. While chicken roasts, whisk vinegar, mustard, remaining ¼ teaspoon salt, and remaining ¼ teaspoon pepper together in small bowl. Slowly whisk in remaining ¼ cup oil. Stir in scallions and currants and set aside. Place arugula in large bowl.

6. Transfer chicken to carving board and let rest, uncovered, for 15 minutes. Run thin metal spatula under bread to loosen from bottom of skillet. (Bread should be mix of softened, golden-brown, and crunchy pieces.) Carve chicken and whisk any accumulated juices into vinaigrette. Add bread and vinaigrette to arugula and toss to evenly coat. Transfer salad to serving platter and serve with chicken.

French Chicken in a Pot

Serves 4

WHY THIS RECIPE WORKS *Poulet en cocotte* (chicken in a pot) is a classic French specialty—at its best, it's a whole chicken baked with root vegetables in a covered pot that delivers incredibly tender and juicy meat. Sounds simple, but it's actually more challenging than throwing chicken in a pot with vegetables. One potential problem is too much moisture in the pot, which washes out the flavor; another pitfall is overcooking. We wanted chicken in a pot that delivered moist meat and satisfying flavor. We removed the vegetables—the liquid they released made the pot too steamy—and cooked the chicken by itself (after browning it in a little oil to prevent it from sticking). We also tightly sealed the pot with foil before adding the lid. To keep the breast meat from drying out and

becoming tough, we cooked the chicken very slowly. After developing the basic technique, we revisited the idea of vegetables, and found that a small amount of potently flavored aromatic vegetables could be added if they were lightly browned with the chicken to erase most of their moisture. Finally, defatting the liquid in the pot rewarded us with a richly flavored sauce. The cooking times in the recipe are for a 4½- to 5-pound bird. A 3½- to 4½-pound chicken will take about an hour to cook, and a 5- to 6-pound bird will take close to 2 hours. We developed this recipe to work with a 5- to 8-quart Dutch oven with a tight-fitting lid. If using a 5-quart pot, do not cook a chicken larger than 5 pounds. If using a kosher chicken, reduce the amount of salt to ½ teaspoon. If you choose not to serve the skin with the chicken, simply remove it before carving. The amount of sauce will vary depending on the size of the chicken; season it with about ¼ teaspoon lemon juice for every ¼ cup.

- 1 (4½- to 5-pound) whole chicken, giblets discarded, wings tucked under back
- 1 teaspoon table salt
- ¼ teaspoon pepper
- 1 tablespoon extra-virgin olive oil
- 1 small onion, chopped
- 1 small celery rib, chopped
- 6 garlic cloves, peeled and trimmed
- 1 bay leaf
- 1 sprig fresh rosemary (optional)
- ½–1 teaspoon lemon juice

1. Adjust oven rack to lowest position and heat oven to 250 degrees. Pat chicken dry with paper towels and season with salt and pepper.

2. Heat oil in Dutch oven over medium heat until just smoking. Add chicken, breast side down, and scatter onion, celery, garlic, bay leaf, and rosemary, if using, around chicken. Cook until breast is lightly browned, about 5 minutes. Flip chicken breast side up and continue to cook until chicken and vegetables are well browned, 6 to 8 minutes.

3. Off heat, place large sheet of aluminum foil over pot and cover tightly with lid. Transfer pot to oven and cook until breast registers 160 degrees and thighs register 175 degrees, 1 hour 20 minutes to 1 hour 50 minutes.

4. Remove pot from oven. Transfer chicken to carving board, tent with foil, and let rest for 20 minutes. Strain chicken juices from pot into fat separator, pressing on solids to extract liquid; discard solids (you should have about ¾ cup juices). Let liquid settle for 5 minutes, then pour into saucepan and cook over low heat until hot. Carve chicken, adding any accumulated juices to saucepan. Season sauce with lemon juice to taste. Serve chicken, passing sauce separately.

High-Roast Butterflied Chicken with Potatoes

Serves 2 to 3

WHY THIS RECIPE WORKS "High roasting"—cooking a bird at temperatures in excess of 450 degrees—is supposed to produce tastier chicken with crisper skin in record time. But recipes we've tried overcook the bird while producing enough smoke to be mistaken for a five-alarm fire. We wanted to improve upon this method for a quick roasted chicken with skin that was crisp and tanned to a deep golden hue and meat that was irresistibly tender and moist. And while we were at it, we wanted roasted potatoes too. We began by brining the chicken for moist, well-seasoned meat. Then we butterflied the chicken, which allowed for more even and faster roasting. We found that we were able to add moisture and flavor to the chicken by rubbing flavored herb butter under the skin. (Some recipes instruct rubbing the butter over the skin, but the herbs burn and the butter doesn't season the meat.) We cooked the chicken on top of a broiler pan with a bottom attached. In the bottom of the pan under the chicken, we placed a layer of potatoes. To ensure that the potatoes cooked through, we sliced them thin—⅛ to ¼ inch thick. As the chicken cooked, the potatoes absorbed the juices from the chicken and became well seasoned. In just 1 hour we had roast chicken with spectacularly crisp skin and moist meat—and potatoes too. If using a kosher bird, skip the brining process and begin with step 2. Because you'll be cooking the chicken under high heat, it's important that you rinse it thoroughly before proceeding—otherwise, the sugar remaining on the skin from the brine will caramelize and ultimately burn. For this cooking technique, russet potatoes offer the best potato flavor, but Yukon Golds develop a beautiful color and retain their shape better after cooking. Either works well in this recipe. A food processor makes quick and easy work of slicing the potatoes.

Chicken
- ½ cup table salt, for brining
- ½ cup sugar
- 1 (3½- to 4-pound) whole chicken, giblets discarded
- 1 recipe Mustard-Garlic Butter with Thyme (recipe follows)
- 1 tablespoon extra-virgin olive oil

Potatoes
- 2½ pounds russet or Yukon Gold potatoes, peeled and sliced ⅛ to ¼ inch thick
- 1 tablespoon extra-virgin olive oil
- ½ teaspoon table salt
- ⅛ teaspoon pepper

1. For the chicken: Dissolve salt and sugar in 2 quarts cold water in large container. Submerge chicken in brine, cover, and refrigerate for 1 hour.

2. Adjust oven rack to lower-middle position and heat oven to 500 degrees. Line broiler-pan bottom with foil. Remove chicken from brine, rinse well, and pat dry with paper towels. Place chicken, breast side down, on cutting board. Using kitchen shears, cut through bones on either side of backbone; discard backbone. Do not trim off any excess fat or skin. Flip chicken over and press on breastbone to flatten. Tuck wings behind back.

3. Use your fingers to gently loosen center portion of skin covering each side of breast. Place butter mixture under skin, directly on meat in center of each side. Gently press on skin to distribute butter over meat. Rub skin with oil and season with pepper. Place chicken on broiler-pan top and push each leg up to rest between thigh and breast.

4. For the potatoes: Toss potatoes with oil, salt, and pepper. Spread potatoes in even layer in prepared broiler-pan bottom. Place broiler-pan top with chicken on top.

5. Roast chicken until just beginning to brown, about 20 minutes. Rotate pan and continue to roast until skin is crisped and deep brown and breasts register 160 degrees and thighs register 175 degrees, 20 to 25 minutes. Transfer chicken to carving board and let rest for 10 minutes.

6. While chicken rests, remove broiler-pan top and, using paper towels, soak up any excess grease from potatoes. Transfer potatoes to serving platter. Carve chicken, transfer to platter with potatoes, and serve.

ACCOMPANIMENT
Mustard-Garlic Butter with Thyme
Makes about 3 tablespoons

- 2 tablespoons unsalted butter, softened
- 1 tablespoon Dijon mustard
- 1 garlic clove, minced
- 1 teaspoon finely chopped fresh thyme
- Pinch pepper

Mash all ingredients together in bowl.

Crispy Fried Chicken

Serves 4 to 6

WHY THIS RECIPE WORKS Frying chicken at home is a daunting task, with its messy preparation and spattering hot fat. The chicken often ends up disappointingly greasy, with a peeling crust and dry, tasteless meat. We wanted fried chicken worthy of the mess and splatter: moist, seasoned meat coated with a delicious, crispy mahogany crust. We

1. *For the chicken:* Dissolve salt, sugar, and paprika in buttermilk in large container. Add garlic and bay leaves, submerge chicken in brine, cover, and refrigerate for 2 to 3 hours.

2. Rinse chicken well and place in single layer on wire rack set in rimmed baking sheet. Refrigerate uncovered for 2 hours. (At this point, chicken can be covered with plastic wrap and refrigerated up to 6 more hours.)

3. Adjust oven rack to middle position and heat oven to 200 degrees. Add oil to large Dutch oven until it measures 2 inches deep and heat over medium-high heat to 375 degrees.

4. *For the coating:* Place flour in shallow dish. Whisk egg, baking powder, and baking soda together in medium bowl, then whisk in buttermilk (the mixture will bubble and foam). Working with 3 chicken pieces at a time, dredge in flour, shaking off excess, then coat with egg mixture, allowing excess to drip off. Finally, coat with flour again, shake off excess, and return to wire rack.

soaked chicken parts in a seasoned buttermilk brine for ultimate flavor and juiciness. Then we air-dried the brined chicken parts to help ensure a crisp skin. Flour made the crispest coating. We found that peanut oil can withstand the demands of frying and has the most neutral flavor of all the oils tested. Vegetable oil was a close runner-up. As for frying the chicken, we found that a Dutch oven worked best. With its high sides and lid, the Dutch oven minimized splatters and retained heat, which helped the chicken cook through. Avoid using kosher chicken in this recipe or it will be too salty. Maintaining an even oil temperature is key. After the chicken is added to the pot, the temperature will drop dramatically, and most of the frying will be done at about 325 degrees. Use an instant-read thermometer with a high upper range; a clip-on candy/deep-fry thermometer is fine, too, though it can be clipped to the pot only for the uncovered portion of frying.

5. When oil is hot, add half of chicken pieces to pot, skin side down, cover, and fry until deep golden brown, 7 to 11 minutes, adjusting heat as necessary to maintain oil temperature of about 325 degrees. (After 4 minutes, check chicken pieces for even browning and rearrange if some pieces are browning faster than others.) Turn chicken pieces over and continue to cook until breasts register 160 degrees and thighs or drumsticks register 175 degrees, 6 to 8 minutes. Drain chicken briefly on paper towel–lined plate, then transfer to clean wire rack set over rimmed baking sheet and keep warm in oven.

6. Return oil to 375 degrees over medium-high heat and repeat with remaining chicken pieces. Serve.

Chicken
- ½ cup table salt, for brining
- ¼ cup sugar, for brining
- 2 tablespoons paprika
- 7 cups buttermilk
- 3 garlic heads, cloves separated and smashed
- 3 bay leaves, crumbled
- 4 pounds bone-in chicken pieces (split breasts cut in half, drumsticks, and/or thighs), trimmed
- 3–4 quarts peanut oil or vegetable oil, for frying

Coating
- 4 cups (20 ounces) all-purpose flour
- 1 large egg
- 1 teaspoon baking powder
- ½ teaspoon baking soda
- 1 cup buttermilk

Oven-Fried Chicken

Serves 4

WHY THIS RECIPE WORKS Oven-fried chicken never seems to taste as good as the real thing. The coating, often plain bread crumbs or cornflakes, just isn't as crunchy or flavorful as a deep-fried coating. We wanted a good alternative to regular fried chicken—one that would have real crunch and good flavor, and wouldn't taste like diet food. We soaked bone-in chicken legs and thighs in a buttermilk brine to achieve maximum juiciness and flavor. And we removed the skin from the chicken before brining because it simply turned flabby in the oven. A mixture of eggs and mustard helped the crumbs stick to the chicken and encouraged the formation of a crunchy crust. Melba toast crumbs made the crispest coating. We baked the chicken on a wire rack set in a baking sheet that we had lined with foil. This method allowed heat to circulate around the chicken during baking, resulting in crisp chicken all over without turning. As a bonus, the foil made cleanup quick and easy. Avoid using kosher chicken in this recipe or it will be too salty. If you don't want to buy whole chicken legs and cut them into drumsticks and thighs, simply buy four drumsticks and four thighs. To crush the Melba toasts, place them in a heavy-duty zipper-lock freezer bag, seal, and pound with a meat pounder or other heavy blunt object. Leave some crumbs in the mixture the size of pebbles, but most should resemble coarse sand.

Chicken

- ½ cup plus 2 tablespoons table salt, for brining
- ¼ cup sugar, for brining
- 2 tablespoons paprika
- 3 heads garlic, cloves separated
- 3 bay leaves, crumbled
- 7 cups buttermilk
- 4 whole chicken legs, separated into drumsticks and thighs and skin removed

Coating

- ¼ cup vegetable oil
- 5 ounces plain Melba toast, crushed
- 2 large eggs
- 1 tablespoon Dijon mustard
- 1 teaspoon dried thyme
- ¾ teaspoon table salt
- ½ teaspoon pepper
- ½ teaspoon dried oregano
- ¼ teaspoon garlic powder
- ¼ teaspoon cayenne pepper (optional)

1. For the chicken: In large zipper-lock bag, combine salt, sugar, paprika, garlic cloves, and bay leaves. With flat meat pounder, smash garlic into salt and spice mixture thoroughly. Pour mixture into large container. Add buttermilk and stir until salt and sugar are completely dissolved. Submerge chicken in brine and refrigerate for 2 to 3 hours. Rinse chicken well and place on wire rack set in rimmed baking sheet. Refrigerate uncovered for 2 hours. (After 2 hours, chicken can be covered with plastic wrap and refrigerated for up to 6 more hours.)

2. Adjust oven rack to upper-middle position and heat oven to 400 degrees. Line rimmed baking sheet with foil and set wire rack in pan.

3. For the coating: Drizzle oil over Melba toast crumbs in pie plate or shallow dish; toss well to coat. Mix eggs, mustard, thyme, salt, pepper, oregano, garlic powder, and cayenne, if using, with fork in second plate.

4. Working with 1 piece at a time, coat chicken on both sides with egg mixture. Set chicken in Melba crumbs, sprinkle crumbs over chicken, and press to coat. Turn chicken over and repeat on other side. Gently shake off excess and place on rack. Bake until chicken is deep nutty brown and registers 175 degrees, about 40 minutes. Serve.

Korean-Style Fried Chicken Wings

Serves 4 to 6

WHY THIS RECIPE WORKS One bite of this exceptionally crunchy, sweet-spicy style of fried chicken and you'll understand its cultlike popularity. The hallmarks of this Korean fried chicken are a thin, crispy exterior and a spicy-sweet-salty sauce. Replicating the sauce would be key but certainly not the hardest part of recipe development. The biggest challenge would be preventing the sauce from destroying the crust. We dunked the wings (which offer a high exterior-to-interior ratio for maximum crunch and also cook quickly) in a loose batter of flour, cornstarch, and water, which clung nicely to the chicken and fried up brown and crispy. To help the coating withstand a wet sauce, we double-fried the wings, which removed more water from the skin than a single fry did, making the coating extra-crispy. The Korean hot red chili paste known as gochujang gave our sauce the proper spicy, fermented notes, while sugar tempered the heat and garlic and ginger—cooked briefly with sesame oil—provided depth. A rasp-style grater makes quick work of turning the garlic into a paste. Gochujang can be found in Asian markets and in some supermarkets. Tailor the heat level of your wings by adjusting its amount. If you can't find gochujang, substitute an equal amount of sriracha and add only 2 tablespoons of water to the sauce. For a complete meal, serve these wings with white rice and a vegetable.

- 1 tablespoon toasted sesame oil
- 1 teaspoon garlic, minced to paste
- 1 teaspoon grated fresh ginger
- 1¾ cups water, divided
- 3 tablespoons sugar
- 2–3 tablespoons gochujang
- 1 tablespoon soy sauce
- 2 quarts vegetable oil
- 1 cup all-purpose flour
- 3 tablespoons cornstarch
- 3 pounds chicken wings, cut at joints, wing tips discarded

1. Combine sesame oil, garlic, and ginger in large bowl and microwave until mixture is bubbly and fragrant but not browned, 40 to 60 seconds. Whisk in ¼ cup water, sugar, gochujang, and soy sauce until smooth and set aside.

2. Heat oil in large Dutch oven over medium-high heat to 350 degrees. While oil heats, whisk flour, cornstarch, and remaining 1½ cups water in second large bowl until smooth. Set wire rack in rimmed baking sheet and set aside.

3. Place half of wings in batter and stir to coat. Using tongs, remove wings from batter one at a time, allowing any excess batter to drip back into bowl, and add to hot oil. Increase heat to high and cook, stirring occasionally to prevent wings from sticking, until coating is light golden and beginning to crisp,

"Years ago I visited a friend I'd made in culinary school back in his home town of Seoul, South Korea. I had expected the trip to be an intensely flavorful education in one of the world's great cuisines (which it was). What I didn't foresee was that I'd take every opportunity I could to sneak another bite of fried chicken after my initial taste. Korean fried wings feature an ultrathin coating that manages to stay audibly crisp under a blanket of spicy, sweet, and deeply savory sauce. That's no easy feat. The incredible crunch staying power is achieved through a clever technique called double frying. Two quick stints in hot oil, versus one longer fry, allow these wings to stay crispy for hours. Which is of course completely unnecessary— they'll be gone in minutes."

—Dan

about 7 minutes. (Oil temperature will drop sharply after adding chicken.) Transfer wings to prepared rack. Return oil to 350 degrees and repeat with remaining wings. Reduce heat to medium and let second batch of chicken rest for 5 minutes.

4. Return oil to 375 degrees. Carefully return all chicken to oil and cook, stirring occasionally, until exterior is deep golden brown and very crispy, about 7 minutes. Transfer to rack and let sit for 2 minutes. Add chicken to reserved sauce and toss until coated. Return chicken to rack and let sit for 2 minutes to allow surface to set. Transfer to platter and serve.

Turkey Breast en Cocotte with Pan Gravy

Serves 6 to 8

WHY THIS RECIPE WORKS Having successfully developed a recipe for chicken *en cocotte*, we wondered if we could use this same method (cooking the poultry in a covered pot over low heat for an extended period of time) to get the same great results with a turkey breast—perfectly cooked, incredibly moist and tender meat. To ensure that a 6- to 7-pound breast fit into the pot, we found it helpful to trim the rib bones. Browning the turkey breast was an essential step in developing deep flavor. Adding some aromatics to the pot further rounded out the flavor, and we settled on a combination of onion, carrot, celery, garlic, thyme, and bay leaf. After 1 hour and 45 minutes, our turkey breast was done—we had an extremely tender, juicy, and moist piece of meat. After removing the turkey from the pot, we reduced the jus until it had all but evaporated, concentrating the turkey flavor, producing a mahogany fond on the bottom of the pot, and separating the fat from the jus. It was into this rendered fat that we stirred flour to make a roux. We then added a full quart of chicken broth to the pot, brought it to a simmer, and reduced it to a proper gravy consistency. The result was a deeply flavored gravy reminiscent of Thanksgiving dinner. Many supermarkets are now selling "hotel-style" turkey breasts. Try to avoid these as they still have the wings attached. If this is the only type of breast you can find, you will simply need to remove the wings before proceeding with the recipe. Be sure to use a 7- to 8-quart Dutch oven here. Don't buy a turkey breast larger than 7 pounds; it won't fit in the pot.

1   **(6- to 7-pound) whole bone-in turkey breast, trimmed**
1   **tablespoon table salt**
1½ **teaspoons pepper**
2   **tablespoons extra-virgin olive oil**
1   **onion, chopped**
1   **carrot, chopped**
1   **celery rib, chopped**
6   **garlic cloves, peeled and crushed**
2   **sprigs fresh thyme**

1   **bay leaf**
¼   **cup all-purpose flour**
4   **cups chicken broth**

1. Adjust oven rack to lowest position and heat oven to 250 degrees. Pat turkey dry with paper towels and season with salt and pepper.

2. Heat oil in Dutch oven over medium-high heat until just smoking. Add turkey, breast side down, and scatter onion, carrot, celery, garlic, thyme sprigs, and bay leaf around turkey. Cook, turning breast on its sides and stirring vegetables as needed, until turkey and vegetables are well browned, 12 to 16 minutes, reducing heat if pot begins to scorch. Turn turkey so breast side is facing up.

3. Off heat, place large sheet of aluminum foil over pot and press to seal, then cover tightly with lid. Transfer pot to oven and cook until breast registers 160 degrees, 1½ to 1¾ hours.

4. Remove pot from oven. Transfer turkey to carving board, tent with foil, and let rest while making gravy.

5. Being careful of hot pot handles, bring remaining juices and vegetables to simmer over medium-high heat and cook until almost all of liquid has evaporated, 15 to 20 minutes. Stir in flour and cook, stirring constantly, until browned, 2 to 5 minutes. Slowly whisk in broth, scraping up any browned bits and smoothing out any lumps, bring to simmer, and cook, stirring often, until gravy is thickened and measures about 2½ cups, 10 to 15 minutes.

6. Strain gravy through fine-mesh strainer; discard solids. Season with salt and pepper to taste. Carve turkey and serve, passing gravy separately.

Classic Roast Turkey

Serves 10 to 12

WHY THIS RECIPE WORKS Few of us want to take chances when cooking the holiday bird. We wanted to find a way that guaranteed moist, flavorful meat and bronzed skin— a true holiday table centerpiece. First we brined our turkey, which helped prevent the meat from drying out and also seasoned it right to the bone. After brining, we let it rest on a wire rack in the refrigerator so that the skin dried out. This step helped ensure the skin would cook up crisp, not flabby. Placing the turkey on a V-rack allowed for air circulation all around so that the bird cooked evenly. And turning the turkey three times also helped to ensure even cooking. Finally, once the turkey was cooked, we waited 30 minutes before carving it. That might seem like a long time, but it allowed the juices in the turkey to redistribute so that, once carved, each slice was moist and full of flavor. Resist the temptation to tent the roasted turkey with foil while it rests on the carving board. Covering the bird will make the skin soggy.

1 cup table salt, for brining
1 (12- to 14-pound) turkey; giblets, neck, and
   tailpiece removed and reserved for gravy
2 onions, chopped, divided
2 carrots, chopped, divided
2 celery ribs, chopped, divided
6 sprigs fresh thyme, divided
3 tablespoons unsalted butter, melted, divided
1 cup water, plus more as needed
1 recipe Giblet Pan Gravy (recipe follows)

1. Dissolve salt in 2 gallons cold water in large container. Submerge turkey in brine, cover, and refrigerate or store in very cool spot (40 degrees or less) for 6 to 12 hours.

2. Set wire rack in rimmed baking sheet. Remove turkey from brine and pat dry, inside and out, with paper towels. Place turkey on prepared sheet. Refrigerate, uncovered, at least 8 hours or overnight.

3. Adjust oven rack to lowest position and heat oven to 400 degrees. Line V-rack with heavy duty foil and poke several holes in foil. Set V-rack in roasting pan and spray foil with vegetable oil spray.

4. Toss half of onions, carrots, celery, and thyme with 1 tablespoon melted butter in medium bowl and place inside turkey. Tie legs together with kitchen twine and tuck wings under bird. Scatter remaining vegetables into roasting pan.

5. Pour 1 cup water over vegetable mixture. Brush turkey breast with 1 tablespoon melted butter, then place turkey, breast side down, on V-rack. Brush with remaining 1 tablespoon melted butter.

6. Roast turkey for 45 minutes. Remove pan from oven; baste with juices from pan. With dish towel in each hand, turn turkey leg/thigh side up. If liquid in pan has totally evaporated, add another ½ cup water. Return turkey to oven and roast for 15 minutes. Remove turkey from the oven again, baste, and turn other leg/thigh side up; roast for another 15 minutes. Remove turkey from oven for final time, baste, and turn breast side up; roast until breast registers 160 degrees and thigh registers 175 degrees, 30 to 45 minutes.

7. Remove turkey from oven. Gently tip turkey so that any accumulated juices in cavity run into roasting pan. Transfer turkey to carving board and let rest, uncovered, for 30 minutes. Carve turkey and serve with gravy.

ACCOMPANIMENT
Giblet Pan Gravy
Makes about 6 cups
Complete step 1 up to a day ahead, if desired. Begin step 3 once the bird has been removed from the oven and is resting on a carving board.

1 tablespoon vegetable oil
   Reserved turkey giblets, neck, and tailpiece
1 onion, chopped
4 cups chicken broth
2 cups water
2 sprigs fresh thyme
8 sprigs fresh parsley
3 tablespoons unsalted butter
¼ cup all-purpose flour
1 cup dry white wine

1. Heat oil in Dutch oven over medium heat until shimmering; add giblets, neck, and tailpiece, and cook until golden and fragrant, about 5 minutes. Add onion and continue to cook until softened, 3 to 4 minutes. Reduce heat to low, cover, and cook until turkey parts and onion release their juices, about 15 minutes. Add broth, water, thyme sprigs, and parsley sprigs and bring to boil; adjust heat to low. Simmer, uncovered, skimming any impurities that may rise to surface, until broth is rich and flavorful, about 30 minutes. Strain broth into large container and reserve giblets. When cool enough to handle, chop giblets. Refrigerate giblets and broth until ready to use. (Broth can be stored in refrigerator for up to 1 day.)

2. While turkey is roasting, return reserved turkey broth to simmer. Melt butter in large saucepan over medium-low heat. Vigorously whisk in flour (mixture will froth and then thin out again). Cook slowly, stirring constantly, until nutty brown and fragrant, 10 to 15 minutes. Vigorously whisk all but 1 cup hot broth into flour mixture, smoothing out any lumps. Bring to boil, then continue to simmer, stirring occasionally, until gravy is lightly thickened and very flavorful, about 30 minutes. Set aside until turkey is done.

3. When turkey has been transferred to carving board to rest, spoon out and discard as much fat as possible from roasting pan, leaving caramelized herbs and vegetables. Place roasting pan over 2 burners set on medium-high heat. Return gravy to simmer. Add wine to roasting pan of caramelized vegetables, scraping up any browned bits, and boil until reduced by half, about 5 minutes. Add remaining 1 cup turkey broth and continue to simmer for 15 minutes; strain pan juices into gravy, pressing as much juice as possible out of vegetables. Stir reserved giblets into gravy and return to boil. Season with salt and pepper to taste.

Easier Roast Turkey and Gravy

Serves 10 to 12

WHY THIS RECIPE WORKS When you want all the advantages of a great roasted turkey with less work, this ingenious recipe delivers. No flipping. No long-simmered gravy. The key is a tool we borrowed from pizza making: a baking stone. But first, to season the meat and help it retain more juices as it cooked, we loosened the skin of the turkey and applied a mixture of salt and sugar to the flesh. We preheated both the baking stone and roasting pan in the oven before placing the turkey in the pan. The stone absorbed heat and delivered it through the pan to the turkey's legs and thighs, which need to cook to a higher temperature than the delicate breast meat (which we protected with a foil shield). After the leg quarters had gotten a jump start on cooking, we reduced the oven temperature from 425 to 325 degrees

and removed the shield to allow the breast to brown while the bird finished cooking. The heat boost provided by the stone also helped the juices brown and reduce into concentrated drippings that we turned into a flavorful gravy in the time that the turkey rested. Note that this recipe requires salting the bird in the refrigerator for 24 to 48 hours. This recipe was developed and tested using Diamond Crystal Kosher Salt. If you have Morton's Kosher Salt, which is denser than Diamond Crystal, reduce the salt in step 1 to 3 tablespoons. Rub 1 tablespoon salt mixture into each side of the breast, 1½ teaspoons into each leg, and the remainder into the cavity. Table salt is too fine and not recommended for this recipe. If you are roasting a kosher or self-basting turkey (such as a frozen Butterball), do not salt it; it already contains a good amount of sodium. The success of this recipe is dependent on saturating the pizza stone and roasting pan with heat. We recommend preheating the stone, pan, and oven for at least 30 minutes.

¼ cup kosher salt
4 teaspoons sugar
1 (12- to 14-pound) turkey, neck and giblets removed and reserved for gravy
2½ tablespoons vegetable oil, divided
1 teaspoon baking powder
1 small onion, chopped fine
1 carrot, peeled and sliced thin
5 sprigs fresh parsley
2 bay leaves
5 tablespoons all-purpose flour
3¼ cups water
¼ cup dry white wine

1. Combine salt and sugar in bowl. Using your fingers, gently loosen skin covering turkey breast and thighs. Rub 4 teaspoons salt mixture under skin of each breast half, 2 teaspoons salt under skin of each leg, and remaining salt mixture into cavity. Tie legs together with kitchen twine. Place turkey on rack set in rimmed baking sheet and refrigerate uncovered for 24 to 48 hours.

2. At least 30 minutes before roasting turkey, adjust oven rack to lowest position and set pizza stone on oven rack. Place roasting pan on pizza stone and heat oven to 500 degrees. Combine 1½ teaspoons oil and baking powder in small bowl. Pat turkey dry with paper towels. Rub oil mixture evenly over turkey. Cover turkey breast with double layer of aluminum foil.

3. Remove roasting pan from oven. Place remaining 2 tablespoons oil in roasting pan. Place turkey into pan breast side up and return pan to oven. Reduce oven temperature to 425 degrees and cook for 45 minutes.

4. Remove foil shield, reduce temperature to 325 degrees, and continue to cook until breast registers 160 degrees and thighs register 175 degrees, 1 to 1½ hours.

Easier Roast Turkey and Gravy

"My Thanksgiving table is usually packed: We have great friends who often join us, along with family who drive and fly in. I've even had a half-dozen extra guests show up at the last minute on turkey day. I say, the more the merrier. I always make too much food anyway. To me, what is appealing about this recipe is its straightforward, step-by-step approach to cooking a truly impressive amount of turkey— plus superflavorful gravy. This makes me happy, and it's not much harder than cooking a single bird. Light and dark meat both come out juicy and just right. And nobody misses waiting for a whole bird to be carved at the table—it's gorgeous and ready to go."

—Lisa

5. Using spatula, loosen turkey from roasting pan; transfer to carving board and let rest uncovered for 45 minutes. While turkey rests, use wooden spoon to scrape any browned bits from bottom of roasting pan. Pour pan drippings through fine-mesh strainer set in bowl. Transfer drippings to fat separator and let rest for 10 minutes. Reserve 3 tablespoons fat and defatted liquid (about 1 cup). Discard remaining fat.

6. Heat reserved fat in large saucepan over medium-high heat until shimmering. Add reserved neck and giblets and cook until well browned, 10 to 12 minutes. Transfer neck and giblets to large plate. Reduce heat to medium; add onion, carrot, parsley, and bay leaves; and cook, stirring frequently, until vegetables are softened, 5 to 7 minutes. Add flour and cook, stirring constantly, until flour is well coated with fat, about 1 minute. Slowly whisk in reserved defatted liquid and cook until thickened, about 1 minute. Whisk in water and wine, return neck and giblets, and bring to simmer. Simmer for 10 minutes. Season with salt and pepper to taste. Discard neck. Strain mixture through fine-mesh strainer and transfer to serving bowl. Carve turkey and arrange on serving platter. Serve with gravy.

Turkey and Gravy for a Crowd

SEASON 20 RECIPE

Serves 18 to 20

WHY THIS RECIPE WORKS For a low-stress holiday meal to feed a crowd, we cooked turkey parts—leg quarters and bone-in breasts—separately rather than roasting two whole birds. The leg quarters benefited from braising them in a flavorful liquid, a step that can be done a few days in advance. We then used the braising liquid as the base for a gravy that could also be made ahead. That left only roasting the breasts (which we salted and refrigerated for 24 hours) and reheating the leg quarters and gravy on Thanksgiving Day. Brushing the skin of the breasts, legs, and thighs with melted butter and heating them in a 500-degree oven ensured that all the parts arrived at the table evenly crisp and bronzed— just as if they'd been carved from two whole roasted birds. This recipe requires refrigerating the salted turkey breasts for 24 hours. If using self-basting or kosher turkey breasts, do not salt in step 7, but season with salt in step 8. We used Diamond Crystal Kosher Salt; if you use Morton Kosher Salt, reduce the salt in step 7 to 2½ teaspoons per breast, rubbing 1 teaspoon onto each side and ½ teaspoon onto the underside of the breast cavity. Covering the turkey with parchment and then foil will prevent the wine in the braising liquid from "pitting" the foil. Please note that in this recipe, the legs and gravy are done three days in advance and the breasts are done one day in advance.

Turkey Legs and Gravy
- 3 onions, chopped
- 4 celery ribs, chopped
- 4 carrots, peeled and chopped
- 10 garlic cloves, crushed and peeled
- 3 tablespoons unsalted butter, melted, plus extra as needed
- 10 sprigs fresh thyme
- 10 sprigs fresh parsley
- 3 bay leaves
- 1 tablespoon black peppercorns
- 4 cups chicken broth
- 1 cup water
- 1 cup dry white wine
- 4 (1½- to 2-pound) turkey leg quarters, trimmed
- 3 tablespoons kosher salt
- ½ teaspoon pepper
- ½ cup all-purpose flour

Turkey Breasts
- 2 (5- to 6-pound) bone-in turkey breasts, trimmed
- 2 tablespoons plus 2 teaspoons kosher salt, divided
- 7 tablespoons unsalted butter, melted, divided

1. *For the turkey legs and gravy (up to 3 days ahead):* Adjust oven rack to lower-middle position and heat oven to 325 degrees. Toss onions, celery, carrots, garlic, melted butter, thyme sprigs, parsley sprigs, bay leaves, and peppercorns together in large roasting pan; spread into even layer. Place pan over medium heat and cook, stirring occasionally, until vegetables are softened and lightly browned and fond forms on bottom of pan, about 15 minutes. Add broth, water, and wine and bring to simmer, scraping up any browned bits. Remove pan from heat.

2. Cut leg quarters at joints into thighs and drumsticks, and sprinkle with salt and pepper. Place pieces skin side up in pan (braising liquid should come about three-quarters of way up legs and thighs). Place 12 by 16-inch piece of parchment paper over turkey pieces. Cover pan tightly with aluminum foil. Cook in oven until thighs register 170 degrees, 2½ to 3 hours. Remove pan from oven. Transfer turkey pieces to large, shallow container and let cool completely, about 1 hour. Once cool, cover and refrigerate.

3. Using spatula, scrape up any browned bits from bottom and sides of pan. Strain contents of pan through fine-mesh strainer set over large bowl, pressing on solids with spatula to extract as much liquid as possible; discard solids.

4. Transfer liquid to fat separator and let settle for 5 minutes. Reserve ½ cup plus 1 tablespoon fat (if there is not enough fat, add extra melted butter to make up difference) and 8 cups liquid; discard remaining liquid.

5. Heat reserved fat in large saucepan over medium-high heat. Add flour and cook, stirring constantly, until flour is medium golden brown and fragrant, about 5 minutes. Slowly whisk in reserved liquid and bring to boil. Reduce heat to medium-low and simmer, stirring occasionally, until gravy is thickened and reduced to 6 cups, 15 to 20 minutes. Off heat, season gravy with salt and pepper to taste. Transfer to large container and let cool completely, about 1 hour. (The legs and gravy can be prepared up to 3 days in advance and refrigerated.)

6. *For the turkey breasts (the day before):* Place breasts on cutting board skin side down. Using kitchen shears, cut through ribs, following vertical lines of fat where breasts meet backs, from tapered ends of breasts to wing joints. Using your hands, bend backs away from breasts to pop shoulder joints out of sockets. Using paring knife, cut through joints between bones to separate backs from breasts.

7. Flip breasts skin side up. Using your fingers, gently loosen skin covering each side of 1 breast. Peel back skin, leaving it attached at top and center. Rub 1 teaspoon salt onto each side of breast, then place skin back over meat. Rub 1 teaspoon salt onto underside of breast cavity. Repeat with second breast. Place breasts on rimmed baking sheet and refrigerate, uncovered, for 24 hours.

8. *Roast the breasts and reheat the dark meat and gravy (serving day):* Adjust oven rack to middle position and heat oven to 325 degrees. Measure out 20-inch piece of foil and roll into loose ball. Unroll foil, place on second rimmed baking sheet, and top with wire rack (crinkled foil will insulate bottom of sheet to keep it from smoking during roasting). Place breasts, skin side up, on prepared wire rack; brush with 4 tablespoons melted butter and sprinkle each whole breast with 1 teaspoon remaining salt. Roast until thickest part of breast registers 130 degrees, about 1½ hours.

9. Remove breasts from oven and increase oven temperature to 500 degrees. When oven reaches temperature, return breasts to oven and roast until skin is deeply browned and thickest part of breast registers 160 degrees, 20 to 30 minutes. Transfer to carving board and let rest, uncovered, for 30 minutes. Pour any juices from sheet into bowl and set aside.

10. Adjust oven rack to upper-middle position. Place thighs and drumsticks skin side up on now-empty wire rack set in sheet and brush with remaining 3 tablespoons melted butter. Place in oven and reheat until skin is well browned and thighs register 110 degrees, 18 to 22 minutes. Transfer thighs and drumsticks to large platter.

11. While thighs reheat, bring gravy to simmer in large saucepan over medium-low heat, whisking occasionally. Add any reserved juices from breasts and season with salt and pepper to taste. Cover and keep warm.

12. Carve breasts and transfer to platter with thighs and drumsticks. Serve, passing gravy separately.

Old-Fashioned Stuffed Turkey

Serves 10 to 12

WHY THIS RECIPE WORKS Perfecting one aspect of a roast turkey often comes at the cost of another. Crisp skin means dry white meat. Brining adds moisture, but can turn the skin soggy. And stuffing the cavity compounds the headache, slowing the roasting time and upping the chance for uneven cooking. We wanted a turkey with juicy meat, crisply burnished skin, and rich-flavored stuffing that cooked inside the bird. For the crispiest possible skin, we opted for salting over brining. Salting initially draws moisture out of the meat, but after a long rest (24 to 48 hours) in the refrigerator, all the moisture gets slowly drawn back in, seasoning the meat and helping it retain moisture. Next we turned to slow roasting and started the bird in a relatively low oven, then cranked the temperature to give it a final blast of skin-crisping heat and to bring the center up to temperature. It worked beautifully, yielding breast meat that was moist and tender. For even crispier skin, we massaged it with a baking powder and salt rub. The baking powder dehydrates the skin and raises its pH, making it more conducive to browning. We also poked holes in the skin to help rendered fat escape. And for extra flavor, we draped the bird with meaty salt pork, which we removed and drained before cranking up the heat so the bird didn't taste too smoky. To make sure the stuffing was cooked through, we started half of it in the bird (in a cheesecloth bag for easy removal) to give it meaty flavor, then combined it with the uncooked batch to finish baking while the turkey rested. Table salt is not recommended for this recipe because it is too fine. To roast a kosher or self-basting turkey (such as a frozen Butterball), do not salt it in step 1. Look for salt pork that is roughly equal parts fat and lean meat. Serve with Make-Ahead Turkey Gravy (recipe follows).

Turkey
- 1 (12- to 14-pound) turkey, giblets and neck reserved for gravy, if making
- 3 tablespoons plus 2 teaspoons kosher salt, divided
- 2 teaspoons baking powder
- 12 ounces salt pork, cut into ¼-inch-thick slices and rinsed

Stuffing
- 1½ pounds hearty white sandwich bread, cut into ½-inch pieces (about 12 cups)
- 4 tablespoons unsalted butter
- 1 onion, chopped fine
- 2 celery ribs, chopped fine
- 2 teaspoons kosher salt
- 1 teaspoon pepper
- 2 tablespoons finely chopped fresh thyme
- 1 tablespoon finely chopped fresh marjoram
- 1 tablespoon finely chopped fresh sage
- 1½ cups chicken broth, divided
- 1 (36-inch) square cheesecloth, folded in quarters
- 2 large eggs

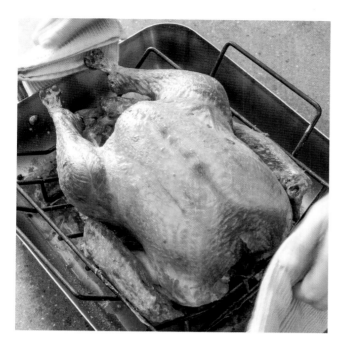

1. For the turkey: Using your fingers, gently loosen skin covering turkey breast, legs, thighs, and back; avoid breaking skin. Rub 1½ teaspoons salt under skin of each breast half, 1½ teaspoons salt under skin of each leg, and 1 tablespoon salt evenly inside cavity. Wrap turkey tightly with plastic wrap and refrigerate for 24 to 48 hours.

2. For the stuffing: Adjust oven rack to lowest position and heat oven to 250 degrees. Spread bread cubes in single layer on rimmed baking sheet; bake until edges have dried but centers are slightly moist (cubes should yield to pressure), about 45 minutes, stirring several times during baking. Transfer to large bowl and increase oven temperature to 325 degrees.

3. While bread dries, melt butter in 12-inch skillet over medium-high heat; add onion, celery, salt, and pepper; and cook, stirring occasionally, until vegetables begin to soften and brown slightly, 7 to 10 minutes. Stir in thyme, marjoram, and sage and cook until fragrant, about 1 minute. Add vegetables to bowl with dried bread; add 1 cup broth and toss until evenly moistened.

4. To roast the turkey: Combine remaining 2 teaspoons salt and baking powder in small bowl. Remove turkey from refrigerator and unwrap. Thoroughly dry turkey inside and out with paper towels. Using skewer, poke 15 to 20 holes in fat deposits on top of breast halves and thighs, 4 or 5 holes in each deposit. Sprinkle surface of turkey with salt–baking powder mixture and rub in mixture with your hands, coating skin evenly. Tuck wings underneath turkey. Line turkey cavity with cheesecloth, pack with 4 to 5 cups stuffing, and tie ends of cheesecloth together. Cover remaining stuffing with plastic wrap and refrigerate. Using kitchen twine, loosely tie turkey legs together. Place turkey breast side down in V-rack set in roasting pan and drape salt pork slices over back.

5. Roast turkey breast side down until breast registers 130 degrees, 2 to 2½ hours. Remove roasting pan from oven and increase oven temperature to 450 degrees. Transfer turkey in V-rack to rimmed baking sheet. Discard salt pork. Using potholders or kitchen towels, rotate turkey breast side up. Cut twine binding legs and remove stuffing bag; empty into reserved stuffing in bowl. Pour drippings from roasting pan into fat separator and reserve for gravy, if making.

6. Once oven has come to temperature, return turkey in V-rack to roasting pan and roast until skin is golden brown and crisp, breast registers 160 degrees, and thighs register 175 degrees, about 45 minutes, rotating pan halfway through roasting. Transfer turkey to carving board and let rest, uncovered, for 30 minutes.

7. While turkey rests, reduce oven temperature to 400 degrees. Whisk eggs and remaining ½ cup broth together in small bowl. Pour egg mixture over stuffing and toss to combine, breaking up any large pieces; spread in greased 13 by 9-inch baking dish. Bake until stuffing registers 165 degrees and top is golden brown, about 15 minutes. Carve turkey and serve with stuffing.

ACCOMPANIMENT
Make-Ahead Turkey Gravy
Makes about 2 quarts
Note that the optional roast turkey drippings may be quite salty—add them carefully to the gravy in step 4 so the gravy does not become too salty.

- 6 turkey thighs, trimmed, or 9 wings, separated at joints
- 2 carrots, chopped
- 2 celery ribs, chopped
- 2 onions, chopped
- 1 head garlic, halved
  Vegetable oil spray
- 10 cups chicken broth, plus extra as needed
- 2 cups dry white wine
- 12 sprigs fresh thyme
  Unsalted butter, as needed
- 1 cup all-purpose flour
  Defatted drippings from Old-Fashioned Stuffed Turkey (page 152; optional)

1. Adjust oven rack to middle position and heat oven to 450 degrees. Toss thighs, carrots, celery, onions, and garlic together in roasting pan and spray with vegetable oil spray. Roast, stirring occasionally, until well browned, 1½ to 1¾ hours.

2. Transfer contents of roasting pan to Dutch oven. Add broth, wine, and thyme sprigs and bring to boil, skimming as needed. Reduce to gentle simmer and cook until broth is brown and flavorful and measures about 8 cups when strained, about 1½ hours. Strain broth through fine-mesh strainer into large container, pressing on solids to extract as much liquid as possible; discard solids. (Turkey broth can be cooled and refrigerated in airtight container for up to 2 days or frozen for up to 1 month.)

3. Let strained turkey broth settle (if necessary) then spoon off and reserve ½ cup of fat that has risen to top (add butter as needed if short on turkey fat). Heat fat in Dutch oven over medium-high heat until bubbling. Whisk in flour and cook, whisking constantly, until well browned, 3 to 7 minutes.

4. Slowly whisk in turkey broth, scraping up any browned bits and smoothing out any lumps, and bring to boil. Reduce to simmer and cook until gravy is very thick, 10 to 15 minutes. (Gravy can be refrigerated for up to 2 days.) To serve, add defatted turkey drippings, if using, and reheat gently, adding additional chicken broth as needed to adjust consistency; season with salt and pepper to taste.

Braised Turkey

Serves 10 to 12

WHY THIS RECIPE WORKS Separating turkey into parts and braising it for the holiday meal? It may sound heretical if you've never presented anything but a whole roasted bird at the table, but this break from tradition has a lot going for it. Roasting a large turkey is always a race to get the denser, fattier thighs and legs to come up to the ideal temperature of around 175 degrees before the leaner, more delicate breast dries out, once its temperature climbs past 160 degrees. An intact, upright bird compounds this problem because the slower-cooking thighs are shielded from the heat. So we wondered if there was an easier way to get perfectly cooked turkey on the table without sacrificing flavor. Turkey parts provided a neat solution to the problem by giving both types of meat more even exposure to the heat—and without any cumbersome turning. Better yet, braising the pieces in a flavorful liquid created rich, ready-made gravy and infused the meat with all of its complex flavors. When we tasted this deeply flavored, moist and tender turkey, we found we didn't miss the traditional whole bird at all. Instead of drumsticks and thighs, you may use 2 whole leg quarters, 1½ to 2 pounds each. The recipe will also work with turkey breast alone; in step 1, reduce the amount of salt and sugar to ½ cup each, and the amount of water to 4 quarts. If you are braising kosher or self-basting turkey parts, skip the brining step, and instead season the turkey parts with 1½ teaspoons salt.

Braised Turkey
- 1 cup table salt, for brining
- 1 cup sugar, for brining
- 1 (5- to 7-pound) whole bone-in turkey breast, trimmed
- 4 pounds turkey drumsticks and thighs, trimmed
- 3 onions, chopped

- 3 celery ribs, chopped
- 2 carrots, peeled and chopped
- 6 garlic cloves, crushed and peeled
- 2 bay leaves
- 6 sprigs fresh thyme
- 6 sprigs fresh parsley
- ½ ounce dried porcini mushrooms, rinsed
- 4 tablespoons unsalted butter, melted, divided
- 4 cups chicken broth
- 1 cup dry white wine

Gravy
- 3 tablespoons all-purpose flour

1. *For the turkey:* Dissolve salt and sugar in 2 gallons cold water in large container. Submerge turkey pieces in brine, cover, and refrigerate for 3 to 6 hours.

2. Adjust oven rack to lower-middle position and heat oven to 500 degrees. Remove turkey pieces from brine and pat dry with paper towels. Toss onions, celery, carrots, garlic, bay leaves, thyme sprigs, parsley sprigs, porcini, and 2 tablespoons melted butter in large roasting pan; arrange in even layer. Brush turkey pieces with remaining 2 tablespoons melted butter and season with pepper. Place turkey pieces, skin side up, over vegetables, leaving at least ¼ inch between pieces. Roast until skin is lightly browned, about 20 minutes.

3. While turkey is roasting, bring broth and wine to simmer in medium saucepan over medium heat. Cover and keep warm.

4. Remove turkey from oven and reduce oven temperature to 325 degrees. Pour broth mixture around turkey pieces (it should come about three-quarters of way up legs and thighs). Place 12 by 16-inch piece of parchment paper over turkey pieces. Cover roasting pan tightly with aluminum foil. Return roasting pan to oven and cook until breast registers 160 degrees and thighs register 175 degrees, 1½ to 2 hours. Transfer turkey to carving board, tent with foil, and let rest for 20 minutes.

5. *For the gravy:* Strain vegetables and liquid from roasting pan through fine-mesh strainer set in large bowl. Press solids with back of spatula to extract as much liquid as possible; discard solids. Transfer liquid to fat separator and let settle for 5 minutes. Reserve 3 tablespoons fat and measure out 3 cups braising liquid (save any remaining liquid for another use).

6. Heat 3 tablespoons reserved turkey fat in medium saucepan over medium-high heat; add flour and cook, stirring constantly, until flour is dark golden brown and fragrant, about 5 minutes. Whisk in 3 cups braising liquid, smoothing out any lumps, and bring to boil. Reduce heat to medium-low and simmer, stirring occasionally, until gravy is thick and reduced to 2 cups, 15 to 20 minutes. Remove gravy from heat and season with salt and pepper to taste

7. Carve turkey and serve, passing gravy separately.

Braised Turkey

Beef

Cast Iron Thick-Cut Steaks with Herb Butter

Cast-Iron Thick-Cut Steaks
with Herb Butter

Cast-Iron Thick-Cut Steaks with Herb Butter

Serves 4

WHY THIS RECIPE WORKS We were looking for a way to make a steak with the ultimate crust entirely on the stovetop—so we turned to a cast-iron skillet, since its heat-retention properties are ideal for a perfect sear. We chose the moderately expensive boneless strip steak for its big, beefy flavor. The first step to a great sear was an evenly heated cooking surface, which we accomplished by preheating the cast-iron skillet in the oven. This also gave us time to prepare a zesty compound butter with shallot, garlic, parsley, and chives—and to let the steaks warm up to room temperature, which helped them cook more quickly and evenly. Salting the outside of the steaks while they rested pulled moisture from the steaks while also seasoning the meat, helping us get a better sear. After testing different flipping techniques and heat levels, we found that flipping the steaks every 2 minutes and transitioning from medium-high to medium-low heat partway through cooking resulted in a perfectly browned, crisp crust and a juicy, evenly cooked interior every time.

- 2 (1-pound) boneless strip steaks,
  1½ inches thick, trimmed
- 1 teaspoon plus pinch table salt, divided
- 4 tablespoons unsalted butter, softened
- 2 tablespoons minced shallot
- 1 tablespoon finely chopped fresh parsley
- 1 tablespoon finely chopped fresh chives
- 1 garlic clove, minced
- ¼ teaspoon pepper
- 2 tablespoons vegetable oil

1. Adjust oven rack to middle position, place 12-inch cast-iron skillet on rack, and heat oven to 500 degrees. Meanwhile, season steaks with 1 teaspoon salt and let sit at room temperature. Mix butter, shallot, parsley, chives, garlic, pepper, and remaining pinch of salt together in bowl; set aside until needed.

2. When oven reaches 500 degrees, pat steaks dry with paper towels and season with pepper. Using potholders, remove skillet from oven and place over medium-high heat; turn off oven. Being careful of hot skillet handle, add oil and heat until just smoking. Cook steaks, without moving, until lightly browned on first side, about 2 minutes. Flip steaks and continue to cook until lightly browned on second side, about 2 minutes.

3. Flip steaks, reduce heat to medium-low, and cook, flipping every 2 minutes, until steaks are well browned and meat registers 120 to 125 degrees (for medium-rare), 7 to 9 minutes.

Transfer steaks to cutting board, dollop 2 tablespoons herb butter on each steak, tent with aluminum foil, and let rest for 5 to 10 minutes. Slice steaks into ½-inch-thick slices and serve.

VARIATION
Cast-Iron Thick-Cut Steaks with Blue Cheese–Chive Butter
Omit shallot and parsley. Increase chives to 2 tablespoons and add ⅓ cup crumbled mild blue cheese to butter with chives.

Pan-Seared Thick-Cut Steaks

Serves 4

WHY THIS RECIPE WORKS A nicely charred thick-cut steak certainly looks appealing. But cutting into the steak to find that the rosy meat is confined to a measly spot in the center—with the rest a thick band of overcooked gray—is a great disappointment. We wanted to find a surefire method for pan-searing thick-cut steaks that could deliver both a flavorful crust and juicy, perfectly pink meat throughout. We found it was essential to sear the steaks quickly to keep the meat directly under the crust from turning gray. But we'd need to take an untraditional approach for these thick-cut steaks and sear them at the end of cooking, rather than at the beginning. We began by moving the steaks straight from the fridge into a 275-degree oven, which not only warmed them to 95 degrees but also dried the meat thoroughly—dry meat is essential for a well-browned crust. At this temperature, when the steak met the hot skillet, it developed a beautiful brown crust in less than four minutes, while the rest of the meat stayed pink, juicy, and tender. Rib-eye or filet mignon of similar thickness can be substituted for strip steaks. If using filet mignon, buying a 2-pound center-cut tenderloin roast and portioning it into four 8-ounce steaks yourself will produce more consistent results. If using filet mignon, increase the oven time by about 5 minutes. When cooking lean strip steaks (without an external fat cap) or filet mignon, add an extra tablespoon of oil to the pan. To serve the steaks with the Red Wine–Mushroom Pan Sauce (recipe follows), prepare all the sauce ingredients while the steaks are in the oven, and don't wash the skillet after cooking the steaks.

- 2 (1-pound) boneless strip steaks,
  each 1½ to 1¾ inches thick, trimmed
- 1 teaspoon table salt
- ½ teaspoon pepper
- 1 tablespoon vegetable oil

1. Adjust oven rack to middle position and heat oven to 275 degrees. Pat steaks dry with paper towels. Cut each steak in half vertically to create four 8-ounce steaks. Season steaks with salt and pepper; using your hands, gently shape into uniform thickness. Place steaks on wire rack set over a rimmed baking sheet; transfer baking sheet to oven. Cook until steaks register 90 to 95 degrees (for rare to medium-rare), 20 to 25 minutes, or 100 to 105 degrees (for medium), 25 to 30 minutes.

2. Heat oil in 12-inch skillet over high heat until smoking. Place steaks in skillet and sear until well browned and crusty, 1½ to 2 minutes, lifting once halfway through to redistribute fat underneath each steak. (Reduce heat if fond begins to burn.) Turn steaks and cook until well browned on second side, 2 to 2½ minutes. Transfer steaks to clean rack and reduce heat under pan to medium. Use tongs to stand 2 steaks on sides. Holding steaks together, return to skillet and sear on all edges until browned, about 1½ minutes. Repeat with remaining 2 steaks.

3. Return steaks to wire rack and let rest, tented with foil, for about 10 minutes. Serve.

ACCOMPANIMENTS

Red Wine–Mushroom Pan Sauce
Makes about 1 cup
Prepare all the ingredients for the pan sauce while the steaks are in the oven.

- 1 tablespoon vegetable oil
- 8 ounces white mushrooms, trimmed and sliced thin
- 1 small shallot, minced
- 1 cup dry red wine
- ½ cup chicken broth
- 1 tablespoon balsamic vinegar
- 1 teaspoon Dijon mustard
- 2 tablespoons cold unsalted butter, cut into 4 pieces
- 1 teaspoon finely chopped fresh thyme

After removing steaks from skillet, pour off fat from skillet. Heat oil over medium-high heat until just smoking. Add mushrooms and cook, stirring occasionally, until beginning to brown and liquid has evaporated, about 5 minutes. Add shallot and cook, stirring frequently, until beginning to soften, about 1 minute. Increase heat to high; add red wine and broth, loosening any browned bits. Simmer rapidly until liquid and mushrooms are reduced to 1 cup, about 6 minutes. Add vinegar, mustard, and any accumulated juices from steaks; cook until thickened, about 1 minute. Off heat, whisk in butter and thyme; season with salt and pepper to taste. Spoon sauce over steaks and serve immediately.

Thai Chili Butter
Makes about ⅓ cup
Prepare all the ingredients for the butter while the steaks are in the oven. If red curry paste isn't available, increase the chili-garlic sauce to 2½ teaspoons.

- 4 tablespoons unsalted butter, softened
- 1 tablespoon finely chopped fresh cilantro
- 2 teaspoons Asian chili-garlic sauce
- 1½ teaspoons thinly sliced scallion greens
- 1 small garlic clove, minced
- ½ teaspoon Thai red curry paste
- 2 teaspoons lime juice

Beat butter vigorously with spoon until soft and fluffy. Add cilantro, chili-garlic sauce, scallion, garlic, and red curry paste; beat to incorporate. Add lime juice a little at a time, beating vigorously between each addition until fully incorporated. Season with salt to taste. Spoon dollop over each steak, giving it time to melt before serving.

Searing Two Steaks at Once

Use tongs to sear sides of 2 steaks at once.

Pepper-Crusted Filet Mignon

Serves 4

WHY THIS RECIPE WORKS Filet mignon is ultratender, but it has only mild beefy flavor. Chefs often compensate by wrapping the delicate meat in bacon or puff pastry, serving it with rich wine sauces or flavored butter, or giving it a crust of cracked black peppercorns. We decided to pursue the peppercorn approach and found several problems to solve: The peppercorns tend to fall off in the pan, interfere with the meat's browning, and—when used in sufficient quantity to create a real crust—deliver punishing pungency. Our first step was to mellow the peppercorns' heat by gently simmering them in olive oil. We then created a well-browned and attractive pepper crust using a two-step process: First, we rubbed the raw steaks with a paste of the cooked cracked peppercorns, salt, and oil, then we pressed the paste into each steak by covering it with a sheet of plastic wrap. We let the steaks sit, covered, for an hour before cooking. The paste not only added flavor to the meat but drew out the meat's own beefy flavor. While the steaks sat wrapped and covered in paste, we had plenty of time to simmer a rich reduction

sauce—though a flavored butter also made an excellent accompaniment. If you prefer a very mild pepper flavor, drain the cooled peppercorns in a fine-mesh strainer in step 1, toss them with 5 tablespoons of fresh oil, add the salt, and proceed. Serve with Port-Cherry Reduction or Blue Cheese–Chive Butter (recipes follow).

- 5 tablespoons black peppercorns, cracked
- 5 tablespoons plus 2 teaspoons extra-virgin olive oil, divided
- 1½ teaspoons table salt
- 4 (7- to 8-ounce) center-cut filets mignons, 1½ to 2 inches thick, trimmed

1. Heat peppercorns and 5 tablespoons oil in small saucepan over low heat until faint bubbles appear. Continue to cook at bare simmer, swirling pan occasionally, until pepper is fragrant, 7 to 10 minutes. Remove from heat and set aside to cool. When mixture is room temperature, add salt and stir to combine. Pat steaks dry with paper towels and rub steaks with pepper mixture, thoroughly coating top and bottom of each steak with peppercorns. Cover steaks with plastic wrap and press gently to make sure peppercorns adhere; let sit at room temperature for 1 hour.

2. Meanwhile, adjust oven rack to middle position, place rimmed baking sheet on oven rack, and heat oven to 450 degrees. Heat remaining 2 teaspoons oil in 12-inch skillet over medium-high heat until just smoking. Add steaks and cook, without moving, until dark brown crust forms, 3 to 4 minutes. Turn steaks and cook until well browned on second side, about 3 minutes. Remove pan from heat and transfer steaks to hot baking sheet. Roast until steaks register 120 degrees (for rare), 3 to 5 minutes, 125 degrees (for medium-rare), 5 to 7 minutes, or 130 degrees (for medium), 7 to 9 minutes. Transfer steaks to wire rack and let rest, tented with foil, for about 10 minutes before serving.

ACCOMPANIMENTS

Port-Cherry Reduction
Makes about 1 cup

- 1½ cups port
- ½ cup balsamic vinegar
- ½ cup dried tart cherries
- 1 large shallot, minced
- 2 sprigs fresh thyme
- 1 tablespoon unsalted butter

1. Combine port, vinegar, cherries, shallot, and thyme sprigs in medium saucepan; simmer over medium-low heat until liquid is reduced to ⅓ cup, about 30 minutes. Set aside, covered.

2. While steaks are resting, reheat sauce. Off heat, remove thyme sprigs, then whisk in butter until melted. Season with salt to taste.

Blue Cheese–Chive Butter
Makes about ½ cup

- 3 tablespoons unsalted butter, softened
- ⅓ cup crumbled mild blue cheese, at room temperature
- ⅛ teaspoon table salt
- 2 tablespoons minced fresh chives

Combine the butter, cheese, and salt in a medium bowl and mix with a stiff rubber spatula until smooth. Fold in the chives. While the steaks are resting, spoon 1 to 2 tablespoons of the butter on each one.

Steak Frites

Serves 4

WHY THIS RECIPE WORKS This recipe re-creates the steak frites of our Parisian dreams, with perfectly cooked steak and fries that are fluffy on the inside and crisp on the outside. For our fries, we liked high-starch russet potatoes and found that double-cooking, or a low-temperature "blanch" in oil followed by a high-temperature "fry," yielded the crispiest exterior and fluffiest interior. Cooking multiple small batches of fries ensured that the oil's temperature wouldn't plunge too much. Soaking the potatoes in cold water before they were cooked further improved their crispiness, and a "rest" between the first and second frying allowed the fries to develop a thin coating of starch, which even further improved their crispiness. Tossing them with additional starch—in the form of cornstarch—made them perfect. In France, steak frites is usually prepared with a cut called entrecôte (literally, "between the ribs"), which is a French cut you won't find in the States, but is actually quite similar to our rib-eye steak.

Choosing the right size—or cutting them to fit—meant we could sear four steaks at once in a large skillet. Capped with a quick herb butter, the steaks tasted just like the bistro classic. Make sure to dry the potatoes well before tossing them with the cornstarch. For safety, use a Dutch oven with a capacity of at least 7 quarts. Use refined peanut oil (such as Planters) to fry the potatoes, not toasted peanut oil. A 12-inch skillet is essential for cooking four steaks at once. The recipe can be prepared through step 4 up to 2 hours in advance; shut off the heat under the oil, turning the heat back to medium when you start step 6. The ingredients can be halved to serve two—keep the oil amount the same and forgo blanching and frying the potatoes in batches.

Herb Butter

- 4 tablespoons unsalted butter, softened
- ½ shallot, minced
- 1 tablespoon finely chopped fresh parsley
- 1 tablespoon finely chopped fresh chives
- 1 garlic clove, minced
- ¼ teaspoon table salt
- ¼ teaspoon pepper

Steak and Potatoes

- 2½ pounds russet potatoes, sides squared off, cut lengthwise into ¼ by ¼-inch fries
- 2 tablespoons cornstarch
- 3 quarts peanut oil
- 1 tablespoon vegetable oil
- 2 (1-pound) boneless rib-eye steaks, trimmed and cut in half
- 1 teaspoon table salt
- ½ teaspoon pepper

1. *For the butter:* Combine all ingredients in medium bowl; set aside.

2. *For the potatoes:* Rinse cut potatoes in large bowl under cold running water until water turns clear. Cover with cold water and refrigerate at least 30 minutes or up to 12 hours.

3. Pour off water, spread potatoes onto clean kitchen towels, and thoroughly dry. Transfer potatoes to large bowl and toss with cornstarch until evenly coated. Transfer potatoes to wire rack set in rimmed baking sheet and let rest until fine white coating forms, about 20 minutes.

4. Meanwhile, heat peanut oil over medium heat to 325 degrees in large Dutch oven.

5. Add half of potatoes, a handful at a time, to hot oil and increase heat to high. Fry, stirring with mesh spider or slotted spoon, until potatoes start to turn from white to blond,

4 to 5 minutes. (Oil temperature will drop about 75 degrees during frying.) Transfer fries to thick paper bag or paper towels. Return oil to 325 degrees and repeat with remaining potatoes. Reduce heat to medium and let fries cool while cooking steaks, at least 10 minutes.

6. *For the steak:* Heat vegetable oil in 12-inch skillet over medium-high heat until smoking. Meanwhile, season steaks with salt and pepper. Lay steaks in pan, leaving ¼ inch between them. Cook, without moving steaks, until well browned, about 4 minutes. Flip steaks and continue to cook until steaks register 120 degrees (for rare to medium-rare), 3 to 7 minutes. Transfer steaks to large plate, top with herb butter, and tent with foil; let rest while finishing fries.

7. Increase heat under Dutch oven to high and heat oil to 375 degrees. Add half of fries, a handful at a time, and fry until golden brown and puffed, 2 to 3 minutes. Transfer to thick paper bag or paper towels. Return oil to 375 degrees and repeat with remaining fries. Season fries with salt to taste and serve immediately with steaks.

Glazed All-Beef Meatloaf

Serves 6 to 8

WHY THIS RECIPE WORKS Every all-beef meatloaf we've tasted has had the same problems—chewy texture and uninteresting flavor, making it more of a hamburger in the shape of a log than bona fide meatloaf. In the past, when we wanted a great meatloaf, we turned to a traditional meatloaf mix consisting of beef, pork, and veal. Could we create an all-beef meatloaf to compete with this classic? Supermarkets offer a wide selection of ground beef, and after testing them alone and in combination we determined that equal parts of chuck (for moisture) and sirloin (for beefy flavor) were best. Beef has a livery taste that we wanted to subdue, and the usual dairy additions to meatloaf didn't work. Chicken broth, oddly enough, neutralized this off-flavor and provided moisture. For additional moisture and richness, we included mild-tasting Monterey Jack cheese, which also helped bind the mixture. To avoid pockets of oozing hot cheese in the meatloaf, we shredded the cheese and froze it briefly. Crushed saltines, our choice for the starchy filler, provided texture, but we felt our meatloaf needed more "sliceability." Surprisingly, gelatin gave us just the smooth, luxurious texture we sought. We seasoned the mixture with onion, celery, garlic (all sautéed), thyme, paprika, soy sauce, and mustard. A traditional ketchup glaze crowned our flavorful all-beef meatloaf. If you can't find chuck and/or sirloin, substitute 85 percent lean ground beef.

Meatloaf

   3 ounces Monterey Jack cheese, shredded on
       small holes of box grater (1 cup)
   1 tablespoon unsalted butter
   1 onion, chopped fine
   1 celery rib, chopped fine
   2 teaspoons finely chopped fresh thyme
   1 teaspoon paprika
   1 garlic clove, minced
  ¼ cup tomato juice
  ½ cup chicken broth
   2 large eggs
  ½ teaspoon unflavored gelatin
  ⅔ cup crushed saltines
   2 tablespoons finely chopped fresh parsley
   1 tablespoon soy sauce
   1 teaspoon Dijon mustard
  ¾ teaspoon table salt
  ½ teaspoon pepper
   1 pound 90 percent lean ground sirloin
   1 pound 80 percent lean ground chuck

Glaze

  ½ cup ketchup
  ¼ cup cider vinegar
   3 tablespoons packed light brown sugar
   1 teaspoon hot sauce
  ½ teaspoon ground coriander

1. *For the meatloaf:* Adjust oven rack to middle position and heat oven to 375 degrees. Spread Monterey Jack on plate and place in freezer until ready to use. Set wire rack in rimmed baking sheet. Fold sheet of aluminum foil to form 10 by 6-inch rectangle. Center foil on rack and poke holes in foil with skewer (about ½ inch apart). Spray foil with vegetable oil spray.

2. Melt butter in 10-inch skillet over medium-high heat; add onion and celery and cook, stirring occasionally, until beginning to brown, 6 to 8 minutes. Add thyme, paprika, and garlic and cook, stirring, until fragrant, about 1 minute. Reduce heat to low and add tomato juice. Cook, scraping up any browned bits, until thickened, about 1 minute. Transfer mixture to small bowl and set aside to cool.

3. Whisk broth and eggs together in large bowl until combined. Sprinkle gelatin over liquid and let sit for 5 minutes. Stir in saltines, parsley, soy sauce, mustard, salt, pepper, and onion mixture. Crumble frozen cheese into coarse powder and sprinkle over mixture. Add sirloin and chuck; mix gently with your hands until thoroughly combined, about 1 minute. Transfer meat to foil rectangle and shape into 10 by 6-inch oval about 2 inches high. Smooth top and edges of meatloaf with moistened spatula. Bake until loaf registers 135 to 140 degrees, 55 minutes to 1 hour 5 minutes. Remove meatloaf from oven and turn on broiler.

4. *For the glaze:* While meatloaf cooks, combine glaze ingredients in small saucepan; bring to simmer over medium heat and cook, stirring, until thick and syrupy, about 5 minutes. Spread half of glaze evenly over cooked meatloaf with rubber spatula; place under broiler and cook until glaze bubbles and begins to brown at edges, about 5 minutes. Remove meatloaf from oven and spread evenly with remaining glaze; place back under broiler and cook until glaze is again bubbling and beginning to brown, about 5 minutes. Let meatloaf cool for about 20 minutes before slicing.

Making a Free-Form Loaf Pan

1. Set wire rack in rimmed baking sheet and top with 10 by 6-inch rectangle of aluminum foil.

2. Using skewer, poke holes in foil, spacing them about half an inch apart.

Juicy Pub-Style Burgers

Serves 4

WHY THIS RECIPE WORKS Few things are as satisfying as a thick, juicy pub-style burger that is evenly rosy from center to edge. Grinding our own meat in the food processor was a must (freezing the meat until just firm helped the processor chop it cleanly), and we found that sirloin steak tips were ideal. To give the burgers just enough structure, we cut the meat into small ½-inch chunks before grinding and lightly packed the meat into patties. Melted butter improved their flavor and juiciness. Transferring the burgers from the stovetop to the oven to finish cooking eliminated the overcooked gray zone. For extra appeal, we came up with flavorful topping combinations to finish off our burgers. Sirloin steak tips are also labeled as "flap meat." When stirring the butter and pepper into the ground meat and shaping the patties, take care not to overwork the meat or the burgers will become dense. For the best flavor, season the burgers aggressively just before cooking. The uncooked patties can be refrigerated for up to one day. Serve with Pub-Style Burger Sauce (recipe follows), if desired.

- 2 pounds sirloin steak tips or boneless beef short ribs, trimmed and cut into ½-inch pieces
- 4 tablespoons unsalted butter, melted and cooled slightly
- 1½ teaspoons pepper, divided
- 1 teaspoon table salt
- 1 teaspoon vegetable oil
- 4 large hamburger buns, toasted and buttered

1. Place beef on baking sheet in single layer. Freeze meat until very firm and starting to harden around edges but still pliable, 15 to 25 minutes.

2. Place one-quarter of meat in food processor and pulse until finely ground into 1/16-inch pieces, about 35 pulses, stopping and redistributing meat around bowl as necessary to ensure beef is evenly ground. Transfer meat to baking sheet by overturning processor bowl and without directly touching meat. Repeat grinding with remaining 3 batches of meat. Spread meat over sheet and inspect carefully, discarding any long strands of gristle or large pieces of hard meat or fat.

3. Adjust oven rack to middle position and heat oven to 300 degrees. Drizzle melted butter over ground meat and add 1 teaspoon pepper. Gently toss with fork to combine. Divide meat into 4 lightly packed balls. Gently flatten into patties ¾ inch thick and about 4½ inches in diameter. Refrigerate patties until ready to cook.

4. Season patties with salt and remaining ½ teaspoon pepper. Heat oil in 12-inch skillet over high heat until just smoking. Using spatula, transfer burgers to skillet and cook without moving for 2 minutes. Using spatula, flip burgers over and cook for 2 minutes. Transfer patties to rimmed baking sheet and bake until burgers register 125 degrees (for medium-rare), 3 to 5 minutes.

5. Transfer burgers to plate and let rest for 5 minutes. Transfer to buns, and serve.

ACCOMPANIMENT
Pub-Style Burger Sauce
Makes about 1 cup, enough to top 4 burgers

- ¾ cup mayonnaise
- 2 tablespoons soy sauce
- 1 tablespoon packed dark brown sugar
- 1 tablespoon Worcestershire sauce
- 1 tablespoon finely chopped fresh chives
- 1 garlic clove, minced
- ¾ teaspoon pepper

Whisk all ingredients together in bowl.

VARIATIONS
Juicy Pub-Style Burgers with Crispy Shallots and Blue Cheese

Heat ½ cup vegetable oil and 3 thinly sliced shallots in medium saucepan over high heat; cook, stirring frequently, until shallots are golden, about 8 minutes. Using slotted spoon, transfer shallots to paper towel–lined plate, season with table salt, and let drain until crisp, about 5 minutes. (Cooled shallots can be stored at room temperature in airtight container for up to 3 days.) In step 4, top each burger with 1 ounce crumbled blue cheese before transferring to oven. Top with crispy shallots just before serving.

Juicy Pub-Style Burgers with Peppered Bacon and Aged Cheddar

Adjust oven rack to middle position and heat oven to 375 degrees. Arrange 6 bacon slices on rimmed baking sheet and sprinkle with 2 teaspoons coarsely ground pepper. Place second rimmed baking sheet on top of bacon and bake until bacon is crisp, 15 to 20 minutes. Transfer bacon to paper towel–lined plate and cool. Cut bacon in half crosswise. In step 4, top each burger with 1 ounce grated aged cheddar cheese before transferring to oven. Top with bacon just before serving.

Juicy Pub-Style Burgers with Sautéed Onions and Smoked Cheddar

Heat 2 tablespoons vegetable oil in 12-inch skillet over medium-high heat until just smoking. Add 1 thinly sliced onion and ¼ teaspoon table salt; cook, stirring frequently, until

softened and lightly browned, 5 to 7 minutes. In step 4, top each burger with 1 ounce grated smoked cheddar cheese before transferring to oven. Top with onion just before serving.

Juicy Pub-Style Burgers with Pan-Roasted Mushrooms and Gruyère

Heat 2 tablespoons vegetable oil in 12-inch skillet over medium-high heat until just smoking. Add 10 ounces thinly sliced cremini mushrooms, ¼ teaspoon table salt, and ¼ teaspoon pepper; cook, stirring frequently, until browned, 5 to 7 minutes. Add 1 minced shallot and 2 teaspoons minced thyme and cook until fragrant. Remove skillet from heat and stir in 2 tablespoons dry sherry. In step 4, top each burger with 1 ounce grated Gruyère cheese before transferring to oven. Top with mushrooms just before serving.

Classic Sloppy Joes

SEASON 20 RECIPE

Serves 4

WHY THIS RECIPE WORKS This recipe is equally loved by adults and children and will earn Sloppy Joes a regular slot in your weeknight meal rotation. Our main objective was to develop a recipe with a more balanced, less sweet flavor and much less greasy meat. We found that treating the ground beef with baking soda (so that it retained more moisture when cooked) and then breaking it down to a fine, uniform texture in the skillet delivered a tender, flavorful, and cohesive mixture that stayed put when placed on a bun. Limiting the aromatics to just onion (also treated with baking soda to soften it) made for a beefier-tasting mixture with a rich, luxurious texture. We made ketchup's sweet-tangy flavor more complex by adding vinegar, red pepper flakes, and sugar and balanced it out with generous amounts of tomato paste, paprika, and Worcestershire sauce. Finally, we served it all up on soft hamburger buns. Tossing the beef with baking soda in step 1 helps keep it tender and juicy; adding baking soda to the skillet with the onion in step 2 helps the onion break down. You may substitute 90 percent lean ground beef in this recipe, but the cooked mixture will be a bit less tender. Serve the Sloppy Joes with pickle chips, if desired

- 2 tablespoons water, divided
- ½ teaspoon plus ⅛ teaspoon baking soda, divided
- 1 pound 85 percent lean ground beef
- ½ teaspoon plus ⅛ teaspoon table salt, divided
- 2 teaspoons vegetable oil
- ½ onion, chopped fine
- 2 garlic cloves, minced
- 2 teaspoons packed brown sugar, plus extra for seasoning
- 2 teaspoons paprika
- ¼ teaspoon red pepper flakes

- ¼ cup tomato paste
- ⅓ cup ketchup
- 1 tablespoon red wine vinegar, plus extra for seasoning
- 1 tablespoon Worcestershire sauce
- ½ teaspoon cornstarch
- 4 hamburger buns

1. Combine 1 tablespoon water and ½ teaspoon baking soda in small bowl. In large bowl, toss beef with baking soda mixture and ½ teaspoon salt until thoroughly combined. Set aside.

2. Heat oil in 12-inch nonstick skillet over medium heat until shimmering. Add onion and remaining ⅛ teaspoon baking soda and stir to coat. Cook, stirring occasionally, until onion is softened, 3 to 4 minutes. Add garlic and cook, stirring constantly, until fragrant, about 30 seconds. Stir in sugar, paprika, pepper flakes, and remaining ⅛ teaspoon salt and cook, stirring constantly, until paprika is fragrant, about 1 minute. Add tomato paste and cook, stirring constantly, until paste is rust-colored, 3 to 4 minutes.

3. Add beef and cook, breaking up meat with wooden spoon, until beef is no longer pink, about 5 minutes. Mash beef with potato masher until fine-textured, about 1 minute. Add ketchup, vinegar, and Worcestershire and stir to combine, scraping up any browned bits.

4. Combine cornstarch and remaining 1 tablespoon water in small bowl, then pour cornstarch mixture over beef and stir to incorporate. Cook, stirring constantly, until sauce thickens and coats beef, about 1 minute. Season with salt, extra sugar, and extra vinegar to taste. Spoon beef mixture onto buns and serve.

Steak Tacos

Serves 4 to 6

WHY THIS RECIPE WORKS Upscale steak tacos usually get their rich, beefy flavor from the grill, but cooking outdoors isn't always possible. We wanted an indoor cooking method that would always yield steak taco meat as tender, juicy, and rich-tasting as the grilled method. We didn't want to wrap a pricey cut of beef in a taco, so we explored inexpensive cuts and chose flank steak for its good flavor and ready availability; when sliced against the grain, it can be just as tender as more expensive cuts. To add flavor, we poked holes in the meat with a fork and rubbed it with a paste of oil, cilantro, jalapeño, garlic, and scallions; salt helped draw all the flavors into the steak and ensured juiciness. Pan searing, with a sprinkling of sugar to enhance browning, gave us a crust that mimicked the char of the grill. To maximize this effect, we cut the steak into four long pieces, which gave us more sides to brown and turn crispy. For additional flavor, we tossed the cooked steak with some marinade that we had reserved and garnished the tacos simply with onion, cilantro, and lime wedges. In Mexico, steak tacos are often served with *curtido*, a relish of pickled vegetables; we devised a quick recipe for pickled onions to accompany our good-as-grilled steak tacos. Our preferred method for warming tortillas is to place each one over the medium flame of a gas burner until slightly charred, about 30 seconds per side. We also like toasting them in a dry skillet over medium-high heat until softened and speckled with brown spots, 20 to 30 seconds per side. For a less spicy dish, remove some or all of the ribs from the jalapeños before chopping them for the marinade. In addition to the toppings suggested in the recipe, try serving the tacos with Sweet and Spicy Pickled Onion (recipe follows), thinly sliced radish or cucumber, or salsa.

Herb Paste
- ½ cup packed fresh cilantro leaves
- 3 scallions, chopped
- 1 jalapeño chile, stemmed, seeded, and chopped
- 3 garlic cloves, chopped
- ½ teaspoon ground cumin
- ¼ cup vegetable oil
- 1 tablespoon lime juice

Steak
- 1 (1½- to 1¾-pound) flank steak, trimmed and cut lengthwise (with grain) into 4 equal pieces
- 1½ teaspoons table salt
- ½ teaspoon sugar
- ½ teaspoon pepper
- 2 tablespoons vegetable oil

Tacos
- 12 (6-inch) corn tortillas, warmed
- Fresh cilantro leaves
- Finely chopped white onion
- Lime wedges

1. *For the herb paste:* Pulse cilantro, scallions, jalapeño, garlic, and cumin in food processor until finely chopped, 10 to 12 pulses, scraping down sides as necessary. Add oil and process until mixture is smooth and resembles pesto, about 15 seconds. Transfer 2 tablespoons herb paste to bowl and whisk in lime juice; set aside for serving.

2. *For the steak:* Using dinner fork, poke each piece of steak 10 to 12 times on each side. Place in large baking dish, rub all sides of steak with salt, then coat with remaining herb paste. Cover with plastic wrap and refrigerate for at least 30 minutes.

3. Scrape herb paste off steak and sprinkle all sides of pieces evenly with sugar and pepper. Heat oil in 12-inch nonstick skillet over medium-high heat until just smoking. Place steak in skillet and cook until well browned, about 3 minutes. Flip steak and sear until second side is well browned, 2 to 3 minutes. Using tongs, stand each piece on cut side and cook, turning as necessary, until all cut sides are well browned and meat registers 125 to 130 degrees, 2 to 7 minutes. Transfer steak to cutting board and let rest for 5 minutes.

4. *For the tacos:* Using sharp chef's knife or carving knife, slice steak pieces against grain into ⅛-inch-thick pieces. Transfer sliced steak to bowl with herb paste–lime juice mixture and toss to coat. Season with salt to taste. Spoon small amount of sliced steak into center of each warm tortilla and serve immediately, passing toppings separately.

ACCOMPANIMENT
Sweet and Spicy Pickled Onion
Makes about 2 cups
The onion can be refrigerated, tightly covered, for up to 1 week.

- 1 red onion, halved and sliced thin
- 1 cup red wine vinegar
- ⅓ cup sugar
- 2 jalapeño chiles, stemmed, seeded, and cut into thin rings
- ¼ teaspoon table salt

Place onion in medium bowl. Bring vinegar, sugar, jalapeños, and salt to simmer in small saucepan over medium-high heat, stirring occasionally, until sugar dissolves. Pour vinegar mixture over onion, cover loosely, and let cool to room temperature, about 30 minutes. Once cool, drain and discard liquid.

Shredded Beef Tacos

Serves 6 to 8

WHY THIS RECIPE WORKS The Mexican taco filling called *carne deshebrada* (shredded meat) is made by braising a large cut of beef (usually brisket, chuck roast, or even flank or skirt steak) until ultratender and then shredding the meat and tossing it with a red or green sauce. We wanted an at-home version, made with a robust *rojo* (red) sauce. Traditionally, the beef is cooked in water, which is then discarded—along with a lot of beefy flavor. Instead, we put the braising liquid to use in the sauce. Having it pull double duty not only ensured more flavor but also streamlined the recipe. We started by swapping out the water for a bright combination of beer and cider vinegar and swapping the large roast for meaty short ribs, cut into cubes to reduce the cooking time. To skip the extra step of browning the meat in batches, we propped up the cubes on slices of onion, which allowed the meat to brown in the ambient heat, contributing deep, meaty flavor to the sauce. Tomato paste lent savory depth, and dried ancho chiles gave it a smoky, spicy kick. Ground cumin, cinnamon, and cloves provided a warm, earthy backbone. We pureed the sauce for a silky, unctuous texture that incorporated into the shredded meat seamlessly. For a bright, fresh topping for our tacos, we made a quick *curtido*, a cabbage slaw from El Salvador. Marinating the shredded vegetables, onion, and jalapeño in a fruity cider vinegar–based pickling liquid gave them just the right amount of punch. A sprinkling of crumbled *queso fresco* introduced the right salty, creamy finish to the tacos. Use a full-bodied lager or ale such as Dos Equis or Sierra Nevada. If you can't find queso fresco, substitute feta. If your Dutch oven does not have a tight-fitting lid, cover the pot tightly with a sheet of heavy-duty aluminum foil and then replace the lid. To warm the tortillas, place them on a plate, cover them with a damp dish towel, and microwave them for 60 to 90 seconds. The shredded beef also makes a great filling for empanadas, tamales, and chiles rellenos.

Beef

- 1½ cups beer
- ½ cup cider vinegar
- 2 ounces (4 to 6) dried ancho chiles, stemmed, seeded, and torn into 1-inch pieces
- 2 tablespoons tomato paste
- 6 garlic cloves, lightly crushed and peeled
- 3 bay leaves
- 2 teaspoons ground cumin
- 2 teaspoons dried oregano
- 2 teaspoons table salt
- ½ teaspoon pepper
- ½ teaspoon ground cloves
- ½ teaspoon ground cinnamon
- 1 large onion, sliced into ½-inch-thick rounds
- 3 pounds boneless beef short ribs, trimmed and cut into 2-inch pieces

Cabbage-Carrot Slaw

- 1 cup cider vinegar
- ½ cup water
- 1 tablespoon sugar
- 1½ teaspoons table salt
- ½ head green cabbage, cored and sliced thin (6 cups)
- 1 onion, sliced thin
- 1 large carrot, peeled and shredded
- 1 jalapeño chile, stemmed, seeded, and minced
- 1 teaspoon dried oregano
- 1 cup chopped fresh cilantro

- 18 (6-inch) corn tortillas, warmed
- 4 ounces queso fresco, crumbled (1 cup)
  Lime wedges

1. *For the beef:* Adjust oven rack to lower-middle position and heat oven to 325 degrees. Combine beer, vinegar, anchos, tomato paste, garlic, bay leaves, cumin, oregano, salt, pepper, cloves, and cinnamon in Dutch oven. Arrange onion rounds in single layer on bottom of pot. Place beef on top of onion rounds in single layer. Cover and cook until meat is well browned and tender, 2½ to 3 hours.

2. *For the cabbage-carrot slaw:* While beef cooks, whisk vinegar, water, sugar, and salt in large bowl until sugar is dissolved. Add cabbage, onion, carrot, jalapeño, and oregano and toss to combine. Cover and refrigerate for at least 1 hour or up to 24 hours. Drain slaw and stir in cilantro right before serving.

3. Using slotted spoon, transfer beef to large bowl, cover loosely with aluminum foil, and set aside. Strain liquid through fine-mesh strainer into 2-cup liquid measuring cup (do not wash pot). Discard onion rounds and bay leaves. Transfer remaining solids to blender. Let strained liquid settle for 5 minutes, then skim any fat off surface. Add water as needed to equal 1 cup. Pour liquid in blender with reserved solids and blend until smooth, about 2 minutes. Transfer sauce to now-empty pot.

4. Using 2 forks, shred beef into bite-size pieces. Bring sauce to simmer over medium heat. Add shredded beef and stir to coat. Season with salt to taste. (Beef can be refrigerated for up to 2 days; gently reheat before serving.)

5. Spoon small amount of beef into each warm tortilla and serve, passing slaw, queso fresco, and lime wedges separately.

"Taco Tuesday is an actual thing at my house, and we even own dinosaur-shaped taco holders to help us enjoy the meal. We change up the taco filling weekly, depending on our moods or what's in the fridge, but this recipe for shredded beef is my personal favorite. I love the tender texture of the braised short ribs and the unique sauce flavored with ancho chiles, cloves, and cinnamon. My daughter, Marta, doesn't like spicy food, so I often reduce the amount of ancho slightly and pull out a selection of hot sauces for serving instead. Also, I love the ease of putting the dish together— just combine all the ingredients in the pot and let it cook in the oven. And if there are any leftovers (which is a big 'if'), try reheating the filling with a fried egg on top—it's the breakfast of champions."

–*Julia*

Ground Beef and Cheese Enchiladas

Serves 4 to 6

WHY THIS RECIPE WORKS Say goodbye to the enchiladas you thought you knew. Techniques from both sides of the border produce a quicker, but still deeply flavorful, take on this Tex-Mex staple. This recipe works by elevating a plain Tex-Mex ground beef filling with melted cheese and spices to give it a richness reminiscent of long-braised beef. When crafting the enchilada sauce, we used whole dried chiles for an authentic, deeper, and more complex flavor than can be achieved when using commercial chili powder. Brushing the tortillas lightly with oil and briefly baking them helped water-proof them so that they didn't get soggy when baked in the enchilada sauce. Fresh herbs and a spritz of lime brightened the dish and provided balance for the rich, cheesy filling. Do not use ground beef that's fattier than 90 percent lean or the dish will be greasy.

Sauce

1½	ounces (3 to 4) dried ancho chiles, stemmed, seeded, and torn into 1-inch pieces
2	cups beef broth
1	tablespoon minced canned chipotle chile in adobo sauce
2	tablespoons vegetable oil
2	onions, chopped fine
6	garlic cloves, minced
¼	cup tomato paste
1	teaspoon ground cumin

Enchiladas

3	tablespoons vegetable oil, divided
1	pound 90 percent lean ground beef
1	teaspoon ground cumin
1	teaspoon ground coriander
½	teaspoon table salt
8	ounces Monterey Jack cheese, shredded (2 cups), divided
4	tablespoons minced fresh cilantro, divided
12	6-inch corn tortillas
2	scallions, sliced thin on bias
	Sour cream
	Lime wedges

1. *For the sauce:* Adjust oven rack to middle position and heat oven to 400 degrees. Heat anchos in 12-inch nonstick skillet over medium-high heat, stirring frequently, until fragrant, 2 to 3 minutes. Transfer anchos to bowl, add broth, and microwave, covered, until steaming, about 2 minutes. Let sit until softened, about 5 minutes. Transfer anchos and broth to blender and add chipotle.

2. Heat oil in now-empty skillet over medium heat until shimmering. Add onions and cook, stirring occasionally, until translucent, about 5 minutes. Add garlic and cook until fragrant, about 1 minute. Transfer half of onion mixture to large bowl and set aside. Return skillet with remaining onion mixture to medium heat and add tomato paste and cumin. Cook, stirring frequently, until tomato paste starts to darken, 3 to 5 minutes. Transfer onion mixture in skillet to blender with ancho mixture and process until smooth, about 1 minute. Season sauce with salt to taste.

3. *For the enchiladas:* Heat 1 tablespoon oil in now-empty skillet over medium heat until shimmering. Add beef, cumin, coriander, and salt and cook for 2 minutes, breaking meat into ¼-inch pieces with wooden spoon. Add reserved onion mixture (do not wash bowl) and continue to cook until beef is no longer pink, 3 to 4 minutes. Return beef mixture to bowl; add 1½ cups Monterey Jack, 2 tablespoons cilantro, and ¼ cup sauce and stir to combine. Season with salt to taste.

4. Spread ½ cup sauce over bottom of 13 by 9-inch baking dish. Brush both sides of tortillas with remaining 2 tablespoons oil. Arrange tortillas, overlapping, on rimmed baking sheet and bake until warm and pliable, about 5 minutes. Spread ¼ cup filling down center of each tortilla. Roll each tortilla tightly around filling and place seam side down in dish, arranging enchiladas in 2 rows across width of dish.

5. Spread remaining sauce over top of enchiladas. Sprinkle with remaining ½ cup Monterey Jack. Bake until cheese is lightly browned and sauce is bubbling at edges, about 15 minutes. Let cool for 10 minutes. Sprinkle with scallions and remaining 2 tablespoons cilantro. Serve, passing sour cream and lime wedges separately.

Old-Fashioned Pot Roast

Serves 6 to 8

WHY THIS RECIPE WORKS Pot roast can be boring and bland, full of dry, stringy meat, stubborn bits of fat, and wan gravy. We wanted a meltingly tender roast sauced in savory, full-bodied gravy. To start, we separated the roast into two lobes, which allowed us to remove the knobs of fat that stubbornly refused to render and also shortened the cooking time. Salting the roast prior to cooking improved its flavor and allowed us to skip browning later. Sautéing the onions, celery, carrot, and garlic before we added them to the pot gave them more depth of flavor. Some recipes use water as a pot roast cooking liquid but when we tried this, the gravy turned out as you'd expect—watery. We had better luck with beef broth. Tomato paste, red wine, thyme, and bay leaf boosted the flavor even further. The resulting gravy boasted a complex character. Finally, sealing the pot with aluminum foil before securing the lid concentrated the steam for a steady simmer and fork-tender meat. To separate the roast into two pieces, simply pull apart at the natural seam and then trim away any large knobs of fat. The roast can be made up to two days ahead: Follow the recipe through step 4, transferring the cooked roasts to a large bowl and straining the liquid as directed in step 5. Transfer the vegetables to the bowl with the roasts, cover with plastic wrap, cut vents in the plastic, and refrigerate overnight or up to 48 hours. One hour before serving, adjust the oven rack to the middle position and heat the oven to 325 degrees. Transfer the cold roasts to a carving board, slice them against the grain into ½-inch-thick slices, place them in a 13 by 9-inch baking dish, cover tightly with foil, and bake until heated through, about 45 minutes. While the roasts heat, puree the sauce and vegetables as directed in step 5. Bring the sauce to a simmer and finish as directed in step 6 before serving with the meat.

- 1 (3½- to 4-pound) boneless chuck-eye roast, pulled into 2 pieces at natural seam and trimmed
- 1½ teaspoons table salt
- 2 tablespoons unsalted butter
- 2 onions, halved and sliced thin
- 1 large carrot, peeled and chopped
- 1 celery rib, chopped
- 2 garlic cloves, minced
- 2–3 cups beef broth, divided
- ¾ cup dry red wine, divided
- 1 tablespoon tomato paste
- 1 bay leaf
- 1 sprig fresh thyme plus ¼ teaspoon finely chopped fresh thyme, divided
- 1 tablespoon balsamic vinegar

1. Sprinkle meat with salt, place on wire rack set in rimmed baking sheet, and let sit at room temperature for 1 hour.

2. Adjust oven rack to lower-middle position and heat oven to 300 degrees. Melt butter in Dutch oven over medium heat. Add onions and cook, stirring occasionally, until softened and beginning to brown, 8 to 10 minutes. Add carrot and celery and continue to cook, stirring occasionally, for 5 minutes. Add garlic and cook until fragrant, about 30 seconds. Stir in 1 cup broth, ½ cup wine, tomato paste, bay leaf, and thyme sprig; bring to simmer.

3. Season beef with pepper. Using 3 pieces of kitchen twine for each piece of beef, tie crosswise to form even roasts.

4. Nestle roasts on top of vegetables. Place large piece of foil over pot and cover tightly with lid; transfer pot to oven. Cook roasts until fully tender and sharp knife easily slips in and out of meat, 3½ to 4 hours, turning roasts halfway through cooking.

5. Transfer roasts to carving board and tent with foil. Strain liquid through fine-mesh strainer into 4-cup liquid measuring cup. Discard thyme sprig and bay leaf. Transfer vegetables to blender. Allow liquid to settle for 5 minutes. Using wide, shallow spoon, skim excess fat from surface of sauce. Add beef broth as necessary to bring total amount of liquid to 3 cups. Place liquid in blender with vegetables and blend until smooth, about 2 minutes. Transfer sauce to medium saucepan and bring to simmer over medium heat.

6. While sauce heats, remove twine from roasts and slice against grain into ½-inch-thick slices. Transfer meat to serving platter. Stir chopped thyme, remaining ¼ cup wine, and balsamic vinegar into sauce and season with salt and pepper to taste. Serve immediately, passing sauce separately.

VARIATION
Old-Fashioned Pot Roast with Root Vegetables
Add 1 pound carrots, peeled and cut into 2-inch pieces; 1 pound parsnips, peeled and cut into 2-inch pieces; and 1½ pounds russet potatoes, peeled, halved lengthwise, and each half quartered, to pot in step 4 after roasts have cooked for 3 hours. Once pot roast and vegetables are fully cooked, transfer any large pieces of carrot, parsnip, and potato to serving platter using slotted spoon, cover tightly with foil, and proceed with recipe as directed.

Sous Vide Rosemary–Mustard Seed Crusted Roast Beef

SEASON 20 RECIPE

Serves 10 to 12

WHY THIS RECIPE WORKS When it comes to holiday beef roasts, chuck isn't really known for being the go-to for medium-rare resplendence (we're looking at you, prime rib). But that's a real shame since chuck is among the most flavorful cuts of beef available—and the cheapest per pound, to boot. This cut has plenty of fat and connective tissue, making it tough and chewy when it's cooked to medium-rare in a conventional oven. With most traditional methods of cooking, you have two options: low and slow until it's tender, or braised and broken down. Neither method gives you pink, tender, juicy meat. But with sous vide we can have it all: A fork-tender, juicy, medium-rare chuck roast. Circulating the roast at a low temperature for 24 hours allows enough time to break down intramuscular collagen, tenderizing the meat while preserving a rosy, medium-rare interior from edge to edge. We were inspired to pair this roast with a generous herb, mustard seed, and peppercorn crust, making it easily customizable and ready to pair with all sorts of sauces. And best of all, it won't break the bank over the holidays. Serve with Yogurt-Herb Sauce (recipe follows), if desired.

- 1 **(5-pound) boneless beef chuck-eye roast, pulled into 2 pieces at natural seam and trimmed of large pieces of fat**
- 4 **teaspoons kosher salt**
- 2 **tablespoons vegetable oil**
- 1¼ **teaspoons pepper**
- 1 **egg white**
- ¼ **cup mustard seeds**
- 3 **tablespoons peppercorns**
- ⅓ **cup finely chopped fresh rosemary**
- 2 **tablespoons flake sea salt**

1. Sprinkle beef with kosher salt. Arrange pieces side by side along natural seam, and then tie together at 1-inch intervals with kitchen twine to create 1 evenly shaped roast. Wrap roast in plastic wrap, transfer to large plate, and refrigerate at least 24 hours or up to 96 hours.

2. Using sous vide circulator, heat water to 133 degrees in 12-quart container.

3. Heat oil in 12-inch skillet over medium-high heat until just smoking. Brown roast on all sides, 6 to 8 minutes. Season roast with pepper and place into 2-gallon zipper-lock freezer bag. Seal bag, pressing out as much air as possible. Gently lower bag into prepared water bath until roast is fully submerged, and then clip top corner of bag to side of water bath container, allowing remaining air bubbles to rise to top of bag. Reopen 1 corner of zipper, release remaining air bubbles, and reseal bag. Cover and cook for at least 18 hours or up to 24 hours.

4. Adjust oven rack to middle position and heat oven to 475 degrees. Set wire rack in aluminum foil–lined rimmed baking sheet and spray with vegetable spray. Transfer roast to prepared rack and let rest for 10 to 15 minutes. Pat roast dry with paper towels.

5. Whisk egg white in bowl until frothy, about 30 seconds. Grind mustard seeds and peppercorns in spice grinder under coarsely ground. Transfer to shallow dish and stir in rosemary and flake sea salt. Brush roast on all sides with egg white, then coat with mustard seed mixture, pressing to adhere. Return roast to prepared rack and roast until surface is evenly browned and fragrant, 15 to 20 minutes, rotating sheet halfway through roasting.

6. Transfer roast to carving board and slice into ½-inch-thick slices, removing pieces of twine as you slice, and serve.

ACCOMPANIMENT
Yogurt-Herb Sauce
Makes about 2 cups
Do not substitute low-fat or nonfat yogurt here.

- 2 **cups plain whole-milk yogurt**
- ¼ **cup finely chopped fresh parsley**
- ¼ **cup finely chopped fresh chives**
- 2 **teaspoons grated lemon zest plus ¼ cup juice**
- 2 **garlic cloves, minced**

Whisk all ingredients together in bowl and season with salt and pepper to taste. Cover and refrigerate for at least 30 minutes to allow flavors to meld. (Sauce can be refrigerated for up to 4 days.)

Simple Pot-au-Feu

Serves 6 to 8

WHY THIS RECIPE WORKS For a pot-au-feu brimming with tradition but suited to today's modern kitchen, we needed a pared-down shopping list. Boneless chuck roast beat out harder-to-find cuts of meat for its relative tenderness and big meaty flavor. Marrow bones gave the broth a buttery, beefy quality when cooked together with the meat, onion, and celery. Gently simmering the broth kept it perfectly clear. We transferred the pot to the oven partially covered to cook low and slow and, in the meantime, stirred together a sauce reminiscent of traditional pot-au-feu accompaniments. The zesty, bright combination of parsley, Dijon, chives, white wine vinegar, minced cornichon pickles, and pepper was deepened with the addition of the soft, beefy marrow extracted from the bones after cooking. Marrow bones (also called soup bones) can be found in the freezer section or the meat counter at most supermarkets. Use small red potatoes measuring 1 to 2 inches in diameter.

Meat

- 1 (3½- to 4-pound) boneless beef chuck-eye roast, pulled apart at seams and trimmed
- 1 tablespoon kosher salt
- 1½ pounds marrow bones
- 1 onion, quartered
- 1 celery rib, sliced thin
- 3 bay leaves
- 1 teaspoon black peppercorns

Parsley Sauce

- ⅔ cup finely chopped fresh parsley
- ¼ cup Dijon mustard
- ¼ cup finely chopped fresh chives
- 3 tablespoons white wine vinegar
- 10 cornichons, minced
- 1½ teaspoons pepper

Vegetables

- 1 pound small red potatoes, unpeeled, halved
- 6 carrots, peeled and halved crosswise, thick halves quartered, thin halves halved
- 1 pound asparagus, trimmed

Flake sea salt

1. For the meat: Adjust oven rack to lower-middle position and heat oven to 300 degrees. Season beef with salt. Using 3 pieces of kitchen twine for each piece of beef, tie crosswise to form even roasts. Place beef, bones, onion, celery, bay leaves, and peppercorns in Dutch oven. Add 4 cups cold water (water should come halfway up roasts). Bring to simmer over high heat. Partially cover pot and transfer to oven. Cook until beef is fully tender and sharp knife easily slips in and out of meat (meat will not be shreddable), 3¼ to 3¾ hours, flipping beef over halfway through cooking.

2. For the parsley sauce: While beef cooks, combine all ingredients in bowl. Cover and set aside.

3. Remove pot from oven and turn off oven. Transfer beef to large platter, cover tightly with aluminum foil, and return to oven to keep warm. Transfer bones to cutting board and use end of spoon to extract marrow. Mince marrow into paste and add 2 tablespoons to parsley sauce (reserve any remaining marrow for other applications). Using wide, shallow spoon, skim excess fat from surface of broth. Strain broth through fine-mesh strainer into large liquid measuring cup; add water to make 6 cups. Return broth to pot. (Meat can be returned to broth, cooled, and refrigerated for up to 2 days. Skim fat from cold broth, then gently reheat and proceed with recipe.)

4. For the vegetables: Add potatoes to broth and bring to simmer over high heat. Reduce heat to medium and simmer for 6 minutes. Add carrots and cook for 10 minutes. Add asparagus and continue to cook until all vegetables are tender, 3 to 5 minutes.

5. Using slotted spoon, transfer vegetables to large bowl. Toss with 3 tablespoons parsley sauce and season with salt and pepper to taste. Season broth with salt to taste.

6. Transfer beef to carving board, remove twine, and slice meat against grain into ½-inch-thick slices. Arrange servings of beef and vegetables in large, shallow bowls. Dollop beef with parsley sauce, drizzle with ⅓ cup broth, and sprinkle with flake sea salt. Serve, passing remaining parsley sauce and flake sea salt separately.

Onion-Braised Beef Brisket

Serves 6

WHY THIS RECIPE WORKS We wanted a way to cook brisket, which is naturally flavorful, so that it would remain moist, and we wanted to serve it with a flavorful sauce that would complement the beef. The fat in a piece of brisket is all on the surface; there's no marbling to keep the interior moist. We needed to find a way to get the moisture inside. We tried many different types and amounts of liquids and a variety of cooking vessels and techniques, but no matter what we did, the meat was still dry. Could the answer lie in adding moisture after the long braise? We left the meat in the sauce after cooking it, and after about an hour there was a noticeable difference. Taking this discovery further, we refrigerated the cooked meat and sauce overnight. The meat reabsorbed some of the liquid, becoming more moist and easier to carve without shredding. The sauce—based on red wine, chicken broth, and lots of onions—had improved as well; the fat had risen to the surface and congealed, making it easier to remove. All we had to do was reheat the sliced meat in the sauce, and this hearty dish was ready. This recipe requires a few hours of unattended cooking. It also requires advance preparation. After cooking, the brisket must stand overnight in the braising liquid that later becomes the sauce. Defatting the sauce is essential. If the fat has congealed into a layer on top of the sauce, it can be easily removed while cold. Sometimes, however, fragments of solid fat are dispersed throughout the sauce; in this case, the sauce should be skimmed of fat after reheating. If you prefer a spicy sauce, increase the amount of cayenne to ¼ teaspoon. You will need 18-inch-wide heavy-duty foil for this recipe. If you would like to make and serve the brisket on the same day, after removing the brisket from the oven in step 4, reseal the foil and let the brisket stand at room temperature for an hour. Then transfer the brisket to a carving board and continue with the recipe to strain, defat, and reheat the sauce and slice the meat; because the brisket will still be hot, there will be no need to put it back into the oven once the reheated sauce is poured over it.

1 (4- to 5-pound) beef brisket, flat cut, fat trimmed to ¼ inch
2¼ teaspoons table salt, divided
1 teaspoon pepper
1 teaspoon vegetable oil, plus extra as needed
2½ pounds onions, halved and sliced ½ inch thick
1 tablespoon packed brown sugar
3 garlic cloves, minced
1 tablespoon tomato paste
1 tablespoon paprika
⅛ teaspoon cayenne pepper
2 tablespoons all-purpose flour
1 cup chicken broth
1 cup dry red wine
3 bay leaves
3 sprigs fresh thyme
2 teaspoons cider vinegar

1. Adjust oven rack to lower-middle position and heat oven to 300 degrees. Line 13 by 9-inch baking dish with two 24-inch-long sheets of 18-inch-wide heavy-duty aluminum foil, positioning sheets perpendicular to each other and allowing excess foil to extend beyond edges of dish. Pat brisket dry with paper towels. Place brisket, fat side up, on cutting board; using fork, poke holes in meat through fat layer about 1 inch apart. Season both sides of brisket with 2 teaspoons salt and pepper.

2. Heat oil in 12-inch skillet over medium-high heat until just smoking. Place brisket, fat side up, in skillet (brisket may climb up sides of skillet); weight brisket with heavy Dutch oven or cast-iron skillet and cook until well browned, about 7 minutes. Remove Dutch oven; using tongs, flip brisket and cook on second side, without weight, until well browned, about 7 minutes. Transfer to platter.

3. Pour off all but 1 tablespoon fat from skillet (or, if brisket was lean, add enough oil to fat in skillet to equal 1 tablespoon). Add onions, sugar, and remaining ¼ teaspoon salt and cook over medium-high heat, stirring occasionally, until onions are softened, 10 to 12 minutes. Add garlic and cook, stirring frequently, until fragrant, about 1 minute. Stir in tomato paste and cook until paste darkens, about 2 minutes. Add paprika and cayenne and cook, stirring constantly, until fragrant, about 1 minute. Add flour and cook, stirring constantly, until well combined, about 2 minutes. Stir in broth, wine, bay leaves, and thyme sprigs, scraping up any browned bits; bring to simmer and cook for 5 minutes to thicken.

4. Pour sauce and onions into prepared dish. Nestle brisket, fat side up, into sauce and onions. Fold foil extensions over brisket and seal (do not tightly crimp foil). Bake until fork slips easily in and out of meat, 3½ to 4 hours. Carefully open foil and let brisket cool for 20 to 30 minutes.

5. Transfer brisket to large bowl; set fine-mesh strainer over bowl and strain sauce over brisket. Discard bay leaves and thyme sprigs and transfer onions to small bowl. Cover both bowls with plastic wrap, cut vents in plastic, and refrigerate for at least 8 hours or up to 2 days.

6. About 45 minutes before serving, adjust oven rack to lower-middle position and heat oven to 350 degrees. Transfer brisket to carving board. Skim fat from surface of sauce, then transfer sauce to medium saucepan and reheat over medium heat until warm, skimming any more fat from surface (you should have about 2 cups sauce without onions; if necessary, simmer sauce over medium-high heat until reduced to 2 cups). Slice brisket against grain ¼ inch thick and place in 13 by 9-inch baking dish. Stir in vinegar and reserved onions and season with salt and pepper to taste. Pour sauce over brisket, cover dish with foil, and bake until heated through, 25 to 30 minutes. Serve immediately.

"Brisket is a very difficult cut to cook so that it turns both tender and moist. We found that time is the key to success here: two days, to be specific. After braising in a rich, oniony broth, the brisket cools overnight in its braising liquid, and then you slice it thin while it's cold and slowly reheat it. The result is tender, juicy meat slathered with tender onions that truly melt in your mouth. Because almost all of the work is done in advance, this has become one of my go-to recipes for entertaining. I like to serve the brisket with a simple side of buttered egg noodles and, of course, a nice bottle of red wine. Sounds like heaven to me."

—*Erin*

Braised Beef Short Ribs

Serves 6

WHY THIS RECIPE WORKS Short ribs have great flavor and luscious texture, but their excess fat can be a problem since so much fat is rendered during the ribs' stint in the oven. Most recipes call for resting them in the braising liquid overnight, so that the fat solidifies into an easy-to-remove layer. However, most people don't plan their dinners days in advance, and skimming such a large amount of fat off with a spoon doesn't work well enough. The meat and sauce come out greasy, no matter how diligent one's spoon-wielding. We wanted a silky, grease-free sauce and fork-tender short rib meat, all in a few hours. The first task was to choose the right rib. Instead of traditional bone-in short ribs, we used boneless short ribs, which rendered significantly less fat than bone-in. While we didn't miss much flavor from the bones, we did want the body that the bones' connective tissue added. To solve this, we sprinkled a bit of gelatin into the sauce to restore suppleness. We also wanted to ramp up the richness of the sauce. We jump-started flavor by reducing wine with browned aromatics (onions, garlic, and carrots) before using the liquid to cook the meat. This added the right intensity, but we needed another cup of liquid to keep the meat half-submerged—the right level for braises. More wine yielded too much wine flavor; we used beef broth instead. As for the excess fat, the level was low enough that we could strain and defat the liquid in a fat separator. Reducing the liquid concentrated the flavors and made for a rich, luxurious sauce for our fork-tender boneless short ribs. Make sure that the ribs are at least 4 inches long and 1 inch thick. If boneless ribs are unavailable, substitute 7 pounds of bone-in beef short ribs at least 4 inches long with 1 inch of meat above the bone and bone them yourself.

3½ **pounds boneless short ribs, trimmed**
1¾ **teaspoons table salt**
¾ **teaspoon pepper**
2 **tablespoons vegetable oil, divided**
2 **large onions, sliced thin**
1 **tablespoon tomato paste**
6 **garlic cloves, peeled**
2 **cups red wine**
1 **cup beef broth**
4 **large carrots, peeled and cut into 2-inch pieces**
4 **sprigs fresh thyme**
1 **bay leaf**
¼ **cup cold water**
½ **teaspoon unflavored gelatin**

1. Adjust oven rack to lower-middle position and heat oven to 300 degrees. Pat beef dry with paper towels and season with salt and pepper. Heat 1 tablespoon oil in Dutch oven over medium-high heat until smoking. Add half of beef and cook until well browned on all sides, 8 to 12 minutes; transfer to bowl. Repeat with remaining 1 tablespoon oil and remaining beef.

2. Add onions to fat left in pot and cook over medium heat, stirring occasionally, until softened and beginning to brown, 12 to 15 minutes. (If onions begin to darken too quickly, add 1 to 2 tablespoons water to pot.) Stir in tomato paste and cook, stirring constantly, until bottom of pan is well browned, about 2 minutes. Stir in garlic and cook until fragrant, about 30 seconds. Stir in wine, scraping up any browned bits. Increase heat to medium-high and simmer until reduced by half, 8 to 10 minutes.

Boning Short Ribs

1. With chef's knife as close as possible to bone, carefully remove meat.

2. Trim excess hard fat and silverskin from both sides of meat.

3. Stir in broth, carrots, thyme sprigs, and bay leaf. Add browned beef and any accumulated juices and bring to simmer. Cover, transfer pot to oven, and cook until fork slips easily in and out of meat, 2 to 2½ hours, turning meat over several times during cooking.

4. Place water in small bowl and sprinkle gelatin on top; let sit at least 5 minutes. Transfer meat and carrots to platter and tent with foil. Pour braising liquid through fine-mesh strainer into fat separator and let settle for 5 minutes. Return defatted juices to now-empty Dutch oven and cook over medium heat until reduced to 1 cup, 5 to 10 minutes. Off heat, stir in gelatin mixture and season with salt and pepper to taste. Pour sauce over meat and serve.

Osso Buco

Serves 6

WHY THIS RECIPE WORKS Osso buco, veal shanks braised in a rich sauce until tender, is incredibly rich and hearty. We felt that this time-honored recipe shouldn't be altered much, but we hoped to identify the keys to flavor so that we could perfect it. To serve one shank per person, we searched for medium-size shanks, and tied them around the equator to keep the meat attached to the bone for an attractive presentation. Most recipes suggest flouring the veal before browning it, but we got better flavor when we simply seared the meat, liberally seasoned with just salt and pepper. Browning in two batches enabled us to deglaze the pan twice, thus enriching the sauce. Celery, onions, and carrots formed the basis of the sauce; for the liquid we used a combination of chicken broth, white wine, and canned tomatoes. The traditional garnish of gremolata—minced garlic, lemon, and parsley—required no changes; we stirred half into the sauce and sprinkled the rest over individual servings for a fresh burst of citrus flavor. To keep the meat attached to the bone during the long simmering process, tie a piece of kitchen twine around the thickest portion of each shank before it is browned. Just before serving, taste the liquid and, if it seems too thin, simmer it on the stovetop as you remove the strings from the osso buco and arrange them in individual bowls. Serve with rice or polenta.

Osso Buco
- 6 (8- to 10-ounce) veal shanks, 1½ inches thick, trimmed and tied around equator
- 2 teaspoons table salt, divided
- 1⅛ teaspoons pepper, divided
- ¼ cup vegetable oil, divided
- 2½ cups dry white wine, divided
- 2 onions, cut into ½-inch pieces
- 2 carrots, cut into ½-inch pieces
- 2 celery ribs, cut into ½-inch pieces
- 6 garlic cloves, minced
- 2 cups chicken broth
- 2 bay leaves
- 1 (14.5-ounce) can diced tomatoes, drained

Gremolata
- ¼ cup finely chopped fresh parsley
- 3 garlic cloves, minced
- 2 teaspoons grated lemon zest

1. *For the osso buco:* Adjust oven rack to lower-middle position and heat oven to 325 degrees. Pat shanks dry with paper towels and season with 1¾ teaspoons salt and 1 teaspoon pepper. Heat 1 tablespoon oil in Dutch oven over medium-high heat until shimmering. Brown half of shanks on all sides, 8 to 10 minutes; transfer to large bowl. Off heat, add ½ cup wine to Dutch oven, scraping up any browned bits. Pour liquid into bowl with browned shanks. Return pot to medium-high heat, add 1 tablespoon oil, and heat until shimmering. Brown remaining shanks, 8 to 10 minutes. Transfer shanks to bowl. Off heat, add 1 cup wine to pot, scraping up any browned bits. Pour liquid into bowl with shanks.

2. Set pot over medium heat. Add remaining 2 tablespoons oil, onions, carrots, celery, remaining ¼ teaspoon salt, and remaining ⅛ teaspoon pepper and cook, stirring occasionally, until soft and lightly browned, about 9 minutes. Stir in garlic and cook until fragrant, about 30 seconds. Increase heat to high and stir in broth, remaining 1 cup wine, and bay leaves. Add tomatoes; return veal shanks to pot along with any accumulated juices (the liquid should just cover the shanks). Bring liquid to simmer. Cover and transfer pot to oven. Cook shanks until meat is easily pierced with fork but not falling off bone, about 2 hours. (Osso buco can be refrigerated for up to 2 days. Bring to a simmer over medium-low heat before continuing.)

3. *For the gremolata:* Combine parsley, garlic, and lemon zest in small bowl. Stir half of gremolata into pot, reserving rest for garnish. Season with salt and pepper to taste. Let osso buco sit, uncovered, for 5 minutes.

4. Remove shanks from pot, discard twine, place 1 veal shank in each of 6 bowls. Ladle some of braising liquid over each shank and sprinkle each serving with remaining gremolata. Serve immediately.

Chinese Braised Beef

Chinese Braised Beef

Serves 6

WHY THIS RECIPE WORKS Chinese braised beef (also called red-cooked beef) is a slow-braised dish in which a thick, ultraflavorful, stew-like sauce envelops tender pieces of beef. We wanted to maintain the deeply complex flavors of the original but simplify the recipe for the home kitchen. We decided to use readily available boneless beef short ribs in place of the traditional shank of beef. To streamline the classic cooking method, we opted to skip blanching the meat, and we moved the pot from the stovetop to the even heat of the oven. A pair of thickeners—gelatin and cornstarch—added body to the sauce. Five-spice powder provided characteristic flavor without the bother of whole spices, and a combination of hoisin sauce and molasses contributed an underlying sweetness that completed the dish. With its generous amount of soy sauce, this dish is meant to taste salty, which is why we pair it with white rice. A simple steamed vegetable like bok choy or broccoli completes the meal. Boneless beef short ribs require little trimming, but you can also use a 4-pound chuck roast. Trim the roast of large pieces of fat and sinew, cut it across the grain into 1-inch-thick slabs, and cut the slabs into 4 by 2-inch pieces.

- 1½ tablespoons unflavored gelatin
- 2½ cups plus 1 tablespoon water, divided
- ½ cup dry sherry
- ⅓ cup soy sauce
- 2 tablespoons hoisin sauce
- 2 tablespoons molasses
- 3 scallions, white and green parts separated, green parts sliced thin on bias
- 1 (2-inch) piece ginger, peeled, halved lengthwise, and crushed
- 4 garlic cloves, peeled and smashed
- 1½ teaspoons five-spice powder
- 1 teaspoon red pepper flakes
- 3 pounds boneless beef short ribs, trimmed and cut into 4-inch lengths
- 1 teaspoon cornstarch

1. Sprinkle gelatin over 2½ cups water in Dutch oven and let sit until gelatin softens, about 5 minutes. Adjust oven rack to middle position and heat oven to 300 degrees.

2. Heat softened gelatin over medium-high heat, stirring occasionally, until melted, 2 to 3 minutes. Stir in sherry, soy sauce, hoisin, molasses, scallion whites, ginger, garlic, five-spice powder, and pepper flakes. Stir in beef and bring to simmer. Remove pot from heat. Cover tightly with sheet of heavy-duty aluminum foil, then lid. Transfer to oven and cook until beef is tender, 2 to 2½ hours, stirring halfway through cooking.

3. Using slotted spoon, transfer beef to cutting board. Strain sauce through fine-mesh strainer into fat separator. Wipe out pot with paper towels. Let liquid settle for 5 minutes, then return defatted liquid to now-empty pot. Cook liquid over medium-high heat, stirring occasionally, until thickened and reduced to 1 cup, 20 to 25 minutes.

4. While sauce reduces, using 2 forks, break beef into 1½-inch pieces. Whisk cornstarch and remaining 1 tablespoon water together in small bowl.

5. Reduce heat to medium-low, whisk cornstarch mixture into reduced sauce, and cook until sauce is slightly thickened, about 1 minute. Return beef to sauce and stir to coat. Cover and cook, stirring occasionally, until beef is heated through, about 5 minutes. Sprinkle scallion greens over top. Serve.

Slow-Roasted Beef

Serves 6 to 8

WHY THIS RECIPE WORKS This inventive recipe turns an inexpensive cut, the eye round, into a tender, beefy-tasting roast worthy of Sunday dinner. The key was keeping the meat's internal temperature below 122 degrees as long as possible, which allowed the meat's enzymes to act as natural tenderizers, breaking down its tough connective tissue (this action stops at 122 degrees). Since most ovens don't heat below 200 degrees, we roasted the meat at 225 degrees (after searing it to give the meat a crusty exterior) and shut off the oven when the roast reached 115 degrees. The meat stayed below 122 degrees an extra 30 minutes, allowing the enzymes to continue their work before the temperature reached 130 degrees for medium-rare. Salting the meat a full 24 hours before roasting made it even more tender and seasoned the roast throughout. We don't recommend cooking this roast past medium. Open the oven door as little as possible and remove the roast from the oven to take its temperature. If the roast has not reached the desired temperature in the time specified in step 3, heat the oven to 225 degrees for 5 minutes, shut it off, and continue to cook the roast to the desired temperature. For a smaller (2½- to 3½-pound) roast, reduce the amount of pepper to 1½ teaspoons. For a 4½- to 6-pound roast, cut in half crosswise before cooking to create two smaller roasts. Slice the roast thinly and serve with Horseradish Cream Sauce (page 181), if desired.

- 1 (3½- to 4½-pound) boneless eye-round roast
- 4 teaspoons kosher salt
- 5 teaspoons vegetable oil, divided
- 2 teaspoons pepper

1. Pat roast dry with paper towels and rub salt evenly over roast. Refrigerate, uncovered, for at least 18 hours or up to 24 hours.

2. Adjust oven rack to middle position and heat oven to 225 degrees. Pat roast dry with paper towels, rub with 2 teaspoons oil, and season with pepper.

Roast Beef Tenderloin

3. Heat remaining 1 tablespoon oil in 12-inch skillet over medium-high heat until just smoking. Brown roast well on all sides, 12 to 16 minutes; reduce heat if pan begins to scorch. Transfer roast to wire rack set in rimmed baking sheet and roast until meat registers 115 degrees (for medium-rare), 1¼ to 1¾ hours, or 125 degrees (for medium), 1¾ to 2¼ hours.

4. Turn off oven and leave roast in oven, without opening door, until meat registers 120 to 125 degrees (for medium-rare), 30 to 50 minutes.

5. Transfer roast to carving board and let rest for 20 minutes. Slice meat as thin as possible. Serve.

ACCOMPANIMENT
Horseradish Cream Sauce
Makes about 1 cup
Our favorite prepared horseradish is Boar's Head Pure Horseradish.

- ½ cup heavy cream, chilled
- ½ cup prepared horseradish
- 1 teaspoon table salt
- ⅛ teaspoon pepper

Whisk cream in medium bowl until thickened but not yet soft peaks, 1 to 2 minutes. Gently fold in horseradish, salt, and pepper. Transfer to serving bowl and refrigerate for at least 30 minutes or up to 1 hour before serving.

Roast Beef Tenderloin

Serves 4

WHY THIS RECIPE WORKS There's nothing like the buttery texture of a roasted beef tenderloin that is rosy all the way through, with a deep brown crust. We opted for a center-cut piece; it's already trimmed and lacks the narrow "tail" of the whole cut. We first tried searing the meat in the oven, but it never browned evenly. Stovetop browning was better for producing a crust, but the roast still came out of the oven with a gray band. The trick was to reverse the process, first roasting the meat in the oven, then searing at the end. Lowering the oven temperature eliminated the ring of overcooked meat altogether. To add flavor to this mild cut of beef, salting it before roasting worked wonders; rubbing the roast with a little softened butter added richness. A flavored butter served alongside was the final touch. Ask your butcher to prepare a trimmed center-cut Châteaubriand from the whole tenderloin, as this cut is not usually available without special ordering. This recipe can be doubled to make two roasts. Both pieces of meat can be roasted on the same rack. Sear the roasts one after the other, wiping out the pan and adding new oil after searing the first roast.

- 1 (2-pound) center-cut beef tenderloin roast, trimmed, tail end tucked, and tied at 1½-inch intervals
- 2 teaspoons kosher salt
- 1 teaspoon pepper
- 2 tablespoons unsalted butter, softened
- 1 tablespoon vegetable oil
- 1 recipe flavored butter (recipes follow)

1. Sprinkle roast evenly with salt, cover loosely with plastic wrap, and let stand at room temperature for 1 hour. Adjust oven rack to middle position and heat oven to 300 degrees.

2. Pat roast dry with paper towels. Sprinkle roast evenly with pepper and spread softened butter evenly over surface. Transfer roast to wire rack set in rimmed baking sheet. Roast until beef registers 120 to 125 degrees (for medium-rare), 40 to 55 minutes, flipping roast halfway through roasting.

3. Heat oil in 12-inch skillet over medium-high heat until just smoking. Brown roast well on all sides, about 8 minutes. Transfer roast to carving board and spread 2 tablespoons flavored butter evenly over top of roast; let rest for 30 minutes. Remove twine and slice into ½-inch-thick slices. Serve, passing remaining flavored butter separately.

ACCOMPANIMENTS
Shallot and Parsley Butter
Makes about ½ cup

- 4 tablespoons unsalted butter, softened
- ½ shallot, minced
- 1 tablespoon finely chopped fresh parsley
- 1 garlic clove, minced
- ¼ teaspoon table salt
- ¼ teaspoon pepper

Combine all ingredients in bowl and let rest to meld flavors, about 10 minutes. Wrap in plastic wrap, roll into log, and refrigerate until serving.

Chipotle and Cilantro Butter
Makes about ½ cup

- 5 tablespoons unsalted butter, softened
- 1 chipotle chile in adobo sauce, minced, with 1 teaspoon adobo sauce
- 1 garlic clove, minced
- 1 teaspoon honey
- 1 teaspoon grated lime zest
- 1 tablespoon finely chopped fresh cilantro
- ½ teaspoon table salt

Combine all ingredients in bowl and let rest to meld flavors, about 10 minutes. Wrap in plastic wrap, roll into log, and refrigerate until serving.

Beef Tenderloin with Smoky Potatoes and Persillade

Serves 6

WHY THIS RECIPE WORKS For special occasions, few cuts top a beef tenderloin. This elegant roast cooks quickly and serves a crowd, and its rich, buttery slices are fork-tender. We found that a hot oven delivered rich, roasted flavor and perfectly rosy meat without overcooking this lean cut. Tying the roast helped to ensure even cooking. The roast needed company, and small whole red potatoes were a perfect pairing. To punch up the flavor, we tossed the potatoes with smoked paprika, which added a pleasant smokiness to complement our meat, along with garlic and scallions for a deep, flavorful backbone. The tender meat needed a sauce, so we made a simple yet bold persillade relish, which featured parsley, capers, and cornichons. We prefer to use extra-small red potatoes measuring less than 1 inch in diameter. Larger potatoes can be used, but it may be necessary to return the potatoes to the oven to finish cooking while the roast is resting in step 5. Center-cut beef tenderloin roasts are sometimes sold as Châteaubriand.

Beef and Potatoes

- 1 (3-pound) center-cut beef tenderloin roast, trimmed
- 3¼ teaspoons kosher salt, divided
- 1¼ teaspoons pepper, divided
- 1 teaspoon baking soda
- 3 tablespoons extra-virgin olive oil, divided
- 3 pounds extra-small red potatoes, unpeeled
- 5 scallions, minced
- 4 garlic cloves, minced
- 1 tablespoon smoked paprika
- ½ cup water

Persillade Relish

- ¾ cup finely chopped fresh parsley
- ½ cup extra-virgin olive oil
- 6 tablespoons minced cornichons plus 1 teaspoon brine
- ¼ cup capers, rinsed and chopped
- 3 garlic cloves, minced
- 1 scallion, minced
- 1 teaspoon sugar
- ¼ teaspoon table salt
- ¼ teaspoon pepper

1. *For the beef and potatoes:* Pat roast dry with paper towels. Combine 2¼ teaspoons salt, 1 teaspoon pepper, and baking soda in small bowl. Rub salt mixture evenly over roast and let stand for 1 hour. Tuck tail end and tie roast with kitchen twine at 1½-inch intervals. Adjust oven rack to middle position and heat oven to 425 degrees.

2. Heat 2 tablespoons oil in large roasting pan over medium-high heat (over 2 burners, if possible) until shimmering. Add potatoes, scallions, garlic, paprika, remaining 1 teaspoon salt, and remaining ¼ teaspoon pepper and cook until scallions are softened, about 1 minute. Off heat, stir in water, scraping up any browned bits. Transfer roasting pan to oven and roast potatoes for 15 minutes.

3. Brush remaining 1 tablespoon oil over surface of roast. Remove roasting pan from oven, stir potato mixture, and lay beef on top. Reduce oven temperature to 300 degrees. Return pan to oven and roast until beef registers 120 to 125 degrees (for medium-rare), 45 to 55 minutes, rotating roasting pan halfway through cooking.

4. *For the persillade relish:* While beef roasts, combine all ingredients in bowl.

5. Remove pan from oven. Transfer roast to carving board, tent with aluminum foil, and let rest for 15 minutes. Cover potatoes in pan with foil to keep warm. Remove twine, slice into ½-inch-thick slices, and serve with potatoes and relish.

Fennel-Coriander Top Sirloin Roast

Serves 8 to 10

WHY THIS RECIPE WORKS For a holiday-caliber roast without the hefty price tag, we set out to bring big flavor to an affordable cut: top sirloin. We began by splitting the roast in half, creating two manageable roasts, salting the halves, and air-drying them in the refrigerator. This seasoned the meat, maximized its juiciness, and dried the surfaces for optimal browning. After 24 hours, we kickstarted the browning by quickly searing all sides of the two roasts in a skillet. Tying the roasts with kitchen twine turned the irregularly shaped roasts into two uniform cylinders. To compensate for the meat's leaner makeup, we created a rich, heavily seasoned paste that would further boost browning. We processed garlic, fennel, olive oil, and umami-boosting anchovy fillets to create a spreadable consistency, then added coriander, paprika, and oregano for extra flavor. After applying the spice paste, we roasted the meat in a 225-degree oven for 2 hours. This initial roast cooked the meat to our liking. To give it an attractive browned crust, we removed the roasts from the oven, ramped up the temperature to 500 degrees, and returned them (with twine removed) for a final crisping. This recipe requires refrigerating the salted meat for at least 24 hours before cooking. Top sirloin roast, also called top butt roast, center-cut roast, spoon roast, shell roast, or shell sirloin roast, should not be confused with a whole top sirloin butt roast or top loin roast. Do not omit the anchovies; they provide great depth of flavor with no overt fishiness. Monitoring the roast with a meat-probe thermometer is best. If you use an instant-read thermometer, open the oven door as little as possible and remove the roast from the oven to take its temperature.

1 (5- to 6-pound) boneless top sirloin center-cut roast, trimmed
2 tablespoons kosher salt
4 teaspoons plus ¼ cup extra-virgin olive oil, divided
4 garlic cloves, minced
6 anchovy fillets, rinsed and patted dry
2 teaspoons ground fennel
2 teaspoons ground coriander
2 teaspoons paprika
1 teaspoon dried oregano
1 teaspoon pepper
Coarse sea salt

1. Cut roast lengthwise along grain into 2 equal pieces. Rub 1 tablespoon kosher salt over each piece. Transfer to large plate and refrigerate, uncovered, for at least 24 hours or up to 4 days.

2. Adjust oven rack to middle position and heat oven to 225 degrees. Heat 2 teaspoons oil in 12-inch skillet over high heat until just smoking. Brown 1 roast on all sides, 6 to 8 minutes. Return browned roast to plate. Repeat with 2 teaspoons oil and remaining roast. Let cool for 10 minutes.

3. While roasts cool, process garlic, anchovies, fennel, coriander, paprika, oregano, and remaining ¼ cup oil in food processor until smooth paste forms, about 30 seconds, scraping down sides of bowl as needed. Add pepper and pulse to combine, 2 or 3 pulses.

4. Using 5 pieces kitchen twine for each piece of beef, tie crosswise to form even roasts. Transfer roasts to wire rack set in rimmed baking sheet and rub roasts evenly with paste.

5. Roast until meat registers 125 degrees (for medium-rare) or 130 degrees (for medium), 2 to 2¼ hours. Remove roasts from oven, leaving on wire rack, and tent with aluminum foil; let rest for 30 to 40 minutes.

6. Heat oven to 500 degrees. Remove foil from roasts and discard twine. Return roasts to oven and cook until exteriors of roasts are well browned, 6 to 8 minutes.

7. Transfer roasts to carving board. Slice meat ¼ inch thick. Season with sea salt to taste, and serve.

VARIATION

Rosemary-Garlic Top Sirloin Roast
Omit fennel, coriander, paprika, and oregano. Add 3 tablespoons chopped fresh rosemary to food processor with oil in step 3. Add ¼ teaspoon red pepper flakes with pepper in step 3.

Beef Top Loin Roast with Potatoes

SEASON 20 RECIPE

Serves 8 to 10

WHY THIS RECIPE WORKS A tender, juicy roast isn't hard to pull off. Neither are creamy, golden-brown potatoes. But merging the two into a holiday centerpiece is where things get tricky. To create a juicy, tender roast and creamy, beefy-tasting potatoes, we started with a top loin roast and trimmed the thick ribbons of fat that run along its sides. Browning the trimmings along with the roast yielded loads of rendered fat (and flavorful fond), which we then used to brown the potatoes. From there, we covered the potatoes with aluminum foil, which trapped steam that helped them cook through and allowed us to roast the beef on top of them (poking holes in the foil let juices drip through). While the cooked roast rested, we flipped the potatoes cut side up; added broth that we fortified with flavor by simmering it with the seared beef scraps, herbs, seasonings, and gelatin for unctuous body; and braised them in a 500-degree oven—our version of the old-school French classic called fondant potatoes. Finally, we strained and defatted the remaining broth to serve as a jus alongside the meat and potatoes.

1 (5- to 6-pound) boneless top loin roast
2 tablespoons plus 2 teaspoons kosher salt, divided
2 teaspoons pepper, divided
5 pounds Yukon Gold potatoes, peeled
¼ cup vegetable oil
5 cups beef broth
6 sprigs fresh thyme
2 small sprigs fresh rosemary
2 tablespoons unflavored gelatin
4 garlic cloves, lightly crushed and peeled

1. Pat roast dry with paper towels. Place roast fat cap side down and trim off strip of meat that is loosely attached to thicker side of roast. Rotate roast 180 degrees and trim off strip of meat and fat from narrow side of roast. (After trimming, roast should be rectangular with roughly even thickness.) Cut trimmings into 1-inch pieces. Transfer trimmings to small bowl, wrap tightly in plastic wrap, and refrigerate.

2. Using sharp knife, cut slits ½ inch apart and ¼ inch deep in crosshatch pattern in fat cap of roast. Sprinkle all sides of roast evenly with 2 tablespoons salt and 1 teaspoon pepper. Wrap in plastic and refrigerate for 6 to 24 hours.

3. Adjust oven rack to lowest position and heat oven to 300 degrees. Trim and discard ¼ inch from end of each potato. Cut each potato in half crosswise. Toss potatoes with remaining 2 teaspoons salt and remaining 1 teaspoon pepper and set aside.

4. Place oil in large roasting pan. Place roast, fat cap side down, in center of pan and scatter trimmings around roast. Cook over medium heat, stirring trimmings frequently but not moving roast, until fat cap is well browned, 8 to 12 minutes. Flip roast and continue to cook, stirring trimmings frequently, until bottom of roast is lightly browned and trimmings are rendered and crisp, 6 to 10 minutes. Remove pan from heat and transfer roast to plate. Using slotted spoon, transfer trimmings to medium saucepan, leaving fat in pan.

5. Arrange potatoes in single layer, broad side down, in pan. Return pan to medium heat and cook, without moving potatoes, until well browned around edges, 15 to 20 minutes. (Do not flip potatoes.) Off heat, lay 22 by 18-inch sheet of aluminum foil over potatoes. Using oven mitts, crimp edges of foil to rim of pan. With paring knife, poke 5 holes in center of foil. Lay roast, fat side up, in center of foil. Transfer pan to oven and cook until meat registers 115 degrees, 1 to 1¼ hours.

6. While roast cooks, add broth, thyme sprigs, rosemary sprigs, gelatin, and garlic to saucepan with trimmings. Bring to boil over medium-high heat. Reduce heat and simmer for 15 minutes. Strain mixture through fine-mesh strainer into 4-cup liquid measuring cup, pressing on solids to extract as much liquid as possible; discard solids. (You should have 4 cups liquid; if necessary, add water to equal 4 cups.)

7. When meat registers 115 degrees, remove pan from oven and increase oven temperature to 500 degrees. Transfer roast to carving board. Remove foil and use to tent roast. Using offset spatula, carefully flip potatoes. Pour strained liquid around potatoes and return pan (handles will be hot) to oven (it's OK if oven has not yet reached 500 degrees). Cook until liquid is reduced by half, 20 to 30 minutes.

8. Carefully transfer potatoes to serving platter. Pour liquid into fat separator and let settle for 5 minutes. Slice roast and transfer to platter with potatoes. Transfer defatted juices to small bowl. Serve, passing juices separately.

Best Prime Rib

Serves 6 to 8

WHY THIS RECIPE WORKS For the perfect prime rib we first cut slits in the layer of fat to help it render efficiently, then salted the roast overnight. The long salting time enhanced the beefy flavor while dissolving some of the proteins, yielding a buttery-tender roast. To further enhance tenderness, we cooked the roast at a very low temperature, which allowed the meat's enzymes to act as natural tenderizers, breaking down its tough connective tissue. A brief stint under the broiler before serving ensured a crisp, flavorful crust. Look for a roast with an untrimmed fat cap (ideally ½ inch thick). We prefer the flavor and texture of Prime beef, but Choice grade will work as well. Monitoring the roast with a meat-probe thermometer is best. If you use an instant-read thermometer, open the oven door as little as possible and remove the roast from the oven while taking its temperature. If the roast has not reached the correct temperature in the time range specified in step 3, heat the oven to 200 degrees, wait for 5 minutes, then shut it off, and continue to cook the roast until it reaches the desired temperature.

1 **(7-pound) first-cut beef standing rib roast (3 bones), meat removed from bones, bones reserved**
2 **tablespoons kosher salt**
2 **teaspoons vegetable oil**

1. Using sharp knife, cut slits in surface layer of fat, spaced 1 inch apart, in crosshatch pattern, being careful to cut down to, but not into, meat. Rub salt over entire roast and into slits. Place meat back on bones (to save space in refrigerator), transfer to large plate, and refrigerate, uncovered, for at least 24 hours or up to 4 days.

2. Adjust oven rack to middle position and heat oven to 200 degrees. Set wire rack in rimmed baking sheet. Heat oil in 12-inch skillet over high heat until just smoking. Sear sides and top of roast (reserving bones) until browned, 6 to 8 minutes total (do not sear side where roast was cut from bones). Place meat back on ribs so bones fit where they were cut and let cool for 10 minutes; tie meat to bones with 2 lengths of kitchen twine between ribs. Transfer roast, fat side up, to prepared wire rack and season with pepper. Roast until meat registers 110 degrees, 3 to 4 hours.

3. Turn off oven; leave roast in oven, opening door as little as possible, until meat registers about 120 degrees (for rare) or about 125 degrees (for medium-rare), 30 minutes to 1¼ hours.

4. Remove roast from oven (leave roast on baking sheet), tent with aluminum foil, and let rest for at least 30 minutes or up to 1¼ hours.

5. Adjust oven rack to about 8 inches from broiler element and heat broiler. Remove foil from roast, form into 3-inch ball, and place under ribs to elevate fat cap. Broil until top of roast is well browned and crisp, 2 to 8 minutes.

6. Transfer roast to carving board; cut twine and remove ribs from roast. Slice meat into ¾-inch-thick slices. Season with salt to taste and serve.

Preparing Best Prime Rib

1. Removing ribs makes it easier to sear prime rib in skillet. Run sharp knife down length of bones, following contours as closely as possible to remove ribs.

2. Score fat cap in 1-inch crosshatch pattern to allow salt to contact meat directly and to improve fat rendering and crisping.

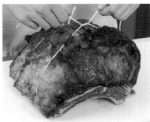

3. After searing meat, place meat back on ribs so bones fit where they were cut and let cool for 10 minutes; tie meat to bones with 2 lengths of kitchen twine between ribs.

Cuban Braised and Shredded Beef

Serves 6 to 8

WHY THIS RECIPE WORKS Tender yet hearty strands of beef napped with a bright and deeply savory sauce define *ropa vieja*. This comforting Cuban specialty with its shredded beef, sliced peppers and onions, chopped green olives, and brothy sauce is as hearty as it is rustic. For braised and shredded beef dishes, we usually turn to chuck roast and short ribs, but this Cuban specialty calls for thicker, more fibrous shreds, so we used brisket; the brisket contains the right mix of beefy flavor and collagen to guarantee tender, flavorful, juicy shreds. Slicing the beef into strips made for faster cooking and easy shredding, and a quick sear before braising gave the meat some ultrasavory browning. The accompanying vegetables would get overly soft if braised, so we cooked them ahead of time, browning sliced onions and red bell peppers and then using their fond (as well as the beef's) to build the sauce. A fragrant combination of minced anchovies, minced garlic, ground cumin, and dried oregano created the meaty, aromatic base to which we added dry white wine for brightness. After letting the mixture reduce, we added chicken broth, tomato sauce, and bay leaves. We cooked the brisket in this seasoned sauce for 2 hours and it emerged juicy and richly flavored. Green olives are a traditional finishing touch, so we chopped and added them to the sauce while the beef cooled, stirring them in with the cooked onions and peppers. A splash of white wine vinegar brought the flavors in our perfectly chewy Cuban shredded beef into sharp focus. Look for a brisket that is 1½ to 2½ inches thick. Serve with steamed white rice and beans.

- 1 (2-pound) beef brisket, fat trimmed to ¼ inch
- 1 teaspoon table salt
- ½ teaspoon pepper
- 5 tablespoons vegetable oil, divided
- 2 onions, halved and sliced thin
- 2 red bell peppers, stemmed, seeded, and sliced into ¼-inch-wide strips
- 2 anchovy fillets, rinsed, patted dry, and minced
- 4 garlic cloves, minced
- 2 teaspoons ground cumin
- 1½ teaspoons dried oregano
- ½ cup dry white wine
- 2 cups chicken broth
- 1 (8-ounce) can tomato sauce
- 2 bay leaves
- ¾ cup pitted green olives, chopped
- ¾ teaspoon white wine vinegar, plus extra for seasoning

1. Adjust oven rack to middle position and heat oven to 300 degrees. Cut brisket against grain into 2-inch-wide strips. Cut any strips longer than 5 inches in half crosswise. Season beef on all sides with salt and pepper. Heat ¼ cup oil in Dutch oven over medium-high heat until just smoking. Brown beef on all sides, 7 to 10 minutes; transfer to large plate and set aside. Add onions and bell peppers and cook until softened and pan bottom develops fond, 10 to 15 minutes. Transfer vegetables to bowl and set aside. Add remaining 1 tablespoon oil to now-empty pot, then add anchovies, garlic, cumin, and oregano and cook until fragrant, about 30 seconds. Stir in wine, scraping up any browned bits, and cook until mostly evaporated, about 1 minute. Stir in broth, tomato sauce, and bay leaves. Return beef and any accumulated juices to pot and bring to simmer over high heat. Transfer to oven and cook, covered, until beef is just tender, 2 to 2¼ hours, flipping beef halfway through cooking.

2. Transfer beef to cutting board; when cool enough to handle, shred into ¼-inch-thick pieces. Meanwhile, add olives and reserved vegetables to pot and bring to boil over medium-high heat; simmer until thickened and measures 4 cups, 5 to 7 minutes. Stir in beef. Add vinegar. Season with salt, pepper, and extra vinegar to taste; serve.

Sichuan Braised Tofu with Beef (Mapo Tofu)

Serves 4 to 6

WHY THIS RECIPE WORKS Our *mapo* tofu recipe is bold in flavor, but not too spicy, and balanced, as all Sichuan dishes should be. We used cubed soft tofu, poached gently in chicken broth to help the cubes stay intact in the braise. For the sauce base, we used plenty of ginger and garlic, along with four Sichuan pantry powerhouses: Asian broad bean chili paste, fermented black beans, Sichuan chili powder, and Sichuan peppercorns. In place of the chili oil often called for, we used a generous amount of vegetable oil, extra Sichuan chili powder, and toasted sesame oil. Finally, just the right amount of cornstarch gave the dish a velvety thickness. Ground pork can be used in place of beef, if desired. Asian broad bean chili paste (or sauce) is also known as *doubanjiang* or *toban djan*; our favorite, Pixian, is available online. Supermarket staple Lee Kum Kee Chili Bean Sauce is also a good option. If you can't find Sichuan chili powder, an equal amount of Korean red pepper flakes (*gochugaru*) is a good substitute. In a pinch, use 2½ teaspoons of ancho chile powder and ½ teaspoon of cayenne pepper. If you can't find fermented black beans, you can use an equal amount of fermented black bean paste or sauce or 2 additional teaspoons of Asian broad bean chili paste. Serve with white rice.

1 tablespoon Sichuan peppercorns
12 scallions
28 ounces soft tofu, cut into ½-inch pieces
2 cups chicken broth
9 garlic cloves, peeled
1 (3-inch) piece ginger, peeled and cut into ¼-inch rounds
⅓ cup Asian broad bean chili paste
1 tablespoon fermented black beans
¼ cup plus 2 tablespoons vegetable oil, divided
1 tablespoon Sichuan chili powder
8 ounces 85 percent lean ground beef
2 tablespoons hoisin sauce
2 teaspoons toasted sesame oil
2 tablespoons water
1 tablespoon cornstarch

1. Place peppercorns in small bowl and microwave until fragrant, 15 to 30 seconds. Let cool completely. Once cool, grind in spice grinder or mortar and pestle (you should have 1½ teaspoons).

2. Using side of chef's knife, lightly crush white parts of scallions, then cut scallions into 1-inch pieces. Place tofu, broth, and scallions in large bowl and microwave, covered, until steaming, 5 to 7 minutes. Let sit while preparing remaining ingredients.

3. Process garlic, ginger, chili paste, and black beans in food processor until coarse paste forms, 1 to 2 minutes, scraping down sides of bowl as needed. Add ¼ cup vegetable oil, chili powder, and 1 teaspoon peppercorns and continue to process until smooth paste forms, 1 to 2 minutes longer. Transfer spice paste to bowl.

4. Heat 1 tablespoon vegetable oil and beef in large saucepan over medium heat; cook, breaking up meat with wooden spoon, until meat just begins to brown, 5 to 7 minutes. Transfer beef to bowl.

5. Add remaining 1 tablespoon vegetable oil and spice paste to now-empty saucepan and cook, stirring frequently, until paste darkens and oil begins to separate from paste, 2 to 3 minutes. Gently pour tofu with broth into saucepan, followed by hoisin, sesame oil, and beef. Cook, stirring gently and frequently, until dish comes to simmer, 2 to 3 minutes. Whisk water and cornstarch together in small bowl. Add cornstarch mixture to saucepan and continue to cook, stirring frequently, until thickened, 2 to 3 minutes. Transfer to serving dish, sprinkle with remaining peppercorns, and serve. (Mapo tofu can be refrigerated for up to 24 hours.)

"This is my kind of food. Give me mapo *tofu* any day of the week, at any time (yep, even for breakfast). The silky tofu and crumbly beef napped with a rich, spicy, mouth-numbing sauce makes for a deeply flavorful, deeply satisfying dish. I recommend doing yourself a favor and ordering any hard-to-find ingredients online so you can make this recipe at the drop of a hat. Sichuan peppercorns, broad bean chili paste, fermented black beans, and Sichuan chili powder all keep indefinitely and their flavors are so robust that you will be happy to have them on hand. This dish reheats beautifully, but that can be our little secret: In my kitchen, the cook (me, of course!) always squirrels away leftovers for a next-day treat."

—*Becky*

Beef Stir-Fry with Bell Peppers and Black Pepper Sauce

Serves 4

WHY THIS RECIPE WORKS We discovered that in order to produce a stir-fry with velvety, tender beef normally only found in Chinese restaurants, we needed to choose the right cut of meat and treat it correctly. Flank steak, cut across the grain into bite-size pieces, delivered great beef flavor and a moderate chew. Then, our combination of meat tenderizing techniques—soaking the meat briefly in a mild baking soda solution and adding some cornstarch to the marinade before flash searing the steak in a very hot pan—finished the job of delivering a supertender, restaurant-quality beef stir-fry. Prepare the vegetables and aromatics while the beef is marinating. Serve with white rice.

- 5 **tablespoons water, divided**
- ¼ **teaspoon baking soda**
- 1 **pound flank steak, trimmed, cut into 2- to 2½-inch strips with grain, each strip cut crosswise against grain into ¼-inch-thick slices**
- 3 **tablespoons soy sauce, divided**
- 3 **tablespoons dry sherry or Chinese rice wine, divided**
- 1 **tablespoon cornstarch, divided**
- 2½ **teaspoons packed light brown sugar, divided**
- 1 **tablespoon oyster sauce**
- 2 **teaspoons rice vinegar**
- 1½ **teaspoons toasted sesame oil**
- 2 **teaspoons coarsely ground pepper**
- 3 **tablespoons plus 1 teaspoon vegetable oil, divided**
- 1 **red bell pepper, stemmed, seeded, and cut into ¼-inch-wide strips**
- 1 **green bell pepper, stemmed, seeded, and cut into ¼-inch-wide strips**
- 6 **scallions, white parts sliced thin on bias, green parts cut into 2-inch pieces**
- 3 **garlic cloves, minced**
- 1 **tablespoon grated fresh ginger**

1. Combine 1 tablespoon water and baking soda in medium bowl. Add beef and toss to coat. Let sit at room temperature for 5 minutes.

2. Whisk 1 tablespoon soy sauce, 1 tablespoon sherry, 1½ teaspoons cornstarch, and ½ teaspoon sugar together in small bowl. Add soy sauce mixture to beef, stir to coat, and let sit at room temperature for 15 to 30 minutes.

3. Whisk remaining ¼ cup water, remaining 2 tablespoons soy sauce, remaining 2 tablespoons sherry, remaining 1½ teaspoons cornstarch, remaining 2 teaspoons sugar, oyster sauce, vinegar, sesame oil, and pepper together in second bowl.

4. Heat 2 teaspoons vegetable oil in 12-inch nonstick skillet over high heat until just smoking. Add half of beef in single layer. Cook without stirring for 1 minute. Continue to cook, stirring occasionally, until spotty brown on both sides, about 1 minute. Transfer to bowl. Repeat with 2 teaspoons vegetable oil and remaining beef.

5. Return skillet to high heat, add 2 teaspoons vegetable oil, and heat until just beginning to smoke. Add bell peppers and scallion greens and cook, stirring occasionally, until vegetables are spotty brown and crisp-tender, about 4 minutes. Transfer vegetables to bowl with beef.

6. Return now-empty skillet to medium-high heat and add remaining 4 teaspoons vegetable oil, scallion whites, garlic, and ginger. Cook, stirring frequently, until lightly browned, about 2 minutes. Return beef and vegetables to skillet and stir to combine.

7. Whisk sauce to recombine. Add to skillet and cook, stirring constantly, until sauce has thickened, about 30 seconds. Serve immediately.

Crispy Orange Beef

Serves 4

WHY THIS RECIPE WORKS Crispy orange beef has long remained a Chinese restaurant standard because its crunchy batter coating and tangy citrus sauce seem impossible to achieve in the home kitchen without a deep fryer. To make this recipe accessible without diminishing its big flavor and shatteringly crisp crust, we started with the beef. We cut tender flap meat into matchsticks to maximize the surface area for extra crunch in each bite. Tossing the beef in soy sauce and cornstarch created a clingy, delicate coating, and 45 minutes in the freezer dried the prepped beef's surface to boost crisping. We only needed 3 cups of oil to fry the beef to a beautiful golden brown, and thanks to the dry cornstarch coating, very little oil was absorbed, so the beef never turned greasy. For a sauce to complement the crispy beef, we recreated the bitter, citrusy tang of hard-to-find dried tangerine peels by using the juice and peels of two oranges. We whisked the fresh juice with soy sauce, molasses, dry sherry, rice vinegar, and sesame oil for a complex, complementary sauce and then, for some bite and heat, browned the peels with jalapeños in a skillet. Garlic, ginger, and red pepper flakes reinforced the spicy bite before the soy sauce mixture was added to the pan. We cooked the mixture until it thickened slightly, and then tossed in our beef along with sliced scallions for a finishing touch of brightness. We prefer to buy flap meat and cut our own steak tips. Use a vegetable peeler on the oranges and make sure that your strips contain some pith. Do not use low-sodium soy sauce. Serve this dish with white rice.

1½ pounds beef flap meat, trimmed
3 tablespoons soy sauce, divided
6 tablespoons cornstarch
10 (3-inch) strips orange peel, sliced thin lengthwise (¼ cup), plus ¼ cup juice (2 oranges)
3 tablespoons molasses
2 tablespoons dry sherry
1 tablespoon rice vinegar
1½ teaspoons toasted sesame oil
3 cups vegetable oil
1 jalapeño chile, stemmed, seeded, and sliced thin lengthwise
3 garlic cloves, minced
2 tablespoons grated fresh ginger
½ teaspoon red pepper flakes
2 scallions, sliced thin on bias

1. Cut beef with grain into 2½- to 3-inch-wide lengths. Slice each piece against grain into ½-inch-thick slices. Cut each slice lengthwise into ½-inch-wide strips. Toss beef with 1 tablespoon soy sauce in bowl. Add cornstarch and toss until evenly coated. Spread beef in single layer on wire rack set in rimmed baking sheet. Transfer sheet to freezer until meat is very firm but not completely frozen, about 45 minutes.

2. Whisk remaining 2 tablespoons soy sauce, orange juice, molasses, sherry, vinegar, and sesame oil together in bowl.

3. Line second rimmed baking sheet with triple layer of paper towels. Heat vegetable oil in large Dutch oven over medium heat until oil registers 375 degrees. Carefully add one-third of beef and fry, stirring occasionally to keep beef from sticking together, until golden brown, about 1½ minutes. Using spider, transfer beef to paper towel–lined sheet. Return oil to 375 degrees and repeat twice more with remaining beef. After frying, reserve 2 tablespoons frying oil.

4. Heat reserved oil in 12-inch skillet over medium-high heat until shimmering. Add orange peel and jalapeño and cook, stirring occasionally, until about half of orange peel is golden brown, 1½ to 2 minutes. Add garlic, ginger, and pepper flakes; cook, stirring frequently, until garlic is beginning to brown, about 45 seconds. Add soy sauce mixture and cook, scraping up any browned bits, until slightly thickened, about 45 seconds. Add beef and scallions and toss. Transfer to platter and serve immediately.

Pork and Lamb

Herb-Crusted Pork Roast

Crispy Pan-Fried Pork Chops

Serves 4

WHY THIS RECIPE WORKS A breaded coating can be just the thing to give lean, bland pork chops a flavor boost—but not when it turns gummy and flakes off the meat. Using boneless chops was fast and easy. Dipping the chops in cornstarch was our first step toward creating an ultracrisp sheath. Buttermilk brought a lighter texture and tangy flavor to the breading, and minced garlic and a bit of mustard perked up the breading's flavor. Crushed cornflakes added a craggy texture to the pork chops, especially once we combined them with more cornstarch. Finally, to ensure that our breading adhered to the chops, we gave the meat a short rest and we lightly scored the pork chops before breading them. We prefer natural to enhanced pork (pork that has been injected with a salt solution to increase moistness and flavor) for this recipe. Don't let the chops drain on the paper towels for longer than 30 seconds, or the heat will steam the crust and make it soggy. You can substitute ¾ cup store-bought cornflake crumbs for the whole cornflakes. If using crumbs, omit the processing step and mix the crumbs with the cornstarch, salt, and pepper.

⅔ cup cornstarch, divided
1 cup buttermilk
2 tablespoons Dijon mustard
1 garlic clove, minced
3 cups cornflakes
1½ teaspoons table salt, divided
1 teaspoon pepper, divided
8 (3- to 4-ounce) boneless pork chops, ½ to ¾ inch thick, trimmed
⅔ cup vegetable oil, divided
Lemon wedges

1. Place ⅓ cup cornstarch in shallow dish. In second shallow dish, whisk buttermilk, mustard, and garlic until combined. Process cornflakes, ½ teaspoon salt, ½ teaspoon pepper, and remaining ⅓ cup cornstarch in food processor until cornflakes are finely ground, about 10 seconds. Transfer cornflake mixture to third shallow dish.

2. Adjust oven rack to middle position and heat oven to 200 degrees. Cut ¹⁄₁₆-inch-deep slits on both sides of chops, spaced ½ inch apart, in crosshatch pattern. Season chops with remaining 1 teaspoon salt and remaining ½ teaspoon pepper. Dredge 1 chop in cornstarch; shake off excess. Using tongs, coat with buttermilk mixture; let excess drip off. Coat with cornflake mixture; gently pat off excess. Transfer coated chop to wire rack set in rimmed baking sheet and repeat with remaining chops. Let chops sit for 10 minutes.

3. Heat ⅓ cup oil in 12-inch nonstick skillet over medium-high heat until shimmering. Place 4 chops in skillet and cook until golden brown and crisp, 2 to 5 minutes. Carefully flip chops and continue to cook until second side is golden brown, crispy, and chops register 140 degrees, 2 to 5 minutes. Transfer chops to paper towel–lined plate and let drain for 30 seconds on each side. Transfer to clean wire rack set in rimmed baking sheet, then transfer to oven to keep warm. Discard oil in skillet and wipe clean with paper towels. Repeat process with remaining ⅓ cup oil and remaining 4 pork chops. Serve with lemon wedges.

Pan-Seared Thick-Cut Pork Chops

Serves 4

WHY THIS RECIPE WORKS This simple skillet-roasting method yields plump, juicy meat and a well-formed crust every time. Instead of brining our chops, we salted the meat and let it rest for almost an hour. This helped to draw out additional moisture, which would be pulled back in later to produce juicy, well-seasoned meat. Instead of cooking our chops only on the stovetop, we turned to the oven. Slow-roasting the chops at a gentle temperature broke down connective tissue and tenderized the meat. This step also dried the exterior of the chops, creating a thin outer layer that, when seared, caramelized and turned into the crisp crust that we were after. For a completely browned crust, we seared the sides of the chops as well, using tongs to hold them up on their edges. While the cooked chops rested, we created a simple wine and garlic sauce using the browned bits left behind in the pan; now we had the perfect rich, tangy accompaniment to our chops' tender meat and crisp surface. We prefer natural to enhanced pork (pork that has been injected with a salt solution to increase moistness and flavor) for this recipe. If using enhanced pork, skip the salting in step 1. If serving the pork chops with the Garlic and Thyme Sauce (recipe follows), have all the sauce ingredients ready to go and don't wash the skillet after browning the chops; begin the sauce, using the fat left behind from browning the chops, when you set them aside to rest.

4 (12-ounce) bone-in rib loin pork chops, 1½ inches thick, trimmed
½ teaspoon table salt
1–2 tablespoons vegetable oil

1. Adjust oven rack to middle position and heat oven to 275 degrees. Pat chops dry with paper towels. Cut 2 slits, about 2 inches apart, through outer layer of fat and silverskin of each chop (do not cut into meat of chops). Sprinkle each chop with salt. Place chops on wire rack set in rimmed baking sheet and let sit at room temperature for 45 minutes.

2. Season chops with pepper; transfer baking sheet to oven. Cook until chops register 120 to 125 degrees, 30 to 45 minutes.

Pan-Seared Thick-Cut Pork Chops

3. Heat 1 tablespoon oil in 12-inch skillet over high heat until smoking. Place 2 chops in skillet and sear until well browned, 2 to 3 minutes, lifting once halfway through to redistribute fat underneath each chop. (Reduce heat if browned bits on pan bottom start to burn.) Flip chops and cook until second side is well browned, 2 to 3 minutes. Transfer chops to plate and repeat with remaining 2 chops, adding 1 tablespoon more oil if pan is dry.

4. Reduce heat to medium. Using tongs, stand 2 pork chops on sides. Hold them together with tongs, return them to skillet, and sear sides (do not sear bone side) until browned and chops register 140 degrees, about 1½ minutes. Repeat with remaining 2 chops. Transfer chops to serving platter, tent with aluminum foil, and let rest for 5 minutes. Serve.

ACCOMPANIMENT
Garlic and Thyme Sauce
Makes about ½ cup

- 1 shallot, minced
- 2 garlic cloves, minced
- ¾ cup chicken broth
- ½ cup white wine
- 1 teaspoon finely chopped fresh thyme
- ¼ teaspoon white wine vinegar
- 3 tablespoons unsalted butter, chilled and cut into 3 pieces

Pour off all but 1 teaspoon oil from skillet and heat over medium heat until shimmering. Add shallot and garlic and cook, stirring constantly, until softened, about 1 minute. Add broth and wine, scraping up any browned bits. Bring to simmer and cook until sauce measures ½ cup, 6 to 7 minutes. Off heat, stir in thyme and vinegar; whisk in butter, 1 tablespoon at a time. Season with salt and pepper to taste.

Smothered Pork Chops

Serves 4

WHY THIS RECIPE WORKS Tender, flavorful chops stand up very well to rich, hearty gravy. But most of the time, the gravy misses the mark—it's either so thick you can't find the pork chop, or so thin and watery that the meat seems to be floating on the plate. We wanted a foolproof recipe for juicy chops smothered in rich gravy with a satiny, thick texture. For a nice balance with the gravy and to allow for the best absorption of the gravy's flavors, we used thin, not thick, rib chops. Searing them well left meaty browned bits in the pan, essential for making a flavorful gravy. To build further flavor, we made a nut-brown, bacony roux. Thinly sliced yellow onions contributed a significant amount of moisture to the gravy. Garlic, thyme, and bay leaves rounded out the flavorful gravy;

we skipped the salt because we had already salted the onions to encourage their browning and so they would give up liquid. For the tenderest chops, we combined the sauce and browned chops in the pan and braised them for half an hour. Not only did the lengthy braise result in moist, tender chops, it also allowed the gravy to thicken and its flavors to meld, so the chops had a rich, velvety coating when served. We prefer natural to enhanced pork (pork that has been injected with a salt solution to increase moistness and flavor) for this recipe, though either will work here. Serve smothered chops with egg noodles or mashed potatoes to soak up the rich gravy.

- 3 slices bacon, cut into ¼-inch pieces
- 2 tablespoons vegetable oil, divided, plus extra as needed
- 2 tablespoons all-purpose flour
- 1¾ cups chicken broth
- 4 (7-ounce) bone-in rib loin pork chops, ½ to ¾ inch thick, trimmed
- 1 teaspoon pepper
- 2 yellow onions, halved and sliced thin
- ¼ teaspoon table salt
- 2 tablespoons water
- 2 garlic cloves, minced
- 1 teaspoon finely chopped fresh thyme
- 2 bay leaves
- 1 tablespoon finely chopped fresh parsley

1. Cook bacon in small saucepan over medium heat, stirring occasionally, until crisp, 8 to 10 minutes. Using slotted spoon, transfer bacon to paper towel–lined plate, leaving fat in saucepan (you should have 2 tablespoons bacon fat; if not, add oil). Whisk in flour and cook over medium-low heat until golden, about 5 minutes. Whisk in broth and bring to boil, stirring occasionally, over medium-high heat. Off heat, cover and set aside.

2. Pat chops dry with paper towels. Cut 2 slits, about 2 inches apart, through outer layer of fat and silverskin of each chop (do not cut into meat of chops). Sprinkle each chop with ½ teaspoon pepper. Heat 1 tablespoon oil in 12-inch skillet over high heat until smoking. Cook chops until browned on first side, about 3 minutes. Flip chops and cook until second side is browned, about 3 minutes. Transfer chops to plate and set aside.

3. Add remaining 1 tablespoon oil to skillet and return to medium heat until shimmering. Add onions, salt, and water, scraping up any browned bits, and cook until lightly browned, about 5 minutes. Stir in garlic and thyme and cook until fragrant, about 30 seconds. Return chops to skillet and cover with onions. Add reserved sauce, bay leaves, and any accumulated juices to skillet. Cover and simmer over low heat until chops are tender and paring knife inserted into chops meets little resistance, about 30 minutes.

4. Transfer chops to serving platter and tent with foil. Simmer sauce over medium-high heat, stirring frequently, until thickened, about 5 minutes. Discard bay leaves, stir in parsley, and season with salt and pepper to taste. Cover chops with sauce, sprinkle with reserved bacon, and serve.

Crunchy Baked Pork Chops

Serves 4

WHY THIS RECIPE WORKS These baked, breaded pork chops are the ultimate comfort food—juicy, tender chops covered with a well-seasoned, crunchy crust. We used center-cut boneless loin chops—which are easy to find and affordable—and brined them so the meat would stay moist and juicy. For the coating, only fresh bread crumbs would do; we toasted them for crispness and doctored them with garlic, shallots, Parmesan cheese, and minced herbs for flavor. To form a strong adhering agent for the crumbs, and prevent the chops from ending up bald in patches, we made a quick batterlike mixture by whisking flour and mustard into egg whites; whole eggs were a no-go because their higher amount of fat made for a soft, puffy layer under the bread crumbs. Baking the breaded chops on a wire rack set in a rimmed baking sheet allowed air to circulate completely around the chops, keeping the bottom crumbs crisp. Out of the oven, these chops were tender and moist, with a crisp coating that stayed put, even through some heavy knife-and-fork action. We prefer natural to enhanced pork (pork that has been injected with a salt solution to increase moistness and flavor) for this recipe. If using enhanced pork, skip the brining in step 1. The breaded chops can be frozen for up to one week. They don't need to be thawed before baking; simply increase the cooking time in step 5 to 35 to 40 minutes.

¼ cup table salt, for brining
4 (6- to 8-ounce) boneless center-cut or loin pork chops, ¾ to 1 inch thick, trimmed
4 slices hearty white sandwich bread, torn into 1-inch pieces
2 tablespoons vegetable oil
1 shallot, minced
3 garlic cloves, minced
¼ teaspoon table salt
¾ teaspoon pepper, divided
2 tablespoons grated Parmesan cheese
2 tablespoons finely chopped fresh parsley
½ teaspoon finely chopped fresh thyme
10 tablespoons all-purpose flour, divided
3 large egg whites
3 tablespoons Dijon mustard
Lemon wedges

1. Adjust oven rack to middle position and heat oven to 350 degrees. Dissolve ¼ cup salt in 4 cups cold water in medium bowl. Submerge chops, cover, and refrigerate for 30 minutes. Remove chops from brine, rinse, and pat dry with paper towels.

2. Meanwhile, pulse bread in food processor to coarse crumbs, about 8 pulses (you should have about 3½ cups crumbs). Transfer crumbs to rimmed baking sheet, add oil, shallot, garlic, ¼ teaspoon salt, and ¼ teaspoon pepper, and toss until crumbs are evenly coated with oil. Bake until golden brown and dry, about 15 minutes, stirring twice. (Do not turn off oven.) Let cool to room temperature. Toss crumbs with Parmesan, parsley, and thyme. (Bread-crumb mixture can be stored for up to 3 days.)

3. Place ¼ cup flour in shallow dish. In second shallow dish, whisk egg whites and mustard together; add remaining 6 tablespoons flour and whisk until almost smooth, with pea-sized lumps remaining.

4. Increase oven temperature to 425 degrees. Spray wire rack with vegetable oil spray and place in rimmed baking sheet. Season chops with remaining ½ teaspoon pepper. Dredge 1 pork chop in flour; shake off excess. Using tongs, coat with egg mixture; let excess drip off. Coat all sides of chop with bread-crumb mixture, pressing gently so that thick layer of crumbs adheres to chop. Transfer breaded chop to wire rack. Repeat with remaining 3 chops.

5. Bake until chops register 140 degrees, about 20 minutes. Let rest on rack for 5 minutes; serve with lemon wedges.

Stuffed Pork Chops

Serves 4

WHY THIS RECIPE WORKS Thick-cut pork chops make the perfect home for a simple stuffing. Unfortunately, most stuffed pork chops are extremely dry and bland, with a filling that looks like it's trying to escape. We wanted the stuffing to be especially flavorful and rich to offset the mildness of the pork, and we wanted the chops to be moist and juicy. Our stuffing was easy enough to make—we used a simple combination of aromatic vegetables, herbs, and fresh bread. But the stuffing was so loose, it crumbled and spilled out over the plate when the chops were served. Clearly, we needed a binder. Instead of eggs, we chose cream, which added richness and enough moisture to bring the stuffing together. Because the stuffing didn't contain eggs, the chops could be cooked to a lower (and more palatable) internal temperature, making for tender and juicy meat. After brining the chops and creating a small "pocket" to hold the stuffing, we started them in a skillet to develop a nice brown crust but finished cooking them through on a baking sheet in a hot oven. A sweet chutney of ginger, apples, and apple cider (recipe follows) provided a nice contrast to the savory filling. For an alternative to chutney, flavorful gravy (sans big roast) was ideal for draping over the stuffed chops (recipe follows). Thoroughly browning both the aromatic vegetables and the flour added significant flavor to the gravy, as did the inclusion of two kinds of broth: beef and chicken. We prefer natural to enhanced pork (pork that has been injected with a salt solution to increase moistness and flavor) for this recipe, though either will work here.

Pork Chops
- 4 (12-ounce) bone-in rib loin pork chops, 1½ inches thick, trimmed
- ¾ cup packed light brown sugar, for brining
- ¼ cup table salt, for brining
- 1 tablespoon vegetable oil

Stuffing
- 3 tablespoons unsalted butter
- 1 small onion, chopped fine
- 1 celery rib, chopped fine
- ½ teaspoon table salt
- 1 tablespoon finely chopped fresh parsley
- 2 garlic cloves, minced
- 2 teaspoons finely chopped fresh thyme
- 2 slices hearty white sandwich bread, cut into ¼-inch pieces
- 2 tablespoons heavy cream
- ⅛ teaspoon pepper

1. *For the pork chops:* Cut small pocket through side of each chop. Dissolve sugar and salt in 6 cups cold water in large bowl or container. Submerge chops in brine, cover with plastic wrap, and refrigerate for 1 hour.

2. *For the stuffing:* Melt butter in 12-inch skillet over medium heat. Add onion, celery, and salt and cook until vegetables are softened, 6 to 8 minutes. Add parsley, garlic, and thyme and cook until fragrant, about 30 seconds. Transfer to medium bowl and toss with bread pieces, cream, and pepper. Mix, lightly pressing mixture against sides of bowl, until it comes together.

3. Adjust oven rack to lower-middle position, place rimmed baking sheet on rack, and heat oven to 450 degrees. Remove chops from brine, rinse, and pat dry with paper towels. Place one-quarter of stuffing (about ⅓ cup) in pocket of each pork chop. Season chops with pepper.

4. Heat oil in 12-inch skillet over high heat until shimmering. Place chops in skillet and cook until well browned, about 3 minutes. Flip chops and cook until second side is well browned, about 2 minutes.

5. Transfer chops to sheet in oven. Roast until chops register 140 degrees, about 15 minutes, turning chops halfway through roasting. Transfer chops to plate, tent with aluminum foil, and let rest for 5 to 10 minutes. Serve.

ACCOMPANIMENTS

Quick All-Purpose Gravy
Makes 2 cups

This gravy can be served with almost any type of meat and with mashed potatoes as well. The recipe can be doubled. If doubling it, use a Dutch oven so that the vegetables brown properly and increase the cooking times by roughly half. The finished gravy can be frozen. To thaw it, place the gravy and 1 tablespoon of water in a saucepan over low heat and slowly bring it to a simmer. It may appear broken or curdled as it thaws, but a vigorous whisking will recombine it.

- 3 tablespoons unsalted butter
- 1 onion, minced
- 1 small carrot, peeled and chopped fine
- 1 celery rib, chopped fine
- ¼ cup all-purpose flour
- 2 cups chicken broth
- 2 cups beef broth
- 1 bay leaf
- ¼ teaspoon dried thyme
- 5 whole black peppercorns

1. Melt butter in large saucepan over medium-high heat. Add onion, carrot, and celery and cook, stirring frequently, until softened, about 7 minutes. Reduce heat to medium, add flour, and cook, stirring constantly, until thoroughly browned, about 5 minutes. Gradually whisk in broths and bring to boil, skimming off any foam that forms on surface. Add bay leaf, thyme, and peppercorns and simmer, stirring occasionally, until thickened and reduced to 3 cups, 20 to 25 minutes.

2. Strain gravy through fine-mesh strainer into clean saucepan, pressing on solids to extract as much liquid as possible; discard solids. Season with salt and pepper to taste.

Ginger-Apple Chutney
Makes about 3½ cups
If you want more heat, add a little more cayenne pepper.

- 1 tablespoon vegetable oil
- 1 small onion, chopped medium
- 2 Granny Smith apples, peeled, cored, and cut into ½-inch pieces
- 1 tablespoon grated fresh ginger
- ¼ teaspoon ground allspice
- ⅛ teaspoon cayenne pepper
- 1 cup apple cider
- ¼ cup packed light brown sugar

After removing chops from pan, pour off any fat left in skillet. Heat oil over medium-high heat until shimmering. Add onion and apples and cook, stirring occasionally, until softened, about 10 minutes. Add ginger, allspice, and cayenne and cook until fragrant, about 30 seconds. Add cider and sugar and bring to boil, scraping up any browned bits, until cider is slightly thickened, about 4 minutes. Season with salt and pepper to taste.

Stuffing Pork Chops

1. Using paring knife, trim away excess fat and connective tissue around edge of meat.

2. With knife positioned as shown, insert blade through center of side of chop until tip touches bone.

3. Swing tip of blade through middle of chop to create pocket (opening should be about 1 inch wide).

4. With your fingers, gently press stuffing mixture into pocket, without enlarging opening.

2 (12- to 16-ounce) pork tenderloins, trimmed
1¼ teaspoons table salt
¾ teaspoon pepper
2 teaspoons vegetable oil

1. Adjust oven rack to middle position and heat oven to 400 degrees. Season tenderloins with salt and pepper; rub seasoning into meat. Heat oil in 12-inch skillet over medium-high heat until smoking. Place both tenderloins in skillet; cook until well browned, about 3 minutes. Using tongs, rotate tenderloins a quarter-turn; cook until well browned, 45 to 60 seconds. Repeat until all sides are browned, about 1 minute. Transfer tenderloins to rimmed baking sheet and place in oven; roast until meat registers 140 degrees, 10 to 16 minutes.

2. Transfer tenderloins to carving board and tent with foil; let rest for 8 to 10 minutes. Cut tenderloins crosswise into ½-inch-thick slices, arrange on serving platter, and serve immediately.

Pan-Seared Oven-Roasted Pork Tenderloin

Serves 4

WHY THIS RECIPE WORKS Because pork tenderloins are so lean, they cook relatively quickly and are therefore a good choice for an easy-to-prepare meal. But that same leanness means that the pork tends to overcook, and there's also less flavor. Simply roasted in the oven, the pork tended to dry out and never achieved the dark brown crust we wanted. We got that crust when we seared the tenderloins on the stovetop—but then the pork wasn't cooked through. A combination of searing the meat in a skillet and transferring the pork to the oven to finish cooking produced a flavorful crust and well-cooked meat. The browned crust added some flavor, but we wanted more. A dry rub of just salt and pepper provided enough seasoning and further encouraged a browned crust, and a pan sauce made with the browned bits left from sautéing gave an additional flavor boost. Not only were these pork tenderloins delicious, they were also on the dinner table in about half an hour. We prefer natural to enhanced pork (pork that has been injected with a salt solution to increase moisture and flavor) for this recipe. Enhanced pork can be used, but the meat won't brown as well. Because two are cooked at once, tenderloins larger than 1 pound apiece will not fit comfortably in a 12-inch skillet. If time permits, season the tenderloins up to 30 minutes before cooking; the seasonings will better penetrate the meat. The recipe will work in a nonstick or a traditional skillet. A pan sauce can be made while the tenderloins are in the oven (recipes follow). If you intend to make a sauce, make sure to prepare all of the sauce ingredients before beginning the recipe and don't wash the skillet after browning the pork.

ACCOMPANIMENTS
Dried Cherry–Port Sauce with Onions and Marmalade
Makes about ½ cup
The flavors in this sauce are especially suited to the winter holiday season. Begin making this sauce as soon as the pork goes into the oven. Spoon the finished sauce over the pork slices just before serving.

1 teaspoon vegetable oil
1 large onion, halved and sliced ½ inch thick
¾ cup port
¾ cup dried cherries
2 tablespoons orange marmalade
3 tablespoons unsalted butter, cut into 3 pieces

1. Add oil to hot skillet, swirl to coat, and set skillet over medium-high heat; add onion and cook, stirring frequently, until softened and browned around edges, 5 to 7 minutes. (If drippings are browning too quickly, add 2 tablespoons water and scrape up browned bits.) Off heat, set skillet aside.

2. While pork is resting, set skillet over medium-high heat and add port and cherries; simmer, scraping up browned bits, until mixture is slightly thickened, 4 to 6 minutes. Add any accumulated pork juices and continue to simmer until thickened and reduced to about ⅓ cup, 2 to 4 minutes. Off heat, whisk in orange marmalade and butter, 1 piece at a time. Season with salt and pepper to taste.

Garlicky Lime Sauce with Cilantro
Makes about ½ cup

This assertive sauce is based on a Mexican sauce called mojo de ajo. A rasp-style grater makes quick work of turning the garlic into a paste. If your garlic cloves contain green sprouts or shoots, remove the sprouts before grating them—their flavor is bitter and hot. The initial cooking of the garlic off the heat will prevent scorching. Begin making this sauce as soon as the pork goes into the oven. Spoon the finished sauce over the pork slices just before serving.

- 10 garlic cloves, minced to paste (2 tablespoons)
- 2 tablespoons water
- 1 tablespoon vegetable oil
- ¼ teaspoon red pepper flakes
- 2 teaspoons packed light brown sugar
- ¼ cup chopped fresh cilantro
- 3 tablespoons lime juice (2 limes)
- 1 tablespoon finely chopped fresh chives
- 4 tablespoons unsalted butter, cut into 4 pieces

1. Mix garlic paste with water in small bowl. Add oil to hot skillet and swirl to coat; off heat, add garlic paste and cook with skillet's residual heat, scraping up browned bits, until sizzling subsides, about 2 minutes. Set skillet over low heat and continue cooking, stirring frequently, until garlic is sticky, 8 to 10 minutes. Off heat, set skillet aside.

2. While pork is resting, set skillet over medium heat; add pepper flakes and sugar to skillet and cook until sticky and sugar is dissolved, about 1 minute. Add cilantro, lime juice, and chives; simmer to meld flavors, 1 to 2 minutes. Add any accumulated pork juices and simmer for 1 minute. Off heat, whisk in butter, 1 piece at a time. Season with salt and pepper to taste.

Maple-Glazed Pork Tenderloin

Serves 6

WHY THIS RECIPE WORKS One way to add flavor to a lean, mild pork tenderloin is to glaze it before roasting. We thought a thick, sweet, fragrant glaze would be just the solution and decided it should feature New England's signature ingredient, maple syrup. Getting the glaze right was comparatively easy: To temper the sweetness of the maple syrup, we added molasses, mustard, and a shot of bourbon; with a little cinnamon, cloves, and cayenne, the glaze was ready. To give the glaze something to hold on to, we rolled the tenderloins in a mixture of cornstarch and sugar before searing them. When we'd built a good crust in the skillet, we painted on some glaze and transferred the pork to the oven.

It occurred to us that the painting analogy was a good one—why not put multiple coats on the tenderloins to get the best coverage? When the meat was nearly done, we put on more glaze, and we added yet another coat when the tenderloins were completely done. Finally, after letting the tenderloins rest, we glazed them one last time. Slicing into this roast revealed success: A thick maple glaze coated the meat. We prefer natural to enhanced pork (pork that has been injected with a salt solution to increase moistness and flavor) for this recipe. If your tenderloins are smaller than 1¼ pounds, reduce the cooking time in step 3 (and use an instant-read thermometer for best results). If the tenderloins don't fit in the skillet initially, let their ends curve toward each other; the meat will eventually shrink as it cooks. Make sure to cook the tenderloins until they turn deep golden brown in step 2 or they will appear pale after glazing. Be sure to pat off the cornstarch mixture thoroughly in step 1, as any excess will leave gummy spots on the tenderloins. Make sure not to use robust or dark molasses or the flavor will be too bitter.

- ¾ cup maple syrup, preferably dark, divided
- ¼ cup molasses
- 2 tablespoons bourbon or brandy
- ⅛ teaspoon ground cinnamon
- Pinch ground cloves
- Pinch cayenne pepper
- ¼ cup cornstarch
- 2 tablespoons sugar
- 1 tablespoon table salt
- 2 teaspoons pepper
- 2 (1¼- to 1½-pound) pork tenderloins, trimmed
- 2 tablespoons vegetable oil
- 1 tablespoon whole-grain mustard

1. Adjust oven rack to middle position and heat oven to 375 degrees. Stir ½ cup maple syrup, molasses, bourbon, cinnamon, cloves, and cayenne together in 2-cup liquid measuring cup; set aside. Whisk cornstarch, sugar, salt, and pepper in small bowl until combined. Transfer cornstarch mixture to rimmed baking sheet. Pat tenderloins dry with paper towels, then roll in cornstarch mixture until evenly coated on all sides. Thoroughly pat off excess cornstarch mixture.

2. Heat oil in 12-inch nonstick skillet over medium-high heat until just smoking. Reduce heat to medium and place both tenderloins in skillet, leaving at least 1 inch between them. Cook until well browned on all sides, 8 to 12 minutes. Transfer tenderloins to wire rack set in rimmed baking sheet.

3. Pour off fat from skillet and return to medium heat. Add syrup mixture to skillet, scraping up any browned bits, and cook until reduced to ½ cup, about 2 minutes. Transfer 2 tablespoons glaze to small bowl and set aside. Using remaining glaze, brush each tenderloin with approximately 1 tablespoon glaze. Roast pork until meat registers 130 degrees, 12 to 20 minutes. Brush each tenderloin with another tablespoon glaze and continue to roast until meat registers 140 degrees, 2 to 4 minutes. Remove tenderloins from oven and brush each with remaining glaze; let rest, uncovered, for about 10 minutes.

4. While tenderloins rest, stir remaining ¼ cup maple syrup and mustard into reserved 2 tablespoons glaze. Brush each tenderloin with 1 tablespoon mustard glaze. Transfer meat to carving board and slice into ¼-inch-thick pieces. Serve, passing extra mustard glaze separately.

Milk-Braised Pork Loin

Serves 4 to 6

WHY THIS RECIPE WORKS Braising pork in milk is an Italian technique that produces moist pork paired with a rich, savory sauce. To maximize the pork loin roast's seasoning and moisture, we brined it in a salt and sugar solution for 90 minutes. We wanted the sauce to be loaded with porky flavor, so we rendered salt pork (simmered in water to prevent burning) before introducing the roast to the pot. We browned the roast on all sides, removed it, and then began to build the sauce, stirring together milk, garlic cloves, and sage. Adding baking soda to the pot deepened the sauce's color and enriched its savory flavors. Once the sauce had thickened, we added the roast back to the pot and transferred it to a 275-degree oven. Adding white wine brightened the sauce, and we finished it with Dijon mustard for heat and parsley for a burst of freshness. The milk will bubble up when added to the pot. If necessary,

remove the pot from the heat and stir to break up the foam before returning it to the heat. We prefer natural pork, but if your pork is enhanced (injected with a salt solution to increase moisture and flavor), do not brine. Instead, skip to step 2.

¼ cup table salt, for brining
¼ cup sugar, for brining
1 (2- to 2½-pound) boneless pork loin roast, trimmed
2 ounces salt pork, chopped
3 cups whole milk
5 garlic cloves, peeled
1 teaspoon finely chopped fresh sage
¼ teaspoon baking soda
½ cup dry white wine
3 tablespoons finely chopped fresh parsley, divided
1 teaspoon Dijon mustard

1. Dissolve ¼ cup salt and sugar in 2 quarts cold water in large container. Submerge roast in brine, cover, and refrigerate for at least 1½ hours or up to 2 hours. Remove roast from brine and pat dry with paper towels.

2. Adjust oven rack to middle position and heat oven to 275 degrees. Bring salt pork and ½ cup water to simmer in Dutch oven over medium heat. Simmer until water evaporates and salt pork begins to sizzle, 5 to 6 minutes. Continue to cook, stirring frequently, until salt pork is lightly browned and fat has rendered, 2 to 3 minutes. Using slotted spoon, discard salt pork, leaving fat in pot.

3. Increase heat to medium-high, add roast to pot, and brown on all sides, 8 to 10 minutes. Transfer roast to large plate. Add milk, garlic, sage, and baking soda to pot and bring to simmer, scraping up any browned bits. Cook, stirring frequently, until milk is lightly browned and has consistency of heavy cream, 14 to 16 minutes. Reduce heat to medium-low and continue to cook, stirring and scraping bottom of pot constantly, until milk thickens to consistency of thin batter, 1 to 3 minutes. Remove pot from heat.

4. Return roast to pot, cover, and transfer to oven. Cook until meat registers 140 degrees, 40 to 50 minutes, flipping roast once halfway through cooking. Transfer roast to carving board, tent with aluminum foil, and let rest for 20 to 25 minutes.

5. Once roast has rested, pour any accumulated juices into pot. Add wine and return sauce to simmer over medium-high heat, whisking vigorously to smooth out sauce. Simmer until sauce has consistency of thin gravy, 2 to 3 minutes. Off heat, stir in 2 tablespoons parsley and mustard and season with salt and pepper to taste. Slice roast into ¼-inch-thick slices. Transfer slices to serving platter. Spoon sauce over slices, sprinkle with remaining 1 tablespoon parsley, and serve.

French-Style Pot-Roasted Pork Loin

Serves 4 to 6

WHY THIS RECIPE WORKS *Enchaud Périgourdine* is a fancy name for what's actually a relatively simple French dish: slow-cooked pork loin. Cooked in the oven in a covered casserole dish, the roast turns out incredibly moist and flavorful, with a rich jus to accompany it. At least it does when it's prepared in France. But while pigs in France are bred to have plenty of fat, their American counterparts are lean, which translates to a bland and stringy roast. To improve the flavor and texture of our center-cut loin, we lowered the oven temperature (to 225 degrees) and removed the roast from the oven when it was medium-rare. Searing just three sides of the roast, rather than all four, prevented the bottom of the roast from overcooking from direct contact with the pot. Butterflying the pork allowed us to salt a maximum amount of surface area for a roast that was thoroughly seasoned throughout. And while we eliminated the hard-to-find trotter (or pig's foot), we added butter for richness, while a sprinkling of gelatin lent body to the sauce. We strongly prefer the flavor of natural pork in this recipe, but enhanced pork (injected with a salt solution to increase moisture and flavor) can be used. If using enhanced pork, reduce the salt to 2 teaspoons (1 teaspoon per side) in step 2.

2 tablespoons unsalted butter, cut into 2 pieces, divided
6 garlic cloves, sliced thin, divided
1 tablespoon kosher salt
1 (2½-pound) boneless center-cut pork loin roast, trimmed and butterflied
1 teaspoon sugar
2 teaspoons herbes de Provence
½ teaspoon pepper
2 tablespoons vegetable oil, divided
1 Granny Smith apple, peeled, cored, and cut into ¼-inch pieces
1 onion, chopped fine
⅓ cup dry white wine
2 sprigs fresh thyme
1 bay leaf
1 tablespoon unflavored gelatin
¼-¾ cup chicken broth, divided
1 tablespoon finely chopped fresh parsley

1. Adjust oven rack to lower-middle position and heat oven to 225 degrees. Melt 1 tablespoon butter in 8-inch skillet over medium-low heat. Add half of garlic and cook, stirring frequently, until golden, 5 to 7 minutes. Transfer mixture to bowl and refrigerate while preparing pork.

2. Sprinkle salt evenly over both sides of loin and thoroughly rub into pork until surface is slightly tacky. Sprinkle sugar evenly over inside of loin and then spread with cooled toasted garlic mixture. Fold roast back together and tie tightly with kitchen twine at 1½-inch intervals. Sprinkle roast with herbes de Provence and pepper. (Pork can be wrapped in plastic wrap and refrigerated for up to 2 days.)

3. Heat 1 tablespoon oil in Dutch oven over medium heat until just smoking. Add roast, fat side down, and brown on top and sides (do not brown bottom of roast), 5 to 8 minutes. Transfer to plate. Add remaining 1 tablespoon oil, apple, and onion; cook, stirring frequently, until onion is softened and browned, 5 to 7 minutes. Stir in remaining sliced garlic and cook until fragrant, about 30 seconds. Stir in wine, thyme sprigs, and bay leaf, and cook for 30 seconds. Return roast, fat side up, to pot; place sheet of aluminum foil over pot and cover tightly with lid. Transfer pot to oven and cook until meat registers 140 degrees, 50 minutes to 1½ hours.

Double-Butterflying a Roast

1. Holding chef's knife parallel to cutting board, insert knife one-third of the way up from bottom of roast and cut horizontally, stopping ½ inch before edge. Open up flap.

2. Make second horizontal cut into thicker portion of roast. Open up this flap, smoothing out butterflied rectangle of meat.

4. Transfer roast to carving board, tent with foil, and let rest for 20 minutes. While pork rests, sprinkle gelatin over ¼ cup chicken broth and let sit until gelatin softens, about 5 minutes. Discard thyme sprigs and bay leaf from jus. Pour jus into 2-cup liquid measuring cup and, if necessary, add chicken broth to measure 1¼ cups. Return jus to pot and bring to simmer over medium heat. Whisk softened gelatin mixture, remaining 1 tablespoon butter, and parsley into jus and season with salt and pepper to taste. Off heat, cover to keep warm. Slice the pork into ½-inch-thick slices, adding any accumulated juices to sauce. Serve pork, passing sauce separately.

Garlic-Studded Roast Pork Loin

Serves 4 to 6

WHY THIS RECIPE WORKS Although it has a little more fat than pork tenderloin, a center loin pork roast is still quite lean and requires special handling to roast without drying out. We sought the best way to roast this cut so that the juices would remain inside the meat, not wind up on the carving board. It turned out that a two-step roasting process was the key to juicy pork loin. After poking slivers of garlic into the meat and rubbing the surface with a mixture of thyme, cloves, salt, and pepper for extra flavor, we refrigerated the roast overnight. The next day we cranked up the oven to 475 degrees and added the pork directly from the fridge, leaving it in the oven for just half an hour before removing it. After we rested the roast, we returned it to the oven, this time at a lower temperature, to finish cooking. The texture of the meat was remarkably tender, and it had lost very little juice. The reason this method worked was that during the rest, the middle of the roast heated by conduction from the heat absorbed by the outside of the roast. When the meat went back into the oven, the center cooked through but the outside didn't overcook. We prefer natural to enhanced pork (pork that has been injected with a salt solution to increase moisture and flavor) for this recipe. For extra flavor and moisture, serve the sliced roast with Mustard-Shallot Sauce with Thyme (recipe follows), if desired.

- 2 **teaspoons dried thyme**
- 2 **teaspoons table salt**
- 1 **teaspoon pepper**
- ¼ **teaspoon ground cloves or allspice**
- 2 **garlic cloves, peeled and sliced thin**
- 1 **(2¼-pound) boneless center loin pork roast, trimmed and tied at 1½-inch intervals**

1. Mix together thyme, salt, pepper, and cloves. Coat garlic slices in spice mixture. Poke slits in roast with point of paring knife; insert garlic slices. Rub remaining spice mixture onto meat. Wrap roast in plastic wrap and refrigerate for at least 2 hours or up to 24 hours.

2. Adjust oven rack to middle position and heat oven to 475 degrees. Take meat directly from refrigerator, remove plastic wrap, and place on wire rack set in shallow roasting pan. Roast for exactly 30 minutes.

3. Remove meat from oven; immediately reduce oven temperature to 325 degrees. Insert instant-read thermometer at 1 end of roast, going into thickest part at center (temperature will range from 80 to 110 degrees); let roast rest at room temperature, uncovered, for exactly 30 minutes. (At this point roast's internal temperature will range from 115 to 140 degrees.) After this 30-minute rest, remove thermometer, return meat to oven, and roast until meat registers 140 degrees, 15 to 30 minutes.

4. Let roast sit at room temperature, uncovered, for 15 to 20 minutes. Remove twine, slice meat thin, and serve.

ACCOMPANIMENT
Mustard-Shallot Sauce with Thyme
Makes about 1 cup
Start making the sauce as soon as the roast comes out of the oven for the second time. Use a grainy, or country-style, mustard in this recipe. For extra body and richness, swirl another tablespoon or two of softened butter into the finished sauce. Serve the sauce immediately with the roast.

- 2 **tablespoons unsalted butter**
- 4 **shallots, chopped fine**
- ¾ **cup dry white wine or dry vermouth**
- 1 **cup chicken broth**
- ¾ **teaspoon finely chopped fresh thyme or**
  ¼ **teaspoon dried thyme**
- ¼ **cup whole-grain mustard**

Melt butter in 10-inch skillet over medium-high heat. Add shallots and sauté until softened, 3 to 4 minutes. Add wine and boil until nearly evaporated, 8 to 10 minutes. Add broth and thyme; boil until reduced by one third, about 5 minutes. Remove pan from heat and stir in mustard.

Maple-Glazed Pork Roast

Serves 4 to 6

WHY THIS RECIPE WORKS Maple-glazed pork roast often falls short of its savory-sweet promise. Many roasts turn out dry, but the glazes often present even bigger problems. Most are too thin to coat the pork properly, some are too sweet, and few have a pronounced maple flavor. We wanted a glistening roast, which, when sliced, would combine the juices from tender, well-seasoned pork with a rich maple glaze to create complex flavor in every bite. For this dish we chose a blade-end loin roast, which has a deposit of fat that helps keep the meat moist. We tied it at intervals to make a neat bundle. Searing the roast first on the stovetop was a must for a flavorful exterior. We then removed the pork so that we could use the browned bits in the skillet to build the glaze. Maple syrup, with complementary spices and cayenne pepper for heat, made a thick, clingy glaze. Instead of brushing the glaze onto the pork, however, we decided to keep things simple and returned the pork to the skillet, rolled it in the glaze to coat it, and put the whole thing into the oven. The smaller area of the skillet kept the glaze from spreading out and burning, and the glaze reduced nicely while the roast cooked. Rolling the roast in the glaze periodically ensured even coverage and resulted in a tender, juicy roast. We prefer natural to enhanced pork (pork that has been injected with a salt solution to increase moisture and flavor) for this recipe. We prefer a nonstick ovensafe skillet because it is much easier to clean than a traditional one. Whichever you use, remember that the handle will be blistering hot when you take it out of the oven, so be sure to use a potholder or oven mitt. Note that you should not trim the pork of its thin layer of fat. This dish is unapologetically sweet, so we recommend side dishes that take well to the sweetness. Garlicky sautéed greens, braised cabbage, and soft polenta are good choices.

⅓ cup maple syrup, preferably dark
⅛ teaspoon ground cinnamon
  Pinch ground cloves
  Pinch cayenne pepper
1 (2½-pound) boneless blade-end pork loin roast, tied at 1½-inch intervals
¾ teaspoon table salt
½ teaspoon pepper
2 teaspoons vegetable oil

1. Adjust oven rack to middle position and heat oven to 325 degrees. Stir maple syrup, cinnamon, cloves, and cayenne together in small bowl and set aside. Pat roast dry with paper towels, then season with salt and pepper.

2. Heat oil in ovensafe 10-inch nonstick skillet over medium-high heat until just smoking. Cook roast until well browned on all sides, 6 to 8 minutes. Transfer roast to large plate. Reduce heat to medium and pour off fat from skillet; add maple syrup mixture and cook until fragrant, about 30 seconds (the syrup will bubble immediately). Off heat, return roast to skillet, rolling roast to coat with glaze on all sides.

3. Place skillet in oven and roast until pork registers 140 degrees, 35 to 45 minutes, rotating pork to coat with glaze twice during roasting time. Transfer roast to carving board; set skillet aside to cool slightly to thicken glaze, about 5 minutes. Pour glaze over roast and let rest for 15 minutes. Remove twine, slice meat ¼ inch thick, and serve immediately.

VARIATIONS

Maple-Glazed Pork Roast with Rosemary
Substitute 2 teaspoons finely chopped fresh rosemary for cinnamon, cloves, and cayenne.

Maple-Glazed Pork Roast with Orange Essence
Add 1 tablespoon grated orange zest to maple syrup along with spices.

Maple-Glazed Pork Roast with Star Anise
Add 4 star anise pods to maple syrup along with spices.

Maple-Glazed Pork Roast with Smoked Paprika
Add 2 teaspoons smoked hot paprika to maple syrup along with spices.

Herb-Crusted Pork Roast

SEASON 20 RECIPE

Serves 6

WHY THIS RECIPE WORKS A fresh herb crust is a classic way to enliven a boneless pork roast and infuse the meat with bold herb presence in every bite. To add flavor from the inside out, we started by cutting a deep, wide pocket in the roast and filling it with a paste packed full of fresh herbs, garlic, and nutty Parmesan. We also scored the fat cap on top of the roast before searing it briefly in a very hot skillet. The seared, crosshatched layer provided the perfect canvas for our bread-crumb and herb-paste crust. It gave the paste something to grip and helped unify the crust and meat. After applying the crust to our seared roast, we transferred the whole dish to a relatively low oven, which allowed the roast to cook evenly and the crust to get beautifully crisp and golden brown. Center-cut pork loin roast is also called center-cut roast. Look for a roast with a thin fat cap (about ¼ inch thick) and don't trim this thin layer of fat. We strongly prefer natural pork in this recipe. If the pork is enhanced (injected with a salt solution to increase moisture and flavor), do not brine and season the exterior of the roast with 1¼ teaspoons salt.

- 1 (2½- to 3-pound) boneless center-cut pork loin roast
- ½ cup table salt, for brining
- ¼ cup sugar, for brining
- 1 slice hearty white sandwich bread, torn into quarters
- 1 ounce Parmesan or Pecorino Romano cheese, grated (½ cup), divided
- 1 shallot, minced
- ¼ cup plus 2 teaspoons extra-virgin olive oil, divided
- ¼ teaspoon table salt
- ¾ teaspoon pepper, divided
- ⅓ cup fresh parsley or basil leaves
- 2 tablespoons finely chopped fresh thyme
- 1 teaspoon finely chopped fresh rosemary or ½ teaspoon dried
- 1 garlic clove, minced

1. Using sharp knife, cut slits ¼ inch apart in crosshatch pattern in fat cap of roast, being careful not to cut into meat. Create pocket in roast by inserting knife ½ inch from end of roast and cutting along side of pork, stopping ½ inch short of other end. Pull open roast and use gentle strokes to cut deeper pocket.

2. Dissolve ½ cup salt and sugar in 2 quarts water in large container; submerge roast, cover, and refrigerate for 1 hour. Remove from brine and pat dry with paper towels.

3. Adjust oven rack to lower-middle position and heat oven to 325 degrees. Set wire rack in rimmed baking sheet lined with aluminum foil. Pulse bread in food processor until coarsely ground, about 16 pulses (you should have 1 cup crumbs). Transfer crumbs to bowl and add 2 tablespoons Parmesan, shallot, 1 tablespoon oil, ⅛ teaspoon salt, and ⅛ teaspoon pepper. Using fork, toss mixture until crumbs are evenly coated with oil.

4. Pulse parsley, thyme, rosemary, garlic, remaining 6 tablespoons Parmesan, 3 tablespoons oil, ⅛ teaspoon salt, and ⅛ teaspoon pepper in now-empty processor until smooth, about 12 pulses. Transfer herb paste to bowl.

5. Spread ¼ cup herb paste inside roast and tie roast at 1½-inch intervals with kitchen twine. Season roast with remaining ½ teaspoon pepper.

6. Heat remaining 2 teaspoons oil in 12-inch skillet over medium-high heat until just smoking. Brown roast well on all sides, about 10 minutes. Transfer roast, fat side up, to prepared sheet.

7. Remove twine from roast. Spread remaining herb paste over roast and top with bread-crumb mixture. Transfer sheet with roast to oven and cook until pork registers 140 degrees, 50 minutes to 1¼ hours. Remove roast from oven and let rest on sheet for 20 minutes. Transfer roast to carving board, taking care not to squeeze juices out of pocket in roast. Slice roast into ½-inch-thick slices. Serve.

Stuffing a Pork Loin Roast

1. Starting ½ inch from end of roast, cut along side of pork, stopping ½ inch short of other end. Pull open roast and use gentle strokes to cut deeper pocket.

2. To stuff roast, spread ¼ cup herb paste evenly into pocket, using spatula and your fingers to make sure paste reaches corners of pocket.

3. Fold roast over to original shape and tie it at 1½-inch intervals along its length with kitchen twine.

Tuscan-Style Roast Pork with Garlic and Rosemary

Tuscan-Style Roast Pork with Garlic and Rosemary (Arista)

Serves 4 to 6

WHY THIS RECIPE WORKS *Arista* means "the best." The Tuscan roast pork dish known as arista turns lean, mild pork loin into a juicy roast flavored with plenty of garlic and rosemary and featuring a deeply browned crust. Though it can be made with a bone-in or boneless roast, we were drawn to the simplicity of using a bonelss loin and the opportunity to turn this everyday cut into something more special. To boost both flavor and juiciness, we salted the meat for 1 hour before cooking, using a double-butterfly technique to expose plenty of surface area and then salting both sides and rolling it back up. This double-butterflied roast and rolling technique also allowed us to maximize the distribution of the garlic and rosemary. Briefly simmering the herb-garlic mixture before spreading it over the pork tempered any raw flavors, and using plenty of oil (which we then strained off) and a nonstick skillet kept the garlic from browning, for a fresher garlic flavor. To boost richness and enhance the overall porky flavor, we processed pancetta with the garlic and rosemary (plus red pepper flakes and lemon zest for brightness) to make a paste. Using a low oven ensured that the meat was evenly cooked from edge to center. And instead of roasting, browning, and then resting the roast under foil, we let it rest after it came out of the oven and then browned it and served it immediately; this approach helped keep the crust crispy. Traditionally arista is served with just juices from the pan but we decided it wouldn't be much more work to put together a more polished sauce. We made a simple, bright, rich sauce by combining the reserved strained oil with the juice from a halved lemon that we quickly caramelized in the skillet for more complex flavor. Bright, slightly sweet, and perfumed with garlic and rosemary, this quick sauce was the perfect finishing touch for the pork. We strongly prefer natural pork in this recipe, but if enhanced pork (injected with a salt solution to increase moisture and flavor) is used, reduce the salt to 2 teaspoons (1 teaspoon per side) in step 3. After applying the seasonings, the pork needs to rest, refrigerated, for 1 hour before cooking.

- 1 lemon
- ⅓ cup extra-virgin olive oil
- 8 garlic cloves, minced
- ¼ teaspoon red pepper flakes
- 1 tablespoon finely chopped fresh rosemary
- 2 ounces pancetta, cut into ½-inch pieces
- 1 (2½-pound) center-cut boneless pork loin roast, trimmed
- 1 tablespoon kosher salt

1. Finely grate 1 teaspoon zest from lemon. Cut lemon in half and reserve. Combine lemon zest, oil, garlic, and pepper flakes in 10-inch nonstick skillet. Cook over medium-low heat, stirring frequently, until garlic is sizzling, about 3 minutes. Add rosemary and cook, about 30 seconds. Drain mixture in fine-mesh strainer set over bowl, pushing on garlic-rosemary mixture to extract oil. Set oil aside and let garlic-rosemary mixture cool. Using paper towels, wipe out skillet.

2. Process pancetta in food processor until smooth paste forms, 20 to 30 seconds, scraping down sides of bowl as needed. Add garlic-rosemary mixture and continue to process until mixture is homogeneous, 20 to 30 seconds, scraping down sides of bowl as needed.

3. Position roast fat side up. Insert knife one-third of way up from bottom of roast along 1 long side and cut horizontally, stopping ½ inch before edge. Open up flap. Keeping knife parallel to cutting board, cut through thicker portion of roast about ½ inch from bottom of roast, keeping knife level with first cut and stopping about ½ inch before edge. Open up this flap. If uneven, cover with plastic wrap and use meat pounder to even out. Sprinkle salt over both sides of roast and rub into meat to adhere. Spread inside of roast evenly with pancetta-garlic paste, leaving about ¼-inch border on all sides. Starting from short side, roll roast (keeping fat on outside) and tie with kitchen twine at 1-inch intervals. Set wire rack in rimmed baking sheet and spray with vegetable oil spray. Set roast fat side up on prepared rack and refrigerate for 1 hour.

4. Adjust oven rack to middle position and heat oven to 275 degrees. Transfer roast to oven and cook until meat registers 140 degrees, 1½ to 2 hours. Remove roast from oven, tent with aluminum foil, and let rest for 20 minutes.

5. Heat 1 teaspoon reserved oil in now-empty skillet over high heat until just smoking. Add reserved lemon halves, cut side down, and cook until softened and cut surfaces are browned, 3 to 4 minutes. Transfer lemon halves to small plate.

6. Pat roast dry with paper towels. Heat 2 tablespoons reserved oil in now-empty skillet over high heat until just smoking. Brown roast on fat side and sides (do not brown bottom of roast), 4 to 6 minutes. Transfer roast to carving board and remove twine.

7. Once lemon halves are cool enough to handle, squeeze into fine-mesh strainer set over bowl. Press on solids to extract all pulp; discard solids. Whisk 2 tablespoons strained lemon juice into bowl with remaining reserved oil. Slice roast into ¼-inch-thick slices and serve, passing vinaigrette separately.

Porchetta

Serves 8 to 10

WHY THIS RECIPE WORKS In this recipe, we took Italy's porchetta—aromatic, tender, rich, slow-cooked pork that is traditionally served with pieces of crisp skin on a crusty roll—and turned it into a holiday-worthy roast. As a substitute for the traditional whole pig, we opted for easy-to-find pork butt (over pork belly or a pork belly–wrapped pork loin) since it cooked up evenly and offered the right balance of meat and fatty richness. To season and flavor the porchetta thoroughly and evenly, we cut slits in the meat every few inches; coated it with salt and an intensely flavored paste of garlic, rosemary, thyme, and fennel seeds; and let it sit overnight in the refrigerator. For quicker cooking and more presentable slices, we cut the roast into two pieces and tied each into a compact cylinder. We used a two-stage cooking method: First, we covered the roasting pan with foil, which trapped steam to cook the meat evenly and more quickly and also helped keep the meat moist. We then uncovered the pan and returned it to a 500-degree oven to brown and crisp the outer layer of the roasts. For the best layer of crisp "skin" on the tops of the roasts, we cut a crosshatch in the fat cap and rubbed it with a mixture of salt, pepper, and baking soda at the same time we applied the paste to help dry it out. Pork butt roast is often labeled Boston butt in the supermarket. Look for a roast with a substantial fat cap. If fennel seeds are unavailable, substitute ¼ cup of ground fennel. The porchetta needs to be refrigerated for 6 to 24 hours once it is rubbed with the paste, but it is best when it sits for a full 24 hours.

3 tablespoons fennel seeds
½ cup fresh rosemary leaves (2 bunches)
¼ cup fresh thyme leaves (2 bunches)
12 garlic cloves, peeled
1 tablespoon plus 1 teaspoon pepper, divided
3 tablespoons kosher salt, divided
½ cup extra-virgin olive oil
1 (5- to 6-pound) boneless pork butt roast, trimmed
¼ teaspoon baking soda

1. Grind fennel seeds in spice grinder or mortar and pestle until finely ground. Transfer fennel to food processor and add rosemary, thyme, garlic, 1 tablespoon pepper, and 2 teaspoons salt. Pulse mixture until finely chopped, 10 to 15 pulses. Add oil and process until smooth paste forms, 20 to 30 seconds.

2. Using sharp knife, cut slits in surface fat of roast, spaced 1 inch apart, in crosshatch pattern, being careful not to cut into meat. Cut roast in half with grain into 2 equal pieces.

3. Turn each roast on its side so fat cap is facing away from you, bottom of roast is facing toward you, and newly cut side is facing up. Starting 1 inch from short end of each roast, use boning or paring knife to make slit that starts 1 inch from top of roast and ends 1 inch from bottom, pushing knife completely

through roast. Repeat making slits, spaced 1 to 1½ inches apart, along length of each roast, stopping 1 inch from opposite end (you should have 6 to 8 slits, depending on size of roast).

4. Turn roast so fat cap is facing down. Rub sides and bottom of each roast with 2 teaspoons salt, taking care to work salt into slits from both sides. Rub herb paste onto sides and bottom of each roast, taking care to work paste into slits from both sides. Flip roast so that fat cap is facing up. Using 3 pieces of kitchen twine per roast, tie each roast into compact cylinder.

5. Combine remaining 1 tablespoon salt, remaining 1 teaspoon pepper, and baking soda in small bowl. Rub fat cap of each roast with salt–baking soda mixture, taking care to work mixture into crosshatches. Transfer roasts to wire rack set in rimmed baking sheet and refrigerate, uncovered, for at least 6 hours or up to 24 hours.

6. Adjust oven rack to middle position and heat oven to 325 degrees. Transfer roasts, fat side up, to large roasting pan, leaving at least 2 inches between roasts. Cover tightly with aluminum foil. Cook until pork registers 180 degrees, 2 to 2½ hours.

7. Remove pan from oven and increase oven temperature to 500 degrees. Carefully remove and discard foil and transfer roasts to large plate. Discard liquid in pan. Line pan with foil. Remove twine from roasts; return roasts to pan, directly on foil; and return pan to oven. Cook until exteriors of roasts are well browned and meat registers 190 degrees, 20 to 30 minutes.

8. Transfer roasts to carving board and let rest for 20 minutes. Slice roasts ½ inch thick, transfer to serving platter, and serve.

Slow-Roasted Bone-In Pork Rib Roast

Serves 6 to 8

WHY THIS RECIPE WORKS The pork equivalent of prime rib, a center-cut pork rib roast is sure to impress but requires some prep work, some tricks, and some time to get it right. To guarantee a juicy, flavorful, and beautifully browned roast (without searing), we applied a brown sugar and salt rub and let it rest overnight. The salt seasoned the meat and drew moisture into the flesh, helping to keep it juicy. The brown sugar contributed deep molasses notes and a gorgeous mahogany color, which allowed us to skip tedious searing. We also removed the bones from the meat so we could season it from all sides, then tied it back onto the bones to roast. Since heat travels more slowly through bone than through flesh, the bones helped keep the center of the roast moist. Another plus was that the finished roast, free of bones, was easier to carve. Scoring deep crosshatch marks into the fat with a sharp knife helped it melt and baste the meat during roasting. Cooking the roast in a gentle 250-degree oven ensured that the pork was evenly cooked all the way through. We crisped up the fat by blasting the roast under the broiler for a couple of minutes just prior to serving. As a finishing touch, a classic *beurre rouge* sauce, made with tawny port and balsamic vinegar and studded with plump dried cherries, balanced the meaty roast with echoes of fruit and herbs. This recipe requires refrigerating the salted meat for at least 6 hours before cooking. For easier carving, ask the butcher to remove the chine bone. Monitoring the roast with an oven probe thermometer is best. If you use an instant-read thermometer, open the oven door as infrequently as possible and remove the roast from the oven while taking its temperature. Serve with Port Wine–Cherry Sauce (recipe follows), if desired. The sauce may be prepared in advance or while the roast rests in step 3.

- 1 (4- to 5-pound) center-cut bone-in pork rib roast, trimmed and chine bone removed
- 2 tablespoons packed dark brown sugar
- 1 tablespoon kosher salt
- 1½ teaspoons pepper

1. Using sharp knife, remove roast from bones, running knife down length of bones and following contours as closely as possible. Reserve bones. Combine sugar and salt in small bowl. Pat roast dry with paper towels. If necessary, trim thick spots of surface fat layer to about ¼-inch thickness. Using sharp knife, cut slits, spaced 1 inch apart and in crosshatch pattern, in surface fat layer, being careful not to cut into meat. Rub roast evenly with sugar mixture. Refrigerate, uncovered, for at least 6 hours or up to 24 hours.

2. Adjust oven rack to lower-middle position and heat oven to 250 degrees. Pat roast dry with paper towels and season with pepper. Place roast back on ribs so bones fit where they were cut; tie roast to bones with lengths of kitchen twine between ribs. Transfer roast, fat side up, to wire rack set in rimmed baking sheet. Roast until pork registers 140 degrees, 3 to 4 hours.

3. Remove roast from oven (leave roast on sheet) and let rest for 30 minutes.

4. Adjust oven rack 8 inches from broiler element and heat broiler. Return roast to oven and broil until top of roast is well browned and crispy, 2 to 6 minutes.

5. Transfer roast to carving board; remove twine and remove meat from ribs. Slice pork ¾ inch thick and serve.

Butchering a Pork Rib Roast

1. Using a sharp knife, remove roast from bones, running knife down length of bones and closely following contours.

2. Trim surface fat to ¼ inch and score with crosshatch slits; rub roast with sugar mixture and refrigerate for at least 6 hours.

3. Pat roast dry, sprinkle with pepper, then place roast back on ribs. Using kitchen twine, tie roast to bones between ribs.

ACCOMPANIMENT
Port Wine–Cherry Sauce
Makes about 1¾ cups

- 2 cups tawny port
- 1 cup dried cherries
- ½ cup balsamic vinegar
- 4 sprigs fresh thyme, plus 2 teaspoons minced
- 2 shallots, finely chopped
- ¼ cup heavy cream
- 16 tablespoons unsalted butter, cut into ½-inch pieces and chilled
- 1 teaspoon table salt
- ½ teaspoon pepper

1. Combine port and cherries in bowl and microwave until steaming, 1 to 2 minutes. Cover and let stand until plump, about 10 minutes. Strain port through fine-mesh strainer into medium saucepan, reserving cherries.

2. Add vinegar, thyme sprigs, and shallots to port and bring to boil over high heat. Reduce heat to medium-high and reduce mixture until it measures ¾ cup, 14 to 16 minutes. Add cream and reduce again to ¾ cup, about 5 minutes. Discard thyme sprigs. Off heat, whisk in butter, a few pieces at a time, until fully incorporated. Stir in cherries, minced thyme, salt, and pepper. Cover pan and hold, off heat, until serving. Alternatively, let sauce cool completely and refrigerate for up to 2 days. Reheat in small saucepan over medium-low heat, stirring frequently, until warm.

Slow-Roasted Pork Shoulder with Peach Sauce

Serves 8 to 12

WHY THIS RECIPE WORKS Slow roasting can take a simple cut of pork and turn it into something magical. We began by rubbing a bone-in pork butt roast with a mixture of salt and sugar and letting it rest overnight. As a result of this extended rest, the salt was able to penetrate deep into the meat, enhancing juiciness and seasoning it throughout, while the sugar caramelized to create a crackling-crisp crust. We then roasted the pork for the better part of a day. Cooking the pork for 5 to 6 hours pushed the meat well beyond its "done" mark, but because there is so much collagen and fat in a pork butt roast, the results were ultratender and moist. Pork butt roast may take longer to cook than other cuts of pork, but it's also inexpensive and loaded with flavorful intramuscular fat; plus, it boasts a thick fat cap that renders to a bronze, bacon-like crust. Elevating the pork on a V-rack and pouring water into the roasting pan kept the pork's drippings from burning as the meat roasted. Finally, a fruity sauce with sweet and tart elements cut the pork's richness. Pork butt roast is often labeled Boston butt in the supermarket. For an accompanying sauce, peaches, white wine, sugar, vinegar, and a couple of sprigs of fresh thyme were added to the drippings and then reduced. To round out the sweetness, we finished it with a spoonful of whole-grain mustard. We prefer natural pork to enhanced pork (pork that has been injected with a salt solution to increase moistness and flavor), though both will work in this recipe. Add more water to the roasting pan as necessary during the last hours of cooking to prevent the fond from burning.

Pork Roast
- 1 (6- to 8-pound) bone-in pork butt roast
- ⅓ cup kosher salt
- ⅓ cup packed light brown sugar

Peach Sauce
- 10 ounces frozen peaches, cut into 1-inch pieces, or 2 fresh peaches, peeled, pitted, and cut into ½-inch wedges
- 2 cups dry white wine
- ½ cup granulated sugar
- 5 tablespoons unseasoned rice vinegar, divided
- 2 sprigs fresh thyme
- 1 tablespoon whole-grain mustard

1. For the pork roast: Using sharp knife, cut slits 1 inch apart in crosshatch pattern in fat cap of roast, being careful not to cut into meat. Combine salt and sugar in bowl. Rub salt mixture over entire roast and into slits. Wrap roast tightly in double layer of plastic wrap and refrigerate for at least 12 hours or up to 24 hours.

2. Adjust oven rack to lowest position and heat oven to 325 degrees. Line large roasting pan with aluminum foil. Unwrap roast and brush any excess salt mixture from surface. Season roast with pepper. Set V-rack in roasting pan, spray with vegetable oil spray, and place roast on rack. Add 1 quart water to roasting pan.

3. Cook roast, basting twice during cooking, until roast is extremely tender and pork near (but not touching) bone registers 190 degrees, 5 to 6 hours. (If pan begins to smoke and sizzle, add additional water.) Transfer roast to carving board and let rest for 1 hour. Transfer liquid in roasting pan to fat separator and let liquid settle for 5 minutes. Pour off ¼ cup jus and set aside; discard fat and reserve remaining jus for another use.

4. For the peach sauce: Bring peaches, wine, sugar, ¼ cup vinegar, ¼ cup defatted jus, and thyme sprigs to simmer in small saucepan; cook, stirring occasionally, until reduced to 2 cups, about 30 minutes. Stir in remaining 1 tablespoon vinegar and mustard. Discard thyme sprigs, cover, and keep warm.

5. Using sharp paring knife, cut around inverted T-shaped bone until it can be pulled free from pork (use clean dish towel to grasp bone). Slice pieces of pork into ¼-inch-thick slices. Serve, passing sauce separately.

VARIATION
Slow-Roasted Pork Shoulder with Cherry Sauce
Substitute 10 ounces fresh or frozen pitted cherries for peaches, red wine for white wine, and red wine vinegar for rice vinegar, and add ¼ cup ruby port along with defatted jus. Increase granulated sugar to ¾ cup, omit thyme sprigs and mustard, and reduce mixture to 1½ cups.

"I'm a Yankee by birth, so where pork is concerned the experience of my youth taught me that apples were its God-given fruity sidekick. Period. Then along came my Georgia-born brother-in-law, who enlightened me as to the pleasures of peaches with pork.

In the summer I tend toward grilled pork with a fresh peach salsa, but as soon as the weather turns cooler I move matters indoors, roasting a pork shoulder slowly in the oven until it's fork-tender and luscious. Salting the roast overnight sets the seasoning right, and a salt–brown sugar rub on the fat cap caramelizes in the oven, turning it into the true definition of 'meat candy.'

Indoors the peaches morph, too. Their naturally seductive tangy sweetness is enhanced with a little sugar, white wine, and rice vinegar, concentrated and reduced to a sauce with a stint on the stove, and highlighted with the essence of fresh thyme and grainy mustard.

Writing that made me hungry. Please pardon me while I go preheat the oven."
—*Adam*

In place of the Sweet and Tangy Barbecue Sauce or the variations that follow, you can use 2 cups of your favorite barbecue sauce thinned with ½ cup of the defatted pork cooking liquid in step 5. The shredded and sauced pork can be cooled, tightly covered, and refrigerated for up to two days. Reheat it gently before serving.

Pork
- 1 cup table salt, for brining
- ½ cup sugar, for brining
- 3 tablespoons liquid smoke, for brining
- 1 5-pound boneless pork butt roast, cut in half horizontally
- ¼ cup yellow mustard
- 2 teaspoons liquid smoke
- 2 tablespoons pepper
- 2 tablespoons smoked paprika
- 2 tablespoons sugar
- 2 teaspoons table salt
- 1 teaspoon cayenne pepper

Sweet and Tangy Barbecue Sauce
- 1½ cups ketchup
- ¼ cup molasses
- 2 tablespoons Worcestershire sauce
- 1 tablespoon hot sauce
- ½ teaspoon table salt
- ½ teaspoon pepper

Indoor Pulled Pork with Sweet and Tangy BBQ Sauce

Serves 6 to 8

WHY THIS RECIPE WORKS In recipes, the phrase "indoor barbecue" is usually code for "braised in a Dutch oven with bottled barbecue sauce." Unfortunately, this results in mushy, waterlogged meat and candy-sweet sauce. We wanted moist, tender, shreddable meat with deep smoke flavor all the way through, plus a dark, richly seasoned crust, often referred to as bark. Be it indoor or outdoor, with barbecue a good amount of fat is necessary for moisture and flavor, so we chose to use boneless Boston butt because of its high level of marbling. To mimic the moist heat of a covered grill, we came up with a dual cooking method: covering the pork for part of the oven time to speed up cooking and keep it moist, then uncovering it for the remainder of the time to help the meat develop a crust. To achieve smoky flavor without an actual barbecue pit, we turned to liquid smoke, a natural product derived from condensing the moist smoke of smoldering wood chips. We found that adding it to our brine infused it with smoky flavor without tasting unnatural. For even more smokiness, we employed a dry rub and a wet rub, which we also fortified with smoky flavorings. To serve alongside our pork, we developed three sauces inspired by the variety of barbecue regions and styles: a classic sweet and tangy sauce, a vinegar sauce, and a mustard sauce, all of which we flavored with some of the pork's defatted cooking liquid. Sweet paprika may be substituted for smoked paprika. Covering the pork with parchment and then foil prevents the acidic mustard from eating holes in the foil. Serve the pork on hamburger rolls with pickle chips and thinly sliced onion.

1. For the pork: Dissolve 1 cup salt, ½ cup sugar, and 3 tablespoons liquid smoke in 1 gallon cold water in large container. Submerge pork in brine, cover, and refrigerate for 2 hours.

2. Meanwhile, combine mustard and 2 teaspoons liquid smoke in small bowl; set aside. Combine pepper, paprika, 2 tablespoons sugar, 2 teaspoons salt, and cayenne in second small bowl; set aside. Adjust oven rack to lower-middle position and heat oven to 325 degrees.

3. Remove pork from brine and dry thoroughly with paper towels. Rub mustard mixture over entire surface of each piece of pork. Sprinkle entire surface of each piece with spice mixture. Place pork on wire rack set over aluminum foil–lined rimmed baking sheet. Place piece of parchment paper over pork, then cover with sheet of foil, sealing edges to prevent moisture from escaping. Roast pork for 3 hours.

4. Remove pork from oven; remove and discard foil and parchment. Carefully pour off liquid in bottom of baking sheet into fat separator and reserve for sauce. Return pork to oven and cook, uncovered, until well browned, tender, and meat registers 200 degrees, about 1½ hours. Transfer pork to serving dish, tent with foil, and let rest for 20 minutes.

5. *For the sauce:* While pork rests, pour ½ cup of defatted cooking liquid from fat separator into medium bowl; whisk in sauce ingredients.

6. *To serve:* Using 2 forks, shred pork into bite-size pieces. Toss with 1 cup sauce and season with salt and pepper to taste. Serve, passing remaining sauce separately.

VARIATIONS
Lexington Vinegar Sauce
Makes about 2½ cups
You can use this sauce instead of the Sweet and Tangy Barbecue Sauce.

- 1 cup cider vinegar
- ½ cup ketchup
- ½ cup water
- 1 tablespoon sugar
- ¾ teaspoon table salt
- ¾ teaspoon red pepper flakes
- ½ teaspoon pepper

Combine all ingredients in medium bowl with ½ cup of defatted cooking liquid in step 5 and whisk to combine.

South Carolina Barbecue Sauce
Makes about 2½ cups
You can use this sauce instead of the Sweet and Tangy Barbecue Sauce.

- 1 cup yellow mustard
- ½ cup white vinegar
- ¼ cup packed light brown sugar
- ¼ cup Worcestershire sauce
- 2 tablespoons hot sauce
- 1 teaspoon table salt
- 1 teaspoon pepper

Combine all ingredients in medium bowl with ½ cup of defatted cooking liquid in step 5 and whisk to combine.

Cutting a Pork Butt in Half

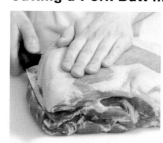

Holding knife parallel to cutting board, press your hand flat against top of pork while cutting horizontally.

Stir-Fried Pork, Eggplant, and Onions with Garlic and Black Pepper

Serves 4

WHY THIS RECIPE WORKS This sophisticated and deeply flavorful stir-fry features tender marinated pork tenderloin, earthy eggplant, wedges of onion, a hefty 12 cloves of garlic, and a sauce that is heady with an abundance of black pepper. Marinating improved the pork's flavor and cooking it quickly over high heat ensured browning. After cooking the thin strips of pork, we transferred them to a bowl to keep warm while we quickly stir-fried the eggplant (adding it to the bowl with the pork) and then the onion. We mashed the mixture of minced garlic, oil, and black pepper into the center of the skillet, pushing the onion off to the side, until fragrant then returned the pork and eggplant to the pan before adding the sauce. For the sauce, we used chicken broth as the backbone along with soy sauce, fish sauce, and brown sugar, and added lime juice to brighten the flavors. Cornstarch created a slightly thickened sauce that lightly cloaked the pork and vegetables. To make slicing the pork easier, freeze it for 15 minutes. This classic Thai stir-fry is not for those with timid palates. Serve with white rice.

Sauce
- 2½ tablespoons soy sauce
- 2½ tablespoons fish sauce
- 2½ tablespoons packed light brown sugar
- 2 tablespoons chicken broth
- 2 teaspoons lime juice
- 1 teaspoon cornstarch

Pork and Vegetables
- 1 (12-ounce) pork tenderloin, trimmed and cut into ¼-inch strips
- 1 teaspoon soy sauce
- 1 teaspoon fish sauce
- 3 tablespoons peanut or vegetable oil, divided
- 12 garlic cloves, minced
- 2 teaspoons pepper
- 1 pound eggplant, cut into ¾-inch pieces
- 1 onion, halved and cut into ¼-inch wedges
- ½ cup finely chopped fresh cilantro

1. *For the sauce:* Combine all ingredients in small bowl; set aside.

2. *For the pork and vegetables:* Toss pork with soy sauce and fish sauce in medium bowl and let marinate at least 10 minutes or up to 1 hour. In small bowl, mix 2 teaspoons oil, garlic, and pepper together.

Sichuan Stir-Fried Pork
in Garlic Sauce

3. Heat 2 teaspoons oil in 12-inch nonstick skillet over high heat until just smoking. Add pork, breaking up any clumps, then cook without stirring until meat is browned at edges, about 1 minute. Stir pork and continue to cook until cooked through, about 1 minute. Transfer pork to clean bowl and cover with foil to keep warm.

4. Add 1 tablespoon oil to skillet and return to high heat until just smoking. Add eggplant and cook, stirring frequently, until browned and no longer spongy, about 5 minutes. Transfer eggplant to bowl with pork. Add remaining 2 teaspoons oil to skillet and return to high heat until just smoking. Add onion and cook until beginning to brown and soften, about 2 minutes.

5. Clear center of skillet, add garlic mixture, and cook, mashing mixture into pan, until fragrant, 15 to 20 seconds. Stir garlic mixture into onion.

6. Stir in eggplant and pork along with any accumulated juices. Whisk sauce to recombine, then add to skillet and cook, tossing constantly, until sauce is thickened, about 30 seconds. Transfer to serving platter, sprinkle with cilantro, and serve.

Sichuan Stir-Fried Pork in Garlic Sauce

Serves 4 to 6

WHY THIS RECIPE WORKS We wanted a version of this hot, sour, salty, and sweet Chinese stir-fry as good as anything we'd order in a Sichuan restaurant. To re-create the succulent pork found in the best restaurant stir-fries (usually achieved by low-temperature deep frying), we chose to use boneless country-style pork ribs instead of leaner pork loin, and soaked the pork in a baking soda solution; this tenderized and moisturized the meat. Then we coated it in a velvetizing cornstarch slurry, which helped it retain moisture as it cooked. For a sauce with just the right balance of salty, sour, sweet, and spicy flavors, we started with a base of soy sauce, Chinese black vinegar, and sesame oil, adding enough chicken broth to amply coat the meat and enough sugar for balance. Ketchup and fish sauce, both high in flavor-enhancing glutamates, rounded out the savory flavor we were looking for while also contributing to the smooth viscosity of the sauce. If Chinese black vinegar is unavailable, substitute 2 teaspoons balsamic vinegar and 2 teaspoons rice vinegar. If Asian broad-bean chili paste is unavailable, substitute 2 teaspoons Asian chili-garlic paste or sriracha. Serve with white rice.

Sauce
- ½ cup chicken broth
- 2 tablespoons sugar
- 2 tablespoons soy sauce
- 4 teaspoons Chinese black vinegar
- 1 tablespoon toasted sesame oil
- 1 tablespoon Chinese rice wine or dry sherry
- 2 teaspoons ketchup
- 2 teaspoons fish sauce
- 2 teaspoons cornstarch

Pork
- 12 ounces boneless country-style pork ribs, trimmed
- 1 teaspoon baking soda
- 2 teaspoons Chinese rice wine or dry sherry
- 2 teaspoons cornstarch

Stir-Fry
- 2 scallions, white parts minced, green parts sliced thin, divided
- 2 tablespoons Asian broad-bean chili paste
- 4 garlic cloves, minced
- ¼ cup vegetable oil, divided
- 6 ounces shiitake mushrooms, stemmed and sliced thin
- 2 celery ribs, cut on bias into ¼-inch slices

1. *For the sauce:* Whisk all ingredients together in bowl; set aside.

2. *For the pork:* Cut pork into 2-inch lengths, then cut each length into ¼-inch matchsticks. Combine pork with ½ cup cold water and baking soda in bowl. Let sit at room temperature for 15 minutes.

3. Rinse pork in cold water. Drain well and pat dry with paper towels. Whisk rice wine and cornstarch together in bowl. Add pork and toss to coat.

4. *For the stir-fry:* Combine scallion whites, chili paste, and garlic in bowl.

5. Heat 1 tablespoon vegetable oil in 12-inch nonstick skillet over high heat until just smoking. Add mushrooms and cook, stirring frequently, until tender, 2 to 4 minutes. Add celery and continue to cook until celery is crisp-tender, 2 to 4 minutes. Transfer vegetables to separate bowl.

6. Add remaining 3 tablespoons vegetable oil to now-empty skillet and place over medium-low heat. Add scallion-garlic mixture and cook, stirring frequently, until fragrant, about 30 seconds. Transfer 1 tablespoon scallion-garlic oil to small bowl and set aside. Add pork to skillet and cook, stirring frequently, until no longer pink, 3 to 5 minutes. Whisk sauce mixture to recombine and add to skillet. Increase heat to high and cook, stirring constantly, until sauce is thickened and pork is cooked through, 1 to 2 minutes. Return vegetables to skillet and toss to combine. Transfer to serving platter, sprinkle with scallion greens and reserved scallion-garlic oil, and serve.

Mu Shu Pork

Serves 4

WHY THIS RECIPE WORKS Mu shu pork's thin, stretchy pancakes are the hallmark of this Chinese restaurant classic, so we started there. Stirring boiling water into flour kept the dough from turning sticky and made it easy to roll. After resting the dough, we rolled it into a log and cut it into 12 pieces, pressing them into rounds and brushing one side of six disks with sesame oil. After placing the unoiled disks on top of the oiled ones, we rolled the doubled-up disks to a 7-inch diameter and cooked each in a warm skillet. These lightly browned, puffed pancakes were easily peeled into two thinner pancakes. We loaded up the filling with flavor-builders, first microwaving dried shiitakes in water to rehydrate them for an earthy component. We saved the shiitakes' soaking liquid to boost our sauce, whisking it with soy sauce, dry sherry, and cornstarch. To season the thinly sliced pork tenderloin, we tossed it in a blend of soy sauce, dry sherry, sugar, fresh ginger, and white pepper. Next, we scrambled two eggs, browned sliced scallion whites, and cooked the pork—a quick 1 to 2 minutes a side. With the pork and scrambled eggs in a bowl to the side, we finished up the vegetables. Simply heating the shiitakes and matchstick-cut bamboo shoots sufficed before adding in sliced green cabbage and scallion greens, cooking them in the mushroom liquid mixture for full umami-rich flavor. A smear of sweet and salty hoisin sauce on the pancakes tied the flavors together. We strongly recommend weighing the flour for the pancakes. For an accurate measurement of boiling water, bring a full kettle to a boil and then measure ¾ cup.

Pancakes

- 1½ cups (7½ ounces) all-purpose flour
- ¾ cup boiling water
- 2 teaspoons toasted sesame oil
- ½ teaspoon vegetable oil

Stir-Fry

- 1 ounce dried shiitake mushrooms, rinsed
- ¼ cup soy sauce, divided
- 2 tablespoons dry sherry, divided
- 1 teaspoon sugar
- 1 teaspoon grated fresh ginger
- ¼ teaspoon white pepper
- 1 (12-ounce) pork tenderloin, trimmed, halved horizontally, and sliced thin against grain
- 2 teaspoons cornstarch
- 2 tablespoons plus 2 teaspoons vegetable oil, divided
- 2 large eggs, beaten
- 6 scallions, white and green parts separated and sliced thin on bias, divided
- 1 (8-ounce) can bamboo shoots, rinsed and sliced into matchsticks
- 3 cups thinly sliced green cabbage
- ¼ cup hoisin sauce

1. *For the pancakes:* Using wooden spoon, mix flour and boiling water in bowl to form rough dough. When cool, transfer dough to lightly floured surface and knead until it forms ball that is tacky but no longer sticky, about 4 minutes (dough will not be perfectly smooth). Cover loosely with plastic wrap and let rest for 30 minutes.

2. Roll dough into 12-inch-long log on lightly floured surface and cut into 12 equal pieces. Turn each piece cut side up and pat into rough 3-inch disk. Brush 1 side of 6 disks with sesame oil; top each oiled side with unoiled disk and press lightly to form 6 pairs. Roll disks into 7-inch rounds, lightly flouring work surface as needed.

3. Heat vegetable oil in 12-inch nonstick skillet over medium heat until shimmering. Using paper towels, carefully wipe out oil. Place pancake in skillet and cook without moving it until air pockets begin to form between layers and underside is dry, 40 to 60 seconds. Flip pancake and cook until few light brown spots appear on second side, 40 to 60 seconds. Transfer to plate and, when cool enough to handle, peel apart into 2 pancakes. Stack pancakes moist side up and cover loosely with plastic. Repeat with remaining pancakes. Cover pancakes tightly and keep warm. Wipe out skillet with paper towel. (Pancakes can be wrapped tightly in plastic wrap, then aluminum foil, and refrigerated for up to 3 days or frozen for up to 2 months. Thaw wrapped pancakes at room temperature. Unwrap and place on plate. Invert second plate over pancakes and microwave until warm and soft, 60 to 90 seconds.)

4. *For the stir-fry:* Microwave 1 cup water and mushrooms in covered bowl until steaming, about 1 minute. Let sit until softened, about 5 minutes. Drain mushrooms through fine-mesh strainer and reserve ⅓ cup liquid. Discard mushroom stems and slice caps thin.

5. Combine 2 tablespoons soy sauce, 1 tablespoon sherry, sugar, ginger, and pepper in large bowl. Add pork and toss to combine. Whisk together reserved mushroom liquid, remaining 2 tablespoons soy sauce, remaining 1 tablespoon sherry, and cornstarch; set aside.

6. Heat 2 teaspoons oil in now-empty skillet over medium-high heat until shimmering. Add eggs and scramble quickly until set but not dry, about 15 seconds. Transfer to bowl and break eggs into ¼- to ½-inch pieces with fork. Return now-empty skillet to medium-high heat and heat 1 tablespoon oil until shimmering. Add scallion whites and cook, stirring frequently, until well browned, 1 to 1½ minutes. Add pork mixture. Spread into even layer and cook without moving it until well browned on 1 side, 1 to 2 minutes. Stir and continue to cook, stirring frequently, until all pork is opaque, 1 to 2 minutes. Transfer to bowl with eggs.

7. Return now-empty skillet to medium-high heat and heat remaining 1 tablespoon oil until shimmering. Whisk mushroom liquid mixture to recombine. Add mushrooms and bamboo shoots to skillet and cook, stirring frequently, until heated through, about 1 minute. Add cabbage, all but 2 tablespoons scallion greens, and mushroom liquid mixture and cook, stirring constantly, until liquid has evaporated and cabbage is wilted but retains some crunch, 2 to 3 minutes. Add pork and eggs and stir to combine. Transfer to platter and top with remaining scallion greens.

8. Spread about 1 teaspoon hoisin in center of each warm pancake. Spoon stir-fry over hoisin and serve.

Making Two Pancakes at a Time

1. Brush 6 disks with sesame oil. Top with unoiled disks. Press pairs together, then roll into thin rounds.

2. Heat each round until air pockets form between layers and underside is dry. Flip and cook second side.

3. When pancakes are cool enough to handle, peel apart into 2 pieces.

Pork Lo Mein

Serves 4

WHY THIS RECIPE WORKS This version of pork lo mein is representative of the best that a good Chinese home cook could turn out: chewy noodles tossed in a salty-sweet sauce and accented with bits of *char siu* (smoky, barbecued pork) and still-crisp cabbage. First we needed to tackle the char siu, preferably perfecting a stir-fried version since we were already stir-frying the vegetables. Country-style pork ribs won for best cut. Though fatty, these meaty ribs have the same rich flavor of pork shoulder—but don't need to be cooked for hours since they're naturally tender. To avoid an overly greasy dish, we trimmed the fat and cut the meat into thin strips that would allow our classic Chinese marinade to penetrate effectively. A few drops of liquid smoke mimicked char siu's characteristic smoky flavor. Turning to the noodles, ones labeled "lo mein" at the Asian market won raves. Fortunately, dried linguine, cooked al dente, also worked beautifully. For the vegetables, we opted for traditional choices—cabbage, scallions, and shiitake mushrooms—stir-frying them with garlic and fresh ginger. We used our meat marinade as a sauce base, with a little chicken broth and a teaspoon of cornstarch added for body. A splash of Asian chili-garlic sauce added a little kick. Use a cast-iron skillet for this recipe if you have one—it will help create the best sear on the pork. If boneless pork ribs are unavailable, substitute 1½ pounds bone-in country-style ribs, followed by the next-best option, pork tenderloin. Liquid smoke provides a flavor reminiscent of the Chinese barbecued pork traditional to this dish. It is important to cook the noodles at the last minute to avoid clumping.

3 tablespoons soy sauce
2 tablespoons oyster sauce
2 tablespoons hoisin sauce
1 tablespoon toasted sesame oil
¼ teaspoon Chinese five-spice powder
1 pound boneless country-style pork ribs, trimmed, sliced crosswise into ⅛-inch pieces
¼ teaspoon liquid smoke (optional)
½ cup chicken broth
1 teaspoon cornstarch
1 teaspoon plus 2 tablespoons peanut or vegetable oil, divided
2 teaspoons grated fresh ginger
2 garlic cloves, minced
¼ cup Chinese rice cooking wine (Shaoxing) or dry sherry, divided
8 ounces shiitake mushrooms, stemmed, wiped clean, caps sliced ¼ inch thick
2 bunches scallions, whites sliced thin, greens cut into 1-inch pieces
1 pound napa cabbage, cored and cut into ½-inch strips
12 ounces fresh Chinese noodles or 8 ounces dried linguine
1 tablespoon Asian chili-garlic sauce

1. Whisk soy sauce, oyster sauce, hoisin, sesame oil, and five-spice powder together in small bowl. Transfer 3 tablespoons mixture to medium bowl and add pork and liquid smoke, if using. Let marinate for at least 10 minutes or up to 1 hour. Whisk broth and cornstarch into remaining soy sauce mixture and set aside. In small bowl, mix 1 teaspoon peanut oil, ginger, and garlic together and set aside.

2. Heat 2 teaspoons peanut oil in 12-inch nonstick skillet over high heat until just smoking. Add half of pork, breaking up any clumps, then cook without stirring until meat is browned at edges, about 1 minute. Stir pork and continue to cook until cooked through, about 1 minute. Add 2 tablespoons wine to skillet and cook, stirring constantly, until liquid is reduced and pork is coated, 30 to 60 seconds. Transfer pork to clean bowl and cover with aluminum foil to keep warm. Repeat with 2 teaspoons peanut oil, remaining pork, and remaining 2 tablespoons wine. Wipe out skillet with paper towels.

3. Add 1 teaspoon peanut oil to skillet and return to high heat until just smoking. Add mushrooms and cook, stirring occasionally, until light golden brown, 4 to 6 minutes. Add scallion whites and greens and cook, stirring occasionally, until wilted, 2 to 3 minutes. Transfer vegetables to bowl with pork.

4. Add remaining 1 teaspoon peanut oil to skillet and heat over high heat until just smoking. Add cabbage and cook, stirring occasionally, until spotty brown, 3 to 5 minutes. Clear center of skillet, add ginger mixture, and cook, mashing mixture into pan, until fragrant, 15 to 20 seconds. Stir ginger mixture into cabbage.

5. Stir in vegetables and pork along with any accumulated juices. Whisk sauce to recombine, then add to skillet and cook, tossing constantly, until sauce is thickened, about 30 seconds.

6. Bring 6 quarts water to boil in large pot. Add noodles and cook, stirring often, until tender, about 4 minutes for fresh and 10 minutes for dried. Drain noodles and return to pot. Add cooked stir-fry mixture and chili-garlic sauce to noodles and toss to combine. Transfer to serving platter and serve.

Fried Brown Rice with Pork and Shrimp

Serves 6

WHY THIS RECIPE WORKS This hearty fried rice dish makes a filling meal and sidesteps tradition in multiple ways: using brown—not white—rice and boiling the rice instead of starting with leftover rice. (Who has multiple cups of brown rice sitting around in their fridge, anyway?) We loved the flavor that nutty brown rice gives this dish, and because of its bran, brown rice holds up well if cooked aggressively in boiling water. The bran acted as a nonstick coating on each grain, so the dish required far less oil for frying—another distinct advantage. To balance the nuttier flavor of brown rice, we used plenty of ginger, garlic, and soy sauce. For a quick version of Chinese barbecued pork to turn our fried rice into a main course, we cut boneless country-style pork ribs across the grain into bite-size slices and tossed them in hoisin sauce, honey, and five-spice powder. We chopped scallions and shrimp, beat some eggs, grated some ginger, and minced some garlic, and we were ready to stir-fry. Preparing these components in batches, starting with the shrimp and eggs and then turning to the pork, yielded perfectly cooked ingredients ready to stir together with the fried brown rice. Boiling the rice gives it the proper texture for this dish. Do not use a rice cooker. The most efficient way to make this dish is to start the rice boiling and then to assemble the remaining ingredients while the rice cooks. The stir-fry portion of this recipe moves quickly, so make sure to have all your ingredients in place before starting. This recipe works best in a nonstick skillet with a slick surface. If your skillet is a bit worn, add an additional teaspoon of oil with the eggs in step 3. Serve with a simple steamed vegetable like broccoli, bok choy, or snow peas if desired.

2 cups short-grain brown rice
¾ teaspoon table salt, divided, plus salt for cooking rice
10 ounces boneless country-style pork ribs, trimmed
1 tablespoon hoisin sauce
2 teaspoons honey
⅛ teaspoon five-spice powder
Small pinch cayenne pepper
4 teaspoons vegetable oil, divided

8 ounces large shrimp (26 to 30 per pound), peeled, deveined, tails removed, and cut into ½-inch pieces

3 large eggs, lightly beaten

1 tablespoon toasted sesame oil

6 scallions, whites and greens separated, sliced thin on bias, divided

1½ teaspoons minced garlic

1½ teaspoons grated fresh ginger

2 tablespoons soy sauce

1 cup frozen peas

1. Bring 3 quarts water to boil in large pot. Add rice and 2 teaspoons salt. Cook, stirring occasionally, until rice is tender, about 35 minutes. Drain well and return to pot. Cover and set aside.

2. While rice cooks, cut pork into 1-inch pieces, and cut each piece into ¼-inch slices against grain. Combine pork with hoisin, honey, five-spice powder, cayenne, and ½ teaspoon salt, and toss to coat; set aside.

3. Heat 1 teaspoon vegetable oil in 12-inch nonstick skillet over medium-high heat until shimmering. Add shrimp in even layer and cook without moving until bottoms are browned, about 90 seconds. Stir and continue to cook until just cooked through, about 90 seconds. Push shrimp to 1 side of skillet. Add 1 teaspoon vegetable oil to cleared side of skillet. Add eggs to clearing and sprinkle with remaining ¼ teaspoon salt. Using rubber spatula, stir eggs gently until set but still wet, about 30 seconds. Stir eggs into shrimp and continue to cook, breaking up large pieces of egg, until eggs are fully cooked, about 30 seconds. Transfer shrimp-egg mixture to clean bowl.

4. Heat remaining 2 teaspoons vegetable oil in now-empty skillet over medium-high heat until shimmering. Add pork in even layer. Cook without moving until pork is well browned on underside, 2 to 3 minutes. Flip pork and cook without moving until pork is cooked through and caramelized on second side, 2 to 3 minutes. Transfer to bowl with shrimp-egg mixture.

5. Heat sesame oil in now-empty skillet over medium-high heat until shimmering. Add scallion whites and cook, stirring frequently, until well-browned, about 1 minute. Add garlic and ginger and cook, stirring frequently, until fragrant and beginning to brown, 30 to 60 seconds. Add soy sauce and half of rice and stir until all ingredients are fully incorporated, making sure to break up clumps of garlic and ginger. Reduce heat to medium-low and add remaining rice, pork, shrimp, eggs, and peas. Stir until all ingredients are evenly incorporated and heated through, 2 to 4 minutes. Remove from heat and stir in scallion greens. Transfer to heated platter and serve.

Cuban-Style Black Beans and Rice

Serves 6 to 8

WHY THIS RECIPE WORKS Salt pork gives Cuban black beans and rice a meaty depth and complex flavor. Also, the rice is cooked in the inky concentrated liquid left over from cooking the beans, which renders the grains superflavorful. For our own version, we expanded on this traditional method, simmering a portion of the *sofrito* (the traditional combination of garlic, bell pepper, and onion) with our beans to infuse them with flavor and then using the liquid to cook our rice and beans together. We used a mixture of chicken broth and water, which gave flavor to the beans as well as to the cooking liquid (which we later used to cook the rice). Lightly browning the remaining sofrito vegetables and spices with rendered salt pork added complex, meaty flavor, and finishing the dish in the oven eliminated the crusty bottom that can form when the dish is cooked on the stove. It is important to use lean—not fatty—salt pork. If you can't find it, substitute six slices of bacon. If using bacon, decrease the cooking time in step 4 to 8 minutes. You will need a Dutch oven with a tight-fitting lid for this recipe. For a vegetarian version of this recipe, use water instead of chicken broth, omit the salt pork, add 1 tablespoon tomato paste with the vegetables in step 4, and increase the amount of salt in step 5 to 1½ teaspoons.

"I have made this recipe—developed by Bryan Roof before he joined team Cook's Country—more than any other dish ever featured on the show. For many years, this was my family's favorite Sunday supper. I like tinga because cooking the pork is mostly hands-off. While it simmers away, I prepare the garnishes. Depending on what's available, I might include a creamy cabbage slaw, fresh tomato salsa, crema (I just thin sour cream with milk), quick pickled radishes with lime juice and salt, slices of buttery avocado, and a bowl of whole fresh cilantro leaves. Everyone at the table can customize their tostadas. If you don't like cilantro, skip it. Want to double up on the avocado? No problem. It's the perfect family recipe. And this hint for busy cooks: Don't fry the tortillas. The test kitchen developed an oven method that's easier and, in my opinion, better. Place 12 corn tortillas on two rimmed baking sheets, brush generously with vegetable oil, and weight with upside-down cooling racks. Then bake in a hot oven until golden brown. Every bit as crisp as the fried version—and because your hands aren't frying tortillas you can enjoy an ice-cold beer."

—*Jack*

1½ tablespoons table salt, for brining
6½ ounces dried black beans (1 cup), picked over and rinsed
2 cups chicken broth
2 cups water
2 large green bell peppers, halved, stemmed, and seeded, divided
1 large onion, halved at equator and peeled, root end left intact, divided
1 head garlic (5 cloves minced, remaining head halved at equator with skin left intact), divided
2 bay leaves
1½ teaspoons table salt, divided
1½ cups long-grain white rice
2 tablespoons extra-virgin olive oil, divided
6 ounces lean salt pork, cut into ¼-inch pieces
4 teaspoons ground cumin
1 tablespoon finely chopped fresh oregano
2 tablespoons red wine vinegar
2 scallions, sliced thin
Lime wedges

1. Dissolve 1½ tablespoons salt in 2 quarts cold water in large bowl or container. Add beans and soak at room temperature for at least 8 hours or up to 24 hours. Drain and rinse well.

2. In Dutch oven, stir together drained beans, broth, water, 1 bell pepper half, 1 onion half (with root end), halved garlic head, bay leaves, and 1 teaspoon salt. Bring to simmer over medium-high heat, cover, and reduce heat to low. Cook until beans are just soft, 30 to 35 minutes. Using tongs, discard pepper, onion, garlic, and bay leaves. Drain beans in colander set over large bowl, reserving 2½ cups bean cooking liquid. (If you don't have enough bean cooking liquid, add water to equal 2½ cups.) Do not clean Dutch oven.

3. Adjust oven rack to middle position and heat oven to 350 degrees. Place rice in fine-mesh strainer and rinse under cold running water until water runs clear, about 1½ minutes. Shake strainer vigorously to remove all excess water; set aside. Cut remaining peppers and onion into 2-inch pieces and process in food processor until broken into rough ¼-inch pieces, about 8 pulses, scraping down bowl as necessary; set aside.

4. In now-empty Dutch oven, heat 1 tablespoon oil and salt pork over medium-low heat and cook, stirring frequently, until lightly browned and rendered, 15 to 20 minutes. Add remaining 1 tablespoon oil, chopped bell peppers and onion, cumin, and oregano. Increase heat to medium and continue to cook, stirring frequently, until vegetables are softened and beginning to brown, 10 to 15 minutes. Add minced garlic and cook, stirring constantly, until fragrant, about 1 minute. Add rice and stir to coat, about 30 seconds.

5. Stir in beans, reserved bean cooking liquid, vinegar, and remaining ½ teaspoon salt. Increase heat to medium-high and bring to simmer. Cover and transfer to oven. Cook until liquid is absorbed and rice is tender, about 30 minutes. Fluff with fork and let rest, uncovered, for 5 minutes. Serve, passing scallions and lime wedges separately.

Spicy Mexican Shredded Pork Tostadas (Tinga)

Serves 4 to 6

WHY THIS RECIPE WORKS The spicy Mexican shredded pork known as *tinga* boasts all the smoke and tenderness of good barbecued pulled pork. Even better—it cooks completely on the stove. And true tinga is a far cry from the bland burrito-joint version often found languishing on steam tables. We set out to perfect the methods that give tinga its characteristic crisp texture and smoky tomato flavor. We wanted tender, full-flavored Mexican shredded pork that we could serve atop crisp corn tortillas or spoon into taco shells. We trimmed and cubed a Boston butt (chosen for its good marbling and little sinew), then simmered the pieces in water that we flavored with garlic, thyme, and onion. Once the pork was tender, we drained the meat (reserving some of the cooking liquid for the sauce) and returned it to the pot to shred. The meat was so tender, it fell apart with nothing more than the pressure of a potato masher. We then sautéed the meat in a hot frying pan along with the requisite additions of finely chopped onion and oregano. Minutes later, the pork had developed crackling edges crisp enough to survive the final step of simmering in tomato sauce. Unlike American barbecue with its sweet and tangy barbecue sauce, tinga relies on a complex smoke-flavored tomato sauce. For our version, we diluted canned tomato sauce with the reserved flavorful cooking liquid from the pork and added bay leaves for herbal complexity. And for tinga's all-important smokiness, we turned to ground chipotle powder, which was a little harder to find than the other option of canned chipotle chiles in adobo sauce, but had a deeper, more complex flavor. The trimmed pork should weigh about 1½ pounds. The shredded pork is traditionally served on tostadas (crisp fried corn tortillas), but you can also use the meat in tacos or burritos or simply serve over rice. Make sure to buy tortillas made only with corn, lime, and salt—preservatives will compromise quality. We prefer the complex flavor of chipotle powder, but two minced canned chipotle chiles can be used in its place. Serve with lime wedges.

Shredded Pork

2 pounds boneless pork butt roast, trimmed and cut into 1-inch pieces

2 onions (1 quartered, 1 chopped fine), divided

5 garlic cloves (3 peeled and smashed, 2 minced), divided

4 sprigs fresh thyme

1 teaspoon table salt

2 tablespoons extra-virgin olive oil

½ teaspoon dried oregano

1 (14.5-ounce) can tomato sauce

1 tablespoon ground chipotle powder

2 bay leaves

Tostadas

12 (6-inch) corn tortillas

¾ cup vegetable oil

Garnishes

Queso fresco or feta cheese

Fresh cilantro leaves

Sour cream

Diced avocado

1. For the shredded pork: Bring pork, quartered onion, smashed garlic cloves, thyme, salt, and 6 cups water to simmer in large saucepan over medium-high heat, skimming off any impurities that rise to surface. Reduce heat to medium-low, partially cover, and cook until pork is tender, 1¼ to 1½ hours. Drain pork, reserving 1 cup cooking liquid. Discard onion, garlic, and thyme. Return pork to saucepan and, using potato masher, mash until shredded into rough ½-inch pieces; set aside. (Pork can be refrigerated for up to 2 days.)

2. Heat olive oil in 12-inch nonstick skillet over medium-high heat until shimmering. Add shredded pork, chopped onion, and oregano; cook, stirring often, until pork is well browned and crisp, 7 to 10 minutes. Add minced garlic and cook until fragrant, about 30 seconds.

3. Stir in tomato sauce, chipotle powder, bay leaves, and reserved pork cooking liquid; simmer until almost all liquid has evaporated, 5 to 7 minutes. Discard bay leaves and season with salt to taste.

4. To bake the tostadas: Adjust oven racks to upper-middle and lower-middle positions and heat oven to 350 degrees. Arrange tortillas in single layer on two rimmed baking sheets; brush both sides of each tortilla with vegetable oil (about 2 tablespoons per tray). Place wire rack upside down on top of the tortillas to keep them flat. Bake until lightly browned and crisp, 15 to 20 minutes, switching and rotating sheets halfway through baking.

5. To serve: Spoon small amount of shredded pork onto center of each tostada and serve, passing garnishes separately.

Roast Fresh Ham

Serves 8 to 10

WHY THIS RECIPE WORKS Fresh ham is not cured like a Smithfield ham or salted and air-dried like prosciutto. It's not pressed or molded like a canned ham, and it's not smoked like a country ham. In fact, some people think there's no such thing as "fresh" ham. There is—and we wanted to find the best way to cook it for a roasted ham that boasted rich, moist meat and crackling crisp skin. Fresh hams are large, so they're usually cut in half and sold as either the sirloin or the shank end; we chose the latter for its ease of carving. But even cut into these smaller roasts, fresh ham needs a long time in the oven, so the danger is drying out the meat. To prevent this, we brined our ham overnight. A garlic and herb rub added further flavor. We positioned the ham face down on a rack in a roasting pan; the rack allowed the heat to circulate all around the ham for more even cooking. A brief roasting at a high temperature followed by longer cooking at a lower temperature produced crunchy skin and succulent meat. The crowning touch was a sweet glaze, which we brushed on periodically while the meat roasted. Fresh ham comes from the pig's hind leg. Because a whole leg is quite large, it is usually cut into two sections. The sirloin, or butt, end is harder to carve than our favorite, the shank end. If you don't have room in your refrigerator, brine the ham in an insulated cooler or a small plastic garbage can; add five or six freezer packs to the brine to keep it well cooled.

Roast

1 (6- to 8-pound) bone-in fresh half ham with skin, preferably shank end

Brine

3 cups packed brown sugar, for brining

2 cups table salt, for brining

2 heads garlic, cloves separated, lightly crushed and peeled, for brining

10 bay leaves, for brining

½ cup black peppercorns, crushed, for brining

Garlic and Herb Rub

1 cup fresh sage leaves

½ cup fresh parsley leaves

¼ cup extra-virgin olive oil

8 garlic cloves, peeled

1½ teaspoons table salt

1½ teaspoons pepper

Glaze

1 recipe glaze (recipes follow)

1. For the roast: Carefully slice through skin and fat with serrated knife, making 1-inch diamond pattern. Be careful not to cut into meat.

Bring sugar, cider, and cloves to boil in small saucepan over high heat; reduce heat to medium-low and simmer until syrupy and reduced to about 1⅓ cups, 5 to 7 minutes. (Glaze will thicken as it cools between bastings; cook over medium heat about 1 minute, stirring once or twice, before using.)

Spicy Pineapple-Ginger Glaze
Makes about 1⅓ cups

- 2 cups packed brown sugar
- 1 cup pineapple juice
- 1 tablespoon grated fresh ginger
- 1 tablespoon red pepper flakes

Bring sugar, pineapple juice, ginger, and pepper flakes to boil in a small saucepan over high heat; reduce heat to medium-low and simmer until syrupy and reduced to about 1⅓ cups, 5 to 7 minutes. (Glaze will thicken as it cools between bastings; cook over medium heat about 1 minute, stirring once or twice, before using.)

Coca-Cola Glaze with Lime and Jalapeño
Makes about 1⅓ cups

- 2 cups packed brown sugar
- 1 cup Coca-Cola
- ¼ cup lime juice (2 limes)
- 2 jalapeño chiles, cut crosswise into ¼-inch-thick slices

Bring sugar, Coca-Cola, lime juice, and jalapeños to boil in small saucepan over high heat; reduce heat to medium-low and simmer until syrupy and reduced to about 1⅓ cups, 5 to 7 minutes. (Glaze will thicken as it cools between bastings; cook over medium heat about 1 minute, stirring once or twice, before using.)

Orange, Cinnamon, and Star Anise Glaze
Makes about 1⅓ cups

- 2 cups packed brown sugar
- 1 tablespoon grated orange zest plus 1 cup juice (2 oranges)
- 4 star anise pods
- 1 cinnamon stick

Bring sugar, orange zest and juice, star anise, and cinnamon stick to boil in small saucepan over high heat; reduce heat to medium-low and simmer until syrupy and reduced to about 1⅓ cups, 5 to 7 minutes. (Glaze will thicken as it cools between bastings; cook over medium heat about 1 minute, stirring once or twice, before using.)

2. _For the brine:_ In large container, dissolve sugar and salt in 2 gallons cold water. Add garlic, bay leaves, and crushed peppercorns. Submerge ham in brine and refrigerate for at least 8 hours or up to 24 hours.

3. Set large disposable aluminum roasting pan on baking sheet for extra support; place flat wire rack in roasting pan. Remove ham from brine; rinse under cold water and dry thoroughly with paper towels. Place ham, wide cut side down, on rack. (If using sirloin end, place ham skin side up.) Let ham sit, uncovered, at room temperature for 1 hour.

4. _For the rub:_ Meanwhile, adjust oven rack to lowest position and heat oven to 500 degrees. Process sage, parsley, oil, garlic, salt, and pepper in food processor until mixture forms smooth paste, about 30 seconds. Rub all sides of ham with paste.

5. Roast ham for 20 minutes. Reduce oven temperature to 350 degrees and continue to roast, brushing ham with glaze every 45 minutes, until ham registers 145 to 150 degrees, about 2½ hours. Remove from oven, tent ham with aluminum foil, and let sit until ham registers 155 to 160 degrees, 30 to 40 minutes. Carve and serve.

ACCOMPANIMENTS
Cider and Brown Sugar Glaze
Makes about 1⅓ cups

- 2 cups packed brown sugar
- 1 cup apple cider
- 5 whole cloves

Glazed Spiral-Sliced Ham

Glazed Spiral-Sliced Ham

Serves 12 to 14

WHY THIS RECIPE WORKS Nothing could be easier than heating up a cured ham, right? Well, we've made enough of them to know that as easy as it may be, the results are often leathery meat with an overly sweet glaze. We wanted to revisit the way to cook this roast to get moist meat accompanied by a glaze that didn't overwhelm it. We have found that bone-in hams, labeled "with natural juices," have the best flavor, and spiral-sliced ones make carving a cinch. We knew that the longer the ham spent in the oven, the greater the chances we'd end up with dried-out meat, so we focused on reducing the cooking time. We soaked the ham in hot water so that it wouldn't be ice-cold when it went into the oven; this step saved a full hour. Roasting the ham in an oven bag further reduced the cooking time, and using the bag had the added advantage of holding in moisture. For the glaze, we threw out the packet that came with our ham and made a fruit-based glaze with just a touch of sweetness to complement the tender meat. This foolproof method will make the perfect holiday ham every time. You can bypass the 90-minute soaking time, but the heating time will increase to 18 to 20 minutes per pound for a cold ham. If there is a tear or hole in the ham's inner covering, wrap the ham in several layers of plastic wrap before soaking it in hot water. Instead of using the plastic oven bag, the ham may be placed cut side down in the roasting pan and covered tightly with foil, but you will need to add 3 to 4 minutes per pound to the heating time. If using an oven bag (you will need a turkey-size bag), be sure to cut slits in the bag so it does not burst. Our favorite spiral-sliced ham is Johnston County Spiral-Sliced Smoked Ham.

- 1 (7- to 10-pound) spiral-sliced bone-in half ham
- 1 large plastic oven bag
- 1 recipe glaze (recipes follow)

1. Leaving ham's inner plastic or foil covering intact, place ham in large container and cover with hot tap water; set aside for 45 minutes. Drain and cover again with hot tap water; set aside for another 45 minutes.

2. Adjust oven rack to lowest position and heat oven to 250 degrees. Unwrap ham; remove and discard plastic disk covering bone. Place ham in oven bag. Gather top of bag tightly so bag fits snugly around ham, tie bag, and trim excess plastic. Set ham, cut side down, in large roasting pan and cut four slits in top of bag with paring knife.

3. Bake ham until meat registers 100 degrees, 1 to 1½ hours (about 10 minutes per pound).

4. Remove ham from oven and increase oven temperature to 350 degrees. Cut open oven bag and roll back sides to expose ham. Brush ham with one-third of glaze and return to oven until glaze becomes sticky, about 10 minutes (if glaze is too thick to brush, return it to heat to loosen).

5. Remove ham from oven, transfer to carving board, and brush entire ham with another third of glaze. Tent ham with aluminum foil and let rest for 15 minutes. While ham rests, heat remaining third of glaze with 4 to 6 tablespoons of ham juices until it forms thick but fluid sauce. Carve and serve ham, passing sauce at table.

ACCOMPANIMENTS
Maple-Orange Glaze
Makes 1 cup

- ¾ cup maple syrup
- ½ cup orange marmalade
- 2 tablespoons unsalted butter
- 1 tablespoon Dijon mustard
- 1 teaspoon pepper
- ¼ teaspoon ground cinnamon

Combine all ingredients in small saucepan. Cook over medium heat, stirring occasionally, until mixture is thick, syrupy, and reduced to 1 cup, 5 to 10 minutes; set aside.

Cherry-Port Glaze
Makes 1 cup

- ½ cup ruby port
- 1 cup packed dark brown sugar
- ½ cup cherry preserves
- 1 teaspoon pepper

Simmer port in small saucepan over medium heat until reduced to 2 tablespoons, about 5 minutes. Add sugar, preserves, and pepper and cook, stirring occasionally, until sugar dissolves and mixture is thick, syrupy, and reduced to 1 cup, 5 to 10 minutes; set aside.

Roast Rack of Lamb with Roasted Red Pepper Relish

Serves 4 to 6

WHY THIS RECIPE WORKS When you really think about it, roasting a rack of lamb is a simple process, but there's a fine line between a showstopper and a dried-out disappointment. For a rack that would make us proud at our next fete, the seasoning needed to be spot-on, the meat had to be juicy, and we'd need a bold relish to serve alongside it. Starting with the lamb, carving a shallow crosshatch into the fat cap and rubbing the racks' surfaces with a blend of kosher salt and ground cumin ensured that our lamb would be loaded with flavor. We heated the oven to 250 degrees and arranged the lamb on a wire rack–lined baking sheet. In just over an hour, our racks emerged at a rosy medium-rare with big flavor to boot. While the racks roasted in the oven, we whipped up a relish to dress up the lamb, combining chopped roasted red pepper, minced parsley, olive oil, fresh lemon juice, and minced garlic. This simple sauce steeped while the lamb cooked. Because meat always tastes best with a bit of char, we browned the racks in a skillet before slicing and serving. We prefer the milder taste and bigger size of domestic lamb, but you may substitute imported lamb from New Zealand and Australia. Since imported racks are generally smaller, in step 1 season each rack with ½ teaspoon of salt and reduce the cooking time to 50 minutes to 1 hour 10 minutes. A rasp-style grater makes quick work of turning the garlic into a paste.

Lamb

- 2 racks of lamb (1¾ to 2 pounds each), fat trimmed to ⅛ to ¼ inch, rib bones frenched
- 2 tablespoons kosher salt
- 1 teaspoon ground cumin
- 1 teaspoon vegetable oil

Relish

- ½ cup jarred roasted red peppers, rinsed, patted dry, and chopped fine
- ½ cup finely chopped fresh parsley
- ¼ cup extra-virgin olive oil
- ¼ teaspoon lemon juice
- ⅛ teaspoon garlic, minced to paste

1. For the lamb: Adjust oven rack to middle position and heat oven to 250 degrees. Using sharp knife, cut slits in surface layer of fat on lamb, spaced ½ inch apart, in cross-hatch pattern, being careful to cut down to, but not into, meat. Combine salt and cumin in bowl. Rub ¾ teaspoon salt mixture over entire surface of each rack and into slits. Reserve remaining salt mixture for serving. Place racks, bone-side down, on wire rack set in rimmed baking sheet. Roast until meat registers 125 degrees (for medium-rare) or 130 degrees (for medium), 1 hour 5 minutes to 1 hour 25 minutes.

2. For the relish: While lamb roasts, combine red peppers, parsley, olive oil, lemon juice, and garlic in bowl. Season with salt and pepper to taste. Let sit at room temperature for at least 1 hour before serving.

3. Heat vegetable oil in 12-inch skillet over high heat until just smoking. Place 1 rack, bone side up, in skillet and cook until well browned, 1 to 2 minutes. Transfer to carving board. Pour off all but 1 teaspoon fat from skillet and repeat with second rack. Tent racks with aluminum foil and let rest for 20 minutes. Cut between ribs to separate chops and sprinkle cut side of chops with ½ teaspoon salt mixture. Serve, passing relish and reserved salt mixture separately.

VARIATION

Roast Rack of Lamb with Sweet Mint-Almond Relish

Substitute ground anise for cumin in salt mixture. Omit red pepper relish. While lamb roasts, combine ½ cup finely chopped fresh mint; ¼ cup sliced almonds, toasted and chopped fine; ¼ cup extra-virgin olive oil; 2 tablespoons red currant jelly; 4 teaspoons red wine vinegar; and 2 teaspoons Dijon mustard in bowl. Season with salt and pepper to taste. Let sit at room temperature for at least 1 hour before serving with lamb.

Roast Boneless Leg of Lamb with Garlic, Herb, and Bread-Crumb Crust

SEASON 20 RECIPE

Serves 6 to 8

WHY THIS RECIPE WORKS A boneless leg of lamb is an easy shortcut to a great roast dinner—as long as you treat it correctly. We started by pounding it to an even thickness. Next we introduced extra flavor and textural interest to the roast. First, we made a potent herb and garlic paste. We spread a portion of the paste over the lamb before rolling up and tying the roast so it would infuse the lamb with flavor from the inside out. The rest of the herb paste was combined with fresh bread crumbs and Parmesan. A quick sear on the stovetop jump-started the cooking process and ensured our lamb would have a golden-brown crust. After searing, we moved the roast to a 375-degree oven, which was perfect for cooking the meat to a juicy, tender medium-rare. Partway through cooking, we took the roast out of the oven, removed the twine, brushed the meat with zingy Dijon mustard, and applied the bread-crumb mixture. This ensured that the crust wouldn't peel off with the twine but also gave the tied lamb enough roasting time to hold its shape when we removed the twine, resulting in perfect slices with a crunchy, savory crust. We prefer the sirloin end rather than the shank end for this recipe, though either will work well. We prefer the subtler flavor and larger size of lamb labeled "domestic" or "American," but you may substitute lamb imported from New Zealand or Australia. Leg of lamb is often sold in elastic netting that must be removed.

- 1 **slice hearty white sandwich bread**
- ¼ **cup extra-virgin olive oil, divided**
- ¼ **cup finely chopped fresh parsley**
- 3 **tablespoons finely chopped fresh rosemary**
- 2 **tablespoons finely chopped fresh thyme**
- 3 **garlic cloves, peeled**
- 1 **ounce Parmesan cheese, grated (½ cup)**
- 1 **(3½- to 4-pound) boneless half leg of lamb, trimmed and pounded to ¾-inch thickness**
- 1 **tablespoon kosher salt, divided**
- 1 **teaspoon pepper, divided**
- 1 **tablespoon Dijon mustard**

1. Adjust oven rack to lower-middle position and heat oven to 375 degrees. Pulse bread in food processor until coarsely ground, about 10 pulses (you should have about 1 cup crumbs). Transfer to bowl and set aside. Process 1 teaspoon oil, parsley, rosemary, thyme, and garlic in now-empty processor until minced, scraping down sides of bowl as needed, about 1 minute. Transfer 1½ tablespoons herb mixture to bowl and reserve. Scrape remaining mixture into bowl of bread crumbs; stir in Parmesan and 1 tablespoon oil and set aside.

2. Lay roast on cutting board with rough interior side (which was against bone) facing up, rub with 2 teaspoons oil, and sprinkle with 1½ teaspoons salt and ½ teaspoon pepper. Spread reserved herb mixture evenly over lamb, leaving 1-inch border around edge. Roll roast and tie with kitchen twine at 1½-inch intervals. Sprinkle roast with remaining 1½ teaspoons salt and remaining ½ teaspoon pepper, then rub with 1 tablespoon oil.

3. Set wire rack in rimmed baking sheet. Heat remaining 1 tablespoon oil in 12-inch skillet over medium-high heat until just smoking. Brown roast well on all sides, about 10 minutes. Transfer to prepared rack and roast until lamb registers 105 to 110 degrees, 30 to 35 minutes. Transfer roast to carving board; remove twine. Brush roast exterior with mustard, then carefully press bread-crumb mixture onto top and sides of roast with your hands, pressing firmly to form solid, even coating that adheres to roast. Return coated roast to prepared rack; roast until lamb registers 125 degrees (for medium-rare), 10 to 15 minutes longer. Transfer roast to carving board and let rest for 20 minutes. Slice roast into ½-inch-thick slices. Serve.

Roast Butterflied Leg of Lamb with Coriander, Cumin, and Mustard Seeds

Serves 8 to 10

WHY THIS RECIPE WORKS Boneless butterflied leg of lamb is pretty much the simplest cut of lamb you can cook. No bones, no tying or rolling, and carving is incredibly simple. The uniform thickness of this cut also encourages even cooking. Our favorite roasting method for boneless butterflied leg of lamb is to start it in a very low oven (just 250 degrees) and then finish with a blast under the broiler for juicy, tender roasted lamb with a burnished, crisp crust. Before cooking, we made sure to remove the sinew and pockets of fat that can hide on this cut. Scoring the fat cap, rubbing the roast with salt and letting it sit for an hour gave us well-seasoned, tender meat. We ditched the usual spice rub (which had a tendency to scorch under the broiler) in favor of a slow-cooked spice-infused oil that both seasoned the lamb during cooking and provided the basis for a quick sauce. We prefer the subtler flavor and larger size of lamb labeled "domestic" or "American," but you may substitute lamb imported from New Zealand or Australia. The 2 tablespoons of salt in step 1 is for a 6-pound leg. If using a larger leg (7 to 8 pounds), add an additional teaspoon of salt for every pound.

Lamb
- 1 (6- to 8-pound) butterflied leg of lamb
- 2 tablespoons kosher salt
- ⅓ cup vegetable oil
- 3 shallots, sliced thin
- 4 garlic cloves, peeled and smashed
- 1 (1-inch) piece ginger, sliced into ½-inch-thick rounds and smashed
- 1 tablespoon coriander seeds
- 1 tablespoon cumin seeds
- 1 tablespoon mustard seeds
- 3 bay leaves
- 2 (2-inch) strips lemon zest

Sauce
- ⅓ cup finely chopped fresh mint
- ⅓ cup finely chopped fresh cilantro
- 1 shallot, minced
- 2 tablespoons lemon juice

1. For the lamb: Place lamb on cutting board with fat cap facing down. Using sharp knife, trim any pockets of fat and connective tissue from underside of lamb. Flip lamb over, trim fat cap so it's between ⅛ and ¼ inch thick, and pound roast to even 1-inch thickness. Cut slits, spaced ½ inch apart, in fat cap in crosshatch pattern, being careful to cut down to but not into meat. Rub salt over entire roast and into slits. Let sit, uncovered, at room temperature for 1 hour.

2. Meanwhile, adjust 1 oven rack to lower-middle position and second rack 4 to 5 inches from broiler element and heat oven to 250 degrees. Stir together oil, shallots, garlic, ginger, coriander seeds, cumin seeds, mustard seeds, bay leaves, and lemon zest on rimmed baking sheet and bake on lower rack until spices are softened and fragrant and shallots and garlic turn golden, about 1 hour. Remove sheet from oven and discard bay leaves.

3. Thoroughly pat lamb dry with paper towels and transfer, fat side up, to sheet (directly on top of spices). Roast on lower rack until lamb registers 120 degrees, 30 to 40 minutes. Remove sheet from oven and heat broiler. Broil lamb on upper rack until surface is well browned and charred in spots and lamb registers 125 degrees (for medium-rare), 3 to 8 minutes.

4. Remove sheet from oven and, using 2 pairs of tongs, transfer lamb to carving board (some spices will cling to bottom of roast); tent with aluminum foil and let rest for 20 minutes.

5. For the sauce: Meanwhile, carefully pour pan juices through fine-mesh strainer into medium bowl, pressing on solids to extract as much liquid as possible; discard solids. Stir in mint, cilantro, shallot, and lemon juice. Add any accumulated lamb juices to sauce and season with salt and pepper to taste.

6. With long side facing you, slice lamb with grain into 3 equal pieces. Turn each piece and slice across grain into ¼-inch-thick slices. Briefly warm sauce in microwave if it has cooled and thickened. Serve lamb with sauce.

VARIATIONS

Roast Butterflied Leg of Lamb with Coriander, Rosemary, and Red Pepper
Omit cumin and mustard seeds. Toss 6 sprigs fresh rosemary and ½ teaspoon red pepper flakes with oil mixture in step 2. Substitute parsley for cilantro in sauce.

Roast Butterflied Leg of Lamb with Coriander, Fennel, and Black Pepper
Substitute 1 tablespoon fennel seeds for cumin seeds and 1 tablespoon black peppercorns for mustard seeds in step 2. Substitute parsley for mint in sauce.

"I didn't grow up eating much lamb, and the next time I see my parents I'm going to give them a hard time about that. Because we all have a limited number of meals in our lifetimes and I've missed out on some important lamb years. To be fair, though, I certainly made up for lost time over the weeks I spent developing this recipe. My goals were perfectly cooked, rosy meat, a burnished crust, and complex spice flavor. That last bit was particularly important to me, as lamb and spice have a special affinity for one another. Whole spices infuse the oil that forms the base of the heady herb sauce; they cling to the lamb itself for bursts of flavor in each bite; and, nearly as important, they perfume the whole kitchen with warmth."

—*Dan*

Fish

Garlicky Roasted Shrimp with Cilantro and Lime

Braised Halibut with Leeks and Mustard

Serves 4

WHY THIS RECIPE WORKS Braising is a technique usually reserved for tough cuts of meat, but the gentle, moist-heat cooking method also works wonders on fish. Halibut's dense flesh made it an easy fillet to manipulate and we knew its clean, sweet flavor would pair well with a simple wine sauce. We began by gently cooking just one side of the fillets in butter in a skillet and then removing the fish to establish the braising liquid. We cooked sliced leeks in Dijon and their exuded moisture added to the thin sauce. Once the leeks had softened, we added some dry white wine, brought it to a simmer, and placed the halibut atop the vegetables with the uncooked side facing down. This arrangement allowed the parcooked side to steam while the rest of the fillet cooked through to perfection. To finish the sauce, we transferred the cooked fish and vegetables to a serving platter and let the wine sauce reduce, adding lemon juice for a burst of bright acidity. We prefer to prepare this recipe with halibut, but a similar firm-fleshed white fish such as striped bass or sea bass that is between ¾ and 1 inch thick can be substituted. To ensure that your fish cooks evenly, purchase fillets that are similarly shaped and uniformly thick.

- 4 **(6- to 8-ounce) skinless halibut fillets, ¾ to 1 inch thick**
- 1 **teaspoon table salt, divided**
- 6 **tablespoons unsalted butter**
- 1 **pound leeks, white and light green parts only, halved lengthwise, sliced thin, and washed thoroughly**
- 1 **teaspoon Dijon mustard**
- ¾ **cup dry white wine**
- 1 **teaspoon lemon juice, plus lemon wedges for serving**
- 1 **tablespoon finely chopped fresh parsley**

1. Sprinkle fish with ½ teaspoon salt. Melt butter in 12-inch skillet over low heat. Place fish in skillet, skinned side up, increase heat to medium, and cook, shaking pan occasionally, until butter begins to brown (fish should not brown), 3 to 4 minutes. Using spatula, carefully transfer fish to large plate, raw side down.

2. Add leeks, mustard, and remaining ½ teaspoon salt to skillet and cook, stirring frequently, until leeks begin to soften, 2 to 4 minutes. Add wine and bring to gentle simmer. Place fish, raw side down, on top of leeks. Cover skillet and cook, adjusting heat to maintain gentle simmer, until fish registers 135 to 140 degrees, 10 to 14 minutes. Remove skillet from heat and, using 2 spatulas, transfer fish and leeks to serving platter or individual plates. Tent with aluminum foil.

3. Return skillet to high heat and simmer briskly until sauce is thickened, 2 to 3 minutes. Remove pan from heat, stir in lemon juice, and season with salt and pepper to taste. Spoon sauce over fish and sprinkle with parsley. Serve immediately with lemon wedges.

VARIATION

Braised Halibut with Carrots and Coriander

Substitute 1 pound carrots, peeled and shaved with vegetable peeler lengthwise into ribbons, and 4 shallots, halved and sliced thin, for leeks. Substitute ½ teaspoon ground coriander for Dijon mustard. Increase lemon juice to 1½ teaspoons and substitute cilantro for parsley.

Poached Fish Fillets with Crispy Artichokes and Sherry-Tomato Vinaigrette

Serves 4

WHY THIS RECIPE WORKS Restaurant-style oil-poached fish requires a potful of pricey olive oil and promises supermoist, delicately cooked fish. Using a small skillet and flipping the fish halfway through cooking allowed us to cut back to ¾ cup of oil, which we employed to crisp flavorful garnishes and finally blended into a vinaigrette. Fillets of meaty white fish like cod, halibut, sea bass, or snapper work best in this recipe. Just make sure the fillets are at least 1 inch thick. A neutral oil such as canola can be substituted for the olive oil. The onion half in step 3 is used to displace the oil; a 4-ounce porcelain ramekin may be used instead. Serve with couscous or steamed white rice.

Fish
- **4 (6-ounce) skinless white fish fillets, 1 inch thick**
- **1 teaspoon kosher salt**
- **1 cup jarred whole baby artichokes packed in water, quartered, rinsed, and patted dry**
- **1 tablespoon cornstarch**
- **¾ cup extra-virgin olive oil, divided**
- **3 garlic cloves, minced**
- **½ onion, peeled**

Vinaigrette
- **6 ounces cherry tomatoes (2 ounces cut into ⅛-inch-thick rounds)**
- **½ small shallot, peeled**
- **4 teaspoons sherry vinegar**
- **½ teaspoon pepper**
- **½ teaspoon kosher salt**
- **1 tablespoon finely chopped fresh parsley**

1. For the fish: Adjust oven racks to middle and lower-middle positions and heat oven to 250 degrees. Pat fish dry with paper towels and season each fillet with ¼ teaspoon salt. Let sit at room temperature for 20 minutes.

2. Meanwhile, toss artichokes with cornstarch in bowl to coat. Heat ½ cup oil in 10-inch nonstick ovensafe skillet over medium heat until shimmering. Shake excess cornstarch from artichokes and add to skillet; cook, stirring occasionally, until crisp and golden, 2 to 4 minutes. Add garlic and continue to cook until garlic is golden, 30 to 60 seconds. Strain oil through fine-mesh strainer into bowl. Transfer artichokes and garlic to ovensafe paper towel–lined plate and season with salt. Do not wash strainer.

3. Return strained oil to skillet and add remaining ¼ cup oil. Place onion half in center of pan. Let oil cool until it registers about 180 degrees, 5 to 8 minutes. Arrange fish fillets, skinned side up, around onion (oil should come roughly halfway up fillets). Spoon a little oil over each fillet, cover skillet, transfer to middle oven rack, and cook for 15 minutes.

4. Being careful of hot skillet handle, remove skillet from oven. Using 2 spatulas, carefully flip fillets. Cover, return to middle rack, and place plate with artichokes and garlic on lower-middle rack. Continue to cook fish until it registers 130 to 135 degrees, 9 to 14 minutes. Gently transfer fish to serving platter, reserving ½ cup oil, and tent with aluminum foil. Turn off oven, leaving plate of artichokes in oven.

5. For the vinaigrette: Process reserved ½ cup fish cooking oil, whole tomatoes, shallot, vinegar, pepper, and salt in blender until smooth, about 2 minutes, scraping down

sides of bowl as needed. Add any accumulated fish juices, season with salt to taste, and blend for 10 seconds. Strain sauce through fine-mesh strainer into bowl; discard solids. To serve, spoon vinaigrette around fish. Garnish each fillet with warmed crisped artichokes and garlic, parsley, and tomato rounds. Serve.

VARIATIONS
Poached Fish Fillets with Jalapeño Vinaigrette
To make this dish spicier, add some of the reserved chile seeds to the vinaigrette in step 5. Serve with steamed white rice.

For fish, substitute 2 seeded jalapeño chiles, cut into ⅛-inch-thick rings, for artichoke hearts and reduce cornstarch to 2 teaspoons. For vinaigrette, process 4 halved and seeded jalapeños (seeds reserved); ½ small shallot, peeled; 6 sprigs fresh cilantro; 8 teaspoons lime juice; and ½ teaspoon kosher salt with ½ cup reserved fish cooking oil as directed in step 5. Garnish fish with 2 tablespoons fresh cilantro leaves and ½ avocado, cut into ¼-inch pieces.

Poached Fish Fillets with Crispy Scallions and Miso-Ginger Vinaigrette
For fish, substitute 8 scallion whites, sliced ¼ inch thick, for artichoke hearts; omit garlic; and reduce cornstarch to 2 teaspoons. For vinaigrette, process 6 scallion greens, 8 teaspoons lime juice, 2 tablespoons mirin, 4 teaspoons white miso paste, 2 teaspoons minced ginger, and ½ teaspoon sugar with ½ cup reserved fish cooking oil as directed in step 5. Garnish fish with 2 thinly sliced scallion greens and 2 halved and thinly sliced radishes.

Chinese-Style Oven-Steamed Fish

Chinese-Style Oven-Steamed Fish

SEASON 20 RECIPE

Serves 4

WHY THIS RECIPE WORKS This inventive, weeknight-friendly recipe captures the essence of the delicious and venerable Chinese tradition of steaming a whole fish while infusing it with the flavor of soy, garlic, and ginger, but using fillets instead (and no bamboo steamer basket or wok required either). We first tried using a perforated metal steamer basket fit into a Dutch oven that had about an inch of water boiling in it but the cooking juices drained into the water below diluting them too much to be of use in the making of a sauce. We also tried simulating a bamboo steamer by placing metal biscuit cutters in the bottom of the Dutch oven with a plate balanced on top to hold the fish and its juices, but it was challenging to lift the steamy, liquid-filled plate out of the pot. Moving the whole operation to the oven proved to be far more promising and effective. To make removing the fish easy, we spread scallions and ginger over the bottom of a baking pan to infuse the fish with flavor as it steamed and then created a foil sling sprayed with vegetable oil spray. After placing the fish on the greased foil strip, we poured in a mixture of soy sauce, rice wine, sesame oil, sugar, salt, and white pepper. After covering the pan we placed it in a hot oven and after just 12 minutes the fish was perfectly cooked. To coat the fish in a fragrant sauce all we needed to do was strain the aromatic liquid left behind in the pan and pour it over the fish. Following the Chinese tradition, to finish we sautéed thin matchsticks of ginger in oil and then poured the mixture over the fish; the ginger added a bit of sweet spiciness and some crisp texture. A smattering of cilantro sprigs over the top provided a final, elegant touch. Haddock, red snapper, halibut, and sea bass will also work in this recipe as long as the fillets are about 1 inch thick. If one end of the fillet is thinner, fold it under when placing it in the pan. This recipe works best in a metal baking pan; if using a glass baking dish, add 5 minutes to the cooking time. To ensure that the fish doesn't overcook, we remove it from the oven between 125 and 130 degrees; it will continue to cook as it is plated. Serve with steamed rice and vegetables.

- 8 scallions, trimmed, divided
- 1 (3-inch) piece ginger, peeled, divided
- 3 garlic cloves, sliced thin
- 4 (6-ounce) skinless cod fillets, about 1 inch thick
- 3 tablespoons soy sauce
- 2 tablespoons rice wine or dry sherry
- 1½ teaspoons toasted sesame oil
- 1½ teaspoons sugar
- ¼ teaspoon table salt
- ¼ teaspoon white pepper
- 2 tablespoons vegetable oil
- ⅓ cup cilantro leaves and thin stems

1. Adjust oven rack to middle position and heat oven to 450 degrees. Chop 6 scallions coarse and spread evenly in 13 by 9-inch baking pan. Slice remaining scallions thin on bias, and set aside. Chop 2 inches of ginger coarse and spread in baking pan with scallions. Slice remaining 1 inch of ginger into thin matchsticks and reserve. Sprinkle garlic over scallions and ginger.

2. Fold 18 by 12-inch piece of aluminum foil lengthwise to create 18 by 6-inch sling and spray lightly with vegetable oil spray. Place in pan lengthwise, allowing excess to hang over each end. Arrange fish on sling. If fillets vary in thickness, place thinner fillets in middle and thicker fillets at ends.

3. Whisk soy sauce, rice wine, sesame oil, sugar, salt, and white pepper in small bowl until combined. Pour around fish. Cover pan tightly with aluminum foil. Bake until fish registers 125 to 130 degrees, 12 to 14 minutes.

4. Grasping sling at each end, carefully transfer sling and fish to deep platter. Place spatula at 1 end of fillet to hold in place, and carefully slide foil out from under fish. Pour cooking liquid into fine-mesh strainer set over bowl and press on solids to extract liquid. Discard solids. Pour cooking liquid over fish. Sprinkle remaining scallions over fish. Heat vegetable oil in skillet over high heat until just smoking. Remove from heat and add remaining ginger (ginger will sizzle). Stir until ginger is beginning to brown and crisp. Drizzle oil and ginger over fish. Top with cilantro and serve.

Fish Meunière with Browned Butter and Lemon

Serves 4

WHY THIS RECIPE WORKS Fish meunière typically features pale, soggy fillets in pools of greasy sauce—that is, if the fish doesn't stick to the pan or fall apart as it is plated. We wanted perfectly cooked fillets that were delicately crisp and golden brown on the outside and moist and flavorful on the inside, napped in a buttery yet light sauce. Whole Dover sole is the most authentic choice, but it was also hard to come by and prohibitively expensive; either sole or flounder fillets were good stand-ins. To prevent the likelihood of overcooking the fish, the fillets needed to be no less than ⅜ inch thick. The fillets must be patted dry before being seasoned with salt and pepper and dredged in flour (no need for eggs and bread crumbs). Using a nonstick skillet for pan-frying meant there was less chance for our fillets to fall apart; lubricating the pan with a mixture of oil and butter added extra insurance. Removing the pan from the heat just before the fish was cooked prevented the fish from being dry (the fish will continue to cook off the heat). Butter browned in a traditional skillet (so the changing color was easy to monitor) and brightened with lemon juice made the ideal accompaniment to our crispy,

"Repeat after me: Browned butter makes everything taste better—even simple fish fillets that are seasoned, dredged in flour, and sautéed for a moment or two on each side. If you want a quick dinner with little fuss, this is your recipe. If you want a dish that's refined and elegant enough to impress your friends, your in-laws, or even your boss, this is your recipe. But don't tell them that it is sautéed fish with browned butter; tell them that they are dining on sautéed fish with beurre noisette. Or even better, call it sole à la meunière. Somehow French terms make food just sound better, and your dining companions will think that you're très cosmopolite!"

—*Bridget*

golden fillets. Try to purchase fillets that are of similar size, and avoid those that weigh less than 5 ounces because they will cook too quickly. When placing the fillets in the skillet, be sure to place them skinned side up so that the opposite side, which had bones, will brown first. To flip the fillets while cooking, use two spatulas; gently lift one side of the fillet with one spatula, then support the fillet with the other spatula and gently flip it so that the browned side faces up. A nonstick skillet ensures that the fillets will release from the pan, but for the sauce a traditional skillet is preferable because its light-colored surface will allow you to monitor the color of the butter as it browns.

Fish

½ cup all-purpose flour
4 (5- to 6-ounce) sole or flounder fillets, ⅜ inch thick
¾ teaspoon table salt
¼ teaspoon pepper
2 tablespoons vegetable oil, divided
2 tablespoons unsalted butter, cut into
   2 pieces, divided

Browned Butter

4 tablespoons unsalted butter, cut into 4 pieces
1 tablespoon finely chopped fresh parsley
1½ tablespoons lemon juice, plus lemon wedges
   for serving

1. For the fish: Adjust oven rack to lower-middle position and heat oven to 200 degrees. Set 4 plates on rack. Spread flour in shallow dish. Pat fillets dry with paper towels, season with salt and pepper, and let sit until fillets are glistening with moisture, about 5 minutes. Coat both sides of fillets with flour, shake off excess, and place in single layer on baking sheet.

2. Heat 1 tablespoon oil in 12-inch nonstick skillet over high heat until shimmering, then add 1 tablespoon butter and swirl to coat pan bottom. Carefully place 2 fillets, skinned side up, in skillet. Immediately reduce heat to medium-high and cook, without moving fish, until edges of fillets are opaque and bottom is golden brown, about 3 minutes. Using 2 spatulas, gently flip fillets and cook until fish flakes apart when gently prodded with paring knife, about 2 minutes. Carefully transfer each fillet to warmed plate, keeping skinned side down, and return plates to oven. Wipe out skillet with paper towels and repeat with remaining 1 tablespoon oil, remaining 1 tablespoon butter, and remaining 2 fillets.

3. For the browned butter: Heat butter in 10-inch skillet over medium-high heat until butter melts, 1 to 1½ minutes. Continue to cook, swirling pan constantly, until butter is golden brown and has nutty aroma, 1 to 1½ minutes. Remove skillet from heat.

4. Remove plates from oven and sprinkle fillets with parsley. Add lemon juice to browned butter and season with salt to taste. Spoon sauce over fillets and serve immediately with lemon wedges.

Crunchy Oven-Fried Fish

Serves 4

WHY THIS RECIPE WORKS The golden-brown coating and moist, flaky flesh of batter-fried fish come at a price: the oil. Cooks have turned to the oven to avoid the bother of deep-fat frying, but oven frying often falls short. The coating never gets very crisp and the fish usually ends up overcooked. We aimed to put the crunch back into oven frying. We used thick fillets so that the fish and coating would finish cooking at the same time. Flaky cod and haddock provided the best contrast to the crunchy exterior we envisioned. A conventional bound breading—flour, egg, and fresh bread crumbs—wasn't as crisp as we wanted, so we toasted the bread crumbs with a little butter. (Precooking the crumbs also ensured that we wouldn't have to overcook the fish to get really crunchy crumbs.) Placing the coated fish on a wire rack while baking allowed air to circulate all around the fish, crisping all sides. We boosted flavor in two ways, adding shallot and parsley to the breading and horseradish, and paprika to the egg wash. As a final touch, we whipped up a creamy tartar sauce with mayonnaise, capers, and sweet relish. To prevent overcooking, buy fish fillets that are at least 1 inch thick. The bread crumbs can be made up to three days in advance and stored at room temperature in a tightly sealed container (allow to cool fully before storing). Serve the dish with Sweet and Tangy Tartar Sauce (page 238), if desired.

4 slices hearty white sandwich bread, torn into
   1-inch pieces
2 tablespoons unsalted butter, melted
¼ teaspoon table salt
½ teaspoon pepper, divided
¼ cup plus 5 tablespoons all-purpose flour, divided
2 large eggs
3 tablespoons mayonnaise
½ teaspoon paprika
2 teaspoons prepared horseradish, drained (optional)
2 tablespoons finely chopped fresh parsley
1 small shallot, minced
4 (6- to 8-ounce) skinless cod fillets,
   1 to 1½ inches thick
   Lemon wedges

1. Adjust oven rack to middle position and heat oven to 350 degrees. Pulse bread, melted butter, salt, and ¼ teaspoon pepper in food processor until bread is coarsely ground, about 8 pulses. Transfer crumb mixture to rimmed baking sheet and bake, stirring occasionally, until deep golden brown, about 15 minutes. Let crumbs cool. (Crumbs can be stored at room temperature for up to 3 days.)

2. Spread ¼ cup flour into shallow dish. In second shallow dish, whisk eggs, mayonnaise, paprika, remaining ¼ teaspoon pepper, and horseradish, if using, together; whisk in remaining 5 tablespoons flour until smooth. In third shallow dish, combine cooled bread-crumb mixture, parsley, and shallot.

3. Increase oven temperature to 425 degrees. Set wire rack in clean rimmed baking sheet and spray with vegetable oil spray. Pat cod dry with paper towels and season with salt and pepper. Working with 1 fillet at a time, dredge in flour, dip in egg mixture, then coat with thick layer of bread-crumb mixture, pressing gently to adhere; transfer to prepared wire rack.

4. Bake until cod registers 140 degrees, 18 to 25 minutes, rotating sheet halfway through baking. Using thin spatula, transfer fillets to individual plates. Serve with lemon wedges.

ACCOMPANIMENT
Sweet and Tangy Tartar Sauce
Makes about 1 cup

- ¾ cup mayonnaise
- 2 tablespoons drained capers, minced
- 2 tablespoons sweet pickle relish
- 1 small shallot, minced
- 1½ teaspoons distilled white vinegar
- ½ teaspoon Worcestershire sauce
- ½ teaspoon pepper

Mix all ingredients together in small bowl. Cover bowl with plastic wrap and let sit until flavors meld, about 15 minutes. Stir again before serving. (Sauce can be refrigerated, covered, for up to 1 week.)

Fish and Chips

Serves 4

WHY THIS RECIPE WORKS The fish and chips served at most American pubs are mediocre at best. But deep-frying fish at home can be a hassle and a mess. Plus, by the time the fries finish frying, the fish is cold. We wanted fish with a light, crisp crust and moist interior, and we wanted to serve both the fish and the fries at their prime. Our first challenge was to come up with a batter that would not only protect the fish as it cooked (allowing it to steam gently) but also provide the fish with a nicely crisp contrast. We discovered that a wet batter was the most effective way to coat and protect the fish. We liked beer—the traditional choice—as the liquid component. What was the best way to keep the coating crisp? The answer was a 3:1 ratio of flour to cornstarch, along with a teaspoon of baking powder. Still, the coating was so tender it puffed away from the fish as it cooked. A final coating of flour on top of the battered fish solved the problem. To solve the second challenge—delivering the fish and fries while both are still hot—we cooked them alternately. First, we precooked the fries in the microwave, which not only lessened cooking time but removed excess moisture that could dilute the oil and diminish crisping. Then we gave the fries their first, quick fry in hot oil. While the potatoes were draining, we battered and fried the fish. Then, as the fish drained, we gave the fries a quick final fry. For safety, use a Dutch oven with at least a 7-quart capacity. Serve with traditional malt vinegar or with Sweet and Tangy Tartar Sauce, if desired.

- 3 pounds russet potatoes, peeled, ends and sides squared off, and cut lengthwise into ½-inch by ½-inch fries
- ¼ cup peanut or vegetable oil
- 1½ cups all-purpose flour
- ½ cup cornstarch
- 2 teaspoons table salt
- ½ teaspoon cayenne pepper
- ½ teaspoon paprika
- ⅛ teaspoon pepper
- 1 teaspoon baking powder
- 3 quarts peanut or vegetable oil for frying, divided
- 1½ pounds cod or other thick white fish fillets, such as hake or haddock, cut into eight 3-ounce pieces about 1 inch thick
- 1½ cups cold beer

1. Place fries in bowl, toss with ¼ cup oil, and cover. Microwave until potatoes are partially translucent and pliable but still offer some resistance when pierced with tip of paring knife, 6 to 8 minutes, tossing them halfway through cooking time. Drain potatoes and rinse well. Spread potatoes on paper towel–lined baking sheet and dry. Let rest until fries have reached room temperature, at least 10 minutes or up to 1 hour.

2. While fries cool, whisk flour, cornstarch, salt, cayenne, paprika, and pepper in bowl; transfer ¾ cup mixture to baking sheet. Add baking powder to bowl and whisk to combine.

3. In large Dutch oven, heat 2 quarts oil over medium heat to 350 degrees. Add fries to oil and increase heat to high. Fry, stirring, until potatoes turn light golden and just begin to brown at corners, 6 to 8 minutes. Transfer fries to paper towels to drain.

4. Reduce heat to medium-high, add remaining 1 quart oil, and heat oil to 375 degrees. Meanwhile, thoroughly dry fish with paper towels and dredge each piece in flour mixture on sheet; transfer pieces to wire rack, shaking off any excess flour. Add 1¼ cups beer to flour in bowl and stir until mixture is just combined (batter will be lumpy). Add remaining ¼ cup beer as needed, 1 tablespoon at a time, whisking after each addition, until batter falls from whisk in thin, steady stream and leaves faint trail across surface of batter. Using tongs, dip 1 piece of fish in batter and let excess run off, shaking gently. Place battered fish back on sheet with flour mixture and turn to coat both sides. Repeat with remaining fish, keeping pieces in single layer on sheet.

"My husband and I are fish and chips fanatics and we think this version knocks it out of the park. The hoppy flavor of the beer really comes through in the batter, and it's spiced up with just the right amount of cayenne, paprika, and black pepper. The chips are impeccable and the fish (I splurge on halibut here) fries up moist as can be with a light, crisp exterior. We like to cover the table with newspaper and pile the fish and chips in the middle. Add a bottle of malt vinegar, a roll of paper towels, and more beer, and dinner is served."

—Becky

5. When oil reaches 375 degrees, increase heat to high and add battered fish to oil, gently shaking off any excess flour. Fry, stirring occasionally, until golden brown, 7 to 8 minutes. Transfer fish to paper towels to drain. Allow oil to return to 375 degrees.

6. Return all of fries to oil and fry until golden brown and crisp, 3 to 5 minutes. Transfer to paper towels to drain. Season fries with salt to taste, and serve immediately with fish.

Pan-Seared Swordfish Steaks

SEASON 20 RECIPE

Serves 4

WHY THIS RECIPE WORKS Swordfish, unlike silky salmon or flaky halibut, offers a unique dense meatiness. This distinctive texture, combined with a sweet mild flavor, makes it an appealing option even for a staunch carnivore. But it isn't that easy to turn out swordfish steaks with a gorgeous brown crust and a tender yet firm interior. The reason is that just like meats, fish contain enzymes called cathepsins. In the right circumstances, such as slow cooking, the cathepsins will break down the proteins that give swordfish its sturdy texture, rendering the dense steaks mushy. So in our testing we learned that the key to perfectly cooked swordfish steaks was to cook them quickly over high heat. To speed up cooking, we seared them in a hot skillet, flipping them frequently so that they cooked from both the bottom up and the top down. To keep each bite juicy, we made sure to remove the steaks from the heat when they reached 130 degrees and let carry-over cooking bring them up to the desired temperature of 140 degrees. For the best results, purchase swordfish steaks that are ¾ to 1 inch thick. Look for four steaks that weigh 7 to 9 ounces each or two steaks that weigh about 1 pound each. If you purchase the latter, cut them in half to create four steaks. We've found that skin-on swordfish often buckles in the hot skillet. Ask your fishmonger to remove the skin or trim it yourself with a thin, sharp knife. Though these rich, meaty, juicy steaks are great with just a squeeze of lemon, we wanted the option of dressing them up a bit so we came up with two sauces (recipes follow). The Caper-Currant Relish is a classic Italian swordfish accompaniment, an *agrodolce*-style relish based on piquant capers and sweet currants; the Spicy Dried Mint–Garlic Sauce is an ultragarlicky sauce with the unique addition of dried mint.

2 teaspoons vegetable oil
2 pounds skinless swordfish steaks,
   ¾ to 1 inch thick
1½ teaspoons kosher salt
   Lemon wedges

1. Heat oil in 12-inch nonstick skillet over medium-high heat until shimmering. While oil heats, pat steaks dry with paper towels and sprinkle on both sides with salt.

2. Place steaks in skillet and cook, flipping every 2 minutes, until golden brown and centers register 130 degrees, 7 to 11 minutes. Transfer to serving platter or individual plates and let rest for 10 minutes. Serve with lemon wedges.

ACCOMPANIMENTS
Caper-Currant Relish
Makes about ½ cup
We balanced sweet currants, salty capers, fresh parsley, and savory garlic in this relish that's perfect for delicately flavored fish and poultry. Golden raisins can be substituted for the currants.

3 tablespoons finely chopped fresh parsley
3 tablespoons extra-virgin olive oil
2 tablespoons capers, rinsed and chopped fine
2 tablespoons currants, chopped fine
1 garlic clove, minced
1 teaspoon grated lemon zest plus
   2 tablespoons juice

Combine all ingredients in bowl. Let sit at room temperature for at least 20 minutes before serving.

Spicy Dried Mint–Garlic Sauce
Makes about ⅓ cup
We pushed dried mint through a strainer to remove any tough stems before moistening the mint powder with bright vinegar and rich olive oil. A hefty dose of raw garlic added a spicy heat and savory flavor to this simple and surprisingly bold sauce. This sauce gets its spiciness from the raw garlic. If you are not using a garlic press, use a fork to bruise the minced garlic when stirring the sauce together.

4 teaspoons dried mint
¼ cup extra-virgin olive oil
2 tablespoons red wine vinegar
4 garlic cloves, minced
⅛ teaspoon table salt

Place mint in fine-mesh strainer and use spoon to rub mint through strainer into bowl. Discard any solids left in strainer. (You should have about 1 tablespoon mint powder.) Add oil, vinegar, garlic, and salt to mint powder and stir to combine.

Poached Salmon with Herb and Caper Vinaigrette

Serves 4

WHY THIS RECIPE WORKS Poaching can deliver supple salmon in under half an hour. Looking for the perfect method, we started our tests with a classic court-bouillon, which is made by boiling water, wine, herbs, vegetables, and aromatics and then straining out the solids. But discarding all those vegetables seemed wasteful for a simple weeknight supper. Using less liquid—just enough to come half an inch up the side of the fillets—allowed us to cut back on the quantity of vegetables and aromatics; in fact, shallot, a few herbs, and some wine were all we needed to solve the flavor issue. However, the low cooking temperature required to poach the salmon evenly didn't create enough steam to cook the part that wasn't submerged in liquid. The solution was to increase the amount of wine. The additional alcohol lowered the liquid's boiling point, producing more vapor even at the lower temperature. Meanwhile, the bottom of the fillets had the opposite problem, overcooking due to direct contact with the pan. Resting the salmon fillets on lemon slices provided insulation. For a finishing touch, after removing the salmon, we reduced the liquid and added a few tablespoons of olive oil to create an easy vinaigrette-style sauce. To ensure even cooking, buy a whole center-cut fillet and cut it into four pieces. If a skinless whole fillet is unavailable, remove the skin yourself or follow the recipe as directed with a skin-on fillet, adding 3 to 4 minutes to the cooking time in step 2. If your knife is too dull to cut through the salmon skin, try a serrated knife.

2 lemons
2 tablespoons chopped fresh parsley, stems reserved
2 tablespoons chopped fresh tarragon, stems reserved
1 large shallot, minced
½ cup dry white wine
½ cup water
1 (1¾ to 2-pound) skinless salmon fillet, 1½ inches thick, sliced crosswise into 4 equal pieces

2 tablespoons capers, rinsed and chopped
2 tablespoons extra-virgin olive oil
1 tablespoon honey

1. Line plate with paper towels. Cut top and bottom off 1 lemon, then cut into eight to ten ¼-inch-thick slices. Cut remaining lemon into 8 wedges and set aside. Arrange lemon slices in single layer across bottom of 12-inch skillet. Scatter herb stems and 2 tablespoons minced shallot evenly over lemon slices. Add wine and water to skillet.

2. Place salmon fillets in skillet, skinned side down, on top of lemon slices. Set pan over high heat and bring liquid to simmer. Reduce heat to low, cover, and cook until sides are opaque but center of thickest part of fillet is still translucent when cut into with paring knife, or until fillet registers 125 degrees (for medium-rare), 11 to 16 minutes. Off heat, use spatula to carefully transfer salmon and lemon slices to prepared plate and tent with aluminum foil.

3. Return pan to high heat and simmer cooking liquid until slightly thickened and reduced to 2 tablespoons, 4 to 5 minutes. Meanwhile, combine capers, oil, honey, chopped parsley and tarragon, and remaining minced shallot in medium bowl. Strain reduced cooking liquid through fine-mesh strainer into bowl with herb mixture, pressing on solids to extract as much liquid as possible. Whisk to combine and season with salt and pepper to taste.

4. Season salmon with salt and pepper to taste. Using spatula, carefully lift and tilt salmon fillets to remove lemon slices. Place salmon on serving platter or individual plates and spoon vinaigrette over top. Serve, passing lemon wedges separately.

How to Skin a Salmon Fillet

1. Insert blade of sharp boning knife just above skin about 1 inch from end of fillet. Cut through nearest end, away from yourself, keeping blade just above skin.

2. Rotate fish and grab loose piece of skin. Run knife between flesh and skin, making sure knife is just above skin, until skin is completely removed.

Pan-Seared Brined Salmon

Serves 4

WHY THIS RECIPE WORKS Harnessing the intense heat of a skillet, you can produce a golden-brown, ultracrisp crust on salmon fillets while keeping their interiors moist. We first brined the fish to season it and to keep it moist. Instead of adding the fish to an already-hot skillet, we placed it in a cold, dry nonstick skillet skin side down and then turned on the heat. The skin protected the fish from drying out while cooking and later was easy to peel off and discard. Also, because the skin released fat into the pan as it cooked, no extra oil was needed to sear the second side of the fish. To ensure even cooking, buy a whole center-cut fillet and cut it into four pieces. Using skin-on salmon is important here, as we rely on the fat underneath the skin as the cooking medium (as opposed to adding extra oil). It is important to keep the skin on during cooking; once the salmon is cooked, the skin will be easy to remove. If using wild salmon, cook it until it registers 120 degrees. Serve with Mango-Mint Salsa or Cilantro-Mint Chutney (recipes follow), if desired.

¼ cup table salt, for brining
1 (1½ to 2-pound) skin-on salmon fillet, 1½ inches thick, sliced crosswise into 4 equal pieces
½ teaspoon table salt, divided
½ teaspoon pepper, divided
Lemon wedges

1. Dissolve ¼ cup salt in 2 quarts cold water in large container. Submerge salmon in brine and let sit at room temperature for 15 minutes. Remove salmon from brine and pat dry with paper towels.

2. Sprinkle bottom of 12-inch nonstick skillet evenly with ¼ teaspoon salt and ¼ teaspoon pepper. Place fillets, skin side down, in skillet and sprinkle tops of fillets with remaining ¼ teaspoon salt and remaining ¼ teaspoon pepper. Heat skillet over medium-high heat and cook fillets without moving them until fat begins to render, skin begins to brown, and bottom ¼ inch of fillets turns opaque, 6 to 8 minutes.

3. Using tongs, flip fillets and continue to cook without moving them until centers are still translucent when checked with tip of paring knife and register 125 degrees, 6 to 8 minutes longer. Transfer fillets skin side down to serving platter and let rest for 5 minutes before serving with lemon wedges.

ACCOMPANIMENTS
Mango-Mint Salsa
Makes about 1 cup
Adjust the salsa's heat level by reserving and adding the jalapeño seeds, if desired.

1 mango, peeled, pitted, and cut into ¼-inch pieces
1 shallot, minced
3 tablespoons lime juice (2 limes)
2 tablespoons chopped fresh mint
1 jalapeño chile, stemmed, seeded, and minced
1 tablespoon extra-virgin olive oil
1 garlic clove, minced
½ teaspoon table salt

Combine all ingredients in bowl.

Cilantro-Mint Chutney
Makes about 1 cup
Adjust the chutney's heat level by reserving and adding the jalapeño seeds, if desired.

2 cups fresh cilantro leaves
1 cup fresh mint leaves
½ cup water
¼ cup sesame seeds, lightly toasted
1 (2-inch) piece ginger, peeled and sliced into ⅛-inch-thick rounds
1 jalapeño chile, stemmed, seeded, and sliced into 1-inch pieces
2 tablespoons vegetable oil
2 tablespoons lime juice
1½ teaspoons sugar
½ teaspoon table salt

Process all ingredients in blender until smooth, about 30 seconds, scraping down sides of jar with spatula after 10 seconds.

Sesame-Crusted Salmon with Lemon and Ginger

Serves 4

WHY THIS RECIPE WORKS The combination of fish and sesame shows up in cuisines from Asia to California to the Middle East and for good reason—the crunch of the sesame seeds is the perfect complement to rich, silky salmon. The simplest approach is to coat fillets with the seeds and then pan-sear the fish. But the duo of salmon and sesame often suffers from a common problem: Both salmon and sesame have a monotonous richness, so finishing a whole serving is a chore. We wanted a lively dish in which the salmon and sesame would be offset with bolder, brighter flavors. Brining the fish for just 15 minutes took care of any dryness. We dunked the seeds in the fish brine, which woke up their nutty flavor by infusing each with salt. Toasting the seeds gave them nice crunch. For extra sesame flavor, we thickened tahini with some lemon juice and used the thick paste to adhere the seeds. We also added scallion whites, lemon zest, fresh ginger, and a dash of cayenne for more layers of flavor. To ensure even cooking, buy a whole center-cut fillet and cut it into four pieces. If any of the pieces have a thin belly flap, fold it over to create a more even thickness.

5 tablespoons table salt, for brining
¾ cup sesame seeds
1 (1½ to 2-pound) skinless salmon fillet, 1½ inches thick, sliced crosswise into 4 equal pieces
2 scallions, white parts minced, green parts sliced thin, divided
1 tablespoon grated lemon zest plus 2 teaspoons juice
4 teaspoons tahini
2 teaspoons grated fresh ginger
⅛ teaspoon cayenne pepper
⅛ teaspoon table salt
1 teaspoon vegetable oil

1. Adjust oven rack to middle position and heat oven to 325 degrees. Dissolve 5 tablespoons salt in 2 quarts water. Transfer 1 cup brine to bowl, stir in sesame seeds, and let sit at room temperature for 5 minutes. Submerge fillets in remaining brine and let sit at room temperature for 15 minutes.

2. Drain seeds and place in 12-inch nonstick skillet. Cook seeds over medium heat, stirring constantly, until golden brown, 2 to 4 minutes. Transfer seeds to shallow dish and wipe out skillet with paper towels. Remove fillets from brine and pat dry.

3. Place scallion whites and lemon zest on cutting board and chop until whites and zest are finely minced and well combined. Transfer scallion-zest mixture to bowl and stir in lemon juice, tahini, ginger, cayenne, and salt.

4. Evenly distribute half of paste over bottoms (skinned sides) of fillets. Press coated sides of fillets in seeds and transfer, seed side down, to plate. Evenly distribute remaining paste over tops of fillets and coat with remaining seeds.

5. Heat oil in now-empty skillet over medium heat until shimmering. Place fillets in skillet, skinned side up, and reduce heat to medium-low. Cook until seeds begin to brown, 1 to 2 minutes. Remove skillet from heat and, using 2 spatulas, carefully flip fillets over. Transfer skillet to oven. Bake until center of fish is translucent when checked with tip of paring knife and registers 125 degrees, 10 to 15 minutes. Transfer to serving platter and let rest for 5 minutes. Sprinkle with scallion greens and serve.

VARIATIONS
Sesame-Crusted Salmon with Lime and Coriander
Substitute 4 teaspoons lime zest for lemon zest, lime juice for lemon juice, and ¼ teaspoon ground coriander for cayenne.

Sesame-Crusted Salmon with Orange and Chili Powder
Substitute orange zest for lemon zest, orange juice for lemon juice, and ¼ teaspoon chili powder for cayenne.

Glazed Salmon

Serves 4

WHY THIS RECIPE WORKS Once you master the simple technique of glazing salmon, you have a nearly endless array of flavor options at your disposal for a quick but elegant weeknight dinner. The traditional method for glazed salmon calls for broiling, but reaching into a broiling-hot oven every minute to baste the fish is a hassle and, even worse, the fillets often burn if your timing isn't spot-on. We wanted a fool-proof method for glazed salmon that was succulent and pink throughout while keeping the slightly crusty, flavorful browned exterior typically achieved with broiling. First we found that reducing the temperature and gently baking the fish, instead of broiling it, cooked the salmon perfectly. Before the fillets went into the oven, we rubbed a mixture of cornstarch, sugar, and salt onto them and quickly pan-seared them on each side. The mixture ensured that the glaze would stay put, and the sugar enabled the fillets to rapidly caramelize before they had a chance to toughen. To ensure even cooking, buy a whole center-cut fillet and cut it into four pieces. If your knife is too dull to cut through the salmon skin, try a serrated knife. Prepare the glaze before you cook the salmon. If your nonstick skillet isn't ovensafe, sear the salmon as directed in step 2, then transfer it to a rimmed baking sheet, glaze it, and bake as directed in step 3. It is important to keep the skin on during cooking; once the salmon is cooked, the skin will be easy to remove.

- 1 teaspoon packed light brown sugar
- ½ teaspoon kosher salt
- ¼ teaspoon cornstarch
- 1 (1½- to 2-pound) skin-on salmon fillet, 1½ inches thick, sliced crosswise into 4 equal pieces
- ½ teaspoon pepper
- 1 teaspoon vegetable oil
- 1 recipe glaze (recipes follow)

1. Adjust oven rack to middle position and heat oven to 300 degrees. Combine sugar, salt, and cornstarch in small bowl. Pat fillets dry with paper towels and season with pepper. Sprinkle sugar mixture evenly over top of flesh side of salmon, rubbing to distribute.

2. Heat oil in 12-inch ovensafe nonstick skillet over medium-high heat until just smoking. Place salmon, flesh side down, in skillet and cook until well browned, about 1 minute. Using tongs, carefully flip salmon and cook on skin side for 1 minute.

3. Remove skillet from heat and spoon glaze evenly over salmon. Transfer skillet to oven and cook until salmon is still translucent when checked with tip of paring knife and registers 125 degrees (for medium-rare), 7 to 10 minutes. Transfer salmon to serving platter or individual plates and serve.

ACCOMPANIMENTS

Pomegranate-Balsamic Glaze
Makes about ½ cup
This fruity, tangy glaze is a perfect match for rich salmon.

- 3 tablespoons packed light brown sugar
- 3 tablespoons pomegranate juice
- 2 tablespoons balsamic vinegar
- 1 tablespoon whole-grain mustard
- 1 teaspoon cornstarch
  Pinch cayenne pepper

Whisk all ingredients together in small saucepan. Bring to boil over medium-high heat; simmer until thickened, about 1 minute. Remove from heat and cover to keep warm.

Asian Barbecue Glaze
Makes about ½ cup
Toasted sesame oil gives this teriyaki-like glaze rich flavor.

- 2 tablespoons ketchup
- 2 tablespoons hoisin sauce
- 2 tablespoons rice vinegar
- 2 tablespoons packed light brown sugar
- 1 tablespoon soy sauce
- 1 tablespoon toasted sesame oil
- 2 teaspoons Asian chili-garlic sauce
- 1 teaspoon grated fresh ginger

Whisk all ingredients together in small saucepan. Bring to boil over medium-high heat; simmer until thickened, about 3 minutes. Remove from heat and cover to keep warm.

Orange-Miso Glaze
Makes about ½ cup

- 1 teaspoon grated orange zest plus ¼ cup juice
- 2 tablespoons white miso
- 1 tablespoon packed light brown sugar
- 1 tablespoon rice vinegar
- 1 tablespoon whole-grain mustard
- ¾ teaspoon cornstarch
- Pinch cayenne pepper

Whisk all ingredients together in small saucepan. Bring to boil over medium-high heat; simmer until thickened, about 1 minute. Remove from heat and cover to keep warm.

Soy-Mustard Glaze
Makes about ½ cup

- 3 tablespoons packed light brown sugar
- 2 tablespoons soy sauce
- 2 tablespoons mirin
- 1 tablespoon sherry vinegar
- 1 tablespoon whole-grain mustard
- 1 tablespoon water
- 1 teaspoon cornstarch
- ⅛ teaspoon red pepper flakes

Whisk all ingredients together in small saucepan. Bring to boil over medium-high heat; simmer until thickened, about 1 minute. Remove from heat and cover to keep warm.

Oven-Roasted Salmon

Serves 4

WHY THIS RECIPE WORKS Roasting a salmon fillet can create a brown exterior, but often at the risk of a dry, overcooked interior. The best roasted salmon should have moist, flavorful flesh inside, with a contrasting crisp texture on the outside. We roasted the fish at a low temperature and achieved the buttery flesh we were after, but no browning—and the fillets were a little mushy from the rendered fat. Taking the opposite approach, we put the fish on a preheated baking sheet and started the oven at a high temperature to firm up and brown the exterior. This gave us a crust, but we still needed to get rid of the fat; cutting slits in the skin released the fat rendered by the high heat. Lowering the temperature as soon as we put the fish in the oven enabled it to cook through gradually after the initial blast of heat, so it didn't dry out.

Now we had the contrast between moist interior and crisp brown exterior that we wanted. Salmon is rich and flavorful all on its own, but we devised a couple of easy no-cook relishes (recipes follow) that can be served alongside for even more flavor and contrast. To ensure even cooking, buy a whole center-cut fillet and cut it into four pieces. If your knife is too dull to cut through the salmon skin, try a serrated knife. It is important to keep the skin on during cooking; once the salmon is cooked, the skin will be easy to remove.

- 1 (1¾- to 2-pound) skin-on salmon fillet, 1½ inches thick, sliced crosswise into 4 equal pieces
- 2 teaspoons extra-virgin olive oil
- 1 teaspoon table salt
- ½ teaspoon pepper

1. Adjust oven rack to lowest position, place aluminum foil–lined rimmed baking sheet on rack, and heat oven to 500 degrees. Make 4 or 5 shallow slashes 1 inch apart along skin side of each salmon piece; do not cut into flesh. Pat salmon dry with paper towels, rub with oil, and season with salt and pepper.

2. Once oven reaches 500 degrees, reduce oven temperature to 275 degrees. Remove sheet from oven and carefully place salmon, skin side down, on hot sheet. Roast until center is still translucent when checked with tip of paring knife and registers 120 degrees (for medium-rare), 4 to 6 minutes.

3. Slide fish spatula along underside of fillets and transfer to individual plates or serving platter, leaving skin behind; discard skin. Serve.

ACCOMPANIMENTS
Tangerine and Ginger Relish
Makes about 1¼ cups

- 4 tangerines, rind and pith removed and segments cut into ½-inch pieces (1 cup)
- 1 scallion, sliced thin
- 2 teaspoons lemon juice
- 2 teaspoons extra-virgin olive oil
- 1½ teaspoons grated fresh ginger

1. Place tangerines in fine-mesh strainer set over medium bowl and drain for 15 minutes.

2. Pour off all but 1 tablespoon tangerine juice from bowl; whisk in the scallion, lemon juice, oil, and ginger. Stir in tangerines and season with salt and pepper to taste.

Roasted Whole Side of Salmon

Fresh Tomato Relish
Makes about 1½ cups

¾ pound ripe tomatoes, cored, seeded, and cut into ¼-inch pieces (1½ cups)
2 tablespoons finely chopped fresh basil
1 shallot, minced
1 tablespoon extra-virgin olive oil
1 teaspoon red wine vinegar
1 garlic clove, minced

Combine tomatoes, basil, shallot, oil, vinegar, and garlic in medium bowl. Season with salt and pepper to taste.

Spicy Cucumber Relish
Makes about 2 cups

1 cucumber, peeled, seeded, and cut into ¼-inch pieces (2 cups)
2 tablespoons finely chopped fresh mint
1 shallot, minced
1 serrano chile, seeded and minced
1 tablespoon lime juice, plus extra as needed
¼ teaspoon table salt

Combine cucumber, mint, shallot, chile, 1 tablespoon lime juice, and salt in medium bowl. Let sit at room temperature until flavors meld, about 15 minutes. Season with lime juice and salt to taste.

Roasted Whole Side of Salmon

Serves 8 to 10

WHY THIS RECIPE WORKS Salmon is ideal for entertaining, especially when you can cook a whole roasted fillet that is evenly moist inside and gorgeously browned on top. To start, we salted it for an hour, which helped the flesh retain moisture and protein. Placing it on a greased aluminum foil sling ensured that it was easy to transfer to a serving platter. We set the salmon on a wire rack set in a rimmed baking sheet to encourage air circulation. Evenly brushing the surface with honey encouraged rapid browning. We preheated the oven to 250 degrees to warm the entire oven, which ensured that cooking happened quickly and evenly. Then, we broiled the fillet until it just began to brown. Lastly, we again turned the oven heat to 250 degrees to allow the fillet to gently cook through. A squeeze of fresh lemon juice was all it took to temper the richness of the salmon, but a pair of vibrant, no-cook condiments—an arugula-based pesto and a crisp cucumber relish—offered even more dress-up potential. This recipe requires salting the fish for at least 1 hour. Look for a fillet that is uniformly thick from end to end. The surface will

continue to brown after the oven temperature is reduced in step 4; if the surface starts to darken too much before the fillet's center registers 125 degrees, shield the dark portion with aluminum foil. If using wild salmon, which contains less fat than farmed salmon, remove it from the oven when the center of the fillet registers 120 degrees. If your knife is too dull to cut through the salmon skin, try a serrated knife. It is important to keep the skin on during cooking; once the salmon is cooked, the skin will be easy to remove. Serve as is or with Arugula and Almond Pesto or Cucumber-Ginger Relish (recipes follow).

1 (4-pound) skin-on side of salmon, pinbones removed
1 tablespoon kosher salt
2 tablespoons honey
   Lemon wedges

1. Sprinkle flesh side of salmon evenly with salt and refrigerate, uncovered, for at least 1 hour or up to 4 hours.

2. Adjust oven rack 7 inches from broiler element and heat oven to 250 degrees. Line rimmed baking sheet with aluminum foil and place wire rack in sheet. Fold 18 by 12-inch piece of foil lengthwise to create 18 by 6-inch sling. Place sling on wire rack and spray with vegetable oil spray.

3. Heat broiler. Pat salmon dry with paper towels and place, skin side down, on foil sling. Brush salmon evenly with honey and broil until surface is lightly but evenly browned, 8 to 12 minutes, rotating sheet halfway through broiling.

4. Return oven temperature to 250 degrees and continue to cook until center of fillet registers 125 degrees, 10 to 15 minutes, rotating sheet halfway through cooking. Using foil sling, transfer salmon to serving platter, then carefully remove foil. Serve, passing lemon wedges separately.

ACCOMPANIMENTS
Arugula and Almond Pesto
Makes about 1½ cups
For a spicier pesto, reserve, mince, and add the ribs and seeds from the chile. The pesto can be refrigerated for up to 24 hours. If refrigerated, let the pesto sit at room temperature for 30 minutes before serving.

¼ cup almonds, lightly toasted
4 garlic cloves, peeled
4 anchovy fillets, rinsed and patted dry
1 serrano chile, stemmed, seeded, and halved lengthwise
6 ounces (6 cups) arugula
¼ cup lemon juice (2 lemons)
¼ cup extra-virgin olive oil
1½ teaspoons kosher salt

Process almonds, garlic, anchovies, and serrano in food processor until finely chopped, about 15 seconds, scraping down sides of bowl as needed. Add arugula, lemon juice, oil, and salt and process until smooth, about 30 seconds.

Cucumber-Ginger Relish
Makes about 2 cups

For a spicier relish, reserve, mince, and add the ribs and seeds from the chile. To keep the cucumbers crisp, serve this relish within 30 minutes of assembling it.

- ½ cup rice vinegar
- 6 tablespoons extra-virgin olive oil
- ¼ cup lime juice (2 limes)
- 2 tablespoons whole-grain mustard
- 1 tablespoon grated fresh ginger
- ½ teaspoon kosher salt
- 1 English cucumber, seeded and cut into ¼-inch dice
- 1 cup finely chopped fresh mint
- 1 cup finely chopped fresh cilantro
- 1 serrano chile, stemmed, seeded, and minced

Whisk vinegar, oil, lime juice, mustard, ginger, and salt in bowl until smooth. Add cucumber, mint, cilantro, and serrano and stir to combine.

Brown Rice Bowls with Vegetables and Salmon

SEASON 20 RECIPE

Serves 4

WHY THIS RECIPE WORKS Rice and grain bowls are all the rage, and no wonder—they are healthy and delicious and offer an array of options for packing proteins and vegetables into a one-bowl meal. The trick is to make the cooking and assembly of all the moving parts reasonably easy. For this brown rice bowl, the chewy, nutty brown rice that forms the base was supereasy to make: We just poured it into plenty of boiling salted water and cooked it like pasta. While the rice cooked, we spread sliced carrots and shiitakes on a baking sheet and started roasting them in a hot oven and prepared pickled cucumbers to add crisp brightness to our bowl. When the vegetables were half-roasted, we cleared a space in the middle of the baking sheet and added four small salmon fillets, brushed with hoisin sauce to boost their flavor and color. We mixed a portion of the pickling liquid with scallion-ginger oil and a bit more hoisin to make a potent dressing. We stirred some into the drained rice to ensure that every bite was flavorful. Topped with pickled cucumbers, roasted vegetables, and salmon and finished with dressing and toasted sesame seeds, this grain bowl makes a satisfying hot dinner or a great packed lunch. If your knife is too dull to cut through the salmon skin, try a serrated knife. It is important to keep the skin on during cooking; once the salmon is cooked, the skin will be easy to remove. Toast the sesame seeds in a dry skillet over medium heat until fragrant (about 1 minute), and then remove the skillet from the heat so the seeds won't scorch.

- ¼ cup vegetable oil, divided
- 3 scallions, white and green parts separated and sliced thin on bias
- 2 teaspoons grated fresh ginger, divided
- ⅓ cup distilled white vinegar
- 1 tablespoon sugar
- 1¾ teaspoons table salt, divided, plus salt for cooking rice
- 1 English cucumber, quartered lengthwise, seeded, and sliced on bias ¼ inch thick
- 1¾ cups short-grain brown rice
- 1 pound carrots, peeled and sliced on bias ½ inch thick
- 1 pound shiitake mushrooms, stemmed, caps larger than 2 inches halved
- 1 (1-pound) skin-on salmon fillet, 1½ inches thick, sliced crosswise into 4 equal pieces
- 4 teaspoons hoisin sauce, divided
- 1 tablespoon sesame seeds, toasted
  Sriracha (optional)

1. Adjust oven rack to lowest position and heat oven to 500 degrees. Heat 2 tablespoons oil in large saucepan over medium heat until shimmering. Add scallion whites and 1½ teaspoons ginger and cook, stirring constantly, until fragrant, about 30 seconds. Transfer scallion mixture to small bowl.

2. Bring 6 cups water to boil in now-empty saucepan. While water is coming to boil, whisk vinegar, sugar, ¾ teaspoon salt, and remaining ½ teaspoon ginger in medium bowl until sugar is dissolved. Add cucumber and stir until coated. Set aside, stirring occasionally.

3. Add rice and 1 teaspoon salt to boiling water. Reduce heat and simmer until rice is tender, about 30 minutes. Drain rice well and return it to saucepan. Cover and set aside.

4. While rice is cooking, toss carrots with 1 tablespoon oil and ½ teaspoon salt. Spread in even layer on half of rimmed baking sheet. Toss mushrooms with 2 tablespoons water, remaining 1 tablespoon oil, and remaining ½ teaspoon salt and spread in even layer on other half of sheet. Roast until vegetables are just beginning to soften and brown, about 10 minutes.

5. While vegetables are cooking, make 2 shallow slashes about 1 inch apart along skin side of each piece of salmon, being careful not to cut into flesh. Brush flesh side of each piece with ½ teaspoon hoisin.

Brown Rice Bowls with
Vegetables and Salmon

6. Reduce oven temperature to 275 degrees and remove sheet. Push vegetables to either side to clear space in middle of sheet. Carefully place salmon, skin side down, in clearing. Return sheet to oven and roast until vegetables are tender and browned and centers of fillets are still translucent when checked with tip of paring knife and register 125 degrees (for medium-rare), 10 to 12 minutes.

7. Measure out ¼ cup cucumber liquid and add to scallion mixture. Whisk in remaining 2 teaspoons hoisin. Stir 2 tablespoons dressing into rice.

8. Spoon rice into 4 wide bowls. Place 1 piece of salmon on top of rice. Arrange carrots, mushrooms, and cucumbers in piles that cover rice. Drizzle salmon and vegetables with remaining dressing. Sprinkle with sesame seeds and scallion greens. Serve, passing sriracha separately, if using.

Pan-Seared Sesame-Crusted Tuna Steaks

Serves 4

WHY THIS RECIPE WORKS Moist and rare in the middle with a seared crust, pan-seared tuna is a popular entrée in restaurants. This dish is so simple that we thought it would be easy to make at home, and set out to determine the best method. Starting with high-quality tuna—sushi grade if possible—is paramount; we prefer the flavor of yellowfin. A thickness of at least an inch is necessary for the center of the tuna to be rare while the exterior browns. Before searing the tuna in a nonstick skillet, we rubbed the steaks with oil, then coated them with sesame seeds; the oil helped the seeds stick to the fish. The sesame seeds browned in the skillet and formed a beautiful, nutty-tasting crust. We learned that tuna, like beef, will continue to cook from residual heat when removed from the stove, so when the interior of the tuna was near the desired degree of doneness (about 110 degrees on an instant-read thermometer), we transferred it to a platter. If you plan to serve the fish with the sauce or salsa (recipes follow), prepare it before cooking the fish. Most members of the test kitchen staff prefer their tuna steaks rare to medium-rare; the cooking times given in this recipe are for tuna steaks cooked to these two degrees of doneness. For tuna steaks cooked medium, observe the timing for medium-rare, then tent the steaks with foil for 5 minutes before slicing. If you prefer tuna steaks cooked so rare that they are still cold in the center, try to purchase steaks that are 1½ inches thick and cook them according to the timing below for rare steaks. Bear in mind, though, that the cooking times below are estimates; check for doneness by nicking the fish with a paring knife. To cook only two steaks, use half as many sesame seeds, reduce the amount of oil to 2 teaspoons both on the fish and in the pan, use a 10-inch nonstick skillet, and follow the same cooking times.

¾ cup sesame seeds
4 (8-ounce) skinless tuna steaks, 1 inch thick
2 tablespoons vegetable oil, divided
1 teaspoon table salt
½ teaspoon pepper

1. Spread sesame seeds in shallow baking dish. Pat tuna steaks dry with paper towels, rub steaks all over with 1 tablespoon oil, then season with salt and pepper. Press both sides of each steak in sesame seeds to coat.

2. Heat remaining 1 tablespoon oil in 12-inch nonstick skillet over high heat until just smoking. Add steaks and cook for 30 seconds without moving them. Reduce heat to medium-high and continue to cook until seeds are golden brown, about 1½ minutes. Using tongs, carefully flip steaks and cook, without moving them, until golden brown on second side and centers register 110 degrees (for rare), about 1½ minutes (steaks will be opaque at perimeters and translucent red at center when checked with tip of paring knife), or 125 degrees (for medium-rare), about 3 minutes (steaks will be opaque at perimeters and reddish pink at center). Serve.

ACCOMPANIMENTS
Ginger-Soy Sauce with Scallions
Makes about 1 cup
If available, serve pickled ginger and wasabi, passed separately, with the tuna and this sauce.

¼ cup soy sauce
¼ cup rice vinegar
¼ cup water
1 scallion, sliced thin
2½ teaspoons sugar

2   teaspoons grated fresh ginger
1½   teaspoons toasted sesame oil
½   teaspoon red pepper flakes

Combine all ingredients in small bowl, stirring to
dissolve sugar.

Avocado-Orange Salsa
Makes about 1 cup
*To keep the avocado from discoloring, prepare this salsa
just before you cook the tuna steaks.*

1   large orange, segmented
1   avocado, halved, pitted, and chopped fine
2   tablespoons finely chopped red onion
2   tablespoons finely chopped fresh cilantro
4   teaspoons lime juice
1   small jalapeño chile, stemmed, seeded, and minced

Combine all ingredients in small bowl. Season with salt
to taste.

Pan-Seared Scallops

Serves 4

WHY THIS RECIPE WORKS Producing crisp-crusted
restaurant-style scallops means overcoming two obstacles:
chemically treated scallops and weak stovetops. We wanted
to achieve superior pan-seared scallops that had a perfectly
brown crust and no hint of off-flavors. We decided to work
with wet scallops (those that are chemically treated with STP,
a solution of water and sodium tripolyphosphate, to increase
shelf life and retain moisture) first. If we could develop a good
recipe for finicky wet scallops, it would surely work with
premium dry (untreated) scallops. We found that waiting to
add the scallops to the skillet until the oil was beginning to
smoke, cooking the scallops in two batches instead of one,
and switching to a nonstick skillet (so that the browned bits
formed a crust on the meat instead of sticking to the skillet)
were all steps in the right direction. But it wasn't until we tried
a common restaurant technique—butter basting—that our
scallops really improved. We seared the scallops in oil on
one side and added butter to the skillet after flipping them.
(Butter contains milk proteins and sugars that brown rapidly
when heated.) We then used a large spoon to ladle the
foaming butter over the scallops. Waiting to add the butter
ensured that it had just enough time to work its browning
magic on the scallops, but not enough time to burn. Next we
addressed the lingering flavor of STP. Unable to rinse it away,
we decided to mask it by soaking the scallops in a saltwater
brine containing lemon juice. For dry scallops, we simply
skipped the soaking step and proceeded with the recipe.

It produced scallops that rivaled those made on a powerful
restaurant range, with golden-brown exteriors and juicy and
tender interiors. We recommend buying "dry" scallops, which
don't have chemical additives and taste better than "wet."
Dry scallops will look ivory or pinkish; wet scallops are bright
white. If you serve the scallops with the browned butter
sauce (page 252), prepare it while the scallops dry (between
steps 1 and 2) and keep it warm while cooking them.

1½   pounds large sea scallops, tendons removed
½   teaspoon table salt
¼   teaspoon pepper
2   tablespoons vegetable oil, divided
2   tablespoons unsalted butter, divided
     Lemon wedges

1. Place scallops on baking sheet lined with clean dish
towel. Place second clean dish towel on top of scallops and
press gently on towel to blot liquid. Let scallops sit at room
temperature for 10 minutes while towels absorb moisture.

2. Remove second towel and season scallops with salt
and pepper. Heat 1 tablespoon oil in 12-inch nonstick skillet
over high heat until just smoking. Add half of scallops in single
layer, flat side down, and cook, without moving, until well
browned, 1½ to 2 minutes.

3. Add 1 tablespoon butter to skillet. Flip scallops and
continue to cook, using large spoon to baste scallops with
melted butter, tilting skillet so butter runs to one side, until
sides of scallops are firm and centers are opaque, 30 to
90 seconds (remove smaller scallops from pan as they finish
cooking). Transfer scallops to large plate and tent with foil.
Wipe out skillet with paper towels and repeat with remaining
1 tablespoon oil, remaining scallops, and remaining 1 tablespoon butter. Serve immediately with lemon wedges.

Lemon Browned Butter Sauce
Makes about ¼ cup

- 4 tablespoons unsalted butter, cut into 4 pieces
- 1 shallot, minced
- 1 tablespoon finely chopped fresh parsley
- ½ teaspoon finely chopped fresh thyme
- 2 teaspoons lemon juice

Heat butter in small saucepan over medium heat and cook, swirling pan constantly, until butter turns dark golden brown and has nutty aroma, 4 to 5 minutes. Add shallot and cook until fragrant, about 30 seconds. Remove pan from heat and stir in parsley, thyme, and lemon juice. Season with salt and pepper to taste. Cover to keep warm.

Pan-Seared Shrimp

Serves 4

WHY THIS RECIPE WORKS A good recipe for pan-seared shrimp is hard to find. Of the handful of recipes we uncovered, the majority resulted in shrimp that were either dry and flavorless or pale, tough, and gummy. We wanted shrimp that were well caramelized but still moist, briny, and tender. We peeled the shrimp first and tried using a brine to add moisture, but found that it inhibited browning. Instead, we seasoned the shrimp with salt, pepper, and sugar, which brought out their natural sweetness and aided in browning. We cooked the shrimp in batches in a large, piping-hot skillet and then paired them with thick, glaze-like sauces with assertive ingredients and plenty of acidity as a foil for the shrimp's richness. This recipe can also be prepared with large shrimp (31 to 40 per pound); the cooking time will be slightly shorter. Either a nonstick or a traditional skillet will work for this recipe, but a nonstick simplifies cleanup.

- 2 tablespoons vegetable oil, divided
- 1½ pounds extra-large shrimp (21 to 25 per pound), peeled and deveined
- ¼ teaspoon table salt
- ¼ teaspoon pepper
- ⅛ teaspoon sugar

1. Heat 1 tablespoon oil in 12-inch skillet over high heat until smoking. Meanwhile, toss shrimp, salt, pepper, and sugar in medium bowl. Add half of shrimp to pan in single layer and cook until spotty brown and edges turn pink, about 1 minute.

2. Off heat, flip each shrimp and let sit until all but very center is opaque, about 30 seconds. Transfer shrimp to large plate. Repeat with remaining 1 tablespoon oil and remaining shrimp. After second batch has stood off heat, return first batch to skillet and toss to combine. Cover skillet and let sit until shrimp are cooked through, 1 to 2 minutes. Serve immediately.

Pan-Seared Shrimp with Garlic-Lemon Butter
Beat 3 tablespoons softened unsalted butter in small bowl until light and fluffy. Stir in 1 minced garlic clove, 1 tablespoon lemon juice, 2 tablespoons finely chopped fresh parsley, and ⅛ teaspoon table salt until combined. Add flavored butter when returning first batch of shrimp to skillet. Serve with lemon wedges, if desired.

Pan-Seared Shrimp with Ginger-Hoisin Glaze
Stir 2 tablespoons hoisin sauce, 1 tablespoon rice vinegar, 1½ teaspoons soy sauce, 2 teaspoons grated fresh ginger, 2 teaspoons water, and 2 thinly sliced scallions together in small bowl. Substitute red pepper flakes for black pepper in step 1, and add hoisin mixture when returning first batch of shrimp to skillet.

Pan-Seared Shrimp with Chipotle-Lime Glaze
Stir 1 minced chipotle chile in adobo, 2 teaspoons adobo sauce, 4 teaspoons packed brown sugar, 2 tablespoons lime juice, and 2 tablespoons finely chopped fresh cilantro together in small bowl. Add chipotle mixture when returning first batch of shrimp to skillet.

Deveining Shrimp

1. After removing shell, use paring knife to make shallow cut along back of shrimp so that vein is exposed.

2. Use tip of knife to lift vein out of shrimp. Discard vein by wiping blade against paper towel.

Spanish-Style Garlic Shrimp

Serves 6

WHY THIS RECIPE WORKS Sizzling *gambas al ajillo* is a tempting dish served in tapas bars. We knew we would have to make some adjustments to re-create this dish as an appetizer to serve at home, but our work would pay off when we could savor the juicy shrimp in spicy, garlic-infused oil. The shrimp in the Spanish original are completely submerged in oil and cooked slowly. We didn't want to use that much oil, so we added just enough to a skillet to come halfway up the sides of the shrimp. We cooked them over very low heat and turned them halfway through; these shrimp cooked as evenly as they would have if completely covered with oil. We built heady garlic flavor in three ways: We added raw minced garlic to a marinade, we browned smashed cloves in the oil in which the shrimp would be cooked, and we cooked slices of garlic along with the shrimp. We included the traditional bay leaf and red chile, and added sherry vinegar (rather than sherry) and parsley, all of which brightened the richness of the oil. Served with plenty of bread to soak up the extra juices and flavorful oil, these garlicky shrimp rival the best restaurant versions. Serve the shrimp with crusty bread for dipping in the richly flavored olive oil. This dish can be served directly from the skillet (make sure to use a trivet) or, for a sizzling effect, transferred to an 8-inch cast-iron skillet that's been heated for 2 minutes over medium-high heat. We prefer the slightly sweet flavor of dried chile in this recipe, but ¼ teaspoon sweet paprika can be substituted. If sherry vinegar is unavailable, use 2 teaspoons dry sherry and 1 teaspoon white vinegar.

14 garlic cloves, peeled
 1 pound large shrimp (31 to 40 per pound), peeled, deveined, and tails removed
 ½ cup extra-virgin olive oil, divided
 ½ teaspoon table salt
 1 bay leaf
 ½ dried New Mexican chile, stemmed, seeds reserved, and torn into ½-inch pieces
1½ teaspoons sherry vinegar
 1 tablespoon finely chopped fresh parsley

1. Mince 2 garlic cloves. Toss minced garlic with shrimp, 2 tablespoons oil, and salt in medium bowl. Let shrimp marinate at room temperature for 30 minutes.

2. Meanwhile, using flat side of chef's knife, smash 4 garlic cloves. Heat smashed garlic with remaining 6 tablespoons oil in 12-inch skillet over medium-low heat, stirring occasionally, until garlic is light golden brown, 4 to 7 minutes. Remove pan from heat and let oil cool to room temperature. Discard smashed garlic, reserving oil.

3. Slice remaining 8 garlic cloves thin. Return skillet to low heat and add sliced garlic, bay leaf, and chile. Cook, stirring occasionally, until garlic is tender but not browned, 4 to 7 minutes. (If garlic has not begun to sizzle after 3 minutes, increase heat to medium-low.) Increase heat to medium-low; add shrimp with marinade to pan in single layer. Cook shrimp, undisturbed, until oil starts to gently bubble, about 2 minutes. Using tongs, flip shrimp and continue to cook until almost cooked through, about 2 minutes. Increase heat to high and add vinegar and parsley. Cook, stirring constantly, until shrimp are cooked through and oil is bubbling vigorously, 15 to 20 seconds. Serve immediately.

Garlicky Roasted Shrimp with Parsley and Anise

Serves 4 to 6

WHY THIS RECIPE WORKS We loved the idea of an easy weeknight meal of juicy roasted shrimp, but getting the lean, quick-cooking shrimp to develop color and roasted flavor before they overcooked and turned rubbery required a few tricks. First we chose jumbo-size shrimp, which were the least likely to dry out and overcook. Butterflying the shrimp increased their surface area, giving us more room to add flavor. After brining the shrimp briefly to help them hold on to more moisture, we tossed them in a potent mixture of aromatic spices, garlic, parsley, butter, and oil. Then we roasted them under the broiler to get lots of color as quickly as possible, elevating them on a wire rack so they'd brown all over. To further protect them as they cooked and to produce a more deeply roasted flavor, we left their shells on; the sugar- and protein-rich shells browned quickly in the heat of the oven and transferred flavor to the shrimp itself. Don't be tempted to use smaller shrimp with this cooking technique; they will be overseasoned and prone to overcook.

1/4 cup table salt, for brining
2 pounds shell-on jumbo shrimp (16 to 20 per pound)
4 tablespoons unsalted butter, melted
1/4 cup vegetable oil
6 garlic cloves, minced
1 teaspoon anise seeds
1/2 teaspoon red pepper flakes
1/4 teaspoon pepper
2 tablespoons finely chopped fresh parsley
Lemon wedges

1. Dissolve salt in 1 quart cold water in large container. Using kitchen shears or sharp paring knife, cut through shell of shrimp and devein but do not remove shell. Using paring knife, continue to cut shrimp 1/2 inch deep, taking care not to cut in half completely. Submerge shrimp in brine, cover, and refrigerate for 15 minutes.

2. Adjust oven rack 4 inches from broiler element and heat broiler. Combine melted butter, oil, garlic, anise seeds, pepper flakes, and pepper in large bowl. Remove shrimp from brine and pat dry with paper towels. Add shrimp and parsley to butter mixture; toss well, making sure butter mixture gets into interior of shrimp. Arrange shrimp in single layer on wire rack set in rimmed baking sheet.

3. Broil shrimp until opaque and shells are beginning to brown, 2 to 4 minutes, rotating sheet halfway through broiling. Flip shrimp and continue to broil until second side is opaque and shells are beginning to brown, 2 to 4 minutes, rotating sheet halfway through broiling. Transfer shrimp to serving platter and serve immediately, passing lemon wedges separately.

VARIATIONS
Garlicky Roasted Shrimp with Cilantro and Lime
Annatto powder, also called achiote, can be found with the Latin American foods at your supermarket. An equal amount of paprika can be substituted.

Omit butter and increase vegetable oil to 1/2 cup. Omit anise seeds and pepper. Add 2 teaspoons lightly crushed coriander seeds, 2 teaspoons grated lime zest, and 1 teaspoon annatto powder to oil mixture in step 2. Substitute 1/4 cup finely chopped fresh cilantro for parsley and lime wedges for lemon wedges.

Garlicky Roasted Shrimp with Cumin, Ginger, and Sesame
Omit butter and increase vegetable oil to 1/2 cup. Decrease garlic to 2 cloves and omit anise seeds and pepper. Add 2 teaspoons toasted sesame oil, 1 1/2 teaspoons grated fresh ginger, and 1 teaspoon cumin seeds to oil mixture in step 2. Substitute 2 thinly sliced scallion greens for parsley and omit lemon wedges.

Ultimate Shrimp Scampi

Serves 4

WHY THIS RECIPE WORKS There is a reason shrimp scampi is a restaurant favorite. When done right, this dish marries tender shrimp with a creamy, garlicky, and lemony sauce. For our recipe, we started by brining the shrimp to season them throughout and to keep them moist and juicy. Then, because sautéing them led to uneven cooking, we poached them in wine, a gentler approach that was more consistent. To get more shrimp flavor into the sauce, we didn't waste the shells; instead, we put them to use as the base of a stock and added wine and thyme. The key was to let it simmer for only 5 minutes, as a longer cooking time resulted in less flavor. For potent but clean garlic flavor, we used a generous amount of sliced, rather than minced, garlic. Just a teaspoon of cornstarch at the end of cooking kept the sauce emulsified and silky. Extra-large shrimp (21 to 25 per pound) can be substituted for jumbo shrimp. If you use them, reduce the cooking time in step 3 by 1 to 2 minutes. We prefer untreated shrimp, but if your shrimp are treated with sodium or preservatives like sodium tripolyphosphate, skip the brining in step 1 and add 1/4 teaspoon of salt to the sauce in step 4. Serve with crusty bread.

3 tablespoons table salt, for brining
2 tablespoons sugar, for brining
1 1/2 pounds jumbo shrimp (16 to 20 per pound), peeled, deveined, and tails removed, shells reserved
2 tablespoons extra-virgin olive oil, divided
1 cup dry white wine
4 sprigs fresh thyme
3 tablespoons lemon juice, plus lemon wedges for serving
1 teaspoon cornstarch
8 garlic cloves, sliced thin
1/2 teaspoon red pepper flakes
1/4 teaspoon pepper
4 tablespoons unsalted butter, cut into 1/2-inch pieces
1 tablespoon finely chopped fresh parsley

1. Dissolve salt and sugar in 1 quart cold water in large container. Submerge shrimp in brine, cover, and refrigerate for 15 minutes. Remove shrimp from brine and pat dry with paper towels.

2. Heat 1 tablespoon oil in 12-inch skillet over high heat until shimmering. Add shrimp shells and cook, stirring frequently, until they begin to turn spotty brown and skillet starts to brown, 2 to 4 minutes. Remove skillet from heat and carefully add wine and thyme sprigs. When bubbling subsides, return skillet to medium heat and simmer gently, stirring occasionally, for 5 minutes. Strain mixture through colander set over large bowl. Discard shells and reserve liquid (you should have about 2/3 cup). Wipe out skillet with paper towels.

"*This recipe holds a special place in my heart because it was the first one I ever cooked after I joined the ATK family. It's also a menu item that my mother and I enjoy ordering when we treat ourselves to dine-out nights. None of the scampi dishes we had in the past ever lived up to the ATK version; they often lacked any depth of flavor and, once the shrimp was out of the butter, the taste was gone. Our recipe offers an abundance of flavor that you don't leave behind on the plate; it also utilizes all the parts of the shrimp so nothing goes to waste. Delicious and sustainable!*"

—Elle

3. Combine lemon juice and cornstarch in small bowl. Heat remaining 1 tablespoon oil, garlic, pepper flakes, and pepper in now-empty skillet over medium-low heat, stirring occasionally, until garlic is fragrant and just beginning to brown at edges, 3 to 5 minutes. Add reserved wine mixture, increase heat to high, and bring to simmer. Reduce heat to medium, add shrimp, cover, and cook, stirring occasionally, until shrimp are just opaque, 5 to 7 minutes. Remove skillet from heat and, using slotted spoon, transfer shrimp to bowl.

4. Return skillet to medium heat, add lemon juice–cornstarch mixture, and cook until slightly thickened, about 1 minute. Remove from heat and whisk in butter and parsley until combined. Return shrimp and any accumulated juices to skillet and toss to combine. Serve, passing lemon wedges separately.

Crispy Salt and Pepper Shrimp

Serves 4 to 6

WHY THIS RECIPE WORKS The shrimp in this Chinese restaurant specialty are noted for their spicy heat and shells so crisp they're good enough to eat. Smaller shrimp are younger and have thinner shells, so we brought home a pound of medium-large shrimp and tossed them in rice wine and salt to infuse them with well-seasoned, savory flavor. We ground black peppercorns and lively Sichuan peppercorns together and combined them with sugar and cayenne to establish the dish's flavor profile. Coating the shrimp with this blend and some cornstarch fused the flavors to the meat while also drawing out excess moisture for maximum crisping. We fried the shrimp in batches to prevent the oil's heat from flagging. Fried jalapeño slices would add extra heat at serving, and we reinforced the dish's big flavors by reserving some of the spicy frying oil and combining it with the spice blend, minced garlic, and grated fresh ginger. We heated this seasoned oil until it browned and tossed the cooked shrimp in it, scattering in sliced scallions for a dose of freshness. In this recipe the shrimp are meant to be eaten shell and all. To ensure that the shells fry up crisp, avoid using shrimp that are overly large or jumbo. We prefer medium-large (31 to 40 per pound) shrimp, but large (26 to 30 per pound) may be substituted. Serve with steamed rice.

1½ **pounds medium-large shell-on shrimp (31 to 40 per pound)**
2 **tablespoons Chinese rice wine or dry sherry**
1½ **teaspoons kosher salt, divided**
2½ **teaspoons black peppercorns**
2 **teaspoons Sichuan peppercorns**
2 **teaspoons sugar**
¼ **teaspoon cayenne pepper**
4 **cups vegetable oil**
5 **tablespoons cornstarch, divided**

2 **jalapeño chiles, stemmed, seeded, and sliced into ⅛-inch-thick rings**
3 **garlic cloves, minced**
1 **tablespoon grated fresh ginger**
2 **scallions, sliced thin on bias**
¼ **head iceberg lettuce, shredded (1½ cups)**

1. Adjust oven rack to upper-middle position and heat oven to 225 degrees. Toss shrimp, rice wine, and 1 teaspoon salt together in large bowl and set aside for 10 to 15 minutes.

2. Grind black peppercorns and Sichuan peppercorns in spice grinder or mortar and pestle until coarsely ground. Transfer peppercorns to small bowl and stir in sugar and cayenne.

3. Heat oil in Dutch oven over medium heat until oil registers 385 degrees. While oil is heating, drain shrimp and pat dry with paper towels. Transfer shrimp to bowl, add 3 tablespoons cornstarch and 1 tablespoon peppercorn mixture, and toss until well combined.

4. Carefully add one-third of shrimp to oil and fry, stirring occasionally to keep shrimp from sticking together, until light brown, 2 to 3 minutes. Using wire skimmer or slotted spoon, transfer shrimp to paper towel–lined plate. Once paper towels absorb any excess oil, transfer shrimp to wire rack set in rimmed baking sheet and place in oven. Return oil to 385 degrees and repeat in 2 more batches, tossing each batch thoroughly with coating mixture before frying.

5. Toss jalapeño rings and remaining 2 tablespoons cornstarch in medium bowl. Shaking off excess cornstarch, carefully add jalapeño rings to oil and fry until crispy, 1 to 2 minutes. Using wire skimmer or slotted spoon, transfer jalapeño rings to paper towel–lined plate. After frying, reserve 2 tablespoons frying oil.

6. Heat reserved oil in 12-inch skillet over medium-high heat until shimmering. Add garlic, ginger, and remaining peppercorn mixture and cook, stirring occasionally, until mixture is fragrant and just beginning to brown, about 45 seconds. Add shrimp, scallions, and remaining ½ teaspoon salt and toss to coat. Line platter with lettuce. Transfer shrimp to platter, sprinkle with jalapeño rings, and serve immediately.

Best Crab Cakes

Serves 4

WHY THIS RECIPE WORKS Our crab cakes are not bound with flavor-muting bread crumbs, gloppy mayo, and eggs. Instead, a delicate shrimp mousse holds everything in place and enhances crabmeat's natural sweetness. To make sure that our fresh crabmeat did not have a fishy smell, we soaked it in milk; the casein in milk binds to a compound called trimethylamine oxide that is found in nearly all seafood, and when the milk is drained away, it takes this culprit with it. Classic components like Old Bay seasoning and lemon juice bolstered the crab's flavor, and panko bread crumbs ensured a crisp crust. Either fresh or pasteurized crabmeat can be used in this recipe. With packaged crab, if the meat smells clean and fresh when you first open the package, skip steps 1 and 4 and simply blot away any excess liquid. Serve with lemon wedges or Sweet and Tangy Tartar Sauce (page 238).

  1 **pound lump crabmeat, picked over for shells**
  1 **cup milk**
1½ **cups panko bread crumbs, divided**
 ¾ **teaspoon table salt, divided**
  2 **celery ribs, chopped**
 ½ **cup chopped onion**
  1 **garlic clove, peeled and smashed**
  1 **tablespoon unsalted butter**
 ⅛ **teaspoon pepper**
  4 **ounces shrimp, peeled, deveined, and tails removed**
 ¼ **cup heavy cream**
  2 **teaspoons Dijon mustard**
  1 **teaspoon lemon juice**
 ½ **teaspoon hot sauce**
 ½ **teaspoon Old Bay seasoning**
 ¼ **cup vegetable oil, divided**

1. Place crabmeat and milk in bowl, making sure crab is totally submerged. Cover and refrigerate for 20 minutes.

2. Meanwhile, place ¾ cup panko in small zipper-lock bag and crush fine with rolling pin. Transfer crushed panko to 10-inch nonstick skillet and add remaining ¾ cup panko. Toast over medium-high heat, stirring constantly, until golden brown, about 5 minutes. Transfer panko to shallow dish and stir in ¼ teaspoon salt and pepper to taste. Wipe out skillet.

3. Pulse celery, onion, and garlic together in food processor until finely chopped, 5 to 8 pulses, scraping down bowl as needed. Transfer vegetables to large bowl. Rinse processor bowl and blade. Melt butter in now-empty skillet over medium heat. Add chopped vegetables, remaining ½ teaspoon salt, and pepper; cook, stirring frequently, until vegetables are softened and all moisture has evaporated, 4 to 6 minutes. Return vegetables to large bowl and let cool to room temperature. Rinse out pan and wipe clean.

4. Strain crabmeat through fine-mesh strainer, pressing firmly to remove milk but being careful not to break up lumps of crabmeat.

5. Pulse shrimp in now-empty food processor until finely ground, 12 to 15 pulses, scraping down bowl as needed. Add cream and pulse to combine, 2 to 4 pulses, scraping down bowl as needed. Transfer shrimp puree to bowl with cooled vegetables. Add mustard, lemon juice, hot sauce, and Old Bay; stir until well combined. Add crabmeat and fold gently with rubber spatula, being careful not to overmix and break up lumps of crabmeat. Divide mixture into 8 balls and firmly press into ½-inch-thick patties. Place cakes in rimmed baking sheet lined with parchment paper, cover tightly with plastic wrap, and refrigerate for 30 minutes.

6. Coat each cake with panko, firmly pressing to adhere crumbs to exterior. Heat 1 tablespoon oil in now-empty skillet over medium heat until shimmering. Place 4 cakes in skillet and cook without moving them until golden brown, 3 to 4 minutes. Using 2 spatulas, carefully flip cakes. Add 1 tablespoon oil, reduce heat to medium-low, and continue to cook until second side is golden brown, 4 to 6 minutes. Transfer cakes to platter. Wipe out skillet and repeat with remaining 2 tablespoons oil and remaining 4 cakes. Serve immediately.

Easy Salmon Cakes

Serves 4

WHY THIS RECIPE WORKS Most salmon cakes are mushy and overly fishy, camouflaged by gluey binders and heavy-handed seasoning. Our goal was a quick and simple recipe for salmon cakes that first and foremost tasted like salmon, with a moist, delicate texture. To simplify preparation, we broke out our food processor. Pulsing small pieces of salmon (we preferred raw over cooked, which turned fishy) allowed for more even chopping and resulted in small, discrete pieces of fish. We also found a way to ditch the egg and flour steps of the breading process. Instead, we coated the salmon cakes with panko, which we had also used as a binder. If buying a skin-on salmon fillet, purchase 1⅓ pounds fish. This will yield 1¼ pounds fish after skinning. When processing the salmon, it is OK to have some pieces that are larger than ¼ inch. It is important to avoid overprocessing the fish. Serve the salmon cakes with lemon wedges and/or Sweet and Tangy Tartar Sauce (page 238).

- 3 tablespoons plus ¾ cup panko bread crumbs, divided
- 2 tablespoons finely chopped fresh parsley
- 2 tablespoons mayonnaise
- 4 teaspoons lemon juice
- 1 scallion, sliced thin
- 1 small shallot, minced
- 1 teaspoon Dijon mustard
- ¾ teaspoon table salt
- ¼ teaspoon pepper
  Pinch cayenne pepper
- 1 (1¼-pound) skinless salmon fillet, cut into 1-inch pieces
- ½ cup vegetable oil

1. Combine 3 tablespoons panko, parsley, mayonnaise, lemon juice, scallion, shallot, mustard, salt, pepper, and cayenne in bowl. Working in 3 batches, pulse salmon in food processor until coarsely chopped into ¼-inch pieces, about 2 pulses, transferring each batch to bowl with panko mixture. Gently mix until uniformly combined.

2. Place remaining ¾ cup panko in shallow dish. Using ⅓-cup measure, scoop level amount of salmon mixture and transfer to baking sheet; repeat to make 8 cakes. Carefully coat each cake with bread crumbs, gently patting into disk measuring 2¾ inches in diameter and 1 inch high. Return coated cakes to baking sheet.

3. Heat oil in 12-inch skillet over medium-high heat until shimmering. Place salmon cakes in skillet and cook without moving until bottoms are golden brown, about 2 minutes.

Carefully flip cakes and cook until second side is golden brown, 2 to 3 minutes. Transfer cakes to paper towel–lined plate to drain for 1 minute. Serve.

VARIATION

Easy Salmon Cakes with Smoked Salmon, Capers, and Dill

Reduce fresh salmon to 1 pound and table salt to ½ teaspoon. Substitute 1 tablespoon finely chopped fresh dill for parsley. Add 4 ounces finely chopped smoked salmon and 1 tablespoon chopped capers to bowl with salmon mixture.

New England Lobster Roll

Serves 6

WHY THIS RECIPE WORKS A true New England–style lobster roll, complete with tender meat coated in a light dressing and tucked into a buttery toasted bun, is the highlight of summer for most of us in the test kitchen, whether they're made at home or eaten at a seafood joint somewhere on the coast of Maine. To develop the perfect recipe, first we had to deal with the lobster. To make things easier, we sedated the lobster by placing it in the freezer for 30 minutes. Boiling was the easiest way to cook it, and removing it from the water when the tail registered 175 degrees ensured that it was perfectly tender. For the lobster roll, we adhered mostly to tradition, tossing our lobster with just a bit of mayonnaise and adding a hint of crunch with lettuce leaves and a small amount of minced celery. Onion and shallot were overpowering, but minced chives offered bright herb flavor. Lemon juice and a pinch of cayenne provided a nice counterpoint to the rich lobster and mayo. This recipe is best when made with lobster you've cooked yourself (recipe follows). Use a very small pinch of cayenne pepper, as it should not make the dressing spicy. We prefer New England–style top-loading hot dog buns, as they provide maximum surface on the sides for toasting. If using other buns, butter, salt, and toast the interior of each bun instead of the exterior.

- 2 tablespoons mayonnaise
- 2 tablespoons minced celery
- 1½ teaspoons lemon juice
- 1 teaspoon finely chopped fresh chives
- ⅛ teaspoon table salt
  Pinch cayenne pepper
- 1 pound lobster meat, tail meat cut into ½-inch pieces and claw meat cut into 1-inch pieces
- 2 tablespoons unsalted butter, softened
- 6 New England–style hot dog buns
- 6 leaves Boston lettuce

"Back when I was in high school, my first job was at a tiny hole-in-the-wall clam shack in a coastal New England town. This is where I tasted my first lobster roll: I was absolutely smitten, and so my journey to find the best lobster roll began. Twenty-three years later, after consuming countless samples, I finally found the best example I could ever hope for: a warm, buttered and toasted top-loaded bun filled with a leaf of Boston lettuce and large chunks of freshly cooked lobster meat that have been lightly dressed with mayonnaise, minimal small bits of celery, fresh chives, a pinch of cayenne, and lemon juice to add brightness. Sheer perfection. My search is over."

—*Erin*

Oven-Steamed Mussels

1. Whisk mayonnaise, celery, lemon juice, chives, salt, and cayenne together in large bowl. Add lobster and gently toss to combine.

2. Place 12-inch nonstick skillet over low heat. Butter both sides of hot dog buns and season lightly with salt to taste. Place buns in skillet, with 1 buttered side down; increase heat to medium-low; and cook until crisp and brown, 2 to 3 minutes. Flip and cook second side until crisp and brown, 2 to 3 minutes. Transfer buns to large platter. Line each bun with lettuce leaf. Spoon lobster salad into buns and serve immediately.

Boiled Lobster

Serves 4; yields 1 pound meat

To cook four lobsters at once, you will need a pot with a capacity of at least 3 gallons. If your pot is smaller, boil the lobsters in batches. Start timing the lobsters from the moment they go into the pot.

4 (1¼-pound) live lobsters
⅓ cup table salt, for cooking lobsters

1. Place lobsters in large bowl and freeze for 30 minutes. Meanwhile, bring 2 gallons water to boil in large pot over high heat.

2. Add lobsters and salt to pot, arranging with tongs so that all lobsters are submerged. Cover pot, leaving lid slightly ajar, and adjust heat to maintain gentle boil. Cook for 12 minutes, until thickest part of tail registers 175 degrees (insert thermometer into underside of tail to take temperature). If temperature registers lower than 175 degrees, return lobster to pot for 2 minutes, until tail registers 175 degrees, using tongs to transfer lobsters in and out of pot.

3. Serve immediately or transfer lobsters to rimmed baking sheet and set aside until cool enough to remove meat, about 10 minutes. (Lobster meat can be refrigerated for up to 24 hours.)

Oven-Steamed Mussels

Serves 2 to 4

WHY THIS RECIPE WORKS Steamed mussels are quick and easy, with their own built-in briny-sweet broth that takes well to lots of different aromatics and flavorings. We wanted to figure out a foolproof way to guarantee that our mussels cooked through at the same rate, so that they were all wide open and perfectly tender, even if they were different sizes. First, we moved them from the stovetop to the oven, where the even heat ensured they cooked through more gently, and we traded the Dutch oven for a large roasting pan so they weren't crowded. Covering the pan with aluminum foil trapped the moisture so the mussels didn't dry out. For a flavorful cooking liquid, we reduced white wine to concentrate its flavor and added thyme, garlic, and red pepper flakes for aromatic complexity. To avoid dirtying another pan, we simply cooked the aromatics and wine on the stovetop in the roasting pan before tossing in our mussels and transferring the pan to the oven. A few pats of butter, stirred in at the end, gave the sauce richness and body. Occasionally, mussels will have a harmless fibrous piece (known as the beard) protruding from between the shells. To remove it easily, trap the beard between the side of a small paring knife and your thumb and pull to remove it. The flat surface of the knife gives you some leverage to remove the beard. Unopened cooked mussels just need more cooking time. To open them, microwave briefly for 30 seconds or so. Serve mussels with crusty bread to sop up the flavorful broth.

1 tablespoon extra-virgin olive oil
3 garlic cloves, minced
  Pinch red pepper flakes
1 cup dry white wine
3 sprigs fresh thyme
2 bay leaves
4 pounds mussels, scrubbed and debearded
¼ teaspoon table salt
2 tablespoons unsalted butter, cut into 4 pieces
2 tablespoons finely chopped fresh parsley

1. Adjust oven rack to lowest position and heat oven to 500 degrees. Heat oil, garlic, and pepper flakes in large roasting pan over medium heat; cook, stirring constantly, until fragrant, about 30 seconds. Add wine, thyme sprigs, and bay leaves and bring to boil. Cook until wine is slightly reduced, about 1 minute. Add mussels and salt. Cover pan tightly with aluminum foil and transfer to oven. Cook until most mussels have opened (a few may remain closed), 15 to 18 minutes.

2. Remove pan from oven. Push mussels to sides of pan. Add butter to center and whisk until melted. Discard thyme sprigs and bay leaves, sprinkle parsley over mussels, and toss to combine. Serve immediately.

VARIATIONS
Oven-Steamed Mussels with Tomato and Chorizo
Omit red pepper flakes and increase oil to 3 tablespoons. Heat oil and 12 ounces Spanish-style chorizo sausage, cut into ½-inch pieces, in roasting pan until chorizo starts to brown, about 5 minutes. Add garlic and cook until fragrant, about 30 seconds. Add 1 (28-ounce) can crushed tomatoes to roasting pan before adding mussels and increase butter to 3 tablespoons.

"I proudly developed this recipe back in 2001 and still make it several times a year for company. I usually assemble the pot during cocktail hour so that everyone can see how clever the cooking method is—shameless, I know. But the Rube Goldberg-esque cooking technique is seriously cool. You start by layering all of the ingredients into a cold pot in the following order—sausage, clams and mussels, potatoes, corn, and lobsters—then put a lid on the pot and cook over high heat for 20 minutes. Here's how it works: The heat first sears the sausage, then moves up to the clams and mussels, causing them to open up and release their liquid. This liquid not only prevents the sausage from scorching, but it creates steam as it hits the bottom of the hot pot, which then cooks the potatoes, corn, and lobsters. The lobsters also release liquid as they begin to cook, which bastes everything with a clean, briny flavor as it makes its way to the bottom of the pot. It's very impressive when you unload the pot onto a large platter ready for serving. All you need to round out the meal is individual ramekins of melted butter, some sort of slaw, and cold beer. Oh, and lots of napkins because eating lobsters is notoriously messy."

–Julia

Oven-Steamed Mussels with Leeks and Pernod

Omit red pepper flakes and increase oil to 3 tablespoons. Heat oil; 1 pound leeks, white and light green parts only, halved lengthwise, sliced thin, and washed thoroughly; and garlic in roasting pan until leeks are wilted, about 3 minutes. Omit thyme sprigs and substitute ½ cup Pernod and ¼ cup water for wine, ¼ cup crème fraîche for butter, and chives for parsley.

Oven-Steamed Mussels with Hard Cider and Bacon

Omit garlic and red pepper flakes. Heat oil and 4 slices thick-cut bacon, cut into ½-inch pieces, in roasting pan until bacon has rendered and is starting to crisp, about 5 minutes. Substitute dry hard cider for wine and ¼ cup heavy cream for butter.

Debearding Mussels

Because of the way they're cultivated, most mussels are free of fibrous strands, or "beards." If your mussel has a beard, hold it and use the back of a paring knife to remove it with a stern yank.

Indoor Clambake

Serves 4 to 6

WHY THIS RECIPE WORKS A clambake is perhaps the ultimate seafood meal: clams, mussels, and lobster, nestled with sausage, corn, and potatoes, all steamed together with hot stones in a sand pit by the sea. A genuine clambake is an all-day affair and, of course, requires a beach. But we wanted to re-create the great flavors of the clambake indoors, so we could enjoy this flavorful feast anywhere, without hours of preparation. A large stockpot was the cooking vessel of choice. Many recipes suggest cooking the ingredients separately before adding them to the pot, but we found that with careful layering, we could cook everything in the same pot and have it all finish at the same time. And we didn't need to add water, because the shellfish released enough liquid to steam everything else. Sliced sausage went into the pot first (we liked kielbasa), so that it could sear before the steam

was generated. Clams and mussels were next, wrapped in cheesecloth for easy removal. Then in went the potatoes, which would take the longest to cook; they were best placed near the heat source, and we cut them into 1-inch pieces to cook more quickly. Corn, with the husks left on to protect it from seafood flavors and lobster foam, was next, followed by the lobsters. It took less than half an hour for everything to cook—and we had all the elements of a clambake (minus the sand and surf) without having spent all day preparing them. Choose a large, narrow stockpot in which you can easily layer the ingredients. The recipe can be cut in half and layered in an 8-quart Dutch oven, but it should cook for the same amount of time. We prefer small littlenecks for this recipe. If your market carries larger clams, use 4 pounds. Mussels sometimes contain a weedy beard protruding from the crack between the two shells. It's fairly small and can be difficult to tug out of place. To remove it easily, trap the beard between the side of a small paring knife and your thumb and pull to remove it. The flat surface of the knife gives you some leverage to remove the beard. Use small red potatoes measuring 1 to 2 inches in diameter.

- 2 **pounds small littleneck or cherrystone clams, scrubbed**
- 2 **pounds mussels, scrubbed and debearded**
- 1 **pound kielbasa, sliced into ⅓-inch-thick rounds**
- 1 **pound small red potatoes, unpeeled, cut into 1-inch pieces**
- 6 **ears corn, silk and all but last layer of husk removed**
- 2 **(1½-pound) live lobsters**
- 8 **tablespoons salted butter, melted**

1. Place clams and mussels on large piece of cheesecloth and tie ends together to secure; set aside. In 12-quart stockpot, layer kielbasa, sack of clams and mussels, potatoes, corn, and lobsters on top of one another. Cover and place over high heat. Cook until potatoes are tender, and lobsters are bright red, 17 to 20 minutes.

2. Off heat, remove lid (watch out for scalding steam). Remove lobsters and set aside until cool enough to handle. Remove corn from pot and peel off husks; arrange ears on large platter. Using slotted spoon, remove potatoes and arrange on platter with corn. Transfer clams and mussels to large bowl and cut open cheesecloth. Using slotted spoon, remove kielbasa from pot and arrange on platter with potatoes and corn. Pour remaining steaming liquid in pot over clams and mussels. Using kitchen towel to protect your hands, twist and remove lobster tails, claws, and legs (if desired). Arrange lobster parts on platter. Serve immediately with melted butter.

Pasta

Pasta all'Amatriciana

1. Pour tomatoes and their juice into strainer set over large bowl. Open tomatoes with your hands and remove seeds and fibrous cores; let excess liquid drain from tomatoes, about 5 minutes. Remove ¾ cup tomatoes from strainer and set aside. Set aside 2½ cups tomato juice and discard remainder.

2. Heat 2 tablespoons oil in 12-inch skillet over medium heat until shimmering. Add onion and cook until softened and lightly browned, 5 to 7 minutes. Stir in garlic and oregano and cook until fragrant, about 30 seconds.

3. Stir in strained tomatoes and increase heat to medium-high. Cook, stirring often, until liquid has evaporated, tomatoes begin to stick to bottom of skillet, and brown fond forms around pan edges, 10 to 12 minutes. Stir in wine and cook until thick and syrupy, about 1 minute. Stir in reserved tomato juice, scraping up any browned bits. Bring to simmer and cook, stirring occasionally, until sauce is thick, 8 to 10 minutes.

4. Pulse sauce and reserved tomatoes in food processor until slightly chunky, about 8 pulses. Return sauce to now-empty skillet and stir in basil and remaining 1 tablespoon oil. Season with sugar, salt, and pepper to taste before serving. (Sauce can be refrigerated for up to 3 days or frozen for up to 1 month.)

Marinara Sauce

Makes 4 cups; enough for 1 pound pasta

WHY THIS RECIPE WORKS Making a tomato sauce with deep, complex flavor usually requires hours of simmering. We wanted to produce a multidimensional marinara sauce in under an hour, perfect for any night of the week. Our first challenge was picking the right tomatoes. We found canned whole tomatoes, which we hand-crushed to remove the hard core, to be the best choice in terms of both flavor and texture. We boosted tomato flavor by sautéing the tomato pieces until they glazed the bottom of the pan, after which we added their liquid. We shortened the simmering time by using a skillet instead of a saucepan (the greater surface area of a skillet encourages faster evaporation and flavor concentration). Finally, we added just the right amount of sugar, red wine, and, just before serving, a few uncooked canned tomatoes for texture, fresh basil for fresh herbal flavor, and olive oil for richness. Chianti or Merlot work well for the dry red wine. Because canned tomatoes vary in acidity and saltiness, it's best to add salt, pepper, and sugar to taste just before serving. If you prefer a chunkier sauce, give it just three or four pulses in the food processor in step 4.

2 (28-ounce) cans whole peeled tomatoes
3 tablespoons extra-virgin olive oil, divided
1 onion, chopped fine
2 garlic cloves, minced
2 teaspoons minced fresh oregano or ½ teaspoon dried
⅓ cup dry red wine
3 tablespoons chopped fresh basil

Pasta Puttanesca

Serves 4 to 6

WHY THIS RECIPE WORKS Puttanesca is a gutsy tomato sauce punctuated by the brash, zesty flavors of garlic, anchovies, olives, and capers. But too often, the sauce comes off as too fishy, too garlicky, too briny, or just plain too salty. We wanted to harmonize the bold flavors in this Neapolitan dish and not let any one preside over the others. For a sauce with the best tomato flavor and a slightly clingy consistency, we used canned diced tomatoes and kept the cooking time to a minimum to retain their fresh flavor and their meaty texture. To tame the garlic and prevent it from burning, we soaked minced garlic in a bit of water before sautéing it. Cooking the garlic and anchovies with red pepper flakes (before adding the tomatoes) helped their flavors bloom and added a subtle heat. We chose to add the olives and capers when the sauce was finished—this prevented them from disintegrating in the sauce. Reserved tomato juice from the canned tomatoes moistened the pasta, and a last-minute addition of minced parsley preserved the fresh flavors of the sauce. The pasta and sauce cook in about the same amount of time, so begin the sauce just after you add the pasta to the boiling water in step 1.

3 garlic cloves, minced
1 pound spaghetti
  Table salt for cooking pasta
1 (28-ounce) can diced tomatoes, drained with
  ½ cup juice reserved
2 tablespoons extra-virgin olive oil, plus extra
  for drizzling
8 anchovy fillets, rinsed and minced
1 teaspoon red pepper flakes
½ cup pitted kalamata olives, chopped
¼ cup finely chopped fresh parsley
3 tablespoons capers, rinsed

1. Combine garlic with 1 tablespoon water in small bowl; set aside. Bring 4 quarts water to boil in large pot. Add pasta and 1 tablespoon salt to water and cook, stirring often, until al dente. Reserve ½ cup cooking water, then drain pasta and return it to pot. Add ¼ cup reserved tomato juice and toss to combine.

2. Meanwhile, heat oil, anchovies, pepper flakes, and garlic mixture in 12-inch skillet over medium heat. Cook, stirring frequently, until garlic is fragrant, 2 to 3 minutes. Add tomatoes and simmer until slightly thickened, about 8 minutes.

3. Stir olives, parsley, and capers into sauce. Pour sauce over pasta and toss to combine; adjust consistency of sauce with remaining reserved tomato juice or reserved pasta cooking water as needed. Season with salt to taste, drizzle with oil, if desired, and serve immediately.

Pasta alla Norma

SEASON 20 RECIPE

Serves 6 to 8

WHY THIS RECIPE WORKS *Pasta alla norma* is Sicily's most iconic pasta dish. It consists of a lively combination of tender eggplant and robust tomato sauce, which is seasoned with herbs, mixed with al dente pasta, and finished with shreds of salty, milky ricotta salata. The dish gets its name from the epic opera *Norma*, which was composed by Vincenzo Bellini, a native of Catania; just as the opera is associated with perfection, so too is the hearty pasta. We salted and microwaved the eggplant to quickly draw out its moisture so that it wouldn't absorb too much oil. We found that it was best to wait until the last minute to combine the eggplant and sauce; this prevented the eggplant from soaking up too much tomato and becoming soggy. If coffee filters are not available, food-safe, undyed paper towels can be substituted when microwaving the eggplant. Be sure to remove the eggplant from the microwave immediately so that the steam can escape. For a spicier dish, use the larger amount of pepper flakes.

1½ pounds eggplant, cut into ½-inch pieces
½ teaspoon table salt, plus salt for cooking pasta
¼ cup extra-virgin olive oil, divided
4 garlic cloves, minced
2 anchovy fillets, minced
¼–½ teaspoon red pepper flakes
1 (28-ounce) can crushed tomatoes
6 tablespoons chopped fresh basil
1 pound ziti, rigatoni, or penne
3 ounces ricotta salata, shredded (1 cup)

1. Toss eggplant with ½ teaspoon salt in bowl. Line entire surface of plate with double layer of coffee filters and lightly spray with vegetable oil spray. Spread eggplant in even layer on coffee filters; wipe out and reserve bowl. Microwave until eggplant is dry and shriveled to one-third of its original size, 8 to 15 minutes (eggplant should not brown). Transfer eggplant immediately to paper towel–lined plate. Let cool slightly.

2. Transfer eggplant to now-empty bowl, drizzle with 1 tablespoon oil, and toss gently to coat; discard coffee filters and reserve plate. Heat 1 tablespoon oil in 12-inch nonstick skillet over medium-high heat until shimmering. Add eggplant and cook, stirring occasionally, until well browned and fully tender, about 10 minutes. Remove skillet from heat and transfer eggplant to now-empty plate.

3. Add 1 tablespoon oil, garlic, anchovies, and pepper flakes to now-empty skillet and cook using residual heat, stirring constantly, until fragrant and garlic becomes pale golden, about 1 minute (if skillet is too cool to cook mixture, set it over medium heat). Add tomatoes and bring to simmer over medium-high heat. Cook, stirring occasionally, until slightly thickened, 8 to 10 minutes.

4. Gently stir in eggplant and cook until heated through and flavors meld, 3 to 5 minutes. Stir in basil and remaining 1 tablespoon oil. Season with salt to taste.

5. Meanwhile, bring 4 quarts water to boil in large pot. Add pasta and 1 tablespoon salt and cook, stirring often, until al dente. Reserve ½ cup cooking water, then drain pasta and return it to pot. Add sauce and toss to combine. Adjust consistency with reserved cooking water as needed. Serve, passing ricotta salata separately.

Pasta all'Amatriciana

Serves 4 to 6

WHY THIS RECIPE WORKS Although the Roman version of this Italian pasta dish is understandably popular, there is another, slightly different version that hails from Amatrice, a town northeast of Rome. Rather than minced onions, the Amatrician version calls for wine in the sauce. We loved the simple concept, and knew we wanted to come up with a version that we could make at home. To create an authentic flavor profile, we first needed an alternative to hard-to-find *guanciale*, or cured pork jowl. Humble salt pork, though an unlikely solution, provided the rich, clean meatiness we were after, and proved to be a perfect foil for the bright acidity of the wine and tomatoes. To ensure tender bites of pork throughout, we first simmered it in water to gently cook it and render fat, a step that allowed the meat to quickly turn golden once the water evaporated. Finally, to ensure that the grated Pecorino Romano didn't clump in the hot sauce, we first mixed it with a little cooled rendered pork fat. Now the flavor of pork, tomato, chili flakes, and Pecorino shone through in each bite. Look for salt pork that is roughly 70 percent fat and 30 percent lean meat; leaner salt pork may not render enough fat. If difficult to slice, the salt pork can be put in the freezer for 15 minutes to firm up. In this dish, it is essential to use high-quality imported Pecorino Romano—not the bland domestic cheese labeled "Romano."

- 8 ounces salt pork, rind removed, rinsed thoroughly, and patted dry
- ½ cup water
- 2 tablespoons tomato paste
- ½ teaspoon red pepper flakes
- ¼ cup red wine
- 1 (28-ounce) can diced tomatoes
- 2 ounces Pecorino Romano, grated fine (1 cup), divided
- 1 pound spaghetti
  Table salt for cooking pasta

1. Slice salt pork into ¼-inch-thick strips, then cut each strip crosswise into ¼-inch pieces. Bring pork and water to simmer in 10-inch nonstick skillet over medium heat; cook until water evaporates and pork begins to sizzle, 5 to 8 minutes. Reduce heat to medium-low and continue to cook, stirring frequently, until fat is rendered and pork turns golden, 5 to 8 minutes. Using slotted spoon, transfer salt pork to bowl. Pour off all but 1 tablespoon fat from skillet. Reserve remaining fat.

2. Return skillet to medium heat and add tomato paste and pepper flakes; cook, stirring constantly, for 20 seconds. Stir in wine and cook for 30 seconds. Stir in tomatoes and their juice and rendered pork and bring to simmer. Cook, stirring frequently, until thickened, 12 to 16 minutes. While sauce simmers, stir 2 tablespoons reserved fat and ½ cup Pecorino together in bowl to form paste.

3. Meanwhile, bring 4 quarts water to boil in Dutch oven. Add pasta and 1 tablespoon salt and cook, stirring often, until al dente. Reserve 1 cup cooking water, then drain pasta and return it to pot.

4. Add sauce, ⅓ cup cooking water, and Pecorino mixture to pasta and toss well to coat, adding cooking water as needed to adjust consistency. Serve, passing remaining ½ cup Pecorino separately.

Pasta alla Gricia (Rigatoni with Pancetta and Pecorino Romano)

SEASON 20 RECIPE

Serves 6

WHY THIS RECIPE WORKS One of Rome's greatest little-known but iconic pasta dishes, *pasta alla gricia* is a simple dish based on cured pork, black pepper, and Pecorino Romano. The fat from the pork (*guanciale* is traditional, but easier-to-find pancetta works well) combines with starchy pasta cooking water and cheese to create a creamy sauce for the pasta. The traditional method is to let parcooked pasta finish cooking in the sauce, where it will release its starch for body, but the technique can be finicky. For consistent results, we cooked the pasta to al dente in half the usual amount of water and then added the extra-starchy pasta cooking water to the rendered pork fat and reduced the mixture to a specific volume. The boiling action further concentrated the starches in the water and emulsified the mixture before we mixed in the pasta. Because this pasta is quite rich, serve it in slightly smaller portions with a green vegetable or salad. For the best results, use the highest-quality pancetta you can find. If you can find guanciale, we recommend using it and increasing the browning time in step 2 to 10 to 12 minutes. Because we call for cutting the pancetta to a specified thickness, we recommend having it cut to order at the deli counter; avoid presliced or prediced products.

Pasta alla Gricia

8 ounces pancetta, sliced ¼ inch thick

1 tablespoon extra-virgin olive oil

1 pound rigatoni

1 teaspoon coarsely ground pepper, plus extra for serving

2 ounces Pecorino Romano cheese, grated fine (1 cup), plus extra for serving

1. Slice each round of pancetta into rectangular pieces that measure about ½ inch by 1 inch.

2. Heat pancetta and oil in Dutch oven over medium-low heat, stirring frequently, until fat is rendered and pancetta is deep golden brown but still has slight pinkish hue, 8 to 10 minutes, adjusting heat as necessary to keep pancetta from browning too quickly. Using slotted spoon, transfer pancetta to bowl; set aside. Pour fat from pot into liquid measuring cup (you should have ¼ to ⅓ cup fat; discard any extra). Return fat to Dutch oven.

3. While pancetta cooks, set colander in large bowl. Bring 2 quarts water to boil in large pot. Add pasta and cook, stirring often, until al dente. Drain pasta in prepared colander, reserving cooking water.

4. Add pepper and 2 cups reserved cooking water to Dutch oven with fat and bring to boil over high heat. Boil mixture rapidly, scraping up any browned bits, until emulsified and reduced to 1½ cups, about 5 minutes. (If you've reduced it too far, add more reserved cooking water to equal 1½ cups.)

5. Reduce heat to low, add pasta and pancetta, and stir to evenly coat. Add Pecorino and stir until cheese is melted and sauce is slightly thickened, about 1 minute. Off heat, adjust sauce consistency with remaining reserved cooking water as needed. Transfer pasta to platter and serve immediately, passing extra pepper and extra Pecorino separately.

Meatless "Meat" Sauce with Chickpeas and Mushrooms

Makes 6 cups; enough for 2 pounds pasta

WHY THIS RECIPE WORKS To create a vegetarian version of an unctuous tomato-meat sauce, we started with cremini mushrooms and tomato paste—both rich sources of savory flavor. We let the food processor do the work for us, using it to chop up our mushrooms, onions, and chickpeas, which added hearty texture. Extra-virgin olive oil did double duty, cooking the mushrooms and the classic Italian aromatics of garlic, dried oregano, and red pepper flakes and enriching the sauce. To loosen the sauce without diluting its flavor, we added vegetable broth. Chopped fresh basil added an authentic finish. Make sure to rinse the chickpeas after pulsing them in the food processor or the sauce will be too thick. Our favorite canned chickpeas are from Goya, our favorite crushed tomatoes are from SMT, and our favorite tomato paste is from Cento.

10 ounces cremini mushrooms, trimmed

6 tablespoons extra-virgin olive oil, divided

1 teaspoon table salt

1 onion, chopped

5 garlic cloves, minced

1¼ teaspoons dried oregano

¼ teaspoon red pepper flakes

¼ cup tomato paste

1 (28-ounce) can crushed tomatoes

2 cups vegetable broth

1 (15-ounce) can chickpeas, rinsed

2 tablespoons chopped fresh basil

1. Pulse mushrooms in 2 batches in food processor until chopped into ⅛- to ¼-inch pieces, 7 to 10 pulses, scraping down sides of bowl as needed. (Do not clean workbowl.)

2. Heat 5 tablespoons oil in Dutch oven over medium-high heat until shimmering. Add mushrooms and salt and cook, stirring occasionally, until mushrooms are browned and fond has formed on bottom of pot, about 8 minutes.

3. While mushrooms cook, pulse onion in food processor until finely chopped, 7 to 10 pulses, scraping down sides of bowl as needed. (Do not clean workbowl.) Transfer onion to pot with mushrooms and cook, stirring occasionally, until onion is soft and translucent, about 5 minutes. Combine remaining 1 tablespoon oil, garlic, oregano, and pepper flakes in bowl.

4. Add tomato paste to pot and cook, stirring constantly, until mixture is rust-colored, 1 to 2 minutes. Reduce heat to medium and push vegetables to sides of pot. Add garlic mixture to center and cook, stirring constantly, until fragrant, about 30 seconds. Stir in tomatoes and broth; bring to simmer over high heat. Reduce heat to low and simmer sauce for 5 minutes, stirring occasionally.

5. While sauce simmers, pulse chickpeas in food processor until chopped into ¼-inch pieces, 7 to 10 pulses. Transfer chickpeas to fine-mesh strainer and rinse under cold running water until water runs clear; drain well. Add chickpeas to pot and simmer until sauce is slightly thickened, about 15 minutes. Stir in basil and season with salt and pepper to taste. (Sauce can be refrigerated for up to 2 days or frozen for up to 1 month.)

Pasta e Ceci (Pasta with Chickpeas)

Serves 4 to 6

WHY THIS RECIPE WORKS *Pasta e ceci*, a sibling of *pasta e fagioli*, is a hearty and fast one-pot meal that's simple to prepare, yet packed full of satisfying flavor. To keep the cooking time to under an hour, we used canned chickpeas—along with their starchy liquid—to add even more body and flavor to the dish. Cooking the chickpeas and ditalini in the same pot blended the dish, and the additional starch released by the pasta created a silky, stick-to-your-ribs texture. We gave the chickpeas a brief head start, simmering them before adding the pasta, to achieve the perfect creamy softness. Using a food processor allowed us to produce a finely minced *soffritto* of onions, garlic, carrot, celery, and pancetta, an addition that gave the dish a meaty backbone. And we achieved depth of flavor by adding anchovy, tomatoes, and Parmesan cheese. A last-minute addition of parsley and lemon juice provided a bright contrast just before serving. Another short pasta, such as orzo, can be substituted for the ditalini, but make sure to substitute by weight and not by volume.

2 ounces pancetta, cut into ½-inch pieces
1 small carrot, peeled and cut into ½-inch pieces
1 small celery rib, cut into ½-inch pieces
4 garlic cloves, peeled
1 onion, halved and cut into 1-inch pieces
1 (14-ounce) can whole peeled tomatoes, drained
¼ cup extra-virgin olive oil, plus extra for serving
1 anchovy fillet, rinsed, patted dry, and minced
¼ teaspoon red pepper flakes
2 teaspoons finely chopped fresh rosemary
2 (15-ounce) cans chickpeas (do not drain)
2 cups water
1 teaspoon table salt
8 ounces (1½ cups) ditalini
1 tablespoon lemon juice
1 tablespoon finely chopped fresh parsley
1 ounce Parmesan cheese, grated (½ cup)

1. Process pancetta in food processor until ground to paste, about 30 seconds, scraping down sides of bowl as needed. Add carrot, celery, and garlic and pulse until finely chopped, 8 to 10 pulses. Add onion and pulse until onion is cut into ⅛- to ¼-inch pieces, 8 to 10 pulses. Transfer pancetta mixture to Dutch oven. Pulse tomatoes in now-empty food processor until coarsely chopped, 8 to 10 pulses. Set aside.

2. Add oil to pancetta mixture in Dutch oven and cook over medium heat, stirring frequently, until fond begins to form on bottom of pot, about 5 minutes. Add anchovy, pepper flakes, and rosemary and cook until fragrant, about 1 minute. Stir in tomatoes, chickpeas and their liquid, water, and salt and bring to boil, scraping up any browned bits. Reduce heat to medium-low and simmer for 10 minutes. Add pasta and cook, stirring frequently, until tender, 10 to 12 minutes. Stir in lemon juice and parsley and season with salt and pepper to taste. Serve, passing Parmesan and extra oil separately.

Orecchiette with Broccoli Rabe and Sausage

Serves 4 to 6

WHY THIS RECIPE WORKS In southern Italy, broccoli rabe and orecchiette (loosely translated as "little ears") is a popular combination. The trick to this pasta dish is cooking the broccoli rabe just right and limiting the number of ingredients so that at the end, you have a moist and flavorful (but not oily) pasta dish. For a hearty, filling dish, we decided to include some Italian sausage. Tasters preferred spicy Italian sausage to the sweet variety, but if you like less heat, the sweet sausage still makes for a satisfying dish. We started by browning the sausage in a skillet. We then added the broccoli rabe and some chicken broth to absorb the rich, meaty flavors in the pan; covering the pan allowed us to steam the rabe with the other sauce ingredients. Besides eliminating the need for a separate pot to blanch the rabe, this cooking method didn't wash away the pleasantly bitter flavor of this Italian vegetable. Some red pepper flakes amplified the heat from the sausage, and a drizzle of olive oil and freshly grated Parmesan cheese brought the whole dish together. If you prefer to use broccoli instead of broccoli rabe in this recipe, use 2 pounds broccoli cut into 1-inch florets and increase the cooking time by several minutes. If you prefer a less spicy dish, use sweet Italian sausage.

1 pound orecchiette
½ teaspoon table salt, plus salt for cooking pasta
8 ounces hot Italian sausage, casings removed
6 garlic cloves, minced
½ teaspoon red pepper flakes
1 pound broccoli rabe, trimmed and cut into 1½-inch pieces
½ cup chicken broth
1 tablespoon extra-virgin olive oil
1 ounce Parmesan cheese, grated (about ½ cup)

1. Bring 4 quarts water to a boil in large pot. Add pasta and 1 tablespoon salt to water and cook, stirring often, until al dente. Reserve ½ cup cooking water, then drain pasta and return it to pot.

2. Meanwhile, cook sausage in 12-inch nonstick skillet over medium-high heat, breaking up meat with wooden spoon, until lightly browned, about 5 minutes. Stir in garlic, pepper flakes, and ½ teaspoon salt. Cook, stirring constantly, until garlic is fragrant, about 1½ minutes. Add broccoli rabe and broth, cover, and cook until broccoli rabe turns bright green, about 2 minutes. Uncover and cook, stirring frequently, until most of broth has evaporated and broccoli rabe is tender, 2 to 3 minutes.

3. Add sausage mixture, oil, and cheese to pasta and toss to combine. Adjust consistency of sauce with reserved pasta cooking water as needed and serve immediately.

Shrimp Fra Diavalo

Serves 4

WHY THIS RECIPE WORKS Shrimp *fra diavolo* is a classic 20th-century Italian American combo of shrimp, tomatoes, garlic, and hot pepper, often served over spaghetti. At its best, it's lively and piquant, the tangy tomatoes countering the sweet and briny shrimp, and the pepper and garlic providing a spirited kick. We wanted to preserve the fiery character of fra diavolo but also heighten the other flavors—particularly the brininess of the shrimp—so that they could stand up to the heat. To build a rich, briny seafood base, we borrowed a technique from shrimp bisque: sautéing the shrimp shells in a little oil until they and the surface of the pan were spotty brown, then deglazing the pan with wine to pick up the flavorful fond. Some canned tomato liquid rounded out our shrimp "stock." To bloom the flavors of our aromatics, we sautéed some garlic, red pepper flakes, oregano, and a couple of anchovy fillets for extra savory (but not fishy) seafood flavor. We added our stock back to the aromatics and used this flavorful sauce to gently poach the shrimp. At the end of cooking, we stirred in some minced pepperoncini and their brine for a boost of tangy heat. Handfuls of chopped basil and parsley lent freshness, and a drizzle of fruity extra-virgin olive oil made for a rich finish. If the shrimp you are using have been treated with salt (check the bag's ingredient list), skip the salting in step 1 and add ¼ teaspoon of salt to the sauce in step 3. Adjust the amount of pepper flakes depending on how spicy you want the dish. Serve the shrimp over spaghetti or with a salad and crusty bread. If serving with spaghetti, adjust the consistency of the sauce with some reserved pasta cooking water.

1½ pounds large shrimp (26 to 30 per pound), peeled and deveined, shells reserved
½ teaspoon table salt
1 (28-ounce) can whole peeled tomatoes
3 tablespoons vegetable oil, divided
1 cup dry white wine
4 garlic cloves, minced
½ teaspoon red pepper flakes
½ teaspoon dried oregano
2 anchovy fillets, rinsed, patted dry, and minced
¼ cup chopped fresh basil
¼ cup chopped fresh parsley
1½ teaspoons minced pepperoncini, plus 1 teaspoon brine
2 tablespoons extra-virgin olive oil

1. Toss shrimp with salt and set aside. Pour tomatoes into colander set over large bowl. Pierce tomatoes with edge of rubber spatula and stir briefly to release juice. Transfer drained tomatoes to small bowl and reserve juice. Do not wash colander.

2. Heat 1 tablespoon vegetable oil in 12-inch skillet over high heat until shimmering. Add shrimp shells and cook, stirring frequently, until they begin to turn spotty brown and skillet starts to brown, 2 to 4 minutes. Remove skillet from heat and carefully add wine. When bubbling subsides, return skillet to heat and simmer until wine is reduced to about 2 tablespoons, 2 to 4 minutes. Add reserved tomato juice and simmer to meld flavors, 5 minutes. Pour contents of skillet into colander set over bowl. Discard shells and reserve liquid. Wipe out skillet with paper towels.

3. Heat remaining 2 tablespoons vegetable oil, garlic, pepper flakes, and oregano in now-empty skillet over medium heat, stirring occasionally, until garlic is straw-colored and fragrant, 1 to 2 minutes. Add anchovies and stir until fragrant, about 30 seconds. Remove from heat. Add drained tomatoes and mash with potato masher until coarsely pureed. Return to heat and stir in reserved tomato juice mixture. Increase heat to medium-high and simmer until mixture has thickened, about 5 minutes.

4. Add shrimp to skillet and simmer gently, stirring and turning shrimp frequently, until they are just cooked through, 4 to 5 minutes. Remove pan from heat. Stir in basil, parsley, and pepperoncini and brine and season with salt to taste. Drizzle with oil and serve.

Beef Short Rib Ragu

Makes 5 cups; enough for 1 pound pasta

WHY THIS RECIPE WORKS This ultrarich and meaty ragu can be on the table in about 2 hours and uses only one cut of beef. We chose a rich, beefy cut of meat—boneless short ribs—and paired it with umami-rich porcini mushrooms, tomato paste, and anchovies. To prevent scorching, we moved the braising operation to the oven, making the dish largely hands-off. Removing the lid partway through cooking helped to thicken the sauce and browned the meat, deepening its flavor and eliminating the messy step of browning it before braising. The addition of five-spice powder contributed subtle background notes that underscored the savory taste of the beef and mushrooms. If you can't find boneless short ribs, don't substitute bone-in short ribs. Instead, use a 2½-pound chuck-eye roast, trimmed and cut into 1-inch pieces. This recipe yields enough to sauce 1 pound of pasta or a batch of No-Fuss Creamy Parmesan Polenta (page 387) (our favorite way to serve it). This recipe can be doubled, and the sauce can be frozen. Better than Bouillon Roasted Beef Broth Base is our taste test winner.

1½ cups beef broth, divided
½ ounce dried porcini mushrooms, rinsed
1 tablespoon extra-virgin olive oil
1 onion, chopped fine
2 garlic cloves, minced
1 tablespoon tomato paste
3 anchovy fillets, rinsed, patted dry, and minced
½ teaspoon five-spice powder
½ cup dry red wine
1 (14.5-ounce) can whole peeled tomatoes, drained with juice reserved, chopped fine
2 pounds boneless beef short ribs, trimmed
¾ teaspoon table salt
½ teaspoon pepper

1. Adjust oven rack to middle position and heat oven to 350 degrees. Microwave ½ cup broth and mushrooms in covered bowl until steaming, about 1 minute. Let sit until softened, about 5 minutes. Drain mushrooms in fine-mesh strainer lined with coffee filter, pressing to extract all liquid; reserve liquid and chop mushrooms fine.

2. Heat oil in Dutch oven over medium heat until shimmering. Add onion and cook, stirring occasionally, until softened, about 5 minutes. Add garlic and cook until fragrant, about 1 minute. Add tomato paste, anchovies, and five-spice powder and cook, stirring frequently, until mixture has darkened and fond forms on pot bottom, 3 to 4 minutes. Add wine, increase heat to medium-high, and bring to simmer, scraping up any browned bits.

Continue to cook, stirring frequently, until wine is reduced and pot is almost dry, 2 to 4 minutes. Add tomatoes and reserved juice, remaining 1 cup broth, reserved mushroom soaking liquid, and mushrooms and bring to simmer.

3. Toss beef with salt and pepper. Add beef to pot, cover, and transfer to oven. Cook for 1 hour.

4. Uncover and continue to cook until beef is tender, 1 to 1¼ hours.

5. Being careful of hot handles, remove pot from oven. Using slotted spoon, transfer beef to cutting board and let cool for 5 minutes. Using 2 forks, shred beef into bite-size pieces; discard any large pieces of fat or connective tissue. Using wide, shallow spoon, skim off any excess fat that has risen to surface of sauce. Return beef to sauce and season with salt and pepper to taste. (Sauce can be refrigerated for up to 3 days or frozen for up to 2 months.)

Weeknight Tagliatelle with Bolognese Sauce

Serves 4 to 6

WHY THIS RECIPE WORKS To create a Bolognese sauce that could come together quickly on a busy weeknight but rival the depth and richness of a long-cooked version, we started by browning the aromatic vegetables (but not the ground beef, which would dry out and toughen if seared) to develop a flavorful fond; we also treated the ground beef with a baking soda solution to ensure that it stayed tender.

Adding pancetta, which we ground and browned deeply with the aromatic vegetables, boosted the sauce's meaty flavor, and a healthy dose of tomato paste added depth and brightness. We also added Parmesan cheese, usually reserved for serving, directly to the sauce as it cooked for its umami richness. To develop concentrated flavor and a consistency that nicely coated the pasta, we boiled beef broth until it was reduced by half and added it to the sauce, which then needed to simmer only 30 minutes longer. Finally, we intentionally made the sauce thin because the eggy noodles (traditionally tagliatelle or pappardelle) absorb a lot of liquid; once they have soaked up some of the sauce, it will coat the noodles beautifully. If you use our recommended beef broth, Better Than Bouillon Roasted Beef Base, you can skip step 2 and make a concentrated broth by adding 4 teaspoons paste to 2 cups water. To ensure the best flavor, be sure to brown the pancetta-vegetable mixture in step 4 until the fond on the bottom of the pot is quite dark. The cooked sauce will look thin but will thicken once tossed with the pasta. Tagliatelle is a long, flat, dry egg pasta that is about ¼ inch wide; if you can't find it, you can substitute pappardelle. Substituting other pasta may result in a too-wet sauce.

1 pound 93 percent lean ground beef
2 tablespoons water
¼ teaspoon baking soda
½ teaspoon pepper, divided
4 cups beef broth
6 ounces pancetta, chopped
1 onion, chopped
1 large carrot, peeled and chopped
1 celery rib, chopped
1 tablespoon unsalted butter
1 tablespoon extra-virgin olive oil
3 tablespoons tomato paste
1 cup dry red wine
1 ounce Parmesan cheese, grated (½ cup), plus extra for serving
1 pound tagliatelle
Table salt for cooking pasta

1. Toss beef with water, baking soda, and ¼ teaspoon pepper in bowl until thoroughly combined. Set aside.

2. Meanwhile, bring broth to boil over high heat in large pot (this pot will be used to cook pasta in step 6) and cook until reduced to 2 cups, about 15 minutes; set aside.

3. Pulse pancetta in food processor until finely chopped, 15 to 20 pulses. Add onion, carrot, and celery and pulse until vegetables are finely chopped and mixture has paste-like consistency, 12 to 15 pulses, scraping down sides of bowl as needed.

4. Heat butter and oil in Dutch oven over medium-high heat until butter is melted and mixture is shimmering. Add pancetta-vegetable mixture and remaining ¼ teaspoon pepper and cook, stirring occasionally, until liquid has evaporated, about 8 minutes. Spread mixture in even layer in bottom of pot and continue to cook, stirring every couple of minutes, until very dark browned bits form on bottom of pot, 7 to 12 minutes. Stir in tomato paste and cook until paste is rust-colored and bottom of pot is dark brown, 1 to 2 minutes.

5. Reduce heat to medium, add beef, and cook, using wooden spoon to break meat into pieces no larger than ¼ inch, until beef has just lost its raw pink color, 4 to 7 minutes. Stir in wine, scraping up any browned bits, and bring to simmer. Cook until wine has evaporated and sauce has thickened, about 5 minutes. Stir in broth and Parmesan. Return sauce to simmer; cover, reduce heat to low, and simmer for 30 minutes (sauce will look thin). Remove from heat and season with salt and pepper to taste.

6. Rinse pot that held broth. While sauce simmers, bring 4 quarts water to boil in now-empty pot. Add pasta and 1 tablespoon salt and cook, stirring occasionally, until al dente. Reserve ¼ cup cooking water, then drain pasta. Add pasta to pot with sauce and toss to combine. Adjust sauce consistency with reserved cooking water as needed. Transfer to platter or individual bowls and serve, passing extra Parmesan separately.

"While my Italian American family never made this exact recipe, it reminds me of the best thing about real Italian cooking: the wonderful, complex flavors in what appears to be a very simple dish. So if you don't have your own Italian grandma to show you the secrets, you do have Bryan Roof, who somehow cracked the Italian Grandma Code. This recipe is now a regular in my rotation, and when guests want to know how I manage to make 'meat sauce' so amazing, I am tempted to just smile and say that it's a family secret."

—Lisa

Ragu alla Bolognese

Makes about 6 cups; enough for 2 pounds pasta

WHY THIS RECIPE WORKS Our goal with this recipe was to develop the richest, most savory interpretation of this famous meat sauce. But how many meats did that require and would the dairy have to go? And what about the tomatoes? Some recipes call for crushed tomatoes to brighten the ragu while others lean toward the more concentrated depth of tomato paste. We settled on six different types of meat for this Bolognese: ground beef, pork, and veal; pancetta; mortadella (bologna-like Italian deli meat); and chicken livers. These meats and the combination of red wine and tomato paste, which we preferred over crushed tomatoes, gave us a rich, complex sauce with balanced acidity. As for milk or cream, we found it muted the meaty flavor of this sauce and was unnecessary. The addition of gelatin lent the sauce an ultrasilky texture. Eight teaspoons of gelatin is equivalent to one 1-ounce box of gelatin. If you can't find ground veal, use an additional 12 ounces of ground beef.

- 1 cup chicken broth
- 1 cup beef broth
- 8 teaspoons unflavored gelatin
- 1 onion, chopped
- 1 large carrot, peeled and chopped
- 1 celery rib, chopped
- 4 ounces pancetta, chopped
- 4 ounces mortadella, chopped
- 6 ounces chicken livers, trimmed
- 3 tablespoons extra-virgin olive oil
- 12 ounces 85 percent lean ground beef
- 12 ounces ground veal
- 12 ounces ground pork
- 3 tablespoons finely chopped fresh sage
- 1 (6-ounce) can tomato paste
- 2 cups dry red wine
- 1 pound pappardelle or tagliatelle
  Table salt for cooking pasta
- 1 ounce Parmesan cheese, grated (½ cup)

1. Combine chicken broth and beef broth in bowl; sprinkle gelatin over top and set aside. Pulse onion, carrot, and celery in food processor until finely chopped, about 10 pulses, scraping down bowl as needed; transfer to separate bowl. Pulse pancetta and mortadella in now-empty food processor until finely chopped, about 25 pulses, scraping down bowl as needed; transfer to second bowl. Process chicken livers in now-empty food processor until pureed, about 5 seconds; transfer to third bowl.

2. Heat oil in Dutch oven over medium-high heat until shimmering. Add beef, veal, and pork; cook, breaking up pieces with wooden spoon, until all liquid has evaporated and meat begins to sizzle, 10 to 15 minutes. Add pancetta mixture and sage; cook, stirring frequently, until pancetta is translucent, 5 to 7 minutes, adjusting heat as needed to keep fond from burning. Add chopped vegetables and cook, stirring frequently, until softened, 5 to 7 minutes. Add tomato paste and cook, stirring constantly, until rust-colored and fragrant, about 3 minutes.

3. Stir in wine, scraping up any browned bits. Simmer until sauce has thickened, about 5 minutes. Stir in broth mixture and return to simmer. Reduce heat to low and cook at bare simmer until thickened (wooden spoon should leave trail when dragged through sauce), about 1½ hours.

4. Stir in pureed chicken livers, bring to boil, and remove from heat. Season with salt and pepper to taste; cover and keep warm.

5. Bring 4 quarts water to boil in large pot. Add pasta and 1 tablespoon salt and cook, stirring often, until al dente. Reserve ¾ cup cooking water, then drain pasta and return it to pot. Add half of sauce and cooking water to pasta and toss to combine. Transfer to serving bowl and serve, passing Parmesan separately. (Leftover sauce may be refrigerated for up to 3 days or frozen for up to 1 month.)

Pasta with Hearty Italian Meat Sauce (Sunday Gravy)

Serves 8 to 10

WHY THIS RECIPE WORKS Traditional "Sunday gravy" is more than just meat sauce—it's a labor of love, an all-day kitchen affair, involving several types of meat, a bunch of tomatoes, and at least one Italian grandmother. We wanted to honor this meaty extravaganza but shortcut the cooking so we could get this traditional dish on the table in a reasonable amount of time. When you're using six or seven types of meat, the browning alone can take up to 40 minutes. Our first step was to limit the dish to just one kind of sausage and one pork cut—plus meatballs. Hot Italian links gave the sauce a mild kick and baby back ribs were our favorite cut of pork because they weren't too fatty and turned moist and tender in just a few hours. Meatloaf mix, a combination of ground beef, pork, and veal, produced juicy, tender meatballs, especially when mixed with a panade of bread and buttermilk. To further bump

Pasta with Hearty Italian
Meat Sauce

up flavor, we mixed in minced garlic, parsley, and red pepper flakes, plus an egg yolk for richness. To help the meatballs retain their shape we browned them first in a skillet before adding them to the sauce. For the tomato sauce, canned crushed tomatoes were a winner, leading to a sauce with nice thickness and bright tomato flavor. Instead of merely browning the tomato paste for 30 seconds, we cooked it until it nearly blackened, which concentrated its sweetness. The sauce was still lacking some beefy undercurrents; the best booster turned out to be the simple, straightforward addition of an ingredient rarely found in tomato sauce: beef broth. We prefer meatloaf mix (a combination of ground beef, pork, and veal) for the meatballs in this recipe. Ground beef may be substituted, but the meatballs won't be as flavorful. Six tablespoons of plain yogurt thinned with 2 tablespoons of milk can be substituted for the buttermilk. Our preferred brand of crushed tomatoes is SMT.

Sauce

- 2 tablespoons extra-virgin olive oil
- 2¼ pounds baby back ribs, cut into 2-rib sections
- 1 teaspoon table salt
- ½ teaspoon pepper
- 1 pound hot Italian sausage
- 2 onions, chopped fine
- 1¼ teaspoons dried oregano
- 3 tablespoons tomato paste
- 4 garlic cloves, minced
- 2 (28-ounce) cans crushed tomatoes
- ⅔ cup beef broth
- ¼ cup chopped fresh basil

Meatballs and Pasta

- 2 slices hearty white sandwich bread, crusts removed, torn into small pieces
- ½ cup buttermilk
- 1 pound meatloaf mix
- 2 ounces thinly sliced prosciutto, chopped fine
- 1 ounce Pecorino Romano cheese, grated (½ cup)
- ¼ cup finely chopped fresh parsley
- 2 garlic cloves, minced
- 1 large egg yolk
- ½ teaspoon table salt, plus salt for cooking pasta
- ¼ teaspoon red pepper flakes
- ½ cup extra-virgin olive oil, for frying meatballs
- 1½ pounds spaghetti or linguine
- 1 ounce Parmesan cheese, grated (½ cup)

1. For the sauce: Adjust oven rack to lower-middle position and heat oven to 325 degrees. Heat oil in Dutch oven over medium-high heat until just smoking. Pat ribs dry with paper towels and season with salt and pepper. Brown half of ribs well on both sides, 5 to 7 minutes. Transfer ribs to large plate and repeat with remaining ribs. After transferring second batch of ribs to plate, brown sausage well on all sides, 5 to 7 minutes; transfer to plate with ribs.

2. Add onions and oregano to fat left in pot and cook over medium heat, stirring occasionally, until onions are softened and lightly browned, 5 to 7 minutes. Add tomato paste and cook, stirring constantly, until very dark, about 3 minutes. Stir in garlic and cook until fragrant, about 30 seconds. Stir in crushed tomatoes and broth, scraping up any browned bits. Nestle browned ribs and sausage into pot. Bring to simmer, cover, and transfer to oven. Cook until ribs are tender, about 2½ hours.

3. For the meatballs and pasta: While sauce cooks, mash bread and buttermilk in large bowl using fork. Let sit for 10 minutes. Using your hands, mix in meatloaf mix, prosciutto, Pecorino, parsley, garlic, egg yolk, ½ teaspoon salt, and pepper flakes. Pinch off and roll mixture into 12 meatballs. Transfer meatballs to plate, cover with plastic wrap, and refrigerate until ready to use.

4. When sauce is 30 minutes from being done, heat oil in 12-inch nonstick skillet over medium-high heat until shimmering. Brown meatballs well on all sides, 5 to 7 minutes; transfer to paper towel–lined plate. Remove sauce from oven and skim fat from surface using wide, shallow spoon. Gently nestle browned meatballs into sauce. Cover, return pot to oven, and continue to cook until meatballs are just cooked through, about 15 minutes. (Sauce can be cooled and refrigerated in Dutch oven for up to 2 days. To reheat, drizzle ½ cup water over sauce [do not stir in] and warm on lower-middle rack of 325-degree oven for 1 hour before proceeding with recipe.)

5. Meanwhile, bring 6 quarts water to boil in large pot. Add pasta and 2 tablespoons salt and cook, stirring often, until al dente. Reserve ½ cup cooking water, then drain pasta and return it to pot.

6. Using tongs, transfer meatballs, ribs, and sausage to serving platter and cut each sausage in half. Stir basil into sauce and season with salt and pepper to taste. Add 1 cup sauce and reserved cooking water to pasta and toss to combine. Serve, passing remaining sauce, meat, and Parmesan separately.

Pasta and Slow-Simmered Tomato Sauce with Meat

Serves 4 to 6

WHY THIS RECIPE WORKS Slow-simmered Italian meat sauce—the kind without meatballs—relies on pork for rich flavor. But the pork found in supermarkets is so lean, we weren't convinced that any of the options could provide enough fat and flavor. So we set out to create a flavorful meat sauce with fall-off-the-bone-tender meat that was made from readily available supermarket products. We used fattier country-style pork ribs, which turned meltingly tender when cooked for a long time and added meaty flavor. Red wine accentuated the meatiness of the sauce, which was built on a simple combination of sautéed onion and canned diced tomatoes. This sauce can be made with either pork ribs or beef ribs; since beef ribs tend to be thicker, it's important to remember to let them cook a little longer. Depending on their size, you will need four or five ribs.

1 tablespoon extra-virgin olive oil
1½ pounds pork spareribs or country-style ribs or beef short ribs, trimmed
½ teaspoon table salt, plus salt for cooking pasta
¼ teaspoon pepper
1 onion, chopped fine
½ cup red wine
1 (28-ounce) can whole peeled tomatoes, drained with juice reserved, chopped fine
1 pound ziti, rigatoni, or other short tubular pasta
1 ounce Parmesan cheese, grated (½ cup)

1. Heat oil in 12-inch skillet over medium-high heat until shimmering. Season ribs with ½ teaspoon salt and pepper and brown on all sides, turning occasionally with tongs, 8 to 10 minutes. Transfer ribs to large plate; pour off all but 1 teaspoon fat from skillet. Add onion and sauté until softened, 2 to 3 minutes. Add wine and simmer briskly, scraping up any browned bits, until wine reduces by half, about 2 minutes.

2. Return ribs and any accumulated juices to skillet; add tomatoes and reserved juice. Bring to boil, then reduce heat to low, cover, and simmer gently, turning ribs several times, until meat is very tender and falling off bones, 1½ hours (for pork spareribs or country-style ribs) to 2 hours (for beef short ribs).

3. Transfer ribs to clean plate. When cool enough to handle, remove meat from bones and shred with your fingers, discarding fat and bones. Return shredded meat to skillet. Bring sauce to simmer over medium heat and cook, uncovered, until heated through and slightly thickened, about 5 minutes. Season with salt and pepper to taste. (Sauce can be refrigerated for up to 4 days or frozen for up to 2 months.)

4. Bring 4 quarts water to boil in large pot. Add pasta and 1 tablespoon salt and cook, stirring often, until al dente. Reserve ½ cup cooking water, then drain pasta and return it to pot. Add sauce to pasta and toss to combine, adjusting consistency with reserved cooking water as needed. Serve immediately, passing Parmesan separately.

Pork, Fennel, and Lemon Ragu with Pappardelle

SEASON 20 RECIPE

Serves 4 to 6

WHY THIS RECIPE WORKS This white ragu, known as *ragu bianco*, skips tomatoes in favor of bright lemon and rich cream. This version features shreds of meltingly tender braised pork punctuated by tart lemon, licorice-y fennel, and salty Pecorino Romano cheese. We ensured plenty of savoriness in the ragu by creating fond twice. We first browned finely chopped pancetta, onion, and fennel in a Dutch oven and then added water and a touch of cream to create a braising liquid. A pork shoulder, which we halved crosswise to make cooking faster and shredding easier, simmered in this liquid in the oven, where a second fond formed on the sides of the pot. After scraping this second fond into the sauce, we brightened its flavor with plenty of lemon juice before adding the pasta. Pork butt roast is often labeled Boston butt in the supermarket. To ensure that the sauce isn't greasy, be sure to trim the roast of all excess surface fat. You can substitute tagliatelle for the pappardelle, if desired.

4 ounces pancetta, chopped
1 large onion, chopped fine
1 large fennel bulb, 2 tablespoons fronds chopped, stalks discarded, bulb halved, cored, and chopped fine, divided
4 garlic cloves, minced
1½ teaspoons table salt, plus salt for cooking pasta
2 teaspoons finely chopped fresh thyme
1 teaspoon pepper
⅓ cup heavy cream
1 (1½-pound) boneless pork butt roast, well trimmed and cut in half across grain
1½ teaspoons grated lemon zest plus ¼ cup juice (2 lemons)
12 ounces pappardelle
2 ounces Pecorino Romano cheese, grated (1 cup), plus extra for serving

"This season 20 recipe has become my new favorite Sunday gravy. It may seem like an unlikely combination: a ragu without tomatoes? My Italian grandmother would certainly have shaken her head. But this ragu bianco (or white sauce) is actually the original recipe, made before Christopher Columbus brought back tomatoes from the New World. Boneless pork butt is braised until fork-tender and then shredded to make this mostly hands-off sauce. Pancetta enhances the savory, meaty notes while fennel and lemon lend brightness and acidity. Pecorino Romano is stirred right into the ragu, adding salty, tangy notes. And did I mention the generous splash of cream, which melds all the big flavors into a cohesive sauce? Rarely does so little effort yield such impressive results. Wide pappardelle noodles are the perfect partner for this chunky ragu. Serve it with a crisp white wine (I like a Vernaccia from Tuscany, but Sauvignon Blanc works well too) and a leafy green salad. Now that's the perfect Sunday supper."

–Jack

1. Adjust oven rack to middle position and heat oven to 350 degrees. Cook pancetta and ⅔ cup water in Dutch oven over medium-high heat, stirring occasionally, until water has evaporated and dark fond forms on bottom of pot, 8 to 10 minutes. Add onion and fennel bulb and cook, stirring occasionally, until vegetables soften and start to brown, 5 to 7 minutes. Stir in garlic, salt, thyme, and pepper and cook until fragrant, about 30 seconds.

2. Stir in cream and 2 cups water, scraping up any browned bits. Add pork and bring to boil over high heat. Cover, transfer to oven, and cook until pork is tender, about 1½ hours.

3. Transfer pork to large plate and let cool for 15 minutes. Cover pot so fond will steam and soften. Using spatula, scrape browned bits from sides of pot and stir into sauce. Stir in lemon zest and juice.

4. While pork cools, bring 4 quarts water to boil in large pot. Using 2 forks, shred pork into bite-size pieces, discarding any large pieces of fat or connective tissue. Return pork and any juices to Dutch oven. Cover and keep warm.

5. Add pasta and 1 tablespoon salt to boiling water and cook, stirring occasionally, until al dente. Reserve 2 cups cooking water, then drain pasta and add it to Dutch oven. Add Pecorino and ¾ cup reserved cooking water and stir until sauce is slightly thickened and cheese is fully melted, 2 to 3 minutes. If desired, stir in remaining reserved cooking water, ¼ cup at a time, to adjust sauce consistency. Season with salt and pepper to taste and sprinkle with fennel fronds. Serve immediately, passing extra Pecorino separately.

Classic Spaghetti and Meatballs for a Crowd

Serves 12

WHY THIS RECIPE WORKS When you want to make a big batch of spaghetti and meatballs but don't want to spend endless amounts of time standing at the stove, this is the recipe to use. Here roasting the meatballs on a wire rack makes the whole process faster. Adding powdered gelatin to a mix of ground chuck and pork served to plump the meatballs and lent them a soft richness. Prosciutto gave the meatballs extra meatiness, and a panade, which we made with panko, kept the meat moist and prevented it from getting tough. To create a rich sauce, we braised the meatballs in marinara sauce for about an hour. To make sure the sauce didn't over-reduce, we swapped half the crushed tomatoes in our marinara recipe for an equal portion of tomato juice. If you don't have buttermilk, you can substitute 1 cup whole-milk plain yogurt

thinned with ½ cup whole milk. Grate the onion on the large holes of a box grater. You can cook the pasta in two separate pots if you do not have a large enough pot to cook all of the pasta together.

Meatballs
2¼ cups panko bread crumbs
1½ cups buttermilk
1½ teaspoons unflavored gelatin
3 tablespoons water
2 pounds 85 percent lean ground beef
1 pound ground pork
6 ounces thinly sliced prosciutto, chopped fine
3 large eggs
3 ounces Parmesan cheese, grated (1½ cups), plus extra for serving
6 tablespoons finely chopped fresh parsley
3 garlic cloves, minced
1½ teaspoons table salt
½ teaspoon pepper

Sauce
3 tablespoons extra-virgin olive oil
1 large onion, grated
6 garlic cloves, minced
1 teaspoon dried oregano
½ teaspoon red pepper flakes
3 (28-ounce) cans crushed tomatoes
6 cups tomato juice
6 tablespoons dry white wine
1½ teaspoons table salt, plus salt for cooking pasta
¼ teaspoon pepper
½ cup finely chopped fresh basil
3 tablespoons finely chopped fresh parsley
   Sugar

3 pounds spaghetti

1. *For the meatballs:* Adjust oven racks to upper-middle and lower-middle positions and heat oven to 450 degrees. Place wire racks in 2 rimmed baking sheets lined with aluminum foil and spray wire racks with vegetable oil spray.

2. Combine panko and buttermilk in large bowl and let sit, mashing occasionally with fork, until smooth paste forms, about 10 minutes. Meanwhile, sprinkle gelatin over water in bowl and let sit until gelatin softens, about 5 minutes.

3. Mix beef, pork, prosciutto, eggs, Parmesan, parsley, garlic, salt, pepper, and gelatin mixture into panko mixture using your hands. Pinch off and roll mixture into 2-inch meatballs (about 40 meatballs total) and arrange on prepared wire racks. Bake until well browned, about 30 minutes, switching and rotating sheets halfway through baking.

4. *For the sauce:* While meatballs bake, heat oil in Dutch oven over medium heat until shimmering. Add onion and cook until softened and lightly browned, 5 to 7 minutes. Stir in garlic, oregano, and pepper flakes and cook until fragrant, about 30 seconds. Stir in tomatoes, tomato juice, wine, 1½ teaspoons salt, and pepper; bring to simmer; and cook until thickened slightly, about 15 minutes.

5. Remove meatballs from oven and reduce oven temperature to 300 degrees. Gently nestle meatballs into sauce. Cover, transfer to oven, and cook until meatballs are firm and sauce has thickened, about 1 hour. (Sauce and meatballs can be cooled and refrigerated for up to 2 days. To reheat, drizzle ½ cup water over sauce, without stirring, and reheat on lower-middle rack of 325-degree oven for 1 hour.)

6. Meanwhile, bring 10 quarts water to boil in 12-quart pot. Add pasta and 2 tablespoons salt and cook, stirring often, until al dente. Reserve ½ cup cooking water, then drain pasta and return it to pot. Gently stir basil and parsley into sauce and season with sugar, salt, and pepper to taste. Add 2 cups sauce (without meatballs) to pasta and toss to combine. Add reserved cooking water as needed to adjust consistency. Serve, topping individual portions with more tomato sauce and several meatballs and passing Parmesan separately.

Sausage Meatballs and Spaghetti

Serves 4 to 6

WHY THIS RECIPE WORKS For a change of pace, we wanted to use Italian sausage to create meatballs that were full of bold flavor but still tender. To temper sausage's springy texture, we added ground pork, brined with baking soda and salt to impart tenderness and help the meat retain juices. A panade made with heavy cream brought more fat into the mix, which would coat the meat's proteins and prevent them from sticking together. Pulsing the meat mixture in a food processor cut the panade into the meat for even incorporation, and processing the meat in stages kept it from turning tough from overworking. To really highlight the bold, seasoned flavors of Italian sausage, we added a reinforcing dose of the classic spices already present in the meat: coarsely ground fennel seeds, oregano, black pepper, and red pepper flakes. We baked the meatballs in a hot oven to quickly brown them in a single batch. A simple tomato sauce was all we needed to complement the spiced-up sausage meatballs, so we sautéed garlic in oil and added both crushed tomatoes and tomato sauce for bright but smooth results. After a quick simmer, we stirred in fresh basil and added the meatballs to the pot to finish cooking. The fennel seeds can be coarsely ground in a

spice grinder or using the bottom of a heavy skillet. Use a light touch when rolling the meatballs to prevent them from being dense. A #30 scoop, loosely filled, works well for portioning the meatballs.

Meatballs
- ½ teaspoon table salt
- ¼ teaspoon baking soda
- 4 teaspoons water
- 12 ounces ground pork
- 2 slices hearty white sandwich bread, crusts removed, torn into ½-inch pieces
- ⅓ cup heavy cream
- ⅓ cup grated Parmesan cheese, plus extra for serving
- 2 large egg yolks
- 2 garlic cloves, minced
- 1 teaspoon fennel seeds, coarsely ground
- 1 teaspoon dried oregano
- 1 teaspoon pepper
- ½ teaspoon red pepper flakes
- 12 ounces sweet Italian sausage, casings removed, broken into 1-inch pieces

Tomato Sauce
- 2 tablespoons extra-virgin olive oil
- 1 garlic clove, minced
- 1 (28-ounce) can crushed tomatoes
- 1 (15-ounce) can tomato sauce
- ¼ teaspoon table salt, plus salt for cooking pasta
- 1 tablespoon chopped fresh basil

- 1 pound spaghetti

1. *For the meatballs:* Adjust oven rack to upper-middle position and heat oven to 500 degrees. Place wire rack in aluminum foil–lined rimmed baking sheet. Spray wire rack with vegetable oil spray.

2. Dissolve salt and baking soda in water in large bowl. Add pork and fold gently to combine; let sit for 10 minutes.

3. Pulse bread, cream, Parmesan, egg yolks, garlic, fennel seeds, oregano, pepper, and pepper flakes in food processor until smooth paste forms, about 10 pulses, scraping down sides of bowl as needed. Add pork mixture and pulse until mixture is well combined, about 5 pulses.

4. Transfer half of pork mixture to now-empty large bowl. Add sausage to food processor and pulse until just combined, 4 to 5 pulses. Transfer sausage-pork mixture to large bowl with pork mixture. Using your hands, gently fold together until mixture is just combined.

5. With your wet hands, lightly shape mixture into 1¾-inch round meatballs (about 1 ounce each); you should have about 24 meatballs. Arrange meatballs, evenly spaced, on prepared rack and bake until browned, about 15 minutes, rotating sheet halfway through baking.

6. *For the tomato sauce:* While meatballs bake, heat oil in Dutch oven over medium heat until shimmering. Add garlic and cook, stirring frequently, until fragrant, about 30 seconds. Stir in crushed tomatoes, tomato sauce, and ¼ teaspoon salt and bring to boil. Reduce heat and simmer gently until slightly thickened, about 10 minutes. Stir in basil and season with salt to taste.

7. Add meatballs to sauce and gently simmer, turning them occasionally, until cooked through, 5 to 10 minutes. Cover and keep warm over low heat.

8. Bring 4 quarts water to boil in large pot. Add pasta and 1 tablespoon salt and cook, stirring often, until al dente. Reserve ½ cup cooking water, then drain pasta and return it to pot.

9. Add ½ cup sauce and ¼ cup reserved cooking water to pasta and toss to combine. Transfer pasta to large serving platter and top with meatballs and remaining sauce, adjusting consistency with remaining reserved cooking water as needed. Serve, passing extra Parmesan separately.

Baked Manicotti

Serves 6 to 8

WHY THIS RECIPE WORKS Despite being composed of a straightforward collection of ingredients (pasta, cheese, and tomato sauce), manicotti is surprisingly fussy to prepare. Blanching, shocking, draining, and stuffing slippery pasta requires a lot of patience and time. We wanted an easy-to-prepare recipe that still produced great-tasting manicotti. Our biggest challenge was filling the slippery manicotti tubes. We solved the problem by discarding the tubes completely and spreading the filling onto a lasagna noodle, which we then rolled up. For the lasagna noodles, we found that the no-boil variety were ideal. We soaked the noodles in boiling water for 5 minutes until pliable and used the tip of a knife to separate them and prevent sticking. For the cheese filling, we taste-tested several ricottas and found that part-skim had an ideal level of richness. Eggs, Parmesan, and an ample amount of mozzarella added richness, flavor, and structure to the ricotta filling. For a quick but brightly flavored tomato sauce, we pureed canned diced tomatoes and simmered them until slightly thickened with sautéed garlic and red pepper flakes, then finished the sauce with fresh basil. We prefer Barilla no-boil lasagna noodles for their delicate texture resembling fresh pasta. Note that Pasta Defino and Ronzoni brands contain only 12 no-boil noodles per package; the recipe requires 16 noodles.

Tomato Sauce

- 2 (28-ounce) cans diced tomatoes
- 2 tablespoons extra-virgin olive oil
- 3 garlic cloves, minced
- ½ teaspoon red pepper flakes (optional)
- ½ teaspoon table salt
- 2 tablespoons chopped fresh basil

Cheese Filling

- 1½ pounds (3 cups) part-skim ricotta cheese
- 8 ounces mozzarella cheese, shredded (2 cups)
- 4 ounces Parmesan cheese, grated (2 cups), divided
- 2 large eggs
- 2 tablespoons chopped fresh parsley
- 2 tablespoons chopped fresh basil
- ¾ teaspoon salt
- ½ teaspoon pepper

- 16 no-boil lasagna noodles

1. For the tomato sauce: Pulse 1 can tomatoes with their juice in food processor until coarsely chopped, 3 or 4 pulses; transfer to bowl. Repeat with remaining can tomatoes.

2. Heat oil, garlic, and pepper flakes, if using, in large saucepan over medium heat. Cook, stirring often, until garlic turns golden but not brown, about 3 minutes. Stir in chopped tomatoes and salt, bring to simmer, and cook until thickened slightly, about 15 minutes. Stir in basil and season with salt to taste.

3. For the cheese filling: Combine ricotta, mozzarella, 1 cup Parmesan, eggs, parsley, basil, salt, and pepper in bowl.

4. Adjust oven rack to middle position and heat oven to 375 degrees. Pour 2 inches boiling water into 13 by 9-inch broiler-safe baking dish. Slip noodles into water, one at a time, and soak until pliable, about 5 minutes, separating noodles with tip of sharp knife to prevent sticking. Remove noodles from water and place in single layer on clean dish towels; discard water and dry dish.

5. Spread 1½ cups sauce evenly over bottom of dish. Using spoon, spread ¼ cup cheese mixture evenly onto bottom three-quarters of each noodle (with short side facing you), leaving top quarter of noodle exposed. Roll into tube shape and arrange in dish seam side down. Top evenly with remaining sauce, making certain that pasta is completely covered.

6. Cover dish tightly with foil and bake until bubbling, about 40 minutes, rotating dish halfway through baking. Remove dish from oven and remove foil. Adjust oven rack 6 inches from broiler element and heat broiler. Sprinkle manicotti evenly with remaining 1 cup Parmesan. Broil until cheese is spotty brown, 4 to 6 minutes. Let manicotti cool for 15 minutes before serving. (Manicotti can be prepared through step 5, covered with sheet of parchment paper, wrapped in aluminum foil, and refrigerated for up to 3 days or frozen for up to 1 month. [If frozen, thaw manicotti in refrigerator for 1 to 2 days.] To bake, remove parchment, replace aluminum foil, and increase baking time to 1 to 1¼ hours.)

VARIATIONS

Baked Manicotti with Sausage

Cook 1 pound hot or sweet Italian sausage, casings removed, in 2 tablespoons extra-virgin olive oil in large saucepan over medium-high heat, breaking sausage into ½-inch pieces with wooden spoon, until no longer pink, about 6 minutes. Omit oil in sauce and cook remaining sauce ingredients in saucepan with sausage.

Baked Manicotti with Prosciutto

Arrange 1 piece very thinly sliced prosciutto on each noodle before spreading cheese filling and rolling manicotti (you will need 16 slices, about 8 ounces total).

Baked Manicotti Puttanesca

Add 3 rinsed and minced anchovy fillets to saucepan with garlic. Add ¼ cup pitted and chopped kalamata olives and 2 tablespoons rinsed and minced capers to ricotta mixture.

Making Baked Manicotti

1. Using spoon, spread about ¼ cup of filling evenly over bottom three-quarters of each noodle, leaving top quarter of noodles exposed.

2. Starting at bottom, roll each noodle up around filling, and lay in prepared baking dish, seam side down.

Hand-Rolled Meat Ravioli with Quick Tomato Sauce

SEASON 20 RECIPE

Serves 4 to 6; makes 36 ravioli plus 3 cups sauce

WHY THIS RECIPE WORKS Handmade ravioli are a treat usually reserved for dinner at a fine Italian restaurant and seldom made at home. But with our supermalleable dough, you don't need a pasta machine or years of pasta-making experience to make tender yet springy ravioli with a delicious meat filling. This dough relies heavily on egg yolks and oil to provide enough fat to limit gluten development so the dough can be rolled without springing back. The easy-to-make ground pork filling is bound with bread, egg, and Parmesan and infused with the flavor of lemon, fennel, and garlic. If using King Arthur All-Purpose Flour, which is higher in protein, increase the number of egg yolks to seven. To ensure the proper dough texture, it's important to use large eggs and to weigh the flour if possible. The longer the dough rests in step 2, the easier it will be to roll out. When rolling out the dough, don't add too much flour; it can cause excessive snapback. Though a pasta machine is not necessary, you may use one if you like. This recipe produces square ravioli with three cut edges and one folded edge. If using a fluted pasta wheel to cut, you can trim the folded edge so that all sides match. If you don't have a pot that holds 6 quarts or more, cook the ravioli in two batches; toss the first batch with some sauce in a serving bowl, cover it with foil, and keep it warm in a 200-degree oven while the second batch cooks.

Pasta Dough
- 2 cups (10 ounces) all-purpose flour, plus extra as needed
- 2 large eggs plus 6 large yolks
- 2 tablespoons extra-virgin olive oil

Filling
- 2 slices hearty white sandwich bread, torn into small pieces
- 1 ounce Parmesan cheese, grated (½ cup), plus extra for serving
- ¼ cup chicken broth
- 1 large egg
- 2 tablespoons minced fresh parsley
- 2 garlic cloves, minced
- 1 teaspoon table salt
- 1 teaspoon ground fennel
- ¾ teaspoon grated lemon zest
- ½ teaspoon pepper
- ½ teaspoon dry mustard
- 1 pound ground pork

Ravioli
- 1 large egg white, lightly beaten
  Table salt for cooking pasta

Tomato Sauce
- 2 tablespoons unsalted butter
- ¼ cup grated onion
- ¼ teaspoon dried oregano
- ½ teaspoon table salt
- 2 garlic cloves, minced
- 1 (28-ounce) can crushed tomatoes
- ¼ teaspoon sugar
- 2 tablespoons chopped fresh basil
- 1 tablespoon extra-virgin olive oil

1. For the pasta dough: Process all ingredients in food processor until mixture forms cohesive dough that is barely tacky to touch, about 45 seconds. (If any dough sticks to your fingers, add up to ¼ cup extra flour, 1 tablespoon at a time. Process until flour is fully incorporated after each addition, 10 to 15 seconds, before retesting. If dough doesn't become cohesive, add up to 1 tablespoon water, 1 teaspoon at a time, until it just comes together; process 30 seconds longer.)

2. Turn out dough onto dry counter and knead until smooth, 1 to 2 minutes. Shape dough into 6-inch-long cylinder. Wrap in plastic wrap and let rest at room temperature for at least 1 hour or up to 4 hours. Wipe processor bowl clean.

3. For the filling: Process bread, Parmesan, broth, egg, parsley, garlic, salt, fennel, lemon zest, pepper, and mustard in now-empty processor until paste forms, 10 to 15 seconds, scraping down sides of bowl as needed. Add pork and pulse until mixture is well combined, about 5 pulses. Transfer filling to medium bowl, cover with plastic, and refrigerate until needed.

4. For the ravioli: Line rimmed baking sheet with parchment paper. Cut dough cylinder crosswise into 6 equal pieces. Working with 1 piece of dough at a time (keep remaining pieces covered), dust both sides with flour, place cut side down on clean counter, and press into 3-inch square. Using heavy rolling pin, roll into 6-inch square.

5. Dust both sides of 1 dough square lightly with flour. Starting at center of square, roll dough away from you in 1 motion. Return rolling pin to center of dough and roll toward you in 1 motion. Repeat rolling steps until dough sticks to counter and measures roughly 12 inches long. Lightly dust both sides of dough with flour and continue to roll out dough until it measures roughly 20 inches long and 6 inches wide, frequently lifting dough to release it from counter. (If dough firmly sticks to counter and wrinkles when rolled out, carefully lift dough and dust counter lightly with flour.) Transfer dough sheet to prepared baking sheet and cover with plastic. Repeat rolling process with remaining 5 dough squares and transfer to prepared sheet (2 dough sheets per layer; place parchment between layers). Keep dough covered with plastic.

6. Line second baking sheet with parchment. Lay 1 dough sheet on clean counter with long side parallel to counter edge (keep others covered). Trim ends of dough with sharp knife so that corners are square and dough is 18 inches long. Brush bottom half of dough with egg white. Starting 1½ inches from left edge of dough and 1 inch from bottom, deposit 1 tablespoon filling. Repeat placing 1-tablespoon mounds of filling, spaced 1½ inches apart, 1 inch from bottom edge of dough. You should be able to fit 6 mounds of filling on 1 dough sheet.

7. Cut dough sheet at center points between mounds of filling, separating it into 6 equal pieces. Working with 1 piece at a time, lift top edge of dough over filling and extend it so that it lines up with bottom edge. Keeping top edge of dough suspended over filling with your thumbs, use your fingers to press dough layers together, working around each mound of filling from back to front, pressing out as much air as possible before sealing completely.

8. Once all edges are sealed, use sharp knife or fluted pastry wheel to cut excess dough from around filling, leaving ¼- to ½-inch border around each mound (it's not necessary to cut folded edge of ravioli, but you may do so, if desired). Transfer ravioli to prepared baking sheet. Refrigerate until ready to cook. Repeat shaping process with remaining dough and remaining filling. (Dough scraps can be frozen and added to soup.)

9. *For the tomato sauce:* Melt butter in medium saucepan over medium heat. Add onion, oregano, and salt; cook, stirring occasionally, until liquid has evaporated and onion is golden brown, about 5 minutes. Add garlic and cook until fragrant, about 30 seconds. Stir in tomatoes and sugar; bring to simmer over high heat. Lower heat to medium-low and simmer until slightly thickened, about 10 minutes. Off heat, stir in basil and oil; season with salt and pepper to taste.

10. Bring 6 quarts water to boil in large pot. Add ravioli and 1 tablespoon salt. Cook, maintaining gentle boil, until ravioli are just tender, about 13 minutes. (To test, pull 1 ravioli from pot, trim off corner without cutting into filling, and taste. Return ravioli to pot if not yet tender.) Drain well. Using spider skimmer or slotted spoon, transfer ravioli to warmed bowls or plates. Serve immediately, passing extra Parmesan separately. (Freeze uncooked ravioli in single layer on parchment paper–lined rimmed baking sheet. Transfer to zipper-lock bag and freeze for up to 1 month. Cook frozen ravioli with no change to cooking time.)

Preparing Pasta Dough and Filling

1. Cut dough cylinder into 6 equal pieces. Working with 1 piece at a time (keeping remaining pieces covered), dust both sides with flour and roll into 6-inch square.

2. Roll from center of dough, dusting with flour if needed, until dough is 6 by 12 inches, lifting frequently to release from counter. Repeat with remaining dough.

3. Lay dough sheet on counter, with long side parallel to edge. Trim and brush with egg white. Deposit 6 equally spaced mounds of filling 1½ inches from left edge of dough and 1 inch from bottom.

4. Cut dough at center points between mounds of filling, separating it into 6 equal pieces. Lift top edge over filling and press to firmly seal in filling, pressing out as much air as possible.

5. Once edges are sealed, use knife or fluted pastry wheel to trim excess dough from ravioli.

6. Boil, maintaining gentle simmer until ravioli are just tender, about 13 minutes.

Skillet Lasagna

Serves 4 to 6

WHY THIS RECIPE WORKS Lasagna isn't usually a dish you can throw together at the last minute. Even with no-boil noodles, it takes a good amount of time to get the components just right. Our goal was to transform traditional baked lasagna into a stovetop skillet dish without losing any of its flavor or appeal. We built a hearty, flavorful meat sauce with onions, garlic, red pepper flakes, and meatloaf mix (a more flavorful alternative to plain ground beef). A large can of diced tomatoes along with tomato sauce provided juicy tomato flavor and a nicely chunky texture. We scattered regular curly-edged lasagna noodles, broken into pieces, over the top of the sauce (smaller pieces are easier to eat and serve). We then diluted the sauce with a little water so that the noodles would cook through. After a 20-minute simmer with the lid on, the pasta was tender, the sauce was properly thickened, and it was time for the cheese. Stirring Parmesan into the dish worked well, but we discovered that the sweet creaminess of ricotta was lost unless we placed it in heaping tablespoonfuls on top of the lasagna. Replacing the lid and letting the cheese warm through for several minutes was the final step for this super-easy one-pan dish. Meatloaf mix is a combination of ground beef, pork, and veal, sold prepackaged in many supermarkets. If it's unavailable, use ground beef. A skillet with a tight-fitting lid works best for this recipe. To make this dish a bit richer, sprinkle lasagna with additional shredded cheese, such as mozzarella or provolone, along with the Parmesan in step 4.

- 1 (28-ounce) can diced tomatoes
- 1 tablespoon extra-virgin olive oil
- 1 onion, chopped fine
- ½ teaspoon table salt
- 3 garlic cloves, minced
- ⅛ teaspoon red pepper flakes
- 1 pound meatloaf mix
- 10 curly-edged lasagna noodles, broken into 2-inch lengths
- 1 (8-ounce) can tomato sauce
- 1 ounce Parmesan cheese, grated (½ cup), plus 2 tablespoons grated, divided
- 8 ounces (1 cup) whole-milk ricotta cheese
- 3 tablespoons chopped fresh basil

1. Place tomatoes and their juice in 4-cup liquid measuring cup. Add water until mixture measures 4 cups.

2. Heat oil in 12-inch nonstick skillet over medium heat until shimmering. Add onion and salt and cook until onion begins to brown, about 5 minutes. Stir in garlic and pepper flakes and cook until fragrant, about 30 seconds. Add meatloaf mix and cook, breaking up meat into small pieces with wooden spoon, until it is no longer pink, about 4 minutes.

3. Scatter noodles over meat, but do not stir. Pour tomato mixture and tomato sauce over noodles, cover, and bring to simmer. Reduce heat to medium-low and simmer, stirring occasionally, until noodles are tender, about 20 minutes.

4. Off heat, stir in ½ cup Parmesan and season with salt and pepper to taste. Dollop heaping tablespoons of ricotta over top, cover, and let sit for 5 minutes. Sprinkle with basil and remaining 2 tablespoons Parmesan. Serve.

Vegetable Lasagna

Serves 8 to 10

WHY THIS RECIPE WORKS For a complex vegetable lasagna with bold flavor, we started with a summery mix of zucchini, yellow squash, and eggplant, salting and microwaving the eggplant and sautéing all of the vegetables to cut down on excess moisture and deepen their flavor. Garlic, spinach, and olives added textural contrast and flavor without much work. We dialed up the typical cheese filling by switching mild-mannered ricotta for tangy cottage cheese mixed with heavy cream for richness and Parmesan and garlic for added flavor. Our creamy, quick no-cook tomato sauce brought enough moisture to our lasagna that we found that we could skip the usual step of soaking the no-boil noodles before assembling the dish. Part-skim mozzarella can also be used in this recipe, but avoid preshredded cheese, as it does not melt well. We prefer kosher salt because it clings best to the eggplant. If using table salt, reduce salt amounts by half. To make assembly easier, the roasted vegetable filling can be made ahead and stored in the refrigerator for up to one day.

Tomato Sauce
- 1 (28-ounce) can crushed tomatoes
- ¼ cup finely chopped fresh basil
- 2 tablespoons extra-virgin olive oil
- 2 garlic cloves, minced
- 1 teaspoon kosher salt
- ¼ teaspoon red pepper flakes

Cream Sauce
- 8 ounces (1 cup) whole-milk cottage cheese
- 4 ounces Parmesan cheese, grated (2 cups)
- 1 cup heavy cream
- 2 garlic cloves, minced
- 1 teaspoon cornstarch
- ½ teaspoon kosher salt
- ½ teaspoon pepper

Vegetable Lasagna

Vegetable Filling

- 1½ pounds eggplant, peeled and cut into ½-inch pieces
- 1¼ teaspoons kosher salt, divided
- 1 pound zucchini, cut into ½-inch pieces
- 1 pound yellow summer squash, cut into ½-inch pieces
- 5 tablespoons plus 1 teaspoon extra-virgin olive oil, divided
- 4 garlic cloves, minced
- 1 tablespoon finely chopped fresh thyme
- ¼ teaspoon pepper
- 12 ounces (12 cups) baby spinach
- ½ cup pitted kalamata olives, minced, divided
- 12 ounces whole-milk mozzarella cheese, shredded (3 cups), divided

- 12 no-boil lasagna noodles
- 2 tablespoons finely chopped fresh basil

1. For the tomato sauce: Whisk all ingredients together in bowl; set aside.

2. For the cream sauce: Whisk all ingredients together in second bowl; set aside.

3. For the vegetable filling: Adjust oven rack to middle position and heat oven to 375 degrees. Toss eggplant with 1 teaspoon salt in large bowl. Line surface of large plate with double layer of coffee filters and lightly spray with vegetable oil spray. Spread eggplant in even layer over coffee filters; wipe out and reserve bowl. Microwave eggplant until dry to touch and slightly shriveled, about 10 minutes, tossing halfway through microwaving. Let cool slightly. Return eggplant to bowl and toss with zucchini and summer squash.

4. Combine 1 tablespoon oil, garlic, and thyme in small bowl. Heat 2 tablespoons oil in 12-inch nonstick skillet over medium-high heat until shimmering. Add half of eggplant mixture, remaining ¼ teaspoon salt, and pepper and cook, stirring occasionally, until vegetables are lightly browned, about 7 minutes. Push vegetables to sides of skillet. Add half of garlic mixture to center and cook, mashing mixture into pan, until fragrant, about 30 seconds. Stir garlic mixture into vegetables and transfer to medium bowl. Repeat with 2 tablespoons oil, remaining eggplant mixture, and remaining garlic mixture; transfer to bowl.

5. Heat remaining 1 teaspoon oil in now-empty skillet over medium-high heat until shimmering. Add spinach and cook, stirring frequently, until wilted, about 3 minutes. Transfer spinach to paper towel–lined plate and let drain for 2 minutes. Stir into eggplant mixture. (Filling can be refrigerated for up to 24 hours.)

6. Grease 13 by 9-inch baking dish. Spread 1 cup tomato sauce evenly over bottom of dish. Arrange 4 noodles on top of sauce (noodles will overlap). Spread half of vegetable mixture over noodles, followed by ¼ cup olives. Spoon half

of cream sauce over top and sprinkle with 1 cup mozzarella. Repeat layering with 4 noodles, 1 cup tomato sauce, remaining vegetable mixture, remaining ¼ cup olives, remaining cream sauce, and 1 cup mozzarella. For final layer, arrange remaining 4 noodles on top and cover noodles completely with remaining tomato sauce. Sprinkle remaining 1 cup mozzarella over top.

7. Cover dish tightly with greased aluminum foil and bake until edges are just bubbling, about 35 minutes, rotating dish halfway through baking. Let lasagna cool for 25 minutes, sprinkle with basil, and serve.

Potato Gnocchi with Browned Butter and Sage Sauce

Serves 4

WHY THIS RECIPE WORKS Good gnocchi with unmistakable potato flavor are something of a culinary paradox; light, airy pillows created from dense, starchy ingredients. Baking russets (parcooked in the microwave for speed and ease) produced intensely flavored potatoes—an excellent start to our gnocchi base. To avoid lumps, which can cause gnocchi to break apart during cooking, we turned to a ricer for a smooth, supple mash. While many recipes offer a range of how much flour to use, which ups the chances of overworking the dough (and producing leaden gnocchi), we used an exact amount based on a ratio of potato to flour that meant our gnocchi dough was mixed as little as possible. And we found that an egg, while not traditional, tenderized our gnocchi further, delivering delicate pillow-like dumplings. Gnocchi require accurate measurement to achieve the proper texture; it's best to weigh the potatoes and flour. After processing, you may have slightly more than the 3 cups (16 ounces) of potatoes required for this recipe; do not be tempted to use more than 3 cups. If you prefer, replace the browned butter sauce with Gorgonzola-Cream Sauce or Parmesan Sauce with Pancetta and Walnuts (recipes follow).

Potato Gnocchi

- 2 pounds russet potatoes
- 1 large egg, lightly beaten
- ¾ cup plus 1 tablespoon (4 ounces) all-purpose flour
- 1 teaspoon table salt, plus salt for cooking gnocchi

Browned Butter and Sage Sauce

- 4 tablespoons unsalted butter, cut into 4 pieces
- 1 small shallot, minced
- 1 teaspoon finely chopped fresh sage
- 1½ teaspoons lemon juice
- ¼ teaspoon table salt

1. For the gnocchi: Adjust oven rack to middle position and heat oven to 450 degrees. Poke each potato 8 times with paring knife over entire surface. Microwave potatoes until slightly softened at ends, about 10 minutes, flipping potatoes

through, about 1½ minutes (gnocchi should float to surface after about 1 minute). Using slotted spoon, transfer cooked gnocchi to skillet with sauce. Repeat with remaining gnocchi. Gently toss gnocchi with sauce and serve.

halfway through microwaving. Transfer potatoes directly to oven rack and bake until skewer glides easily through flesh and potatoes yield to gentle pressure, 18 to 20 minutes.

2. Holding each potato with potholder or dish towel, peel with paring knife. Process potatoes through ricer or food mill onto rimmed baking sheet. Gently spread potatoes into even layer on sheet and let cool for 5 minutes.

3. Transfer 3 cups (16 ounces) warm potatoes to bowl. Using fork, gently stir in egg until just combined. Sprinkle flour and 1 teaspoon salt over potato mixture. Using fork, gently combine until no pockets of dry flour remain. Press mixture into rough ball, transfer to lightly floured counter, and gently knead until smooth but slightly sticky, about 1 minute, lightly dusting counter with flour as needed to prevent sticking.

4. Line 2 rimmed baking sheets with parchment paper and dust liberally with flour. Cut dough into 8 pieces. Lightly dust counter with flour. Gently roll 1 piece of dough into ½-inch-thick rope, dusting with flour to prevent sticking. Cut rope into ¾-inch lengths. Holding fork with tines facing down in your hand, press each dough piece, cut side down, against tines with thumb of your other hand to create indentation. Roll dough down tines to form ridges on sides. If dough sticks, dust your thumb or fork with flour. Transfer formed gnocchi to prepared sheets and repeat with remaining dough.

5. *For the sauce:* Melt butter in 12-inch skillet over medium-high heat, swirling occasionally, until butter is browned and releases nutty aroma, about 1½ minutes. Off heat, add shallot and sage, stirring until shallot is fragrant, about 1 minute. Stir in lemon juice and salt; cover to keep warm.

6. Bring 4 quarts water to boil in large pot. Add 1 tablespoon salt. Using parchment, gently lower gnocchi from 1 sheet into water and cook until firm and just cooked

ACCOMPANIMENTS
Gorgonzola-Cream Sauce
Makes about 1 cup
Adjust the consistency of the sauce with up to 2 tablespoons cooking water before adding the gnocchi to it.

- ¾ cup heavy cream
- ¼ cup dry white wine
- 4 ounces Gorgonzola cheese, crumbled (about 1 cup)
- 2 tablespoons finely chopped fresh chives

Bring cream and wine to simmer in 12-inch skillet over medium-high heat. Gradually add Gorgonzola while whisking constantly and cook until melted and sauce is thickened, 2 to 3 minutes. Stir in chives and season with salt and pepper to taste. Off heat, cover to keep warm.

Parmesan Sauce with Pancetta and Walnuts
Makes about 1 cup
Serve gnocchi prepared with this sauce with extra grated Parmesan cheese on the side.

- ½ cup chicken broth
- 1 ounce Parmesan cheese, grated (½ cup)
- ¼ cup heavy cream
- 2 large egg yolks
- ⅛ teaspoon pepper
- 2 teaspoons extra-virgin olive oil
- 3 ounces pancetta, chopped fine
- ½ cup walnuts, chopped

Whisk broth, Parmesan, cream, yolks, and pepper together in bowl until smooth. Heat oil in 12-inch skillet over medium heat until shimmering. Add pancetta and cook until crisp, 5 to 7 minutes. Stir in walnuts and cook until golden and fragrant, about 1 minute. Off heat, gradually add broth mixture, whisking constantly. Return skillet to medium heat and cook, stirring often, until sauce is thickened slightly, 2 to 4 minutes. Season with salt to taste. Off heat, cover to keep warm.

Making Ridges on Gnocchi

To make ridges on gnocchi, hold fork with tines facing down. Press each dough piece (cut side down) against tines with your thumb to make indentation. Roll dough down tines to create ridges on sides.

Grown-Up Stovetop Macaroni and Cheese

Serves 4

WHY THIS RECIPE WORKS Inspired by an innovative macaroni and cheese recipe that calls for adding sodium citrate, an emulsifying salt, to cheese to keep it smooth when heated (instead of adding flour to make a béchamel), we based our sauce on American cheese, which contains a similar ingredient. Because American cheese has plenty of emulsifier but not a lot of flavor, we combined it with more-flavorful Gruyère and blue cheeses. A bit of mustard and cayenne pepper added piquancy. We cooked the macaroni in a smaller-than-usual amount of water (along with some milk), so we didn't have to drain it; the liquid that was left after the elbows were hydrated was just enough to form the base of the sauce. Rather than bake the mac and cheese, we sprinkled crunchy, cheesy toasted panko bread crumbs on top. Barilla makes our favorite elbow macaroni. Because the macaroni is cooked in a measured amount of liquid, we don't recommend using different shapes or sizes of pasta. Use a 4-ounce block of American cheese from the deli counter rather than presliced cheese.

1¾ cups water
1 cup milk
8 ounces elbow macaroni
4 ounces American cheese, shredded (1 cup)
½ teaspoon Dijon mustard
   Small pinch cayenne pepper
3½ ounces Gruyère cheese, shredded (¾ cup)
2 tablespoons crumbled blue cheese
⅓ cup panko bread crumbs
1 tablespoon extra-virgin olive oil
⅛ teaspoon table salt
⅛ teaspoon pepper
2 tablespoons grated Parmesan cheese

1. Bring water and milk to boil in medium saucepan over high heat. Stir in macaroni and reduce heat to medium-low. Cook, stirring frequently, until macaroni is soft (slightly past al dente), 6 to 8 minutes. Add American cheese, mustard, and cayenne and cook, stirring constantly, until cheese is completely melted, about 1 minute. Off heat, stir in Gruyère and blue cheese until evenly distributed but not melted. Cover saucepan and let sit for 5 minutes.

2. Meanwhile, combine panko, oil, salt, and pepper in 8-inch nonstick skillet until panko is evenly moistened. Cook over medium heat, stirring frequently, until evenly browned, 3 to 4 minutes. Off heat, sprinkle Parmesan over panko mixture and stir to combine. Transfer panko mixture to small bowl.

3. Stir macaroni until sauce is smooth (sauce may look loose but will thicken as it cools). Season with salt and pepper to taste. Transfer to warm serving dish and sprinkle panko mixture over top. Serve immediately.

Everyday Pad Thai

Serves 4

WHY THIS RECIPE WORKS To create a truly authentic version of pad thai with distinct sweet, sour, and salty flavors and a mix of textures, it is necessary to source hard-to-find ingredients like preserved daikon, palm sugar, and dried shrimp. We wanted a recipe that maintained the integrity of the dish while using accessible ingredients. Soaking rice noodles in boiling water softened them quickly, and a sauce of sugar, fish sauce, and tamarind concentrate (increasingly available in supermarkets) resulted in balanced flavor. Shrimp and egg bulked up the dish while bean sprouts, scallion greens, and peanuts added crunch. Finally, we pickled regular red radishes to use in place of hard-to-find preserved daikon, and we created our own faux dried shrimp by microwaving and then frying small pieces of fresh shrimp. Since pad thai cooks very quickly, prepare everything before you begin to cook. Use the time during which the radishes and noodles soak to prepare the other ingredients. We recommend using a tamarind juice concentrate made in Thailand in this recipe. If you cannot find tamarind, substitute 1½ tablespoons lime juice and 1½ tablespoons water and omit the lime wedges.

Chile Vinegar
⅓ cup distilled white vinegar
1 serrano chile, stemmed and sliced into thin rings

Stir-Fry
½ teaspoon plus ⅛ teaspoon table salt, divided
¼ teaspoon plus 3 tablespoons plus ⅛ teaspoon sugar, divided
2 radishes, trimmed and cut into 1½-inch by ¼-inch matchsticks
8 ounces (¼-inch-wide) rice noodles
3 tablespoons plus 2 teaspoons vegetable oil, divided

- ¼ cup fish sauce
- 3 tablespoons tamarind juice concentrate
- 1 pound large shrimp (26 to 30 per pound), peeled and deveined
- 4 scallions, white and light green parts minced, dark green parts cut into 1-inch lengths
- 1 garlic clove, minced
- 4 large eggs, beaten
- 4 ounces (2 cups) bean sprouts
- ¼ cup roasted unsalted peanuts, chopped
  Lime wedges

1. *For the chile vinegar:* Combine vinegar and chile in bowl and let sit at room temperature for at least 15 minutes.

2. *For the stir-fry:* Combine ¼ cup water, ½ teaspoon salt, and ¼ teaspoon sugar in small bowl. Microwave until steaming, about 30 seconds. Add radishes and let sit for 15 minutes. Drain and pat dry with paper towels.

3. Bring 6 cups water to boil. Place noodles in large bowl. Pour boiling water over noodles. Stir, then let soak until noodles are almost tender, about 8 minutes, stirring once halfway through soaking. Drain noodles and rinse with cold water. Drain noodles well, then toss with 2 teaspoons oil.

4. Combine fish sauce, tamarind concentrate, and 3 tablespoons sugar in bowl and whisk until sugar is dissolved; set aside.

5. Remove tails from 4 shrimp. Cut shrimp in half lengthwise, then cut each half into ½-inch pieces. Toss shrimp pieces with remaining ⅛ teaspoon salt and remaining ⅛ teaspoon sugar. Arrange pieces in single layer on large plate and microwave at 50 percent power until shrimp are dried and have reduced in size by half, 4 to 5 minutes. (Check halfway through microwaving and separate any pieces that may have stuck together.)

6. Heat 2 teaspoons oil in 12-inch nonstick skillet over medium heat until shimmering. Add dried shrimp and cook, stirring frequently, until golden brown and crispy, 3 to 5 minutes. Transfer to large bowl.

7. Heat 1 teaspoon oil in now-empty skillet over medium heat until shimmering. Add minced scallions and garlic and cook, stirring constantly, until garlic is golden brown, about 1 minute. Transfer to bowl with dried shrimp.

8. Heat 2 teaspoons oil in now-empty skillet over high heat until just smoking. Add remaining whole shrimp and spread into even layer. Cook, without stirring, until shrimp turn opaque and brown around edges, 2 to 3 minutes, flipping halfway through cooking. Push shrimp to sides of skillet. Add 2 teaspoons oil to center, then add eggs to center. Using rubber spatula, stir eggs gently and cook until set but still wet. Stir eggs into shrimp and continue to cook, breaking up large pieces of egg, until eggs are fully cooked, 30 to 60 seconds. Transfer shrimp-egg mixture to bowl with scallion-garlic mixture and dried shrimp.

9. Heat remaining 2 teaspoons oil in now-empty skillet over high heat until just smoking. Add noodles and sauce and toss with tongs to coat. Cook, stirring and tossing often, until noodles are tender and have absorbed sauce, 2 to 4 minutes. Transfer noodles to bowl with shrimp mixture. Add 2 teaspoons chile vinegar, drained radishes, scallion greens, and bean sprouts and toss to combine.

10. Transfer to platter and sprinkle with peanuts. Serve immediately, passing lime wedges and remaining chile vinegar separately.

Flat Hand-Pulled Noodles (Biang Biang Mian) with Chili Oil Vinaigrette

Serves 4

WHY THIS RECIPE WORKS Biang biang noodles are a popular dish from the Shaanxi province of China. They are handmade, flat, belt-like noodles often served with lots of hot peppers and chili oil in the cold winter months. The name describes the sound made when the noodles are slapped against a table to stretch them. To achieve the perfect chew and texture, we used high-protein bread flour and an extended resting time, which allowed the strong gluten network to relax and make the stretching process easier. We then dressed the noodles in a simple Sichuan-inspired chili oil vinaigrette. A sprinkle of fresh cilantro and scallions just before serving added a pop of freshness and burst of color. Bird chiles are dried red chiles, and are pretty spicy; scale back according to your taste. Black vinegar can be found at Asian markets or online. In step 1, you can mix the dough in a food processor instead of a stand mixer. Process the flour and salt in food processor until combined, about 2 seconds. With the processor running, add the water and oil and process until the dough forms a satiny ball that clears the sides of the workbowl, about 90 seconds. It is critical to rest the dough for at least 12 hours (and up to 48 hours). During this long rest, the gluten network becomes more extensible, making it easier to pull long, flat noodles by hand. Note that after 24 hours the surface of the dough may develop small black speckles. This oxidation has no impact on flavor or safety.

Dough
- 2⅓ cups (12¾ ounces) bread flour
- ¾ teaspoon table salt
- 1 cup (8 ounces) water
- 1 tablespoon vegetable oil

Flat Hand-Pulled Noodles
with Chili Oil Vinaigrette

Chili Oil Vinaigrette

10–20 bird chiles, ground fine
 ½ cup vegetable oil
 2 garlic cloves, sliced thin
 1 (1-inch) piece fresh ginger, peeled and
    sliced thin
 1 tablespoon Sichuan peppercorns
 ½ cinnamon stick
 1 star anise pod
 2 tablespoons soy sauce
 2 tablespoons black vinegar
 1 tablespoon toasted sesame oil
 1 teaspoon sugar

 Table salt for cooking noodles
12 fresh cilantro sprigs, trimmed and
    cut into 2-inch pieces
 6 scallions, sliced thin on bias

1. *For the dough:* Whisk flour and salt together in bowl of stand mixer. Add water and oil. Fit stand mixer with dough hook and mix on low speed until all flour is moistened, 1 to 2 minutes. Increase speed to medium and knead until dough is smooth and satiny, 10 to 12 minutes. (Alternatively, mix dough in food processor.) Transfer dough to counter, knead for 30 seconds, and shape into 9-inch log. Wrap log in plastic wrap and refrigerate for at least 12 hours or up to 48 hours.

2. *For the chili oil vinaigrette:* Place chiles in large heatproof bowl. Place fine-mesh strainer over bowl and set aside. Combine vegetable oil, garlic, ginger, peppercorns, cinnamon, and star anise pod in small saucepan and heat over medium-high heat until sizzling. Reduce heat to low and gently simmer until garlic and ginger are slightly browned, 10 to 12 minutes. Pour through strainer into bowl with chiles; discard solids in strainer. Stir chile oil to combine and let cool for 5 minutes. Stir in soy sauce, vinegar, sesame oil, and sugar until combined; set aside.

3. Unwrap dough, transfer to lightly oiled counter, and, using bench scraper or knife, divide into 6 equal pieces (each 1½ inches wide). Cover with plastic and let rest for 5 minutes. Meanwhile, bring 4 quarts water and 1 tablespoon salt to boil in large pot; reduce heat to low and cover to keep hot. Working with 1 piece at a time, oil both sides of dough and flatten into 7 by 3-inch rectangle, with long side parallel to edge of counter. With both hands, gently grasp short ends of dough. Stretch dough and slap against counter until noodle is 32 to 36 inches long (noodle will be between 1/16 and 1/8 inch thick). Place noodle on counter. Pinch center of noodle with forefingers and thumbs of both hands and pull apart with even pressure in both directions to rip seam in middle of noodle and create 1 continuous loop. Cut loop to create 2 equal-length noodles. Set noodles aside on lightly oiled counter (do not let noodles touch) and cover with plastic. Repeat stretching and cutting with remaining pieces of dough.

4. Return water to boil over high heat. Add half of noodles to water and cook, stirring occasionally, until noodles float and turn chewy-tender, 45 to 60 seconds. Using wire skimmer, transfer noodles to bowl with chili vinaigrette; toss to combine. Return water to boil and repeat with remaining noodles. Divide noodles among individual bowls, top with cilantro and scallions, and serve.

Pulling Flat Noodles By Hand

1. Flatten 1 piece of oiled dough into 7 by 3-inch rectangle, with long side parallel to edge of counter.

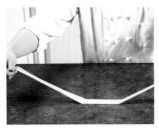

2. Gently grasp short ends of dough. Using quick repetitive flapping motion, stretch and slap center of dough strand against counter until noodle is 32 to 36 inches long.

3. Pinch center of noodle with forefingers and thumbs of both your hands and pull apart in both directions to create 1 continuous loop. Cut loop to create 2 equal-length noodles.

Steamed Chinese Dumplings (Shu Mai)

Makes about 40 dumplings

WHY THIS RECIPE WORKS Every so often we'll land on an exemplary version of *shu mai* (steamed Chinese dumplings)—one that boasts a tender, thin skin and a moist, flavorful filling. Our goal was to replicate this version at home. Our favorite restaurant dumplings rely on coarse-ground pork and shrimp. To ensure proper flavor and texture, we chose to chop the pork (boneless country-style spareribs) in a food processor rather than relying on supermarket ground pork, which is often inconsistent. To prevent the meat from drying out during steaming, we mixed in a little powdered gelatin dissolved in soy sauce. As for the shrimp, we added that to the food processor, too. Dried shiitake mushrooms, minced cilantro, fresh ginger, and water chestnuts were just a few of the ingredients we relied on to round out our flavorful filling.

We chose widely available egg roll skins and cut them into rounds with a biscuit cutter. Once we added the filling and gathered the edges of the wrappers up around each one, we steamed our dumplings in a steamer basket. Served with a hot chili oil, our dumplings were full-flavored and virtually foolproof. Do not trim the excess fat from the spareribs, as the fat contributes flavor and moistness. Use any size shrimp except popcorn shrimp; there's no need to halve shrimp smaller than 26 to 30 per pound before processing. The dumplings may be frozen for up to three months; cook straight from the freezer for about an extra 5 minutes. Shu mai are traditionally served with a spicy chili oil; you can make your own (recipe follows) or use store-bought.

2 tablespoons soy sauce
½ teaspoon unflavored gelatin
1 pound boneless country-style pork ribs, cut into 1-inch pieces, divided
8 ounces shrimp, peeled and deveined, tails removed, halved lengthwise
¼ cup chopped water chestnuts
4 dried shiitake mushroom caps (¾ ounce), soaked in hot water for 30 minutes, squeezed dry, and chopped fine
2 tablespoons cornstarch
2 tablespoons finely chopped fresh cilantro
1 tablespoon toasted sesame oil
1 tablespoon Chinese rice wine or dry sherry
1 tablespoon rice vinegar
2 teaspoons sugar
2 teaspoons grated fresh ginger
½ teaspoon table salt
½ teaspoon pepper
1 (1-pound) package 5½-inch-square egg roll wrappers
¼ cup finely grated carrot (optional)

1. Combine soy sauce and gelatin in small bowl. Set aside to allow gelatin to bloom, about 5 minutes.

2. Meanwhile, pulse half of pork in food processor until coarsely ground into ⅛-inch pieces, about 10 pulses; transfer to large bowl. Add shrimp and remaining pork to food processor and pulse until coarsely chopped into ¼-inch pieces, about 5 pulses. Add to finely ground pork. Stir in soy sauce mixture, water chestnuts, mushrooms, cornstarch, cilantro, sesame oil, rice wine, vinegar, sugar, ginger, salt, and pepper.

3. Divide egg roll wrappers into 3 stacks. Using 3-inch biscuit cutter, cut two rounds from each stack. Cover with moist paper towels to prevent drying.

4. Working with 6 rounds at a time, brush edges of each round lightly with water. Place heaping tablespoon of filling in center of each round. Form dumplings by pinching opposing sides of wrapper with your fingers until you have 8 equidistant pinches. Gather up sides of dumpling and squeeze gently to create "waist." Hold dumpling in your hand and gently but

firmly pack down filling with butter knife. Transfer to parchment paper–lined baking sheet, cover with damp dish towel, and repeat with remaining wrappers and filling. Top center of each dumpling with pinch of grated carrot, if using.

5. Cut piece of parchment paper slightly smaller than diameter of steamer basket and place in basket. Poke about 20 small holes in parchment and lightly coat with vegetable oil spray. Place batches of dumplings on parchment, making sure they are not touching. Set steamer over simmering water and cook, covered, until no longer pink, 8 to 10 minutes. Serve immediately.

ACCOMPANIMENT
Chili Oil
Makes about ½ cup

1 tablespoon soy sauce
2 teaspoons sugar
½ teaspoon table salt
½ cup peanut oil
¼ cup red pepper flakes
2 garlic cloves, peeled

Combine soy sauce, sugar, and salt in small bowl; set aside. Heat oil in small saucepan over medium heat until just shimmering and it registers 300 degrees. Off heat, stir in pepper flakes, garlic, and soy mixture. Let cool to room temperature, stirring occasionally, about 1 hour. Discard garlic before storing.

Filling and Forming Shu Mai

1. Brush edges of dumpling wrapper lightly with water. Place heaping tablespoon of filling in center of each wrapper.

2. Pinch 2 opposing sides of wrapper with your fingers. Rotate dumpling 90 degrees; repeat pinching. Continue until you have 8 equidistant pinches around circumference of dumpling.

3. Gather up sides of dumpling and squeeze gently at top to create "waist." Holding dumpling in your hand, gently but firmly pack filling into dumpling with butter knife.

"Homemade dumplings can feel like a lot of work. The skins, the folding, the stuffing—sometimes the payoff isn't worth the effort. Not with these shu mai. These don't require advanced folding techniques, which makes them perfect for beginners. But what makes them really special is the filling. Instead of starting with supermarket ground pork, we grind country-style pork ribs, which are more flavorful. We also add a mixture of gelatin and cornstarch to ensure that the filling stays moist and tender."

—*Keith*

Grilling

Grill-Smoked Herb-Rubbed Flat-Iron Steaks

Grilled Glazed Boneless, Skinless Chicken Breasts

Serves 4

WHY THIS RECIPE WORKS Grilled glazed boneless chicken breasts are a quick and easy summer dinner, but too often the glaze burns or the chicken overcooks. To produce perfectly cooked chicken, we briefly brined the meat to keep it moist during cooking, and used a two-level grill fire to prevent the glaze from singeing. Lightly coating the chicken with milk powder hastened browning during the quick cooking time. We developed a variety of sweet-savory glazes that complemented but didn't overpower the chicken. A small amount of corn syrup provided a mild sweetness and just enough viscosity to help the glaze cling to the meat.

- ¼ cup table salt, for brining
- ¼ cup sugar, for brining
- 4 (6- to 8-ounce) boneless, skinless chicken breasts, trimmed
- 2 teaspoons nonfat dry milk powder
- ¼ teaspoon pepper
  Vegetable oil spray
- 1 recipe glaze (recipes follow)

1. Dissolve salt and sugar in 1½ quarts cold water. Submerge chicken in brine, cover, and refrigerate for at least 30 minutes or up to 1 hour. Remove chicken from brine and pat dry with paper towels. Combine milk powder and pepper in bowl.

2A. *For a charcoal grill:* Open bottom vent completely. Light large chimney starter mounded with charcoal briquettes (7 quarts). When top coals are partially covered with ash, pour two-thirds evenly over half of grill, then pour remaining coals over other half of grill. Set cooking grate in place, cover, and open lid vent completely. Heat grill until hot, about 5 minutes.

2B. *For a gas grill:* Turn all burners to high, cover, and heat grill until hot, about 15 minutes. Leave primary burner on high and turn other burner(s) to medium-high.

3. Clean and oil cooking grate. Sprinkle half of milk powder mixture over 1 side of chicken. Lightly spray coated side of chicken with oil spray until milk powder is moistened. Flip chicken and sprinkle remaining milk powder mixture over second side. Lightly spray with oil spray.

4. Place chicken, skinned side down, on hotter side of grill and cook until browned on first side, 2 to 2½ minutes. Flip chicken, brush with 2 tablespoons glaze, and cook until browned on second side, 2 to 2½ minutes. Flip chicken, move to cooler side of grill, brush with 2 tablespoons glaze, and cook for 2 minutes. Repeat flipping and brushing 2 more times, cooking for 2 minutes on each side. Flip chicken, brush with remaining glaze, and cook until chicken registers 160 degrees, 1 to 3 minutes. Transfer chicken to plate and let rest for 5 minutes before serving.

Spicy Hoisin Glaze
Makes about ⅔ cup
For a spicier glaze use the larger amount of sriracha.

- 2 tablespoons rice vinegar
- 1 teaspoon cornstarch
- ⅓ cup hoisin sauce
- 2 tablespoons light corn syrup
- 1–2 tablespoons sriracha
- 1 teaspoon grated fresh ginger
- ¼ teaspoon five-spice powder

Whisk vinegar and cornstarch together in small saucepan until cornstarch has dissolved. Whisk in hoisin, corn syrup, sriracha, ginger, and five-spice powder. Bring mixture to boil over high heat. Cook, stirring constantly, until thickened, about 1 minute. Transfer glaze to bowl.

Honey-Mustard Glaze
Makes about ⅔ cup

- 2 tablespoons cider vinegar
- 1 teaspoon cornstarch
- 3 tablespoons Dijon mustard
- 3 tablespoons honey
- 2 tablespoons corn syrup
- 1 garlic clove, minced
- ¼ teaspoon ground fennel seeds

Whisk vinegar and cornstarch together in small saucepan until cornstarch has dissolved. Whisk in mustard, honey, corn syrup, garlic, and fennel seeds. Bring mixture to boil over high heat. Cook, stirring constantly, until thickened, about 1 minute. Transfer glaze to bowl.

Coconut-Curry Glaze
Makes about ⅔ cup

- 2 tablespoons lime juice
- 1½ teaspoons cornstarch
- ⅓ cup canned coconut milk
- 3 tablespoons corn syrup
- 1 tablespoon fish sauce
- 1 tablespoon red curry paste
- 1 teaspoon grated fresh ginger
- ¼ teaspoon ground coriander

Whisk lime juice and cornstarch together in small saucepan until cornstarch has dissolved. Whisk in coconut milk, corn syrup, fish sauce, curry paste, ginger, and coriander. Bring mixture to boil over high heat. Cook, stirring constantly, until thickened, about 1 minute. Transfer glaze to bowl.

Miso-Sesame Glaze
Makes about ⅔ cup

- 3 tablespoons rice vinegar
- 1 teaspoon cornstarch
- 3 tablespoons white miso paste
- 2 tablespoons corn syrup
- 1 tablespoon sesame oil
- 2 teaspoons ground ginger
- ¼ teaspoon ground coriander

Whisk vinegar and cornstarch together in small saucepan until cornstarch has dissolved. Whisk in miso, corn syrup, sesame oil, ginger, and coriander. Bring mixture to boil over high heat. Cook, stirring constantly, until thickened, about 1 minute. Transfer glaze to bowl.

Grilled Chicken Souvlaki

Serves 4

WHY THIS RECIPE WORKS Souvlaki is basically a Greek term for meat grilled on a stick. In modern Greece, souvlaki is usually made with pork, but at Greek restaurants here in the United States, boneless, skinless chicken breast is common. The chunks of white meat are marinated in a tangy mixture of lemon juice, olive oil, oregano, parsley, and garlic before being skewered and grilled until charred. The chicken is often placed on a lightly grilled pita, slathered with a yogurt-based tzatziki sauce, wrapped snugly, and eaten out of hand. At least as appealing as the dish itself is how easily it translates to a home grill. The ingredients are readily available, and small chunks of boneless chicken cook quickly, making souvlaki a prime candidate for weeknight fare. Instead of a long marinating time, which made the meat mushy and didn't add much flavor, we brined the chicken for a mere 30 minutes and then tossed it with olive oil, lemon juice, dried oregano, parsley, black pepper, and honey. The honey added complexity and encouraged browning. We also reserved a bit of the mixture to season the meat after cooking. We found that the meat on the outside of the skewers cooked faster than the chunks in the middle, so we made "shields" by threading bell peppers and onions onto the ends of the skewers. For soft pita, we wrapped a stack of four pitas tightly in foil after moistening the top and bottom surfaces of the stack with water. They steamed and softened while the chicken cooked. Topped with a cool, creamy tzatziki, our chicken souvlaki makes a perfect summer dinner. This tzatziki is fairly mild; for a more assertive flavor, double the garlic. A rasp-style grater makes quick work of turning the garlic into a paste. We like the chicken as a wrap, but you may skip the pita and serve the chicken, vegetables, and tzatziki with rice. You will need four 12-inch metal skewers.

Tzatziki Sauce
- 1 tablespoon lemon juice
- 1 small garlic clove, minced to paste
- ¾ cup plain Greek yogurt
- ½ cucumber, peeled, halved lengthwise, seeded, and diced fine (½ cup)
- 3 tablespoons finely chopped fresh mint
- 1 tablespoon finely chopped fresh parsley
- ⅜ teaspoon table salt

Chicken
- 2 tablespoons table salt, for brining
- 1½ pounds boneless, skinless chicken breasts, trimmed and cut into 1-inch pieces
- ⅓ cup extra-virgin olive oil
- 2 tablespoons finely chopped fresh parsley
- 1 teaspoon lemon zest plus ¼ cup juice (2 lemons)
- 1 teaspoon honey
- 1 teaspoon dried oregano
- ½ teaspoon pepper
- 1 green bell pepper, quartered, stemmed, and seeded, each quarter cut into 4 pieces
- 1 small red onion, ends trimmed, peeled, and halved lengthwise, each half cut into 4 pieces
- 4 (8-inch) pita breads

1. *For the tzatziki sauce:* Whisk lemon juice and garlic together in small bowl. Let sit for 10 minutes. Stir in yogurt, cucumber, mint, parsley, and salt. Cover and set aside.

2. *For the chicken:* Dissolve salt in 1 quart cold water. Submerge chicken in brine, cover, and refrigerate for 30 minutes. While chicken is brining, combine oil, parsley, lemon zest and juice, honey, oregano, and pepper in medium bowl. Transfer ¼ cup oil mixture to large bowl and set aside to toss with cooked chicken.

3. Remove chicken from brine and pat dry with paper towels. Toss chicken with remaining oil mixture. Thread 4 pieces of bell pepper, concave side up, onto one 12-inch metal skewer. Thread one-quarter of chicken onto skewer. Thread 2 pieces of onion onto skewer, and place skewer on plate. Repeat skewering remaining chicken and vegetables on 3 more skewers. Lightly moisten 2 pita breads with water. Sandwich 2 unmoistened pita breads between moistened pita breads and wrap stack tightly in lightly greased heavy-duty aluminum foil.

4A. *For a charcoal grill:* Open bottom vent completely. Light large chimney starter mounded with charcoal briquettes (7 quarts). When top coals are partially covered with ash, pour evenly over half of grill. Set cooking grate in place, cover, and open lid vent completely. Heat grill until hot, about 5 minutes.

4B. *For a gas grill:* Turn all burners to high, cover, and heat grill until hot, about 15 minutes. Leave primary burner on high and turn off other burner(s).

5. Clean and oil cooking grate. Place skewers on hotter side of grill and cook, turning occasionally, until chicken and vegetables are well browned on all sides and chicken registers 160 degrees, 15 to 20 minutes. Using fork, push chicken and vegetables off skewers into bowl of reserved oil mixture. Stir gently, breaking up onion pieces; cover with foil and let sit for 5 minutes.

6. Meanwhile, place packet of pitas on cooler side of grill. Flip occasionally to heat, about 5 minutes.

7. Lay each warm pita on 12-inch square of foil. Spread each pita with 2 tablespoons tzatziki. Place one-quarter of chicken and vegetables in middle of each pita. Roll into cylindrical shape and serve.

Charcoal-Grilled Barbecued Chicken Kebabs

SEASON 20 RECIPE

Serves 6

WHY THIS RECIPE WORKS In theory, barbecued chicken kebabs sound pretty great: char-streaked chunks of juicy meat lacquered with sweet and tangy barbecue sauce. But without an insulating layer of skin, even the fattiest thigh meat can dry out and toughen when exposed to the blazing heat of the grill—and forget about ultralean skinless breast meat. Our goal was simple: juicy, tender chicken with plenty of sticky-sweet, smoke-tinged flavor. Brining is one common way to safeguard against dry meat, but in this case the brine made the meat so slick that the barbecue sauce refused to stick.

A salt rub worked much better; the rub crisped up on the chicken's exterior as it cooked, forming a craggy surface that the sauce could really cling to. For incredible depth of flavor as well as juicy meat, we turned to an unusual technique: grinding bacon to a paste and applying it to the salted meat. Combined with both sweet and smoked paprika and a little sugar, our bacony rub created chicken that was juicy, tender, and full-flavored, with a smoky depth that complemented the barbecue sauce. We prefer flavorful thigh meat for these kebabs, but you can use white meat. Whichever you choose, don't mix white and dark meat on the same skewer since they cook at different rates. If you have thin pieces of chicken, cut them larger than 1 inch and roll or fold them into approximately 1-inch cubes. Use the large holes on a box grater to grate the onion.

Sauce

- ½ cup ketchup
- ¼ cup light or mild molasses
- 2 tablespoons grated onion
- 2 tablespoons Worcestershire sauce
- 2 tablespoons Dijon mustard
- 2 tablespoons cider vinegar
- 1 tablespoon packed light brown sugar

Kebabs

- 2 pounds boneless, skinless chicken thighs or breasts, trimmed and cut into 1-inch cubes
- 2 teaspoons kosher salt
- 2 tablespoons sweet paprika
- 4 teaspoons sugar
- 2 teaspoons smoked paprika
- 2 slices bacon, cut into ½-inch pieces
- 4 12-inch metal skewers

1. *For the sauce:* Bring all ingredients to simmer in small saucepan over medium heat; cook, stirring occasionally, until sauce reaches ketchup-like consistency and is reduced to about 1 cup, 5 to 7 minutes. Transfer ½ cup sauce to small bowl and set aside remaining sauce to serve with cooked chicken.

2. *For the kebabs:* Toss chicken and salt in large bowl; cover with plastic wrap and refrigerate for at least 30 minutes and up to 1 hour.

3. Open bottom vent completely. Light large chimney starter three-quarters filled with charcoal (4½ quarts). When top coals are partially covered with ash, pour evenly over half of grill. Set cooking grate in place, cover, and open lid vent completely. Heat grill until hot, about 5 minutes.

4. While grill heats, pat chicken dry with paper towels. Combine sweet paprika, sugar, and smoked paprika in small bowl. Process bacon in food processor until smooth paste forms, 30 to 45 seconds, scraping down bowl twice during

Charcoal-Grilled Barbecued
Chicken Kebabs

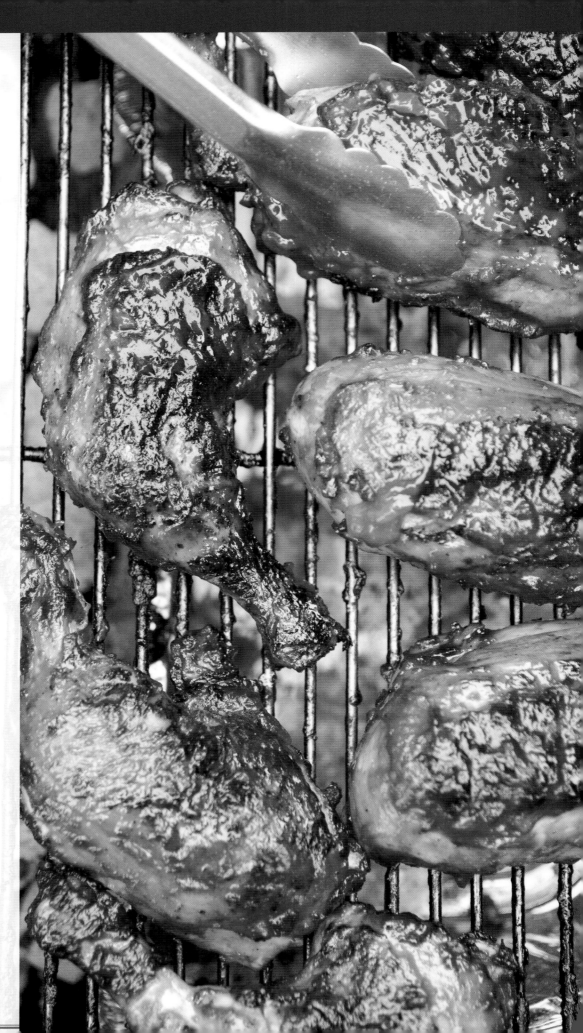

"*Before starting at ATK, I'd grilled three things: hot dogs, hamburgers, and buns. It wasn't until I started working on this recipe that I learned how much you can do with a grill. What was the breakthrough moment? The grill setup. Whether you're cooking with charcoal or gas, concentrate the heat on one side to create two cooking zones. Over the flames, food sears quickly and picks up that tantalizing grill flavor. Over the cooler side, it cooks gently and evenly. If you've ever had trouble with burnt exteriors and undercooked interiors give this setup a try.*"

–Lan

processing. Add bacon paste and spice mixture to chicken; mix with hands or rubber spatula until ingredients are thoroughly blended and chicken is completely coated. Thread meat onto skewers, rolling or folding meat as necessary to maintain 1-inch cubes.

5. Clean and oil cooking grate. Place kebabs over coals and cook, turning one-quarter turn every 2 to 2½ minutes until well browned and slightly charred, 8 minutes for breasts or 10 minutes for thighs. (If flare-ups occur, slide kebabs to cool side of grill until fire dies down.) Brush top surface of kebabs with ¼ cup sauce; flip and cook until sauce is brown in spots, about 1 minute. Brush second side with remaining ¼ cup sauce; flip and continue to cook until brown in spots and breasts register 160 degrees or thighs register 175 degrees, about 1 minute. Remove kebabs from grill and let rest for 5 minutes. Serve, passing reserved barbecue sauce separately.

Sweet and Tangy Barbecued Chicken

Serves 6 to 8

WHY THIS RECIPE WORKS To produce juicy, evenly cooked chicken parts on the grill, indirect cooking is key, as it provides a hotter side for briefly searing the parts and a cooler side for them to cook through gently. We lined up the fattier leg quarters closer to the coals and the leaner white meat farther from the heat, as well as adding a water pan underneath the cooler side, to help the dark and white pieces cook slowly and evenly. Applying a simple spice rub deeply seasoned the meat, and the salt in it helped retain moisture, while brushing on a homemade sauce in stages allowed it to cling nicely to the skin and also develop layers of tangy-sweet flavor. When browning the chicken over the hotter side of the grill, move it away from any flare-ups. Try to select similar-size chicken parts for even cooking.

Chicken

- 2 tablespoons packed dark brown sugar
- 1½ tablespoons kosher salt
- 1½ teaspoons onion powder
- 1½ teaspoons garlic powder
- 1½ teaspoons paprika
- ¼ teaspoon cayenne pepper
- 6 pounds bone-in chicken pieces (split breasts and/or leg quarters), trimmed

Sauce

- 1 cup ketchup
- 5 tablespoons molasses
- 3 tablespoons cider vinegar
- 2 tablespoons Worcestershire sauce
- 2 tablespoons Dijon mustard
- ¼ teaspoon pepper
- 2 tablespoons vegetable oil

- ⅓ cup grated onion
- 1 garlic clove, minced
- 1 teaspoon chili powder
- ¼ teaspoon cayenne pepper
- 1 large disposable aluminum roasting pan (if using charcoal) or 2 disposable aluminum pie plates (if using gas)

1. *For the chicken:* Combine sugar, salt, onion powder, garlic powder, paprika, and cayenne in bowl. Arrange chicken on rimmed baking sheet and sprinkle both sides evenly with spice rub. Cover with plastic wrap and refrigerate for at least 6 hours or up to 24 hours.

2. *For the sauce:* Whisk ketchup, molasses, vinegar, Worcestershire, mustard, and pepper together in bowl. Heat oil in medium saucepan over medium heat until shimmering. Add onion and garlic; cook until onion is softened, 2 to 4 minutes. Add chili powder and cayenne and cook until fragrant, about 30 seconds. Whisk in ketchup mixture and bring to boil. Reduce heat to medium-low and simmer gently for 5 minutes. Set aside ⅔ cup sauce to baste chicken and reserve remaining sauce for serving. (Sauce can be refrigerated for up to 1 week.)

3A. *For a charcoal grill:* Open bottom vent halfway and place disposable pan filled with 3 cups water on 1 side of grill. Light large chimney starter filled with charcoal briquettes (6 quarts). When top coals are partially covered with ash, pour evenly over other half of grill (opposite disposable pan). Set cooking grate in place, cover, and open lid vent halfway. Heat grill until hot, about 5 minutes.

3B. *For a gas grill:* Place 2 disposable pie plates, each filled with 1½ cups water, directly on 1 burner of gas grill (opposite primary burner). Turn all burners to high, cover, and heat grill until hot, about 15 minutes. Turn primary burner to medium-high and turn off other burner(s). (Adjust primary burner as needed to maintain grill temperature of 325 to 350 degrees.)

4. Clean and oil cooking grate. Place chicken, skin side down, over hotter part of grill and cook until browned and blistered in spots, 2 to 5 minutes. Flip chicken and cook until second side is browned, 4 to 6 minutes. Move chicken to cooler side of grill and brush both sides of chicken with ⅓ cup sauce. Arrange chicken, skin side up, with leg quarters closest to fire and breasts farthest away. Cover (positioning lid vent over chicken if using charcoal) and cook for 25 minutes.

5. Brush both sides of chicken with remaining ⅓ cup sauce and continue to cook, covered, until breasts register 160 degrees and leg quarters register 175 degrees, 25 to 35 minutes.

6. Transfer chicken to serving platter, tent with aluminum foil, and let rest for 10 minutes. Serve, passing reserved sauce separately.

Barbecued Pulled Chicken

Serves 6 to 8

WHY THIS RECIPE WORKS This recipe takes pulled chicken sandwiches seriously—using tender, smoky meat pulled off the bone in moist, soft shreds and then tossed with a tangy, sweet sauce—and it doesn't take all day to make them. We chose whole chicken legs for great flavor, low cost, and resistance to overcooking. The legs cooked gently but thoroughly over indirect heat, absorbing plenty of smoke flavor along the way. Cooking the chicken to a higher-than-usual temperature also dissolved connective tissue and rendered more fat, making the meat tender and less greasy. Once the chicken finished cooking, we hand-shredded half and machine-processed the other half to produce the perfect texture—one similar to pulled pork. The chicken then just had to be combined with a thin but tangy barbecue sauce to become truly bun-worthy. Chicken leg quarters consist of drumsticks attached to thighs; often also attached are backbone sections that must be trimmed away. If you'd like to use wood chunks instead of wood chips when using a charcoal grill, substitute two medium wood chunks, soaked in water for 1 hour, for the wood chip packets. Serve the pulled chicken on hamburger rolls or sandwich bread, with pickles and coleslaw.

Chicken

    2 cups wood chips, soaked in water for
       15 minutes and drained
    1 (16 by 12-inch) disposable aluminum
       roasting pan (if using charcoal)
    1 tablespoon vegetable oil
    8 (14-ounce) chicken leg quarters, trimmed
 3½ teaspoons table salt
 1¾ teaspoons pepper

Sauce

    1 large onion, peeled and quartered
   ¼ cup water
 1½ cups ketchup
 1½ cups apple cider
   ¼ cup molasses
   ¼ cup apple cider vinegar, divided
    3 tablespoons Worcestershire sauce
    3 tablespoons Dijon mustard
   ½ teaspoon pepper
    1 tablespoon vegetable oil
 1½ tablespoons chili powder
    2 garlic cloves, minced
   ½ teaspoon cayenne pepper
       Hot sauce

1. For the chicken: Using large piece of heavy-duty aluminum foil, wrap soaked chips in 8 by 4½-inch foil packet. (Make sure chips do not poke holes in sides or bottom of packet.) Cut 2 evenly spaced 2-inch slits in top of packet.

2A. For a charcoal grill: Open bottom vent halfway and place roasting pan in center of grill. Light large chimney starter three-quarters filled with charcoal briquettes (4½ quarts). When top coals are partially covered with ash, pour into 2 even piles on either side of roasting pan. Place wood chip packet on 1 pile of coals. Set cooking grate in place, cover, and open lid vent halfway. Heat grill until hot and wood chips are smoking, about 5 minutes.

2B. For a gas grill: Place wood chip packet directly on primary burner. Turn all burners to high, cover, and heat grill until hot and wood chips are smoking, about 15 minutes. Turn all burners to medium. (Adjust burners as needed during cooking to maintain grill temperature between 250 and 300 degrees.)

3. Clean and oil cooking grate. Pat chicken dry with paper towels and season with salt and pepper. Place chicken in single layer on center of grill (over roasting pan if using charcoal), skin side up, or evenly over grill (if using gas). Cover (position lid vent over meat if using charcoal) and cook until chicken registers 185 degrees, 1 to 1½ hours, rotating chicken pieces halfway through cooking. Transfer chicken to cutting board, tent with foil, and let rest until cool enough to handle.

4. For the sauce: Meanwhile, process onion and water in food processor until mixture resembles slush, about 30 seconds. Pass through fine-mesh strainer into liquid measuring cup, pressing on solids with rubber spatula (you should have ¾ cup strained onion juice). Discard solids.

5. Whisk onion juice, ketchup, cider, molasses, 3 tablespoons vinegar, Worcestershire, mustard, and pepper together in bowl. Heat oil in large saucepan over medium heat until shimmering. Stir in chili powder, garlic, and cayenne and cook until fragrant, about 30 seconds. Stir in ketchup mixture, bring to simmer, and cook over medium-low heat until slightly thickened, about 15 minutes (you should have about 4 cups of sauce). Transfer 2 cups sauce to serving bowl; leave remaining sauce in saucepan.

6. To serve: Remove and discard skin from chicken legs. Using your fingers, pull meat off bones, separating larger pieces (which should fall off bones easily) from smaller, drier pieces into 2 equal piles.

7. Pulse smaller chicken pieces in food processor until just coarsely chopped, 3 or 4 pulses, stirring chicken with rubber spatula after each pulse. Add chopped chicken to sauce in saucepan. Using your fingers or 2 forks, pull larger chicken pieces into long shreds and add to saucepan. Stir in remaining 1 tablespoon vinegar, cover, and heat chicken over medium-low heat, stirring occasionally, until heated through, about 10 minutes. Add hot sauce to taste, and serve, passing remaining sauce separately.

VARIATION
Barbecued Pulled Chicken for a Crowd
Serves 10 to 12
This technique works well on a charcoal grill but not so well on a gas grill. If your gas grill is large and can accommodate more than eight legs, follow the master recipe, adding as many legs as will comfortably fit in a single layer.

Increase amount of charcoal briquettes to 6 quarts. Use 12 chicken legs and slot them into V-shaped roasting rack set on top of cooking grate over disposable aluminum pan. Increase cooking time in step 3 to 1½ to 1¾ hours. In step 5, remove only 1 cup of sauce from saucepan. In step 7, pulse chicken in food processor in 2 batches.

Smoked Chicken

Serves 6 to 8

WHY THIS RECIPE WORKS Smoked chicken needs to be cooked for a long time to be imbued with smoke flavor, but the meat dries out easily. We wanted perfectly cooked meat with a pervasive smoky flavor and crisp skin. A salt and sugar brine guaranteed moist, well-seasoned meat. Chicken parts were easier than whole chickens; the breasts could cook evenly on the coolest part of the grill and more of the bird was exposed to the smoke and heat, adding flavor and rendering more fat from the skin. To keep the skin moist, we brushed it with oil and added a pan of water to the grill. Two wood chip packets produced the ideal amount of smoke. If using kosher chicken, do not brine in step 1. If you'd like to use wood chunks instead of wood chips when using a charcoal grill, substitute two medium wood chunks, soaked in water for 1 hour, for the wood chip packets.

1 cup table salt, for brining
1 cup sugar, for brining
6 pounds bone-in chicken parts (breasts, thighs, and/or drumsticks), trimmed
3 tablespoons vegetable oil
1½ teaspoons pepper
3 cups wood chips (1½ cups soaked in water for 15 minutes and drained plus 1½ cups unsoaked)
1 (16 by 12-inch) disposable aluminum roasting pan (if using charcoal) or 1 disposable aluminum pie plate (if using gas)

1. Dissolve salt and sugar in 4 quarts cold water in large container. Submerge chicken pieces in brine, cover, and refrigerate for 30 minutes to 1 hour. Remove chicken from brine and pat dry with paper towels. Brush chicken evenly with oil and season with pepper.

2. Using large piece of heavy-duty aluminum foil, wrap soaked chips in 8 by 4½-inch foil packet. (Make sure chips do not poke holes in sides or bottom of packet.) Cut 2 evenly spaced 2-inch slits in top of packet. Repeat with another sheet of foil and unsoaked wood chips.

3A. For a charcoal grill: Open bottom vent halfway. Arrange 2 quarts unlit charcoal banked against 1 side of grill and disposable pan filled with 2 cups water on empty side of grill. Light large chimney starter half filled with charcoal briquettes (3 quarts). When top coals are partially covered with ash, pour on top of unlit charcoal, to cover one-third of grill with coals steeply banked against side of grill. Place wood chip packets on top of coals. Set cooking grate in place, cover, and open lid vent halfway. Heat grill until hot and wood chips begin to smoke, about 5 minutes.

3B. *For a gas grill:* Place wood chip packets directly on primary burner. Place disposable pie plate filled with 2 cups water on other burner(s). Turn all burners to high, cover, and heat grill until hot and wood chips begin to smoke, about 15 minutes. Turn primary burner to medium-high and turn off other burner(s). (Adjust primary burner as needed to maintain grill temperature around 325 degrees.)

4. Clean and oil cooking grate. Place chicken on cool side of grill, skin side up, as far away from heat as possible with thighs closest to heat and breasts farthest away. Cover (positioning lid vent over chicken if using charcoal) and cook until breasts register 160 degrees and thighs/drumsticks register 175 degrees, 1¼ to 1½ hours.

5. Transfer chicken to serving platter, tent with foil, and let rest for 5 to 10 minutes before serving.

Peri Peri Grilled Chicken

Serves 6 to 8

WHY THIS RECIPE WORKS To bring this bold African chicken dish home, we started with a spice paste. We first blended garlic, shallot, bay leaves, lemon zest and juice, and pepper. Five-spice powder and tomato paste promised complexity, depth, and richness. Fruity-tasting arbol chiles, along with some cayenne pepper, replaced hard-to-find peri peri peppers. We tossed chicken pieces in the mixture along with chopped peanuts and let it sit overnight. The paste seasoned the meat and helped it stay juicy when cooked. We set up the grill with a cooler side and a hotter side, as well as a pan of water to help regulate the temperature. After rendering and charring the skin on the hotter side of the grill, we finished cooking the chicken on the cooler side. This recipe requires refrigerating the spice paste–coated chicken for at least 6 hours or up to 24 hours prior to cooking. When browning the chicken over the hotter side of the grill, move it away from the direct heat if any flare-ups occur. Serve with white rice.

4–10 arbol chiles, stemmed
   3 tablespoons extra-virgin olive oil
   2 tablespoons table salt
   8 garlic cloves, peeled
   2 tablespoons tomato paste
   1 shallot, chopped
   1 tablespoon sugar
   1 tablespoon paprika
   1 tablespoon five-spice powder
   2 teaspoons grated lemon zest plus
     ¼ cup juice (2 lemons), plus lemon
     wedges for serving

   1 teaspoon pepper
  ½ teaspoon cayenne pepper
   3 bay leaves, crushed
   6 pounds bone-in chicken pieces (breasts, thighs, and/or drumsticks), trimmed
  ½ cup dry-roasted peanuts, chopped fine
   1 (13 by 9-inch) disposable aluminum pan (if using charcoal) or 2 (9-inch) disposable aluminum pie plates (if using gas)

1. Process 4 arbols, oil, salt, garlic, tomato paste, shallot, sugar, paprika, five-spice powder, lemon zest and juice, pepper, cayenne, and bay leaves in blender until smooth, 10 to 20 seconds. Taste paste and add up to 6 additional arbols, depending on desired level of heat (spice paste should be slightly hotter than desired heat level of cooked chicken), and process until smooth. Using metal skewer, poke skin side of each chicken piece 8 to 10 times. Place chicken pieces, peanuts, and spice paste in large bowl or container and toss until chicken is evenly coated. Cover and refrigerate for at least 6 hours or up to 24 hours.

2A. *For a charcoal grill:* Open bottom vent halfway and place disposable pan filled with 3 cups water on 1 side of grill. Light large chimney starter filled with charcoal briquettes (6 quarts). When top coals are partially covered with ash, pour evenly over other half of grill (opposite disposable pan). Set cooking grate in place, cover, and open lid vent halfway. Heat grill until hot, about 5 minutes.

2B. *For a gas grill:* Place 2 disposable pie plates, each filled with 1½ cups water, directly on 1 burner of gas grill (opposite primary burner). Turn all burners to high, cover, and heat grill until hot, about 15 minutes. Turn primary burner to medium-high and turn off other burner(s). (Adjust primary burner as needed to maintain grill temperature between 325 and 350 degrees.)

3. Clean and oil cooking grate. Place chicken, skin side down, on hotter side of grill and cook until browned and blistered in spots, 2 to 5 minutes. Flip chicken and cook until second side is browned, 4 to 6 minutes. Move chicken to cooler side of grill and arrange, skin side up, with legs and thighs closest to fire and breasts farthest away. Cover (positioning lid vent over chicken if using charcoal) and cook until breasts register 160 degrees and legs and thighs register 175 degrees, 50 minutes to 1 hour.

4. Transfer chicken to serving platter, tent with aluminum foil, and let rest for 10 minutes before serving, passing lemon wedges separately.

Peri Peri Grilled Chicken

Italian-Style Grilled Chicken

Serves 4

WHY THIS RECIPE WORKS Anyone who has tried to grill a whole chicken knows that it's challenging at best, and the results are often inedible. Many cuisines have developed methods to overcome the problems of chicken cooked over a fire; the Italian way is to cook the chicken under bricks. This was one method we had to try. One attempt to grill a butterflied chicken the Italian way was enough to let us know that we needed more than just bricks to make this recipe work. We thought of brining to keep the meat moist, but it produced burnt chicken when the liquid dripped into the fire. Another way to retain moisture in meat is salting; we rubbed the flesh under the skin with salt mixed with garlic, red pepper flakes, and herbs for Italian flavor. We built a half-grill fire and then cooked the chicken under preheated bricks on the cooler side, skin side down, to firm up the flesh and release fat and liquid where the fire wouldn't cause flare-ups. We flipped the chicken and finished cooking it on the hot side; another flip and a few minutes without the bricks crisped up the skin. The combination of flipping and moving the chicken from the cool side to the hot side guaranteed even cooking, and the salting had kept the meat juicy. With the embellishment of a quick vinaigrette, we had perfectly cooked chicken with zesty Italian flavor, and not a burnt piece in sight. Use an oven mitt or kitchen towel to safely grip and maneuver the hot bricks. You will need two standard-size bricks for this recipe. Placing the bricks on the chicken while it cooks ensures that the skin will be evenly browned and well rendered. A cast-iron skillet or other heavy pan can be used in place of the bricks.

- ⅓ cup extra-virgin olive oil
- 8 garlic cloves, minced
- 1 teaspoon grated lemon zest plus 2 tablespoons juice, divided
  Pinch red pepper flakes
- 4 teaspoons finely chopped fresh thyme, divided
- 1 tablespoon finely chopped fresh rosemary, divided
- 1 (3½- to 4-pound) whole chicken, giblets discarded
- 1½ teaspoons table salt
- 1 teaspoon pepper

1. Heat oil, garlic, lemon zest, and pepper flakes in small saucepan over medium-low heat until sizzling, about 3 minutes. Stir in 1 tablespoon thyme and 2 teaspoons rosemary and continue to cook for 30 seconds. Strain mixture through fine-mesh strainer set over small bowl, pushing on solids to extract oil. Transfer solids to bowl and cool; set oil and solids aside.

2. Use kitchen shears to cut along both sides of backbone to remove it. Flatten breastbone and tuck wings behind back. Use your hands or handle of wooden spoon to loosen skin over breast and thighs and remove any excess fat.

3. Combine salt and pepper in bowl. Mix 2 teaspoons salt mixture with cooled garlic solids. Spread salt-garlic mixture evenly under skin over chicken breast and thighs. Sprinkle remaining ½ teaspoon salt mixture on exposed meat of bone side. Place chicken skin side up on wire rack set in rimmed baking sheet and refrigerate for 1 to 2 hours.

4A. *For a charcoal grill:* Open bottom vent halfway. Light large chimney starter three-quarters filled with charcoal briquettes (4½ quarts). When top coals are partially covered with ash, pour evenly over half of grill. Set cooking grate in place, wrap 2 bricks tightly in aluminum foil, and place on cooking grate. Cover and open lid vent halfway. Heat grill until hot, about 5 minutes.

4B. *For a gas grill:* Wrap 2 bricks tightly in aluminum foil and place on cooking grate. Turn all burners to high, cover, and heat grill until hot, about 15 minutes. Leave primary burner on high and turn off other burner(s). (Adjust primary burner as needed during cooking to maintain grill temperature around 350 degrees.)

5. Clean and oil cooking grate. Place chicken on cooler side of grill, skin side down, with legs facing coals and flames. Place hot bricks lengthwise over each breast half, cover, and cook until skin is lightly browned and faint grill marks appear, 22 to 25 minutes. Remove bricks from chicken. Using tongs, grip legs and flip chicken (chicken should release freely from grill; use thin metal spatula to loosen if stuck), then transfer to hot side of grill, skin side up. Place bricks over breast, cover, and cook until chicken is well browned, 12 to 15 minutes.

6. Remove bricks, flip chicken skin side down, and continue to cook until skin is well browned and breast registers 160 degrees and thighs register 175 degrees, 5 to 10 minutes. Transfer chicken to carving board, tent with foil, and let rest for 15 minutes.

7. Whisk lemon juice, remaining 1 teaspoon thyme, and remaining 1 teaspoon rosemary into reserved oil and season with salt and pepper to taste. Carve chicken and serve, passing sauce separately.

Grill-Roasted Whole Chicken
SEASON 20 RECIPE

Serves 4

WHY THIS RECIPE WORKS This recipe delivers our grill-roasted chicken ideal: succulent, distinctly but subtly smoky meat encased in a well-rendered and deeply golden skin. There's no brining, no salting, no tedious knifework, and no dirtying of the dishes that such tasks require. But cooking a whole chicken that hasn't been flattened by spatchcocking over direct heat can be disastrous: Thanks to the bird's bulbous shape, its exterior can easily dry out before the interior cooks through. And while some measure of fatty juices dripping onto the coals creates desirable grill flavor, too much triggers significant flare-ups that leave a layer of black carbon on the bird's exterior that overwhelms its delicate flavor. That's why most recipes for grilling a whole bird use indirect heat, which cooks it gently and evenly—but also why the results usually lack grill flavor. Our solution was a method that incorporated both indirect and direct heat. We built a two-zone fire with heat sources on either side of the grill and a cooler zone down the middle and cooked the chicken breast side up over indirect heat until it hit 130 degrees; at that point, it had rendered most of its fat, so flareups wouldn't be an issue. Then we finished cooking it directly over the fire, flipping it breast side down after a few minutes so that both sides saw direct heat. The trick was calibrating the smoke's effect to keep it from overwhelming the clean chicken taste. We smoked various amounts of wood chips per our standard method—wrapped in aluminum foil with a pair of slits cut in the packet to allow the smoke to escape—and found that we needed just ¼ to ½ cup of chips (depending on whether we used charcoal or gas) to generate the understated flavor we wanted. We also made sure to use dry wood chips, since they ignite quickly while the bird is still relatively cold and best able to absorb smoke flavor. We developed this recipe on a three-burner gas grill where the burners run from front-to-back, and refer to the two outside burners as the primary burners and the center one as the secondary burner. If using a two-burner grill, use one side—the side with the wood chips—as the primary burner and the other as the secondary burner. Adjust the primary burner to maintain a grill temperature of 375 to 400 degrees. Place the chicken 6 inches from the primary burner and rotate it after 25 minutes of cooking in step 4 so that it cooks evenly.

1 tablespoon kosher salt
½ teaspoon pepper
1 (3½- to 4½-pound) whole chicken, giblets discarded
1 tablespoon vegetable oil
¼–½ cup wood chips

1. Combine salt and pepper in bowl. Pat chicken dry with paper towels. Rub entire surface with oil. Sprinkle evenly all over with salt mixture and rub in mixture with your hands to coat evenly. Tie legs together with twine and tuck wing tips behind back.

2. Using large piece of heavy-duty aluminum foil, wrap chips (½ cup if using gas; ¼ cup if using charcoal) in 8 by 4½-inch foil packet. (Make sure chips do not poke holes in sides or bottom of packet.) Cut 2 evenly spaced 2-inch slits in top of packet.

3A. *For a charcoal grill:* Open bottom vent halfway. Light large chimney starter mounded with charcoal briquettes (7 quarts). When top coals are partially covered with ash, pour into 2 even banked piles on either side of grill. Place wood chip packet on 1 pile of coals. Set cooking grate in place, cover, and open lid vent halfway. Heat grill until hot and wood chips are smoking, about 5 minutes. (Temperature of grill will start around 400 degrees and will fall to about 350 degrees by end of cooking.)

3B. *For a gas grill:* Place wood chip packet directly on primary burner. Turn all burners to high, cover, and heat grill until hot and wood chips are smoking, about 15 minutes. Turn primary burners (2 outside burners) to medium-high and turn off center (secondary) burner. (Adjust primary burners as needed to maintain grill temperature between 400 and 425 degrees.)

4. Clean and oil cooking grate. Place chicken, breast side up with cavity facing toward you, in center of grill, making sure bird is centered between heat sources on either side. Cover (placing vent over chicken on charcoal grill) and cook until breast registers 130 degrees, about 45 to 55 minutes.

5. Using long grill tongs, reach into cavity and carefully lift chicken by breast. Holding chicken over bowl or container, tilt toward you to allow fat and juices to drain from cavity. Transfer chicken, breast side up, to hotter side of grill (without wood chip packet) and cook, covered, until back is deep golden brown, about 5 minutes. Using tongs, flip chicken breast side down; cover and continue to cook over hotter side of grill until breast is deep golden brown, about 5 minutes longer. Using tongs, flip chicken breast side up, return to center of grill; take internal temperature of breast. If breast registers 155 degrees, transfer chicken to carving board. If breast registers less than 155 degrees, cover and continue to cook in center of grill, checking temperature every 2 minutes until it registers 155 degrees, 2 to 10 minutes longer. Let chicken rest, uncovered, for 20 minutes. Carve chicken and serve.

Thai Grilled Cornish Game Hens with Chili Dipping Sauce (Gai Yang)

Serves 4

WHY THIS RECIPE WORKS For our take on Thai grilled chicken, we started with Cornish hens, which are similar in size to the hens traditionally used by street vendors in Thailand. Butterflying and flattening the hens helped them cook more quickly and evenly on the grill. We created a marinade consisting of cilantro leaves and stems (a substitute for hard-to-find cilantro root), lots of garlic, white pepper, ground coriander, brown sugar, and fish sauce; thanks to its pesto-like consistency, it clung to the hens instead of sliding off. We set up a half-grill fire and started cooking the hens skin side up over the cooler side of the grill so the fatty skin had time to slowly render while the meat cooked; we then finished them over the hotter side to crisp the skin. We whipped up a version of the traditional sweet-tangy-spicy dipping sauce by combining equal parts white vinegar and sugar and simmering the mixture until it was slightly thickened and would cling nicely to the chicken. Plenty of minced garlic and Thai chiles balanced the sauce with savory, fruity heat. The hens need to marinate for at least 6 hours before cooking (a longer marinating time is preferable). If your hens weigh 1½ to 2 pounds, grill three hens instead of four and extend the initial cooking time in step 6 by 5 minutes. If you can't find Thai chiles, substitute Fresno or red jalapeño chiles. Serve with steamed white rice.

Hens
- 4 Cornish game hens (1¼ to 1½ pounds each), giblets discarded
- 1 cup fresh cilantro leaves and stems, chopped
- 12 garlic cloves, peeled
- ¼ cup packed light brown sugar
- 2 teaspoons ground white pepper
- 2 teaspoons ground coriander
- 2 teaspoons table salt
- ¼ cup fish sauce

Dipping Sauce
- ½ cup distilled white vinegar
- ½ cup granulated sugar
- 1 tablespoon minced Thai chiles
- 3 garlic cloves, minced
- ¼ teaspoon table salt

1. For the hens: Place 1 hen breast side down on cutting board and use kitchen shears to cut through bones on either side of backbone; discard backbone. Flip hen and press on breastbone to flatten. Trim off any excess fat and skin. Repeat with remaining 3 hens.

2. Pulse cilantro leaves and stems, garlic, sugar, pepper, coriander, and salt in food processor until finely chopped, 10 to 15 pulses; transfer to small bowl. Add fish sauce and stir until marinade has consistency of loose paste.

3. Rub hens all over with marinade. Transfer hens and any excess marinade to large zipper-lock bag and refrigerate for at least 6 hours or up to 24 hours, turning bag halfway through marinating.

4. For the dipping sauce: Bring vinegar to boil in small saucepan. Add sugar and stir to dissolve. Reduce heat to medium-low and simmer until vinegar mixture is slightly thickened, 5 minutes. Remove from heat and let vinegar mixture cool to room temperature. Add chiles, garlic, and salt and stir until combined. Transfer sauce to airtight container and refrigerate until ready to use. (Sauce can be refrigerated for up to 2 weeks. Bring to room temperature before serving.)

5A. For a charcoal grill: Open bottom vent completely. Light large chimney starter filled with charcoal briquettes (6 quarts). When top coals are partially covered with ash, pour evenly over half of grill. Set cooking grate in place, cover, and open lid vent completely. Heat grill until hot, about 5 minutes.

5B. For a gas grill: Turn all burners to high, cover, and heat grill until hot, about 15 minutes. Leave primary burner and secondary burner (next to primary burner) on high and turn off other burner(s). Adjust secondary burner as needed to maintain grill temperature between 400 and 450 degrees.

6. Clean and oil cooking grate. Remove hens from bag, leaving any marinade that sticks to hens in place. Tuck wingtips behind backs and turn legs so drumsticks face inward toward breasts. Place hens, skin side up, on cooler side of grill (if using charcoal, arrange hens so that legs and thighs are facing coals). Cover and cook until skin has browned and breasts register 145 to 150 degrees, 30 to 35 minutes, rotating hens halfway through cooking.

7. Using tongs, carefully flip hens and place skin side down on hotter side of grill. Cover and cook until skin is crisp, deeply browned, and charred in spots and breasts register 160 degrees, 3 to 5 minutes, being careful to avoid burning.

8. Transfer hens, skin side up, to cutting board, tent with aluminum foil, and let rest for 10 minutes. Carve each hen in half or into 4 pieces and serve, passing dipping sauce separately.

Grill-Roasted Turkey

Serves 10 to 12

WHY THIS RECIPE WORKS Grill roasting a turkey can be hard to manage. Cooking times can vary depending on the weather, and it's much easier to burn the bird's skin on a grill. There also remain the usual problems inherent to roasting a turkey: dry, overcooked breast meat and undercooked thighs. But grill roasting can produce the best-tasting, best-looking turkey ever, with crispy skin and moist meat wonderfully perfumed with smoke. We wanted to take the guesswork out of preparing the holiday bird on the grill. Because the skin on larger birds will burn before the meat is done, we chose a small turkey (less than 14 pounds). We ditched stuffing the turkey or trussing it—both can lead to burnt skin and undercooked meat. To season the meat and help prevent it from drying out on the grill, we brined the turkey. To protect the skin and promote slow cooking, we placed the turkey on the opposite side of the glowing coals or lit gas burner. Using a V-rack also helped, as it improved air circulation. And we turned the turkey three times instead of twice; this way, all four sides received equal exposure to the hot side of the grill for evenly bronzed skin. If using a self-basting turkey or kosher turkey, do not brine in step 1, and season with salt after brushing with melted butter in step 2. If you'd like to use wood chunks instead of wood chips when using a charcoal grill, substitute six medium wood chunks, soaked in water for 1 hour, for the wood chip packets. The total cooking time is 2 to 2½ hours, depending on the size of the bird, the ambient conditions (the bird will require more time on a cool, windy day), and the intensity of the fire.

- 1 **cup table salt, for brining**
- 1 **(12- to 14-pound) turkey, neck and giblets removed, wings tucked behind back**
- 2 **tablespoons unsalted butter, melted**
- 6 **cups wood chips**

1. Dissolve salt in 2 gallons cold water in large container. Submerge turkey in brine, cover, and refrigerate or store in very cool spot (40 degrees or less) for 6 to 12 hours.

2. Lightly spray V-rack with vegetable oil spray. Remove turkey from brine and pat dry, inside and out, with paper towels. Brush both sides of turkey with melted butter and place breast side down in prepared V-rack.

3. Just before grilling, soak wood chips in water for 15 minutes, then drain. Using 3 large pieces of heavy-duty aluminum foil, wrap soaked chips in three 8 by 4½-inch foil packets. (Make sure chips do not poke holes in sides or bottom of packets.) Cut 2 evenly spaced 2-inch slits in top of each packet.

4A. *For a charcoal grill:* Open bottom vent halfway. Light large chimney mounded with charcoal briquettes (7 quarts). When top coals are partially covered with ash, pour into steeply banked pile against side of grill. Place 1 wood chip packet on pile of coals. Set cooking grate in place, cover, and open lid vent halfway. Heat grill until hot and wood chips are smoking, about 5 minutes.

4B. *For a gas grill:* Place 1 wood chip packet directly on primary burner. Turn all burners to high, cover, and heat grill until hot and wood chips are smoking, about 15 minutes. Turn primary burner to medium-high and turn off other burner(s). (Adjust primary burner as needed during cooking to maintain grill temperature around 325 degrees.)

5. Clean and oil cooking grate. Place V-rack with turkey on cool side of grill with leg and wing facing coal, cover (position lid vent over turkey if using charcoal), and cook for 1 hour.

6. Using potholders, transfer V-rack with turkey to rimmed baking sheet or roasting pan. If using charcoal, remove cooking grate and add 12 new briquettes and second wood chip packet to pile of coals; set cooking grate in place. If using gas, place remaining wood chip packets directly on primary burner. With wad of paper towels in each hand, flip turkey breast side up in rack and return V-rack with turkey to cool side of grill, with other leg and wing facing heat. Cover (position lid vent over turkey if using charcoal) and cook for 45 minutes.

7. Using potholders, carefully rotate V-rack with turkey (breast remains up) 180 degrees. Cover and continue to cook until breast registers 160 degrees and thighs register 175 degrees, 15 to 45 minutes. Transfer turkey to carving board, tent with foil, and let rest for 20 to 30 minutes. Carve and serve.

Grill-Smoked Herb-Rubbed Flat-Iron Steaks

Serves 4 to 6

WHY THIS RECIPE WORKS We often smoke chicken, turkey, pork, and fish—but beef, not so much. There are some notable exceptions, such as Texas-style barbecued ribs and brisket. But we wanted to look into smoking quicker-cooking cuts; for example, steak. Smoking steaks can lend them complexity, but treating them like larger, collagen-rich barbecue cuts like brisket can overwhelm the meat's delicate flavor with too much smoke. We were intrigued by the notion of smoking flat-iron steak, a cut we don't use much in the test kitchen. It's a beefy-tasting steak from the shoulder that's decently marbled and tender and also relatively inexpensive. We found that the key to success was using a small amount of wood chips and cooking the steaks quickly over direct heat so that they were just kissed with smoke. To make sure we had a consistent amount of smoke, we weighed the wood chips for more control over the smoke quantity. Salting the steaks for an hour before cooking ensured that the seasoning penetrated below the meat's surface, and coating them with an herb-spice rub lent an extra layer of flavor that complemented the smoke. We also grilled lemons to serve with the steaks for a hit of brightness. This recipe requires rubbing the steaks with salt and letting them sit at room temperature for 1 hour before cooking. You can substitute blade steaks for the flat-iron steaks, if desired. We like both cuts cooked to medium (130 to 135 degrees). We like hickory chips in this recipe, but other kinds of wood chips will work. Gas grills are not as efficient at smoking meat as charcoal grills, so we recommend using 1½ cups of wood chips if using a gas grill. Wood chunks are not recommended for this recipe.

2 teaspoons dried thyme
1 teaspoon dried rosemary
¾ teaspoon fennel seeds
½ teaspoon black peppercorns
¼ teaspoon red pepper flakes
4 (6- to 8-ounce) flat-iron steaks, ¾ to 1 inch thick, trimmed
1 tablespoon kosher salt
1–1½ cups wood chips
Vegetable oil spray
2 lemons, quartered lengthwise

1. Grind thyme, rosemary, fennel seeds, peppercorns, and pepper flakes in spice grinder or with mortar and pestle until coarsely ground. Transfer to small bowl. Pat steaks dry with paper towels. Rub steaks evenly on both sides with salt and place on wire rack set in rimmed baking sheet. Let sit at room temperature for 1 hour. (After 30 minutes, prepare grill.)

2. Using large piece of heavy-duty aluminum foil, wrap wood chips (1 cup if using charcoal; 1½ cups if using gas) in 8 by 4½-inch foil packet. (Make sure chips do not poke holes in sides or bottom of packet.) Cut 2 evenly spaced 2-inch slits in top of packet.

3A. *For a charcoal grill:* Open bottom vent completely. Light large chimney starter filled with charcoal briquettes (6 quarts). When top coals are partially covered with ash, pour evenly over half of grill. Place wood chip packet on coals. Set cooking grate in place, cover, and open lid vent completely. Heat grill until hot and wood chips are smoking, about 5 minutes.

3B. *For a gas grill:* Place wood chip packet directly on primary burner. Turn all burners to high, cover, and heat grill until hot and wood chips are smoking, about 15 minutes. Leave primary burner on high and turn other burner(s) to medium.

4. Clean and oil cooking grate. Sprinkle half of herb rub evenly over 1 side of steaks and press to adhere. Lightly spray herb-rubbed side of steaks with oil spray, about 3 seconds. Flip steaks and repeat process of sprinkling and pressing steaks with remaining herb rub and coating with oil spray on second side.

5. Place lemons and steaks on hotter side of grill, cover (position lid vent over steaks if using charcoal), and cook until lemons and steaks are well browned on both sides and meat registers 130 to 135 degrees (for medium), 4 to 6 minutes per side. (If steaks are fully charred before reaching desired temperature, move to cooler side of grill, cover, and continue to cook.) Transfer lemons and steaks to clean wire rack set in rimmed baking sheet, tent with foil, and let rest for 10 minutes. Slice steaks thin against grain and serve, passing lemons separately.

Grill-Smoked Herb-Rubbed
Flat-Iron Steaks

Grilled Flank Steak Tacos

SEASON 20 RECIPE

Serves 4 to 6

WHY THIS RECIPE WORKS *Tacos al carbón*, or grilled steak tacos, feature meat seasoned with a marinade or spices, cooked over a live fire, tucked into soft corn tortillas, and topped with garnishes like charred scallions and lime juice. Two cuts of steak are common for tacos al carbón: skirt and flank. We chose flank. Like skirt steak, flank steak is thin and beefy, cooks quickly, and has lots of surface area for picking up flavor. But flank is less expensive and more widely available. We decided to skip a marinade, which needs about an hour to season the exterior of the meat; instead, we opted for a spice paste made with chipotle chiles in adobo sauce for spicy, smoky, and savory notes. Cumin, oil, and a little salt turned the minced chipotles into a paste. Grilled directly over the coals (a gas grill works, too), the thickest part of the steak was medium-rare (125 degrees) in 10 minutes. After giving the meat a brief rest, we sliced it thin across the grain. The chipotle paste was a keeper, but the thinner areas of the steak were overdone. What's more, it was unevenly browned and didn't have much grill flavor. So next time around we divided the steak into thirds lengthwise. This separated the thinner portions from the thicker ones so we could grill each to the proper doneness. These narrow strips, once sliced, also fit nicely into 6-inch tortillas. The mediocre browning was because the steak's fibers contracted during the first few minutes of cooking. When meat cooks evenly from the top and bottom, both sides seize at the same rate, leaving the meat flat. But in this case, the hot grill was only cooking one side at a time; thus, buckling happened. Frequent flipping helped the top and bottom shrink at about the same rate so the steaks stayed flat and browned evenly. As for the deficit of grill flavor, if we wanted deep grill flavor, we needed drippings. Next time around, we trimmed less fat. Problem solved. Inspired by

the charred scallions that often adorn tacos al carbón, we whipped up a grilled scallion salsa. For the sake of efficiency, we decided to grill the vegetables alongside the steak. As an added benefit, they picked up some flavor from the meat vapors. Finally, we blistered the corn tortillas on the hot side of the grill until they developed a toasty, popcorn-like aroma and then wrapped them tightly in foil so they would stay warm and soft. This steak's grill flavor is created when some of the fat and juices land on the fire and create small, controlled flare-ups. For this reason, choose a steak that has some fat deposits. For a spicier scallion salsa, add the reserved jalapeño seeds in step 5.

> 3 tablespoons extra-virgin olive oil, divided
> 2 teaspoons minced canned chipotle chile in adobo sauce, plus 1 teaspoon adobo sauce, divided
> 2 teaspoons kosher salt, divided
> ¾ teaspoon ground cumin
> 1 (1½- to 1¾-pound) flank steak
> 2 jalapeño chiles
> 20 scallions
> 12 (6-inch) corn tortillas
> 1½ tablespoons lime juice plus more to taste, plus lime wedges for serving
> Fresh cilantro
> Sour cream

1. Combine 1 tablespoon oil, chipotles, 1½ teaspoons salt, and cumin in bowl. Trim fat deposits on steak to ⅛-inch thickness. Cut steak lengthwise (with grain) into three 2- to 3-inch-wide strips. Rub chipotle mixture into all surfaces of steak and transfer to rimmed baking sheet.

2A. *For a charcoal grill:* Open bottom vent completely. Light large chimney starter mounded with charcoal briquettes (7 quarts). When top coals are partially covered with ash, pour evenly over half of grill. Set cooking grate in place, cover, and open lid vent completely. Heat grill until hot, about 5 minutes.

2B. *For a gas grill:* Turn all burners to high, cover, and heat grill until hot, about 15 minutes. Turn off 1 burner (if using grill with more than 2 burners, turn off burner farthest from primary burner) and leave other burner(s) on high.

3. Clean and oil cooking grate. Arrange steaks and jalapeños on hotter side of grill. (If using gas, cover grill.) Cook steaks, flipping every 2 minutes, until meat is well browned and registers 125 to 130 degrees, 7 to 12 minutes. Cook jalapeños until skins are blistered and charred in spots, 7 to 10 minutes. Transfer steaks to clean cutting board and tent with aluminum foil. Transfer jalapeños to medium bowl and cover tightly with plastic wrap.

4. Grill scallions on hotter side of grill until greens are well charred on 1 side, 1 to 2 minutes. Flip scallions, arranging so that greens are on cooler side while white and pale green parts are on hotter side. Continue to cook until whites are well charred, 1 to 2 minutes. Transfer to bowl with jalapeños and cover tightly with plastic wrap. Arrange half of tortillas over hotter side of grill and cook until lightly charred, about 45 to 60 seconds per side. Tightly wrap warmed tortillas in foil. Repeat with remaining tortillas.

5. Without peeling, stem and seed jalapeños and reserve seeds. Chop jalapeños fine, chop scallions coarse, and transfer to bowl. Stir in remaining 2 tablespoons oil, lime juice, remaining adobo sauce, and remaining ½ teaspoon salt. Season with lime juice, salt, and jalapeño seeds to taste. Slice steaks thin across grain and transfer to serving platter. Serve, passing scallion salsa, tortillas, lime wedges, cilantro, and sour cream separately.

Grilled Steak Tips

Serves 4 to 6

WHY THIS RECIPE WORKS Steak tips have long been the darling of all-you-can-eat restaurant chains where quantity takes precedence over quality. If they're not mushy, they land on the table tough and dry. We wanted to improve this classic bar food and instill it with deep flavor and a tender texture. To stay true to the inexpensive nature of this dish, we set our sights on finding the best affordable (read: cheap) cut of meat that would stay tender and moist during a brief stint on the grill. The best cut, we found, is what butchers call flap meat. To tenderize and flavor the meat, we used a soy sauce–based marinade and let the meat marinate for at least an hour—just enough time to allow the thicker parts of the meat to become tender while preventing the thinner sections from becoming too salty. Grilling the tips over a two-level fire, which has hotter and cooler areas, helps to cook this often unevenly shaped cut evenly. We let the meat rest for 5 minutes after grilling to ensure juicy meat and then sliced it thin so the meat would be tender and flavorful. Lime, orange, or lemon wedges provided a bright acidic counterpoint to the steak tips. Sirloin steak tips are sometimes labeled "flap meat." A two-level fire allows you to brown the steak over the hot side of the grill and then move it to the cooler side if it is not yet cooked through. If your steak is thin, however, you may not need to use the cooler side of the grill. Serve lime wedges with the southwestern-marinated tips and orange wedges with the tips marinated in garlic, ginger, and soy sauce.

    1 recipe marinade (recipes follow)
    2 pounds sirloin steak tips, trimmed
       Lime, orange, or lemon wedges

1. Combine marinade and beef in 1-gallon zipper-lock bag and toss to coat; press out as much air as possible and seal bag. Refrigerate for 1 hour, flipping bag halfway through marinating.

2A. *For a charcoal grill:* Open bottom vent completely. Light large chimney starter filled with charcoal briquettes (6 quarts). When top coals are partially covered with ash, pour two-thirds evenly over grill, then pour remaining coals over half of grill. Set cooking grate in place, cover, and open lid vent completely. Heat grill until hot, about 5 minutes.

2B. *For a gas grill:* Turn all burners to high, cover, and heat grill until hot, about 15 minutes.

3. Clean and oil cooking grate. Remove beef from bag and pat dry with paper towels. Place steak tips on grill (on hotter side if using charcoal) and cook (covered if using gas) until well browned on first side, about 4 minutes. Flip steak tips and continue to cook (covered if using gas) until meat registers 120 to 125 degrees (for medium-rare) or 130 to 135 degrees (for medium), 6 to 10 minutes. If exterior of meat is browned but steak is not yet cooked through, move to cooler side of grill (if using charcoal) or turn down burners to medium (if using gas) and continue to cook to desired doneness.

4. Transfer steak tips to cutting board, tent with aluminum foil, and let rest for 5 to 10 minutes. Slice steak tips very thin on bias and serve with lime, orange, or lemon wedges.

Southwestern Marinade
Makes about ¾ cup

    ⅓ cup soy sauce
    ⅓ cup vegetable oil
    3 garlic cloves, minced
    1 tablespoon packed dark brown sugar
    1 tablespoon tomato paste
    1 tablespoon chili powder
    2 teaspoons ground cumin
    ¼ teaspoon cayenne pepper

Combine all ingredients in bowl.

Garlic, Ginger, and Soy Marinade
Makes about ⅔ cup

    ⅓ cup soy sauce
    3 tablespoons vegetable oil
    3 tablespoons toasted sesame oil
    2 tablespoons packed dark brown sugar
    1 tablespoon grated fresh ginger
    2 teaspoons grated orange zest
    1 scallion, sliced thin
    3 garlic cloves, minced
    ½ teaspoon red pepper flakes

Combine all ingredients in bowl.

"I have a confession to make: I'm not a big fan of steak. Now before I'm forced to renounce my American citizenship, I need to report that I rank burgers in my top 10 favorite foods of all time. Burgers are beefy like a good steak, but they aren't only about the beef. There are condiments that add sweetness, savoriness, and spice; vegetables that contribute freshness and texture; and a bun to sop up all the juices. This recipe is the burger of the steak dish world, and I love it. You start by grilling a flank steak to a rosy medium-rare, but then you layer on complexity with a deeply savory, tart, spicy dressing laced with fish sauce and lime juice, a mountain of fresh herbs, and thinly sliced shallots. Then you serve it with a mound of steamed jasmine rice, perfect for sopping up all the juices."

—*Dan*

Grilled Thai Beef Salad

Serves 4 to 6

WHY THIS RECIPE WORKS This traditional Thai salad features slices of charred steak tossed with shallots, mint, and cilantro in a bright dressing. We chose flank steak for its marbling and moderate price. Grilling the steak over a modified two-level fire and flipping it just when moisture beaded on the surface yielded perfectly charred, juicy meat. Adding a fresh Thai chile, toasted cayenne, and paprika gave the dressing a fruity, fiery heat. Toasted rice powder, a traditional Thai tableside condiment that gives the dressing fuller body and a subtle crunch, is not widely available here, but we made our own by toasting rice in a skillet on the stovetop and then grinding it in a spice grinder (a mini food processor or a mortar and pestle also work). If fresh Thai chiles are unavailable, substitute half of a serrano chile. Don't skip the toasted rice; it's integral to the texture and flavor of the dish. Any variety of white rice can be used. Toasted rice powder (*kao kua*) can also be found in many Asian markets; substitute 1 tablespoon rice powder for the white rice. Serve with steamed rice, if desired.

- 1 teaspoon paprika
- 1 teaspoon cayenne pepper
- 1 tablespoon white rice
- 3 tablespoons lime juice (2 limes)
- 2 tablespoons fish sauce
- 2 tablespoons water
- ½ teaspoon sugar
- 1 (1½-pound) flank steak, trimmed
- ½ teaspoon table salt
- ¼ teaspoon ground white pepper
- 1 seedless English cucumber, sliced ¼ inch thick on bias
- 4 shallots, sliced thin
- 1½ cups fresh mint leaves, torn
- 1½ cups fresh cilantro leaves
- 1 Thai chile, stemmed, seeded, and sliced thin into rounds

1. Heat paprika and cayenne in 8-inch skillet over medium heat; cook, shaking pan, until fragrant, about 1 minute. Transfer to small bowl. Return skillet to medium-high heat, add rice and toast, stirring constantly, until deep golden brown, about 5 minutes. Transfer to small bowl and let cool for 5 minutes. Grind rice with spice grinder, mini food processor, or mortar and pestle until it resembles fine meal, 10 to 30 seconds (you should have about 1 tablespoon rice powder).

2. Whisk lime juice, fish sauce, water, sugar, and ¼ teaspoon toasted paprika mixture in large bowl and set aside.

3A. *For a charcoal grill:* Open bottom vent completely. Light large chimney starter filled with charcoal briquettes (6 quarts). When top coals are partially covered with ash, pour in even layer over half of grill. Set cooking grate in place, cover, and open lid vent completely. Heat grill until hot, about 5 minutes.

3B. *For a gas grill:* Turn all burners to high, cover, and heat grill until hot, about 15 minutes. Leave primary burner on high and turn off other burner(s).

4. Clean and oil cooking grate. Season steak with salt and pepper. Place steak on grate over hot part of grill and cook until beginning to char and beads of moisture appear on outer edges of meat, 5 to 6 minutes. Flip steak and continue to cook on second side until meat registers 125 degrees (for medium-rare), about 5 minutes. Transfer to cutting board, tent with aluminum foil, and let rest for 10 minutes (or allow to cool to room temperature, about 1 hour).

5. Line large platter with cucumber slices. Slice meat, against grain, on bias, into ¼-inch-thick slices. Transfer sliced steak to bowl with fish sauce mixture, add shallots, mint, cilantro, chile, and half of rice powder, and toss to combine. Arrange steak over cucumber-lined platter. Serve, passing remaining rice powder and toasted paprika mixture separately.

Tender, Juicy Grilled Burgers

Serves 4

WHY THIS RECIPE WORKS For us, the ideal burger has an ultracraggy charred crust, a rich beefy taste, and an interior so juicy and tender that it practically falls apart at the slightest pressure—a particularly difficult achievement when grilling. The problem is, such a burger is pretty hard to come by. While the typical specimen may have a nicely browned crust, it's also heavy and dense with a pebbly texture that comes from using preground beef. We knew we wanted to grind our own meat to make the ultimate burger. In the test kitchen, we've found it easy to grind meat ourselves with a food processor. We trim gristle and excess fat from the meat, cut the meat into ½-inch pieces, freeze it for about 30 minutes to firm it up so that the blades cut it cleanly, and finally process it in small batches to ensure an even, precise grind. We chose to use beefy steak tips since they are decently tender, require virtually no trimming, and are relatively inexpensive. Adding a bit of butter to the food processor when grinding added richness but not buttery flavor. To form the burgers so that they wouldn't fall apart on the grate but at the same time achieve that essential open texture, we froze them briefly before putting them on the grill. By the time they'd thawed at their centers, they had developed enough crust to ensure that they held together. A few minutes over a hot grill was all our burgers needed to achieve a perfect medium-rare. Whether served with the classic fixings like lettuce and tomato or one of our creamy grilled-vegetable toppings, this was a grilled burger that lived up to our ideal. This recipe requires freezing the meat twice, for a total of 65 to 80 minutes, before grilling.

When stirring the salt and pepper into the ground meat and shaping the patties, take care not to overwork the meat or the burgers will become dense. Sirloin steak tips are also sold as flap meat. Serve the burgers with your favorite toppings or one of our grilled-vegetable toppings (recipes follow).

1½ pounds sirloin steak tips, trimmed and cut into ½-inch pieces
4 tablespoons unsalted butter, cut into ¼-inch pieces
1 teaspoon pepper
¾ teaspoon kosher salt
1 (13 by 9-inch) disposable aluminum pan (if using charcoal)
4 hamburger buns

1. Place beef pieces and butter on large plate in single layer. Freeze until meat is very firm and starting to harden around edges but still pliable, about 35 minutes.

2. Place one-quarter of meat and one-quarter of butter cubes in food processor and pulse until finely ground into pieces size of rice grains (about ⅟₃₂ inch), 15 to 20 pulses, stopping and redistributing meat around bowl as necessary to ensure beef is evenly ground. Transfer meat to baking sheet. Repeat grinding with remaining 3 batches of meat and butter. Spread mixture over sheet and inspect carefully, discarding any long strands of gristle or large pieces of hard meat, fat, or butter.

3. Sprinkle pepper and salt over meat and gently toss with fork to combine. Divide meat into 4 balls. Toss each between your hands until uniformly but lightly packed. Gently flatten into patties ¾ inch thick and about 4½ inches in diameter. Using your thumb, make 1-inch-wide by ¼-inch-deep depression in center of each patty. Transfer patties to platter and freeze for 30 to 45 minutes.

4A. *For a charcoal grill:* Using skewer, poke 12 holes in bottom of disposable pan. Open bottom vent completely and place disposable pan in center of grill. Light large chimney starter two-thirds filled with charcoal briquettes (4 quarts). When top coals are partially covered with ash, pour into disposable pan. Set cooking grate in place, cover, and open lid vent completely. Heat grill until hot, about 5 minutes.

4B. *For a gas grill:* Turn all burners to high, cover, and heat grill until hot, about 15 minutes. Leave all burners on high.

5. Clean and oil cooking grate. Season 1 side of patties liberally with salt and pepper. Using spatula, flip patties and season other side. Grill patties (directly over coals if using charcoal), without moving them, until browned and meat easily releases from grill, 4 to 7 minutes. Flip burgers and continue to grill until browned on second side and meat registers 125 degrees (for medium-rare) or 130 degrees (for medium), 4 to 7 minutes.

6. Transfer burgers to plate and let rest for 5 minutes. While burgers rest, lightly toast buns on grill, 1 to 2 minutes. Transfer burgers to buns and serve.

ACCOMPANIMENTS
Grilled Scallion Topping
Makes about ½ cup

2 tablespoons sour cream
2 tablespoons mayonnaise
2 tablespoons buttermilk
1 tablespoon cider vinegar
1 tablespoon minced fresh chives
2 teaspoons Dijon mustard
½ teaspoon table salt
¼ teaspoon sugar
⅛ teaspoon pepper
20 scallions
2 tablespoons vegetable oil

1. Combine sour cream, mayonnaise, buttermilk, vinegar, chives, mustard, salt, sugar, and pepper in medium bowl.

2. Toss scallions with oil in large bowl (do not wash out bowl). Grill scallions over hot fire until lightly charred and softened, 2 to 4 minutes per side. Return to bowl and let cool for 5 minutes. Slice scallions thin, then transfer to bowl with sour cream mixture. Toss to combine and season with salt and pepper to taste.

Grilled Shiitake Mushroom Topping
Makes about ¾ cup

2 tablespoons sour cream
2 tablespoons mayonnaise
2 tablespoons buttermilk
1 tablespoon cider vinegar
1 tablespoon minced fresh chives
2 teaspoons Dijon mustard
½ teaspoon table salt
¼ teaspoon sugar
⅛ teaspoon pepper
8½ ounces shiitake mushrooms, stems removed
2 tablespoons vegetable oil

1. Combine sour cream, mayonnaise, buttermilk, vinegar, chives, mustard, salt, sugar, and pepper in medium bowl.

2. Toss mushrooms with oil in large bowl (do not wash out bowl). Grill mushrooms over hot fire until lightly charred and softened, 2 to 4 minutes per side. Return to bowl and let cool for 5 minutes. Slice mushrooms thin, then transfer to bowl with sour cream mixture. Toss to combine and season with salt and pepper to taste.

Grilled Napa Cabbage and Radicchio Topping
Makes about ¾ cup

- 2 tablespoons sour cream
- 2 tablespoons mayonnaise
- 2 tablespoons buttermilk
- 1 tablespoon cider vinegar
- 1 tablespoon minced fresh parsley
- 2 teaspoons Dijon mustard
- ½ teaspoon table salt
- ¼ teaspoon sugar
- ⅛ teaspoon pepper
- ¼ small head napa cabbage
- ½ small head radicchio, cut into 2 wedges
- 2 tablespoons vegetable oil

1. Combine sour cream, mayonnaise, buttermilk, vinegar, parsley, mustard, salt, sugar, and pepper in medium bowl.

2. Place cabbage and radicchio wedges on rimmed baking sheet and brush with oil (do not wash sheet). Grill over hot fire until lightly charred and beginning to wilt, 2 to 4 minutes on each cut side. Return to baking sheet and let cool for 5 minutes. Slice cabbage and radicchio thin, then transfer to bowl with sour cream mixture. Toss to combine and season with salt and pepper to taste.

Grilled Lamb Kofte

Serves 4 to 6

WHY THIS RECIPE WORKS In the Middle East, kebabs called *kofte* feature ground meat, not chunks, mixed with lots of spices and fresh herbs. For ours, we started with preground lamb for convenience. Kneading the meat ensured that the kofte had a sausage-like spring. To help keep the meat firm, we added a small amount of gelatin and then refrigerated it. Ground pine nuts ensured a perfect texture and prevented toughness; plus, they gave the kofte a noticeably richer flavor. Hot smoked paprika, cumin, and cloves contributed warm spice notes, while parsley and mint offered bright, grassy flavors. Adding a little tahini to the tangy garlic and yogurt serving sauce gave it more complexity. You will need eight 12-inch metal skewers for this recipe. Serve with rice pilaf or make sandwiches with warm pita bread, sliced red onion, and chopped fresh mint.

Yogurt-Garlic Sauce
- 1 cup plain whole-milk yogurt
- 2 tablespoons lemon juice
- 2 tablespoons tahini
- 1 garlic clove, minced
- ½ teaspoon table salt

Kofte
- ½ cup pine nuts
- 4 garlic cloves, peeled
- 1½ teaspoons hot smoked paprika
- 1 teaspoon table salt
- 1 teaspoon ground cumin
- ½ teaspoon pepper
- ¼ teaspoon ground coriander
- ¼ teaspoon ground cloves
- ⅛ teaspoon ground nutmeg
- ⅛ teaspoon ground cinnamon
- 1½ pounds ground lamb
- ½ cup grated onion, drained
- ⅓ cup finely chopped fresh parsley
- ⅓ cup finely chopped fresh mint
- 1½ teaspoons unflavored gelatin
- 1 large disposable aluminum roasting pan (if using charcoal)

1. *For the yogurt-garlic sauce:* Whisk all ingredients together in bowl. Set aside.

2. *For the kofte:* Process pine nuts, garlic, paprika, salt, cumin, pepper, coriander, cloves, nutmeg, and cinnamon in food processor until coarse paste forms, 30 to 45 seconds. Transfer mixture to large bowl. Add lamb, onion, parsley, mint, and gelatin; knead with your hands until thoroughly combined and mixture feels slightly sticky, about 2 minutes. Divide mixture into 8 equal portions. Shape each portion into 5-inch-long cylinder about 1 inch in diameter. Using 8 (12-inch) metal skewers, thread 1 cylinder onto each skewer, pressing gently to adhere. Transfer skewers to lightly greased baking sheet, cover with plastic wrap, and refrigerate for at least 1 hour or up to 24 hours.

3A. *For a charcoal grill:* Using skewer, poke 12 holes in bottom of disposable pan. Open bottom vent completely and place pan in center of grill. Light large chimney starter two-thirds filled with charcoal briquettes (4 quarts). When top coals are partially covered with ash, pour into pan. Set cooking grate in place, cover, and open lid vent completely. Heat grill until hot, about 5 minutes.

3B. *For a gas grill:* Turn all burners to high, cover, and heat grill until hot, about 15 minutes. Leave all burners on high.

4. Clean and oil cooking grate. Place skewers on grill (directly over coals if using charcoal) at 45-degree angle to grate. Cook (covered if using gas) until browned and meat easily releases from grill, 4 to 7 minutes. Flip skewers and continue to cook until browned on second side and meat registers 160 degrees, about 6 minutes. Transfer skewers to platter and serve, passing yogurt-garlic sauce separately.

VARIATION
Grilled Beef Kofte

Substitute 80 percent lean ground beef for lamb. Increase garlic to 5 cloves, paprika to 2 teaspoons, and cumin to 2 teaspoons.

Grill-Smoked Pork Chops

Serves 4

WHY THIS RECIPE WORKS These chops have it all: charred crust, ultramoist meat, and true smoke flavor. We decided to employ a technique we had used in previous pork chop recipes: reversing the cooking by starting low and finishing with a quick sear. To reap the benefits of both high and low heat on a charcoal grill, we used a double-banked fire (made by placing a disposable aluminum pan between two mounds of coals) and started our chops under cover on the cooler center of the grill, allowing the smoke to do its job for about 25 minutes. We then applied a few coats of sauce and finished by searing them, uncovered, over hot coals. As for arranging the chops on the grill, we found it best to rest each chop on its bone instead of laying it flat. To keep them from toppling over, we speared the chops together with skewers, making sure to leave a good inch between them to allow smoke to circulate, then stood them upright in the center of the grill with bone, not meat, touching the grill. This allowed us to keep the chops over the fire for a full 30 minutes, after which we removed the skewers, applied the glaze, and finished the chops over hot coals for that crusty char. Buy chops of the same thickness so they will cook uniformly. Use the large holes on a box grater to grate the onion for the sauce.

If you'd like to use wood chunks instead of wood chips when using a charcoal grill, substitute two medium wood chunks, soaked in water for 1 hour, for the wood chip packet. You'll need two 10-inch metal skewers for this recipe.

Sauce
- ½ cup ketchup
- ¼ cup molasses
- 2 tablespoons grated onion
- 2 tablespoons Worcestershire sauce
- 2 tablespoons Dijon mustard
- 2 tablespoons cider vinegar
- 1 tablespoon packed light brown sugar

Chops
- 2 cups wood chips, soaked in water for 15 minutes and drained
- 4 (12-ounce) bone-in pork rib chops, 1½ inches thick, trimmed
- 2 teaspoons table salt
- 2 teaspoons pepper
- 1 (13 by 9-inch) disposable aluminum roasting pan (if using charcoal)

1. *For the sauce:* Bring all ingredients to simmer in small saucepan over medium heat and cook, stirring occasionally, until reduced to about 1 cup, 5 to 7 minutes. Transfer ½ cup sauce to small bowl and set aside remaining sauce for serving.

2. *For the chops:* Using large piece of heavy-duty aluminum foil, wrap soaked chips in 8 by 4½-inch foil packet. (Make sure chips do not poke holes in sides or bottom of packet.) Cut 2 evenly spaced 2-inch slits in top of packet.

Pat pork chops dry with paper towels. Use sharp knife to cut 2 slits about 1 inch apart through outer layer of fat and connective tissue. Season each chop with ½ teaspoon salt and ½ teaspoon pepper. Place chops side by side, facing in same direction, on cutting board with curved rib bone facing down. Pass 2 skewers through loin muscle of each chop, close to bone, about 1 inch from each end, then pull apart to create 1-inch space between each.

3A. *For a charcoal grill:* Open bottom vent halfway and place roasting pan in center of grill. Light large chimney starter filled with charcoal briquettes (6 quarts). When top coals are partially covered with ash, pour into 2 even piles on either side of roasting pan. Place wood chip packet on 1 pile of coals. Set cooking grate in place, cover, and open lid vent halfway. Heat grill until hot and wood chips are smoking, about 5 minutes.

3B. *For a gas grill:* Place wood chip packet over primary burner. Turn all burners to high, cover, and heat grill until hot and wood chips are smoking, about 15 minutes. Turn all burners to medium-high. (Adjust burners as needed during cooking to maintain grill temperature between 300 and 325 degrees.)

4. Clean and oil cooking grate. Place skewered chops bone side down on grill (over pan if using charcoal). Cover and cook until meat registers 120 degrees, 28 to 32 minutes.

5. Remove skewers from chops, tip chops onto flat side and brush surface of each with 1 tablespoon sauce. Transfer chops, sauce side down, to hotter parts of grill (if using charcoal) or turn all burners to high (if using gas) and cook until browned on first side, 2 to 6 minutes. Brush top of each chop with 1 tablespoon sauce, flip, and continue to cook until browned on second side and meat registers 140 degrees, 2 to 6 minutes.

6. Transfer chops to serving platter, tent with aluminum foil, and let rest for 5 to 10 minutes. Serve, passing reserved sauce separately.

Skewering Pork Chops for the Grill

1. Pass 2 skewers through loin muscle of each chop to provide stability when standing on grill.

2. Stand skewered chops, bone side down, on cooking grate in center of grill so smoke can reach all sides.

Grilled Glazed Pork Tenderloin Roast

Serves 6

WHY THIS RECIPE WORKS Pork tenderloin is wonderfully tender and versatile, it doesn't require much prep, and it's relatively inexpensive. That said, too often, delicate pork tenderloin turns out disappointing: The lean meat dries out easily, and it is plagued by uneven cooking because of its tapered shape. By the time the large end hits a perfect medium (140 degrees), the skinnier tail is guaranteed to be overdone. To make the pork cook more evenly and to create a more presentation-worthy roast, we tied two tenderloins together. Scraping the insides of the tenderloins with a fork created a sticky protein network that helped the tenderloins bind together. To ensure that our pork retained maximum juiciness, we brined the meat and cooked it mostly over indirect heat. Finally, we put together a few flavorful glazes. We made sure to use enough sugar (or ingredients containing sugar) to encourage browning, giving the pork a beautiful crust along with a flavor boost. Since brining is a key step in having the two tenderloins stick together, we don't recommend using enhanced pork (injected with a salt solution) in this recipe.

2 (1-pound) pork tenderloins, trimmed
3 tablespoons table salt, for brining
2 tablespoons vegetable oil
1 recipe glaze (recipes follow)

1. Lay tenderloins on cutting board, flat side (side opposite where silverskin was) up. Holding thick end of 1 tenderloin with paper towels and using dinner fork, scrape flat side lengthwise from end to end 5 times, until surface is completely covered with shallow grooves. Repeat with second tenderloin. Dissolve salt in 1½ quarts cold water in large container. Submerge tenderloins in brine and let sit at room temperature for 1 hour.

2. Remove tenderloins from brine and pat completely dry with paper towels. Lay 1 tenderloin, scraped side up, on cutting board and lay second tenderloin, scraped side down, on top so that thick end of 1 tenderloin matches up with thin end of other. Spray five 14-inch lengths of kitchen twine thoroughly with vegetable oil spray; evenly space twine underneath tenderloins and tie. Brush roast with vegetable oil and season with pepper. Transfer ⅓ cup glaze to bowl for grilling; reserve remaining glaze for serving.

3A. *For a charcoal grill:* Open bottom vent completely. Light large chimney starter filled with charcoal briquettes (6 quarts). When top coals are partially covered with ash, pour into steeply banked pile against side of grill. Set cooking grate in place, cover, and open lid vent completely. Heat grill until hot, about 5 minutes.

3B. *For a gas grill:* Turn all burners to high, cover, and heat grill until hot, about 15 minutes. Leave primary burner on high and turn off other burner(s).

4. Clean and oil cooking grate. Place roast on cooler side of grill, cover, and cook until meat registers 115 degrees, 22 to 28 minutes, flipping and rotating halfway through cooking.

5. Slide roast to hotter side of grill and cook until lightly browned on all sides, 4 to 6 minutes. Brush top of roast with about 1 tablespoon glaze and grill, glaze side down, until glaze begins to char, 2 to 3 minutes; repeat glazing and grilling with remaining 3 sides of roast, until meat registers 140 degrees.

6. Transfer roast to carving board, tent with aluminum foil, and let rest for 10 minutes. Carefully remove twine and slice roast into ½-inch-thick slices. Serve with remaining glaze.

Miso Glaze
Makes about ¾ cup

- 3 tablespoons sake
- 3 tablespoons mirin
- ⅓ cup white miso paste
- ¼ cup sugar
- 2 teaspoons Dijon mustard
- 1 teaspoon rice vinegar
- ¼ teaspoon grated fresh ginger
- ¼ teaspoon toasted sesame oil

Bring sake and mirin to boil in small saucepan over medium heat. Whisk in miso and sugar until smooth, about 30 seconds. Remove pan from heat and continue to whisk until sugar is dissolved, about 1 minute. Whisk in mustard, vinegar, ginger, and sesame oil until smooth.

Sweet and Spicy Hoisin Glaze
Makes about ¾ cup

- 1 teaspoon vegetable oil
- 3 garlic cloves, minced
- 1 teaspoon grated fresh ginger
- ½ teaspoon red pepper flakes
- ½ cup hoisin sauce
- 2 tablespoons soy sauce
- 1 tablespoon rice vinegar

Heat oil in small saucepan over medium heat until shimmering. Add garlic, ginger, and pepper flakes; cook until fragrant, about 30 seconds. Whisk in hoisin and soy sauce until smooth. Remove pan from heat and stir in vinegar.

Satay Glaze
Makes about ¾ cup

- 1 teaspoon vegetable oil
- 1 tablespoon red curry paste
- 2 garlic cloves, minced
- ½ teaspoon grated fresh ginger
- ½ cup canned coconut milk
- ¼ cup packed dark brown sugar
- 2 tablespoons peanut butter
- 1 tablespoon lime juice
- 2½ teaspoons fish sauce

Heat oil in small saucepan over medium heat until shimmering. Add curry paste, garlic, and ginger; cook, stirring constantly, until fragrant, about 1 minute. Whisk in coconut milk and sugar and bring to simmer. Whisk in peanut butter until smooth. Remove pan from heat and whisk in lime juice and fish sauce.

Grilled Pork Loin with Apple-Cranberry Filling
Serves 6

WHY THIS RECIPE WORKS Center-cut pork loin is an especially lean cut, making it difficult to cook without drying out. We wanted to cook our pork loin on the grill but keep it moist using an approach other than traditional brines or sauces. We decided to use a moist, well-seasoned stuffing (and careful cooking) so our grilled pork loin would be juicy and flavorful. We bought a short and wide roast, more square than cylindrical. This shape only required a few straight, short cuts to open to a long, flat sheet that was easy to fill and roll up. The best stuffing required both a deep flavor to counter the pork's rather bland taste and a texture thick enough to stay put. Poaching apples and cranberries in a blend of apple cider, apple cider vinegar, and spices developed a filling with the dense, chewy consistency we wanted. And this process had an added bonus—we had ample poaching liquid left, which could be reduced to a glaze. We had already decided not to give the loin a preliminary sear, which can create a tough exterior, but found we missed the brown color that searing produces. Rolling the loin in our glaze gave it a beautifully burnished finish. This recipe is best prepared with a loin that is 7 to 8 inches long and 4 to 5 inches wide and not enhanced (injected with a salt solution). To make cutting the pork easier, freeze it for 30 minutes. If mustard seeds are unavailable, stir an equal amount of whole-grain mustard into the filling after the apples have been processed. For a spicier stuffing, use the larger amount of cayenne. If you'd like to use wood chunks instead of wood chips when using a charcoal grill, substitute two medium wood chunks, soaked in water for 1 hour, for the wood chip packet. The pork loin can be stuffed and tied a day ahead of time, but don't season the exterior until you are ready to grill.

Grilled Pork Loin with
Apple-Cranberry Filling

Filling

- 1½ cups (4 ounces) dried apples
- 1 cup apple cider
- ¾ cup packed light brown sugar
- ½ cup cider vinegar
- ½ cup dried cranberries
- 1 large shallot, halved lengthwise and sliced thin crosswise
- 1 tablespoon grated fresh ginger
- 1 tablespoon yellow mustard seeds
- ½ teaspoon ground allspice
- ⅛–¼ teaspoon cayenne pepper

Pork

- 1 (2½-pound) boneless center-cut pork loin roast, trimmed
- 1¼ teaspoons table salt, divided
- ½ teaspoon pepper, divided
- 2 cups wood chips, soaked in water for 15 minutes and drained

1. For the filling: Bring all ingredients to simmer in medium saucepan over medium-high heat. Cover, reduce heat to low, and cook until apples are very soft, about 20 minutes. Pour mixture through fine-mesh strainer set over bowl, pressing with back of spoon to extract as much liquid as possible. Return liquid to saucepan and simmer over medium-high heat until reduced to ⅓ cup, about 5 minutes; reserve for glazing. Pulse apple mixture in food processor until coarsely chopped, about 15 pulses. Transfer filling to bowl and refrigerate until needed.

2. For the pork: Position roast fat side up. Insert knife ½ inch from bottom of roast and cut horizontally, stopping ½ inch before edge. Open up this flap. Cut through thicker half of roast about ½ inch from bottom, stopping about ½ inch before edge. Open up this flap. Repeat until pork is even ½-inch thickness throughout. If uneven, cover with plastic wrap and use meat pounder to even out. Season interior with ½ teaspoon salt and ¼ teaspoon pepper and spread filling in even layer, leaving ½-inch border. Roll tightly and tie with kitchen twine at 1-inch intervals. Season with remaining ¾ teaspoon salt and remaining ¼ teaspoon pepper.

3. Using large piece of heavy-duty aluminum foil, wrap soaked chips in 8 by 4½-inch foil packet. (Make sure chips do not poke holes in sides or bottom of packet.) Cut 2 evenly spaced 2-inch slits in top of packet.

4A. For a charcoal grill: Open bottom vent halfway. Light large chimney starter three-quarters filled with charcoal briquettes (4½ quarts). When top coals are partially covered with ash, pour evenly over half of grill. Place wood chip packet on coals. Set cooking grate in place, cover, and open lid vent halfway. Heat grill until hot and wood chips are smoking, about 5 minutes.

4B. For a gas grill: Place wood chip packet over primary burner. Turn all burners to high, cover, and heat grill until hot and wood chips are smoking, about 15 minutes. Leave primary burner on medium-high and turn off other burner(s). (Adjust primary burner as needed to maintain grill temperature of 300 to 325 degrees.)

5. Clean and oil cooking grate. Place pork, fat side up, on cooler side of grill, cover (position lid vent over roast if using charcoal), and cook until meat registers 130 to 135 degrees, 55 minutes to 1 hour 10 minutes, flipping halfway through cooking.

6. Brush roast evenly with reserved glaze. (Reheat glaze, if necessary, to make it spreadable.) Continue to cook until glaze is glossy and meat registers 145 degrees, 5 to 10 minutes. Transfer to carving board, tent with foil, and let rest for 15 minutes. Remove twine, cut roast into ½-inch-thick slices, and serve.

How to Stuff a Pork Loin

1. Position roast fat side up. Insert knife ½ inch from bottom of roast and cut horizontally, stopping ½ inch before edge. Open up this flap.

2. Cut through thicker half of roast ½ inch from bottom, stopping about ½ inch before edge. Open up this flap. Repeat until pork loin is even ½-inch thickness throughout.

3. With long side of meat facing you, season meat and spread filling, leaving ½-inch border on all sides.

4. Starting from short side, roll pork loin tightly, then tie roast with kitchen twine at 1-inch intervals.

Grill-Roasted Bone-In Pork Rib Roast

Serves 6 to 8

WHY THIS RECIPE WORKS A tender, quick-cooking center-cut rib roast and a simple salt rub were all that we needed for a juicy grilled roast with a mahogany crust. We grilled it over indirect heat so it could cook through slowly, adding a small amount of wood chips to the fire to produce a subtle smoke flavor. After a little more than an hour, our roast was tender with plenty of rich, deep flavor. For the perfect counterpoint to the roast's richness, we made a fresh orange salsa with bright citrus and fresh herbs, jalapeño, and a touch of cumin. If you buy a blade-end roast (sometimes called a rib-end roast), tie it into a uniform shape with kitchen twine at 1-inch intervals; this step is unnecessary with a center-cut roast. For easier carving, ask the butcher to remove the tip of the chine bone and to cut the remainder of the chine bone between each rib. If you'd like to use wood chunks instead of wood chips when using a charcoal grill, substitute one medium wood chunk, soaked in water for 1 hour, for the wood chip packet. Serve the roast with Orange Salsa with Cuban Flavors (recipe follows) if desired.

- 1 **(4- to 5-pound) bone-in center-cut pork rib roast, tip of chine bone removed, fat trimmed to ¼-inch thickness**
- 4 **teaspoons kosher salt**
- 1 **cup wood chips**
- 1½ **teaspoons pepper**

1. Pat roast dry with paper towels. Using sharp knife, cut slits in surface fat layer, spaced 1 inch apart, in crosshatch pattern, being careful not to cut into meat. Season roast with salt. Wrap with plastic wrap and refrigerate for at least 6 hours or up to 24 hours.

2. Just before grilling, soak wood chips in water for 15 minutes, then drain. Using large piece of heavy-duty aluminum foil, wrap soaked chips in 8 by 4½-inch foil packet. (Make sure chips do not poke holes in sides or bottom of packet.) Cut 2 evenly spaced 2-inch slits in top of packet.

3A. *For a charcoal grill:* Open bottom vent halfway. Light large chimney starter filled with charcoal briquettes (6 quarts). When top coals are partially covered with ash, pour into steeply banked pile against side of grill. Place wood chip packet on coals. Set cooking grate in place, cover, and open lid vent halfway. Heat grill until hot and wood chips are smoking, about 5 minutes.

3B. *For a gas grill:* Place wood chip packet over primary burner. Turn all burners to high, cover, and heat grill until hot and wood chips are smoking, about 15 minutes. Turn primary burner to medium-high and turn off other burner(s). (Adjust primary burner as needed during cooking to maintain grill temperature around 325 degrees.)

4. Clean and oil cooking grate. Unwrap roast and season with pepper. Place roast on grate with meat near, but not over, coals and flames and bones facing away from coals and flames. Cover (position lid vent over meat if using charcoal) and cook until meat registers 140 degrees, 1¼ to 1½ hours.

5. Transfer roast to carving board, tent with foil, and let rest for 30 minutes. Carve into thick slices by cutting between ribs. Serve.

ACCOMPANIMENT
Orange Salsa with Cuban Flavors
Makes about 2½ cups
To make this salsa spicier, add the reserved chile seeds.

- ½ **teaspoon grated orange zest plus 5 oranges peeled and segmented; each segment quartered crosswise**
- ½ **cup finely chopped red onion**
- 1 **jalapeño chile, stemmed, seeds reserved, and minced**
- 2 **tablespoons lime juice**
- 2 **tablespoons finely chopped fresh parsley**
- 1 **tablespoon extra-virgin olive oil**
- 2 **teaspoons packed brown sugar**
- 1½ **teaspoons distilled white vinegar**
- 1½ **teaspoons finely chopped fresh oregano**
- 1 **garlic clove, minced**
- ½ **teaspoon ground cumin**
- ½ **teaspoon table salt**
- ½ **teaspoon pepper**

Combine all ingredients in medium bowl.

Barbecued Pulled Pork on a Charcoal Grill

Serves 8

WHY THIS RECIPE WORKS There is no getting around the fact that deeply flavored, smoky pulled pork is best made on a charcoal grill, and this recipe perfects the technique for doing just that. (Though if you don't have a charcoal grill, see our inventive recipe that follows for making it using a gas grill.) However, many barbecue procedures demand the regular attention of the cook for 8 hours or more. We wanted to find a way to make moist, fork-tender pulled pork without the marathon cooking time and constant attention to the grill. After testing shoulder roasts (also called Boston butt), fresh ham, and picnic roasts, we determined that the shoulder roast, which has the most fat, retained the most moisture and flavor during a long, slow cook. We massaged a spicy chili rub into the meat; then we wrapped the roast in plastic wrap and refrigerated it for at least 3 hours to "marinate." We cooked the roast first on the grill to absorb smoky flavor (from wood chips—no smoker required) and then in the oven to finish. Finally, we let the pork rest in a paper bag so the meat would steam and any remaining collagen would break down, allowing the flavorful juices to be reabsorbed. We also developed a pair of sauce recipes to please barbecue fans with different tastes. Pulled pork can be made with a fresh ham or picnic roast, although our preference is for Boston butt. If using a fresh ham or picnic roast, remove the skin by cutting through it with the tip of a chef's knife; slide the blade just under the skin and work around to loosen it while pulling it off with your other hand. If you'd like to use wood chunks instead of wood chips when using a charcoal grill, substitute four medium wood chunks, soaked in water for 1 hour, for the wood chip packet. Serve on plain white bread or warmed rolls with dill pickle chips and coleslaw.

- 1 (6- to 8-pound) bone-in Boston butt roast
- ¾ cup Dry Rub for Barbecue (recipe follows)
- 4 cups wood chips
- 1 (13 by 9-inch) disposable aluminum roasting pan
- 2 cups barbecue sauce (recipes follow)

1. Pat pork dry with paper towels, then massage dry rub into meat. Wrap meat in plastic wrap and refrigerate for at least 3 hours or up to 3 days.

2. At least 1 hour prior to cooking, remove roast from refrigerator, unwrap, and let sit at room temperature. Soak wood chips in water for 15 minutes, then drain. Using 2 large piece of heavy-duty aluminum foil, wrap soaked chips in two 8 by 4½-inch foil packets. (Make sure chips do not poke holes in sides or bottom of packets.) Cut 2 evenly spaced 2-inch slits in top of each packet.

3. Open bottom vent halfway. Light large chimney starter three-quarters filled with charcoal briquettes (4½ quarts). When top coals are partially covered with ash, pour evenly over half of grill. Place wood chip packets on coals. Set cooking grate in place, cover, and open lid vent halfway. Heat grill until hot and wood chips are smoking, about 5 minutes.

4. Set roast in disposable pan, place on cool side of grill, and cook for 3 hours. During final 20 minutes of cooking, adjust oven rack to lower-middle position and heat oven to 325 degrees.

5. Wrap disposable pan with heavy-duty foil and cook in oven until meat is fork-tender, about 2 hours.

6. Carefully slide foil-wrapped pan with roast into brown paper bag. Crimp end shut and let rest for 1 hour.

7. Transfer roast to carving board and unwrap. Separate roast into muscle sections, removing fat, if desired, and tearing meat into shreds with your fingers. Place shredded meat in large bowl and toss with 1 cup barbecue sauce. Serve, passing remaining sauce separately.

Dry Rub for Barbecue
Makes about 1 cup
You can adjust the proportions of spices in this all-purpose rub or add or subtract a spice, as you wish.

- ¼ cup paprika
- 2 tablespoons chili powder
- 2 tablespoons ground cumin
- 2 tablespoons packed dark brown sugar
- 2 tablespoons table salt
- 1 tablespoon dried oregano
- 1 tablespoon granulated sugar
- 1 tablespoon black pepper
- 1 tablespoon white pepper
- 1–2 teaspoons cayenne pepper

Combine all ingredients in small bowl.

Eastern North Carolina Barbecue Sauce
Makes about 2 cups

- 1 cup distilled white vinegar
- 1 cup cider vinegar
- 1 tablespoon sugar
- 1 tablespoon red pepper flakes
- 1 tablespoon hot sauce

Mix all ingredients together in bowl and season with salt and pepper to taste. (Sauce can be refrigerated for up to 4 days.)

Mid–South Carolina Mustard Sauce
Makes about 2½ cups

- 1 cup cider vinegar
- 1 cup vegetable oil
- 6 tablespoons Dijon mustard
- 2 tablespoons maple syrup or honey
- 4 teaspoons Worcestershire sauce
- 1 teaspoon hot sauce

Mix all ingredients together in bowl and season with salt and pepper to taste. (Sauce can be refrigerated for up to 4 days.)

Smoky Pulled Pork on a Gas Grill

SEASON 20 RECIPE

Serves 8 to 10

WHY THIS RECIPE WORKS Pulled pork is traditionally best made on a charcoal grill. But the reality is that most home cooks rely on a gas grill. And simply using a charcoal recipe on a gas grill—a solution that often works for other dishes—is a total failure in this case. That's because it is so difficult to imbue pulled pork with rich, smoky flavor when cooking on a gas grill. We cut our pork butt into three pieces to increase the surface area that the smoke could cling to. After salting the pork overnight, we took it directly from the fridge to the grill: The meat's cool temperature allowed more smoke to condense onto its surface. Instead of inundating the meat with smoke at the beginning, we got the most out of the wood chips by soaking half of them in water to delay when they began to smoke. We fashioned foil packets that were the right size and shape to sit on the grill, with just the right size and number of openings to allow in enough oxygen so that the chips smoldered, but not so much that they caught fire. Finally, we stirred together a bright and spicy vinegar sauce that high-lighted the pungent smoke flavors of our pulled pork. As we developed this recipe, the only thing that wasn't up for debate was what cut of pork to use. Pork butt is ideal because it's collagen-rich and has the right amount of intramuscular fat. During cooking, that fat is rendered while the collagen trans-forms into water-retaining gelatin, together giving pulled pork its tender texture. Pork butt roast is often labeled Boston butt in the supermarket. We developed this recipe with hickory chips, though other varieties of hardwood can be used. (We do not recommend mesquite chips.) Before beginning, check your propane tank to make sure that you have at least a half-tank of fuel. If you happen to run out of fuel, you can move the pork to a preheated 300-degree oven to finish cooking. Serve the pulled pork on white bread or hamburger buns with pickles and coleslaw.

Pork
- 5 teaspoons kosher salt
- 2½ teaspoons pepper
- 2 teaspoons paprika
- 2 teaspoons packed light brown sugar
- 1 (5-pound) boneless pork butt roast, trimmed
- 4 cups wood chips
- 2 (9-inch) disposable aluminum pie plates
- 1 (13 by 9-inch) disposable aluminum roasting pan

Vinegar Sauce
- 2 cups cider vinegar
- 2 tablespoons ketchup
- 2 teaspoons packed light brown sugar
- 1 teaspoon red pepper flakes
- 1 teaspoon kosher salt

1. *For the pork:* Combine salt, pepper, paprika, and sugar in small bowl. Cut pork against grain into 3 equal slabs. Rub salt mixture into pork, making sure meat is evenly coated. Wrap pork tightly in plastic wrap and refrigerate for at least 6 hours or up to 24 hours.

2. Just before grilling, soak 2 cups wood chips in water for 15 minutes, then drain. Using large piece of heavy-duty aluminum foil, wrap soaked chips in 8 by 4½-inch foil packet. (Make sure chips do not poke holes in sides or bottom of packet.) Repeat with remaining 2 cups unsoaked chips. Cut 2 evenly spaced 2-inch slits in top of each packet.

3. Remove cooking grate and place wood chip packets directly on primary burner. Place disposable pie plates, each filled with 3 cups water, directly on other burner(s). Set grate in place, turn all burners to high, cover, and heat grill until hot

"Pork chops are a big thing at my house. My husband, Ian, loves them so much, that his nick name is actually 'Pork Chop'. But sometimes, I like to take a little break from chops and buy country-style ribs instead. Not only are they less expensive, but I think they have more flavor. My favorite way to cook them is on the grill with a little glaze. I like this ribs recipe because it's so darn easy and I can easily change up the flavors by using other spices in the rub and/or a different style of barbecue sauce. Seasoning the meat for at least an hour before cooking is key, and the longer you can let it rest at this stage, the better the flavor. Be sure to trim the ribs well of excess fat around the edges to help prevent flare-ups during cooking."

–*Julia*

and wood chips are smoking, about 15 minutes. Turn primary burner to medium and turn off other burner(s). (Adjust primary burner as needed to maintain grill temperature of 300 degrees.)

4. Clean and oil cooking grate. Place pork on cooler side of grill, directly over water pans; cover and smoke for 1½ hours.

5. Transfer pork to disposable pan. Place pork in pan on cooler side of grill and continue to cook until meat registers 200 degrees, 2½ to 3 hours.

6. Transfer pork to carving board and let rest for 20 minutes. Pour juices from disposable pan into fat separator and let sit for 5 minutes.

7. *For the vinegar sauce:* While pork rests, whisk all ingredients together in bowl. Using 2 forks, shred pork into bite-size pieces. Stir ⅓ cup defatted juices and ½ cup sauce into pork. Serve, passing remaining sauce separately.

Sweet and Tangy Grilled Country-Style Pork Ribs

Serves 4 to 6

WHY THIS RECIPE WORKS Country-style pork ribs are a favorite in the test kitchen—we've sliced them into small pieces for stir-fries and braised and shredded them for hearty ragus. But this cut is rarely prepared on its own, perhaps because the name causes confusion. In many ways, country-style ribs are actually more like pork chops—a point that can make them a little confusing for home cooks. They're a knife-and-fork cut, sold either boneless or with a portion of bone attached, containing both light, lean loin meat and a section from the dark, richly pork-flavored shoulder. Because they feature a combination of two kinds of meat, the trick is figuring out how to grill them so that the white meat is juicy and the dark meat is tender. We applied a salty dry rub to boost the ribs' seasoning and help them stay moist, particularly the faster-drying light meat. We found that a doneness temperature of 150 degrees—a compromise between the usual 135 to 140 degrees required for light meat and 175 degrees for dark meat—delivered optimal results. Starting the ribs over high heat and then finishing on the cooler side of the grill ensured good browning and an evenly cooked interior. While the ribs were on the cooler side of the grill, we basted them with a sweet and tangy sauce of ketchup, molasses, Worcestershire sauce, cider vinegar, and Dijon mustard. Stirring in grated onion, minced garlic, chili powder, cayenne, and black pepper gave the sauce some depth. Be sure to carefully trim the pork to reduce the number of flare-ups when the pork is grilled. This recipe requires refrigerating the spice-rubbed ribs for at least 1 hour or up to 24 hours before grilling.

Pork
- 4 teaspoons packed brown sugar
- 1 tablespoon kosher salt
- 1 tablespoon chili powder
- ⅛ teaspoon cayenne pepper
- 4 pounds bone-in country-style pork ribs, trimmed

Sauce
- 1 cup ketchup
- 5 tablespoons molasses
- 3 tablespoons cider vinegar
- 2 tablespoons Worcestershire sauce
- 2 tablespoons Dijon mustard
- ¼ teaspoon pepper
- 2 tablespoons vegetable oil
- ⅓ cup grated onion
- 1 garlic clove, minced
- 1 teaspoon chili powder
- ¼ teaspoon cayenne pepper

1. *For the pork:* Combine sugar, salt, chili powder, and cayenne in bowl. Rub mixture all over ribs. Wrap tightly in plastic wrap and refrigerate for at least 1 hour or up to 24 hours.

2. *For the sauce:* Whisk ketchup, molasses, vinegar, Worcestershire, mustard, and pepper together in bowl. Heat oil in medium saucepan over medium heat until shimmering. Add onion and garlic; cook until onion is softened, 2 to 4 minutes. Add chili powder and cayenne and cook until fragrant, about 30 seconds. Whisk in ketchup mixture and bring to boil. Reduce heat to medium-low and simmer gently for 5 minutes. Set aside ½ cup of sauce for basting pork and reserve remaining sauce for serving. (Sauce can be refrigerated for up to 1 week.)

3A. *For a charcoal grill:* Open bottom vent halfway. Light large chimney starter filled with charcoal briquettes (6 quarts). When top coals are partially covered with ash, pour evenly over half of grill. Set cooking grate in place, cover, and open lid vent halfway. Heat grill until hot, about 5 minutes.

3B. *For a gas grill:* Turn all burners to high, cover, and heat grill until hot, about 15 minutes. Leave primary burner on high and turn other burner(s) off to maintain grill temperature around 350 degrees.

4. Clean and oil cooking grate. Place ribs over hotter part of grill and cook until well browned on both sides, 4 to 7 minutes. Move ribs to cooler part of grill and brush top sides with ¼ cup sauce. Cover and cook for 6 minutes. Flip ribs and brush with remaining ¼ cup sauce. Cover and continue to cook until pork registers 150 degrees, 5 to 10 minutes. Transfer ribs to serving platter, tent with aluminum foil, and let rest for 10 minutes. Serve, passing reserved sauce separately.

Tuscan Grilled Pork Ribs (Rosticciana)

SEASON 20 RECIPE

Serves 4 to 6

WHY THIS RECIPE WORKS *Rosticciana,* or Tuscan grilled pork spareribs, will be unlike any others you've had. In fact, with no barbecue sauce or spice rub, it might be like tasting ribs for the first time. Their preparation falls in line with the less-is-more ethos of Tuscan cuisine, where ingredients are seasoned sparingly to allow their natural flavors to shine. In this case, it's all about the pork, so the seasonings are restricted to salt, pepper, and maybe a hint of garlic or rosemary. Then the ribs are grilled quickly—typically for only 15 to 30 minutes—over a hot fire until the meat is browned and crisp but still succulent. To re-create juicy, deeply porky, chewy-tender Tuscan-style ribs, we started by removing the tough, papery membranes from two racks of St. Louis–style spareribs. Cutting the ribs into two-rib sections created more surface area for flavorful browning, and salting them for an hour prior to grilling ensured that they would cook up juicy and well seasoned. We grilled the ribs over a medium-hot (rather than blazing) fire to help prevent the meat from drying out, and removed them promptly when their temperature reached between 175 and 185 degrees—which took only about 20 minutes. Drizzling the pork with a vinaigrette made from minced rosemary, garlic, and lemon juice balanced its richness without obscuring its meaty flavor. When portioning the meat into two-rib sections, start at the thicker end of the rack. If you are left with a three-rib piece at the tapered end, grill it as such. Take the temperature of the meat between the bones. Since these ribs cook quickly, we like to use the still-hot fire to grill a vegetable. Radicchio's pleasant bitterness and crunch make it a perfect partner for the rich meat.

Ribs

- 2 (2½- to 3-pound) racks St. Louis–style spareribs, trimmed, membrane removed, and each rack cut into 2-rib sections
- 2 teaspoons kosher salt
- 1 tablespoon vegetable oil
- 1 teaspoon pepper

Vinaigrette

- ¼ cup extra-virgin olive oil
- 2 garlic cloves, minced
- 1 teaspoon finely chopped fresh rosemary
- 2 tablespoons lemon juice

1. *For the ribs:* Pat ribs dry with paper towels. Rub evenly on both sides with salt and place on wire rack set in rimmed baking sheet. Let sit at room temperature for 1 hour. Brush meat side of ribs with oil and sprinkle with pepper.

2. *For the vinaigrette:* Combine oil, garlic, and rosemary in small bowl and microwave until fragrant and just starting to bubble, about 30 seconds. Stir in lemon juice and set aside.

3A. *For a charcoal grill:* Open bottom vent completely. Light large chimney starter filled with charcoal briquettes (6 quarts). When top coals are partially covered with ash, pour evenly over grill. Set cooking grate in place, cover, and open lid vent completely. Heat grill until hot, about 5 minutes.

3B. *For a gas grill:* Turn all burners to high, cover, and heat grill until hot, about 15 minutes. Turn all burners to medium-high.

4. Clean and oil cooking grate. Place ribs meat side down on grill. Cover and cook until meat side begins to develop spotty browning and light but defined grill marks, 4 to 6 minutes. Flip ribs and cook, covered, until second side is lightly browned, 4 to 6 minutes, moving ribs as needed to ensure even browning. Flip again and cook, covered, until meat side is deeply browned with slight charring and thick ends of ribs register 175 to 185 degrees, 4 to 6 minutes.

5. Transfer ribs to cutting board and let rest for 10 minutes. Cut ribs between bones and serve, passing vinaigrette separately.

ACCOMPANIMENT
Grilled Radicchio
Serves 4
Turning the wedges during cooking ensures that all sides, including the rounded one, spend time facing the fire.

- 3 heads radicchio (10 ounces each), quartered
- ¼ cup extra-virgin olive oil
   Balsamic vinegar

1. Place radicchio on rimmed baking sheet, brush with oil, and season with salt and pepper to taste.

2. Grill radicchio over medium-hot fire (covered if using gas), turning every 1½ minutes, until edges are browned and wilted but centers are still slightly firm, about 5 minutes. Transfer radicchio to serving dish, drizzle with vinegar, and serve.

Removing the Membrane from Spareribs

The papery membrane on the rack's underside is chewy and unpleasant to eat. Here's how to remove it.

1. Slip tip of paring knife under edge of membrane on each rack.

2. Gripping loosened edge with paper towel, slowly pull off membrane. It should come off in single piece.

Cutting Ribs Two by Two

Cutting the racks into two-rib sections increases the meat's surface area for flavorful browning and provides a meaty pocket between the two bones for easily taking the pork's temperature.

Starting at the thicker end of the rack, portion the meat into two-rib sections. You might be left with a three-rib piece at the tapered end of the rack, which can be grilled as such.

Memphis-Style Barbecued Spareribs

Serves 4 to 6

WHY THIS RECIPE WORKS Memphis pit masters pride themselves on their all-day barbecued pork ribs with a dark bark-like crust and distinctive chew. Up for a challenge, we decided to come up with our own version, but one that wouldn't involve tending a grill all day. After failing to grill the ribs in a reasonable amount of time (less than 7 hours), we opted for a grill-to-oven approach. We started first with the grill. For a fire that would maintain the key amount of indirect heat (roughly 250 to 275 degrees), we turned to a half-grill fire where the hot coals are arranged over half the grill. In addition, we stowed a pan of water underneath the cooking grate on the cooler side of the grill, where it would absorb heat and work to keep the temperature stable, as well as help keep the meat moister. Then we transferred the ribs to a wire rack set in a rimmed baking sheet and cooked them in a moderate oven until tender and thick-crusted. We even mimicked our grill setup by pouring 1½ cups water into the rimmed baking sheet. In all, we'd shaved more than 3 hours off of our shortest recipe. Don't remove the membrane that runs along the bone side of the ribs; it prevents some of the fat from being rendered and is authentic to this style of ribs.

- 1 recipe Spice Rub (page 334)
- 2 (2½- to 3-pound) racks St. Louis–style spareribs, trimmed
- ½ cup apple juice
- 3 tablespoons cider vinegar
- 1 (13 by 9-inch) disposable aluminum roasting pan (if using charcoal) or 2 (9-inch) disposable aluminum pie plates (if using gas)
- ¾ cup wood chips, soaked in water for 15 minutes and drained

1. Rub 2 tablespoons spice rub on each side of each rack of ribs. Let ribs sit at room temperature while preparing grill.

2. Combine apple juice and vinegar in small bowl and set aside.

3A. *For a charcoal grill:* Open bottom vent halfway and evenly space 15 unlit charcoal briquettes on 1 side of grill. Place disposable pan filled with 2 cups water on other side of grill. Light large chimney starter one-third filled with charcoal briquettes (2 quarts). When top coals are partially covered with ash, pour evenly over unlit coals. Sprinkle soaked wood chips over lit coals. Set cooking grate in place, cover, and open lid vent halfway. Heat grill until hot and wood chips are smoking, about 5 minutes.

3B. *For a gas grill:* Place soaked wood chips in pie plate with ¼ cup water and set over primary burner. Place second pie plate filled with 2 cups water on other burner(s). Turn all burners to high, cover, and heat grill until hot and wood chips are smoking, about 15 minutes. Turn primary burner to medium-high and turn off other burner(s). (Adjust primary burner as needed to maintain grill temperature of 250 to 275 degrees.)

4. Clean and oil cooking grate. Place ribs meat side down on cooler side of grill over water-filled pan. Cover (position lid vent over meat if using charcoal) and cook until ribs are deep red and smoky, about 1½ hours, brushing with apple juice mixture and flipping and rotating racks halfway through cooking. About 20 minutes before removing ribs from grill, adjust oven rack to lower-middle position and heat oven to 300 degrees.

5. Set wire rack in rimmed baking sheet and transfer ribs to rack. Brush top of each rack with 2 tablespoons apple juice mixture. Pour 1½ cups water into bottom of sheet; roast for 1 hour. Brush ribs with remaining apple juice mixture and continue to cook until meat is tender and registers 195 degrees, 1 to 2 hours. Transfer ribs to cutting board and let rest for 15 minutes. Slice ribs between bones and serve.

Spice Rub
Makes about ½ cup
For less spiciness, reduce the amount of cayenne to ½ teaspoon.

- 2 tablespoons paprika
- 2 tablespoons packed light brown sugar
- 1 tablespoon table salt
- 2 teaspoons chili powder
- 1½ teaspoons pepper
- 1½ teaspoons garlic powder
- 1½ teaspoons onion powder
- 1½ teaspoons cayenne pepper
- ½ teaspoon dried thyme

Combine all ingredients in bowl.

Grilled Swordfish Skewers with Tomato-Scallion Caponata

Serves 4 to 6

WHY THIS RECIPE WORKS Swordfish has a robust taste all its own and needs co-starring ingredients with just as much oomph. Here we paired swordfish with a Sicilian-inspired grilled caponata relish. As a base, we grilled cherry tomatoes, lemons, and scallions alongside the swordfish and added an aromatic blend of warm spices for a potent sauce to complement the fish. Once grilled, the lemon transformed from tart and acidic to sweet. Rubbing the swordfish with ground coriander added complexity that popped with the tomato, scallions, and fresh basil. If swordfish isn't available, you can substitute halibut. You will need six 12-inch metal skewers for this recipe.

- 1½ pounds skinless swordfish steaks, 1¼ to 1½ inches thick, cut into 1¼-inch pieces
- 5 teaspoons ground coriander, divided
- 1¼ teaspoons table salt, divided
- ½ teaspoon pepper, divided
- 12 ounces cherry tomatoes
- 1 small eggplant (12 ounces), cut crosswise on bias into ½-inch-thick ovals
- 6 scallions, trimmed
- ¼ cup extra-virgin olive oil, divided
- 1 tablespoon grated lemon zest, plus 2 lemons, halved
- 1½ tablespoons honey
- 2 garlic cloves, minced
- 1 teaspoon ground cumin
- ¼ teaspoon ground cinnamon
- ⅛ teaspoon ground nutmeg
- ¼ cup pitted kalamata olives, chopped
- 2 tablespoons finely chopped fresh basil

1. Pat swordfish dry with paper towels, rub with 1 tablespoon coriander, and season with ½ teaspoon salt and ¼ teaspoon pepper. Thread fish onto three 12-inch metal skewers. Thread tomatoes onto three 12-inch metal skewers. Brush swordfish, tomatoes, eggplant, and scallions with 2 tablespoons oil.

2A. *For a charcoal grill:* Open bottom vent completely. Light large chimney starter filled with charcoal briquettes (6 quarts). When top coals are partially covered with ash, pour evenly over grill. Set cooking grate in place, cover, and open lid vent completely. Heat grill until hot, about 5 minutes.

2B. *For a gas grill:* Turn all burners to high, cover, and heat grill until hot, about 15 minutes. Leave all burners on high.

3. Clean cooking grate, then repeatedly brush grate with well-oiled paper towels until black and glossy, 5 to 10 times. Place swordfish, tomatoes, eggplant, scallions, and lemon halves on grill. Cook (covered if using gas), turning as needed, until swordfish flakes apart when gently prodded with paring knife and registers 140 degrees and tomatoes, eggplant, scallions, and lemon halves are softened and lightly charred, 5 to 15 minutes. Transfer items to serving platter as they finish grilling and tent with aluminum foil. Let swordfish rest while finishing caponata.

4. Whisk lemon zest, honey, garlic, cumin, cinnamon, nutmeg, remaining 2 teaspoons coriander, remaining ¾ teaspoon salt, remaining ¼ teaspoon pepper, and remaining 2 tablespoons oil together in large bowl. Microwave, stirring occasionally, until fragrant, about 1 minute. Once lemons are cool enough to handle, squeeze into fine-mesh strainer set over bowl with oil-honey mixture, extracting as much juice as possible; whisk to combine. Stir in olives.

5. Using tongs, slide tomatoes off skewers onto cutting board. Chop tomatoes, eggplant, and scallions coarse, transfer to bowl with dressing, and gently toss to combine. Season with salt and pepper to taste. Remove swordfish from skewers, sprinkle with basil, and serve with caponata.

Grilled Swordfish Skewers with
Tomato-Scallion Caponata

"With a kitchen renovation at home a few years ago, I finally got a proper vent hood over the stove, thus ending my days of setting off the fire alarm whenever I seared something. Still and all, the prospect of cooking New Orleans–style blackened anything, which can get impressively smoky, indoors gives me pause. Move the action outdoors to the grill, however, and I'm all in!

Red snapper is a fave among fishes because it's meaty and it grills beautifully. Scoring the skin keeps the fillets flat as they cook, and superheating the grill and oiling the grate both hedge against sticking. Best of all, the butter-bloomed spice mixture (heavy on the cayenne when I'm in charge) gives the fish an unmistakable essence of the Crescent City. Invite the firefighters to dinner, not to a false alarm!"

—*Adam*

Grilled Blackened Red Snapper

Serves 4

WHY THIS RECIPE WORKS Blackened fish is usually prepared in a cast-iron skillet, but it can lead to one smoky kitchen. We thought we'd solve this issue by throwing our fish on the grill. Unfortunately, this created a host of other problems, including fish stuck to the grate, the outside of the fish being way overdone by the time the flesh had cooked through, and the skin-on fillets curling midway through cooking. We were done with the smoke—and were ready for our fillets to have a dark brown, crusty, sweet-smoky, toasted spice exterior, providing a rich contrast to the moist, mild-flavored fish inside. The curling problem was easy to fix: We simply needed to score the skin. To prevent sticking, we made sure the grill was hot when we put the fish on and oiled the grate multiple times. Finally, to give the fish its flavorful "blackened but not burned" coating, we bloomed our spice mixture in melted butter, allowed it to cool, and then applied the coating to the fish. Once on the grill, the spice crust acquired the proper depth and richness while the fish cooked through. Striped bass, halibut, or grouper can be substituted for the snapper; if the fillets are thicker or thinner, they will have slightly different cooking times. Serve the fish with lemon wedges, Rémoulade, or Pineapple and Cucumber Salsa with Mint (recipes follow).

- 2 tablespoons paprika
- 2 teaspoons onion powder
- 2 teaspoons garlic powder
- ¾ teaspoon ground coriander
- ¾ teaspoon table salt
- ¼ teaspoon cayenne pepper
- ¼ teaspoon black pepper
- ¼ teaspoon white pepper
- 3 tablespoons unsalted butter
- 4 (6- to 8-ounce) skin-on red snapper fillets, ¾ inch thick

1. Combine paprika, onion powder, garlic powder, coriander, salt, cayenne, pepper, and white pepper in bowl. Melt butter in 10-inch skillet over medium heat. Stir in spice mixture and cook, stirring frequently, until fragrant and spices turn dark rust color, 2 to 3 minutes. Transfer mixture to pie plate and let cool to room temperature. Use fork to break up any large clumps.

2A. *For a charcoal grill:* Open bottom vent completely. Light large chimney starter two-thirds filled with charcoal briquettes (4 quarts). When top coals are partially covered with ash, pour evenly over half of grill. Set cooking grate in place, cover, and open lid vent completely. Heat grill until hot, about 5 minutes.

2B. *For a gas grill:* Turn all burners to high, cover, and heat grill until hot, about 15 minutes.

3. Clean cooking grate, then repeatedly brush grate with well-oiled paper towels until black and glossy, 5 to 10 times.

4. Meanwhile, pat fillets dry with paper towels. Using sharp knife, make shallow diagonal slashes every inch along skin side of fish, being careful not to cut into flesh. Place fillets skin side up on large plate. Using your fingers, rub spice mixture in thin, even layer on top and sides of fish. Flip fillets over and repeat on other side (you should use all of spice mixture).

5. Place fish skin side down on grill (hot side if using charcoal) with fillets diagonal to grate. Cook until skin is very dark brown and crisp, 3 to 5 minutes. Carefully flip fish and continue to cook until dark brown and beginning to flake and center is opaque but still moist, about 5 minutes longer. Serve.

ACCOMPANIMENTS
Rémoulade
Makes about ½ cup

- ½ cup mayonnaise
- 1½ teaspoons sweet pickle relish
- 1 teaspoon hot sauce
- 1 teaspoon lemon juice
- 1 teaspoon minced fresh parsley
- ½ teaspoon capers, rinsed
- ½ teaspoon Dijon mustard
- 1 small garlic clove, minced

Pulse all ingredients in food processor until well combined but not smooth, about 10 pulses. Season with salt and pepper to taste. Transfer to serving bowl. (Rémoulade can be refrigerated for up to 3 days.)

Pineapple and Cucumber Salsa with Mint
Makes about 3 cups
To make this dish spicier, add the reserved chile seeds.

- ½ large pineapple, peeled, cored, and cut into ¼-inch pieces
- ½ cucumber, peeled, halved lengthwise, seeded, and cut into ¼-inch pieces
- 1 small shallot, minced
- 1 serrano chile, stemmed, seeds reserved, and minced
- 2 tablespoons chopped fresh mint
- 1–2 tablespoons lime juice, divided
- ½ teaspoon grated fresh ginger
- ½ teaspoon table salt

Combine pineapple, cucumber, shallot, serrano, mint, 1 tablespoon lime juice, ginger, and salt in bowl and let sit at room temperature for 15 to 30 minutes. Season with lime juice, salt, and sugar to taste. Transfer to serving bowl.

Grill-Smoked Salmon

Serves 6

WHY THIS RECIPE WORKS We wanted to capture the intense, smoky flavor of hot-smoked fish and the firm but silky texture of the cold-smoked type, but we also wanted to skip specialized equipment and make this dish less of a project. We quick-cured the fish with a mixture of salt and sugar to draw moisture from the flesh, and we seasoned it inside and out. We then cooked it over a gentle fire with ample smoke to produce salmon that was sweet, smoky, and tender. We also cut our large fillet into individual serving-size portions. This ensured more thorough smoke exposure by creating more surface area. Plus, the smaller pieces of salmon were far easier to get off the grill intact than one large fillet. Use center-cut salmon fillets of similar thickness so that they cook at the same rate. The best way to ensure uniformity is to buy a 2½- to 3-pound whole center-cut fillet and cut it into six pieces. If you'd like to use wood chunks instead of wood chips when using a charcoal grill, substitute two medium wood chunks, soaked in water for 1 hour, for the wood chips. Avoid mesquite wood chunks for this recipe. Serve the salmon with lemon wedges or with our "Smoked Salmon Platter" Sauce or Apple-Mustard Sauce (recipes follow).

    2 tablespoons sugar
    1 tablespoon kosher salt
    6 (6- to 8-ounce) center-cut skin-on salmon fillets
    2 cups wood chips

1. Combine sugar and salt in bowl. Set wire rack in rimmed baking sheet, set salmon on rack, and sprinkle flesh side evenly with sugar mixture. Refrigerate, uncovered, for 1 hour. With paper towels, brush any excess salt and sugar from salmon and blot dry. Return fish on wire rack to refrigerator, uncovered, while preparing grill. Just before grilling, soak 1 cup wood chips in water for 15 minutes, then drain. Using large piece of heavy-duty aluminum foil, wrap soaked and unsoaked chips together in 8 by 4½-inch foil packet. (Make sure chips do not poke holes in sides or bottom of packet.) Cut 2 evenly spaced 2-inch slits in top of packet.

2A. *For a charcoal grill:* Open bottom vent halfway. Light large chimney starter one-third filled with charcoal briquettes (2 quarts). When top coals are partially covered with ash, pour into steeply banked pile against side of grill. Place wood chip packet on top of coals. Set coowking grate in place, cover, and open lid vent halfway. Heat grill until hot and wood chips begin to smoke, about 5 minutes.

2B. *For a gas grill:* Place wood chip packet directly on primary burner. Turn primary burner to high (leave other burners off), cover, and heat grill until hot and wood chips begin to smoke, 15 to 25 minutes. Turn primary burner to medium. (Adjust primary burner as needed to maintain grill temperature of 275 to 300 degrees.)

3. Fold piece of heavy-duty foil into 18 by 6-inch rectangle. Place foil rectangle over cool side of grill and place salmon pieces on foil, spaced at least ½ inch apart. Cover grill (positioning lid vent over fish if using charcoal) and cook until center of thickest part of fillet registers 125 degrees and is still translucent when checked with tip of paring knife, 30 to 40 minutes. Transfer to platter and serve or allow to cool to room temperature.

ACCOMPANIMENTS
"Smoked Salmon Platter" Sauce
Makes 1½ cups
This sauce incorporates the three garnishes that are commonly served on a smoked salmon platter—hard-cooked egg, capers, and dill.

    1 large egg yolk, plus 1 large hard-cooked egg,
       chopped fine
    2 teaspoons Dijon mustard
    2 teaspoons sherry vinegar
    ½ cup vegetable oil
    2 tablespoons capers, rinsed, plus 1 teaspoon
       caper brine
    2 tablespoons minced shallot
    2 tablespoons finely chopped fresh dill

Whisk egg yolk, mustard, and vinegar together in medium bowl. Whisking constantly, slowly drizzle in oil until emulsified, about 1 minute. Gently fold in capers and brine, hard-cooked egg, shallot, and dill.

Apple-Mustard Sauce
Makes 1½ cups

- 2 Honeycrisp or Granny Smith apples, peeled, cored, and cut into ¼-inch pieces
- ¼ cup whole-grain mustard
- 2 tablespoons Dijon mustard
- 2 tablespoons finely chopped fresh chervil or parsley
- 1 tablespoon cider vinegar
- 1 tablespoon honey
- ¼ teaspoon table salt

Combine all ingredients in bowl.

Grilled Shrimp Skewers

Serves 4

WHY THIS RECIPE WORKS Great grilled shrimp—tender, moist, and flavorful—are hard to come by. Grilling shrimp in their shells can guarantee juiciness, but the seasoning tends to be lost when the shells are pulled off. We wanted tender, juicy, boldly seasoned grilled shrimp, with the flavor in the shrimp and not on our fingers. Our decision to use peeled shrimp for this recipe meant we had to revisit how we traditionally grilled shrimp. First we eliminated brining, which created waterlogged shrimp and hindered caramelization. Then we set the shrimp over a screaming-hot fire. This worked well with jumbo shrimp, but smaller shrimp overcooked before charring. With jumbo shrimp costing as much as $25 per pound, we decided against them. They did give us an idea, though. For our next step, we created faux jumbo shrimp by cramming a skewer with several normal-sized shrimp pressed tightly together. And we took the shrimp off the fire before they were completely cooked (but after they had picked up attractive grill marks). We finished cooking them in a heated sauce waiting on the cool side of the grill; this final simmer gave them tons of flavor. The shrimp and sauce finish cooking together on the grill, so prepare the sauce ingredients while the grill is heating. To fit all of the shrimp on the cooking grate at once, you will need three 14-inch metal skewers. Serve with grilled bread.

- 1½ pounds extra-large shrimp (21 to 25 per pound), peeled and deveined
- 2–3 tablespoons extra-virgin olive oil
- ½ teaspoon table salt
- ¼ teaspoon pepper
- ¼ teaspoon sugar
- 1 recipe sauce (page 341)
  Lemon wedges

1. Pat shrimp dry with paper towels. Thread shrimp onto 3 skewers, alternating direction of heads and tails. Brush both sides of shrimp with oil and season with salt and pepper. Sprinkle 1 side of each skewer evenly with sugar.

2A. *For a charcoal grill:* Open bottom vent completely. Light large chimney starter filled with charcoal briquettes (6 quarts). When top coals are partially covered with ash, pour evenly over half of grill. Set cooking grate in place, cover, and open lid vent completely. Heat grill until hot, about 5 minutes.

2B. *For a gas grill:* Turn all burners to high, cover, and heat grill until hot, about 15 minutes. Leave primary burner on high and turn other burner(s) to medium-low.

3. Clean cooking grate, then repeatedly brush grate with well-oiled paper towels until grate is black and glossy, 5 to 10 times. Place disposable pan with sauce ingredients on hot side of grill and cook, stirring occasionally, until hot, 1 to 3 minutes. Move pan to cool side of grill.

4. Place shrimp skewers sugared side down on hot side of grill and use tongs to push shrimp together on skewers if they have separated. Cook shrimp until lightly charred, 4 to 5 minutes. Using tongs, flip and continue to cook until second side is pink and slightly translucent, 1 to 2 minutes.

5. Using potholder, carefully lift each skewer from grill and use tongs to slide shrimp off skewers into pan with sauce. Toss shrimp and sauce to combine. Place pan on hot side of

Arranging Shrimp on a Skewer

Pass skewer through center of each shrimp. As you add shrimp to skewer, alternate directions of heads and tails for compact arrangement of shrimp. Shrimp should fit snugly against each other.

"It's a good idea to have a few recipes that you can count on to reliably impress company at a casual get-together. In the summer and into the fall, this is the recipe that I go back to year after year. Now, usually I like to have most of the meal done before company arrives, but this is a dish that's interesting to watch come together. I do get some of the components done ahead—I make the clam juice–tomato broth, season the shrimp, and season and brown the chicken thighs—but then I get my company to help out with the rest. People get a real rush cooking a dish with seafood, chicken, rice and sausage all on the grill.

Now I get requests to make this dish and I've had to buy a second paella pan in order to make enough to send people home with leftovers."

—*Bridget*

grill and cook, stirring, until shrimp are opaque throughout, about 30 seconds. Remove from grill, add remaining sauce ingredients, and toss to combine. Transfer to serving platter and serve with lemon wedges.

Spicy Lemon-Garlic Sauce
Makes about ½ cup

    4 tablespoons unsalted butter, cut into 4 pieces
    ¼ cup lemon juice (2 lemons)
    3 garlic cloves, minced
    ½ teaspoon red pepper flakes
    ⅛ teaspoon table salt
    1 (10-inch) disposable aluminum pie pan
    ⅓ cup finely chopped fresh parsley

Combine butter, lemon juice, garlic, pepper flakes, and salt in aluminum pan. Cook over hot side of grill, stirring occasionally, until butter melts, about 1½ minutes. Move to cool side of grill and proceed to grill shrimp, adding parsley just before serving.

Fresh Tomato Sauce with Feta and Olives
Makes about ½ cup

    ¼ cup extra-virgin olive oil
    1 large tomato, cored, seeded, and minced
    1 tablespoon finely chopped fresh oregano
    ⅛ teaspoon table salt
    1 (10-inch) disposable aluminum pie pan
    4 ounces feta cheese, crumbled (1 cup)
    ⅓ cup kalamata olives, pitted and chopped fine
    2 tablespoons lemon juice
    3 scallions, sliced thin

Combine oil, tomato, oregano, and salt in aluminum pan. Cook over hot side of grill, stirring occasionally, until hot, about 1½ minutes. Move to cool side of grill and proceed to grill shrimp, adding feta, olives, lemon juice, and scallions just before serving.

Paella on the Grill

Serves 8

WHY THIS RECIPE WORKS Grilling paella lends the dish subtle smoke flavor and a particularly rich crust and makes it a great dish for summer entertaining. In place of a traditional paella pan, we used a large, sturdy roasting pan that maximized the amount of *socarrat*, the prized caramelized rice crust that forms on the bottom of the pan. Building a large (7-quart) fire and fueling it with fresh coals (which ignited during cooking) ensured that the heat output would last throughout cooking, but we also shortened the outdoor cooking time by using roasted red peppers and tomato paste (instead of fresh peppers and tomatoes), making an infused broth with the seasonings, and grilling (rather than searing) the chicken thighs. To ensure that the various components finished cooking at the same time, we staggered the addition of the proteins—first, the chicken thighs, followed by the shrimp, clams, and chorizo. We also deliberately placed the chicken on the perimeter of the pan, where it would finish cooking gently after grilling, and the sausage and seafood in the center, where they were partially submerged in the liquid so that they cooked through; once the liquid reduced, the steam kept them warm. This recipe was developed with a light-colored 16 by 13½-inch tri-ply roasting pan; however, it can be made in any heavy roasting pan that measures at least 14 by 11 inches. If your roasting pan is dark in color, the cooking times will be on the lower end of the ranges given. The recipe can also be made in a 15- to 17-inch paella pan. If littlenecks are unavailable, use 1½ pounds shrimp in step 1 and season it with ½ teaspoon table salt.

    1½ pounds boneless, skinless chicken thighs, trimmed and halved crosswise
    1¾ teaspoons table salt, divided
    1 teaspoon pepper
    12 ounces jumbo shrimp (16 to 20 per pound), peeled and deveined
    6 tablespoons extra-virgin olive oil, divided
    6 garlic cloves, minced, divided
    1¾ teaspoons smoked hot paprika, divided
    3 tablespoons tomato paste
    4 cups chicken broth
    ⅔ cup dry sherry
    1 (8-ounce) bottle clam juice
      Pinch saffron threads (optional)
    1 onion, chopped fine
    ½ cup roasted red peppers, chopped fine
    3 cups Arborio rice
    1 pound littleneck clams, scrubbed
    1 pound Spanish-style chorizo, cut into ½-inch pieces
    1 cup frozen peas, thawed
      Lemon wedges

1. Place chicken on large plate and sprinkle both sides with 1 teaspoon salt and 1 teaspoon pepper. Toss shrimp with 1 tablespoon oil, ½ teaspoon garlic, ¼ teaspoon paprika, and ¼ teaspoon salt in bowl until evenly coated. Set aside.

2. Heat 1 tablespoon oil in medium saucepan over medium heat until shimmering. Add remaining garlic and cook, stirring constantly, until garlic sticks to bottom of saucepan and begins to brown, about 1 minute. Add tomato paste and remaining 1½ teaspoons paprika and continue to cook, stirring constantly, until dark brown bits form on bottom of saucepan, about 1 minute. Add broth, sherry, clam juice, and saffron, if using. Increase heat to high and bring to boil. Remove pan from heat and set aside.

3A. *For a charcoal grill:* Open bottom vent completely. Light large chimney starter mounded with charcoal briquettes (7 quarts). When top coals are partially covered with ash, pour evenly over grill. Using tongs, arrange 20 unlit briquettes evenly over coals. Set cooking grate in place, cover, and open lid vent completely. Heat grill until hot, about 5 minutes.

3B. *For a gas grill:* Turn all burners to high, cover, and heat grill until hot, about 15 minutes. Leave all burners on high.

4. Clean and oil cooking grate. Place chicken on grill and cook until both sides are lightly browned, 5 to 7 minutes. Return chicken to plate. Clean cooking grate.

5. Place roasting pan on grill (turning burners to medium-high if using gas) and add remaining ¼ cup oil. When oil begins to shimmer, add onion, red peppers, and remaining ½ teaspoon salt. Cook, stirring frequently, until onion begins to brown, 4 to 7 minutes. Add rice (turning burners to medium if using gas) and stir until grains are well coated with oil.

6. Arrange chicken around perimeter of pan. Pour broth mixture and any accumulated juices from chicken over rice. Smooth rice into even layer, making sure nothing sticks to sides of pan and no rice rests atop chicken. When liquid reaches gentle simmer, place shrimp in center of pan in single layer. Arrange clams in center of pan, evenly distributing with shrimp and pushing hinge sides of clams into rice slightly so they stand up. Distribute chorizo evenly over surface of rice. Cook, moving and rotating pan to maintain gentle simmer across entire surface of pan, until rice is almost cooked through, 12 to 18 minutes. (If using gas, heat can also be adjusted to maintain simmer.)

7. Sprinkle peas evenly over paella, cover grill, and cook until liquid is fully absorbed and rice on bottom of pan sizzles, 5 to 8 minutes. Continue to cook, uncovered, checking frequently, until uniform golden-brown crust forms on bottom of pan, 8 to 15 minutes. (Rotate and slide pan around grill as necessary to ensure even crust formation.) Remove from grill, cover with foil, and let sit for 10 minutes. Serve with lemon wedges.

Mexican-Style Grilled Corn

Serves 6

WHY THIS RECIPE WORKS In Mexico, street vendors add kick to grilled corn by slathering it with a creamy, spicy sauce. The corn takes on a sweet, charred flavor, which is heightened by the lime juice and chili powder in the cheesy sauce. For our own rendition of this south-of-the-border street fare we ditched the husks, coated the ears with oil to prevent sticking, and grilled them directly on the grate.

Over a single-level fire, the corn emerged nicely smoky but insufficiently charred, so we pushed all the coals to one side to create a half-grill fire, allowing the ears to cook closer to the coals. The traditional base for the sauce is crema, a thick, soured Mexican cream. But given its spotty availability, we replaced the crema with a combination of mayonnaise and sour cream. Most recipes call for *queso fresco* or Cotija, but these can be hard to find. Pecorino Romano made a good substitute. We included the usual seasonings of cilantro, lime juice, garlic, and chili powder. To provide more depth, we added chili powder to the oil used for coating the corn; once heated on the grill, the chili powder bloomed with a full flavor that penetrated the corn kernels. If you can find queso fresco or Cotija, use either in place of the Pecorino Romano. If you prefer the corn spicy, add the optional cayenne pepper.

1½ ounces Pecorino Romano cheese, grated (¾ cup)
¼ cup mayonnaise
3 tablespoons sour cream
3 tablespoons finely chopped fresh cilantro
4 teaspoons lime juice
1 garlic clove, minced
¾ teaspoon chili powder, divided
¼ teaspoon pepper
¼ teaspoon cayenne pepper (optional)
4 teaspoons vegetable oil
¼ teaspoon table salt
6 ears corn, husks and silk removed

1A. *For a charcoal grill:* Open bottom vent completely. Light large chimney starter filled with charcoal briquettes (6 quarts). When top coals are partially covered with ash, pour evenly over half of grill. Set cooking grate in place, cover, and open lid vent completely. Heat grill until hot, about 5 minutes.

1B. *For a gas grill:* Turn all burners to high, cover, and heat grill until hot, about 15 minutes.

2. Meanwhile, combine Pecorino, mayonnaise, sour cream, cilantro, lime juice, garlic, ¼ teaspoon chili powder, pepper, and cayenne, if using, in large bowl and set aside. In second large bowl, combine oil, salt, and remaining ½ teaspoon chili powder. Add corn to oil mixture and toss to coat evenly.

3. Clean and oil cooking grate. Place corn on grill (hot side if using charcoal) and cook (covered if using gas) until lightly charred on all sides, 7 to 12 minutes, turning as needed. Place corn in bowl with cheese mixture, toss to coat evenly, and serve.

Grilled Baba Ghanoush

Makes 2 cups

WHY THIS RECIPE WORKS A great way to ensure this appealing dip is full of smoky eggplant flavor is start off by grilling the eggplant. For the best flavor, it's imperative to start out with firm, shiny, and unblemished eggplants. We grilled the eggplants directly over a hot fire until they were wrinkled and soft. To avoid a watery texture and any bitterness, we drained the pulp of excess fluid, but didn't bother spending time deseeding the eggplants. We processed the pulp with a modest amount of garlic, tahini, and lemon juice for the creaminess and bright flavor that baba ghanoush is known for. When buying eggplants, select those with shiny, taut, and unbruised skins and an even shape (eggplants with a bulbous shape won't cook evenly). Grill until the eggplant walls have collapsed and the insides feel sloshy when pressed with tongs. We prefer to serve baba ghanoush only lightly chilled; if cold, let it stand at room temperature for about 20 minutes before serving. Baba ghanoush does not keep well, so plan to make it the day you want to serve it. Serve with pita bread, black olives, tomato wedges, or cucumber slices.

- 2 **pounds eggplant (about 2 large globe eggplants, 5 medium Italian eggplants, or 12 medium Japanese eggplants), pricked all over with fork**
- 2 **tablespoons tahini**
- 1 **tablespoon lemon juice**
- 1 **tablespoon extra-virgin olive oil, plus extra for serving**
- 1 **small garlic clove, minced**
- ¼ **teaspoon table salt**
- ¼ **teaspoon pepper**
- 2 **teaspoons chopped fresh parsley**

1A. *For a charcoal grill:* Open bottom vent completely. Light large chimney starter filled with charcoal briquettes (6 quarts). When top coals are partially covered with ash, pour evenly over grill. Set cooking grate in place, cover, and open lid vent completely. Heat grill until hot, about 5 minutes.

1B. *For a gas grill:* Turn all burners to high, cover, and heat grill until hot, about 15 minutes. Turn all burners to medium. (Adjust burners as needed to maintain grill temperature around 350 degrees.)

2. Clean and oil cooking grate. Set eggplants on cooking grate and cook until skins darken and wrinkle on all sides and eggplants are uniformly soft when pressed with tongs, about 25 minutes for large globe eggplants, 20 minutes for Italian eggplants, and 15 minutes for Japanese eggplants, turning every 5 minutes and reversing direction of eggplants on grill with each turn. Transfer eggplants to rimmed baking sheet and let cool for 5 minutes.

3. Set small colander over bowl. Trim top and bottom off each eggplant. Slit eggplants lengthwise and use spoon to scoop hot pulp from skins and place pulp in colander (you should have about 2 cups packed pulp); discard skins. Let pulp drain for 3 minutes.

4. Transfer pulp to food processor. Add tahini, lemon juice, oil, garlic, salt, and pepper. Pulse until mixture has coarse, choppy texture, about 8 pulses. Season with salt and pepper to taste. Transfer to serving bowl, press plastic wrap flush to surface of dip, and refrigerate for 45 minutes to 1 hour. Make trough in center of dip using large spoon and spoon olive oil into it. Sprinkle with parsley and serve.

Sides

Quick Green Bean "Casserole"

Pan-Roasted Asparagus

Serves 3 to 4

WHY THIS RECIPE WORKS Recipes for pan-roasted asparagus promise ease and flavor, but the results are usually disappointing: limp, greasy, and shriveled spears. We wanted a simple stovetop method that would deliver crisp, nicely browned spears. We quickly learned to choose thick spears because thinner spears overcooked too quickly. Taking a cue from restaurant chefs who blanch asparagus first, we developed a method to lightly steam and then brown the asparagus in the same skillet. For both flavor and browning, we used olive oil and butter. Positioning half the spears in one direction and the other half in the opposite direction ensured a better fit in the pan. Browning just one side of the asparagus provided a contrast in texture and guaranteed that the asparagus was firm and tender, never limp. This recipe works best with asparagus that is at least ½ inch thick near the base. If using thinner spears, reduce the covered cooking time to 3 minutes and the uncovered cooking time to 5 minutes. Do not use pencil-thin asparagus; it cannot withstand the heat and overcooks too easily.

1 tablespoon extra-virgin olive oil
1 tablespoon unsalted butter
2 pounds thick asparagus, trimmed
½ lemon (optional)

1. Heat oil and butter in 12-inch skillet over medium-high heat. When butter has melted, add half of asparagus to skillet with tips pointed in 1 direction; add remaining asparagus with tips pointed in opposite direction. Using tongs, distribute spears in even layer (spears will not quite fit into single layer); cover and cook until asparagus is bright green and still crisp, about 5 minutes.

2. Uncover and increase heat to high; season asparagus with salt and pepper to taste. Cook until spears are tender and well browned along 1 side, 5 to 7 minutes, using tongs to occasionally move spears from center of pan to edge of pan to ensure all are browned. Transfer asparagus to serving dish, season with salt and pepper to taste, and squeeze lemon half, if using, over spears. Serve.

Stir-Fried Asparagus with Shiitake Mushrooms

Serves 4

WHY THIS RECIPE WORKS This elegant stir-fry pairs asparagus with earthy shiitake mushrooms and a classic Asian stir-fry sauce. To achieve stir-fried asparagus with a flavorful browned exterior and a crisp-tender texture, we had to start with a hot pan and only stir the asparagus occasionally. This allowed the vegetables to char and caramelize. To ensure that the asparagus cooked evenly, we diluted the sauce with water. This diluted sauce created a small amount of steam, cooking the spears through, before evaporating and leaving behind a flavorful glaze. To allow it to brown, stir the asparagus only occasionally. Look for spears that are no thicker than ½ inch.

2 tablespoons water
1 tablespoon soy sauce
1 tablespoon dry sherry
2 teaspoons packed brown sugar
2 teaspoons grated fresh ginger
1 teaspoon toasted sesame oil
1 tablespoon vegetable oil
1 pound asparagus, trimmed and cut on bias into 2-inch lengths
4 ounces shiitake mushrooms, stemmed and sliced thin
2 scallions, green parts only, sliced thin on bias

1. Combine water, soy sauce, sherry, sugar, ginger, and sesame oil in bowl.

2. Heat vegetable oil in 12-inch nonstick skillet over high heat until smoking. Add asparagus and mushrooms and cook, stirring occasionally, until asparagus is spotty brown, 3 to 4 minutes. Add soy sauce mixture and cook, stirring once or twice, until pan is almost dry and asparagus is crisp-tender, 1 to 2 minutes. Transfer to serving platter, sprinkle with scallion greens, and serve.

Stir-Fried Asparagus with Red Bell Pepper

Omit soy sauce, sherry, brown sugar, ginger, and sesame oil. Reduce water to 1 tablespoon. Whisk 1 tablespoon orange juice, 1 tablespoon rice vinegar, 1 tablespoon granulated sugar, 1 teaspoon ketchup, and ½ teaspoon table salt into water. Substitute 1 red bell pepper cut into 2-inch-long matchsticks for shiitakes.

Stir-Fried Asparagus with Red Onion

Omit soy sauce, sherry, ginger, and sesame oil. Whisk 4 teaspoons fish sauce, 1 tablespoon lime juice, 2 teaspoons minced fresh lemon grass, and ⅛ teaspoon red pepper flakes into water, along with sugar. Substitute ½ red onion sliced through root end into ¼-inch-thick pieces for shiitakes and 2 tablespoons chopped fresh mint for scallion greens.

Beets with Lemon and Almonds

Serves 4 to 6

WHY THIS RECIPE WORKS This streamlined recipe for beets maximizes their sweet, earthy flavor with minimal mess. Roasting the beets took over an hour, and boiling washed away their flavor, but braising worked perfectly. We partially submerged the beets in just 1¼ cups of water so that they partially simmered and partially steamed. Halving the beets cut down our cooking time even further. In just 45 minutes the beets were tender and their skins slipped off easily. To further amplify their flavor, we reduced the braising liquid and added brown sugar and vinegar to make a glossy sauce. Shallot, toasted almonds, fresh mint and thyme, and a little lemon zest finished the dish. Look for beets that are roughly 2 to 3 inches in diameter. The beets can be served warm or at room temperature. If serving at room temperature, add the nuts, seeds, and fresh herbs right before serving.

1½ **pounds beets, trimmed and halved horizontally**
1¼ **cups water**
 ¾ **teaspoon table salt, divided**
  3 **tablespoons distilled white vinegar**
  1 **tablespoon packed light brown sugar**
  1 **shallot, sliced thin**
  1 **teaspoon grated lemon zest**
 ¼ **teaspoon pepper**
 ½ **cup whole almonds, toasted and chopped**
  2 **tablespoons chopped fresh mint**
  1 **teaspoon chopped fresh thyme**

1. Place beets, cut side down, in single layer in 11-inch straight-sided sauté pan or Dutch oven. Add water and ¼ teaspoon salt; bring to simmer over high heat. Reduce heat to low, cover, and simmer until beets are tender and tip of paring knife inserted into beets meets no resistance, 45 to 50 minutes.

2. Transfer beets to cutting board. Increase heat to medium-high and reduce cooking liquid, stirring occasionally, until pan is almost dry, 5 to 6 minutes. Add vinegar and sugar, return to boil, and cook, stirring constantly with heat-resistant spatula, until spatula leaves wide trail when dragged through glaze, 1 to 2 minutes. Remove pan from heat.

3. When beets are cool enough to handle, rub off skins with paper towel or clean dish towel and cut into ½-inch wedges. Add beets, shallot, lemon zest, remaining ½ teaspoon salt, and pepper to glaze and toss to coat. Transfer beets to serving dish; sprinkle with almonds, mint, and thyme; and serve.

Beets with Lime and Pepitas

Omit thyme. Substitute lime zest for lemon zest, toasted pepitas for almonds, and cilantro for mint.

Beets with Orange and Walnuts

Substitute orange zest for lemon zest; walnuts, toasted and chopped, for almonds; and parsley for mint.

Roasted Broccoli

Serves 4

WHY THIS RECIPE WORKS Roasting is a great way to deepen the flavor of vegetables, but broccoli can be tricky to roast given its awkward shape, dense woody stalks, and shrubby florets. We wanted to figure out how to roast broccoli so that it turned out perfectly browned and deeply flavorful every time. To ensure that the broccoli would brown evenly, we cut the crown into uniform wedges that lay flat on the baking sheet, increasing contact with the pan. To promote even cooking of the stem, we sliced away the exterior and cut the stalk into rectangular pieces slightly smaller than the more delicate wedges. After trial and error, we discovered that preheating the baking sheet helped the broccoli cook faster, crisping but not charring the florets, while a very hot oven delivered the best browning. Sprinkling a little sugar over the broccoli along with the salt and pepper helped it brown even more deeply. We finally had roasted broccoli with crispy-tipped florets and sweet, browned stems. It is important to trim away the outer peel from the broccoli stalks; otherwise they will turn tough when cooked.

1¾ pounds broccoli
3 tablespoons extra-virgin olive oil
½ teaspoon table salt
½ teaspoon sugar
 Lemon wedges

1. Adjust oven rack to lowest position, place rimmed baking sheet on rack, and heat oven to 500 degrees. Cut broccoli at juncture of florets and stems; remove outer peel from stalk. Cut stalk into 2- to 3-inch lengths and each length into ½-inch-thick pieces. Cut crowns into 4 wedges (if 3 to 4 inches in diameter) or 6 wedges (if 4 to 5 inches in diameter). Place broccoli in large bowl; drizzle with oil and toss well until evenly coated. Season with salt, sugar, and pepper to taste and toss to combine.

2. Carefully remove sheet from oven. Working quickly, transfer broccoli to sheet and spread into even layer, placing flat sides down. Return sheet to oven and roast until stalks are well browned and tender and florets are lightly browned, 9 to 11 minutes. Transfer to serving dish and serve with lemon wedges.

VARIATION
Roasted Broccoli with Garlic
Add 1 garlic clove, minced, to oil before drizzling it over broccoli in step 1.

Skillet-Roasted Brussels Sprouts with Lemon and Pecorino Romano

Serves 4

WHY THIS RECIPE WORKS All too often, Brussels sprouts wind up either overcooked or undercooked and rarely receive the praise they deserve. We wanted a foolproof stovetop recipe that would produce Brussels sprouts that were deeply browned on the cut sides, while still bright green on the uncut sides and crisp-tender within. After several unsuccessful attempts in a hot skillet, we tried starting the sprouts in a cold skillet (which also made it easier to arrange them), adding plenty of oil and cooking them covered. This gently heated the sprouts and created a steamy environment that cooked them through without adding any extra moisture. We then removed the lid and continued to cook the sprouts cut sides down so they had time to develop a substantial, caramelized crust. Using enough oil to completely coat the skillet ensured that all the sprouts made full contact with the fat to brown from edge to edge, resulting in gorgeously, evenly browned sprouts that weren't greasy. To balance their nutty sweetness, we stirred in some lemon juice and sprinkled Pecorino Romano as a finishing touch. Look for Brussels sprouts that are similar in size, with small, tight heads that are no more than 1½ inches in diameter, as they're likely to be sweeter and more tender than larger sprouts. Parmesan cheese can be substituted for the Pecorino, if desired.

1 pound small (1 to 1½ inches in diameter) Brussels sprouts, trimmed and halved
5 tablespoons extra-virgin olive oil
1 tablespoon lemon juice
¼ teaspoon table salt
¼ cup shredded Pecorino Romano cheese

1. Arrange Brussels sprouts in single layer, cut sides down, in 12-inch nonstick skillet. Drizzle oil evenly over sprouts. Cover skillet, place over medium-high heat, and cook until sprouts are bright green and cut sides have started to brown, about 5 minutes.

2. Uncover and continue to cook until cut sides of sprouts are deeply and evenly browned and paring knife slides in with little to no resistance, 2 to 3 minutes, adjusting heat and moving sprouts as necessary to prevent them from overbrowning. While sprouts cook, combine lemon juice and salt in small bowl.

Skillet-Roasted Brussels Sprouts with
Lemon and Pecorino Romano

3. Off heat, add lemon juice mixture to skillet and stir to evenly coat sprouts. Season with salt and pepper to taste. Transfer sprouts to large plate, sprinkle with Pecorino, and serve.

VARIATIONS
Skillet-Roasted Brussels Sprouts with Cider Vinegar and Honey
Substitute 2 teaspoons cider vinegar, 2 teaspoons honey, and ¼ teaspoon red pepper flakes for lemon juice and omit pepper and Pecorino.

Skillet-Roasted Brussels Sprouts with Maple Syrup and Smoked Almonds
Omit pepper. Substitute 1 tablespoon maple syrup and 1 tablespoon sherry vinegar for lemon juice and ¼ cup smoked almonds, chopped fine, for Pecorino.

Skillet-Roasted Brussels Sprouts with Pomegranate and Pistachios
Substitute 1 tablespoon pomegranate molasses and ½ teaspoon ground cumin for lemon juice. Omit pepper. Substitute ¼ cup shelled pistachios, toasted and chopped fine, and 2 tablespoons pomegranate seeds for Pecorino.

Skillet-Roasted Brussels Sprouts with Chile, Peanuts, and Mint
Substitute 1 Fresno chile, minced; 2 teaspoons lime juice; and 1 teaspoon fish sauce for lemon juice. Omit pepper. Substitute 2 tablespoons finely chopped dry-roasted peanuts and 2 tablespoons chopped fresh mint for Pecorino.

Skillet-Roasted Brussels Sprouts with Gochujang and Sesame Seeds
Omit pepper. Substitute 1 tablespoon gochujang and 1 tablespoon rice vinegar for lemon juice and 2 teaspoons toasted sesame seeds for Pecorino.

Skillet-Roasted Brussels Sprouts with Mustard and Brown Sugar
Substitute 1 tablespoon Dijon mustard, 1 tablespoon packed brown sugar, 2 teaspoons white wine vinegar, and ⅛ teaspoon cayenne pepper for lemon juice. Omit pepper and Pecorino.

Slow-Cooked Whole Carrots

Serves 4 to 6

WHY THIS RECIPE WORKS Here's a technique for cooking whole carrots that yields a sweet and meltingly tender vegetable from one end to the other without the carrots becoming mushy or waterlogged. Gently "steeping" the carrots in warm water, butter, and salt before cooking them firmed up the vegetable's cell walls so that they could be cooked for a long time without falling apart. We also took a tip from restaurant cooking and topped the carrots with a cartouche (a circle of parchment that sits directly on the food) during cooking to regulate the reduction of moisture. An easy relish finished the dish on a high note. Use carrots that measure ¾ to 1¼ inches across at the thickest end. The carrots can be served plain, but we recommend topping them with Pine Nut Relish (recipe follows).

3 cups water
1 tablespoon unsalted butter
½ teaspoon table salt
12 carrots (1½ to 1¾ pounds), peeled

1. Fold 12-inch square of parchment paper into quarters to create 6-inch square. Fold bottom right corner of square to top left corner to create triangle. Fold triangle again, right side over left, to create narrow triangle. Cut off ¼ inch of tip of triangle to create small hole. Cut base of triangle straight across where it measures 5 inches from hole. Open paper round.

2. Bring water, butter, and salt to simmer in 12-inch skillet over high heat. Remove pan from heat, add carrots in single layer, and place parchment round on top of carrots. Cover skillet and let sit for 20 minutes.

3. Remove lid from skillet, leaving parchment round in place, and bring to simmer over high heat. Reduce heat to medium-low and simmer until almost all water has evaporated and carrots are very tender, about 45 minutes.

4. Discard parchment round, increase heat to medium-high, and continue to cook carrots, shaking pan frequently, until they are lightly glazed and no water remains in skillet, 2 to 4 minutes longer. Transfer carrots to platter and serve.

ACCOMPANIMENT
Pine Nut Relish
Makes about ¾ cup
Pine nuts burn easily, so be sure to shake the pan frequently while toasting them.

- ⅓ cup pine nuts, toasted
- 1 shallot, minced
- 1 tablespoon sherry vinegar
- 1 tablespoon finely chopped fresh parsley
- 1 teaspoon honey
- ½ teaspoon finely chopped fresh rosemary
- ¼ teaspoon smoked paprika
- ¼ teaspoon table salt
   Pinch cayenne pepper

Combine all ingredients in bowl.

Modern Cauliflower Gratin

Serves 8 to 10

WHY THIS RECIPE WORKS To create a cauliflower gratin that was flavorful and fresh, not rich and stodgy, we relied on cauliflower's ability to become an ultracreamy puree, using it as a sauce to bind the florets together. To ensure that we had enough cauliflower to use in two ways, we used two heads. We removed the cores and stems and steamed them until soft; then blended them to make the sauce. We cut each cored head into slabs, which made for a more compact casserole and helped the florets cook more evenly. For an efficient cooking setup, we placed the cauliflower cores and stems in water in the bottom of a Dutch oven and set a steamer basket filled with the florets on top. Butter and Parmesan, plus a little cornstarch, gave the sauce a richer flavor and texture without making it too heavy, and a few pantry spices lent complexity. Tossing the florets in the sauce before placing them in the dish ensured that they were completely coated. A crisp topping of Parmesan and panko gave the gratin savory crunch, while a final garnish of minced chives added color. When buying cauliflower, look for heads without many leaves. Alternatively, if your cauliflower does have a lot of leaves, buy slightly larger heads—about 2¼ pounds each. This recipe can be halved to serve four to six; cook the cauliflower in a large saucepan and bake the gratin in an 8-inch square baking dish.

- 2 heads cauliflower (2 pounds each)
- 8 tablespoons unsalted butter, divided
- ½ cup panko bread crumbs
- 2 ounces Parmesan cheese, grated (1 cup), divided
- 2 teaspoons table salt
- ½ teaspoon pepper
- ½ teaspoon dry mustard
- ⅛ teaspoon ground nutmeg
   Pinch cayenne pepper
- 1 teaspoon cornstarch dissolved in 1 teaspoon water
- 1 tablespoon finely chopped fresh chives

1. Adjust oven rack to middle position and heat oven to 400 degrees.

2. Pull off outer leaves of 1 head of cauliflower and trim stem. Using paring knife, cut around core to remove; halve core lengthwise and slice thin crosswise. Slice head into ½-inch-thick slabs. Cut stems from slices to create florets that are about 1½ inches tall; slice stems thin and reserve along with sliced core. Transfer florets to bowl, including any small pieces that may have been created during trimming, and set aside. Repeat with remaining head of cauliflower. (After trimming you should have about 3 cups of sliced stems and cores and 12 cups of florets.)

3. Combine sliced stems and cores, 2 cups florets, 3 cups water, and 6 tablespoons butter in Dutch oven and bring to boil over high heat. Place remaining florets in steamer basket (do not rinse bowl). Once mixture is boiling, place steamer basket in pot, cover, and reduce heat to medium. Steam florets in basket until translucent and stem ends can be easily pierced with paring knife, 10 to 12 minutes. Remove steamer basket and drain florets. Re-cover pot, reduce heat to low, and continue to cook stem mixture until very soft, about 10 minutes. Transfer drained florets to now-empty bowl.

4. While stem mixture is cooking, melt remaining 2 tablespoons butter in 10-inch skillet over medium heat. Add panko and cook, stirring frequently, until golden brown, 3 to 5 minutes. Transfer to second bowl and let cool. Once cool, add ½ cup Parmesan and toss to combine.

5. Transfer stem mixture and cooking liquid to blender and add salt, pepper, mustard, nutmeg, cayenne, and remaining ½ cup Parmesan. Process until smooth and velvety, about 1 minute (puree should be pourable; adjust consistency with additional water as needed). With blender running, add cornstarch slurry. Season with salt and pepper to taste. Pour puree over cauliflower florets and toss gently to evenly coat. Transfer mixture to 13 by 9-inch baking dish (it will be quite loose) and smooth top with spatula.

6. Scatter bread-crumb mixture evenly over top. Transfer dish to oven and bake until sauce bubbles around edges, 13 to 15 minutes. Let sit for 20 to 25 minutes. Sprinkle with chives and serve.

"As a child, cauliflower was my least favorite vegetable; I just couldn't accept the 'pale broccoli' concept. Every time I ate it, it was a soggy pile of flavorless veggie. As time has gone on and my taste buds have matured, I now know what a treasure cauliflower really is. It can be made into steaks and roasted, topped with cheese or chimichurri, pureed into a soup, and it even makes a pretty tasty pizza crust. However, its greatest transformation is into these Buffalo bites.

This recipe turns bite-size pieces of cauliflower into what is the next best thing to actual chicken. I'm a weekday vegan/weekend carnivore so these bites are just the perfect snack for midweek game days. I also love to impress my vegan friends with these but I can never make enough of them because the non-vegans can't keep away! The bites are coated with coconut milk and fried in a mixture of flour and cornmeal so they really pack a crunch. They are tossed in a hot sauce and coconut oil mixture that gently coats them and never becomes soggy. These bites are an all-around surprise and will impress even the biggest cauliflower critic."

—Elle

Vegan Buffalo Cauliflower Bites

Serves 4 to 6

WHY THIS RECIPE WORKS These crunchy, tangy, spicy, and just plain addictive cauliflower bites will be the new star of your game day table. The key was to come up with a crunchy coating that would hold up under the Buffalo sauce. A mixture of cornstarch and cornmeal gave us an ultracrisp exterior. But because cauliflower is not naturally moist, the mixture didn't adhere; so we dunked the florets in canned coconut milk, which had the right viscosity. We got decent results when we baked our bites, but we absolutely flipped over the crust and tender interior we achieved through frying. Since these cauliflower bites are vegan, we developed a ranch dressing that uses our homemade vegan mayonnaise, though of course you can use store-bought vegan mayonnaise or regular mayonnaise if you wish. We used Frank's RedHot Original Cayenne Pepper Sauce. Use a Dutch oven that holds 6 quarts or more for this recipe. When you open the can of coconut milk, there may be a more solid mass above the watery liquid. If so, be sure to mix it together before measuring.

Buffalo Sauce
- ¼ cup coconut oil
- ½ cup hot sauce
- 1 tablespoon packed organic dark brown sugar
- 2 teaspoons cider vinegar

Cauliflower
- 1–2 quarts peanut or vegetable oil
- ¾ cup cornstarch
- ¼ cup cornmeal
- ½ teaspoon table salt
- ¼ teaspoon pepper
- ⅔ cup canned coconut milk
- 1 tablespoon hot sauce
- 1 pound cauliflower florets, cut into 1½-inch pieces
- 1 recipe Vegan Ranch Dressing (recipe follows)

1. For the buffalo sauce: Melt coconut oil in small saucepan over low heat. Whisk in hot sauce, sugar, and vinegar until combined. Remove from heat and cover to keep warm; set aside.

2. For the cauliflower: Line platter with triple layer of paper towels. Add oil to large Dutch oven until it measures about 1½ inches deep and heat over medium-high heat to 400 degrees.

3. While oil heats, combine cornstarch, cornmeal, salt, and pepper in small bowl. Whisk coconut milk and hot sauce together in large bowl. Add cauliflower to coconut milk mixture and toss to coat well. Sprinkle cornstarch mixture over cauliflower and fold with rubber spatula until cauliflower is thoroughly coated.

4. Fry half of cauliflower, adding 1 or 2 pieces to oil at a time, until golden and crispy, gently stirring as needed to prevent pieces from sticking together, about 3 minutes. Using slotted spoon, transfer fried cauliflower to prepared platter. Return oil to 400 degrees and repeat with remaining cauliflower.

5. Transfer ½ cup sauce to clean large bowl, add fried cauliflower, and gently toss to coat. Serve immediately with remaining sauce and dressing.

ACCOMPANIMENTS

Vegan Ranch Dressing
Makes about ½ cup
We strongly prefer our favorite store-bought vegan mayonnaise, Hampton Creek Just Mayo, Original or our homemade Vegan Mayonnaise (recipe follows).

- ½ cup vegan mayonnaise
- 2 tablespoons unsweetened plain coconut milk yogurt
- 1 teaspoon white wine vinegar
- 1½ teaspoons finely chopped fresh chives
- 1½ teaspoons finely chopped fresh dill
- ¼ teaspoon garlic powder
- ⅛ teaspoon table salt
- ⅛ teaspoon pepper

Whisk all ingredients in bowl until smooth. (Dressing can be refrigerated for up to 4 days.)

Vegan Mayonnaise
Makes about 1 cup
Aquafaba, the liquid found in a can of chickpeas, gives our mayo volume and emulsified body.

- ⅓ cup aquafaba
- 1½ teaspoons lemon juice
- ½ teaspoon table salt
- ½ teaspoon sugar
- ½ teaspoon Dijon mustard
- 1¼ cups vegetable oil
- 3 tablespoons extra-virgin olive oil

1. Process aquafaba, lemon juice, salt, sugar, and mustard in food processor for 10 seconds. With processor running, gradually add vegetable oil in slow, steady stream until mixture is thick and creamy, scraping down sides of bowl as needed, about 3 minutes.

2. Transfer mixture to bowl. Whisking constantly, slowly add olive oil until emulsified. If pools of oil form on surface, stop addition of oil and whisk mixture until well combined, then resume adding oil. Mayonnaise should be thick and glossy with no oil pools on surface. (Mayonnaise can be refrigerated for up to 1 week.)

Boiled Corn

Serves 4 to 6

WHY THIS RECIPE WORKS You might think that you don't need a recipe for boiled corn, but who hasn't pulled out the ears too early only to reveal underdone, starchy kernels or let them sit in the cooling water too long, turning mushy and shriveled? Corn season is so fleeting that we wanted a foolproof method for perfect corn every time. There are two key variables at play: starches and pectin. As corn heats, the starches in the kernels absorb water, swell, and gelatinize, and the corn "milk" becomes smoother, silkier, and more translucent. Simultaneously, the pectin, (essentially the glue holding together the cell walls inside each kernel) dissolves, so the corn softens. The more pectin that dissolves, the mushier the corn becomes. To produce perfectly done, juicy corn every time, we learned that the ideal doneness range is 150 to 170 degrees—when the starches have gelatinized but a minimum amount of the pectin has dissolved. Consistently cooking the corn to that temperature was easy once we realized we could use a sous vide method: bringing water to a boil, dropping in six ears of corn, and shutting off the heat. The temperature of the water decreased quickly so the corn didn't overcook, while the temperature of the corn increased to the ideal zone. Even better, this method can accommodate from six to eight ears of different sizes, and the corn can sit in the water for as long as 30 minutes without overcooking. This recipe's success depends on using the proper ratio of hot water to corn. Use a Dutch oven with a capacity of at least 7 quarts, and bring the water to a rolling boil. Eight ears of corn can be prepared using this recipe, but let the corn sit for at least 15 minutes before serving. Serve with a flavored salt (recipes follow), if desired.

6 ears corn, husks and silk removed
Unsalted butter, softened

1. Bring 4 quarts water to boil in large Dutch oven. Turn off heat, add corn to water, cover, and let sit for at least 10 minutes or up to 30 minutes.

2. Transfer corn to large platter and serve immediately, passing butter, salt, and pepper separately.

ACCOMPANIMENTS
Chili-Lime Salt
Makes 3 tablespoons

2 tablespoons kosher salt
4 teaspoons chili powder
¾ teaspoon grated lime zest

Combine all ingredients in small bowl.

Pepper-Cinnamon Salt
Makes 2 tablespoons

1 tablespoon kosher salt
1 tablespoon pepper
¼ teaspoon ground cinnamon

Combine all ingredients in small bowl.

Cumin-Sesame Salt
Makes 3 tablespoons

1 tablespoon cumin seeds
1 tablespoon sesame seeds
1 tablespoon kosher salt

Toast cumin seeds and sesame seeds in 8-inch skillet over medium heat, stirring occasionally, until fragrant and sesame seeds are golden brown, 3 to 4 minutes. Transfer mixture to cutting board and let cool for 2 minutes. Mince mixture fine until well combined. Transfer mixture to small bowl and stir in salt.

Buttery Spring Vegetables

Serves 6

WHY THIS RECIPE WORKS Crisp-tender spring vegetables coated in a rich yet light butter sauce sounds ideal, but many of these recipes wind up dull, waterlogged, and ultimately lacking in buttery flavor. We wanted spring vegetables that retained their vibrant colors and crisp textures and a butter sauce that would cling to the vegetables, not the platter. To prevent our medley of vegetables from becoming waterlogged, we cooked them in a steamer basket, staggering their additions so that each ended up perfectly crisp-tender.

are crisp-tender, about 2 minutes. Add radishes, cover, and cook for 1 minute. Lift basket out of saucepan and transfer vegetables to platter. Spread into even layer to allow steam to dissipate. Discard all but 3 tablespoons liquid from saucepan.

2. Return saucepan to medium heat. Add shallot, vinegar, salt, and sugar and cook until mixture is reduced to 1½ tablespoons (it will barely cover bottom of saucepan), about 2 minutes. Reduce heat to low. Add butter, 1 piece at a time, whisking vigorously after each addition, until butter is incorporated and sauce has consistency of heavy cream, 4 to 5 minutes. Remove saucepan from heat. Add vegetables and stir to coat. Dry platter and return vegetables to platter. Sprinkle with chives and serve.

Skillet-Charred Green Beans with Crispy Bread-Crumb Topping

SEASON 20 RECIPE

Serves 4

WHY THIS RECIPE WORKS Sichuan cooks have a method for preparing green beans called "dry frying," which is a two-step process where the beans are deep-fried, and then stir-fried with aromatics and maybe a little ground pork. We love this restaurant dish and wanted to re-create what we love about it—deeply browned, blistered green beans with a satisfying chew and concentrated flavor—without all the hassle. The secret, we learned, to truly charred beans was to steam the beans first (which we did in the microwave to keep things easy and avoid having to wash out the skillet before cooking them, as steaming them leaves a residue in the pan). Then we charred them in a skillet with just a couple of tablespoons of hot oil. We didn't stir the beans for the first few minutes so that they developed deep color and flavor on one side; then we tossed them in the pan so that they blistered all over. Once they were charred, we seasoned them with a crispy bread-crumb topping, which offered great contrast to their tender chew. Microwave thinner, more tender beans for 6 to 8 minutes and thicker, tougher beans for 10 to 12 minutes. To make the beans without a microwave, bring ¼ cup of water to a boil in a skillet over high heat. Add the beans, cover, and cook for 5 minutes. Transfer the beans to a paper towel–lined plate to drain and wash the skillet before proceeding with the recipe.

Spreading the vegetables on a platter immediately after cooking allowed excess heat to dissipate, so the vegetables didn't overcook while we made the sauce. Instead of plain melted butter, which had a tendency to slip off the vegetables and pool on the platter below, we made a version of the creamy, tangy French butter sauce beurre blanc by emulsifying chilled butter into a mixture of sautéed shallot, vinegar, salt, sugar, and water. The emulsified sauce clung to and coated each vegetable. A sprinkle of chives made this simple platter of vegetables worthy of a special occasion. To ensure that the turnips are tender, peel them thoroughly to remove not only the tough outer skin but also the fibrous layer of flesh just beneath. This recipe works best with thick asparagus spears that are between ½ and ¾ inch in diameter.

    1 **pound turnips, peeled and cut into**
       ½-inch by ½-inch by 2-inch batons
    1 **pound asparagus, trimmed and cut on**
       bias into 2-inch lengths
    8 **ounces sugar snap peas, strings**
       removed, trimmed
    4 **large radishes, halved and sliced thin**
    1 **tablespoon minced shallot**
  1½ **teaspoons white wine vinegar**
    ¾ **teaspoon table salt**
    ¼ **teaspoon sugar**
    6 **tablespoons unsalted butter, cut into**
       6 pieces and chilled
    1 **tablespoon finely chopped fresh chives**

1. Bring 1 cup water to boil in large saucepan over high heat. Place steamer basket over boiling water. Add turnips and asparagus to basket, cover saucepan, and reduce heat to medium. Cook until vegetables are slightly softened, about 2 minutes. Add snap peas, cover, and cook until snap peas

    2 **tablespoons panko bread crumbs**
    3 **tablespoons vegetable oil, divided**
    ¾ **teaspoon kosher salt**
    ¼ **teaspoon pepper**
    ¼ **teaspoon red pepper flakes**
    1 **pound green beans, trimmed**

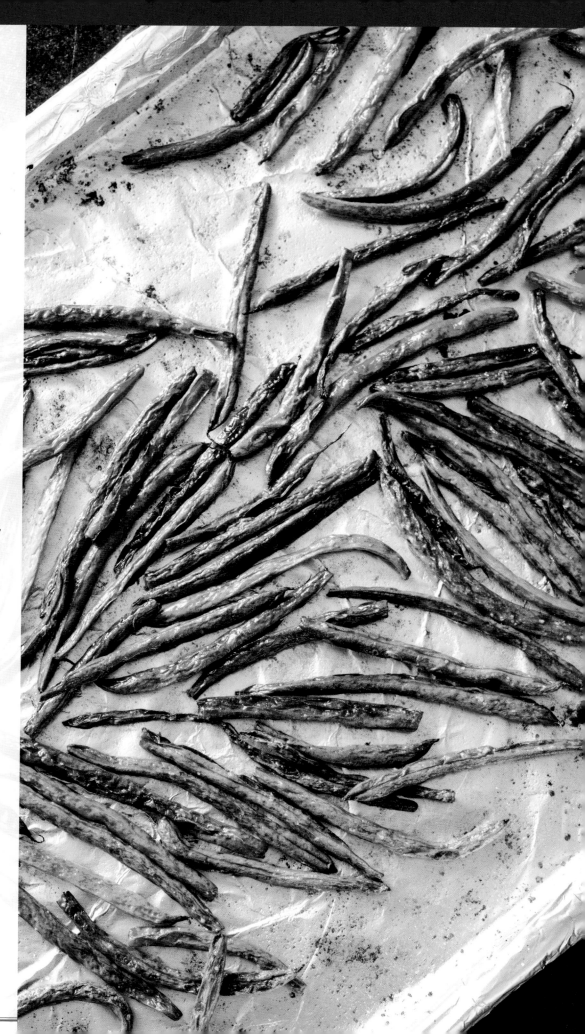

"It's been nearly 15 years since I developed this recipe, but I still recall lingering in the test kitchen with my colleagues after taste tests, devouring the hot, salty beans as if they were French fries. (They really are that good. So good, in fact, that I can, on occasion, get away with offering them as an after-school snack.) Since then, roasting has become my default method for weeknight dinner veggies. It's a mostly hands-off technique, so it frees me up to work on the rest of the meal. More importantly, it imparts deep browning—and deep flavor—to the vegetable."

—Becky

1. Process panko in spice grinder or mortar and pestle until uniformly ground to medium-fine consistency that resembles couscous. Transfer panko to 12-inch skillet, add 1 tablespoon oil, and stir to combine. Cook over medium-low heat, stirring frequently, until light golden brown, 5 to 7 minutes. Remove skillet from heat; add salt, pepper, and pepper flakes; and stir to combine. Transfer panko mixture to bowl and set aside. Wash out skillet thoroughly and dry with paper towels.

2. Rinse green beans but do not dry. Place in medium bowl, cover, and microwave until tender, 6 to 12 minutes, stirring every 3 minutes. Using tongs, transfer green beans to paper towel–lined plate and let drain.

3. Heat remaining 2 tablespoons oil in now-empty skillet over high heat until just smoking. Add green beans in single layer. Cook, without stirring, until green beans begin to blister and char, 4 to 5 minutes. Toss green beans and continue to cook, stirring occasionally, until green beans are softened and charred, 4 to 5 minutes longer. Using tongs, transfer green beans to serving bowl, leaving any excess oil in skillet. Sprinkle with panko mixture and toss to coat. Serve.

Roasted Green Beans

Serves 4

WHY THIS RECIPE WORKS Here roasting transforms mature supermarket green beans, giving them a flavor comparable to sweet, fresh-picked beans. We were pleased when a remarkably simple test produced outstanding results: Beans roasted in a 450-degree oven with only oil, salt, and pepper transformed aged specimens into deeply caramelized, full-flavored beans. Just 20 minutes of roasting reversed the aging process (converting starch back to sugar) and encouraged flavorful browning. Just 1 tablespoon of oil was enough to lend flavor and moisture without making the beans greasy. Lining the baking sheet with foil prevents scorching and makes for easy cleanup.

1 pound green beans, trimmed
1 tablespoon extra-virgin olive oil
½ teaspoon table salt

1. Adjust oven rack to middle position and heat oven to 450 degrees. Line rimmed baking sheet with foil; spread green beans on sheet. Drizzle with oil; using your hands, toss to coat evenly. Sprinkle with salt, toss to coat, and distribute in even layer. Roast for 10 minutes.

2. Remove sheet from oven. Using tongs, redistribute green beans. Continue roasting until green beans are dark golden brown in spots and have started to shrivel, 10 to 12 minutes. Season with salt and pepper to taste, and serve.

Quick Green Bean "Casserole"

Serves 8

WHY THIS RECIPE WORKS We love a traditional green bean casserole, but we wanted a streamlined technique for preparing the dish—one with tender beans in a tasty sauce worthy of a holiday spread yet speedy enough for a last-minute supper. Rather than using two pots—one for the beans and one for the sauce—we cooked both in a skillet. First, we built a sauce with onion, garlic, chicken broth, cream, and a little flour. Next, we added the green beans along with thyme and bay leaves, covered them, and allowed them to steam until the beans were almost done. We then stirred in meaty browned cremini mushrooms and thickened the sauce by uncovering the skillet during the final phase of cooking. Crunchy fried sliced shallots were the finishing touch.

3 large shallots, sliced thin
3 tablespoons all-purpose flour, divided
½ teaspoon table salt, divided
⅛ teaspoon pepper
5 tablespoons vegetable oil, divided
10 ounces cremini mushrooms, trimmed and sliced ¼ inch thick
2 tablespoons unsalted butter
1 onion, chopped fine
2 garlic cloves, minced
1½ pounds green beans, trimmed
3 sprigs fresh thyme
2 bay leaves
¾ cup heavy cream
¾ cup chicken broth

1. Toss shallots with 2 tablespoons flour, ¼ teaspoon salt, and pepper in bowl. Heat 3 tablespoons oil in 12-inch nonstick skillet over medium-high heat until smoking; add shallots and cook, stirring frequently, until golden and crisp, about 5 minutes. Transfer shallots with oil to baking sheet lined with paper towels.

2. Wipe out skillet and return to medium-high heat. Add remaining 2 tablespoons oil, mushrooms, and remaining ¼ teaspoon salt; cook, stirring occasionally, until mushrooms are well browned, about 8 minutes. Transfer to plate and set aside.

3. Wipe out skillet. Melt butter in skillet over medium heat, add onion and cook, stirring occasionally, until edges begin to brown, about 2 minutes. Stir in garlic and remaining 1 tablespoon flour; toss in green beans, thyme sprigs, and bay leaves. Add cream and broth, increase heat to medium-high, cover, and cook until green beans are partly tender but still crisp at center, about 4 minutes. Add mushrooms and continue to cook, uncovered, until green beans are tender, about 4 minutes. Off heat, discard bay leaves and thyme sprigs; season with salt and pepper to taste. Transfer to serving dish, sprinkle evenly with shallots, and serve.

Eggplant Involtini

Serves 4 to 6

WHY THIS RECIPE WORKS Eggplant *involtini* ("little bundles" in Italian) can be so complicated and messy that it makes the cook wonder whether these cheese-filled eggplant bundles are worth making. But the resulting dish—charmingly tidy involtini with homemade tomato sauce and a pleasantly cheesy filling—was too good to give up on. We wanted to come up with a version of involtini that would emphasize the eggplant and minimize the fuss. First up for fixing: the eggplant. Generally this recipe calls for frying, but in order to fry eggplant, you must first get rid of the excess water or the eggplant will turn mushy and oily. Salting can fix this problem, but it's time-consuming. Instead, we opted for a lighter and more hands-off option: baking. We brushed the planks with oil, seasoned them with salt and pepper, and then baked them for about 30 minutes. They emerged light brown and tender, with a compact texture that was neither mushy nor sodden. To lighten up our involtini filling, we decreased the amount of ricotta and replaced it with more flavorful Pecorino Romano, and brightened the filling with a squeeze of lemon juice. To ensure that our filling stayed creamy and didn't toughen up, we added bread crumbs to the mix. We made a bare-bones tomato sauce while the eggplant baked, and then added the eggplant rolls directly to the sauce. Using a skillet meant that we could easily transfer the whole operation to the oven. We crowned the dish with an additional dusting of Pecorino and a sprinkling of basil before serving directly from the skillet. Select shorter, wider eggplants for this recipe. Part-skim ricotta may be used, but do not use fat-free ricotta. Serve the eggplant with crusty bread and a salad.

- 2 large eggplants (1½ pounds each), peeled
- 6 tablespoons vegetable oil, divided
- 2 teaspoons kosher salt, divided
- ½ teaspoon pepper, divided
- 2 garlic cloves, minced
- ¼ teaspoon dried oregano
  Pinch red pepper flakes
- 1 (28-ounce) can whole peeled tomatoes, drained with juice reserved, chopped
- 1 slice hearty white sandwich bread, torn into 1-inch pieces
- 8 ounces (1 cup) whole-milk ricotta cheese
- 1½ ounces grated Pecorino Romano (¾ cup), divided
- ¼ cup plus 1 tablespoon chopped fresh basil, divided
- 1 tablespoon lemon juice

1. Slice each eggplant lengthwise into ½-inch-thick planks (you should have 12 planks). Trim rounded surface from each end piece so it lies flat.

2. Adjust 1 oven rack to lower-middle position and second rack 8 inches from broiler element. Heat oven to 375 degrees. Line 2 rimmed baking sheets with parchment paper and spray generously with vegetable oil spray. Arrange eggplant slices in single layer on prepared sheets. Brush 1 side of eggplant slices with 2½ tablespoons oil and sprinkle with ½ teaspoon salt and ¼ teaspoon pepper. Flip eggplant slices and brush with 2½ tablespoons oil and sprinkle with ½ teaspoon salt and remaining ¼ teaspoon pepper. Bake until tender and lightly browned, 30 to 35 minutes, switching and rotating sheets halfway through baking. Let cool for 5 minutes. Using thin spatula, flip each slice over. Heat broiler.

3. While eggplant cooks, heat remaining 1 tablespoon oil in 12-inch broiler-safe skillet over medium-low heat until just shimmering. Add garlic, oregano, pepper flakes, and ½ teaspoon salt and cook, stirring occasionally, until fragrant, about 30 seconds. Stir in tomatoes and their juice. Increase heat to high and bring to simmer. Reduce heat to medium-low and simmer until thickened, about 15 minutes. Cover and set aside.

4. Pulse bread in food processor until finely ground, 10 to 15 pulses. Combine bread crumbs, ricotta, ½ cup Pecorino, ¼ cup basil, lemon juice, and remaining ½ teaspoon salt in medium bowl.

5. With widest short sides of eggplant slices facing you, evenly distribute ricotta mixture on bottom third of each slice. Gently roll up each eggplant slice and place seam side down in tomato sauce.

6. Bring sauce to simmer over medium heat. Simmer for 5 minutes. Transfer skillet to oven and broil until eggplant is well browned and cheese is heated through, 5 to 10 minutes. Sprinkle with remaining ¼ cup Pecorino and let sit for 5 minutes. Sprinkle with remaining 1 tablespoon basil and serve.

Sautéed Mushrooms with Red Wine and Rosemary

SEASON 20 RECIPE

Serves 4

WHY THIS RECIPE WORKS These deeply flavored mushrooms are a game changer—they make a fantastic side dish, or a topping for steak, polenta, or crostini, just to name a few uses. And it is a counterintuitive trick—starting by adding water, not oil—that makes all the difference. Usually, sautéing mushrooms means piling them in a skillet slicked with a couple of tablespoons of oil and waiting patiently for them to release their moisture, which then must evaporate before the mushrooms can brown. Instead, we accelerated the process by adding a small amount of water to the pan to steam the mushrooms, which allowed them to release their moisture more quickly. The added benefit of steaming them was that the collapsed mushrooms didn't absorb much oil; in fact, ½ teaspoon of oil was enough to prevent sticking and encourage browning. And because we used so little fat to sauté the mushrooms, we were able to sauce them with a

Eggplant Involtini

butter-based reduction without making them overly rich. Adding broth to the sauce and simmering the mixture ensured that the butter emulsified, creating a flavorful glaze that clung well to the mushrooms. Use one variety of mushroom or a combination. Stem and halve portobello mushrooms and cut each half crosswise into ½-inch pieces. Trim white or cremini mushrooms; quarter them if large or medium or halve them if small. Tear trimmed oyster mushrooms into 1- to 1½-inch pieces. Stem shiitake mushrooms; quarter large caps and halve small caps. Cut trimmed maitake (hen-of-the-woods) mushrooms into 1- to 1½-inch pieces. You can substitute vegetable broth for the chicken broth, if desired.

1¼ pounds mushrooms
¼ cup water
½ teaspoon vegetable oil
1 tablespoon unsalted butter
1 shallot, minced
1 teaspoon finely chopped fresh rosemary
¼ teaspoon table salt
¼ teaspoon pepper
¼ cup red wine
1 tablespoon cider vinegar
½ cup chicken broth

1. Cook mushrooms and water in 12-inch nonstick skillet over high heat, stirring occasionally, until skillet is almost dry and mushrooms begin to sizzle, 4 to 8 minutes. Reduce heat to medium-high. Add oil and toss until mushrooms are evenly coated. Continue to cook, stirring occasionally, until mushrooms are well browned, 4 to 8 minutes longer. Reduce heat to medium.

2. Push mushrooms to sides of skillet. Add butter to center. When butter has melted, add shallot, rosemary, salt, and pepper to center and cook, stirring constantly, until aromatic, about 30 seconds. Add wine and vinegar and stir mixture into mushrooms. Cook, stirring occasionally, until liquid has evaporated, 2 to 3 minutes. Add broth and cook, stirring occasionally, until glaze is reduced by half, about 3 minutes. Season with salt and pepper to taste, and serve.

Roasted Mushrooms with Parmesan and Pine Nuts

Serves 4

WHY THIS RECIPE WORKS Serving up a side of juicy, full-flavored roasted mushrooms started with an unusual step: brining. Soaking earthy cremini and meaty, smoky shiitakes in salty water for 10 minutes allowed the mushrooms' water-resistant proteins to break down, inviting in moisture and perfect seasoning. To cook the mushrooms

evenly, we bypassed our stovetop in favor of oven-roasting. We spread the mushrooms on a baking sheet, drizzled them with olive oil, and roasted them for 35 minutes. After a quick stir and 10 more minutes in the oven, the mushrooms emerged deeply browned but still supremely juicy. As a final flourish before serving, we glossed them with butter and a touch of lemon juice and added Parmesan, pine nuts, and parsley to round out the side's hearty, herbal notes. Quarter large cremini mushrooms (more than 2 inches), halve medium (1- to 2-inch) ones, and leave small (under 1-inch) ones whole.

5 teaspoons table salt, for brining
1½ pounds cremini mushrooms, trimmed and left whole if small, halved if medium, or quartered if large
1 pound shiitake mushrooms, stemmed, caps larger than 3 inches halved
2 tablespoons extra-virgin olive oil
2 tablespoons unsalted butter, melted
1 teaspoon lemon juice
1 ounce Parmesan cheese, grated (½ cup)
2 tablespoons pine nuts, toasted
2 tablespoons chopped fresh parsley

1. Adjust oven rack to lowest position and heat oven to 450 degrees. Dissolve salt in 2 quarts room-temperature water in large container. Add cremini mushrooms and shiitake mushrooms to brine, cover with plate or bowl to submerge, and let sit for 10 minutes.

2. Drain mushrooms in colander and pat dry with paper towels. Spread mushrooms evenly on rimmed baking sheet, drizzle with oil, and toss to coat. Roast until liquid from mushrooms has completely evaporated, 35 to 45 minutes.

3. Remove sheet from oven (be careful of escaping steam when opening oven) and, using thin metal spatula, carefully stir mushrooms. Return to oven and continue to roast until mushrooms are deeply browned, 5 to 10 minutes.

4. Combine melted butter and lemon juice in large bowl. Add mushrooms and toss to coat. Add Parmesan, pine nuts, and parsley and toss. Season with salt and pepper to taste; serve immediately.

Crispy Potato Latkes

Serves 4 to 6

WHY THIS RECIPE WORKS Latkes come in all shapes and sizes, but the textural goal is always the same: delicate and light throughout, with a creamy, soft interior surrounded by a shatteringly crispy outer shell. Unfortunately, many recipes produce latkes that soak up oil like sponges, leaving them greasy and limp. Others are crispy outside but gluey inside or are simply undercooked. To achieve latkes that were light and not greasy, with flavorful tender interiors and a pleasingly crispy outer shell, we needed to do two things: First, we removed as much water as possible from the potato shreds by wringing them out in a dish towel. Then, we briefly microwaved them. This caused the starches in the potatoes to form a gel that held on to the potatoes' moisture so it didn't leach out during cooking. With the water taken care of, the latkes crisped up quickly and absorbed minimal oil. We prefer shredding the potatoes on the large holes of a box grater, but you can also use the large shredding disk of a food processor; cut the potatoes into 2-inch lengths first so you are left with short shreds. Serve with applesauce, sour cream, or gravlax.

- 2 **pounds russet potatoes, unpeeled, scrubbed, and shredded**
- ½ **cup grated onion**
- 1 **teaspoon table salt**
- 2 **large eggs, lightly beaten**
- 2 **teaspoons finely chopped fresh parsley**
- ¼ **teaspoon pepper**
  Vegetable oil for frying

1. Adjust oven rack to middle position, place rimmed baking sheet on rack, and heat oven to 200 degrees. Toss potatoes, onion, and salt in bowl. Place half of potato mixture in center of clean dish towel. Gather ends together and twist tightly to drain as much liquid as possible, reserving liquid in liquid measuring cup. Transfer drained potato mixture to second bowl and repeat process with remaining potato mixture. Set potato liquid aside and let sit so starch settles to bottom, at least 5 minutes.

2. Cover potato mixture and microwave until just warmed through but not hot, 1 to 2 minutes, stirring mixture with fork every 30 seconds. Spread potato mixture evenly over second rimmed baking sheet and let cool for 10 minutes. Don't wash out bowl.

3. Pour off water from reserved potato liquid, leaving potato starch in measuring cup. Add eggs and stir until smooth. Return cooled potato mixture to bowl. Add parsley, pepper, and potato starch mixture and toss until evenly combined.

4. Set wire rack in clean rimmed baking sheet and line with triple layer of paper towels. Add oil to 12-inch skillet to a depth of ¼ inch and heat over medium-high heat until shimmering but not smoking (350 degrees). Place ¼-cup mound of potato mixture in oil and press with nonstick spatula into ⅓-inch-thick disk. Repeat until 5 latkes are in pan. Cook, adjusting heat so fat bubbles around latke edges, until golden brown on bottom, about 3 minutes. Turn and continue cooking until golden brown on second side, about 3 minutes. Drain on paper towels and transfer to baking sheet in oven. Repeat with remaining potato mixture, adding oil to maintain ¼-inch depth and returning oil to 350 degrees between batches. Season with salt and pepper to taste, and serve immediately. (Cooled latkes can be covered loosely with plastic wrap and held at room temperature for up to 4 hours. Alternatively, they can be frozen on baking sheet until firm, transferred to zipper-lock bag, and frozen for up to 1 month. Reheat latkes in 375-degree oven until crisp and hot, 3 minutes per side for room-temperature latkes and 6 minutes per side for frozen latkes.)

Easier French Fries

Serves 4

WHY THIS RECIPE WORKS Traditional methods of making French fries involve rinsing, soaking, double-frying, and then draining and salting them—not an easy process. We challenged ourselves to devise a shortcut that would give us crisp, golden fries with less work. Oven-frying is the usual "quick" method, but we wanted real french fries. We began with an unorthodox procedure of starting the cut potatoes in a few cups of cold oil. To our surprise, the fries were pretty good, if a little dry. Because russets are fairly dry, we wondered if a different type of potato would work better. Sure enough, Yukon Golds, which have more water and less starch, came out creamy and smooth inside and crisp outside. We found that leaving the fries undisturbed for 15 minutes, then stirring them, kept them from sticking and from breaking apart. Thinner batons were also less likely to stick. These fries had all the qualities of classic French fries, without all the bother. For those who like it, flavoring the oil with bacon fat gives the fries a mild meaty flavor. We prefer peanut oil for frying, but vegetable oil can be substituted. This recipe will not work with sweet potatoes or russets. Serve with a dipping sauce (recipes follow), if desired.

- 2½ pounds Yukon Gold potatoes, unpeeled, sides squared off, and cut lengthwise into ¼-inch by ¼-inch batons
- 6 cups peanut or vegetable oil for frying
- ¼ cup bacon fat, strained (optional)

1. Combine potatoes, oil, and bacon fat, if using, in Dutch oven. Cook over high heat until oil has reached rolling boil, about 5 minutes. Continue to cook, without stirring, until potatoes are pale golden and exteriors are beginning to crisp, about 15 minutes.

2. Using tongs, stir potatoes, gently scraping up any that stick, and continue to cook, stirring occasionally, until golden and crisp, 5 to 10 minutes. Using skimmer or slotted spoon, transfer fries to paper towels. Season with salt to taste, and serve immediately.

ACCOMPANIMENTS
Chive and Black Pepper Dipping Sauce
Makes about ½ cup

- 5 tablespoons mayonnaise
- 3 tablespoons sour cream
- 2 tablespoons chopped fresh chives
- 1½ teaspoons lemon juice
- ¼ teaspoon table salt
- ¼ teaspoon pepper

Whisk all ingredients together in small bowl.

Belgian-Style Dipping Sauce
Makes about ½ cup

- 5 tablespoons mayonnaise
- 3 tablespoons ketchup
- 1 garlic clove, minced
- ½ teaspoon hot sauce, plus extra as needed
- ¼ teaspoon table salt

Whisk all ingredients together in small bowl. Season with extra hot sauce to taste.

Thick-Cut Oven Fries

Serves 4

WHY THIS RECIPE WORKS Most people's alternative to deep-fried fries is oven fries, which are usually less fussy to make, often less greasy—but usually a disappointment. We wanted the flavor and crispiness of deep-fried fries with no more work than roasting potatoes. Taking a closer look at how French fries cook, we discovered that when traditional fries are fried, water is rapidly driven out of the starch cells at the surface of the potato, leaving behind tiny cavities; it's these cavities that create a delicate, crispy crust. Since oven fries don't heat fast enough for air pockets to form, we looked to alternatives and instead coated the potatoes in a cornstarch slurry that crisped up like a deep-fried fry would. We arranged the coated planks on a rimmed baking sheet that we coated with both vegetable oil spray and vegetable oil; the former contains a surfactant called lecithin, which prevented the oil from pooling and, in turn, prevented the potatoes from sticking. Using the oil spray also allowed us to use only 3 tablespoons of oil, just enough to evenly coat the fries. Covering the baking sheet with aluminum foil for the first half of cooking ensured that the potatoes were fully tender by the time they browned to perfection. Choose potatoes that are 4 to 6 inches in length to ensure well-proportioned fries. Trimming thin slices from the ends of the potatoes in step 2 ensures that each fry has two flat surfaces for even browning. This recipe's success is dependent on a heavy-duty rimmed baking sheet that will not warp in the heat of the oven. Spraying the sheet with vegetable oil spray will help the oil spread evenly and prevent sticking. The rate at which the potatoes brown is dependent on your baking sheet and oven. After removing the foil from the baking sheet in step 5, monitor the color of the potatoes carefully to prevent scorching.

- 3 tablespoons vegetable oil
- 2 pounds Yukon Gold potatoes, unpeeled
- 3 tablespoons cornstarch
- ½ teaspoon table salt

1. Adjust oven rack to lowest position and heat oven to 425 degrees. Generously spray rimmed baking sheet with vegetable oil spray. Pour oil into prepared sheet and tilt sheet until surface is evenly coated with oil.

2. Halve potatoes lengthwise and turn halves cut sides down on cutting board. Trim thin slice from both long sides of each potato half; discard trimmings. Slice potatoes lengthwise into ⅓- to ½-inch-thick planks.

3. Combine ¾ cup water and cornstarch in large bowl, making sure no lumps of cornstarch remain on bottom of bowl. Microwave, stirring every 20 seconds, until mixture begins to thicken, 1 to 3 minutes. Remove from microwave and continue to stir until mixture thickens to pudding-like consistency. (If necessary, add up to 2 tablespoons water to achieve correct consistency.)

4. Transfer potatoes to bowl with cornstarch mixture and toss until each plank is evenly coated. Arrange planks on prepared sheet, leaving small gaps between planks. (Some cornstarch mixture will remain in bowl.) Cover sheet tightly with lightly greased aluminum foil and bake for 12 minutes.

5. Remove foil from sheet and bake until bottom of each fry is golden brown, 10 to 18 minutes. Remove sheet from oven and, using thin metal spatula, carefully flip each fry. Return sheet to oven and continue to bake until second sides are golden brown, 10 to 18 minutes. Sprinkle fries with salt. Using spatula, carefully toss fries to distribute salt. Transfer fries to paper towel–lined plate and season with salt to taste. Serve.

Patatas Bravas

Serves 4 to 6

WHY THIS RECIPE WORKS The best versions of *patatas bravas*, a Spanish tapas preparation, showcase crispy, well-browned potatoes served with a smoky, spicy tomato-based sauce. To create an ultracrispy crust without the need for double frying, we first parboiled russet potatoes with baking soda, which helped develop into a thick crust. We also tossed the parcooked potatoes with kosher salt, which roughed up the surfaces of the potatoes, creating nooks and crannies through which steam could escape. As the steam escaped, the nooks and crannies trapped oil, making an even more substantial crust. For our sauce, tomato paste, cayenne, smoked sweet paprika, garlic, and water made a smooth, smoky, and spicy mixture, which we finished with sherry vinegar for tang. Finally, adding mayonnaise allowed us to combine the bravas sauce and another common accompaniment, aioli, into a single sauce. While this dish is traditionally served as part of a tapas spread, it can also be served as a side dish with grilled or roasted meat. Bittersweet or smoked hot paprika can be used in place of sweet, if desired. If you make this substitution, be sure to taste the sauce before deciding how much cayenne to add, if any. A rasp-style grater makes quick work of turning the garlic into a paste.

Sauce

- 1 tablespoon vegetable oil
- 2 teaspoons garlic, minced to paste
- 1 teaspoon smoked sweet paprika
- ½ teaspoon kosher salt
- ½–¾ teaspoon cayenne pepper
- ¼ cup tomato paste
- ½ cup water
- 2 teaspoons sherry vinegar
- ¼ cup mayonnaise

Potatoes

- 2¼ pounds russet potatoes, peeled and cut into 1-inch pieces
- ½ teaspoon baking soda
- 1½ teaspoons kosher salt
- 3 cups vegetable oil for frying

1. **For the sauce:** Heat oil in small saucepan over medium-low heat until shimmering. Add garlic, paprika, salt, and cayenne and cook until fragrant, about 30 seconds. Add tomato paste and cook for 30 seconds. Whisk in water and bring to boil over high heat. Reduce heat to medium-low and simmer until slightly thickened, 4 to 5 minutes. Transfer sauce to bowl, stir in vinegar, and let cool completely. Once cool, whisk in mayonnaise. (Sauce can be refrigerated for up to 24 hours. Bring to room temperature before serving.)

2. **For the potatoes:** Bring 8 cups water to boil in large saucepan over high heat. Add potatoes and baking soda. Return to boil and cook for 1 minute. Drain potatoes.

"*Leave it to my colleague Lan, a scientist turned master cook, to transform this basic recipe (do you even need a recipe for baked potatoes?) into something transcendent. Honestly, as a recipe developer, it's not that hard to create something memorable if you're assigned a complicated dish with multiple components and a dozen or more ingredients. But how do you improve on baked potatoes, the ultimate one-ingredient recipe? Lan's answer: Think like a scientist who cooks. To start, the spuds are dipped in salt water before baking so the skin is well seasoned (you can't get salt to stick otherwise!). Baking the potatoes on a rack set in a baking sheet ensures even cooking, and a hot oven and long baking time gets the centers nice and fluffy. Lan insists on temping the potatoes—they are done when the temperature reaches a minimum of 205 degrees. (Trust Lan on this one.) For exceptionally crisp skin, apply a light coating of oil during the last minutes of baking—if applied earlier the oil slows moisture evaporation, which is key for a fluffy texture. If you think all baked potatoes are the same, make this recipe to prove yourself wrong.*"

—Jack

3. Return potatoes to saucepan and place over low heat. Cook, shaking saucepan occasionally, until any surface moisture has evaporated, 30 seconds to 1 minute. Remove from heat. Add salt and stir with rubber spatula until potatoes are coated with thick, starchy paste, about 30 seconds. Transfer potatoes to rimmed baking sheet in single layer to cool. (Potatoes can sit at room temperature for up to 2 hours.)

4. Heat oil in Dutch oven over high heat to 375 degrees. Add all potatoes (they should just be submerged in oil) and cook, stirring occasionally with wire skimmer or slotted spoon, until deep golden brown and crispy, 20 to 25 minutes.

5. Set wire rack in rimmed baking sheet and line with paper towels. Transfer potatoes to sheet and season with salt to taste. Spoon ½ cup sauce onto bottom of large platter or 1½ tablespoons sauce onto individual plates. Arrange potatoes over sauce and serve immediately, passing remaining sauce separately.

Best Baked Potatoes

Serves 4

WHY THIS RECIPE WORKS Baked potatoes, like boiled corn, are one of those dishes that most home cooks think they don't need a recipe for, but following our precise roasting technique guarantees a perfect potato—with a fluffy interior, crispy skin, and even seasoning—every time. For starters, our testing pointed us to an ideal doneness temperature: 205 degrees. Baking russet potatoes in a hot oven propped up on a wire rack prevented a leathery ring from forming beneath the peel, and taking the potato's temperature with an instant-read thermometer ensured we hit the 205-degree sweet spot every time. To season the potato skin, we coated the potatoes in salty water before baking them. We also achieved crisp skin by painting the potatoes with vegetable oil once they were cooked through and then baking the potatoes for an additional 10 minutes. Potatoes this good deserve an accompaniment, so we came up with some simple but sophisticated toppings to serve with them (recipes follow). Open up the potatoes immediately after removal from the oven in step 3 so steam can escape.

2 tablespoons table salt, for brining
4 (7- to 9-ounce) russet potatoes, unpeeled, each lightly pricked with fork in 6 places
1 tablespoon vegetable oil

1. Adjust oven rack to middle position and heat oven to 450 degrees. Dissolve salt in ½ cup water in large bowl. Place potatoes in bowl and toss so exteriors of potatoes are evenly moistened. Transfer potatoes to wire rack set in rimmed baking sheet and bake until center of largest potato registers 205 degrees, 45 minutes to 1 hour.

2. Remove potatoes from oven and brush tops and sides with oil. Return potatoes to oven and continue to bake for 10 minutes.

3. Remove potatoes from oven and, using paring knife, make 2 slits, forming X, in each potato. Using clean dish towel, hold ends and squeeze slightly to push flesh up and out. Season with salt and pepper to taste. Serve immediately.

ACCOMPANIMENTS
Creamy Egg Topping
Makes 1 cup

3 hard-cooked large eggs (page 25), chopped
4 tablespoons sour cream
1½ tablespoons minced cornichons
1 tablespoon finely chopped fresh parsley
1 tablespoon Dijon mustard
1 tablespoon capers, rinsed and minced
1 tablespoon minced shallot

Stir together eggs, sour cream, cornichons, parsley, mustard, capers, and shallot. Season with salt and pepper to taste.

Herbed Goat Cheese Topping
Makes ¾ cup
Our favorite goat cheese is Laura Chenel's Pure Goat Milk Cheese Original Log.

4 ounces goat cheese, softened
2 tablespoons extra-virgin olive oil
2 tablespoons finely chopped fresh parsley
1 tablespoon minced shallot
½ teaspoon grated lemon zest

Mash goat cheese with fork. Stir in oil, parsley, shallot, and lemon zest. Season with salt and pepper to taste.

Smoked Trout Topping
Makes 1 cup
We prefer trout for this recipe, but any hot-smoked fish, such as salmon or bluefish, may be substituted.

5 ounces smoked trout, chopped
⅓ cup crème fraîche
2 tablespoons finely chopped fresh chives
4 teaspoons minced shallot
1¼ teaspoons grated lemon zest plus
¾ teaspoon lemon juice

Stir together trout, crème fraîche, chives, shallot, and lemon zest and juice and season with salt and pepper to taste.

Creamy Mashed Potatoes

Serves 8 to 10

WHY THIS RECIPE WORKS Sometimes we want a luxurious mash, one that is silky smooth and loaded with cream and butter. But there's a fine line between creamy and gluey. We wanted lush, creamy mashed potatoes, with so much richness and flavor they could stand on their own—no gravy necessary. For a creamier, substantial mash, we found that Yukon Golds were perfect—creamier than russets but not as heavy as red potatoes. Slicing the peeled potatoes into rounds and then rinsing away the surface starch before boiling helped intensify their creamy texture without making them gluey. Setting the boiled and drained potatoes in their pot over a low flame helped further evaporate any excess moisture. Using 1½ sticks of butter and 1½ cups of heavy cream gave these potatoes luxurious flavor and richness without making the mash too thin. We found that melting the butter and warming the cream before adding them to the potatoes ensured that the finished dish arrived at the table piping hot. This recipe can be cut in half, if desired.

    4   pounds Yukon Gold potatoes,
        peeled and sliced ¾ inch thick
 1½   cups heavy cream
  12   tablespoons unsalted butter,
        cut into 6 pieces
    2   teaspoons table salt

1. Place potatoes in colander and rinse under cool running water, tossing with your hands, for 30 seconds. Transfer potatoes to Dutch oven, add cold water to cover by 1 inch, and bring to boil over high heat. Reduce heat to medium and boil until potatoes are tender, 20 to 25 minutes.

2. Meanwhile, heat heavy cream and butter in small saucepan over medium heat until butter is melted, about 5 minutes. Set aside and keep warm.

3. Drain potatoes and return to Dutch oven. Stir over low heat until potatoes are thoroughly dried, 1 to 2 minutes. Set ricer or food mill over large bowl and press or mill potatoes into bowl. Gently fold in warm cream mixture and salt with rubber spatula until cream is absorbed and potatoes are thick and creamy. Serve.

Smashed Potatoes

Serves 4

WHY THIS RECIPE WORKS Bold flavors and a rustic, chunky texture make smashed potatoes a satisfying side dish. But good smashed potatoes are hard to find. We were after a nice contrast of textures, with the rich, creamy puree of mashed potatoes accented by chunks of potato and skins. Testing revealed that low-starch, high-moisture red potatoes were the best choice for this dish. Their compact structure held up well under pressure, maintaining its integrity. The thin skins were pleasantly tender and paired nicely with the chunky potatoes. Cooked whole in salted water, the potatoes became lightly seasoned while also retaining their naturally creamy texture, as the skins protected the potato flesh from the water. For the best chunky texture, we smashed the potatoes with a rubber spatula or the back of a wooden spoon. Cream cheese and butter lent tang and body to the dish, and stirring in a little of the potato cooking water added moisture to give it a creamy consistency. Seasoned with salt, freshly ground black pepper, and chopped chives, these potatoes are a quick, no-fuss side dish. Try to get potatoes of equal size; if that's not possible, test the larger potatoes for doneness (use a paring knife). If only large potatoes are available, increase the cooking time by about 10 minutes.

    2   pounds red potatoes, scrubbed
 1½   teaspoons table salt, divided
    1   bay leaf
    4   tablespoons unsalted butter, melted
    4   ounces cream cheese, room temperature
    3   tablespoons finely chopped fresh chives (optional)
   ½   teaspoon pepper

1. Place potatoes in large saucepan and add cold water to cover by 1 inch; add 1 teaspoon salt and bay leaf. Bring to boil over high heat, then reduce heat to medium-low and simmer gently until paring knife can be inserted into potatoes with no resistance, 35 to 45 minutes. Reserve ½ cup cooking water, then drain potatoes. Return potatoes to pot, discard bay leaf, and allow potatoes to sit in pot, uncovered, until surfaces are dry, about 5 minutes.

2. Meanwhile, whisk melted butter and softened cream cheese in medium bowl until smooth and fully incorporated. Add ¼ cup reserved cooking water, chives, if using, pepper, and remaining ½ teaspoon salt. Using rubber spatula or back of wooden spoon, smash potatoes just enough to break skins. Fold in butter–cream cheese mixture until most of liquid has been absorbed and chunks of potatoes remain. Add more cooking water as needed, 1 tablespoon at a time, until potatoes are slightly looser than desired (potatoes will thicken slightly with sitting). Season with salt and pepper to taste, and serve.

Crispy Roasted Potatoes

Serves 4 to 6

WHY THIS RECIPE WORKS The aroma of roasting potatoes draws everyone into the kitchen come mealtime. Too often, though, the potatoes turn out brown and leathery with a mealy interior, or worse, soft with no crisp crust at all. We wanted oven-roasted potatoes that had a crisp crust with a silky interior. We tested different potatoes and found that we liked Yukon Golds best. Parcooking the potatoes before subjecting them to high oven temperatures helped them develop a somewhat crisper exterior, but the browning was uneven and they still weren't crispy enough. When we switched from cubing the potatoes to slicing them thick, we created more surface area for crisping but enough heft for a creamy interior. As an added bonus, with only two surfaces to cook, we now only had to flip the potatoes once halfway through roasting. Boiling the potatoes very briefly before roasting prevented them from breaking up on the baking sheet, and we tossed the precooked potatoes with some olive oil to rough up the exteriors and increase crispiness. Note that the potatoes should be just undercooked when removed from the boiling water—this helps ensure that they will roast up crispy.

2½ pounds Yukon Gold potatoes, unpeeled,
     cut into ½-inch-thick slices
1   tablespoon plus 1 teaspoon table salt, divided
5   tablespoons extra-virgin olive oil, divided
     Ground black pepper

1. Adjust oven rack to lowest position, place rimmed baking sheet on rack, and heat oven to 450 degrees. Place potatoes and 1 tablespoon salt in Dutch oven; add cold water to cover by 1 inch. Bring to boil over high heat; reduce heat and gently simmer until exterior of potato has softened, but center offers resistance when pierced with paring knife, about 5 minutes. Drain potatoes well, and transfer to large bowl. Drizzle with 2 tablespoons oil and sprinkle with ½ teaspoon salt; using rubber spatula, toss to combine. Drizzle with 2 tablespoons oil and remaining ½ teaspoon salt; continue to toss until exteriors of potato slices are coated with starchy paste.

2. Working quickly, remove sheet from oven and drizzle remaining 1 tablespoon oil over surface. Carefully transfer potatoes to sheet and spread them into even layer (skin side up for end pieces). Bake until bottoms of potatoes are golden brown and crisp, 15 to 25 minutes, rotating sheet after 10 minutes.

3. Remove sheet from oven and, using metal spatula and tongs, loosen potatoes from pan and carefully flip each slice. Continue to roast until second side is golden and crisp, 10 to 20 minutes, rotating sheet as needed to brown potatoes evenly. Season with salt and pepper to taste, and serve.

Roasted Fingerling Potatoes with Mixed Herbs
SEASON 20 RECIPE

Serves 4

WHY THIS RECIPE WORKS Roasting is a great way to enhance the nutty flavor of fingerling potatoes, and their diminutive shape means they can be cooked whole. The only problem is, they can vary widely in shape (from crescent-like to knobby) and length (from 1 inch to nearly 5 inches). Our challenge would be to get a typical bag of assorted sizes to cook at the same rate. We first tried tossing the potatoes with oil and salt and roasting them in a very hot oven, but at such high heat, the exteriors were drying out before the larger potatoes had a chance to cook through. Instead we moved the fingerlings to a 13 by 9-inch baking pan, where they fit snugly in a single layer. To solve the textural problems, we covered the pan with foil to trap steam: Since the potatoes were crowded together, they would be bathed in moist air from their neighbors, helping them cook evenly without turning leathery. After 15 minutes, the tip of a knife easily pierced the largest potato, so we removed the foil to let the skins take on some color, shaking the pan a couple of times so they browned evenly. To dress up these perfectly roasted fingerlings, we coated them with seasonings that would stick to their skins. For a simple yet classic combination, we tossed chopped thyme and sage leaves with the potatoes in a bowl after roasting, where their heady fragrances wafted up as they hit the hot spuds. But it was tricky to evenly disperse the small amount of herbs. For the next batch, we held off on adding salt prior to roasting and instead sprinkled salt onto the herbs as we chopped them. The increased volume made both ingredients easier to distribute evenly. Two more potent toppings included a zippy mix of lemon zest, garlic, and parsley, and a salty-sharp take on *cacio e pepe* pasta with Pecorino Romano and black pepper. Fingerlings vary in size; to ensure that they are all cooked through, check the doneness of the largest potato. If using a glass or ceramic baking dish, increase the baking time in step 1 by 5 minutes. This recipe can be doubled; use two 13 by 9-inch baking pans on the same oven rack.

2 pounds fingerling potatoes, scrubbed, unpeeled
3 tablespoons vegetable oil
2 teaspoons chopped fresh thyme
2 teaspoons chopped fresh sage
½ teaspoon table salt

1. Adjust oven rack to middle position and heat oven to 450 degrees. In 13 by 9-inch baking pan, toss potatoes with oil until evenly coated. Arrange potatoes in even layer. Cover pan tightly with aluminum foil. Transfer to oven and cook for 15 minutes.

2. Carefully remove foil (steam will escape). Shake pan and continue to roast until potatoes are spotty brown and tender, and largest potato can be pierced easily with tip of paring knife, about 20 minutes, shaking pan halfway through cooking. While potatoes roast, chop thyme, sage, and salt together until finely minced and well combined. Transfer potatoes to bowl, along with oil, and toss with topping until evenly coated. Transfer potatoes and topping to platter. Let cool for 5 minutes and serve.

VARIATIONS

Roasted Fingerling Potatoes with Parsley, Lemon, and Garlic

Substitute 2 tablespoons chopped fresh parsley, 2 teaspoons grated lemon zest, and 1 minced garlic clove for thyme and sage. Finely mince ingredients with salt as directed in step 2 and toss with cooked potatoes.

Roasted Fingerling Potatoes with Pecorino and Black Pepper

Omit thyme and sage. Once cooked potatoes have been transferred to bowl in step 2, toss with salt, 2 teaspoons pepper, and 2 tablespoons grated Pecorino Romano cheese. Sprinkle potatoes with another 2 tablespoons grated Pecorino Romano before serving.

Braised Red Potatoes with Lemon and Chives

Serves 4 to 6

WHY THIS RECIPE WORKS What if you could get red potatoes with the creamy interiors created by steaming and the crispy browned exteriors produced by roasting—without doing either? That's the result promised by recipes for braised red potatoes, but they rarely deliver. To make good on the promise, we combined halved small red potatoes, butter, and

salted water (plus thyme for flavoring) in a 12-inch skillet and simmered the spuds until their interiors were perfectly creamy and the water was fully evaporated. Then we let the potatoes continue to cook in the now-dry skillet until their cut sides browned in the butter, developing the rich flavor and crisp edges of roasted potatoes. These crispy, creamy potatoes were so good they needed only a minimum of seasoning: We simply tossed them with some minced garlic (softened in the simmering water along with the potatoes), thyme, lemon juice, chives, and pepper. Use small red potatoes measuring about 1½ inches in diameter.

1½ pounds small red potatoes, unpeeled, halved
2 cups water
3 tablespoons unsalted butter
3 garlic cloves, peeled
3 sprigs fresh thyme
¾ teaspoon table salt
1 teaspoon lemon juice
¼ teaspoon pepper
2 tablespoons finely chopped fresh chives

1. Arrange potatoes in single layer, cut side down, in 12-inch nonstick skillet. Add water, butter, garlic, thyme sprigs, and salt and bring to simmer over medium-high heat. Reduce heat to medium, cover, and simmer until potatoes are just tender, about 15 minutes.

2. Remove lid and use slotted spoon to transfer garlic to cutting board; discard thyme sprigs. Increase heat to medium-high and vigorously simmer, swirling pan occasionally, until water evaporates and butter starts to sizzle, 15 to 20 minutes. When cool enough to handle, mince garlic to paste. Transfer paste to bowl and stir in lemon juice and pepper.

3. Continue to cook potatoes, swirling pan frequently, until butter browns and cut sides of potatoes turn spotty brown, 4 to 6 minutes. Off heat, add garlic mixture and chives and toss to thoroughly coat. Serve immediately.

VARIATIONS

Braised Red Potatoes with Dijon and Tarragon

Substitute 2 teaspoons Dijon mustard for lemon juice and 1 tablespoon minced fresh tarragon for chives.

Braised Red Potatoes with Miso and Scallions

Reduce salt to ½ teaspoon. Substitute 1 tablespoon red miso paste for lemon juice and 3 thinly sliced scallions for chives.

Braised Red Potatoes with
Lemon and Chives

Twice-Baked Potatoes

Serves 6 to 8

WHY THIS RECIPE WORKS Twice-baked potatoes are not difficult to make, but the process can be time-consuming, and they're plagued by chewy skins and pasty, bland fillings. We wanted to perfect the process and have twice-baked potatoes with slightly crisp, chewy skins and a rich, creamy filling. To start, we oiled the potatoes before baking for a crisp skin, and we let the baked potatoes cool slightly before slicing them open and removing the flesh. We found that we could prevent the hollowed-out shells from turning soggy by keeping them in the oven while making the filling. And for the filling we found it best to combine the potato with tangy dairy ingredients—sour cream and buttermilk, a small amount of butter, and sharp cheddar cheese for its bold flavor. For a perfect finish, we placed the filled potatoes under the broiler, where they turned brown and crisp. Most potatoes have two relatively flat, blunt sides and two curved sides. Halve the baked potatoes lengthwise so the blunt sides are down once the shells are stuffed, making the potatoes much more stable in the pan during final baking. To vary the flavor a bit, try substituting other types of cheese, such as Gruyère, fontina, or feta, for the cheddar. Yukon Gold potatoes can be substituted for the russets.

- 4 russet potatoes (8 ounces each), unpeeled, rubbed lightly with vegetable oil
- 4 ounces sharp cheddar cheese, shredded (about 1 cup)
- ½ cup sour cream
- ½ cup buttermilk
- 2 tablespoons unsalted butter, softened
- 3 scallions, sliced thin
- ½ teaspoon table salt

1. Adjust oven rack to upper-middle position and heat oven to 400 degrees. Bake potatoes on aluminum foil–lined baking sheet until skin is crisp and deep brown and skewer easily pierces flesh, about 1 hour. Transfer potatoes to wire rack and cool slightly, about 10 minutes. (Leave oven on.)

2. Using oven mitt or folded dish towel to handle hot potatoes, cut each potato in half so that long, blunt sides rest on work surface. Using small spoon, scoop flesh from each half into medium bowl, leaving ⅛- to ¼-inch thickness of flesh in each shell. Arrange shells on sheet and return to oven until dry and slightly crisp, about 10 minutes. Meanwhile, mash potato flesh with fork until smooth. Stir in remaining ingredients, including pepper to taste, until well combined.

3. Remove shells from oven and heat broiler. Using oven mitt or dish towel to protect your hand, spoon mixture into crisped shells, mounding it slightly at center, and return potatoes to oven. Broil until spotty brown and crisp on top, 10 to 15 minutes. Let cool for 10 minutes and serve warm.

Crispy Smashed Potatoes

Serves 4 to 6

WHY THIS RECIPE WORKS Crispy smashed potatoes give you the best of both worlds, delivering mashed potato creaminess with the crackling crisp crust of roasted potatoes. The technique looks straightforward: Skin-on spuds are parcooked in seasoned water, drained, and squashed just shy of an inch thick. Then the potatoes are oiled, and either pan-fried on the stovetop or spread out on a baking sheet in the oven to render the roughened edges browned and crispy and the interior flesh creamy and sweet. But parcooking the potatoes (waxy, thin-skinned Red Bliss) in water diluted their flavor, so they tasted flat, rather than rich and earthy. To fix the flavor problem and streamline the cooking method, we turned to a baking sheet to get the job done. The baking sheet's roomy cooking surface allowed us to easily prepare potatoes for four at once rather than pan-frying them in fussy batches. To soften the potatoes, we spread them out on the baking sheet, added a little water, covered the pan with foil, and baked them until tender. To smash all the potatoes at once, we used a second baking sheet, which we simply pressed evenly and firmly on top of the pan of parcooked potatoes. To crisp the potatoes we opted for olive oil to coat the baking sheet and to drizzle over the broken spuds. The result? Browned and crunchy potato patties, full of deep, earthy flavor. This recipe is designed to work with potatoes that are 1½ to 2 inches in diameter. Do not attempt it with potatoes that are over 2 inches. Remove the potatoes from the baking sheet as soon as they are done browning—they will toughen if left on the baking sheet for too long. A potato masher can also be used to "smash" the potatoes.

- 2 pounds small red potatoes, unpeeled
- 6 tablespoons extra-virgin olive oil, divided
- 1 teaspoon chopped fresh thyme

1. Adjust oven racks to highest and lowest positions and heat oven to 500 degrees. Spread potatoes on rimmed baking sheet, pour ¾ cup water into baking sheet, and wrap tightly with aluminum foil. Cook on bottom rack until skewer or paring knife slips in and out of potatoes easily, 25 to 30 minutes (poke skewer through foil to test). Remove foil and let cool for 10 minutes. If any water remains on pan, blot dry with paper towel.

2. Drizzle 3 tablespoons oil over potatoes and roll to coat. Space potatoes evenly on sheet. Place second sheet on top; press down uniformly on sheet until potatoes are roughly ⅓ to ½ inch thick. Sprinkle with thyme and season with salt and pepper; drizzle evenly with remaining 3 tablespoons oil. Roast potatoes on top rack for 15 minutes. Transfer potatoes to bottom rack and continue to roast until well browned, 20 to 30 minutes. Serve immediately.

Making Crispy Smashed Potatoes

You can smash each potato by hand with a potato masher, but we found that a baking sheet smashes the potatoes all at once.

1. After rolling cooled, oven-steamed potatoes in olive oil, space potatoes evenly on baking sheet and place second baking sheet on top; press down uniformly on baking sheet until potatoes are roughly ⅓ to ½ inch thick.

2. Sprinkle smashed potatoes with thyme and season generously with salt and pepper; drizzle evenly with remaining 3 tablespoons oil. Roast as directed.

Candied Sweet Potato Casserole

Serves 10 to 12

WHY THIS RECIPE WORKS Sweet potato casserole is often claimed as a must-have at the Thanksgiving table. Kids love this sweet, sticky dish, but adults long for a side dish with more restrained sweetness, rather than one that could double as dessert. We set out to develop a sweet potato casserole with a bit of a savory accent to please everyone. For the best texture and flavor, we steamed the sweet potatoes on the stovetop with a little water, butter, and brown sugar. We kept the other flavorings simple—just salt and pepper. In the topping, we used whole pecans instead of chopped; this gave

the casserole a better texture and appearance. And a little cayenne and cumin lent a hit of spice to the topping that offset the sweetness of the potato. For a more intense molasses flavor, use dark brown sugar in place of light brown sugar.

Sweet Potatoes
- 8 tablespoons unsalted butter, cut into 1-inch pieces
- 5 pounds sweet potatoes, peeled and cut into 1-inch cubes
- 1 cup packed light brown sugar
- ½ cup water
- 1½ teaspoons table salt
- ½ teaspoon pepper

Pecan Topping
- 2 cups pecan halves
- ½ cup packed light brown sugar
- 1 egg white, lightly beaten
- ⅛ teaspoon table salt
  Pinch cayenne pepper
  Pinch ground cumin

1. *For the sweet potatoes:* Melt butter in Dutch oven over medium-high heat. Add sweet potatoes, sugar, water, salt, and pepper; bring to simmer. Reduce heat to medium-low, cover, and cook, stirring often, until sweet potatoes are tender (paring knife can be slipped into and out of center of potatoes with very little resistance), 45 minutes to 1 hour.

2. When sweet potatoes are tender, remove lid and bring sauce to rapid simmer over medium-high heat. Continue to simmer until sauce has reduced to glaze, 7 to 10 minutes.

3. *For the topping:* Meanwhile, mix all topping ingredients together in medium bowl; set aside.

4. Adjust oven rack to middle position and heat oven to 450 degrees. Pour potato mixture into 13 by 9-inch baking dish (or shallow casserole dish of similar size). Spread topping over potatoes. Bake until pecans are toasted and crisp, 10 to 15 minutes. Serve immediately.

Mashed Sweet Potatoes

Serves 4

WHY THIS RECIPE WORKS Mashed sweet potatoes often turn out overly thick and gluey or, at the other extreme, sloppy and loose. We wanted a recipe that would push sweet potatoes' deep, earthy sweetness to the fore and that would produce a silky puree with enough body to hold its shape on a fork. We braised the sweet potatoes in a mixture of butter and heavy cream to impart a smooth richness. Adding a little salt brought out the sweet potatoes' delicate flavor, and just a teaspoon of sugar bolstered their sweetness. Once the potatoes were tender, we mashed them in the saucepan with a potato masher. We skipped the typical pumpkin pie seasoning and instead let the simple sweet potato flavor shine through. Cutting the sweet potatoes into slices of even thickness is important so that they cook at the same rate. The potatoes are best served immediately, but they can be covered tightly with plastic wrap and kept warm for 30 minutes. This recipe can be doubled and prepared in a Dutch oven; the cooking time will need to be doubled as well.

 4 tablespoons unsalted butter, cut into 4 pieces
 2 tablespoons heavy cream
 1 teaspoon sugar
 ½ teaspoon table salt
 2 pounds sweet potatoes, peeled, quartered lengthwise, and cut crosswise into ¼-inch-thick slices

1. Melt butter in large saucepan over low heat. Stir in cream, sugar, and salt; add sweet potatoes and cook, covered, stirring occasionally, until potatoes fall apart when poked with fork, 35 to 45 minutes.

2. Off heat, mash sweet potatoes in saucepan with potato masher or transfer mixture to food mill and process into warmed serving bowl. Season with pepper to taste, and serve.

VARIATIONS
Maple-Orange Mashed Sweet Potatoes
Stir 2 tablespoons maple syrup and ½ teaspoon grated orange zest into potatoes before mashing.

Garlic-Scented Mashed Sweet Potatoes with Coconut Milk and Cilantro
Substitute ½ cup coconut milk for butter and cream. Add ¼ teaspoon red pepper flakes and 1 minced garlic clove to saucepan with potatoes. Stir 1 tablespoon minced fresh cilantro into mashed potatoes before serving.

Thick-Cut Sweet Potato Fries

Serves 4 to 6

WHY THIS RECIPE WORKS Too often, sweet potato fries simply don't do justice to their namesake. We wanted thick-cut fries with crispy exteriors and creamy interiors. Taking a cue from commercial frozen fries, we dunked the potato wedges in a slurry of water and cornstarch. Blanching the potatoes with salt and baking soda before dipping them in the slurry helped the coating stick to the potatoes, giving the fries a supercrunchy crust that stayed crispy. To keep the fries from sticking to the pan, we used a nonstick skillet, which had the added benefit of allowing us to use less oil. For a finishing touch to complement the natural sweetness of the fries, we made a spicy Belgian-style dipping sauce. If your sweet potatoes are shorter than 4 inches in length, do not cut the wedges crosswise. We prefer peanut oil for frying, but vegetable oil may be used instead. Leftover frying oil may be saved for further use; strain the cooled oil into an airtight container and store it in a cool, dark place for up to one month or in the freezer for up to two months. We like these fries with our Spicy Fry Sauce (recipe follows), but they are also good served plain.

 ½ cup cornstarch
 ¼ cup kosher salt
 1 teaspoon baking soda
 3 pounds sweet potatoes, peeled and cut into ¾-inch-thick wedges, wedges cut in half crosswise
 3 cups peanut oil

1. Adjust oven rack to middle position and heat oven to 200 degrees. Set wire rack in rimmed baking sheet. Whisk cornstarch and ½ cup cold water together in large bowl.

2. Bring 2 quarts water, salt, and baking soda to boil in Dutch oven. Add potatoes and return to boil. Reduce heat to simmer and cook until exteriors turn slightly mushy (centers will remain firm), 3 to 5 minutes. Whisk cornstarch slurry to recombine. Using wire skimmer or slotted spoon, transfer potatoes to bowl with slurry.

3. Using rubber spatula, fold potatoes with slurry until slurry turns light orange, thickens to paste, and clings to potatoes.

4. Heat oil in 12-inch nonstick skillet over high heat to 325 degrees. Using tongs, carefully add one-third of potatoes to oil, making sure that potatoes aren't touching one another. Fry until crispy and lightly browned, 7 to 10 minutes, using tongs to flip potatoes halfway through frying (adjust heat as necessary to maintain oil temperature between 280 and 300 degrees). Using wire skimmer or slotted spoon, transfer fries to prepared wire rack (fries that stick together can be separated with tongs or forks). Season with salt to taste and transfer to oven to keep warm. Return oil to 325 degrees and repeat in 2 more batches with remaining potatoes. Serve immediately.

ACCOMPANIMENT
Spicy Fry Sauce
Makes about ½ cup
For a less spicy version, use only 2 teaspoons of Asian chili-garlic sauce.

 6 tablespoons mayonnaise
 1 tablespoon Asian chili-garlic sauce
 2 teaspoons white vinegar

Whisk all ingredients together in small bowl. (Sauce can be refrigerated for up to 4 days.)

"When I finally finished developing this recipe back in 2014, sweet potatoes and I weren't on the best of terms. But it didn't start out that way. In fact, I'd gone in excited and optimistic. I've always enjoyed the lush creaminess of sweet potatoes and I love French fries. What could go wrong? Well, over the weeks that I spent working on this recipe, quite a bit went wrong: oily exteriors, burnt edges, fleeting crispiness. But through my many failed tests I learned a great deal about the science of frying and the secrets to making high-sugar sweet potato fries emerge from the oil crisp, and never burnt. I call for cutting these fries nice and thick for the best contrast of creamy interior to crisp outer shell and, now that we are back on good terms, I love dunking them in a spicy fry sauce."

—Dan

Sautéed Baby Spinach with Almonds and Golden Raisins

Serves 4

WHY THIS RECIPE WORKS Baby spinach is convenient—no stems to remove or grit to rinse out—but cooking often turns this tender green into a watery, mushy mess. We were determined to find a method for cooking baby spinach that would give us a worthwhile side dish. Wilting, blanching, and steaming proved to be ineffective in removing excess water, but parcooking the spinach in the microwave with a little water added to the bowl worked great. After 3 minutes, the spinach had softened and shrunk to half its size, thanks to the release of a great deal of liquid. But there was still more water to remove. We found that pressing the spinach against the colander before roughly chopping it on a cutting board and then pressing it again removed any remaining excess liquid. The spinach was now tender, sweet, and ready to be combined with complementary ingredients. Almonds and raisins introduced bold flavors and textures that enlivened this quick-cooking green. If you don't have a microwave-safe bowl large enough to accommodate the entire amount of spinach, cook it in a smaller bowl in two batches. Reduce the amount of water to 2 tablespoons per batch and cook each batch for about 1½ minutes.

- 18 ounces (18 cups) baby spinach
- ¼ cup water
- 2 tablespoons plus 2 teaspoons extra-virgin olive oil, divided
- ½ cup golden raisins
- 4 garlic cloves, sliced thin crosswise
- ¼ teaspoon red pepper flakes
- ¼ teaspoon table salt
- 2 teaspoons sherry vinegar
- ⅓ cup slivered almonds, toasted

1. Place spinach and water in large bowl. Cover bowl with plate (plate should completely cover bowl and not rest on spinach). Microwave until spinach is wilted and decreased in volume by half, 3 to 4 minutes. Using potholders, remove bowl from microwave and keep covered for 1 minute. Carefully remove plate and transfer spinach to colander set in sink. Using back of rubber spatula, gently press spinach against colander to release excess liquid. Transfer spinach to cutting board and roughly chop. Return to colander and press second time.

2. Heat 2 tablespoons oil, raisins, garlic, and pepper flakes in 10-inch skillet over medium-high heat. Cook, stirring constantly, until garlic is light golden brown and beginning to sizzle, 3 to 6 minutes. Add spinach to skillet, using tongs to stir and coat with oil. Sprinkle with salt and continue stirring with tongs until spinach is uniformly wilted and glossy, about 2 minutes. Sprinkle with vinegar and almonds; stir to combine. Drizzle with remaining 2 teaspoons oil and season with salt to taste. Serve.

Braised Greens with Bacon and Onion

SEASON 20 RECIPE

Serves 4

WHY THIS RECIPE WORKS This one-pot approach to turning meaty greens like kale and collards tender works perfectly and doesn't require hours of braising or leaving the greens awash in liquid. And these greens are also deeply flavored with smoky bacon and red onion. To start, we cooked the pieces of bacon until crisp, removing them to add later. The onion went into the skillet next and once it was softened we added garlic and some red pepper flakes. At this point we added half the greens and cooked them until they were beginning to wilt before adding the rest of the greens, along with broth and water. We covered the pot to let them cook through; when the greens had the tender-firm texture we wanted, we removed the lid to allow the liquid to cook off. The result: a winter greens recipe that highlights the greens' cabbage-like flavor and firm texture. A bit of cider vinegar added a sharp brightness to our greens and the crisp bacon pieces added big flavor and texture. For the best results, be sure the greens are fully cooked and tender in step 1 before moving on to step 2.

- 6 slices bacon, cut into ¼-inch pieces
- 1 red onion, halved and cut into ¼-inch slices
- 5 garlic cloves, minced
- ⅛ teaspoon red pepper flakes
- 2 pounds kale or collard greens, stemmed and leaves chopped into 3-inch pieces
- 1 cup chicken broth
- 1 cup water
- ¼ teaspoon table salt
- 1 tablespoon extra-virgin olive oil
- 3–4 teaspoons cider vinegar

1. Cook bacon in Dutch oven over medium heat until crisp, 5 to 7 minutes. Transfer bacon to paper towel–lined plate and pour off all but 2 tablespoons fat. Add onion and cook, stirring frequently, until softened and beginning to brown, 4 to 5 minutes. Add garlic and pepper flakes and cook until garlic is fragrant, about 1 minute. Add half of greens and stir until beginning to wilt, about 1 minute. Add remaining greens, broth, water, and salt. Quickly cover pot and reduce heat to medium-low. Cook, stirring occasionally, until greens are tender, 25 to 35 minutes for kale or 35 to 45 minutes for collards.

2. Remove lid and increase heat to medium-high. Cook, stirring occasionally, until most of liquid has evaporated (bottom of pot will be almost dry and greens will begin to sizzle), 8 to 12 minutes. Off heat, stir in oil, vinegar, and reserved bacon. Season with salt, pepper, and vinegar to taste, and serve.

Braised Greens with
Bacon and Onion

"This rich and hearty ratatouille is surprisingly versatile. It tastes great hot or at room temperature. Make it ahead, let its flavors meld, and serve it the next day. Pair it with grilled or roasted meat, pile it on creamy polenta, or top it with a soft-cooked egg. Best of all, make it year-round. Of course, ratatouille is great in the summer when tomatoes, eggplant, zucchini, and bell peppers are at their peak, but I love serving it in winter. Oven roasting concentrates the flavors, helping midwinter produce shine. And the herbes de Provence perfume the kitchen with soothing aromas that temporarily transport you to the summer fields of southern France."

—*Lan*

Walkaway Ratatouille

Serves 6 to 8

WHY THIS RECIPE WORKS Classic ratatouille recipes call for cutting vegetables into small pieces, labor- and time-intensive pretreatments like salting and/or pressing the vegetables to remove excess moisture, and cooking them in batches on the stovetop. Our secret to great yet easy ratatouille? Overcook some of the vegetables, barely cook the others—and let the oven do the work. We started our streamlined recipe by sautéing onions and aromatics and then adding chunks of eggplant and tomatoes before moving the pot to the oven, where the dry, ambient heat thoroughly evaporated moisture, concentrated flavors, and caramelized some of the veggies. After 45 minutes, the tomatoes and eggplant became meltingly soft and could be mashed into a thick, silky sauce. Zucchini and bell peppers went into the pot last so that they retained some texture. Finishing the dish with fresh herbs, a splash of sherry vinegar, and a drizzle of extra-virgin olive oil tied everything together. This dish is best prepared using ripe, in-season tomatoes. If good tomatoes are not available, substitute one 28-ounce can of whole peeled tomatoes that have been drained, rinsed, and chopped coarse. Ratatouille can be served as an accompaniment to meat or fish. It can also be served on its own with crusty bread, topped with an egg, or over pasta or rice. This dish can be served warm, at room temperature, or chilled.

⅓ cup plus 1 tablespoon extra-virgin olive oil, divided
2 large onions, cut into 1-inch pieces
8 large garlic cloves, peeled and smashed
1¾ teaspoons table salt, divided
¾ teaspoon pepper, divided
1½ teaspoons herbes de Provence
¼ teaspoon red pepper flakes
1 bay leaf
1½ pounds eggplant, peeled and cut into 1-inch pieces
2 pounds plum tomatoes, peeled, cored, and chopped
2 small zucchini, halved lengthwise and cut into 1-inch pieces
1 red bell pepper, stemmed, seeded, and cut into 1-inch pieces
1 yellow bell pepper, stemmed, seeded, and cut into 1-inch pieces
2 tablespoons chopped fresh basil, divided
1 tablespoon finely chopped fresh parsley
1 tablespoon sherry vinegar

1. Adjust oven rack to middle position and heat oven to 400 degrees. Heat ⅓ cup oil in Dutch oven over medium-high heat until shimmering. Add onions, garlic, 1 teaspoon salt, and ¼ teaspoon pepper and cook, stirring occasionally, until onions are translucent and starting to soften, about 10 minutes.

Add herbes de Provence, pepper flakes, and bay leaf and cook, stirring frequently, for 1 minute. Stir in eggplant and tomatoes. Sprinkle with ½ teaspoon salt and ¼ teaspoon pepper and stir to combine.

2. Transfer pot to oven and cook, uncovered, until vegetables are very tender and spotty brown, 40 to 45 minutes.

3. Remove pot from oven and, using potato masher or heavy wooden spoon, smash and stir eggplant mixture until broken down to sauce-like consistency. Stir in zucchini, bell peppers, remaining ¼ teaspoon salt, and remaining ¼ teaspoon pepper and return to oven. Cook, uncovered, until zucchini and bell peppers are just tender, 20 to 25 minutes.

4. Remove pot from oven, cover, and let sit until zucchini is translucent and easily pierced with tip of paring knife, 10 to 15 minutes. Using wooden spoon, scrape any browned bits from sides of pot and stir back into ratatouille. Discard bay leaf.

5. Stir in 1 tablespoon basil, parsley, and vinegar. Season with salt and pepper to taste. Transfer to large platter, drizzle with remaining 1 tablespoon oil, sprinkle with remaining 1 tablespoon basil, and serve.

Roasted Butternut Squash with Browned Butter and Hazelnuts

Serves 4 to 6

WHY THIS RECIPE WORKS Taking a cue from famed chef Yotam Ottolenghi, we sought to create a simple, savory, and presentation-worthy recipe for roasted butternut squash. We chose to peel the squash thoroughly to remove not only the tough outer skin but also the rugged fibrous layer of white flesh just beneath, ensuring supremely tender squash. To encourage the squash slices to caramelize, we placed the squash on the lowest rack in a 425-degree oven, and increased the baking time to evaporate the water. We also swapped in melted butter for olive oil to promote the flavorful Maillard reaction. Finally, we selected a mix of toppings that added crunch, creaminess, brightness, and visual appeal. For plain roasted squash omit the topping. This dish can be served warm or at room temperature. For the best texture it's important to remove the fibrous flesh just below the squash's skin.

Squash
1 large (2½- to 3-pound) butternut squash
3 tablespoons unsalted butter, melted
½ teaspoon table salt
½ teaspoon pepper

Topping
- 3 tablespoons unsalted butter, cut into 3 pieces
- ⅓ cup hazelnuts, toasted, skinned, and chopped
- 1 tablespoon water
- 1 tablespoon lemon juice
- Pinch table salt
- 1 tablespoon finely chopped fresh chives

1. **For the squash:** Adjust oven rack to lowest position and heat oven to 425 degrees. Using sharp vegetable peeler or chef's knife, remove skin and fibrous threads from squash just below skin (peel until squash is completely orange with no white flesh remaining, roughly ⅛ inch deep). Halve squash lengthwise and scrape out seeds. Place squash, cut side down, on cutting board and slice crosswise ½ inch thick.

2. Toss squash with melted butter, salt, and pepper until evenly coated. Arrange squash on rimmed baking sheet in single layer. Roast squash until side touching sheet toward back of oven is well browned, 25 to 30 minutes. Rotate sheet and continue to bake until side touching sheet toward back of oven is well browned, 6 to 10 minutes. Remove squash from oven and use metal spatula to flip each piece. Continue to roast until squash is very tender and side touching sheet is browned, 10 to 15 minutes longer.

3. **For the topping:** While squash roasts, melt butter with hazelnuts in 8-inch skillet over medium-low heat. Cook, stirring frequently, until butter and hazelnuts are brown and fragrant, about 2 minutes. Immediately remove skillet from heat and stir in water (butter will foam and sizzle). Let cool for 1 minute; stir in lemon juice and salt.

4. Transfer squash to large serving platter. Drizzle butter mixture evenly over squash. Sprinkle with chives and serve.

VARIATIONS
Roasted Butternut Squash with Radicchio and Parmesan
Omit topping. Whisk 1 tablespoon sherry vinegar, ½ teaspoon mayonnaise, and pinch table salt together in small bowl; gradually whisk in 2 tablespoons extra-virgin olive oil until smooth. Before serving, drizzle vinaigrette over squash and sprinkle with ½ cup coarsely shredded radicchio; ½ ounce Parmesan cheese, shaved into thin strips; and 3 tablespoons toasted pine nuts.

Roasted Butternut Squash with Goat Cheese, Pecans, and Maple
Omit topping. Stir 2 tablespoons maple syrup and pinch cayenne pepper together in small bowl. Before serving, drizzle maple mixture over squash and sprinkle with ⅓ cup crumbled goat cheese; ⅓ cup pecans, toasted and chopped; and 2 teaspoons fresh thyme leaves.

Roasted Butternut Squash with Tahini and Feta
Omit topping. Whisk 1 tablespoon tahini, 1 tablespoon extra-virgin olive oil, 1½ teaspoons lemon juice, 1 teaspoon honey, and pinch table salt together in small bowl. Before serving, drizzle tahini mixture over squash and sprinkle with ¼ cup finely crumbled feta cheese; ¼ cup shelled pistachios, toasted and chopped fine; and 2 tablespoons chopped fresh mint.

Best Summer Tomato Gratin
SEASON 20 RECIPE

Serves 6 to 8

WHY THIS RECIPE WORKS A summer tomato gratin should burst with concentrated, bright tomato flavor and contrasting firm texture from the bread, but most recipes lead to mushy results. Starting our gratin on the stovetop initiated the breakdown of the tomatoes, drove off some moisture that would otherwise have sogged out the bread, and shortened the overall cooking time. We finished the dish in the dry, even heat of the oven. Toasting large cubes of crusty artisan-style baguette ensured that the bread didn't get too soggy once combined with the tomatoes. After toasting the bread, we added the coarsely chopped tomatoes as well as garlic, a small amount of sugar, and salt and pepper. Just before moving the skillet to the oven, we folded in most of the toasted bread and scattered the remainder over the top along with some Parmesan to create a crusty, savory topping that contrasted with the custardy interior. A scattering of fresh basil provided color and bright flavor. For the best results, use the ripest in-season tomatoes you can find. Supermarket vine-ripened tomatoes will work, but the gratin won't be as flavorful as one made with locally grown tomatoes. Do not use plum tomatoes, which contain less juice than regular round tomatoes and will result in a dry gratin. For the bread, we prefer a crusty baguette with a firm, chewy crumb. You can serve the gratin hot, warm, or at room temperature.

- 6 tablespoons extra-virgin olive oil, divided
- 6 ounces crusty baguette, cut into ¾-inch cubes (4 cups)
- 3 garlic cloves, sliced thin
- 3 pounds tomatoes, cored and cut into ¾-inch pieces
- 2 teaspoons sugar
- 1 teaspoon table salt
- 1 teaspoon pepper
- 1½ ounces Parmesan cheese, grated (¾ cup)
- 2 tablespoons chopped fresh basil

1. Adjust oven rack to middle position and heat oven to 350 degrees. Heat ¼ cup oil in 12-inch ovensafe skillet over medium-low heat until shimmering. Add bread and stir to coat. Cook, stirring constantly, until bread is browned and toasted, about 5 minutes. Transfer bread to bowl.

2. Return now-empty skillet to low heat and add remaining 2 tablespoons oil and garlic. Cook, stirring constantly, until garlic is golden at edges, 30 to 60 seconds. Add tomatoes, sugar, salt, and pepper and stir to combine. Increase heat to medium-high and cook, stirring occasionally, until tomatoes have started to break down and have released enough juice to be mostly submerged, 8 to 10 minutes.

3. Remove skillet from heat and gently stir in 3 cups bread until completely moistened and evenly distributed. Using spatula, press down on bread until completely submerged. Arrange remaining 1 cup bread evenly over surface, pressing to partially submerge. Sprinkle evenly with Parmesan.

4. Bake until top of gratin is deeply browned, tomatoes are bubbling, and juice has reduced, 40 to 45 minutes; after 30 minutes, run spatula around edge of skillet to loosen crust and release any juice underneath. (Gratin will appear loose and jiggle around outer edges but will thicken as it cools.)

5. Remove skillet from oven and let sit for 15 minutes. Sprinkle gratin with basil and serve.

Wild Rice Pilaf with Pecans and Dried Cranberries

Serves 6 to 8

WHY THIS RECIPE WORKS Sometimes wild rice turns out undercooked and difficult to chew, and other times the rice is overcooked and gluey. We wanted to figure out how to turn out properly cooked wild rice every time. Through trial and error, we learned to simmer the rice slowly in plenty of liquid, making sure to stop the cooking process at just the right moment by checking it for doneness every couple of minutes past the 35-minute mark. For a simmering liquid, we used chicken broth—its mild yet rich profile tempered the rice's muddy flavor to a pleasant earthiness and affirmed its subdued nuttiness. To further tame the strong flavor of the wild rice, we added some white rice to the mixture, then added onion, carrot, dried cranberries, and toasted pecans for a winning pilaf. Wild rice quickly goes from tough to pasty, so begin testing the rice at the 35-minute mark and drain the rice as soon as it is tender.

¾ cup plus 2 tablespoons chicken broth
1 bay leaf
4 sprigs fresh thyme, divided
½ cup wild rice, picked over and rinsed
¾ cup long-grain white rice
1½ tablespoons unsalted butter
½ onion, chopped fine
½ large carrot, peeled and chopped fine
1½ teaspoons table salt
6 tablespoons dried cranberries
6 tablespoons pecans, toasted and chopped
2¼ teaspoons finely chopped fresh parsley

1. Bring broth, 2 tablespoons water, bay leaf, and 2 thyme sprigs to boil in medium saucepan over medium-high heat. Add wild rice, cover, and reduce heat to low; simmer until rice is plump and tender and has absorbed most of liquid, about 35 minutes. Drain wild rice in fine-mesh strainer. Discard bay leaf and thyme sprigs. Return wild rice to now-empty saucepan, cover, and set aside.

2. While wild rice is cooking, place white rice in fine-mesh strainer and rinse under cold running water until water runs clear. Place strainer over bowl and set aside. Melt butter in medium saucepan over medium-high heat. Add onion, carrot, and salt and cook, stirring frequently, until vegetables are softened but not browned, about 4 minutes. Add white rice and stir to coat grains with butter; cook, stirring frequently, until grains begin to turn translucent, about 3 minutes.

Meanwhile, bring 1 cup plus 2 tablespoons water to boil in small saucepan. Add boiling water and remaining 2 thyme sprigs to white rice mixture and return to boil. Reduce heat to low, sprinkle cranberries evenly over white rice, and cover. Simmer until all liquid is absorbed, about 15 minutes. Off heat, discard thyme sprigs and fluff white rice with fork.

3. Combine wild rice, white rice mixture, pecans, and parsley in bowl and toss with rubber spatula to combine. Season with salt and pepper to taste; serve immediately.

Rice and Lentils with Crispy Onions (Mujaddara)

Serves 4 to 6

WHY THIS RECIPE WORKS *Mujaddara*, the rice and beans of the Middle East, is a hearty, warm-spiced rice and lentil pilaf containing large brown or green lentils and crispy fried onion strings. We wanted a version of this dish in which all of the elements were cooked perfectly. We found that precooking the lentils and soaking the rice in hot water before combining them ensured that both components cooked evenly. For the crispiest possible onions, we removed some moisture by salting and microwaving them before frying. This allowed us to pare down the fussy process of batch-frying in several cups of oil to a single batch. And using some of the oil from the onions to dress our pilaf gave it ultrasavory depth. Large green or brown lentils will work interchangeably in this recipe; do not substitute smaller French lentils. When preparing the Crispy Onions, be sure to reserve 3 tablespoons of the onion cooking oil for cooking the rice and lentils.

Yogurt Sauce
- 1 cup plain whole-milk yogurt
- 2 tablespoons lemon juice
- ½ teaspoon minced garlic
- ½ teaspoon table salt

Rice and Lentils
- 8½ ounces (1¼ cups) green or brown lentils, picked over and rinsed
- 2 teaspoons table salt, divided
- 1¼ cups basmati rice
- 1 recipe Crispy Onions, plus 3 tablespoons reserved oil (recipe follows)
- 3 garlic cloves, minced
- 1 teaspoon ground coriander
- 1 teaspoon ground cumin
- ½ teaspoon ground cinnamon
- ½ teaspoon ground allspice
- ¼ teaspoon pepper
- ⅛ teaspoon cayenne pepper
- 1 teaspoon sugar
- 3 tablespoons finely chopped fresh cilantro

1. *For the yogurt sauce:* Whisk all ingredients together in bowl. Refrigerate while preparing rice and lentils.

2. *For the rice and lentils:* Bring lentils, 4 cups water, and 1 teaspoon salt to boil in medium saucepan over high heat. Reduce heat to low and cook until lentils are tender, 15 to 17 minutes. Drain and set aside. While lentils cook, place rice in medium bowl and cover by 2 inches with hot tap water; let sit for 15 minutes.

3. Using your hands, gently swish rice grains to release excess starch. Carefully pour off water, leaving rice in bowl. Add cold tap water to rice and pour off water. Repeat adding and pouring off cold tap water 4 or 5 times, until water runs almost clear. Drain rice in fine-mesh strainer.

4. Heat reserved onion oil, garlic, coriander, cumin, cinnamon, allspice, pepper, and cayenne in Dutch oven over medium heat until fragrant, about 2 minutes. Add rice and cook, stirring occasionally, until edges of rice begin to turn translucent, about 3 minutes. Add 2¼ cups water, sugar, and remaining 1 teaspoon salt and bring to boil. Stir in lentils, reduce heat to low, cover, and cook until all liquid is absorbed, about 12 minutes.

5. Off heat, remove lid, fold clean dish towel in half, and place over pot; replace lid. Let sit for 10 minutes. Fluff rice and lentils with fork and stir in cilantro and half of crispy onions. Transfer to serving platter, top with remaining crispy onions, and serve, passing yogurt sauce separately.

Crispy Onions
Makes 1½ cups
It is crucial to thoroughly dry the microwaved onions after rinsing. The best way to accomplish this is to use a salad spinner. Reserve 3 tablespoons of oil when draining the onions to use in Rice and Lentils with Crispy Onions. Remaining oil may be stored in an airtight container and refrigerated for up to four weeks.

- 2 pounds onions, halved and sliced crosswise into ¼-inch-thick pieces
- 2 teaspoons table salt
- 1½ cups vegetable oil for frying

1. Toss onions and salt together in large bowl. Microwave for 5 minutes. Rinse thoroughly, transfer to paper towel–lined baking sheet, and dry well.

2. Heat onions and oil in Dutch oven over high heat, stirring frequently, until onions are golden brown, 25 to 30 minutes. Drain onions in colander set in large bowl; reserve oil. Transfer onions to paper towel–lined baking sheet to drain.

Rice and Lentils with
Crispy Onions

Persian-Style Rice with Golden Crust (Chelow)

Serves 6

WHY THIS RECIPE WORKS *Chelow* is a classic Iranian dish that marries a light and fluffy rice pilaf with a golden-brown, crispy crust (known as *tahdig*). Rinsing the rice and then soaking it for 15 minutes in hot salted water produced fluffy grains. Parboiling the rice and then steaming it was also essential to creating the best texture for the pilaf and the perfect crust. Steaming the grains for 45 minutes rather than the traditional hour was enough; we also wrapped the lid with a towel to absorb extra moisture. Combining a portion of the rice with thick Greek yogurt and oil created a flavorful crust, while chunks of butter enriched the pilaf portion. The yogurt also made the tahdig easier to remove from the pot, as did brushing the bottom of the pot with extra oil. Adding cumin seeds and parsley to the dish made for a more interesting and well-rounded flavor profile. We prefer the nutty flavor and texture of basmati rice, but Texmati or another long-grain rice will work. For the best results, use a Dutch oven with a bottom diameter between 8½ and 10 inches. It is important not to overcook the rice during the parboiling step, as it will continue to cook during steaming. Begin checking the rice at 3 minutes. Do not skip placing the pot on a damp towel in step 7—doing so will help free the crust from the pot. Serve this pilaf alongside stews or kebabs.

- 2 **cups basmati rice**
- ¼ **teaspoon table salt, plus salt for soaking and cooking rice**
- 1 **tablespoon plus ¼ cup vegetable oil, divided**
- ¼ **cup plain Greek yogurt**
- 1½ **teaspoons cumin seeds, divided**
- 2 **tablespoons unsalted butter, cut into 8 cubes**
- ¼ **cup finely chopped fresh parsley, divided**

1. Place rice in fine-mesh strainer and rinse under cold running water until water runs clear. Place rinsed rice and 1 tablespoon salt in medium bowl and cover with 4 cups hot tap water. Stir gently to dissolve salt; let sit for 15 minutes. Drain rice in fine-mesh strainer.

2. Meanwhile, bring 8 cups water to boil in Dutch oven over high heat. Add rice and 2 tablespoons salt. Boil briskly, stirring frequently, until rice is mostly tender with slight bite in center and grains are floating toward top of pot, 3 to 5 minutes (begin timing from when rice is added to pot).

3. Drain rice in large fine-mesh strainer and rinse with cold water to stop cooking, about 30 seconds. Rinse and dry pot well to remove any residual starch. Brush bottom and 1 inch up sides of pot with 1 tablespoon oil.

4. Whisk remaining ¼ cup oil, yogurt, 1 teaspoon cumin seeds, and ¼ teaspoon salt together in medium bowl. Add 2 cups parcooked rice and stir until combined. Spread yogurt-rice mixture evenly over bottom of prepared pot, packing it down well.

5. Stir remaining ½ teaspoon cumin seeds into remaining rice. Mound rice in center of pot on top of yogurt-rice base (it should look like small hill). Poke 8 equally spaced holes through rice mound but not into yogurt-rice base. Place 1 butter cube in each hole. Drizzle ⅓ cup water over rice mound.

6. Wrap pot lid with clean dish towel and cover pot tightly, making sure towel is secure on top of lid and away from heat. Cook over medium-high heat until rice on bottom is crackling and steam is coming from sides of pot, about 10 minutes, rotating pot halfway through for even cooking.

7. Reduce heat to medium-low and continue to cook until rice is tender and fluffy and crust is golden brown around edges, 30 to 35 minutes. Remove covered pot from heat and place on damp dish towel set in rimmed baking sheet; let sit for 5 minutes.

8. Stir 2 tablespoons parsley into rice, making sure not to disturb crust on bottom of pot, and season with salt to taste. Gently spoon rice onto serving platter.

9. Using thin metal spatula, loosen edges of crust from pot, then break crust into large pieces. Transfer pieces to serving platter, arranging evenly around rice. Sprinkle with remaining 2 tablespoons parsley and serve.

Almost Hands-Free Risotto with Parmesan and Herbs

Serves 6

WHY THIS RECIPE WORKS Classic risotto can demand half an hour of stovetop tedium for the best creamy results. Our goal was 5 minutes of stirring, tops. First, we chose to cook our risotto in a Dutch oven rather than a saucepan. A Dutch oven's thick, heavy bottom, deep sides, and tight-fitting lid are made to trap and distribute heat as evenly as possible. Typical recipes dictate adding the broth in small increments after the wine has been absorbed (and stirring constantly after each addition), but we added most of the broth at once. Then we covered the pan and simmered the rice until almost all the broth had been absorbed, stirring just twice during this time. After adding the second and final addition of broth, we stirred the pot for just a few minutes to ensure that the bottom wouldn't cook more quickly than the top and turned off the heat. Without sitting over a direct flame, the sauce turned out perfectly creamy and the rice was thickened, velvety, and just barely chewy. To finish, we simply stirred in butter, herbs, and a squeeze of lemon juice to brighten the flavors. This more hands-off method does require precise timing, so we strongly recommend using a timer. The consistency of risotto is largely a matter of personal taste; if you prefer a brothy risotto, add extra broth in step 4. This makes a great side dish for braised meats.

5 cups chicken broth
1½ cups water
4 tablespoons unsalted butter, divided
1 large onion, finely chopped
¾ teaspoon table salt
1 garlic clove, minced
2 cups Arborio rice
1 cup dry white wine
2 ounces Parmesan cheese, grated (1 cup)
1 teaspoon lemon juice
2 tablespoons chopped fresh parsley
2 tablespoons chopped fresh chives

1. Bring broth and water to boil in large saucepan over high heat. Reduce heat to medium-low to maintain gentle simmer.

2. Heat 2 tablespoons butter in Dutch oven over medium heat. When butter has melted, add onion and salt. Cook, stirring frequently, until onion is softened but not browned, 5 to 7 minutes. Add garlic and stir until fragrant, about 30 seconds. Add rice and cook, stirring frequently, until grains are translucent around edges, about 3 minutes.

3. Add wine and cook, stirring constantly, until fully absorbed, 2 to 3 minutes. Stir 5 cups warm broth mixture into rice, reduce heat to medium-low, cover, and simmer until almost all liquid has been absorbed and rice is just al dente, 16 to 19 minutes, stirring twice during cooking.

4. Add ¾ cup more broth mixture and stir gently and constantly until risotto becomes creamy, about 3 minutes. Stir in Parmesan. Remove pot from heat, cover, and let sit for 5 minutes. Stir in remaining 2 tablespoons butter, lemon juice, parsley, and chives. Season with salt and pepper to taste. If desired, add up to ½ cup remaining broth mixture to loosen texture of risotto. Serve immediately.

Simple Israeli Couscous

Makes about 4 cups

WHY THIS RECIPE WORKS Israeli couscous is nuttier than its North African cousin, thanks to the practice of drying the pasta-like pearls over a flame. To accentuate the earthy, nutty flavor of Israeli couscous, we started by toasting the spheres in oil. We then added water, brought it to a boil, and cooked the couscous covered and at a simmer, allowing it to slowly and evenly absorb the liquid. To turn the finished couscous into a salad, we spread it out on a baking sheet to cool, which prevented it from cooking further in its own steam. Meanwhile, we quickly pickled shallot slices, dissolving sugar in red wine vinegar over medium-high heat before removing the pan from heat, stirring in the shallots, and letting them take on more flavor as the liquid cooled. We dressed the couscous in a bold vinaigrette, whisking together olive oil, lemon juice, Dijon, and red pepper flakes. Once the couscous was coated in the vinaigrette, we finished off the salad with mint, peas, toasted pistachios, and feta. We also created a version with tomatoes, olives, and ricotta salata. Plain warm couscous can be tossed with butter or extra-virgin olive oil and salt and pepper for a simple side dish. If you're using it in a salad (recipes follow), transfer the couscous to a rimmed baking sheet and let it cool completely, about 15 minutes.

"I don't have the time to develop recipes anymore since my job has grown over the years, but it's something that I truly loved to do. This was the last recipe that I developed, and it was an especially fun one to create. It's a twist on pasta salad that uses tender, bouncy, lightly toasted Israeli couscous as its base. The pearl-like pasta is elevated by fresh, bright, and lively ingredients, including spicy arugula, briny and creamy feta, green peas, sweet-and-sour pickled shallots, toasted pistachios, and a healthy dose of fresh mint leaves—all tossed with a lemon and extra-virgin olive oil dressing. This is exactly the type of dish that I love to eat because each bite is complex, and it's visually inviting. I make this for just about any occasion: parties, packed for a weekend getaway, or even just a simple picnic at the beach."

—Erin

2 cups Israeli couscous
1 tablespoon extra-virgin olive oil
2½ cups water
½ teaspoon table salt

Heat couscous and oil in medium saucepan over medium heat, stirring frequently, until about half of grains are golden brown, 5 to 6 minutes. Carefully add water and salt; stir briefly to combine. Increase heat to high and bring to boil. Reduce heat to medium-low, cover, and simmer, stirring occasionally, until water is absorbed, 9 to 12 minutes. Remove saucepan from heat and let sit, covered, for 3 minutes. Serve.

VARIATIONS

Israeli Couscous with Lemon, Mint, Peas, Feta, and Pickled Shallots
Serves 6

For efficiency, let the shallots pickle while you prepare the remaining ingredients.

⅓ cup red wine vinegar
2 tablespoons sugar
Pinch plus ⅛ teaspoon table salt
2 shallots, sliced thin
3 tablespoons extra-virgin olive oil
3 tablespoons lemon juice
1 teaspoon Dijon mustard
⅛ teaspoon red pepper flakes
1 recipe Simple Israeli Couscous (page 383), cooled
4 ounces (4 cups) baby arugula, chopped coarse
1 cup fresh mint leaves, torn
½ cup frozen peas, thawed
½ cup shelled pistachios, toasted and chopped, divided
3 ounces feta cheese, crumbled (¾ cup), divided

1. Bring vinegar, sugar, and pinch salt to simmer in small saucepan over medium-high heat, stirring occasionally, until sugar dissolves. Remove pan from heat, add shallots, and stir to combine. Cover and let cool completely, about 30 minutes. Drain and discard liquid.

2. Whisk oil, lemon juice, mustard, pepper flakes, and remaining ⅛ teaspoon salt together in large bowl. Add cooled couscous, arugula, mint, peas, 6 tablespoons pistachios, ½ cup feta, and shallots and toss to combine. Season with salt and pepper to taste, and transfer to serving bowl. Let stand for 5 minutes. Sprinkle with remaining ¼ cup feta and remaining 2 tablespoons pistachios and serve.

Israeli Couscous with Tomatoes, Olives, and Ricotta Salata
Serves 6

Crumbled feta cheese can be substituted for the ricotta salata.

3 tablespoons extra-virgin olive oil
3 tablespoons red wine vinegar
1 teaspoon Dijon mustard
⅛ teaspoon table salt
1 recipe Simple Israeli Couscous (page 383), cooled
12 ounces grape tomatoes, quartered
3 ounces ricotta salata, crumbled (¾ cup)
2 ounces (2 cups) baby spinach, sliced ¼ inch thick
⅔ cup pitted kalamata olives, sliced
1 bunch chives, cut into ¼-inch pieces (¼ cup)
1½ cups fresh basil leaves, chopped
½ cup pine nuts, toasted, divided

Whisk oil, vinegar, mustard, and salt together in large bowl. Add cooled couscous, tomatoes, ricotta salata, spinach, olives, chives, basil, and 6 tablespoons pine nuts and toss to combine. Season with salt and pepper to taste and transfer to serving bowl. Let sit for 5 minutes. Sprinkle with remaining 2 tablespoons pine nuts and serve.

Quinoa Pilaf with Herbs and Lemon
Serves 4 to 6

WHY THIS RECIPE WORKS Most recipes for quinoa pilaf turn out woefully overcooked because they call for nearly twice as much liquid as they should. We cut the water back to ensure tender grains with a satisfying bite, and gave it a stir partway through cooking to ensure that the grains cooked evenly. We let the quinoa rest for several minutes before fluffing to help further improve the texture. We also pre-toasted the quinoa in a dry saucepan before simmering to develop its natural nutty flavor, and finished our pilaf with a judicious amount of boldly flavored ingredients. If you buy unwashed quinoa, rinse the grains in a fine-mesh strainer, drain them, and then spread them on a rimmed baking sheet lined with a clean dish towel and let them dry for 15 minutes before proceeding with the recipe. Any soft herbs, such as cilantro, parsley, chives, mint, and tarragon, can be used.

1½ cups prewashed white quinoa
2 tablespoons unsalted butter, cut into 2 pieces
1 small onion, chopped fine
¾ teaspoon table salt
1¾ cups water
3 tablespoons chopped fresh herbs
1 tablespoon lemon juice

1. Toast quinoa in medium saucepan over medium-high heat, stirring frequently, until quinoa is very fragrant and makes continuous popping sound, 5 to 7 minutes. Transfer quinoa to bowl and set aside.

2. Return now-empty pan to medium-low heat and melt butter. Add onion and salt; cook, stirring frequently, until onion is softened and light golden, 5 to 7 minutes.

3. Increase heat to medium-high, stir in water and quinoa, and bring to simmer. Cover, reduce heat to low, and simmer until grains are just tender and liquid is absorbed, 18 to 20 minutes, stirring once halfway through cooking. Remove pan from heat and let sit, covered, for 10 minutes. Fluff quinoa with fork, stir in herbs and lemon juice, and serve.

VARIATIONS
Quinoa Pilaf with Chipotle, Queso Fresco, and Peanuts

Add 1 teaspoon chipotle chile powder and ¼ teaspoon ground cumin with onion and salt. Substitute ½ cup crumbled queso fresco; ½ cup roasted unsalted peanuts, chopped; and 2 thinly sliced scallions for herbs. Substitute 4 teaspoons lime juice for lemon juice.

Quinoa Pilaf with Apricots, Aged Gouda, and Pistachios

Add ½ teaspoon grated lemon zest, ½ teaspoon ground coriander, ¼ teaspoon ground cumin, and ⅛ teaspoon pepper with onion and salt. Stir in ½ cup dried apricots, chopped, before letting quinoa sit for 10 minutes in step 3. Substitute ½ cup shredded aged gouda; ½ cup shelled pistachios, toasted and chopped coarse; and 2 tablespoons chopped fresh mint for herbs.

Farro Salad with Asparagus, Sugar Snap Peas, and Tomatoes

Serves 6

WHY THIS RECIPE WORKS Nutty, chewy farro is a popular grain in Italian cuisine and makes for a satisfying side. When we decided to turn farro into a hearty, fresh salad, we wondered if we could bypass the traditional step of soaking the grains overnight and then cooking them gradually for over an hour in favor of a simpler, quicker method. After testing out a few cooking techniques, we learned that boiling the grains in plenty of salted water and then draining them yielded nicely firm but tender farro—no soaking necessary. To make sure this salad looked as good as it tasted, we briefly boiled bite-size

pieces of asparagus and snap peas to bring out their vibrant color and crisp-tender bite. A lemon-dill dressing served as a citrusy herbal complement to the earthy farro. Cherry tomatoes and feta cheese offered a fresh, full-flavored finish. We prefer the flavor and texture of whole-grain farro. Pearl farro can be used, but cooking times vary, so start checking for doneness after 10 minutes. Do not use quick-cooking farro in this recipe.

1½ cups whole farro, rinsed
¼ teaspoon table salt, plus salt for cooking farro and vegetables
6 ounces asparagus, trimmed and cut into 1-inch lengths
6 ounces sugar snap peas, strings removed, cut into 1-inch lengths
3 tablespoons extra-virgin olive oil
2 tablespoons lemon juice
2 tablespoons minced shallot
1 teaspoon Dijon mustard
¼ teaspoon pepper
6 ounces cherry tomatoes, halved
3 tablespoons chopped fresh dill
2 ounces feta cheese, crumbled (½ cup), divided

1. Bring 2 quarts water to boil in large saucepan. Add farro and 1 tablespoon salt. Return to boil, reduce heat, and simmer until grains are tender with slight chew, 15 to 20 minutes. Drain well.

2. Bring 2 quarts water to boil in large saucepan. Add asparagus, snap peas, and 1 tablespoon salt. Cook until vegetables are crisp-tender, 2 to 3 minutes. Using slotted spoon, transfer vegetables to rimmed baking sheet and let cool for 15 minutes.

3. Whisk oil, lemon juice, shallot, mustard, ¼ teaspoon salt, and pepper together in large bowl. Add tomatoes, dill, ¼ cup feta, cooled vegetables, and farro to dressing and toss to combine. Season with salt and pepper to taste, and transfer to serving bowl. Sprinkle salad with remaining ¼ cup feta and serve.

No-Fuss Creamy Parmesan Polenta

Serves 6 to 8

WHY THIS RECIPE WORKS If you don't stir polenta almost constantly, it forms intractable lumps. Our goal was creamy, smooth polenta with rich corn flavor, but we wanted to find a way around the fussy process. The prospect of stirring continuously for an hour made our arms ache, so we set out to find a way to give the water a head start on penetrating the cornmeal (we prefer the soft texture and nutty flavor of degerminated cornmeal in polenta). Our research led us to consider the similarities between cooking dried beans and dried corn. With beans, water has to penetrate the hard outer skin to gelatinize the starch within. In a corn kernel, the water has to penetrate the endosperm. To soften bean skins and speed up cooking, baking soda is sometimes added to the cooking liquid. Sure enough, a pinch was all it took to cut the cornmeal's cooking time in half without affecting the texture or flavor. Baking soda also helped the granules break down and release their starch in a uniform way, so we could virtually eliminate the stirring if we covered the pot and adjusted the heat to low. Parmesan cheese and butter stirred in at the last minute made the finished polenta satisfying and rich. Coarse-ground degerminated cornmeal such as yellow grits (with grains the size of couscous) works best in this recipe. Avoid instant and quick-cooking products, as well as whole grain, stone-ground, and regular cornmeal. Do not omit the baking soda—it reduces the cooking time and makes for a creamier polenta. The polenta should do little more than release wisps of steam. If it bubbles or sputters even slightly after the first 10 minutes, the heat is too high and you may need a flame tamer. A flame tamer can be purchased at most kitchen supply stores, or you can improvise your own (see "Making a Flame Tamer"). For a main course, serve the polenta with a wedge of rich cheese, meat sauce, or cooked leafy greens. Served plain, the polenta makes a great accompaniment to stews and braises.

7½ **cups water**
1½ **teaspoons table salt**
    Pinch baking soda
1½ **cups coarse-ground cornmeal**
 4 **ounces Parmesan cheese, grated (2 cups),**
    plus extra for serving
 2 **tablespoons unsalted butter**

1. Bring water to boil in 4-quart saucepan over medium-high heat. Stir in salt and baking soda. Slowly pour cornmeal into water in steady stream, while stirring back and forth with wooden spoon or rubber spatula. Bring mixture to boil, stirring constantly, about 1 minute. Reduce heat to lowest possible setting and cover.

2. After 5 minutes, whisk polenta to smooth out any lumps that may have formed, about 15 seconds. (Make sure to scrape sides and bottom of pan.) Cover and continue to cook, without stirring, until grains of polenta are tender but slightly al dente, about 25 minutes. (Polenta should be loose and barely hold its shape; it will continue to thicken as it cools.)

3. Remove from heat, stir in Parmesan and butter, and season with pepper to taste. Let sit, covered, for 5 minutes. Serve, passing extra Parmesan separately.

Making a Flame Tamer

A flame tamer keeps risotto, polenta, and sauces from simmering too briskly. To make one, shape a sheet of heavy-duty aluminum foil into a 1-inch-thick ring of even thickness the size of your burner.

Bread and Pizza

Pizza al Taglio with Prosciutto and Figs

Easiest-Ever Biscuits

Easiest-Ever Biscuits

SEASON 20 RECIPE

Makes 10 biscuits

WHY THIS RECIPE WORKS A fresh, warm biscuit instantly doubles the coziness quotient of practically anything you serve it with: chicken stew, vegetable soup, fried eggs, just to name a few. We wanted to combine the ease of cream biscuits (which eliminate the step of cutting cold fat into dry ingredients) with the ease of drop biscuits (which skip the rolling and cutting) to create the easiest biscuits ever. But the most obvious solution—increasing the amount of cream in a cream biscuit recipe until the dough had a droppable consistency—produced biscuits that spread too much and were greasy. Instead of increasing the amount of cream, we found a way to increase its fluidity: We heated it to between 95 and 100 degrees, which melted the solid particles of butterfat dispersed throughout. This made a dough that was moister and scoopable but that rose up instead of spreading out in the oven, producing biscuits that were appropriately rich and tender but not greasy. These biscuits come together very quickly, so in the interest of efficiency, start heating your oven before gathering your ingredients. We like these biscuits brushed with a bit of melted butter, but you can skip that step if you're serving the biscuits with a rich accompaniment such as sausage gravy.

- 3 cups (15 ounces) all-purpose flour
- 4 teaspoons sugar
- 1 tablespoon baking powder
- ¼ teaspoon baking soda
- 1¼ teaspoons table salt
- 2 cups heavy cream
- 2 tablespoons unsalted butter, melted (optional)

1. Adjust oven rack to upper-middle position and heat oven to 450 degrees. Line rimmed baking sheet with parchment paper. In medium bowl, whisk together flour, sugar, baking powder, baking soda, and salt. Microwave cream until just warmed to body temperature (95 to 100 degrees), 60 to 90 seconds, stirring halfway through microwaving. Stir cream into flour mixture until soft, uniform dough forms.

2. Spray ⅓-cup dry measuring cup with vegetable oil spray. Drop level scoops of batter 2 inches apart on prepared sheet (biscuits should measure about 2½ inches wide and 1¼ inches tall). Respray measuring cup after every 3 or 4 scoops. If portions are misshapen, use your fingertips to gently reshape dough into level cylinders. Bake until tops are light golden brown, 10 to 12 minutes, rotating sheet halfway through baking. Brush hot biscuits with melted butter, if using. Serve warm. (Biscuits can be stored in zipper-lock bag at room temperature for up to 24 hours. Reheat biscuits in 300-degree oven for 10 minutes.)

Pumpkin Bread

Serves 16 (Makes 2 loaves)

WHY THIS RECIPE WORKS Although recipes for pumpkin bread are pleasantly sweet and spicy, they're nothing to write home about. We wanted a bread that had just the right texture—neither too dense nor too cakey—and a rich pumpkin flavor that was properly tempered with sweetness and gently enhanced rather than obscured by spices. We wanted to skip roasting and pureeing canned pumpkin because after all, this is supposed to be a "quick" bread. But canned pumpkin has a raw flavor, a problem we easily remedied by cooking it on top of the stove just until it started to caramelize. This also drove off moisture. To restore that moisture, we added buttermilk. And since caramelizing the pumpkin added sweetness, to restore the balance we added tangy cream cheese, which also added richness. We liked toasted walnuts added to the batter but we still wanted something to complement the bread's crumb and flavor. Sprinkled on just before baking, a simple streusel gives the perfect amount of sweet crunch to each slice. The test kitchen's preferred loaf pan measures 8½ by 4½ inches; if using 9 by 5-inch loaf pans, start checking for doneness 5 minutes earlier than advised in the recipe.

Topping
- 5 tablespoons packed (2¼ ounces) light brown sugar
- 1 tablespoon all-purpose flour
- 1 tablespoon unsalted butter, softened
- 1 teaspoon ground cinnamon
- ⅛ teaspoon table salt

Bread
- 2 cups (10 ounces) all-purpose flour
- 1½ teaspoons baking powder
- ½ teaspoon baking soda
- 1 (15-ounce) can unsweetened pumpkin puree
- 1 teaspoon table salt
- 1½ teaspoons ground cinnamon
- ¼ teaspoon ground nutmeg
- ⅛ teaspoon ground cloves
- 1 cup (7 ounces) granulated sugar
- 1 cup packed (7 ounces) light brown sugar
- ½ cup vegetable oil
- 4 ounces cream cheese, cut into 12 pieces
- 4 large eggs
- ¼ cup buttermilk
- 1 cup walnuts, toasted and chopped fine

1. *For the topping:* Using your fingers, mix all ingredients in bowl until well combined and topping resembles wet sand; set aside.

2. For the bread: Adjust oven rack to middle position and heat oven to 350 degrees. Grease two 8½ by 4½-inch loaf pans. Whisk flour, baking powder, and baking soda together in bowl.

3. Combine pumpkin puree, salt, cinnamon, nutmeg, and cloves in large saucepan over medium heat. Cook mixture, stirring constantly, until reduced to 1½ cups, 6 to 8 minutes. Remove pot from heat; stir in granulated sugar, brown sugar, oil, and cream cheese until combined. Let mixture sit for 5 minutes. Whisk until no visible pieces of cream cheese remain and mixture is homogeneous.

4. Whisk together eggs and buttermilk. Add egg mixture to pumpkin mixture and whisk to combine. Fold flour mixture into pumpkin mixture until combined (some small lumps of flour are OK). Fold walnuts into batter. Scrape batter into prepared pans. Sprinkle topping evenly over top of each loaf. Bake until skewer inserted in center of loaf comes out clean, 45 to 50 minutes. Let loaves cool in pans on wire rack for 20 minutes. Remove loaves from pans and let cool for at least 1½ hours before serving. (Pumpkin bread is best served on day it is baked but can be cooled completely and stored, covered tightly with plastic wrap, for up to 3 days.)

VARIATION

Pumpkin Bread with Candied Ginger

Substitute ½ teaspoon ground ginger for cinnamon in topping. Fold ⅓ cup minced crystallized ginger into batter after flour mixture has been added in step 4.

Ultimate Banana Bread

Serves 8

WHY THIS RECIPE WORKS Our ideal banana bread is a moist, tender loaf that really tastes like bananas. We discovered that doubling the bananas in our favorite recipe was both a blessing and a curse. The abundance of fruit made for intense flavor, but the weight and moisture sank the loaf. Looking to add banana flavor without moisture, we placed our bananas in a bowl and microwaved them for a few minutes; we then transferred the fruit to a strainer to drain. We simmered the exuded banana liquid in a saucepan until it was reduced and incorporated it into the batter. Brown sugar complemented the bananas better than granulated sugar, and vanilla worked well with the bananas' faintly boozy, rum-like flavor, as did swapping out the oil for the nutty richness of butter. As a final embellishment, we sliced a sixth banana and shingled it on top of the loaf. A sprinkle of granulated sugar helped the slices

caramelize and gave the loaf an enticingly crunchy top. Be sure to use very ripe, heavily speckled or even black bananas in this recipe. This recipe can be made using five thawed frozen bananas; since they release a lot of liquid naturally, they can bypass the microwaving in step 2 and go directly into the fine-mesh strainer. Do not use a thawed frozen banana in step 4; it will be too soft to slice. Instead, simply sprinkle the top of the loaf with sugar. The test kitchen's preferred loaf pan measures 8½ by 4½ inches; if you use a 9 by 5-inch loaf pan, start checking for doneness 5 minutes earlier than advised in the recipe.

1¾ cups (8¾ ounces) all-purpose flour
1 teaspoon baking soda
½ teaspoon table salt
6 very ripe large bananas (2¼ pounds), peeled
8 tablespoons unsalted butter, melted and cooled
2 large eggs
¾ cup packed (5¼ ounces) light brown sugar
1 teaspoon vanilla extract
½ cup walnuts, toasted and chopped coarse (optional)
2 teaspoons granulated sugar

1. Adjust oven rack to middle position and heat oven to 350 degrees. Grease 8½ by 4½-inch loaf pan. Whisk flour, baking soda, and salt together in large bowl.

2. Place 5 bananas in separate bowl, cover, and microwave until bananas are soft and have released liquid, about 5 minutes. Drain bananas in fine-mesh strainer set over medium bowl, stirring occasionally, for 15 minutes; you should have ½ to ¾ cup liquid.

3. Transfer drained liquid to medium saucepan and cook over medium-high heat until reduced to ¼ cup, about 5 minutes. Return drained bananas to bowl. Stir reduced liquid into bananas and mash with potato masher until mostly smooth. Whisk in melted butter, eggs, brown sugar, and vanilla.

4. Pour banana mixture into flour mixture and stir until just combined, with some streaks of flour remaining. Gently fold in walnuts, if using. Scrape batter into prepared loaf pan and smooth top. Slice remaining 1 banana on bias into ¼-inch-thick slices and shingle down both sides of loaf pan, leaving center clear to ensure even rise. Sprinkle granulated sugar over top.

5. Bake until skewer inserted in center comes out clean, 55 minutes to 1¼ hours, rotating pan halfway through baking. Let loaf cool in pan for 15 minutes, then turn out onto wire rack and continue to cool. Serve warm or at room temperature. (Banana bread is best served on day it is baked but can be cooled completely and stored, covered tightly with plastic wrap, for up to 3 days.)

"I didn't grow up eating banana bread, and by the time I understood what it was, I had developed high standards. This recipe is the only one that meets the mark for me because it has serious banana flavor but doesn't have a mushy texture. And I love that the solution to this otherwise simple quick bread is very test kitchen-y. Just reduce the banana liquid so you get all the flavor but less moisture—easy and brilliant. I store up superripe bananas in the freezer until I have enough for the batter, and then I just need one fresh banana for the top. The nice thing about using frozen bananas is that they shed their liquid as they thaw— no microwave needed."

–Julia

Boston Brown Bread

Serves 6 to 8 (Makes 2 small loaves)

WHY THIS RECIPE WORKS When colonists started making this unyeasted, one-bowl bread in the 18th century, most cooking was done over an open hearth—a tricky environment for bread baking. To get around this, brown bread was steamed in lidded tin pudding molds in a kettle of simmering water over an open fire, giving the loaves a distinctive shape and a smooth, crustless exterior—and keeping the whole-grain crumb remarkably moist. To get the right balance of flavor in our brown bread, we combined whole-wheat flour, rye flour, and finely ground cornmeal in equal amounts. Molasses, the traditional sweetener, added the right hint of bitterness. Baking soda and baking powder reacted with the acid in the batter to lighten the bread, and melted butter added some richness. We steamed the batter on the stovetop in two 28-ounce tomato cans, which produced moist loaves inside and out. Tomato cans are a good substitute for traditional (but increasingly uncommon) coffee cans. This recipe requires two empty 28-ounce cans. Make sure to use cans that are labeled "BPA-free." We prefer Quaker white cornmeal in this recipe, though other types will work; do not use coarse grits. Any style of molasses will work except for blackstrap. This recipe requires a 10-quart or larger stockpot that is at least 7 inches deep. Brown bread is traditionally served with baked beans but is also good toasted and buttered.

- ¾ cup (4⅛ ounces) rye flour
- ¾ cup (4⅛ ounces) whole-wheat flour
- ¾ cup (3¾ ounces) fine white cornmeal
- 1¾ teaspoons baking soda
- ½ teaspoon baking powder
- 1 teaspoon table salt
- 1⅔ cups buttermilk
- ½ cup molasses
- 3 tablespoons butter, melted and cooled slightly
- ¾ cup raisins

1. Bring 3 quarts water to simmer in large stockpot over high heat. Fold two 16 by 12-inch pieces of aluminum foil in half to yield 2 rectangles that measure 8 by 12 inches. Spray 4-inch circle in center of each rectangle with vegetable oil spray. Spray insides of 2 clean 28-ounce cans with vegetable oil spray.

2. Whisk rye flour, whole-wheat flour, cornmeal, baking soda, baking powder, and salt together in large bowl. Whisk buttermilk, molasses, and melted butter together in second bowl. Stir raisins into buttermilk mixture. Add buttermilk mixture to flour mixture and stir until combined and no dry flour remains. Evenly divide batter between cans. Wrap tops of cans tightly with prepared foil, positioning sprayed side of foil over can openings.

3. Place cans in stockpot (water should come about halfway up sides of cans). Cover pot and cook, maintaining gentle simmer, until skewer inserted in center of loaves comes out clean, about 2 hours. Check pot occasionally and add hot water as needed to maintain water level.

4. Using jar lifter, carefully transfer cans to wire rack set in rimmed baking sheet and let cool for 20 minutes. Slide loaves from cans onto rack and let cool completely, about 1 hour, before serving. (Bread can be wrapped tightly in plastic wrap and stored at room temperature for up to 3 days or frozen for up to 2 weeks.)

Irish Soda Bread

Serves 8

WHY THIS RECIPE WORKS Authentic Irish soda bread has a tender, dense crumb and a rough-textured, thick crust—definitely a departure from the more common Americanized soda bread, which is closer to a supersize scone. We wanted to try our hand at the authentic version of this bread, which relies on a simple ingredient list of flour, baking soda, salt, and buttermilk. A loaf made with all-purpose flour produced a doughy, heavy bread with an overly thick crust. To soften the crumb, we added some cake flour. A version made with all cake flour, however, was heavy and compact. A ratio of 3 parts all-purpose flour to 1 part cake flour proved best. With only the flour, buttermilk, baking soda, and salt, our bread was lacking in flavor and still tough. Traditionally, very small amounts of butter and sugar are sometimes added, so we felt justified in using a minuscule amount of each. The sugar added flavor without making the bread sweet, and the butter softened the dough without making it overly rich. If you do not have a cast-iron skillet, the bread can be baked on a baking sheet,

although the crust won't be quite as crunchy. Soda bread is best eaten on the day it is baked but does keep well covered and stored at room temperature for a couple of days, after which time it will become dry.

3 cups (15 ounces) all-purpose flour
1 cup (4 ounces) cake flour
2 tablespoons sugar
1½ teaspoons baking soda
1½ teaspoons cream of tartar
1½ teaspoons table salt
2 tablespoons unsalted butter, softened, plus 1 tablespoon melted butter for brushing loaf (optional)
1¾ cups buttermilk, divided

1. Adjust oven rack to middle position and heat oven to 400 degrees. Whisk all-purpose flour, cake flour, sugar, baking soda, cream of tartar, and salt together in large bowl. Add softened butter and rub it into flour using your fingers until it is completely incorporated. Make well in center of flour mixture and add 1½ cups buttermilk. Work buttermilk into flour mixture using fork until dough comes together in large clumps and there is no dry flour in bottom of bowl, adding up to ¼ cup more buttermilk, 1 tablespoon at a time, until all loose flour is just moistened. Turn dough onto lightly floured work surface and pat together to form 6-inch round. Dough will be scrappy and uneven.

2. Place dough in 12-inch cast-iron skillet. Score deep cross, about 5 inches long and ¾ inch deep, on top of loaf and place in oven. Bake until nicely browned and knife inserted in center of loaf comes out clean, 40 to 45 minutes. Remove from oven and brush with melted butter (if using). Let cool for at least 30 minutes before serving.

VARIATION
Whole-Wheat Soda Bread
This variation is known as brown bread in Ireland. The dough will be sticky and you may need to add a small amount of all-purpose flour as you mix it.

Reduce all-purpose flour to 1½ cups (7½ ounces) and cake flour to ½ cup (2 ounces) and increase sugar to 3 tablespoons. Add 1½ cups (8¼ ounces) whole-wheat flour and ½ cup toasted wheat germ with flours, sugar, baking soda, cream of tartar, and salt in step 1.

Quick Cheese Bread

Serves 8

WHY THIS RECIPE WORKS This rich and easy-to-make cheese bread is packed with flavor and topped with a bold crust. It makes an excellent accompaniment to chili or soup and is fantastic toasted and buttered. We started with all-purpose flour and added whole milk and sour cream for a creamy flavor and moist texture. Just a few tablespoons of butter added enough richness without greasiness, and using less fat made the texture heartier. A single egg gave rise and structure without an overly eggy flavor. As for cheese, small chunks of Asiago or cheddar mixed into the dough offered rich, cheesy pockets throughout the bread; a moderate amount added plenty of flavor without weighing it down. For added cheesy flavor and a crisp crust, we coated the pan and sprinkled the top of the loaf with shredded Parmesan. If using Asiago, choose a mild supermarket cheese that yields to pressure when pressed. Aged Asiago that is as firm as Parmesan is too sharp and piquant for this bread. If, when testing the bread for doneness, the toothpick comes out with what looks like uncooked batter clinging to it, try again in a different, but still central, spot; if the toothpick hits a pocket of cheese, it may give a false indication. The test kitchen's preferred loaf pan measures 8½ by 4½ inches; if you use a 9 by 5-inch loaf pan, start checking for doneness 5 minutes earlier than advised in the recipe.

3 ounces Parmesan cheese, shredded on large holes of box grater (1 cup), divided
3 cups (15 ounces) all-purpose flour
1 tablespoon baking powder
1 teaspoon table salt
¼ teaspoon cayenne pepper
⅛ teaspoon pepper
4 ounces extra-sharp cheddar cheese, cut into ½-inch cubes, or mild Asiago, crumbled into ¼- to ½-inch pieces (1 cup)
1¼ cups whole milk
¾ cup sour cream
1 large egg, lightly beaten
3 tablespoons unsalted butter, melted

1. Adjust oven rack to middle position and heat oven to 350 degrees. Spray 8½ by 4½-inch loaf pan with vegetable oil spray; sprinkle ½ cup Parmesan evenly over bottom of pan.

2. Whisk flour, baking powder, salt, cayenne, and pepper together in large bowl. Using rubber spatula, mix in cheddar, breaking up clumps. Whisk milk, sour cream, egg, and melted butter together in medium bowl. Using rubber spatula, gently fold wet ingredients into dry ingredients until just combined (batter will be heavy and thick); do not overmix. Scrape batter into prepared loaf pan; smooth surface with rubber spatula. Sprinkle remaining ½ cup Parmesan evenly over surface.

3. Bake until deep golden brown and toothpick inserted in center comes out clean, 45 to 50 minutes. Let cool on wire rack for 5 minutes; invert loaf onto wire rack, then turn right side up and continue to let cool until warm, about 45 minutes, before serving.

VARIATION

Quick Cheese Bread with Bacon, Onion, and Gruyère

Cook 5 slices bacon, cut into ½-inch pieces, in 10-inch nonstick skillet over medium heat, stirring occasionally, until crisp, about 8 minutes. Using slotted spoon, transfer bacon to paper towel–lined plate and pour off all but 3 tablespoons fat from skillet. Add ½ cup finely chopped onion to skillet and cook, stirring frequently, until softened, about 3 minutes; set skillet with onion aside. Substitute Gruyère for cheddar, add bacon and onion to flour mixture with cheese, and omit butter.

All-Purpose Cornbread

Serves 6

WHY THIS RECIPE WORKS Cornbread can be sweet and cakey (the Northern version) or savory and light (the Southern version). We wanted a combination of the two. And most important, we wanted our cornbread to be bursting with corn flavor. The secret to cornbread with real corn flavor was pretty simple: Use corn, not just cornmeal. While fresh corn was best, we wanted to be able to make this cornbread year round. We found that frozen kernels were nearly as good as fresh, and pureeing the kernels in a food processor made them easy to use while minimizing tough, chewy kernels. For flavoring, buttermilk provided tang, while light brown sugar enhanced the natural sweetness of the corn. Baking the bread at a higher than conventional temperature produced a crunchy crust full of toasted corn flavor. Before preparing the baking dish or any of the other ingredients, measure out the frozen

corn kernels and let them stand at room temperature until thawed. When corn is in season, fresh cooked kernels can be substituted for the frozen corn. This recipe was developed with Quaker yellow cornmeal; a stone-ground whole-grain cornmeal will work but will yield a drier and less tender cornbread. We prefer a Pyrex glass baking dish because it yields a nice golden brown crust, but a metal baking dish (nonstick or traditional) will also work. The cornbread is best served warm; leftovers can be wrapped in foil and reheated in a 350-degree oven for 10 to 15 minutes.

1½ cups (7½ ounces) all-purpose flour
1 cup (5 ounces) yellow cornmeal
2 teaspoons baking powder
¼ teaspoon baking soda
¾ teaspoon table salt
1 cup buttermilk
¾ cup frozen corn kernels, thawed
¼ cup packed (1¾ ounces) light brown sugar
2 large eggs
8 tablespoons unsalted butter, melted and cooled slightly

1. Adjust oven rack to middle position and heat oven to 400 degrees. Spray 8-inch square baking dish with vegetable oil spray. Whisk flour, cornmeal, baking powder, baking soda, and salt in medium bowl until combined; set aside.

2. Process buttermilk, corn kernels, and brown sugar in food processor or blender until combined, about 5 seconds. Add eggs and process until well combined (corn lumps will remain), about 5 seconds.

3. Using rubber spatula, make well in center of dry ingredients; pour wet ingredients into well. Begin folding dry ingredients into wet ingredients, giving mixture only a few turns to barely combine; add melted butter and continue folding until dry ingredients are just moistened. Pour batter into prepared dish, smoothing surface. Bake until deep golden brown and toothpick inserted in center comes out clean, 25 to 35 minutes. Let cool on wire rack for 10 minutes; invert cornbread onto wire rack, then turn right side up and continue to let cool until warm, about 10 minutes, before serving.

VARIATION

Spicy Jalapeño-Cheddar Cornbread

Reduce salt to ½ teaspoon; add ⅜ teaspoon cayenne pepper, 1 seeded and minced jalapeño chile, and ½ cup shredded sharp cheddar cheese to flour mixture in step 1 and toss well to combine. Reduce brown sugar to 2 tablespoons and sprinkle ½ cup more shredded sharp cheddar over batter in baking dish just before baking.

"I will say it plainly: I'm a child of the north (raised near New York City), and the Southern style of cornbread, revered for being savory, dense, and crumbly, just isn't my thing. My suspicion of it is likely exacerbated by the fact that cake is, hands down, my favorite food. Northern-style cornbread, with some flour in the batter to lighten the texture of the bread, as well as some sweetener, is cakier, and thus comes closer to my cornbread ideal.

This cornbread recipe splits the difference, and I love it. The bread hits a textural sweet spot, light yet substantial, and nicely crumbly. Sweetness is present but restrained, buttermilk provides depth and balance, and there's plenty of butter for a lovely flavor and showstopper crust (adding it late in the mixing helps). Most revelatory of all, this cornbread tastes of… corn!… because the batter includes not just cornmeal but actual pureed corn (fresh if you have it, and frozen if you don't). It's a modest extra step that elevates this cornbread recipe to cherished keeper status—I've made it regularly for years."

–Adam

Rosemary Focaccia

Serves 12 (Makes 2 loaves)

WHY THIS RECIPE WORKS This focaccia has a crisp bottom, a deeply browned top, and an airy interior. As we started our recipe development, we settled on the flavor benefits of a long fermentation. It is an approach many bakers use, and it involves a "pre-ferment" (also known as a "sponge," "starter," or *biga* in Italian): a mixture of flour, water, and a small amount of yeast that rests (often overnight) before being incorporated into the dough. But the interiors of the loaves weren't as tender and airy as we wanted. We wondered if our stand mixer was developing too much gluten, so we turned to a more gentle approach. We increased the hydration level and relied on a long dough resting process (called autolyse) to take advantage of the enzymes naturally present in the wheat to produce the same effect as kneading. But although our loaves were light and airy, they were squat. To improve the structure, we turned the dough at regular intervals while it proofed. To cut back on the long proofing time (3 hours) and hasten gluten development, we held back the salt when mixing our dough, adding it later. If you don't have a baking stone, bake the bread on an overturned, preheated rimmed baking sheet set on the upper-middle oven rack. The bread can be kept for up to two days well wrapped at room temperature or frozen for several months wrapped in foil and placed in a zipper-lock bag.

Sponge
- ½ cup (2½ ounces) all-purpose flour
- ⅓ cup water, room temperature
- ¼ teaspoon instant or rapid-rise yeast

Dough
- 2½ cups (12½ ounces) all-purpose flour
- 1¼ cups water, room temperature
- 1 teaspoon instant or rapid-rise yeast
- 1 teaspoon kosher salt
- ¼ cup extra-virgin olive oil, divided
- 2 tablespoons chopped fresh rosemary

1. *For the sponge:* Stir all ingredients in large bowl with wooden spoon until well combined. Cover tightly with plastic wrap and let sit at room temperature until sponge has risen and begins to collapse, about 6 hours or up to 24 hours.

2. *For the dough:* Stir flour, water, and yeast into sponge with wooden spoon until well combined. Cover bowl tightly with plastic and let dough rest for 15 minutes.

3. Stir 2 teaspoons salt into dough with wooden spoon until thoroughly incorporated, about 1 minute. Cover bowl tightly with plastic and let dough rest for 30 minutes.

4. Using greased bowl scraper (or rubber spatula), fold dough over itself by gently lifting and folding edge of dough toward middle. Turn bowl 45 degrees and fold dough again; repeat turning bowl and folding dough 6 more times (total of 8 folds). Cover tightly with plastic and let rise for 30 minutes. Repeat folding and rising. Fold dough again, then cover bowl tightly with plastic and let dough rise until nearly doubled in size, 30 minutes to 1 hour.

5. One hour before baking, adjust oven rack to upper-middle position, place baking stone on rack, and heat oven to 500 degrees. Coat two 9-inch round cake pans with 2 tablespoons oil each. Sprinkle each pan with ½ teaspoon salt. Transfer dough to lightly floured counter and dust top with flour. Divide dough in half and cover loosely with greased plastic. Working with 1 piece of dough at a time (keep remaining piece covered), shape into 5-inch round by gently tucking under edges.

6. Place dough rounds seam side up in prepared pans, coat bottoms and sides with oil, then flip rounds over. Cover loosely with greased plastic and let dough rest for 5 minutes.

7. Using your fingertips, gently press each dough round into corners of pan, taking care not to tear dough. (If dough resists stretching, let it relax for 5 to 10 minutes before trying to stretch it again.) Using fork, poke surface of dough 25 to 30 times, popping any large bubbles. Sprinkle 1 tablespoon rosemary evenly over top of each loaf, cover loosely with greased plastic, and let dough rest until slightly bubbly, about 10 minutes.

8. Place pans on baking stone and reduce oven temperature to 450 degrees. Bake until tops are golden brown, 25 to 30 minutes, rotating pans halfway through baking. Let loaves cool in pans for 5 minutes. Remove loaves from pans and transfer to wire rack. Brush tops with any oil remaining in pans and let cool for 30 minutes. Serve warm or at room temperature.

Focaccia with Caramelized Red Onion, Pancetta, and Oregano

Cook 4 ounces finely chopped pancetta in 12-inch skillet over medium heat, stirring occasionally, until well rendered, about 10 minutes. Using slotted spoon, transfer pancetta to medium bowl. Add 1 chopped red onion and 2 tablespoons water to fat left in skillet and cook over medium heat until onion is softened and lightly browned, about 12 minutes. Transfer onion to bowl with pancetta and stir in 2 teaspoons minced fresh oregano; let mixture cool completely before using. Substitute pancetta mixture for rosemary.

Making Focaccia

1. Fold partially risen dough over itself by gently lifting and folding edge of dough toward middle. Turn bowl 90 degrees; fold again. Turn bowl and fold dough 6 more times (for a total of 8 turns).

2. Cover with plastic wrap and let rise for 30 minutes. Repeat turning, folding, and rising 2 more times, for a total of three 30-minute rises.

3. Divide floured dough in half. Shape halves into 5-inch rounds. Place rounds in oiled pans and slide to coat dough. Flip and repeat. Cover pans with plastic wrap and let rest for 5 minutes.

4. Using your fingertips, press dough out toward edges of pan, taking care not to tear it. (If dough resists stretching, let it relax for 5 to 10 minutes before trying to stretch it again.)

5. Using fork, poke dough 25 to 30 times. Deflate any remaining bubbles of dough with fork. Sprinkle rosemary over dough. Let rest until slightly bubbly, about 10 minutes, before baking.

Rustic Dinner Rolls

Makes 16 rolls

WHY THIS RECIPE WORKS European-style dinner rolls are different from their rich, tender American cousins. The dough for these rustic rolls is lean and the crumb is open, with a yeasty, savory flavor. But the best part might be their crust—so crisp it practically shatters when you bite into it, yet chewy enough to offer satisfying resistance. It is this crust that keeps European-style dinner rolls in the domain of professionals, who use steam-injected ovens to expose the developing crust to moisture. We wanted a reliable recipe for rolls as good as any from a European bakery. Unfortunately, when we tasted our first batch, we found a dense, bland crumb beneath a leathery crust. The flavor was easy enough to improve: We added whole-wheat flour for earthiness (just 3 tablespoons did the trick) and honey for sweetness. Extra yeast opened the crumb slightly, but it wasn't enough. The crumb structure of artisan-style loaves is achieved with a wet dough so we ultimately found success when we upped the hydration of our roll dough. The water created steam during baking, opening up the crumb and making it airier. For an ultracrisp crust, we came up with a two-step process that mimicked a steam-injected oven: First we misted the rolls with water before starting them in a cake pan at a high temperature to help set their shape (since the dough was soft, individually baked rolls turned out squat). Next, we lowered the temperature, pulled the rolls apart, and returned them to the oven on a baking sheet until they were golden on all sides. We do not recommend mixing this dough by hand. Because this dough is sticky, keep your hands well floured when handling it. Use a spray bottle to mist the rolls with water.

3 cups (16½ ounces) bread flour
3 tablespoons whole-wheat flour
1½ teaspoons instant or rapid-rise yeast
1½ cups plus 1 tablespoon water, room temperature
2 teaspoons honey
1½ teaspoons table salt

1. Whisk bread flour, whole-wheat flour, and yeast together in bowl of stand mixer. Whisk water and honey in 4-cup liquid measuring cup until honey has dissolved.

2. Using dough hook on low speed, slowly add water mixture to flour mixture and mix until cohesive dough starts to form and no dry flour remains, about 2 minutes, scraping down bowl and hook as needed. Cover bowl tightly with plastic wrap and let dough rest for 30 minutes.

3. Add salt to dough and mix on low speed for 5 minutes. Increase speed to medium and knead until dough is smooth and slightly sticky, about 1 minute. Transfer dough to lightly greased large bowl or container, cover tightly with plastic, and let rise until doubled in size, 1 to 1½ hours.

4. Using greased bowl scraper (or your fingertips), fold dough over itself by gently lifting and folding edge of dough toward middle. Turn bowl 90 degrees and fold dough again; repeat turning bowl and folding dough 2 more times (total of 4 folds). Cover tightly with plastic and let rise for 30 minutes. Repeat folding, then cover bowl tightly with plastic and let dough rise until doubled in size, about 30 minutes.

5. Grease two 9-inch round cake pans. Press down on dough to deflate. Transfer dough to well-floured counter, sprinkle lightly with flour, and divide in half. Stretch each half into even 16-inch log and cut into 8 equal pieces (about 2 ounces each). Using your well-floured hands, gently pick up each piece and roll in your palms to coat with flour, shaking off excess.

6. Arrange rolls in prepared pans, placing 1 in center and 7 around edges, with cut side facing up and long side of each piece running from center to edge of pan. Cover loosely with greased plastic and let rolls rise until nearly doubled in size and dough springs back minimally when poked gently with your knuckle, about 30 minutes. (Unrisen rolls can be refrigerated for at least 8 hours or up to 16 hours; let rolls sit at room temperature for 1½ hours before baking.)

7. Adjust oven rack to middle position and heat oven to 500 degrees. Mist rolls with water and bake until tops are brown, about 10 minutes. Remove rolls from oven and reduce oven temperature to 400 degrees.

Folding and Shaping Dinner Rolls

1. Fold dough over itself by gently lifting and folding edge of dough toward middle. Turn bowl 90 degrees and fold dough again; repeat turning bowl and folding dough 2 more times.

2. After rising, divide dough in half. Stretch each floured half into even 16-inch log and cut into 8 equal pieces. Using floured hands, roll each piece in your palms to coat with flour, shaking off excess.

3. Arrange rolls in prepared pans, placing one in center and seven around edges, with cut side facing up and long side of each piece running from center to edge of pan. Let rise for 30 minutes.

8. Carefully invert rolls out of pans onto baking sheet and let cool slightly. Turn rolls right side up, pull apart, and arrange evenly on sheet. Continue to bake until deep golden brown, 10 to 15 minutes, rotating sheet halfway through baking. Transfer rolls to wire rack and let cool completely, about 1 hour, before serving. (Rolls will keep for up to 2 days at room temperature stored in zipper-lock bag. To recrisp crust, place rolls in 450-degree oven for 6 to 8 minutes. Rolls will keep frozen for several months wrapped in foil and placed in large zipper-lock freezer bag. Thaw rolls at room temperature and recrisp using instructions above.)

Almost No-Knead Bread

Serves 6

WHY THIS RECIPE WORKS Artisan-style bakery loaves—beautifully browned *boules* with a thick, crisp crust that breaks to a chewy open interior—take professional skills to make, right? Wrong. Not only is it possible to make a rustic loaf for your table, it's easy, too, with the no-knead method of bread baking. This technique replaces the kneading that develops gluten to give bread structure with a high hydration level—around 85 percent (8½ ounces of water for every 10 ounces of flour)—and an 8- to 18-hour-long (and hands-off) resting period, or autolyse. During autolyse, the flour hydrates and enzymes work to break up the proteins so that the dough requires only a brief turn to develop gluten. The dough is then baked in a Dutch oven; the humid environment gives the loaf a dramatic open crumb and a crisp crust. But the breads we tested needed more structure and flavor. To strengthen the dough, we lowered the hydration and added less than a minute of kneading to compensate. We introduced an acidic tang from vinegar and a shot of yeasty flavor from beer. We prefer to use a mild American lager, such as Budweiser, here; strongly flavored beers will make this bread taste bitter. Do not wait until the oven has preheated to start your timer or the bread will burn.

      3 cups (15 ounces) all-purpose flour
    1½ teaspoons table salt
      ¼ teaspoon instant or rapid-rise yeast
      ¾ cup plus 2 tablespoons water, room temperature
      6 tablespoons mild-flavored lager
      1 tablespoon distilled white vinegar

1. Whisk flour, salt, and yeast together in large bowl. Add water, lager, and vinegar. Using rubber spatula, fold mixture, scraping up dry flour from bottom of bowl, until shaggy ball forms. Cover bowl with plastic wrap and let dough sit at room temperature for at least 8 hours or up to 18 hours.

2. Lay 18 by 12-inch sheet of parchment paper on counter and coat lightly with vegetable oil spray. Transfer dough to lightly floured counter and knead by hand to form smooth,

"This standout recipe has really taken off to become a sensation with our readers. And for good reason: After putting in very little effort, you are rewarded with an amazing loaf. There just isn't an easier bread recipe out there. I know several cooks who bake this bread as their weekly loaf because it's so incredibly simple and full of flavor. It's the type of recipe that you end up memorizing after you make it a few times and then muscle memory just takes over. Before you know it, you are churning out bakery-quality loaves over and over again!"

—Erin

round ball, 10 to 15 times. Shape dough into ball by pulling edges into middle. Transfer dough, seam side down, to center of parchment. Pick up dough by lifting parchment overhang and lower into heavy-bottomed Dutch oven (let any excess parchment hang over pot edge). Cover loosely with plastic and let rise at room temperature until dough has doubled in size and does not readily spring back when poked with your finger, 1½ to 2 hours.

3. Adjust oven rack to middle position. Remove plastic from pot. Lightly flour top of dough and, using razor blade or sharp knife, make two 5-inch-long, ½-inch-deep slashes with swift, fluid motion along top of loaf to form cross. Cover pot and place in oven. Turn oven to 425 degrees. Bake bread for 30 minutes.

4. Remove lid and continue to bake until loaf is deep brown and registers 205 to 210 degrees, 25 to 30 minutes. Using parchment sling, carefully remove bread from pot; transfer to wire rack, discard parchment and let cool completely, about 3 hours, before serving. Bread is best eaten on day it is baked, but can be wrapped in aluminum foil and stored in a cool, dry place for up to 2 days.

Making Almost No-Knead Bread

1. Mix dough by stirring wet ingredients into dry ingredients with rubber spatula, then leave dough to rest for 8 to 18 hours.

2. Turn dough out onto lightly floured surface and knead 10 to 15 times. After kneading dough, shape into ball by pulling edges into middle.

3. Transfer loaf, seam side down, to large sheet of greased parchment and, using paper, transfer to Dutch oven. Cover loosely with plastic and let rise until doubled in size, 1½ to 2 hours.

4. Sprinkle dough with flour and cut ½-inch-deep X into loaf. Cover pot, place in oven, and turn oven to 425 degrees. Bake for 30 minutes, then remove lid and bake until loaf registers 205 to 210 degrees.

No-Knead Brioche

Serves 12 to 16 (Makes 2 loaves)

WHY THIS RECIPE WORKS The average brioche recipe is 50 percent butter, and the high fat content can make the brioche incredibly tender—or it can cause the dough to separate into a greasy mess. For rich, tender brioche without the hassle of painstakingly adding softened butter to the dough little by little as it is kneaded, we added melted butter directly to the eggs. Then we dispensed with the stand mixer and opted for a no-knead approach that lets time do most of the work: An overnight rest in the fridge developed both structure and flavor. We used two loaf pans and then, to build structure and ensure an even, fine crumb, we shaped the dough into four tight balls before placing two in each pan. The dough can also be divided to make brioche buns or traditionally shaped loaves using fluted brioche molds. High-protein King Arthur Bread Flour works best with this recipe, though other bread flours will suffice. The test kitchen's preferred loaf pan measures 8½ by 4½ inches; if you use 9 by 5-inch pans, start checking for doneness 5 minutes earlier than advised in the recipe. If you don't have a baking stone, bake the bread on a preheated rimmed baking sheet.

3¼ cups (17¾ ounces) bread flour
2¼ teaspoons instant or rapid-rise yeast
1½ teaspoons table salt
 7 large eggs (1 lightly beaten with pinch salt)
 ½ cup water, room temperature
 ⅓ cup (2⅓ ounces) sugar
16 tablespoons unsalted butter, melted and cooled slightly

1. Whisk flour, yeast, and salt together in large bowl. Whisk 6 eggs, water, and sugar together in medium bowl until sugar has dissolved. Whisk in butter until smooth. Add egg mixture to flour mixture and stir with wooden spoon until uniform mass forms and no dry flour remains, about 1 minute. Cover bowl with plastic wrap and let sit for 10 minutes.

2. Holding edge of dough with your fingertips, fold dough over itself by gently lifting and folding edge of dough toward middle. Turn bowl 45 degrees; fold again. Turn bowl and fold dough 6 more times (total of 8 folds). Cover with plastic and let rise for 30 minutes. Repeat folding and rising every 30 minutes, 3 more times. After fourth set of folds, cover bowl tightly with plastic and refrigerate for at least 16 hours or up to 2 days.

3. Transfer dough to well-floured counter and divide into 4 equal pieces. Working with 1 piece of dough at a time, pat dough into 4-inch disk. Working around circumference of dough, fold edges of dough toward center until ball forms. Flip dough over and, without applying pressure, move your hands in small circular motions to form dough into smooth, taut round. (If dough sticks to your hands, lightly dust top of dough with flour.) Repeat with remaining dough. Cover dough rounds loosely with plastic and let rest for 5 minutes.

4. Grease two 8½ by 4½-inch loaf pans. After 5 minutes, flip each dough ball so seam side is facing up, pat into 4-inch disk, and repeat rounding step. Place 2 rounds, seam side down, side by side into prepared pans and press gently into corners. Cover loaves loosely with plastic and let rise at room temperature until almost doubled in size (dough should rise to about ½ inch below top edge of pan), 1½ to 2 hours. Thirty minutes before baking, adjust oven rack to middle position, place baking stone on rack, and heat oven to 350 degrees.

5. Remove plastic and brush loaves gently with beaten egg. Set loaf pans on stone and bake until golden brown and internal temperature registers 190 degrees, 35 to 45 minutes, rotating pans halfway through baking. Transfer pans to wire rack and let cool for 5 minutes. Remove loaves from pans, return to wire rack, and let cool completely, about 2 hours, before serving.

Ciabatta

Serves 12 (Makes 2 loaves)

WHY THIS RECIPE WORKS Unless you buy them from an artisanal bakery, most loaves of ciabatta available just aren't any good. Ideally, this Italian loaf should boast a crisp, flavorful crust, a full and tangy flavor, and a chewy, open crumb. Uninterested in yet another lackluster loaf from the supermarket, we decided to make our own. We started with the flour selection—whole-wheat, bread, or all-purpose? We preferred all-purpose, which is made from both hard and soft wheat and has less protein than bread flour, producing loaves with a more open, springy texture. The next step was to build flavor through the sponge (or *biga* in Italian), which we also used in our Rosemary Focaccia (page 398). As it ferments, the yeast in the biga produces lactic and acetic acids as by-products, which give the bread its characteristic sourness. Kneading the sponge and remaining dough ingredients in a stand mixer for only a few minutes produced loaves that spread out instead of rising, so we turned to a combination of kneading and folding the dough over itself a few times before letting it rest. This two-step process gave the dough structure but also supported oversize holes. Adding a small amount of milk, which contains a protein that slightly weakens the gluten strands, remedied the problem and took down the size of those big bubbles. To avoid extra handling of the dough, we formed the loaves, then moved them to parchment paper and slid the parchment onto the baking surface after another rest. We opted to bake the loaves at a cooler temperature than 500 degrees (as most recipes recommend). A final enhancement was to spray the loaves with water in the first minutes of baking for a crisper crust and loaves that rose a bit higher. As you make this bread, keep in mind that the dough is wet and very sticky. The key to manipulating it is working quickly and gently; rough handling will result in flat, tough loaves. When possible, use a large rubber spatula or bowl scraper to move the dough. If you have to

use your hands, make sure they are well floured. Because the dough is so sticky, it must be prepared in a stand mixer. If you don't have a baking stone, bake the bread on an overturned and preheated rimmed baking sheet set on the lowest oven rack.

Sponge
- 1 cup (5 ounces) all-purpose flour
- ½ cup water, room temperature
- ⅛ teaspoon instant or rapid-rise yeast

Dough
- 2 cups (10 ounces) all-purpose flour
- 1½ teaspoons salt
- ½ teaspoon instant or rapid-rise yeast
- ¾ cup water, room temperature
- ¼ cup whole milk, room temperature

1. *For the sponge:* Stir all ingredients in 4-cup liquid measuring cup with wooden spoon until well combined. Cover tightly with plastic wrap and let sit at room temperature until sponge has risen and begins to collapse, about 6 hours (sponge can sit at room temperature for up to 24 hours).

2. *For the dough:* Whisk flour, salt, and yeast together in bowl of stand mixer. Stir water and milk into sponge with wooden spoon until well combined. Using paddle on low speed, slowly add sponge mixture to flour mixture and mix until cohesive dough starts to form and no dry flour remains, about 2 minutes, scraping down bowl as needed. Increase speed to medium-low and continue to mix until dough becomes uniform mass that collects on paddle and pulls away from sides of bowl, 4 to 6 minutes.

3. Remove paddle and fit stand mixer with dough hook. Knead on medium-low speed until dough is smooth and shiny (dough will be very sticky), about 10 minutes. Transfer dough to lightly greased large bowl or container, cover tightly with plastic, and let rise until doubled in size, 30 minutes to 1 hour.

4. Using greased bowl scraper (or rubber spatula), fold dough over itself by gently lifting and folding edge of dough toward middle. Turn bowl 45 degrees and fold dough again; repeat turning bowl and folding dough 6 more times (total of 8 folds). Cover tightly with plastic and let rise for 30 minutes. Repeat folding, then cover bowl tightly with plastic and let dough rise until nearly doubled in size, about 30 minutes.

5. One hour before baking, adjust oven racks to lower-middle and lowest positions. Place baking stone on upper rack and heat oven to 450 degrees. Dust two 12 by 6-inch pieces of parchment paper liberally with flour. Transfer dough to well-floured counter (side of dough that was against bowl should now be against counter). Liberally dust top of dough with flour and divide in half. Turn 1 piece of dough cut side up and dust with flour. Using your well-floured hands, press and stretch dough into 12 by 6-inch rectangle, with short side parallel to counter edge, being careful not to deflate dough completely.

6. Stretch and fold top and bottom thirds of dough over middle like business letter to form rough 7 by 4-inch loaf. Pinch seams closed. Transfer loaf seam side down to 1 sheet of prepared parchment and cover loosely with greased plastic. Repeat with second piece of dough. Let loaves sit until puffy and surface of loaves develops small bubbles, about 30 minutes.

7. Transfer parchment with loaves to pizza peel. Using your floured fingertips, evenly poke entire surface of each loaf to form 10 by 6-inch rectangle. Mist loaves with water.

8. Working quickly, slide each piece of parchment with loaf onto baking stone. Bake, misting loaves with water twice more during first 5 minutes of baking time, until crust is deep golden brown and loaves register 210 to 212 degrees, 25 to 30 minutes, rotating loaves halfway through baking. Transfer loaves to wire rack, discard parchment, and let cool completely, about 2 hours, before serving.

Making Ciabatta Bread

1. Using greased spatula or bowl scraper, fold dough over itself by gently lifting and folding edge of dough toward middle. Turn bowl 45 degrees and fold dough again; repeat 6 more times (total of 8 folds).

2. After rising, divide dough in half on well-floured counter. Press and stretch each half into a 12 by 6-inch rectangle, being careful not to deflate dough completely.

3. Fold top and bottom thirds of dough over middle to form 7 by 4-inch loaf. Pinch seams closed. Transfer loaf seam side down to prepared parchment; cover with greased plastic. Repeat with remaining dough.

4. Transfer parchment with loaves to pizza peel. Using your floured fingertips, evenly poke entire surface of each loaf to form 10 by 6-inch rectangle.

Fougasse

SEASON 20 RECIPE

Serves 8 (Makes 2 loaves)

WHY THIS RECIPE WORKS If ever there was a bread made for crust lovers, it has to be *fougasse*. This relatively unknown loaf, first created in Provence, is related by name and pedigree to Italian *focaccia*. But unlike its Italian cousin, fougasse gets an elegant twist: After being stretched and flattened, the dough is given a series of cuts, usually in fanciful geometric patterns, to create multiple openings in the finished flatbread and give it a leaf shape. As pretty as the sculpted breads are, the openings are not just for aesthetics: They dramatically increase the crust-to-crumb ratio so that nearly every bite includes an equal share of crisp crust and tender, airy interior. The cuts also help the bread bake very quickly. Most bakeries don't make a separate dough for fougasse. Instead, they simply repurpose extra dough from some other product, such as baguettes. We decided to follow suit and used our bakery-style French baguette recipe as a starting point, eliminating the diastatic malt powder, and then changing up the shaping. To make shaping the fougasse easy, we rolled it out with a rolling pin so that the dough was level, transferred it to parchment, and cut into it with a pizza cutter, which proved the perfect-size implement. The fougasse looked flawless, but the substantial crust was too hard and tough. We tried adding olive oil to the dough, as we'd seen in some recipes, to soften it, but this eliminated any crispness. Brushing the dough with oil before it went into the oven worked much better, producing a delicate, almost fried crunch and even browning that complemented a rosemary and sea salt topping. You'll need to plan ahead: The dough needs to rise in the refrigerator for at least 16 hours. If you can't find King Arthur all-purpose flour, you can substitute bread flour. The fougasses are best eaten within 4 hours of baking. If you don't have a baking stone, bake the bread on an overturned and preheated rimmed baking sheet set on the lowest oven rack.

¼ cup (1⅓ ounces) whole-wheat flour
3 cups (15 ounces) King Arthur all-purpose flour
1½ teaspoons table salt
1 teaspoon instant or rapid-rise yeast
1½ cups water, room temperature
Cornmeal or semolina flour
¼ cup extra-virgin olive oil, divided
1 tablespoon chopped fresh rosemary, divided
2 teaspoons coarse sea salt, divided

1. Sift whole-wheat flour through fine-mesh strainer into bowl of stand mixer; discard bran remaining in strainer. Add all-purpose flour, salt, and yeast to mixer bowl. Using dough hook on low speed, slowly add water to flour mixture and mix until cohesive dough starts to form and no dry flour remains, 5 to 7 minutes, scraping down bowl as needed. Transfer dough to lightly oiled large bowl or container, cover tightly with plastic wrap, and let rise for 30 minutes.

Fougasse

2. Holding edge of dough with your fingertips, fold dough over itself by gently lifting and folding edge of dough toward center. Turn bowl 45 degrees and fold dough again; repeat turning bowl and folding dough 6 more times (total of 8 folds). Cover tightly with plastic and let rise for 30 minutes. Repeat folding and rising every 30 minutes, 3 more times. After fourth set of folds, cover bowl tightly with plastic and refrigerate for at least 16 hours or up to 2 days.

3. Transfer dough to lightly floured counter, stretch gently into 8-inch round (do not deflate), and divide in half. Working with 1 piece of dough at a time, gently stretch and fold over 3 sides of dough to create rough triangle with 5-inch sides. Transfer triangles seam side down to lightly floured rimmed baking sheet, cover loosely with lightly oiled plastic, and let rest until no longer cool to the touch, 30 minutes to 1 hour.

4. Place baking stone on lower-middle rack of oven and heat oven to 450 degrees. Line 2 overturned rimmed baking sheets with parchment paper, and dust liberally with cornmeal. Transfer 1 piece of dough to lightly floured counter and gently roll into triangular shape with 8-inch base and 10-inch sides, about ½ inch thick. Transfer dough to prepared sheet, with base facing short side of sheet.

5. Using pizza cutter, make 6-inch-long cut down center of triangle, through dough to sheet, leaving about 1½ inches at either end. Make three 2- to 3-inch diagonal cuts through dough on each side of center cut, leaving 1-inch border on each end of cuts, to create leaf-vein pattern (cuts should not connect to one another or to edges of dough).

6. Gently stretch dough toward sides of sheet to widen cuts and emphasize leaf shape; overall size of loaf should measure about 10 by 12 inches. Cover loosely with lightly oiled plastic and let rise until nearly doubled in size, 30 to 45 minutes. Twenty minutes after shaping first loaf, repeat rolling, cutting, and shaping with second piece of dough. (Staggering shaping of loaves will allow them to be baked in succession.)

7. Brush top and sides of first loaf with 2 tablespoons oil. Sprinkle loaf evenly with 1½ teaspoons rosemary and 1 teaspoon coarse salt. Slide parchment with loaf onto baking stone and bake until golden brown, 18 to 22 minutes, rotating loaf halfway through baking. Transfer loaf to wire rack, discard parchment, and let cool for 20 minutes. Repeat topping and baking with second loaf. Serve warm or at room temperature.

VARIATIONS
Fougasse with Bacon and Gruyère
Cook 4 slices thick-cut bacon, cut into ½-inch pieces, in 10-inch nonstick skillet over medium heat, stirring occasionally, until crispy, 6 to 8 minutes. Using slotted spoon, transfer bacon to paper towel–lined plate. Omit rosemary and sea salt. Add bacon to mixer bowl with flour in step 1. Sprinkle each loaf with ½ cup shredded Gruyère cheese before baking.

Fougasse with Asiago and Black Pepper
Omit rosemary and sea salt. Sprinkle each loaf with 1 teaspoon coarsely ground pepper and ½ cup finely grated Asiago cheese before baking.

Olive Fougasse
Add 1 cup coarsely chopped pitted kalamata olives to mixer bowl with flour in step 1.

Shaping Fougasse

1. Working with one 8-inch round of dough at a time, stretch and fold over 3 sides of dough to create triangle with 5-inch sides. Transfer to baking sheet, cover with plastic, and let rest 30 minutes to 1 hour.

2. Transfer 1 piece of dough to floured counter and roll into triangular shape with 8-inch base and 10-inch sides, about ½ inch thick. Transfer to parchment-lined baking sheet dusted with cornmeal.

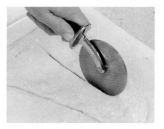

3. Using pizza cutter, make 6-inch-long cut down center of triangle, through dough to sheet, leaving about 1½ inches at either end.

4. Make three 2- to 3-inch diagonal cuts through dough on each side of center cut, leaving 1-inch border on each side to create leaf-vein pattern.

5. Gently stretch dough toward sides of sheet to widen cuts and emphasize leaf shape; overall leaf should measure about 10 by 12 inches. Let rise 30 to 45 minutes.

Authentic Baguettes at Home

Serves 8 to 12 (Makes four 15-inch-long baguettes)

WHY THIS RECIPE WORKS A great baguette is hard to come by outside of France. The idea is a moist, wheaty interior punctuated with irregular holes, and a deeply browned crust so crisp it shatters into shards. But home cooks rarely attempt to make baguettes since existing recipes provide little instruction. We wanted to create a detailed, authentic recipe for the home oven. First order of business: the mixing method. We chose a hybrid approach for the ideal structure and open crumb: We mixed the dough in a stand mixer and then folded the dough several times during the first rising period. We got the best flavor when we then gave the folded dough a slow rise—16 to 48 hours—in the fridge. We added a little diastatic malt powder to our dough to boost exterior browning and flavor; during the dough's long refrigerator stay, the yeast consumed nearly all of the available sugars, and the malt powder unlocked more sugar by converting starches in the flour. A little whole-wheat flour provided even more depth. For a shatteringly crisp, flavorful crust, we covered the bread with a disposable roasting pan while it baked so it could cook in its own steam. We recommend using a *couche, lame,* flipping board, and diastatic malt powder for this recipe. You will also need a baking stone and a baking peel. If you can't find King Arthur all-purpose flour, substitute bread flour, not another all-purpose flour. This recipe makes enough dough for four loaves, which can be baked anytime during the 24- to 72-hour window after placing the dough in the refrigerator in step 3. The baguettes are best eaten within 4 hours of baking.

- ¼ cup (1⅓ ounces) whole-wheat flour
- 3 cups (15 ounces) King Arthur all-purpose flour
- 1 teaspoon instant or rapid-rise yeast
- 1 teaspoon diastatic malt powder (optional)
- 1½ teaspoons table salt
- 1½ cups water, room temperature
- 2 (16 by 12-inch) disposable aluminum roasting pans

1. Sift whole-wheat flour through fine-mesh strainer into bowl of stand mixer; discard bran remaining in strainer. Add all-purpose flour; yeast; malt, if using; and salt to mixer bowl. Fit stand mixer with dough hook, add water, and knead on low speed until cohesive dough forms and no dry flour remains, 5 to 7 minutes. Transfer dough to lightly oiled large bowl, cover with plastic wrap, and let rest at room temperature for 30 minutes.

2. Holding edge of dough with your fingertips, fold dough over itself by gently lifting and folding edge of dough toward center. Turn bowl 45 degrees; fold again. Turn bowl and fold dough 6 more times (total of 8 folds). Cover with plastic and let rise for 30 minutes. Repeat folding and rising every 30 minutes, 3 more times. After fourth set of folds, cover bowl tightly with plastic and refrigerate for at least 24 hours or up to 3 days.

3. Transfer dough to lightly floured counter, pat into 8-inch square (do not deflate), and divide in half. Return 1 piece of dough to container, wrap tightly with plastic, and refrigerate (dough can be shaped and baked anytime within 3-day window). Divide remaining dough in half crosswise, transfer to lightly floured rimmed baking sheet, and cover loosely with plastic. Let rest for 45 minutes.

4. On lightly floured counter, roll each piece into loose 3- to 4-inch-long cylinder; return to floured baking sheet and cover with plastic. Let rest at room temperature for 30 minutes.

5. Lightly mist underside of couche with water, drape over inverted baking sheet and dust with flour. Gently press 1 piece of dough into 6 by 4-inch rectangle on lightly floured counter, with long edge facing you. Fold upper quarter of dough toward center and press gently to seal. Rotate dough 180 degrees and repeat folding step to form 8 by 2-inch rectangle.

6. Fold dough in half toward you, using thumb of your other hand to create crease along center of dough, sealing with heel of your hand as you work your way along loaf. Without pressing down on loaf, use heel of your hand to reinforce seal (do not seal ends of loaf).

7. Cup your hand over center of dough and roll dough back and forth gently to tighten (it should form dog-bone shape).

8. Starting at center of dough and working toward ends, gently and evenly roll and stretch dough until it measures 15 inches long by 1¼ inches wide. Moving your hands in opposite directions, use back-and-forth motion to roll ends of loaf under your palms to form sharp points.

9. Transfer dough to floured couche, seam side up. Gather edges of couche into 2 pleats on either side of loaf, then cover loosely with large plastic garbage bag.

10. Repeat steps 4 through 9 with second piece of dough and place on opposite side of pleat. Fold edges of couche over loaves to cover completely, then carefully place sheet inside bag, and tie or fold under to enclose.

11. Let stand until loaves have nearly doubled in size and dough springs back minimally when poked gently with your fingertip, 45 minutes to 1 hour. While bread rises, adjust oven rack to middle position, place baking stone on rack, and heat oven to 500 degrees.

12. Line pizza peel with 16 by 12-inch piece parchment paper with long edge perpendicular to handle. Unfold couche, pulling from ends to remove pleats. Gently pushing with side of flipping board, roll 1 loaf over, away from other loaf, so it is seam side down. Using your hand, hold long edge of flipping board between loaf and couche at 45-degree angle, then lift couche with your other hand and flip loaf seam side up onto board.

"Baking bread at home is usually about the experience, not the end result. Truth be told, most of the bread you make at home isn't as good as the artisan loaves you can buy at a good local bakery. This classic recipe with a few clever tricks is a project (it's a two-day recipe), but the finished loaves are the real deal, as good as any baguette you will eat in Paris. The small amount of whole-wheat flour amps up the wheaty flavor and the slow rise in the refrigerator delivers complex, yeasty flavors. And did I mention the marvelous crumb? It's moist, it's chewy, and it has plenty of holes that are neither too big nor too small. The crispy, crackly crust will give your jaws a good workout, like only the best baguettes can. You will need some special equipment to make this recipe, but the investment is modest. In return, baking bread this good will make you feel like a rock star. Plus, you get to share four truly amazing loaves."

–Jack

13. Invert loaf onto parchment-lined peel, seam side down, about 2 inches from long edge of parchment, then use flipping board to straighten loaf. Repeat with remaining loaf, leaving at least 3 inches between loaves.

14. Holding lame concave side up at 30-degree angle to loaf, make series of three 4-inch-long, ½-inch-deep slashes along length of loaf, using swift, fluid motion, overlapping each slash slightly. Repeat with second loaf.

15. Transfer loaves, on parchment, to baking stone, cover with stacked inverted disposable pans, and bake for 5 minutes. Carefully remove pans and bake until loaves are evenly browned, 12 to 15 minutes longer, rotating parchment halfway through baking. Transfer to wire rack and let cool for at least 20 minutes before serving.

Shaping and Baking Baguettes

Once your dough has gone through the initial rising, folding, and resting stages, it's ready to be shaped.

1. On lightly floured counter, roll each piece of refrigerated and rested dough into 3- to 4-inch-long cylinder. Move dough to floured baking sheet and cover with plastic. Let rest for 30 minutes.

2. Press 1 piece of dough into 6 by 4-inch rectangle. Fold upper quarter of dough toward center; press to seal. Rotate 180 degrees and repeat folding to form 8 by 2-inch rectangle.

3. Fold dough in half toward you, using thumb of your other hand to create crease along center of dough, sealing with heel of your hand as you work your way along the loaf. Do not seal ends of loaf.

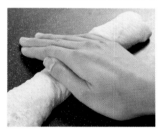

4. Cup your hand over center of dough and roll to form dog-bone shape. Working toward ends, gently roll and stretch dough until it measures 15 inches long by 1¼ inches wide.

5. Moving your hands in opposite directions, use back-and-forth motion to roll ends of loaf under your palms to form sharp points.

6. Transfer dough to floured couche, seam side up. On either side of loaf, pinch edges of couche into pleat. Cover loosely with large plastic garbage bag.

7. Place second loaf on opposite side of pleat. Fold edges of couche over loaves then place sheet inside bag, and tie or fold under to enclose. Let rise for 45 minutes to 1 hour.

8. Use flipping board to roll loaf so it is seam side down. Hold flipping board between loaf and couche at 45-degree angle. Lift couche and flip loaf seam side up onto board. Invert loaf onto peel.

9. Holding lame concave side up at 30-degree angle to loaf, make series of three 4-inch-long, ½-inch-deep slashes along length of each loaf, using swift, fluid motion, overlapping each slash slightly.

10. Transfer loaves, on parchment, to baking stone, cover with stacked inverted disposable pans, and bake for 5 minutes. Remove pans and continue to bake until loaves are evenly browned.

Easy Sandwich Bread

Serves 8

WHY THIS RECIPE WORKS Many people who might enjoy making homemade sandwich bread (which beats any store-bought loaf) don't even try because they think it takes most of a day. Not so. It's true, however, that "quicker" yeasted breads can lack the structure necessary for a satisfactory rise and that their interiors are often coarse. But we found that we could bake soft, well-risen, even-crumbed bread that was perfect for any sandwich without kneading or shaping—and it took just 2 hours to make (with most of that time being hands-off). To encourage maximum gluten development in a short amount of time, we used higher-protein bread flour and made a wet, batter-like dough; increasing the amount of water enhanced the gluten structure without requiring prolonged kneading. We also reduced the fat and sugar slightly and with-held salt until the second mix, which gave our bread more spring and lift. Using our mixer's paddle instead of the dough hook and increasing the speed to medium not only shortened our mixing time but also gave our loose dough enough struc-ture to rise into a dome shape—plus, we didn't need to handle the dough or determine when it was perfectly kneaded. We highlighted the crust by brushing the loaf with an egg wash before baking and painting it with melted butter afterward. The test kitchen's preferred loaf pan measures 8½ by 4½ inches; if you use a 9 by 5-inch loaf pan, start checking for doneness 5 minutes earlier than advised in the recipe. To prevent the loaf from deflating as it rises, do not let the batter come in contact with the plastic wrap. We do not recommend mixing this dough by hand.

2 cups (11 ounces) bread flour
6 tablespoons (2 ounces) whole-wheat flour
2¼ teaspoons instant or rapid-rise yeast
1¼ cups plus 2 tablespoons warm water (120 degrees), divided
3 tablespoons unsalted butter, melted, divided
1 tablespoon honey
¾ teaspoon table salt
1 large egg, lightly beaten with 1 teaspoon water and pinch salt

1. In bowl of stand mixer, whisk bread flour, whole-wheat flour, and yeast together. Add 1¼ cups warm water, 2 table-spoons melted butter, and honey. Fit stand mixer with paddle and mix on low speed for 1 minute. Increase speed to medium and mix for 2 minutes. Scrape down bowl and paddle with greased rubber spatula. Continue to mix 2 minutes longer. Remove bowl and paddle from mixer. Scrape down bowl and paddle, leaving paddle in batter. Cover with plastic wrap and let batter rise in warm place until doubled in size, about 20 minutes.

2. Adjust oven rack to lower-middle position and heat oven to 375 degrees. Spray 8½ by 4½-inch loaf pan with vegetable oil spray. Dissolve salt in remaining 2 tablespoons warm water. When batter has doubled, attach bowl and paddle to mixer. Add salt-water mixture and mix on low speed until water is mostly incorporated, about 40 seconds. Increase speed to medium and mix until thoroughly combined, about 1 minute, scraping down paddle if necessary. Transfer batter to prepared pan and smooth surface with greased rubber spatula. Cover and leave in warm place until batter reaches ½ inch below edge of pan, 15 to 20 minutes. Uncover and let rise until center of batter is level with edge of pan, 5 to 10 minutes.

3. Gently brush top of risen loaf with egg mixture. Bake until deep golden brown and center of loaf registers 208 to 210 degrees, 40 to 45 minutes, rotating pan halfway through baking. Using clean dish towels, carefully invert bread onto wire rack. Reinvert loaf and brush top and sides with remaining 1 tablespoon melted butter. Let cool completely before serving. (Loaf is best eaten on day it is baked, but leftovers may be wrapped in plastic wrap and stored for up to 2 days at room temperature or frozen for up to 1 month.)

Best Whole-Wheat Sandwich Bread

Serves 16 (Makes 2 loaves)

WHY THIS RECIPE WORKS Most whole-wheat bread recipes turn out either squat bricks or white bread in disguise. We wanted a nutty, light-textured sandwich loaf. We started with a good white-flour recipe and worked our way backward to "unrefine" it. We made a series of white bread loaves, replacing different amounts of all-purpose flour with whole-wheat to find the highest percentage of whole-wheat flour we could use before the texture suffered, landing on 60 percent. We also substituted bread flour for the all-purpose flour. Next, we soaked the flour overnight in milk, with some wheat germ for added flavor. This softened the grain's fiber, kept the dough moist, and coaxed out some sweetness. Finally, we turned to a sponge, a mixture of flour, water, and yeast left to sit overnight to develop a full range of flavor. Adding honey lent complexity and swapping out some of the butter for vegetable oil cut the richness. If you don't have a baking stone, bake the bread on an overturned and preheated rimmed baking sheet set on the lowest oven rack. The test kitchen's preferred loaf pan measures 8½ by 4½ inches; if you use a 9 by 5-inch loaf pan, start checking for doneness 5 minutes earlier than advised in the recipe.

Sponge
- 2 cups (11 ounces) bread flour
- 1 cup warm water (110 degrees)
- ½ teaspoon instant or rapid-rise yeast

Soaker
- 3 cups (16½ ounces) whole-wheat flour
- ½ cup wheat germ
- 2 cups whole milk

Dough
- 6 tablespoons unsalted butter, softened
- ¼ cup honey
- 2 tablespoons instant or rapid-rise yeast
- 2 tablespoons vegetable oil
- 4 teaspoons table salt

1. For the sponge: Combine flour, water, and yeast in large bowl and stir with wooden spoon until uniform mass forms and no dry flour remains, about 1 minute. Cover bowl tightly with plastic wrap and let sit at room temperature for at least 8 hours or up to 24 hours.

2. For the soaker: Combine flour, wheat germ, and milk in separate large bowl and stir with wooden spoon until shaggy mass forms, about 1 minute. Transfer dough to lightly floured work surface and knead by hand until smooth, 2 to 3 minutes. Return soaker to bowl, cover tightly with plastic wrap, and refrigerate for at least 8 hours or up to 24 hours.

3. For the dough: Tear soaker apart into 1-inch pieces and place in bowl of stand mixer fitted with dough hook. Add sponge, butter, honey, yeast, oil, and salt and mix on low speed until cohesive mass starts to form, about 2 minutes. Increase speed to medium and knead until dough is smooth and elastic, 8 to 10 minutes. Transfer dough to lightly floured work surface and knead by hand to form smooth, round ball, about 1 minute. Place dough in lightly greased large bowl. Cover tightly with plastic wrap and let rise at room temperature for 45 minutes.

4. Gently press down on center of dough to deflate. Spray rubber spatula or bowl scraper with vegetable oil spray; fold partially risen dough over itself by gently lifting and folding the edge of dough toward middle. Turn bowl 90 degrees; fold again. Turn bowl and fold dough 6 more times (total of 8 folds). Cover tightly with plastic wrap and allow to rise at room temperature until doubled in size, about 45 minutes.

5. Grease two 8½ by 4½-inch loaf pans. Transfer dough to well-floured work surface and divide in half. Press 1 piece dough into 17 by 8-inch rectangle, with short side facing you. Roll dough toward you into firm cylinder, keeping roll taut by tucking it under itself as you go. Turn loaf seam side up and pinch it closed. Place loaf seam side down in prepared pan, pressing gently into corners. Repeat with second piece of dough. Cover loaves loosely with greased plastic wrap and let rise at room temperature until nearly doubled in size, 1 to 1½ hours (top of the loaves should rise about 1 inch over lip of pan).

6. Thirty minutes before baking, adjust oven racks to middle and lowest positions, place baking stone on upper rack, place empty loaf pan or other heatproof pan on lower rack, and heat oven to 400 degrees. Bring 2 cups water to boil.

7. Using sharp serrated knife or a single-edge razor blade, make one ¼-inch-deep slash lengthwise down center of each loaf. Working quickly, pour boiling water into empty loaf pan in oven and set loaves on baking stone. Reduce oven temperature to 350 degrees. Bake until crust is dark brown and center of loaves registers 200 degrees, 40 to 50 minutes, rotating pans halfway through baking. Transfer pans to wire rack and let cool for 5 minutes. Remove loaves from pans, return to rack, and let cool to room temperature, about 2 hours, before slicing and serving. (Bread can be wrapped in double layer of plastic wrap and stored at room temperature for up to 3 days, or wrapped with additional layer of aluminum foil and frozen for up to 1 month.)

Forming Whole-Wheat Sandwich Bread

1. Deflate center of dough, then fold it in on itself. Turn bowl 90 degrees; fold again. Repeat for a total of 8 folds. Let rise for 45 minutes.

2. Halve dough and pat each portion into 8 by 17-inch rectangle, with short side facing you.

3. Roll each sheet toward you into tight cylinder. Keep roll taut by tucking it under itself as you go. Pinch seams to seal.

4. Place loaves seam side down in prepared loaf pans. Let dough rise until almost doubled in size, 1 to 1½ hours.

5. Using serrated knife, make ¼-inch shallow slash down center of each loaf to stop bread from tearing when it rises. Bake for 40 to 50 minutes.

Multigrain Bread

Serves 16 (Makes 2 loaves)

WHY THIS RECIPE WORKS Although multigrain bread often has great flavor, the quantity of ingredients weighs it down so much that the loaf becomes dense and heavy. On the other end of the spectrum are loaves with a sandwich-style texture but so little grain that they're hard to distinguish from white bread. We wanted a multigrain bread with great flavor and balanced texture. Our first challenge was to develop more gluten in the dough. Because the protein content of any flour is an indicator of how much gluten it will produce, we thought first to switch out all-purpose flour for bread flour, but this move only made the bread chewier. The solution was twofold: long kneading preceded by an autolyse, a resting period just after the initial mixing of water and flour that gives flour time to hydrate. This method also made the dough easier to work with. The result was a loaf that baked up light yet chewy, without being tough. To incorporate grains into the bread, we used a one-stop-shopping alternative: packaged seven-grain hot cereal. To soften the grains, we made a thick porridge with the cereal before adding it to the dough. A final step of rolling the shaped loaves in oats yielded a finished, professional look. Don't confuse seven-grain hot cereal mix with boxed, cold breakfast cereals that may also be labeled "seven-grain." Our favorite brands of seven-grain mix are Bob's Red Mill and Arrowhead Mills. For an accurate measurement of boiling water, bring a kettle of water to a boil, then measure out the desired amount.

1¼ cups (6¼ ounces) seven-grain hot cereal mix
2½ cups boiling water
3 cups (15 ounces) all-purpose flour, plus extra as needed
1½ cups (8¼ ounces) whole-wheat flour
¼ cup honey
4 tablespoons unsalted butter, melted and cooled slightly
2¼ teaspoons instant or rapid-rise yeast
1 tablespoon table salt
¾ cup unsalted pumpkin seeds or sunflower seeds
½ cup old-fashioned rolled oats or quick oats

1. Place cereal mix in bowl of stand mixer and pour boiling water over it; let sit, stirring occasionally, until mixture cools to 100 degrees and resembles thick porridge, about 1 hour. Whisk flours together in medium bowl.

2. Once grain mixture has cooled, add honey, melted butter, and yeast and stir to combine. Attach bowl to stand mixer fitted with dough hook. With mixer running on low speed, add flour mixture, ½ cup at a time, and knead until dough forms ball, 1½ to 2 minutes; cover bowl with plastic wrap and let dough rest for 20 minutes. Add salt and knead

New York Bagels

Makes 8 bagels

WHY THIS RECIPE WORKS Proper New York bagels have a fine, uniform crumb, a substantial chew, a complex sweetness (derived from the addition of malt syrup), and a thin, crackly crust. We wanted to be able to enjoy New York bagels anywhere. To get the right amount of chew, we supplemented high-protein bread flour with vital wheat gluten. We also incorporated some gluten-strengthening shaping techniques: We rolled the dough, formed it into a rope, and twisted the rope before shaping it into a ring. Formed bagels are usually refrigerated for about a day to minimize the yeast's gas production and create lots of flavor. It's traditional to then boil them before baking to "wake up" the yeast. This process also hydrates and cooks the starches on the bagel's exterior to create the glossy, crisp crust. We spiked our boiling water with baking soda and sugar, which helped the bagels brown quickly. To build on that crust, we baked the bagels on a wire rack set in a rimmed baking sheet that we then placed on a preheated baking stone. And we poured boiling water into the pan to create steam. This recipe works best with King Arthur bread flour, although other bread flours will work. Vital wheat gluten and malt syrup are available in most supermarkets in the baking and syrup aisles, respectively. If you cannot find malt syrup, substitute 4 teaspoons of molasses. We do not recommend mixing this dough by hand. You can customize the toppings of your bagels with ½ cup poppy seeds, sesame seeds, caraway seeds, dehydrated onion flakes, dehydrated garlic flakes, or coarse/pretzel salt. Press the tops of the just-boiled bagels (the side without cornmeal) gently into the topping and return to the wire rack topping side up.

  1 **cup plus 2 tablespoons ice water (9 ounces)**
  2 **tablespoons malt syrup**
2⅔ **cups (14⅔ ounces) bread flour**
  4 **teaspoons vital wheat gluten**
  2 **teaspoons instant or rapid-rise yeast**
  2 **teaspoons table salt**
  ¼ **cup (1¼ ounces) cornmeal**
  ¼ **cup (1¾ ounces) sugar**
  1 **tablespoon baking soda**

1. Stir ice water and malt syrup together in 2-cup liquid measuring cup until malt syrup has fully dissolved. Process flour, wheat gluten, and yeast in food processor until combined, about 2 seconds. With processor running, slowly add ice water mixture; process until dough is just combined and no dry flour remains, about 20 seconds. Let dough sit for 10 minutes.

on medium-low speed until dough clears sides of bowl, 3 to 4 minutes (if it does not clear sides, add 2 to 3 tablespoons additional all-purpose flour and continue mixing); continue to knead dough for 5 more minutes. Add seeds and knead for another 15 seconds. Transfer dough to floured work surface and knead by hand until seeds are dispersed evenly and dough forms smooth, taut ball. Place dough in greased container with 4-quart capacity; cover with plastic wrap and allow to rise until doubled in size, 45 minutes to 1 hour.

3. Adjust oven rack to middle position and heat oven to 375 degrees. Spray two 9 by 5-inch loaf pans with vegetable oil spray. Transfer dough to lightly floured work surface and pat into 12 by 9-inch rectangle; cut dough in half crosswise with knife or bench scraper. With short side facing you, starting at farthest end, roll 1 dough piece into log, keeping roll taut by tucking it under itself as you go. Seal loaf by pinching seam together gently with your thumb and forefinger; repeat with remaining dough. Spray loaves lightly with water. Roll each dough log in oats to coat evenly and place, seam side down, in greased loaf pans, pressing gently into corners; cover lightly with plastic wrap and let rise until almost doubled in size, 30 to 40 minutes. (Dough should barely spring back when poked with your knuckle.) Bake until center of loaves registers 200 degrees, 35 to 40 minutes, rotating pans halfway through baking. Remove loaves from pans and let cool on wire rack for about 3 hours before serving. (Bread can be wrapped in double layer of plastic wrap and stored at room temperature for up to 3 days, or wrapped with additional layer of aluminum foil and frozen for up to 1 month.)

2. Add salt to dough and process, stopping processor and redistributing dough as needed, until dough forms shaggy mass that clears sides of workbowl (dough may not form 1 single mass), 45 to 90 seconds. Transfer dough to unfloured counter and knead until smooth, about 1 minute. Divide dough into 8 equal pieces (3½ ounces each) and cover loosely with plastic wrap.

3. Working with 1 piece of dough at a time and keeping remaining pieces covered, form dough pieces into smooth, taut rounds. (To round, set piece of dough on unfloured counter. Loosely cup your hand around dough and, without applying pressure to dough, move your hand in small circular motions. Tackiness of dough against counter and circular motion should work dough into smooth, even ball, but if dough sticks to your hands, lightly dust your fingers with flour.) Let dough balls rest on counter, covered, for 15 minutes.

4. Sprinkle rimmed baking sheet with cornmeal. Working with 1 dough ball at a time and keeping remaining pieces covered, coat dough balls lightly with flour and then, using your hands and rolling pin, pat and roll dough balls into 5-inch rounds. Starting with edge of dough farthest from you, roll into tight cylinder. Starting at center of cylinder and working toward ends, gently and evenly roll and stretch dough into 8- to 9-inch-long rope. Do not taper ends. Rolling ends of dough under your hands in opposite directions, twist rope to form tight spiral. Without unrolling spiral, wrap rope around your fingers, overlapping ends of dough by about 2 inches under your palm, to create ring shape. Pinch ends of dough gently together. With overlap under your palm, press and roll seam using circular motion on counter to fully seal. Transfer rings to prepared sheet and cover loosely with plastic, leaving at least 1 inch between bagels. Let bagels sit at room temperature for 1 hour. Cover sheet tightly with plastic and refrigerate for at least 16 hours or up to 24 hours.

5. One hour before baking, adjust oven rack to upper-middle position, place baking stone on rack, and heat oven to 450 degrees.

6. Bring 4 quarts water, sugar, and baking soda to boil in large Dutch oven. Set wire rack in rimmed baking sheet and spray rack with vegetable oil spray.

7. Transfer 4 bagels to boiling water and cook for 20 seconds. Using wire skimmer or slotted spoon, flip bagels over and cook 20 seconds longer. Using wire skimmer or slotted spoon, transfer bagels to prepared wire rack, with cornmeal side facing down. Repeat with remaining 4 bagels.

8. Place sheet with bagels on preheated baking stone and pour ½ cup boiling water into bottom of sheet. Bake until tops of bagels are beginning to brown, 10 to 12 minutes. Using metal spatula, flip bagels and continue to bake until golden brown, 10 to 12 minutes. Remove sheet from oven and let bagels cool on wire rack for at least 15 minutes. Serve warm or at room temperature. (Bagels are best eaten on day they are baked but can be cooled completely, transferred to heavy-duty zipper-lock bags, and frozen for up to 1 month.)

VARIATIONS
Everything Bagels
Combine 2 tablespoons poppy seeds, 2 tablespoons sesame seeds, 1 tablespoon dehydrated onion flakes, 2 teaspoons dehydrated garlic flakes, 2 teaspoons caraway seeds, and ½ teaspoon coarse sea salt in bowl. Press tops of just-boiled bagels (side without cornmeal) gently into topping mixture and return to wire rack, topping side up.

Cinnamon-Raisin Bagels
After transferring dough to counter in step 3, sprinkle ⅔ cup raisins over top and knead by hand until raisins are evenly distributed and dough forms smooth, round ball, about 1 minute. Divide and shape dough into balls as directed. Combine 1 teaspoon sugar and 1 teaspoon ground cinnamon in bowl. Before rolling dough rounds into cylinders in step 5, sprinkle ¼ teaspoon sugar-cinnamon mixture over each round, leaving ½-inch border around edges.

Shaping Bagels
Thoroughly working the dough during shaping helps a New York bagel develop its characteristic chew.

1. Pat and roll dough ball (lightly coated with flour) with rolling pin into 5-inch round. Roll into tight cylinder, starting with far side of dough.

2. Roll and stretch dough into 8- to 9-inch-long rope, starting at center of cylinder (don't taper ends). Twist rope to form tight spiral by rolling ends of dough under hands in opposite directions.

3. Wrap rope around your fingers, overlapping ends by 2 inches, to create ring. Pinch ends together. Press and roll seam (positioned under your palm) using circular motion on counter to fully seal.

New York Bagels

Pita Bread

SEASON 20 RECIPE

Makes eight 7-inch pita breads

WHY THIS RECIPE WORKS The tender chew and complex flavor of fresh-baked pitas are revelatory. Our recipe creates tender, chewy pitas with perfect pockets, every time. We started with high-protein bread flour, which encouraged pocket formation and increased the pita's chew. A high hydration level and a generous amount of oil helped keep the pita tender, and honey added a touch of sweetness. After quickly making the dough in the stand mixer, we shaped it into balls and let them proof overnight in the refrigerator to develop complex flavor. We then rolled the dough balls into thin, even disks before baking them on a hot baking stone placed on the lowest oven rack, which ensured that they would puff up quickly and fully. We prefer King Arthur bread flour for this recipe for its high protein content. If using another bread flour, reduce the amount of water in the dough by 2 tablespoons (1 ounce). If you don't have a baking stone, bake the pitas on an overturned and preheated rimmed baking sheet.

2⅔ cups (14⅔ ounces) bread flour
2¼ teaspoons instant or rapid-rise yeast
1⅓ cups (10½ ounces) ice water
 ¼ cup extra-virgin olive oil
 4 teaspoons honey
1¼ teaspoons table salt
    Vegetable oil spray

1. Whisk flour and yeast together in bowl of stand mixer. Add ice water, oil, and honey on top of flour mixture. Fit stand mixer with dough hook and mix on low speed until all flour is moistened, 1 to 2 minutes. Let dough sit for 10 minutes.

2. Add salt to dough and mix on medium speed until dough forms satiny, sticky ball that clears sides of bowl, 6 to 8 minutes. Transfer dough to lightly oiled counter and knead until smooth, about 1 minute. Divide dough into 8 equal pieces (about 3⅜ ounces each). Shape dough pieces into tight, smooth balls and transfer, seam side down, to rimmed baking sheet coated with oil spray. Spray tops of balls lightly with oil spray, then cover tightly with plastic wrap and refrigerate for at least 16 hours or up to 24 hours.

3. One hour before baking pitas, adjust oven rack to lowest position, set baking stone on rack, and heat oven to 425 degrees.

4. Remove dough from refrigerator. Coat 1 dough ball generously on both sides with flour and place on well-floured counter, seam side down. Use heel of your hand to press dough ball into 5-inch circle. Using rolling pin, gently roll into 7-inch circle, adding flour as necessary to prevent sticking. Roll slowly and gently to prevent any creasing. Repeat with second dough ball. Brush both sides of each dough round with pastry brush to remove any excess flour. Transfer dough rounds to unfloured peel, making sure side that was facing up when you began rolling is faceup again.

5. Slide both dough rounds carefully onto stone and bake until evenly inflated and lightly browned on undersides, 1 to 3 minutes. Using peel, slide pitas off stone and, using your hands or spatula, gently invert. (If pitas do not puff after 3 minutes, flip immediately to prevent overcooking.) Return pitas to stone and bake until lightly browned in center of second side, 1 minute. Transfer pitas to wire rack to cool, covering loosely with clean dish towel. Repeat shaping and baking with remaining 6 pitas in 3 batches. Let pitas cool for 10 minutes before serving. (The pitas are best eaten within 24 hours of baking. Reheat leftover pitas by wrapping them in aluminum foil, placing them in a cold oven, setting the temperature to 300 degrees, and baking for 15 to 20 minutes.)

One-Hour Pizza

Serves 4 to 6

WHY THIS RECIPE WORKS We were determined to make a really good pizza from scratch in just 1 hour. Doing so required a handful of tricks to get a crust that was crisp, tender, and light without prolonged proofing. First, we used a high percentage of yeast and warm water in the dough to make sure it proofed in 30 minutes. We also found that a combination of semolina and all-purpose flours worked best, providing crispness, stretch, and enough structure. Finally, we rolled the dough between sheets of oiled parchment paper immediately after mixing so that the air bubbles that developed during proofing wouldn't be knocked out by shaping.

We made our quick no-cook pizza sauce in the food processor. The last step was the cheese: We sprinkled grated Parmesan on top of the sauce, followed by creamy shredded mozzarella. Just a few minutes in the oven browned the crust to perfection, while the cheese melted and turned bubbly. For the best results, weigh your ingredients. We like the depth anchovies add to the sauce, but you can omit them, if desired. For the mild lager, we recommend Budweiser or Stella Artois. Extra sauce can be refrigerated for up to a week or frozen for up to a month. Some baking stones can crack under the intense heat of the broiler. Our recommended stone from Old Stone Oven won't, but if you're using another stone, check the manufacturer's website. If you don't have a pizza peel, use an overturned rimmed baking sheet instead.

Dough

- 1⅓ cups (7⅓ ounces) bread flour
- ½ cup (3 ounces) semolina flour
- 2 teaspoons instant or rapid-rise yeast
- 2 teaspoons sugar
- ½ cup plus 2 tablespoons (5 ounces) warm water (115 degrees)
- ¼ cup (2 ounces) mild lager
- 2 teaspoons distilled white vinegar
- 1½ teaspoons extra-virgin olive oil
- 1 teaspoon table salt
  Vegetable oil spray

Sauce

- 1 (28-ounce) can whole peeled tomatoes, drained
- 1 tablespoon extra-virgin olive oil
- 3 anchovy fillets, rinsed and patted dry (optional)
- 1 teaspoon table salt
- 1 teaspoon dried oregano
- ½ teaspoon sugar
- ¼ teaspoon pepper
- ⅛ teaspoon red pepper flakes

Pizza

- 1 ounce Parmesan cheese, grated fine (½ cup), divided
- 6 ounces whole-milk mozzarella, shredded (1½ cups), divided

1. For the dough: Adjust oven rack 4 to 5 inches from broiler element, set pizza stone on rack, and heat oven to 500 degrees.

2. While oven heats, process bread flour, semolina flour, yeast, and sugar in food processor until combined, about 2 seconds. With processor running, slowly pour warm water, lager, vinegar, and oil through feed tube; process until dough is just combined and no dry flour remains, about 10 seconds. Let dough sit for 10 minutes.

3. Add salt to dough and process until dough forms satiny, sticky ball that clears sides of workbowl, 30 to 60 seconds. Transfer dough to lightly floured counter and gently knead until smooth, about 15 seconds. Divide dough into 2 equal pieces and shape each into smooth ball.

4. Spray 11-inch circle in center of large sheet of parchment paper with oil spray. Place 1 ball of dough in center of parchment. Spray top of dough with oil spray. Using rolling pin, roll dough into 10-inch circle. Cover with second sheet of parchment. Using rolling pin and your hands, continue to roll and press dough into 11½-inch circle. Set aside and repeat rolling with second ball of dough. Let dough sit at room temperature until slightly puffy, 30 minutes.

5. For the sauce: Process all ingredients in food processor until smooth, about 30 seconds. Transfer to medium bowl.

6. For the pizza: When dough has rested for 20 minutes, heat broiler for 10 minutes. Remove top piece of parchment from 1 disk of dough and dust top of dough lightly with all-purpose flour. Using your hands or pastry brush, spread flour evenly over dough, brushing off any excess. Liberally dust pizza peel with all-purpose flour. Flip dough onto peel, parchment side up. Carefully remove parchment and discard.

7. Using back of spoon or ladle, spread ½ cup sauce in thin layer over surface of dough, leaving ¾-inch border around edge. Sprinkle ¼ cup Parmesan evenly over sauce, followed by ¾ cup mozzarella. Slide pizza carefully onto stone and return oven to 500 degrees. Bake until crust is well browned and cheese is bubbly and beginning to brown, 8 to 12 minutes, rotating pizza halfway through baking.

8. Transfer pizza to wire rack and let cool for 5 minutes before serving. Repeat steps 6 and 7 to top and bake second pizza.

"If you open my freezer you will find the following: ice cream (lots of that), frozen homemade stock, and a stack of homemade, parbaked pizzas that I make using this recipe. I had made a lot of homemade pizza before this recipe was developed—none of them were great. Usually the crust was tough or hard to roll out. This recipe changed all of that.

So, Wednesday night is the time that I start the pizza dough because I like the way that it tastes after 48 hours in the fridge. Each time, I double the recipe (at least) in order to make a minimum of four pizzas. There are four of us in our house and on more than one occasion there is not a single slice left over. It's just that good. That stack of frozen pizzas acts as backup in case after devouring all four pizzas someone asks, 'Is there any more?'"

–Bridget

New York–Style Thin-Crust Pizza

Serves 4 to 6

WHY THIS RECIPE WORKS New York–style pizza is something special: It has a thin, crisp, and spottily charred exterior, and it's tender yet chewy within. But with home ovens that reach only 500 degrees and dough that's impossible to stretch thin, the savviest cooks struggle to produce parlor-quality pies. In pursuit of the perfect crust at home, we made the dough fairly wet so it was easy to stretch. However, it puffed in the oven and was a little bland. The solution was to employ a slow, cold fermentation by chilling the dough in the refrigerator for a day or so instead of letting it rise on the counter. This kept the bubbles in the dough tighter, and it created more flavor via the prolonged production of sugar, alcohol, and acids. Situating the baking stone on the highest rack mimicked the shallow chamber of a commercial pizza oven, in which heat rises, radiates off the top of the oven, and browns the pizza before the interior dries out. Shape the second dough ball while the first pizza bakes, but don't top the pizza until right before you bake it. The sauce will yield more than is needed in the recipe; extra sauce can be refrigerated for up to one week or frozen for up to one month. It's important to use ice water in the dough to prevent it from overheating in the food processor. Semolina flour is ideal for dusting the peel; use it in place of bread flour if you have it.

Dough

- 3 cups (16½ ounces) bread flour
- 2 tablespoons sugar
- ½ teaspoon instant or rapid-rise yeast
- 1⅓ cups ice water
- 1 tablespoon vegetable oil
- 1½ teaspoons table salt

Sauce

- 1 (28-ounce) can whole peeled tomatoes, drained
- 1 tablespoon extra-virgin olive oil
- 1 teaspoon red wine vinegar
- 2 garlic cloves, minced
- 1 teaspoon table salt
- 1 teaspoon dried oregano
- ¼ teaspoon pepper

Pizza

- 1 ounce Parmesan cheese, grated fine (½ cup), divided
- 8 ounces whole-milk mozzarella, shredded (2 cups), divided

1. *For the dough:* Pulse flour, sugar, and yeast in food processor (fitted with dough blade if possible) until combined, about 5 pulses. With processor running, slowly add ice water; process until dough is just combined and no dry flour remains, about 10 seconds. Let dough sit for 10 minutes.

2. Add oil and salt to dough and process until dough forms satiny, sticky ball that clears sides of bowl, 30 to 60 seconds. Transfer dough to lightly oiled counter and briefly knead by hand until smooth, about 1 minute. Shape dough into tight ball and place in lightly oiled large bowl; cover bowl tightly with plastic wrap and refrigerate for at least 24 hours or up to 3 days.

3. *For the sauce:* Process tomatoes, oil, vinegar, garlic, salt, oregano, and pepper in clean, dry workbowl until smooth, about 30 seconds. Transfer to bowl and refrigerate until ready to use.

4. *For the pizza:* One hour before baking, adjust oven rack to upper-middle position (rack should be 4 to 5 inches from broiler), set baking stone on rack, and heat oven to 500 degrees. Transfer dough to clean counter and divide in half. Using your cupped palms, form each half into smooth, tight ball. Place balls of dough on lightly greased baking sheet, spacing them at least 3 inches apart; cover loosely with greased plastic and let sit for 1 hour.

5. Coat 1 ball of dough generously with flour and place on well-floured counter (keep other ball covered). Use your fingertips to gently flatten dough into 8-inch disk, leaving 1 inch of edge slightly thicker than center. Using your hands, gently stretch disk into 12-inch round, working along edges and giving disk quarter turns. Transfer dough to well-floured pizza peel and stretch into 13-inch round. Using back of spoon or ladle, spread ½ cup sauce in thin layer over surface of dough, leaving ¼-inch border around edge. Sprinkle ¼ cup Parmesan evenly over sauce, followed by 1 cup mozzarella. Slide pizza carefully onto baking stone and bake until crust is well browned and cheese is bubbly and beginning to brown, 10 to 12 minutes, rotating pizza halfway through baking.

6. Transfer pizza to wire rack and let cool for 5 minutes before serving. Repeat step 5 to shape, top, and bake second pizza.

Pizza Bianca

Serves 6 to 8

WHY THIS RECIPE WORKS The Roman version of pizza has a crust like no other we've ever tasted: crisp but extraordinarily chewy. It's so good on its own that it is usually topped with just olive oil, rosemary, and kosher salt. We wanted to figure out how we could enjoy this marvel without taking a trip to Italy. This pizza dough contains significantly more water than other styles, which is the secret to its chewy texture. But extra-wet doughs require more kneading, and we wanted to make this dish at home in a reasonable amount of time. Instead of a long knead, we let the dough rest for 20 minutes, which let us get away with just 10 minutes of kneading. After an initial rise, the dough was still sticky; we couldn't roll it out, but it was easy to pour out and then press onto a baking sheet. After letting the dough rest briefly, we baked the crust, adding just kosher salt, oil, and rosemary to remain true to the authentic version. While kneading the dough on high speed, the mixer tends to wobble and walk on the countertop. Place a towel or shelf liner under the mixer and watch it at all times while mixing. Handle the dough with lightly oiled hands. Resist flouring your fingers or the dough might stick further. This recipe was developed using an 18 by 13-inch baking sheet. Smaller baking sheets can be used, but because the pizza will be thicker, baking times will be longer. If you don't have a pizza stone, bake the pizza on a rimless or over-turned baking sheet that has been preheated just like the pizza stone. Serve the pizza by itself as a snack, or with soup or salad as a light entrée.

3 cups (15 ounces) all-purpose flour
1⅔ cups (13⅓ ounces) water, room temperature
1¼ teaspoons salt
1½ teaspoons instant or rapid-rise yeast
1¼ teaspoons sugar
5 tablespoons extra-virgin olive oil
1 teaspoon kosher salt
2 tablespoons fresh rosemary leaves

1. Using stand mixer fitted with dough hook, mix flour, water, and salt together on low speed until no areas of dry flour remain, 3 to 4 minutes, scraping down bowl as needed. Turn off mixer and let dough rest for 20 minutes.

2. Sprinkle yeast and sugar over dough. Knead on low speed until fully combined, 1 to 2 minutes. Increase mixer speed to high and knead until dough is glossy and smooth and pulls away from sides of bowl, 6 to 10 minutes. (Dough will pull away from sides only while mixer is on. When mixer is off, dough will fall back to sides.)

3. Using your fingers, coat large bowl with 1 tablespoon oil, rubbing excess oil from your fingers onto blade of rubber spatula. Using oiled spatula, transfer dough to prepared bowl and pour 1 tablespoon oil over top. Flip dough over once so that it is well coated with oil; cover bowl tightly with plastic wrap and let dough rise at room temperature until nearly tripled in volume and large bubbles have formed, 2 to 2½ hours. (Dough can be refrigerated for up to 24 hours. Bring dough to room temperature, 2 to 2½ hours, before proceeding with step 4.)

4. One hour before baking, adjust oven rack to middle position, place baking stone on rack, and heat oven to 450 degrees. Coat rimmed baking sheet with 2 tablespoons oil. Using rubber spatula, turn dough out onto prepared baking sheet along with any oil in bowl. Using your fingertips, press dough out toward edges of baking sheet, taking care not to tear dough. (Dough will not fit snugly into corners. If dough resists stretching, let it relax for 5 to 10 minutes before trying to stretch it again.) Let dough rest until slightly bubbly, 5 to 10 minutes. Using dinner fork, poke surface of dough 30 to 40 times and sprinkle with kosher salt.

5. Bake until golden brown, 20 to 30 minutes, sprinkling rosemary over top and rotating baking sheet halfway through baking. Using metal spatula, transfer pizza to cutting board. Brush dough lightly with remaining 1 tablespoon oil. Serve immediately.

Thick-Crust Sicilian-Style Pizza

Serves 6 to 8

WHY THIS RECIPE WORKS Sicilian-style pizza boasts a thick crust with a tight, even crumb and a delicately crisp underside. To replicate it, we created a dough with all-purpose and semolina flours, the latter contributing the distinct yellow color and cake-like crumb. We took things slowly, adding ice water and 3 tablespoons of olive oil for a tender texture, then letting the dough rest before adding salt and kneading and shaping it into a ball. Letting the dough proof for 24 hours in the refrigerator helped create flavor: The cold kept carbon dioxide from forming bubbles while the extended fermentation allowed an array of flavor compounds to form. To ensure that bubbles wouldn't form during the second proof, we rolled the dough out with a rolling pin, moved it onto a rimmed baking sheet, and covered it with plastic wrap and a second baking sheet. Before baking, we topped the dough with a boldly seasoned homemade tomato sauce and a blend of gooey mozzarella and Parmesan. King Arthur all-purpose flour and Bob's Red Mill semolina flour work best in this recipe. Using ice water prevents overheating during mixing.

Dough
2¼ cups (11¼ ounces) all-purpose flour
2 cups (12 ounces) semolina flour
1 teaspoon sugar
1 teaspoon instant or rapid-rise yeast
1⅔ cups (13⅓ ounces) ice water
3 tablespoons extra-virgin olive oil
2¼ teaspoons table salt

Sauce
1 (28-ounce) can whole peeled tomatoes, drained
2 teaspoons sugar
¼ teaspoon table salt
¼ cup extra-virgin olive oil
3 garlic cloves, minced
1 tablespoon tomato paste
3 anchovy fillets, rinsed, patted dry, and minced
1 teaspoon dried oregano
¼ teaspoon red pepper flakes

Pizza
¼ cup extra-virgin olive oil
2 ounces Parmesan cheese, grated (1 cup)
12 ounces whole-milk mozzarella, shredded (3 cups)

5. Remove top baking sheet and plastic wrap. Gently stretch and lift dough to fill pan. Using back of spoon or ladle, spread sauce in even layer over surface of dough, leaving ½-inch border. Sprinkle Parmesan evenly over entire surface of dough to edges followed by mozzarella.

6. Place pizza on stone; reduce oven temperature to 450 degrees and bake until bottom crust is evenly browned and cheese is bubbly and browned, 20 to 25 minutes, rotating pizza halfway through baking. Remove pan from oven and let cool on wire rack for 5 minutes. Run knife around rim of pan to loosen pizza. Transfer pizza to cutting board, cut into squares, and serve.

Pizza al Taglio with Arugula and Fresh Mozzarella

SEASON 20 RECIPE

Serves 4 to 6

WHY THIS RECIPE WORKS Tender and airy yet substantial, this Roman pie is often topped like an open-faced sandwich. Roman pizzerias adorn it in a variety of ways and display it behind glass in deli-style cases, where it is sold by the length and cut with scissors (*al taglio* means "by the cut"). It's also one of the easiest pizzas you'll ever make. Our Pizza al Taglio recipe uses a dough containing lots of water and olive oil to create a tender and airy crust with a crisp, light underside. Because the dough is so wet, we folded it by hand (rather than employ a stand mixer) to develop gluten. We placed the dough in a baking pan to proof overnight in the refrigerator to develop flavor and allow the dough to relax for easy stretching to its final dimensions. We then coated the top of the dough with olive oil and turned it out onto a baking sheet. We stretched it to the edges of the sheet and allowed it to proof for an hour until it was bubbly and risen. Finally, we topped the pizza and baked it on the lowest rack of a 450-degree oven until the bottom was evenly browned and crisp before adding the toppings. The dough for this pizza requires a 16- to 24-hour rest in the refrigerator. You'll get the crispest texture by using high-protein King Arthur bread flour, but other bread flours will also work. For the best results, weigh your flour and water. The bread flour should weigh 14⅔ ounces regardless of which brand of flour is used. Anchovies give the sauce depth, so don't omit them; they won't make the sauce taste fishy. Use the large holes of a box grater to shred the Parmesan.

Dough

2⅔ cups (14⅔ ounces) bread flour
1 teaspoon instant or rapid-rise yeast
1½ cups (12 ounces) water, room temperature
2 tablespoons extra-virgin olive oil
1¼ teaspoons table salt
Vegetable oil spray

1. *For the dough:* Using stand mixer fitted with dough hook, mix all-purpose flour, semolina flour, sugar, and yeast on low speed until combined, about 10 seconds. With machine running, slowly add water and oil until dough forms and no dry flour remains, 1 to 2 minutes. Cover with plastic wrap and let dough sit for 10 minutes.

2. Add salt to dough and mix on medium speed until dough forms satiny, sticky ball that clears sides of bowl, 6 to 8 minutes. Remove dough from bowl and knead briefly on lightly floured counter until smooth, about 1 minute. Shape dough into tight ball and place in large, lightly oiled bowl. Cover tightly with plastic wrap and refrigerate for at least 24 hours or up to 2 days.

3. *For the sauce:* Process tomatoes, sugar, and salt in food processor until smooth, about 30 seconds. Heat oil and garlic in medium saucepan over medium-low heat, stirring occasionally, until garlic is fragrant and just beginning to brown, about 2 minutes. Add tomato paste, anchovies, oregano, and pepper flakes and cook until fragrant, about 30 seconds. Add tomato mixture and cook, stirring occasionally, until sauce measures 2 cups, 25 to 30 minutes. Transfer to bowl, let cool, and refrigerate until needed.

4. *For the pizza:* One hour before baking pizza, place baking stone on upper-middle rack and heat oven to 500 degrees. Spray rimmed baking sheet (including rim) with vegetable oil spray, then coat bottom of a second baking sheet with oil. Remove dough from refrigerator and transfer to lightly floured counter. Lightly flour top of dough and gently press into 12 by 9-inch rectangle. Using rolling pin, roll dough into 18 by 13-inch rectangle. Transfer dough to prepared baking sheet, fitting dough into corners. Spray top of dough with oil spray and lay sheet of plastic wrap over dough. Place second baking sheet on dough and let stand for 1 hour.

Sauce

- 1 (14.5-ounce) can whole peeled tomatoes, drained
- 1 tablespoon extra-virgin olive oil
- 2 anchovy fillets, rinsed
- 1 teaspoon dried oregano
- ½ teaspoon table salt
- ¼ teaspoon red pepper flakes

Topping

- ¼ cup extra-virgin olive oil, divided
- 4 ounces (4 cups) baby arugula
- 8 ounces fresh mozzarella cheese, torn into bite-size pieces (about 2 cups)
- 1½ ounces Parmesan cheese, shredded (½ cup)

1. *For the dough:* Whisk flour and yeast together in medium bowl. Add room-temperature water and oil and stir with wooden spoon until shaggy mass forms and no dry flour remains. Cover bowl with plastic wrap and let sit for 10 minutes. Sprinkle salt over dough and mix until fully incorporated. Cover bowl with plastic and let dough rest for 20 minutes.

2. Using your wet hands, fold dough over itself by gently lifting and folding edge of dough toward middle. Turn bowl 90 degrees; fold again. Turn bowl and fold dough 4 more times (total of 6 turns). Cover bowl with plastic and let dough rest for 20 minutes. Repeat folding technique, turning bowl each time, until dough tightens slightly, 3 to 6 turns total. Cover bowl with plastic and let dough rest for 10 minutes.

3. Spray bottom of 13 by 9-inch baking pan liberally with oil spray. Transfer dough to prepared pan and spray top of dough lightly with oil spray. Gently press dough into 10 by 7-inch oval of even thickness. Cover pan tightly with plastic and refrigerate for at least 16 hours or up to 24 hours.

4. *For the sauce:* While dough rests, process all ingredients in blender until smooth, 20 to 30 seconds. Transfer sauce to bowl, cover, and refrigerate until needed. (Sauce can be refrigerated for up to 2 days.)

5. *For the topping:* Brush top of dough with 2 tablespoons oil. Spray rimmed baking sheet (including rim) with oil spray. Invert prepared sheet on top of pan and flip, allowing dough to fall onto sheet (you may need to lift pan and nudge dough at 1 end to release). Using your fingertips, gently dimple dough into even thickness and stretch toward edges of sheet to form 15 by 11-inch oval. Spray top of dough lightly with oil spray, cover loosely with plastic, and let rest until slightly puffy, 1 to 1¼ hours.

6. Thirty minutes before baking, adjust oven rack to lowest position and heat oven to 450 degrees. Just before baking, use your fingertips to gently dimple dough into even thickness, pressing into corners of sheet. Using back of spoon or ladle, spread ½ cup sauce in even layer over surface of dough. (Remaining sauce can be frozen for up to 2 months.)

7. Drizzle 1 tablespoon oil over top of sauce and use back of spoon to spread evenly over surface. Transfer sheet to oven and bake until bottom of crust is evenly browned and top is lightly browned in spots, 20 to 25 minutes, rotating sheet halfway through baking. Transfer sheet to wire rack and let cool for 5 minutes. Run knife around rim of sheet to loosen pizza. Transfer pizza to cutting board and cut into 8 rectangles. Toss arugula with remaining 1 tablespoon oil in bowl. Top pizza with arugula, followed by mozzarella and Parmesan, and serve.

VARIATIONS

Pizza al Taglio with Potatoes and Soppressata

Decrease oil in topping to 3 tablespoons and omit arugula, mozzarella, and Parmesan. After spreading sauce over dough, lay 6 ounces thinly sliced soppressata in even layer over sauce, followed by 10 ounces thinly sliced provolone. Toss 1 pound peeled and thinly sliced small Yukon Gold potatoes with ½ teaspoon pepper and remaining 1 tablespoon oil. Starting in 1 corner, shingle potatoes to form even row across bottom of pizza, overlapping each slice by about one-quarter. Continue to layer potatoes in rows, overlapping each row by about one-quarter. Bake pizza as directed until bottom of crust is evenly browned and potatoes are browned around edges. Sprinkle pizza with 2 teaspoons chopped fresh parsley before serving.

Pizza al Taglio with Prosciutto and Figs

Omit sauce ingredients as well as arugula, mozzarella, and Parmesan in topping. Spread remaining 2 tablespoons oil evenly over dough. Bake pizza as directed until bottom of crust is evenly browned and top is lightly browned in spots. Let pizza cool, then cut as directed. Top slices of pizza with 4 ounces thinly sliced prosciutto, followed by 8 thinly sliced figs and 2 ounces thinly shaved ricotta salata.

How to Fold Dough

Instead of kneading the dough, our recipe calls for folding it in on itself, letting it rest, and then folding and letting it rest again. This allows gluten to develop. Here's how we do it.

1. Grasp section of dough with your wet fingertips and gently lift.

2. Place edge down in middle of dough. Rotate bowl 90 degrees and repeat for total of 6 turns.

Pizza al Taglio with Arugula
and Fresh Mozzarella

Cookies

Chocolate Chip Cookie Ice Cream Sandwiches

Brown Sugar Cookies

Makes 24 cookies

WHY THIS RECIPE WORKS Simple sugar cookies, while classic, can seem too basic—even dull—at times. We wanted to turn up the volume on the sugar cookie by switching out the granulated sugar in favor of brown sugar. We had a clear vision of this cookie: It would be oversize, with a crackling crisp exterior and a chewy interior. And, like Mick Jagger, this cookie would scream "brown sugar." We wanted butter for optimal flavor, but the traditional creaming method (creaming softened butter with sugar until fluffy, beating in an egg, and then adding the dry ingredients) gave us a cakey texture. Cutting the butter into the flour produced crumbly cookies. What worked was first melting the butter. We then tweaked the amount of eggs, dark brown sugar, flour, and leavener to give us a good cookie, but we wanted even more brown sugar flavor. We made progress by rolling the dough balls in a combination of brown and granulated sugar and adding a healthy amount of vanilla and table salt. But our biggest success came from an unlikely refinement. Browning the melted butter added a complex nuttiness that made a substantial difference. Avoid using a nonstick skillet to brown the butter. The dark color of the nonstick coating makes it difficult to gauge when the butter is sufficiently browned. Use fresh brown sugar, as hardened brown sugar will make the cookies too dry. Achieving the proper texture—crisp at the edges and chewy in the middle—is critical to this recipe. Because the cookies are so dark, it's hard to judge doneness by color. Instead, gently press halfway between the edge and center of the cookie. When it's done, it will form an indentation with slight resistance. Check early and err on the side of underdone.

- 14 tablespoons unsalted butter, divided
- 2 cups plus 2 tablespoons (10⅔ ounces) all-purpose flour
- ½ teaspoon baking soda
- ¼ teaspoon baking powder
- 1¾ cups packed (12¼ ounces) dark brown sugar, plus ¼ cup for rolling
- ½ teaspoon table salt
- 1 large egg plus 1 large yolk
- 1 tablespoon vanilla extract
- ¼ cup granulated sugar

1. Melt 10 tablespoons butter in 10-inch skillet over medium-high heat. Continue to cook, swirling skillet constantly, until butter is dark golden brown and has nutty aroma, 1 to 3 minutes. Transfer browned butter to large bowl and stir in remaining 4 tablespoons butter until melted; let cool for 15 minutes.

2. Meanwhile, adjust oven rack to middle position and heat oven to 350 degrees. Line 2 baking sheets with parchment paper. Whisk flour, baking soda, and baking powder together in bowl.

3. Whisk 1¾ cups brown sugar and salt into cooled browned butter until smooth and no lumps remain, about 30 seconds. Whisk in egg and yolk and vanilla until incorporated, about 30 seconds. Using rubber spatula, stir in flour mixture until just combined, about 1 minute.

4. Combine remaining ¼ cup brown sugar and granulated sugar in shallow dish. Working with 2 tablespoons dough at a time, roll into balls, then roll in sugar to coat; space dough balls 2 inches apart on prepared sheets. (Dough balls can be frozen for up to 1 month; bake frozen dough balls on 1 baking sheet set inside second sheet in 325-degree oven for 20 to 25 minutes.)

5. Bake cookies, 1 sheet at a time, until edges have begun to set but centers are still soft, puffy, and cracked (cookies will look raw between cracks and seem underdone), 12 to 14 minutes, rotating sheet halfway through baking. Let cookies cool on sheet for 5 minutes, then transfer to wire rack. Let cookies cool completely before serving.

Molasses Spice Cookies

Makes 24 cookies

WHY THIS RECIPE WORKS The best molasses spice cookies combine a homespun crinkled appearance with a chewy texture and a deep, gently spiced molasses flavor. We wanted to create the ultimate molasses spice cookie—soft, chewy, and gently spiced with deep, dark molasses flavor. We also wanted it to have the traditional cracks and crinkles so characteristic of these charming cookies. We started with all-purpose flour and butter for full, rich flavor. Using just the right amount of molasses and brown sugar and flavoring the cookies with a combination of vanilla, ginger, cinnamon, cloves, black pepper, and allspice gave these spiced cookies the warm tingle that we were after. We found that to keep the cookies mild, using a light or mild molasses was imperative; but if it's a stronger flavor you want, dark molasses is in order. We pulled the cookies from the oven when they still looked a bit underdone; residual heat finished the baking and kept the cookies chewy and moist. For best flavor, make sure that your spices are fresh. Light or mild molasses gives the cookies a milder flavor; for a stronger flavor, use dark molasses. Either way, measure the molasses in a liquid measuring cup. If you find that the dough sticks to your palms as you shape the balls, moisten your hands occasionally in a bowl filled with cold tap water and shake off the excess. Bake the cookies one sheet at a time; if baked two sheets at a time, the cookies started on the bottom rack won't develop attractive crackly tops. Remove the cookies from the oven when they still look slightly raw and underbaked.

"If you love cookies (yes, I do!), and if you really love chewy cookies (yes, that's me!!), this humble recipe is going to make you very, very happy. The technique is dead simple—this recipe is all about the right ratio of ingredients. Dark brown sugar supplements the molasses flavor and helps provide maximum chew. The spices—cinnamon, ginger, cloves, and allspice— are perfectly balanced, with the cinnamon and ginger in the fore. Black pepper adds subtle heat that helps keep all the sweet stuff in check. Rolling the balls of dough in granulated sugar gives the baked cookies a sparkly exterior. And, for the ultimate treat, make the variation with the dark rum glaze. It's your standard confectioners' sugar glaze but with rum in place of the usual milk. We have developed dozens of amazing cookies in the test kitchen during the past two decades, but this one gets my vote for number one all-time-best cookie."

–Jack

"I have to admit, I once thought there was nothing wrong with regular old chocolate chip cookies. Since I've tasted our Perfect Chocolate Chip Cookies, I've changed my tune. The browned butter heightens and deepens all the other flavors with a toffee-caramel background, and the cookies have my favorite texture: chewy in the middle with crispy golden edges. They're not too sweet, too big, or too small—and they have an ideal ratio of cookie to chip, too. I'm probably overly familiar with this recipe, since I used it in my recent tasting of 14 brands of dark-chocolate chips. From early morning to late evening on one very long day, I carefully baked nearly 400 Perfect Chocolate Chip Cookies, batch after batch, trying to carry out each step exactly the same way, except for switching out the brand of chocolate chips. (It helped that I was surrounded by heavenly scents, though I could not eat the cookies; I had to save them all for the tasting!) The stampede when I summoned tasters to try them was memorable; I've never seen the tables fill so fast. This cookie is legendary."

—Lisa

2¼ cups (11¼ ounces) all-purpose flour
1½ teaspoons ground cinnamon
1½ teaspoons ground ginger
1 teaspoon baking soda
½ teaspoon ground cloves
¼ teaspoon ground allspice
¼ teaspoon pepper
¼ teaspoon table salt
12 tablespoons unsalted butter, softened
⅓ cup packed (2⅓ ounces) dark brown sugar
⅓ cup (2⅓ ounces) granulated sugar,
plus ½ cup for rolling
1 large egg yolk
1 teaspoon vanilla extract
½ cup mild or robust molasses

1. Adjust oven rack to middle position and heat oven to 375 degrees. Line 2 baking sheets with parchment paper. Whisk flour, cinnamon, ginger, baking soda, cloves, allspice, pepper, and salt together in bowl.

2. Using stand mixer fitted with paddle, beat butter, brown sugar, and ⅓ cup granulated sugar on medium speed until pale and fluffy, about 3 minutes. Reduce speed to medium-low, add egg yolk and vanilla, and beat until combined, about 30 seconds. Beat in molasses until incorporated, about 30 seconds, scraping down bowl as needed. Reduce speed to low and slowly add flour mixture until combined, about 30 seconds (dough will be soft). Give dough final stir by hand to ensure that no flour pockets remain.

3. Spread remaining ½ cup granulated sugar in shallow dish. Working with 2 tablespoons dough at a time, roll into balls with your dampened hands, then roll in sugar to coat; space dough balls 2 inches apart on prepared sheets. (Dough balls can be frozen for up to 1 month; bake frozen dough balls in 300-degree oven for 30 to 35 minutes.)

4. Bake cookies, 1 sheet at a time, until edges are set but centers are still soft, puffy, and cracked (cookies will look raw between cracks and seem underdone), 10 to 12 minutes, rotating sheet halfway through baking. Let cookies cool on sheet for 10 minutes. Serve warm or transfer to wire rack and let cool completely.

VARIATION
Molasses Spice Cookies with Dark Rum Glaze
If the glaze is too thick to drizzle, whisk in up to an additional ½ tablespoon rum.

Whisk 1 cup (4 ounces) confectioners' sugar and 2½ tablespoons dark rum together in medium bowl until smooth. Drizzle or spread glaze using back of spoon on cooled cookies. Allow glazed cookies to dry for at least 15 minutes.

Perfect Chocolate Chip Cookies
Makes 16 cookies

WHY THIS RECIPE WORKS Rich and buttery, with their soft cores and crispy edges, chocolate chip cookies are the American cookie-jar standard. Since Nestlé first began printing the recipe for Toll House cookies on the back of chocolate chip bags in 1939, generations of bakers have packed them into lunches and taken them to potlucks. But we wanted something more than the standard bake sale offering; we wanted a moist and chewy cookie with crisp edges and deep notes of toffee and butterscotch to balance its sweetness. Melting the butter before combining it with the other ingredients gave us the chewy texture we wanted, and browning a portion of it added nutty flavor. Upping the brown sugar enhanced chewiness, while a combination of one whole egg and one egg yolk gave us supremely moist cookies. For the crisp edges and deep toffee flavor, we allowed the sugar to dissolve and rest in the melted butter. We baked the cookies until golden brown and just set, but still soft in the center. The resulting cookies were crisp, chewy, and gooey with chocolate and boasted a complex medley of sweet, buttery, caramel, and toffee flavors. Avoid using a nonstick skillet to brown the butter; the dark color of the nonstick coating makes it difficult to gauge when the butter is browned. Use fresh, moist brown sugar instead of hardened brown sugar, which will make the cookies dry. This recipe works with light brown sugar, but the cookies will be less full-flavored. If you're using smaller baking sheets, put fewer cookies on each sheet and bake them in batches.

1¾ cups (8¾ ounces) all-purpose flour
½ teaspoon baking soda
14 tablespoons unsalted butter, divided
¾ cup packed (5¼ ounces) dark brown sugar
½ cup (3½ ounces) granulated sugar
2 teaspoons vanilla extract
1 teaspoon table salt
1 large egg plus 1 large yolk
1¼ cups (7½ ounces) semisweet or bittersweet chocolate chips
¾ cup pecans or walnuts, toasted and chopped (optional)

1. Adjust oven rack to middle position and heat oven to 375 degrees. Line 2 baking sheets with parchment paper. Whisk flour and baking soda together in bowl.

2. Melt 10 tablespoons butter in 10-inch skillet over medium-high heat. Continue to cook, swirling skillet constantly, until butter is dark golden brown and has nutty aroma, 1 to 3 minutes. Transfer browned butter to large bowl and stir in remaining 4 tablespoons butter until melted. Whisk in brown sugar, granulated sugar, vanilla, and salt until incorporated. Whisk in egg and yolk until smooth and no lumps remain, about 30 seconds.

"In our family, my sister is the undisputed cookie goddess. Her holiday cookie trays are exquisite by any measure, and the number of types she bakes borders on masochistic— 15 to 20 is not unusual. Her cookie aesthetic skews elegant, delicate, crisp, and European, but she welcomes representatives from the American cookie canon with open arms, so I swoop in with one of my favorites, chocolate crinkles.

Often crinkles look more dramatic than they taste; overly sweet and underly chocolaty is the norm. Happily, the ATK recipe bucks that trend by using a flavorful trifecta: unsweetened chocolate, cocoa powder, and espresso powder (which, technically, is optional in the recipe, but which I highly recommend). Sweetness comes from brown sugar, adding more nuance than white granulated, which is reserved for coating along with confectioners' sugar for the telltale striking white exterior with dark, almost black, fissures."

—Adam

3. Let mixture sit for 3 minutes, then whisk for 30 seconds. Repeat process of resting and whisking 2 more times until mixture is thick, smooth, and shiny. Using rubber spatula, stir in flour mixture until just combined, about 1 minute. Stir in chocolate chips and pecans, if using.

4. Working with 3 tablespoons dough at a time, roll into balls and space them 2 inches apart on prepared sheets. (Dough balls can be frozen for up to 1 month; bake frozen dough balls in 300-degree oven for 30 to 35 minutes.)

5. Bake cookies, 1 sheet at a time, until golden brown and edges have begun to set but centers are still soft and puffy, 10 to 14 minutes, rotating sheet halfway through baking. Transfer baking sheet to wire rack. Let cookies cool completely before serving.

Chocolate Crinkle Cookies

Makes 22 cookies

WHY THIS RECIPE WORKS The name says it all—these cookies are as much about looks as they are about flavor. Rolled in powdered sugar before going in the oven, chocolate crinkle cookies (aka earthquakes) form dark chocolaty fissures that break through the bright white surface during baking. They're eye-catching, with an irresistible deep chocolaty richness to back it up. Or at least, that's how they should be. Too often, these cookies turn out tooth-achingly sweet, with just a couple of wide gaping cracks instead of a crackly surface. We wanted a cookie with deep chocolate flavor and only enough sweetness to balance the chocolate's bitterness; a moist and tender—but not gooey—interior; and plenty of small irregular crinkly fissures breaking through a bright-white surface. For the best chocolate flavor, we used a combination of unsweetened chocolate and cocoa powder, which got an additional flavor boost from espresso powder. Using brown sugar instead of granulated lent a more complex, tempered sweetness with a bitter molasses edge that complemented the chocolate. A combination of both baking powder and baking soda gave us cookies with the right amount of lift and spread and contributed to a crackly surface. But the real key was rolling the cookies in granulated sugar before the traditional powdered sugar. It not only helped produce the perfect crackly exterior by creating a "shell" that broke into numerous fine fissures as the cookie rose and spread, but it also helped the powdered sugar coating stay in place. We finally had chocolate crinkle cookies that lived up to their name. Both natural and Dutch-processed cocoa will work in this recipe. Our favorite brand of cocoa powder is Droste Cacao.

1 cup (5 ounces) all-purpose flour
½ cup (1½ ounces) unsweetened cocoa powder
1 teaspoon baking powder
¼ teaspoon baking soda
½ teaspoon table salt
1½ cups packed (10½ ounces) brown sugar
3 large eggs
4 teaspoons instant espresso powder (optional)
1 teaspoon vanilla extract
4 ounces unsweetened chocolate, chopped
4 tablespoons unsalted butter
½ cup granulated sugar
½ cup confectioners' sugar

1. Adjust oven rack to middle position and heat oven to 325 degrees. Line 2 baking sheets with parchment paper. Whisk flour, cocoa, baking powder, baking soda, and salt together in bowl.

2. Whisk brown sugar; eggs; espresso powder, if using; and vanilla together in large bowl. Microwave chocolate and butter in bowl at 50 percent power, stirring occasionally, until melted, 2 to 3 minutes.

3. Whisk chocolate mixture into egg mixture until combined. Fold in flour mixture until no dry streaks remain. Let dough sit at room temperature for 10 minutes.

4. Spread granulated sugar in shallow dish. Spread confectioners' sugar in second shallow dish. Working in batches, drop 2-tablespoon mounds of dough (or use #30 scoop) directly into granulated sugar and roll to coat. Transfer dough balls to confectioners' sugar and roll to coat; space dough balls evenly on prepared sheets, 11 per sheet.

5. Bake cookies, 1 sheet at a time, until they are puffed and cracked and edges have begun to set but centers are still soft (cookies will look raw between cracks and seem underdone), about 12 minutes, rotating sheet halfway through baking. Let cookies cool on sheet for 5 minutes, then transfer to wire rack. Let cookies cool completely before serving.

Big and Chewy Oatmeal-Raisin Cookies

Makes 18 large cookies

WHY THIS RECIPE WORKS Big, moist, and craggy, oatmeal-raisin cookies are so good and so comforting, but also so hard to get just right. Too often, they have textural issues and other times the flavor is off, with cookies that lack any sign of oatiness. We wanted an oversize, chewy cookie with buttery oat flavor. After numerous rounds of testing, we discovered three key changes that made a significant difference in the research recipes we uncovered. First, we substituted baking powder for baking soda, which gave the dough more lift and made the cookies less dense and a bit chewier. Second, we eliminated the cinnamon recommended in lots of recipes; by taking away the cinnamon, we revealed more oat flavor. We wanted some spice, however, and chose nutmeg, which has a cleaner, subtler flavor that we like with oats. Finally, we increased the sugar in our cookies, and this made a huge difference in terms of texture and moistness. If you prefer a less sweet cookie, you can reduce the granulated sugar to ¾ cup, but you will lose some crispness. Do not overbake these cookies. The edges should be brown, but the rest of the cookie should be very light in color.

1½ cups (7½ ounces) all-purpose flour
½ teaspoon table salt
½ teaspoon baking powder
¼ teaspoon ground nutmeg
16 tablespoons unsalted butter, softened
1 cup packed (7 ounces) light brown sugar
1 cup (7 ounces) granulated sugar
2 large eggs
3 cups (9 ounces) old-fashioned oats
1½ cups raisins (optional)

1. Adjust oven racks to upper-middle and lower-middle positions and heat oven to 350 degrees. Line 2 baking sheets with parchment paper. Whisk flour, salt, baking powder, and nutmeg together in medium bowl; set aside.

2. In stand mixer fitted with paddle, beat butter, brown sugar, and granulated sugar at medium speed until light and fluffy, about 2 minutes. Add eggs, one at a time, and mix until combined, about 30 seconds.

3. Decrease speed to low and slowly add flour mixture until combined, about 30 seconds. Mix in oats and raisins (if using) until just incorporated.

4. Divide dough into 18 portions, each a generous 2 tablespoons, and roll them between your hands into balls about 2 inches in diameter. Place dough balls on prepared sheets, spacing them about 2 inches apart.

5. Bake, switching and rotating sheets halfway through baking time, until cookies turn golden brown around edges, 22 to 25 minutes. Let cookies cool on sheets for 2 minutes; using wide metal spatula, transfer cookies to wire rack and let cool to room temperature.

VARIATION
Big and Chewy Oatmeal-Date Cookies
Substitute 1½ cups chopped dates for raisins.

Chocolate-Chunk Oatmeal Cookies with Pecans and Dried Cherries

Makes 16 cookies

WHY THIS RECIPE WORKS Oatmeal cookies provide an ideal backdrop for almost any addition. But in pursuit of the ultimate oatmeal cookie, it's easy to lapse into a kitchen sink mentality, overloading the dough with a crazy jumble of ingredients. We wanted the perfect combination of oats, nuts, chocolate, and fruit in a superlatively chewy package. Bittersweet chocolate, dried sour cherries (or cranberries), and toasted pecans gave the right balance of flavors. We also analyzed the cookie dough ingredients and discovered that cookies made with brown sugar were moister and chewier than cookies made with granulated sugar. A combination of baking powder and baking soda (we doubled the usual amount) produced cookies that were light and crisp on the outside, but chewy, dense, and soft in the center. Finally, we focused on appearance to decide when to remove the cookies from the oven—they should be set but still look wet between the fissures; if they look matte rather than shiny, they've been overbaked. We like these cookies made with pecans and dried sour cherries, but walnuts or skinned hazelnuts can be substituted for the pecans, and dried cranberries for the cherries. Quick oats used in place of the old-fashioned oats will yield a cookie with slightly less chewiness. These cookies keep for four to five days stored in an airtight container or zipper-lock bag, but they will lose their crisp exterior and become uniformly chewy after a day or so. To recrisp the cookies, place them on a baking sheet and bake in a 425-degree oven for 4 to 5 minutes. Make sure to let the cookies cool on the baking sheet for a few minutes before removing them, and eat them while they're warm.

1¼ cups (6¼ ounces) all-purpose flour
¾ teaspoon baking powder
½ teaspoon baking soda
½ teaspoon table salt
1¼ cups (3¾ ounces) old-fashioned rolled oats
1 cup pecans, toasted and chopped
1 cup (4 ounces) dried sour cherries, chopped coarse
4 ounces bittersweet chocolate, chopped into chunks about size of chocolate chips
12 tablespoons unsalted butter, softened
1½ cups packed (10½ ounces) dark brown sugar
1 large egg
1 teaspoon vanilla extract

1. Adjust oven racks to upper-middle and lower-middle positions and heat oven to 350 degrees. Line 2 baking sheets with parchment paper. Whisk flour, baking powder, baking soda, and salt together in bowl. Stir oats, pecans, cherries, and chocolate together in second bowl.

2. Using stand mixer fitted with paddle, beat butter and sugar on medium speed until no sugar lumps remain, about 1 minute, scraping down bowl as needed. Reduce speed to medium-low, add egg and vanilla, and beat until fully incorporated, about 30 seconds, scraping down bowl as needed. Reduce speed to low, add flour mixture, and mix until just combined, about 30 seconds. Gradually add oat mixture until just incorporated. Give dough final stir by hand to ensure that no flour pockets remain and ingredients are evenly distributed.

3. Working with ¼ cup dough at a time, roll into balls and space them 2½ inches apart on prepared sheets. Using bottom of greased dry measuring cup, press each ball to 1-inch thickness.

4. Bake cookies until medium brown and edges have begun to set but centers are still soft (cookies will look raw between cracks and seem underdone), 20 to 22 minutes, switching and rotating sheets halfway through baking. Let cookies cool on sheets for 5 minutes, then transfer to wire rack. Let cookies cool completely before serving.

Peanut Butter Sandwich Cookies

Makes 24 cookies

WHY THIS RECIPE WORKS We love a thick, chewy peanut butter cookie, but we also have an undeniable soft spot for peanut butter sandwich cookies. Our ideal sandwich would feature thin, crunchy cookies and a smooth filling, both packed with peanut flavor—basically a Nutter Butter made better. The first task: giving the cookie rounds big flavor. In addition to the obvious inclusion of peanut butter in the dough, we cut a portion of the flour with finely chopped peanuts—a simple substitution that boosted flavor dramatically.

To make the cookies thin and crisp, we added some milk; the increased moisture made a thinner dough that spread more readily during baking. This was a great start, but baking soda took our intentions further. Adding a full teaspoon to the recipe encouraged air bubbles within the dough to inflate so rapidly that they burst before the cookies set, leaving the cookies flat. A creamy filling of peanut butter, confectioners' sugar, and butter tasted great but was too thick to spread without breaking the cookies. We didn't want to lose any peanut flavor in an effort to soften the filling, so we warmed the peanut butter and butter in the microwave to make the filling easy to sandwich. Do not use unsalted peanut butter. Take care when processing the peanuts—you want to chop them, not turn them into a paste.

Cookies
1¼ cups raw or dry-roasted peanuts, toasted and cooled
¾ cup (3¾ ounces) all-purpose flour
1 teaspoon baking soda
½ teaspoon table salt
3 tablespoons unsalted butter, melted
½ cup creamy peanut butter
½ cup (3½ ounces) granulated sugar
½ cup packed (3½ ounces) light brown sugar
3 tablespoons whole milk
1 large egg

Filling
¾ cup creamy peanut butter
3 tablespoons unsalted butter
1 cup (4 ounces) confectioners' sugar

1. *For the cookies:* Adjust oven racks to upper-middle and lower-middle positions and heat oven to 350 degrees. Line 2 baking sheets with parchment paper. Pulse peanuts in food processor until finely chopped, about 8 pulses. Whisk flour, baking soda, and salt together in bowl. Whisk melted butter, peanut butter, granulated sugar, brown sugar, milk, and egg together in second bowl. Using rubber spatula, stir flour mixture into peanut butter mixture until combined. Stir in chopped peanuts until evenly distributed.

2. Using 1 tablespoon measure or #60 scoop, drop 12 mounds evenly onto each prepared sheet. Using your dampened hand, press each mound until 2 inches in diameter.

3. Bake cookies until deep golden brown and firm to touch, 15 to 18 minutes, switching and rotating sheets halfway through baking. Let cookies cool on sheets for 5 minutes, then transfer to wire rack. Repeat with remaining dough. Let cookies cool completely.

4. *For the filling:* Microwave peanut butter and butter until melted and warm, about 40 seconds. Using rubber spatula, stir in confectioners' sugar until combined.

5. Place 1 tablespoon (or #60 scoop) warm filling in center of bottom of half of cookies, then top with remaining cookies, pressing gently until filling spreads to edges. Let filling set for 1 hour before serving.

VARIATIONS

Peanut Butter Sandwich Cookies with Honey-Cinnamon Filling

Omit butter from filling. Stir 5 tablespoons honey and ½ teaspoon ground cinnamon into warm peanut butter before adding confectioners' sugar.

Peanut Butter Sandwich Cookies with Milk Chocolate Filling

Reduce peanut butter to ½ cup and omit butter from filling. Stir 6 ounces finely chopped milk chocolate into warm peanut butter until melted, microwaving for 10 seconds at a time if necessary, before adding confectioners' sugar.

Filling Cookies Evenly

1. Using #60 scoop or tablespoon measure, portion warm filling onto bottom cookies (turned upside down).

2. Rather than spreading filling with knife or offset spatula, top bottom cookie with second cookie and press gently until filling spreads to edges.

Gingersnaps

Makes 80 cookies

WHY THIS RECIPE WORKS We wanted to put the "snap" back in gingersnap cookies. This meant creating a cookie that not only breaks cleanly in half and crunches satisfyingly with every bite but also has an assertive ginger flavor and heat. The key to texture was reducing the moisture in the final baked cookie. We achieved this by reducing the amount of sugar (which holds on to moisture), increasing the baking soda (which created cracks in the dough where more moisture could escape), and lowering the oven temperature (which increased the baking time). For flavor we doubled the normal amount of dried ginger but also added fresh ginger, black pepper, and cayenne to ensure that our cookies had real "snap." For the best results, use fresh spices. For efficiency, form the second batch of cookies while the first batch bakes. The 2 teaspoons of baking soda are essential to getting the right texture.

2½ cups (12½ ounces) all-purpose flour
 2 teaspoons baking soda
 ½ teaspoon table salt
12 tablespoons unsalted butter
 2 tablespoons ground ginger
 1 teaspoon ground cinnamon
 ¼ teaspoon ground cloves
 ¼ teaspoon pepper
     Pinch cayenne pepper
1¼ cups packed (8¾ ounces) dark brown sugar
 ¼ cup molasses
 2 tablespoons finely grated fresh ginger
 1 large egg plus 1 large yolk
 ½ cup granulated sugar

1. Whisk flour, baking soda, and salt together in bowl; set aside.

2. Melt butter in 10-inch skillet over medium heat. Reduce heat to medium-low and continue to cook, swirling skillet frequently, until butter is just beginning to brown, 2 to 4 minutes. Transfer browned butter to large bowl and whisk in ground ginger, cinnamon, cloves, pepper, and cayenne. Let cool slightly, about 2 minutes.

3. Whisk brown sugar, molasses, and fresh ginger into butter mixture until combined. Whisk in egg and yolk until combined. Stir in flour mixture until just combined. Cover bowl tightly with plastic wrap and refrigerate until dough is firm, about 1 hour. (Dough can be refrigerated for up to 2 days or frozen for up to 1 month. Let frozen dough thaw overnight in refrigerator before proceeding with recipe. Let dough stand at room temperature for 30 minutes before shaping.)

4. Adjust oven racks to upper-middle and lower-middle positions and heat oven to 300 degrees. Line 2 baking sheets with parchment paper. Spread granulated sugar in shallow dish. Divide dough into heaping teaspoon portions; roll dough into 1-inch balls. Working in batches of 10, roll balls in sugar to coat; space dough balls evenly on prepared sheets, 20 dough balls per sheet.

5. Place 1 sheet on upper rack and bake for 15 minutes. Transfer partially baked top sheet to lower rack, rotating sheet, and place second sheet of dough balls on upper rack. Continue to bake until cookies on lower sheet just begin to darken around edges, 10 to 12 minutes longer. Remove lower sheet of cookies and transfer upper sheet to lower rack, rotating sheet; continue to bake until cookies begin to darken around edges, 15 to 17 minutes longer.

6. Slide baked cookies, still on parchment, onto wire rack and let cool completely before serving. Repeat with remaining dough balls. (Cooled cookies can be stored at room temperature for up to 2 weeks.)

Belgian Spice Cookies (Speculoos)

SEASON 20 RECIPE

Makes 32 cookies

WHY THIS RECIPE WORKS The enthusiasm for these humble cookies is understandable: *Speculoos* boast warm spice notes, nuanced caramel flavor, and a crisp, open texture that crumbles easily. Imagine something between a delicate graham cracker and a hard gingersnap that nearly melts in your mouth. The widely available packaged version of these Belgian treats, Biscoff cookies, gained a huge following when Delta Airlines started giving them away during flights. We aimed to create a homemade version that mimicked their caramel taste but improved the spice flavor. To achieve the appropriate texture, we rolled the dough thin so it would bake up dry and crisp, used only enough sugar to lightly sweeten the dough since sugar is hygroscopic and makes cookies moist, and added baking powder along with the usual baking soda to produce an open, airy crumb. For a subtle caramel taste, we chose turbinado sugar rather than molasses-based brown sugar or traditional (but hard-to-find) Belgian brown sugar. To nail the spice flavor, we used a large amount of cinnamon along with small amounts of cardamom and cloves for complexity. For the proper flavor, we strongly recommend using turbinado sugar (commonly sold as Sugar in the Raw). If you can't find it, use ¾ cup plus 2 tablespoons (6 ounces) of packed light brown sugar and skip the sugar grinding in step 2. In step 3, use a rolling pin and a combination of rolling

and a smearing motion to form the rectangle. If the dough spreads beyond the rectangle, trim it and use the scraps to fill in the corners; then, replace the parchment and continue to roll. Do not use cookie molds or an embossed rolling pin for the speculoos; they will not hold decorations.

1½ cups (7½ ounces) all-purpose flour
5 teaspoons ground cinnamon
1 teaspoon ground cardamom
¼ teaspoon ground cloves
¼ teaspoon baking soda
¼ teaspoon baking powder
¼ teaspoon table salt
¾ cup (6 ounces) turbinado sugar
8 tablespoons unsalted butter, cut into ½-inch pieces and chilled
1 large egg

1. Whisk flour, cinnamon, cardamom, cloves, baking soda, baking powder, and salt together in bowl. Using pencil and ruler, draw 10 by 12-inch rectangle in center of each of 2 large sheets of parchment paper, crisscrossing lines at corners. (Use crisscrosses to help line up top and bottom sheets as dough is rolled.)

2. Process sugar in food processor for 30 seconds (some grains will be smaller than granulated sugar; others will be larger). Add butter and process until uniform mass forms and no large pieces of butter are visible, about 30 seconds, scraping down sides of bowl as needed. Add egg and process until smooth and paste-like, about 10 seconds, scraping down sides of bowl as needed. Add flour mixture and process until no dry flour remains but mixture remains crumbly, about 30 seconds, scraping down sides of bowl as needed.

3. Transfer dough to bowl and knead gently with spatula until uniform and smooth, about 10 seconds. Place 1 piece of parchment on counter with pencil side facing down (you should be able to see rectangle through paper). Place dough in center of marked rectangle and press into 6 by 9-inch rectangle. Place second sheet of parchment over dough, with pencil side facing up, so dough is in center of marked rectangle. Using pencil marks as guide, use rolling pin and bench scraper to shape dough into 10 by 12-inch rectangle of even ⅜-inch thickness. Transfer dough with parchment to rimmed baking sheet. Refrigerate until dough is firm, at least 1½ hours (or freeze for 30 minutes). (Rolled dough can be wrapped in plastic wrap and refrigerated for up to 5 days.)

4. Adjust oven racks to upper-middle and lower-middle positions and heat oven to 300 degrees. Line 2 rimless baking sheets with parchment. Transfer chilled dough to counter. Gently peel off top layer of parchment from dough. Using fluted pastry wheel (or sharp knife or pizza cutter) and ruler, trim off rounded edges of dough that extend over marked edges of 10 by 12-inch rectangle. Cut dough lengthwise into 8 equal strips about 1¼ inches wide. Cut each strip crosswise into 4 equal pieces about 3 inches long. Transfer cookies to prepared sheets, spacing them at least ½ inch apart. Bake until cookies are lightly and evenly browned, 30 to 32 minutes, switching and rotating sheets halfway through baking. Let cookies cool completely on sheets, about 20 minutes. (Cookies can be stored at room temperature for up to 3 weeks.)

Triple-Coconut Macaroons

Makes 48 cookies

WHY THIS RECIPE WORKS Not that long ago, macaroons (cone-shaped cookies flavored with shredded coconut) were quite elegant and very popular. But today, they have deteriorated into lackluster mounds of beaten egg whites and coconut shreds or, at their worst, nothing more than a baked mixture of condensed milk and sweetened coconut. We set out to create a great coconut macaroon, with a pleasing texture and real, honest coconut flavor. When we began looking at recipes for modern coconut macaroons, we found that they varied widely, some calling for vanilla or almond extract in addition to different kinds of coconut and sweeteners. We knew that narrowing the field when it came to the coconut and other flavorings would make a big difference in both taste and texture. After rounds of testing, we determined that unsweetened shredded coconut resulted in a less sticky, more appealing texture. But sweetened shredded coconut packed more flavor than the unsweetened coconut, so we decided to use both; together they worked very well in the cookie. To add one more layer of coconut flavor, we tried cream of coconut and hit the jackpot. As for the structure of our cookie, a few egg whites and some corn syrup ensured

that the macaroons held together well and were moist and pleasantly chewy. Cream of coconut, available canned, is a very sweet product commonly used in piña colada cocktails. Be sure to mix the can's contents thoroughly before using, as the mixture separates upon standing. Unsweetened desiccated coconut is commonly sold in natural foods stores and Asian markets. If you are unable to find any, use all sweetened flaked or shredded coconut, but reduce the amount of cream of coconut to ½ cup, omit the corn syrup, and toss 2 tablespoons cake flour with the coconut before adding the liquid ingredients. For larger macaroons, shape haystacks from a generous ¼ cup of batter and increase the baking time to 20 minutes.

- 1 cup cream of coconut
- 4 large egg whites
- 2 tablespoons light corn syrup
- 2 teaspoons vanilla extract
- ½ teaspoon table salt
- 3 cups (9 ounces) unsweetened shredded coconut
- 3 cups (9 ounces) sweetened shredded coconut

1. Adjust oven racks to upper-middle and lower-middle positions and heat oven to 375 degrees. Line 2 baking sheets with parchment paper.

2. Whisk cream of coconut, egg whites, corn syrup, vanilla, and salt together in bowl; set aside. Toss unsweetened coconut and sweetened coconut together in large bowl, breaking up clumps with your fingertips. Pour cream of coconut mixture over coconut and mix until evenly moistened; transfer bowl to refrigerator for 15 minutes.

3. Drop 1-tablespoon mounds of dough onto prepared sheets, spacing them 1 inch apart. Using your moistened fingertips, form dough into loose haystacks. Bake until light golden brown, about 15 minutes, switching and rotating sheets halfway through baking.

4. Let cookies cool on sheets until slightly set, about 2 minutes, then transfer cookies to wire rack and let cool completely before serving.

VARIATION
Chocolate-Dipped Triple-Coconut Macaroons
Let baked macaroons cool completely. Line 2 baking sheets with parchment paper. Chop 10 ounces semisweet chocolate. Microwave 8 ounces chocolate at 50 percent power, stirring occasionally, until melted, 2 to 4 minutes. Remove melted chocolate from microwave and stir in remaining 2 ounces chocolate until smooth. Holding macaroon by pointed top, dip bottom ½ inch up sides in chocolate, scrape off excess, and place macaroon on prepared baking sheet. Repeat with remaining macaroons. Refrigerate until chocolate sets, about 15 minutes, before serving.

Chocolate-Dipped
Triple-Coconut Macaroons

Sablés (French Butter Cookies)

Makes 40 cookies

WHY THIS RECIPE WORKS During the holidays, these French butter cookies offer sophistication and style. That is, if you can capture their elusive sandy texture (*sablé* is French for "sandy"), which separates them from sturdy American butter cookies. They are often made as icebox cookies, in which the dough is shaped into a log, chilled, sliced into rounds and baked, so there's no need to fuss with cookie cutters. And because they are delicate and refined, they require only a sprinkle of sugar to be ready for the holiday table. Most of the sablé recipes we came across had only slight differences in ingredient proportions—but they all baked up without the delicate crumbliness that defines this cookie. To create the hallmark sandy texture of sablés—light, with an inviting granular quality similar to shortbread—we would have to do some detective work. We started with a basic recipe using the typical method of creaming butter and sugar, then adding egg and flour. We found that we needed to decrease the liquid in the dough so there would be less moisture to dissolve the sugar particles. Cutting back on butter helped, as did the inclusion of a hard-cooked egg yolk, an addition we came across in our research. Adding the mashed yolk during creaming eliminated moisture and perfected the texture of the cookies. Brushing the cookies with a beaten egg white and sprinkling them with coarse sugar before baking added a delicate crunch and an attractive sparkle. Turbinado sugar is commonly sold as Sugar in the Raw. Demerara sugar, sanding sugar, or another coarse sugar can be substituted. Make sure the cookie dough is well chilled and firm so that it can be uniformly sliced.

- 1 large egg, plus 1 large white lightly beaten with 1 teaspoon water
- 10 tablespoons unsalted butter, softened
- ⅓ cup plus 1 tablespoon (2¾ ounces) granulated sugar
- ¼ teaspoon table salt
- 1 teaspoon vanilla extract
- 1½ cups (7½ ounces) all-purpose flour
- 4 teaspoons turbinado sugar

1. Place whole egg in small saucepan, cover with 1 inch water, and bring to boil over high heat. Remove pan from heat, cover, and let sit for 10 minutes. Meanwhile, fill small bowl halfway with ice and water. Using slotted spoon, transfer egg to ice bath and let stand for 5 minutes. Crack egg and peel shell. Separate yolk from white; discard white. Press yolk through fine-mesh strainer into small bowl.

2. Using stand mixer fitted with paddle, beat butter, granulated sugar, salt, and cooked egg yolk on medium speed until light and fluffy, about 4 minutes, scraping down bowl as needed. Reduce speed to low, add vanilla, and mix until incorporated. Turn off mixer. Add flour and mix on low speed until just combined, about 30 seconds. Using rubber spatula, press dough into cohesive mass.

3. Divide dough in half and roll each half into log about 6 inches long and 1¾ inches in diameter. Wrap each log in 12-inch square of parchment paper and twist ends to seal and firmly compact dough into tight cylinder. Refrigerate until firm, about 1 hour. (After the dough has been wrapped in parchment, it can be double-wrapped in plastic wrap and frozen for up to 2 weeks.)

4. Adjust oven racks to upper-middle and lower-middle positions and heat oven to 350 degrees. Line 2 rimmed baking sheets with parchment. Using chef's knife, slice dough into ¼-inch-thick rounds, rotating dough so that it won't become misshapen from weight of knife. Space cookies 1 inch apart on prepared sheets. Using pastry brush, gently brush cookies with egg white mixture and sprinkle evenly with turbinado sugar.

5. Bake until centers are pale golden brown with edges slightly darker than centers, about 15 minutes, switching and rotating sheets halfway through baking. Let cookies cool on sheets for 5 minutes, then transfer to wire rack. Let cookies cool completely before serving. (Cookies can be stored between parchment for up to 1 week.)

VARIATIONS
Chocolate Sablés

Reduce flour to 1⅓ cups and add ¼ cup Dutch-processed cocoa with flour.

Black and White Spiral Cookies
Makes 80 cookies

Follow recipes for Sablés and Chocolate Sablés through step 2, omitting egg white mixture and turbinado sugar. Halve each batch of dough; roll out each on parchment into 8 by 6-inch rectangle, ¼ inch thick. Briefly chill dough until firm enough to handle. Using bench scraper, place 1 plain dough rectangle on top of 1 chocolate dough rectangle. Repeat to make 2 double rectangles. Roll out each double rectangle on parchment into 9 by 6-inch rectangle. Starting at long end, roll each into tight log. Twist ends of parchment to seal. Chill logs for 1 hour. Slice logs into ¼-inch-thick rounds and bake as directed.

Chocolate Sandwich Cookies

In step 4, slice 1 dough log into ⅛-inch-thick rounds; omit egg white mixture and turbinado sugar. Bake cookies as directed, reducing baking time to 10 to 13 minutes. Repeat with second dough log. When all cookies are completely cool, melt 3½ ounces dark or milk chocolate and cool slightly. Spread melted chocolate on bottom of one cookie. Place second cookie on top, slightly off-center, so some chocolate shows. Repeat with remaining melted chocolate and cookies.

Vanilla Pretzel Cookies

Increase vanilla extract to 1 tablespoon and reduce chilling time to 30 minutes (dough will not be fully hardened). Slice dough into ¼-inch-thick rounds and roll into balls. Roll each ball into 6-inch rope, tapering ends. Form ropes into pretzel shapes. Proceed with recipe, brushing with egg white mixture, sprinkling with turbinado sugar, and baking as directed.

Forming Spiral Cookies

1. Halve each batch of dough. Roll out each portion on parchment paper into 8 by 6-inch rectangle, ¼ inch thick. Briefly chill dough until firm enough to handle.

2. Using bench scraper, place 1 plain cookie dough rectangle on top of 1 chocolate dough rectangle. Repeat to make 2 double rectangles.

3. Roll out each double rectangle on parchment into 9 by 6-inch rectangle (if too firm, let rest until malleable). Starting at long end, roll each into tight log.

4. Twist ends of parchment to seal. Chill logs for 1 hour. Slice logs into ¼-inch-thick rounds.

Forming Pretzel Cookies

1. Slice slightly chilled dough into ¼-inch-thick rounds and roll into balls.

2. Roll each ball into 6-inch rope, tapering ends.

3. Pick up 1 end of rope and cross it over to form half of pretzel shape.

4. Bring second end over to complete pretzel shape.

"This sugar cookie recipe, which rolls out the dough immediately after mixing, is the best—hands down. It's downright rebellious, and I can imagine old-school bakers shaking their heads at the reversed method of rolling before chilling. But this makes the dough a dream to work with so that anyone, even my young daughter, can roll it out with ease. Plus, if you use cookie cutters, the shape stays true during baking. And the cookies are tender without being overly sweet, so that they're still edible after being glazed and decorated."

–*Julia*

Easy Holiday Sugar Cookies

Makes forty 2½-inch cookies

WHY THIS RECIPE WORKS Our holiday roll-and-cut sugar cookies are as good to eat as they are easy to make. For a crisp and sturdy texture with no hint of graininess, we made superfine sugar by grinding granulated sugar briefly in the food processor, and we added small amounts of baking powder and baking soda to the dough. A touch of almond extract, added along with the usual vanilla, made these cookies taste more interesting without giving them overt almond flavor. We skipped creaming softened butter and sugar in favor of whizzing cold butter with sugar in the food processor, which let the dough come together in just minutes. The just-made dough was cold enough to be rolled out immediately, and we chilled it after rolling. For an even, golden color; minimal browning; and a crisp, crunchy texture from edge to edge, we baked the cookies at a gentle 300 degrees on a rimless cookie sheet (to promote air circulation) on the oven's lower-middle rack. For the dough to have the proper consistency when rolling, make sure to use cold butter directly from the refrigerator. In step 3, use a rolling pin and a combination of rolling and a pushing or smearing motion to form the soft dough into an oval. A rimless cookie sheet helps achieve evenly baked cookies; if you do not have one, use an over-turned rimmed baking sheet. Dough scraps can be combined and rerolled once, though the cookies will be slightly less tender. If desired, stir 1 or 2 drops of food coloring into the icing. For a pourable icing, whisk in milk, 1 teaspoon at a time, until the desired consistency is reached. You can also decorate the shapes with sanding sugar or sprinkles before baking.

Cookies
- 1 large egg
- 1 teaspoon vanilla extract
- ¾ teaspoon table salt
- ¼ teaspoon almond extract
- 2½ cups (12½ ounces) all-purpose flour
- ¼ teaspoon baking powder
- ¼ teaspoon baking soda
- 1 cup (7 ounces) granulated sugar
- 16 tablespoons unsalted butter, cut into ½-inch pieces and chilled

Royal Icing
- 2⅔ cups (10⅔ ounces) confectioners' sugar
- 2 large egg whites
- ½ teaspoon vanilla extract
- ⅛ teaspoon table salt

1. For the cookies: Whisk egg, vanilla, salt, and almond extract together in small bowl. Whisk flour, baking powder, and baking soda together in second bowl.

2. Process sugar in food processor until finely ground, about 30 seconds. Add butter and process until uniform mass forms and no large pieces of butter are visible, about 30 seconds, scraping down sides of bowl as needed. Add egg mixture and process until smooth and paste-like, about 10 seconds. Add flour mixture and process until no dry flour remains but mixture remains crumbly, about 30 seconds, scraping down sides of bowl as needed.

3. Turn out dough onto counter and knead gently by hand until smooth, about 10 seconds. Divide dough in half. Place 1 piece of dough in center of large sheet of parchment paper and press into 7 by 9-inch oval. Place second large sheet of parchment over dough and roll dough into 10 by 14-inch oval of even ⅛-inch thickness. Transfer dough with parchment to rimmed baking sheet. Repeat pressing and rolling with second piece of dough, then stack on top of first piece on sheet. Refrigerate until dough is firm, at least 1½ hours (or freeze for 30 minutes). (Rolled dough can be wrapped in plastic wrap and refrigerated for up to 5 days.)

4. Adjust oven rack to lower-middle position and heat oven to 300 degrees. Line rimless cookie sheet with parchment. Working with 1 piece of rolled dough, gently peel off top layer of parchment. Replace parchment, loosely covering dough. (Peeling off parchment and returning it will make cutting and removing cookies easier.) Turn over dough and parchment and gently peel off and discard second piece of parchment. Using cookie cutter, cut dough into shapes. Transfer shapes to prepared cookie sheet, spacing them about ½ inch apart. Bake until cookies are lightly and evenly browned around edges, 14 to 17 minutes, rotating sheet halfway through baking. Let cookies cool on sheet for 5 minutes. Using wide metal spatula, transfer cookies to wire rack and let cool completely. Repeat cutting and baking with remaining dough. (Dough scraps can be patted together, rerolled, and chilled once before cutting and baking.)

5. For the royal icing: Using stand mixer fitted with whisk, whip all ingredients on medium-low speed until combined, about 1 minute. Increase speed to medium-high and whip until glossy, soft peaks form, 3 to 4 minutes, scraping down bowl as needed.

6. Spread icing onto cooled cookies. Let icing dry completely, about 1½ hours, before serving.

VARIATION

Easy Holiday Cocoa Sugar Cookies

Reduce vanilla extract to ½ teaspoon and substitute 1½ teaspoons espresso powder for almond extract. Add ⅓ cup Dutch-processed cocoa powder to flour mixture in step 1.

Pecan or Walnut Crescent Cookies

Makes 48 cookies

WHY THIS RECIPE WORKS When nut crescent cookies are well made, they can be delicious: buttery, nutty, slightly crisp, slightly crumbly, with a melt-in-your-mouth quality. Too often, however, they turn out bland and dry. We wanted to develop a recipe that would put them back in their proper place. The ratio of 1 cup butter to 2 cups flour in almost all of the recipes we looked at is what worked for us. We tried three kinds of sugar in the batter: granulated, confectioners', and superfine. The last resulted in just what we wanted: cookies that melted in our mouths. In determining the amount, we had to remember that the cookies would be sweetened once more by their traditional coating of confectioners' sugar. Before rolling them, we let the cookies cool to room temperature; coating them with sugar while still warm results in the pasty outer layer we wanted to avoid. If you cannot find superfine sugar, you can obtain a close approximation by processing regular granulated sugar in a food processor for about 30 seconds. If you don't have a food processor, you can finely grind the chopped nuts by rolling them between two large sheets of plastic wrap with a rolling pin, applying moderate pressure, until broken down to a coarse cornmeal-like texture.

- 2 cups (10 ounces) all-purpose flour
- 2 cups pecans or walnuts, chopped fine, divided
- ½ teaspoon table salt
- 16 tablespoons unsalted butter, softened
- ⅓ cup (2⅓ ounces) superfine sugar
- 1½ teaspoons vanilla extract
- 1½ cups confectioners' sugar

1. Adjust oven racks to upper-middle and lower-middle positions and heat oven to 325 degrees. Line 2 baking sheets with parchment paper.

2. Whisk flour, 1 cup pecans, and salt together in medium bowl; set aside. Process remaining 1 cup pecans in food processor until they are texture of coarse cornmeal, 10 to 15 seconds (do not overprocess). Stir pecans into flour mixture; set aside.

3. Using stand mixer fitted with paddle, beat butter and superfine sugar on medium-low speed until pale and fluffy, about 2 minutes; add vanilla, scraping down bowl as needed. Add flour mixture and beat on low speed until dough just begins to come together but still looks scrappy, about 15 seconds. Scrape down bowl as needed and continue to beat until dough is cohesive, 6 to 9 seconds (do not overbeat).

4. Working with 1 tablespoon dough at a time, roll into balls. Roll each ball of dough between your palms into rope that measures 3 inches long. Space ropes 1 inch apart on prepared sheets and turn ends to form crescent shape. Bake until tops of cookies are pale golden and bottoms are just beginning to brown, 17 to 19 minutes, switching and rotating sheets halfway through baking.

5. Let cookies cool on sheets for 2 minutes, then transfer cookies to wire rack and let cool completely. Spread confectioners' sugar in shallow dish. Working with 3 or 4 cookies at a time, roll cookies in sugar to coat thoroughly; gently tap off excess. (Cookies can be stored at room temperature for up to 5 days.) When ready to serve, reroll cookies in confectioners' sugar to ensure thick coating and gently tap off excess.

VARIATION

Almond or Hazelnut Crescent Cookies

Almonds can be used raw for cookies that are light in both color and flavor or toasted to enhance the almond flavor and darken the crescents.

Follow recipe for Pecan or Walnut Crescent Cookies, substituting 1¾ cups whole blanched almonds (toasted, if desired) or 2 cups toasted, skinned hazelnuts for pecans or walnuts. If using almonds, add ½ teaspoon almond extract along with vanilla extract.

Almond Biscotti

Makes 30 cookies

WHY THIS RECIPE WORKS Biscotti means "twice-baked"; the dough is formed into a loaf and baked and then sliced on the bias into planks, which are returned to the oven to dry. The result: nutty cookies that are perfect alongside coffee or a glass of vin santo. Italians like their biscotti dry and hard, whereas Americans tend to favor a buttery, tender version. We wanted a cookie that fell in between, one that had plenty of crunch but wasn't tooth-breaking. Batches of biscotti made with little (or no) fat were rocks, while doughs enriched with a full stick of butter baked up too soft. Four tablespoons of butter struck just the right balance, for a cookie that was both crunchy and tender. Whipping the eggs before adding the other ingredients provided lift, and swapping out ¼ cup of flour for an equal amount of ground almonds made the cookies more tender by breaking up the crumb and interrupting gluten development. The almonds will continue to toast during baking, so toast them just until they're fragrant.

1¼ cups whole almonds, lightly toasted, divided
1¾ cups (8¾ ounces) all-purpose flour
2 teaspoons baking powder
¼ teaspoon table salt
2 large eggs, plus 1 large white beaten with pinch salt
1 cup (7 ounces) sugar
4 tablespoons unsalted butter, melted and cooled
1½ teaspoons almond extract
½ teaspoon vanilla extract
Vegetable oil spray

1. Adjust oven rack to middle position and heat oven to 325 degrees. Using ruler and pencil, draw two 8 by 3-inch rectangles, spaced 4 inches apart, on piece of parchment paper. Grease baking sheet and place parchment on it, marked side down.

2. Pulse 1 cup almonds in food processor until coarsely chopped, 8 to 10 pulses; transfer to bowl and set aside. Process remaining ¼ cup almonds in food processor until finely ground, about 45 seconds. Add flour, baking powder, and salt; process to combine, about 15 seconds. Transfer flour mixture to second bowl. Process 2 eggs in now-empty food processor until lightened in color and almost doubled in volume, about 3 minutes. With processor running, slowly add sugar until thoroughly combined, about 15 seconds. Add melted butter, almond extract, and vanilla and process until combined, about 10 seconds. Transfer egg mixture to medium bowl. Sprinkle half of flour mixture over egg mixture and, using spatula, gently fold until just combined. Add remaining flour mixture and chopped almonds and gently fold until just combined.

3. Divide batter in half. Using your floured hands, form each half into 8 by 3-inch rectangle, using lines on parchment as guide. Spray each loaf lightly with oil spray. Using rubber spatula lightly coated with oil spray, smooth tops and sides of rectangles. Gently brush tops of loaves with egg white wash. Bake until loaves are golden and just beginning to crack on top, 25 to 30 minutes, rotating pan halfway through baking.

4. Let loaves cool on baking sheet for 30 minutes. Transfer loaves to cutting board. Using serrated knife, slice each loaf on slight bias into ½-inch-thick slices. Lay slices, cut side down, about ¼ inch apart on wire rack set in rimmed baking sheet. Bake until crisp and golden brown on both sides, about 35 minutes, flipping slices halfway through baking. Let cool completely before serving. (Biscotti can be stored in airtight container for up to 1 month.)

VARIATIONS
Anise Biscotti
Add 1½ teaspoons anise seeds to flour mixture in step 2. Substitute anise-flavored liqueur for almond extract.

Hazelnut-Orange Biscotti
Substitute lightly toasted and skinned hazelnuts for almonds. Add 2 tablespoons finely chopped fresh rosemary to flour mixture in step 2. Substitute orange-flavored liqueur for almond extract and add 1 tablespoon grated orange zest to egg mixture with butter.

Hazelnut-Lavender Biscotti
Substitute lightly toasted and skinned hazelnuts for almonds. Add 2 teaspoons dried lavender flowers to flour mixture in step 2. Substitute 1½ teaspoons water for almond extract and add 2 tablespoons grated lemon zest to egg mixture with butter.

Pistachio-Spice Biscotti
Substitute shelled pistachios for almonds. Add 1 teaspoon ground cardamom, ½ teaspoon ground cloves, ½ teaspoon pepper, ¼ teaspoon ground cinnamon, and ¼ teaspoon ground ginger to flour mixture in step 2. Substitute 1 teaspoon water for almond extract and increase vanilla extract to 1 teaspoon.

Browned Butter Blondies

Makes 24 blondies

WHY THIS RECIPE WORKS There is a reason people go crazy for blondies: the best ones are moist, chewy, complex, butterscotchy, and not too sweet. We learned quickly that making a great blondie would take some finessing. First up was the mixing method. Blondie recipes typically call either for creaming butter and sugar and then adding the eggs and dry ingredients or for mixing melted butter with the sugar and eggs before incorporating the dry ingredients. Since creaming the butter and sugar incorporates air that results in a cakey texture, we settled on the second method, which leads to a denser, chewier bar. But our biggest breakthrough was finding that instead of just melting the butter, browning it boosted the underlying toffee notes of our bars. Next order of business: boosting butterscotch flavor. Most blondie recipes call for light brown sugar, and we wondered if using dark brown sugar instead would help just a little. Interestingly, most tasters panned the dark brown sugar for making the blondies taste more like molasses than butterscotch. So we stuck with light brown sugar, and to tone down the sweetness we replaced a portion of it with corn syrup, which is actually less sweet. Vanilla extract played a key role too: A whopping 2 tablespoons deepened the warm caramel flavors in the bars enormously. A generous amount of salt in the batter and flaky sea salt sprinkled on top brought all the flavors into sharp focus. Chopped pecans and milk chocolate chips complemented the butterscotch flavor without overwhelming it. We developed this recipe using a metal baking pan; using a glass baking dish may cause the blondies to overbake. Toast the pecans on a rimmed baking sheet in a 350-degree oven until fragrant, 8 to 12 minutes, stirring them halfway through.

2¼ cups (11¼ ounces) all-purpose flour
1¼ teaspoons table salt
½ teaspoon baking powder
12 tablespoons unsalted butter
1¾ cups packed (12¼ ounces) light brown sugar
3 large eggs
½ cup corn syrup
2 tablespoons vanilla extract
1 cup pecans, toasted and chopped
½ cup (3 ounces) milk chocolate chips
¼–½ teaspoon flake sea salt, crumbled (optional)

1. Adjust oven rack to middle position and heat oven to 350 degrees. Make foil sling for 13 by 9-inch baking pan by folding 2 long sheets of aluminum foil; first sheet should be 13 inches wide and second sheet should be 9 inches wide. Lay sheets of foil in pan perpendicular to each other, with extra foil hanging over edges of pan. Push foil into corners and up sides of pan, smoothing foil flush to pan. Grease foil.

2. Whisk flour, table salt, and baking powder together in medium bowl.

3. Heat butter in 10-inch skillet over medium-high heat until melted, about 2 minutes. Continue to cook, swirling skillet and stirring constantly with rubber spatula, until butter is dark golden brown and has nutty aroma, 1 to 3 minutes. Remove skillet from heat and transfer browned butter to large heatproof bowl.

4. Add sugar to hot butter and whisk until combined. Add eggs, corn syrup, and vanilla and whisk until smooth. Using rubber spatula, stir in flour mixture until fully incorporated. Stir in pecans and chocolate chips. Transfer batter to prepared pan; using spatula, spread batter into corners of pan and smooth surface. Sprinkle with sea salt, if using. Bake until top is deep golden brown and springs backs when lightly pressed, 35 to 40 minutes, rotating pan halfway through baking (blondies will firm as they cool).

5. Let blondies cool completely in pan on wire rack, about 2 hours. Using foil overhang, lift blondies out of pan and transfer to cutting board. Remove foil. Cut into 24 bars. (Blondies can be wrapped tightly in plastic wrap and stored at room temperature for up to 5 days.)

Chewy Brownies

Makes 24 brownies

WHY THIS RECIPE WORKS Brownies are a tricky business: Homemade recipes have better flavor, while boxed mixes claim best texture. Our goal was clear: a homemade brownie with chewiness to rival the boxed-mix standard—but flush with a rich, deep chocolate flavor. Boxed brownie mixes derive their chewy texture from the right combination of saturated (solid) and unsaturated (liquid) fats. Unsaturated vegetable oil and powdered solid fat combine in a ratio designed to deliver maximum chew. To get the same chew at home, we tested and tested until we finally homed in on the ratio that produced the chewiest brownie. By using both butter (a predominently saturated fat) and unsaturated vegetable oil, we were able to approximate the same 1:3 ratio found in commercially engineered specimens to mimic their satisfying chew. To combat greasiness, we replaced some of the oil with egg yolks, whose emulsifiers prevented fat from separating and leaking out during baking. We focused on flavor next. Because unsweetened chocolate contains a similar ratio of saturated and unsaturated fat to butter, we could replace some of the butter with unsweetened chocolate, thereby providing more chocolate flavor. Espresso powder improved the chocolate taste as well. And finally, folding in bittersweet chocolate

"I have to admit I was concerned when we started development of this recipe. Given that we already had a blondie recipe in the ATK archives, I was dubious that we could improve upon what was a really great recipe. I was wrong. The first improvement we made was to replace some of the sugar with corn syrup. The corn syrup upped the chewiness, but also made the bars less sweet, which is also a bonus. A healthy dose of vanilla and a sprinkle of coarse sea salt on the top gave them a more sophisticated flavor. But my favorite improvement was the browned butter. In addition to adding a complex nutty flavor, the melted butter helped to create a dense, chewy texture, a texture that beats any blondie recipe— even ours."

—Keith

chunks just before baking gave our chewy, fudgy brownies gooey pockets of melted chocolate and rounded out their complex chocolate flavor. For an accurate measurement of boiling water, bring a full kettle of water to a boil, then measure out the desired amount. For the chewiest texture, it is important to let the brownies cool thoroughly before cutting. If your baking dish is glass, cool the brownies for 10 minutes, then remove them promptly from the pan (otherwise, the superior heat retention of glass can lead to overbaking). While any high-quality chocolate can be used, our preferred brands of bittersweet chocolate are Callebaut Intense Dark Chocolate and Ghirardelli Bittersweet Chocolate. Our preferred brand of unsweetened chocolate is Baker's.

⅓ cup (1 ounce) Dutch-processed cocoa powder
1½ teaspoons instant espresso powder (optional)
½ cup plus 2 tablespoons boiling water
2 ounces unsweetened chocolate, chopped fine
½ cup plus 2 tablespoons vegetable oil
4 tablespoons unsalted butter, melted
2 large eggs plus 2 large yolks
2 teaspoons vanilla extract
2½ cups (17½ ounces) sugar
1¾ cups (8¾ ounces) all-purpose flour
¾ teaspoon table salt
6 ounces bittersweet chocolate, cut into ½-inch pieces

1. Adjust oven rack to lowest position and heat oven to 350 degrees. Make foil sling for 13 by 9-inch baking pan by folding 2 long sheets of aluminum foil; first sheet should be 13 inches wide and second sheet should be 9 inches wide. Lay sheets of foil in pan perpendicular to each other, with extra foil hanging over edges of pan. Push foil into corners and up sides of pan, smoothing foil flush to pan. Grease foil.

2. Whisk cocoa; espresso powder, if using; and boiling water in large bowl until smooth. Add unsweetened chocolate and whisk until chocolate is melted. Whisk in oil and melted butter. (Mixture may look curdled.) Whisk in eggs and yolks and vanilla until smooth and homogeneous. Whisk in sugar until fully incorporated. Using rubber spatula, stir in flour and salt until combined. Fold in chocolate pieces.

3. Transfer batter to prepared pan and smooth top. Bake until toothpick inserted halfway between edge and center comes out with few moist crumbs attached, 30 to 35 minutes, rotating pan halfway through baking. Let brownies cool in pan on wire rack for 1½ hours. Using foil overhang, remove brownies from pan. Transfer to wire rack and let cool completely, about 1 hour. Cut into 24 pieces before serving. (Brownies can be stored at room temperature for up to 4 days.)

Ultranutty Pecan Bars

Makes 24 bars

WHY THIS RECIPE WORKS Most pecan bars consist of a single layer of nuts dominated by a thick, gooey, ultrasweet filling sitting atop the crust—essentially, pecan pie in bar form. Our ideal pecan bar would feature a buttery crust piled high with the star ingredient. The pecans would be held in place by a not-too-sweet glaze that enhanced their flavor and glued them to the crust. We tried making glazes from a variety of sweeteners, but most were problematic: Corn syrup coated the nuts nicely but had a flat flavor; maple syrup dried out and crystallized; and honey had a flavor that overwhelmed the pecans. The best glaze was made with a combination of brown sugar and corn syrup, melted butter, vanilla, and salt. Into the glaze we stirred a whole pound of pecans; with that many pecans, the nuts were layered on top of one another, allowing for a variety of textures—some nuts were slicked with glaze and chewy, while those sitting on top were crisp. Since the topping wasn't wet, we didn't need to parbake our crust. A final sprinkling of flaky sea salt as the bars came out of the oven elevated the flavor and appearance of this nutty treat. The edges will be slightly firmer than the center. If desired, trim ¼ inch from the edges before cutting into bars. Toast the pecans on a rimmed baking sheet in a 350-degree oven until fragrant, 8 to 12 minutes, shaking the sheet halfway through. It is important to use pecan halves, not pieces.

Crust
1¾ cups (8¾ ounces) all-purpose flour
6 tablespoons (2⅔ ounces) granulated sugar
½ teaspoon table salt
8 tablespoons unsalted butter, melted

Topping

- ¾ cup packed (5¼ ounces) light brown sugar
- ½ cup light corn syrup
- 7 tablespoons unsalted butter, melted and hot
- 1 teaspoon vanilla extract
- ½ teaspoon table salt
- 4 cups (1 pound) pecan halves, toasted
- ½ teaspoon flake sea salt (optional)

1. For the crust: Adjust oven rack to lowest position and heat oven to 350 degrees. Make foil sling for 13 by 9-inch baking pan by folding 2 long sheets of aluminum foil; first sheet should be 13 inches wide, and second sheet should be 9 inches wide. Lay sheets of foil in pan perpendicular to each other, with extra foil hanging over edges of pan. Push foil into corners and up sides of pan, smoothing foil flush to pan. Grease foil.

2. Whisk flour, sugar, and salt together in bowl. Stir in melted butter with wooden spoon until dough begins to form. Using your hands, continue to combine until no dry flour remains and small portion of dough holds together when squeezed in palm of your hand. Evenly scatter 1-tablespoon pieces of dough over surface of pan. Using your fingertips and palm of your hand, press and smooth dough into even thickness in bottom of pan.

3. For the topping: Whisk sugar, corn syrup, melted butter, vanilla, and table salt in bowl until smooth (mixture will look separated at first but will become homogeneous), about 20 seconds. Fold pecans into sugar mixture until nuts are evenly coated.

4. Pour topping over crust and spread into even layer with spatula, pushing to edges and into corners (there will be bare patches). Bake until topping is evenly distributed and rapidly bubbling across entire surface, 23 to 25 minutes.

5. Transfer pan to wire rack and sprinkle bars with sea salt, if using. Let bars cool completely in pan, about 1½ hours. Using foil overhang, remove bars from pan. Cut into 24 pieces before serving. (Bars can be stored at room temperature for up to 5 days.)

Millionaire's Shortbread

Makes 40 bars

WHY THIS RECIPE WORKS Millionaire's shortbread is a fitting name for this impressively rich British cookie/confectionery hybrid. And it has a lot going for it: a crunchy shortbread base; a chewy, caramel-like filling; and a shiny, snappy chocolate top. The only thing that could make it better would be foolproof methods for producing all three layers. We started by making a quick shortbread with melted butter

rather than pulling out the mixer or food processor—after all, we had two more layers to work on. Sweetened condensed milk is important to the flavor of the caramel filling, but it also makes the filling vulnerable to breaking because the whey proteins it includes, crucial to keeping the mixture emulsified, have been damaged by heat both during processing and during the cooking of the filling. We added fresh cream to supply just enough whey to keep it together. Melting the chocolate very carefully so that it never got too hot and stirring in grated chocolate at the end created a smooth, firm top layer, which made a suitably elegant finish for this rich yet refined cookie. Grating a portion of the chocolate is important for getting the chocolate to set properly; the small holes on a box grater work well for this task. Stir often while melting the chocolate and don't overheat it. We prefer Ghirardelli 60% Cacao Bittersweet Chocolate Premium Baking Bar for this recipe.

Crust

- 2½ cups (12½ ounces) all-purpose flour
- ½ cup (3½ ounces) granulated sugar
- ¾ teaspoon table salt
- 16 tablespoons unsalted butter, melted

Filling

- 1 (14-ounce) can sweetened condensed milk
- 1 cup packed (7 ounces) brown sugar
- ½ cup heavy cream
- ½ cup corn syrup
- 8 tablespoons unsalted butter
- ½ teaspoon table salt

Chocolate

- 8 ounces bittersweet chocolate (6 ounces chopped fine, 2 ounces grated), divided

1. *For the crust:* Adjust oven rack to lower-middle position and heat oven to 350 degrees. Make foil sling for 13 by 9-inch baking pan by folding 2 long sheets of aluminum foil; first sheet should be 13 inches wide and second sheet should be 9 inches wide. Lay sheets of foil in pan perpendicular to each other, with extra foil hanging over edges of pan. Push foil into corners and up sides of pan, smoothing foil flush to pan. Combine flour, sugar, and salt in medium bowl. Add melted butter and stir with rubber spatula until flour is evenly moistened. Crumble dough evenly over bottom of prepared pan. Using your fingertips and palm of your hand, press and smooth dough into even thickness. Using fork, pierce dough at 1-inch intervals. Bake until light golden brown and firm to touch, 25 to 30 minutes. Transfer pan to wire rack. Using sturdy metal spatula, press on entire surface of warm crust to compress (this will make finished bars easier to cut). Let crust cool until it is just warm, at least 20 minutes.

2. *For the filling:* Stir all ingredients together in large, heavy-bottomed saucepan. Cook over medium heat, stirring frequently, until mixture registers between 236 and 239 degrees (temperature will fluctuate), 16 to 20 minutes. Pour over crust and spread to even thickness (mixture will be very hot). Let cool completely, about 1½ hours.

3. *For the chocolate:* Microwave chopped chocolate in bowl at 50 percent power, stirring every 15 seconds, until melted but not much warmer than body temperature (check by holding in palm of your hand), 1 to 2 minutes. Add grated chocolate and stir until smooth, returning to microwave for no more than 5 seconds at a time to finish melting if necessary. Spread chocolate evenly over surface of filling. Refrigerate shortbread until chocolate is just set, about 10 minutes.

4. Using foil overhang, lift shortbread out of pan and transfer to cutting board; discard foil. Using serrated knife and gentle sawing motion, cut shortbread in half crosswise to create two 6½ by 9-inch rectangles. Cut each rectangle in half to make four 3½ by 9-inch strips. Cut each strip crosswise into 10 equal pieces. (Shortbread can be stored at room temperature, between layers of parchment, for up to 1 week.)

Best Lemon Bars

Makes 12 bars

WHY THIS RECIPE WORKS A great lemon bar is all about the interplay between a crisp buttery crust and a tart, silky filling, but achieving that perfect balance isn't easy. The more lemon juice you add, the more flavor-deadening thickeners you need so the filling holds its shape. It's a vicious cycle, which is why most lemon bars have a gooey filling that tastes overly eggy rather than irresistibly lemony. First, we focused on the crust, opting for the standard pat-in-the-pan variety. Our crust is made with melted—not cold—butter, which allowed us to stir it together, no food processor required.

For a crisp texture, we used granulated sugar instead of confectioners' sugar and baked the crust until it was dark golden brown to ensure that it retained its crispness even after we topped it with the lemon filling. Cooking our lemon filling on the stove shortened the oven time and kept it from curdling or browning at the edges when it baked. The combination of lemon juice and lemon zest provided complex flavor, and a couple of teaspoons of cream of tartar, the magic ingredient, gave it a bright, lingering finish. Do not substitute bottled lemon juice for fresh here.

Crust
- 1 cup (5 ounces) all-purpose flour
- ¼ cup (1¾ ounces) granulated sugar
- ½ teaspoon table salt
- 8 tablespoons unsalted butter, melted

Filling
- 1 cup (7 ounces) granulated sugar
- 2 tablespoons all-purpose flour
- 2 teaspoons cream of tartar
- ¼ teaspoon table salt
- 3 large eggs plus 3 large yolks
- 2 teaspoons grated lemon zest plus ⅔ cup juice (4 lemons)
- 4 tablespoons unsalted butter, cut into 8 pieces Confectioners' sugar (optional)

1. *For the crust:* Adjust oven rack to middle position and heat oven to 350 degrees. Make foil sling for 8-inch square baking pan by folding 2 long sheets of aluminum foil so each is 8 inches wide. Lay sheets of foil in pan perpendicular to each other, with extra foil hanging over edges of pan. Push foil into corners and up sides of pan, smoothing foil flush to pan.

2. Whisk flour, sugar, and salt together in bowl. Add melted butter and stir until combined. Transfer mixture to prepared pan and press into even layer over entire bottom of pan (do not wash bowl). Bake crust until dark golden brown, 19 to 24 minutes, rotating pan halfway through baking.

3. *For the filling:* While crust bakes, whisk granulated sugar, flour, cream of tartar, and salt together in now-empty bowl. Whisk in eggs and yolks until no streaks of egg remain. Whisk in lemon zest and juice. Transfer mixture to saucepan and cook over medium-low heat, stirring constantly, until mixture thickens and registers 160 degrees, 5 to 8 minutes. Off heat, stir in butter. Strain filling through fine-mesh strainer set over bowl.

4. Pour filling over hot crust and tilt pan to spread evenly. Bake until filling is set and barely jiggles when pan is shaken, 8 to 12 minutes. (Filling around perimeter of pan may be slightly raised.) Let bars cool completely, at least 1½ hours. Using foil overhang, lift bars out of pan and transfer to cutting board. Cut into bars, wiping knife clean between cuts as necessary. Before serving, dust bars with confectioners' sugar, if using.

Best Lemon Bars

Chocolate Chip Cookie Ice Cream Sandwiches

SEASON 20 RECIPE

Makes 12 sandwiches

WHY THIS RECIPE WORKS The stars of this nostalgic and delicious treat are the thin, rich chocolate chip cookies we engineered for just the right texture and pliability to make them the perfect partner for the ice cream. There were several reasons why just using our favorite chocolate chip cookies didn't work: The freezer dulled their flavor, their texture was all wrong when paired with ice cream, and their dimensions were not quite right. We found that making a moister cookie was key, and to that end, we replaced the white sugar with dark brown sugar, since the molasses it contains is a source of both water and simple sugars (glucose and fructose) that are hygroscopic—that is, very effective at attracting water. (It also added appealing toffee-like notes to the cookies.) So by using all brown sugar, we boosted the dough's water content and its ability to retain water. The all–brown sugar dough was encouragingly moist, and the frozen cookies noticeably more tender, though still harder than we wanted. So next we went straight to the source and added various amounts of water along with the egg and vanilla. Ultimately, we settled on 2 tablespoons of water, which, when combined with a good 8 hours in the freezer, made for cookies that were sturdy enough to sandwich the ice cream, but tender enough to bite through with just a hint of snap. In addition

to using all dark brown sugar, we browned all of the butter, which maximized the amount of browned flecks and aromatic compounds that make its flavor rich and round, and we upped the amount of vanilla and salt. The resulting cookies boasted big toffee-like, hazelnut-y richness even after spending hours in the freezer. Mini chips added delicately crunchy bursts of chocolate. These sandwiches should be made at least 8 hours before serving. We prefer the deeper flavor of dark brown sugar here, but light brown will also work. Use your favorite ice cream. If using a premium brand like Ben and Jerry's or Häagen-Dazs, which tend to be harder when frozen, let the ice cream soften slightly in the refrigerator before scooping. If you have it, a #16 scoop works well for portioning the ice cream. We like these sandwiches with chocolate chips pressed into the sides, but the garnish is optional.

- 10 **tablespoons unsalted butter**
- ¾ **cup (5¼ ounces) dark brown sugar**
- ¾ **teaspoon table salt**
- 1 **cup plus 2 tablespoons (5⅔ ounces) all-purpose flour**
- ¼ **teaspoon baking soda**
- 1 **large egg**
- 2 **tablespoons water**
- 2 **teaspoons vanilla extract**
- ½ **cup (3 ounces) mini semisweet chocolate chips, plus 1 cup for optional garnish**
- 3 **pints ice cream**

1. Adjust oven rack to middle position and heat oven to 325 degrees. Heat butter in 10-inch skillet over medium-high heat until melted, about 2 minutes. Continue cooking, stirring and scraping constantly with rubber spatula until milk solids are dark golden brown and butter has nutty aroma, 1 to 3 minutes. Immediately transfer to large heatproof bowl. Whisk in sugar and salt until fully incorporated and let mixture cool for 10 minutes. Meanwhile, line 2 rimmed baking sheets with parchment paper. Stir flour and baking soda together in bowl; set aside.

2. Add egg, water, and vanilla to browned butter mixture and whisk until smooth, about 30 seconds. Using rubber spatula, stir in flour mixture until combined. Stir in ½ cup chocolate chips. (Dough will be very soft.)

3. Using #60 scoop or 1-tablespoon measure, place 12 mounds of dough, evenly spaced, on each prepared baking sheet. Bake, 1 sheet at a time, until cookies are puffed and golden brown, 9 to 12 minutes, rotating sheet halfway through baking. Let cookies cool on sheet for 5 minutes, then transfer cookies to wire rack and let cool completely, about 45 minutes. Place 1 sheet, without discarding parchment, in freezer.

4. Place 4 cookies upside down on work surface. Quickly deposit 2-inch tall and 2-inch wide scoop of ice cream onto center of each cookie. Place 1 cookie from rack, right side up, on top of each scoop. Gently press and twist each sandwich between your hands until ice cream spreads to edges (this doesn't have to be perfect; ice cream can be neatened after chilling). Transfer sandwiches to sheet in freezer. Repeat with remaining cookies and ice cream. Place 1 cup chocolate chips, if using, in shallow bowl or pie plate.

5. Remove first 4 sandwiches from freezer. Hold 1 sandwich at a time over bowl of chips and gently press chips into sides with your other hand, neatening ice cream if needed. Return garnished sandwiches to freezer, and repeat with remaining 8 sandwiches in 2 batches. Freeze sandwiches for at least 8 hours before serving. (For longer storage, wrap each sandwich tightly with plastic wrap. Transfer wrapped sandwiches to zipper-lock bag and freeze for up to 2 months.)

Holiday Eggnog

SEASON 20 RECIPE

Serves 12 to 16

WHY THIS RECIPE WORKS The rich, deep, creamy flavor of a really fine eggnog is just too good to pass up. It's well worth knowing how to make this indulgent treat for the holidays, just about the only time it is served; the homemade version beats store-bought by a mile. We wanted a rich eggnog recipe with a relatively thick, creamy texture. Starting with a standard custard recipe (six eggs to 4 cups milk to ½ cup sugar), we tinkered around to find improvements. To enhance the custard's flavor and richness, we added two extra egg yolks; a little more sugar and a bit of salt also improved the flavor. Many eggnog recipes, though not all, call for the milk to be added to the beaten eggs very gradually. Upon trying this, we found that it did indeed make for a smoother texture. Last, but not least, were the flavorings. We tested recipes that used everything from blades of mace and split vanilla beans to whole cloves and cinnamon sticks. Call us traditionalists, but in the end we felt that nothing beat vanilla extract and nutmeg for true holiday eggnog flavor. Adding the milk to the eggs in small increments and blending thoroughly after each addition helps ensure a smooth custard. To prevent curdling, do not heat the custard beyond 165 degrees. If it does begin to curdle, remove it from the heat immediately, pour it into a bowl set over a larger bowl of ice water to stop the cooking, and proceed with the recipe. You can omit the brandy to make a nonalcoholic eggnog, but you should also decrease the cream to ¼ cup to keep the right consistency. For the same reason, increase the cream to ¾ cup if you choose to add another ½ cup alcohol for a high-test eggnog.

6 large eggs plus 2 large yolks
½ cup plus 2 tablespoons sugar
4 cups whole milk
¼ teaspoon table salt
½ cup brandy, bourbon, or dark rum
1 tablespoon vanilla extract
½ teaspoon fresh grated nutmeg, plus extra for serving
½ cup heavy cream

1. Whisk eggs, yolks, and sugar together in medium bowl until thoroughly combined, about 30 seconds; set aside. Bring milk and salt to simmer in large saucepan over medium-high heat, stirring occasionally.

2. When milk mixture comes to simmer, remove from heat and, whisking constantly, slowly pour into yolk mixture to temper. Return milk-yolk mixture to saucepan. Place over medium-low heat and cook, stirring constantly, until mixture reaches 160 to 165 degrees, 2 to 5 minutes.

3. Immediately pour custard through fine-mesh strainer into large bowl; stir in liquor, vanilla, and nutmeg. Cover with plastic wrap and refrigerate until well chilled, at least 3 hours and up to 3 days.

4. Just before serving, using stand mixer fitted with whisk attachment, whip cream on medium-low speed until foamy, about 1 minute. Increase speed to high and whip until soft peaks form, 1 to 3 minutes. Whisk whipped cream into chilled eggnog. Serve, garnished with extra nutmeg.

Pies, Tarts, and Fruit Desserts

Fresh Plum-Ginger Pie with Whole-Wheat Lattice-Top Crust

Foolproof All-Butter Dough for Single-Crust Pie

Makes one 9-inch single crust

WHY THIS RECIPE WORKS This is our go-to dough: It's supremely supple and extremely easy to roll out. Even better, it bakes up buttery, tender, and flaky. How did we do it? First we used the food processor to coat two-thirds of the flour with butter, creating a water-resistant paste-like mixture. Next we broke that dough into pieces, coated the pieces with the remaining flour, and tossed in grated butter. By doing this, we ensured that the water we folded in was absorbed only by the dry flour that coated the butter-flour chunks. Since gluten can develop only when flour is hydrated, the resulting crust was supertender but had enough structure to support flakes. After a 2-hour chill, the dough was completely hydrated and easy to roll out. Be sure to weigh the flour. This dough will be more moist than most pie doughs, but it will absorb a lot of excess moisture as it chills. Roll out the dough on a well-floured counter.

10   tablespoons unsalted butter, chilled, divided
1¼ cups (6¼ ounces) all-purpose flour, divided
1   tablespoon sugar
½   teaspoon table salt
¼   cup ice water, divided

1. Grate 2 tablespoons butter on large holes of box grater and place in freezer. Cut remaining 8 tablespoons butter into ½-inch cubes.

2. Pulse ¾ cup flour, sugar, and salt in food processor until combined, 2 pulses. Add cubed butter and process until homogeneous paste forms, about 30 seconds. Using your hands, carefully break paste into 2-inch pieces and redistribute evenly around processor blade. Add remaining ½ cup flour and pulse until mixture is broken into pieces no larger than 1 inch (most pieces will be much smaller), 4 or 5 pulses. Transfer mixture to medium bowl. Add grated butter and toss until butter pieces are separated and coated with flour.

3. Sprinkle 2 tablespoons ice water over mixture. Toss with rubber spatula until mixture is evenly moistened. Sprinkle remaining 2 tablespoons ice water over mixture and toss to combine. Press dough with spatula until dough sticks together. Transfer dough to sheet of plastic wrap. Draw edges of plastic over dough and press firmly on sides and top to form compact, fissure-free mass. Wrap in plastic and form into 5-inch disk. Refrigerate dough for at least 2 hours or up to 2 days. Let chilled dough sit on counter to soften slightly, about 10 minutes, before rolling. (Wrapped dough can be frozen for up to 1 month. If frozen, let dough thaw completely on counter before rolling.)

VARIATION
Foolproof Whole-Wheat Dough for Single-Crust Pie
Substitute ¾ cup (4⅛ ounces) whole-wheat flour for first addition of all-purpose flour, using ½ cup all-purpose flour (2½ ounces) for second addition of flour.

Making Foolproof All-Butter Pie Dough

1. Pulse portion of flour, plus sugar and salt, in food processor until combined, 2 pulses. Add cubed butter and process until homogeneous paste forms, about 30 seconds.

2. Carefully break paste into 2-inch chunks and redistribute evenly around processor blade. Add remaining flour and pulse until mixture is broken into pieces no larger than 1 inch (most pieces will be much smaller), 4 or 5 pulses. Transfer mixture to bowl.

3. Add grated butter and toss until butter pieces are separated and coated with flour. Sprinkle 2 tablespoons ice water over mixture. Toss with spatula until mixture is evenly moistened. Sprinkle remaining 2 tablespoons ice water over mixture and toss to combine.

4. Transfer dough to sheet of plastic wrap. Draw edges of plastic over dough and press firmly on sides and top to form compact, fissure-free mass. Wrap in plastic and form into 5-inch disk.

Foolproof All-Butter Dough
for Single-Crust Pie

Rolling and Fitting Pie Dough

1. Lay disk of dough on lightly floured work surface and roll dough outward from its center into 12-inch circle. Between every few rolls, give dough a quarter turn to help keep circle nice and round.

2. Loosely roll dough around rolling pin, then gently unroll it over pie plate.

3. Lift dough and gently press it into pie plate, letting excess hang over plate. For double-crust pie, cover crust lightly with plastic wrap and refrigerate for at least 30 minutes.

Crimping a Single-Crust Pie Dough

For a traditional single-crust pie, you need to make an evenly thick edge before crimping. Trim the pie dough so that it hangs over the pie plate by ½ inch, then tuck the dough underneath itself to form a tidy, even edge that sits on the lip of the pie plate.

For Fluted Edge Use index finger of 1 hand and thumb and index finger of other hand to create fluted ridges perpendicular to edge of pie plate.

For Ridged Edge Press tines of fork into dough to flatten it against rim of pie plate.

Foolproof All-Butter Dough for Double-Crust Pie

Makes one 9-inch double crust

WHY THIS RECIPE WORKS Be sure to weigh the flour for this recipe. This dough will be more moist than most pie doughs, but as it chills it will absorb a lot of excess moisture. Roll the dough on a well-floured counter. If your recipe requires rolling your dough piece(s) to a rectangle after chilling, as when making a lattice top for a pie, form the dough into a 5-inch square instead of a disk.

20 tablespoons (2½ sticks) unsalted butter, chilled, divided
2½ cups (12½ ounces) all-purpose flour, divided
2 tablespoons sugar
1 teaspoon table salt
½ cup ice water, divided

1. Grate 4 tablespoons butter on large holes of box grater and place in freezer. Cut remaining 16 tablespoons butter into ½-inch cubes.

2. Pulse 1½ cups flour, sugar, and salt in food processor until combined, 2 pulses. Add cubed butter and process until homogeneous paste forms, 40 to 50 seconds. Using your hands, carefully break paste into 2-inch pieces and redistribute evenly around processor blade. Add remaining 1 cup flour and pulse until mixture is broken into pieces no larger than 1 inch (most pieces will be much smaller), 4 or 5 pulses. Transfer mixture to medium bowl. Add grated butter and toss until butter pieces are separated and coated with flour.

3. Sprinkle ¼ cup ice water over mixture. Toss with rubber spatula until mixture is evenly moistened. Sprinkle remaining ¼ cup ice water over mixture and toss to combine. Press dough with spatula until dough sticks together. Use spatula to divide dough into 2 portions. Transfer each portion to sheet of plastic wrap. Working with 1 portion at a time, draw edges of plastic over dough and press firmly on sides and top to form compact, fissure-free mass. Wrap in plastic and form into 5-inch disk (or square). Repeat with remaining portion; refrigerate dough for at least 2 hours or up to 2 days. Let chilled dough sit on counter to soften slightly, about 10 minutes, before rolling. (Dough, wrapped tightly in plastic wrap, can be refrigerated for up to 2 days or frozen for up to 1 month. If frozen, let dough thaw completely on counter before rolling it out.)

VARIATION
Foolproof Whole-Wheat Dough for Double-Crust Pie
Substitute 1½ cups (8¼ ounces) whole-wheat flour for first addition of all-purpose flour, using 1 cup all-purpose flour (5 ounces) for second addition of flour.

Making a Double-Crust Pie

1. Loosely roll chilled top crust around rolling pin, then gently unroll it over filled pie crust bottom.

2. Using scissors, trim all but ½ inch of dough overhanging edge of pie plate.

3. Press top and bottom crusts together, then tuck edges underneath.

4. Crimp dough evenly around edge of pie, using your fingers. Cut vent holes attractively in center of top crust with paring knife (drier pies only require 4 vents, while very juicy pies require 8 vents).

Graham Cracker Crust

Makes one 9-inch crust

WHY THIS RECIPE WORKS This fresh-tasting graham cracker crust couldn't be easier to make: After combining crushed crumbs with sugar and a little melted butter to bind them, we simply used a measuring cup to pack the crumbs into the pie plate. Producing a perfect graham cracker crust has a lot to do with the type of graham crackers used. After experimenting with the three leading brands, we discovered subtle but distinct differences among them and found that these differences carried over into crumb crusts made with each kind of cracker. In the end, we preferred Keebler Grahams Crackers Original in our crust. We don't recommend using store-bought graham cracker crumbs here, as they can often be stale.

8   whole graham crackers, broken into 1-inch pieces
5   tablespoons unsalted butter, melted and cooled
3   tablespoons sugar

1. Adjust oven rack to middle position and heat oven to 325 degrees. Process graham cracker pieces in food processor to fine, even crumbs, about 30 seconds. Sprinkle melted butter and sugar over crumbs and pulse to incorporate.

2. Sprinkle mixture into 9-inch pie plate. Use bottom of measuring cup to press crumbs into even layer on bottom and sides of pie plate. Bake until crust is fragrant and beginning to brown, 13 to 18 minutes. Following particular pie recipe, use crust while it is still warm or let it cool completely.

Classic Tart Dough

Makes one 9-inch tart crust

WHY THIS RECIPE WORKS The problem with most tarts is the crust—it's usually either too tough or too brittle. While regular pie crust is tender and flaky, classic tart crust should be fine-textured, buttery-rich, crisp, and crumbly— it is often described as being shortbread-like. We set out to achieve the perfect tart dough, one that we could use in several of our tart recipes. We found that using a full stick of butter made tart dough that tasted great and was easy to handle, yet still had a delicate crumb. Instead of using the hard-to-find pastry flour and superfine sugar that many other recipes call for, we used all-purpose flour and confectioners' sugar to achieve a crisp texture. Rolling the dough and fitting it into the tart pan was easy, and we had ample dough to patch any holes. Tart crust is sweeter, crisper, and less flaky than pie crust—it is more similar in texture to a cookie.

1   large egg yolk
1   tablespoon heavy cream
½   teaspoon vanilla extract
1¼   cups (6¼ ounces) all-purpose flour
⅔   cup (2⅔ ounces) confectioners' sugar
¼   teaspoon table salt
8   tablespoons unsalted butter, cut into ¼-inch pieces and chilled

1. Whisk egg yolk, cream, and vanilla together in bowl. Process flour, sugar, and salt in food processor until combined, about 5 seconds. Scatter butter over top and pulse until mixture resembles coarse cornmeal, about 15 pulses. With processor running, add egg yolk mixture and continue to process until dough just comes together around processor blade, about 12 seconds.

2. Turn dough onto sheet of plastic wrap and form into 6-inch disk. Wrap tightly in plastic and refrigerate for at least 1 hour or up to 2 days. Let chilled dough sit on counter to soften slightly, about 10 minutes, before rolling. (Wrapped dough can be frozen for up to 1 month. If frozen, let dough thaw completely on counter before rolling.)

Classic Apple Pie

Serves 8

WHY THIS RECIPE WORKS We have found that it's difficult to produce an apple pie with a filling that is tart as well as sweet and juicy. We wanted to develop a classic apple pie recipe—one with the clean, bright taste of apples that could be made year-round, based on apple types that are always available in the supermarket. To arrive at the tartness and texture we were after, we had to use two kinds of apples in our pie, Granny Smith and McIntosh. The Grannies could be counted on for tartness and for keeping their shape during cooking; the Macs added flavor, and their otherwise frustrating tendency to become mushy was a virtue, providing a nice, juicy base for the harder Grannies. While many bakers add butter to their apple pie fillings, we found that it dulled the fresh taste of the apples so we did without it. Lemon juice, however, was essential, counterbalancing the sweetness of the apples. To give the apples the upper hand, we settled on quite modest amounts of cinnamon, nutmeg, and allspice. The pie is best eaten when cooled to room temperature, or even the next day. Serve with vanilla ice cream or lightly sweetened whipped cream.

- 1 recipe Foolproof All-Butter Dough for Double-Crust Pie (page 456)
- 2 tablespoons all-purpose flour
- 3/4 cup (5 1/4 ounces) plus 1 tablespoon sugar, divided
- 1 teaspoon grated lemon zest plus 1 tablespoon juice
- 1/4 teaspoon table salt
- 1/4 teaspoon ground nutmeg
- 1/4 teaspoon ground cinnamon
- 1/8 teaspoon ground allspice
- 2 pounds McIntosh apples, peeled, cored, and sliced 1/4 inch thick
- 1 1/2 pounds Granny Smith apples, peeled, cored, and sliced 1/4 inch thick
- 1 large egg, lightly beaten with 1 tablespoon water

1. Roll 1 disk of dough into 12-inch circle on well-floured counter. Loosely roll dough around rolling pin and gently unroll it into 9-inch pie plate, letting excess dough hang over edge. Ease dough into plate by gently lifting edge of dough with your hand while pressing into plate bottom with your other hand. Leave any dough that overhangs plate in place. Wrap dough-lined plate loosely in plastic wrap and refrigerate until firm, about 30 minutes.

2. Roll other disk of dough into 12-inch circle on well-floured counter, then transfer to parchment paper–lined baking sheet; cover with plastic and refrigerate for 30 minutes.

3. Adjust oven rack to lowest position and heat oven to 500 degrees. Whisk flour, 3/4 cup sugar, lemon zest, salt, nutmeg, cinnamon, and allspice together in large bowl. Add lemon juice and apples and toss until combined. Spread apples and their juices into dough-lined plate, mounding them slightly in middle. Loosely roll remaining dough round around rolling pin and gently unroll it onto filling.

4. Trim overhang to 1/2 inch beyond lip of plate. Pinch edges of top and bottom dough firmly together. Tuck overhang under itself; folded edge should be flush with edge of plate. Crimp dough evenly around edge of plate. Cut four 2-inch slits in top of dough. Brush surface with egg wash and sprinkle evenly with remaining 1 tablespoon sugar.

5. Place pie on aluminum foil–lined rimmed baking sheet, reduce oven temperature to 425 degrees, and bake until crust is golden, about 25 minutes. Reduce oven temperature to 375 degrees, rotate sheet, and continue to bake until juices are bubbling and crust is deep golden brown, 35 to 45 minutes longer. Let pie cool on wire rack until filling has set, about 4 hours. Serve.

VARIATIONS
Apple Pie with Crystallized Ginger
Add 3 tablespoons chopped crystallized ginger to apple mixture.

Apple Pie with Dried Fruit
Toss 1 cup raisins, dried sweet cherries, or dried cranberries with lemon juice plus 1 tablespoon applejack, brandy, or cognac. Add dried fruit and liquid to apple mixture.

Apple Pie with Fresh Cranberries
Increase sugar to 1 cup and add 1 cup fresh or frozen cranberries to apple mixture.

Deep-Dish Apple Pie

Serves 8

WHY THIS RECIPE WORKS If you find yourself with a surplus of fruit after a fall apple-picking extravaganza, we recommend you enjoy them in a towering deep-dish pie. But the problem with deep-dish apple pie is that the apples are often unevenly cooked and the exuded juice leaves the apples swimming in liquid, producing a bottom crust that is pale and soggy. Then there is the gaping hole left between the apples (which are shrunken from the loss of all that moisture) and the arching top crust, making it impossible to slice and serve a neat piece of pie. We wanted each piece of our deep-dish pie to be a towering wedge of tender, juicy apples, fully framed by a buttery, flaky crust. Precooking the apples solved the shrinking problem, helped the apples hold their shape, and

prevented juices from collecting in the bottom of the pie plate, giving us a nicely browned bottom crust. All that was left to do was to choose the right combination of apples and stir in a little brown sugar, salt, lemon, and cinnamon for flavor and sweetness. Use a combination of tart and sweet apples for this pie. Good choices for tart are Granny Smiths, Empires, or Cortlands; for sweet we recommend Golden Delicious, Jonagolds, or Braeburns. Serve with vanilla ice cream or lightly sweetened whipped cream.

1 recipe Foolproof All-Butter Dough for Double-Crust Pie (page 456)
2½ pounds tart apples, peeled, cored, and sliced ¼ inch thick
2½ pounds sweet apples, peeled, cored, and sliced ¼ inch thick
½ cup (3½ ounces) plus 1 tablespoon granulated sugar, divided
¼ cup packed (1¾ ounces) light brown sugar
½ teaspoon grated lemon zest plus 1 tablespoon juice
¼ teaspoon table salt
⅛ teaspoon ground cinnamon
1 large egg, lightly beaten with 1 tablespoon water

1. Roll 1 disk of dough into 12-inch circle on well-floured counter. Loosely roll dough around rolling pin and gently unroll it into 9-inch pie plate, letting excess dough hang over edge. Ease dough into plate by gently lifting edge of dough with your hand while pressing into plate bottom with your other hand. Leave any dough that overhangs plate in place. Wrap dough-lined plate loosely in plastic wrap and refrigerate until firm, about 30 minutes.

2. Roll other disk of dough into 12-inch circle on well-floured counter, then transfer to parchment paper–lined baking sheet; cover with plastic and refrigerate for 30 minutes.

3. Toss apples, ½ cup granulated sugar, brown sugar, lemon zest, salt, and cinnamon together in Dutch oven. Cover and cook over medium heat, stirring frequently, until apples are tender when poked with fork but still hold their shape, 15 to 20 minutes.

4. Spread apples and their juice on rimmed baking sheet and let cool completely, about 30 minutes.

5. Adjust oven rack to lowest position and heat oven to 425 degrees. Drain cooled apples thoroughly in colander set over bowl, reserving ¼ cup of juice. Stir lemon juice into reserved juice. Spread apples into dough-lined plate, mounding them slightly in middle, and drizzle with lemon juice mixture. Loosely roll remaining dough round around rolling pin and gently unroll it onto filling.

6. Trim overhang to ½ inch beyond lip of plate. Pinch edges of top and bottom dough firmly together. Tuck overhang under itself; folded edge should be flush with edge of plate. Crimp dough evenly around edge of plate. Cut four 2-inch slits in top of dough. Brush surface with egg wash and sprinkle evenly with remaining 1 tablespoon granulated sugar.

7. Place pie on aluminum foil–lined rimmed baking sheet and bake until crust is golden, about 25 minutes. Reduce oven temperature to 375 degrees, rotate sheet, and continue to bake until juices are bubbling and crust is deep golden brown, 30 to 40 minutes longer. Let pie cool on wire rack until filling has set, about 4 hours. Serve.

Skillet Apple Pie

Serves 6 to 8

WHY THIS RECIPE WORKS Who says a pie needs to bake in a special plate—or even have a bottom crust? It can come in a skillet, and it can be just about the easiest pie you can make. Unlike the filling for a double-crust pie, which needs to be juicy enough to flatter the fresh fruit but tight enough to keep the crust from becoming soggy, the filling for a skillet apple pie can be saucy. Apple cider provided resonant apple flavor and, when thickened with cornstarch, it yielded a juicy filling with just the right body. We used ⅓ cup of maple syrup to further sweeten the filling, and it complemented the natural sweetness of the apples without being cloying. Working in a heavy skillet allowed us to sauté the apples just long enough to caramelize them before we transferred the dough-topped pie to the oven, where the crust developed a lovely deep brown hue. Cutting the dough into six pieces prior to baking allowed the crust to develop multiple crisp, flaky edges that contrasted with the saucy, caramelized, and tender apples. Serve warm or at room temperature with vanilla ice cream or whipped cream. Use a combination of sweet, crisp apples such as Golden Delicious and firm, tart apples such as Cortland or Empire.

- ½ cup apple cider
- ⅓ cup maple syrup
- 2 tablespoons lemon juice
- 2 teaspoons cornstarch
- ⅛ teaspoon ground cinnamon (optional)
- 2 tablespoons unsalted butter
- 2½ pounds sweet and tart apples, peeled, cored, and cut into ½-inch-thick wedges
- 1 recipe Foolproof All-Butter Dough for Single-Crust Pie (page 454)
- 2 teaspoons sugar

1. Adjust oven rack to upper-middle position and heat oven to 500 degrees. Whisk cider, syrup, lemon juice, cornstarch, and cinnamon, if using, in bowl until smooth.

2. Melt butter in 12-inch ovensafe skillet over medium-high heat. Add apples and cook, stirring 2 or 3 times, until apples begin to caramelize, about 5 minutes. (Do not fully cook apples.) Off heat, add cider mixture and gently stir until apples are well coated. Set aside to cool slightly.

3. Roll dough into 11-inch circle on well-floured counter. Loosely roll dough around rolling pin and gently unroll it onto apple filling. Brush dough with water and sprinkle evenly with sugar. Using sharp knife, gently cut dough into 6 pieces by making 1 vertical cut followed by 2 evenly spaced horizontal cuts (perpendicular to first cut).

4. Bake until apples are tender and crust is deep golden brown, 15 to 20 minutes, rotating skillet halfway through baking. Let cool for 30 minutes; serve warm.

Fresh Peach Pie

Serves 8

WHY THIS RECIPE WORKS Juicy summer peaches often produce soupy peach pies, and the amount of moisture changes from pie to pie. To control the moisture, we macerated the peaches to draw out some of their juices and then added a measured amount back to the filling. Cornstarch and pectin helped hold the filling together without making it gluey or bouncy, and mashing some of the peaches helped make neat, attractive slices. For an impressive presentation, we wanted a buttery lattice top on our pie, as this would allow moisture to evaporate, but to keep things super easy, we used a cheater's lattice-making method, no weaving required. If your peaches are too soft to withstand the pressure of a peeler, cut a shallow X in the bottom of the fruit, blanch them in a pot of simmering water for 15 seconds, and then shock them in a bowl of ice water before peeling. For fruit pectin we recommend both Sure-Jell for Less or No Sugar Needed Recipes and Ball Real Fruit Low or No-Sugar Needed Pectin.

- 1 recipe Foolproof All-Butter Dough for Double-Crust Pie (page 456)
- 3 pounds peaches, peeled, quartered, and pitted, each quarter cut into thirds
- ½ cup (3½ ounces) plus 3 tablespoons sugar, divided
- 1 teaspoon grated lemon zest plus 1 tablespoon juice
- ⅛ teaspoon table salt
- 2 tablespoons low- or no-sugar-needed fruit pectin
- ¼ teaspoon ground cinnamon
  - Pinch ground nutmeg
- 1 tablespoon cornstarch

1. Roll 1 disk of dough into 12-inch circle on well-floured counter. Loosely roll dough around rolling pin and gently unroll it onto 9-inch pie plate, letting excess dough hang over edge. Ease dough into plate by gently lifting edge of dough with your hand while pressing into plate bottom with your other hand. Leave any dough that overhangs plate in place. Wrap dough-lined plate loosely in plastic wrap and refrigerate until firm, about 30 minutes.

2. Roll other piece of dough into 12-inch circle on well-floured counter, then transfer to parchment paper–lined rimmed baking sheet. Using pizza wheel, fluted pastry wheel, or paring knife, cut dough into ten 1¼-inch-wide strips. Cover loosely with plastic and refrigerate until firm, about 30 minutes. Adjust oven rack to middle position and heat oven to 400 degrees.

3. Toss peaches, ½ cup sugar, lemon zest and juice, and salt in bowl and let sit for 30 minutes to 1 hour. Combine pectin, cinnamon, nutmeg, and 2 tablespoons sugar in small bowl; set aside. Measure out 1 cup peach pieces and mash with fork to coarse paste. Drain remaining peach pieces in colander set in bowl, reserving ½ cup peach juice. Return peach pieces to now-empty bowl and toss with cornstarch.

4. Whisk reserved peach juice and pectin mixture together in 12-inch skillet. Cook over medium heat, stirring occasionally, until thickened slightly and pectin is dissolved (liquid should become less cloudy), 3 to 5 minutes. Transfer peach-pectin mixture and peach paste to bowl with peach pieces and stir to combine. Spread peach mixture into dough-lined plate.

5. Remove dough strips from refrigerator; if too stiff to be workable, let sit at room temperature until softened slightly but still very cold. Lay 2 longest strips across center of pie, perpendicular to each other. Arrange 4 shortest strips around edge of pie in shape of square. Lay remaining 4 strips between strips in center and around edge to make lattice design.

6. Trim overhang to ½ inch beyond lip of plate. Pinch edges of bottom crust and lattice strips together firmly to seal. Tuck overhang under itself; folded edge should be flush with edge of plate. Crimp dough evenly around edge of plate. (If dough is very soft, refrigerate for 10 minutes before baking.) Brush surface with water and sprinkle with remaining 1 tablespoon sugar.

Fresh Peach Pie

7. Place pie on aluminum foil–lined rimmed baking sheet and bake until crust is light golden, 20 to 25 minutes. Reduce oven temperature to 350 degrees, rotate sheet, and continue to bake until juices are bubbling and crust is deep golden brown, 30 to 50 minutes longer. Let pie cool on wire rack until filling has set, about 4 hours. Serve.

Building a "No-Weave" Lattice Top

1. Roll dough into 12-inch circle, transfer to parchment paper–lined baking sheet, and cut into ten 1¼-inch-wide strips with fluted pastry wheel, pizza wheel, or paring knife. Refrigerate for 30 minutes.

2. Lay 2 longest strips perpendicular to each other across center of pie to form cross. Place 4 shorter strips along edges of pie, parallel to center strips.

3. Lay 4 remaining strips between each edge strip and center strip. Trim off excess lattice ends, press edges of bottom crust and lattice strips together, and fold under.

Strawberry-Rhubarb Pie

Serves 8

WHY THIS RECIPE WORKS Strawberries and rhubarb aren't the perfect couple you might think they are. The trouble lies not in their differences, but in a similarity: Both are loaded with water. During baking, all this water heats up and causes the rhubarb to blow out, releasing its moisture into the filling and collapsing into mush, while the strawberries become bloated. To fix these problems, we microwaved the rhubarb with sugar to draw out some liquid and then stirred a portion of the strawberries into the warm liquid to soften; we then cooked the liquid down with the remaining strawberries to make a jam that we folded into the filling. This allowed us to use less thickener and more fruit than most pies for an intense filling that was chunky and softly gelled. Brushing the dough with a generous amount of water and sprinkling it with sugar gave it a crackly finish.

1 recipe Foolproof All-Butter Dough for Double-Crust Pie (page 456)
2 pounds rhubarb, trimmed and cut into ½-inch pieces (7 cups)
1¼ cups (8¾ ounces) sugar, plus 3 tablespoons for sprinkling
1 pound strawberries, hulled, halved if less than 1 inch, quartered if more than 1 inch (3 to 4 cups), divided
3 tablespoons instant tapioca

1. Roll 1 disk of dough into 12-inch circle on well-floured counter. Loosely roll dough around rolling pin and gently unroll it onto 9-inch pie plate, letting excess dough hang over edge. Ease dough into plate by gently lifting edge of dough with your hand while pressing into plate bottom with your other hand. Leave any dough that overhangs plate in place. Wrap dough-lined plate loosely in plastic wrap and refrigerate until firm, about 30 minutes.

2. Roll other disk of dough into 12-inch circle on well-floured counter, then transfer to parchment paper–lined rimmed baking sheet; cover loosely with plastic and refrigerate until firm, about 30 minutes.

3. Combine rhubarb and sugar in bowl and microwave for 1½ minutes. Stir and continue to microwave until sugar is mostly dissolved, about 1 minute longer. Stir in 1 cup strawberries and set aside for 30 minutes, stirring once halfway through. Drain rhubarb mixture in fine-mesh strainer set over large saucepan. Return drained rhubarb mixture to bowl; set aside. Add remaining strawberries to rhubarb liquid and cook over medium-high heat until strawberries are very soft and mixture is reduced to 1½ cups, about 10 to 15 minutes. Mash berries with fork (mixture does not have to be smooth). Add strawberry mixture and tapioca to drained rhubarb mixture and stir to combine; set aside.

4. Adjust oven rack to lowest position and heat oven to 425 degrees. Spread filling into dough-lined plate. Loosely roll remaining dough round around rolling pin and gently unroll it onto filling.

5. Trim overhang to ½ inch beyond lip of plate. Pinch edges of top and bottom crusts firmly together. Tuck overhang under itself; folded edge should be flush with edge of plate. Crimp dough evenly around edge of plate. Cut eight 2-inch slits in top of dough. Brush surface thoroughly with water and sprinkle with remaining 3 tablespoons sugar.

6. Place pie on aluminum foil–lined rimmed baking sheet and bake until crust is set and begins to brown, about 25 minutes. Rotate pie and reduce oven temperature to 375 degrees; continue to bake until crust is deep golden brown and filling is bubbling, 30 to 40 minutes longer. Let pie cool on wire rack until filling has set, about 4 hours. Serve.

Blueberry Pie

Serves 8

WHY THIS RECIPE WORKS If the filling for blueberry pie doesn't gel, a sliced wedge can collapse into a soupy puddle topped by a sodden crust. But use too much thickener and cutting through the filling is like slicing through gummi bears. We wanted a pie with a firm, glistening filling full of fresh, bright flavor and still-plump berries. To thicken the pie, we favored tapioca because it didn't mute the fresh yet subtle blueberry flavor as cornstarch and flour did; but as with the other thickeners, too much made the filling stiff and congealed. Cooking and reducing half of the berries helped us cut down on the tapioca required, but not enough. A second inspiration came from a peeled and grated Granny Smith apple. Apples are high in pectin, a type of carbohydrate that acts as a thickener when cooked. Combined with a modest 2 tablespoons of instant tapioca, the apple helped the filling take on a soft, even consistency. We still needed a bit of moisture evaporation as more liquid was released during baking; cutouts atop the pie were a simple and attractive alternative to a more advanced lattice crust. This recipe was developed using fresh blueberries, but unthawed frozen blueberries will work as well. In step 3, cook half the frozen berries over medium-high heat, without mashing, until reduced to 1¼ cups, 12 to 15 minutes. Grind the tapioca to a powder in a spice grinder or mini food processor. If using pearl tapioca, reduce the amount to 5 teaspoons. Serve with vanilla ice cream or lightly sweetened whipped cream.

1 **recipe Foolproof All-Butter Dough for Double-Crust Pie (page 456)**
6 **cups (30 ounces) fresh blueberries, divided**
1 **Granny Smith apple, peeled, cored, and shredded on large holes of box grater**
¾ **cup (5¼ ounces) sugar**
2 **tablespoons instant tapioca, ground**
2 **teaspoons grated lemon zest plus 2 teaspoons juice Pinch table salt**
2 **tablespoons unsalted butter, cut into ¼-inch pieces**
1 **large egg, lightly beaten with 1 tablespoon water**

1. Roll 1 disk of dough into 12-inch circle on well-floured counter. Loosely roll dough around rolling pin and gently unroll it onto 9-inch pie plate, letting excess dough hang over edge. Ease dough into plate by gently lifting edge of dough with your hand while pressing into plate bottom with your other hand. Leave any dough that overhangs plate in place. Wrap dough-lined plate loosely in plastic wrap and refrigerate until firm, about 30 minutes.

2. Roll other disk of dough into 12-inch circle on well-floured counter. Using 1¼-inch round biscuit cutter, cut round from center of dough. Cut 6 more rounds from dough, 1½ inches from edge of center hole and equally spaced around center hole. Transfer dough to parchment paper–lined baking sheet; cover with plastic and refrigerate until firm, about 30 minutes.

3. Place 3 cups berries in medium saucepan and set over medium heat. Using potato masher, mash berries several times to release juices. Continue to cook, stirring often and mashing occasionally, until about half of blueberries have broken down and mixture is thickened and reduced to 1½ cups, about 8 minutes; let cool slightly.

4. Adjust oven rack to lowest position and heat oven to 400 degrees. Place apple in clean dish towel and wring dry. Transfer apple to large bowl and stir in sugar, tapioca, lemon zest and juice, salt, cooked berries, and remaining 3 cups uncooked berries until combined. Spread mixture into dough-lined plate and scatter butter over top. Loosely roll remaining dough round around rolling pin and gently unroll it onto filling.

5. Trim overhang to ½ inch beyond lip of plate. Pinch edges of top and bottom dough firmly together. Tuck overhang under itself; folded edge should be flush with edge of plate. Crimp dough evenly around edge of plate. Brush surface with egg wash.

6. Place pie on aluminum foil–lined rimmed baking sheet and bake until crust is light golden brown, about 25 minutes. Reduce oven temperature to 375 degrees, rotate sheet, and continue to bake until juices are bubbling and crust is deep golden brown, 35 to 50 minutes longer. Let pie cool on wire rack until filling has set, about 4 hours. Serve.

"I have a strong memory of the afternoon that we filmed this recipe for TV back in 2003. At that point, I was not a cast member but a 'runner' for the show: My main task was to arrange cookware and ingredients on the set between scenes. I was also in charge of shuttling any leftovers from the back kitchen to share with the film crew. All of the food always disappeared, but this pie in particular got more oohs, ahhs, and compliments than any other dish I can remember. I wasn't surprised: It celebrates the flavors, shapes, and colors of berries in a beautiful, simple way. It's been a regular part of my summer rotation ever since."

—Becky

Summer Berry Pie

Serves 8

WHY THIS RECIPE WORKS This delicious fruit pie captures the flavors of summer in a simple pat-in-the-pan crust. There's no bouncy gelatin or dairy-heavy pudding here to overshadow the sweet-tart flavor of perfectly ripe berries. Rather, the filling is simply fresh whole berries piled on a puree of more berries that we cooked down with some sugar and just enough cornstarch to hold the filling together. A flavorful graham cracker crust provided the perfect complement to the bright mix of berries. The result was a pie that sliced neatly and had great berry texture and flavor. Tossing the whole berries with a bit of jelly gave them a beautiful sheen and contributed the perfect amount of sweetness. Feel free to vary the amount of each berry as desired as long as you have 6 cups of berries total; do not substitute frozen berries here. Serve with lightly sweetened whipped cream.

- 2 cups (10 ounces) raspberries
- 2 cups (10 ounces) blackberries
- 2 cups (10 ounces) blueberries
- ½ cup (3½ ounces) sugar
- 3 tablespoons cornstarch
- ⅛ teaspoon table salt
- 1 tablespoon lemon juice
- 1 recipe Graham Cracker Crust (page 457), baked and cooled
- 2 tablespoons red currant or apple jelly

1. Gently toss berries together in large bowl. Process 2½ cups berries in food processor until very smooth, about 1 minute (do not underprocess). Strain puree through fine-mesh strainer into small saucepan, pressing on solids to extract as much liquid as possible (you should have about 1½ cups); discard solids.

2. Whisk sugar, cornstarch, and salt together in bowl, then whisk into strained puree. Bring puree mixture to boil, stirring constantly, and cook until thickened to consistency of pudding, about 7 minutes. Off heat, stir in lemon juice and let cool slightly.

3. Pour warm berry puree into cooled crust. Melt jelly in clean, dry small saucepan over low heat, then pour over remaining 3½ cups berries and toss to coat. Spread berries evenly over puree and lightly press them into puree. Cover pie loosely with plastic wrap and refrigerate until filling is chilled and set, at least 3 hours or up to 24 hours. Serve chilled or at room temperature.

Fresh Plum-Ginger Pie with Whole-Wheat Lattice-Top Crust

SEASON 20 RECIPE

Serves 8

WHY THIS RECIPE WORKS Plum pies have a problem: They're either a mushy disappointment or a dense brick of overcooked, dried-out, leathery fruit. We wanted tender bites of plum in a fresh but slightly jammy filling. Leaving the skins on the plums and cutting them into ¼-inch-thick slices resulted in perfectly cooked fruit and filling. Plums, while plenty juicy, release less liquid during baking than fruit such as blueberries or cherries, so using tapioca for the thickener gave our filling a slightly sticky quality; cornstarch was a much better choice. Another key step to nailing our pie's texture was letting the filling sit for 15 minutes before adding it to the pie shell; this drew out some of the plums' juices, which ensured that the cornstarch was evenly absorbed and eliminated any clumps of thickener. A bit of spicy, tangy ginger complemented the sweetness of the plums. We think our whole-grain pie crust made with whole-wheat flour pairs particularly well with this filling, but you can use our classic Foolproof All-Butter Dough for Double-Crust Pie recipe (page 456) if you prefer. If at any point the dough is too stiff to be workable, let it sit at room temperature until it is slightly softened but still very cold. Conversely, if the dough becomes too soft to work with, refrigerate it for 30 minutes to let it firm up.

- 1 recipe Foolproof Whole-Wheat Dough for Double-Crust Pie (page 456)
- ¾ cup (5¼ ounces) sugar
- 3 tablespoons cornstarch
- 2 teaspoons grated lemon zest plus 1 tablespoon juice
- 1 teaspoon grated fresh ginger
- ¼ teaspoon ground ginger
- ¼ teaspoon table salt
- 2½ pounds plums, pitted and cut into ¼-inch-thick wedges
- 1 large egg, lightly beaten with 1 tablespoon water

1. Roll 1 disk of dough into 12-inch circle on well-floured counter. Loosely roll dough around rolling pin and gently unroll it onto 9-inch pie plate, letting excess dough hang over edge. Ease dough into plate by gently lifting edge of dough with your hand while pressing into plate bottom with your other hand. Leave any dough that overhangs plate in place. Wrap dough-lined plate loosely in plastic wrap and refrigerate until firm, about 30 minutes.

Weaving a Lattice Top

1. Evenly space 4 dough strips across top of pie, parallel to counter edge.

2. Fold back first and third strips almost completely. Lay 1 strip across pie, perpendicular to counter edge.

3. Unfold first and third strips over top of perpendicular strip.

4. Fold back second and fourth strips and add second perpendicular strip. Unfold second and fourth strips.

5. Repeat, alternating between folding back first and third strips and second and fourth strips and laying remaining strips evenly across pie.

6. Trim lattice ends, press edges of bottom crust and lattice strips together, and fold under. Crimp dough evenly around edge of pie.

2. Roll other piece of dough into 13 by 10½-inch rectangle on well-floured counter, then transfer to parchment paper–lined rimmed baking sheet; cover loosely with plastic and refrigerate until firm, about 30 minutes.

3. Using pizza wheel, fluted pastry wheel, or paring knife, trim ¼ inch dough from long sides of rectangle, then cut rectangle lengthwise into eight 1¼-inch-wide strips. Cover loosely with plastic and refrigerate until firm, about 30 minutes. Adjust oven rack to middle position and heat oven to 400 degrees.

4. Whisk sugar, cornstarch, lemon zest, fresh ginger, ground ginger, and salt together in large bowl. Stir in plums and lemon juice and let sit for 15 minutes. Spread plum mixture into chilled dough-lined plate.

5. Remove dough strips from refrigerator; if too stiff to be workable, let sit at room temperature until softened slightly but still very cold. Space 4 strips evenly across top of pie, parallel to counter edge. Fold back first and third strips almost completely. Lay 1 strip across pie, perpendicular to second and fourth strips, keeping it snug to folded edges of dough strips, then unfold first and third strips over top.

6. Fold back second and fourth strips and add second perpendicular strip, keeping it snug to folded edge. Unfold second and fourth strips over top. Repeat weaving remaining strips evenly across pie, alternating between folding back first and third strips and second and fourth strips to create lattice pattern. Shift strips as needed so they are evenly spaced over top of pie. (If dough becomes too soft to work with, refrigerate pie and dough strips until firm.)

7. Trim overhang to ½ inch beyond lip of plate. Pinch edges of bottom crust and lattice strips together firmly to seal. Tuck overhang under itself; folded edge should be flush with edge of plate. Crimp dough evenly around edge of plate. (If dough is very soft, refrigerate for 10 minutes before baking.) Brush surface with egg wash.

8. Place pie on aluminum foil–lined rimmed baking sheet and bake until crust is light golden, 20 to 25 minutes. Reduce oven temperature to 350 degrees, rotate sheet, and continue to bake until juices are bubbling and crust is deep golden brown, 30 to 50 minutes longer. Let pie cool on wire rack until filling has set, about 4 hours. Serve.

Pumpkin Pie

Serves 8

WHY THIS RECIPE WORKS Our pumpkin pie sets the standard: It's velvety smooth (not stodgy or dense), packed with pumpkin flavor (not diluted), and perfectly spiced (not like potpourri). Canned pumpkin puree contains flavor-muting moisture, so to eliminate some of the liquid and concentrate the pumpkin's flavor we cooked the puree with sugar and spices before whisking in heavy cream, milk, and eggs to enrich it. Working with this hot filling and a warm prebaked crust helped the custard firm up quickly in the oven and prevented it from soaking into the crust. For spices, we used ground nutmeg and cinnamon—just enough to provide warmth without being distracting—and added some fresh grated ginger to awaken the mix. This autumnal pie was better than most, but it still didn't taste distinctly like sugar pumpkins. Granulated sugar and maple syrup sweetened things, but, surprisingly, it was another vegetable that really put our pie's flavor over the top. The addition of mashed candied sweet potatoes actually made our filling taste more like pumpkin than when it was made from pumpkin puree alone. Starting the pie in a hot oven and then dropping the temperature partway through baking prevented curdling. If candied sweet potatoes or yams are unavailable, regular canned sweet potatoes or yams can be substituted. When the pie is properly baked, the center 2 inches of the pie should look firm but jiggle slightly. Serve with lightly sweetened whipped cream.

 1 recipe Foolproof All-Butter Dough for
   Single-Crust Pie (page 454)
 1 cup heavy cream
 1 cup whole milk
 3 large eggs plus 2 large yolks
 1 teaspoon vanilla extract
 1 (15-ounce) can pumpkin puree
 1 cup candied sweet potatoes, drained
 ¾ cup (5¼ ounces) sugar
 ¼ cup maple syrup
 2 teaspoons grated fresh ginger
 1 teaspoon table salt
 ½ teaspoon ground cinnamon
 ¼ teaspoon ground nutmeg

1. Roll dough into 12-inch circle on well-floured counter. Loosely roll dough around rolling pin and gently unroll it onto 9-inch pie plate, letting excess dough hang over edge. Ease dough into plate by gently lifting edge of dough with your hand while pressing into plate bottom with your other hand.

2. Trim overhang to ½ inch beyond lip of plate. Tuck overhang under itself; folded edge should be flush with edge of plate. Crimp dough evenly around edge of plate.

Wrap dough-lined plate loosely in plastic wrap and refrigerate until firm, about 30 minutes. Adjust oven rack to middle position and heat oven to 350 degrees.

3. Line chilled pie shell with double layer of aluminum foil, covering edges to prevent burning, and fill with pie weights. Bake on foil-lined rimmed baking sheet until edges are set and just beginning to turn golden, 25 to 30 minutes, rotating sheet halfway through baking.

4. Remove foil and weights, rotate sheet, and continue to bake crust until golden brown and crisp, 10 to 15 minutes longer. Transfer sheet to wire rack. (Crust must still be warm when filling is added.) Increase oven temperature to 400 degrees.

5. While crust is baking, whisk cream, milk, eggs and yolks, and vanilla together in bowl; set aside. Bring pumpkin, sweet potatoes, sugar, maple syrup, ginger, salt, cinnamon, and nutmeg to simmer in large saucepan over medium heat and cook, stirring constantly and mashing sweet potatoes against sides of saucepan, until thick and shiny, 15 to 20 minutes.

6. Remove saucepan from heat and whisk in cream mixture until fully incorporated. Strain mixture through fine-mesh strainer into bowl, using back of ladle or spatula to press solids through strainer.

7. Whisk mixture; then, with pie still on sheet, pour into warm crust. Bake for 10 minutes. Reduce oven temperature to 300 degrees and continue to bake until edges of pie are set and center registers 175 degrees, 20 to 35 minutes longer, rotating sheet halfway through baking. Let pie cool completely on wire rack, about 4 hours. Serve.

Pecan Pie

Pecan Pie

Serves 8

WHY THIS RECIPE WORKS Pecan pie is a classic for good reason—rich, buttery pecans mingle with a custardy, deeply flavored sugar filling in a crisp crust for an irresistible treat. That's the ideal, at least. Pecan pies are often overwhelmingly sweet and lacking in their namesake flavor. What's more, the custard often curdles and separates, resulting in a weepy filling that makes the bottom crust soggy and leathery. We tackled this classic pie's classic problems by using dark brown sugar rather than granulated for deeper flavor; we also reduced the amount, which helped tame the saccharine bite and allowed the pecan flavor to shine. Some butter added a lush texture to the filling and underscored the richness of the pecans. After partially baking the crust, we found it important to add the hot filling to the warm pie crust to keep the crust from getting soggy. Melting the butter and cooking the filling over a simulated double-boiler was an easy way to maintain gentle heat and prevent the eggy filling from curdling. Finally, we avoided overbaking the pie—further insurance against curdling—by removing it from the oven when the center was still jiggly. As the pie cooled, the residual heat of the filling cooked the center through, so each slice of pie was silky and tender rather than marred by sugary curds. We recommend chopping the toasted pecans by hand. The crust must still be warm when the filling is added. To serve the pie warm, cool it thoroughly so that it sets completely, then warm it in a 250-degree oven for about 15 minutes and slice. Serve with vanilla ice cream or lightly sweetened whipped cream.

- 1 recipe Foolproof All-Butter Dough for Single-Crust Pie (page 454)
- 6 tablespoons unsalted butter, cut into 1-inch pieces
- 1 cup packed (7 ounces) dark brown sugar
- ½ teaspoon table salt
- 3 large eggs
- ¾ cup light corn syrup
- 1 tablespoon vanilla extract
- 2 cups (8 ounces) pecans, toasted and chopped fine

1. Roll dough into 12-inch circle on well-floured counter. Loosely roll dough around rolling pin and gently unroll it onto 9-inch pie plate, letting excess dough hang over edge. Ease dough into plate by gently lifting edge of dough with your hand while pressing into plate bottom with your other hand.

2. Trim overhang to ½ inch beyond lip of plate. Tuck overhang under itself; folded edge should be flush with edge of plate. Crimp dough evenly around edge of plate. Wrap dough-lined plate loosely in plastic wrap and refrigerate until firm, about 30 minutes. Adjust oven rack to lowest position and heat oven to 425 degrees.

3. Line chilled pie shell with double layer of aluminum foil, covering edges to prevent burning, and fill with pie weights. Bake on foil-lined rimmed baking sheet until pie dough looks dry and is pale in color, about 15 minutes.

4. Remove foil and weights, rotate sheet, and continue to bake until crust is light golden brown, 4 to 7 minutes longer. Transfer sheet to wire rack. (Crust must still be warm when filling is added.)

5. While crust is baking, melt butter in heatproof bowl set over saucepan filled with 1 inch of barely simmering water, making sure that water does not touch bottom of bowl. Off heat, stir in sugar and salt until butter is absorbed. Whisk in eggs, then corn syrup and vanilla, until smooth. Return bowl to saucepan and stir until mixture is shiny, hot to touch, and registers 130 degrees. Off heat, stir in pecans.

6. As soon as pie crust comes out of oven, adjust oven rack to lower-middle position and reduce oven temperature to 275 degrees. With pie still on sheet, pour pecan mixture into warm crust. Bake until filling looks set but yields like gelatin when gently pressed with back of spoon, 50 minutes to 1 hour, rotating sheet halfway through baking. Let pie cool completely on wire rack, about 4 hours. Serve.

VARIATION
Triple Chocolate Chunk Pecan Pie
After pouring pecan mixture into warm crust in step 6, sprinkle 6 ounces chopped semisweet, milk, and/or white chocolate over top, pressing lightly into filling with back of a spoon.

Blind Baking a Pie Crust

1. Line chilled pie shell with double layer of aluminum foil, covering edges to prevent burning.

2. Fill shell with pie weights and bake until dry and pale in color. After baking, carefully remove weights and let crust cool (for partially baked crust) or continue to bake until deep golden brown (for fully baked crust).

Key Lime Pie

Serves 8

WHY THIS RECIPE WORKS Key lime pie should remind us of the warm breezes of the Florida Keys. Unfortunately, when we're not on vacation it often disappoints us with its harsh, artificial flavor. We wanted a recipe for classic Key lime pie with fresh flavor and a silky filling. Traditional Key lime pie is usually not baked; instead, the combination of egg yolks, lime juice, and sweetened condensed milk firms up when chilled because the juice's acidity causes the proteins in the eggs and milk to bind. We found that just one simple swap—from the typical bottled, reconstituted lime juice to fresh lime juice and zest—gave us a pie that was pungent and refreshing, cool yet creamy, and very satisfying. We also discovered that while the pie filling will set without baking (most recipes call only for mixing and then chilling), it set much more nicely after being baked for just 15 minutes. These two seemingly minor adjustments to the classic recipe made all the difference. Despite this pie's name, we found that most tasters could not tell the difference between pies made with regular supermarket limes (called Persian limes) and true Key limes. Since Persian limes are easier to find and to juice we recommend using them instead.

- 1 (14-ounce) can sweetened condensed milk
- 4 large egg yolks
- 4 teaspoons grated lime zest plus ½ cup juice (4 limes)
- 1 recipe Graham Cracker Crust (page 457), baked and still warm
- 1 cup heavy cream
- ¼ cup (1 ounce) confectioners' sugar

1. Adjust oven rack to middle position and heat oven to 325 degrees. Whisk condensed milk, egg yolks, and lime zest and juice together in bowl. Let sit at room temperature until thickened, about 30 minutes.

2. Pour thickened filling into warm crust. Bake pie until center is firm but jiggles slightly when shaken, 15 to 20 minutes. Let pie cool slightly on wire rack, about 1 hour. Cover pie loosely with plastic wrap and refrigerate until filling is chilled and set, at least 3 hours or up to 24 hours.

3. Before serving, using stand mixer fitted with whisk attachment, whip cream and sugar on medium-low speed until foamy, about 1 minute. Increase speed to high and whip until soft peaks form, 1 to 3 minutes. Spread whipped cream attractively over top of pie and serve.

Lemon Meringue Pie

Serves 8

WHY THIS RECIPE WORKS Most everybody loves lemon meringue pie—at least the bottom half of it. The most controversial part is the meringue. On any given day it can shrink, bead, puddle, deflate, burn, sweat, break down, or turn rubbery. We wanted a pie with a crisp, flaky crust and a rich filling that would balance the airy meringue, without blocking the clear lemon flavor. The filling should be soft but not runny; firm enough to cut but not stiff and gelatinous. Most important, we wanted a meringue that didn't break down and puddle on the bottom or "tear" on top. We consulted a food scientist, who told us that the puddling underneath the meringue is from undercooking. The beading on top of the pie is from overcooking. We discovered that if the filling is piping hot when the meringue is applied, the underside of the meringue will not undercook; if the oven temperature is relatively low, the top of the meringue won't overcook. Baking the pie in a relatively cool (325-degree) oven also produces the best-looking, most evenly baked meringue. To further stabilize the meringue and keep it from weeping (even on hot, humid days), we beat in a small amount of cornstarch. Make the pie crust, let it cool, and then begin work on the filling. As soon as the filling is made, cover it with parchment paper to keep it hot and then start working on the meringue topping. You want to add the hot filling to the pie crust, apply the meringue topping, and then quickly get the pie into the oven.

1 recipe Foolproof All-Butter Dough for
  Single-Crust Pie (page 454)

Filling
1½ cups water
 1 cup (7 ounces) sugar
 ¼ cup (1 ounce) cornstarch
 ⅛ teaspoon table salt
 6 large egg yolks
 1 tablespoon grated lemon zest plus ½ cup
   juice (3 lemons)
 2 tablespoons unsalted butter, cut into 2 pieces

Meringue
 ⅓ cup water
 1 tablespoon cornstarch
 4 large egg whites
 ½ teaspoon vanilla extract
 ¼ teaspoon cream of tartar
 ½ cup (3½ ounces) sugar

1. Roll dough into 12-inch circle on well-floured counter.
Loosely roll dough around rolling pin and gently unroll it onto
9-inch pie plate, letting excess dough hang over edge. Ease
dough into plate by gently lifting edge of dough with your hand
while pressing into plate bottom with your other hand.

2. Trim overhang to ½ inch beyond lip of plate. Tuck
overhang under itself; folded edge should be flush with edge
of plate. Crimp dough evenly around edge of plate. Wrap
dough-lined plate loosely in plastic wrap and refrigerate until
firm, about 30 minutes. Adjust oven rack to middle position
and heat oven to 350 degrees.

3. Line chilled pie shell with double layer of aluminum foil,
covering edges to prevent burning, and fill with pie weights.
Bake on foil-lined rimmed baking sheet until edges are set
and just beginning to turn golden, 25 to 30 minutes, rotating
sheet halfway through baking. Remove foil and weights,
rotate sheet, and continue to bake crust until golden brown
and crisp, 10 to 15 minutes longer. Transfer sheet to wire
rack and let cool completely, about 45 minutes. Reduce oven
temperature to 325 degrees.

4. *For the filling:* Bring water, sugar, cornstarch, and
salt to simmer in large saucepan over medium heat, whisking
constantly. When mixture starts to turn translucent, whisk in
yolks, two at a time. Whisk in lemon zest and juice and butter.
Return mixture to brief simmer, then remove from heat. Spray
piece of parchment paper with vegetable oil spray and press
directly against surface of filling to keep warm and prevent
skin from forming.

5. *For the meringue:* Bring water and cornstarch to
simmer in small saucepan and cook, whisking occasionally,
until thickened and translucent, 1 to 2 minutes. Remove from
heat and let cool slightly.

6. Using stand mixer fitted with whisk attachment, whip
egg whites, vanilla, and cream of tartar on medium-low speed
until foamy, about 1 minute. Increase speed to medium-high
and beat in sugar, 1 tablespoon at a time, until incorporated and
mixture forms soft, billowy mounds. Add cornstarch mixture,
1 tablespoon at a time, and continue to beat to glossy, stiff
peaks, 2 to 3 minutes.

7. Meanwhile, remove parchment from filling and return to
very low heat during last minute or so of beating meringue
(to ensure filling is hot).

8. With pie still on sheet, pour warm filling into cooled
crust. Using rubber spatula, immediately dollop meringue
evenly around edge of crust, spreading meringue so it touches
crust (this will prevent the meringue from shrinking), then fill
in center with remaining meringue. Using back of spoon, create
attractive swirls and peaks in meringue. Bake until meringue
is light golden brown, about 20 minutes. Let pie cool on wire
rack until filling has set, about 2 hours. Serve.

Chocolate Cream Pie

Serves 8 to 10

WHY THIS RECIPE WORKS There is a reason this
old-fashioned pie is still crave-worthy because, honestly, what
could be more satisfying than a pie with a rich chocolate
filling and a pillowy topping of whipped cream all nestled in
a flaky pie crust? But this staple of the diner or deli dessert
case often fails to deliver. Gluey (rather than creamy) and
overly sweet fillings can belie even the best-looking cream
pies. For a deeply chocolaty mixture that wasn't too heavy,
we made a milk-based cocoa pudding and then whisked in
bittersweet chocolate, along with vanilla for extra depth.
A few tablespoons of butter helped the filling set up with a
silky consistency once it was poured into the prebaked pie
shell and refrigerated. Finally, we finished off the pie with a
complementary topping of lightly sweetened whipped cream.
We developed this recipe with whole milk, but you can use
2 percent low-fat milk, if desired. Avoid using 1 percent low-fat
or skim milk, as the filling will be too thin.

1 recipe Foolproof All-Butter Dough for Single-Crust Pie (page 454)

Filling
⅓ cup (2⅓ ounces) sugar
¼ cup (1 ounce) cornstarch
2 tablespoons unsweetened cocoa powder
¼ teaspoon salt
3 cups whole or 2 percent low-fat milk
6 ounces bittersweet chocolate, chopped fine
3 tablespoons unsalted butter, cut into 3 pieces
2 teaspoons vanilla extract

Topping
1 cup heavy cream
1 tablespoon confectioners' sugar

1. Roll dough into 12-inch circle on well-floured counter. Loosely roll dough around rolling pin and gently unroll it onto 9-inch pie plate, letting excess dough hang over edge. Ease dough into plate by gently lifting edge of dough with your hand while pressing into plate bottom with your other hand.

2. Trim overhang to ½ inch beyond lip of plate. Tuck overhang under itself; folded edge should be flush with edge of plate. Crimp dough evenly around edge of plate. Wrap dough-lined plate loosely in plastic wrap and refrigerate until firm, about 30 minutes. Adjust oven rack to middle position and heat oven to 350 degrees.

3. Line chilled pie shell with double layer of aluminum foil, covering edges to prevent burning, and fill with pie weights. Bake on foil-lined rimmed baking sheet until edges are set and just beginning to turn golden, 25 to 30 minutes, rotating sheet halfway through baking. Remove foil and weights, rotate sheet, and continue to bake crust until golden brown and crisp, 10 to 15 minutes longer. Transfer sheet to wire rack and let cool completely, about 45 minutes.

4. *For the filling:* Whisk sugar, cornstarch, cocoa, and salt together in large saucepan. Whisk in milk until incorporated, making sure to scrape corners of saucepan. Place saucepan over medium heat; cook, whisking constantly, until mixture is thickened and bubbling over entire surface, 8 to 10 minutes. Cook 30 seconds longer; remove from heat. Add chocolate and butter and whisk until melted and fully incorporated. Whisk in vanilla. Pour filling into cooled pie crust. Press lightly greased parchment paper against surface of filling and let cool completely, about 1 hour. Refrigerate until filling is firmly set, at least 2½ hours or up to 24 hours.

5. *For the topping:* Using stand mixer fitted with whisk attachment, whip cream and sugar on medium-low speed until foamy, about 1 minute. Increase speed to high and whip until stiff peaks form, 1 to 2 minutes. Spread whipped cream evenly over chilled pie and serve.

Lemon Tart

Serves 8 to 10

WHY THIS RECIPE WORKS Shiny lemon filling and buttery crust: These are the two components of a classic lemon tart. But despite the tart's minimal ingredients, lemon curd can be tricky to get right. It can easily slip over the edge of perfectly sweet into cloying, or its tartness can grab at your throat; it can be gluey or eggy or, even worse, metallic-tasting. We wanted a proper tart, one with a filling that's baked with the tart shell (rather than spread into a finished, prebaked shell) for a cohesive finish. For just enough sweetness to offset the lemons' acidity, we used 3 parts sugar to 2 parts lemon juice, while a whopping ¼ cup of floral lemon zest provided well-rounded citrus flavor. To achieve a curd that was creamy and dense with a vibrant hue, we used a combination of whole eggs and egg yolks. We cooked the curd and then strained it and stirred in a lick of cream just before baking to ensure a smooth, light texture. Once the lemon curd ingredients have been combined, cook it immediately; otherwise, its finished texture will be grainy.

1 recipe Classic Tart Dough (page 457)
2 large eggs plus 7 large yolks
1 cup (7 ounces) granulated sugar
¼ cup grated lemon zest plus ⅔ cup juice (4 lemons)
   Pinch table salt
4 tablespoons unsalted butter, cut into 4 pieces
3 tablespoons heavy cream
   Confectioners' sugar

1. Roll dough into 11-inch circle on lightly floured counter, then transfer to parchment paper–lined rimmed baking sheet; cover loosely with plastic wrap and refrigerate until firm but pliable, about 10 minutes.

2. Loosely roll dough around rolling pin and gently unroll it onto 9-inch tart pan with removable bottom, letting excess dough hang over edge. Ease dough into pan by gently lifting edge of dough with your hand while pressing into corners and fluted sides of pan with your other hand. Run rolling pin over top of pan to remove any excess dough. Wrap loosely in plastic, place on large plate, and freeze until fully firm, about 30 minutes. (Dough-lined tart pan can be frozen for up to 1 month.) Adjust oven rack to middle position and heat oven to 375 degrees.

3. Line chilled tart shell with double layer of aluminum foil and fill with pie weights. Bake on foil-lined rimmed baking sheet until tart shell is golden and set, about 30 minutes, rotating sheet halfway through baking. Remove foil and weights and transfer sheet to wire rack. (Tart shell must still be warm when filling is added.)

4. Whisk eggs and yolks together in medium saucepan. Whisk in granulated sugar until combined, then whisk in lemon zest and juice and salt. Add butter and cook over medium-low heat, stirring constantly, until mixture thickens slightly and registers 170 degrees, about 5 minutes. Immediately pour mixture through fine-mesh strainer into bowl. Stir in cream.

5. Pour warm lemon filling into warm tart shell. Bake tart on sheet until filling is shiny and opaque and center jiggles slightly when shaken, 10 to 15 minutes, rotating sheet halfway through baking.

6. Let tart cool completely on sheet on wire rack, about 2 hours. Remove outer ring of tart pan, slide thin metal spatula between tart and tart pan bottom, and carefully slide tart onto serving platter or cutting board. Dust with confectioners' sugar. Serve.

Lemon Olive Oil Tart

SEASON 20 RECIPE

Serves 8

WHY THIS RECIPE WORKS An unorthodox ingredient is the key to this simple, elegant, and brightly flavored tart. Most lemon tart recipes feature butter in both the crust and the filling, but here we used extra-virgin olive oil instead. It makes the crust a snap: Just mix the flour, sugar, and salt with the oil and a little water until a soft dough forms; crumble it into the tart pan; press it into the sides and bottom; and bake it right away—no rolling or chilling required. Using olive oil in the filling doesn't compromise its firmness or sliceability because the filling gets plenty of structure from the protein in

the eggs. Olive oil does, however, allow lemons' acidity to come to the fore in a way that butter doesn't. That means we could use a bit less juice and still enjoy plenty of bright lemon flavor. For the best flavor, use a fresh, high-quality extra-virgin olive oil. Make sure that all your metal equipment—saucepan, strainer, and whisk—is nonreactive, or the filling may have a metallic flavor.

Crust
1½ cups (7½ ounces) all-purpose flour
5 tablespoons (2¼ ounces) sugar
½ teaspoon table salt
½ cup extra-virgin olive oil
2 tablespoons water

Filling
1 cup (7 ounces) sugar
2 tablespoons all-purpose flour
¼ teaspoon table salt
3 large eggs plus 3 large yolks
1 tablespoon grated lemon zest plus
½ cup juice (3 lemons)
¼ cup extra-virgin olive oil

1. *For the crust:* Adjust oven rack to middle position and heat oven to 350 degrees. Whisk flour, sugar, and salt together in bowl. Add oil and water and stir until uniform dough forms. Using your hands, crumble three-quarters of dough over bottom of 9-inch tart pan with removable bottom. Press dough to even thickness in bottom of pan. Crumble remaining dough and scatter evenly around edge of pan, then press crumbled dough into fluted sides of pan. Press dough to even thickness. Bake on rimmed baking sheet until crust is deep golden brown and firm to touch, 30 to 35 minutes, rotating sheet halfway through baking. Transfer sheet to wire rack. (Tart shell must still be warm when filling is added.)

2. *For the filling:* About 5 minutes before crust is finished baking, whisk sugar, flour, and salt in medium saucepan until combined. Whisk in eggs and yolks until no streaks of egg remain, then whisk in lemon zest and juice. Cook over medium-low heat, whisking constantly and scraping corners of saucepan, until mixture thickens slightly and registers 160 degrees, 5 to 8 minutes.

3. Off heat, whisk in oil until incorporated. Strain curd through fine-mesh strainer into bowl. Pour curd into warm tart shell.

4. Bake until filling is set and barely jiggles when pan is shaken, 8 to 12 minutes. Let tart cool completely on sheet on wire rack, about 2 hours. Remove outer ring of tart pan, slide thin metal spatula between tart and tart pan bottom, and carefully slide tart onto serving platter or cutting board. Serve. (Leftovers can be wrapped loosely in plastic wrap and refrigerated for up to 3 days.)

The Best Summer Fruit Tart

Serves 8

WHY THIS RECIPE WORKS By trading the traditional rolled pastry and pastry cream filling for easier, faster alternatives, we produced a fresh fruit tart that is as appealing to make as it is to eat. Stirring melted butter into the dry ingredients yielded a malleable dough that could be pressed into the pan; for extra flavor, we browned the butter first and added back water that we lost so that there was enough moisture to help the flour form gluten (the protein network that would give the dough structure). A mix of mascarpone cheese, melted white baking chips, and lime juice and zest gave us a quick-to-make filling that was lush and creamy but also tangy and firm enough to slice cleanly. Arranging thin-sliced peaches in lines that radiated from the center of the tart to its outer edge created cutting guides between which we artfully arranged a mix of berries. These cutting guides ensured that we could slice the tart into neat portions without marring the arrangement of the fruit. An apricot preserves and lime juice glaze brightened the fruit, and gave the tart a polished, professional look. This recipe calls for extra berries to account for any bruising. Ripe, unpeeled nectarines can be substituted for the peaches, if desired. Use white baking chips here, not white chocolate bars, which contain cocoa butter and will result in a loose filling. Be sure to use a light hand when dabbing on the glaze, as too much force will dislodge the fruit. If the glaze begins to solidify while dabbing, microwave it for 5 to 10 seconds.

Crust
- 1 cup (6 ounces) all-purpose flour
- ¼ cup (1¾ ounces) sugar
- ⅛ teaspoon table salt
- 10 tablespoons unsalted butter
- 2 tablespoons water

Tart
- ⅓ cup (2 ounces) white baking chips
- ¼ cup heavy cream
- 1 teaspoon grated lime zest plus 7 teaspoons juice (2 limes), divided
  Pinch table salt
- 6 ounces (¾ cup) mascarpone, room temperature
- 2 ripe peaches, peeled
- 20 ounces (4 cups) raspberries, blackberries, and blueberries
- ⅓ cup apricot preserves

1. *For the crust:* Adjust oven rack to middle position and heat oven to 350 degrees. Whisk flour, sugar, and salt together in bowl. Melt butter in small saucepan over medium-high heat, swirling pan occasionally, until foaming subsides.

Continue to cook, stirring and scraping bottom of pan with spatula, until milk solids are dark golden brown and butter has nutty aroma, 1 to 3 minutes. Remove pan from heat and add water. When bubbling subsides, transfer butter to bowl with flour mixture, scraping pan with spatula. Stir until mixture is well combined. Transfer dough to 9-inch tart pan with removable bottom and let dough rest until warm to the touch, about 10 minutes.

2. Use your hands to evenly press and smooth dough over bottom and up side of pan (using two-thirds of dough for bottom crust and remaining third for side). Place tart pan on wire rack set in rimmed baking sheet. Bake until crust is golden brown, 25 to 30 minutes, rotating pan halfway through baking. Let cool completely, about 1 hour. (Cooled crust can be wrapped loosely in plastic wrap and stored at room temperature for up to 24 hours before filling.)

3. *For the tart:* Microwave baking chips, cream, lime zest, and salt in bowl, stirring every 10 seconds, until baking chips are melted, 30 seconds to 1 minute. Whisk in one-third of mascarpone, then whisk in 6 teaspoons lime juice and remaining mascarpone until smooth. Spread filling evenly over bottom of cooled tart shell.

4. Place 1 peach, stem side down, on cutting board. Placing knife just to side of pit, cut down to remove 1 side of peach. Turn peach 180 degrees and cut off opposite side. Cut off remaining 2 sides. Place pieces cut side down and slice ¼ inch thick. Repeat with second peach. Select best 24 slices.

5. Evenly space 8 berries around outer edge of tart. Using berries as guide, arrange 8 sets of 3 peach slices in filling, slightly overlapping slices with rounded side up, starting at center and ending on right side of each berry. Arrange remaining berries in attractive pattern between peach slices, covering as much of filling as possible and keeping fruit in even layer.

6. Microwave preserves and remaining 1 teaspoon lime juice in small bowl until fluid, 20 to 30 seconds. Strain mixture through fine-mesh strainer into bowl. Using pastry brush, gently dab mixture over fruit, avoiding crust. Refrigerate tart for 30 minutes.

7. Remove outer ring of tart pan, slide thin metal spatula between tart and tart pan bottom, and carefully slide tart onto serving platter or cutting board. Let tart sit at room temperature for 15 minutes. Using peaches as guide, cut tart into wedges and serve. (Tart can be refrigerated for up to 24 hours. If refrigerated for more than 1 hour, let tart sit at room temperature for 1 hour before serving.)

"I loved working on this recipe because it was fulfilling intellectually and artistically. Finding substitutes for pâte sucrée and crème pâtissière, the traditional crust and filling for the fruit tarts that adorn pastry cases, required brainstorming sessions with my team and a couple weeks of baking. Working out a strategy for cutting and arranging the fruit in a pattern that looks gorgeous when the tart is whole and sliced was pure fun. I got to try a variety of fruits and patterns, some symmetrical and others abstract. All of them were gorgeous!"

—Lan

Free-Form Summer Fruit Tart

Serves 6

WHY THIS RECIPE WORKS Few things are better than a summer fruit pie, but that takes time (and skill). What we wanted was simpler: a buttery, flaky crust paired with juicy summer fruit—with half the work of a regular pie. A free-form tart (a single layer of buttery pie dough folded up around fresh fruit) seemed the obvious solution. Without the support of a pie plate, tender crusts are prone to leak juice, and this results in soggy bottoms. For our crust, we used a high proportion of butter to flour, which provided the most buttery flavor and tender texture without compromising the structure. We then turned to a French technique in pastry making called *fraisage*. To begin, butter is only partially cut into the dry ingredients. Then, with the heel of the hand, the cook presses the barely mixed dough firmly against the counter. As a result, the chunks of butter are pressed into long, thin sheets that create lots of flaky layers when the dough is baked. We rolled the dough into a 12-inch circle for a crust that was thick enough to contain a lot of fruit but thin enough to bake evenly and thoroughly. We placed the fruit in the middle, then lifted the dough up and back over the fruit and pleated it loosely to allow for shrinkage. The bright summer fruit needed only the simple addition of sugar. Though we prefer a tart made with a mix of stone fruits and berries, you can use only one type of fruit if you prefer. Taste the fruit before adding sugar to it; use the lesser amount if the fruit is very sweet, more if it is tart. However much sugar you use, do not add it to the fruit until you are ready to fill and form the tart. Serve with vanilla ice cream, lightly sweetened whipped cream, or crème fraîche.

Rustic Tart Dough

- 1½ cups (7½ ounces) all-purpose flour
- ½ teaspoon table salt
- 10 tablespoons unsalted butter, cut into ½-inch pieces and chilled
- 3–6 tablespoons ice water

Filling

- 1 pound peaches, nectarines, apricots, or plums, pitted and sliced into ½-inch-thick wedges
- 5 ounces (1 cup) blueberries, raspberries, or blackberries
- 4–6 tablespoons sugar, divided

1. *For the rustic tart dough:* Process flour and salt in food processor until combined, about 5 seconds. Scatter butter over top and pulse until mixture resembles coarse sand and butter pieces are about size of small peas, about 10 pulses. Continue to pulse, adding water 1 tablespoon at a time, until dough begins to form small curds that hold together when pinched with your fingers, about 10 pulses.

2. Transfer mixture to lightly floured counter and gather into rectangular-shaped pile. Starting at farthest end, use heel of your hand to smear small amount of dough against counter. Continue to smear dough until all crumbs have been worked. Gather smeared crumbs together in another rectangular-shaped pile and repeat process. Form dough into 6-inch disk, wrap tightly in plastic wrap, and refrigerate for at least 1 hour or up to 2 days. Let chilled dough sit on counter to soften slightly, about 10 minutes, before rolling. (Wrapped dough can be frozen for up to 1 month. If frozen, let dough thaw completely on counter before rolling.)

Mixing a Flaky Dough

1. Starting at 1 end of rectangular pile of dough, smear small amount of dough against counter with heel of your hand. Repeat process (called fraisage) until rest of buttery crumbs have been worked.

2. Gather smeared bits into another rectangular pile and repeat smearing process until all of crumbs have been worked again.

3. Roll dough into 12-inch circle between 2 large sheets of floured parchment paper. (If dough sticks to parchment, gently loosen dough with bench scraper and dust parchment with additional flour.) Slide dough, still between parchment, onto rimmed baking sheet and refrigerate until firm, 15 to 30 minutes.

4. *For the filling:* Adjust oven rack to middle position and heat oven to 375 degrees. Gently toss peaches, blueberries, and 3 to 5 tablespoons sugar together in bowl. Remove top sheet of parchment from dough. Mound fruit in center of dough, leaving 2½-inch border around edge of fruit. Fold outermost 2 inches of dough over fruit, pleating it every 2 to 3 inches as needed; be sure to leave ½-inch border of dough between fruit and edge of tart. Gently pinch pleated dough to secure, but do not press dough into fruit. Brush top and sides of dough lightly with water and sprinkle with remaining 1 tablespoon sugar.

5. Bake until crust is deep golden brown and fruit is bubbling, about 1 hour, rotating sheet halfway through baking.

6. Let tart cool on sheet on wire rack for 10 minutes. Using parchment, carefully slide tart onto wire rack and let tart cool until filling thickens, about 25 minutes. Serve slightly warm or at room temperature.

Linzertorte

SEASON 20 RECIPE

Serves 10 to 12

WHY THIS RECIPE WORKS The components of a Linzertorte couldn't be easier to prepare. A buttery, nut-enhanced crust comes together easily in the food processor, and the raspberry jam filling is something you buy. Making this holiday tart look special is what takes precision. The hazelnut-and-almond-enriched dough is extra-delicate, so we simply patted it into the tart pan in pieces rather than rolling it. As for the lattice, we cut the strips on parchment paper so we could use the parchment to transfer the soft strips to the jam-filled tart, peeling the paper back as we placed the strips. A brush of cream and a sprinkling of turbinado sugar gave the golden-brown tart glitter and glow. Make sure to buy blanched almonds and use an 11-inch tart pan here. You will have some extra dough when cutting out the lattice strips; we suggest cutting out a few extra lattice strips as backup (they are delicate and could break). If the dough becomes too soft while forming the lattice, refrigerate it for 15 minutes before continuing. The Linzertorte may be served at room temperature the day it is baked, but it's at its best after a night in the refrigerator.

Tart dough
- 1 large egg
- 1 teaspoon vanilla extract
- 1 cup hazelnuts, toasted and skinned
- ½ cup plus 2 tablespoons (4⅓ ounces) granulated sugar
- ½ cup blanched almonds
- ½ teaspoon table salt
- 1 teaspoon grated lemon zest
- 1½ cups (7½ ounces) all-purpose flour
- ½ teaspoon ground cinnamon
- ⅛ teaspoon ground allspice
- 12 tablespoons unsalted butter, cut into ½-inch pieces and chilled

Filling
- 1¼ cups raspberry preserves
- 1 tablespoon lemon juice
- 1 tablespoon heavy cream
- 1½ teaspoons turbinado or Demerara sugar (optional)

1. *For the tart dough:* Whisk egg and vanilla together in bowl. Process hazelnuts, sugar, almonds, and salt in food processor until very finely ground, 45 to 60 seconds. Add lemon zest and pulse to combine, about 5 pulses. Add flour, cinnamon, and allspice and pulse to combine, about 5 pulses. Scatter butter over top and pulse until mixture resembles coarse cornmeal, about 15 pulses. With processor running, add egg mixture and continue to process until dough just comes together, about 12 seconds longer.

2. Transfer dough to counter and form into cohesive mound. Divide dough in half and form each half into 5-inch disk. (If not using immediately, wrap disks tightly in plastic wrap and refrigerate for up to 2 days. Let chilled dough sit at room temperature until soft and malleable, about 1 hour, before using.)

3. Tear 1 disk into walnut-size pieces, then pat pieces into 11-inch tart pan with removable bottom, pressing dough into corners and ¾ inch up sides of pan. Cover dough with plastic and smooth out any bumps using bottom of measuring cup. Set pan on large plate and freeze until firm, about 30 minutes.

4. Roll second disk into 12-inch square between 2 large sheets of floured parchment paper. (If dough sticks to parchment, gently loosen and lift sticky area with bench scraper and dust parchment with additional flour.) Slide dough, still between parchment, onto rimmed baking sheet and refrigerate until firm, about 15 minutes. Remove top layer of parchment and trim edges of dough to form perfect square, then cut ten ¾-inch-wide strips, cutting through underlying parchment. Cover with parchment and freeze until dough is fully chilled and firm, about 20 minutes.

Making a Linzertorte Lattice

1. Pick up 1 strip of dough by parchment ends, then flip it over onto tart, positioning it near edge of pan. Remove parchment strip and trim ends of dough strip by pressing down on top edge of pan.

2. Place 2 more strips parallel to first, spacing them evenly so that one is across center and other is near opposite edge of pan.

3. Rotate pan 90 degrees, then place 3 more strips, spacing as with first three.

4. Rotate pan 90 degrees again, then place 2 strips across pan, spaced evenly between first three.

5. Rotate pan again and complete lattice by placing last 2 strips between second set of three.

6. Use small scraps of dough to fill in crust around edges between lattice strips.

5. Meanwhile, adjust oven rack to middle position and heat oven to 350 degrees. Set dough-lined tart pan on rimmed baking sheet. Spray 1 side of double layer of aluminum foil with vegetable oil spray. Press foil, greased side down, into frozen tart shell, covering edges to prevent burning, and fill with pie weights. Bake until tart shell is golden brown and set, about 30 minutes, rotating sheet halfway through baking. Remove foil and weights, transfer sheet to wire rack, and let cool completely, about 1 hour.

6. *For the filling:* Stir raspberry preserves and lemon juice together in bowl. Spread filling evenly over bottom of tart shell. Pick up 1 strip of dough by parchment ends, then flip it over onto tart, positioning it near edge of pan. Remove parchment strip and trim ends of dough strip by pressing down on top edge of pan; reserve all dough scraps. Place 2 more strips parallel to first, spacing them evenly so that one is across center and other is near opposite edge of pan. Rotate pan 90 degrees, then place 3 more strips, spacing as with first three. Rotate pan 90 degrees again, then place 2 strips across pan, spaced evenly between first three. Rotate pan again and complete lattice by placing last 2 strips between second set of three. Use small scraps of dough to fill in crust around edges between lattice strips. Top of crust should be just below top of pan.

7. Gently brush lattice strips with cream and sprinkle with sugar, if using. Bake on sheet until crust is deep golden brown, 40 to 45 minutes. Let tart cool completely on sheet on wire rack, about 2 hours. Remove outer ring of tart pan, slide thin metal spatula between tart and tart pan bottom, and carefully slide tart onto serving platter or cutting board. Serve or refrigerate overnight.

Apple Galette

Serves 10 to 12

WHY THIS RECIPE WORKS The French tart known as an apple galette should have a flaky crust and a layer of shingled caramelized apples. But it's challenging to make a crust strong enough to hold the apples and still be eaten out of hand—most recipes create a tough, bland crust. Choosing the right flour put us on the right track. All-purpose flour contained too much gluten; it made the pastry tough. Lower-protein pastry flour created a flaky and sturdy pastry. As pastry flour is hard to find, we mixed regular all-purpose flour with instant flour. Technique also proved to be important. We found that any thinly sliced apple would work, although we slightly preferred Granny Smith. The most common brand of instant flour is Wondra; it is sold in a canister in the baking aisle. The galette can be made without instant flour, using 2 cups unbleached all-purpose flour and 2 tablespoons cornstarch; however, you might have to increase the amount of ice water. Serve with ice cream, whipped cream, or crème fraîche.

Linzertorte

"I'm not a big fan of cakes, but I love fruit desserts and this galette is an all-time favorite. It's simple—just apples and a crust—but both are done perfectly. The crust has the ultimate texture of delicate yet sturdy, like a croissant dough crossed with a pie dough. Using the French fraisage method can seem tricky at first, but there is really no wrong way to do it, as long as you get a few good smears of butter. It's those butter smears that turn into flaky bits of pastry during baking. I almost always use Granny Smith apples because I like their tangy flavor and they hold their shape well during baking, but Golden Delicious and Empire also work well. Also, it's important that the apples are sliced as thin as possible, so take your time with their prep. If they are cut thicker than ⅛ inch, they will be hard to shingle."

—*Julia*

Dough

- 1½ cups (7½ ounces) all-purpose flour
- ½ cup (2½ ounces) instant flour
- ½ teaspoon table salt
- ½ teaspoon sugar
- 12 tablespoons unsalted butter, cut into ¼-inch pieces and chilled
- 7–9 tablespoons ice water

Topping

- 1½ pounds Granny Smith apples, peeled, cored, and sliced ⅛ inch thick
- 2 tablespoons unsalted butter, cut into ¼-inch pieces
- ¼ cup (1¾ ounces) sugar
- 3 tablespoons apple jelly

1. For the dough: Process all-purpose flour, instant flour, salt, and sugar in food processor until combined. Scatter butter over top and pulse until mixture resembles coarse cornmeal, about 15 pulses. Continue to pulse, adding water 1 tablespoon at a time, until dough begins to form small curds that hold together when pinched with your fingers, about 10 pulses.

Preparing Apple Galette

1. Cut piece of parchment to measure exactly 16 by 12 inches, then roll dough out on top of the parchment until it just overhangs the edge and is about ⅛ inch thick.

2. Trim dough so edges are even with parchment.

3. Roll up 1 inch of each edge to create ½-inch-thick border.

4. Slide parchment and dough onto rimmed baking sheet. Starting in one corner, shingle apple slices in tidy rows on diagonal over dough, overlapping each row by a third.

2. Transfer mixture to lightly floured counter and gather into rectangular-shaped pile. Starting at farthest end, use heel of your hand to smear small amount of dough against counter. Continue to smear dough until all crumbs have been worked. Gather smeared crumbs together in another rectangular-shaped pile and repeat process. Form dough into 6-inch disk, wrap tightly in plastic wrap, and refrigerate for at least 1 hour or up to 2 days. Let chilled dough sit on counter to soften slightly, about 10 minutes, before rolling. (Wrapped dough can be frozen for up to 1 month. If frozen, let dough thaw completely on counter before rolling.)

3. Adjust oven rack to middle position and heat oven to 400 degrees. Cut piece of parchment into 16 by 12-inch rectangle. Roll dough out over parchment, dusting with flour as needed, until it just overhangs parchment. Trim edges of dough even with parchment. Roll outer 1 inch of dough up to create ½-inch-thick border. Slide parchment paper with dough onto rimmed baking sheet.

4. For the topping: Starting in 1 corner of tart, shingle apple slices onto crust in tidy diagonal rows, overlapping them by one-third. Dot with butter and sprinkle evenly with sugar. Bake tart until bottom is deep golden brown and apples have caramelized, 45 minutes to 1 hour, rotating sheet halfway through baking.

5. Melt jelly in small saucepan over medium-high heat, stirring occasionally to smooth out any lumps. Brush glaze evenly over apples, avoiding tart crust, then let tart cool on sheet for 10 minutes. Slide tart onto platter or cutting board. Serve slightly warm or at room temperature.

French Apple Tart

Serves 8

WHY THIS RECIPE WORKS French apple tart is a visually stunning centerpiece dessert that's little more than, well, apples—half of which are cooked down to an applesauce-like mixture—and pastry. For intense fruit flavor, we packed our tart with a whopping 5 pounds of Golden Delicious apples; we found this variety broke down easily to make the puree. To concentrate the apple flavor, we cooked the puree until it measured about 2 cups. A little butter enriched the lean filling. For a beautiful presentation—and even more apple flavor—we parcooked apple slices until they were just pliable and arranged them on top of the tart in beautiful concentric circles to form a flower-like design. A thin coat of preserves and a final run under the broiler provided a caramelized finish. If you don't have a potato masher, you can puree the apples in a food processor. You may have extra apple slices after arranging the apples in step 6. To ensure that the outer ring of the pan releases easily from the tart, avoid getting apple puree and apricot glaze on the edge of the crust. The tart is best served the day it is assembled.

Crust

1⅓ cups (6⅔ ounces) all-purpose flour
5 tablespoons (2¼ ounces) sugar
½ teaspoon table salt
10 tablespoons unsalted butter, melted

Filling

10 large Golden Delicious apples (8 ounces each), peeled and cored, divided
3 tablespoons unsalted butter, divided
1 tablespoon water
½ cup apricot preserves
¼ teaspoon table salt

1. For the crust: Adjust 1 oven rack to lowest position and second rack 5 to 6 inches from broiler element. Heat oven to 350 degrees. Whisk flour, sugar, and salt together in bowl. Add melted butter and stir until dough forms. Using your hands, press two-thirds of dough into bottom of 9-inch tart pan with removable bottom. Press remaining dough into fluted sides of pan. Press and smooth dough with your hands to even thickness. Place pan on wire rack set in rimmed baking sheet and bake on lowest rack until crust is deep golden brown and firm to touch, 30 to 35 minutes, rotating sheet halfway through baking. Set aside until ready to fill.

2. For the filling: Cut 5 apples lengthwise into quarters and cut each quarter lengthwise into 4 slices. Melt 1 tablespoon butter in 12-inch skillet over medium heat. Add apple slices and water and toss to combine. Cover and cook, stirring occasionally, until apples begin to turn translucent and are slightly pliable, 3 to 5 minutes. Transfer apples to large plate, spread into single layer, and set aside to cool.

3. While apples cook, microwave apricot preserves until fluid, about 30 seconds. Strain preserves through fine-mesh strainer into small bowl, reserving solids. Set aside 3 tablespoons strained preserves for brushing tart.

4. Cut remaining 5 apples into ½-inch-thick wedges. Melt remaining 2 tablespoons butter in now-empty skillet over medium heat. Add remaining strained apricot preserves, reserved apricot solids, apple wedges, and salt. Cover and cook, stirring occasionally, until apples are very soft, about 10 minutes.

5. Mash apples to puree with potato masher. Continue to cook, stirring occasionally, until puree is reduced to 2 cups, about 5 minutes.

6. Transfer apple puree to baked tart shell and smooth surface. Select 5 thinnest slices of sautéed apple and set aside. Starting at outer edge of tart, arrange remaining slices, tightly overlapping in concentric circles. Bend reserved slices to fit in center. Bake tart, still on wire rack in sheet, on lowest rack, for 30 minutes. Remove tart from oven and heat broiler.

7. While broiler heats, warm reserved preserves in microwave until fluid, about 20 seconds. Brush evenly over surface of apples, avoiding tart crust. Broil tart, checking every 30 seconds and turning as necessary, until apples are attractively caramelized, 1 to 3 minutes. Let tart cool for at least 1½ hours. Remove outer metal ring of tart pan, slide thin metal spatula between tart and pan bottom, and carefully slide tart onto serving platter. Cut into wedges and serve. (Baked crust, apple slices, and apple puree can be made up to 24 hours in advance. Apple slices and puree should be refrigerated separately. Assemble tart with refrigerated apple slices and puree and bake as directed, adding 5 minutes to baking time.)

Making an Apple Rosette

1. Starting at edges and working toward center, arrange most of the cooled sautéed apple slices in tightly overlapping concentric circles.

2. Bend remaining slices to fit in center.

Best Chocolate Tart

Serves 10 to 12

WHY THIS RECIPE WORKS For us, a great chocolate tart should possess deep chocolate flavor, a rich, lush texture, and a sophisticated presentation. First we made a custardy filling by melting intense dark chocolate into hot cream, adding eggs, and baking. To enrich the filling's flavor, we added some butter and a little instant espresso to echo the bittersweetness of the chocolate. Because custards tend to curdle under high heat, we baked the tart in a very low 250-degree oven for a smooth and silky texture. To make our tart a showstopper, we topped it with a simple glossy glaze of chocolate, cream, and corn syrup. A classic sweet pastry dough flavored with ground almonds made the perfect complement to the chocolate filling. Toasted and skinned hazelnuts can be substituted for the almonds. Use good-quality dark chocolate containing a cacao percentage between 60 and 65 percent; our favorites are Ghirardelli 60% Cacao Bittersweet Chocolate and Callebaut Intense Dark Chocolate, L-60–40NV. Let tart sit at room temperature for 30 minutes before glazing in step 7. The tart can be garnished with chocolate curls or with a flaky coarse sea salt, such as Maldon. Serve with lightly sweetened whipped cream; if you like, flavor the whipped cream with cognac or vanilla extract.

Crust
- 1 large egg yolk
- 2 tablespoons heavy cream
- ½ cup sliced almonds, toasted
- ¼ cup (1¾ ounces) sugar
- 1 cup (5 ounces) all-purpose flour
- ¼ teaspoon table salt
- 6 tablespoons unsalted butter, cut into ½-inch pieces

Filling
- 9 ounces bittersweet chocolate, chopped fine
- 1¼ cups heavy cream
- ½ teaspoon instant espresso powder
- ¼ teaspoon table salt
- 4 tablespoons unsalted butter, cut into thin slices and softened
- 2 large eggs, lightly beaten, room temperature

Glaze
- 3 tablespoons heavy cream
- 1 tablespoon light corn syrup
- 2 ounces bittersweet chocolate, chopped fine
- 1 tablespoon hot water

1. For the crust: Beat egg yolk and cream together in bowl. Process almonds and sugar in food processor until nuts are finely ground, 15 to 20 seconds. Add flour and salt and pulse to combine, about 10 pulses. Scatter butter over top and pulse until mixture resembles coarse meal, about 15 pulses. With processor running, add egg yolk mixture and continue to process until dough forms ball, about 10 seconds. Transfer dough to large sheet of plastic wrap and form into 6-inch disk. Wrap tightly in plastic and refrigerate until firm but malleable, at least 30 minutes or up to 3 days. Let chilled dough sit on counter to soften slightly, about 10 minutes, before rolling.

2. Roll dough into 11-inch circle between 2 large sheets of plastic. (If dough becomes too soft to work with, transfer to rimmed baking sheet and refrigerate until chilled.) Slide dough, still between plastic, onto rimmed baking sheet and refrigerate until firm but pliable, 15 to 30 minutes.

3. Adjust oven rack to middle position and heat oven to 375 degrees. Spray 9-inch tart pan with removable bottom with vegetable oil spray. Keeping dough on sheet, remove top layer of plastic. Invert tart pan (with bottom) on top of dough round. Press on tart pan to cut dough. Using both hands, pick up sheet and tart pan and carefully invert both, setting tart pan right side up. Remove sheet and peel off plastic; reserve plastic. Roll over edges of tart pan with rolling pin to cut dough. Gently ease and press dough into bottom of pan, reserving scraps. Roll dough scraps into ¾-inch rope (various lengths are OK). Line edge of tart pan with rope(s) and gently press into fluted sides. Line tart pan with reserved plastic and, using measuring cup, gently press and smooth dough to even thickness (sides should be about ¼ inch thick). Using paring knife, trim any excess dough above rim of tart; discard scraps. Freeze dough-lined pan until dough is firm, 20 to 30 minutes.

Fitting Delicate Pastry into a Tart Pan
This novel method works with any tart dough, but it is especially helpful when working with higher-fat, more fragile pastry.

1. Invert tart pan onto dough round. Press down on pan to perforate dough. Invert baking sheet, holding tart pan in place, then set down so tart pan is right side up. Remove baking sheet and plastic wrap.

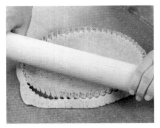

2. Roll over dough edges with rolling pin to cut off excess, reserving scraps. Gently press dough into bottom of pan in even layer.

3. Roll dough scraps into ¾-inch rope(s). Line fluted edges of pan with ropes and press evenly into sides.

4. Line chilled tart shell with greased double layer of aluminum foil and fill with pie weights. Bake on foil-lined rimmed baking sheet until tart shell is light golden and dough is dry, about 25 minutes, rotating sheet halfway through baking. Remove foil and weights and continue to bake until tart shell is rich golden brown and fragrant, 8 to 10 minutes longer. Let cool completely on sheet on wire rack.

5. *For the filling:* Reduce oven temperature to 250 degrees. Place chocolate in large bowl. Bring cream, espresso powder, and salt to simmer in small saucepan over medium heat, whisking to dissolve espresso powder and salt, then pour over chocolate. Cover and let sit until chocolate is softened, about 5 minutes, then whisk to combine. Whisk in butter until smooth, then pour beaten eggs through fine-mesh strainer into chocolate mixture and whisk until combined and glossy.

6. Pour filling into cooled tart shell and spread into even layer with rubber spatula, popping any large bubbles with toothpick. Bake until edge of filling is just set but center jiggles slightly and very faint cracks appear on surface, 30 to 35 minutes. Let tart cool completely on sheet on wire rack, about 2 hours. Refrigerate, uncovered, until filling is chilled and set, at least 3 hours or up to 18 hours.

7. *For the glaze:* Remove tart from refrigerator and let sit at room temperature for 30 minutes. Bring cream and corn syrup to simmer in small saucepan over medium heat, stirring occasionally. Off heat, add chocolate, cover, and let sit until chocolate is softened, about 5 minutes. Whisk to combine, then whisk in hot water (glaze should be homogenous, shiny, and pourable). Working quickly, pour glaze onto center of tart and tilt tart to allow glaze to run to edge. Pop any large bubbles with toothpick. Let sit at room temperature until glaze is set, at least 1 hour or up to 3 hours.

8. Remove outer ring of tart pan, slide thin metal spatula between tart and tart pan bottom, and carefully slide tart onto serving platter or cutting board. Serve.

Strawberry Shortcakes

Serves 6

WHY THIS RECIPE WORKS While some cooks like to spoon strawberries over pound cake, sponge cake, and even angel food cake, our idea of strawberry shortcake definitely involves a biscuit. We wanted a juicy strawberry filling and mounds of freshly whipped cream sandwiched in between a lightly sweetened, tender biscuit. While eggs are not traditional, we found that one whole egg gave our biscuits a light, tender texture. And we used just enough dairy (half-and-half or milk) to bind the dough together. A modest amount of sugar yielded a lightly sweetened biscuit. For the strawberries, we wanted to avoid both a mushy puree and dry chunks of fruit.

We found our solution in a compromise—mashing a portion of the berries and slicing the rest for a chunky, juicy mixture that didn't slide off the biscuit. And lightly sweetened whipped cream, flavored with vanilla, provided a cool, creamy contrast to the berries and biscuits. Start the recipe by preparing the fruit, then set the fruit aside while preparing the biscuits to allow the juices to become syrupy.

Fruit
8   cups (40 ounces) strawberries, hulled, divided
6   tablespoons sugar

Shortcake
2   cups (10 ounces) all-purpose flour
5   tablespoons sugar, divided
1   tablespoon baking powder
½   teaspoon table salt
8   tablespoons unsalted butter, cut into ½-inch pieces and chilled
½   cup plus 1 tablespoon half-and-half or milk, divided
1   large egg, lightly beaten, plus 1 large egg white, lightly beaten

Whipped Cream
1   cup heavy cream, chilled
1   tablespoon sugar
1   teaspoon vanilla extract

1. *For the fruit:* Crush 3 cups strawberries in large bowl with potato masher. Slice remaining 5 cups of berries and stir into crushed berries along with sugar. Set aside until sugar has dissolved and berries are juicy, at least 30 minutes or up to 2 hours.

2. *For the shortcake:* Adjust oven rack to lower-middle position and heat oven to 425 degrees. Line baking sheet with parchment paper. Pulse flour, 3 tablespoons sugar, baking powder, and salt in food processor until combined. Sprinkle butter pieces over top and pulse until mixture resembles coarse meal, about 15 pulses. Transfer mixture to large bowl.

3. Whisk half-and-half and lightly beaten egg together in small bowl, then stir into flour mixture with rubber spatula until large clumps form. Turn dough onto lightly floured work surface and knead lightly until it comes together.

4. Pat dough into 9 by 6-inch rectangle, about ¾ inch thick. Do not overwork dough. Using floured 2¾-inch biscuit cutter, cut out six dough rounds. Arrange shortcakes on prepared sheet, spaced about 1½ inches apart. Brush tops with lightly beaten egg white and sprinkle evenly with remaining 2 tablespoons sugar. (Unbaked shortcakes can be covered with plastic wrap and refrigerated for up to 2 hours.)

5. Bake until shortcakes are golden brown, 12 to 14 minutes, rotating sheet halfway through baking. Transfer sheet to wire rack and let shortcakes cool until warm, about 10 minutes.

Strawberry Shortcakes

6. *For the whipped cream:* In medium bowl, whip cream, sugar, and vanilla with an electric mixer on medium-low speed until frothy, about 1 minute. Increase speed to high and continue to whip until cream forms soft peaks, 1 to 3 minutes.

7. *To assemble:* When shortcakes have cooled slightly, split in half horizontally. Place each shortcake bottom on individual plate, spoon portion of berries over each bottom, dollop with whipped cream, and cap with shortcake tops. Serve immediately.

Sour Cherry Cobbler

Serves 12

WHY THIS RECIPE WORKS Most cherry cobblers are no more than canned pie filling topped with dry, heavy biscuits. We wanted a filling that highlighted the unique, sweet-tart flavor of sour cherries and, on top, we wanted a tender, feather-light biscuit crust. Because fresh sour cherries are so hard to find most of the year, we picked jarred Morello cherries—easy to find and available year-round. Embellishing the cherries with cherry juice, cinnamon, and vanilla was a step in the right direction but the filling still tasted a bit flat, so we switched out some of the juice for red wine and replaced the vanilla with almond extract. The resulting sauce was better, but a little thin. A small amount of cornstarch thickened the filling nicely. As for the biscuits, we favored buttermilk biscuits, which have a light and fluffy texture. To ensure nicely browned biscuits that didn't become soggy over the filling, we par-baked them on their own ahead of time, then slid the biscuits over the warm cherry filling and put it in the oven to finish cooking. Use the smaller amount of sugar in the filling if you prefer your fruit desserts on the tart side and the larger amount if you like them sweet. Serve with vanilla ice cream or lightly sweetened whipped cream.

Biscuit Topping

- 2 cups (10 ounces) all-purpose flour
- ½ cup (3½ ounces) sugar, divided
- ½ teaspoon baking powder
- ½ teaspoon baking soda
- ½ teaspoon table salt
- 6 tablespoons unsalted butter, cut into ½-inch pieces and chilled
- 1 cup buttermilk

Filling

- 8 cups jarred Morello cherries from 4 (24-ounce) jars, drained, 2 cups juice reserved
- ¾–1 cup (5¼–7 ounces) sugar
- 3 tablespoons plus 1 teaspoon cornstarch
  Pinch table salt
- 1 cup dry red wine
- 1 (3-inch) cinnamon stick
- ¼ teaspoon almond extract

1. Adjust oven rack to middle position and heat oven to 425 degrees. Line baking sheet with parchment paper.

2. *For the biscuit topping:* Pulse flour, 6 tablespoons sugar, baking powder, baking soda, and salt in food processor until combined. Sprinkle butter pieces over top and pulse until mixture resembles coarse meal, about 15 pulses. Transfer mixture to large bowl; add buttermilk and stir with rubber spatula until combined. Using greased ¼-cup measure ice cream scoop, scoop 12 biscuits onto prepared sheet, spacing them 1½ inches apart. Sprinkle biscuits evenly with remaining 2 tablespoons sugar and bake until lightly browned, about 15 minutes, rotating sheet halfway through baking. (Do not turn oven off.)

3. *For the filling:* Meanwhile, arrange drained cherries in even layer in 13 by 9-inch baking dish. Combine sugar, cornstarch, and salt in medium saucepan. Stir in reserved cherry juice and wine and add cinnamon stick; cook over medium-high heat, stirring frequently, until mixture simmers and thickens, about 5 minutes. Discard cinnamon stick, stir in almond extract, and pour hot liquid over cherries in baking dish.

4. *To bake:* Arrange hot biscuits in 3 rows of 4 biscuits over warm filling. Bake cobbler until filling is bubbling and biscuits are deep golden brown, about 10 minutes. Transfer baking dish to wire rack and let cool for 10 minutes; serve.

VARIATION
Fresh Sour Cherry Cobbler
Morello or Montmorency cherries can be used in this cobbler made with fresh sour cherries. Do not use sweet Bing cherries. If the cherries do not release enough juice after 30 minutes in step 1, add cranberry juice to make up the difference.

- 1¼ cups (8¾ ounces) sugar
- 3 tablespoons plus 1 teaspoon cornstarch
  Pinch table salt
- 8 cups (4 pounds) fresh sour cherries, pitted, juice reserved
- 1 cup dry red wine
  Cranberry juice, as needed
- 1 recipe Biscuit Topping
- 1 (3-inch) cinnamon stick
- ¼ teaspoon almond extract

1. Whisk sugar, cornstarch, and salt together in large bowl; add cherries and toss well to combine. Pour wine over cherries; let sit for 30 minutes. Drain cherries in colander set over medium bowl. Combine drained and reserved juices (from pitting cherries); you should have 3 cups (if not, add cranberry juice to make this amount).

2. Meanwhile, prepare and bake biscuit topping.

3. Arrange drained cherries in even layer in 13 by 9-inch baking dish. Bring juices, wine, and cinnamon stick to simmer in medium saucepan over medium-high heat, stirring frequently, until mixture thickens, about 5 minutes. Discard cinnamon stick, stir in almond extract, and pour hot juices over cherries in baking dish.

4. Arrange hot biscuits in 3 rows of 4 biscuits over warm filling. Bake cobbler until filling is bubbling and biscuits are deep golden brown, about 10 minutes. Transfer baking dish to wire rack and let cool for 10 minutes; serve.

Blueberry Cobbler

Serves 6 to 8

WHY THIS RECIPE WORKS Too often, blueberry cobbler means a filling that is too sweet, overspiced, and unappealingly thick. We wanted a not-too-thin, not-too-thick filling where the blueberry flavor would be front and center. And over the fruit, we wanted a light, tender biscuit topping that could hold its own against the fruit filling, with an ingredient list simple enough to allow the blueberries to play a starring role. We prepared a not-too-sweet filling using 6 cups of fresh berries and less than a cup of sugar. Cornstarch worked well as a thickener—it thickened the fruit's juice without leaving a starchy texture behind. A little lemon and cinnamon were all that were needed to enhance the filling without masking the blueberry flavor. For the topping, we made light, rustic drop biscuits enriched with a little cornmeal. Adding the biscuit topping to the cobbler after the filling had baked on its own allowed the biscuits to brown evenly and cook through. A sprinkling of cinnamon sugar on the dropped biscuit dough added a pleasing sweet crunch. While the blueberries are baking, prepare the ingredients for the topping, but do not stir the wet ingredients into the dry ingredients until just before the berries come out of the oven. A standard or deep-dish 9-inch pie plate works well; an 8-inch square baking dish can also be used. To reheat leftovers, put the cobbler in a 350-degree oven for 10 to 15 minutes, until heated through.

Filling
- ½ cup (3½ ounces) sugar
- 1 tablespoon cornstarch
   Pinch ground cinnamon
   Pinch table salt
- 6 cups (30 ounces) fresh blueberries, rinsed and picked over
- 1½ teaspoons grated lemon zest plus 1 tablespoon juice

Biscuit Topping
- 1 cup (5 ounces) all-purpose flour
- ¼ cup (1¾ ounces) plus 2 teaspoons sugar, divided
- 2 tablespoons stone-ground cornmeal

- 2 teaspoons baking powder
- ¼ teaspoon baking soda
- ¼ teaspoon table salt
- 4 tablespoons unsalted butter, melted
- ⅓ cup buttermilk
- ½ teaspoon vanilla extract
- ⅛ teaspoon ground cinnamon

1. Adjust oven rack to lower-middle position and heat oven to 375 degrees.

2. *For the filling:* Whisk sugar, cornstarch, cinnamon, and salt together in large bowl. Add berries and mix gently with rubber spatula until evenly coated; add lemon zest and juice and mix to combine. Transfer berry mixture to 9-inch glass pie plate, place pie plate on rimmed baking sheet, and bake until filling is hot and bubbling around edges, about 25 minutes.

3. *For the biscuit topping:* Meanwhile, whisk flour, ¼ cup sugar, cornmeal, baking powder, baking soda, and salt together in large bowl. Whisk melted butter, buttermilk, and vanilla together in small bowl. Mix remaining 2 teaspoons sugar with cinnamon in second small bowl and set aside. One minute before berries come out of oven, add wet ingredients to dry ingredients; stir with rubber spatula until just combined and no dry pockets remain.

4. *To assemble and bake:* Remove berries from oven; increase oven temperature to 425 degrees. Divide biscuit dough into 8 equal pieces and place them on hot berry filling, spacing them at least ½ inch apart (they should not touch). Sprinkle each mound of dough evenly with cinnamon sugar. Bake until filling is bubbling and biscuits are golden brown on top and cooked through, 15 to 18 minutes. Transfer cobbler to wire rack; let cool for 20 minutes and serve.

Peach Crisp

Serves 4 to 6

WHY THIS RECIPE WORKS There is seldom anything crisp about most crisps. This simple fruit dessert usually comes out of the oven with a soggy, mushy topping—quite a letdown from the ideal of a warm, fruity filling covered in a crunchy, sweet topping. We set out to make peach crisp with the perfect balance of nicely thickened filling and a lightly sweetened, crisp topping. We tried everything from Grape-Nuts to cookie crumbs and found the ideal topping mixture to be chopped nuts, sugar, butter, and flour. Cutting the butter into the flour was crucial for creating a crisp topping, and we found that a food processor was ideally suited to producing a mixture that resembled crumbly wet sand. Another issue to tackle was sugar: what kind and how much. White sugar alone was too bland, while brown sugar on its own tasted too strong. A 50–50 mix of the two proved to be the perfect combination. We decided not to use too much sugar in the fruit filling so there would be some contrast with the topping. And we nixed the idea of a thickener—the filling without one had a nicely bright fresh fruit flavor and the topping remained crisp whether we used one or not. Lightly sweetened whipped cream or vanilla ice cream is the perfect accompaniment, especially if serving the crisp warm. A standard or deep-dish 9-inch pie plate works well; an 8-inch square baking dish can also be used.

Topping
- 6 tablespoons all-purpose flour
- ¼ cup packed (1¾ ounces) light brown sugar
- ¼ cup (1¾ ounces) granulated sugar
- ¼ teaspoon ground cinnamon
- ¼ teaspoon ground nutmeg
- ¼ teaspoon table salt
- 5 tablespoons unsalted butter, cut into ½-inch pieces and chilled
- ¾ cup coarsely chopped pecans, walnuts, or almonds

Filling
- 3 pounds peaches, peeled, pitted, and cut into ½-inch slices
- ¼ cup (1¾ ounces) granulated sugar
- ½ teaspoon grated lemon zest plus 1½ tablespoons juice

1. For the topping: Pulse flour, brown sugar, granulated sugar, cinnamon, nutmeg, and salt in food processor until combined. Sprinkle butter pieces over top and pulse until mixture resembles coarse meal, about 15 pulses. Add nuts and pulse until mixture clumps together and resembles wet sand, about 5 pulses; do not overmix. Transfer mixture to bowl and refrigerate while preparing filling, at least 15 minutes.

2. For the filling: Adjust oven rack to lower-middle position and heat oven to 375 degrees. Combine peaches, sugar, and lemon zest and juice in large bowl and toss gently to combine. Transfer peach mixture to 9-inch glass pie plate, place pie plate on rimmed baking sheet, and sprinkle chilled topping evenly over top.

3. Bake for 40 minutes. Increase oven temperature to 400 degrees and continue to bake until filling is bubbling and topping is deep golden brown, about 5 minutes. Serve warm.

VARIATION
Peach Crisp for a Crowd
Serves 10

Double all ingredients and use 13 by 9-inch baking dish. Increase baking time to 55 minutes and bake at 375 degrees without increasing oven temperature.

Pear Crisp
SEASON 20 RECIPE

Serves 6

WHY THIS RECIPE WORKS The delicate texture and subtle flavor of pears make this homey dessert a bit more sophisticated and the perfect ending to an elegant fall dinner. But as we learned quickly, simply substituting pears for apples is a recipe for disaster. Our first step was to determine why pears react to baking so differently than apples. It turns out that pears and apples contain the same amount of moisture, but their cell walls are of very different strengths. During the ripening process, the moisture-retaining cell walls in pears break down much faster than apples, and cooking accelerates this process. Using pears that were just becoming ripe helped, as did using less sugar. Also, because pears release more juice than apples do, our pear crisp needed a thickener. A teaspoon of cornstarch mixed into a slurry with lemon juice thickened the juices enough and didn't leave a starchy taste or texture. For a crunchy, sweet topping, the usual combination of cold butter cut into sugar, flour, and nuts didn't work—it simply washed down into the filling. A topping made with melted butter was more cohesive and stayed in place. We prefer a crisp made with Bartlett pears, but Bosc pears can also be used. The pears should be ripe but firm, which means the flesh at the base of the stem should give slightly when gently pressed with your finger. Bartlett pears will turn from green to greenish yellow when ripe. Although almost any unsalted nut may be used in the topping, we prefer almonds or pecans. Serve the crisp with lightly sweetened whipped cream or vanilla ice cream, if desired.

Topping

- ¾ cup nuts, chopped
- ½ cup (2½ ounces) all-purpose flour
- ¼ cup packed (1¾ ounces) light brown sugar
- 2 tablespoons granulated sugar
- ¼ teaspoon ground cinnamon
- ⅛ teaspoon ground nutmeg
- ⅛ teaspoon table salt
- 5 tablespoons unsalted butter, melted and cooled

Filling

- 2 tablespoons granulated sugar
- 2 teaspoons lemon juice
- 1 teaspoon cornstarch
  Pinch table salt
- 3 pounds pears, peeled, halved, cored, each half quartered lengthwise, and each quarter cut in half crosswise

1. Adjust oven rack to lower-middle position and heat oven to 425 degrees. Line rimmed baking sheet with aluminum foil.

2. *For the topping:* Pulse nuts, flour, brown sugar, granulated sugar, cinnamon, nutmeg, and salt in food processor until nuts are finely chopped, about 9 pulses. Drizzle melted butter over nut mixture and pulse until mixture resembles crumbly wet sand, about 5 pulses, scraping down sides of bowl halfway through pulsing. Set aside.

3. *For the filling:* Whisk sugar, lemon juice, cornstarch, and salt together in large bowl. Gently toss pears with sugar mixture and transfer to 8-inch square baking dish.

4. Sprinkle topping evenly over filling, breaking up any large pieces. Transfer dish to prepared sheet. Bake until fruit is bubbling around edges and topping is deep golden brown, about 30 minutes, rotating sheet halfway through baking. Transfer dish to wire rack and let cool until warm, about 15 minutes. Serve.

Roasted Pears with Dried Apricots and Pistachios

Serves 4 to 6

WHY THIS RECIPE WORKS Tender, caramelized roasted pears are a delightfully simple dessert, but it took a two-step cooking process to perfect their texture. To eliminate any excess moisture that might weigh down the fruit, we cooked our peeled, halved pears in butter in a hot skillet. Once the pears began to brown, we transferred the skillet to the oven for 30 minutes. We plated the fork-tender fruit and started in on the sauce, deglazing the pan with white wine and adding sweet dried apricots, sugar, cardamom, and salt, plus a pat of butter for a creamy dimension. A touch of lemon juice stirred in once the liquid had thickened contributed citrusy brightness, and a sprinkling of pistachios, added right at serving, gave the dessert some toasty, textural contrast. Select pears that yield slightly when pressed. We prefer Bosc pears in this recipe, but Comice and Bartlett pears also work. The fruit can be served as is or with vanilla ice cream or plain Greek yogurt.

- 2½ tablespoons unsalted butter, divided
- 4 ripe but firm Bosc pears (6 to 7 ounces each), peeled, halved, and cored
- 1¼ cups dry white wine
- ½ cup dried apricots, quartered
- ⅓ cup (2⅓ ounces) sugar
- ¼ teaspoon ground cardamom
- ⅛ teaspoon table salt
- 1 teaspoon lemon juice
- ⅓ cup shelled pistachios, toasted and chopped

1. Adjust oven rack to middle position and heat oven to 450 degrees. Melt 1½ tablespoons butter in ovensafe 12-inch skillet over medium-high heat. Place pear halves, cut side down, in skillet. Cook, without moving them, until pears are just beginning to brown, 3 to 5 minutes.

2. Transfer skillet to oven and roast pears for 15 minutes. Using tongs, flip pears and continue to roast until fork easily pierces fruit, 10 to 15 minutes (skillet handle will be hot).

"This clafouti recipe is quintessential America's Test Kitchen: It's straightforward to make, lovely to behold, and best of all, utterly delicious. Well, it is now. But having been one of the tasters during Dan Souza's testing journey to develop that recipe, I shudder to recall how difficult it was to achieve this sweet, flavorful, creamy result. Dan tortured us all with lots of very bad cherry clafouti on his way to (dare I say) bonafide clafouti genius. I lost hope. Thought maybe this wasn't my thing. But then slowly and surely he worked through each element of the dish, scientifically drilling down and nailing each part. The result? Perfection."

—*Lisa*

3. Using tongs, transfer pears to platter. Return skillet to medium-high heat and add wine, apricots, sugar, cardamom, salt, and remaining 1 tablespoon butter. Bring to vigorous simmer, whisking to scrape up any browned bits. Cook until sauce is reduced and has consistency of maple syrup, 7 to 10 minutes. Remove pan from heat and stir in lemon juice.

4. Pour sauce over pears, sprinkle with pistachios, and serve.

VARIATION

Roasted Apples with Dried Figs and Walnuts

Substitute Gala apples for pears, red wine for white wine, dried figs for apricots, ¾ teaspoon pepper for cardamom, and walnuts for pistachios.

Cherry Clafouti

Serves 6 to 8

WHY THIS RECIPE WORKS A clafouti is France's answer to a simple crisp or cobbler: a rustic yet graceful baked custard that is studded with fresh fruit, most often (and our favorite choice) cherries. For a clafouti that featured juicy cherries in every bite (and no pits to get in the way, as most traditional recipes have), we pitted and halved the cherries. To concentrate their flavor and prevent excess moisture from leaking into the custard, we roasted them in a hot oven for 15 minutes and then tossed them with a couple of teaspoons of absorbent flour. To recover the slightly spicy, floral flavor the pits contributed, we added ⅛ teaspoon of cinnamon to the flour. We found that too much flour made the custard too bready, whereas an excess of dairy made it too loose. Ultimately, we settled on a moderate amount of each for a tender yet slightly resilient custard void of pastiness. Switching from a casserole dish to a preheated 12-inch skillet gave us better browning and made the custard easy to slice and serve. A last-minute sprinkle of granulated sugar added a touch of sweetness and a delicate crunch. We prefer whole milk in this recipe, but 1 or 2 percent low-fat milk may be substituted. Do not substitute frozen cherries for the fresh cherries.

    1½ pounds fresh sweet cherries, pitted and halved
     1 teaspoon lemon juice
     2 teaspoons plus ½ cup (2½ ounces) all-purpose flour, divided
    ⅛ teaspoon ground cinnamon
     4 large eggs
    ⅔ cup (4⅔ ounces) plus 2 teaspoons sugar, divided
    2½ teaspoons vanilla extract
    ¼ teaspoon table salt
     1 cup heavy cream
    ⅔ cup whole milk
     1 tablespoon unsalted butter

1. Adjust oven racks to upper-middle and lowest positions; place 12-inch ovensafe skillet on lower rack and heat oven to 425 degrees. Line rimmed baking sheet with aluminum foil and place cherries, cut side up, on sheet. Roast cherries on upper rack until just tender and cut sides look dry, about 15 minutes. Transfer cherries to medium bowl, toss with lemon juice, and let cool for 5 minutes. Combine 2 teaspoons flour and cinnamon in small bowl; dust flour mixture evenly over cherries and toss to coat thoroughly.

2. While cherries roast, whisk eggs, ⅔ cup sugar, vanilla, and salt in large bowl until smooth and pale, about 1 minute. Whisk in remaining ½ cup flour until smooth. Whisk in cream and milk until incorporated.

3. Remove skillet (skillet handle will be hot) from oven and set on wire rack. Add butter and swirl to coat bottom and sides of skillet (butter will melt and brown quickly). Pour batter into skillet and place cherries evenly over top (some will sink). Transfer skillet to lower rack and bake until clafouti puffs and surface is golden brown (edges will be dark brown), and center registers 195 degrees, 18 to 22 minutes, rotating skillet halfway through baking. Transfer skillet to wire rack and let cool for 25 minutes. Sprinkle evenly with remaining 2 teaspoons sugar. Slice into wedges and serve.

Simple Raspberry Gratin

Serves 4 to 6

WHY THIS RECIPE WORKS Quicker than a crisp and dressier than a shortcake, a gratin is a layer of fresh fruit piled into a shallow baking dish, dressed up with bread crumbs, and run under a broiler. The topping browns and the fruit is warmed just enough to release a bit of juice. We wanted to find the quickest, easiest route to this pleasing dessert. We started with perfect raspberries: ripe, dry, unbruised, and clean. Tossing the sweet-tart berries with just a bit of sugar and kirsch (a clear cherry brandy; vanilla extract can be substituted) provided enough additional flavor and sweetness. For the topping, we combined soft white bread, brown sugar, cinnamon, and butter in the food processor and topped the berries with the fluffy crumbs. Instead of broiling the gratin, which can produce a crust that's burnt in spots, we simply baked it. We found that a moderately hot oven gave the berries more time to soften and browned the crust more evenly. If you prefer, you can substitute blueberries, blackberries, or strawberries for part or all of the raspberries. If using strawberries, hull them and slice them in half lengthwise if small or into quarters if large. Later in the summer season, ripe, peeled peaches or nectarines, sliced, can be used in combination with the blueberries or raspberries.

4 cups (20 ounces) fresh or frozen (not thawed) raspberries
1 tablespoon granulated sugar
1 tablespoon kirsch or vanilla extract (optional)
  Pinch table salt
3 slices hearty white sandwich bread, torn into quarters
¼ cup packed (1¾ ounces) brown sugar
2 tablespoons unsalted butter, softened
  Pinch ground cinnamon

1. Adjust oven rack to lower-middle position and heat oven to 400 degrees. Gently toss raspberries; granulated sugar; kirsch, if using; and salt in medium bowl. Transfer mixture to 9-inch glass pie plate.

2. Pulse bread, brown sugar, butter, and cinnamon in food processor until mixture resembles coarse crumbs, about 10 pulses. Sprinkle crumbs evenly over fruit and bake until crumbs are deep golden brown, 15 to 20 minutes. Transfer to wire rack; let cool for 5 minutes and serve.

Apple Strudel

Serves 6

WHY THIS RECIPE WORKS Most modern phyllo-based versions of strudel have tough layers of phyllo on the underside, while the sheets on top shatter before you even cut a slice. Meanwhile, fillings collapse and leak everywhere, despite the bread crumbs supposedly added to soak up liquid and prevent leaking (instead, they just make the filling taste pasty). We parcooked the apples in the microwave to activate an enzyme that sets the pectin in the fruit and allows them to bake without collapsing. We stirred in ultradry panko bread crumbs instead of homemade toasted crumbs since we could use less of them to soak up a comparable amount of liquid (thus avoiding pastiness). To prevent a compressed, tough underside, we used fewer sheets of phyllo and changed the typical wrapping technique so the seam was on the top instead of on the bottom. We were able to minimize the flyaways on top by dusting a small amount of confectioners' sugar between the phyllo layers so that they fused in the oven, and by slicing our strudel while it was warm. Making two smaller strudels simplified assembly. Gala apples can be substituted for Golden Delicious. Phyllo dough is also available in larger 18 by 14-inch sheets; if using, cut them in half to make 14 by 9-inch sheets. Thaw phyllo in the refrigerator overnight or on the counter for 4 to 5 hours; don't thaw it in the microwave.

1¾ pounds Golden Delicious apples, peeled, cored, and cut into ½-inch pieces
3 tablespoons granulated sugar
½ teaspoon grated lemon zest plus 1½ teaspoons juice
¼ teaspoon ground cinnamon
¼ teaspoon ground ginger
¼ teaspoon table salt, divided
3 tablespoons golden raisins
1½ tablespoons panko bread crumbs
7 tablespoons unsalted butter, melted
14 (14 by 9-inch) phyllo sheets, thawed
1 tablespoon confectioners' sugar, divided, plus extra for serving

1. Toss apples, granulated sugar, lemon zest and juice, cinnamon, ginger, and ⅛ teaspoon salt together in large bowl. Cover and microwave until apples are warm to touch, about 2 minutes, stirring once halfway through microwaving. Let apples sit, covered, for 5 minutes. Transfer apples to colander set in second large bowl and let drain, reserving liquid. Return apples to bowl; stir in raisins and panko.

2. Adjust oven rack to upper-middle position and heat oven to 375 degrees. Spray rimmed baking sheet with vegetable oil spray. Stir remaining ⅛ teaspoon salt into melted butter.

3. Place 16½ by 12-inch sheet of parchment paper on counter with long side parallel to edge of counter. Place 1 phyllo sheet on parchment with long side parallel to edge of counter. Place 1½ teaspoons confectioners' sugar in fine-mesh strainer (rest strainer in bowl to prevent making mess). Lightly brush sheet with melted butter and dust sparingly with confectioners' sugar. Repeat with 6 more phyllo sheets, melted butter, and confectioners' sugar, stacking sheets one on top of another as you go.

4. Arrange half of apple mixture in 2½ by 10-inch rectangle 2 inches from bottom of phyllo and about 2 inches from each side. Using parchment, fold sides of phyllo over filling, then fold bottom edge of phyllo over filling. Brush folded portions of phyllo with reserved apple liquid. Fold top edge over filling, making sure top and bottom edges overlap by about 1 inch.

(If they do not overlap, unfold, rearrange filling into slightly narrower strip, and refold.) Press firmly to seal. Using thin metal spatula, transfer strudel to 1 side of prepared baking sheet, facing seam toward center of sheet. Lightly brush top and sides of strudel with half of remaining apple liquid. Repeat process with remaining phyllo, melted butter, confectioners' sugar, filling, and apple liquid. Place second strudel on other side of prepared sheet, with seam facing center of sheet.

5. Bake strudels until golden brown, 27 to 35 minutes, rotating sheet halfway through baking. Using thin metal spatula, immediately transfer strudels to cutting board. Let cool for 3 minutes. Slice each strudel into thirds and let cool for at least 20 minutes. Serve warm or at room temperature, dusting with extra confectioners' sugar before serving.

Individual Summer Berry Puddings

Serves 6

WHY THIS RECIPE WORKS If any food speaks of summer, the English dessert called summer pudding does. Ripe, fragrant, lightly sweetened berries are gently cooked to coax out their juices and then packed into a bowl lined with slices of bread. The berry juices soak and soften the bread to make it meld with the fruit. We set out to master this summertime classic. Instead of lining the mold with bread and then filling it with berries, we opted to layer bread (cut out with a biscuit cutter) and berries together in ramekins; this way, the layers of bread on the inside would almost melt into the fruit. Combining the berries—we used strawberries, raspberries, blueberries, and blackberries—with sugar and lemon juice, and gently cooking the mixture for just 5 minutes, released just the right amount of juice and offset the tartness of the berries. Fresh bread became too gummy in the pudding, but day-old bread had just the right consistency. We used potato bread; its even, tight-crumbed, tender texture and light sweetness was a perfect match for the berries (challah makes a good substitute). To ensure that the puddings would come together and hold their shape, we weighted and refrigerated them for at least 8 hours. The bread should be dry to the touch but not brittle. If working with fresh bread, dry the slices by heating them on an oven rack in a single layer in a 200-degree oven for about 1 hour, flipping them once halfway through the time. For this recipe, you will need six 6-ounce ramekins and a round cookie cutter of a slightly smaller diameter than the ramekins. If you don't have the right size cutter, use a paring knife and the bottom of a ramekin (most ramekins taper toward the bottom) as a guide for trimming the rounds. Challah will need to be cut into slices about ½ inch thick; if both potato bread and challah are unavailable, use high-quality white sandwich bread. Lightly sweetened whipped cream is the perfect accompaniment.

4 cups (20 ounces) strawberries, hulled and sliced
2 cups (10 ounces) raspberries
1 cup (5 ounces) blueberries
1 cup (5 ounces) blackberries
¾ cup (5¼ ounces) sugar
2 tablespoons lemon juice
12 slices stale potato bread, challah, or hearty white sandwich bread

1. Cook strawberries, raspberries, blueberries, blackberries, and sugar in large saucepan over medium heat, stirring occasionally, until berries begin to release their juice and sugar has dissolved, about 5 minutes. Off heat, stir in lemon juice; let cool to room temperature.

2. While berries are cooling, spray six 6-ounce ramekins with vegetable oil spray and place on rimmed baking sheet. Use cookie cutter to cut out 12 bread rounds that are slightly smaller in diameter than ramekins.

3. Using slotted spoon, place ¼ cup fruit mixture in each ramekin. Lightly soak 1 bread round in fruit juice in saucepan and place on top of fruit in ramekin; repeat with 5 more bread rounds and remaining ramekins. Diving remaining fruit among ramekins. Lightly soak 1 bread round in juice and place on top of fruit in ramekin (it should sit above lip of ramekin); repeat with remaining 5 bread rounds and remaining ramekins. Pour remaining fruit juice over bread and cover ramekins loosely with plastic wrap. Place second baking sheet on top of ramekins and weight it with heavy cans. Refrigerate puddings for at least 8 hours or up to 24 hours.

4. Remove cans and baking sheet and uncover puddings. Loosen puddings by running paring knife around edge of each ramekin, unmold into individual bowls, and serve immediately.

VARIATION
Large Summer Berry Pudding
Serves 6 to 8
You will need a 9 by 5-inch loaf pan for this recipe. Because there is no need to cut out rounds for this version, you will need only about 8 slices bread, depending on their size.

While berries are cooling, spray 9 by 5-inch loaf pan with vegetable oil spray, line it with plastic wrap, and place it on rimmed baking sheet. Trim crusts from bread and trim slices to fit in single layer in loaf pan (you will need about 2½ slices per layer; there will be 3 layers). Using slotted spoon, spread about 2 cups of fruit mixture evenly over bottom of prepared pan. Lightly soak enough bread slices for 1 layer in fruit juice in saucepan and place on top of fruit. Repeat with 2 more layers of fruit and bread. Pour remaining fruit juice over bread and cover loosely with plastic wrap. Place second baking sheet on top of loaf pan and weight it with heavy cans. Refrigerate pudding for at least 8 hours or up to 24 hours. Remove cans and baking sheet and uncover pudding. Invert pudding onto serving platter, remove loaf pan and plastic wrap, slice, and serve.

Lemon Posset with Berries

Serves 6

WHY THIS RECIPE WORKS This classic English specialty transforms cream, sugar, and lemon into a lush pudding with clean citrus flavor. It is the easiest dessert you've never made. There are no tempermental egg yolks or add-ins like gelatin, flour, or cornstarch needed to help the mixture thicken or set or interfere with the bright taste of citrus. We found that using just the right proportions of sugar and lemon juice was the key to custard with a smooth, luxurious consistency and a bright enough flavor to balance the richness of the cream. Lemon zest was essential to making the lemon flavor even more prominent. For a posset with an optimally dense, firm set, we reduced the cream-sugar mixture to 2 cups to evaporate some of the water before adding the lemon juice, which in turn caused the mixture to solidify. Letting the warm mixture rest for 20 minutes before straining and portioning allowed the flavors to meld even more and ensured a silky-smooth consistency. Pairing the dessert with fresh berries for textural contrast helps keep it from feeling overly rich. This dessert requires portioning into individual servings. Reducing the cream mixture to exactly 2 cups creates the best consistency. Transfer the liquid to a 2-cup heatproof liquid measuring cup once or twice during boiling to monitor the amount. Do not leave the cream unattended, as it can boil over easily.

2 cups heavy cream
⅔ cup (4⅔ ounces) sugar
1 tablespoon grated lemon zest plus
   6 tablespoons juice (2 lemons)
1½ cups (7½ ounces) blueberries or raspberries

1. Combine cream, sugar, and lemon zest in medium saucepan and bring to boil over medium heat. Continue to boil, stirring frequently to dissolve sugar. If mixture begins to boil over, briefly remove from heat. Cook until mixture is reduced to 2 cups, 8 to 12 minutes.

2. Remove saucepan from heat and stir in lemon juice. Let sit until mixture is cooled slightly and skin forms on top, about 20 minutes. Strain through fine-mesh strainer into bowl; discard zest. Divide mixture evenly among 6 individual ramekins or serving glasses.

3. Refrigerate, uncovered, until set, at least 3 hours. (Once chilled, possets can be wrapped in plastic wrap and refrigerated for up to 2 days.) Unwrap and let sit at room temperature for 10 minutes before serving. Garnish with berries and serve.

Fresh Strawberry Mousse

Serves 4 to 6

WHY THIS RECIPE WORKS There's a good reason that strawberry mousse recipes aren't very prevalent: The berries contain lots of juice that can easily ruin the texture of a mousse that should be creamy and rich. Plus, the fruit flavor produced by most strawberry mousse recipes is too subtle. To achieve a creamy yet firm texture without losing the strawberry flavor, we replaced some of the cream with cream cheese. We processed the berries into small pieces and macerated them with sugar and a little salt to draw out their juice. We then reduced the released liquid to a syrup before adding it to the mousse, which standardized the amount of moisture in the dessert and also concentrated the berry flavor. Fully pureeing the juiced berries contributed bright, fresh berry flavor. A dollop of lemon whipped cream made for a tangy finish, and extra diced strawberries made for a pretty presentation. This recipe works well with supermarket strawberries and farmers' market strawberries. In step 1, be careful not to overprocess the berries. If you like, substitute 1½ pounds (5¼ cups) of thawed frozen strawberries for fresh strawberries. If using frozen strawberries skip step 1 (do not process berries). Proceed with the recipe, adding the ½ cup of sugar and the salt to the whipped cream in step 4. For more complex berry flavor, replace the 3 tablespoons of raw strawberry juice in step 2 with strawberry or raspberry liqueur. In addition to the diced berries, or if you're using frozen strawberries, you can serve the mousse with Lemon Whipped Cream (recipe follows).

2 pounds strawberries, hulled (6½ cups), divided
½ cup (3½ ounces) sugar, divided
   Pinch table salt
1¾ teaspoons unflavored gelatin
4 ounces cream cheese, cut into 8 pieces and softened
½ cup heavy cream, chilled

1. Cut enough strawberries into ¼-inch dice to measure 1 cup; refrigerate until ready to garnish. Pulse remaining strawberries in food processor in 2 batches until most pieces are ¼ to ½ inch thick (some larger pieces are fine), 6 to 10 pulses. Transfer strawberries to bowl and toss with ¼ cup sugar and salt. (Do not clean processor.) Cover bowl and let strawberries sit for 45 minutes, stirring occasionally.

2. Strain processed strawberries through fine-mesh strainer into bowl (you should have about ⅔ cup juice). Measure out 3 tablespoons juice into small bowl, sprinkle gelatin over juice, and let sit until gelatin softens, about 5 minutes. Place remaining juice in small saucepan and cook over medium-high heat until reduced to 3 tablespoons, about 10 minutes. Remove pan from heat, add softened gelatin mixture, and stir until gelatin has dissolved. Add cream cheese and whisk until smooth. Transfer mixture to large bowl.

3. While juice is reducing, return strawberries to now-empty processor and process until smooth, 15 to 20 seconds. Strain puree through fine-mesh strainer into medium bowl, pressing on solids to remove seeds and pulp (you should have about 1⅔ cups puree). Discard any solids in strainer. Add strawberry puree to juice-gelatin mixture and whisk until incorporated.

4. Using stand mixer fitted with whisk, whip cream on medium-low speed until foamy, about 1 minute. Increase speed to high and whip until soft peaks form, 1 to 3 minutes. Gradually add remaining ¼ cup sugar and whip until stiff peaks form, 1 to 2 minutes. Whisk whipped cream into strawberry mixture until no white streaks remain. Portion into dessert dishes and chill for at least 4 hours or up to 2 days. (If chilled longer than 6 hours, let mousse sit at room temperature for 15 minutes before serving.) Serve, garnishing with reserved diced strawberries.

ACCOMPANIMENT
Lemon Whipped Cream
Makes about 1 cup
If preferred, you can replace the lemon with lime.

½ cup heavy cream
2 tablespoons sugar
1 teaspoon grated lemon zest plus
  1 tablespoon juice

Using stand mixer fitted with whisk, whip cream on medium-low speed until foamy, about 1 minute. Add sugar and lemon zest and juice, increase speed to medium-high, and whip until soft peaks form, 1 to 3 minutes.

Pavlova with Fruit and Whipped Cream
SEASON 20 RECIPE

Serves 10

WHY THIS RECIPE WORKS Pavlova is a drop-dead gorgeous dessert of marshmallowy, crisp-shelled meringue piled high with lightly whipped cream and fresh fruit. For a foolproof pavlova, we switched from the typical French meringue—which requires precise timing when adding the sugar to the egg whites—to a Swiss meringue, which is made by dissolving the sugar in the egg whites as they are heated over a simmering water bath and then whipping the mixture to stiff peaks. Cornstarch and vinegar produced a meringue that was marshmallowy within, with a slight chew at the edge; a generous amount of sugar ensured a crisp exterior. We shaped the meringue into a wide, flat disk and then baked it and let it dry in a turned-off oven. Lightly sweetened whipped cream and fresh fruit balanced the meringue's sweetness and made for a beautiful presentation of colors and textures. Letting the finished meringue sit for a few minutes before serving helped soften the crust for neater slices. Because eggs can vary in size, measuring the egg whites by weight or volume is essential to ensure that you are working with the correct ratio of egg whites to sugar. Open the oven door as infrequently as possible while the meringue is inside. Don't worry when the meringue cracks; it is part of the dessert's charm. The inside of the meringue will remain soft.

Meringue
1½ cups (10½ ounces) sugar
¾ cup (6 ounces) egg whites (5 to 7 large eggs)
1½ teaspoons distilled white vinegar
1½ teaspoons cornstarch
1 teaspoon vanilla extract

Whipped Cream
2 cups heavy cream, chilled
2 tablespoons sugar

1 recipe fruit topping (recipes follow)

1. ***For the meringue:*** Adjust oven rack to middle position and heat oven to 250 degrees. Using pencil, draw 10-inch circle in center of 18 by 13-inch piece of parchment paper.

2. Combine sugar and egg whites in bowl of stand mixer and place bowl over saucepan filled with 1 inch simmering water, making sure that water does not touch bottom of bowl. Whisking gently but constantly, heat until sugar is dissolved and mixture registers 160 to 165 degrees, 5 to 8 minutes.

Pavlova with Fruit and
Whipped Cream

3. Fit stand mixer with whisk attachment and whip mixture on high speed until meringue forms stiff peaks, is smooth and creamy, and is bright white with sheen, about 4 minutes (bowl may still be slightly warm to touch). Stop mixer and scrape down bowl with spatula. Add vinegar, cornstarch, and vanilla and whip on high speed until combined, about 10 seconds.

4. Spoon about ¼ teaspoon meringue onto each corner of rimmed baking sheet. Press parchment, marked side down, onto sheet to secure. Pile meringue in center of circle on parchment. Using circle as guide, spread and smooth meringue with back of spoon or spatula from center outward, building 10-inch disk that is slightly higher around edges. Finished disk should measure about 1 inch high with ¼-inch depression in center.

5. Bake meringue until exterior is dry and crisp and meringue releases cleanly from parchment when gently lifted at edge with thin metal spatula, 1 to 1½ hours. Meringue should be quite pale (a hint of creamy color is OK). Turn off oven, prop door open with wooden spoon, and let meringue cool in oven for 1½ hours. Remove from oven and let cool completely before topping, about 15 minutes. (Cooled meringue can be wrapped tightly in plastic wrap and stored at room temperature for up to 1 week.)

6. *For the whipped cream:* Before serving, whip cream and sugar in chilled bowl of stand mixer fitted with whisk attachment on low speed until small bubbles form, about 30 seconds. Increase speed to medium and whip until whisk leaves trail, about 30 seconds. Increase speed to high and continue to whip until cream is smooth, thick, and nearly doubled in volume, about 20 seconds longer for soft peaks. If necessary, finish whipping by hand to adjust consistency.

7. Carefully peel meringue away from parchment and place on large serving platter. Spoon whipped cream into center of meringue. Top whipped cream with fruit topping. Let stand for at least 5 minutes or up to 1 hour, then slice and serve.

Orange, Cranberry, and Mint Topping
Serves 10 (Makes 4½ cups)
You can substitute tangelos or Cara Cara oranges for the navel oranges, if desired. Valencia or blood oranges can also be used, but since they are smaller, increase the number of oranges to six.

- 1½ cups (10½ ounces) sugar, divided
- 6 ounces (1½ cups) frozen cranberries
- 5 navel oranges
- ⅓ cup chopped fresh mint, plus 10 small mint leaves, divided

1. Bring 1 cup sugar and 1 cup water to boil in medium saucepan over medium heat, stirring to dissolve sugar. Off heat, stir in cranberries. Let cranberries and syrup cool completely, about 30 minutes. (Cranberries in syrup can be refrigerated for up to 24 hours.)

2. Place remaining ½ cup sugar in shallow dish. Drain cranberries, discarding syrup. Working in 2 batches, roll ½ cup cranberries in sugar and transfer to large plate or tray. Let stand at room temperature to dry, about 1 hour.

3. Cut away peel and pith from oranges. Cut each orange into quarters from pole to pole, then cut crosswise into ¼-inch-thick pieces (you should have 3 cups). Just before serving, toss oranges with non-sugared cranberries and chopped mint in bowl until combined. Using slotted spoon, spoon fruit in even layer over pavlova. Garnish with sugared cranberries and mint leaves. Before serving, drizzle pavlova slices with any juice from bowl.

Mango, Kiwi, and Blueberry Topping
Serves 10 (Makes 5 cups)
Do not use frozen blueberries in this recipe.

- 3 large mangos, peeled, pitted, and cut into ½-inch pieces (3 cups)
- 2 kiwis, peeled, quartered lengthwise, and sliced crosswise ¼ inch thick (about 1 cup)
- 5 ounces (1 cup) blueberries
- 1 tablespoon sugar

Toss all ingredients together in large bowl. Set aside for 30 minutes. Using slotted spoon, spoon fruit in even layer over pavlova. Before serving, drizzle pavlova slices with any juice from bowl.

VARIATION
Individual Pavlovas with Fruit and Whipped Cream
Adjust oven racks to upper-middle and lower-middle positions and heat oven to 250 degrees. In step 4, spoon about ¼ teaspoon meringue onto each corner of 2 rimmed baking sheets. Line sheets with parchment paper. Spoon heaping ½ cup meringue into 5 evenly spaced piles on each sheet. Spread each meringue pile with back of spoon to form 3½-inch disk with slight depression in center. Decrease baking time in step 5 to 50 minutes. Top each meringue with ½ cup whipped cream, followed by ½ cup fruit topping.

Cakes and More

Olive Oil Cake

Rich Chocolate Bundt Cake

Serves 12

WHY THIS RECIPE WORKS A Bundt cake is the pinnacle of cake-baking simplicity. With its decorative shape, this cake doesn't require frosting or fussy finishing techniques. We wanted a cake that would deliver that moment of pure chocolate ecstasy with the first bite—a chocolate Bundt cake that tastes every bit as good as it looks, with a fine crumb, moist texture, and rich chocolate flavor. We intensified the chocolate flavor by using both bittersweet chocolate and natural cocoa and dissolving them in boiling water, which "bloomed" their flavor. We used sour cream and brown sugar instead of white to add moisture and flavor. Finally, we further enhanced flavor with a little espresso powder and a generous amount of vanilla extract, both of which complemented the floral nuances of the chocolate. We prefer natural cocoa here because Dutch-processed cocoa will result in a compromised rise. For an accurate measurement of boiling water, bring a kettle of water to a boil, then measure out the desired amount. The cake can be served with just a dusting of confectioners' sugar or lightly sweetened whipped cream and raspberries.

¾ cup (2¼ ounces) natural unsweetened cocoa powder, plus 1 tablespoon for pan
12 tablespoons unsalted butter, cut into 12 pieces and softened, plus 1 tablespoon, melted, for pan
6 ounces bittersweet chocolate, chopped
1 teaspoon instant espresso powder (optional)
¾ cup boiling water
1 cup sour cream, room temperature
1¾ cups (8¾ ounces) all-purpose flour
1 teaspoon table salt
1 teaspoon baking soda
2 cups packed (14 ounces) light brown sugar
1 tablespoon vanilla extract
5 large eggs, room temperature
Confectioners' sugar (optional)

1. Adjust oven rack to lower-middle position and heat oven to 350 degrees. Mix 1 tablespoon cocoa and melted butter into paste. Using pastry brush, thoroughly coat interior of 12-cup nonstick Bundt pan.

2. Combine chocolate; espresso powder, if using; and remaining ¾ cup cocoa in bowl. Pour boiling water over mixture and let sit, covered, for 5 minutes. Whisk mixture gently until smooth. Let cool completely, then whisk in sour cream. Whisk flour, salt, and baking soda together in second bowl.

3. Using stand mixer fitted with paddle, beat softened butter, brown sugar, and vanilla on medium-high speed until pale and fluffy, about 3 minutes. Add eggs, one at a time, and beat until combined. Reduce speed to low and add flour mixture in 3 additions, alternating with chocolate–sour cream mixture in 2 additions, scraping down bowl as needed. Give batter final stir by hand.

4. Transfer batter to prepared pan and smooth top with rubber spatula. Bake until skewer inserted in center comes out with few crumbs attached, 45 to 50 minutes, rotating pan halfway through baking. Let cake cool in pan on wire rack for 10 minutes. Invert cake onto rack, remove pan, and let cool completely, about 3 hours. Dust with confectioners' sugar, if using, before serving. (Cake can be stored at room temperature for up to 24 hours.)

Cider-Glazed Apple Bundt Cake

Serves 12 to 16

WHY THIS RECIPE WORKS We managed to pack the equivalent of 4½ pounds of fruit into our apple cake and its glaze. Minimizing the spices allowed the apples' true flavor to shine. Baking the thick, dense batter in a Bundt pan rather than a round pan allowed heat to flow through the center of the cake, ensuring that it baked evenly edge to edge. To reinforce the apple flavor throughout the cake, we mixed reduced apple cider into the batter, brushed it onto the cake, and used it to flavor the icing drizzled on top. For the sake of efficiency, we recommend that you begin boiling the cider before assembling the batter. Reducing the cider to exactly 1 cup is important to the success of this recipe. If you accidentally overreduce the cider, make up the difference with water. Baking spray that contains flour can be used to grease and flour the pan. We like the tartness of Granny Smith apples in this recipe, but any variety of apple will work. You may shred the apples with the large shredding disk of a food processor or with the large holes of a box grater.

4 cups apple cider
3¾ cups (18¾ ounces) all-purpose flour
1½ teaspoons table salt
1½ teaspoons baking powder
½ teaspoon baking soda
¾ teaspoon ground cinnamon
¼ teaspoon ground allspice
¾ cup (3 ounces) confectioners' sugar
16 tablespoons unsalted butter, melted
1½ cups packed (10½ ounces) dark brown sugar
3 large eggs
2 teaspoons vanilla extract
1½ pounds Granny Smith apples, peeled and shredded (3 cups)

1. Bring cider to boil in 12-inch skillet over high heat; cook until reduced to 1 cup, 20 to 25 minutes. While cider is reducing, adjust oven rack to middle position and heat oven to 350 degrees. Spray 12-cup nonstick Bundt pan with baking spray with flour. Whisk flour, salt, baking powder, baking soda, cinnamon, and allspice in large bowl until combined. Place confectioners' sugar in small bowl.

"As an avid fan of both apples and cake, rarely have I encountered a combination of the two that I didn't like. However, just as rarely have I had an apple cake that truly put me over the moon, as this one from baker extraordinaire Andrea Geary does. How do I love this cake? Let me count the ways. Beautifully moist and not soggy in the slightest: check! Lovely, even texture: check! An irresistible form factor (who doesn't love a Bundt?): check! And best of all, true apple flavor: check plus!

The flavor is this cake's real genius. Grated apples, rather than the chunks used commonly, integrate seamlessly into the batter. Better yet, the clever triple use of a concentrated apple cider reduction—in the batter, brushed over the cake as it cools, and in a simple glaze—guarantees a potent apple presence."

—*Adam*

2. Add 2 tablespoons cider reduction to confectioners' sugar and whisk to form smooth icing. Cover with plastic wrap and set aside. Set aside 6 tablespoons cider reduction.

3. Pour remaining ½ cup cider reduction into large bowl; add melted butter, brown sugar, eggs, and vanilla and whisk until smooth. Pour cider mixture over flour mixture and stir with rubber spatula until almost fully combined (some streaks of flour will remain). Stir in apples and any accumulated juice until evenly distributed. Transfer mixture to prepared pan and smooth top. Bake until skewer inserted in center comes out clean, 55 minutes to 1 hour 5 minutes, rotating pan halfway through baking.

4. Transfer pan to wire rack set in rimmed baking sheet. Brush exposed surface of cake lightly with 1 tablespoon reserved cider reduction. Let cake cool for 10 minutes. Invert cake onto rack, remove pan, and brush top and sides of cake with remaining 5 tablespoons reserved cider reduction. Let cake cool for 20 minutes. Stir icing to loosen, then drizzle evenly over cake. Let cake cool completely, at least 2 hours, before serving. (Cake can be stored at room temperature for up to 3 days.)

Lemon Pound Cake

Serves 8

WHY THIS RECIPE WORKS A rich, golden pound cake is a must in any baker's repertoire. But pound cakes often turn out spongy, rubbery, heavy, and dry—and lemon pound cakes often lack true lemon flavor. We wanted to produce a superior pound cake (fine-crumbed, rich, moist, and buttery) while making the process as simple and foolproof as possible. After less-than-successful results with a stand mixer and a hand mixer, we turned to the food processor to mix our cake. It ensured a perfect emulsification of the eggs, sugar, and melted butter. Cake flour produced a tender crumb, but our cake was still a bit heavy. We fixed matters with the addition of baking powder, which increased lift and produced a consistent, fine crumb. Finally, in addition to mixing lemon zest into the cake batter, we glazed the finished cake with lemon sugar syrup—but first we poked holes all over the cake to ensure that the tangy, sweet glaze infused the cake with a blast of bright lemon flavor. You can use a blender instead of a food processor to mix the batter. To add the butter, remove the center cap of the lid so it can be drizzled into the whirling blender with minimal splattering. This batter looks almost like a thick pancake batter and is very fluid. The test kitchen's preferred loaf pan measures 8½ by 4½ inches; if you use a 9 by 5-inch loaf pan, start checking for doneness 5 minutes earlier than advised in the recipe.

Cake
- 16 tablespoons unsalted butter, plus 1 tablespoon, softened, for pan
- 1½ cups (6 ounces) cake flour, plus 1 tablespoon for pan
- 1 teaspoon baking powder
- ½ teaspoon table salt
- 1¼ cups (8¾ ounces) sugar
- 2 tablespoons grated lemon zest plus 2 teaspoons juice
- 4 large eggs, room temperature
- 1½ teaspoons vanilla extract

Glaze
- ½ cup (3½ ounces) sugar
- ¼ cup lemon juice

1. *For the cake:* Adjust oven rack to middle position and heat oven to 350 degrees. Grease 8½ by 4½-inch loaf pan with 1 tablespoon softened butter; dust with 1 tablespoon flour, tapping out excess. In medium bowl, whisk together the remaining 1½ cups flour, baking powder, and salt; set aside.

2. Melt remaining 16 tablespoons butter in small saucepan over medium heat. Whisk melted butter thoroughly to reincorporate any separated milk solids.

3. In food processor, pulse sugar and zest until combined, about 5 pulses. Add lemon juice, eggs, and vanilla; process until combined, about 5 seconds. With machine running, add melted butter through feed tube in steady stream (this should take about 20 seconds). Transfer mixture to large bowl. Sift flour mixture over egg mixture in 3 additions, whisking gently after each addition until just combined.

4. Pour batter into prepared pan and bake for 15 minutes. Reduce oven temperature to 325 degrees and continue to bake until deep golden brown and toothpick inserted in center comes out clean, about 35 minutes, rotating pan halfway through baking time. Let cool in pan for 10 minutes, then turn onto wire rack. Poke top and sides of cake throughout with toothpick. Let cool to room temperature, at least 1 hour. (Cooled cake can be wrapped tightly in plastic wrap and stored at room temperature for up to 5 days.)

5. *For the glaze:* While cake is cooling, bring sugar and lemon juice to boil in small saucepan, stirring occasionally to dissolve sugar. Reduce heat to low and simmer until thickened slightly, about 2 minutes. Brush top and sides of cake with glaze and let cool to room temperature.

Pear-Walnut Upside-Down Cake

Serves 8 to 10

WHY THIS RECIPE WORKS Pears are sometimes referred to as the queen of fruit, but, despite their subtle floral flavor and graceful shape, their popularity in desserts has always been a distant second to apples. We were determined to create an elegant cake that really showcased the pears. We settled on Bosc pears; since they have dense flesh, they hold their shape after baking. Cutting the pears into wedges allowed them to be baked raw but still be manageable to eat with the cake. Instead of a sweet, somewhat dense yellow cake, we made a walnut-based cake, which was light but sturdy, earthy-tasting and less sweet, and visually attractive. Lining the cake pan (a light-colored pan helped the cake cook more evenly) with parchment and removing the cake from the pan after 15 minutes—good practice for any upside-down cake—allowed the top to set while preventing the bottom of the cake from steaming and turning soggy. We strongly recommend baking this cake in a light-colored cake pan with sides that are at least 2 inches tall. If using a dark-colored pan, start checking for doneness at 1 hour, and note that the cake may dome in the center and the topping may become too sticky. Serve with crème fraîche or lightly sweetened whipped cream.

Topping
- 4 **tablespoons unsalted butter, melted**
- ½ **cup packed (3½ ounces) dark brown sugar**
- 2 **teaspoons cornstarch**
- ⅛ **teaspoon table salt**
- 3 **ripe but firm Bosc pears (8 ounces each)**

Cake
- 1 **cup walnuts, toasted**
- ½ **cup (2½ ounces) all-purpose flour**
- ½ **teaspoon table salt**
- ¼ **teaspoon baking powder**
- ⅛ **teaspoon baking soda**
- 3 **large eggs**
- 1 **cup (7 ounces) sugar**
- 4 **tablespoons unsalted butter, melted**
- ¼ **cup vegetable oil**

1. *For the topping:* Adjust oven rack to middle position and heat oven to 300 degrees. Grease 9-inch round cake pan and line with parchment paper. Pour melted butter over bottom of pan and swirl to evenly coat. Combine sugar, cornstarch, and salt in small bowl and sprinkle evenly over melted butter.

2. Peel, halve, and core pears. Set aside 1 pear half and reserve for other use. Cut remaining 5 pear halves into 4 wedges each. Arrange pears in circular pattern around prepared pan with tapered ends pointing inward. Arrange 2 smallest pear wedges in center.

3. *For the cake:* Pulse walnuts, flour, salt, baking powder, and baking soda in food processor until walnuts are finely ground, 8 to 10 pulses. Transfer walnut mixture to bowl.

4. Process eggs and sugar in now-empty processor until very pale yellow, about 2 minutes. With processor running, add melted butter and oil in steady stream until incorporated. Add walnut mixture and pulse to combine, 4 to 5 pulses. Pour batter evenly over pears (some pears may show through; cake will bake up over fruit).

5. Bake until center of cake is set and bounces back when gently pressed and toothpick inserted in center comes out clean, 1 hour 10 minutes to 1¼ hours, rotating pan after 40 minutes. Let cake cool in pan on wire rack for 15 minutes. Run thin knife around edge of pan to loosen cake. Invert cake onto rack set in rimmed baking sheet and remove pan, discarding parchment. Let cake cool for 2 hours. Serve.

Apple Upside-Down Cake

Serves 8

WHY THIS RECIPE WORKS Ever since canned pineapple was introduced into this country in the early 1900s, pineapple has been synonymous with upside-down cake. But at one time, upside-down cakes were made with seasonal fruit, such as apples. We loved the idea of resurrecting apple upside-down cake. We wanted a rich, buttery cake topped with tightly packed burnished sweet apples. We started our testing with choosing the type of apple. Most apples turned mushy and watery and were simply too sweet, but crisp, tart Granny Smiths made the cut. Following the lead of recipes found in our research, we shingled the apples in the pan and poured the cake batter over the top. But once baked and inverted, our apple layer was shrunken and dry. The solution turned out to be increasing the number of apples, for a hefty layer of fruit. This effort yielded better results, but we found the apples to be overcooked, so we turned to a method uncovered in our recipe for Deep-Dish Apple Pie (page 458)—we precooked half the apples by sautéing them on the stovetop and we cut the remainder thin, so they baked through evenly. For the butter cake, we tested milk, buttermilk, yogurt, and sour cream. Sour cream won hands down—its subtle tang balanced the sweetness of the cake and complemented the caramelized apples. And another addition—cornmeal—gave the cake a hint of earthy flavor and a pleasantly coarse texture. Our final discovery came when we attempted to release the cake cleanly from the pan. Typical recipes instruct a 5- to 10-minute cooling period, but we found that a full 20 minutes was required to allow the apple filling to set. And turning the cake out onto a rack to finish cooling let the bottom of the cake breathe, preventing the sogginess that is typical of so many upside-down cakes. We like the slight coarseness that

cornmeal adds to the cake, but it's fine to omit it. Golden Delicious apples can be substituted for the Granny Smiths. You will need a 9-inch nonstick cake pan with sides that are at least 2 inches high; anything shallower and the cake will overflow. Alternatively, a 10-inch ovensafe stainless steel skillet (don't use cast iron) can be used to both cook the apples and bake the cake, with the following modifications: Cook the apples in the skillet and set them aside while mixing the batter (it's OK if the skillet is still warm when the batter is added) and increase the baking time by 7 to 9 minutes. If you don't have either a 2-inch-high cake pan or an ovensafe skillet, use an 8-inch square pan.

Topping

- 2 pounds Granny Smith or Golden Delicious apples, peeled and cored
- 4 tablespoons unsalted butter, cut into 4 pieces
- ⅔ cup packed (4⅔ ounces) light brown sugar
- 2 teaspoons lemon juice

Cake

- 1 cup (5 ounces) all-purpose flour
- 1 tablespoon cornmeal (optional)
- 1 teaspoon baking powder
- ½ teaspoon salt
- ¾ cup (5¼ ounces) granulated sugar
- ¼ cup packed (1¾ ounces) light brown sugar
- 2 large eggs
- 6 tablespoons unsalted butter, melted and slightly cooled
- ½ cup sour cream
- 1 teaspoon vanilla extract

1. Adjust oven rack to lowest position and heat oven to 350 degrees. Grease 9-inch round cake pan.

2. *For the topping:* Cut half of apples into ¼-inch-thick slices. Cut remaining apples into ½-inch-thick slices. Melt butter in 12-inch skillet over medium-high heat. Add ½-inch-thick apple slices and cook, stirring occasionally, until they begin to caramelize, 4 to 6 minutes (do not fully cook apples).

3. Add ¼-inch-thick apple slices, sugar, and lemon juice. Cook, stirring constantly, until sugar dissolves and apples are coated, about 1 minute. Transfer apple mixture to prepared pan and lightly press into even layer.

4. *For the cake:* Whisk flour; cornmeal, if using; baking powder; and salt together in bowl. Whisk granulated sugar, brown sugar, and eggs in large bowl until thick and homogeneous, about 45 seconds. Slowly whisk in melted butter until combined. Whisk in sour cream and vanilla until combined. Add flour mixture and whisk until just combined. Transfer batter to prepared pan and spread evenly over apples. Bake until cake is golden brown and toothpick inserted in center comes out clean, 35 to 40 minutes, rotating pan halfway through baking.

5. Let cake cool in pan on wire rack for 20 minutes. Run thin knife around edge of pan to loosen cake. Invert cake onto rack set in rimmed baking sheet. Let sit until cake releases itself from pan, about 1 minute. Remove pan and gently scrape off any fruit stuck in pan and arrange on top of cake. Let cake cool on rack for at least 20 minutes before serving.

VARIATIONS

Apple Upside-Down Cake with Almond
Combine ⅓ cup finely ground toasted almonds with flour and add 1 teaspoon almond extract with sour cream and vanilla in step 4.

Apple Upside-Down Cake with Lemon and Thyme
Add 1 teaspoon finely grated lemon zest and 1 teaspoon finely chopped fresh thyme with sour cream and vanilla in step 4.

French Apple Cake

Serves 8 to 10

WHY THIS RECIPE WORKS The French have a remarkable apple cake featuring butter-soft yet perfectly intact apple slices surrounded by a rich—but not heavy—custard base. Above the custard sits a layer of airy cake with a golden, crisp top. We opted for firm, tart Granny Smith apples in our recipe to provide a nice foil to the sweet cake. To ensure that the apple slices softened fully, we gave them a head start in the microwave. Next we needed to find a way to create two cake layers with different textures from one batter. Fortunately, this step was easier than we thought; we simply divided the batter, adding egg yolks to one portion to make the custardy base and then adding flour to the rest to form the cake layer above it. Sprinkling the cake with granulated sugar just before it went into the oven gave the cake an appealingly crisp top. The microwaved apples should be pliable but not completely soft when cooked. To test for doneness, take one apple slice and try to bend it. If it snaps in half, it's too firm; microwave it for an additional 30 seconds and test again. If Calvados is unavailable, 1 tablespoon of apple brandy or white rum can be substituted.

1½   pounds Granny Smith apples, peeled, cored, cut into 8 wedges, and sliced ⅛ inch thick crosswise
1   tablespoon Calvados
1   teaspoon lemon juice
1   cup (5 ounces) plus 2 tablespoons all-purpose flour, divided
1   cup (7 ounces) plus 1 tablespoon granulated sugar, divided
2   teaspoons baking powder
½   teaspoon table salt

1   cup vegetable oil
1   cup whole milk
1   large egg plus 2 large yolks
1   teaspoon vanilla extract
Confectioners' sugar

1. Adjust oven rack to lower-middle position and heat oven to 325 degrees. Spray 9-inch springform pan with vegetable oil spray. Place prepared pan on aluminum foil–lined rimmed baking sheet. Place apples in pie plate, cover, and microwave until apples are pliable and slightly translucent, about 3 minutes. Toss apples with Calvados and lemon juice and let cool for 15 minutes.

2. Whisk 1 cup flour, 1 cup granulated sugar, baking powder, and salt together in bowl. Whisk oil, milk, whole egg, and vanilla in second large bowl until smooth. Add flour mixture to milk mixture and whisk until just combined. Transfer 1 cup batter to third bowl and set aside.

3. Add egg yolks to remaining batter and whisk to combine. Using spatula, gently fold in cooled apples. Transfer batter to prepared pan; using offset spatula, spread batter evenly to pan edges, gently pressing on apples to create even, compact layer and smooth surface.

4. Whisk remaining 2 tablespoons flour into reserved batter. Pour over batter in pan, spread batter evenly to pan edges, and smooth surface. Sprinkle remaining 1 tablespoon granulated sugar evenly over cake. Bake until center of cake is set, toothpick inserted in center comes out clean, and top is golden brown, about 1¼ hours. Let cake cool in pan on wire rack for 5 minutes. Run thin knife around edge of pan to loosen cake, then let cool completely, 2 to 3 hours. Remove sides of pan and slide thin metal spatula between cake bottom and pan bottom to loosen, then slide cake onto platter. Dust cake lightly with confectioners' sugar before serving.

"My mother liked to sneak vegetables into desserts so you'll understand why I was a carrot cake skeptic. Why ruin a perfectly good cake with carrots? My stance eventually softened to ambivalence. Then I tried this layer cake. If I could only have one cake for the rest of my life, this is it. The recipe has clever tricks that ensure that the carrots are tender but present. And its impressive appearance is pretty easy to achieve because the cake is baked in a thin layer, quartered, and stacked. But it's the combination of tangy, silky frosting and sweet, spiced, faintly earthy cake that makes it shine."

–Lan

Carrot Layer Cake

Serves 10 to 12

WHY THIS RECIPE WORKS This American classic has a lot going for it: moist cake, delicate spices, tangy cream cheese frosting. But we wanted to reengineer humble carrot cake as a four-tier, nut-crusted confection that could claim its place among the most glamorous desserts. To start, we found that baking it in a half sheet pan meant that it baked and cooled in far less time than a conventional layer cake, and—cut into quarters—it produced four thin, level layers that did not require splitting or trimming. Extra baking soda raised the pH of the batter, so the coarsely shredded carrots softened during the shortened baking time. Buttermilk powder in the frosting reinforced the tangy flavor of the cream cheese. Shred the carrots on the large holes of a box grater or in a food processor fitted with the shredding disk. Do not substitute liquid buttermilk for the buttermilk powder. If your baked cake is of an uneven thickness, adjust the orientation of the layers as they are stacked to produce a level cake. Assembling this cake on a cardboard cake round trimmed to about a 6 by 8-inch rectangle makes it easy to press the pecans onto the sides of the frosted cake.

Cake
- 1¾ cups (8¾ ounces) all-purpose flour
- 2 teaspoons baking powder
- 1 teaspoon baking soda
- 1½ teaspoons ground cinnamon
- ¾ teaspoon ground nutmeg
- ½ teaspoon table salt
- ¼ teaspoon ground cloves
- 1¼ cups packed (8¾ ounces) light brown sugar
- ¾ cup vegetable oil
- 3 large eggs
- 1 teaspoon vanilla extract
- 2⅔ cups shredded carrots (4 carrots)
- ⅔ cup dried currants

Frosting and Nuts
- 16 tablespoons unsalted butter, softened
- 3 cups (12 ounces) confectioners' sugar
- ⅓ cup (1 ounce) buttermilk powder
- 2 teaspoons vanilla extract
- ¼ teaspoon table salt
- 12 ounces cream cheese, cut into 12 equal pieces and chilled
- 2 cups pecans, toasted and chopped coarse

1. *For the cake:* Adjust oven rack to middle position and heat oven to 350 degrees. Grease 18 by 13-inch rimmed baking sheet, line with parchment paper, and grease parchment.

2. Whisk flour, baking powder, baking soda, cinnamon, nutmeg, salt, and cloves together in large bowl. Whisk sugar, oil, eggs, and vanilla in second large bowl until mixture is smooth. Stir in carrots and currants. Add flour mixture and fold with rubber spatula until mixture is just combined.

3. Transfer batter to prepared sheet and smooth top with offset spatula. Bake until center is firm to touch, 15 to 18 minutes, rotating sheet halfway through baking. Let cake cool in pan on wire rack for 5 minutes. Invert cake onto rack (do not remove parchment), then reinvert onto second rack. Let cake cool completely, about 30 minutes.

4. *For the frosting and nuts:* Using stand mixer fitted with paddle, beat butter, sugar, buttermilk powder, vanilla, and salt on low speed until smooth, about 2 minutes, scraping down bowl as needed. Increase speed to medium-low, add cream cheese, 1 piece at a time, and mix until smooth, about 2 minutes.

5. Transfer cooled cake to cutting board, parchment side down. Using sharp chef's knife, cut cake and parchment in half crosswise, then lengthwise, making 4 equal rectangles, about 8 by 6 inches each.

6. Place 1 cake layer, parchment side up, on 8 by 6-inch cardboard rectangle and carefully remove parchment. Spread ⅔ cup frosting evenly over top, right to edge of cake. Repeat with 2 more cake layers, pressing lightly to adhere and spreading ⅔ cup frosting evenly over each layer. Top with remaining cake layer and spread 1 cup frosting evenly over top. Spread remaining frosting evenly over sides of cake. (It's fine if some crumbs show through frosting on sides, but if you go back to smooth top of cake, be sure that spatula is free of crumbs.)

7. Hold cake with your hand and gently press pecans onto sides with your other hand. Refrigerate for at least 1 hour. Transfer cake to platter and serve. (Cake can be refrigerated for up to 24 hours; bring to room temperature before serving.)

Olive Oil Cake

Serves 8 to 10

WHY THIS RECIPE WORKS We wanted our simple olive oil cake to have a light yet plush crumb, with a subtle but noticeable olive oil flavor. Whipping the sugar with whole eggs, rather than just the whites, produced a fine texture that was airy but sturdy enough to support the olive oil–rich batter. To emphasize the defining flavor, we opted for a good-quality extra-virgin olive oil and accentuated its fruitiness with a tiny bit of lemon zest. Sugar created a crackly topping that added a touch of sweetness and sophistication. For the best flavor, use a fresh, high-quality extra-virgin olive oil. If your springform pan is prone to leaking, place a rimmed baking sheet on the oven floor to catch any drips. Leftover cake can be wrapped in plastic wrap and stored at room temperature for up to three days.

1¾ cups (8¾ ounces) all-purpose flour
1 teaspoon baking powder
¾ teaspoon table salt
3 large eggs
1¼ cups (8¾ ounces) plus 2 tablespoons
    sugar, divided
¼ teaspoon grated lemon zest
¾ cup extra-virgin olive oil
¾ cup milk

1. Adjust oven rack to middle position and heat oven to 350 degrees. Grease 9-inch springform pan. Whisk flour, baking powder, and salt together in bowl.

2. Using stand mixer fitted with whisk attachment, whip eggs on medium speed until foamy, about 1 minute. Add 1¼ cups sugar and lemon zest, increase speed to high, and whip until mixture is fluffy and pale yellow, about 3 minutes. Reduce speed to medium and, with mixer running, slowly pour in oil. Mix until oil is fully incorporated, about 1 minute. Add half of flour mixture and mix on low speed until incorporated, about 1 minute, scraping down bowl as needed. Add milk and mix until combined, about 30 seconds. Add remaining flour mixture and mix until just incorporated, about 1 minute, scraping down bowl as needed.

3. Transfer batter to prepared pan; sprinkle remaining 2 tablespoons sugar over entire surface. Bake until cake is deep golden brown and toothpick inserted in center comes out with few crumbs attached, 40 to 45 minutes. Transfer pan to wire rack and let cool for 15 minutes. Remove side of pan and let cake cool completely, about 1½ hours. Cut into wedges and serve.

Italian Almond Cake

Serves 8 to 10

WHY THIS RECIPE WORKS Simple, rich almond cake makes a sophisticated dessert, but traditional European versions can be heavy and dense. For a slightly cakier version with plenty of nutty flavor, we swapped out traditional almond paste for toasted blanched sliced almonds and added a bit of almond extract for extra depth. Lemon zest in the batter provided citrusy brightness. For a lighter crumb, we increased the flour slightly and added baking powder. Making the batter in a food processor broke down some of the protein structure in the eggs, ensuring that the cake had a level, not domed, top. We swapped some butter for oil and lowered the oven temperature to produce an evenly baked, moist cake. For a crunchy finishing touch, we topped the cake with sliced almonds and a sprinkle of lemon zest–infused sugar. If you can't find blanched sliced almonds, grind slivered almonds for the batter and use unblanched sliced almonds for the topping. Serve plain or with Orange Crème Fraîche (recipe follows).

1½ cups plus ⅓ cup blanched sliced almonds,
    toasted, divided
¾ cup (3¾ ounces) all-purpose flour
¾ teaspoon table salt
¼ teaspoon baking powder
⅛ teaspoon baking soda
4 large eggs
1¼ cups (8¾ ounces) plus 2 tablespoons
    sugar, divided
1 tablespoon plus ½ teaspoon grated lemon
    zest (2 lemons), divided
¾ teaspoon almond extract
5 tablespoons unsalted butter, melted
⅓ cup vegetable oil

1. Adjust oven rack to middle position and heat oven to 300 degrees. Grease 9-inch round cake pan and line with parchment paper. Pulse 1½ cups almonds, flour, salt, baking powder, and baking soda in food processor until almonds are finely ground, 5 to 10 pulses. Transfer almond mixture to bowl.

2. Process eggs, 1¼ cups sugar, 1 tablespoon lemon zest, and almond extract in now-empty processor until very pale yellow, about 2 minutes. With processor running, add melted butter and oil in steady stream, until incorporated. Add almond mixture and pulse to combine, 4 to 5 pulses. Transfer batter to prepared pan.

3. Using your fingers, combine remaining 2 tablespoons sugar and remaining ½ teaspoon lemon zest in small bowl until fragrant, 5 to 10 seconds. Sprinkle top of cake evenly with remaining ⅓ cup almonds followed by sugar-zest mixture.

4. Bake until center of cake is set and bounces back when gently pressed and toothpick inserted in center comes out clean, 55 minutes to 1 hour 5 minutes, rotating pan after 40 minutes. Let cake cool in pan on wire rack for 15 minutes. Run paring knife around sides of pan. Invert cake onto greased wire rack, discard parchment, and reinvert cake onto second wire rack. Let cake cool, about 2 hours. Cut into wedges and serve. (Cooled cake can be wrapped in plastic wrap and stored at room temperature for up to 3 days.)

ACCOMPANIMENT
Orange Crème Fraîche
Makes about 2 cups

2 oranges
1 cup crème fraîche
2 tablespoons sugar
⅛ teaspoon table salt

Remove 1 teaspoon zest from 1 orange. Cut away peel and pith from oranges. Slice between membranes to release segments and cut segments into ¼-inch pieces. Combine orange pieces and zest, crème fraîche, sugar, and salt in bowl and mix well. Refrigerate for 1 hour.

Italian Almond Cake

Gâteau Breton with Apricot Filling

Serves 8

WHY THIS RECIPE WORKS Hailing from France's Brittany coast, where butter is king, *gâteau Breton* is a simple yet stately cake, rich in flavor, with a dense yet tender crumb that falls somewhere between shortbread cookie and pound cake. Most recipes call for creaming the butter and sugar before incorporating egg yolks and flour, with some specifying upward of 10 minutes of creaming. But extended creaming incorporated too much air into the batter and resulted in a light, fluffy crumb—the opposite of what we wanted. Creaming the butter for a more reasonable 4 to 5 minutes (only 3 minutes of which was with the sugar) produced an ultrathick batter that baked into a firm yet tender cake. Briefly freezing a layer of the batter in the cake pan made easy work of spreading on a bright apricot filling, and a second stint in the freezer firmed up the apricot-topped batter so we could cleanly apply the top layer. We strongly prefer the flavor of California apricots in the filling. Mediterranean or Turkish apricots can be used, but increase the amount of lemon juice to 2 tablespoons. This cake is traditionally served plain with coffee or tea but can be dressed up with fresh berries, if desired.

Filling
- ⅔ cup water
- ½ cup dried California apricots, chopped
- ⅓ cup (2⅓ ounces) sugar
- 1 tablespoon lemon juice

Cake
- 16 tablespoons unsalted butter, cut into 16 pieces and softened
- ¾ cup plus 2 tablespoons (6⅛ ounces) sugar
- 6 large egg yolks (1 lightly beaten with 1 teaspoon water)
- 2 tablespoons dark rum
- 1 teaspoon vanilla extract
- 2 cups (10 ounces) all-purpose flour
- ½ teaspoon table salt

1. For the filling: Process water and apricots in blender until uniformly pureed, about 2 minutes. Transfer puree to 10-inch nonstick skillet and stir in sugar. Set skillet over medium heat and cook, stirring frequently, until puree has darkened slightly and rubber spatula leaves distinct trail when dragged across bottom of skillet, 10 to 12 minutes. Transfer filling to bowl and stir in lemon juice. Refrigerate filling until cool to touch, about 15 minutes.

2. For the cake: Adjust oven rack to lower-middle position and heat oven to 350 degrees. Grease 9-inch round cake pan.

3. Using stand mixer fitted with paddle, beat butter on medium-high speed until smooth and lightened in color, 1 to 2 minutes. Add sugar and continue to beat until pale

and fluffy, about 3 minutes longer. Add 5 egg yolks, one at a time, and beat until combined. Scrape down bowl, add rum and vanilla, and mix until incorporated, about 1 minute. Reduce speed to low, add flour and salt, and mix until flour is just incorporated, about 30 seconds. Give batter final stir by hand.

4. Spoon half of batter into bottom of prepared pan. Using small offset spatula, spread batter into even layer. Freeze for 10 minutes. Spread ½ cup filling in even layer over chilled batter, leaving ¾-inch border around edge (reserve remaining filling for another use). Freeze for 10 minutes.

5. Gently spread remaining batter over filling. Using offset spatula, carefully smooth top of batter. Brush with egg yolk wash. Using tines of fork, make light scores in surface of cake, spaced about 1½ inches apart, in diamond pattern, being careful not to score all the way to sides of pan. Bake until top is golden brown and edges of cake start to pull away from sides of pan, 45 to 50 minutes, rotating pan halfway through baking. Let cake cool in pan on wire rack for 30 minutes. Run thin knife around edge of pan, remove cake from pan, and let cool completely on rack, about 1 hour, before serving.

VARIATION

Gâteau Breton with Prune Filling
Increase water to 1 cup, substitute 1 cup pitted prunes for apricots, and omit sugar. Bring water and prunes to simmer in small saucepan over medium heat. Reduce heat to medium-low and cook until all liquid is absorbed and prunes are very soft, 10 to 12 minutes. Remove saucepan from heat, add lemon juice, and stir with wooden spoon, pressing prunes against side of saucepan, until coarsely pureed. Transfer filling to bowl and refrigerate until cool to touch, about 15 minutes.

Summer Peach Cake

Serves 8

WHY THIS RECIPE WORKS Marrying cake with fresh summer peaches, this dessert is a bakery favorite, yet most versions are plagued by soggy cake and barely noticeable peach flavor. We wanted a buttery cake that was moist and not at all soggy, with a golden-brown exterior and plenty of peach flavor. Roasting chunks of peaches tossed in sugar and a little lemon juice helped concentrate their flavor and expel excess moisture before we combined them with our cake batter. However, during roasting, the peach chunks became swathed in a flavorful but unpleasantly gooey film. Coating our roasted peaches in panko bread crumbs before combining them with the batter ensured the film was absorbed by the crumbs, which then dissolved into the cake during baking. To amplify the peach flavor, we tossed the fruit with peach schnapps before roasting, and a little almond extract added to the batter lent a subtle complementary note. Fanning peach slices (macerated with a little more of the schnapps) over the

"Gâteau Breton is a classic French butter cake. It's a simple yet pretty cake, rich in butter, with a dense, tender crumb. I have to be honest, I was very intimidated by this recipe. I'm not a pastry chef so it always takes some Jedi mind tricks to get me feeling bold enough to tackle anything that must be baked but after the first time I made the cake properly, I was in love.

Making this cake requires a bit of patience because it has multiple levels: There's the base of the cake, the delicious apricot jam in the middle, and then the top layer that has to be (and it is) firm enough to not taint the jam. There's time in the freezer and then baking time; seemingly laborious but actually it's a masterpiece. It's the Sistine Chapel of cakes, right down to its decorative top."

—*Elle*

top, sprinkled with almond extract–flavored sugar for a light glaze, ensured our cake looked as good as it tasted. To crush the panko bread crumbs, place them in a zipper-lock bag and smash them with a rolling pin. If you can't find panko, ¼ cup of plain, unseasoned bread crumbs can be substituted. Orange liqueur can be substituted for the peach schnapps. If using peak-of-season, farm-fresh peaches, omit the peach schnapps.

Peaches

- 2½ pounds peaches, peeled, halved, pitted, and cut into ½-inch wedges, divided
- 5 tablespoons peach schnapps, divided
- 4 teaspoons lemon juice, divided
- 3 tablespoons granulated sugar, divided

Cake

- 1 cup (5 ounces) all-purpose flour
- 1¼ teaspoons baking powder
- ¾ teaspoon table salt
- ½ cup packed (3½ ounces) light brown sugar
- ⅓ cup (2⅓ ounces) plus 3 tablespoons granulated sugar, divided
- 2 large eggs, room temperature
- 8 tablespoons unsalted butter, melted and cooled
- ¼ cup sour cream
- 1½ teaspoons vanilla extract
- ⅜ teaspoon almond extract, divided
- ⅓ cup panko bread crumbs, crushed fine

1. For the peaches: Adjust oven rack to middle position and heat oven to 425 degrees. Line rimmed baking sheet with aluminum foil and spray with vegetable oil spray. Grease and flour 9-inch springform pan. Gently toss 24 peach wedges with 2 tablespoons schnapps, 2 teaspoons lemon juice, and 1 tablespoon sugar in bowl; set aside.

2. Cut remaining peach wedges crosswise into 3 chunks and gently toss with remaining 3 tablespoons schnapps, remaining 2 teaspoons lemon juice, and remaining 2 tablespoons sugar in second bowl. Spread peach pieces onto prepared baking sheet and bake until exuded juices begin to thicken and caramelize at edges of pan, 20 to 25 minutes. Let peaches cool completely on pan, about 30 minutes. Reduce oven temperature to 350 degrees.

3. For the cake: Whisk flour, baking powder, and salt together in bowl. Whisk brown sugar, ⅓ cup granulated sugar, and eggs in large bowl until thick and thoroughly combined, about 45 seconds. Slowly whisk in melted butter until combined. Whisk in sour cream, vanilla, and ¼ teaspoon almond extract until combined. Add flour mixture and whisk until just combined.

4. Pour half of batter into prepared pan and spread to pan edges with rubber spatula. Sprinkle crushed panko over roasted peaches and toss gently to combine. Arrange peaches evenly in pan and press gently into batter. Gently spread remaining batter over peaches, smooth top, and arrange reserved peaches attractively over top, also placing wedges in center. Combine remaining 3 tablespoons granulated sugar and remaining ⅛ teaspoon almond extract in bowl; sprinkle over top.

5. Bake cake until golden brown and toothpick inserted in center comes out clean, 50 minutes to 1 hour, rotating pan halfway through baking. Let cake cool in pan on wire rack for 5 minutes. Run thin knife around edge of pan to loosen cake, then remove sides of pan. Let cake cool completely on rack, 2 to 3 hours. Slide thin metal spatula between cake bottom and pan bottom to loosen, then slide cake onto platter. Serve.

Applesauce Snack Cake

Serves 9

WHY THIS RECIPE WORKS Applesauce cakes run the gamut from dense, chunky fruitcakes to gummy "health" cakes without much flavor. We wanted a moist and tender cake that actually tasted like its namesake. It was easy to achieve the looser, more casual crumb that is best suited to a rustic snack cake. Since this texture is similar to that of quick breads and muffins, we used the same technique, i.e., mixing the wet ingredients separately and then gently adding the dry ingredients by hand. The challenge was to develop more apple flavor—simply adding more applesauce made for a gummy cake and fresh apples added too much moisture. But apple cider, reduced to a syrup, contributed a pleasing sweetness and a slight tang without excess moisture. And plumping dried apples in the cider while it was reducing added even more apple taste without making the cake chunky. With such great apple flavor, we didn't want the cake to be too sweet or rich, so we rejected the idea of topping the cake with a glaze or frosting. But we found we liked the modicum of textural contrast provided by a simple sprinkling of spiced granulated sugar. The cake is very moist, so it is best to err on the side of overdone when testing its doneness. The test kitchen prefers the rich flavor of cider, but apple juice can be substituted.

- 1 cup apple cider
- ¾ cup dried apples, cut into ½-inch pieces
- 1 cup unsweetened applesauce, room temperature
- ⅔ cup (4⅔ ounces) sugar
- ½ teaspoon ground cinnamon
- ¼ teaspoon ground nutmeg
- ⅛ teaspoon ground cloves
- 1½ cups (7½ ounces) all-purpose flour
- 1 teaspoon baking soda
- 1 large egg, room temperature
- ½ teaspoon table salt
- 8 tablespoons unsalted butter, melted and cooled
- 1 teaspoon vanilla extract

1. Adjust oven rack to middle position and heat oven to 325 degrees. Make foil sling for 8-inch square baking pan by folding 2 long sheets of aluminum foil so each is 8 inches wide. Lay sheets of foil in pan perpendicular to each other, with extra foil hanging over edges of pan. Push foil into corners and up sides of pan, smoothing foil flush to pan.

2. Combine cider and dried apples in small saucepan and simmer over medium heat until liquid evaporates and mixture appears dry, about 15 minutes. Let mixture cool completely, then process with applesauce in food processor until smooth, 20 to 30 seconds.

3. Whisk sugar, cinnamon, nutmeg, and cloves together in bowl; set aside 2 tablespoons mixture for topping. Whisk flour and baking soda together in second bowl.

4. Whisk egg and salt together in large bowl. Whisk in sugar mixture until well combined and light-colored, about 20 seconds. Whisk in melted butter in 3 additions, whisking after each addition until incorporated. Whisk in applesauce mixture and vanilla. Using rubber spatula, fold in flour mixture until just combined.

5. Transfer batter to prepared pan and smooth top with rubber spatula. Gently tap pan on counter to settle batter. Sprinkle reserved sugar mixture evenly over top. Bake until toothpick inserted in center comes out clean, 35 to 40 minutes, rotating pan halfway through baking. Let cake cool completely in pan on wire rack, 1 to 2 hours. Using foil overhang, lift cake from pan. Serve. (Cake can be stored at room temperature for up to 2 days.)

Fluffy Yellow Layer Cake with Milk Chocolate Frosting

Serves 10 to 12

WHY THIS RECIPE WORKS It's easy to create a supremely fluffy layer cake with additives, but most cakes made entirely from natural ingredients are either unpleasantly dense or too fragile to support layers of frosting. We wanted a frosted yellow layer cake with an ethereal texture and the great flavor of real butter and eggs. Chiffon cakes are especially weightless, springy, and moist. But unlike butter cakes, they are too light to stand up to a serious slathering of frosting. We decided to blend the two types of cake. We adapted a chiffon technique (using a large quantity of whipped egg whites to get a high volume and light texture) to combine the ingredients from our butter cake recipe. This worked beautifully, creating a light, porous cake that was hefty enough to hold the frosting's weight. But the cake lacked moistness and some tenderness. A combination of fats (butter plus vegetable oil) kept the butter flavor intact while improving the moistness of

the cake. For extra tenderness, we increased the sugar and substituted buttermilk for milk. The buttermilk not only introduced a new flavor dimension, but also allowed us to replace some of the baking powder with a little baking soda to ensure an even rise. As for the frosting, a fluffy chocolate frosting is the perfect partner to this cake. A hefty amount of cocoa powder combined with melted chocolate gave the frosting a deep chocolate flavor. A combination of confectioners' sugar and corn syrup made it smooth and glossy. To keep the frosting from separating and turning greasy, we moved it out of the stand mixer and into the food processor. The faster machine minimized any risk of overbeating, as it blended the ingredients quickly without melting the butter or incorporating too much air. The result is a thick, fluffy chocolate frosting that spreads like a dream. Bring all the ingredients to room temperature before beginning. For the frosting, cool the chocolate to between 85 and 100 degrees before adding it to the butter mixture. The frosting can be made 3 hours in advance. For longer storage, refrigerate the frosting, covered, and let it stand at room temperature for 1 hour before using.

Cake
2½ cups (10 ounces) cake flour
1¼ teaspoons baking powder
¼ teaspoon baking soda
¾ teaspoon table salt
1¾ cups (12¼ ounces) sugar, divided
1 cup buttermilk, room temperature
10 tablespoons unsalted butter, melted and cooled
3 large eggs, separated, plus 3 large yolks, room temperature
3 tablespoons vegetable oil
2 teaspoons vanilla extract
Pinch cream of tartar

Frosting
- 30 tablespoons (3¾ sticks) unsalted butter, softened
- 1½ cups (6 ounces) confectioners' sugar
- 1 cup Dutch-processed cocoa powder
- ⅛ teaspoon table salt
- 1 cup light corn syrup
- 1½ teaspoons vanilla extract
- 12 ounces milk chocolate, melted and cooled slightly

1. *For the cake:* Adjust oven rack to middle position and heat oven to 350 degrees. Grease two 9-inch round cake pans, line with parchment paper, grease parchment, and flour pans. Whisk flour, baking powder, baking soda, salt, and 1½ cups sugar together in bowl. Whisk buttermilk, melted butter, egg yolks, oil, and vanilla together in second bowl.

2. Using stand mixer fitted with whisk attachment, whip egg whites and cream of tartar on medium-low speed until foamy, about 1 minute. Increase speed to medium-high and whip whites to soft, billowy mounds, about 1 minute. Gradually add remaining ¼ cup sugar and whip until glossy and stiff peaks form, 2 to 3 minutes; transfer to third bowl.

3. Add flour mixture to now-empty mixer bowl and mix on low speed, gradually adding buttermilk mixture and mixing until almost incorporated (few streaks of dry flour will remain), about 15 seconds. Scrape down bowl, then mix on medium-low speed until smooth and fully incorporated, 10 to 15 seconds.

4. Using rubber spatula, stir one-third of whites into batter. Gently fold remaining whites into batter until no white streaks remain. Divide batter evenly between prepared pans and smooth tops with rubber spatula. Gently tap pans on counter to settle batter. Bake until toothpick inserted in center comes out clean, 20 to 22 minutes, rotating pans halfway through baking. Let cakes cool in pans on wire rack for 10 minutes. Remove cakes from pans, discarding parchment, and let cool completely on rack, about 2 hours. (Cake layers can be stored at room temperature for up to 24 hours or frozen for up to 1 month; defrost at room temperature.)

5. *For the frosting:* In food processor, process butter, confectioners' sugar, cocoa, and salt until smooth, about 30 seconds, scraping down sides of bowl as needed. Add corn syrup and vanilla and process until just combined, 5 to 10 seconds. Scrape down sides of bowl, then add chocolate and process until smooth and creamy, 10 to 15 seconds. (Frosting can be held at room temperature for up to 3 hours or refrigerated for up to 3 days. If refrigerated, let sit at room temperature for 1 hour before using.)

6. Line edges of cake platter with 4 strips of parchment paper to keep platter clean. Place 1 cake layer on platter. Spread 1½ cups frosting evenly over top, right to edge of cake. Top with second cake layer, press lightly to adhere, then spread remaining frosting evenly over top and sides of cake. Carefully remove parchment strips before serving.

Frosting a Layer Cake

1. Dollop portion of frosting in center of cake and spread into even layer right to edge.

2. Lay second layer on top. Brush away any large crumbs, dollop more frosting in center, and spread slightly over edge.

3. Gather few tablespoons of frosting onto top of spatula, then gently smear it onto side of cake. Repeat to frost sides completely.

4. For smooth sides, gently run edge of spatula around cake. Or, to create billows in frosting, press back of soup spoon into frosting, then twirl spoon as you lift it away.

Chocolate Sheet Cake with Easy Chocolate Frosting

Serves 15 to 18

WHY THIS RECIPE WORKS Sheet cakes, for all their simplicity, can still turn out dry, sticky, or flavorless and, on occasion, can even sink in the middle. We wanted a simple, dependable recipe that delivered a moist yet tender cake. We started with the mixing method—testing everything from creaming butter to beating yolks, whipping whites, and gently folding together everything in the end. The best of the lot was the most complicated to make, so we took a step back. The simplest technique we tried was just whisking all the ingredients together without beating, creaming, or whipping. The recipe needed work, but the approach was clearly a good match for the simple all-purpose nature of a sheet cake. First we added buttermilk and baking soda to lighten the batter. To increase the chocolate flavor, we reduced the sugar, flour, and butter. To further deepen the chocolate taste, we used semisweet chocolate in addition to the cocoa. We baked the cake at a low temperature for 40 minutes to produce a perfect cake with a flat top. Though this cake can be frosted with almost anything, we like a classic American milk chocolate frosting, which pairs well with the darker flavor of the cake. We prefer Dutch-processed cocoa for the deeper chocolate flavor it gives the cake. The frosting needs about an hour to cool before it can be used, so begin making it when the cake comes out of the oven. You can also serve the cake lightly dusted with confectioners' sugar or with lightly sweetened whipped cream.

Cake

- ¾ cup (2¼ ounces) Dutch-processed cocoa powder
- 1¼ cups (6¼ ounces) all-purpose flour
- ½ teaspoon baking soda
- ¼ teaspoon table salt
- 8 ounces semisweet chocolate, chopped
- 12 tablespoons unsalted butter
- 4 large eggs, room temperature
- 1½ cups (10½ ounces) granulated sugar
- 1 teaspoon vanilla extract
- 1 cup buttermilk

Frosting

- ½ cup heavy cream
- 1 tablespoon corn syrup
  Pinch table salt
- 10 ounces milk chocolate, chopped
- ½ cup (2 ounces) confectioners' sugar
- 8 tablespoons unsalted butter, cut into 8 pieces, cold

1. For the cake: Adjust oven rack to middle position and heat oven to 325 degrees. Grease 13 by 9-inch baking pan, then line bottom with parchment paper.

2. Sift together cocoa, flour, baking soda, and salt in medium bowl; set aside. Melt chocolate and butter in bowl set over saucepan filled with 1 inch of barely simmering water, stirring occasionally until smooth. Whisk together eggs, sugar, and vanilla in medium bowl. Whisk in buttermilk until smooth.

3. Whisk chocolate into egg mixture until combined. Whisk in dry ingredients until batter is smooth and glossy. Pour batter into prepared pan; bake until firm in center when lightly pressed and toothpick inserted in center comes out clean, about 40 minutes, rotating pan halfway through baking time. Let cake cool completely in pan, set on wire rack, about 2 hours. Run small knife around cake and flip cake out onto wire rack. Peel off parchment paper, then flip cake right side up onto serving platter.

4. For the frosting: Heat cream, corn syrup, and salt in measuring cup on high power until simmering, about 1 minute, or bring to simmer in small saucepan over medium heat.

5. Place chocolate in food processor. With machine running, gradually add hot cream mixture through feed tube; process for 1 minute after cream has been added. Stop machine; add confectioners' sugar and process to combine, about 30 seconds. With machine running, add butter through feed tube 1 piece at a time; process until incorporated and smooth, about 20 seconds.

6. Transfer frosting to medium bowl and let cool at room temperature, stirring frequently, until thick and spreadable, about 1 hour. Spread frosting evenly over top and sides of cake and serve.

Easy Vanilla Bean Buttercream
Makes about 3 cups
If you prefer to skip the vanilla bean, increase the extract to 1½ teaspoons. Any of the buttercream frostings can be made ahead and refrigerated; if refrigerated, however, the frosting must stand at room temperature to soften before use. If using a handheld mixer, increase mixing times significantly (by at least 50 percent).

- 20 tablespoons unsalted butter, softened
- 1 vanilla bean, halved lengthwise
- 2½ cups (10 ounces) confectioners' sugar
  Pinch table salt
- 2 tablespoons heavy cream
- 1 teaspoon vanilla extract

In stand mixer fitted with whisk, beat butter at medium-high speed until smooth, about 20 seconds. Using paring knife, scrape seeds from vanilla bean into butter and beat mixture at medium-high speed to combine, about 15 seconds. Add confectioners' sugar and salt and beat at medium-low speed until most of sugar is moistened, about 45 seconds. Scrape down bowl and beat at medium speed until mixture is fully combined, about 15 seconds. Scrape down bowl, add heavy cream and vanilla extract, and beat at medium speed until incorporated, about 10 seconds, then increase speed to medium-high and beat until light and fluffy, about 4 minutes, scraping down bowl once or twice.

VARIATIONS
Easy Chocolate Buttercream
Omit vanilla bean and heavy cream and reduce sugar to 2 cups. After beating in vanilla extract, reduce speed to low and gradually beat in 8 ounces melted and cooled semisweet or bittersweet chocolate.

Easy Coffee Buttercream
Omit vanilla bean and dissolve 3 teaspoons instant espresso powder in heavy cream and vanilla extract.

Classic Gingerbread Cake

Serves 8

WHY THIS RECIPE WORKS Most recipes for gingerbread suffer from a dense, sunken center, and flavors range from barely gingery to spicier than a curry dinner. Our ideal gingerbread is moist through and through and utterly simple. Focusing on flavor first, we bumped up the ginger with both a hefty dose of ground ginger and grated fresh ginger. Cinnamon and freshly ground pepper produced a complex, lingering heat. Dark stout, gently heated to minimize its booziness, had a bittersweet flavor that brought out the caramel undertones of the molasses. Finally, swapping out the butter for vegetable oil and replacing some of the brown sugar with granulated let the spice flavors come through. To prevent a sunken center, we looked at our leaveners first. Baking powder isn't as effective at leavening if too many other acidic ingredients are present in the batter. Incorporating baking soda with the wet ingredients instead of the other dry ones helped to neutralize those acidic ingredients before they got incorporated into the batter and allowed the baking powder to do a better job. While stirring is typically the enemy of tenderness since it develops the flour's gluten, our batter was so loose that vigorous stirring actually gave our gingerbread the structure necessary to further ensure the center didn't collapse. With that, we had a flawless cake with plenty of spice and warmth. This cake packs potent yet well-balanced spice. If you prefer less spice, you can decrease the amount of ground ginger to 1 tablespoon. Avoid opening the oven door, except to rotate the cake, until the minimum baking time has elapsed. Serve the gingerbread plain or with lightly sweetened whipped cream.

- ¾ **cup stout**
- ½ **teaspoon baking soda**
- ¾ **cup packed (5¼ ounces) light brown sugar**
- ⅔ **cup molasses**
- ¼ **cup (1¾ ounces) granulated sugar**
- 1½ **cups (7½ ounces) all-purpose flour**
- 2 **tablespoons ground ginger**
- ½ **teaspoon baking powder**
- ½ **teaspoon table salt**
- ¼ **teaspoon ground cinnamon**
- ¼ **teaspoon pepper**
- 2 **large eggs**
- ⅓ **cup vegetable oil**
- 1 **tablespoon finely grated fresh ginger**

1. Adjust oven rack to middle position and heat oven to 350 degrees. Grease and flour 8-inch square baking pan.

2. Bring stout to boil in medium saucepan over medium heat, stirring occasionally. Off heat, stir in baking soda (mixture will foam vigorously). When foaming subsides, stir in brown sugar, molasses, and granulated sugar until dissolved; set aside. Whisk flour, ground ginger, baking powder, salt, cinnamon, and pepper together in large bowl; set aside.

3. Transfer stout mixture to second large bowl. Whisk in eggs, oil, and grated ginger until combined. Whisk stout-egg mixture into flour mixture in 3 additions, stirring vigorously until completely smooth after each addition.

4. Transfer batter to prepared pan and gently tap on counter to release air bubbles. Bake until top of cake is just firm to touch and toothpick inserted in center comes out clean, 35 to 45 minutes, rotating pan halfway through baking. Let cake cool in pan on wire rack, about 1½ hours. Cut into 2-inch squares and serve warm or at room temperature. (Leftover cake can be wrapped in plastic wrap and stored at room temperature for up to 2 days.)

Coconut Layer Cake

Serves 10 to 12

WHY THIS RECIPE WORKS The ideal coconut cake is perfumed inside and out with the subtle essence of coconut. We wanted a four-layer affair featuring moist, tender cake with a delicate, yielding crumb and silky, gently sweetened frosting covered with a deep drift of downy coconut. For the cake layers, we preferred a rich and moist butter cake made with low-protein cake flour for a supertender crumb. To infuse this base with maximum coconut flavor, we tried a combination of coconut extract and coconut milk, but found that the fat content among brands of coconut milk varied too much—enough to throw off our cake's carefully balanced formula. Using cream of coconut in place of the coconut milk gave us more consistent results; plus, cream of coconut simply delivered fuller coconut flavor. For a light yet rich frosting we chose an egg white–based buttercream that we flavored with more coconut extract and cream of coconut. A woolly coating of toasted shredded coconut provided textural interest and delivered a final dose of flavor. Be sure to use cream of coconut (such as Coco López) and not coconut milk here. One 15-ounce can of cream of coconut is enough for both the cake and the frosting.

Cake
- 1 **large egg plus 5 large whites**
- ¾ **cup cream of coconut**
- ¼ **cup water**
- 1 **teaspoon coconut extract**
- 1 **teaspoon vanilla extract**
- 2¼ **cups (9 ounces) cake flour**
- 1 **cup (7 ounces) sugar**
- 1 **tablespoon baking powder**
- ¾ **teaspoon table salt**
- 12 **tablespoons unsalted butter, cut into 12 pieces and softened**
- 2 **cups (6 ounces) sweetened shredded coconut**

"If there's a cake to be frosted on the season's TV lineup, I will be first to raise my hand and volunteer for the job. Just ask my cast mates, frosting cakes is a moment of zen for me. The lights are beating down on the set, and I've got at least four cameras pointed on me, but I just get lost in the process.

Now, some cakes need extra care and finesse to look suitable for company (or to a discerning viewing audience), but cakes like this coconut confection are so much less fussy. That's thanks to the massive snowfall of toasted coconut that coats the thick layer of coconut-flavored buttercream and hides any marring or other imperfections in the frosting.

If you are a fan of coconut then you need to make this cake. It's got an old-fashioned style that evokes a time when such a cake would have been served at a garden club meeting, or featured in a local bakery window."

—*Bridget*

Frosting

- 4 large egg whites
- 1 cup (7 ounces) sugar
  Pinch table salt
- 1 pound (4 sticks) unsalted butter, cut into 24 pieces and softened
- ¼ cup cream of coconut
- 1 teaspoon coconut extract
- 1 teaspoon vanilla extract

1. **For the cake:** Adjust oven rack to lower-middle position and heat oven to 325 degrees. Grease two 9-inch round cake pans, line with parchment paper, grease parchment, and flour pans. Whisk egg and whites together in 4-cup liquid measuring cup. Whisk in cream of coconut, water, coconut extract, and vanilla.

2. Using stand mixer fitted with paddle, mix flour, sugar, baking powder, and salt on low speed until combined. Add butter, 1 piece at a time, mixing until only pea-size pieces remain, about 1 minute. Add half of egg mixture, increase speed to medium-high, and beat until light and fluffy, about 1 minute. Reduce speed to medium-low, add remaining egg mixture, and beat until incorporated, about 30 seconds. Give batter final stir by hand.

3. Divide batter evenly between prepared pans and smooth tops with rubber spatula. Gently tap pans on counter to settle batter. Bake until toothpick inserted in center comes out clean, about 30 minutes, rotating pans halfway through baking.

4. Let cakes cool in pans on wire rack for 10 minutes. Remove cakes from pans, discarding parchment, and let cool completely on rack, about 2 hours. (Cake layers can be stored at room temperature for up to 24 hours or frozen for up to 1 month; defrost cakes at room temperature.) Meanwhile, spread shredded coconut on rimmed baking sheet and toast in oven until shreds are mix of golden brown and white, 15 to 20 minutes, stirring 2 or 3 times; let cool.

5. **For the frosting:** Combine egg whites, sugar, and salt in bowl of stand mixer and set over medium saucepan filled with 1 inch barely simmering water, making sure that water does not touch bottom of bowl. Cook, whisking constantly, until mixture is opaque and registers 120 degrees, about 2 minutes.

6. Remove bowl from heat and transfer to stand mixer fitted with whisk attachment. Whip egg white mixture on high speed until glossy, sticky, and barely warm (80 degrees), about 7 minutes. Reduce speed to medium-high and whip in butter, 1 piece at a time, followed by cream of coconut, coconut extract, and vanilla, scraping down bowl as needed. Continue to whip until combined, about 1 minute.

7. Using long serrated knife, cut 1 horizontal line around sides of each layer; then, following scored lines, cut each layer into 2 even layers.

8. Line edges of cake platter with 4 strips of parchment to keep platter clean. Place 1 cake layer on platter. Spread ¾ cup frosting evenly over top, right to edge of cake. Repeat with 2 more cake layers, pressing lightly to adhere and spreading ¾ cup frosting evenly over each layer. Top with remaining cake layer and spread remaining frosting evenly over top and sides of cake. Sprinkle top of cake evenly with toasted coconut, then gently press remaining toasted coconut onto sides. Carefully remove parchment strips before serving. (Frosted cake can be refrigerated for up to 24 hours; bring to room temperature before serving.)

Wicked Good Boston Cream Pie

Serves 8 to 10

WHY THIS RECIPE WORKS This triple-component dessert deserved a revival—if only we could make the filling foolproof and keep the glaze from cracking off. A hot-milk sponge cake made a good base because it didn't require any finicky folding or separating of eggs. Baking the batter in two pans eliminated the need to slice a single cake horizontally before adding the filling. We used butter to firm up our pastry cream, and added corn syrup to heavy cream and melted chocolate to make a smooth glaze that clung to the top of our Boston Cream Pie and dripped artistically down its sides. Chill the assembled cake for at least 3 hours to make it easy to cut and serve.

Pastry Cream

- 2 cups half-and-half
- 6 large egg yolks, room temperature
- ½ cup (3½ ounces) sugar
  Pinch table salt
- ¼ cup (1¼ ounces) all-purpose flour
- 4 tablespoons unsalted butter, cut into 4 pieces and chilled
- 1½ teaspoons vanilla extract

Cake

- 1½ cups (7½ ounces) all-purpose flour
- 1½ teaspoons baking powder
- ¾ teaspoon table salt
- ¾ cup whole milk
- 6 tablespoons unsalted butter
- 1½ teaspoons vanilla extract
- 3 large eggs, room temperature
- 1½ cups (10½ ounces) sugar

Glaze

- ½ cup heavy cream
- 2 tablespoons corn syrup
- 4 ounces bittersweet chocolate, chopped fine

1. *For the pastry cream:* Heat half-and-half in medium saucepan over medium heat until just simmering. Meanwhile, whisk egg yolks, sugar, and salt in medium bowl until smooth. Add flour to yolk mixture and whisk until incorporated. Remove half-and-half from heat and, whisking constantly, slowly add ½ cup to yolk mixture to temper. Whisking constantly, return tempered yolk mixture to half-and-half in saucepan.

2. Return saucepan to medium heat and cook, whisking constantly, until mixture thickens slightly, about 1 minute. Reduce heat to medium-low and continue to simmer, whisking constantly, 8 minutes.

3. Increase heat to medium and cook, whisking vigorously, until bubbles burst on surface, 1 to 2 minutes. Remove saucepan from heat; whisk in butter and vanilla until butter is melted and incorporated. Strain pastry cream through fine-mesh strainer set over medium bowl. Press lightly greased parchment paper directly on surface and refrigerate until set, at least 2 hours or up to 24 hours.

4. *For the cake:* Adjust oven rack to middle position and heat oven to 325 degrees. Lightly grease two 9-inch round cake pans with vegetable oil spray and line with parchment. Whisk flour, baking powder, and salt together in medium bowl. Heat milk and butter in small saucepan over low heat until butter is melted. Remove from heat, add vanilla, and cover to keep warm.

5. In stand mixer fitted with whisk attachment, whip eggs and sugar at high speed until light and airy, about 5 minutes. Remove mixer bowl from stand. Add hot milk mixture and whisk by hand until incorporated. Add dry ingredients and whisk until incorporated.

6. Working quickly, divide batter evenly between prepared pans. Bake until tops are light brown and toothpick inserted in center of cakes comes out clean, 20 to 22 minutes.

7. Transfer cakes to wire rack and let cool completely in pan, about 2 hours. Run small plastic knife around edge of pans, then invert cakes onto wire rack. Carefully remove parchment, then reinvert cakes.

8. Place 1 cake round on large plate. Whisk pastry cream briefly, then spoon onto center of cake. Using offset spatula, spread evenly to cake edge. Place second layer on pastry cream, bottom side up, making sure layers line up properly. Press lightly on top of cake to level. Refrigerate cake while preparing glaze.

9. *For the glaze:* Bring cream and corn syrup to simmer in small saucepan over medium heat. Remove from heat and add chocolate. Whisk gently until smooth, 30 seconds. Let stand, whisking occasionally, until thickened slightly, about 5 minutes.

10. Pour glaze onto center of cake. Use offset spatula to spread glaze to edge of cake, letting excess drip decoratively down sides. Chill finished cake for 3 hours before serving. (Cake may be made up to 24 hours before serving.)

Chocolate-Caramel Layer Cake

Serves 12

WHY THIS RECIPE WORKS Many chocolate-caramel cakes barely contain enough caramel flavor to merit the name. To ensure a hit of caramel flavor in each and every bite, we sandwiched three layers of thick but spreadable caramel filling between layers of deep, dark, moist chocolate cake. We started with a simple chocolate cake recipe, added a little extra water, and swapped melted butter for more neutral-tasting vegetable oil. Combining the dry ingredients and wet ingredients separately before whisking them together could not have been easier, and greasing and then lining two cake pans with parchment paper made for a clean release after baking. For a not-too-sweet caramel that was spreadable but thick enough to stand out between the layers, we cooked it until it turned dark (but not burnt) and added extra butter to ensure that it set up at room temperature without any unpleasant oozing. Because the cake and filling both had deep, rich flavors, we determined that the frosting could afford to be on the slightly sweeter side. Using a food processor, we combined softened butter, confectioners' sugar, cocoa powder, corn syrup (for a guaranteed smooth texture), vanilla, and melted bittersweet chocolate. For a dramatic layered look, we split our two cake rounds in half, creating four layers, and sandwiched our lush

"I'm not much of cake person. I find most layer cakes boring and typically ask for a lattice-top blueberry or peach pie to celebrate my summer birthday. But this cake is altogether another matter and has changed my mind about my birthday celebration. The problem with most layer cakes? Yellow cake is boring. Chocolate is where it's at. And vanilla buttercream? No thanks. I want chocolate ganache and the frosting in this recipe has both cocoa powder and bittersweet chocolate so it screams chocolate. But it's the three layers of caramel that make this cake extraordinary. The caramel is cooked until quite dark to bring out the bittersweet notes in the sugar. A healthy amount of butter ensures that the caramel sets up and stays put between the cake layers. And the final embellishment—a sprinkle of coarse sea salt (use flaky Maldon, please)—seals the deal. The crunchy, salty notes are the perfect contrast to all that sweetness and creaminess. Make this cake for someone you love. Make this cake to celebrate a holiday. Make this cake for a swank dinner party. Make this cake because I don't really like cake and I love this recipe!"

–*Jack*

caramel filling between each before spreading the thick chocolate frosting over the sides and top of the cake. Baking spray with flour can be used to grease and flour the pans. Both natural and Dutch-processed cocoa will work in this recipe. Our favorite natural cocoa is Hershey's Natural Cocoa Unsweetened; our favorite Dutch-processed cocoa is Droste Cacao. When taking the temperature of the caramel in steps 3 and 4, remove the pot from the heat and tilt the pan to one side. Use your thermometer to stir the caramel back and forth to equalize hot and cool spots and make sure you are getting an accurate reading. When cooking the caramel in step 4, be sure the caramel is between 240 and 245 degrees to ensure a filling with the correct consistency.

Cake
1½	cups (7½ ounces) all-purpose flour
¾	cup (2¼ ounces) unsweetened cocoa powder
1½	cups (10½ ounces) granulated sugar
1¼	teaspoons baking soda
¾	teaspoon baking powder
¾	teaspoon table salt
¾	cup buttermilk
½	cup water
¼	cup vegetable oil
2	large eggs
1	teaspoon vanilla extract

Caramel Filling
1¼	cups (8¾ ounces) granulated sugar
¼	cup light corn syrup
¼	cup water
1	cup heavy cream
8	tablespoons unsalted butter, cut into 8 pieces
1	teaspoon vanilla extract
¾	teaspoon table salt

Frosting
16	tablespoons unsalted butter, softened
¾	cup (3 ounces) confectioners' sugar
½	cup (1½ ounces) unsweetened cocoa powder
	Pinch table salt
½	cup light corn syrup
¾	teaspoon vanilla extract
6	ounces bittersweet chocolate, melted and cooled
¼–½	teaspoon coarse sea salt (optional)

1. For the cake: Adjust oven rack to middle position and heat oven to 325 degrees. Grease two 9-inch round cake pans, line with parchment paper, grease parchment, and flour pans. Sift flour and cocoa into large bowl. Whisk in sugar, baking soda, baking powder, and salt. Whisk buttermilk, water, oil, eggs, and vanilla together in second bowl. Whisk buttermilk mixture into flour mixture until smooth batter forms. Divide batter evenly between prepared pans and smooth tops with rubber spatula.

2. Bake until toothpick inserted in center comes out clean, 22 to 28 minutes, rotating pans halfway through baking. Let cakes cool in pans on wire rack for 15 minutes. Remove cakes from pans, discard parchment, and let cool completely on rack, at least 2 hours.

3. For the caramel filling: Lightly grease 8-inch square baking pan. Combine sugar, corn syrup, and water in medium saucepan. Bring to boil over medium-high heat and cook, without stirring, until mixture is amber colored, 8 to 10 minutes. Reduce heat to low and continue to cook, swirling saucepan occasionally, until dark amber, 2 to 5 minutes. (Caramel will register between 375 and 380 degrees.)

4. Off heat, carefully stir in cream, butter, vanilla, and salt (mixture will bubble and steam). Return saucepan to medium heat and cook, stirring frequently, until smooth and caramel reaches 240 to 245 degrees, 3 to 5 minutes. Carefully transfer caramel to prepared pan and let cool until just warm to touch (100 to 105 degrees), 20 to 30 minutes.

5. For the frosting: Process butter, sugar, cocoa, and salt in food processor until smooth, about 30 seconds, scraping down sides of bowl as needed. Add corn syrup and vanilla and process until just combined, 5 to 10 seconds. Scrape down sides of bowl, then add chocolate and pulse until smooth and creamy, 10 to 15 seconds. (Frosting can be made 3 hours in advance. For longer storage, cover and refrigerate frosting. Let stand at room temperature for 1 hour before using.)

6. Using long serrated knife, score 1 horizontal line around sides of each cake layer; then, following scored lines, cut each layer into 2 even layers.

7. Using rubber spatula or large spoon, transfer one-third of caramel to center of 1 cake layer and use small offset spatula to spread over surface, leaving ½-inch border around edge. Repeat with remaining caramel and 2 more cake layers. (Three of your cake layers should be topped with caramel.)

8. Line edges of cake platter with 4 strips of parchment to keep platter clean. Place 1 caramel-covered cake layer on platter. Top with second caramel-covered layer. Repeat with third caramel-covered layer and top with final layer. Spread frosting evenly over sides and top of cake. Carefully remove parchment strips. Let cake stand for at least 1 hour. (Cake can be made up to 2 days in advance and refrigerated. Let stand at room temperature for at least 5 hours before serving.) Sprinkle with sea salt, if using, then serve.

Chocolate-Raspberry Torte

Chocolate-Raspberry Torte

Serves 12 to 16

WHY THIS RECIPE WORKS Sachertorte, the classic Viennese dessert with layers of chocolate cake sandwiching apricot jam and enrobed in a creamy-rich chocolate glaze, always sounds more promising than it typically is in reality— dry, flavorless cake and sweet jam with little fruity complexity, all covered in a glaze that is nothing more than a thin, overly sugary coating. We set out to create a rich, deeply chocolaty dessert using Sachertorte as the inspiration, giving it our own spin by pairing the chocolate with raspberries. For a rich, fudgy base, we started by baking a dense flourless chocolate cake batter in two 9-inch pans, so we could sandwich the two cakes together rather than deal with halving a single delicate cake. But when we tried to stack the layers, the dense cake tore and fell apart. Adding ground nuts gave it the structure it needed, plus a good boost of flavor. Since we were using the food processor to grind the nuts, we tweaked our cake recipe so that it could be prepared using the same appliance. The winning approach for our filling was to combine jam with lightly mashed fresh berries for a tangy-sweet mixture that clung to the cake. For the glaze, we kept things simple, melting bittersweet chocolate with heavy cream to create a rich-tasting, glossy ganache that poured smoothly over the cake. For simple but tasty decorating, we dotted fresh raspberries around the top of the torte and pressed toasted sliced almonds along its sides. Be sure to use cake pans with at least 2-inch-tall sides.

Cake
- 8 ounces bittersweet chocolate, chopped fine
- 12 tablespoons unsalted butter, cut into ½-inch pieces
- 2 teaspoons vanilla extract
- ¼ teaspoon instant espresso powder
- 1¾ cups sliced almonds, toasted, divided
- ¼ cup (1¼ ounces) all-purpose flour
- ½ teaspoon table salt
- 5 large eggs, room temperature
- ¾ cup (5¼ ounces) sugar
- 2 (9-inch) cardboard rounds

Filling
- 2½ ounces (½ cup) raspberries, plus 16 raspberries for garnishing, divided
- ¼ cup seedless raspberry jam

Glaze
- 5 ounces bittersweet chocolate, chopped fine
- ½ cup plus 1 tablespoon heavy cream

1. *For the cake:* Adjust oven rack to middle position and heat oven to 325 degrees. Grease two 9-inch round cake pans, line with parchment paper, grease parchment, and flour pans. Melt chocolate and butter in large heatproof bowl set over saucepan filled with 1 inch barely simmering water, making sure that water does not touch bottom of bowl and stirring occasionally until smooth. Let cool completely, about 30 minutes. Stir in vanilla and espresso powder.

2. Pulse ¾ cup almonds in food processor until coarsely chopped, 6 to 8 pulses; transfer to bowl and set aside. Process remaining 1 cup almonds until very finely ground, about 45 seconds. Add flour and salt and continue to process until combined, about 15 seconds. Transfer almond mixture to second bowl. Process eggs in now-empty processor until lightened in color and almost doubled in volume, about 3 minutes. With processor running, slowly add sugar and process until thoroughly combined, about 15 seconds. Using whisk, gently fold egg mixture into chocolate mixture until some streaks of egg remain. Sprinkle half of ground almond mixture over chocolate mixture and gently whisk until just combined. Sprinkle with remaining ground almond mixture and gently whisk until just combined.

3. Divide batter evenly between prepared pans and smooth tops with rubber spatula. Bake until centers are firm and toothpick inserted in center comes out with few moist crumbs attached, 14 to 16 minutes, switching and rotating pans halfway through baking. Let cakes cool completely in pans on wire rack, about 30 minutes.

4. Run thin knife around edges of pans to loosen cakes, then invert onto cardboard rounds, discarding parchment. Using wire rack, turn 1 cake right side up, then slide from rack back onto cardboard round.

Decorating Chocolate-Raspberry Torte

1. With fully assembled cake placed on cardboard round, hold bottom of cake in your hand and gently press chopped nuts onto its side with your other hand.

2. Place 1 raspberry on cake at 12 o'clock, then another at 6 o'clock. Place third berry at 9 o'clock and fourth at 3 o'clock. Continue to place raspberries directly opposite each other until all have been arranged in evenly spaced circle.

5. For the filling: Place ½ cup raspberries in bowl and mash coarse with fork. Stir in jam until just combined.

6. Spread raspberry mixture onto cake layer that is right side up. Top with second cake layer, leaving it upside down. Transfer assembled cake, still on cardboard round, to wire rack set in rimmed baking sheet.

7. For the glaze: Melt chocolate and cream in bowl set over saucepan filled with 1 inch barely simmering water, making sure that water does not touch bottom of bowl and stirring occasionally until smooth. Off heat, gently whisk until very smooth. Pour glaze onto center of assembled cake. Using offset spatula, spread glaze evenly over top of cake, letting it drip down sides. Spread glaze along sides of cake to coat evenly.

8. Using fine-mesh strainer, sift reserved chopped almonds to remove any fine bits. Gently press sifted almonds onto cake sides. Arrange remaining 16 raspberries around outer edge. Refrigerate cake on rack until glaze is set, at least 1 hour or up to 24 hours. (If refrigerated for more than 1 hour, let cake sit at room temperature for about 30 minutes before serving.) Transfer cake to platter and serve.

Torta Caprese

SEASON 20 RECIPE

Serves 12 to 14

WHY THIS RECIPE WORKS This torte, a classic dessert along the Amalfi Coast, is a showstopper that packs in all the richness and depth of flourless chocolate cake. It features finely ground almonds in the batter that subtly break up the fudgy crumb, making it lighter and less cloying to eat. Our version contains melted butter and bittersweet chocolate as well as vanilla, cocoa powder, and salt to boost the chocolate's complexity. Instead of grinding almonds in a food processor, we used commercial almond flour (commercial "almond meal," which may or may not be made from skin-on nuts, also works well). All flourless cakes are aerated with whipped eggs instead of chemical leaveners, and we found that whipping the whites and yolks separately in a stand mixer, each with half the sugar, created strong, stable egg foams that lightened the rich, heavy batter and prevented it from collapsing after baking. For the best results, use a good-quality bittersweet chocolate and Dutch-processed cocoa here. We developed this recipe using our favorite bittersweet chocolate, Ghirardelli 60% Cacao Bittersweet Chocolate Premium Baking Bar, and our favorite Dutch-processed cocoa, Droste Cacao. Either almond flour or almond meal will work in this recipe; we used Bob's Red Mill. Serve with lightly sweetened whipped cream or with Amaretto Whipped Cream or Orange Whipped Cream (recipes follow).

12 tablespoons unsalted butter, cut into 12 pieces
6 ounces bittersweet chocolate, chopped
1 teaspoon vanilla extract
4 large eggs, separated
1 cup (7 ounces) granulated sugar, divided
2 cups (7 ounces) almond flour
2 tablespoons Dutch-processed cocoa powder
½ teaspoon table salt
Confectioners' sugar (optional)

1. Adjust oven rack to middle position and heat oven to 325 degrees. Lightly spray 9-inch springform pan with vegetable oil spray.

2. Microwave butter and chocolate in medium bowl at 50 percent power, stirring often, until melted, 1½ to 2 minutes. Stir in vanilla and set aside.

3. Using stand mixer fitted with whisk attachment, whip egg whites on medium-low speed until foamy, about 1 minute. Increase speed to medium-high and continue to whip, slowly adding ½ cup granulated sugar, until whites are glossy and thick and hold stiff peaks, about 4 minutes longer. Transfer whites to large bowl.

4. Add egg yolks and remaining ½ cup granulated sugar to now-empty mixer bowl and whip on medium-high speed until thick and pale yellow, about 3 minutes, scraping down bowl as necessary. Add chocolate mixture and mix on medium speed until incorporated, about 15 seconds. Add almond flour, cocoa, and salt and mix until incorporated, about 30 seconds.

5. Remove bowl from mixer and stir few times with large rubber spatula, scraping bottom of bowl to ensure almond flour is fully incorporated. Add one-third of whipped whites to bowl, return bowl to mixer, and mix on medium speed until no streaks of white remain, about 30 seconds, scraping down bowl halfway through mixing. Transfer batter to bowl with remaining whites. Using large rubber spatula, gently fold whites into batter until no streaks of white remain. Pour batter into prepared pan, smooth top with spatula, and place pan on rimmed baking sheet.

6. Bake until toothpick inserted in center comes out with few moist crumbs attached, about 50 minutes, rotating pan halfway through baking. Let cake cool in pan on wire rack for 20 minutes. Remove side of pan and let cake cool completely, about 2 hours. (Cake can be wrapped in plastic wrap and stored at room temperature for up to 3 days.)

7. Dust top of cake with confectioners' sugar, if using. Using offset spatula, transfer cake to serving platter. Cut into wedges and serve.

Amaretto Whipped Cream

Serves 12 to 14 (Makes 2 cups)

For the best results, chill the bowl and the whisk attachment before whipping the cream.

- 1 cup heavy cream, chilled
- 2 tablespoons Amaretto
- 1 tablespoon confectioners' sugar

Using stand mixer fitted with whisk attachment, whip all ingredients on medium-low speed until foamy, about 1 minute. Increase speed to high and whip until soft peaks form, 1 to 3 minutes.

Orange Whipped Cream

Serves 12 to 14 (Makes 2 cups)

You can substitute Grand Marnier for the Cointreau, if desired.

- 1 cup heavy cream, chilled
- 2 tablespoons Cointreau
- 1 tablespoon confectioners' sugar
- ¼ teaspoon grated orange zest

Using stand mixer fitted with whisk attachment, whip all ingredients on medium-low speed until foamy, about 1 minute. Increase speed to high and whip until soft peaks form, 1 to 3 minutes.

Triple-Chocolate Mousse Cake

Serves 12 to 16

WHY THIS RECIPE WORKS Triple-chocolate mousse cake, sometimes called tuxedo cake, is a triple-decker stunner that becomes incrementally lighter in texture and richness from bottom to top. For a base layer that had the heft to support the upper two tiers, we chose flourless chocolate cake instead of the typical mousse cake. For the middle layer, we started with a traditional chocolate mousse but found it a little heavy; removing the eggs resulted in a lighter, creamier layer. And for the top tier, we made an easy white chocolate mousse by folding whipped cream into melted white chocolate. To prevent the soft top mousse from oozing during slicing, we added a little gelatin to the mix. This recipe requires a springform pan that is at least 3 inches high. It is imperative that each layer is made in sequential order. Cool the base completely before topping with the middle layer. We recommend using our favorite dark chocolate, Ghirardelli 60% Cacao Bittersweet

Chocolate Premium Baking Bar, for the bottom and middle layers; the test kitchen's other highly recommended dark chocolate, Callebaut Intense Dark Chocolate, L-60-40NV, may be used, but it will produce drier, slightly less sweet results. For the best results, chill the mixer bowl before whipping the heavy cream in steps 5 and 8. To slice, use a cheese wire or dip a sharp knife in hot water and wipe dry before and after each cut. Top servings with shaved chocolate if desired.

Bottom Layer
- 6 tablespoons unsalted butter, cut into 6 pieces
- 7 ounces bittersweet chocolate, chopped fine
- ¾ teaspoon instant espresso powder
- 4 large eggs, separated
- 1½ teaspoons vanilla extract
  Pinch cream of tartar
  Pinch table salt
- ⅓ cup packed (2⅓ ounces) light brown sugar

Middle Layer
- 5 tablespoons hot water
- 2 tablespoons Dutch-processed cocoa powder
- 7 ounces bittersweet chocolate, chopped fine
- 1½ cups heavy cream, chilled
- 1 tablespoon granulated sugar
- ⅛ teaspoon table salt

Top Layer
- ¾ teaspoon unflavored gelatin
- 1 tablespoon water
- 1 cup (6 ounces) white chocolate chips
- 1½ cups heavy cream, chilled, divided
  Shaved semisweet chocolate (optional)

1. For the bottom layer: Adjust oven rack to middle position and heat oven to 325 degrees. Grease 9-inch springform pan. Combine butter, chocolate, and espresso powder in large bowl set over saucepan filled with 1 inch barely simmering water, making sure that water does not touch bottom of bowl and stirring occasionally until butter and chocolate are melted. Remove from heat and let cool slightly, about 5 minutes. Whisk in egg yolks and vanilla; set aside.

2. Using stand mixer fitted with whisk attachment, whip egg whites, cream of tartar, and salt on medium-low speed until foamy, about 1 minute. Add half of sugar and whip until combined, about 15 seconds. Add remaining sugar, increase speed to high, and whip until soft peaks form, about 1 minute, scraping down bowl halfway through whipping. Using whisk, fold one-third of whipped whites into chocolate mixture to lighten. Using rubber spatula, fold in remaining whites until no white streaks remain. Carefully pour batter into prepared pan and smooth top with rubber spatula.

3. Bake until cake has risen, is firm around edges, and center springs back when pressed gently with your finger, 13 to 18 minutes, rotating pan halfway through baking. Let cake cool completely in pan on wire rack, about 1 hour, before filling. (Cake will collapse as it cools.) Do not remove cake from pan.

4. For the middle layer: Combine hot water and cocoa in small bowl; set aside. Melt chocolate in large bowl set over saucepan filled with 1 inch barely simmering water, making sure that water does not touch bottom of bowl and stirring occasionally until smooth. Remove from heat and let cool slightly, 2 to 5 minutes.

5. Using clean, dry mixer bowl and whisk attachment, whip cream, sugar, and salt on medium-low speed until foamy, about 1 minute. Increase speed to high and whip until soft peaks form, 1 to 3 minutes.

6. Whisk cocoa mixture into melted chocolate until smooth. Using whisk, fold one-third of whipped cream into chocolate mixture to lighten. Using rubber spatula, fold in remaining whipped cream until no white streaks remain. Spoon mousse into pan over cooled cake and smooth top with offset spatula. Gently tap pan on counter to release air bubbles. Wipe inside edge of pan with damp cloth to remove any drips. Refrigerate cake for at least 15 minutes.

7. For the top layer: Sprinkle gelatin over water in small bowl and let sit until gelatin softens, about 5 minutes. Place chocolate chips in medium bowl. Bring ½ cup cream to simmer in small saucepan over medium-high heat. Remove from heat, add gelatin mixture, and stir until gelatin is fully dissolved. Pour cream mixture over chocolate chips and let sit, covered, for 5 minutes. Whisk mixture gently until smooth. Let cool completely, stirring occasionally (mixture will thicken slightly).

8. Using clean, dry mixer bowl and whisk attachment, whip remaining 1 cup cream on medium-low speed until foamy, about 1 minute. Increase speed to high and whip until soft peaks form, 1 to 3 minutes. Using hand whisk, fold one-third of whipped cream into white chocolate mixture to lighten. Using rubber spatula, fold in remaining whipped cream until no white streaks remain. Spoon white chocolate mousse into pan over middle layer and smooth top with offset spatula. Refrigerate cake until set, at least 2½ hours. (Cake can be refrigerated for up to 24 hours; let sit at room temperature for up to 45 minutes before releasing from pan and serving.)

9. Garnish top of cake with shaved chocolate, if using. Run thin knife around edge of pan to loosen cake, then remove sides of pan. Run clean knife along outside of cake to smooth. Serve.

Chocolate-Espresso Dacquoise

Serves 10 to 12

WHY THIS RECIPE WORKS It's possible there is no more stunning finale to a meal than a dacquoise, a multilayered showpiece of crisp meringue and rich, silky buttercream coated in a glossy ganache. But preparing one is typically a project to rival all projects. For a more approachable dacquoise, we swapped the traditional individually piped meringue layers for a single sheet that we trimmed into layers; we also shortened the usual 4-plus hours of oven time by increasing the temperature. For the filling, we opted for a German buttercream. Unlike some other buttercreams, it requires no thermometer or hot sugar syrup. And because it calls for equal parts pastry cream and butter, this option enabled us to use the egg yolks left over from the meringue. Flavoring the buttercream with espresso powder and amaretto contributed another element of sophistication. Use a rimless baking sheet or an overturned rimmed baking sheet to bake the meringue. Instant coffee may be substituted for the espresso powder. To skin the hazelnuts, simply place the warm toasted nuts in a clean dish towel and rub gently. We recommend Ghirardelli 60% Cacao Bittersweet Chocolate Premium Baking Bar for this recipe. To slice, dip a sharp knife in hot water and wipe it dry before and after each cut.

Meringue
- ¾ cup blanched sliced almonds, toasted
- ½ cup hazelnuts, toasted and skinned
- 1 tablespoon cornstarch
- ⅛ teaspoon table salt
- 1 cup (7 ounces) sugar, divided
- 4 large egg whites, room temperature
- ¼ teaspoon cream of tartar

Buttercream

- ¾ cup whole milk
- 4 large egg yolks
- ⅓ cup (2⅓ ounces) sugar
- 1½ teaspoons cornstarch
- ¼ teaspoon table salt
- 2 tablespoons amaretto or water
- 1½ tablespoons instant espresso powder
- 16 tablespoons unsalted butter, cut into 16 pieces and softened

Ganache

- 6 ounces bittersweet chocolate, chopped fine
- ¾ cup heavy cream
- 2 teaspoons corn syrup

- 12 whole hazelnuts, toasted and skinned
- 1 cup blanched sliced almonds, toasted

1. For the meringue: Adjust oven rack to middle position and heat oven to 250 degrees. Using ruler and pencil, draw 13 by 10½-inch rectangle on piece of parchment paper. Grease baking sheet and place parchment on it, marked side down.

2. Process almonds, hazelnuts, cornstarch, and salt in food processor until nuts are finely ground, 15 to 20 seconds. Add ½ cup sugar and pulse to combine, 1 to 2 pulses.

3. Using stand mixer fitted with whisk, whip egg whites and cream of tartar on medium-low speed until foamy, about 1 minute. Increase speed to medium-high and whip whites to soft, billowy mounds, about 1 minute. With mixer running at medium-high speed, slowly add remaining ½ cup sugar and continue to whip until glossy, stiff peaks form, 2 to 3 minutes. Fold nut mixture into egg whites in 2 batches. With offset spatula, spread meringue evenly into 13 by 10½-inch rectangle on parchment, using lines on parchment as guide. Using spray bottle, evenly mist surface of meringue with water until glistening. Bake for 1½ hours. Turn off oven and allow meringue to cool in oven for 1½ hours. (Do not open oven during baking and cooling.) Remove from oven and let cool to room temperature, about 10 minutes. (Cooled meringue can be kept at room temperature, tightly wrapped in plastic wrap, for up to 2 days.)

4. For the buttercream: Heat milk in small saucepan over medium heat until just simmering. Meanwhile, whisk egg yolks, sugar, cornstarch, and salt in bowl until smooth. Remove milk from heat and, whisking constantly, add half of milk to yolk mixture to temper. Whisking constantly, return tempered yolk mixture to remaining milk in saucepan. Return saucepan to medium heat and cook, whisking constantly, until mixture is bubbling and thickens to consistency of warm pudding, 3 to 5 minutes. Transfer pastry cream to bowl. Cover and refrigerate until set, at least 2 hours or up to 24 hours. Before using, warm gently to room temperature in microwave at 50 percent power, stirring every 10 seconds.

5. Stir together amaretto and espresso powder; set aside. Using stand mixer fitted with paddle, beat butter at medium speed until smooth and light, 3 to 4 minutes. Add pastry cream in 3 batches, beating for 30 seconds after each addition. Add amaretto mixture and continue to beat until light and fluffy, about 5 minutes, scraping down bowl thoroughly halfway through mixing.

6. For the ganache: Place chocolate in bowl. Bring cream and corn syrup to simmer in small saucepan over medium heat. Pour cream mixture over chocolate and let sit for 1 minute. Stir mixture until smooth. Set aside to cool until chocolate mounds slightly when dripped from spoon, about 5 minutes.

7. Carefully invert meringue and peel off parchment. Reinvert meringue and place on cutting board. Using serrated knife and gentle, repeated scoring motion, trim edges of meringue to form 12 by 10-inch rectangle. Discard trimmings. With long side of rectangle parallel to counter, use ruler to mark both long edges of meringue at 3-inch intervals. Using serrated knife, score surface of meringue by drawing knife toward you from mark on top edge to corresponding mark on bottom edge. Repeat scoring until meringue is fully cut through. Repeat until you have four 10 by 3-inch rectangles. (If any rectangles break during cutting, use them as middle layers.)

8. Place 3 rectangles on wire rack set in rimmed baking sheet. Using offset spatula, spread ¼ cup ganache evenly over surface of each meringue. Refrigerate until ganache is firm, about 15 minutes. Set aside remaining ganache.

9. Using offset spatula, spread top of remaining rectangle with ½ cup buttercream; place on wire rack with ganache-coated meringues. Invert 1 ganache-coated meringue, place on top of buttercream, and press gently to level. Repeat, spreading meringue with ½ cup buttercream and topping with inverted ganache-coated meringue. Spread top with buttercream. Invert final ganache-coated meringue on top of cake. Use 1 hand to steady top of cake and spread half of remaining buttercream to lightly coat sides of cake, then use remaining buttercream to coat top of cake. Smooth until cake resembles box. Refrigerate until buttercream is firm, about 2 hours. (Once buttercream is firm, assembled cake may be wrapped tightly in plastic and refrigerated for up to 2 days.)

10. Warm remaining ganache in heatproof bowl set over barely simmering water, stirring occasionally, until mixture is very fluid but not hot. Keeping assembled cake on wire rack, pour ganache over top of cake. Using offset spatula, spread ganache in thin, even layer over top of cake, letting excess flow down sides. Spread ganache over sides in thin layer (top must be completely covered, but some small gaps on sides are OK).

11. Garnish top of cake with hazelnuts. Holding bottom of cake with your hand, gently press almonds onto sides with your other hand. Chill on wire rack, uncovered, for at least 3 hours or up to 12 hours. Transfer to platter. Cut into slices with sharp knife that has been dipped in hot water and wiped dry before each slice. Serve.

Assembling Chocolate-Espresso Dacquoise

1. Using offset spatula, spread ¼ cup ganache evenly over 3 meringue rectangles and refrigerate until firm. Spread top of remaining rectangle with ½ cup buttercream.

2. Invert 1 ganache-coated meringue, place on top of buttercream-coated meringue, and level. Repeat spreading meringue with buttercream; top with inverted ganache-coated meringue.

3. Spread top with buttercream. Invert final ganache-coated meringue on top of cake. Coat sides and top with remaining buttercream.

Paris-Brest

SEASON 20 RECIPE

Serves 8 to 10

WHY THIS RECIPE WORKS If you are looking for the ultimate Christmas Eve dessert, look no further than this elegant French dessert. *Paris-Brest* is a showstopper that consists of a large ring of pate a choux that is filled with hazelnut praline pastry cream and then sprinkled with chopped almonds and powdered sugar. Its name dates back to 1910 when an enterprising baker whose shop was located along the route of the Paris-Brest-Paris bicycle race—from Paris to the city of Brest, in Brittany, and back again—invented the dessert to honor the cyclists. (His creation was in the shape of a bicycle tire.) To make this dessert foolproof, we started with our pate a choux recipe, which created a tender but strong "case" for the cream filling. For the cream filling, we started with a flour-thickened pastry cream (which was more stable than the normal cornstarch-thickened version), added pulverized caramel-coated hazelnuts, and then folded in whipped cream that had been enriched with gelatin. An equal amount of slivered almonds can be substituted for the hazelnuts. To skin the hazelnuts, simply place them in a clean dish towel after toasting, while they are still warm, and rub gently. Use a serrated knife to cut the dessert.

Praline
½ cup (3½ ounces) sugar
¼ cup water
1 teaspoon lemon juice
1 cup hazelnuts, toasted and skinned
1 tablespoon vegetable oil
½ teaspoon table salt

Pastry Dough
4 large eggs
8 tablespoons unsalted butter, cut into 16 pieces
½ cup whole milk
⅓ cup water
2¾ teaspoons sugar
¾ teaspoon salt
1 cup (5 ounces) all-purpose flour
2 tablespoons toasted, skinned, and chopped hazelnuts

Cream Filling
2 teaspoons unflavored gelatin
¼ cup water
1½ cups half-and-half
5 large egg yolks
⅓ cup (2⅓ ounces) sugar
3 tablespoons all-purpose flour
3 tablespoons unsalted butter, cut into 3 pieces and chilled
1½ teaspoons vanilla extract
1 cup heavy cream, chilled
Confectioners' sugar

Paris-Brest

1. *For the praline:* Line rimmed baking sheet with parchment paper; spray parchment with vegetable oil spray and set aside. Bring sugar, water, and lemon juice to boil in medium saucepan over medium heat, stirring once or twice to dissolve sugar. Cook, without stirring, until syrup is golden brown, 10 to 15 minutes. Remove saucepan from heat, stir in hazelnuts, and immediately pour mixture onto prepared sheet. Place sheet on wire rack and allow caramel to harden, about 30 minutes.

2. Break hardened caramel into 1- to 2-inch pieces; process pieces in food processor until finely ground, about 30 seconds. Add oil and salt and process until uniform paste forms, 1 to 2 minutes. Transfer mixture to bowl, cover with plastic wrap, and set aside.

3. *For the pastry dough:* Adjust oven racks to upper-middle and lower-middle positions and heat oven to 400 degrees. Draw or trace 8-inch circle in center of two 12 by 18-inch sheets of parchment paper; flip parchment over. Spray 2 baking sheets with vegetable oil spray and line with parchment (keeping guide rings on underside).

4. Beat eggs in measuring cup or small bowl; you should have about 1 cup (discard any excess over 1 cup). Heat butter, milk, water, sugar, and salt in medium saucepan over medium heat, stirring occasionally. When butter mixture reaches full boil (butter should be fully melted), immediately remove saucepan from heat and stir in flour with heat-resistant spatula or wooden spoon until combined and no mixture remains on sides of pan. Return saucepan to low heat and cook, stirring

Putting Together Paris-Brest

1. As soon as caramel turns golden brown, stir in toasted hazelnuts and pour mixture onto parchment paper–lined baking sheet to set.

2. Process broken caramel pieces in food processor until finely ground, about 30 seconds. Add salt and vegetable oil and process again until uniform paste forms, 1 to 2 minutes longer.

3. Using bag fitted with ⅜-inch round tip, pipe narrow circle of pastry dough directly on top of guide ring traced on parchment. Set aside.

4. Use ½-inch star tip to pipe circle of dough around inside of remaining guide ring. Then pipe second circle around first so they overlap slightly.

5. Finish outer ring by piping third circle on top of other 2 circles, directly over seam. Sprinkle with nuts and bake.

6. After letting outer ring cool, halve horizontally using serrated knife.

7. Using pastry bag fitted with ½-inch star tip, pipe narrow zigzag of praline cream onto bottom half of outer ring.

8. Place inner ring on top of praline cream and press down gently.

9. Pipe remaining praline cream over inner ring in zigzag pattern to cover.

10. Gently place top half of outer ring over filling and dust with confectioners' sugar.

constantly, using smearing motion, until mixture is slightly shiny and tiny beads of fat appear on bottom of saucepan, about 3 minutes.

5. Immediately transfer butter mixture to food processor and process with feed tube open for 30 seconds to cool slightly. With processor running, gradually add eggs in steady stream. When all eggs have been added, scrape down sides of bowl, then process for 30 seconds until smooth, thick, sticky paste forms.

6. Transfer ¾ cup dough to pastry bag fitted with ⅜-inch round tip. To make narrow inner ring, pipe single ½-inch-wide circle of dough directly on traced guide ring on 1 baking sheet. For large outer ring, squeeze out any excess dough in pastry bag and change pastry bag tip to ½-inch star tip. Put all remaining dough into pastry bag. Pipe ½-inch-wide circle of dough around inside of traced guide ring on remaining baking sheet. Pipe second ½-inch circle of dough around first so they overlap slightly. Pipe third ½-inch circle on top of other 2 circles directly over seam. Discard any excess dough. Sprinkle hazelnuts evenly over surface of ring.

7. Place sheet with larger outer ring on upper rack and sheet with narrow inner ring on lower rack and bake until narrow ring is golden brown and firm, 22 to 26 minutes. Remove narrow ring and transfer to wire rack. Reduce oven temperature to 350 degrees and continue to bake larger ring for 10 minutes. Remove sheet from oven and turn off oven. Using paring knife, cut 4 equally spaced ¾-inch-wide slits around edges of larger ring to release steam. Return larger ring to oven and prop oven door open with handle of wooden spoon. Let ring stand in oven until exterior is crisp, about 45 minutes. Transfer ring to wire rack to cool, about 15 minutes.

8. *For the cream filling:* Sprinkle gelatin over water in small bowl and let sit until gelatin softens, about 5 minutes. Heat half-and-half in medium saucepan over medium heat until just simmering. Meanwhile, whisk egg yolks and sugar in medium bowl until smooth. Add flour to yolk-sugar mixture and whisk until incorporated. Remove half-and-half from heat and, whisking constantly, slowly add ½ cup to yolk-sugar mixture to temper. Whisking constantly, add tempered yolk-sugar mixture back to half-and-half in saucepan.

9. Return saucepan to medium heat and cook, whisking constantly, until yolk-sugar mixture thickens slightly, 1 to 2 minutes. Reduce heat to medium-low and continue to cook, whisking constantly, for 8 minutes.

10. Increase heat to medium and cook, whisking vigorously, until bubbles burst on surface, 1 to 2 minutes. Remove saucepan from heat; whisk in butter, vanilla, and softened gelatin until butter is melted and incorporated. Strain pastry cream through fine-mesh strainer set over large bowl. Press lightly greased parchment paper directly on surface and refrigerate until chilled but not set, about 45 minutes.

11. Using stand mixer fitted with whisk, whip cream on medium-low speed until foamy, about 1 minute. Increase speed to high and whip until soft peaks form, 1 to 3 minutes. Whisk praline paste and half of whipped cream into pastry cream until combined. Gently fold in remaining whipped cream until incorporated. Cover and refrigerate until set, at least 3 hours or up to 24 hours.

12. Using serrated knife, slice larger outer ring in half horizontally; place bottom on large serving plate. Fill pastry bag fitted with ½-inch star tip with cream filling. Pipe ½-inch-wide strip of cream filling in narrow zigzag pattern around center of bottom half of ring. Press narrow inner ring gently into cream filling. Pipe cream filling over narrow ring in zigzag pattern to cover. Place top half of larger ring over cream filling, dust with confectioners' sugar, and serve. (Cooled pastry rings can be wrapped tightly in plastic wrap and stored at room temperature for up to 24 hours or frozen for up to 1 month. Before using, recrisp rings in 300-degree oven for 5 to 10 minutes. Praline can be made up to 1 week in advance and refrigerated. Let praline come to room temperature before using. Pastry dough can be transferred to bowl, with surface covered with sheet of lightly greased parchment paper, and stored at room temperature for up to 2 hours. Dessert can be assembled and kept in refrigerator up to 3 hours in advance.)

Tiramisu

Serves 10 to 12

WHY THIS RECIPE WORKS There's a reason restaurant menus (Italian or not) offer tiramisu. Delicate ladyfingers soaked in a spiked coffee mixture layered with a sweet, creamy filling make an irresistible combination. Preparing tiramisu, however, can be labor intensive, and some versions are overly rich with ladyfingers that turn soggy. We wanted to avoid these issues and find a streamlined approach—one that highlights the luxurious combination of flavors and textures that have made this dessert so popular. Instead of hauling out a double boiler to make the fussy custard-based filling (called zabaglione), we instead simply whipped egg yolks, sugar, salt, rum, and mascarpone together. Salt heightened the filling's subtle flavors. And to lighten the filling, we chose whipped cream instead of egg whites. For the coffee soaking mixture, we combined strong brewed coffee and espresso powder (along with more rum). To moisten the ladyfingers so that they were neither too dry nor too saturated, we dropped them one at a time into the spiked coffee mixture and rolled them over to moisten the other side for just a couple of seconds. For the best flavor and texture, it is important to chill the tiramisu for at least 6 hours. Brandy and even whiskey can stand in for the dark rum. We prefer tiramisu with a pronounced rum flavor; for a less potent rum flavor, halve the amount of rum added to the coffee mixture in step 1. Do not allow the mascarpone to warm to room temperature before using it; it has a tendency to break if allowed to do so.

2½ cups strong brewed coffee, room temperature
½ cup plus 1 tablespoon dark rum, divided
1½ tablespoons instant espresso powder
6 large egg yolks
⅔ cup (4⅔ ounces) sugar
¼ teaspoon table salt
1½ pounds (3 cups) mascarpone cheese
¾ cup heavy cream, chilled
14 ounces dried ladyfingers (savoiardi)
3½ tablespoons Dutch-processed cocoa powder, divided
¼ cup grated semisweet or bittersweet chocolate (optional)

1. Stir coffee, 5 tablespoons rum, and espresso powder in wide bowl or baking dish until espresso powder dissolves; set aside.

2. Using stand mixer fitted with whisk attachment, mix egg yolks on low speed until just combined. Add sugar and salt and whip on medium-high speed until pale yellow, 1½ to 2 minutes, scraping down bowl as needed. Add remaining ¼ cup rum and whip on medium speed until just combined, 20 to 30 seconds; scrape down bowl. Add mascarpone and whip until no lumps remain, 30 to 45 seconds, scraping down bowl once or twice. Transfer mixture to large bowl and set aside.

3. In now-empty mixer bowl, whip cream on medium-low speed until foamy, about 1 minute. Increase speed to high and whip until stiff peaks form, 1 to 3 minutes. Using rubber spatula, fold one-third of whipped cream into mascarpone mixture to lighten it, then gently fold in remaining whipped cream until no white streaks remain. Set aside mascarpone mixture.

4. Working with 1 cookie at a time, drop half of ladyfingers into coffee mixture, roll to coat, and transfer to 13 by 9-inch baking dish. (Do not submerge ladyfingers in coffee mixture; entire process should take no longer than 2 to 3 seconds per cookie.) Arrange coated cookies in single layer in baking dish, breaking or trimming ladyfingers as needed to fit neatly in dish.

5. Using offset spatula, spread half of mascarpone mixture evenly over ladyfingers to sides and into corners of dish, then smooth surface. Place 2 tablespoons cocoa in fine-mesh strainer and dust mascarpone mixture with cocoa.

6. Repeat dipping and arranging with remaining ladyfingers; spread remaining mascarpone mixture over ladyfingers and dust with remaining 1½ tablespoons cocoa. Wipe edges of dish clean with paper towel.

7. Wrap dish tightly in plastic wrap and refrigerate until set, at least 6 hours or up to 24 hours. (Chilled tiramisu can be frozen for up to 1 month; defrost in refrigerator.)

8. Remove plastic and sprinkle top of tiramisu with grated chocolate, if using; cut into pieces and serve chilled.

VARIATION
Tiramisu with Cooked Eggs
This recipe involves cooking the egg yolks in a double boiler, which requires a little more effort and makes for a slightly thicker mascarpone filling, but the results are just as good as with our traditional method. You will need an additional ⅓ cup of heavy cream.

In step 2, add ⅓ cup cream to egg yolks after whipping in sugar and salt and whip for 20 to 30 seconds; do not add rum. Set bowl with egg yolk mixture over medium saucepan filled with 1 inch barely simmering water and cook, constantly scraping bottom and sides of bowl with heat-resistant rubber spatula, until mixture coats back of spoon and registers 160 degrees, 4 to 7 minutes. Remove from heat and stir vigorously to cool slightly, then set aside and let cool completely, about 15 minutes. Whisk in remaining ¼ cup rum until combined. Using stand mixer fitted with whisk, whip egg yolk mixture and mascarpone on medium speed until no lumps remain, 30 to 45 seconds. Transfer mixture to large bowl and set aside. Proceed with recipe from step 3, using full amount of cream specified (¾ cup).

Foolproof New York Cheesecake

Serves 12 to 16

WHY THIS RECIPE WORKS New York cheesecake has a plush, luxurious texture, a golden-brown surface, and a buttery graham cracker crust. But it's hard to get right: Different ovens yield different cakes. We started by creating a hybrid pastry–graham cracker crust that wouldn't become soggy beneath the moist, dense filling. Adding sour cream to our rich cream cheese filling contributed more tang, and straining and resting the filling eliminated any lumps or air pockets. Traditionally, New York–style cheesecakes start in a hot oven so that a burnished outer skin develops before the temperature is dropped to finish, but we found that the time it took for the oven temperature to change varied. We flipped the order, baking at a low temperature to set the filling and then removing it before turning up the heat. Once the oven hit 500 degrees, we put the cheesecake on the upper rack to brown the surface. These tweaks may defy convention, but you can count on this cheesecake to have the same texture, flavor, and appearance no matter what oven is used to bake it. This cheesecake takes at least 12 hours to make (including chilling), so we recommend making it the day before serving. An accurate oven thermometer and instant-read thermometer are essential. To ensure proper baking, check that the oven thermometer is holding steady at 200 degrees and refrain from frequently taking the temperature of the cheesecake (unless it is within a few degrees of 165, allow 20 minutes between checking). Keep a close eye on the cheesecake in step 5 to prevent overbrowning.

"My sister and I would always fight over the last bite of cheesecake. It was our top dessert choice at any restaurant that served it and my parents would often get us one decadent slice to share. We didn't see eye to eye on much as kids, but we agreed that cheesecake's plush creaminess, buttery crust, and sweet strawberry sauce was the ultimate way to end a meal. This recipe approaches the most beloved and most difficult style of cheesecake with smart solutions. To achieve that classic New York–style burnished crust, the gently baked cheesecake gets a short blast in a hot oven at the very end. The result of this reversed approach is a cheesecake as foolproof as it is decadent. But the best part of this recipe is that when I make it myself, my sister and I can each have our own slice."

—Dan

Crust

6   whole graham crackers, broken into pieces
⅓   cup packed (2⅓ ounces) dark brown sugar
½   cup (2½ ounces) all-purpose flour
¼   teaspoon table salt
7   tablespoons unsalted butter, melted, divided

Filling

2½   pounds cream cheese, cut into pieces and softened
1½   cups (10½ ounces) granulated sugar, divided
⅛   teaspoon table salt
⅓   cup sour cream
2   teaspoons lemon juice
2   teaspoons vanilla extract
6   large eggs plus 2 large yolks

1. For the crust: Adjust oven racks to upper-middle and lower-middle positions and heat oven to 325 degrees. Process crackers and sugar in food processor until finely ground, about 30 seconds. Add flour and salt and pulse to combine, about 2 pulses. Add 6 tablespoons melted butter and pulse until crumbs are evenly moistened, about 10 pulses. Brush bottom of 9-inch springform pan with ½ tablespoon melted butter. Using your hands, press crumb mixture evenly into pan bottom. Using bottom of measuring cup, firmly pack crust into pan. Bake on lower rack until fragrant and beginning to brown around edges, about 13 minutes. Transfer to rimmed baking sheet; set aside and let cool completely. Reduce oven temperature to 200 degrees.

2. For the filling: Using stand mixer fitted with paddle, beat cream cheese, ¾ cup sugar, and salt on medium-low speed until combined, about 1 minute. Beat in remaining ¾ cup sugar until combined, about 1 minute. Scrape paddle and bowl well; add sour cream, lemon juice, and vanilla and beat at low speed until combined, about 1 minute. Add egg yolks and beat on medium-low speed until thoroughly combined, about 1 minute. Scrape bowl and paddle. Add whole eggs, two at a time, beating until thoroughly combined, about 30 seconds after each addition. Strain filling through fine-mesh strainer set in large bowl, pressing against strainer with rubber spatula or back of ladle to help filling pass through strainer.

3. Brush sides of springform pan with remaining ½ tablespoon melted butter. Pour filling into crust and set aside for 10 minutes to allow air bubbles to rise to top. Gently draw tines of fork across surface of cake to pop air bubbles that have risen to surface.

4. When oven thermometer reads 200 degrees, bake cheesecake on lower rack until center registers 165 degrees, 3 to 3½ hours. Remove cake from oven and increase oven temperature to 500 degrees.

5. When oven is at 500 degrees, bake cheesecake on upper rack until top is evenly browned, 4 to 12 minutes. Let cool for 5 minutes, then run thin knife around edge of pan. Let cheesecake cool in pan on wire rack until barely warm, 2½ to 3 hours. Wrap cheesecake tightly in plastic wrap and refrigerate until cold and firmly set, at least 6 hours or up to 24 hours.

6. To unmold cheesecake, remove sides of pan and slide thin metal spatula between crust and pan bottom to loosen, then slide cheesecake onto platter. Let sit at room temperature for about 30 minutes before serving. (Leftovers can be refrigerated for up to 4 days.)

Lemon Cheesecake

Serves 12

WHY THIS RECIPE WORKS Trust us, if you make this special cheesecake for your friends, they will ask for the recipe. It features a classic and rich cheesecake base that is very easy to make, but it is the bracing lemon curd, which you add after the cheesecake is baked, that puts it in a category all its own. The curd offers a welcome (and almost luminescent) contrast to the creamy richness of the cheesecake. Fully assembled and placed on a cake stand, it is drop-dead gorgeous. As we were developing this recipe in the test kitchen, we started by grinding lemon zest with some of the sugar we were adding to the cream cheese mixture, a step that released its flavorful oils and infused the base of the cake with lemony essence too. Heavy cream provided a silky richness, and vanilla rounded out the flavors. But when we paired our cheesecake filling with the traditional graham cracker crust, we found that the graham flavor overwhelmed the lemon. Instead, we turned to biscuit-type cookies, such as animal crackers, for a mild-tasting crust that allowed the lemon flavor to shine. Baking the cake in a water bath gave us an ultracreamy cake that wasn't as dense as New York–style cheesecake. Be sure to zest the lemons before juicing them. For neater slices, clean the knife thoroughly between slices.

Crust

5   ounces Nabisco Barnum's Animals Crackers or Social Tea Biscuits
3   tablespoons sugar
5   tablespoons unsalted butter, melted, divided

Filling

1¼ cups (8¾ ounces) sugar, divided
1 tablespoon grated lemon zest plus ¼ cup juice (2 lemons)
1½ pounds cream cheese, cut into pieces and softened
¼ teaspoon table salt
½ cup heavy cream
2 teaspoons vanilla extract
4 large eggs, room temperature

Lemon Curd

⅓ cup lemon juice (2 lemons)
2 large eggs plus 1 large yolk
½ cup (3½ ounces) sugar
2 tablespoons unsalted butter, cut into ½-inch pieces and chilled
1 tablespoon heavy cream
¼ teaspoon vanilla extract
Pinch table salt

1. For the crust: Adjust oven rack to lower-middle position and heat oven to 325 degrees. Process cookies and sugar in food processor until finely ground, about 30 seconds. Add 4 tablespoons melted butter and pulse until crumbs are evenly moistened, about 10 pulses. Using your hands, press crumb mixture evenly into bottom of 9-inch springform pan. Using bottom of measuring cup, firmly pack crust into pan. Bake until fragrant and golden brown, 15 to 18 minutes.

2. Let crust cool completely on wire rack, about 30 minutes, then wrap outside of pan with two 18-inch square pieces heavy-duty aluminum foil. Brush inside of pan with remaining 1 tablespoon melted butter. Set springform pan in roasting pan. Bring kettle of water to boil.

3. For the filling: Process ¼ cup sugar and lemon zest in food processor until sugar is yellow and zest is broken down, about 15 seconds; transfer to small bowl and stir in remaining 1 cup sugar.

4. Using stand mixer fitted with paddle, beat cream cheese, salt, and half of lemon-sugar mixture on medium-low speed until combined, about 1 minute. Add remaining lemon-sugar mixture and beat until combined, about 1 minute. Scrape bowl and paddle. Add cream, lemon juice, and vanilla and beat on low speed until combined and smooth, 1 to 3 minutes. Add eggs, two at a time, beating until thoroughly combined, about 30 seconds after each addition.

5. Pour filling into crust. Set roasting pan on oven rack and pour enough boiling water into roasting pan to come about halfway up sides of springform pan. Bake until center jiggles slightly, sides just start to puff, surface is no longer shiny, and center of cake registers 150 degrees, 55 minutes to 1 hour.

6. Turn off oven and prop open oven door with potholder or wooden spoon handle; let cake cool in water bath in oven for 1 hour. Transfer springform pan to wire rack, discarding foil. Run thin knife around edge of pan and let cheesecake cool for 2 hours.

7. For the lemon curd: While cheesecake bakes, heat lemon juice in small saucepan over medium heat until hot but not boiling. Whisk eggs and yolk together in bowl, then gradually whisk in sugar. Whisking constantly, slowly pour hot lemon juice into eggs, then return mixture to saucepan and cook over medium heat, stirring constantly with wooden spoon, until mixture is thick enough to cling to spoon and registers 170 degrees, about 3 minutes. Immediately remove pan from heat and stir in cold butter until incorporated. Stir in cream, vanilla, and salt, then strain curd through fine-mesh strainer into small bowl. Place plastic wrap directly on surface of curd and refrigerate until needed.

8. When cheesecake is cool, scrape lemon curd onto cheesecake still in springform pan. Using offset spatula, spread curd evenly over top of cheesecake. Wrap cheesecake tightly in plastic and refrigerate for at least 4 hours or up to 24 hours. To unmold cheesecake, wrap hot, damp dish towel around pan and let sit for 1 minute. Remove sides of pan and slide thin metal spatula between crust and pan bottom to loosen, then slide cheesecake onto platter. Serve.

Spiced Pumpkin Cheesecake

Serves 12

WHY THIS RECIPE WORKS This is a spectacular cheesecake. Make it for your Thanksgiving dessert spread and we guarantee it will be a huge hit. Although spiced pumpkin may be a well-trod flavor profile, it really shines in cheesecake—the tangy cream cheese is a beautiful foil to the earthy pumpkin and warm spices. The only problem? Pumpkin puree holds a lot of moisture that interferes with the creaminess of this custard-based cake, usually resulting in a wet cake and soggy crust. Fortunately, the solution was easy: We thoroughly blotted the pumpkin with paper towels until it became paste-like. To match the pumpkin flavor profile, many recipes call for brown sugar, but we liked white here; its cleaner flavor let the pumpkin take center stage. The addition of some heavy cream fortified the richness of our filling and resulted in an ultracreamy cake. For a complementary crust, we wanted to use spicy gingersnaps, but they refused to retain their crispness when baked beneath the filling, so we spiced up reliable graham crackers with ginger, cinnamon, and cloves. Be sure to buy unsweetened canned pumpkin, not pumpkin pie filling, which is preseasoned and sweetened. For neater slices, clean the knife thoroughly between slices. Serve with Brown Sugar and Bourbon Whipped Cream (recipe follows), if desired.

Crust

- 9 whole graham crackers, broken into 1-inch pieces
- 3 tablespoons sugar
- ½ teaspoon ground ginger
- ½ teaspoon ground cinnamon
- ¼ teaspoon ground cloves
- 7 tablespoons unsalted butter, melted, divided

Filling

- 1⅓ cups (9⅓ ounces) sugar
- 1 teaspoon ground cinnamon
- ½ teaspoon ground ginger
- ½ teaspoon table salt
- ¼ teaspoon ground nutmeg
- ¼ teaspoon ground cloves
- ¼ teaspoon ground allspice
- 1 (15-ounce) can unsweetened pumpkin puree
- 1½ pounds cream cheese, cut into chunks and softened
- 1 tablespoon vanilla extract
- 1 tablespoon lemon juice
- 5 large eggs, room temperature
- 1 cup heavy cream

1. *For the crust:* Adjust oven rack to lower-middle position and heat oven to 325 degrees. Pulse crackers, sugar, ginger, cinnamon, and cloves in food processor until finely ground, about 15 pulses. Transfer crumbs to bowl, drizzle with 6 tablespoons melted butter, and mix with rubber spatula until evenly moistened. Using your hands, press crumb mixture evenly into bottom of 9-inch springform pan. Using bottom of measuring cup, firmly pack crust into pan. Bake until browned around edges, about 15 minutes, rotating pan halfway through baking. Let crust cool completely on wire rack, about 30 minutes, then wrap outside of pan with two 18-inch square pieces of heavy-duty aluminum foil. Brush inside of pan with remaining 1 tablespoon melted butter. Set springform pan in roasting pan. Bring kettle of water to boil.

2. *For the filling:* Whisk sugar, cinnamon, ginger, salt, nutmeg, cloves, and allspice together in bowl. Line rimmed baking sheet with triple layer of paper towels. Spread pumpkin on paper towels in roughly even layer and press with second triple layer of paper towels to wick away moisture. Peel back top layer of paper towels and discard. Grasp bottom layer of paper towels and fold pumpkin in half; peel back paper towels. Repeat and flip pumpkin onto sheet.

3. Using stand mixer fitted with paddle, beat cream cheese on medium-low speed until smooth, about 1 minute. Scrape down bowl, then beat in half of sugar mixture until combined, about 1 minute. Repeat with remaining sugar mixture. Add vanilla, lemon juice, and pumpkin and beat until combined, about 1 minute; scrape down bowl and paddle. Add eggs, one at a time, and beat until combined, about 1 minute. Beat in cream until combined, about 1 minute. Give filling final stir by hand.

4. Pour filling into crust and smooth top with spatula. Set roasting pan on oven rack and pour enough boiling water into roasting pan to come about halfway up sides of springform pan. Bake until cheesecake registers 150 degrees, about 1½ hours. Let cake cool in water bath on wire rack for 45 minutes. Transfer springform pan to rack, discarding foil, and let cheesecake cool until barely warm, about 3 hours. Wrap cheesecake tightly in plastic wrap and refrigerate until cold, at least 3 hours or up to 24 hours.

5. To unmold cheesecake, wrap hot, damp dish towel around springform pan and let sit for 1 minute. Remove sides of pan and slide thin metal spatula between crust and pan bottom to loosen, then slide cheesecake onto platter. Let sit at room temperature for 30 minutes before serving.

VARIATION
Pumpkin-Bourbon Cheesecake with Graham-Pecan Crust
Reduce graham crackers to 5 whole crackers, process ½ cup chopped pecans with crackers, and reduce melted butter to 5 tablespoons. Use 4 tablespoons in crust and 1 tablespoon to grease pan. Omit lemon juice from filling, reduce vanilla extract to 1 teaspoon, and add ¼ cup bourbon along with heavy cream.

ACCOMPANIMENT
Brown Sugar and Bourbon Whipped Cream
Makes 2½ cups
Refrigerating the mixture in step 1 gives the brown sugar time to dissolve.

 1 **cup heavy cream, chilled**
 ½ **cup sour cream**
 ½ **cup packed (3½ ounces) light brown sugar**
 2 **teaspoons bourbon**
 ⅛ **teaspoon salt**

1. Using stand mixer fitted with whisk attachment, mix heavy cream, sour cream, sugar, bourbon, and salt until combined. Transfer to separate bowl, cover with plastic wrap, and refrigerate until ready to serve, at least 4 hours or up to 24 hours, stirring once or twice during chilling to ensure that sugar dissolves.

2. Using clean, dry mixer bowl and whisk attachment, whip mixture on medium-low speed until foamy, about 1 minute. Increase speed to high and whip until soft peaks form, 1 to 3 minutes.

Lemon Pudding Cakes

Serves 6

WHY THIS RECIPE WORKS The appeal of lemon pudding cake—aside from its vibrant citrus flavor—lies in the magic of a single batter producing two texturally distinct layers. But all too often, it emerges from the oven as an under-baked cake sitting atop a grainy pudding. We wanted tender cake, rich and creamy pudding, and lots of lemon flavor in one individual-size dessert. Whipping the egg whites to stiff peaks produced a too-tall, tough cake layer, while barely whipping the whites resulted in a squat, rubbery cake; the midpoint, soft peaks, produced a tender cake with moderate lift. Baking the cakes in a water bath prevented the pudding from curdling while still allowing the cake to cook through. With the most challenging piece of the puzzle—the texture—solved, we turned to the lemon flavor. Lemon zest, in addition to plenty of juice, was essential for balanced flavor, but the pieces of zest marred the pudding's silky texture. Instead, we infused the milk and cream with subtle lemon flavor by steeping the zest in the liquid. To take the temperature of the pudding layer, touch the probe tip of a thermometer to the bottom of the ramekin and pull it up ¼ inch. We like this dessert served at room temperature, but it can also be chilled (the texture will be firmer). Serve with Blueberry Compote (page 538) or simply dust with confectioners' sugar.

1 cup whole milk
½ cup heavy cream
3 tablespoons grated lemon zest plus
   ½ cup juice (3 lemons)
1 cup (7 ounces) sugar, divided
¼ cup (1¼ ounces) all-purpose flour
½ teaspoon baking powder
⅛ teaspoon table salt
2 large eggs, separated, plus 2 large whites
½ teaspoon vanilla extract

1. Adjust oven rack to middle position and heat oven to 325 degrees. Bring milk and cream to simmer in medium saucepan over medium-high heat. Remove pan from heat, whisk in lemon zest, cover pan, and let sit for 15 minutes. Meanwhile, fold dish towel in half and place in bottom of large roasting pan. Place six 6-ounce ramekins on top of towel and set aside pan.

2. Strain milk mixture through fine-mesh strainer into bowl, pressing on lemon zest to extract liquid; discard lemon zest. Whisk ¾ cup sugar, flour, baking powder, and salt in second bowl until combined. Add egg yolks, vanilla, lemon juice, and milk mixture and whisk until combined. (Batter will have consistency of milk.)

3. Using stand mixer fitted with whisk, whip egg whites on medium-low speed until foamy, about 1 minute. Increase speed to medium-high and whip whites to soft, billowy mounds, about 1 minute. Gradually add remaining ¼ cup sugar and whip until glossy, soft peaks form, 1 to 2 minutes.

4. Whisk one-quarter of whites into batter to lighten. With rubber spatula, gently fold in remaining whites until no clumps or streaks remain. Ladle batter into ramekins (ramekins should be nearly full). Pour enough cold water into roasting pan to come one-third of way up sides of ramekins. Bake until cake is set and pale golden brown and pudding layer registers 172 to 175 degrees at center, 50 to 55 minutes.

5. Remove pan from oven and let ramekins sit in water bath for 10 minutes. Transfer ramekins to wire rack and let cool completely. Serve.

ACCOMPANIMENT
Blueberry Compote
Makes about 1 cup
To use fresh blueberries, crush one-third of them against the side of the saucepan with a wooden spoon after adding them to the butter and then proceed as directed.

1 tablespoon unsalted butter
10 ounces (2 cups) frozen blueberries
2 tablespoons sugar, plus extra for seasoning
   Pinch table salt
½ teaspoon lemon juice

Melt butter in small saucepan over medium heat. Add blueberries, 2 tablespoons sugar, and salt; bring to boil. Lower heat and simmer, stirring occasionally, until thickened and about one-quarter of juice remains, 8 to 10 minutes. Remove pan from heat and stir in lemon juice. Season with extra sugar to taste.

Baked Alaska

Serves 8

WHY THIS RECIPE WORKS Though making a baked Alaska can be intimidating to some, the dessert is essentially a dressed-up ice cream cake that's no more difficult to make than any other version. Plenty of insulation was the key to a baked Alaska that was toasty on the outside but still firm at the center. Most recipes use cake only as a base, but we used it to encase the ice cream entirely, thereby decreasing the amount of meringue by more than one-third without sacrificing heat resistance. To further improve the balance, we added cocoa to our cake, boosting flavor without adding sweetness. Rather than packing softened ice cream into a mold (refrozen ice cream can be icy, and it can be hard to match cake pans and bowls), we simply cut the cardboard off two pints of firm ice cream and stuck them together to form the core of our dessert. We opted for coffee ice cream, which complements the flavor of the cake and the sweetness of the meringue perfectly. Coffee ice cream provides the best contrast with sweet meringue in this recipe, but other flavors may be substituted, if desired. A high-quality ice cream such as Häagen-Dazs works best because it is slower to melt. To ensure the proper texture when serving, it is necessary to remove the cake from the freezer before making the meringue. This recipe leaves just enough leftover cake and ice cream to make a bonus for-two version (see page 541).

2 (1-pint) containers coffee ice cream

Cake
1 cup (4 ounces) cake flour
⅔ cup (4⅔ ounces) sugar, divided
⅓ cup (1 ounce) unsweetened cocoa powder
1½ teaspoons baking powder
¼ teaspoon table salt
½ cup vegetable oil
6 tablespoons water
4 large eggs, separated

Meringue
¾ cup (5¼ ounces) sugar
⅓ cup light corn syrup
3 large egg whites
2 tablespoons water
   Pinch table salt
1 teaspoon vanilla extract

Baked Alaska

1. Lay 12-inch square sheet of plastic wrap on counter and remove lids from ice cream. Use scissors to cut cardboard tubs from top to bottom. Peel away cardboard and discard. Place ice cream blocks on their sides in center of plastic with wider ends facing each other. Grasp each side of plastic and firmly press blocks together to form barrel shape. Wrap plastic tightly around ice cream and roll briefly on counter to form uniform cylinder. Place cylinder, standing on end, in freezer until completely solid, at least 1 hour.

2. *For the cake:* Adjust oven rack to middle position and heat oven to 350 degrees. Lightly grease 18 by 13-inch rimmed baking sheet, line with parchment paper, and lightly grease parchment. Whisk flour, ⅓ cup sugar, cocoa, baking powder, and salt together in large bowl. Whisk oil, water, and egg yolks into flour mixture until smooth batter forms.

3. Using stand mixer fitted with whisk, whip egg whites on medium-low speed until foamy, about 1 minute. Increase speed to medium-high and whip whites to soft, billowy mounds, about 1 minute. Gradually add remaining ⅓ cup sugar and whip until glossy, soft peaks form, 1 to 2 minutes. Transfer one-third of whites to batter; whisk gently until mixture is lightened. Using rubber spatula, gently fold remaining egg whites into batter until no white streaks remain.

4. Pour batter into prepared sheet and spread into even layer. Bake until cake springs back when pressed lightly in center, 10 to 13 minutes. Let cake cool in baking sheet on wire rack for 5 minutes. Run knife around edge of sheet, then invert cake onto wire rack. Carefully remove parchment, then reinvert cake onto second wire rack and let cool completely, at least 15 minutes.

5. Transfer cake to cutting board with long side of rectangle parallel to edge of counter. Using serrated knife, trim ¼ inch off left side of cake and discard. Using ruler, measure 4½ inches from cut edge and make mark with knife. Using mark as guide, cut 4½-inch rectangle from cake. Trim piece to create 4½ by 11-inch rectangle and set aside. (Depending on pan size and how much cake has shrunk during baking, it may not be necessary to trim piece to measure 11 inches.) Measure 4 inches from new cut edge and make mark. Using mark as guide, cut 4-inch rectangle from cake. Trim piece to create 4 by 10-inch rectangle, wrap rectangle in plastic, and set aside. Cut 3½-inch round from remaining cake and set aside (biscuit cutter works well); discard scraps.

6. Unwrap ice cream. Trim cylinder to 4½ inches in length; discard scraps. Place ice cream cylinder on 4½ by 11-inch cake rectangle and wrap cake around ice cream. (Cake may crack slightly.) Place cake circle on 1 end of cylinder. Wrap entire cylinder tightly in plastic. Place cylinder, standing on cake-covered end, in freezer until cake is firm, at least 30 minutes. Unwrap cylinder and place on cutting board, standing on cake-covered end, and cut in half lengthwise. Unwrap reserved 4 by 10-inch cake rectangle and place halves on top, ice cream side down, with open ends meeting in middle. Wrap tightly in plastic and press ends gently to close gap between halves. Return to freezer for at least 2 hours or up to 2 weeks.

7. *For the meringue:* Adjust oven rack to upper-middle position and heat oven to 500 degrees. Spray wire rack set in rimmed baking sheet with vegetable oil spray. Unwrap cake and place on rack. Combine sugar, corn syrup, egg whites, water, and salt in bowl of stand mixer; place bowl over saucepan filled with 1 inch barely simmering water, making sure that water does not touch bottom of bowl. Whisking gently but constantly, heat until sugar is dissolved and mixture registers 160 degrees, 5 to 8 minutes.

Assembling Baked Alaska

1. Place ice cream cylinder on 4½ by 11-inch cake rectangle and wrap cake around ice cream.

2. Place cake circle on 1 end of cylinder. Wrap entire cylinder tightly in plastic. Place cylinder, standing on cake-covered end, in freezer until cake is firm, at least 30 minutes.

3. Unwrap cylinder and place on cutting board, standing on cake-covered end, and cut in half lengthwise.

4. Unwrap reserved cake rectangle and place halves on top, ice cream side down, with open ends in middle. Wrap in plastic and press ends to close gap between halves. Return to freezer.

8. Transfer bowl to stand mixer fitted with whisk attachment. Whip mixture on medium speed until bowl is only slightly warm to touch, about 5 minutes. Increase speed to high and beat until mixture begins to lose its gloss and forms stiff peaks, about 5 minutes. Add vanilla and mix until combined. Using offset spatula, spread meringue over top and sides of cake, avoiding getting meringue on rack. Use back of spoon to create peaks all over meringue.

9. Bake until browned and crisp, about 5 minutes. Run offset spatula or thin knife under dessert to loosen from rack, then use 2 spatulas to transfer to platter. Serve immediately.

VARIATION
Bonus Baked Alaska
Serves 2
Our Baked Alaska recipe leaves just enough leftover cake and ice cream to make an additional for-two version.

From remaining cake scraps, cut two 3⅓-inch rounds and one 11 by 2-inch strip. Place leftover ice cream disk on top of 1 cake round. Wrap strip of cake around sides of disk. Place remaining cake round on top, wrap tightly in plastic, and freeze. Following step 8, spread meringue over cake and bake as directed.

Sous Vide Crème Brûlée

SEASON 20 RECIPE

Serves 4

WHY THIS RECIPE WORKS While sous vide is not the answer for most baked desserts, it most definitely is when it comes to custard. Conventional custard recipes require care and attention with temperature-sensitive steps like tempering the eggs with the hot cream to avoid curdling and arranging a water bath in the oven. The precise temperature control of sous vide cooking makes custardy desserts like crème brûlée easier to execute. We whisked the base together, portioned it into Mason jars, and circulated for 1 hour. It was that easy. Once the custards finished cooking, we chilled them before the finale of a torched sugar topping. We found that crunchy turbinado sugar made for a satisfyingly crackly crust. A vanilla bean gives the crème brûlée the deepest flavor, but 1 teaspoon vanilla extract can be substituted. For the caramelized sugar crust, we recommend turbinado or Demerara sugar; regular granulated sugar will work, but use only 1 scant teaspoon (4 grams) for each Mason jar portion. You will need four 8-ounce widemouthed Mason jars and a kitchen torch for this recipe. Be careful not to overtighten the jars before placing them in the water bath; it can cause the glass to crack.

½ vanilla bean
2 cups heavy cream
5 large egg yolks
⅓ cup granulated sugar
  Pinch table salt
4 teaspoons turbinado or Demerara sugar

1. Using sous vide circulator, bring water to 180 degrees in 7-quart container.

2. Cut vanilla bean in half lengthwise. Using tip of paring knife, scrape out seeds. Whisk vanilla bean and seeds, cream, egg yolks, granulated sugar, and salt in bowl until sugar has dissolved. Strain custard through fine-mesh strainer into 4-cup liquid measuring cup, then divide evenly among four 8-ounce widemouthed Mason jars. Gently tap jars on counter to remove any air bubbles, then seal; do not overtighten lids.

3. Gently lower jars into water bath until fully submerged. Cover and cook for at least 1 hour or up to 1¼ hours.

4. Transfer jars to wire rack and let cool to room temperature, about 1 hour. Refrigerate until chilled, at least 4 hours. (Custards can be refrigerated for up to 3 days.)

5. Gently blot away condensation on top of custards using paper towels. Sprinkle each custard with 1 teaspoon turbinado sugar. Tilt and tap each jar to distribute sugar evenly, then wipe rims of jars clean. Ignite torch and caramelize sugar by sweeping flame of torch from perimeter of custard toward middle, keeping flame about 2 inches above jar, until sugar is bubbling and deep golden brown. Let sit for 5 minutes to allow sugar crust to harden, then serve.

Chocolate Pots de Crème

Chocolate Pots de Crème

Serves 8

WHY THIS RECIPE WORKS When you want a make-ahead dessert that is easy to orchestrate but also elegant enough for a special dinner, look no further than this intensely chocolate custard. Classic *pots de crème,* however, can be finicky and laborious, requiring a hot water bath that threatens to splash the custards every time the pan is moved. In addition, the individual custards don't always cook at the same rate. We set out to develop a user-friendly recipe that delivered a decadent dessert with a satiny texture and intense chocolate flavor. First we moved the dish out of the oven, concentrating on an unconventional approach in which the custard is cooked on the stovetop in a saucepan and then poured into ramekins. Our next challenge was developing the right amount of richness and body, which we did by choosing a combination of heavy cream and half-and-half, along with egg yolks only, for maximum richness. For intense chocolate flavor, we focused on bittersweet chocolate—and a lot of it. Our chocolate content was at least 50 percent more than in any other recipe we had encountered. We prefer pots de crème made with 60 percent bittersweet chocolate (our favorite is Ghirardelli 60% Cacao Bittersweet Chocolate Premium Baking Bar), but 70 percent bittersweet chocolate can also be used. If using a 70 percent bittersweet chocolate, reduce the amount of chocolate to 8 ounces. An instant-read thermometer is the most reliable way to judge when the custard has reached the proper temperature. However, you can also judge the progress of the custard by its thickness. Dip a wooden spoon into the custard and run your finger across the back. The custard is ready when it coats the spoon and a line drawn maintains neat edges. The pots de crème (minus the whipped cream garnish) can be covered tightly with plastic wrap and refrigerated for up to three days.

Pots de Crème
- 10 ounces bittersweet chocolate, chopped fine
- 1 tablespoon vanilla extract
- 1 tablespoon water
- ½ teaspoon instant espresso powder
- 5 large egg yolks
- 5 tablespoons (2¼ ounces) sugar
- ¼ teaspoon table salt
- 1½ cups heavy cream
- ¾ cup half-and-half

Whipped Cream and Garnish
- ½ cup heavy cream, chilled
- 2 teaspoons sugar
- ½ teaspoon vanilla extract
- Cocoa powder and/or chocolate shavings (optional)

1. *For the pots de crème:* Place chocolate in medium bowl and set fine-mesh strainer over top. Combine vanilla, water, and espresso powder in small bowl.

2. Whisk egg yolks, sugar, and salt in separate bowl until combined. Whisk in cream and half-and-half. Transfer mixture to medium saucepan and cook over medium-low heat, stirring constantly and scraping bottom of pot with wooden spoon, until thickened and silky and registers 175 to 180 degrees, 8 to 12 minutes. (Do not let custard overcook or simmer.)

3. Immediately pour custard through fine-mesh strainer over chocolate. Let mixture sit to melt chocolate, about 5 minutes. Add espresso-vanilla mixture and whisk mixture until smooth. Divide mixture evenly among eight 5-ounce ramekins. Gently tap ramekins against counter to settle custard.

4. Let pots de crème cool to room temperature, then cover with plastic wrap and refrigerate until chilled, at least 4 hours or up to 3 days. Before serving, let pots de crème stand at room temperature for 20 to 30 minutes.

5. *For the whipped cream and garnish:* Using stand mixer fitted with whisk, whip cream, sugar, and vanilla on medium-low speed until foamy, about 1 minute. Increase speed to high and whip until stiff peaks form, 1 to 3 minutes. Dollop each pot de crème with about 2 tablespoons whipped cream and garnish with cocoa and/or chocolate shavings, if using. Serve.

VARIATION
Milk Chocolate Pots de Crème
Milk chocolate behaves differently in this recipe than bittersweet chocolate, and more of it must be used to ensure that the custard sets. And because of the increased amount of chocolate, it's necessary to cut back on the amount of sugar so that the custard is not overly sweet.

Substitute 12 ounces milk chocolate for bittersweet chocolate. Reduce amount of sugar to 2 tablespoons.

Nutritional Information for Our Recipes

We calculate the nutritional values of our recipes per serving; if there is a range in the serving size, we used the highest number of servings to calculate the nutritional values. We entered all the ingredients, using weights for important ingredients such as most vegetables. We also used our preferred brands in these analyses. We did not include additional salt or pepper for food that's "seasoned to taste."

	CALORIES	TOTAL FAT (G)	SAT FAT (G)	CHOL (MG)	SODIUM (MG)	TOTAL CARB (G)	DIETARY FIBER (G)	TOTAL SUGARS (G)	PROTEIN (G)
BREAKFAST AND BRUNCH									
Fluffy Scrambled Eggs	189	14	6	385	148	1	0	1	13
Hearty Scrambled Eggs with Asparagus and Salmon	263	20	4	375	384	3	1	1	16
Hearty Scrambled Eggs with Pinto Beans and Cotija Cheese	384	22	5	379	538	23	6	1	21
Hearty Scrambled Eggs with Shiitake Mushrooms and Feta Cheese	282	21	5	378	360	7	1	3	15
Perfect Fried Eggs	219	18	5	382	142	0	0	0	12
Perfect Poached Eggs	145	9	3	372	142	0	0	0	12
Eggs Benedict with Foolproof Hollandaise	594	39	20	644	778	27	2	1	32
Eggs in Spicy Tomato and Roasted Red Pepper Sauce (Shakshuka)	463	27	6	378	739	38	6	6	20
Zhoug (Spicy Middle Eastern Herb Sauce)	88	9	1	0	64	1	0	0	0
Soft-Cooked Eggs	72	4	1	186	71	0	0	0	6
Soft-Cooked Eggs with Salad	347	30	5	372	323	5	1	2	14
Soft-Cooked Eggs with Sautéed Mushrooms	203	23	5	372	152	8	1	3	16
Soft-Cooked Eggs with Steamed Asparagus	354	26	7	381	340	8	3	3	21
Curry Deviled Eggs with Easy-Peel Hard-Cooked Eggs	120	10	2.5	190	125	1	0	0	6
Easy-Peel Hard-Cooked Eggs	72	4	1	186	71	0	0	0	6
French Omelets	383	31	14	603	420	1	0	0	23
Asparagus, Ham, and Gruyère Frittata	203	13	5	300	348	3	1	1	15
Quiche Lorraine	501	40	19	185	374	19	0	4	13
Home Fries for a Crowd	255	9	3	11	90	38	3	2	4
Everyday French Toast	316	13	6	160	394	34	2	9	12
Blueberry Pancakes	310	11	5	54	402	44	1	10	8
Lemon Ricotta Pancakes	339	18	9	139	338	31	0	13	12
Apple-Cranberry Topping	223	0	0	0	151	54	7	41	0
Pear-Blackberry Topping	110	0	0	0	74	28	6	18	1
Plum-Apricot Topping	113	0	0	0	73	28	3	24	1
100 Percent Whole-Wheat Pancakes	127	6	0	26	157	15	1	3	4
Ten-Minute Steel-Cut Oatmeal	74	1	0	0	155	13	1	0	2
Apple-Cinnamon Steel-Cut Oatmeal	155	4	1	3	314	25	2	10	4
Carrot-Spice Steel-Cut Oatmeal	284	11	1	3	491	43	4	25	5
Cranberry-Orange Steel-Cut Oatmeal	297	11	1	3	315	44	5	25	7
Banana-Coconut Steel-Cut Oatmeal	297	17	14	0	336	34	3	12	4
Peanut, Honey, and Banana Steel-Cut Oatmeal	418	22	5	10	320	47	5	24	12
British-Style Currant Scones	270	9	5	53	210	40	1	12	5
Blueberry Muffins	301	9	3	41	267	49	1	27	4
Corn Muffins	275	12	7	59	201	37	1	13	4
Corn and Apricot Muffins with Orange Essence	322	12	7	59	273	49	2	23	5
New York–Style Crumb Cake	397	17	10	80	146	55	0	23	4
Cream Cheese Coffee Cake	393	21	11	103	268	45	1	26	6
Perfect Sticky Buns	405	18	8	47	279	54	1	28	6

	CALORIES	TOTAL FAT (G)	SAT FAT (G)	CHOL (MG)	SODIUM (MG)	TOTAL CARB (G)	DIETARY FIBER (G)	TOTAL SUGARS (G)	PROTEIN (G)
SOUPS, STEWS, CHILIS, AND CURRIES									
Hearty Chicken Noodle Soup	316	19	5	94	685	10	1	1	23
Avgolemono	397	8	2	154	534	38	1	5	38
Tortilla Soup	520	32	10	90	1530	28	3	6	32
Thai-Style Chicken Soup	340	24	19	41	619	16	1	5	19
Thai Hot and Sour Noodle Soup with Shrimp (Guay Tiew Tom Yum Goong)	318	5	1	104	1642	47	4	11	23
Thai Chili Jam (Nam Prik Pao) (per tablespoon)	100	9	0.5	0	115	5	0	3	1
Classic French Onion Soup	426	20	11	56	713	39	4	8	22
Quick Beef and Vegetable Soup	424	23	8	80	590	26	6	8	27
Vietnamese Beef Pho	390	4	1.5	40	2250	63	1	3	25
Caldo Verde	415	24	7	41	719	30	5	3	17
Creamy Cauliflower Soup	175	15	9	40	40	8	2	2	2
Carrot-Ginger Soup	156	4	2	10	1018	29	5	16	2
Buttery Croutons	120	8	4	15	92	8	0	1	2
Super Greens Soup with Lemon Tarragon Cream	143	6	3	16	172	19	3	3	5
Rustic Leek and Potato Soup	267	12	5	22	193	31	2	3	9
Sweet Potato Soup	180	7	4.5	20	660	27	4	10	2
Buttery Rye Croutons	77	8	3	15	14	1	0	0	0
Candied Bacon Bits	85	7	2	12	128	1	0	1	2
Maple Sour Cream (per tablespoon)	30	2	1	5	0	2	0	3	0
Creamless Creamy Tomato Soup	159	8	1	0	316	17	4	7	4
Classic Croutons	79	3	0	0	92	8	0	1	1
Classic Gazpacho	76	4	0	0	494	9	1	5	1
Garlic Croutons	80	3	0	0	92	9	0	1	1
Provençal Vegetable Soup (Soupe au Pistou)	299	16	2	3	427	30	6	4	10
Farmhouse Vegetable and Barley Soup	249	4	2	7	190	45	8	7	8
Lemon-Thyme Butter (per tablespoon)	100	11	7	30	25	0	0	0	0
Herbed Croutons	69	2	1	5	98	9	0	1	2
Italian Pasta and Bean Soup (Pasta e Fagioli)	210	5	1.5	5	890	32	3	5	9
Black Bean Soup	410	8	1	0	1220	66	4	14	18
Red Lentil Soup with North African Spices	320	10	5	25	259	41	6	5	17
Best Chicken Stew	493	22	8	193	627	25	2	5	40
Chicken and Dumplings	965	62	19	300	746	41	3	5	56
Chicken and Sausage Gumbo	370	14	3.5	165	940	20	2	3	40
Hungarian Beef Stew	644	38	14	177	374	23	6	10	53
Catalan-Style Beef Stew	950	81	31	143	135	14	3	4	31
Modern Beef Burgundy	754	46	19	168	1028	20	2	5	47
Daube Provençal	650	24	6	175	1180	21	3	7	61
Carbonnade	674	40	12	164	260	22	3	6	50
Cioppino	551	29	7	119	1160	18	4	6	45
Brazilian Shrimp and Fish Stew (Moqueca)	422	29	14	127	562	15	4	6	27
Hearty Tuscan Bean Stew	434	12	3	14	371	59	13	6	23
Our Favorite Chili	632	32	9	123	164	38	9	5	45
Beef Chili with Kidney Beans	396	18	5	61	623	33	10	10	26
Best Vegetarian Chili	226	9	0	0	410	33	8	10	6
Thai Chicken Curry with Potatoes	448	26	13	72	696	34	5	8	23
Thai Green Curry with Chicken, Broccoli, and Mushrooms	694	49	38	127	991	23	3	7	47
Green Curry Paste (per tablespoon)	50	3.5	0	0	490	4	1	2	1
Panang Beef Curry	602	52	25	111	478	7	1	2	30
Lamb Curry	439	26	7	88	159	21	8	3	30

	CALORIES	TOTAL FAT (G)	SAT FAT (G)	CHOL (MG)	SODIUM (MG)	TOTAL CARB (G)	DIETARY FIBER (G)	TOTAL SUGARS (G)	PROTEIN (G)
SOUPS, STEWS, CHILIS, AND CURRIES (continued)									
Thai Red Curry with Shrimp, Pineapple, and Peanuts	720	53	39	160	1370	41	4	22	29
Red Curry Paste (per tablespoon)	60	3.5	0	0	300	6	1	1	1
Indian Curry with Potatoes, Cauliflower, Peas, and Chickpeas	340	15	3	13	270	42	11	10	10
Onion Relish (per tablespoon)	5	0	0	0	20	1	0	0	0
Cilantro-Mint Chutney (per tablespoon)	5	0	0	0	40	1	0	1	0
Vegetable Broth Base (per tablespoon)	10	0	0	0	350	2	0	1	0
SALADS									
Foolproof Vinaigrette (per tablespoon)	100	11	1.5	0	90	0	0	0	0
Foolproof Lemon Vinaigrette (per tablespoon)	100	11	1.5	0	90	0	0	0	0
Foolproof Balsamic-Mustard Vinaigrette (per tablespoon)	110	11	1.5	0	135	1	0	1	0
Foolproof Walnut Vinaigrette (per tablespoon)	100	11	1	0	90	0	0	0	0
Foolproof Herb Vinaigrette (per tablespoon)	100	11	1.5	0	90	0	0	0	0
Salad with Herbed Baked Goat Cheese and Vinaigrette	411	31	11	119	643	15	2	1	17
Arugula Salad with Figs, Prosciutto, Walnuts, and Parmesan	187	13	3	13	395	8	1	5	7
Kale Caesar Salad	551	47	8	23	715	21	3	3	12
Classic Greek Salad	397	33	10	43	618	16	5	8	10
Mediterranean Chopped Salad	368	21	6	25	630	34	10	9	13
Wilted Spinach Salad with Warm Bacon Dressing	211	17	5	118	314	3	0	1	8
Italian Bread Salad (Panzanella)	501	29	4	0	465	51	4	10	10
Pita Bread Salad with Tomatoes and Cucumber	315	24	3	0	115	22	4	5	4
Creamy Buttermilk Coleslaw	120	7	1	7	139	12	3	7	3
Confetti Cabbage Salad with Spicy Peanut Dressing	83	5	1	0	218	7	2	3	2
Chopped Carrot Salad with Fennel, Orange, and Hazelnuts	232	19	2	0	72	13	5	5	3
Chopped Carrot Salad with Mint, Pistachios, and Pomegranate Seeds	237	16	2	0	54	20	5	11	4
Chopped Carrot Salad with Celery and Raisins	183	9	1	0	73	26	3	17	1
Chopped Carrot Salad with Radishes and Sesame Seeds	171	11	1	0	68	16	3	10	2
Smashed Cucumbers (Pai Huang Gua)	61	2	0	0	493	8	1	4	1
Sichuan Chili Oil (per tablespoon)	90	10	1	0	125	1	1	0	0
Mexican Style Corn Salad (Esquites)	176	11	3	17	229	16	1	5	5
Crispy Thai Eggplant Salad	560	38	4	0	1330	52	12	31	13
Fried Shallots (per 2 tablespoons)	70	4.5	0	0	50	6	1	3	1
Lentil Salad with Olives, Mint, and Feta	271	14	2	4	157	26	5	2	11
Lentil Salad with Spinach, Walnuts, and Parmesan	286	15	3	4	150	26	4	2	13
Lentil Salad with Hazelnuts and Goat Cheese	317	18	3	4	101	26	5	2	13
Lentil Salad with Carrots and Cilantro	244	12	1	0	51	25	4	1	10
Cool and Creamy Macaroni Salad	413	27	4	14	224	35	2	2	6
Italian Pasta Salad	390	20	7	40	790	36	1	2	16
Pasta Salad with Pesto	372	20	3	6	115	37	2	2	9
American Potato Salad with Hard-Cooked Eggs and Sweet Pickles	294	16	2	69	213	30	2	3	5
Classic Chicken Salad	306	18	2	104	192	2	0	1	30
Curried Chicken Salad with Cashews	459	25	4	139	207	12	1	6	43
Waldorf Chicken Salad	398	21	3	139	214	7	1	3	41

	CALORIES	TOTAL FAT (G)	SAT FAT (G)	CHOL (MG)	SODIUM (MG)	TOTAL CARB (G)	DIETARY FIBER (G)	TOTAL SUGARS (G)	PROTEIN (G)
SALADS (continued)									
Chicken Salad with Red Grapes and Smoked Almonds	452	25	3	139	214	10	2	5	44
Classic Tuna Salad	280	23	3	41	387	1	0	0	16
Tuna Salad with Balsamic Vinegar and Grapes	356	26	3	41	436	12	2	8	18
Curried Tuna Salad with Apples and Currants	333	23	3	41	444	15	2	11	17
Tuna Salad with Lime and Horseradish	285	23	3	41	434	2	0	1	16
POULTRY									
Perfect Poached Chicken Breasts	210	4.5	1	125	440	1	0	1	38
Warm Tomato-Ginger Vinaigrette (per ½ cup)	150	14	2	0	150	6	1	4	1
Cumin-Cilantro Yogurt Sauce (per ¼ cup)	90	8	1.5	5	15	3	0	2	1
Quick Sun-Dried Tomato Sauce (per ¼ cup)	180	15	1.5	0	350	11	1	4	3
Pan-Seared Chicken Breasts	230	12	4.5	100	630	2	0	0	26
Lemon and Chive Pan Sauce	150	12	7	30	570	9	0	2	2
Better Chicken Marsala	630	35	10	160	1980	27	2	5	50
Sweet and Tangy Oven-Barbecued Chicken	508	11	1	198	859	38	1	31	62
Chicken Piccata	381	19	5	113	187	18	1	2	33
Pan-Fried Chicken Cutlets (Chicken Katsu)	418	24	2	158	111	14	0	0	33
Tonkatsu Sauce (per tablespoon)	25	0	0	0	330	5	0	4	0
Garlic-Curry Sauce (per tablespoon)	70	6	1	5	100	2	0	1	0
Best Chicken Parmesan	607	40	9	155	905	23	4	9	38
Thai-Style Chicken with Basil	350	11	1	124	918	18	2	10	41
Skillet-Roasted Chicken Breasts with Harissa-Mint Carrots	575	30	7	159	1253	19	5	9	54
Crispy-Skinned Chicken Breasts with Vinegar-Pepper Pan Sauce	664	43	11	176	251	11	2	3	55
Crispy-Skinned Chicken Breasts with Lemon-Rosemary Pan Sauce	673	44	11	177	291	11	1	4	55
Crispy-Skinned Chicken Breasts with Maple–Sherry Vinegar Pan Sauce	695	44	11	176	249	18	2	9	55
Chicken Enchiladas with Red Chile Sauce	705	44	18	145	1899	48	12	12	36
Three-Cup Chicken	404	21	3	159	1338	13	1	4	36
Kung Pao Chicken	339	18	2	106	715	16	3	8	28
Chicken Provençal	799	55	14	292	495	11	2	3	52
Filipino Chicken Adobo	884	70	31	292	1425	8	0	0	53
Skillet-Roasted Chicken in Lemon Sauce (Rao's Famous Lemon Chicken)	841	58	18	272	1011	8	1	2	65
Braised Chicken with Mustard and Herbs	563	35	9	207	726	5	0	1	50
Braised Chicken with Basil and Tomato	564	35	9	207	725	5	0	1	50
Spice-Rubbed Picnic Chicken	635	43	12	212	677	5	1	3	53
Tandoori Chicken	872	66	17	341	976	7	1	3	59
Slow Roasted Chicken Parts with Shallot-Garlic Pan Sauce	720	49	16	229	302	9	1	3	56
Weeknight Roast Chicken	600	43	12	195	1020	0	0	0	49
Tarragon-Lemon Pan Sauce	60	6	3.5	15	200	2	0	1	0
Thyme–Sherry Vinegar Pan Sauce	60	6	3.5	15	200	2	0	1	1
Peruvian Roast Chicken with Garlic and Lime	700	50	13	195	1940	9	2	4	50
Spicy Mayonnaise	520	57	4.5	45	190	1	0	0	2
Roast Chicken with Warm Bread Salad	680	47	11	150	960	21	1	5	40
French Chicken in a Pot	850	61	17	324	949	4	0	0	65
High-Roast Butterflied Chicken with Potatoes	924	45	14	187	1300	79	4	26	49
Mustard-Garlic Butter with Thyme	73	7	4	20	56	0	0	0	0
Crispy Fried Chicken	790	34	7	125	940	73	1	14	45
Oven-Fried Chicken	904	71	16	412	806	2	0	0	59

	CALORIES	TOTAL FAT (G)	SAT FAT (G)	CHOL (MG)	SODIUM (MG)	TOTAL CARB (G)	DIETARY FIBER (G)	TOTAL SUGARS (G)	PROTEIN (G)
POULTRY (continued)									
Korean-Style Fried Chicken Wings	730	50	10	250	460	24	0	8	42
Turkey Breast en Cocotte with Pan Gravy	525	24	6	183	213	8	1	1	65
Classic Roast Turkey	690	28	8	335	1300	4	1	2	99
Giblet Pan Gravy (per ½ cup)	70	4	2	10	190	3	0	1	1
Easier Roast Turkey and Gravy	700	29	7	325	1670	5	0	2	99
Turkey and Gravy for a Crowd	564	27	9	222	981	8	1	2	65
Old-Fashioned Stuffed Turkey	1024	53	17	365	1603	31	3	4	99
Make-Ahead Turkey Gravy	100	4.5	0	0	410	8	0	1	2
Braised Turkey	1014	53	15	404	407	28	2	18	99
BEEF									
Cast Iron Thick-Cut Steaks with Herb Butter	655	53	21	197	113	1	0	0	39
Cast Iron Thick-Cut Steaks with Blue Cheese–Chive Butter	691	56	23	206	241	1	0	0	42
Pan-Seared Thick-Cut Steaks	389	29	10	123	81	0	0	0	29
Red Wine–Mushroom Pan Sauce	159	9	3	15	30	6	0	2	2
Thai Chili Butter	110	11	7	30	100	1	0	0	0
Pepper-Crusted Filet Mignon	606	48	15	150	470	5	2	0	35
Port-Cherry Reduction	141	2	1	7	14	16	1	10	1
Blue Cheese–Chive Butter	58	5	3	15	61	0	0	0	1
Steak Frites	880	52	16	165	890	47	0	0	52
Glazed All-Beef Meatloaf	341	17	7	139	508	16	0	9	29
Juicy Pub-Style Burgers	717	46	20	207	327	21	1	2	49
Pub-Style Burger Sauce	319	33	4	16	731	4	0	2	0
Juicy Pub-Style Burgers with Crispy Shallots and Blue Cheese	1087	81	27	228	657	29	2	6	56
Juicy Pub-Style Burgers with Peppered Bacon and Aged Cheddar	1017	73	32	265	798	23	1	3	61
Juicy Pub-Style Burgers with Sautéed Onions and Smoked Cheddar	907	63	26	236	511	25	1	4	56
Juicy Pub-Style Burgers with Pan-Roasted Mushrooms and Gruyère	934	62	26	238	536	28	2	5	60
Classic Sloppy Joes	492	25	7	77	695	38	2	13	27
Steak Tacos	294	18	2	22	265	23	3	1	10
Sweet and Spicy Pickled Onion	310	0	0	0	590	79	3	73	1
Shredded Beef Tacos	350	18	7	100	730	8	2	1	34
Ground Beef and Cheese Enchiladas	549	33	11	82	579	34	6	4	30
Old-Fashioned Pot Roast	223	14	4	58	148	4	0	2	18
Old-Fashioned Pot Roast with Root Vegetables	362	14	4	58	228	37	7	10	21
Sous Vide Rosemary–Mustard Seed Crusted Roast Beef	370	25	9	115	1450	1	1	0	36
Yogurt-Herb Sauce (per tablespoon)	10	0.5	0	0	5	1	0	1	1
Simple Pot-au-Feu	551	29	12	156	418	20	5	5	50
Onion-Braised Beef Brisket	530	13	4.5	195	1320	25	4	11	68
Braised Beef Short Ribs	590	32	12	155	990	8	1	3	52
Osso Buco	824	32	6	375	483	13	3	5	99
Chinese Braised Beef	619	43	18	165	1048	12	0	6	42
Slow-Roasted Beef	270	9	2.5	115	680	0	0	0	45
Horseradish Cream Sauce (per tablespoon)	30	3	1.5	10	180	1	0	1	0
Roast Beef Tenderloin with Shallot Butter	530	35	16	190	830	1	0	0	50
Shallot and Parsley Butter	100	11	7	30	150	1	0	0	0
Chipotle and Cilantro Butter	130	14	9	40	150	2	0	1	0
Beef Tenderloin with Smoky Potatoes and Persillade	580	22	7	145	980	38	5	3	55

	CALORIES	TOTAL FAT (G)	SAT FAT (G)	CHOL (MG)	SODIUM (MG)	TOTAL CARB (G)	DIETARY FIBER (G)	TOTAL SUGARS (G)	PROTEIN (G)
BEEF (continued)									
Fennel-Coriander Top Sirloin Roast	430	23	5	140	890	1	1	0	51
Rosemary-Garlic Top Sirloin Roast	430	23	5	140	890	1	0	0	51
Beef Top Loin Roast with Potatoes	783	44	16	184	1412	42	5	2	51
Best Prime Rib	650	34	13	235	1090	0	0	0	80
Cuban Braised and Shredded Beef	476	36	11	109	369	10	2	4	23
Sichuan Braised Tofu with Beef (Mapo Tofu)	384	27	4	28	390	16	2	5	19
Beef Stir-Fry with Bell Peppers and Black Pepper Sauce	366	21	4	77	930	12	2	4	26
Crispy Orange Beef	560	32	1.5	120	780	27	1	13	39
PORK AND LAMB									
Crispy Pan-Fried Pork Chops	1085	66	8	220	514	41	1	5	76
Pan-Seared Thick-Cut Pork Chops	120	5	1	55	340	0	0	0	18
Garlic and Thyme Sauce (per 2 tablespoons)	110	8	5	25	100	3	0	1	1
Smothered Pork Chops	534	32	9	151	285	11	1	2	47
Crunchy Baked Pork Chops	512	24	4	113	493	24	2	2	46
Stuffed Pork Chops	696	33	13	170	728	53	1	42	44
Quick All-Purpose Gravy (per ½ cup)	120	8	5	25	100	3	0	1	1
Ginger-Apple Chutney	620	15	1	0	35	117	11	96	2
Pan-Seared Oven-Roasted Pork Tenderloin	110	4	1	55	770	0	0	0	18
Dried Cherry–Port Sauce with Onions and Marmalade	257	10	5	22	13	36	1	29	0
Garlicky Lime Sauce with Cilantro	154	15	7	30	4	5	0	1	0
Maple-Glazed Pork Tenderloin	450	9	1.5	125	1330	46	0	38	40
Milk-Braised Pork Loin	330	15	6	120	650	8	0	6	36
French-Style Pot-Roasted Pork Loin	380	18	6	115	700	8	1	5	43
Garlic-Studded Roast Pork Loin	350	22	8	100	920	1	0	0	36
Mustard-Shallot Sauce with Thyme	90	3.5	2.5	10	330	4	1	2	1
Maple-Glazed Pork Roast	330	13	4	110	430	12	0	11	40
Maple-Glazed Pork Roast with Rosemary	330	13	4	110	430	12	0	11	40
Maple-Glazed Pork Roast with Orange Essence	330	13	4	110	430	12	0	11	40
Maple-Glazed Pork Roast with Star Anise	695	32	5	234	466	18	0	15	78
Maple-Glazed Pork Roast with Smoked Paprika	330	13	4	110	430	12	0	11	40
Herb-Crusted Pork Roast	573	36	11	134	203	14	1	9	43
Tuscan-Style Roast Pork with Garlic and Rosemary (Arista)	447	34	9	99	137	2	0	0	30
Porchetta	467	34	9	117	150	3	1	0	33
Slow-Roasted Bone-In Pork Rib Roast	200	7	2	75	500	4	0	3	30
Port Wine–Cherry Sauce	364	25	16	71	265	25	1	19	1
Slow Roasted Pork Shoulder with Peach Sauce	520	28	10	140	1670	18	0	17	40
Slow Roasted Pork Shoulder with Cherry Sauce	550	28	10	140	1640	24	0	22	40
Indoor Pulled Pork with Sweet and Tangy BBQ Sauce	222	5	1	22	610	39	1	33	7
Lexington Vinegar Sauce (per 5 tablespoons)	35	0	0	0	380	7	0	6	0
South Carolina Barbecue Sauce (per 5 tablespoons)	60	1	0	0	810	10	1	8	1
Stir-Fried Pork, Eggplant, and Onions with Garlic and Black Pepper	306	15	1	55	1677	21	4	11	21
Chinese-Style Pork in Garlic Sauce	230	15	2	40	980	9	0	6	14
Mu Shu Pork	487	16	2	132	1230	54	5	9	28
Pork Lo Mein	738	27	4	155	1250	80	7	8	40
Fried Brown Rice with Pork and Shrimp	464	15	2	162	639	56	3	4	23

	CALORIES	TOTAL FAT (G)	SAT FAT (G)	CHOL (MG)	SODIUM (MG)	TOTAL CARB (G)	DIETARY FIBER (G)	TOTAL SUGARS (G)	PROTEIN (G)
PORK AND LAMB (continued)									
Cuban-Style Black Beans and Rice	318	21	6	18	598	23	5	2	8
Spicy Mexican Shredded Pork Tostadas (Tinga)	740	54	9	95	820	35	2	7	31
Roast Fresh Ham	520	19	5	120	680	48	0	46	39
Cider and Brown Sugar Glaze	180	0	0	0	15	46	0	45	0
Spicy Pineapple-Ginger Glaze	180	0	0	0	15	47	0	45	0
Coca-Cola Glaze with Lime and Jalapeño	180	0	0	0	15	47	0	46	0
Orange, Cinnamon, and Star Anise Glaze	180	0	0	0	15	46	0	45	0
Glazed Spiral-Sliced Ham	460	20	8	140	2940	33	0	28	40
Maple-Orange Glaze	90	1.5	1	5	35	19	0	17	0
Cherry-Port Glaze	100	0	0	0	0	23	0	22	0
Roast Rack of Lamb with Roasted Red Pepper Relish	370	23	7	115	1300	1	0	1	38
Roast Rack of Lamb with Sweet Mint-Almond Relish	410	25	7	115	1280	6	1	4	39
Roast Boneless Leg of Lamb with Garlic, Herb, and Bread-Crumb Crust	330	17	5	110	690	4	0	0	37
Roast Butterflied Leg of Lamb with Coriander, Cumin, and Mustard Seeds	440	22	6	175	330	1	1	0	56
Roast Butterflied Leg of Lamb with Coriander, Rosemary, and Red Pepper	440	22	6	175	330	1	1	0	56
Roast Butterflied Leg of Lamb with Coriander, Fennel, and Black Pepper	440	22	6	175	330	1	1	0	56
FISH									
Braised Halibut with Leeks and Mustard	442	20	11	143	176	18	2	4	38
Braised Halibut with Carrots and Coriander	462	20	11	143	225	23	5	10	39
Poached Fish Fillets with Crispy Artichokes and Sherry-Tomato Vinaigrette	566	43	6	85	120	9	2	2	35
Poached Fish Fillets with Jalapeño Vinaigrette	538	46	6	57	67	8	2	2	24
Poached Fish Fillets with Crispy Scallions and Miso-Ginger Vinaigrette	583	43	6	85	316	11	2	3	36
Chinese-Style Oven-Steamed Fish	315	10	1	99	791	8	1	2	43
Fish Meunière with Browned Butter and Lemon	262	18	8	79	324	9	0	0	14
Crunchy Oven-Fried Fish	452	18	6	173	373	34	2	3	34
Sweet and Tangy Tartar Sauce (per tablespoon)	70	8	1	5	120	1	0	1	0
Fish and Chips	1060	62	5	75	800	83	4	2	40
Pan-Seared Swordfish Steaks	359	18	3	149	543	0	0	0	44
Caper-Currant Relish (per tablespoon)	50	5	0.5	0	50	1	0	0	0
Spicy Dried Mint–Garlic Sauce (per tablespoon)	100	11	1.5	0	55	1	0	0	0
Poached Salmon with Herb and Caper Vinaigrette	334	20	4	54	167	12	1	6	21
Pan-Seared Brined Salmon	415	26	6	109	117	0	0	0	40
Mango-Mint Salsa (per ¼ cup)	110	4	0	0	330	20	0	2	0
Cilantro-Mint Chutney (per ¼ cup)	130	12	1	0	330	6	2	2	2
Sesame-Crusted Salmon with Lemon and Ginger	612	43	8	109	127	8	4	0	46
Sesame-Crusted Salmon with Lime and Coriander	612	43	8	109	127	8	4	0	46
Sesame-Crusted Salmon with Orange and Chili Powder	613	43	8	109	132	8	4	0	46
Glazed Salmon	370	24	5	95	240	1	0	1	35
Pomegranate-Balsamic Glaze	70	0	0	0	95	15	0	14	0
Asian Barbecue Glaze	90	4	0.5	0	490	13	0	11	1
Orange-Miso Glaze	40	0	0	0	330	7	0	5	1
Soy-Mustard Glaze	70	0	0	0	550	13	0	12	1

	CALORIES	TOTAL FAT (G)	SAT FAT (G)	CHOL (MG)	SODIUM (MG)	TOTAL CARB (G)	DIETARY FIBER (G)	TOTAL SUGARS (G)	PROTEIN (G)
FISH (continued)									
Oven-Roasted Salmon	430	29	6	110	700	0	0	0	41
Tangerine and Ginger Relish (per ¼ cup)	60	2	0	0	0	10	1	8	1
Fresh Tomato Relish (per ¼ cup)	35	2.5	0	0	0	3	1	2	1
Spicy Cucumber Relish (per ¼ cup)	5	0	0	0	75	1	0	1	0
Roasted Whole Side of Salmon	391	24	5	99	107	3	0	3	37
Arugula and Almond Pesto (per 2 tablespoons)	80	8	1	0	230	2	1	1	2
Cucumber-Ginger Relish (per ¼ cup)	110	11	1.5	0	160	2	1	1	1
Brown Rice Bowls with Vegetables and Salmon	802	33	5	62	1266	91	9	14	34
Pan-Seared Sesame-Crusted Tuna Steaks	404	21	2	66	79	6	3	0	46
Ginger-Soy Sauce with Scallions (per tablespoon)	10	0	0	0	230	1	0	1	1
Avocado-Orange Sauce (per tablespoon)	25	2	0	0	10	2	1	1	0
Pan-Seared Scallops	232	13	4	56	667	5	0	0	20
Lemon Browned Butter Sauce	110	11	7	30	3	1	0	0	0
Pan-Seared Shrimp	184	8	0	214	962	1	0	0	23
Pan-Seared Shrimp with Garlic-Lemon Butter	263	17	6	237	965	2	0	0	23
Pan-Seared Shrimp with Ginger-Hoisin Glaze	206	9	0	214	1202	6	0	2	23
Pan-Seared Shrimp with Chipotle-Lime Glaze	201	8	0	214	1178	6	0	3	23
Spanish-Style Garlic Shrimp	232	19	2	95	431	4	0	0	11
Garlicky Roasted Shrimp with Parsley and Anise	265	18	5	210	858	2	0	0	20
Garlicky Roasted Shrimp with Cilantro and Lime	282	20	1	190	857	3	0	0	21
Garlicky Roasted Shrimp with Cumin, Ginger, and Sesame	291	21	1	190	857	2	0	0	20
Ultimate Shrimp Scampi	371	20	8	244	969	13	0	7	23
Crispy Salt and Pepper Shrimp	290	20	1.5	145	500	10	0	2	16
Best Crab Cakes	448	26	7	179	923	23	1	5	29
Easy Salmon Cakes	526	47	5	57	370	4	0	1	20
Easy Salmon Cakes with Smoked Salmon, Capers, and Dill	559	48	5	63	438	4	0	1	26
New England Lobster Roll	245	9	3	108	560	21	1	2	16
Boiled Lobster	116	1	0	190	634	0	0	0	24
Oven-Steamed Mussels	525	19	6	142	1302	19	0	0	54
Oven-Steamed Mussels with Tomato and Chorizo	710	41	14	150	1910	23	3	6	52
Oven-Steamed Mussels with Leeks and Pernod	645	23	4	134	1473	34	2	4	56
Oven-Steamed Mussels with Hard Cider and Bacon	622	30	9	166	1498	20	0	0	58
Indoor Clambake	670	36	15	235	2030	40	3	6	50
PASTA									
Marinara Sauce	126	7	1	0	305	12	5	8	2
Pasta Puttanesca	360	7	1	5	600	61	2	4	12
Pasta alla Norma	694	19	4	12	471	111	12	17	23
Pasta all'Amatriciana	634	34	12	42	1211	62	5	6	16
Pasta alla Gricia (Rigatoni with Pancetta and Pecorino Romano)	496	20	7	34	390	57	2	2	17
Meatless "Meat" Sauce with Chickpeas and Mushrooms	176	9	1	0	523	19	5	7	5
Pasta e Ceci (Pasta with Chickpeas)	507	18	3	10	594	67	12	9	19
Orecchiette with Broccoli Rabe and Sausage	565	26	8	40	432	60	4	2	20
Shrimp Fra Diavolo	363	19	2	216	1279	11	4	5	25
Beef Short Rib Ragu	680	55	22	120	820	9	1	4	30

	CALORIES	TOTAL FAT (G)	SAT FAT (G)	CHOL (MG)	SODIUM (MG)	TOTAL CARB (G)	DIETARY FIBER (G)	TOTAL SUGARS (G)	PROTEIN (G)
PASTA (continued)									
Weeknight Tagliatelle with Bolognese Sauce	664	25	9	76	756	65	3	5	34
Ragu alla Bolognese	520	25	8	135	640	33	0	3	30
Pasta with Hearty Italian Meat Sauce (Sunday Gravy)	886	48	14	134	1088	70	6	11	43
Pasta and Slow-Simmered Tomato Sauce with Meat	470	11	4	35	650	64	0	7	25
Pork, Fennel, and Lemon Ragu with Pappardelle	559	26	11	93	648	49	3	4	29
Classic Spaghetti and Meatballs for a Crowd	993	30	10	141	1039	128	9	25	51
Sausage Meatballs and Spaghetti	733	31	11	141	1138	77	6	11	36
Baked Manicotti	576	28	15	128	733	48	5	7	31
Baked Manicotti with Sausage	772	46	21	171	1070	49	5	7	39
Baked Manicotti with Prosciutto	634	31	16	149	1324	48	5	7	39
Baked Manicotti Puttanesca	584	29	15	130	955	49	5	7	32
Hand-Rolled Meat Ravioli with Quick Tomato Sauce	245	12	4	90	212	18	0	0	12
Skillet Lasagna	420	18	8	55	1330	50	3	8	24
Vegetable Lasagna	544	32	14	74	965	44	7	9	22
Potato Gnocchi with Browned Butter and Sage Sauce	535	17	10	102	903	83	5	3	12
Gorgonzola-Cream Sauce	355	32	20	109	456	3	0	2	9
Parmesan Sauce with Pancetta and Walnuts	162	15	5	87	171	1	0	0	5
Grown-Up Stovetop Macaroni and Cheese	549	25	13	62	684	52	2	4	27
Everyday Pad Thai	580	24	3.5	295	1280	66	2	14	26
Flat Hand-Pulled Noodles (Biang Biang Mian) with Chili Oil Vinaigrette	738	27	4	155	1250	80	7	8	40
Steamed Chinese Dumplings (Shu Mai)	336	9	1	82	745	38	1	1	21
Chili Oil (per teaspoon)	45	4.5	1	0	85	1	0	0	0
GRILLING									
Grilled Glazed Boneless, Skinless Chicken Breasts	210	4.5	1	125	380	1	0	1	39
Spicy Hoisin Glaze	90	1	0	0	430	19	0	15	1
Honey-Mustard Glaze	100	0	0	0	280	22	0	20	0
Coconut-Curry Glaze	100	4	3.5	0	440	17	0	13	1
Miso-Sesame Glaze	90	4	0.5	0	360	14	0	11	1
Grilled Chicken Souvlaki	564	26	5	131	529	34	5	5	47
Charcoal-Grilled Barbecued Chicken Kebabs	319	10	3	148	514	23	1	20	31
Sweet and Tangy Barbecued Chicken	859	55	14	255	958	24	0	19	64
Barbecued Pulled Chicken	230	6	1	45	1800	32	1	26	10
Barbecued Pulled Chicken for a Crowd	650	21	4.5	360	2130	32	1	26	77
Smoked Chicken	380	12	2	200	410	1	0	1	61
Peri Peri Grilled Chicken	870	61	16	255	961	11	2	5	67
Italian-Style Grilled Chicken	895	71	16	231	217	3	0	0	57
Grill-Roasted Whole Chicken	527	38	10	172	543	0	0	0	42
Thai Grilled Cornish Game Hens with Chili Dipping Sauce (Gai Yang)	858	47	13	339	1627	44	1	39	59
Grill-Roasted Turkey	670	27	8	330	900	1	0	0	98
Grill-Smoked Herb-Rubbed Flat-Iron Steaks	199	11	3	76	360	2	0	0	22
Grilled Flank Steak Tacos	240	11	2	22	349	25	4	1	10
Grilled Steak Tips	260	14	5	105	75	0	0	0	31
Southwestern Marinade	202	19	1	0	1259	6	1	2	2
Garlic, Ginger, and Soy Marinade	920	84	9	0	4920	34	1	27	12
Grilled Thai Beef Salad	120	3	1	22	505	14	3	5	9

	CALORIES	TOTAL FAT (G)	SAT FAT (G)	CHOL (MG)	SODIUM (MG)	TOTAL CARB (G)	DIETARY FIBER (G)	TOTAL SUGARS (G)	PROTEIN (G)
GRILLING (continued)									
Tender, Juicy Grilled Burgers	520	29	13	145	510	22	0	3	39
Grilled Scallion Topping	155	14	2	6	256	6	2	2	1
Grilled Shiitake Mushroom Topping	150	14	2	6	213	4	1	2	1
Grilled Napa Cabbage and Radicchio Topping	139	14	2	6	200	2	0	1	1
Grilled Lamb Kofte	469	38	13	88	459	8	1	3	23
Grilled Beef Kofte	440	34	10	85	462	8	1	3	24
Grill-Smoked Pork Chops	210	2.5	1	30	1790	32	1	28	11
Grilled Glazed Pork Tenderloin Roast	290	9	1.5	100	590	16	0	13	33
Miso Glaze	90	0.5	0	0	420	16	0	13	1
Sweet and Spicy Hoisin Glaze	60	1.5	0	0	650	10	0	6	1
Satay Glaze	120	7	4	0	220	12	0	10	2
Grilled Pork Loin with Apple-Cranberry Filling	610	25	8	110	670	58	3	52	41
Grill-Roasted Bone-In Pork Rib Roast	190	8	2.5	100	650	0	0	0	28
Orange Salsa with Cuban Flavors (per ¼ cup)	50	1.5	0	0	130	10	2	7	1
Barbecued Pulled Pork on a Charcoal Grill	550	33	11	160	2020	12	3	7	46
Dry Rub for Barbecue	50	1	0	0	1810	10	3	5	1
Eastern North Carolina Barbecue Sauce	20	0	0	0	50	2	0	2	0
Mid–South Carolina Mustard Sauce	280	28	2	0	320	4	0	4	0
Smoky Pulled Pork on a Gas Grill	320	13	4.5	135	850	4	0	3	43
Sweet and Tangy Grilled Country-Style Pork Ribs	420	15	4	130	1290	31	1	27	37
Tuscan Grilled Pork Ribs (Rosticciana)	204	19	4	28	124	0	0	0	5
Grilled Radicchio	130	14	2	0	0	0	0	0	0
Memphis-Style Barbecued Spareribs	780	62	20	210	1410	10	1	7	42
Spice Rub	35	0	0	0	1190	8	1	5	1
Grilled Swordfish Skewers with Tomato-Scallion Caponata	308	17	3	74	137	14	4	8	24
Grilled Blackened Red Snapper	344	15	6	103	555	4	1	0	45
Rémoulade (per tablespoon)	90	10	1.5	5	125	1	0	0	0
Pineapple and Cucumber Salsa with Mint (per ¼ cup)	20	0	0	0	100	5	1	4	0
Grill-Smoked Salmon	320	20	4.5	85	180	1	0	1	31
"Smoked Salmon Platter" Sauce (per 2 tablespoons)	100	10	1	30	60	0	0	0	1
Apple-Mustard Sauce (per 2 tablespoons)	30	0	0	0	170	5	0	5	0
Grilled Shrimp Skewers	260	19	8	190	560	4	0	1	18
Spicy Lemon-Garlic Sauce	110	11	7	30	75	2	0	0	0
Fresh Tomato Sauce with Feta and Olives	220	21	6	25	390	5	1	3	5
Paella on the Grill	898	38	11	204	1792	75	4	4	56
Mexican-Style Grilled Corn	236	13	2	8	329	28	3	9	6
Grilled Baba Ghanoush (per ¼ cup)	70	4	0.5	0	75	8	3	4	2
SIDES									
Pan-Roasted Asparagus	70	4	1	5	3	6	3	2	3
Stir-Fried Asparagus with Shiitake Mushrooms	93	4	0	0	227	9	3	5	3
Stir-Fried Asparagus with Red Bell Pepper	81	3	0	0	306	10	3	7	2
Stir-Fried Asparagus with Red Onion	73	3	0	0	475	8	2	5	3
Beets with Lemon and Almonds	137	6	0	0	92	17	5	11	4
Beets with Lime and Pepitas	128	5	0	0	93	16	4	10	5
Beets with Orange and Walnuts	84	1	0	0	93	15	3	10	2
Roasted Broccoli	130	7	0	0	211	13	5	3	5
Roasted Broccoli with Garlic	158	10	1	0	353	13	5	3	5

	CALORIES	TOTAL FAT (G)	SAT FAT (G)	CHOL (MG)	SODIUM (MG)	TOTAL CARB (G)	DIETARY FIBER (G)	TOTAL SUGARS (G)	PROTEIN (G)
SIDES (continued)									
Skillet-Roasted Brussels Sprouts with Lemon and Pecorino Romano	232	19	3	8	147	10	4	2	6
Skillet-Roasted Brussels Sprouts with Cider Vinegar and Honey	210	18	2.5	0	170	12	4	5	3
Skillet-Roasted Brussels Sprouts with Maple Syrup and Smoked Almonds	264	21	2	0	29	15	5	5	5
Skillet-Roasted Brussels Sprouts with Pomegranate and Pistachios	263	20	2	0	31	17	5	7	5
Skillet-Roasted Brussels Sprouts with Chile, Peanuts, and Mint	230	19	2	0	148	12	4	3	5
Skillet-Roasted Brussels Sprouts with Gochujang and Sesame Seeds	216	18	2	0	189	11	4	2	4
Skillet-Roasted Brussels Sprouts with Mustard and Brown Sugar	214	17	2	0	71	13	4	5	3
Slow-Cooked Whole Carrots	67	2	1	5	282	11	3	5	1
Pine Nut Relish (per 2 tablespoons)	50	4.5	0	0	100	3	0	2	1
Modern Cauliflower Gratin	144	11	6	28	115	8	2	2	4
Vegan Buffalo Cauliflower Bites	570	53	19	0	690	25	2	4	2
Vegan Ranch Dressing (per tablespoon)	90	10	1	0	120	0	0	0	0
Vegan Mayonnaise (per tablespoon)	180	20	1.5	0	75	0	0	0	0
Boiled Corn	99	2	1	2	15	19	2	6	3
Chili-Lime Salt	5	0	0	0	1170	1	1	0	0
Pepper-Cinnamon Salt	5	0	0	0	560	1	0	0	0
Cumin-Sesame Salt	15	1	0	0	560	1	0	0	0
Buttery Spring Vegetables	158	11	7	30	349	11	4	6	3
Skillet Charred Green Beans with Crispy Bread-Crumb Topping	140	11	1	0	220	10	3	4	2
Roasted Green Beans	66	3	0	0	6	8	3	3	2
Quick Green Bean "Casserole"	260	20	7	38	27	17	4	6	4
Eggplant Involtini	314	21	5	26	315	23	9	11	10
Sautéed Mushrooms with Red Wine and Rosemary	97	4	2	8	198	8	1	4	5
Roasted Mushrooms with Parmesan and Pine Nuts	246	17	5	20	120	16	4	5	10
Crispy Potato Latkes	172	4	0	62	32	29	2	1	5
Easier French Fries	400	19	1.5	0	15	50	0	0	7
Chive and Black Pepper Dipping Sauce (per tablespoon)	70	7	1.5	5	130	0	0	0	0
Belgian-Style Dipping Sauce (per tablespoon)	60	6	1	5	200	2	0	2	0
Thick-Cut Oven Fries	291	10	0	0	14	45	5	1	4
Patatas Bravas	290	19	2	5	630	29	2	2	4
Best Baked Potatoes	167	3	0	0	8	31	2	1	3
Creamy Egg Topping	82	6	2	145	152	1	0	0	5
Herbed Goat Cheese Topping	137	12	5	13	131	0	0	0	5
Smoked Trout Topping	89	5	2	30	27	1	0	0	7
Creamy Mashed Potatoes	385	27	17	85	491	32	3	2	4
Smashed Potatoes	253	14	8	41	80	27	3	1	4
Crispy Roasted Potatoes	247	11	1	0	11	33	4	1	3
Roasted Fingerling Potatoes with Mixed Herbs	240	11	1	0	290	36	6	3	3
Roasted Fingerling Potatoes with Parsley, Lemon, and Garlic	250	11	1	0	290	37	6	3	3
Roasted Fingerling Potatoes with Pecorino and Black Pepper	260	11	1.5	5	330	37	6	3	4

	CALORIES	TOTAL FAT (G)	SAT FAT (G)	CHOL (MG)	SODIUM (MG)	TOTAL CARB (G)	DIETARY FIBER (G)	TOTAL SUGARS (G)	PROTEIN (G)
SIDES (continued)									
Braised Red Potatoes with Lemon and Chives	135	5	3	15	315	19	2	1	2
Braised Red Potatoes with Dijon and Tarragon	137	6	3	15	334	19	2	1	2
Braised Red Potatoes with Miso and Scallions	143	6	3	15	325	20	2	1	2
Twice-Baked Potatoes	223	3	0	0	12	44	3	1	5
Crispy Smashed Potatoes	237	13	1	0	9	26	3	1	3
Candied Sweet Potato Casserole	451	19	5	20	431	67	7	35	4
Mashed Sweet Potatoes	327	14	9	40	419	46	6	10	3
Maple-Orange Mashed Sweet Potatoes	350	14	9	40	420	54	7	17	4
Garlic-Scented Mashed Sweet Potatoes with Coconut Milk and Cilantro	260	6	5	0	420	48	7	11	4
Thick-Cut Sweet Potato Fries	1191	108	18	0	335	55	6	9	3
Spicy Fry Sauce (per tablespoon)	70	8	1	5	125	0	0	0	0
Sautéed Baby Spinach with Almonds and Golden Raisins	201	11	1	0	104	22	4	11	6
Braised Winter Greens with Bacon and Onion	381	26	8	34	406	25	9	6	17
Walkaway Ratatouille	161	9	1	0	13	18	5	8	3
Roasted Butternut Squash with Browned Butter and Hazelnuts	188	16	7	30	247	11	2	2	2
Roasted Butternut Squash with Radicchio and Parmesan	173	14	4	17	251	10	1	2	2
Roasted Butternut Squash with Goat Cheese, Pecans, and Maple	164	11	5	18	231	15	2	6	2
Roasted Butternut Squash with Tahini and Feta	170	12	5	19	251	13	2	3	3
Best Summer Tomato Gratin	206	12	2	3	488	19	2	6	5
Wild Rice Pilaf with Pecans and Dried Cranberries	232	11	3	11	25	29	3	9	5
Rice and Lentils with Crispy Onions (Mujaddara)	460	14	2.5	5	810	70	9	9	14
Crispy Onions	100	5	0	0	100	13	2	6	1
Persian-Style Rice with Golden Crust (Chelow)	293	7	3	11	11	50	0	0	5
Almost Hands-Free Risotto with Parmesan and Herbs	421	11	6	26	198	59	2	1	12
Simple Israeli Couscous	178	1	0	0	152	33	2	0	5
Israeli Couscous with Lemon, Mint, Peas, Feta, and Pickled Shallots	211	14	3	12	164	15	3	8	6
Israeli Couscous with Tomatoes, Olives, and Ricotta Salata	464	23	4	14	219	50	5	2	13
Quinoa Pilaf with Herbs and Lemon	197	6	2	10	297	28	3	0	6
Quinoa Pilaf with Chipotle, Queso Fresco, and Peanuts	297	14	4	16	368	31	4	1	11
Quinoa Pilaf with Apricots, Aged Gouda, and Pistachios	314	13	4	20	371	38	5	7	11
Farro Salad with Asparagus, Sugar Snap Peas, and Tomatoes	113	8	2	8	100	5	1	3	3
No-Fuss Creamy Parmesan Polenta	384	14	8	34	1256	48	2	1	14

	CALORIES	TOTAL FAT (G)	SAT FAT (G)	CHOL (MG)	SODIUM (MG)	TOTAL CARB (G)	DIETARY FIBER (G)	TOTAL SUGARS (G)	PROTEIN (G)
BREAD AND PIZZA									
Easiest-Ever Biscuits	347	20	12	71	223	35	1	3	5
Pumpkin Bread	294	12	2	56	239	41	1	25	4
Pumpkin Bread with Candied Ginger	326	12	2	56	261	49	1	33	4
Ultimate Banana Bread	410	12	7	75	320	71	3	34	6
Boston Brown Bread	287	5	3	13	406	56	3	26	5
Irish Soda Bread	300	3.5	2	10	720	56	0	6	9
Whole-Wheat Soda Bread	320	5	2	10	720	58	4	8	11
Quick Cheese Bread	390	17	10	70	770	42	0	2	16
Quick Cheese Bread with Bacon, Onion, and Gruyère	430	20	9	70	890	42	0	3	19
All-Purpose Cornbread	430	18	10	105	560	58	2	11	10
Spicy Jalapeño-Cheddar Cornbread	490	24	14	125	600	55	2	7	15
Rosemary Focaccia	170	4.5	0.5	0	95	26	0	0	4
Focaccia with Caramelized Red Onion, Pancetta, and Oregano	257	10	2	7	255	33	1	0	6
Rustic Dinner Rolls	104	0	0	0	120	20	0	0	3
Almost No-Knead Bread	250	0	0	0	580	52	0	0	7
No-Knead Brioche	252	14	8	111	176	24	0	4	6
Ciabatta	130	0	0	0	290	26	0	0	4
Fougasse	260	7	1	0	920	42	1	0	6
Fougasse with Bacon and Gruyère	360	16	4.5	15	580	44	2	0	10
Fougasse with Asiago and Black Pepper	290	9	1.5	5	480	44	2	0	7
Olive Fougasse	270	8	1	0	970	42	1	0	6
Authentic Baguettes at Home	130	0	0	0	290	28	0	0	4
Easy Sandwich Bread	220	5	3	35	250	35	2	2	7
Best Whole-Wheat Sandwich Bread	270	8	3.5	15	600	43	4	6	9
Multigrain Bread	260	7	2.5	10	440	44	2	4	9
New York Bagels	253	1	0	0	477	51	1	10	8
Everything Bagels	260	2.5	0	0	740	49	3	5	10
Cinnamon-Raisin Bagels	268	1	0	0	478	55	2	11	8
Pita Bread	251	8	1	0	227	36	1	3	5
One-Hour Pizza	350	12	5	25	1340	43	3	5	16
New York–Style Thin-Crust Pizza	495	15	6	33	736	66	4	8	20
Pizza Bianca	251	8	1	0	247	36	1	0	5
Thick-Crust Sicilian-Style Pizza	649	31	9	39	706	68	4	4	23
Pizza al Taglio with Arugula and Fresh Mozzarella	593	32	9	39	651	54	2	2	20
Pizza al Taglio with Potatoes and Soppressata	771	42	13	56	1115	67	4	2	29
Pizza al Taglio with Prosciutto and Figs	505	20	3	18	559	64	3	11	15
COOKIES									
Brown Sugar Cookies	182	7	4	33	88	28	0	19	1
Molasses Spice Cookies	153	6	4	25	83	22	0	12	1
Molasses Spice Cookies with Dark Rum Glaze	174	6	4	25	88	26	0	16	1
Perfect Chocolate Chip Cookies	312	18	9	49	153	36	1	23	3
Chocolate Crinkle Cookies	155	5	3	31	95	24	1	16	2
Big and Chewy Oatmeal-Raisin Cookies	295	11	6	44	87	45	1	26	3
Big and Chewy Oatmeal-Date Cookies	310	11	6	44	86	50	2	31	3
Chocolate-Chunk Oatmeal Cookies with Pecans and Dried Cherries	301	16	7	34	141	38	2	25	3

	CALORIES	TOTAL FAT (G)	SAT FAT (G)	CHOL (MG)	SODIUM (MG)	TOTAL CARB (G)	DIETARY FIBER (G)	TOTAL SUGARS (G)	PROTEIN (G)
COOKIES (continued)									
Peanut Butter Sandwich Cookies	214	13	3	15	104	19	1	13	5
Peanut Butter Sandwich Cookies with Honey-Cinnamon Filling	215	12	2	11	109	23	1	17	5
Peanut Butter Sandwich Cookies with Milk Chocolate Filling	223	13	3	13	110	23	1	16	5
Gingersnaps	50	1	1	6	33	7	0	4	0
Belgian Spice Cookies (Speculoos)	69	3	1	12	33	9	0	4	0
Triple-Coconut Macaroons	81	5	4	0	48	7	0	6	0
Chocolate-Dipped Triple-Coconut Macaroons	109	7	5	0	48	11	1	10	1
Sablés (French Butter Cookies)	55	3	1	12	17	6	0	2	0
Chocolate Sablés	54	3	1	12	17	5	0	2	0
Black and White Spiral Cookies	52	3	1	12	16	5	0	2	0
Chocolate Sandwich Cookies	66	3	2	12	18	7	0	3	0
Vanilla Pretzel Cookies	56	3	1	12	18	6	0	2	0
Easy Holiday Sugar Cookies	123	4	2	16	66	18	0	12	1
Easy Holiday Cocoa Sugar Cookies	125	4	3	16	66	19	0	12	1
Pecan or Walnut Crescent Cookies	102	6	2	10	37	9	0	5	0
Almond or Hazelnut Crescent Cookies	109	7	2	10	37	10	0	5	1
Almond Biscotti	113	5	1	16	48	14	0	6	2
Anise Biscotti	114	5	1	16	48	14	0	7	2
Hazelnut-Orange Biscotti	109	5	1	16	48	14	0	6	2
Hazelnut-Lavender Biscotti	108	5	1	16	48	13	0	6	2
Pistachio-Spice Biscotti	108	4	1	16	48	14	0	7	2
Browned Butter Blondies	218	10	4	39	123	29	0	18	2
Chewy Brownies	299	14	4	43	98	41	1	29	3
Ultranutty Pecan Bars	266	19	5	19	117	23	1	13	2
Millionaire's Shortbread	195	10	6	25	91	24	0	17	1
Best Lemon Bars	260	13	8	125	170	32	0	21	4
Chocolate Chip Cookie Ice Cream Sandwiches	355	19	11	69	236	1	1	31	4
Holiday Eggnog	165	7	4	119	106	12	0	12	5
PIES, TARTS, AND FRUIT DESSERTS									
Foolproof All-Butter Dough for Single-Crust Pie	210	14	9	40	150	18	0	2	2
Foolproof Whole-Wheat Dough for Single-Crust Pie	210	14	9	40	150	17	2	2	3
Foolproof All-Butter Dough for Double-Crust Pie	410	28	18	75	290	35	0	3	5
Foolproof Whole-Wheat Dough for Double-Crust Pie	410	28	18	75	290	35	3	3	5
Graham Cracker Crust	100	7	4.5	20	20	7	0	6	0
Classic Tart Dough	230	12	8	55	75	26	0	9	3
Classic Apple Pie	618	30	14	45	375	82	6	43	5
Apple Pie with Crystallized Ginger	620	30	14	45	375	82	6	43	5
Apple Pie with Dried Fruit	684	30	14	45	377	99	7	57	5
Apple Pie with Fresh Cranberries	630	28	18	100	380	89	3	49	6
Deep-Dish Apple Pie	475	19	12	50	304	71	6	39	4
Skillet Apple Pie	318	15	8	30	156	45	3	26	2
Fresh Peach Pie	574	26	12	38	331	80	3	40	6

	CALORIES	TOTAL FAT (G)	SAT FAT (G)	CHOL (MG)	SODIUM (MG)	TOTAL CARB (G)	DIETARY FIBER (G)	TOTAL SUGARS (G)	PROTEIN (G)
PIES, TARTS, AND FRUIT DESSERTS (continued)									
Strawberry-Rhubarb Pie	631	30	14	45	300	80	4	38	6
Blueberry Pie	625	34	16	76	341	72	4	34	5
Summer Berry Pie	305	16	9	47	99	39	4	25	2
Fresh Plum-Ginger Pie with Whole-Wheat Lattice-Top Crust	559	30	18	99	378	69	4	36	6
Pumpkin Pie	530	29	18	195	520	58	2	37	8
Pecan Pie	644	39	12	107	347	71	2	51	7
Triple Chocolate Chunk Pecan Pie	584	36	16	114	307	61	2	43	6
Key Lime Pie	449	24	13	158	165	53	0	41	7
Lemon Meringue Pie	450	20	12	185	220	61	0	39	6
Chocolate Cream Pie	290	20	13	40	50	26	1	12	5
Lemon Tart	302	17	7	184	149	35	0	25	3
Lemon–Olive Oil Tart	437	22	3	69	243	54	0	32	5
The Best Summer Fruit Tart	410	25	14	71	161	43	5	19	5
Free-Form Summer Fruit Tart	368	19	12	50	197	45	2	19	4
Linzertorte	413	22	8	47	117	49	2	28	5
Apple Galette	299	16	10	42	121	36	2	14	2
French Apple Tart	453	19	11	49	233	67	5	38	3
Best Chocolate Tart	415	32	18	114	126	31	2	20	4
Strawberry Shortcakes	624	34	20	129	422	73	4	36	8
Sour Cherry Cobbler	392	6	3	16	229	78	5	53	5
Fresh Sour Cherry Cobbler	368	6	3	16	229	72	3	49	4
Blueberry Cobbler	263	6	3	15	261	50	3	30	3
Peach Crisp	390	20	7	25	100	55	5	45	4
Peach Crisp for a Crowd	470	23	8	30	120	66	6	53	5
Pear Crisp	424	18	7	25	8	64	8	39	4
Roasted Pears with Dried Apricots and Pistachios	273	8	3	12	53	41	5	30	2
Roasted Apples with Dried Figs and Walnuts	209	6	3	12	52	31	3	26	0
Cherry Clafouti	291	15	8	139	131	33	1	32	4
Simple Raspberry Gratin	180	5	2.5	10	105	33	6	16	3
Apple Strudel	374	16	9	35	220	53	4	23	3
Individual Summer Berry Puddings	358	2	0	0	242	76	11	42	9
Large Summer Berry Pudding	226	1	0	0	121	49	7	30	5
Lemon Posset with Berries	382	29	18	108	30	29	0	28	1
Fresh Strawberry Mousse	248	14	8	47	127	29	3	25	3
Lemon Whipped Cream	64	5	3	20	5	3	0	3	0
Pavlova with Fruit and Whipped Cream	300	17	11	55	40	34	0	34	3
Orange, Cranberry, and Mint Topping	160	0	0	0	0	41	2	36	1
Mango, Kiwi, and Blueberry Topping	80	0.5	0	0	0	21	2	18	1
Individual Pavlovas with Fruit and Whipped Cream	300	17	11	55	40	34	0	34	3

	CALORIES	TOTAL FAT (G)	SAT FAT (G)	CHOL (MG)	SODIUM (MG)	TOTAL CARB (G)	DIETARY FIBER (G)	TOTAL SUGARS (G)	PROTEIN (G)
CAKES AND MORE									
Rich Chocolate Bundt Cake	407	20	11	103	296	55	2	39	5
Cider-Glazed Apple Bundt Cake	401	14	8	74	358	62	2	33	5
Lemon Pound Cake	520	27	16	157	230	64	0	44	5
Pear-Walnut Upside-Down Cake	342	18	6	80	195	42	2	32	3
Apple Upside-Down Cake	455	18	11	92	225	68	2	52	4
Apple Upside-Down Cake with Almond	480	20	11	92	225	69	3	52	4
Apple Upside-Down Cake with Lemon and Thyme	456	18	11	92	225	69	2	52	4
French Apple Cake	395	23	2	21	207	42	2	29	2
Carrot Layer Cake	771	52	17	118	461	71	3	52	7
Olive Oil Cake	353	18	3	57	225	42	0	25	4
Italian Almond Cake	362	22	5	89	197	36	2	25	6
Orange Crème Fraîche (per 2 tablespoons)	70	6	3.5	10	30	4	0	4	1
Gâteau Breton with Apricot Filling	491	26	15	200	203	52	1	28	8
Gâteau Breton with Prune Filling	493	26	15	199	157	57	2	27	5
Summer Peach Cake	272	11	6	64	243	38	2	24	4
Applesauce Snack Cake	200	8	5	35	210	30	1	18	2
Fluffy Yellow Layer Cake with Milk Chocolate Frosting	910	53	31	200	310	105	0	80	8
Chocolate Sheet Cake with Easy Chocolate Frosting	778	52	25	131	222	74	4	56	9
Easy Vanilla Bean Buttercream	209	15	9	40	39	18	0	18	0
Easy Chocolate Buttercream	255	18	11	38	40	24	0	22	0
Easy Coffee Buttercream	208	15	9	40	39	18	0	18	0
Classic Gingerbread Cake	311	8	0	37	225	54	0	36	3
Coconut Layer Cake	777	52	35	127	340	74	1	52	5
Wicked Good Boston Cream Pie	585	29	17	233	322	73	1	52	8
Chocolate-Caramel Layer Cake	751	41	23	119	483	98	4	78	6
Chocolate-Raspberry Torte	424	30	14	105	118	37	3	28	6
Torta Caprese	310	22	9	79	106	26	2	22	5
Amaretto Whipped Cream	70	6	4	20	0	2	0	2	0
Orange Whipped Cream	110	11	7	35	25	3	0	3	1
Triple-Chocolate Mousse Cake	458	36	22	137	94	32	2	28	4
Chocolate-Espresso Dacquoise	503	38	17	124	111	38	3	32	7
Paris-Brest	507	37	16	222	288	34	1	22	9
Tiramisu	482	31	16	248	315	37	1	15	9
Tiramisu with Cooked Eggs	505	33	18	257	318	37	1	15	9
Foolproof New York Cheesecake	510	37	20	186	358	36	0	29	8
Lemon Cheesecake	435	28	15	172	316	38	0	32	6
Spiced Pumpkin Cheesecake	437	30	17	156	341	35	1	27	6
Pumpkin-Bourbon Cheesecake with Graham-Pecan Crust	466	31	16	151	326	38	3	28	7
Brown Sugar and Bourbon Whipped Cream	106	7	4	27	33	8	0	8	0
Lemon Pudding Cakes	270	10	5	93	128	40	0	35	4
Blueberry Compote (per tablespoon)	20	1	0	0	10	4	0	3	0
Baked Alaska	467	19	3	104	264	68	1	51	7
Bonus Baked Alaska	467	19	3	104	264	68	1	51	7
Sous Vide Crème Brûlée	560	49	30	365	80	25	0	25	7
Chocolate Pots de Crème	490	41	25	190	110	30	2	11	6
Milk Chocolate Pots de Crème	510	39	24	200	140	32	1	28	7

Conversions and Equivalents

Some say cooking is a science and an art. We would say geography has a hand in it, too. Flours and sugars manufactured in the United Kingdom and elsewhere will feel and taste different from those manufactured in the United States. So we cannot promise that a loaf of bread you bake in Canada or England will taste the same as a loaf baked in the States, but we can offer guidelines for converting weights and measures. We also recommend that you rely on your instincts when making our recipes. Refer to the visual cues provided. If the dough hasn't come together as described, you may need to add more flour—even if the recipe doesn't tell you to. You be the judge.

The recipes in this book were developed using standard U.S. measures following U.S. government guidelines. The charts below offer equivalents for U.S. and metric measures. All conversions are approximate and have been rounded up or down to the nearest whole number.

EXAMPLE

1 teaspoon = 4.9292 milliliters, rounded up to 5 milliliters
1 ounce = 28.3495 grams, rounded down to 28 grams

Volume Conversions

U.S.	METRIC
1 teaspoon	5 milliliters
2 teaspoons	10 milliliters
1 tablespoon	15 milliliters
2 tablespoons	30 milliliters
¼ cup	59 milliliters
⅓ cup	79 milliliters
½ cup	118 milliliters
¾ cup	177 milliliters
1 cup	237 milliliters
1¼ cups	296 milliliters
1½ cups	355 milliliters
2 cups (1 pint)	473 milliliters
2½ cups	591 milliliters
3 cups	710 milliliters
4 cups (1 quart)	0.946 liter
1.06 quarts	1 liter
4 quarts (1 gallon)	3.8 liters

Weight Conversions

OUNCES	GRAMS
½	14
¾	21
1	28
1½	43
2	57
2½	71
3	85
3½	99
4	113
4½	128
5	142
6	170
7	198
8	227
9	255
10	283
12	340
16 (1 pound)	454

Conversions For Common Baking Ingredients

Because measuring by weight is far more accurate than measuring by volume, and thus more likely to produce reliable results, in our recipes we provide ounce measures in addition to cup measures for many ingredients. Refer to the chart below to convert these measures into grams.

INGREDIENT	OUNCES	GRAMS
FLOUR		
1 cup all-purpose flour*	5	142
1 cup cake flour	4	113
1 cup whole-wheat flour	5½	156
SUGAR		
1 cup granulated (white) sugar	7	198
1 cup packed brown sugar (light or dark)	7	198
1 cup confectioners' sugar	4	113
COCOA POWDER		
1 cup cocoa powder	3	85
BUTTER†		
4 tablespoons (½ stick or ¼ cup)	2	57
8 tablespoons (1 stick or ½ cup)	4	113
16 tablespoons (2 sticks or 1 cup)	8	227

* U.S. all-purpose flour, the most frequently used flour in this book, does not contain leaveners, as some European flours do. These leavened flours are called self-rising or self-raising. If you are using self-rising flour, take this into consideration before adding leaveners to a recipe.

† In the United States, butter is sold both salted and unsalted. We recommend unsalted butter. If you are using salted butter, take this into consideration before adding salt to a recipe.

Oven Temperature

FAHRENHEIT	CELSIUS	GAS MARK
225	105	¼
250	120	½
275	135	1
300	150	2
325	165	3
350	180	4
375	190	5
400	200	6
425	220	7
450	230	8
475	245	9

Converting Temperatures from an Instant-Read Thermometer

We include doneness temperatures in many of the recipes in this book. We recommend an instant-read thermometer for the job. Refer to the table above to convert Fahrenheit degrees to Celsius. Or, for temperatures not represented in the chart, use this simple formula:

Subtract 32 degrees from the Fahrenheit reading, then divide the result by 1.8 to find the Celsius reading.

EXAMPLE

"Flip chicken, brush with remaining glaze, and cook until breast registers 160 degrees, 1 to 3 minutes."

To convert:
160°F − 32 = 128°
128° ÷ 1.8 = 71.11°C, rounded down to 71°C

Index

Note: Page references in *italics* indicate photographs.

C

F

Farmhouse Vegetable and Barley Soup, 62, *62*
Farro Salad with Asparagus, Sugar Snap Peas, and Tomatoes, *386,* 386–87
Fennel
    Coriander, and Black Pepper, Roast Butterflied Rack of Lamb with, 228
    -Coriander Top Sirloin Roast, 182–83
    Orange, and Hazelnuts, Chopped Carrot Salad with, 100–101
    Pork, and Lemon Ragu with Pappardelle, 280–82, *281*
Feta
    Cheese and Shiitake Mushrooms, Scrambled Eggs with, 20
    Classic Greek Salad, 95–96
    Lemon, Mint, Peas, and Pickled Shallots, Israeli Couscous with, *384,* 385
    Mediterranean Chopped Salad, 96, *96*
    Olives, and Mint, Lentil Salad with, 106
    and Olives, Fresh Tomato Sauce with, 341
    and Tahini, Roasted Butternut Squash with, 378
Figs
    Dried, and Walnuts, Roasted Apples with, 491
    Prosciutto, Walnuts, and Parmesan, Arugula Salad with, 94
    and Prosciutto, Pizza al Taglio with, *388,* 422
Filipino Chicken Adobo, 130, *130*
Fish
    Braised Halibut with Carrots and Coriander, 232
    Braised Halibut with Leeks and Mustard, 232, *232*
    Chinese-Style Oven-Steamed, *234,* 235
    and Chips, 238–40, *239*
    Cioppino, 75, *75*
    Crunchy Oven-Fried, 237–38
    Fillets, Poached, with Crispy Artichokes and Sherry-Tomato Vinaigrette, 232–33, *233*
    Fillets, Poached, with Crispy Scallions and Miso-Ginger Vinaigrette, 233
    Fillets, Poached, with Jalapeño Vinaigrette, 233
    Grilled Blackened Red Snapper, *336,* 337
    Grilled Swordfish Skewers with Tomato-Scallion Caponata, 334, *335*
    Meunière with Browned Butter and Lemon, 235–37, *236*
    Pan-Seared Swordfish Steaks, 240, *240*
    and Shrimp Stew, Brazilian, 76, *76*
    Smoked Trout Topping, 365
    see also Anchovies; Salmon; Tuna
Flame tamer, improvising, 387

Flat Hand-Pulled Noodles with Chili Oil Vinaigrette, 293–95, *294*
Fluffy Scrambled Eggs, 19
Fluffy Yellow Layer Cake with Milk Chocolate Frosting, *513,* 513–14
Focaccia
    with Caramelized Red Onion, Pancetta, and Oregano, 399
    Rosemary, 398, *398*
Foolproof All-Butter Dough for Double-Crust Pie, 456
Foolproof All-Butter Dough for Single-Crust Pie, 454, *455*
Foolproof New York Cheesecake, 532–34, *533*
Foolproof Vinaigrette, 93
    Balsamic-Mustard, 93
    Herb, 93
    Lemon, 93
    Walnut, 93
Foolproof Whole-Wheat Dough for Double-Crust Pie, 456
Foolproof Whole-Wheat Dough for Single-Crust Pie, 454
Fougasse, 404–6, *405*
    with Asiago and Black Pepper, 406
    with Bacon and Gruyère, 406
    Olive, 406
Free-Form Summer Fruit Tart, *476,* 476–77
French Apple Cake, 505, *505*
French Apple Tart, 481–82, *482*
French Chicken in a Pot, *140,* 141
French Fries, Easier, 362
French Omelets, 26–27
French Onion Soup, Classic, 50–51, *51*
French-Style Pot Roasted Pork Loin, *202,* 202–3
French Toast, Everyday, 29, *29*
Fresh Peach Pie, 460–62, *461*
Fresh Plum-Ginger Pie with Whole-Wheat Lattice-Top Crust, *452,* 465–66
Fresh Sour Cherry Cobbler, 486–87
Fresh Strawberry Mousse, 494–95, *495*
Fresh Tomato Relish, 247
Fresh Tomato Sauce with Feta and Olives, 341
Fried Brown Rice with Pork and Shrimp, 218–19
Fried Shallot Oil, 105–6
Fried Shallots, *104,* 105–6
Fries
    French, Easier, 362
    Oven, Thick-Cut, 362–63, *363*
    Sweet Potato, Thick-Cut, 372, *373*
Frittata, Asparagus, Ham, and Gruyère, 27, *27*
Frostings
    applying to layer cakes, 514
    Chocolate, Easy, Chocolate Sheet Cake with, 514–15
    Easy Chocolate Buttercream, 515

Frostings *(cont.)*
    Easy Coffee Buttercream, 515
    Easy Vanilla Bean Buttercream, 515
    Milk Chocolate, Fluffy Yellow Layer Cake with, *513,* 513–14
Fruit
    Dried, Apple Pie with, 458
    Summer, Tart, The Best, 474, *475*
    Summer, Tart, Free-Form, *476,* 476–77
    and Whipped Cream, Individual Pavlovas with, 497
    and Whipped Cream, Pavlova with, 495–97, *496*
    see also Berry(ies); *specific fruits*

G

Galette, Apple, 478–81, *480*
Garlic
    Croutons, 60
    -Curry Sauce, 120
    –Dried Mint Sauce, Spicy, 240–41
    Everything Bagels, 414, *415*
    Garlicky Lime Sauce with Cilantro, 199
    Garlicky Roasted Shrimp with Cilantro and Lime, *230,* 254
    Garlicky Roasted Shrimp with Cumin, Ginger, and Sesame, 254
    Garlicky Roasted Shrimp with Parsley and Anise, 253–54
    Ginger, and Soy Marinade, 317
    Gremolata, 177
    Herb, and Bread-Crumb Crust, Roast Boneless Leg of Lamb with, 227, *227*
    -Lemon Butter, Pan-Seared Shrimp with, 252
    -Lemon Sauce, Spicy, 341
    and Lime, Peruvian Roast Chicken with, 138, *138*
    -Mustard Butter with Thyme, 142
    Roasted Broccoli with, 348
    and Rosemary, Tuscan-Style Roast Pork with, *206,* 207
    -Rosemary Top Sirloin Roast, 183
    Sauce, Sichuan Stir-Fried Pork in, *214,* 215
    -Scented Mashed Sweet Potatoes with Coconut Milk and Cilantro, 372
    -Shallot Pan Sauce, Slow-Roasted Chicken Parts with, 135
    Shrimp, Spanish-Style, 253, *253*
    -Studded Roast Pork Loin, 203
    and Thyme Sauce, 194
    Ultimate Shrimp Scampi, 254–56, *255*
    -Yogurt Sauce, 321
Gâteau Breton with Apricot Filling, 510, *511*
Gâteau Breton with Prune Filling, 510
Gazpacho, Classic, 59, *59*–60
Giblet Pan Gravy, *147,* 147–48

U

V

W

Y

Z

Copyright © 2019 by America's Test Kitchen

Library of Congress Cataloging-in-Publication Data has been applied for.

ISBN 978-1-945256-88-2

AMERICA'S TEST KITCHEN
21 Drydock Avenue, Boston, MA 02210

Manufactured in Canada
10 9 8 7 6 5 4 3 2

Distributed by Penguin Random House
Publisher Services
Tel: 800.733.3000

Editorial Director, Books Elizabeth Carduff

Executive Editor Adam Kowit

Executive Food Editor Dan Zuccarello

Senior Editor Sara Mayer

Executive Managing Editor Debra Hudak

Editorial Assistants Brenna Donovan and Sara Zatopek

Art Director, Books Lindsey Timko Chandler

Deputy Art Directors Allison Boales, Courtney Lentz, and Janet Taylor

Associate Art Director Katie Barranger

Photography Director Julie Bozzo Cote

Photography Producer Meredith Mulcahy

Contributing Photography Direction Greg Galvan

Senior Staff Photographers Steve Klise and Daniel J. van Ackere

Staff Photographer Kevin White

Additional Photography Keller + Keller and Carl Tremblay

Food Styling Catrine Kelty, Chantal Lambeth, Kendra McKnight, Ashley Moore, Marie Piraino, Elle Simone Scott, and Sally Staub

Photoshoot Kitchen Team

    Photo Team Manager Timothy McQuinn

    Assistant Test Cooks Sarah Ewald, Hannah Fenton, Jacqueline Gochenouer, and Eric Haessler

Senior Manager, Publishing Operations Taylor Argenzio

Imaging Manager Lauren Robbins

Production and Imaging Specialists Dennis Noble, Jessica Voas, and Amanda Yong

Copy Editor Cheryl Redmond

Proofreader Christine Corcoran Cox

Indexer Elizabeth Parson

Chief Creative Officer Jack Bishop

Executive Editorial Directors Julia Collin Davison and Bridget Lancaster